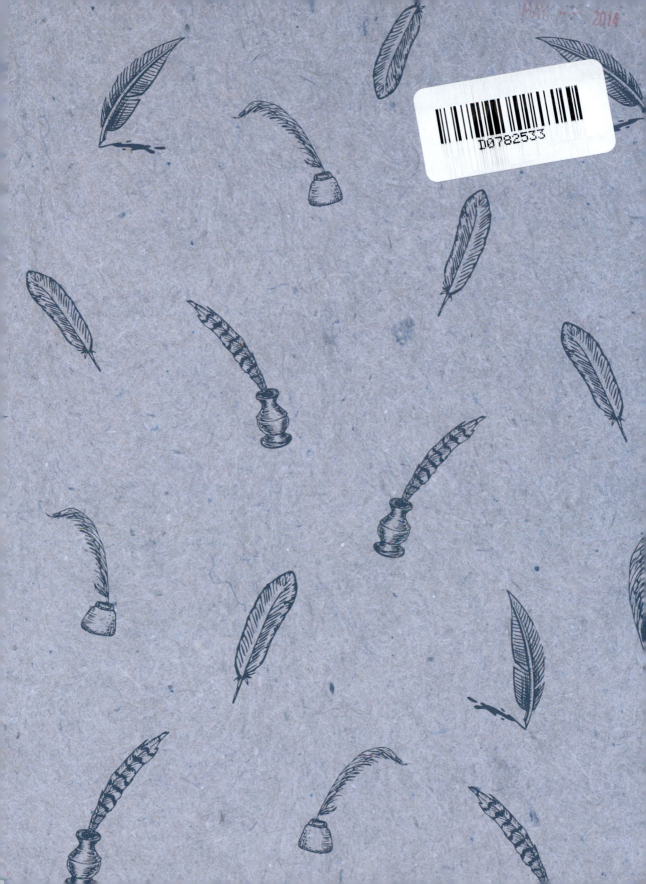

The RSC Shakespeare

William Shakespeare and Others

COLLABORATIVE PLAYS

General Introduction and Play Introductions: Jonathan Bate

Textual Editing: Eric Rasmussen and Jan Sewell, assisted by Sarah Stewart
and checked by Peter Kirwan and Will Sharpe

Explanatory Notes: Jan Sewell

'Authorship and Attribution': Will Sharpe

Key Facts and 'From Script to Stage' Interviews: Peter Kirwan

The London Prodigal adapted from a text edited and annotated by Paul Edmondson

The research for this edition was funded by a generous grant
from the Arts and Humanities Research Council

 Arts & Humanities
Research Council

The RSC Shakespeare

William Shakespeare and Others

COLLABORATIVE PLAYS

Edited by

**Jonathan Bate and Eric Rasmussen
with Jan Sewell and Will Sharpe**

Associate Editors

Peter Kirwan and Sarah Stewart

palgrave
macmillan

First published 2013 by
PALGRAVE MACMILLAN

Palgrave Macmillan in the UK is an imprint of Macmillan Publishers Limited,
registered in England, company number 785998, of Houndmills, Basingstoke,
Hampshire RG21 6XS.

Palgrave Macmillan in the US is a division of St Martin's Press LLC,
175 Fifth Avenue, New York, NY 10010.

Palgrave Macmillan is the global academic imprint of the above companies
and has companies and representatives throughout the world.

Palgrave® and Macmillan® are registered trademarks in the United States,
the United Kingdom, Europe and other countries.

ISBN-13: 978–1–137–27144–0 hardback
ISBN-10: 1–137–27144–2   hardback

This book is printed on paper suitable for recycling and made from fully managed
and sustained forest sources. Logging, pulping and manufacturing processes are
expected to conform to the environmental regulations of the country of origin.

A catalogue record for this book is available from the British Library.

A catalog record for this book is available from the Library of Congress.

Printed and bound in the Eurepean Union by TJ International, Padstow, Cornwall,
England

The RSC Shakespeare

William Shakespeare and Others
COLLABORATIVE PLAYS

Among the plays staged at the Globe and published in Shakespeare's lifetime were *The London Prodigal by William Shakespeare*, *A Yorkshire Tragedy written by W. Shakespeare* and *Thomas Lord Cromwell written by W. S.*

Could Shakespeare really have written these plays? Why were they excluded from the First Folio of his collected works? As a companion to their award-winning *The RSC Shakespeare: The Complete Works*, renowned scholars Jonathan Bate and Eric Rasmussen, supported by a dynamic team of co-editors, now present *William Shakespeare and Others: Collaborative Plays*.

This is the first edition for over a hundred years of the fascinatingly varied body of plays that has become known as 'The Shakespeare Apocrypha'. Among the highlights are the whole text of *Sir Thomas More*, which includes the only scene from any play to survive in Shakespeare's own handwriting; the history play *Edward III*, including a superb seduction scene by Shakespeare; and the domestic murder tragedy *Arden of Faversham*, in which Shakespeare's hand has been detected by recent computer-assisted analysis. This is also the first ever Shakespeare edition to include the 1602 edition of Thomas Kyd's pioneering *The Spanish Tragedy*, with 'additions' that the latest research attributes to Shakespeare. A magisterial essay by Will Sharpe provides a comprehensive account of the Authorship and Attribution of each play.

William Shakespeare and Others: Collaborative Plays has all the features of the bestselling RSC Shakespeare series: inimitable introductions by Jonathan Bate, rigorous textual editing led by Eric Rasmussen, Key Facts boxes with information on sources and the distribution of parts, on-page notes explaining difficult or obsolete vocabulary, and interviews with directors and actors who have staged the plays, including RSC Artistic Directors Terry Hands, Michael Boyd and Gregory Doran.

ABOUT THE EDITORS

Jonathan Bate is Provost of Worcester College and Professor of English Literature in the University of Oxford. Well known as a critic, biographer and broadcaster, he has held visiting posts at Harvard, Yale and UCLA, and was previously King Alfred Professor at the University of Liverpool and Professor of Shakespeare at the University of Warwick. Among his many books are a biography of Shakespeare, *Soul of the Age*, and a history of his fame, *The Genius of Shakespeare*. His biography of the poet John Clare won Britain's two oldest literary awards, the Hawthornden Prize and the James Tait Black Prize. His one-man play for Simon Callow, *Being Shakespeare*, was performed in Edinburgh, London, New York and Chicago, and he was consultant curator for the British Museum's major exhibition for the London 2012 Cultural Olympiad, *Shakespeare Staging the World*. He is a Governor of the Royal Shakespeare Company, Vice-President (Humanities) of the British Academy, and a Fellow of the Royal Society of Literature.

Eric Rasmussen is Foundation Professor of English and Chair at the University of Nevada. His recent publications include the award-winning catalogue raisonné *The Shakespeare First Folios: A Descriptive Catalogue*, co-edited with Anthony James West, and its companion volume *The Shakespeare Thefts: In Search of the First Folios* (Palgrave Macmillan). He is co-author, with Lars Engle, of *Studying Shakespeare's Contemporaries* (Wiley Blackwell) and is an editor of *The Norton Anthology of English Renaissance Drama*, and of plays in the Arden Shakespeare series, the New Variorum Shakespeare, the Oxford World's Classics series, the Revels Plays series, and the Cambridge complete *Works of Ben Jonson*. He has served on the Board of Trustees of the Shakespeare Association of America, on the General Council of the Malone Society, and as General Textual Editor of the Internet Shakespeare Editions Project – one of the most visited Shakespearean websites in the world.

Jan Sewell is a freelance writer and academic who worked as an Associate Editor on the RSC *Complete Works of Shakespeare* and as Chief Associate Editor on the RSC single volume editions of Shakespeare's plays.

Will Sharpe is a visiting lecturer at The Shakespeare Institute, University of Birmingham. He has taught at the University of Warwick and at the University of Leeds completed postdoctoral work on the Cambridge complete *Works of Ben Jonson*. In the *RSC Shakespeare* series, he was Lead Editor of *Cymbeline* and Chief Associate Editor for several other plays. He contributed to *A Year of Shakespeare* (Arden), and is one of the General Editors of *Digital Renaissance Editions*.

Peter Kirwan is Lecturer in Shakespeare and Early Modern Drama at the University of Nottingham. He has published on the text and stage history of disputed Shakespeare plays in several journals and book collections. He is a critic of contemporary Shakespearean performance, a prolific blogger and co-editor of a forthcoming collection entitled *Shakespeare and the Digital World*. He is a trustee of the British Shakespeare Association.

Sarah Stewart is Associate Editor of *The Shakespeare First Folios: A Descriptive Catalogue* (Palgrave Macmillan) and served as an editorial assistant on Sonia Massai's edition of *'Tis Pity She's a Whore* in the Arden Early Modern Drama Series.

THE RSC SHAKESPEARE
WILLIAM SHAKESPEARE AND OTHERS
COLLABORATIVE PLAYS

Contents

LIST OF ILLUSTRATIONS

Illustration acknowledgements: 1–7, 10–11 Jonathan Bate collection; 8 British Library; 9 Ian McKellen; 12–13 Clwyd Theatr Cymru; 14–19 Shakespeare Birthplace Trust/Royal Shakespeare Company.

GENERAL INTRODUCTION
Jonathan Bate

Collaborative Plays?

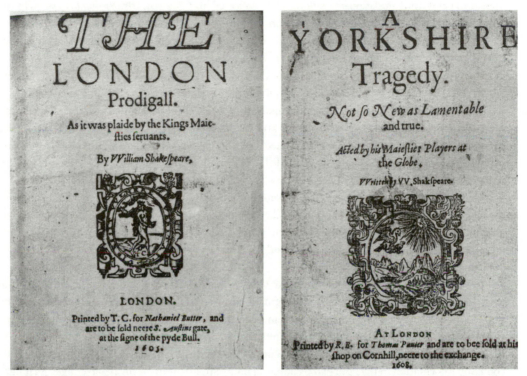

1. *The London Prodigal*　　　　2. *A Yorkshire Tragedy*

Imagine, to begin, that you are a keen playgoer in London early in the reign of King James I. You know that the most admired acting company in the land is the King's Men, formerly known as the Lord Chamberlain's Men. You have seen some of their most famous recent plays – let us say *Othello*, *Macbeth* and *King Lear*. You have heard that these tragedies were written by the acting company's in-house dramatist, Master William Shakespeare. You know that certain playbooks are available in print, in cheap pocket 'Quarto'-sized format, available unbound for a couple of shillings from the bookstalls in St Paul's churchyard under the tower of the old cathedral.

So you go along to St Paul's Yard, in search of plays with the name 'William Shakespeare' on the title page. What will you find? Let us suppose that the year is 1608. If you are lucky enough to find and buy copies of every play bearing the name of W. Shakespeare, you will now own eleven plays that will in future years be numbered among his best-known works, all of them written by

Shakespeare alone.* But you will also be in possession of *The London Prodigal, by William Shakespeare* (1605) and *A Yorkshire Tragedy, written by W. Shakspeare* (1608).

If you were in the know about the theatre, you might have been aware that certain dramatic scripts lacking an author's name on the title page were also by Shakespeare. In 1608, you could have picked up a further five anonymously published plays that everyone in the theatre world linked to Shakespeare (*Titus Andronicus, Romeo and Juliet, Henry V, The First Part of the Contention betwixt the two famous houses of York and Lancaster,* and *The True Tragedy of Richard Duke of York* – these two were later redescribed as parts two and three of *Henry VI*). You would have looked in vain for such tragedies as *Coriolanus* and *Macbeth* or such comedies as *Twelfth Night* and *As You Like It*: they did not appear in print until Shakespeare's fellow-actors collected his *Comedies, Histories and Tragedies* in the large format 'First Folio', published seven years after his death.

As far as the world of print – of the reader – was concerned, in 1608 Shakespeare was the author not only of such acknowledged masterpieces as *A Midsummer Night's Dream, Richard III,* the two parts of *Henry IV, Hamlet* and *King Lear,* but also of *The London Prodigal* and *A Yorkshire Tragedy.* Readers would not have had the slightest reason to question the attributions. After all, the identification of a play's original acting company was as important a mark of its authenticity as the playwright's name. Just as *A Midsummer Night's Dream* and *King Lear* were ascribed to Shakespeare's acting company, so *The London Prodigal* was published '*as it was played by the King's Majesty's Servants*' and the title page of *A Yorkshire Tragedy* carried the information that the play had been '*acted by his Majesty's Players at the Globe*'.

If one was a very keen Shakespearean, snouting around for every available text that might be associated with him, one might also have taken a punt on the purchase of a couple of play scripts attributed to a certain 'W. S.' Thus *The Lamentable Tragedy of Locrine,* published in 1595, was '*newly set forth, overseen and corrected, by W. S.*', while *The true chronicle history of Thomas Lord Cromwell,* published in 1602, was '*Written by W. S.*'

The latter, in particular, would have looked like a good bet, since the title page added 'As it hath been sundry times publicly Acted by the Right Honorable the Lord Chamberlain his Servants.' By 1602 William Shakespeare's name had appeared on the title page of several plays belonging to the Chamberlain's Men. No other 'W. S.' had a single play in print. You could be forgiven for jumping to the obvious conclusion as to the author's identity. A second edition, dated 1613, duly updated the company information in the light of the change of name attendant upon royal patronage: 'As it hath been sundry times publicly Acted by the King's Majesty's Servants.' The initials 'W. S.' remained. If our imaginary reader accepted these ascriptions, he or she might have gone away from the bookstalls with the impression that these two plays were also Shakespeare's work.

Whether or not William Shakespeare wrote a word of *The London Prodigal* and *A Yorkshire Tragedy,* they were among the plays ascribed to him in print in his own lifetime. Whether or not he had any association with *Locrine* and *Thomas Lord Cromwell,* there is a strong probability that the initials 'W. S.' were intended to give the impression that he was the author. These facts alone make the plays worth reading: even if they are not by Shakespeare, they are plays that were plausibly

---

* *A Pleasant conceited comedy called Love's Labours Lost newly corrected and augmented by W. Shakespeare* (1598); *The Tragedy of King Richard the Second by W. Shakespeare* (1598); *The Tragedy of King Richard the Third by William Shakespeare* (1598); *The History of Henry the Fourth with the Battle at Shrewsbury newly corrected by W. Shakespeare* (1599); *A Midsummer Night's Dream written by William Shakespeare* (1600); *The Second Part of Henry the Fourth written by William Shakespeare* (1600); *Much Ado about Nothing written by William Shakespeare* (1600); *The Merchant of Venice written by William Shakespeare* (1600); *A most pleasant and excellent conceited Comedy of Sir John Falstaff and the Merry Wives of Windsor by William Shakespeare* (1602); *The Tragical History of Hamlet Prince of Denmark by William Shakespeare* (1603); *Master William Shakespeare: his true chronicle history of the life and death of King Lear and his three daughters* (1608).

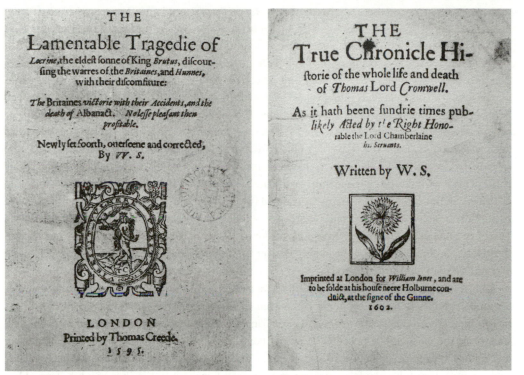

3. *Locrine*   4. *Thomas Lord Cromwell*

passed off as his. Three of the four came from the repertoire of the acting company in which he was a shareholder. He might have commissioned them. He might have polished up the raw scripts. As a key member of the company, he explicitly or implicitly signed them off for performance. He might have acted in them. He did not, as far as we are aware, dissociate himself or his company from them, as he did from the 1612 edition of the poetry anthology called *The Passionate Pilgrim* which was erroneously attributed to him. In that instance the poet and dramatist Thomas Heywood recorded that Shakespeare was 'much offended with Mr Jaggard [the publisher] that altogether unknown to him presumed to make so bold with his name'.

It was common for dramatists to be identified with initials before their full names appeared on title pages. George Peele and Thomas Middleton were dramatists with whom Shakespeare seems to have collaborated. The first publication of one of Peele's plays written for the public stage bore the initials 'G. P.' – it was printed in 1595, the same year as W. S.'s *Locrine*. Only in 1599 did the name 'George Peele' make it to the title page of a play script. Only in 1598 did the name 'William Shakespeare' make it to the title page of a play script. So too with Middleton: first he was identified as 'T. M.' and only once well established did he become 'Thomas Middleton.' Ben Jonson and John Marston were rivals to Shakespeare. They too made their first appearance in print in the form of initials, with several years passing before their full names were given on the title pages of their plays. Given that this was the pattern, the inference has to be that 'W. S.' was intended to mean William Shakespeare. Scholars have proposed alternative candidates, such as a certain Wentworth Smith, who received script payments from theatre manager Philip Henslowe, but no more than one of his plays survives and there is no evidence that he was active until after 1600. Shakespeare is the only candidate for W. S. conforming to the model of initials on an early play and then full name on the title page once he was established.

Precisely what role is being claimed for W. S. in relation to *The Lamentable Tragedy of Locrine?* The phrasing 'Newly set forth, overseen and corrected' may suggest that he was not the original playwright. The implication is rather that W. S. revised the play or corrected it or prepared it for the press, or some combination of these interventions. This possibility coheres neatly with a manuscript note on one of the surviving copies of the 1595 text, written in the hand of Sir George Buc, who later became Master of the Revels, the court officer in charge of the licensing of plays. Elsewhere, Buc reveals that he knew a lot about the London theatre world – on one occasion, he made a particular point of asking Shakespeare the identity of the author of a play called *George a Greene, the Pinner of Wakefield*. So Buc is a reliable witness. He claimed that *Locrine* was originally written under the title *Estrild*, the name of one of the female characters. And he said that the original author was Charles Tilney, cousin of Edmund Tilney, Buc's predecessor as Master of the Revels. Buc also claimed that he himself wrote 'dumb shows' (mimed interludes) for the play. Presumably he was referring to Tilney's original version, not the 1595 text.

Charles Tilney died, aged just twenty-five, in 1586. *Locrine* may therefore have gone through a number of mutations, beginning as an academic or court drama, much influenced by the old neo-Roman tragedy of *Gorboduc*, then disappearing for a while, then being revived in the public theatre in the early 1590s, when there was a considerable vogue for dramas of ancient history and bloody revenge. The published text includes an epilogue, clearly composed for a particular performance, that takes the form of a prayer for Queen Elizabeth in the thirty-eighth year of her reign, a year that began in November 1595. If Buc was telling the truth, the role of W. S. might have been to revise the play for the public stage, though there is no way of knowing whether that would have meant an extensive reworking or a quick tidying up. Alternatively, or additionally, his role might have been to write the 1595 epilogue and/or to prepare a script for publication.

We cannot be sure about any of this, just as we cannot be sure that W. S. really was Shakespeare. There is, however, plenty of other evidence that Shakespeare initially made his mark in the London theatre world as a fixer-up of other men's plays. Notoriously, the earliest clear allusion to his theatre work casts him in precisely this role. He had started out as an actor, arriving in London without a university degree to give him the status of 'gentleman'. Late in 1592, a pamphlet was published under the title *Greene's Groatsworth of Wit, bought with a Million of Repentance*. Prepared for the press by the playwright and printer Henry Chettle, it purportedly contained the dying wishes of the prolific writer Robert Greene, whose life had ended in squalor and poverty a few months before. One section took the form of a letter addressed 'To those Gentlemen his *quondam* acquaintance, that spend their wits in making plays.' The gentlemen in question are recognizable as Christopher Marlowe, Thomas Nashe and George Peele. The first two had, like Greene, graduated from Cambridge University, while Peele was an Oxford man. Collectively known by modern scholars as the 'university wits', they had written many of the best plays of the late 1580s and early 1590s, often working in collaboration with each other. The *Groatsworth* complains that the players – 'those puppets, I mean, that spake from our mouths, those antics garnished in our colours' – were getting rich on the back of the university men's labour, yet offering them minimal reward. Stop writing for the theatre, warns the voice of the dying Greene, or you will end up in my sorry condition. What is more, there is a new threat to the professional writers coming from within the acting trade:

Trust them not, for there is an upstart crow beautified with our feathers that, with his 'Tiger's heart wrapped in a player's hide', supposes he is as well able to bombast out a blank verse as the best of you: and being an absolute *Johannes Factotum*, is in his own conceit the only Shake-scene in a country. O that I might entreat your rare wits to be employed in more profitable courses: and let those apes imitate your past excellence and never more acquaint them with your admired inventions... whiles you may, seek you better masters, for it is a pity men of such rare wits should be subject to the pleasure of such rude grooms.

In the most famous scene in the early Shakespeare play *The True Tragedy of Richard Duke of York* (later known as *Henry VI Part 3*), the redoubtable Queen Margaret, 'she-wolf of France', taunts York with a paper crown and he responds by excoriating her 'tiger's heart wrapt in a woman's hide' (*Henry VI Part 3*, 1.4.111–49). The allusion to this line, with 'woman's hide' wittily changed to 'player's hide', together with the pun 'Shake-scene', leaves no room for doubt that the person under attack here is Shakespeare, the actor turned 'mender' of plays. The implication is that the actors, who are not gentlemen but lowly 'grooms' in the service of their patrons, are taking the 'inventions' of the freelance playwrights and altering them at their 'pleasure', particularly through the agency of the 'upstart crow'.

'Upstart' suggests Shakespeare's inferior social origin. *Johannes Factotum* means 'jack of all trades', an allusion to the perceived breach of decorum whereby he has dabbled in both the vulgar trade of acting and the genteel profession of writing. The jibe in the voice of Greene seems to have stung Shakespeare. He couldn't get that word 'beautified' out of his head: '"To the celestial and my soul's idol, the most beautified Ophelia"—That's an ill phrase, a vile phrase: "beautified" is a vile phrase', says Polonius in *Hamlet* (2.2.114–15).

Regardless of the unresolved question of W. S.'s hand in *Locrine*, the famous passage in the Chettle/Greene pamphlet takes us to the heart of the question of Shakespeare and collaborative playwriting. Shakespeare, says Greene, was one of the 'apes'. Actors were apes because they imitated the actions of real-life people. Shakespeare's double offence was to be an ape as an actor, then to be one as a writer: Greene's claim is that the 'upstart crow' has started writing in a style that ignobly imitated the literary elegance of his better-educated predecessors. 'Beautified with our feathers' is a pointed allusion to a passage in the Roman poet Horace concerning a crow ('cornicula') decked out in the stolen, coloured feathers of brighter birds ('furtivis coloribus'). The context in Horace's third epistle is a warning against poetic plagiarism. For our purposes, it does not matter whether Greene and Chettle were referring to some particular act of plagiarism or a more general sense in which Shakespeare was imitating his betters: the point is that Shakespeare was gaining a reputation as someone who 'newly set forth' material that was not originally his own.

In a poem called 'Greene's Funeral' (1594), one 'R. B.' (probably Richard Barnfield), repeated the accusation that had appeared in the *Groatsworth*: 'Greene gave the ground to all that wrote upon him; / Nay more, the men that so eclipsed his fame, / Purloined his plumes, can they deny the same?' There are indeed many senses in which Shakespeare's predecessors 'gave the ground' and that he 'wrote upon' them. Ever since the late eighteenth century, scholars have debated – lengthily, fiercely, without resolution – as to the extent to which the plays that really made Shakespeare's name, the three parts of *Henry VI* and the tragedy of *Titus Andronicus*, were revisions of older plays by others, collaborative works involving several playwrights, or the achievement of Shakespeare alone.

So, for example, in 1849 the German scholar G. G. Gervinus proposed that *The First Part of the Contention betwixt the two famous houses of York and Lancaster* and *The True Tragedy of Richard Duke of*

York were not in fact by Shakespeare. Other scholars picked up on the suggestion and over the years Greene and various other Oxbridge-educated dramatists – Peele, Thomas Lodge, even Christopher Marlowe – were put forward as the authors. If Shakespeare subsequently revised those anonymously published histories into the *Henry VI* plays of his First Folio, one would see the force of the accusation that he had stolen plumes that were not his own and 'eclipsed' Greene's 'fame'. In the twentieth century, however, this theory fell out of favour and the early versions of the second and third parts of *Henry VI* were more commonly regarded as 'Bad Quartos' – abbreviated and inaccurately reported acting texts – of genuine Shakespearean originals. But the debate remains open.

As for *Henry VI Part 1*, the consensus of early twenty-first-century scholars is that very little of it is by Shakespeare and quite a lot of it by Thomas Nashe, another of the 'university wits'. Equally, there is a widespread view that the first act of *Titus Andronicus* is by George Peele, but there is no consensus as to whether Shakespeare and Peele wrote in active collaboration or whether Shakespeare took over a play by Peele and made it more and more his own as the action progressed.

The precise details of the young Shakespeare's status as reviser, collaborator and possible purloiner will probably never be resolved. But here are some uncontested facts regarding a number of his other plays. A tragedy about Hamlet Prince of Denmark was in the London theatrical repertoire long before the earliest record of Shakespeare's *Hamlet*. Old plays from the 1580s about *The Famous Victories of Henry the Fifth* and *King Leir* were – together with various history books – among the sources that Shakespeare stitched together as he invented his *Henry V* and *King Lear*. There is a close but baffling relationship between Shakespeare's *The Taming of the Shrew*, only published in the 1623 First Folio, and an anonymous play called *The Taming of a Shrew*, published in 1594. There is an equally close but equally baffling relationship between Shakespeare's *The Life and Death of King John*, again only published in the 1623 First Folio, and an anonymous two-part play called *The Troublesome Reign of King John*, which was published in 1591 but reprinted in 1611 as 'Written by W. Sh.' and again in 1622 as 'Written by W. Shakespeare.' Both reprints were blatant attempts to pass the play off as Shakespeare's version of the story, which it wasn't.

Something similar happened with a later history play. The character of Sir John Falstaff in *Henry IV* was originally called Sir John Oldcastle. A descendant of the real historical Oldcastle happened to be Lord Chamberlain at the time, and it was because of the perceived insult to his illustrious ancestor that the name was changed to Falstaff. This controversy gave a rival acting company, the Lord Admiral's Men, the opportunity to stage their own two-part play, *The Life of Sir John Oldcastle*, which treated the historical character with much more respect. When the first part of that play was reprinted in 1619 it too was passed off as being 'Written by William Shakespeare' – which, of course, it wasn't. The publisher was clearly trying to con prospective purchasers into thinking that they were getting their hands on a Falstaff play.

The various forms of 'newly setting forth' implied in these cases run the gamut from imitating to borrowing to revising to wholly reworking, and perhaps from locally plagiarizing to broadly imitating. But they also include actively parodying, resisting and inverting, giving alternative treatment to the same story. The most thoroughgoing example of this latter process is the contrast between the happy 'romance' ending of the old *King Leir*, where the king is restored and Cordelia saved, and the almost apocalyptic tragic ending of Shakespeare's *King Lear*.

For the purposes of this edition, our working definition of 'collaborative plays' is not so broad as to include Shakespeare's source plays or such parallel works as *The Taming of a Shrew*, or indeed such acts of publishing legerdemain as the fraudulent ascription of *The Troublesome Reign* and *Sir John Oldcastle* to Shakespeare. So what is the basis for our inclusions and exclusions?

In answering that question, the broader context must be considered. Where do we draw the borders of the Shakespearean 'canon'?* How much can we know about the extent, and the kinds, of his collaborative work? What has been, and is now, the status of those plays outside the 'authorized' First Folio which have, either in their own time or since, been attributed or part-attributed to Shakespeare?

These are questions which have been debated ever since the eighteenth century, but in which there has been considerable new interest in the last twenty years, for two principal reasons. Firstly, there has been a renewed willingness to approach Shakespeare as a working man of the theatre and a collaborative author, not a solitary genius. And, secondly, the advent of large digitized online databases of early modern corpora, together with sophisticated computerized search techniques, has brought new rigour to the science of 'stylometry' – the identification of authorship on the basis of what might be called 'linguistic fingerprinting'.

Surprisingly though, given the huge amount of Shakespeare-related publication in recent decades, the primary prerequisite for the discussion of the collaborative or non-canonical Shakespeare beyond the specialized arena of stylometric scholarship, remains startlingly absent: there has not been a collected edition of this group of plays since C. F. Tucker Brooke's *The Shakespeare Apocrypha*, published in 1908. Indeed, until now there has *never* been a modern spelling (and thus theatrically usable), or an annotated, or a critically and theatrically introduced, edition of the so-called apocrypha. This gap – perhaps the single most significant lacuna in twenty-first-century Shakespearean scholarship – is what we seek to fill here, in a volume intended as a supplement and companion to our RSC *William Shakespeare: Complete Works* (2007). In order to keep the many unresolved questions open and to avoid the quasi-biblical (and thus unhelpfully bardolatrous) associations of the word 'apocrypha', we call our edition *William Shakespeare and Others: Collaborative Plays*.

The First Folio and the Creation of the Shakespeare Canon

The Elizabethan and Jacobean era was the time when the business of professional acting and writing came into being. Permanent playhouses were built in London for the first time. Professional acting companies operated as profitable capitalist enterprises. Star actors made their fortunes. Audiences could go to the theatre almost every day and see several different plays each week. Writers could (just about) make a living through commercial transactions as opposed to aristocratic patronage. It was a new world of public entertainment, in which product – in the form of new scripts – was as hungrily consumed as it would be in the golden age of the Hollywood studios.

Just as the studio names and the star actors dominated the public perception of twentieth-century Hollywood, with the scriptwriting teams very much in the background, so in Shakespeare's time celebrity belonged to the acting companies – most notably the Chamberlain's/King's Men at the Globe and the Lord Admiral's at the Rose – and the lead players (Edward Alleyn and Richard Burbage in tragedy, Will Kempe and Robert Armin in comedy). Especially in the earlier years, it

---

* The word 'canon', together with its corollary 'apocrypha', was originally theological. The terms were not applied to Shakespeare or other secular authors until the nineteenth century. In AD 393 the Synod of Hippo, under the authority of St Augustine, approved the canon of books that made up the New Testament. All other Gospels and Epistles were henceforth deemed apocryphal or non-canonical. The New Testament canon was thus closed, though during the Reformation Martin Luther tried to remove several books. The Old Testament canon was unstable for longer, but was dogmatically articulated (for the Roman Catholic Church) by the Council of Trent in 1546. The Church of England's – slightly different – canon was fixed seventeen years later among the Thirty-Nine Articles of Anglican faith. In both Roman and Protestant traditions, a selection of apocryphal books continued to be printed along with the Holy Scripture. In Luther's German translation of the Bible (1534) these were placed between the Old and New Testaments, with the title 'Apocrypha, that is, books which are not held equal to the sacred Scriptures, and nevertheless are useful and good to read.' A similar judgement could perhaps be applied to the plays edited here.

was the exception rather than the rule for a scriptwriter to be given any kind of billing. Posters advertising new plays do not, alas, survive, but all the evidence suggests that they would have given company, theatre and title, but not scriptwriter's name. It appears that no author's name appeared on a playbill until 1693, when William Congreve was advertised as author of *The Double-Dealer.* John Dryden noted that 'the printing of an Author's name, in a Play bill, is a new manner of proceeding, at least in England'.

Since many plays were published anonymously, it is often exceptionally difficult to work out which playwright or playwrights wrote which script. *The Spanish Tragedy* is widely regarded as one of the foundational plays of the Elizabethan theatrical repertoire. We know that the two greatest tragic actors of the age, first Edward Alleyn and then Richard Burbage, played the lead part of Hieronimo. But the only reason why we know that the original author was Thomas Kyd is a passing remark to this effect in Thomas Heywood's defence of theatre against the strictures of the Puritans, *An Apology for Actors* (1612). Nobody noticed the reference until 1773: in its own time, and for nearly two centuries more, *The Spanish Tragedy* was an anonymous play. Similarly, another hugely influential drama, the mighty two-part *Tamburlaine the Great*, was published in 1590 with an elaborate title page, talking up the Lord Admiral's Servants and the many performances of the show 'upon stages in the city of London'. But there is no mention of the playwright. The author did not live to see his name in print: the attribution 'Chri. Marlow *Gent.*' appeared on a published playbook for the first time in 1598, the same year as Shakespeare's first such naming. For Marlowe, several years dead in Deptford, it was on the title page of his *Edward II*.

We do know about the authorship of many lesser plays – the vast majority of them never printed and thus lost for ever – because of the survival of the account books of Philip Henslowe, owner of the Rose Theatre in the 1590s. The Henslowe documents, now at Dulwich College, are stuffed with suggestive entries: 'Lent unto Harry Chettle at the request of Robert Shaw the 25 of November 1598 in earnest of his comedy called *'Tis No Desert to Deserve the Deserver* and for mending of *Robin Hood* for the court – 10 shillings'; 'Paid unto Mr Drayton and Mr Dickers [Dekker] the 30 of December 1598 for a book called *The Three Parts of the Civil Wars of France* the sum of – five pounds'; 'Lent unto Benjamin Jonson at the appointment of E. Alleyn and William Bird the 22 of June 1602 in earnest of a book called *Richard Crookback* and for new additions to *Jeronimo* the sum of – ten pounds.' Henslowe's records give an incomparable insight into the working life of the London theatre. Sums loaned to hard-pressed playwrights in a manner analogous to a modern publisher's 'advance' upon a promised work. The 'mending' of old plays for new performances, whether in response to a command appearance at court or simply a desire to refit an old perennial with 'additions'. The commissioning of new works to compete with successful titles in the rival repertoire: if the Lord Chamberlain's Men were still going strong with Burbage as Shakespeare's hunchbacked Richard III, the Lord Admiral's would have to mount their own *Richard Crookback*, from the pen of a rising young scriptwriter called Ben Jonson (we don't know if he ever finished or delivered it). Above all, Henslowe's meticulous records reveal that the prevailing model of playwriting was collaboration: in the mind's eye, one sees Drayton and Dekker poring over source material together as they hammer out the three parts of their history of the French civil wars, or Munday, Drayton, Chettle and Smythe sharing out the meagre proceeds of four pounds (one up front and three on delivery) for *The First Part of Cardinal Wolsey*. If only there survived a similar account book in the hand of Shakespeare's intimate friend John Hemings, business manager of the Lord Chamberlain's and later King's Men, so many of the unanswered questions about the extent of Shakespeare's collaborations would be answered.

The first dramatist who seems to have been seriously interested in publishing his own plays, and distinguishing between his own work and that of his collaborators, was Ben Jonson. He introduced onto his title pages such formulations as 'The Author', 'Composed by Ben Jonson' and 'Made by Ben Jonson', all terms newly suggestive of a higher degree of both proprietorship and creative craft than had been claimed for other plays. In the case of his tragedy *Sejanus his Fall*, he made a point of excluding the work of his collaborator from the printed text: 'I would inform you that this Book, in all numbers, is not the same with that which was acted on the public Stage, wherein a second pen had good share; in place of which I have rather chosen to put weaker (and no doubt less pleasing) of mine own, than to defraud so happy a *Genius* of his right, by my loathed usurpation.' Since *Sejanus* was acted by the King's Men in 1603, with 'Will Shakespeare' among the 'principal Tragedians', there has to be a strong possibility that the 'happy *Genius*' who wielded the 'second pen' was Shakespeare himself (though George Chapman has also been proposed).

In 1616, Jonson collected a selection of his plays, poems and court entertainments in the high-end publishing format known by bibliographers as a Folio. He gave his volume the title *The Works of Benjamin Jonson*. This was considered by many to be somewhat self-promoting. The range of genres and the title suggested an attempt to replicate in the vernacular a collection along the lines of the *opera* ('complete works') of a classical poet such as Virgil or Horace. The publication that same year, and in a very similar format, of *The Works of the most high and mighty Prince, James by the grace of God, King of Great Britain, France and Ireland, Defender of the Faith*, added to the sense of presumption.

The Jonson Folio established two key ideas: the play as a *work*, which is to say a literary composition as opposed to a raw script for performance, and the contemporary playwright as an *author* with what we now call a *canon*. That is to say, Jonson excluded not only his hackwork (there are no 'new additions to *Jeronimo*') but also his collaborative plays: the Folio does not include *The Isle of Dogs* (co-written with Nashe), *Hot Anger soon Cold* (with Chettle and Porter), *Page of Plymouth* (with Dekker), *Robert II King of Scots* (with Chettle, Dekker and 'another Gentleman'), or *Eastward Ho!* (with Chapman and Marston). This decision would have momentous consequences for the afterlife of Shakespeare, who died in that same year of 1616.

In 1619, a publisher of somewhat mixed repute called Thomas Pavier printed editions of *Henry V*, the two *Henry VI* plays (with the joint title *The whole contention between the two famous houses, Lancaster and York*), *King Lear*, *The Merchant of Venice*, *The Merry Wives of Windsor*, *A Midsummer Night's Dream*, *Pericles* and two other plays attributed to Shakespeare, *The First Part of Sir John Oldcastle* and *A Yorkshire Tragedy*. An element of through-pagination suggests that this was intended as some kind of 'collected Shakespeare', following the precedent of the Jonson Folio. With the assistance of their patron, the Earl of Pembroke, the leading players of the King's Men (Richard Burbage, John Hemings and Henry Condell) obtained an order preventing Pavier, or anyone else, from going any further with such an enterprise. It was probably at this time that the actors began considering the possibility of a collected Shakespeare of their own. Burbage died later in 1619, so Hemings and Condell carried forward the project. Materials were gathered and printing began in 1621. The First Folio (so named for the large size and single fold of its paper) eventually appeared in 1623. Jonson and others provided prefatory poems in celebration of Shakespeare's genius. The volume included thirty-six plays, but not – in contrast to the Jonson Folio – any of the non-dramatic poems. Among the thirty-six were seventeen that had been published in Shakespeare's lifetime, *Othello* (which had appeared independently, in a variant text, in 1622), and eighteen hitherto unpublished plays, a couple of which had been licensed for earlier publication that did not materialize.

Given that the Folio was modelled on the Jonsonian precedent and authorized by the foremost survivors of Shakespeare's acting company, it is hardly surprising that the contents of this great book have often been considered his 'complete works'. The thirty-six Folio plays represent the Shakespeare 'canon'. The general assumption is that in the case of any play *included* in the First Folio the burden of proof is on the sceptic to show that it is *not* by Shakespeare, whereas in the case of any play *excluded* from the First Folio the burden of proof is on the collaborationist to prove that it *is*, albeit partly, by Shakespeare. No play outside the First Folio has gained widespread acceptance as being wholly by Shakespeare.

However, the moment one begins to investigate the publishing history of the Folio, matters become a great deal more complicated. Shakespeare was not around to supervise the question of inclusions and exclusions, as Jonson had been for his Folio. Jonson had made a point of including poems as well as plays, and had Shakespeare been alive he would almost certainly have pressed for the same policy. After all, he had fully authorized the publication of his early narrative poems, *Venus and Adonis* and *The Rape of Lucrece*, complete with dedicatory epistles signed in his own name. Scholars are divided as to whether or not Shakespeare also authorized the publication of his *Sonnets*, but given the emphasis in so many of them on the idea of cheating death and achieving immortality through poetry, it would have been natural to include them in a 'complete works' destined for posterity.

With those plays that had already appeared in print, there was also the question of publishing rights. Several different publishers held the rights to the Quartos. In some cases, those rights had been passed from one owner to another, or were a matter of dispute. So, for example, it seems that the publishers of the Folio intended to include *Troilus and Cressida* among the tragedies, but then discovered that the rights were not available. *Timon of Athens*, which it would seem they did not originally intend to include at all, was therefore put into the space left by this omission, but since it was a lot shorter than *Troilus* several blank pages were left at the end once it had been set up in type. Then, at the last minute, even after the printing of the contents list of all the plays in the book (the 'catalogue'), *Troilus and Cressida* was obtained after all. The printers squeezed the text in between the Histories and Tragedies, but did not amend the contents list, from which this title remains absent. Was *Timon of Athens* to be left out because it was unfinished or in an unsatisfactory manuscript, because it was never performed, or because it was a collaboration between Shakespeare and Thomas Middleton? We will never know, but what this story shows is that chance and circumstance played a role in the shaping of the First Folio canon.

Where is *Love's Labour's Won*? There is firm evidence that Shakespeare wrote such a comedy and a strong suggestion, in the form of a fragment of a bookseller's catalogue, that it was printed in Quarto. Why was *Henry VIII* included but *The Two Noble Kinsmen* and the lost *Cardenio* excluded, given that all three were collaborations with John Fletcher? If the Jonson Folio was the model, and it excluded the dramatist's early collaborative works, why did the Shakespeare Folio include such early and probably collaborative works as *Henry VI Part 1* and *Titus Andronicus*? Since it included these, why did it exclude other probable early and collaborative works such as *Edward III* and possibly *Arden of Faversham*? How confident can we be that Hemings and Condell remembered, or even knew, every detail of Shakespeare's early career as a 'mender' of plays prior to the formation of the Lord Chamberlain's Men in 1594, at which point he became shareholder and company dramatist, embarking, at least initially, on a process of solo-authoring that was a highly innovative form of scriptwriting?

The exclusion of *The London Prodigal* and *A Yorkshire Tragedy* is usually taken to be firm evidence of their inauthenticity. The frequently played and oft reprinted *The late and much admired play, called Pericles, Prince of Tyre, by William Shakespeare* (1609), was also excluded, and yet all scholars now agree that its second half is authentically Shakespearean. Could these three omissions have been because the plays were collaborative, not because they were inauthentic? At the very least, the omission of *Pericles* had the effect of moving a collaborative play to the margin of the canon for nearly two hundred years.

A decade after its first publication, the Folio went into a second edition. There was a new printer: the huge job that had been undertaken the first time by the Jaggard family together with Edward Blount now went into the printing shop of a man named Thomas Cotes. Two years later, Cotes printed an edition of *The Two Noble Kinsmen* with the title-page ascription,

> Written by the memorable Worthies of their time;
> Mr *John Fletcher*, and
> Mr *William Shakespeare*. } Gent.

This could be described as the moment when the persona of 'collaborative Shakespeare' definitively came into being. Yet the following year Cotes printed a new edition of *Pericles*, continuing the ascription of it to Shakespeare alone. So here are two collaborative plays, appearing in quick succession as a kind of supplement to the Second Folio, but one described as jointly written and the other as solo-authored. Both are included in almost all modern editions of Shakespeare's collected plays. We now turn our attention to the later history of the uncollected plays: those that were given neither to the Jaggards and Blount in the early 1620s, nor to Cotes in the early 1630s.

A Brief History of the Shakespeare Apocrypha

King Charles I was a great fan of Shakespeare. He owned a copy of the Second Folio and personally annotated its catalogue of plays with the names of his favourite characters, writing 'Bennedike and Beatrice' beside *Much Ado about Nothing* and 'Malvolio' beside *Twelfth Night*. Perhaps stimulated by His Majesty's enthusiasm, the royal librarian bound together a group of other plays and labelled them 'Shakespeare Vol. 1'. The collection consisted of four plays that had been published in quarto under the name William Shakespeare or W. S. (*Thomas Lord Cromwell*, *The London Prodigal*, *The Puritan or the Widow of Watling Street* and *The First Part of Sir John Oldcastle*), two anonymous comedies from the repertoire of the King's Men (*The Merry Devil of Edmonton* and *Mucedorus*), a comedy called *Fair Em* dating from the early 1590s, and, curiously, given the presence of the play within the Folio, a recent reprint of the Quarto of *Love's Labour's Lost* (was this in some sense standing in for the lost *Love's Labour's Won*?). It has recently been argued that this 'nonce' volume, broken up in the eighteenth century, was the first attempt to create a collection of 'doubtful' Shakespeare plays – what would later come to be called an 'apocrypha' – to stand alongside the Folio.*

Something similar happened on a grander scale with the second issue of the Third Folio in 1664. As the title page reveals, the publisher Philip Chetwind added to the thirty-six Folio plays a further

---

* Peter Kirwan, 'The First Collected "Shakespeare Apocrypha"', *Shakespeare Quarterly*, 62(4) (2011), pp. 594–601. This whole section of our General Introduction is much indebted to Kirwan's doctoral thesis and forthcoming book, researched as an integral part of our project, *Shakespeare and the Idea of Apocrypha: Negotiating the Boundaries of the Dramatic Canon* (University of Warwick, 2011).

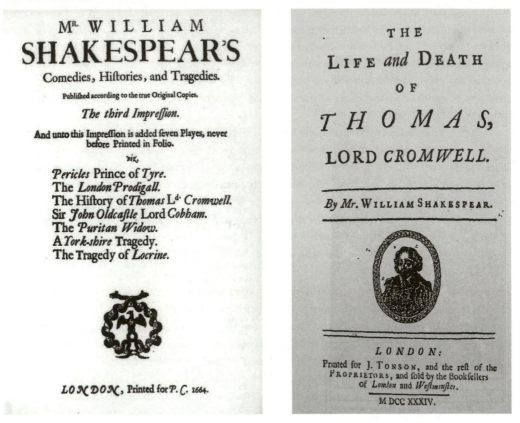

5. Title page of the 1664 Third Folio   6. 1734 edition of *Thomas Lord Cromwell*

seven, all of which had been printed in Quarto with either 'Shakespeare' or 'W. S.' on their title page. Those seven plays remained part of the Shakespeare canon in the Fourth Folio of 1685.

Interestingly, Chetwind did not include two plays published as collaborative works: *The Two Noble Kinsmen* by Shakespeare and Fletcher, and *The Birth of Merlin*, published in 1662 with the claim that it was 'written by William Shakespeare and William Rowley'. The exclusion may have been a matter of rights, but it suggests a continuation of the pattern whereby collaborative works were somehow valued less than supposedly solo-authored plays.

The first editor to regularize Shakespeare's texts and modernize his spelling – Nicholas Rowe in 1709 – duly included the seven extra plays in his edition. It was only with the editions of Alexander Pope and Lewis Theobald in the 1720s and 1730s that the canon shrank back down to thirty-six plays. Even then, the additional plays appeared in small format, cheap editions from the rival publishers Tonson and Walker, who were battling for market share in popular Shakespeare. It still gives pause for thought when we see a title page such as that of *The Life and Death of Thomas Lord Cromwell by Mr William Shakespear*, which appeared under the imprint of the powerful Tonson publishing house in 1734.

Some of the non-Folio plays also had a continuing life on the London stage, albeit usually in adapted form. *Pericles* was revived as *Marina* and *The London Prodigal* loosely adapted as *The Spendthrift*. The process was no different from that entailed in the rewriting of many of the Folio plays in versions that conformed to the conventions of the Restoration and eighteenth-century stage (*Macbeth* with all-singing, all-dancing witches and *Lear* with a happy ending).

Pope had been the first to dismiss the seven extra works as 'wretched plays' which could not possibly have been by Shakespeare. By the late eighteenth century this had become a settled opinion. Scholars such as Edward Capell and Edmond Malone examined Shakespeare's texts and language with new rigour, while the authority of the Folio took on new force. Most of the non-Folio plays were consigned to outer darkness. *Pericles* was the one exception: Malone's influential edition of 1790 did not distinguish it from the Folio plays, and from this point on it effectively became part of the canon.

During this same period, serious gentleman scholars began looking closely at the wider body of anonymously published Elizabethan plays. In 1760 Edward Capell published an edition of the historical drama of *Edward III*, with an attribution to Shakespeare based not on any external evidence but on an instinctive sense that it had strong resemblances of language and dramatic style to Shakespeare's early plays. Other scholars noticed that the memorable line 'Lilies that fester smell far worse than weeds' appears both in this play (published 1596) and at the climax of Shakespeare's Sonnet 94 (not published until 1609). The phrase was not in common or proverbial usage – in Elizabethan English, it was usually wounds or souls that 'festered', not flowers. The precise verbal parallel could hardly have been a coincidence: it might have been a casual borrowing, but could it also have been a sign of Shakespeare's hand in the play? The argument has rumbled on for 250 years, but it is now widely believed by scholars that Shakespeare did indeed contribute the tightly-written scenes in which King Edward attempts to seduce the Countess of Salisbury. The Royal Shakespeare Company staged *Edward III* in the Swan Theatre in Stratford-upon-Avon in 2002. Our edition includes interviews with the actors who played the king and the Countess.

Ten years after Capell's *Edward III*, a gentleman-scholar called Edward Jacob, from Faversham in Kent, published an edition of a superb Elizabethan domestic tragedy set in his home town: *The Lamentable and True Tragedy of Mr Arden of Feversham ... with a Preface in which some reasons are offered in favour of its being the earliest dramatic work of Shakespear now remaining.* Jacob's argument was based partly on a subjective sense of quality: what other dramatist working in the early 1590s could have written such a good tragedy? (A question to which one answer might be Christopher Marlowe, a man of Kent.) But it was also grounded in the comparison of parallel passages, a technique that would become the staple of authorship studies in the field – something which remains the case, albeit now using more 'objective' methods involving computer software, lexical scatter charts and statistical probability. The most recent analyses lean strongly towards support for Jacob's instinctive feel that Shakespeare's hand is somewhere in *Arden*, most probably in the powerful scene when Alice Arden quarrels with her love, Mosby. Regardless of the possible Shakespearean contribution, *Arden of Faversham* is a murder story that merits its continuing place in the repertory. Our edition includes an interview with Terry Hands, who has directed the play at both the RSC and Clwyd Theatr Cymru.

The Countess of Salisbury and Alice Arden are two of the strongest female roles in the drama of the early 1590s. It would be fitting if indeed they were both creations of Shakespeare's early pen, given how he went on to create the vast majority of the most memorable female roles in the entire repertoire of Elizabethan and Jacobean drama.

Among the other features for which Shakespeare became especially notable were scenes in which a skilful politician manipulates a crowd (think of *Richard III* or *Julius Caesar*) and speeches in

> ARDEN, Page 6. *Ile send from London such a taunting letter.*
> As you like it, Act III. Sc. 11. *I will write to him such a tau⌐*
> *ing letter.*
> Page 6. *With a verse or two stolen from a painted cloth.*
> As you like it, A. III. S. 7. *But I answer you right in the stile*
> *the painted cloth.*
> Page 8. *So lifts the sailor to the Mermaid's song.*
> Com. of Errors, A. III. S. 4. *I'll stop my ears against the M⌐*
> *maid's song.*
> Page 8. *So looks the travellour to the Basiliske.*
> Winter's Tale. *Make me not sighted like the Basiliske.*
> Page 25. *A lean faced writhin knave, &c.*
> Com. of Errors. A. V. S. 5. *A hungry, lean faced villain, &c.*
> Page 40. *The white livered peasant.*
> Mer. of Ven. A. III. S. 2. *Liver as white as Milk.*
> Page 40. *And he shall buy his merriment as dear.*
> Com. of Errors, A. IV. S. 1. *But, Sirrah, you shall buy this s⌐*
> *as dear.*
> Page 40. *How now, Will, become a Precisian?*
> Mer. Wiv. of Windsor. A. II. S. 1. *Use Reason for his Precis⌐*
> Page 47. *That shews my heart a Raven for a Dove.*
> Mids. N. Dr. A. II. S. 7. *Who will not change a Raven for a D⌐*
> Page 55. *Home is a wild cat to a wandering Wit.*
> Othel. S. 5. *Wild cats in your kitchens.*
> Page 50. *You were best swear me on the in'errogatories.*
> Mer. of Ver. last. Sc. *And charge us there on interrogatories.*

7. Attribution on the basis of parallel passages: from the Preface to Jacob's 1770 edition of *Arden of Faversham*

which an audience is invited to imagine itself in the situation of someone very different from itself (at one extreme, Henry V showing us what it is like to be a king; at the other, King Lear sympathizing with homeless beggars in a storm). It was these characteristics, together with some very striking features of poetic vocabulary, that led an exceptionally intelligent Victorian critic, Richard Simpson, to suggest that Shakespeare was responsible for some of the 'additions' in a play called *Sir Thomas More* that survived in manuscript, having, it seems, been suppressed from the stage for reasons of political censorship (the first printed edition was published in 1844).

London apprentices are rioting on the streets, complaining that immigrants are taking their jobs. Sir Thomas More, sheriff of the city, calms them with a speech in which he forces them to confront the image of the 'strangers' being deported:

> Grant them removed, and grant that this your noise
> Hath chid down all the majesty of England.
> Imagine that you see the wretched strangers,
> Their babies at their backs, with their poor luggage
> Plodding to th'ports and coasts for transportation,
> And that you sit as kings in your desires,
> Authority quite silenced by your brawl,
> And you in ruff of your opinions clothed:
> What had you got? I'll tell you: you had taught
> How insolence and strong hand should prevail,
> How order should be quelled, and by this pattern
> Not one of you should live an agèd man,

> For other ruffians, as their fancies wrought,
> With selfsame hand, self-reasons, and self-right,
> Would shark on you, and men like ravenous fishes
> Would feed on one another.   (2.4.68–83)

The language here has all the features of Shakespeare's unique poetic intensity: look at the way in which the metaphor of dress ('in ruff of your opinions clothed') mutates via verbal play into the figure of 'other ruffians', which in turn leads to a noun ('shark') becoming a verb, which then leads to a further development of the image-cluster as the whole complex sentence and intricate thought ends with a simile run across the line ending ('and men like ravenous fishes – [momentary pause] – Would feed on one another'). Sharks entered the English language via mid-Elizabethan maritime travel narratives. 'Shark' becomes a verb for the first time with Shakespeare. He was master of this linguistic device of grammatical 'conversion'.

Early in the twentieth century, the handwriting of this added scene in the collaborative play of *Sir Thomas More* was submitted to minute forensic examination. Sir Walter Greg, the greatest Shakespearean bibliographer of the twentieth century, had established that no fewer than five different authorial hands (dubbed Hands A–E) had been involved in the process of making additions and revisions to the original version of the play. Then Sir Edward Maunde Thompson of the British Museum, the world's leading palaeographer, pronounced that Hand D truly was the Holy Grail of Shakespeare studies: an original working manuscript from the author's own pen. Maunde Thompson and a procession of subsequent experts have undertaken comparative analysis of the handwriting in hundreds of Elizabethan and Jacobean documents. As Will Sharpe reports in our detailed account of 'Authorship and Attribution', scholars have identified 'four orthographic features in Shakespeare's six acknowledged signatures which are totally unique, not found in any other document ... except for the Hand D passage, in which all four features (a "spurred *a*", a unique *w* form, a strange flourish in the *k* formation, and unique upstrokes in the *m* and *w* of Shakespeare's sixth signature) appear'.

Of all the claims we make about Shakespeare as a collaborator, the closest to a racing certainty is the remarkable fact that the only working manuscript in his hand is a single scene not from one of his solo-authored plays but from a multiple collaboration. Why did it survive when all his other working manuscripts are lost? Precisely because the play was never staged or printed. With other plays, there would have been no reason to keep the original manuscript once it was transcribed by the 'book-holder' (prompter/stage manager) in the theatre or set up in type by the compositor in the printing house.

Sir Thomas More has been staged on a number of occasions during the last fifty years. In 1964 a production at the Nottingham Playhouse starred the young Ian McKellen, his costume resembling the famous Holbein portrait of More.

The speech to the rioters has remained a favourite of McKellen's, used as a set-piece in his one-man showcase of Shakespeare's language, as it was to equally striking effect on audiences in Simon Callow's biographical theatre event *Being Shakespeare* (2010–12). The RSC staged a production in the Swan Theatre in 2005. We include interviews with the director and the actor who played More.

Paradoxically, then, there is a greater likelihood of Shakespeare having contributed to three plays on which his name does not appear – *Edward III*, *Arden of Faversham* and *Sir Thomas More* – than to several of those on which his name did appear in his lifetime. Equally, his almost certain contribution to the revision of *Sir Thomas More* strongly suggests that in his capacity as resident

8. Hand D in *Sir Thomas More*: a unique record of Shakespeare in the act of writing
© The British Library Board 11765.s.11

9. Ian McKellen as Thomas More, 1964
© Ian McKellen

playwright for the Chamberlain's/King's Men he was responsible for writing or, to use the term on the title page of *Locrine*, 'overseeing', the reworking of old plays for new occasions.

It has often been suggested that the brilliantly-written 'new additions' in the 1602 edition of Kyd's *Spanish Tragedy* were synonymous with Henslowe's payment to Ben Jonson for 'new additions to *Jeronimo*', but chronology, style and several other considerations make this most unlikely. We know that the role of Hieronimo was in the repertoire of Shakespeare's leading man Burbage. It is quite probable that the popularity of *The Spanish Tragedy* was such that the two principal rival acting companies each had their own version of the play, and that the amendments, enlargements and additions in the 1602 text were those of the Chamberlain's Men. Recent computer-assisted analysis has added strong support to a suggestion that goes all the way back to the infinitely subtle Romantic poet and critic Samuel Taylor Coleridge: 'The parts pointed out in Hieronimo as Ben Jonson's bear no traces of his style; but they are very like Shakespeare's; and it is very remarkable that every one of them reappears in full form and development, and tempered with mature judgment, in some one or other of Shakespeare's great pieces' (*Specimens of the Table Talk of S. T. Coleridge*, 5 April 1833).

Again, is it a coincidence that *Mucedorus* – probably the most popular comedy of the age, as *The Spanish Tragedy* was the most popular tragedy – was revived by the King's Men in about 1610 with new additions incorporating a live bear, at precisely the time when the company first staged a new Shakespeare play, *The Winter's Tale*, written very much in the 'romance' style of *Mucedorus* and featuring the direction '*Exit pursued by a Bear*'? Shakespeare and the author of the *Mucedorus* additions were writing for the same beast, quite possibly a young polar bear borrowed from Henslowe. It is just possible, though the extent of the additions is too small for stylometric conclusions to be robust one way or the other, that Shakespeare himself was the reviser of the old romance. The links with his acting company are sufficiently strong and the linguistic evidence sufficiently open for us to include both the 1602 edition of *The Spanish Tragedy* and the 1610 edition of *Mucedorus* in this volume.

In the course of the nineteenth century, numerous other dramas were considered as possible 'Doubtful Plays of Shakespeare'. His German translators A. W. von Schlegel and Ludwig Tieck had a

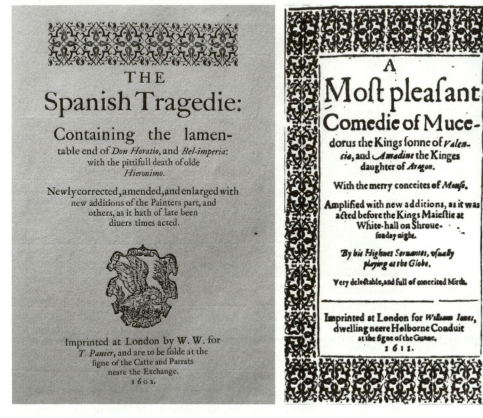

10. *The Spanish Tragedy*   11. *Mucedorus*

particularly capacious view of the extent of the canon. Then in 1908 C. F. Tucker Brooke produced an original spelling edition of *The Shakespeare Apocrypha, being a Collection of Fourteen Plays which have been ascribed to Shakespeare*. The Bard had by this time become a secular god (in 1901 George Bernard Shaw mockingly coined the word 'bardolatry'). If Shakespeare's work constituted a kind of English literary Holy Scripture, the *Comedies, Histories and Tragedies* of the Folio being his Old and New Testament, then there must also be an Apocrypha, and this was it. With *Pericles* having entered the canon, the fourteen apocryphal plays identified by Brooke were the other six from the Third Folio, three from Charles I's 'Shakespeare Vol. 1' (wrongly identified as Charles II's), the three attributed on the basis of internal evidence, and the two originally published as collaborative works (*The Two Noble Kinsmen* and *The Birth of Merlin*). But in his introduction Brooke listed about thirty other plays that had at one time or another been ascribed to Shakespeare.

In the course of the twentieth century, several more were added to this list, ranging from a hoary old history play in manuscript called *Edmond Ironside* to an interesting 'prequel' to *Richard II* that has become known as *Thomas of Woodstock*. None has gained wide favour, with the exception of *Double Falsehood; or the Distressed Lovers*. This is a special case because nobody believes that in itself it really is Shakespearean. It was first published in 1728 by the scholar and editor Lewis Theobald. He claimed that it was a lost Shakespeare play, which has subsequently been conjecturally identified with the *Cardenio* of Shakespeare and Fletcher that was performed at court in 1613. Some people thought (and some still do) that it was a forgery by Theobald. But the weight of modern scholarly opinion inclines to the view that the claim was genuine and that *Double Falsehood* does indeed bear the traces of Shakespeare and, predominantly, Fletcher, but only in the shadow form of a rewriting analogous to the other Restoration and early eighteenth-century adaptations of the plays. In 2011 director Gregory Doran 'reimagined' *Cardenio* for the Royal Shakespeare Company, making use of both *Double Falsehood* and the story's source, a sequence in Miguel de Cervantes' *Don Quixote*. Several other conjectural and semi-invented 'reconstructions' of *Cardenio* have also appeared in recent years. Rather than printing the Doran version, we provide texts of both Theobald's adaptation (or invention?) and the source material: the story of Cardenio's love-madness in Thomas Shelton's lively 1612 translation of the incomparable *Don Quixote*. We thus leave it to the reader to imagine Shakespeare and Fletcher's collaboration in the gap between source and vestige.

This Edition: Texts and Editorial Conventions

Our edition of *The RSC Shakespeare: Complete Works* began from the First Folio. Given Hemings and Condell's authorization of that book, inclusion therein is sufficient evidence for Shakespeare having had a major hand in thirty-six plays. Our policy for inclusion of non-Folio plays in the *Complete Works* edition was conservative: we required strong evidence, both external (attribution when first printed) and internal (stylistic and stylometric analysis), for Shakespeare's part-authorship. Only two plays met this rigorous test: *Pericles* (co-author George Wilkins) and *The Two Noble Kinsmen* (co-author John Fletcher). The riot-quelling scene from *Sir Thomas More* was also included: recent scholarship has reinforced the identification of Shakespeare with Hand D, but the limited and self-contained nature of the contribution meant that we did not see a case for including the whole play, as one or two other recent editions have.

Now, in the context of Shakespeare's collaborative plays, we restore Hand D to the full text of *Sir Thomas More*. We treat the revised version as a unified text, though in the footnotes we note the distribution of hands in the additions. So too with *Edward III* and *Arden of Faversham*: though Shakespeare's possible contributions are probably confined to a few scenes, we treat each play as a single work of art. With *The Spanish Tragedy* and *Mucedorus*, by contrast, we indicate the self-contained 'additions' – the moments of possible Shakespearean intervention in a prior non-Shakespearean text – by printing them in a different typeface from the rest of the play.

As far as the seven extra plays included in the 1664 Third Folio are concerned, we have excluded those that have decisively been shown *not* to be by Shakespeare. That is to say, *Sir John Oldcastle Lord Cobham* is clearly an Admiral's Men play by Drayton, Hathaway, Munday and Wilson; the ascription to Shakespeare was a blatant attempt to cash in on Falstaff's fame. Equally, *The Puritan Widow* was, as its original title page proclaimed, written for 'the Children of Paul's', one of the companies of boy actors who rivalled the adult professionals. Shakespeare never wrote for the boys' companies and, besides, a wealth of stylistic evidence reveals an exceptionally strong case for Thomas Middleton's authorship. With *Pericles* having been subsumed within the core canon, that leaves *The London Prodigal*, *A Yorkshire Tragedy*, *Thomas Lord Cromwell* and *Locrine*, all of which we include for consideration. Texts are edited from First Quartos, though we have collated later Quartos and Third Folio, and adopted some emendations, as indicated in our textual notes.

We include the 1610 edition of *Mucedorus* because of the close association between its revisions and the shift to a 'romance' style in Shakespeare's work and the repertoire of the King's Men more generally at this time. We regard the Charles I library attribution as tentative supporting evidence for its inclusion, but we do not follow Tucker Brooke in also including *Fair Em* and *The Merry Devil of Edmonton*. We thought long and hard about these two plays. The Charles I Second Folio reveals some inside knowledge of the work of the King's Men ('acted the part of Hamlet' is written against the name of their actor Joseph Taylor), so the librarian's attribution to Shakespeare may have had some foundation. A well-attested theatre story from the period *might* suggest that Shakespeare played the part of William the Conqueror in *Fair Em*, but that is not enough to suggest his part-authorship of the play. *The Merry Devil*, meanwhile, was a highly popular (and rather good) King's Men comedy. If it was by Shakespeare it would surely have been included in the Folio. Stylistically, it reads as a solo-authored play, not a collaborative work. The prolific Thomas Dekker is the likeliest author. We also exclude *The Birth of Merlin*, since recently-discovered evidence shows that it was licensed as a new play in 1622, well after Shakespeare's death. Detailed reasoning for all our inclusions and exclusions is provided in Will Sharpe's extended essay on 'Authorship and Attribution'.

Each **text** is freshly edited from its first printed editions or from the revised manuscript in the case of *Sir Thomas More* and the first printed edition with 'additions' in the cases of *The Spanish Tragedy* and *Mucedorus*. That is to say, our base text is the version of the play that reflects the moment of putative Shakespearean intervention.

Textual Notes at the end of each play indicate major departures from the base text. They take the following form: the line reference and reading of our text are given first, with its source following an equals sign, 'Q' indicating that it derives from the principal Quarto (or 'MS' in the case of *More*) and 'Ed' that it derives from the editorial tradition. Where we emend, the rejected Q or MS reading is also given.

Lists of Parts are in most but not all cases editorial, arranged by groups of characters. Capitals indicate the part of the name that is used for speech headings in the script (thus in *Edward III*, 'COUNTESS of Salisbury'). At the head of *Mucedorus* we also include a fascinating doubling chart from the Quarto ('Ten persons may easily play it').

Speakers' Names are often inconsistent in the original scripts; we have regularized for ease of use, but where appropriate have retained the wording of original entry directions.

Locations are rarely provided in original Elizabethan and Jacobean drama scripts. Eighteenth-century editors, working in an age of elaborately realistic stage sets, were the first to provide detailed locations. Given that Shakespeare and his contemporaries wrote for a bare stage and often an imprecise sense of place, we have relegated locations to the explanatory notes at the foot of the page, where they are given at the beginning of each scene where the imaginary location is different from the one before. We have emphasized broad geographical settings rather than specifics of the kind that suggest anachronistically realistic staging.

Act and Scene Divisions were treated very variably in the original scripts of these plays. Our practice has been to follow the convention that seems best for each work. Thus in some cases (e.g. *Locrine*) there is a clear five-act division on the classical model, while in others (for example, *The London Prodigal*) there is a straight run of scenes that is best treated as a single sequence rather than divided into acts.

Verse is indicated by lines that do not run to the right margin and by capitalization of the first letter of each line. Compositors sometimes set verse as prose, and vice versa (either out of misunderstanding or for reasons of space). We have silently corrected in such cases, although in some instances there is ambiguity, in which case we have leaned towards the preservation of the original layout. Most printed play texts used contraction ('turnd' rather than 'turned') to indicate whether or not the final '-ed' of a past participle is sounded, an area where there is variation for the sake of the five-beat iambic pentameter rhythm. We use the convention of a grave accent to indicate sounding (thus 'turnèd' would be two syllables), but would urge actors not to overstress. In cases where one speaker ends with a verse half-line and the next begins with the other half of the pentameter, editors since the late eighteenth century have indented the second line. We have abandoned this convention, since the original scripts do not use it, and nor did actors' cues in the Shakespearean theatre. An exception is made when the second speaker actively interrupts or completes the first speaker's sentence.

Spelling is modernized, but older forms are occasionally maintained where necessary for rhythm or aural effect.

Punctuation in Shakespeare's time was as much rhetorical as grammatical. 'Colon' was originally a term for a unit of thought in an argument. The semi-colon was a new unit of punctuation (some of the Quartos lack them altogether). We have modernized punctuation throughout, but have given more weight to original punctuation than many editors since, though not authorial, it reflects the usage of the period. In particular, we have used the colon far more than many editors: it is exceptionally useful as a way of indicating how dramatic speeches unfold clause by clause in a developing argument that gives the illusion of enacting the process of thinking in the moment. We have also kept in mind the origin of punctuation in classical times as a way of assisting the actor and orator: the comma suggests the briefest of pauses for breath, the colon a middling one and a full stop or period a longer pause. Semi-colons, by contrast, belong to an era of punctuation that was only just coming in during Shakespeare's time and that is coming to an end now: we have accordingly only used them where they occur in our copy-texts (and not always then). Dashes are sometimes used for parenthetical interjections where the original texts have brackets. They are also used for interruptions and changes in train of thought. Where a change of addressee occurs within a speech, we have used a dash preceded by a full stop (or occasionally another form of punctuation). Often the identity of the respective addressees is obvious from the context. When it is not, this has been indicated in a marginal stage direction.

Entrances and Exits are fairly thorough in most of the original texts, which have accordingly been followed as faithfully as possible. Where characters are omitted or corrections are necessary, this is indicated by square brackets (e.g. '[*and Attendants*]').

Editorial Stage Directions such as stage business, asides, indication of addressee and of characters' position on the gallery stage, are only used sparingly in the original texts. We have sought to distinguish what could be described as *directorial* interventions of this kind from more basic exit and entrance directions (either original or supplied) by placing them in the right margin in a different typeface. There is a degree of subjectivity about which directions are of which kind, but the procedure is intended as a reminder to the reader and the actor that theatrical stage directions are often dependent upon editorial inference alone and are not set in stone.

Line Numbers in the left margin are editorial, for reference and to key the explanatory and textual notes.

Explanatory Notes at the foot of each page explain allusions and gloss obsolete and difficult words, confusing phraseology, occasional major textual cruces, and so on. Particular attention is given to non-standard usage, bawdy innuendo, dialect and technical terms (e.g. legal and military language). Where more than one sense is given, commas indicate shades of related meaning, slashes alternative or double meanings.

Key Facts boxes at the beginning of each work give information on plot, sources, proportion of verse and prose, textual issues, authorial attribution, date of composition and first performance. They also include lists of substantial parts (characters who speak more than about forty lines) in descending order of size. Since the definition of a line spoken is variable (because of prose and half-lines), figures are given in terms of a percentage of the whole, the number of speeches delivered and the number of scenes the character is on stage. These lists make it possible to distinguish between works that are more ensemble-based (e.g. *Mucedorus*) and those that are dominated by a single character (e.g. *The Spanish Tragedy* and *Sir Thomas More*). Though there is a degree of imprecision about these lists as a result of editorial interventions, they offer much valuable information, not least with regard to the relative prominence of female roles.

Theatre was, and remains, an essentially collaborative art form. As actor, Shakespeare was collaborator in other men's plays. As shareholder, he was collaborator in the overall management of his theatre company, including choice and adjustment of repertoire. As principal shaper of 'company style' he steered the Chamberlain's/King's Men through two decades of ensemble work and inter-theatrical rivalry. As 'director' (of a kind – one imagines his role in rehearsal as akin to that of Peter Quince in *A Midsummer Night's Dream*), he was collaborator in the transformation of script to performance. And as scriptwriter, we know that he was a frequent collaborator, especially at the beginning and end of his career.

The full – or limited or even non-existent – extent of Shakespeare's involvement in the actual writing or rewriting of each of the ten plays edited here will probably never be known. But if we accept this broader definition of 'collaborative plays' we can say with certainty that these works represent a fascinating part of the repertoire in which he participated so centrally. *The Spanish Tragedy, Arden of Faversham* and *Locrine* take us to the foundations of Elizabethan tragedy, leading us on the path towards *Hamlet, Othello* and *King Lear. Edward III* complements the English history plays. *Thomas Lord Cromwell* and *Sir Thomas More*, like Shakespeare and Fletcher's later *Henry VIII*, stand among a group of intriguing plays about Tudor politics. *The London Prodigal* in comedy and *A Yorkshire Tragedy* in darker vein are excellent examples of the work of the King's Men at the height of their fame. *Mucedorus* and *Cardenio/Double Falsehood* are intimately bound to the turn to romance in the last years of Shakespeare's career. Whether or not some or all of them were indeed part-written or 'newly set forth' or 'overseen' by Shakespeare, the reading of them cannot fail to illuminate his theatrical world.

ARDEN OF FAVERSHAM

In classical times, tragedy meant the fall of a great hero or the tale of a larger-than-life figure out of mythology. At school, Shakespeare and his contemporaries would have learnt about Achilles and Hector, Hercules and Medea. The tragedies that set the pattern for popular theatre in the Elizabethan age told of mighty Tamburlaine the Great and Hieronimo the Knight Marshall of Spain. Shakespeare began his career in tragedy with the gory demise of a legendary Roman general called Titus Andronicus and the epic tale of the rise and fall of England's kings and dukes during the Wars of the Roses. But the early 1590s also witnessed a new phenomenon: tragedy at home, in the near-present and in a world akin to that of ordinary theatre-goers.

The story of the murder, in February 1551, of Thomas Arden of Faversham, a small but prosperous market town in Kent, appeared in the most famous history book of the age of Queen Elizabeth, Holinshed's *Chronicles*. It was soon dramatized for the London stage, providing the earliest (and best) example of the genre that scholars call 'domestic tragedy' – a breach of the classical idea that you can write comedies about ordinary people but must confine tragedy to kings and lords and heroes. The play was also the first detective procedural in English literature: in the final act, virtuous Franklin turns detective, tracing footprints and bloodstains.

The play's theatrical strengths have been revealed in a number of successful modern stage revivals: it has a unified and pacy plot, vivid and highly functional poetry, excitement in both the crime of passion and the process of detection, comedy in the serial incompetence of Black Will and Shakebag, and, above all, strong central characters – especially the figure of Alice Arden. Few other tragedies bring alive so vividly the ordinary matter of Elizabethan life. The stage-play world is made real through details of dress and diet, place names and customs. Black Will and Shakebag deploy a rich vernacular language as they tell of their track record of violence and mayhem: 'Sirrah Shakebag, canst thou remember since we trolled the bowl at Sittingburgh, where I broke the tapster's head of the Lion with a cudgel-stick?' They also dish out a good portion of salty humour: 'Didst thou ever see better weather to run away with another man's wife or play with a wench at potfinger'. The latter is a game that involves making popping sounds by rapidly removing a finger from the corner of the mouth, but playing it with a wench suggests another kind of finger and a different orifice.

'Two rougher ruffians never lived in Kent' says Michael, a line which sounds and looks even better in the original spelling and pronunciation, 'Ruffer Ruffins'. Hilariously, though, banal reality keeps foiling their plans. An apprentice is shutting up shop before the crowd comes out of St Paul's, bringing along potential shoplifters. He pulls down his shutters and breaks Black Will's head. Later, the English weather plays its part: fog causes another botch in the murder plan.

Self-consciously poetic language is generally avoided, though Arden evokes his past love for Alice by means of an allusion to the Roman erotic poet Ovid, as if to remind his wife that he is better educated than her new low-born lover:

> Sweet love, thou knowst that we two, Ovid-like,
> Have often chid the morning, when it 'gan to peep.
> And often wished that dark night's purblind steeds
> Would pull her by the purple mantle back.

And when servant Michael, getting cold feet about his participation in the plot, warns of the murderers' presence, there is a clear borrowing from a famous theatrical moment in Thomas Kyd's *The Spanish Tragedy*: Franklin's 'What dismal outcry calls me from my rest?' is an echo of Hieronimo's famous line 'What outcries pluck me from my naked bed?' But these moments are exceptional. Generally, the author keeps a focus on the story in Holinshed and the texture of the everyday world, rather than his literary and dramatic inheritance.

The drama opens a window onto the various strata of Elizabethan society. Mosby is of humble origin. He has become a servingman and then, as Arden sees it, wheedled his way to the position of steward in a nobleman's house. His status even allows him to wear clothes of silk, the very idea of which infuriates Arden. Mosby is not, however, entitled to wear a sword, as Arden reminds him when they draw to fight: there was a statute decreeing that only true gentlemen, not 'artificers', could bear arms. Arden's animosity towards Mosby is driven as much by class prejudice as sexual jealousy. Franklin offers some cold comfort by reminding him that women are often 'false and wavering'. Arden replies, 'Ay, but to dote on such a one as he / Is monstrous, Franklin, and intolerable.' He almost seems to be saying that he wouldn't mind if his wife were having an affair with someone richer or of higher status than himself.

The social spectrum of the stage-world of Faversham runs from a brief encounter with a lord via the measured presence of the well-to-do Franklin, through upwardly-mobile Arden himself to less well-off neighbours such as Greene and Reede, and down to his servant Michael and ultimately the masterless drifters, Black Will and Shakebag. Arden himself is a man on the make. Greene complains to Alice,

> Your husband doth me wrong
> To wring me from the little land I have.
> My living is my life, only that
> Resteth remainder of my portion.
> Desire of wealth is endless in his mind,
> And he is greedy gaping still for gain:
> Nor cares he though young gentlemen do beg,
> So he may scrape and horde up in his pouch.

And Dick Reede the sailor laments,

> Master Arden, I am now bound to the sea.
> My coming to you was about the plot of ground
> Which wrongfully you detain from me.
> Although the rent of it be very small,
> Yet will it help my wife and children
> Which here I leave in Faversham, God knows,
> Needy and bare. For Christ's sake, let them have it.

It is hard to sympathize with Arden, given his treatment of others as he grabs land and racks up rents.

At times, the play almost anticipates modern 'kitchen sink' drama in its portrayal of a marriage on the rocks and a messy love affair. The husband and wife are always at each other's throats.

'If well-attired, thou thinks I will be gadding: / If homely, I seem sluttish in thine eye', complains Alice, which is as if to say 'I can't win with you: if I dress up, you accuse me of wanting to attract other men, but if I don't, you accuse me of looking a mess.' On the other hand, she is in the game of attracting another man. Again, lines such as 'Husband sit down, your breakfast will be cold' and 'There's nothing that I do can please your taste' could be spoken by any disaffected wife, but in this instance they have piquancy because the breakfast in question has been poisoned. Alice describes herself to her husband as 'abused by thy misgovernment'. A dysfunctional household was often compared to a disrupted state; in the little kingdom of the Arden home, neither party is behaving as they should.

Unsympathetic as Arden frequently is, his jealousy is portrayed with conviction. He can't rest at home because he sees Alice's desire for Mosby in her every look and gesture, but can't rest in London because he can't stop imagining Mosby in his bed at home, making love to Alice. 'Then that base Mosby doth usurp my room, / And makes his triumph of my being thence': 'base' and 'usurp' continue the language of class antagonism, the suggestion that the love affair is a breach of the social order.

Alice, meanwhile, is a woman of strong will: 'he shall be mine'. She unashamedly speaks out against convention, dismissing marriage as a mere tie rather than a spiritual obligation: 'Love is a god and marriage is but words, / And therefore, Mosby's title is the best' (a nicely ironic use of 'title' in a play where questions of land ownership are central). Inevitably, this brazenness will bring her to a sticky end. In the final act, her guilt is quickly established. And the blood sticks to her hands in a manner that foreshadows Lady Macbeth. 'Susan, fetch water and wash away this blood', asks Alice. But they can't get rid of it: 'But with my nails I'll scrape away the blood: / The more I strive the more the blood appears.'

For the sake of social decorum, Alice must be brought to penitence and judgement. But that does not mean that we side with Arden. In the final speech of the play, Franklin becomes a chorus passing judgement and he finds a kind of divine justice in the greedy landowner's end: 'Arden lay murdered in that plot of ground / Which he by force and violence held from Reede'. The print of his body remains on the grass for two years after the deed, serving as admonition to all who pass by.

In the very final lines, Franklin describes the play as a 'naked tragedy' in which 'no filed points are foisted in'. It has presented 'simple truth' and no 'glossing stuff'. No fancy language here, this is as if to say, and the judgement is for the most part true. But one scene stands out for the much more multi-layered quality of its language and psychology.

Scene 8, the quarrel between Alice and Mosby, is drawn from imagination, not taken from Holinshed. Stylistically, it feels remarkably different from the rest of the play. Mosby enters with a self-revelatory soliloquy in which the dramatist seems to enact the very process of thought:

> Disturbèd thoughts drives me from company
> And dries my marrow with their watchfulness:
> Continual trouble of my moody brain
> Feebles my body by excess of drink
> And nips me as the bitter north-east wind
> Doth check the tender blossoms in the spring.

This is indeed a 'filed', closely worked language, combining the device of synecdoche (substitution of the part for the whole, marrow and brain for the body and the mind) with that of simile (comparison of the troubled self to spring blossoms nipped by late frost). Psychological realism is achieved with casual ease: Mosby has started drinking because he is stressed.

The writer is inside the character, thinking as a poet, making rapid connections, moving at speed from image to image, immediate detail to universalizing aphorism ('Well fares the man, howe'er his cates do taste, / That tables not with foul suspicion'), then back to the self, out to the process of social mobility and its consequences ('My golden time was when I had no gold. / Though then I wanted, yet I slept secure'), and then to the dilemma as to future action:

> The way I seek to find where pleasure dwells
> Is hedged behind me that I cannot back
> But needs must on although to danger's gate.

The rich vein of metaphor continues: from corn to beeswax and sting, to action as theatre ('Chief actors to Arden's overthrow'). And the future is vividly imagined:

> But what for that I may not trust you, Alice?
> You have supplanted Arden for my sake,
> And will extirpen me to plant another.

How is Mosby to know that she will not do to him what she has done to Arden?

At this point, Alice enters, with a prayerbook in hand. She is trying to be good, to resist temptation, but when she sees Mosby the fire of her desire is rekindled. There is then a brilliant enactment of the kind of row that adulterous lovers are always having. Each has it in mind to call off the affair, but the moment the other sounds as if they are going to do so, they change their mind and want it to carry on. They twist and turn until Mosby is won back by Alice's 'sweet-set tongue'. They embrace and one senses that if Bradshaw had not entered at this point they would have been making passionate love a moment later. It is a riveting piece of theatre.

A number of rare words in the scene such as 'copesmate' and 'sland'rous', together with some very distinctive image-clusters (notably a comparison of a troubled mind to a muddied fountain), have led some very sophisticated stylistic analysts to suggest that this scene is by Shakespeare. There are especially close collocations with the language of *The Rape of Lucrece*, written just a year or two after *Arden of Faversham* was published.

The jury remains out and a great deal of uncertainty still surrounds the play. Some have detected the hand of Thomas Kyd. The Kentish setting brings to mind the name of Christopher Marlowe of Canterbury. Others have suggested that *Arden* is the work of an amateur and that it may never have been staged by the professional London companies. The published text of 1592 is disappointingly lacking in any theatrical provenance. But Shakespeare's involvement remains a genuine possibility. Could it be that an amateur Kentish author with a real eye for local detail wrote a script and passed it to whatever London acting company Shakespeare was with in the early 1590s? And that, in his capacity as patcher of plays, he improved it for performance and inserted the quarrel scene? We will probably never know, but such a scenario is as plausible as any, and we should be grateful for the presence of such a powerful and original play on the fringe of the Shakespearean canon.

┌─ KEY FACTS ─

AUTHORSHIP: The play was published anonymously, and continues to resist consensus over authorship. Shakespeare's authorship was first posited by Edward Jacob (a Faversham resident) in 1770 and continues to be a possibility. Christopher Marlowe and Thomas Kyd have both been championed, the latter most recently by Brian Vickers. Independent recent studies by MacDonald P. Jackson and Arthur F. Kinney, on the other hand, claim that the middle section of the play, particularly the quarrel scene (scene 8) is by Shakespeare. Other critics including Martin Wiggins prefer to see the play as the sole surviving work of an amateur. Regardless of authorship, most critics agree on the play's general quality and theatrical effectiveness.

PLOT: Master Arden, a provincial landowner, has recently come into possession of lands formerly belonging to a local abbey. His young wife Alice, meanwhile, is having an affair with Mosby, a tailor-turned-steward. Arden is suspicious, but Alice angrily counters his accusations. Alice and Mosby plot to murder Arden and, after a failed poisoning attempt by Alice, employ several willing assistants: Arden's manservant Michael and Clarke the painter (both suitors to Mosby's sister Susan); Greene, a local landowner dispossessed of his lands by Arden; and Black Will and Shakebag, two notorious criminals. Arden is cursed by Dick Reede, a poor man dispossessed by Arden. As Arden and his friend Franklin travel to and from London, Will and Shakebag make several attempts to murder Arden, each time being comically thwarted. In Faversham, meanwhile, Alice and Mosby quarrel over their mutual lack of trust. Upon Arden and Franklin's return, Mosby is wounded in another failed murder attempt, but Alice tricks Arden into believing he was at fault and arranges for Mosby to be invited to dinner by way of apology. Franklin is delayed by Greene from joining the dinner, at which the conspirators kill Arden and hide his body. Franklin and the Justice are led to the body by telltale bloodstains, and the conspirators – including Bradshaw, an innocent bystander – are sentenced to death or die abroad. The impression of Arden's body, however, remains on Reede's land for more than two years.

MAJOR PARTS: Alice (25%/171/8), Arden (13%/87/9), Mosby (12%/100/8), Black Will (11%/79/9), Michael (9%/59/8), Franklin (8%/62/11), Greene (6%/52/9), Shakebag (5%/44/9), Clarke (3%/23/2), Bradshaw (2%/16/4), Reede (2%/3/1), Ferryman (1%/17/2), Susan (1%/14/3), Lord Cheyne (1%/7/1), Mayor (1%/12/3).

LINGUISTIC MEDIUM: 95% verse, 5% prose.

DATE: c.1590. The play was first printed in 1592, and the primary source, Holinshed's *Chronicles*, was revised and republished in 1587. The play is the earliest extant English domestic tragedy, and is stylistically similar to the drama of the late 1580s.

SOURCES: The play is based on the real-life murder of Thomas Arden of Faversham in Kent. His murder by his wife was recorded in local accounts and picked up by some of the major Tudor chroniclers. The dramatist(s) used Raphael Holinshed's account in *Chronicles of England, Scotland and Ireland* (first published 1577; second edition 1587), which particularly coincides with the play in its spellings of names. The most significant addition is the character of Franklin.

▷

TEXT: The First Quarto of 1592 was followed by fresh editions in 1599 and 1633, each set from its predecessor. The title-page wording is unusually didactic, drawing morals against wanton wives and murderers. Opinions on the state of the text range wildly, but most scholars now accept that it was prepared for the press reasonably carefully, particularly in respect to its stage directions. Mislineation of verse and prose is the most significant editorial difficulty, particularly in the Will/Shakebag scenes.

THE LAMENTABLE AND TRUE TRAGEDY OF MASTER ARDEN OF FAVERSHAM IN KENT. Who was Most Wickedly Murdered, by the Means of His Disloyal and Wanton Wife, Who for the Love She Bare to One Mosby, Hired Two Desperate Ruffians, Black Will and Shakebag, to Kill Him. Wherein is Showed the Great Malice and Dissimulation of a Wicked Woman, the Insatiable Desire of Filthy Lust and the Shameful End of All Murderers.

Thomas ARDEN, a gentleman of Faversham

ALICE Arden, his wife

FRANKLIN, his friend

MOSBY, Alice's lover

SUSAN, Mosby's sister and Alice's maid

MICHAEL, Arden's servant, in love with Susan

CLARKE, a painter in love with Susan

BLACK WILL } villains hired to murder Arden
SHAKEBAG }

Richard GREENE, a tenant whose land Arden has taken

A PRENTICE of a shop in London

LORD CHEYNE and his Men

ADAM Fowle, landlord of the Flower-de-Luce

BRADSHAW, a goldsmith

A FERRYMAN

DICK REEDE, a sailor from Faversham

A SAILOR, his friend

The MAYOR of Faversham

The Watch

[Scene 1]

Enter Arden and Franklin

FRANKLIN   Arden, cheer up thy spirits and droop no more.

My gracious Lord the Duke of Somerset

Hath freely given to thee and to thy heirs,

By letters patents from his majesty,

ARDEN was coincidentally the surname of Shakespeare's mother's family   **Faversham** or Feversham is a town in Kent in south-east England; at this time it was the leading port for the export of wool as well as the centre for explosives, having the first English gunpowder plant   **FRANKLIN** his surname signifies a landowner of free but not noble birth, ranking below the gentry   **CLARKE** his surname signifies one able to read and write   **Flower-de-Luce** name of a public house; anglicization of 'fleur-de-lis', a species of lily used as a heraldic device, notably in the coat of arms of the French royal family   **The Watch** group of citizens responsible for law and order in their neighbourhood   **[Scene 1]**   There are no scene numbers or locations given in the Quarto of the play. *Location: Arden's house in Faversham*   **2 Duke of Somerset** Edward Seymour was named Lord Protector when his nephew, Edward VI, who was a minor, became king; he was subsequently executed for treason   **4 letters patents** open letters from the monarch or government conferring legal rights, especially in relation property   **his majesty** Edward VI

5   All the lands of the Abbey of Faversham.
         Here are the deeds,   *Gives deeds*
         Sealed and subscribed with his name and the king's.
         Read them, and leave this melancholy mood.
ARDEN   Franklin, thy love prolongs my weary life,
10   And but for thee, how odious were this life
         That shows me nothing but torments my soul,
         And those foul objects that offend my eyes,
         Which makes me wish that for this veil of heaven,
         The earth hung over my head and covered me.
15   Love letters passed 'twixt Mosby and my wife,
         And they have privy meetings in the town.
         Nay, on his finger did I spy the ring
         Which at our marriage day the priest put on.
         Can any grief be half so great as this?
20 FRANKLIN Comfort thyself, sweet friend: it is not strange,
         That women will be false and wavering.
ARDEN   Ay, but to dote on such a one as he
         Is monstrous, Franklin, and intolerable.
FRANKLIN Why, what is he?
25 ARDEN   A botcher, and no better at the first,
         Who, by base brokage getting some small stock,
         Crept into service of a nobleman,
         And by his servile flattery and fawning
         Is now become the steward of his house
30   And bravely jets it in his silken gown.
FRANKLIN No nobleman will count'nance such a peasant.
ARDEN   Yes, the Lord Clifford, he that loves not me.
         But through his favour let not him grow proud,
         For, were he by the Lord Protector backed,
35   He should not make me to be pointed at.
         I am by birth a gentleman of blood,
         And that injurious ribald that attempts
         To violate my dear wife's chastity,
         (For dear I hold her love, as dear as heaven)
40   Shall, on the bed which he thinks to defile,
         See his dissevered joints and sinews torn,

---

5 lands ... Faversham at the dissolution of the monastery in 1536, Henry VIII awarded the lands to Sir Thomas Culpeper. They passed to Lord Cheyne who later transferred them to Arden 7 subscribed signed 11 shows offers/teaches 13 veil of heaven sky, plays on sense of earthly life as a 'vale of tears' 15 'twixt abbreviation of betwixt, i.e. between 16 privy secret 22 dote be infatuated with 25 botcher mender, patcher/bungler, shoddy workman 26 base brokage dishonest dealing/trading in secondhand goods/pimping stock fund, store/sum of capital/property/livestock (farm animals)/thrusting sword 29 steward official who controls the domestic affairs of a household 30 bravely boldly/showily jets struts, swaggers silken gown sign of his steward's office; Tudor sumptuary laws laid down the appropriate clothing for different social classes 31 count'nance favour, patronize 32 Lord Clifford the historical Baron de Clifford (Earl of Cumberland) does not figure in this story; Mosby served Sir Edward North, Alice's stepfather and Arden's former master 36 gentleman of blood one entitled to bear arms although not of the nobility 37 injurious ribald insulting menial/knave, rascal 41 dissevered separated, divided

Whilst on the planchers pants his weary body,

Smeared in the channels of his lustful blood.

FRANKLIN Be patient, gentle friend, and learn of me

45   To ease thy grief and save her chastity.

Entreat her fair: sweet words are fittest engines

To race the flint walls of a woman's breast.

In any case, be not too jealous,

Nor make no question of her love to thee.

50   But as securely, presently take horse,

And lie with me at London all this term.

For women when they may, will not,

But being kept back, straight grow outrageous.

ARDEN Though this abhors from reason, yet I'll try it,

55   And call her forth, and presently take leave.

How, Alice!

Here enters Alice

ALICE Husband, what mean you to get up so early?

Summer nights are short, and yet you rise ere day,

Had I been wake, you had not rise so soon.

60   **ARDEN** Sweet love, thou knowst that we two, Ovid-like,

Have often chid the morning, when it 'gan to peep.

And often wished that dark night's purblind steeds

Would pull her by the purple mantle back

And cast her in the ocean to her love.

65   But this night, sweet Alice, thou hast killed my heart:

I heard thee call on Mosby in thy sleep.

ALICE 'Tis like I was asleep when I named him,

For being awake he comes not in my thoughts.

ARDEN Ay, but you started up and suddenly,

70   Instead of him, caught me about the neck.

ALICE Instead of him? Why, who was there but you,

And where but one is, how can I mistake?

FRANKLIN Arden leave to urge her overfar.   *Aside?*

ARDEN Nay, love, there is no credit in a dream.

75   Let it suffice I know thou lov'st me well.

ALICE Now I remember whereupon it came:

Had we no talk of Mosby yesternight?

FRANKLIN Mistress Alice, I heard you name him once or twice.

ALICE And thereof came it, and therefore blame not me.

---

42 planchers floorboards   **46 Entreat her fair** treat her gently/speak to her kindly   **fittest engines** the most appropriate instruments   **47 race** penetrate, playing on 'raze' tear down   **49 make no question** raise doubts about/debate   **50 as securely** as though confident   **51 lie** lodge   **term** session of the law courts   **52 For … outrageous** when women are allowed freedom they will refrain from immoral behaviour but when they are restrained they become immediately shameless   **54 abhors from** is at variance with   **56 How** exclamation to attract attention   **58 ere** before   **59 wake** awake   **rise** risen, got up   **60 Ovid-like** like the poet of love   **61 chid** reproved, scolded   **62 purblind** completely blind   **steeds** horses; in classical mythology, Nyx, goddess of night was depicted as winged or as driving a chariot drawn by horses   **63 mantle** cloak   **64 love** Erebus, god of darkness, by whom Nyx bore Aether (the sky) and Hemera (day)   **72 but one is** there is only one   **73 leave to urge** refrain from pressing   **overfar** too far   **74 credit** truth, belief   **76 whereupon** for what reason

80   ARDEN   I know it did, and therefore let it pass,

I must to London, sweet Alice, presently.

ALICE   But tell me, do you mean to stay there long?

ARDEN   No longer there till my affairs be done.

FRANKLIN   He will not stay above a month at most.

85   ALICE   A month? Ay me! Sweet Arden, come again

Within a day or two or else I die.

ARDEN   I cannot long be from thee gentle Alice,

Whilst Michael fetch our horses from the field,

Franklin and I will down unto the quay,

90   For I have certain goods there to unload.

Meanwhile prepare our breakfast, gentle Alice,

For yet ere noon we'll take horse and away.   *Exeunt Arden and Franklin*

ALICE   Ere noon he means to take horse and away.

Sweet news is this. O, that some airy spirit

95   Would in the shape and likeness of a horse

Gallop with Arden 'cross the ocean

And throw him from his back into the waves.

Sweet Mosby is the man that hath my heart,

And he usurps it, having nought but this,

100   That I am tied to him by marriage.

Love is a god and marriage is but words,

And therefore, Mosby's title is the best.

Tush! Whether it be or no, he shall be mine,

In spite of him, of Hymen, and of rites.

Here enters Adam of the Flower-de-Luce

105   And here comes Adam of the Flower-de-Luce.

I hope he brings me tidings of my love.

How now Adam, what is the news with you?

Be not afraid, my husband is now from home.

ADAM   He whom you wot of, Mosby, Mistress Alice,

110   Is come to town and sends you word by me.

In any case, you may not visit him.

ALICE   Not visit him?

ADAM   No, nor take no knowledge of his being here.

ALICE   But tell me, is he angry or displeased?

115   ADAM   Should seem so, for he is wondrous sad.

ALICE   Were he as mad as raving Hercules,

I'll see him. Ay, and were thy house of force,

These hands of mine should raze it to the ground

Unless that thou wouldst bring me to my love.

---

84 **above** longer than   85 **Ay me!** Alas!, expression of regret   99 **he** i.e. Arden   102 **title** claim, legal right to possess   104 **Hymen** god of marriage in Greek mythology   **rites** ceremonies, plays on 'rights', i.e. legal rights   ***Flower-de-Luce*** name of a public house in Faversham, from the heraldic lily associated with the coat of arms of the French monarchy   106 **tidings** news   109 **wot** know   113 **take no knowledge** know anything about   115 **Should seem** it appears   **wondrous** exceedingly   116 **raving Hercules** mythological hero driven mad by the poisoned shirt given to him by his wife Deianeira who believed it would make him faithful   118 **raze** demolish, tear down

120	ADAM	Nay, and you be so impatient, I'll be gone.
	ALICE	Stay, Adam, stay. Thou wert wont to be my friend.

Ask Mosby how I have incurred his wrath.

Bear him from me these pair of silver dice   *Gives dice*

With which we played for kisses many a time,

125   And when I lost, I won, and so did he.

Such winning and such losing Jove send me!

And bid him if his love do not decline,

Come this morning but along my door

And as a stranger but salute me there.

130   This may he do without suspect or fear.

ADAM   I'll tell him what you say, and so farewell.   *Exit Adam*

ALICE   Do, and one day I'll make amends for all.

I know he loves me well but dares not come

Because my husband is so jealous,

135   And these my narrow, prying neighbours blab,

Hinder our meetings when we would confer.

But, if I live, that block shall be removed.

And Mosby, thou that comes to me by stealth,

Shalt neither fear the biting speech of men

140   Nor Arden's looks. As surely shall he die,

As I abhor him, and love only thee.

Here enters Michael

How now Michael, whither are you going?

MICHAEL   To fetch my master's nag,

I hope you'll think on me.

145   ALICE   Ay, but Michael, see you keep your oath,

And be as secret as you are resolute.

MICHAEL   I'll see he shall not live above a week.

ALICE   On that condition, Michael, here is my hand.

None shall have Mosby's sister but thyself.

150   MICHAEL   I understand the painter here hard by

Hath made report that he and Sue is sure.

ALICE   There's no such matter, Michael: believe it not.

MICHAEL   But he hath sent a dagger sticking in a heart,

With a verse or two stolen from a painted cloth,

155   The which I hear the wench keeps in her chest.

Well let her keep it. I shall find a fellow

That can both write and read, and make rhyme too:

And if I do, well, I say no more.

I'll send from London such a taunting letter

120 and if   **121 wert wont** used, were accustomed   **126 Jove** chief of the Roman gods   **128 along** by   **129 salute** greet   **135 blab** talk indiscreetly   **137 block** obstacle/blockhead, i.e. Arden   **138 by stealth** in secret   **141 abhor** detest   **142 whither** to where   **143 nag** horse   **144 on** of/about   **150 hard by** near, close by   **151 sure** engaged to be married   **154 painted cloth** cheap substitute for woven tapestry used as wall decoration; they often featured mottoes or a line of verse   **155 wench** girl, young woman

160   As shall eat the heart he sent with salt
          And fling the dagger at the painter's head.

ALICE   What needs all this? I say that Susan's thine.

MICHAEL   Why, then I say that I will kill my master
          Or anything that you will have me do.

165 ALICE   But, Michael, see you do it cunningly.

MICHAEL   Why, say I should be took, I'll ne'er confess
          That you know anything: and Susan, being a maid,
          May beg me from the gallows of the shrieve.

ALICE   Trust not to that, Michael.

170 MICHAEL   You cannot tell me, I have seen it, I.
          But mistress, tell her whether I live or die,
          I'll make her more worth than twenty painters can,
          For I will rid mine elder brother away:
          And then the farm of Bolton is mine own.

175   Who would not venture upon house and land
          When he may have it for a right-down blow?

Here enters Mosby

ALICE   Yonder comes Mosby, Michael get thee gone,
          And let not him nor any know thy drifts.   *Exit Michael*
          Mosby, my love!

180 MOSBY   Away I say, and talk not to me now.

ALICE   A word or two sweetheart, and then I will.
          'Tis yet but early days, thou need'st not fear.

MOSBY   Where is your husband?

ALICE   'Tis now high water, and he is at the quay.

185 MOSBY   There let him be: henceforward know me not.

ALICE   Is this the end of all thy solemn oaths?
          Is this the fruit thy reconcilement buds?
          Have I, for this, given thee so many favours,
          Incurred my husband's hate, and out alas,

190   Made shipwreck of mine honour for thy sake?
          And dost thou say, 'Henceforward know me not'?
          Remember when I locked thee in my closet:
          What were thy words and mine? Did we not both
          Decree to murder Arden in the night?

195   The heavens can witness and the world can tell,
          Before I saw that falsehood look of thine,
          Fore I was tangled with thy ticing speech,
          Arden to me was dearer than my soul —

---

162 **What ... this?** What's all this for?   165 **cunningly** skilfully/secretly   166 **took** caught, arrested   167 **maid ... gallows** referring to the belief
that a virgin might save a man from hanging by offering to marry him   168 **shrieve** sheriff, officer who represented the authority of the king
172 **more worth** richer/more highly respected   176 **right-down** positive   178 **any** anyone else   **drifts** plots/intentions   184 **high water** i.e. high
tide   190 **Made ... honour** lost my reputation/acted immorally, i.e. committed adultery   192 **closet** private room, inner chamber   194 **Decree**
decide, resolve   196 **falsehood** lying (the *OED* records no use as an adjective. Perhaps a Shakespearean coinage)   197 **Fore** before   **tangled** trapped/
confused   **ticing** beguiling, seductive

And shall be still. Base peasant, get thee gone!

200 And boast not of thy conquest over me,

Gotten by witchcraft, and mere sorcery.

For what hast thou to countenance my love,

Being descended of a noble house,

And matched already with a gentleman

205 Whose servant thou mayst be, and so farewell!

MOSBY   Ungentle and unkind Alice, now I see

That which I ever feared and find too true:

A woman's love is as the lightning flame

Which even in bursting forth consumes itself.

210 To try thy constancy have I been strange.

Would I had never tried, but lived in hope.

ALICE   What needs thou try me whom thou never found false?

MOSBY   Yet pardon me, for love is jealous.

ALICE   So list the sailor to the mermaid's song:

215 So looks the traveller to the basilisk.

I am content for to be reconciled,

And that I know will be mine overthrow.

MOSBY   Thine overthrow? First let the world dissolve!

ALICE   Nay, Mosby, let me still enjoy thy love,

220 And, happen what will, I am resolute.

My saving husband hordes up bags of gold

To make our children rich, and now is he

Gone to unload the goods that shall be thine,

And he and Franklin will to London straight.

225 MOSBY   To London, Alice? If thou'lt be ruled by me,

We'll make him sure enough for coming there.

ALICE   Ah, would we could!

MOSBY   I happened on a painter yesternight,

The only cunning man of Christendom,

230 For he can temper poison with his oil

That who so looks upon the work he draws

Shall, with the beams that issue from his sight,

Suck venom to his breast and slay himself.

Sweet Alice, he shall draw thy counterfeit

235 That Arden, may by gazing on it, perish.

ALICE   Ay, but Mosby, that is dangerous,

For thou, or I, or any other else,

Coming into the chamber where it hangs, may die.

199 Base lowly born/mean, cowardly – social and moral values are typically confused   **peasant** member of agricultural class dependent on subsistence farming/term of abuse for one of low social status   **202 countenance** pretend to, have claims on   **203 noble house** aristocratic family   **204 matched** married   **206 Ungentle** harsh, punning on sense of 'ignoble'   **unkind** unnatural/ungrateful/wicked/ungenerous, ill-tempered   **210 try** test   **strange** cold, reserved   **211 Would ... never** I wish I had never   **214 list** listened   **mermaid's song** a reference to the song of the Sirens in Homer's *Odyssey* who lured sailors to their deaths   **215 basilisk** fabulous reptile whose gaze was fatal   **217 overthrow** ruin, that which brings a person down   **226 sure** safe   **228 happened on** met by chance with   **229 only cunning** most knowledgeable   **230 temper** mix   **232 beams ... sight** one early theory of sight suggested that rays or beams were emitted from the eye which were intercepted by visual objects   **234 counterfeit** portrait   **235 That** in such a way that

MOSBY   Ay, but we'll have it covered with a cloth,

240   And hung up in the study for himself.

ALICE   It may not be, for when the picture's drawn,

Arden, I know, will come and show it me.

MOSBY   Fear not: we'll have that shall serve the turn.

This is the painter's house: I'll call him forth.

245   ALICE   But Mosby, I'll have no such picture, I.

MOSBY   Ay, pray thee leave it to my discretion. How, Clarke!

Here enters Clarke

O, you are an honest man of your word: you served me well.

CLARKE   Why sir, I'll do it for you at any time,

Provided, as you have given your word,

250   I may have Susan Mosby to my wife.

For as sharp-witted poets, whose sweet verse

Make heavenly gods break off their nectar draughts

And lay their ears down to the lowly earth,

Use humble promise to their sacred Muse,

255   So we that are the poets' favourites

Must have a love. Ay, love is the painter's Muse.

That makes him frame a speaking countenance,

A weeping eye that witnesses heart's grief.

Then tell me, Master Mosby, shall I have her?

260   ALICE   'Tis pity but he should: he'll use her well.   *To Mosby*

MOSBY   Clarke here's my hand: my sister shall be thine.

CLARKE   Then, brother, to requite this courtesy,

You shall command my life, my skill and all.

ALICE   Ah, that thou could'st be secret!

265   MOSBY   Fear him not. Leave: I have talked sufficient.

CLARKE   You know not me, that ask such questions.

Let it suffice I know you love him well

And fain would have your husband made away,

Wherein, trust me, you show a noble mind,

270   That rather than you'll live with him you hate

You'll venture life, and die with him you love.

The like will I do for my Susan's sake.

ALICE   Yet nothing could enforce me to the deed

But Mosby's love. Might I without control

275   Enjoy thee still, then Arden should not die:

But seeing I cannot, therefore let him die.

MOSBY   Enough, sweet Alice. Thy kind words makes me melt.

Your trick of poisoned pictures we dislike: *To Clarke*

---

243 **serve the turn** do the job   252 **break off** stop in the middle of drinking   **nectar** delicious mythical drink of the classical gods   254 **Use** are accustomed to make   **Muse** one of nine classical goddesses regarded as presiding over and inspiring the arts   257 **speaking countenance** expressive face   260 **'Tis ... should** it's a pity if he doesn't have her for his wife/it would be a pity if he did – the phrase may be deliberately ambiguous since Alice has already promised Susan to her servant, Michael   262 **requite** repay   268 **fain** gladly   277 **makes** singular form of verbs were sometimes used with plural nouns

Some other poison would do better far.

280 ALICE   Ay, such as might be put into his broth,

And yet in taste not to be found at all.

CLARKE   I know your mind, and here I have it for you.   *Shows poison*

Put but a dram of this into his drink,

Or any kind of broth that he shall eat,

285 And he shall die within an hour after.

ALICE   As I am a gentlewoman, Clarke, next day

Thou and Susan shall be married.

MOSBY   And I'll make her dowry more than I'll talk of, Clarke.

CLARKE   Yonder's your husband: Mosby, I'll be gone.   *Exit Clarke*

290 ALICE   In good time — see where my husband comes!

Here enters Arden and Franklin [and Michael]

Master Mosby, ask him the question yourself.

MOSBY   Master Arden, being at London yesternight,

The Abbey lands whereof you are now possessed

Were offered me on some occasion

295 By Greene, one of Sir Antony Ager's men.

I pray you sir, tell me, are not the lands yours?

Hath any other interest herein?

ARDEN   Mosby, that question we'll decide anon.

Alice, make ready my breakfast: I must hence.   *Exit Alice*

300 As for the lands, Mosby, they are mine,

By letters patents from his majesty.

But I must have a mandate for my wife:

They say you seek to rob me of her love.

Villain, what makes thou in her company?

305 She's no companion for so base a groom.

MOSBY   Arden, I thought not on her. I came to thee,

But rather than I pocket up this wrong—

FRANKLIN   What will you do, sir?

MOSBY   Revenge it on the proudest of you both.

Then Arden draws forth Mosby's sword

310 ARDEN   So, sirrah, you may not wear a sword.

The statute makes against artificers:

I warrant that I do. Now use your bodkin,

Your Spanish needle and your pressing iron.

For this shall go with me, and mark my words,

315 You, goodman botcher, 'tis to you I speak.

---

283 dram small draught; in medicine one eighth of a fluid ounce   **288 dowry** money or property the wife brings to her husband on marriage   **295 Sir Anthony Ager's** Ager was Greene's liege lord, i.e. his feudal superior to whom he owed allegiance and services   **297 interest** legal right or title   **298 anon** straight away/presently   **302 mandate** contract/order   **304 what makes thou** what are you doing? Arden changes from polite 'you' to the intimate/insulting 'thou' in addressing Mosby   **305 groom** fellow/servingman   **307 pocket up** swallow, submit to   *draws forth* pulls out, removes   **310 sirrah** term of address expressing contempt   **311 statute** law (passed under Edward VI) forbidding those under the rank of gentleman to wear a sword   **artificers** craftsmen/tricksters   **312 warrant** have legal sanction for (since he is a gentleman)   **bodkin** small pointed instrument for making holes in cloth (Mosby had been a tailor)/short dagger   **313 Spanish needle** the finest steel was from Spain   **315 goodman botcher** an insult; **goodman** was a term of address for one below the level of gentleman; **botcher** a patcher and mender of clothes/shoddy workman

The next time that I take thee near my house,
Instead of legs, I'll make thee crawl on stumps.

MOSBY   Ah, Master Arden, you have injured me.
I do appeal to God and to the world.

320 FRANKLIN   Why can'st thou deny thou wert a botcher once?

MOSBY   Measure me what I am, not what I was.

ARDEN   Why what art thou now, but a velvet drudge,
A cheating steward and base-minded peasant?

MOSBY   Arden, now thou hast belched and vomited
325 The rancorous venom of thy mis-swoll'n heart,
Hear me but speak. As I intend to live
With God and his elected saints in heaven,
I never meant more to solicit her:
And that she knows, and all the world shall see,
330 I loved her once. Sweet Arden, pardon me.
I could not choose: her beauty fired my heart.
But time hath quenched these overraging coals:
And Arden, though I now frequent thy house,
'Tis for my sister's sake, her waiting-maid,
335 And not for hers. Mayst thou enjoy her long.
Hell fire and wrathful vengeance light on me
If I dishonour her or injure thee.

ARDEN   Mosby, with these thy protestations,
The deadly hatred of my heart is appeased,
340 And thou and I'll be friends, if this prove true.
As for the base terms I gave thee late,
Forget them Mosby. I had cause to speak
When all the knights and gentlemen of Kent
Make common table talk of her and thee.

345 MOSBY   Who lives that is not touched with sland'rous tongues?

FRANKLIN   Then Mosby, to eschew the speech of men,
Upon whose general bruit all honour hangs,
Forbear his house.

ARDEN   Forbear it, nay rather frequent it more:
350 The world shall see that I distrust her not.
To warn him on the sudden from my house
Were to confirm the rumour that is grown.

MOSBY   By faith, my sir, you say true.
And therefore will I sojourn here a while,
355 Until our enemies have talked their fill.
And then I hope they'll cease, and at last confess
How causeless they have injured her and me.

---

321 **Measure** judge   322 **velvet drudge** hack or servant employed in menial work despite now wearing velvet (considered appropriate only for the upper classes)   325 **mis-swoll'n** morbidly, excessively swollen, inflated   333 **frequent** visit   341 **base terms** insults   346 **eschew** avoid   347 **bruit** rumour, report   348 **Forbear** avoid, keep away from   354 **sojourn** stay, remain

ARDEN   And I will lie at London all this term

To let them see how light I weigh their words.

Here enters Alice

360   ALICE   Husband sit down, your breakfast will be cold.

ARDEN   Come, Master Mosby, will you sit with us.

MOSBY   I cannot eat, but I'll sit for company.

ARDEN   Sirrah Michael, see our horse be ready.   *[Exit Michael]*

ALICE   Husband, why pause ye, why eat you not?

365   ARDEN   I am not well: there's something in this broth

That is not wholesome. Didst thou make it Alice?

ALICE   I did, and that's the cause it likes not you.

Then she throws down the broth on the ground

There's nothing that I do can please your taste:

You were best to say I would have poisoned you.

370   I cannot speak or cast aside my eye

But he imagines I have stepped awry.

Here's he that you cast in my teeth so oft.

Now will I be convinced or purge myself.

I charge thee speak to this mistrustful man—   *To Mosby*

375   Thou that wouldst see me hang, thou, Mosby thou,

What favour hast thou had more than a kiss

At coming or departing from the town?

MOSBY   You wrong yourself and me to cast these doubts:

Your loving husband is not jealous.

380   ARDEN   Why, gentle Mistress Alice, cannot I be ill

But you'll accuse yourself?

Franklin, thou hast a box of mithridate,

I'll take a little to prevent the worst.

[Enter Michael]

FRANKLIN   Do so, and let us presently take horse: *Gives medicine*

385   My life for yours, ye shall do well enough.

ALICE   Give me a spoon, I'll eat of it myself,

Would it were full of poison to the brim,

Then should my cares and troubles have an end.

Was ever silly woman so tormented?

390   ARDEN   Be patient, sweet love: I mistrust not thee.

ALICE   God will revenge it, Arden, if thou dost:

For never woman loved her husband better than I do thee.

ARDEN   I know it, sweet Alice, cease to complain:

Lest that in tears I answer thee again.

---

367 likes not doesn't agree with   **371 I ... awry** Alice is complaining that her husband becomes jealous and convinced that she is unfaithful if she so much as speaks to or looks at another man   **372 cast ... teeth** throw up at me, i.e. accuse me of having an illicit relationship with   **373 purge myself** clear my name, establish my innocence; puns on the sense of vomit, rid the body of harmful substances   **382 mithridate** medicine believed to be a universal antidote to poison   **385 ye ... enough** you'll be all right   **389 silly** weak, foolish, helpless

395 FRANKLIN Come, leave this dallying and let us away.

ALICE   Forbear to wound me with that bitter word:

Arden shall go to London in my arms.

ARDEN   Loath am I to depart: yet I must go.

ALICE   Wilt thou to London then, and leave me here?

400 Ah, if thou love me, gentle Arden, stay:

Yet, if thy business be of great import,

Go if thou wilt, I'll bear it as I may,

But write from London to me every week.

Nay, everyday and stay no longer there

405 Than thou must needs, lest that I die for sorrow.

ARDEN   I'll write unto thee every other tide,

And so farewell, sweet Alice, till we meet next.

ALICE   Farewell, husband, seeing you'll have it so.

And Master Franklin, seeing you take him hence

410 In hope you'll hasten him home I'll give you this.

And then she kisseth him

FRANKLIN And if he stay, the fault shall not be mine.—

Mosby, farewell, and see you keep your oath.

MOSBY   I hope he is not jealous of me now.

ARDEN   No, Mosby, no, hereafter think of me

415 As of your dearest friend, and so, farewell.   *Exeunt Arden, Franklin*
                                                              and Michael

ALICE   I am glad he is gone: he was about to stay.

But did you mark me then how I break off?

MOSBY   Ay Alice, and it was cunningly performed:

But what a villain is this painter Clarke?

420 ALICE   Was it not a goodly poison that he gave?

Why he's as well now as he was before.

It should have been some fine confection

That might have given the broth some dainty taste.

This powder was too gross and populous.

425 MOSBY   But had he eaten but three spoonfuls more,

Then had he died and our love continued.

ALICE   Why, so it shall Mosby, albeit he live.

MOSBY   It is impossible, for I have sworn

Never hereafter to solicit thee,

430 Or whilst he lives, once more importune thee.

ALICE   Thou shalt not need: I will importune thee.

What, shall an oath make thee forsake my love?

As if I have not sworn as much myself

And given my hand unto him in the church.

435 Tush, Mosby, oaths are words, and words is wind,

---

395 **dallying** idle chatting/lingering   406 **every other tide** i.e. once a day; the letters would be carried by boat   422 **confection** preparation; the term could refer to both a sweetmeat and a deadly poison   424 **gross** coarse/obvious   **populous** abundant   427 **albeit he** even though he continues to   430 **importune** trouble, pester

And wind is mutable. Then I conclude,
'Tis childishness to stand upon an oath.

MOSBY   Well proved, Mistress Alice, yet by your leave,
I'll keep mine unbroken whilst he lives.

440 ALICE   Ay, do, and spare not, his time is but short:
For, if thou be'st as resolute as I,
We'll have him murdered as he walks the streets.
In London many ale-house ruffians keep,
Which as I hear will murder men for gold,
445 They shall be soundly fee'd to pay him home.

Here enters Greene

MOSBY   Alice, what's he that comes yonder, knowst thou him?

ALICE   Mosby be gone: I hope 'tis one that comes
To put in practice our intended drifts.   *Exit Mosby*

GREENE   Mistress Arden, you are well met.
450 I am sorry that your husband is from home
Whenas my purposed journey was to him.
Yet all my labour is not spent in vain,
For I suppose that you can full discourse
And flat resolve me of the thing I seek.

455 ALICE   What is it, Master Greene? If that I may
Or can with safety, I will answer you.

GREENE   I heard your husband hath the grant of late,
Confirmed by letters patents from the king,
Of all the lands of the Abbey of Faversham,
460 Generally entitled, so that all former grants
Are cut off, whereof I myself had one,
But now my interest by that is void.
This is all, Mistress Arden: is it true nor no?

ALICE   True, Master Greene, the lands are his in state:
465 And whatsoever leases were before
Are void for term of Master Arden's life.
He hath the grant under the Chancery seal.

GREENE   Pardon me, Mistress Arden: I must speak,
For I am touched. Your husband doth me wrong
470 To wring me from the little land I have.
My living is my life, only that
Resteth remainder of my portion.
Desire of wealth is endless in his mind,
And he is greedy gaping still for gain:
475 Nor cares he though young gentlemen do beg,

---

438 proved demonstrated (by her logical argument)   **439 mine** i.e. oath   **443 keep** reside/lie in wait for   **448 drifts** schemes   **451 Whenas** seeing that   **454 flat resolve** answer fully   **467 Chancery seal** wax imprint of heraldic device as evidence of authority from the Lord Chancellor's court   **469 touched** affected/injured   **470 wring** force   **471 living** tenement, holding of land   **only ... portion** that is all that is left of my inheritance

So he may scrape and horde up in his pouch.
But seeing he hath taken my lands, I'll value life
As careless, as he is careful for to get:
And tell him this from me, I'll be revenged.

480 And so, as he shall wish the Abbey lands
Had rested still within their former state.

ALICE   Alas, poor gentleman, I pity you:
And woe is me that any man should want.
God knows 'tis not my fault: but wonder not

485 Though he be hard to others, when to me,
Ah, Master Greene, God knows how I am used.

GREENE   Why, Mistress Arden, can the crabbed churl
Use you unkindly? Respects he not your birth,
Your honourable friends, nor what you brought?

490 Why, all Kent knows your parentage, and what you are.

ALICE   Ah, Master Greene, be it spoken in secret here.
I never live good day with him alone.
When he is at home, then have I froward looks,
Hard words and blows, to mend the match withal.

495 And, though I might content as good a man,
Yet doth he keep in every corner trulls.
And, weary with his trugs at home,
Then rides he straight to London. There, forsooth,
He revels it among such filthy ones

500 As counsels him to make away his wife:
Thus live I daily in continual fear.
In sorrow, so despairing of redress
As every day I wish with hearty prayer,
That he or I were taken forth the world.

505 GREENE   Now, trust me Mistress Alice, it grieveth me
So fair a creature should be so abused.
Why, who would have thought the civil sir so sullen?
He looks so smoothly now. Fie upon him churl!
And if he live a day, he lives too long.

510 But frolic, woman: I shall be the man
Shall set you free from all this discontent.
And if the churl deny my interest
And will not yield my lease into my hand,
I'll pay him home, whatever hap to me.

515 ALICE   But speak you as you think?

---

476 **pouch** purse   481 **rested ... state** remained as they were before   483 **want** be destitute   487 **crabbed** harsh, bad-tempered   **churl** villain/
low-born fellow   489 **what you brought** i.e. your dowry   493 **froward** perverse, ill-humoured   494 **mend** complete   **withal** along with the
rest   496 **trulls** trollops, whores   497 **trugs** prostitutes   498 **forsooth** in truth   507 **civil** educated, well-governed, polite, civilized   **sullen**
ill-natured   508 **smoothly** mild, plausible   **Fie upon** exclamation of disgust   **churl** base fellow, villain/one who is mean with money   510 **frolic** make
merry   511 **discontent** misery, unhappiness   512 **deny my interest** refuses to accept my claim   514 **pay him home** be revenged on him   **hap** happens

GREENE   Ay, God's my witness, I mean plain dealing:

For I had rather die than lose my land.

ALICE   Then, Master Greene, be counsellèd by me

Endanger not yourself for such a churl,

520   But hire some cutter for to cut him short,

And here's ten pound, to wager them withal.   *Gives money*

When he is dead you shall have twenty more:

And the lands whereof my husband is possessed,

Shall be entitled as they were before.

525   GREENE   Will you keep promise with me?

ALICE   Or count me false and perjured, whilst I live.

GREENE   Then here's my hand I'll have him so dispatched,

I'll up to London straight: I'll thither post

And never rest till I have compassed it.

530   Till then, farewell.

ALICE   Good fortune follow all your forward thoughts.   *Exit Greene*

And whosoever doth attempt the deed,

A happy hand I wish and so farewell.

All this goes well. Mosby, I long for thee

535   To let thee know all that I have contrived.

Here enters Mosby and Clarke

MOSBY   How now Alice, what's the news?

ALICE   Such as will content thee well, sweetheart.

MOSBY   Well, let them pass awhile, and tell me, Alice,

How have you dealt and tempered with my sister?

540   What, will she have my neighbour Clarke or no?

ALICE   What, Master Mosby, let him woo himself.

Think you that maids look not for fair words?

Go to her, Clarke: she's all alone within.

Michael, my man, is clean out of her books.

545   CLARKE   I thank you, Mistress Arden, I will in,

And, if fair Susan and I can make a gree,

You shall command me to the uttermost,

As far as either goods or life may stretch.   *Exit Clarke*

MOSBY   Now, Alice, let's hear thy news?

550   ALICE   They be so good that I must laugh for joy

Before I can begin to tell my tale.

MOSBY   Let's hear them that I may laugh for company.

ALICE   This morning, Master Greene — Dick Greene, I mean,

From whom my husband had the Abbey land —

555   Came hither railing for to know the truth

Whether my husband had the lands by grant.

---

520 cutter cut-throat   **521 wager** pay   **526 Or** if not   **528 post** ride with haste   **529 compassed** contrived   **539 tempered** prepared, brought to a suitable condition   **543 within** in the house   **544 clean … books** completely out of her good books, out of favour with her   **546 make a gree** come to terms   **555 railing** ranting, complaining

I told him all, whereat he stormed amain,

And swore he would cry quittance with the churl:

And if he did deny his interest,

560   Stab him, whatsoever did befall himself.

When as I saw his choler thus to rise,

I whetted on the gentleman with words

And to conclude, Mosby, at last we grew

To composition for my husband's death.

565   I gave him ten pound to hire knaves

By some device to make away the churl.

When he is dead, he should have twenty more

And repossess his former lands again.

On this we greed and he is ridden straight

570   To London to bring his death about.

MOSBY   But call you this good news?

ALICE   Ay, sweetheart, be they not?

MOSBY   'Twere cheerful news, to hear the churl were dead.

But trust me Alice, I take it passing ill

575   You would be so forgetful of our state

To make recount of it to every groom.

What, to acquaint each stranger with our drifts,

Chiefly in case of murder! Why, 'tis the way

To make it open unto Arden's self

580   And bring thyself and me to ruin both.

Forewarned, forearmed, who threats his enemy

Lends him a sword to guard himself withal.

ALICE   I did it for the best.

MOSBY   Well, seeing 'tis done, cheerily let it pass.

585   You know this Greene, is he not religious,

A man I guess of great devotion?

ALICE   He is.

MOSBY   Then, sweet Alice, let it pass. I have a drift

Will quiet all, whatever is amiss.

Here enters Clarke and Susan

590   **ALICE**   How now Clarke, have you found me false?

Did I not plead the matter hard for you?

CLARKE   You did.

MOSBY   And what, will't be a match?

CLARKE   A match, i'faith, sir. Ay, the day is mine,

595   The painter lays his colours to the life,

His pencil draws no shadows in his love.

Susan is mine.

557 **amain** violently   558 **cry quittance** declare himself even with   559 **interest** right, entitlement   561 **choler** bile, anger; one of the four humours of early physiology believed to cause ill temper   562 **whetted on** sharpened, encouraged   564 **composition** an agreement/arrangement   565 **knaves** villains   569 **greed** agreed   574 **passing** extremely   577 **drifts** intentions, plans   578 **Chiefly** especially   579 **open** known   588 **drift** plan   596 **shadows** what is fleeting or ephemeral, plays on 'shadow' meaning 'portrait'

	ALICE	You make her blush.
	MOSBY	What, sister, is it Clarke must be the man?
600	SUSAN	It resteth in your grant. Some words are passed,

ALICE   You make her blush.

MOSBY   What, sister, is it Clarke must be the man?

600 SUSAN   It resteth in your grant. Some words are passed,
And happily we be grown unto a match
If you be willing that it shall be so?

MOSBY   Ah, Master Clarke, it resteth at my grant.
You see my sister's yet at my dispose,
605 But so you'll grant me one thing I shall ask,
I am content my sister shall be yours.

CLARKE   What is it, Master Mosby?

MOSBY   I do remember once in secret talk
You told me how you could compound by art
610 A crucifix empoisonèd.
That whoso look upon it should wax blind,
And with the scent be stifled, that ere long,
He should die poisoned that did view it well.
I would have you make me such a crucifix,
615 And then I'll grant my sister shall be yours.

CLARKE   Though I am loath because it toucheth life,
Yet, rather or I'll leave sweet Susan's love,
I'll do it, and with all the haste I may.
But for whom is it?

620 ALICE   Leave that to us. Why, Clarke, is it possible
That you should paint and draw it out yourself,
The colours being baleful and empoisoned,
And no ways prejudice yourself withal?

MOSBY   Well questioned Alice.— Clarke, how answer you that?

625 CLARKE   Very easily, I'll tell you straight,
How I do work of these empoisoned drugs.
I fasten on my spectacles so close
As nothing can any way offend my sight.
Then as I put a leaf within my nose,
630 So put I rhubarb to avoid the smell,
And, softly as another work, I paint.

MOSBY   'Tis very well, but against when shall I have it?

CLARKE   Within this ten days.

MOSBY   'Twill serve the turn.
635 Now, Alice, let's in and see what cheer you keep:
I hope, now Master Arden is from home,
You'll give me leave to play your husband's part.

ALICE   Mosby, you know who's master of my heart,
He well may be the master of the house.   *Exeunt*

---

600 **your grant** i.e. the consent or permission of Mosby, her closest male relative   **passed** spoken between us   604 **at my dispose** within my power, control   605 **so** if   611 **wax** grow, become   612 **stifled** suffocated   **ere** before   616 **loath** reluctant   617 **or** than   622 **baleful** deadly, noxious   623 **prejudice** harm, damage   **withal** as well   631 **softly** as carefully   632 **against** by   633 **this** i.e. these   635 **cheer** entertainment

[Scene 2]

Here enters Greene and Bradshaw

BRADSHAW   See you them that comes yonder, Master Greene?

GREENE   Ay, very well: do you know them?

Here enters Black Will and Shakebag

BRADSHAW   The one I know not: but he seems a knave,
  Chiefly for bearing the other company.
5 For such a slave, so vile a rogue as he,
  Lives not again upon the earth,
  Black Will is his name. I tell you Master Greene,
  At Boulogne he and I were fellow soldiers,
  Where he played such pranks,
10 As all the camp feared him for his villainy.
  I warrant you he bears so bad a mind
  That for a crown he'll murder any man.

GREENE   The fitter is he for my purpose, marry.   *Aside*

BLACK WILL   How now, fellow Bradshaw,
15 Whither away so early?

BRADSHAW   O Will, times are changed, no fellows now,
  Though we were once together in the field.
  Yet, thy friend to do thee any good I can.

BLACK WILL   Why, Bradshaw, was not thou and I fellow soldiers at Boulogne, where
20   I was a corporal and thou but a base mercenary groom? No fellows now, because
you are a goldsmith and have a little plate in your shop. You were glad to call me
'fellow Will,' and with a curtsy to the earth, 'One snatch good corporal' when I stole
the half ox from John the victualler and domineered with it amongst good fellows
in one night.

25   **BRADSHAW**   Ay, Will, those days are past with me.

BLACK WILL   Ay, but they be not past with me, for I keep that same honourable mind
still. Good neighbour Bradshaw, you are too proud to be my fellow. But were it
not that I see more company coming down the hill, I would be fellows with you
once more, and share crowns with you too. But let that pass, and tell me whither
30   you go.

BRADSHAW   To London, Will, about a piece of service
  Wherein happily thou mayst pleasure me.

BLACK WILL   What is it?

BRADSHAW   Of late, Lord Cheyne lost some plate,
35 Which one did bring, and sold it at my shop,
  Saying he served Sir Anthony Cooke.
  A search was made, the plate was found with me,

[Scene 2]   *Location: London*   **3 knave** rogue, villain   **8 Boulogne** a French port on the English Channel captured by the English in 1544   **12 crown** coin worth five shillings, one quarter of one pound   **13 marry** truly, literally 'by the Virgin Mary'   **18 Yet** but still   **20 groom** inferior fellow   **21 plate** items of precious metal   **22 curtsy** customary gesture of respect   **23 victualler** innkeeper/seller of provisions   **domineered** swaggered, lorded it   **34 Of late** recently   **Lord Cheyne** Sir Thomas (not Lord) Cheyne was Lord Warden of the Cinque Ports and MP for Kent   **36 Sir Anthony Cooke** was tutor to Edward VI

And I am bound to answer at the 'size.

Now Lord Cheyne solemnly vows

40 If law will serve him, he'll hang me for his plate.

Now I am going to London upon hope,

To find the fellow. Now Will, I know

Thou art acquainted with such companions.

BLACK WILL   What manner of man was he?

45 BRADSHAW   A lean-faced, writhen knave,

Hawk-nosed, and very hollow-eyed,

With mighty furrows in his stormy brows,

Long hair down his shoulders curled:

His chin was bare, but on his upper lip,

50 A mutchado, which he wound about his ear.

BLACK WILL   What apparel had he?

BRADSHAW   A watchet satin doublet all to-torn:

The inner side did bear the greater show:

A pair of threadbare velvet hose, seam rent,

55 A worsted stocking rent above the shoe,

A livery cloak, but all the lace was off.

'Twas bad, but yet it served to hide the plate.

BLACK WILL   Sirrah Shakebag, canst thou remember since we trolled the bowl at Sittingburgh, where I broke the tapster's head of the Lion with a cudgel-stick?

60 SHAKEBAG   Ay, very well, Will.

BLACK WILL   Why, it was with the money that the plate was sold for. Sirrah Bradshaw what wilt thou give him that can tell thee who sold thy plate?

BRADSHAW   Who? I pray thee, good Will.

BLACK WILL   Why 'twas one Jack Fitten. He's now in Newgate for stealing a horse,

65 and shall be arraigned the next 'size.

BRADSHAW   Why then, let Lord Cheyne seek Jack Fitten forth, for I'll back and tell him who robbed him of his plate. This cheers my heart.— Master Greene, I'll leave you, for I must to the Isle of Sheppey with speed.

GREENE   Before you go let me entreat you to carry this letter to Mistress Arden of

70 Faversham and humbly recommend me to herself.

BRADSHAW   That will I, Master Greene, and so farewell.

Here Will, there's a crown for thy good news.   *Gives money*

Exit Bradshaw

BLACK WILL   Farewell, Bradshaw, I'll drink no water for thy sake, whilst this lasts.

Now gentleman, shall we have your company to London?

75 GREENE   Nay, stay sirs, a little more I needs must use your help,

And in a matter of great consequence,

---

38 'size assize, trial   **45 writhen** twisted   **50 mutchado** moustache   **51 apparel** clothing   **52 watchet** light blue   **doublet** close-fitting body garment worn by men   **all to-torn** badly torn   **53 inner side** lining   **bear ... show** was more prominent   **54 hose** leggings   **rent** torn   **55 worsted** woollen fabric   **56 livery** uniform indicating service to a particular family   **58 trolled the bowl** played at bowls   **59 Sittingburgh** Sittingbourne, a town in Kent nine miles east of Faversham   **tapster's** innkeeper's   **Lion** name of a public house   **cudgel-stick** short stick or club used in contests   **64 Newgate** London's main prison   **68 Isle of Sheppey** island off the coast of northern Kent in the Thames estuary

Wherein if you'll be secret and profound,

I'll give you twenty angels for your pains.

BLACK WILL   How? Twenty angels? Give my fellow George Shakebag and me twenty

80   angels, and if thou'lt have thy own father slain, that thou mayst inherit his land,

we'll kill him.

SHAKEBAG   Ay, thy mother, thy sister, thy brother, or all thy kin.

GREENE   Well this it is, Arden of Faversham

Hath highly wronged me about the Abbey land,

85   That no revenge but death will serve the turn.

Will you two kill him? Here's the angels down,   *Offers money*

And I will lay the platform of his death.

BLACK WILL   Plat me no platforms! Give me the money, and I'll stab him as he stands

pissing against a wall, but I'll kill him.

90   SHAKEBAG   Where is he?

GREENE   He is now at London, in Aldersgate Street.

SHAKEBAG   He's dead, as if he had been condemned by an act of Parliament, if once

Black Will and I swear his death.

GREENE   Here is ten pound, and when he is dead,   *Gives money*

95   Ye shall have twenty more.

BLACK WILL   My fingers itches to be at the peasant. Ah, that I might be set a work

thus through the year, and that murder would grow to an occupation that a man

might without danger of law. Zounds, I warrant I should be warden of the company.

Come let us be going, and we'll bait at Rochester, where I'll give thee a gallon of sack

100   to handsel the match withal.   *Exeunt*

[Scene 3]

Here enters Michael

MICHAEL   I have gotten such a letter,

As will touch the painter, and thus it is:

Here enters Arden and Franklin, and hears Michael read this letter:

'My duty remembered Mistress Susan, hoping in God you be in good health, as I,

Michael, was at the making hereof. This is to certify you, that as the turtle true,

5   when she hath lost her mate, sitteth alone, so I mourning for your absence, do walk

up and down Paul's, till one day I fell asleep and lost my master's pantofles. Ah,

Mistress Susan, abolish that paltry painter: cut him off by the shins with a frowning

look of your crabbed countenance and think upon Michael, who, drunk with the

dregs of your favour, will cleave as fast to your love, as a plaster of pitch to a galled

78 angels coins, worth ten shillings, half a pound at this time   87 lay the platform set out the basis/devise the plan   91 Aldersgate Street important
street running westwards from the Aldersgate, one of the original gates of the city   98 might i.e. might follow   Zounds, I warrant by God's wounds I
swear   warden … company master of the guild (of murderers)   99 bait stop to take refreshments, originally to feed horses   Rochester cathedral city
in Kent between London and Faversham   sack white wine (from Spain or the Canary Isles)   100 handsel inaugurate with some ceremony   match
agreement   [Scene 3]   *Location: London*   2 touch affect injuriously   4 turtle turtle dove, symbol of conjugal affection and constancy   6 Paul's St Paul's
Cathedral in London; the old cathedral and its precincts were public places frequented by gossips, idlers and disreputable characters   pantofles slippers, loose
shoes   7 abolish put an end to   8 crabbed ill-tempered   9 plaster of pitch bandage or dressing soaked in resin to treat galled (chafed) skin

10   horseback. Thus hoping you will let my passions penetrate, or rather impetrate
       mercy of your meek hands, I end. Yours, Michael, or else not Michael.'

       ARDEN   Why, you paltry knave,
           Stand you here loitering, knowing my affairs,
           What haste my business craves to send to Kent?

15   FRANKLIN   Faith, friend Michael, this is very ill.
           Knowing your master hath no more but you,
           And do ye slack his business for your own?

       ARDEN   Where is the letter, sirrah, let me see it,

       Then he [Michael] gives him the letter
           See Master Franklin, here's proper stuff:

20   Susan, my maid, the painter, and my man,
           A crew of harlots all in love forsooth.—
           Sirrah, let me hear no more of this.
           Now for thy life, once write to her a word.

       Here enters Greene, Will, and Shakebag   *Unseen by the others*
           Wilt thou be married to so base a trull?

25   'Tis Mosby's sister! Come I once at home,
           I'll rouse her from remaining in my house.
           Now Master Franklin, let us go walk in Paul's,
           Come, but a turn or two and then away.   *Exeunt*

       GREENE   The first is Arden, and that's his man,   [*Arden, Franklin and Michael*]

30   The other is Franklin, Arden's dearest friend.

       BLACK WILL   Zounds! I'll kill them all three!

       GREENE   Nay, sirs, touch not his man in any case:
           But stand close, and take you fittest standing,
           And at his coming forth speed him.

35   To the Nag's Head: there is this coward's haunt.
           But now I'll leave you till the deed be done.   *Exit Greene*

       SHAKEBAG   If he be not paid his own, ne'er trust Shakebag.

       BLACK WILL   Sirrah Shakebag, at his coming forth
           I'll run him through, and then to the Blackfriars,

40   And there take water and away.

       SHAKEBAG   Why that's the best, but see thou miss him not.

       BLACK WILL   How can I miss him, when I think on the forty
           Angels I must have more.

       Here enters a Prentice

---

10 passions penetrate with bawdy innuendo   **impetrate** beg for   **12 paltry** worthless   **16 no more** no other servant   **17 slack** neglect   **21 harlots**
rascals/sexually loose persons, applied to men and women   **24 trull** whore   **25 Come ... home** when I return home   **26 rouse** startle from a state
of security   **33 fittest standing** the best position   **34 speed** kill, despatch   **35 Nag's Head** London tavern in Cheapside   **37 his own** what he
deserves   **39 run him through** i.e. with a sword   **Blackfriars** to claim sanctuary at the Dominican monastery there: fugitives from justice were entitled
to immunity from arrest at religious sites; after the dissolution of the monasteries some of the buildings were later leased – the King's Men performed
there from until 1642   **40 take water** get a boat across the river Thames   **away** escape   **42 forty Angels** a total of twenty pounds, a large sum of
money   *Prentice* an apprentice

PRENTICE 'Tis very late, I were best shut up my stall, for here will be old filching
45   when the press comes forth of Paul's.

Then lets he down his window, and it breaks Black Will's head

BLACK WILL Zounds! Draw, Shakebag, draw! I am almost killed!

PRENTICE We'll tame you, I warrant.

BLACK WILL Zounds, I am tame enough already.

Here enters Arden, Franklin and Michael

ARDEN   What troublesome fray or mutiny is this?

50   FRANKLIN 'Tis nothing but some brabbling paltry fray,

Devised to pick men's pockets in the throng.

ARDEN   Is't nothing else? Come, Franklin, let us away.   *Exeunt [Arden, Franklin*

BLACK WILL What mends shall I have for my broken head?   *and Michael]*

PRENTICE Marry, this mends, that if you get you not away all the sooner, you shall be
55   well beaten and sent to the Counter.   *Exit Prentice*

BLACK WILL Well, I'll be gone: but look to your signs,

For I'll pull them down all.

Shakebag, my broken head grieves me not so much,

As by this means Arden hath escaped.

Here enters Greene

60   I had a glimpse of him and his companion.

GREENE   Why, sirs, Arden's as well as I.

I met him and Franklin going merrily to the ordinary.

What, dare you not do it?

BLACK WILL   Yes sir, we dare do it, but were my consent to give again,
65   We would not do it under ten pound more.

I value every drop of my blood at a French crown.

I have had ten pound to steal a dog:

And we have no more here to kill a man.

But that a bargain is a bargain, and so forth,
70   You should do it yourself.

GREENE   I pray thee how came thy head broke?

BLACK WILL   Why, thou see'st it is broke, dost thou not?

SHAKEBAG   Standing against a stall, watching Arden's coming,

A boy let down his shop window and broke his head,
75   Whereupon arose a brawl and in the tumult

Arden escaped us, and passed by unthought on.

But forbearance is no acquittance.

Another time we'll do it, I warrant thee.

GREENE   I pray thee, Will, make clean thy bloody brow,
80   And let us bethink us on some other place,

Where Arden may be met with handsomely.

---

44 old filching clever, experienced thieving   **45 press** crowd   **49 fray** conflict, disturbamce   **50 brabbling** quarrelsome, riotous   **53 mends** recompense/remedy   **55 Counter** sheriff's court or the prison attached to it   **56 signs** i.e. shop signs   **62 ordinary** inn or tavern where meals are served at a fixed price   **66 French crown** English name for the French coin, the écu; punningly used with reference to the baldness produced by the 'French disease', syphilis   **69 But that** however since   **77 forbearance ... acquittance** refraining from carrying out the deed is no satisfaction/ payment   **81 handsomely** conveniently

Remember how devoutly thou hast sworn
To kill the villain: think upon thine oath.

BLACK WILL   Tush, I have broken five hundred oaths,
85   But wouldst thou charm me to effect this deed?
Tell me of gold my resolution's fee,
Say thou see'st Mosby kneeling at my knees,
Off'ring me service for my high attempt:
And sweet Alice Arden with a lap of crowns
90   Comes with a lowly curtsy to the earth
Saying, 'Take this, but for thy quarterage,
Such yearly tribute will I answer thee.'
Why this would steel soft-mettled cowardice,
With which Black Will was never tainted with.
95   I tell thee, Greene, the forlorn traveller,
Whose lips are glued with summer's parching heat,
Ne'er longed so much to see a running brook,
As I to finish Arden's tragedy.
See'st thou this gore that cleaveth to my face?
100   From hence ne'er will I wash this bloody stain,
Till Arden's heart be panting in my hand.

GREENE   Why, that's well said, but what saith Shakebag?

SHAKEBAG   I cannot paint my valour out with words,
But give me place and opportunity:
105   Such mercy as the starven lioness
When she is dry sucked of her eager young
Shows to the prey that next encounters her,
On Arden so much pity would I take.

GREENE   So should it fare with men of firm resolve.
110   And now, sirs, seeing this accident
Of meeting him in Paul's hath no success,
Let us bethink us on some other place,
Whose earth may swallow up this Arden's blood.

Here enters Michael

See yonder comes his man, and wot you what?
115   The foolish knave is in love with Mosby's sister,
And for her sake, whose love he cannot get
Unless Mosby solicit his suit,
The villain hath sworn the slaughter of his master.
We'll question him, for he may stead us much.
120   How now, Michael, whither are you going?

MICHAEL   My master hath new supped:
And I am going to prepare his chamber.

---

89 lap of crowns skirt filled with coins   **91 quarterage** quarterly payment   **93 steel** harden   **soft-mettled** gentle-tempered, playing on **steel** and 'metal'   **99 gore** blood   **cleaveth** sticks   **102 saith** says   **105 starven** starved   **114 wot you what?** what do you know?   **wot** know   **119 stead** be useful to, profit   **121 new** recently

GREENE   Where supped Master Arden?

MICHAEL   At the Nag's Head, at the eighteenpence ordinary,

125   How now, Master Shakebag. What, Black Will?

           God's dear Lady, how chance your face is so bloody?

BLACK WILL   Go to, sirrah, there is a chance in it.

           This sauciness in you will make you be knocked.

MICHAEL   Nay, and you be offended: I'll be gone.   *Starts to go*

130   GREENE   Stay, Michael: you may not scape us so.

           Michael, I know you love your master well.

MICHAEL   Why so I do, but wherefore urge you that?

GREENE   Because I think you love your mistress better.

[MICHAEL]   So think not I. But say, i'faith, what if I should?

135   SHAKEBAG   Come to the purpose.— Michael, we hear   *To Greene*

           You have a pretty love in Faversham.

MICHAEL   Why, have I two or three, what's that to thee?

BLACK WILL   You deal too mildly with the peasant. Thus it is,   *To Shakebag*

           'Tis known to us you love Mosby's sister.

140   We know, besides, that you have ta'en your oath

           To further Mosby to your mistress' bed,

           And kill your master for his sister's sake.

           Now sir, a poorer coward than yourself

           Was never fostered in the coast of Kent.

145   How comes it then, that such a knave as you

           Dare swear a matter of such consequence?

GREENE   Ah, Will!

BLACK WILL   Tush give me leave, there's no more but this.

           Sith thou hast sworn, we dare discover all:

150   And hadst thou or shouldst thou utter it,

           We have devised a complot underhand,

           Whatever shall betide to any of us,

           To send thee roundly to the devil of hell.

           And therefore thus, I am the very man,

155   Marked in my birth hour by the Destinies,

           To give an end to Arden's life on earth.

           Thou but a member, but to whet the knife,

           Whose edge must search the closet of his breast.

           Thy office is but to appoint the place

160   And train thy master to his tragedy:

           Mine to perform it when occasion serves.

           Then be not nice, but here devise with us

           How and what way we may conclude his death.

SHAKEBAG   So shalt thou purchase Mosby for thy friend

---

124 **eighteenpence ordinary** tavern where the fixed price for food was eighteen old pence   126 **God's dear Lady** i.e. by the Virgin Mary   127 **Go to** expression of protest   129 **and** if   130 **scape** escape, get away from   132 **urge** mention, bring up   144 **fostered** brought up   149 **Sith** since   **dare discover** are bold to tell   151 **complot** plot, conspiracy   **underhand** secret   152 **betide** happen   153 **roundly** straight, promptly   155 **Destinies** Fates, three classical goddesses who determine the course of human life   157 **whet** sharpen   159 **office** task   162 **nice** foolish/fastidious/morally scrupulous

165   And by his friendship gain his sister's love.

GREENE   So shall thy mistress be thy favourer,

     And thou disburdened of the oath thou made.

MICHAEL   Well, gentlemen, I cannot but confess,

     Sith you have urged me so apparently,

170   That I have vowed my Master Arden's death:

     And he whose kindly love and liberal hand,

     Doth challenge nought but good deserts of me,

     I will deliver over to your hands.

     This night come to his house at Aldersgate,

175   The doors I'll leave unlocked against you come.

     No sooner shall ye enter through the latch,

     Over the threshold to the inner court

     But on your left hand shall you see the stairs

     That leads directly to my master's chamber.

180   There take him and dispose him as ye please.

     Now, it were good we parted company:

     What I have promised, I will perform.

BLACK WILL   Should you deceive us, 'twould go wrong with you.

MICHAEL   I will accomplish all I have revealed.

185 BLACK WILL   Come: let's go drink! Choler makes me as dry as a dog.

                          Exeunt Will, Greene and Shakebag. Michael remains

MICHAEL   Thus feeds the lamb securely on the down,

     Whilst through the thicket of an arbour brake,

     The hunger-bitten wolf o'erpries his haunt

     And takes advantage to eat him up.

190   Ah, harmless Arden how, how hast thou misdone,

     That thus thy gentle life is levelled at?

     The many good turns that thou hast done to me

     Now must I quittance with betraying thee:

     I that should take the weapon in my hand

195   And buckler thee from ill-intending foes,

     Do lead thee with a wicked, fraudful smile,

     As unsuspected to the slaughterhouse.

     So have I sworn to Mosby and my mistress:

     So have I promised to the slaughtermen.

200   And should I not deal currently with them,

     Their lawless rage would take revenge on me.

     Tush, I will spurn at mercy for this once.

     Let pity lodge where feeble women lie.

     I am resolved: and Arden needs must die.   *Exit Michael*

---

169 apparently clearly   **171 liberal** generous   **172 challenge** claim   **175 against** in preparation for when   **185 Choler** anger, one of the four humours early physiology believed regulated the body and the character; choler was characteristically hot and dry   **186 down** hill   **187 arbour brake** plot of ground with ferns, clumps of bushes; perhaps playing on 'arber' (windpipe) and 'break'   **188 o'erpries** overlooks, spies on   **191 levelled** aimed   **193 quittance** repay   **195 buckler** shield, protect   **200 currently** readily

[Scene 4]

Here enters Arden and Franklin

ARDEN   No, Franklin, no! If fear or stormy threats,
     If love of me, or care of womanhood,
     If fear of God, or common speech of men,
     Who mangle credit with their wounding words,
5   And couch dishonour as dishonour buds,
     Might join repentance in her wanton thoughts,
     No question, then, but she would turn the leaf
     And sorrow for her dissolution.
     But she is rooted in her wickedness:
10   Perverse and stubborn, not to be reclaimed.
     Good counsel is to her as rain to weeds
     And reprehension makes her vice to grow,
     As Hydra's head that perished by decay.
     Her faults methink are painted in my face
15   For every searching eye to overread.
     And Mosby's name, a scandal unto mine,
     Is deeply trenchèd in my blushing brow.
     Ah, Franklin, Franklin, when I think on this,
     My heart's grief rends my other powers
20   Worse than the conflict at the hour of death.
FRANKLIN   Gentle Arden, leave this sad lament.
     She will amend, and so your griefs will cease:
     Or else she'll die, and so your sorrows end.
     If neither of these two do haply fall,
25   Yet let your comfort be that others bear
     Your woes twice doubled all with patience.
ARDEN   My house is irksome: there I cannot rest.
FRANKLIN   Then stay with me in London: go not home.
ARDEN   Then that base Mosby doth usurp my room,
30   And makes his triumph of my being thence.
     At home, or not at home, where'er I be,
     Here, here it lies. Ah, Franklin here it lies,   *Indicating his breast*
     That will not out till wretched Arden dies.
Here enters Michael
FRANKLIN   Forget your griefs awhile, here comes your man.
35   ARDEN   What o'clock is't, sirrah?   *To Michael*
MICHAEL   Almost ten.
ARDEN   See, see how runs away the weary time!
     Come, Master Franklin, shall we go to bed?   *Exeunt Arden and Michael.*
FRANKLIN   I pray you go before: I'll follow you.   *Franklin remains*

[Scene 4] *Location:* London   **4 mangle credit** destroy truth/reputation   **5 couch** lower/conceal, cover up   **8 dissolution** dissolute, immoral behaviour
12 reprehension censure, reproof   **13 Hydra's head** in Greek mythology, as soon as one of the fabulous many-headed creature's heads was cut off two grew in its
place   **17 trenchèd** cut, carved   **19 rends** tears apart   **22 amend** reform   **24 haply** perhaps, playing on 'happily'   **29 usurp my room** take my place

40   Ah, what a hell is fretful jealousy?
         What pity-moaning words, what deep-fetched sighs,
         What grievous groans, and overlading woes
         Accompanies this gentle gentleman!
         Now will he shake his care-oppressèd head,
45   Then fix his sad eyes on the sullen earth,
         Ashamed to gaze upon the open world.
         Now will he cast his eyes up towards the heavens
         Looking that ways for redress of wrong.
         Sometimes he seeketh to beguile his grief,
50   And tells a story with his careful tongue.
         Then comes his wife's dishonour in his thoughts,
         And in the middle cutteth off his tale,
         Pouring fresh sorrow on his weary limbs.
         So woebegone, so inly charged with woe:
55   Was never any lived and bore it so.

         Here enters Michael

         MICHAEL   My master would desire you come to bed.

         FRANKLIN   Is he himself already in his bed?

         MICHAEL   He is and fain would have the light away.—   *Exit Franklin. Michael remains*
         Conflicting thoughts encampèd in my breast
60   Awake me with the echo of their strokes
         And I, a judge to censure either side,
         Can give to neither wishèd victory.
         My master's kindness pleads to me for life
         With just demand and I must grant it him.
65   My mistress she hath forced me with an oath,
         For Susan's sake, the which I may not break,
         For that is nearer than a master's love.
         That grim-faced fellow, pitiless Black Will
         And Shakebag, stern in bloody stratagem —
70   Two rougher ruffians never lived in Kent —
         Have sworn my death if I infringe my vow,
         A dreadful thing to be considered of.
         Methinks I see them with their boltered hair,
         Staring and grinning in thy gentle face,
75   And in their ruthless hands, their daggers drawn,
         Insulting o'er thee with a peck of oaths,
         Whilst thou, submissive, pleading for relief,
         Art mangled by their ireful instruments.
         Methinks I hear them ask where Michael is

---

42 **overlading** too heavy   50 **careful** full of grief   54 **inly** inwardly   **charged** full, laden   58 **fain** gladly   **away** put out   61 **a … side** i.e. two conflicting advisers in his head – the good and bad angels of self-interest and conscience, a technique literalized in the psychomachia of medieval morality plays   73 **boltered** padded/matted with blood   76 **peck** pile, heap

80   And pitiless Black Will cries, 'Stab the slave.

The peasant will detect the tragedy.'

The wrinkles in his foul, death-threatening face

Gapes open wide, like graves to swallow men.

My death to him is but a merriment,

85   And he will murder me to make him sport.

He comes, he comes! Ah, Master Franklin help!

Call up the neighbours or we are but dead!

Here enters Franklin and Arden

FRANKLIN   What dismal outcry calls me from my rest?

ARDEN   What hath occasioned such a fearful cry?

90   Speak Michael! Hath any injured thee?

MICHAEL   Nothing sir, but as I fell asleep,

Upon the threshold leaning to the stairs,

I had a fearful dream that troubled me:

And in my slumber thought I was beset

95   With murderer thieves that came to rifle me.

My trembling joints witness my inward fear.

I crave your pardons for disturbing you.

ARDEN   So great a cry for nothing, I ne'er heard.

What, are the doors fast locked and all things safe?

100   MICHAEL   I cannot tell, I think I locked the doors.

ARDEN   I like not this, but I'll go see myself.   *He checks the door*

Ne'er trust me, but the doors were all unlocked!

This negligence not half contenteth me.

Get you to bed: and if you love my favour,

105   Let me have no more such pranks as these.

Come, Master Franklin, let us go to bed.

FRANKLIN   Ay, by my faith, the air is very cold.

Michael, farewell: I pray thee dream no more.   *Exeunt*

[Scene 5]

Here enters Will, Greene and Shakebag

SHAKEBAG   Black night hath hid the pleasures of the day,

And sheeting darkness overhangs the earth,

And with the black fold of her cloudy robe

Obscure us from the eyesight of the world

5   In which sweet silence such as we triumph.

The lazy minutes linger on their time,

---

81 detect expose   **94 beset** set upon/surrounded   **95 rifle** rob, plunder   **[Scene 5]**   *Location: London, near Franklin's house*   **5 such as we** i.e. thieves, murderers

Loth to give due audit to the hour
Till in the watch our purpose be complete,
And Arden sent to everlasting night.

10   Greene, get you gone, and linger here about,
And at some hour hence, come to us again,
Where we will give you instance of his death.

GREENE   Speed to my wish whose will soe'er says no:
And so I'll leave you for an hour or two.   *Exit Greene*

15   BLACK WILL   I tell thee Shakebag, would this thing were done.
I am so heavy that I can scarce go:
This drowsiness in me bodes little good.

SHAKEBAG   How now Will, become a precisian?
Nay, then let's go sleep when bugs and fears
20   Shall kill our courages with their fancy's work.

BLACK WILL   Why, Shakebag, thou mistakes me much
And wrongs me too in telling me of fear.
Were't not a serious thing we go about
It should be slipped till I had fought with thee,
25   To let thee know I am no coward, I:
I tell thee, Shakebag, thou abusest me.

SHAKEBAG   Why thy speech bewrayed an inly kind of fear
And savoured of a weak, relenting spirit.
Go forward now in that we have begun:
30   And afterwards attempt me when thou dar'st.

BLACK WILL   And if I do not, heaven cut me off.
But let that pass, and show me to this house
Where thou shalt see I'll do as much as Shakebag.

SHAKEBAG   This is the door. But soft, methinks 'tis shut.   *Trying the door*
35   The villain Michael hath deceivèd us.

BLACK WILL   Soft let me see, Shakebag. 'Tis shut indeed.   *Trying the door*
Knock with thy sword, perhaps the slave will hear.

SHAKEBAG   It will not be. The white-livered peasant   *Knocking*
Is gone to bed and laughs us both to scorn.

40   BLACK WILL   And he shall buy his merriment as dear,
As ever coistrel bought so little sport.
Ne'er let this sword assist me when I need
But rust and canker after I have sworn
If I, the next time that I meet the hind,

---

7 Loth reluctant   **due audit** a true account; also a biblical allusion to the Judgement Day   **8 watch** period into which the night was divided; between three and five, collectively known as 'the watches of the night'   **11 some hour hence** in an hour's time   **12 instance** token of proof   **13 Speed** success/ grant   **whose will soe'er** despite whoever's will   **15 would** I wish   **17 bodes** presages, foretells   **18 precisian** one of strict religious observance, a puritan   **19 bugs** bugbears, imaginary fears   **20 fancy's work** imagination effects/afflictions   **22 telling** telling lies about/accusing   **27 bewrayed** exposed   **inly** inward   **28 savoured** has the appearance of proceeding from   **30 attempt** try to fight   **38 white-livered** cowardly   **41 coistrel** knave, base fellow   **44 hind** rustic, boor/fellow

45   Lop not away his leg, his arm or both.

SHAKEBAG   And let me never draw a sword again,
            Nor prosper in the twilight, cock-shut light,
            When I would fleece the wealthy passenger,
            But lie and languish in a loathsome den,
50   Hated and spit at by the goers-by,
            And in that death may die unpitièd
            If I, the next time that I meet the slave,
            Cut not the nose from off the coward's face,
            And trample on it for this villainy.

55   BLACK WILL   Come, let's go seek out Greene: I know he'll swear.

SHAKEBAG   He were a villain and he would not swear.
            'Twould make a peasant swear amongst his boys,
            That ne'er durst say before but 'yea' and 'no'
            To be thus flouted of a coisterel.

60   BLACK WILL   Shakebag, let's seek out Greene, and in the morning
            At the ale-house butting Arden's house,
            Watch the outcoming of that prick-eared cur,
            And then let me alone to handle him.   *Exeunt*

[Scene 6]

Here enters Arden, Franklin and Michael

ARDEN   Sirrah, get you back to Billingsgate
            And learn what time the tide will serve our turn.
            Come to us in Paul's. First go make the bed,
            And afterwards go harken for the flood.   *Exit Michael*
5   Come, Master Franklin, you shall go with me.
            This night I dreamed that being in a park,
            A toil was pitched to overthrow the deer
            And I, upon a little rising hill,
            Stood whistly watching for the herd's approach.
10   Even there, methoughts, a gentle slumber took me
            And summoned all my parts to sweet repose.
            But in the pleasure of this golden rest
            An ill-thewed foster had removed the toil
            And rounded me with that beguiling home,
15   Which late, methought, was pitched to cast the deer.

---

47 **cock-shut** twilight   48 **passenger** traveller (on foot)   56 **and** if   59 **coisterel** i.e. coistrel, see above, line 41   61 **butting** abutting, adjacent to   62 **prick-eared cur** a term of abuse, plays on **prick** i.e. penis, literally a dog with erect ears   **[Scene 6]**   *Location: London*   1 **Billingsgate** one of the gates of the City of London and the fishmarket nearby   2 **tide … turn** i.e. when the tide will suit us; the Thames is a tidal river and the journey to Faversham was made by boat   4 **harken** make enquiries   **flood** flowing in of the tide; perhaps suggesting a biblical reference to Noah's Flood   7 **toil** net   **pitched** put in place   9 **whistly** silently   13 **ill-thewed** ill-natured   **foster** forester   14 **rounded** surrounded   **home** sense is unclear, perhaps referring to the net

With that he blew an evil-sounding horn,
And at the noise another herdman came
With falchion drawn, and bent it at my breast,
Crying aloud, 'Thou art the game we seek!'
20 With this I waked and trembled every joint,
Like one obscurèd in a little bush
That sees a lion foraging about.
And when the dreadful forest king is gone,
He pries about with timorous suspect
25 Throughout the thorny casements of the brake,
And will not think his person dangerless,
But quakes and shivers though the cause be gone.
So trust me, Franklin, when I did awake
I stood in doubt whether I waked or no,
30 Such great impression took this fond surprise.
God grant this vision bedeem me any good.

FRANKLIN This fantasy doth rise from Michael's fear,
Who being awaked with the noise he made,
His troubled senses yet could take no rest:
35 And this, I warrant you, procured your dream.

ARDEN   It may be so. God frame it to the best,
But oftentimes my dreams presage too true.

FRANKLIN To such as note their nightly fantasies,
Some one in twenty may incur belief.
40 But use it not: 'tis but a mockery.

ARDEN   Come, Master Franklin, we'll now walk in Paul's
And dine together at the ordinary,
And by my man's direction draw to the quay
And with the tide go down to Faversham.
45 Say, Master Franklin, shall it not be so?

FRANKLIN At your good pleasure sir: I'll bear you company.   *Exeunt*

[Scene 7]

Here enters Michael at one door. Here enters Greene, Will, and Shakebag, at another door

BLACK WILL   Draw, Shakebag, for here's that villain Michael.

GREENE   First, Will, let's hear what he can say.

BLACK WILL   Speak, milksop slave, and never after speak!

MICHAEL   For God's sake sirs, let me excuse myself!
5 For hear I swear by heaven and earth and all,

---

18 **falchion** curved broadsword   **bent** aimed   24 **pries** peers   25 **casements** coverings   **brake** clump of bushes   30 **fond** foolish   **surprise** fear caused by unexpected terror of his dream   31 **bedeem** decree/signify   **any** some   35 **procured** brought about   37 **presage** foretell   40 **use** practise   **mockery** deceptive counterfeit   42 **ordinary** tavern   **[Scene 7]**   *Location: London*   1 **Draw** take out your sword   3 **milksop** feeble, timid

I did perform the outmost of my task

And left the doors unbolted and unlocked.

But see the chance: Franklin and my master

Were very late conferring in the porch,

10   And Franklin left his napkin where he sat,

With certain gold knit in it, as he said.

Being in bed, he did bethink himself,

And coming down, he found the doors unshut.

He locked the gates and brought away the keys.

15   For which offence my master rated me,

But now I am going to see what flood it is

For with the tide my master will away,

Where you may front him well on Rainham Down,

A place well-fitting such a stratagem.

20   BLACK WILL   Your excuse hath somewhat mollified my choler.—

Why now, Greene, 'tis better now nor e'er it was.

GREENE   But Michael, is this true?

MICHAEL   As true as I report it to be true.

SHAKEBAG   Then, Michael, this shall be your penance:

25   To feast us all at the Salutation,

Where we will plot our purpose throughly.

GREENE   And Michael, you shall bear no news of this tide

Because they two may be in Rainham Down down before your master.

MICHAEL   Why I'll agree to anything you'll have me:

30   So you will accept of my company.   *Exeunt*

[Scene 8]

Here enters Mosby

MOSBY   Disturbèd thoughts drives me from company

And dries my marrow with their watchfulness,

Continual trouble of my moody brain

Feebles my body by excess of drink

5   And nips me, as the bitter north-east wind

Doth check the tender blossoms in the spring.

Well fares the man, howe'er his cates do taste,

That tables not with foul suspicion:

And he but pines amongst his delicates

10   Whose troubled mind is stuffed with discontent.

My golden time was when I had no gold.

---

6 **outmost** utmost   10 **napkin** small piece of cloth: table napkin, small towel, handkerchief   11 **knit** tied up   15 **rated** scolded berated   16 **flood** high tide   18 **front** confront   **Rainham Down** open country around the small town in Kent between Rochester and Faversham situated on the slope of the North Downs   20 **mollified my choler** softened my anger   21 **nor e'er** than ever   25 **Salutation** a public house in Newgate Street   26 **throughly** thoroughly   28 **Because** so that   30 **accept of** agree to   [Scene 8]   *Location: Faversham*   2 **marrow** innermost part of his being   7 **cates** choice foods, delicacies   8 **tables** tabulates, enters in a list   9 **pines** suffers/starves

Though then I wanted, yet I slept secure:
My daily toil begat me night's repose,
My night's repose made daylight fresh to me.
15 But since I climbed the top bough of the tree
And sought to build my nest among the clouds,
Each gentle starry gale doth shake my bed
And makes me dread my downfall to the earth.
But whither doth contemplation carry me?
20 The way I seek to find where pleasure dwells
Is hedged behind me that I cannot back
But needs must on although to danger's gate.
Then, Arden, perish thou by that decree,
For Greene doth ear the land and weed thee up
25 To make my harvest nothing but pure corn.
And for his pains I'll heave him up awhile
And after smother him to have his wax.
Such bees as Greene must never live to sting.
Then is there Michael and the painter too,
30 Chief actors to Arden's overthrow,
Who, when they shall see me sit in Arden's seat,
They will insult upon me for my meed
Or fright me by detecting of his end.
I'll none of that, for I can cast a bone
35 To make these curs pluck out each other's throat,
And then am I sole ruler of mine own.
Yet Mistress Arden lives: but she's myself,
And holy church rites makes us two but one.
But what for that I may not trust you, Alice?
40 You have supplanted Arden for my sake,
And will extirpen me to plant another.
'Tis fearful sleeping in a serpent's bed
And I will cleanly rid my hands of her.

Here enters Alice   *Carrying a prayerbook*

But here she comes and I must flatter her—
45 How now, Alice? What, sad and passionate?
Make me partaker of thy pensiveness:
Fire divided burns with lesser force.
ALICE   But I will damn that fire in my breast:
Till by the force thereof my part consume.
50 Ah, Mosby!
MOSBY   Such deep pathaires like to a cannon's burst
Discharged against a ruinated wall,

---

13 begat brought, generated   **24 ear** plough   **25 corn** small, hard particles, i.e. unprofitable   **26 heave** lift   **27 wax** growth, stature, playing on 'beeswax'   **32 meed** reward/merit   **33 detecting** exposing   **34 bone** i.e. Susan   **41 extirpen** extirpate, root out   **48 damn** condemn, with religious connotation 'eternal punishment in hell' but also puns on homophone 'dam' meaning confine   **51 pathaires** passionate outbursts

Breaks my relenting heart in thousand pieces.

Ungentle Alice, thy sorrow is my sore:

55   Thou knowst it well and 'tis thy policy

To forge distressful looks, to wound a breast

Where lies a heart that dies where thou art sad:

It is not love that loves to anger love.

ALICE   It is not love that loves to murder love.

60 MOSBY   How mean you that?

ALICE   Thou knowst how dearly Arden lovèd me.

MOSBY   And then?

ALICE   And then — conceal the rest, for 'tis too bad,

Lest that my words be carried with the wind

65   And published in the world to both our shames.

I pray thee, Mosby, let our springtime wither:

Our harvest else will yield but loathsome weeds.

Forget, I pray thee, what hath passed betwixt us,

For now I blush and tremble at the thoughts.

70 MOSBY   What, are you changed?

ALICE   Ay, to my former happy life again,

From title of an odious strumpet's name

To honest Arden's wife, not Arden's honest wife.

Ha, Mosby, 'tis thou hast rifled me of that,

75   And made me sland'rous to all my kin.

Even in my forehead is thy name engraven,

A mean artificer, that low-born name.

I was bewitched. Woe worth the hapless hour

And all the causes that enchanted me.

80 MOSBY   Nay, if thou ban, let me breath curses forth,

And if you stand so nicely at your fame,

Let me repent the credit I have lost.

I have neglected matters of import

That would have stated me above thy state,

85   Forslowed advantages, and spurned at time.

Ay, Fortune's right hand Mosby hath forsook

To take a wanton giglot by the left.

I left the marriage of an honest maid,

Whose dowry would have weighed down all thy wealth,

90   Whose beauty and demeanour far exceeded thee.

This certain good I lost for changing bad

And wrapped my credit in thy company.

I was bewitched — that is no theme of thine! —

---

66 wither shrivel up and die   **72 strumpet's** whore's   **74 rifled** plundered, despoiled   **75 sland'rous** a source of shame or disgrace   **77 mean** inferior, of low social status   **artificer** artisan, craftsman/trickster   **78 hapless** unlucky   **80 ban** curse   **81 stand so nicely** position yourself in such a fastidious way   **fame** reputation   **84 stated** raised me socially   **85 Forslowed** neglected, delayed   **spurned** rejected with contempt   **86 Fortune's** of Fortune, imagined as a goddess with a wheel which she turns and which brings good or bad luck   **87 wanton** lascivious, unchaste   **giglot** lewd woman   **92 wrapped** covered up/entangled   **credit** honour, reputation

And thou unhallowed hast enchanted me.
95   But I will break thy spells and exorcisms,
And put another sight upon these eyes
That showed my heart a raven for a dove.
Thou art not fair, I viewed thee not till now:
Thou art not kind: till now I knew thee not.
100   And now the rain hath beaten off thy gilt,
Thy worthless copper shows thee counterfeit.
It grieves me not to see how foul thou art,
But mads me that ever I thought thee fair.
Go, get thee gone, a copesmate for thy hinds!
105   I am too good to be thy favourite.

ALICE   Ay, now I see, and too soon find it true,
Which often hath been told me by my friends,
That Mosby loves me not but for my wealth,
Which, too incredulous I ne'er believed.
110   Nay, hear me speak, Mosby, a word or two: *Mosby tries to interrupt*
I'll bite my tongue if it speak bitterly.
Look on me, Mosby, or I'll kill myself.
Nothing shall hide me from thy stormy look.
If thou cry war, there is no peace for me.
115   I will do penance for offending thee
And burn this prayerbook, where I here use
The holy word that had converted me.
See, Mosby, I will tear away the leaves,   *She tears out leaves from the prayerbook?*
And all the leaves, and in this golden cover
120   Shall thy sweet phrases and thy letters dwell;
And thereon will I chiefly meditate,
And hold no other sect but such devotion.
Wilt thou not look? Is all thy love o'erwhelmed?
Wilt thou not hear? What malice stops thine ears?
125   Why speaks thou not? What silence ties thy tongue?
Thou hast been sighted as the eagle is,
And heard as quickly as the fearful hare,
And spoke as smoothly as an orator.
When I have bid thee hear or see or speak,
130   And art thou sensible in none of these?
Weigh all thy good turns with this little fault,
And I deserve not Mosby's muddy looks.
A fount once troubled is not thickened still:
Be clear again, I'll ne'er more trouble thee.
135   MOSBY   O, no, I am a base artificer:

---

94 **unhallowed** wicked, impious   95 **exorcisms** calling up of spirits   100 **gilt** thin veneer of gold leaf, plays on 'guilt'   104 **copesmate** companion/ accomplice/paramour   **hinds** servants   108 **but** except   122 **sect** adherence to religious faith   130 **sensible** able to perceive   132 **muddy** sullen, glowering   133 **fount** spring   **still** always

My wings are feathered for a lowly flight.

Mosby? Fie, no! Not for a thousand pound.

Make love to you? Why, 'tis unpardonable:

We beggars must not breathe where gentles are.

140 ALICE   Sweet Mosby is as gentle as a king,

And I too blind to judge him otherwise.

Flowers do sometimes spring in fallow lands,

Weeds in gardens, roses grow on thorns:

So whatsoe'er my Mosby's father was,

145   Himself is valued gentle by his worth.

MOSBY   Ah, how you women can insinuate,

And clear a trespass with your sweet-set tongue.

I will forget this quarrel, gentle Alice,

Provided I'll be tempted so no more.

Here enters Bradshaw

150 ALICE   Then with thy lips seal up this new-made match.   *She goes to kiss him*

MOSBY   Soft, Alice, for here comes somebody.

ALICE   How now, Bradshaw, what's the news with you?

BRADSHAW   I have little news but here's a letter

That Master Greene importuned me to give you.

155 ALICE   Go in, Bradshaw, call for a cup of beer.

'Tis almost suppertime: thou shalt stay with us.   *Exit [Bradshaw]*

Then she reads the letter

'We have missed of our purpose at London, but shall perform it by the way. We thank our neighbour Bradshaw. Yours, Richard Greene.'

How likes my love the tenor of this letter?

160 MOSBY   Well, were his date complete and expired.

ALICE   Ah, would it were! Then comes my happy hour:

Till then my bliss is mixed with bitter gall.

Come, let us in to shun suspicion.

MOSBY   Ay, to the gates of death to follow thee.   *Exeunt*

[Scene 9]

Here enters Greene, Will and Shakebag

SHAKEBAG   Come, Will, see thy tools be in a readiness?

Is not thy powder dank, or will thy flint strike fire?

BLACK WILL   Then ask me if my nose be on my face

Or whether my tongue be frozen in my mouth.

5   Zounds, here's a coil!

---

139 **gentles** those of noble or gentle birth/rank   149 **tempted** tried, tested   154 **importuned** urged, pressed   159 **tenor** substance   162 **gall** bile/ spirit of resentment   163 **shun** avoid   **[Scene 9]** *Location: the road near Rainham Down*   2 **powder** gunpowder   **dank** damp   5 **Zounds** By God's wounds   **coil** fuss

You were best swear me on the intergatories
How many pistols I have took in hand,
Or whether I love the smell of gunpowder
Or dare abide the noise the dag will make,
10 Or will not wink at flashing of the fire.
I pray thee, Shakebag, let this answer thee:
That I have took more purses in this down
Than e'er thou handled'st pistols in thy life.

SHAKEBAG   Ay, haply thou hast picked more in a throng.
15 But should I brag what booties I have took:
I think the overplus that's more than thine
Would mount to a greater sum of money
Than either thou or all thy kin are worth.
Zounds, I hate them as I hate a toad
20 That carry a muscado in their tongue,
And scarce a hurting weapon in their hand.

BLACK WILL   O, Greene, intolerable!   *To Greene*
It is not for mine honour to bear this.
Why, Shakebag, I did serve the King at Boulogne
25 And thou canst brag of nothing that thou hast done.

SHAKEBAG   Why, so can Jack of Faversham,
That swooned for a fillip on the nose,
When he that gave it him hollowed in his ear,
And he supposed a cannon bullet hit him.

Then they fight

30 GREENE   I pray you, sirs, list to Aesop's talk:
Whilst two stout dogs were striving for a bone,
There comes a cur and stole it from them both.
So while you stand striving on these terms of manhood,
Arden escapes us and deceives us all.

35 SHAKEBAG   Why, he begun.

BLACK WILL   And thou shalt find I'll end.
I do but slip it until better time,
But if I do forget—

Then he kneels down and holds up his hands to heaven

GREENE   Well, take your fittest standings, and once more
40 Lime your twigs to catch this weary bird.
I'll leave you, and at your dag's discharge,
Make towards like the longing water-dog
That coucheth till the fowling-piece be off

---

6 **intergatories** i.e. interrogatories, formal questions   9 **dag** heavy pistol   10 **wink** blink, close my eyes   14 **haply** perhaps   **throng** crowd   15 **booties** prizes   16 **overplus** surplus   19 **toad** loathsome creature/fellow   20 **muscado** a kind of herb/musket; presumably a jibe at Will who talks a good fight   27 **fillip** smart tap   28 **hollowed** shouted, hollered   30 **Aesop's talk** moral of one of the tales of the sixth-century BC Greek writer Aesop   32 **cur** dog/worthless fellow   40 **Lime** smear with birdlime, a sticky substance spread on twigs, used for catching birds   **weary** wearisome, tedious   42 **longing** eager   43 **fowling-piece** light gun for shooting wildfowl

Then seizeth on the prey with eager mood.
45   Ah, might I see him stretching forth his limbs
As I have seen them beat their wings ere now,
SHAKEBAG   Why, that thou shalt see if he come this way.
GREENE   Yes, that he doth, Shakebag, I warrant thee.
But brawl not when I am gone in any case,
50   But, sirs, be sure to speed him when he comes:
And in that hope I'll leave you for an hour.   *Exit Greene*

Black Will and Shakebag hide

Here enters Arden, Franklin and Michael
MICHAEL   'Twere best that I went back to Rochester.
The horse halts downright: it were not good
He travelled in such pain to Faversham.
55   Removing of a shoe may happily help it.
ARDEN   Well, get you back to Rochester, but, sirrah, see
Ye overtake us ere we come to Rainham Down,
For it will be very late ere we get home.
MICHAEL   Ay, God he knows, and so doth Will and Shakebag,   *Aside*
60   That thou shalt never go further than that down,
And therefore have I pricked the horse on purpose,
Because I would not view the massacre.   *Exit Michael*
ARDEN   Come, Master Franklin, onwards with your tale.
FRANKLIN   I assure you sir, you task me much.
65   A heavy blood is gathered at my heart
And, on the sudden, is my wind so short
As hindereth the passage of my speech.
So fierce a qualm yet ne'er assailèd me.
ARDEN   Come, Master Franklin, let us go on softly.
70   The annoyance of the dust, or else some meat
You ate at dinner, cannot brook you.
I have been often so and soon amended.
FRANKLIN   Do you remember where my tale did leave?
ARDEN   Ay, where the gentleman did check his wife.
75   FRANKLIN   She, being reprehended for the fact,
Witness produced that took her with the deed,
Her glove brought in, which there she left behind,
And many other assured arguments:
Her husband asked her whether it were not so.
80   ARDEN   Her answer then? I wonder how she looked
Having forsworn it with such vehement oaths
And at the instant so approved upon her.

---

46 ere before   50 speed assist/hasten   53 halts limps, is lame   downright outright, completely   61 pricked injured   66 on the sudden all at once   wind breath   67 hindereth prevents   68 qualm fit/fear, misgiving   69 softly gently, quietly   70 meat food   71 brook be tolerated or digested by   74 check rebuke, reproach/reject/strike   75 reprehended rebuked – perhaps meaning 'apprehended', arrested   81 forsworn perjured, falsely sworn   82 approved proved

	FRANKLIN	First, did she cast her eyes down to the earth,
		Watching the drops that fell amain from thence,
85		Then softly draws she forth her handkercher
		And modestly she wipes her tear-stained face.
		Then, hemmed she out, to clear her voice should seem,
		And with a majesty addressed herself
		To encounter all their accusations.
90		Pardon me, Master Arden, I can no more:
		This fighting at my heart, makes short my wind.
	ARDEN	Come, we are almost now at Rainham Down:
		Your pretty tale beguiles the weary way.
		I would you were in state to tell it out.

90 **FRANKLIN** First, did she cast her eyes down to the earth,
Watching the drops that fell amain from thence,
85 Then softly draws she forth her handkercher
And modestly she wipes her tear-stained face.
Then, hemmed she out, to clear her voice should seem,
And with a majesty addressed herself
To encounter all their accusations.
90 Pardon me, Master Arden, I can no more:
This fighting at my heart, makes short my wind.
ARDEN Come, we are almost now at Rainham Down:
Your pretty tale beguiles the weary way.
I would you were in state to tell it out.
95 **SHAKEBAG** Stand close, Will, I hear them coming.   *Aside*

Here enters Lord Cheyne with his men

BLACK WILL Stand to it, Shakebag, and be resolute.   *Aside*
LORD CHEYNE Is it so near night as it seems,
Or will this black-faced evening have a shower?
What, Master Arden, you are well met.
100 I have longed this fortnight's day to speak with you:
You are a stranger, man, in the Isle of Sheppey.
ARDEN Your honour's always, bound to do you service.
LORD CHEYNE Come you from London and ne'er a man with you?
ARDEN My man's coming after:
105 But here's my honest friend that came along with me.
LORD CHEYNE My Lord Protector's man, I take you to be.   *To Franklin*
FRANKLIN Ay, my good lord, and highly bound to you.
LORD CHEYNE You and your friend come home and sup with me.
ARDEN I beseech your honour pardon me:
110 I have made a promise to a gentleman,
My honest friend, to meet him at my house.
The occasion is great, or else would I wait on you.
LORD CHEYNE Will you come tomorrow and dine with me?
And bring your honest friend along with you:
115 I have diverse matters to talk with you about.
ARDEN Tomorrow we'll wait upon your honour.
LORD CHEYNE One of you stay my horse at the top of the hill.
What, Black Will, for whose purse wait you?   *He sees Black Will*
Thou wilt be hanged in Kent when all is done.
120 **BLACK WILL** Not hanged, God save your honour.
I am your beadsman, bound to pray for you.
LORD CHEYNE I think thou ne'er said'st prayer in all thy life.
One of you, give him a crown:

---

84 **amain** with such force   85 **handkercher** handkerchief   87 **hemmed she out** she coughed quietly out loud   102 **Your honour's always** at your honour's service – a polite greeting to a superior   103 **man** servant   108 **sup** have supper   112 **great** important   115 **diverse** various   121 **beadsman** term of respect used to a superior, equivalent to 'your humble servant'; originally one paid to pray for the soul or spiritual welfare of another   123 **crown** coin worth five shillings, one quarter of a pound

And, sirrah, leave this kind of life.

125 If thou be'st 'tainted for a penny matter,

And come in question surely thou wilt truss.

Come, Master Arden, let us be going:

Your way and mine lies four mile together.   *Exeunt. Black Will and*

BLACK WILL   The devil break all your necks, at four miles end.   *Shakebag remain*

130 Zounds, I could kill myself for very anger!

His lordship chops me in, even when

My dag was levelled at his heart.

I would his crown were molten down his throat.

SHAKEBAG   Arden, thou hast wondrous holy luck!

135 Did ever man escape as thou hast done?

Well, I'll discharge my pistol at the sky,   *Fires pistol*

For by this bullet Arden might not die.

Here enters Greene

GREENE   What, is he down, is he dispatched?

SHAKEBAG   Ay, in health towards Faversham, to shame us all.

140 GREENE   The devil he is. Why, sirs, how escaped he?

SHAKEBAG   When we were ready to shoot,

Comes my Lord Cheyne to prevent his death.

GREENE   The lord of heaven hath preserved him.

BLACK WILL   Preserved, a fig! The Lord Cheyne hath preserved him

145 And bids him to a feast to his house at Shorlow.

But by the way, once more I'll meet with him,

And if all the Cheynes in the world say no,

I'll have a bullet in his breast tomorrow.

Therefore, come Greene, and let us to Faversham.

150 GREENE   Ay, and excuse ourselves to Mistress Arden.

O, how she'll chafe when she hears of this!

SHAKEBAG   Why, I'll warrant you she'll think we dare not do it.

BLACK WILL   Why, then, let us go, and tell her all the matter

And plot the news to cut him off tomorrow.   *Exeunt*

[Scene 10]

Here enters Arden and his wife, Franklin and Michael

ARDEN   See how the Hours, the guardant of heaven's gate,

Have by their toil removed the darksome clouds

That Sol may well deserve the trampled pace,

Wherein he's wont to guide his golden car:

125 **be'st 'tainted** should be accused   **a penny matter** even a trivial offence   **126 in question** before the court   **wilt truss** will hang   **131 chops me in** interrupts me   **144 a fig!** term signifying contempt   **145 Shorlow** Shurland, Lord Cheyne's house on the Isle of Sheppey   **151 chafe** rage, fume/scold   **[Scene 10]** *Location: Faversham*   **1 Hours** in classical mythology, the female divinities supposed to preside over the changes of the seasons   **guardant** guardian, protector   **heaven's** of Olympus   **3 Sol** sun-god in classical mythology   **pace** path   **4 wont** is accustomed   **golden car** the sun god was imagined as driving a golden chariot across the sky

5   The season fits. Come Franklin, let's away.

ALICE   I thought you did pretend some special hunt

           That made you thus cut short the time of rest.

ARDEN   It was no chase that made me rise so early,

           But as I told thee yesternight, to go

10   To the Isle of Sheppey, there to dine with my Lord Cheyne:

           For so his honour late commanded me.

ALICE   Ay, such kind husbands seldom want excuses:

           Home is a wild cat to a wand'ring wit.

           The time hath been, would God it were not past,

15   That honour's title nor a lord's command

           Could once have drawn you from these arms of mine.

           But my deserts, or your desires decay,

           Or both, yet if true love may seem desert,

           I merit still to have thy company.

20 FRANKLIN Why, I pray you, sir, let her go along with us.

           I am sure his honour will welcome her

           And us the more for bringing her along.

ARDEN   Content.— Sirrah, saddle your mistress' nag.   *To Michael*

ALICE   No, begged favour merits little thanks.

25   If I should go, our house would run away

           Or else be stolen: therefore I'll stay behind.

ARDEN   Nay, see how mistaking you are:

           I pray thee go.

ALICE   No, no, not now.

30 ARDEN   Then let me leave thee satisfied in this,

           That time nor place, nor persons alter me,

           But that I hold thee dearer than my life.

ALICE   That will be seen by your quick return.

ARDEN   And that shall be ere night and if I live.

35   Farewell, sweet Alice: we mind to sup with thee.   *Exit Alice*

FRANKLIN Come, Michael, are our horses ready?

MICHAEL   Ay, your horse are ready: but I am not ready,

           For I have lost my purse

           With six and thirty shillings in it

40   With taking up of my master's nag.

FRANKLIN Why, I pray you, let us go before,   *To Arden*

           Whilst he stays behind to seek his purse.

ARDEN   Go to, sirrah, see you follow us to the Isle of Sheppey   *To Michael*

           To my Lord Cheyne's where we mean to dine.

           Exeunt Arden and Franklin. Michael remains

45 MICHAEL So, fair weather after you:

---

5 fits is suitable   **6 pretend** claim/use as an excuse   **11 late** recently   **12 kind** sort of/amiable   **want** lack/need   **13 Home … wit** the general sense seems to be that home is a disagreeable place to one who is inconstant and has a roving eye   **wild cat** term of contempt, especially used of a woman   **wand'ring wit** one who is inconstant, roving, restless   **15 That** that neither   **18 desert** merit, deserving   **33 quick** rapid punning on 'live'   **35 mind to sup** plan to be back in time to have supper, the last meal of the day

For before you lies Black Will and Shakebag

In the broom close, too close for you.

They'll be your ferrymen to long home.

Here enters the Painter [Clarke]

But who is this? The painter, my corrival,

50   That would needs win Mistress Susan?

CLARKE   How now, Michael, how doth my mistress

And all at home?

MICHAEL   Who, Susan Mosby? She is your mistress too?

CLARKE   Ay, how doth she, and all the rest?

55 MICHAEL   All's well but Susan: she is sick.

CLARKE   Sick? Of what disease?

MICHAEL   Of a great fear.

CLARKE   A fear, of what?

MICHAEL   A great fever.

60 CLARKE   A fever, God forbid!

MICHAEL   Yes, faith, and of a lurdan, too,

As big as yourself.

CLARKE   O, Michael, the spleen prickles you.

Go to, you carry an eye over Mistress Susan.

65 MICHAEL   Ay, faith, to keep her from the painter.

CLARKE   Why more from a painter than from a serving creature like yourself?

MICHAEL   Because you painters make but a painting-table of a pretty wench and spoil her beauty with blotting.

CLARKE   What mean you by that?

70 MICHAEL   Why, that you painters paint lambs, in the lining of wenches' petticoats:

And we servingmen put horns to them to make them become sheep.

CLARKE   Such another word will cost you a cuff or a knock.

MICHAEL   What, with a dagger made of a pencil?

Faith 'tis too weak,

75   And therefore thou too weak to win Susan.

CLARKE   Would Susan's love lay upon this stroke!

Then he breaks Michael's head

Here enters Mosby, Greene and Alice

ALICE   I'll lay my life, this is for Susan's love.

Stayed you behind your master to this end?

Have you no other time to brabble in

80   But now when serious matters are in hand?

Say Clarke, hast thou done the thing thou promised?

CLARKE   Ay, here it is: the very touch is death.   *Shows the poisoned crucifix*

ALICE   Then this I hope, if all the rest do fail,

Will catch Master Arden,

---

47 broom close shrubbery containing yellow broom, *Sarothamnus* (or *Cytisus*) *Scoparius*   **48 long home** death   **49 corrival** rival suitor   **61 lurdan** lazy rascal; 'fever-lurdan' was the disease of laziness   **63 spleen** organ of the body associated with violent ill-humour   **prickles** pricks, goads   **64 carry … over** have an eye for   **71 horns** penises   **sheep** obedient wives – as opposed to 'shrews'   **79 brabble** quarrel, brawl

85 And make him wise in death, that lived a fool.

Why should he thrust his sickle in our corn,

Or what hath he to do with thee, my love?

Or govern me that am to rule myself,

Forsooth for credit sake I must leave thee.

90 Nay he must leave to live, that we may love,

May live, may love, for what is life but love?

And love shall last as long as life remains,

And life shall end, before my love depart.

MOSBY   Why what's love, without true constancy?

95 Like to a pillar built of many stones.

Yet neither with good mortar, well compact,

Nor cement, to fasten it in the joints,

But that it shakes with every blast of wind,

And being touched, straight falls unto the earth,

100 And buries all his haughty pride in dust.

No let our love be rocks of adamant,

Which time nor place, nor tempest can asunder.

GREENE   Mosby, leave protestations now

And let us bethink us what we have to do.

105 Black Will and Shakebag I have placed

In the broom close watching Arden's coming.

Let's to them and see what they have done.   *Exeunt*

[Scene 11]

Here enters Arden and Franklin

ARDEN   O, ferryman, where art thou?

Here enters the Ferryman

FERRYMAN   Here, here, go before to the boat

And I will follow you.

ARDEN   We have great haste: I pray thee come away.

5 FERRYMAN   Fie, what a mist is here!

ARDEN   This mist, my friend, is mystical,

Like to a good companion's smoky brain,

That was half-drowned with new ale overnight.

FERRYMAN   'Twere pity but his skull were opened, to make more chimney room.

10 FRANKLIN   Friend, what's thy opinion of this mist?

---

86 **sickle … corn** interfere in our affairs, an agricultural metaphor   **sickle** curved instrument for reaping corn   89 **credit** reputation's   90 **leave** leave off, cease   96 **compact** knit, firmly put together   101 **adamant** hard rock, diamond or loadstone but confusingly it can also refer to the natural opposite; the ambiguity may be deliberately ironic   102 **Which** which neither   **asunder** separate, divide   106 **broom close** thicket, enclosure of broom shrubs   **[Scene 11]** *Location: the Harty Ferry across the Swale to the Isle of Sheppey*   9 **but … were** that his skull wasn't

FERRYMAN I think 'tis like to a cursed wife in a little house that never leaves her husband till she have driven him out at doors with a wet pair of eyes, then looks he as if his house were afire, or some of his friends dead.

ARDEN   Speaks thou this of thine own experience?

15 **FERRYMAN**   Perhaps ay, perhaps no: for my wife is as other women are,

   That is to say, governed by the moon.

FRANKLIN By the moon, how I pray thee?

FERRYMAN   Nay, thereby lies a bargain, and you shall not have it fresh and fasting.

ARDEN   Yes, I pray thee, good ferryman.

20 **FERRYMAN**   Then for this once, let it be midsummer moon, but yet my wife has

   another moon.

FRANKLIN Another moon?

FERRYMAN   Ay, and it hath influences and eclipses.

ARDEN   Why, then, by this reckoning, you sometimes

25   Play the man in the moon.

FERRYMAN   Ay, but you had not best to meddle with that moon

   Lest I scratch you by the face with my bramble bush.

ARDEN   I am almost stifled with this fog: come, let's away.

FRANKLIN And sirrah, as we go, let us have some more of your bold yeomanry.

30 **FERRYMAN**   Nay, by my troth sir, but flat knavery.   *Exeunt*

[Scene 12]

Here enters Will at one door and Shakebag at another

SHAKEBAG   O Will, where art thou?

BLACK WILL   Here Shakebag, almost in hell's mouth, where I cannot see my way for smoke.

SHAKEBAG   I pray thee speak still, that we may meet by the sound, for I shall fall into

5   some ditch or other, unless my feet see better than my eyes.

BLACK WILL   Didst thou ever see better weather to run away with another man's wife or play with a wench at potfinger.

SHAKEBAG   No! This were a fine world for chandlers

   If this weather would last, for then a man

10   Should never dine nor sup without candlelight.

   But, sirrah Will, what horses are those that passed?

BLACK WILL   Why, didst thou hear any?

SHAKEBAG   Ay, that I did.

BLACK WILL   My life for thine, 'twas Arden and his companion

16 **moon** i.e. fickle, changeable, with an oblique reference to the menses, periods   17 **how** in what way/what do you mean   18 **bargain** transaction with unpleasant consequences/combat   19 **fresh and fasting** on an empty stomach   21 **let it be** even if it was   22 **moon** slang term for genitals   28 **bramble bush** the man in the moon was popularly imaged as having a dog and a thorn bush   29 **stifled** suffocated, presumably the talk of adultery has oppressed him   30 **bold yeomanry** blunt speech befitting a yeoman, a respectable countryman who cultivates his own land   31 **troth** word, truth   **flat knavery** plain roguery, waggishness   [Scene 12]   *Location: open country near the ferry*   2 **hell's mouth** likening the mist to the smoke associated with hell but also perhaps referring to the medieval theatrical device of a 'hellmouth', a scene painted to suggest the horrors of hell, or the physical staging in which hell was represented as below the stage through the trapdoor; all these play on Will's moral situation   7 **potfinger** a game involving making popping sounds by rapidly removing a finger from the corner of the mouth   8 **chandlers** those who make or sell candles

15   And then all our labour's lost.

SHAKEBAG   Nay, say not so, for if it be they, they may haply lose their way as we have done and then we may chance meet with them.

BLACK WILL   Come, let us go on like a couple of blind pilgrims.

Then Shakebag falls into a ditch

SHAKEBAG   Help, Will, help! I am almost drowned!

Here enters the Ferryman

20 FERRYMAN   Who's that that calls for help?

BLACK WILL   'Twas none here: 'twas thou thyself.

FERRYMAN   I came to help him that called for help.

Why, how now? Who is this that's in the ditch?

You are well enough served to go without a guide, such weather as this.

25 BLACK WILL   Sirrah, what companies hath past your ferry this morning?

FERRYMAN   None but a couple of gentlemen that went to dine at my Lord Cheyne's.

BLACK WILL   Shakebag, did not I tell thee as much?

FERRYMAN   Why sir, will you have any letters carried to them?

BLACK WILL   No, sir: get you gone.

30 FERRYMAN   Did you ever see such a mist as this?

BLACK WILL   No, nor such a fool as will rather be hought than get his way.

FERRYMAN   Why sir, this is no Hock Monday, you are deceived. What's his name, I pray you, sir?

SHAKEBAG   His name is Black Will.

35 FERRYMAN   I hope to see him one day hanged upon a hill.   *Exit Ferryman*

SHAKEBAG   See how the sun hath cleared the foggy mist:

Now we have missed the mark of our intent.

Here enters Greene, Mosby and Alice

MOSBY   Black Will and Shakebag, what make you here?

What is the deed done? Is Arden dead?

40 BLACK WILL   What could a blinded man perform in arms?

Saw you not how till now the sky was dark,

That neither horse nor man could be discerned?

Yet did we hear their horses as they passed.

GREENE   Have they escaped you then and passed the ferry?

45 SHAKEBAG   Ay, for a while, but here we two will stay,

And at their coming back meet with them once more.

Zounds, I was ne'er so toiled in all my life

In following so slight a task as this.

MOSBY   How cam'st thou so bewrayed?   *To Shakebag*

50 BLACK WILL   With making false footing in the dark:

He needs would follow them without a guide.

ALICE   Here's to pay for a fire and good cheer   *Gives money*

---

16 **haply** perhaps   24 **You … served** it serves you right   31 **hought** hamstrung, lamed or crippled by cutting the hamstring/used to suggest sexual disability, being controlled by a woman   32 **Hock Monday** first Monday after Easter; the earlier custom was to seize and bind persons of the opposite sex (by women on Monday, and by men on Tuesday) who released themselves by a small payment   37 **mark** target   38 **make you** are you doing   47 **toiled** exhausted   49 **bewrayed** exposed, revealed   51 **He needs would** he (Greene or perhaps Shakebag) insisted that we

Get you to Faversham to the Flower-de-Luce,

And rest yourselves until some other time.

55   GREENE   Let me alone: it most concerns my state.

BLACK WILL   Ay, Mistress Arden: this will serve the turn

In case we fall into a second fog.   *Exeunt Greene, Will and Shakebag*

MOSBY   These knaves will never do it: let us give it over.

ALICE   First, tell me how you like my new device?

60   Soon when my husband is returning back,

You and I both, marching arm in arm

Like loving friends, we'll meet him on the way.

And boldly beard and brave him to his teeth.

When words grow hot, and blows begin to rise,

65   I'll call those cutters forth your tenement,

Who, in a manner to take up the fray,

Shall wound my husband Hornsby to the death.

MOSBY   Ah, fine device. Why, this deserves a kiss.   *Exeunt*   *Kisses her*

[Scene 13]

Here enters Dick Reede and a Sailor

SAILOR   Faith, Dick Reede it is to little end.

His conscience is too liberal and he too niggardly

To part from anything may do thee good.

DICK REEDE   He is coming from Shorlow as I understand.

5   Here I'll intercept him, for at his house

He never will vouchsafe to speak with me.

If prayers and fair entreaties will not serve

Or make no batt'ry in his flinty breast,

Here enters Franklin, Arden and Michael

I'll curse the carl and see what that will do.

10   See where he comes: to further my intent—

Master Arden, I am now bound to the sea.

My coming to you was about the plot of ground

Which wrongfully you detain from me.

Although the rent of it be very small,

15   Yet will it help my wife and children

Which here I leave in Faversham, God knows,

Needy and bare. For Christ's sake, let them have it.

---

59 device plan   **63 beard** oppose openly (as in **beard** a lion in his den)   **brave** challenge, defy   **teeth** face   **65 cutters** cut-throats   **forth your tenement** out of your house   **66 fray** attack   **67 Hornsby** slang for a cuckold, a man whose wife was unfaithful, popularly imaged as growing horns on his forehead   **[Scene 13]**   *Location: Faversham, near Arden's house*   **1 end** purpose   **2 liberal** easygoing, unscrupulous   **niggardly** mean, miserly   **4 Shorlow** Shurland, Lord Cheyne's house   **6 vouchsafe** deign, condescend   **7 fair entreaties** polite requests, supplications   **9 carl** churl, villain, especially one who is mean in money matters   **13 detain** withold

ARDEN   Franklin, hearest thou this fellow speak?

That which he craves I dearly bought of him,

20   Although the rent of it was ever mine.—

Sirrah, you, that ask these questions,

If with thy clamorous impeaching tongue

Thou rail on me, as I have heard thou dost,

I'll lay thee up so close a twelvemonth's day,

25   As thou shalt neither see the sun nor moon.

Look to it, for as surely as I live,

I'll banish pity if thou use me thus.

DICK REEDE   What, wilt thou do me wrong and threat me too?

Nay, then I'll tempt thee, Arden, do thy worst.

30   God, I beseech thee show some miracle

On thee or thine in plaguing thee for this.

That plot of ground, which thou detains from me —

I speak it in an agony of spirit —

Be ruinous and fatal unto thee!

35   Either there be butchered by thy dearest friends,

Or else be brought for men to wonder at,

Or thou or thine miscarry in that place,

Or there run mad and end thy cursèd days.

FRANKLIN   Fie, bitter knave! Bridle thine envious tongue,

40   For curses are like arrows shot upright,

Which falling down light on the suitor's head.

DICK REEDE   Light where they will. Were I upon the sea,

As oft I have in many a bitter storm,

And saw a dreadful southern flaw at hand,

45   The pilot quaking at the doubtful storm,

And all the sailors praying on their knees,

Even in that fearful time would I fall down

And ask of God whate'er betide of me,

Vengence on Arden or some mis-event

50   To show the world what wrong the carl hath done.

This charge I'll leave with my distressful wife:

My children shall be taught such prayers as these.

And thus I go, but leave my curse with thee.   *Exeunt Reede and Sailor*

ARDEN   It is the railingest knave in Christendom,

55   And oftentimes the villain will be mad.

It greatly matters not what he says,

But I assure you, I ne'er did him wrong.

---

19 **craves** wants, asks for   **dearly** at a high price   20 **rent ... mine** the money for renting it was always due to me   22 **impeaching** accusing   24 **lay ... close** imprison   **a twelvemonth's day** for a whole year   27 **use** treat   28 **threat** threaten   37 **miscarry** come to grief   41 **suitor's** petitioner's, one who seeks   44 **flaw** squall, sudden burst of rough weather   48 **betide** became   49 **mis-event** evil fortune   50 **carl** villain, miser   54 **railingest** most complaining, abusive

FRANKLIN I think so, Master Arden.

ARDEN   Now that our horses are gone home before,

60   My wife may haply meet me on the way:

For God knows she is grown passing kind of late

And greatly changèd from the old humour

Of her wonted frowardness

And seeks by fair means to redeem old faults.

65   FRANKLIN Happy the change that alters for the best.

But see in any case you make no speech,

Of the cheer we had at my Lord Cheyne's.

Although most bounteous and liberal,

For that will make her think herself more wronged,

70   In that we did not carry her along:

For sure she grieved that she was left behind.

ARDEN   Come, Franklin, let us strain to mend our pace

And take her unawares playing the cook.

Here enters Alice and Mosby [arm in arm]

For I believe she'll strive to mend our cheer.

75   FRANKLIN Why, there's no better creatures in the world

Than women are when they are in good humours.

ARDEN   Who is that? Mosby? What, so familiar?

Injurious strumpet and thou, ribald knave,

Untwine those arms!

80   ALICE   Ay, with a sugared kiss, let them untwine.   *She kisses Mosby*

ARDEN   Ah, Mosby! Perjured beast! Bear this and all!

MOSBY   And yet no hornèd beast: the horns are thine.

FRANKLIN O monstrous! Nay, then, 'tis time to draw.

ALICE   Help! Help! They murder my husband!

Here enters Will and Shakebag   *They fight, Shakebag and Mosby are injured*

85   SHAKEBAG Zounds! Who injures Master Mosby? Help, Will, I am hurt.

MOSBY   I may thank you, Mistress Arden, for this wound.   *Exeunt Mosby,*

ALICE   Ah, Arden, what folly blinded thee?   *Will and Shakebag*

Ah, jealous, hare-brain man what hast thou done?

When we, to welcome thee, intended sport,

90   Came lovingly to meet thee on thy way,

Thou drew'st thy sword enraged with jealousy,

And hurt thy friend whose thoughts were free from harm.

All for a worthless kiss and joining arms:

Both done but merrily to try thy patience.

95   And me, unhappy, that devised the jest,

Which though begun in sport, yet ends in blood.

FRANKLIN Marry, God defend me from such a jest.

---

61 passing more than, extremely   **63 wonted** usual, customary   **frowardness** perverseness, ill-humour   **67 cheer** entertainment   **72 strain ... pace** make an effort to hurry   **74 mend our cheer** remedy our welcome, hospitality   **78 Injurious strumpet** wicked whore   **ribald knave** base, dissolute villain   **82 hornèd beast** cuckold   **83 draw** i.e. their swords   **88 hare-brain** reckless

	ALICE	Couldst thou not see us friendly smile on thee

ALICE   Couldst thou not see us friendly smile on thee
         When we joined arms and when I kissed his cheek?
100   Hast thou not lately found me overkind?
         Did'st thou not hear me cry they murder thee?
         Called I not help to set my husband free?
         No, ears and all were witched. Ah, me accursed,
         To link in liking with a frantic man!
105   Henceforth I'll be thy slave, no more thy wife:
         For with that name I never shall content thee.
         If I be merry, thou straightways thinks me light:
         If sad, thou say'st the sullens trouble me:
         If well-attired, thou thinks I will be gadding:
110   If homely, I seem sluttish in thine eye.
         Thus am I still, and shall be while I die,
         Poor wench abused by thy misgovernment.

ARDEN   But is it for truth, that neither thou nor he,
         Intended'st malice in your misdemeanour?
115 ALICE The heavens can witness of our harmless thoughts.

ARDEN   Then pardon me sweet Alice
         And forgive this fault.
         Forget but this, and never see the like.
         Impose me penance, and I will perform it:
120   For in thy discontent I find a death,
         A death tormenting more than death itself.

ALICE   Nay, hadst thou loved me as thou dost pretend,
         Thou wouldst have marked the speeches of thy friend,
         Who going wounded from the place, he said
125   His skin was pierced only through my device.
         And if sad sorrow taint thee for this fault,
         Thou wouldst have followed him and seen him dressed,
         And cried him mercy whom thou hast misdone:
         Ne'er shall my heart be eased till this be done.

130 ARDEN Content thee, sweet Alice: thou shalt have thy will
         Whate'er it be, for that I injured thee
         And wronged my friend, shame scourgeth my offence.
         Come, thou thyself, and go along with me,
         And be a mediator 'twixt us two.

135 FRANKLIN Why, Master Arden, know you what you do?
         Will you follow him that hath dishonoured you?

ALICE   Why, can'st thou prove I have been disloyal?

FRANKLIN Why, Mosby taunts your husband with the horn!

---

100 **overkind** extremely, excessively kind   107 **light** wanton, unchaste   108 **sullens** sulks   109 **well-attired** nicely dressed   **gadding** roving idly, with sexual implication   110 **homely** plainly-dressed   **sluttish** dirty, untidy, disgusting   112 **misgovernment** ill-treatment   118 **but this** just this one fault   119 **penance** punishment, usual in religious sense   123 **marked** noted   126 **taint** attaint, convict   127 **dressed** i.e. his wound treated   128 **misdone** wronged, done harm to   132 **scourgeth** punishes, chastises   138 **the horn** being a cuckold and hence wearing horns

ALICE   Ay, after he had reviled him

140   By the injurious name of perjured beast.

He knew no wrong could spite a jealous man

More than the hateful naming of the horn.

FRANKLIN   Suppose 'tis true, yet is it dangerous

To follow him whom he hath lately hurt.

145   ALICE   A fault confessed is more than half amends,

But men of such ill spirit as yourself

Work crosses and debates 'twixt man and wife.

ARDEN   I pray thee, gentle Franklin, hold thy peace:

I know my wife counsels me for the best.

150   I'll seek out Mosby, where his wound is dressed

And salve his hapless quarrel if I may.   *Exeunt Arden and Alice*

FRANKLIN   He whom the devil drives must go perforce,

Poor gentleman how soon he is bewitched,

And yet because his wife is the instrument,

155   His friends must not be lavish in their speech.   *Exit Franklin*

[Scene 14]

Here enters Will, Shakebag and Greene

BLACK WILL   Sirrah Greene, when was I so long in killing a man?

GREENE   I think we shall never do it: let us give it over.

SHAKEBAG   Nay, zounds! We'll kill him though we be hanged at his door for our labour.

5   BLACK WILL   Thou know'st, Greene, that I have lived in London this twelve years. Where I have made some go upon wooden legs, for taking the wall on me, divers with silver noses, for saying, 'There goes Black Will.' I have cracked as many blades, as thou hast done nuts.

GREENE   O, monstrous lie!

10   BLACK WILL   Faith, in a manner I have. The bawdy houses have paid me tribute: there durst not a whore set up, unless she have agreed with me first, for opening her shop windows. For a cross word of a tapster, I have pierced one barrel after another, with my dagger, and held him by the ears till all his beer hath run out. In Thames Street a brewer's cart was like to have run over me, I made no more ado, but went to the

15   clerk and cut all the notches off his tallies, and beat them about his head. I and my company have taken the constable from his watch and carried him about the fields on a coltstaff. I have broken a sergeant's head with his own mace and bailed whom I list with my sword and buckler. All the tenpenny ale-houses would stand every

---

147 Work ... debates create conflicts and arguments   148 hold thy peace say no more   151 salve heal   hapless unfortunate   [Scene 14]   *Location: Faversham, near Arden's house*   6 taking the wall walking by the wall therefore forcing him to walk in the gutter   divers various, several   7 silver false; implying he had cut the originals off for insulting him   10 bawdy houses brothels   tribute tax   12 tapster tavern keeper   15 notches ... tallies accounts were kept by making notches in a tally stick, so Black Will wiped out his accounts   17 coltstaff cowl-staff, a stout stick on which the offender was hoisted and carried about the streets in derision; a popular form of rough punishment, especially on a husband whose wife abused him   mace staff of office   bailed freed   18 list liked, chose

morning, with a quart pot in his hand, saying, 'Will it please your worship drink?'

20 He that had not done so had been sure to have had his sign pulled down, and his lattice borne away the next night. To conclude, what have I not done? Yet cannot do this? Doubtless he is preserved by miracle.

Here enters Alice and Michael

GREENE   Hence, Will, here comes Mistress Arden.

ALICE   Ah, gentle Michael, art thou sure they're friends?

25 MICHAEL   Why, I saw them when they both shook hands.

When Mosby bled, he even wept for sorrow

And railed on Franklin that was cause of all.

No sooner came the surgeon in at doors,

But my master took to his purse and gave him money.

30 And to conclude, sent me to bring you word,

That Mosby, Franklin, Bradshaw, Adam Fowle,

With divers of his neighbours, and his friends,

Will come and sup with you at our house this night.

ALICE   Ah, gentle Michael, run thou back again,

35 And when my husband walks into the fair,

Bid Mosby steal from him and come to me:

And this night shall thou and Susan be made sure.

MICHAEL   I'll go tell him.

ALICE   And as thou goest, tell John Cook of our guests,

40 And bid him lay it on: spare for no cost.   *Exit Michael*

BLACK WILL   Nay, an there be such cheer, we will bid ourselves

Mistress Arden: Dick Greene and I do mean to sup with you.

ALICE   And welcome shall you be. Ah, gentlemen,

How missed you of your purpose yesternight?

45 GREENE   'Twas long of Shakebag, that unlucky villain.

SHAKEBAG   Thou dost me wrong: I did as much as any.

BLACK WILL   Nay, then, Mistress Alice, I'll tell you how it was:

When he should have locked with both his hilts, he, in a bravery, flourished over his head. With that comes Franklin at him lustily and hurts the slave:

50 with that he slinks away. Now his way had been to have come hand and feet, one and two round at his costard. He, like a fool, bears his sword point half a yard out of danger, I lie here for my life. If the devil come and he have no more strength than sense, he shall never beat me from this ward, I'll stand to it, a buckler in a skilful hand is as good as a castle. Nay, 'tis better than a

55 sconce, for I have tried it. Mosby, perceiving this, began to faint. With that comes Arden with his arming-sword and thrust him through the shoulder in a trice.

ALICE   Ay, but I wonder why you both stood still.

BLACK WILL   Faith, I was so amazed I could not strike.

19 **quart** two pints   21 **lattice** screen for windows   27 **railed on** loudly complained about   36 **steal** creep away   37 **made sure** engaged   40 **lay it on** prepare   41 **an** if   **cheer** hospitality   **bid** invite   45 **long of** because of   48 **locked ... hilts** hemmed him in with both his weapons   **bravery** act of bravado   50 **his ... been** what he ought to have done   51 **costard** head   53 **ward** duty/defensive position   54 **buckler** shield   55 **sconce** small fort, earthwork   56 **arming-sword** war sword, a light, versatile weapon which could cut and thrust   57 **trice** moment

60	ALICE	Ah, sirs, had he yesternight been slain:
		For every drop of his detested blood
		I would cram in angels in thy fist,
		And kissed thee too and hugged thee in my arms.
	BLACK WILL	Patient yourself, we cannot help it now,
65		Greene and we two, will dog him through the fair
		And stab him in the crowd and steal away.

Here enters Mosby

	ALICE	It is unpossible, but here comes he
		That will I hope invent some surer means.
		Sweet Mosby hide thy arm: it kills my heart.
70	MOSBY	Ay, Mistress Arden, this is your favour.
	ALICE	Ah, say not so: for when I saw thee hurt,
		I could have took the weapon thou let'st fall,
		And run at Arden, for I have sworn
		That these mine eyes, offended with his sight,
75		Shall never close till Arden's be shut up.
		This night I rose and walked about the chamber,
		And twice or thrice I thought to have murdered him.
	MOSBY	What, in the night? Then had we been undone.
	ALICE	Why, how long shall he live?
80	MOSBY	Faith, Alice no longer than this night.
		Black Will and Shakebag, will you two
		Perform the complot that I have laid?
	BLACK WILL	Ay, or else think me as a villain.
	GREENE	And rather than you shall want, I'll help myself.
85	MOSBY	You, Master Greene, shall single Franklin forth,
		And hold him with a long tale of strange news:
		That he may not come home till suppertime.
		I'll fetch Master Arden home, and we like friends
		Will play a game or two at tables here.
90	ALICE	But what of all this? How shall he be slain?
	MOSBY	Why, Black Will and Shakebag locked within the counting-house,
		Shall, at a certain watchword given, rush forth.
	BLACK WILL	What shall the watch word be?
	MOSBY	'Now I take you', that shall be the word.
95		But come not forth before in any case.
	BLACK WILL	I warrant you: but who shall lock me in?
	ALICE	That will I do: thou'st keep the key thyself.
	MOSBY	Come, Master Greene, go you along with me.
		See all things ready, Alice, against we come.
100	ALICE	Take no care for that: send you him home. *Exeunt Mosby and Greene*

---

62 angels gold coins   **65 dog** follow   **78 undone** ruined   **82 complot** plot   **85 single Franklin forth** get Franklin out of the way   **89 tables** board games, especially backgammon   **91 counting-house** office   **96 warrant** assure   **97 thou'st** thou shouldst, i.e. you should   **99 against** until

And if he e'er go forth again blame me.

Come, Black Will, that in mine eyes art fair:

Next unto Mosby do I honour thee.

Instead of fair words and large promises

105 My hands shall play you golden harmony.

How like you this? Say, will you do it, sirs?

BLACK WILL   Ay, and that bravely too: mark my device.

Place Mosby, being a stranger, in a chair,

And let your husband sit upon a stool,

110 That I may come behind him cunningly

And with a towel pull him to the ground,

Then stab him till his flesh be as a sieve,

That done, bear him behind the Abbey,

That those that find him murdered may suppose

115 Some slave or other killed him for his gold.

ALICE   A fine device! You shall have twenty pound,

And when he is dead you shall have forty more.

And lest you might be suspected staying here:

Michael shall saddle you two lusty geldings.

120 Ride whither you will, to Scotland or to Wales:

I'll see you shall not lack where e'er you be.

BLACK WILL   Such words would make one kill a thousand men!

Give me the key: which is the counting-house?

ALICE   Here would I stay, and still encourage you,

125 But that I know how resolute you are.

SHAKEBAG   Tush, you are too faint-hearted: we must do it.

ALICE   But Mosby will be there, whose very looks

Will add unwonted courage to my thought,

And make me the first that shall adventure on him.

130 BLACK WILL   Tush, get you gone: 'tis we must do the deed.

When this door opens next, look for his death.

ALICE   Ah, would he now were here, that it might open.

I shall no more be closed in Arden's arms,

That like the snakes of black Tisiphone

135 Sting me with their embracings. Mosby's arms

Shall compass me, and, were I made a star,

I would have none other spheres but those.

There is no nectar but in Mosby's lips.

Had chaste Diana kissed him, she like me

140 Would grow lovesick, and from her watery bower

---

105 **golden harmony** agreement in gold   107 **bravely** handsomely, excellently   **device** scheme/ingenuity   108 **stranger** guest; even well-to-do houses had little furniture at this time   110 **cunningly** secretly   119 **geldings** riding horses which were castrated   128 **unwonted** unaccustomed   129 **adventure** take the risk/dare to attack   134 **Tisiphone** one of the classical Furies, depicted with snakes growing out of her head; she punished the crime of murder   136 **compass** encircle   138 **nectar** drink of the gods   139 **Diana** goddess of chastity, hunting and the moon   140 **lovesick** overwhelmed by love   **watery bower** the moon

Fling down Endymion and snatch him up.

Then blame not me that slay a silly man

Not half so lovely as Endymion.

Here enters Michael

MICHAEL   Mistress, my master is coming hard by.

145 ALICE   Who comes with him?

MICHAEL   Nobody but Mosby.

ALICE   That's well Michael. Fetch in the tables:

And when thou hast done, stand before the counting-house door.

MICHAEL   Why so?

150 ALICE   Black Will is locked within to do the deed.

MICHAEL   What, shall he die tonight?

ALICE   Ay, Michael.

MICHAEL   But shall not Susan know it?

ALICE   Yes, for she'll be as secret as ourselves.

155 MICHAEL   That's brave: I'll go fetch the tables.

ALICE   But Michael hark to me a word or two,

When my husband is come in lock the street door,

He shall be murdered ere the guests come in.   *Exit Michael*

Here enters Arden and Mosby

Husband, what mean you to bring Mosby home?

160   Although I wished you to be reconciled,

'Twas more for fear of you than love of him.

Black Will and Greene are his companions,

And they are cutters and may cut you short.

Therefore, I thought it good to make you friends.

165   But wherefore do you bring him hither now?

You have given me my supper with his sight.   *Aside*

[*Enter Michael, with the gaming tables*]

MOSBY   Master Arden, methinks your wife would have me gone.

ARDEN   No, good Master Mosby, women will be prating.

Alice, bid him welcome: he and I are friends.

170 ALICE   You may enforce me to it, if you will,

But I had rather die than bid him welcome:

His company hath purchased me ill friends,

And therefore will I ne'er frequent it more.

MOSBY   O, how cunningly she can dissemble.   *Aside*

175 ARDEN   Now he is here, you will not serve me so.   *To Alice*

ALICE   I pray you be not angry or displeased.

I'll bid him welcome, seeing you'll have it so:

You are welcome, Master Mosby. Will you sit down?

MOSBY   I know I am welcome to your loving husband,   *Sits*

180   But for yourself, you speak not from your heart.

141 Endymion beautiful youth loved by Diana **him** i.e. Mosby **142 silly** foolish, simple **144 hard** close **147 tables** board games **155 brave**
fine **163 cutters** cutthroats **168 prating** prattling, talking idly **172 purchased** brought/bought **173 frequent** resort to/be familiar
with **174 dissemble** conceal her true opinions **175 serve** behave/speak to

ALICE	And if I do not, sir, think I have cause.	
MOSBY	Pardon me, Master Arden, I'll away.	
ARDEN	No, good Master Mosby.	
ALICE	We shall have guests enough, though you go hence.	
185 MOSBY	I pray you, Master Arden, let me go.	
ARDEN	I pray thee, Mosby, let her prate her fill.	
ALICE	The doors are open, sir: you may be gone.	
MICHAEL	Nay, that's a lie: for I have locked the doors.	*Aside*
ARDEN	Sirrah, fetch me a cup of wine.	

190   I'll make them friends.   *[Exit Michael]*

      And gentle Mistress Alice, seeing you are so stout,

      You shall begin. Frown not: I'll have it so.

ALICE   I pray you meddle with that you have to do.

ARDEN   Why Alice? How can I do too much for him,

195   Whose life I have endangered without cause.

      [Enter Michael with wine]

ALICE   'Tis true, and seeing 'twas partly through my means

      I am content to drink to him for this once.

      Here, Master Mosby, and I pray you henceforth,

      Be you as strange to me, as I to you.

200   Your company hath purchased me ill friends.

      And I for you, God knows, have undeserved

      Been ill-spoken of in every place.

      Therefore henceforth frequent my house no more.

MOSBY   I'll see your husband in despite of you,

205   Yet, Arden, I protest to thee by heaven,

      Thou ne'er shalt see me more, after this night.

      I'll go to Rome rather than be forsworn.

ARDEN   Tush, I'll have no such vows made in my house.

ALICE   Yes, I pray you husband, let him swear:

210   And on that condition, Mosby, pledge me here.

MOSBY   Ay, as willingly as I mean to live.

ARDEN   Come, Alice, is our supper ready yet?

ALICE   It will by then you have played a game at tables.

ARDEN   Come, Master Mosby, what shall we play for?

215 MOSBY   Three games for a French crown, sir,

      An't please you.

ARDEN   Content.

      Then they play at the tables

      [Black Will and Shakebag enter, unobserved]

BLACK WILL   Can he not take him yet? What a spite is that?   *Aside to Alice*

ALICE   Not yet, Will. Take heed he see thee not.   *Aside to Black Will*

220 BLACK WILL   I fear he will spy me as I am coming.   *Aside to Michael*

---

186 prate her fill chatter as much as she likes   **191 stout** proud, resolute   **193 meddle** concern yourself   **that ... do** your own business   **199 strange** distant   **207 I'll ... Rome** become a (Roman) Catholic   **forsworn** perjured, made a liar of   **213 then** the time that   **215 French crown** English name for French coin, the écu   **216 An't** if it

MICHAEL	To prevent that creep betwixt my legs.	*Aside to Black Will*
MOSBY	One ace, or else I lose the game.	*Throws the dice*
ARDEN	Marry, sir, there's two for failing.	
MOSBY	Ah, Master Arden, now I can take you.	

Then Will pulls him down with a towel

225 ARDEN   Mosby! Michael! Alice! What will you do?

BLACK WILL   Nothing but take you up, sir, nothing else.   *Kills Arden*

MOSBY   There's for the pressing iron you told me of.

SHAKEBAG   And there's for the ten pound in my sleeve,

ALICE   What, groans thou? Nay, then give me the weapon.

230   Take this for hindering Mosby's love and mine.

MICHAEL   O, Mistress!

BLACK WILL   Ah, that villain will betray us all.

MOSBY   Tush, fear him not: he will be secret.

MICHAEL   Why dost thou think I will betray myself?

235 SHAKEBAG   In Southwark dwells a bonny northern lass,

The widow Chambley: I'll to her house now,

And if she will not give me harborough,

I'll make booty of the quean, even to her smock.

BLACK WILL   Shift for yourselves: we two will leave you now.

240 ALICE   First, lay the body in the counting-house.

Then they lay the body in the counting-house

BLACK WILL   We have our gold. Mistress Alice, adieu.

Mosby, farewell: and Michael farewell too.   *Exeunt [Black Will and Shakebag]*

Enter Susan

SUSAN   Mistress, the guests are at the doors.   *Knocking heard*

Harken, they knock. What, shall I let them in?

245 ALICE   Mosby, go thou and bear them company.   *Exit Mosby*

And, Susan, fetch water and wash away this blood.

SUSAN   The blood cleaveth to the ground and will not out.   *Tries to wash away the blood*

ALICE   But with my nails I'll scrape away the blood: *Tries to scrape away the blood*

The more I strive the more the blood appears.

250 SUSAN   What's the reason, Mistress, can you tell?

ALICE   Because I blush not at my husband's death.

Here enters Mosby

MOSBY   How now, what's the matter? Is all well?

ALICE   Ay, well, if Arden were alive again!

In vain we strive, for here his blood remains.

255 MOSBY   Why, strew rushes on it, can you not?

This wench doth nothing.— Fall unto the work!   *To Susan*

ALICE   'Twas thou that made me murder him.

---

235 **Southwark** area of London, south of the river Thames in the liberties, i.e. outside the jurisdiction of the City Fathers   **bonny** pretty   237 **harborough** harbour, shelter   238 **booty** prize taken by force   **quean** whore   **smock** underwear, i.e. he'll strip her   239 **Shift** manage/move (the body)   241 **adieu** goodbye (French)   244 **Harken** listen   247 **cleaveth** clings   255 **strew rushes** cover with rushes; reed stems were commonly used as floor covering on bare earth floors and replaced regularly

MOSBY   What of that?

ALICE   Nay, nothing, Mosby, so it be not known.

260   MOSBY   Keep thou it close, and 'tis unpossible.

ALICE   Ah, but I cannot, was he not slain by me?

My husband's death torments me at the heart.

MOSBY   It shall not long torment thee, gentle Alice,

I am thy husband, think no more of him.

Here enters Adam Fowle and Bradshaw

265   BRADSHAW   How now Mistress Arden? What ail, you weep?

MOSBY   Because her husband is abroad so late.

A couple of ruffians threatened him yesternight,

And she, poor soul, is afraid he should be hurt.

ADAM   Is't nothing else? Tush, he'll be here anon.

Here enters Greene

270   GREENE   Now, Mistress Arden, lack you any guests.

ALICE   Ah, Master Greene, did you see my husband lately?

GREENE   I saw him walking behind the Abbey even now.

Here enters Franklin

ALICE   I do not like this being out so late:

Master Franklin, where did you leave my husband?

275   FRANKLIN   Believe me I saw him not since morning,

Fear you not, he'll come anon. Meantime,

You may do well to bid his guests sit down.

ALICE   Ay, so they shall.— Master Bradshaw, sit you there.

I pray you be content: I'll have my will.

280   Master Mosby, sit you in my husband's seat.

MICHAEL   Susan, shall thou and I wait on them,   *Susan and Michael converse apart*

Or, an thou say'st the word, let us sit down too.

SUSAN   Peace, we have other matters now in hand.

I fear me, Michael, all will be bewrayed.

285   MICHAEL   Tush, so it be known that I shall marry thee in the morning. I care not though I be hanged ere night. But to prevent the worst, I'll buy some ratsbane.

SUSAN   Why, Michael, wilt thou poison thyself?

MICHAEL   No, but my Mistress, for I fear she'll tell.

290   SUSAN   Tush, Michael, fear not her: she's wise enough.

MOSBY   Sirrah Michael, give's a cup of beer.

Mistress Arden, here's to your husband.   *Offers a toast with the cup*

ALICE   My husband?

FRANKLIN   What ails you woman, to cry so suddenly?

295   ALICE   Ah, neighbours, a sudden qualm came over my heart:

My husband's being forth torments my mind.

I know something's amiss: he is not well.

---

259 **so … not** as long as it isn't   260 **close** secret   **unpossible** impossible, that it will be discovered   265 **ail** trouble   266 **abroad** out   269 **anon** presently   272 **even now** just recently   282 **an** if   284 **bewrayed** disclosed   287 **ratsbane** poison   295 **qualm** fear, misgiving/moral scruple

Or else I should have heard of him ere now.

MOSBY   She will undo us through her foolishness.   *Aside*

300 GREENE   Fear not, Mistress Arden: he's well enough.

ALICE   Tell not me, I know he is not well,

He was not wont for to stay thus late.

Good, Master Franklin, go and seek him forth,

And if you find him send him home to me

305   And tell him what a fear he hath put me in.

FRANKLIN   I like not this, I pray God all be well.   *Aside*

I'll seek him out and find him if I can.   *Exeunt Franklin, Mosby and Greene*

ALICE   Michael, how shall I do to rid the rest away?   *Aside to Michael*

MICHAEL   Leave that to my charge: let me alone.—   *Aside to Alice*

310   'Tis very late, Master Bradshaw,

And there are many false knaves abroad

And you have many narrow lanes to pass.

BRADSHAW   Faith, friend Michael, and thou say'st true.

Therefore I pray thee light's forth and lend's a link.

315 ALICE   Michael, bring them to the doors, but do not stay.

You know I do not love to be alone.   *Exeunt Bradshaw, Adam and Michael*

Go, Susan, and bid thy brother come,

But wherefore should he come? Here is nought but fear.

Stay Susan stay, and help to counsel me.

320 SUSAN   Alas, I counsel? Fear frights away my wits.

Then they open the counting-house door and look upon Arden

ALICE   See, Susan, where thy quondam master lies:

Sweet Arden smeared in blood and filthy gore.

SUSAN   My brother, you and I shall rue this deed.

ALICE   Come, Susan, help to lift his body forth

325   And let our salt tears be his obsequies.   *They bring out the body*

Here enters Mosby and Greene

MOSBY   How now, Alice, whither will you bear him?

ALICE   Sweet Mosby, art thou come? Then weep that will.

I have my wish in that I joy thy sight.

GREENE   Well it 'hooves us to be circumspect.

330 MOSBY   Ay, for Franklin thinks that we have murdered him.

ALICE   Ay, but he cannot prove it for his life.

We'll spend this night in dalliance and in sport.

Here enters Michael

MICHAEL   O, mistress, the Mayor and all the watch

Are coming towards our house with glaives and bills.

---

302 wont used, accustomed   308 rid ... away get rid of the others   314 light's forth light us on our way   lend's a link lend us a torch   link torch made of tallow and pitch   315 bring ... doors take them as far as their front doors   321 quondam former, sometime (Latin)   323 rue regret   325 obsequies funeral rites   327 that will those who wish to   328 joy enjoy   329 'hooves behooves, requires   332 dalliance light-hearted talk, pleasure   333 Mayor chief officer of the town   watch citizens appointed to maintain law and order   334 glaives lances or spears   bills bill-hooks, thick, heavy knives with curved end

| 335 | ALICE | Make the door fast: let them not come in. |

335   **ALICE**   Make the door fast: let them not come in.

MOSBY   Tell me, sweet Alice, how shall I escape?

ALICE   Out at the back door, over the pile of wood.
And for one night lie at the Flower-de-Luce.

MOSBY   That is the next way to betray myself.

340   **GREENE**   Alas, Mistress Arden, the watch will take me here,
And cause suspicion where else would be none.

ALICE   Why, take that way that Master Mosby doth:
But first convey the body to the fields.

Then they bear the body into the fields [and return]

MOSBY   Until tomorrow, sweet Alice, now farewell,

345   And see you confess nothing in any case.

GREENE   Be resolute, Mistress Alice: betray us not,
But cleave to us as we will stick to you.   *Exeunt Mosby and Greene*

ALICE   Now let the judge and juries do their worst:
My house is clear and now I fear them not.

350   **SUSAN**   As we went it snowed all the way,
Which makes me fear our footsteps will be spied.

ALICE   Peace, fool! The snow will cover them again.

SUSAN   But it had done before we came back again.

ALICE   Hark! Hark! They knock! Go, Michael, let them in.   *Knocking heard*

Here enters the Mayor and the watch

355   How now, Master Mayor, have you brought my husband home?

MAYOR   I saw him come into your house an hour ago.

ALICE   You are deceived: it was a Londoner.

MAYOR   Mistress Arden, know you not one that is called Black Will?

ALICE   I know none such. What mean these questions?

360   **MAYOR**   I have the Council's warrant to apprehend him.

ALICE   I am glad it is no worse.—   *Aside*
Why, Master Mayor, think you I harbour any such?

MAYOR   We are informed that here he is,
And therefore pardon us, for we must search.

365   **ALICE**   Ay, search, and spare you not, through every room.
Were my husband at home, you would not offer this.

Here enters Franklin   *with a towel and a knife*

Master Franklin, what mean you come so sad?

FRANKLIN   Arden, thy husband and my friend, is slain.

ALICE   Ah! By whom, Master Franklin, can you tell?

370   **FRANKLIN**   I know not: but behind the Abbey
There he lies murdered in most piteous case.

MAYOR   But, Master Franklin, are you sure 'tis he.

---

335 **Make ... fast** secure, lock the door   360 **apprehend** arrest   362 **harbour** shelter   366 **offer** propose, attempt

FRANKLIN I am too sure: would God I were deceived.

ALICE   Find out the murderers! Let them be known!

375 FRANKLIN Ay, so they shall. Come you along with us.

ALICE   Wherefore?

FRANKLIN Know you this handtowel and this knife?

SUSAN   Ah, Michael, through this thy negligence   *Aside to Michael*

Thou hast betrayed and undone us all.

380 MICHAEL I was so afraid, I knew not what I did: *Aside to Susan*

I thought I had thrown them both into the well.

ALICE   It is the pig's blood we had to supper.   *To Franklin*

But wherefore stay you? Find out the murderers.

MAYOR   I fear me you'll prove one of them yourself.

385 ALICE   I, one of them? What mean such questions?

FRANKLIN I fear me he was murdered in this house

And carried to the fields: for from that place,

Backwards and forwards, may you see

The print of many feet within the snow.

390 And look about this chamber where we are

And you shall find part of his guiltless blood:

For in his slip-shoe did I find some rushes,

Which argueth he was murdered in this room.

MAYOR   Look in the place where he was wont to sit.

395 See, see! His blood! It is too manifest.

ALICE   It is a cup of wine that Michael shed.

MICHAEL Ay, truly.

FRANKLIN It is his blood which, strumpet, thou hast shed.

But if I live, thou and thy complices

400 Which have conspired and wrought his death shall rue it.

ALICE   Ah, Master Franklin, God and heaven can tell

I loved him more than all the world beside.

But bring me to him: let me see his body.

FRANKLIN Bring that villain and Mosby's sister too: *To the watch*

405 And one of you go to the Flower-de-Luce

And seek for Mosby and apprehend him too.   *Exeunt*

[Scene 15]

Here enters Shakebag solus

SHAKEBAG The widow Chambley in her husband's days I kept:

And now he's dead, she is grown so stout

She will not know her old companions.

---

392 **slip-shoe** light shoe, slipper 395 **manifest** apparent 399 **complices** accomplices 400 **wrought** carried out **rue** regret, repent **[Scene 15]**
Location: London ***solus*** 'alone' (Latin) 1 **kept** i.e. as a mistress, maintained for pleasure 2 **stout** proud, haughty

I came thither, thinking to have had

5 Harbour as I was wont,

And she was ready to thrust me out at doors.

But whether she would or no I got me up,

And as she followed me, I spurned her down the stairs

And broke her neck, and cut her tapster's throat:

10 And now I am going to fling them in the Thames.

I have the gold: what care I though it be known?

I'll cross the water and take sanctuary.   *Exit Shakebag*

[Scene 16]

Here enters the Mayor, Mosby, Alice, Franklin, Michael and Susan

MAYOR   See, Mistress Arden, where your husband lies.

Confess this foul fault and be penitent.

ALICE   Arden, sweet husband, what shall I say?

The more I sound his name, the more he bleeds.

5 This blood condemns me, and in gushing forth

Speaks as it falls, and asks me why I did it.

Forgive me, Arden, I repent me now:

And would my death save thine, thou shouldst not die.

Rise up, sweet Arden, and enjoy thy love,

10 And frown not on me when we meet in heaven:

In heaven I love thee, though on earth I did not.

MAYOR   Say, Mosby, what made thee murder him?

FRANKLIN Study not for an answer, look not down.

His purse and girdle found at thy bed's head

15 Witness sufficiently thou didst the deed.

It bootless is to swear thou didst it not.

MOSBY   I hired Black Will and Shakebag, ruffians both,

And they and I have done this murd'rous deed.

But wherefore stay we? Come and bear me hence.

20 FRANKLIN Those ruffians shall not escape. I will up to London

and get the Council's warrant to apprehend them.   *Exeunt*

[Scene 17]

Here enters Will

BLACK WILL   Shakebag, I hear, hath taken sanctuary:

But I am so pursued with hues and cries

---

8 **spurned** kicked   9 **tapster's** serving-man's in a tavern   **[Scene 16]**   *Location: Faversham*   5 **This ... me** refers to a popular superstition that a corpse bled in the presence of the killer   16 **bootless** pointless   **[Scene 17]**   *Location: unspecified*   2 **hues and cries** outcries for the pursuit of a felon by the aggrieved parties

For petty robberies that I have done,

That I can come unto no sanctuary.

5   Therefore must I in some oyster boat

At last be fain to go aboard some hoy,

And so to Flushing. There is no staying here.

At Sittingburgh the watch was like to take me

And, had I not with my buckler covered my head,

10   And run full blank at all adventures,

I am sure I had ne'er gone further than that place,

For the constable had twenty warrants to apprehend me:

Besides that, I robbed him and his man once at Gadshill.

Farewell, England: I'll to Flushing now.   *Exit Will*

[Scene 18]

Here enters the Mayor, Mosby, Alice, Michael, Susan and Bradshaw [guarded by the watch]

MAYOR   Come, make haste, and bring away the prisoners.   *To the watch*

BRADSHAW   Mistress Arden, you are now going to God,

And I am, by the law, condemned to die

About a letter I brought from Master Greene.

5   I pray you, Mistress Arden, speak the truth,

Was I ever privy to your intent or no?

ALICE   What should I say? You brought me such a letter.

But I dare swear thou knew'st not the contents.

Leave now to trouble me with worldly things

10   And let me meditate upon my Saviour Christ,

Whose blood must save me for the blood I shed.

MOSBY   How long shall I live in this hell of grief?

Convey me from the presence of that strumpet!

ALICE   Ah, but for thee I had never been strumpet!

15   What cannot oaths and protestations do

When men have opportunity to woo?

I was too young to sound thy villainies,

But now I find it, and repent too late.

SUSAN   Ah, gentle brother, wherefore should I die?   *To Mosby*

20   I knew not of it till the deed was done.

MOSBY   For thee I mourn more than for myself,

But let it suffice, I cannot save thee now.

---

4 **sanctuary** religious establishment offering protection from arrest   **5 oyster boat** boat used in oyster fishing   **6 fain** glad under the circumstances   **hoy** small seagoing boat for goods and passengers   **7 Flushing** coastal port of Vlissingen in the Netherlands, across the North Sea   **8 Sittingburgh** Sittingbourne in Kent   **9 buckler** round shield   **10 full blank** headlong/at full tilt   **adventures** all those who came towards me   **13 Gadshill** hill on the road between London and Kent well known for highway robbery   **[Scene 18]** *Location: Faversham*   **6 privy** to familiar, acquainted with   **intent** intentions, plan   **13 strumpet** whore   **17 sound** get to the bottom of

MICHAEL   And if your brother and my mistress   *To Susan*

      Had not promised me you in marriage,

25   I had ne'er given consent to this foul deed.

MAYOR   Leave to accuse each other now,

      And listen to the sentence I shall give.

      Bear Mosby and his sister to London straight,

      Where they in Smithfield must be executed:

30   Bear Mistress Arden unto Canterbury,

      Where her sentence is she must be burned.

      Michael and Bradshaw in Faversham must suffer death.

ALICE   Let my death make amends for all my sins.

MOSBY   Fie upon women! This shall be my song.

35   But bear me hence, for I have lived too long.

SUSAN   Seeing no hope on earth, in heaven is my hope.

MICHAEL   Faith, I care not, seeing I die with Susan.

BRADSHAW   My blood be on his head that gave the sentence!

MAYOR   To speedy execution with them all!   *Exeunt*

[Epilogue]

Here enters Franklin

FRANKLIN   Thus have you seen the truth of Arden's death.

      As for the ruffians, Shakebag and Black Will,

      The one took sanctuary and being sent for out,

      Was murdered in Southwark as he passed

5   To Greenwich where the Lord Protector lay.

      Black Will was burnt in Flushing on a stage:

      Greene was hanged at Osbridge in Kent:

      The painter fled, and how he died we know not.

      But this above the rest is to be noted:

10   Arden lay murdered in that plot of ground

      Which he by force and violence held from Reede:

      And in the grass his body's print was seen

      Two years and more after the deed was done.

      Gentlemen, we hope you'll pardon this naked tragedy

15   Wherein no filed points are foisted in

      To make it gracious to the ear or eye.

      For simple truth is gracious enough,

      And needs no other points of glossing stuff.   *[Exit]*

FINIS

---

26 Leave cease   **29 Smithfield** large open area just outside the walls of the city used as a livestock market and for public executions   **[Epilogue]**
7 Osbridge village in Kent, a mile outside Faversham   **15 filed points** sophisticated rhetorical tricks   **foisted** introduced surreptitiously   **18 glossing stuff** material, apparatus that comments upon/explains away/gives a fair appearance to

Textual Notes

Q = First Quarto text of 1592

Ed = a correction introduced by a later editor

List of parts = Ed

1.12 my = Ed. Q = myne   **13 veil** *spelled* vale *in* Q   **14 head** *spelled* heed *in* Q   **37 ribald** = Ed. Q = riball   **118 raze** *spelled* race *in* Q   **135 narrow** = Ed. Q = marrow   **142 whither** *spelled* whether *in* Q   **215 basilisk** *spelled* Bauliske *in* Q

2.55 worsted = Ed. Q = wosted

3.6 pantofles *spelled* Pantophelles *in* Q   **114 See** *spelled* Se *in* Q   **wot** = Ed. Q = wat   **188 haunt** *spelled* hant *in* Q

4.51 wife's *spelled* wives *in* Q   **55 bore** = Ed. Q = bare   **73 boltered** = Ed. Q = bolstred

6.18 falchion = Ed. Q = fauchon   **27 shivers** = Ed. Q = shewers

7.18 front = Ed. Q = frons   **30 accept** *spelled* except *in* Q

8.12 Though = Ed. Q = thought   **24 ear** *spelled* erre *in* Q   **32 meed** *spelled* mede *in* Q   **61 lovèd** = Ed. Q = knowest   **64 Lest** *spelled* Least *in* Q   **95 exorcisms** = Ed. Q = excirsimes   **133 fount once troubled** = Ed. Q = fence of trouble   **145 is** = Ed. *Not in* Q

9.24 Boulogne *spelled* Bulloyne *in* Q   **27 swooned** = Ed. Q = sounded   **fillip** *spelled* phillope *in* Q   **54 travelled** *spelled* trauailed *in* Q

10.17 desires = Ed. Q = deserues   **23 mistress** = Ed. Q = M   **61 lurdan** *spelled* lordaine *in* Q   **67 table** = Ed. Q = fable   **97 cement** = Ed. Q = semel

11.20 has = Ed. Q = as

12.32 Hock = Ed. Q = hough

13.89 thee = Ed. Q = thy   **138 taunts** = Ed. Q = truant

14.13 Thames *spelled* Temes *in* Q   **15 tallies** = Ed. Q = tales   **112 sieve** = Ed. Q = sine   **118 lest** = Ed. Q = least   **141 snatch** = Ed. Q = snath   **158 ere** *spelled* or *in* Q   **216 An't** = Ed. Q = And   **282 an** = Ed. Q = and

15.10 Thames *spelled* Temes *in* Q

18.16 woo = Ed. Q = woe

An aged British king is carried onto the stage in a chair, accompanied by his courtiers and his three children. He speaks of his impending death and his worries for the future of his kingdom. In order to forestall possible disputes over the inheritance of the throne, he divides the kingdom into three. He also arranges a royal marriage, again for the purpose of holding the state together and avoiding possible civil war.

To those who know their Shakespeare, this sounds like an account of the beginning of *King Lear*. But it is also a description of the opening scene (following a theme-setting prologue in dumb-show) of *Locrine*, published a decade before Shakespeare wrote *King Lear*. When old King Brutus asks his children and his courtiers to listen to his 'latest words', in which he will 'unfold / Our royal mind and resolute intent', readers of Shakespeare cannot help but hear a pre-echo of Lear's 'fast intent / To shake all cares and business from our age' (*King Lear*, 1.1.29–30). Similarly, when Brutus refers to his beloved son Locrine as the 'only pillar of my weakened age' and asks him to 'draw near unto thy sire / And take thy latest blessings at his hands', there is an unmistakable resemblance to the language in which Lear addresses his beloved Cordelia.

Locrine is the eldest of three sons, Cordelia the youngest of three daughters. There is also a key difference between the particular historical moments when the two plays were written and first performed. *King Lear* belongs to the early years of the reign of King James, who in 1603 had ascended the throne of England to add to that of Scotland. A play about the disastrous consequences of a legendary ancient British monarch dividing his kingdom would have had a particular resonance when acted in the presence of a king who was making it his business to *unite* two distinct kingdoms. By contrast, *Locrine* – like the older, anonymously-written, play about King Lear which Shakespeare's version completely reworks – belongs to the earlier time when English courtiers and politicians were beginning to worry about the succession to Queen Elizabeth I, who had remained unmarried all her reign and grown too old to bear a child.

Equally, King James fashioned peace with Spain, whereas in the early 1590s the Spanish Armada was a fresh memory and the prospect of invasion, perhaps via rebellious Ireland, remained a genuine threat. In the latter years of Elizabeth's reign there would have been a particular frisson to any play in which the inhabitants of Britain found themselves up against an enemy from continental Europe. It is not only the possibility of internal strife that troubles old King Brutus, but also an external foe in the form of Humber, King of the Scythians (otherwise known as the Huns), and his warlike son Hubba.

King Brutus's division of the kingdoms goes as follows. His eldest son Locrine gets the best territory, roughly corresponding to England. This is the equivalent of Cordelia's 'third more opulent' than her sisters' (*King Lear*, 1.1.77). Youngest son Albanact gets the north, which is to say Scotland, for his dominion: 'A country full of hills and ragged rocks, / Replenished with fierce untamèd beasts, / As correspondent to thy martial thoughts'. In the medieval chronicler Geoffrey of Monmouth's *History of Britain*, from which these mythical stories of the nation's origins derive, it is as a result of Albanact's name that Scotland became known as Albania (thus in *King Lear* it is the domain of the Duke of Albany). Middle son Camber, meanwhile, gets the west – which is why Wales was known as Cambria. The equivalent share in *King Lear* is another western territory, the Duchy of Cornwall, but *Locrine* has a significant variation whereby Cornwall has been passed as a reward to a loyal councillor called Corineus, whose daughter Gwendolyn is given in marriage to Locrine, a seemingly shrewd political union.

The twist in the action occurs when the opposing forces of love and war get mixed up with each other. After the defeat and death of Humber the invader, Locrine falls in love with his widow Estrild, who has been taken prisoner. His infidelity to Gwendolyn inevitably alienates Corineus and brings about precisely the civil war that Brutus begins the play by seeking to avoid. The tragedy ends with multiple suicides and Gwendolyn taking the crown: though she is a widow rather than a virgin queen, Elizabeth and her courtiers would perhaps have taken pleasure in the ultimate victory of a female monarch who shows herself to be at once firm and magnanimous. Despite his infidelity, Locrine is to be 'buried in a stately tomb, / Close by his agèd father Brutus' bones', while Sabren, his plucky daughter by Estrild, is celebrated for her courage. Estrild, however, is to be denied a proper burial – her body is thrown to the dogs and birds, a similar fate to that bestowed on the comparable figure of Tamora Queen of the Goths in Shakespeare's contemporaneous *Titus Andronicus*, a tragedy very much in the style of *Locrine*.

Though the subject matter of war and invasion, political alliance and betrayal, national unity and royal succession, was of great interest when *Locrine* entered the theatrical repertoire, the play is not in any direct sense an allegory of contemporary history. It is very deliberately set in a mythical distant past. It is an *etiological* narrative, a story about origins. That is to say, the river Humber and the river Severn were regarded as important borderlines, so the narrative of the aftermath of Brutus' death – as first told by Geoffrey of Monmouth, retold in various Elizabethan historical poems, and dramatized in this play – becomes an occasion to put a story behind their names. Humber in the north is so called because the invader drowns there. The girl Sabren commits suicide by drowning herself in a western river, which thus becomes Severn – which translates as Sabrina in Latin (or 'Hafren' in Celtic, which seems to be why on a couple of occasions Sabren is called 'Habren').

Another etiological dimension is the derivation of the name of Britain itself from 'Brutus'. Here the story goes that after the destruction of Troy, Aeneas escaped to Italy and eventually had a grandson (or great-grandson, according to which version of the legend you read) called Brutus, who went into exile, married a girl called Innogen, wandered the world and eventually landed at Totnes in the west country of an island inhabited by giants, whom he and his companions slew. The land thus became Britain and he named his capital (the future London) Troynovant, 'new Troy'. This story served to support a claim about the westward shift of empire: as Troy was once great, so it was succeeded by Rome, which could trace its origins to Aeneas (as described in the foundational epic narrative of Virgil's *Aeneid*), and so in the future Rome would be succeeded by Britain, which could trace its origins to Brutus. These were matters of great interest to Shakespeare as well as great importance to the action of *Locrine*. 'Innogen' seems to have been the name he intended for the heroine of another of his British-Roman-Celtic plays, *Cymbeline*.

The Romans had taken their literary forms as well as some of their myths of origin from the Greeks: the epics and tragedies of the Trojan war and its aftermath, as told by Homer and Euripides, were reworked by Virgil in poetry and Seneca in drama. By the same account, in order to establish a national literature in the English language, Elizabethan writers poeticized and dramatized their own mythical history in similar forms. A poet called William Warner wrote a hugely popular epic called *Albion's England*, telling of the line of Brutus, at exactly the same time that such plays as *Locrine* were being performed. Edmund Spenser's great *Faerie Queene* also tells the story in passing.

Locrine proclaims its allegiance to Seneca and classical tragedy by means of its weight of allusion to classical mythology (it is hosted by Ate, spirit of revenge, and comes replete with mini-enactments of grim tales in dumb shows), its long speeches and formal rhetoric, and most obviously its ghosts calling in Latin for revenge: 'Revenge, revenge for blood! / *Vindicta, vindicta!*' The neo-Senecan ghostly language was intended to split the ears of the groundlings. There is plenty of evidence that Elizabethan audiences could be excited by the alliteration and adjectival accumulation that fills this 'Lamentable Tragedy':

> The snarling curs of darkened Tartarus,
> Sent from Avernus' ponds by Rhadamanth,
> With howling ditties pester every wood:
> The wat'ry ladies and the lightfoot fawns,
> And all the rabble of the woody nymphs,
> All trembling hide themselves in shady groves,
> And shroud themselves in hideous hollow pits.
> The boisterous Boreas thund'reth forth revenge.

It is hard for us to take this ghastly ghostly poetry seriously, precisely because Shakespeare went on to parody such language – one thinks of Nick Bottom's 'part to tear a cat in', with its 'raging rocks / And shivering shocks' (*A Midsummer Night's Dream*, 1.2.21–2) – and then to create a much more complex and flexible, yet quieter and more conversational, style of verse tragedy. But we must remember that *Locrine* was written before Shakespeare's innovations, which were only made possible through the act of reacting against the older style. Besides, it can add to our pleasure in, say, the bombastic language of Pistol in *Henry IV Part 2* if we know that a few years before he appeared on the stage of the Globe, Elizabethan audiences were relishing such lines as 'The Scythians slain with great occision / Do equalize the grass in multitude'.

Linguistically, *Locrine* is also under the influence of Christopher Marlowe's ear for exotic names and tribes:

> If the brave nation of the Troglodytes,
> If all the coal-black Ethiopians,
> If all the forces of the Amazons,
> If all the hosts of the barbarian lands,
> Should dare to enter this our little world

And it tunes into a vein of what might be described as 'Orphic lyricism' of a kind that Shakespeare would soon perfect:

> O that I had the Thracian Orpheus' harp,
> For to awake out of the infernal shade
> Those ugly devils of black Erebus
> That might torment the damnèd traitor's soul:
> O that I had Amphion's instrument,
> To quicken with his vital notes and tunes
> The flinty joints of every stony rock

The mature Shakespeare would never have suffered the tautology of a rock being stony, so one can see why, when introducing the play in his 1908 collection of *Shakespeare Apocrypha*, the editor Tucker Brooke complained that 'No reader will fail to note the infinity of classical allusion, the craze for mouth-filling but meaningless adjectival epithets, the ranting bombast of the heroic figures, the wearisome lyrical repetition of high-sounding words and phrases, or the childish delight in such freaks of verbiage as *agnominated* and *contention*.' Tucker Brooke did, nevertheless, recognize that the comic scenes are rather well done. The action involving the cobbler clown Strumbo offers an early reminder of the thing that makes Shakespearean drama utterly unlike ancient Roman or neo-classical theatre: the action habitually moves, at vertiginous speed, from tragedy to comedy, verse to prose, high to low.

The comic sub-plot offers parallels to the main action, making the audience think twice about the assumptions and postures of the elevated characters. Received ideas are called into question through parody. Consider Strumbo's 'Either the four elements, the seven planets and all the particular stars of the Pole Antastick, are adversative against me, or else I was begotten and born in the wane of the moon, when everything, as saith Lactantius in his fourth book of constultations doth say, goeth arseward'. Here is a seed for the scornful dismissal of astrological prognostication voiced by the Edmund of *King Lear*. Throughout, Strumbo's language is irreverent and inventive. Drunken horseplay and the sight of a commoner fleeing from a burning town provide vivid contrasts to the grandiose heroic language, pulling the action down to earth. We are not, after all, so far from the mingled yarn of Shakespearean theatre.

┌─ **KEY FACTS** ───

AUTHORSHIP: The play was first published 'newly set forth, overseen and corrected by W. S.'. While the possibility of 'W. S.' referring to Shakespeare is usually ignored or dismissed as a deliberately misleading attempt, it is not impossible that Shakespeare was involved in revising the play. The usual candidates advanced for the main play are Robert Greene or George Peele, though a manuscript note also suggests that the substrate play may have been devised by Charles Tilney.

PLOT: Até, the Goddess of Revenge, introduces the tragedy. The dying King Brutus, King of Britain, bequeaths his kingdom to his eldest son, Locrine, and instructs him to marry Gwendolyn, daughter of his counsellor Corineus. Shortly after, the country is invaded by Humber, King of the Scythians. Battle is joined with Locrine's army, led by his brother Albanact, but despite initially having the better, Albanact's army is overrun and he kills himself. Corineus leads a second army and defeats the invaders. The Ghost of Albanact pursues Humber himself to his eventual drowning in a river, which takes his name. Humber's queen, Estrild, is taken prisoner, and Locrine falls in love with her. Corineus is enraged at this slight on his daughter, and Locrine pledges faith to Gwendolyn. He keeps Estrild as a secret mistress, however, and she bears him a daughter, Sabren. Some years pass, and Corineus dies. Locrine dismisses Gwendolyn and crowns Estrild in her place. Gwendolyn raises an army and conquers her husband. Locrine, Estrild and Sabren commit suicide, and Gwendolyn takes the crown. In the sub-plot, a comic cobbler, Strumbo, has a love affair with a wench called

▷

└───

Dorothy, but is called up to the war, and Dorothy is killed. After fighting in the war, Strumbo takes a new wife, Margery. He later attempts to relieve the dying Humber, but is prevented by the ghost of Albanact.

MAJOR PARTS: Locrine (16%/43/9), Humber (13%/22/8), Strumbo (9%/46/7), Corineus (8%/13/6), Thrasimachus (7%/25/11), Albanact (7%/18/9), Brutus (7%/8/1), Gwendolyn (6%/11/5), Estrild (5%/18/7), Até (5%/6/6), Hubba (3%/6/6), Sabren (3%/4/3), Trompart (2%/13/6), Dorothy (2%/10/2), Camber (2%/8/6), Assaracus (2%/5/8), Captain (1%/6/1), Segar (1%/3/5).

LINGUISTIC MEDIUM: 91% verse, 9% prose.

DATE: c.1586? If Tilney was involved in the original play, his execution in 1586 gives us the latest possible date. The question of the play's relationship to a stylistically similar tragedy called *Selimus* has complicated the dating issue, but the play was certainly revised after the publication of Edmund Spenser's *Complaints* in 1591. The Epilogue refers to the thirty-eighth year of Elizabeth's reign, which suggests that the play was indeed newly fitted up in 1595.

SOURCES: The play is heavily influenced by the rhetorical Senecan-inflected tragedy of its day, particularly Sackville and Norton's *Gorboduc*, and draws classical allusions from a range of sources. The historical story of Locrine was well known, and was retold contemporaneously by Edmund Spenser in *The Faerie Queene* (1590).

TEXT: The only early text is the 1595 Quarto, which claims to have been 'newly set forth'. The text shows signs of revisions but is largely well-printed. There is some possible repetition in Act 2 scene 2 and Act 3 scene 3 that suggests the printed text retains elements of a draft as well as the final version: we indicate such 'first thoughts' by enclosing them in solidi (//).

THE LAMENTABLE TRAGEDY OF LOCRINE, the Eldest Son of King Brutus Discoursing the Wars of the Britons and Huns with their Discomfiture: the Britons' Victory with their Accidents and the Death of Albanact. No Less Pleasant than Profitable. Newly Set Forth, Overseen and Corrected by W. S.

ATÉ, Chorus, Greek goddess of ruin, folly and revenge

BRUTUS, King of Britain

LOCRINE
CAMBER } his sons
ALBANACT

ASSARACUS
DEBON } loyal followers of Brutus
CORINEUS

GWENDOLYN, daughter of Corineus, married to Locrine

THRASIMACHUS, her brother

MADAN, son of Locrine and Gwendolyn

HUMBER, King of Scythia

ESTRILD, his queen, later beloved of Locrine

HUBBA, son of Humber and Estrild

SEGAR
TRUSSIER } followers of Humber

SABREN, daughter of Estrild and Locrine

STRUMBO, a cobbler

TROMPART, his man

DOROTHY, Strumbo's first wife

MARGERY, Strumbo's second wife

OLIVER, her father

WILLIAM, her brother

CAPTAIN in Albanact's army

Two SOLDIERS

PAGE

GHOST of Albanact

GHOST of Corineus

Lords, Soldiers

Dumb Shows: 1 Lion, Bear, Archer

2 Perseus, Andromeda, Cepheus, Phineus, Ethiopians

3 Crocodile, Snake

4 Omphale, Hercules

5 Jason, Medea, Creon's daughter

Act 1 Scene 1

Enter Até with thunder and lightning, all in black, with a burning torch in one hand, and a bloody sword in the other hand and presently let there come forth a lion running after a bear or any other beast, then come forth an archer, who must kill the lion in a dumb show, and then depart. Remain Até

ATÉ *In poenam sectatur et umbra.*

  A mighty lion, ruler of the woods,

1.1 Each act opens with a dumb show: a dramatic device of medieval theatre, ultimately derived from Greek drama that rehearsed the plot in silent pantomimed actions. Act 1's emblematic dumb show suggests the death of the king, signified by the *lion*. After the dumb show **Até**, originally the Greek goddess of ruin and folly who later became associated with revenge, speaks a prologue explaining its meaning. The pre-Christian setting is reflected in the numerous references to the deities, characters and events from classical mythology **1** *In … umbra* 'The shade too pursues him to retribution' (Latin)

Of wondrous strength and great proportion,

With hideous noise scaring the trembling trees,

5 With yelling clamours shaking all the earth,

Traversed the groves, and chased the wand'ring beasts:

Long did he range amidst the shady trees,

And drave the silly beasts before his face:

When suddenly from out a thorny bush

10 A dreadful archer with his bow y-bent,

Wounded the lion with a dismal shaft,

So he him struck, that it drew forth the blood

And filled his furious heart with fretting ire:

But all in vain he threat'neth teeth and paws,

15 And sparkleth fire from forth his flaming eyes,

For the sharp shaft gave him a mortal wound.

So valiant Brute, the terror of the world,

Whose only looks did scare his enemies,

The archer, Death, brought to his latest end.

20 O, what may long abide above this ground

In state of bliss and healthful happiness?   *Exit*

Act 1 Scene 2

Enter Brutus, carried in a chair, Locrine, Camber, Albanact, Corineus, Gwendolyn,
Assaracus, Debon, Thrasimachus

BRUTUS   Most loyal lords and faithful followers

That have with me, unworthy general,

Passèd the greedy gulf of Ocĕan,

Leaving the confines of fair Italy,

5 Behold, your Brutus draweth nigh his end

And I must leave you though against my will.

My sinews shrunk, my numbèd senses fail,

A chilling cold possesseth all my bones,

Black ugly Death, with visage pale and wan,

10 Presents himself before my dazzled eyes,

And with his dart preparèd is to strike.

These arms, my lords, these never-daunted arms,

That oft have quelled the courage of my foes

And eke dismayed my neighbour's arrogance,

15 Now yield to death, o'erlaid with crooked age,

Devoid of strength and of their proper force.

8 drave drove   **silly** simple, defenceless   **11 dismal** fatal, disastrous   **12 So** in such a way   **13 fretting ire** impatient anger   **17 Brute** King Brutus, mythical first king of Britain, according to Geoffrey of Monmouth's *Historia Regum Britanniae* (*The History of the Kings of Britain* c.1136) was supposedly descended from the Trojan prince, Aeneas, hero of Virgil's *Aeneid*, who escaped from the burning flames of Troy at the end of the Trojan war and after much wandering around the Mediterranean and many hardships eventually founded Rome   **18 only looks** looks alone   **1.2   3 Ocĕan** Oceanus, in Greek mythology the god of the wide river which encircled the whole plain of earth   **5 nigh** near to   **14 eke** also   **dismayed … arrogance** i.e. successfully defeated the presumptuous attempts of neighbouring kings to invade Britain   **15 o'erlaid** covered over   **16 their proper force** their own/appropriate power or strength, referring to his '**never-daunted arms**' (line 12)

Even as the lusty cedar worn with years,
That far abroad her dainty odour throws,
'Mongst all the daughters of proud Lebanon,
20   This heart, my lords, this ne'er-appallèd heart,
That was a terror to the bord'ring lands,
A doleful scourge unto my neighbour kings,
Now by the weapons of unpartial death
Is clove asunder and bereft of life,
25   As when the sacred oak with thunderbolts,
Sent from the fiery circuit of the heavens,
Sliding along the air's celestial vaults,
Is rent and cloven to the very roots.
In vain therefore I struggle with this foe,
30   Then welcome, Death, since God will have it so.

ASSARACUS   Alas, my lord, we sorrow at your case
And grieve to see your person vexèd thus,
But whatsoe'er the Fates determined have,
It lieth not in us to disannul,
35   And he that would annihilate his mind,
Soaring with Icarus too near the sun,
May catch a fall with young Bellerophon.
For when the fatal sisters have decreed
To separate us from this earthly mould,
40   No mortal force can countermand their minds:
Then, worthy lord, since there's no way but one,
Cease your laments, and leave your grievous moan.

CORINEUS   Your highness knows how many victories,
How many trophies I erected have
45   Triumphantly in every place we came:
The Grecian monarch, warlike Pandrassus,
And all the crew of the Molossians:
Goffarius the arm-strong king of Gauls,
And all the borders of great Aquitaine
50   Have felt the force of our victorious arms,
And to their cost beheld our chivalry.

---

17 lusty vigorous   cedar the evergreen conifer, *Pinus Cedrus*, native to the Mediterranean region, famed for strength and beauty as well as longevity, hence 'worn with years' and its pine fragrance; Brutus likens his heart and thus himself to such a tree   18 abroad afield   19 daughters … Lebanon in the Bible, the sons of Israel married the daughters of Lebanon and forsook their own God (Judges 3:1–7)   20 ne'er-appallèd never daunted   22 doleful sorrowful/causing grief   scourge whip/instrument of divine punishment   23 unpartial impartial   24 clove asunder split apart   bereft deprived   25 As … roots Brutus likens his impending death to an oak tree struck down and split apart by lightning   sacred oak tree sacred to Jupiter/ Jove, whose weapon was the 'thunderbolt'; the oak is also an emblem of Englishness   26 fiery … heavens lightning   33 Fates the three sisters of classical mythology responsible for human destiny; Clotho, the spinner; Lachesis, the measurer; Atropos who cut the thread of human life   34 disannul cancel, make null and void   36 Icarus in Greek mythology, son of Daedalus, the skilled craftsman and inventor who built King Minos' labyrinth. When Minos refused to let him go Daedalus made wings of wax for himself and his son so that they could fly away but Icarus flew too close to the sun, the wings melted and he fell into the sea and was drowned   37 Bellerophon a hero of Greek myth who performed labours similar to Hercules with the help of the winged horse Pegasus but when he tried to ride Pegasus to heaven, the gods were angry and the horse threw him; he died a lonely outcast   38 fatal sisters the Fates (as in line 33)   46 Pandrassus Greek king who imprisoned the descendants of Helenus (a brother of Aeneas) until Brutus freed them   47 Molossians ancient Greek tribe   48 Goffarius Goffarius Pictus, King of Aquitaine, was defeated by Brutus' army and Corineus' courage   49 Aquitaine now a province of south-western France, then an independent kingdom

Where'er Aurora, handmaid of the sun,

Where'er the sun-bright guardian of the day,

Where'er the joyful day with cheerful light,

55 Where'er the light illuminates the world,

The Trojans' glory flies with golden wings,

Wings that do soar beyond fell envious flight.

The fame of Brutus and his followers

Pierceth the skies, and with the skies the throne

60 Of mighty Jove, commander of the world.

Then, worthy Brutus, leave these sad laments:

Comfort yourself with this your great renown,

And fear not Death, though he seem terrible.

BRUTUS   Nay, Corineus, you mistake my mind

65 In construing wrong the cause of my complaints,

I feared not t'yield myself to fatal death!

God knows it was the least of all my thoughts:

A greater care torments my very bones

And makes me tremble at the thought of it,

70 And in you, lordings, doth the substance lie.

THRASIMACHUS   Most noble lord, if aught your loyal peers

Accomplish may, to ease your ling'ring grief,

I, in the name of all, protest to you,

That we will boldly enterprise the same,

75 Were it to enter to black Tartarus,

Where triple Cerberus with his venomous throat,

Scareth the ghosts with high resounding noise;

We'll either rent the bowels of the earth,

Searching the entrails of the brutish earth,

80 Or with his Ixion's over-daring son

Be bound in chains of ever-during steel.

BRUTUS   Then harken to your sovereign's latest words,

In which I will unto you all unfold

Our royal mind and resolute intent.

85 When golden Hebe, daughter to great Jove,

Covered my manly cheeks with youthful down,

Th'unhappy slaughter of my luckless sire,

Drove me and old Assaracus, mine eme,

As exiles from the bounds of Italy

90 So that perforce we were constrained to fly

---

52 **Where'er** wherever; the repetition beginning each phrase is an example of the rhetorical figure 'anaphora'   **Aurora** Roman goddess of the dawn
53 **guardian** guardian   57 **fell** fierce/keen/great   60 **Jove** supreme Roman god   71 **aught** anything   75 **Tartarus** part of the classical Underworld
where the wicked were punished for their misdeeds on earth   76 **triple Cerberus** in Greek myth the monstrous three-headed dog guarding the
entrance to the Underworld – in some versions he has as many as fifty heads   78 **rent** rend, tear   80 **Ixion's over-daring son** Ixion was king of the
centaurs in Greek mythology; his son Pirithous tried to steal Persephone, wife of Hades, god of the Underworld, and was punished by being held there for
eternity   81 **ever-during** everlasting   84 **Our** Brutus is using the plural royal pronoun   85 **Hebe** Greek goddess of youth   87 **Th'unhappy … sire**
Brutus mistook his father for a deer whilst hunting, fulfilling a prophecy that he would kill his father   88 **eme** uncle/friend; he is later referred to as
'brother'   90 **perforce** of necessity

To Grecians' monarch, noble Pandrassus.
There I alone did undertake your cause,
There I restored your antique liberty,
Though Grecia frowned, and all Molossia stormed,
95   Though brave Antigonus with martial band
In pitchèd field encountered me and mine,
Though Pandrassus and his contributaries
With all the rout of their confederates,
Sought to deface our glorious memory
100   And wipe the name of Trojans from the earth,
Him did I captivate with this mine arm
And by compulsion forced him to agree
To certain articles which there we did propound.
From Grecia through the boisterous Hellespont,
105   We came into the fields of Lestrigon,
Whereas our brother Corineus was:
Which when we passed the Sicilian gulf,
And so transfretting the Illyrian sea,
Arrivèd on the coasts of Aquitaine:
110   Where with an army of his barbarous Gauls
Goffarius and his brother Gathelus
Encount'ring with our host, sustained the foil,
And for your sakes my Turnus there I lost—
Turnus that slew six hundred men at arms
115   All in an hour with his sharp battle-axe.
From thence upon the stronds of Albion
To Corus' haven happily we came,
And quelled the giants come of Albion's race
With Gogmagog, son to Samotheus,
120   The cursèd captain of that damnèd crew,
And in that isle at length I placèd you.
Now let me see if my laborious toils,
If all my care, if all my grievous wounds,
If all my diligence were well employed.
125   CORINEUS When first I followed thee and thine, brave king,
I hazarded my life and dearest blood
To purchase favour at your princely hands,
And for the same in dangerous attempts

---

92 There … cause i.e. to release the descendants of Helenus held captive by Pandrassus – see note to line 1.2.46   **93 antique** former/ancient
94 Molossia province of north-western Greece   **95 Antigonus** brother of Pandrassus   **96 pitchèd field** battle ground   **encountered** i.e. fought
97 contributaries those who pay (Pandrassus) tribute   **101 captivate** capture   **103 propound** propose, set forward   **104 Hellespont** ancient name
for the Dardanelles, the narrow strait of water which separates Greece and Turkey with a strong current, hence **boisterous**   **105 Lestrigon** region of
southern Italy; the inhabitants famously ate Odysseus' companions in Homer's *Odyssey*   **106 Whereas** where   **108 transfretting** crossing   **Illyrian
sea** most likely the modern Adriatic   **112 sustained the foil** suffered defeat   **113 Turnus** nephew to Brutus, after whom Tours was supposedly named
116 stronds strands, shores   **Albion** original name for Britain; in Greek mythology a **giant** son of Poseidon killed by Hercules   **117 Corus' haven** port/
refuge of the Roman god of the north-west wind, i.e. Britain   **119 Gogmagog** giant thrown into the sea by Corineus

In sundry conflicts and in divers broils,
130   I showed the courage of my manly mind.
For this I combated with Gathelus,
The brother to Goffarius of Gaul:
For this I fought with furious Gogmagog,
A savage captain of a savage crew:
135   And for these deeds brave Cornwall I received,
A grateful gift given by a gracious king:
And for this gift, this life and dearest blood,
Will Corineus spend for Brutus' good.

DEBON   And what my friend, brave prince, hath vowed to you,
140   The same will Debon do unto his end.

BRUTUS   Then, loyal peers, since you are all agreed,
And resolute to follow Brutus' hosts,
Favour my sons, favour these orphans, lords,
And shield them from the dangers of their foes.
145   Locrine, the column of my family,
And only pillar of my weakened age:
Locrine, draw near, draw near unto thy sire,
And take thy latest blessings at his hands:
And for thou art the eldest of my sons,
150   Be thou a captain to thy bretheren,
And imitate thy agèd father's steps
Which will conduct thee to true honour's gate:
For if thou follow sacred virtue's lore,
Thou shalt be crownèd with a laurel branch,
155   And wear a wreath of sempiternal fame,
Sorted amongst the glorious happy ones.

LOCRINE   If Locrine do not follow your advice
And bear himself in all things like a prince
That seeks to amplify the great renown
160   Left unto him for an inheritage
By those that were his ancestors,
Let me be flung into the ocean,
And swallowed in the bowels of the earth:
Or let the ruddy lightning of great Jove
165   Descend upon this, my devolted head.

BRUTUS   But for I see you all to be in doubt   *Brutus taking Gwendolyn*
Who shall be matchèd with our royal son—   *by the hand*
Locrine, receive this present at my hand:
A gift more rich than are the wealthy mines

---

129 divers various/separate   **broils** quarrels   **135 brave** could qualify '**deeds**' hence meaning 'courageous' or '**Cornwall**' and mean 'fine, splendid'
Cornwall supposedly named after Corineus   **142 hosts** armies   **145 column** prop, support   **147 sire** father   **148 latest** last, final   **149 for** since,
because   **150 bretheren** brethren, brothers; the extra 'e' is to make three syllables to fit the metre   **154 laurel branch** wreaths of *Laurus Nobilis* were worn
as an emblem of victory   **155 sempiternal** everlasting   **156 Sorted** chosen   **160 inheritage** inheritance   **165 devolted** bowed down/legally succeeding
or inheriting   **167 matchèd with** married to

170   Found in the bowels of America.

Thou shalt be spousèd to fair Gwendolyn.

Love her, and take her, for she is thine own,

If so thy uncle and herself do please.

CORINEUS   And herein how your highness honours me,

175   It cannot be in my speech expressed:

For careful parents glory not so much

At their honour and promotion,

As for to see the issue of their blood

Seated in honour and prosperity.

180   GWENDOLYN   And far be it from my maiden's thoughts

To contradict her agèd father's will.

Therefore since he to whom I must obey

Hath given me now unto your royal self,

I will not stand aloof from off the lure,

185   Like crafty dames that most of all deny

That which they most desire to possess.

BRUTUS   Then now, my son, thy part is on the stage,   *Turning to Locrine*
                                                         Locrine kneeling

For thou must bear the person of a king.   *Puts the crown on his head*

Locrine, stand up and wear the regal crown,

190   And think upon the state of majesty,

That thou with honour well may'st wear the crown.

And if thou tend'rest these my latest words,

As thou requir'st my soul to be at rest,

As thou desir'st thine own security,

195   Cherish and love thy new betrothèd wife.

LOCRINE   No longer let me well enjoy the crown,

Than I do peerless Gwendolyn.

BRUTUS   Camber.

CAMBER   My lord.

200   BRUTUS   The glory of mine age,

And darling of thy mother, Innogen,

Take thou the south for thy dominion.

From thee there shall proceed a royal race

That shall maintain the honour of this land,

205   That sway the regal sceptre with their hands.   *Turning to Albanact*

And Albanact, thy father's only joy,

Youngest in years, but not the young'st in mind,

A perfect pattern of all chivalry,

Take thou the north for thy dominion,

210   A country full of hills and ragged rocks,

---

171 spousèd espoused, married   **184 I … possess** Gwendolyn means she's not going to play hard to get and pretend she doesn't want to marry Locrine   **stand aloof** hold back, show no sympathy with   **lure** apparatus containing bait used by falconers to train hawks   **187 Then … king** Brutus means the role his son must play in the drama of life – a meta-theatrical moment   **192 tend'rest** offer to discharge a debt (legal term)/hold dear, care about   **201 Innogen** was the daughter of Pandrassus

Replenished with fierce untamèd beasts,

As correspondent to thy martial thoughts.

Live long, my sons, with endless happiness,

And bear firm concordance amongst yourselves:

215   Obey the counsels of these fathers grave,

That you may better bear out violence.

But suddenly through weakness of my age,

And the defect of youthful puissance,

My malady increaseth more and more,

220   And cruel death hast'neth his quickened pace,

To dispossess me of my earthly shape;

Mine eyes wax dim, o'ercast with clouds of age;

The pangs of death compass my crazèd bones.

Thus to you all my blessings I bequeath,

225   And with my blessings, this my fleeting soul.

My glass is run, and all my miseries

Do end with life: death closeth up mine eyes,

My soul in haste flies to the Elysian fields.   *He dies*

LOCRINE Accursèd stars, damned and accursèd stars,

230   To abbreviate my noble father's life!

Hard-hearted gods, and too envious fates,

Thus to cut off my father's fatal thread!

Brutus that was a glory to us all,

Brutus that was a terror to his foes,

235   Alas too soon by Demogorgon's knife,

The martial Brutus is bereft of life.

[CORINEUS] No sad complaints may move just Aeacus.

No dreadful threats can fear judge Rhadamanth.

Wert thou as strong as mighty Hercules,

240   That tamed the hugy monsters of the world,

Play'd'st thou as sweet on the sweet-sounding lute

As did the spouse of fair Eurydice,

That did enchant the waters with his noise

And made stones, birds, and beasts to lead a dance,

245   Constrained the hilly trees to follow him,

Thou could'st not move the judge of Erebus,

Nor move compassion in grim Pluto's heart

---

212 **correspondent** appropriate, matching   214 **bear firm concordance** remain strongly in agreement, i.e. don't fall out with each other   215 **counsels** advice   **fathers grave** experienced elder statesmen   216 **bear out** successfully endure   218 **defect** absence, lack   **puissance** power, strength   223 **compass** plan, contrive/embrace, seize   **crazèd** diseased, infirm   225 **fleeting** swiftly passing   226 **glass** i.e. the hourglass measuring his life   228 **Elysian fields** where heroes in classical mythology went after death   235 **Demogorgon's knife** the knife belonging to the mysterious and infernal deity of classical mythology used to cut the thread of Brutus' life   237 **Aeacus ... Rhadamanth** judges of hell; Minos was the third   239 **Hercules** mythological hero who famously achieved twelve seemingly impossible labours   240 **hugy** huge – the extra 'y' has been added to make up the pentameter beat of the line   241 **lute** stringed instrument, associated with love songs   242 **spouse ... Eurydice** Orpheus was Eurydice's husband in classical myth; his musical skill was such that he could charm wild beasts and move rocks and trees. When she died he went to the Underworld to beg that she be restored to him and Hades agreed that she could return to earth with Orpheus as long as he did not look back at her but as they approached the land of the living Orpheus forgot the condition, turned around and Eurydice was lost for ever   246 **Erebus** darkness: part of the Underworld in Greek mythology   247 **Pluto's** belonging to Pluto, the Roman god of the Underworld, equivalent to Greek Hades

For fatal Mors expecteth all the world,

And every man must tread the way of death.

250 Brave Tantalus, the valiant Pelops' sire,

Guest to the gods, suffered untimely death,

And old Tithonus, husband to the morn,

And eke grim Minos whom just Jupiter

Deigned to admit unto his sacrifice.

255 The thund'ring trumpets of bloodthirsty Mars,

The fearful rage of fell Tisiphone,

The boist'rous waves of humid Ocëan,

Are instruments and tools of dismal death.

Then, noble cousin, cease to mourn his chance,

260 Whose age and years were signs that he should die.

It resteth now that we inter his bones,

That was a terror to his enemies.

Take up the corpse and princes hold him dead,

Who, while he lived, upheld the Troyan state.

265 Sound drums and trumpets, march to Troynovant,

There to provide our chieftain's funeral.   *Exeunt*

Act 1 Scene 3

Enter Strumbo above in a gown, with ink and paper in his hand, saying

STRUMBO   Either the four elements, the seven planets and all the particular stars of the Pole Antastick, are adversative against me, or else I was begotten and born in the wane of the moon, when everything, as saith Lactantius in his fourth book of constultations doth say, goeth arseward. Ay, masters, ay, you may laugh, but I must

5 weep: you may joy, but I must sorrow: shedding salt tears from the wat'ry fountains of my most dainty fair eyes, along my comely and smooth cheeks, in as great plenty as the water runneth from the bucking-tubs, or red wine out of the hogsheads: for trust me, gentlemen and my very good friends, and so forth: the little god, nay the

248 **Mors** Greek god personifying death   250 **Tantalus ... sire** in Greek mythology Tantalus, King of Lydia, was entertained on Mount Olympus by the **gods** but he stole nectar and ambrosia from them to give to his people. The gods were offended and Tantalus offered his son **Pelops** as a sacrifice, serving him to them as food but Zeus ordered that he should be restored to life. Tantalus was punished by standing in a pool of water and having food and drink placed just out of reach, hence 'tantalize'   252 **Tithonus** in Greek mythology was beloved of Eos, the dawn; she asked Zeus to make him immortal but forgot to ask for eternal youth   253 **eke** also   **Minos ... sacrifice** Minos, mythical king of Crete, was sent a bull to sacrifice to confirm his kingship but it was so handsome he declined to kill it and his wife, Pasiphaë fell in love with it and gave birth to the Minotaur; after his death Minos was made one of the judges of the Underworld by **Jupiter**, chief of the Roman gods   255 **Mars** Roman god of war   256 **Tisiphone** one of the Furies, who punished crimes of murder   257 **Ocean** Oceanus, in Greek mythology the god of the wide river which encircled the whole plain of earth   259 **cousin** kinsman, used to a close friend or relative   263 **hold** carry   264 **Troyan** Trojan   265 **Troynovant** new Troy (London)   **1.3**   *above* Strumbo appears in the gallery or balcony   1 **STRUMBO** a comic name, perhaps from a 'strum', the contraption used to strain liquor; his language contains a significant number of references to alcohol and perhaps he is supposed to be drunk   **seven planets** according to the geocentric system of planetary motion devised by Ptolemy, there were seven planets which travelled around the earth: the moon, Mercury, Venus, the sun, Mars, Jupiter, Saturn   2 **Antastick** i.e. 'Antarctic'; malapropism is one of the characteristics of Strumbo's speech   **adversative** adverse, contrary   3 **wane** i.e. waning   **Lactantius** a fourth-century teacher of Latin rhetoric who was popular in the Renaissance; his best known works were his *Divinae Institutiones* (Divine Institutions) which are perhaps what Strumbo means by the '**book of constultations**'; the name suggests a play on consultations/constellations/stultifications   4 **arseward** backwards, contrariwise   **masters** flattering form of direct address to the audience   7 **bucking-tubs** wash-tubs; buck or lye was used in bleaching   **hogsheads** large casks holding sixty-three old wine-gallons

desperate god Cuprit, with one of his vengible bird-bolts, hath shot me unto the
heel: so not only, but also, O, fine phrase! I burn, I burn, and I burn ah, in love,
in love, and in love. Ah, ah Strumbo, what hast thou seen? Not Dina with the ass
Tom? Yea, with these eyes thou hast seen her, and therefore pull them out: for they
will work thy bale. Ah, Strumbo, hast thou heard, not the voice of the nightingale,
but a voice sweeter than hers, yea with these ears hast thou heard them, and
therefore cut them off, for they have caused thy sorrow. Nay, Strumbo, kill thyself,
drown thyself, hang thyself, starve thyself. O, but then I shall leave my sweetheart.
O, my heart! Now, pate, for thy master, I will dite an aliquant love-pistle to her,
and then she hearing the grand verbosity of my scripture, will love me presently.

Let him write a little, and then read

My pen is naught, gentlemen, lend me a knife: I think the more haste the worst
speed.   *Then write again, and after read*
'So it is, Mistress Dorothy, and the sole essence of my soul, that the little sparkles
of affection kindled in me towards your sweet self, hath now increased to a great
flame, and will ere it be long consume my poor heart, except you with the pleasant
water of your secret fountain, quench the furious heat of the same. Alas, I am a
gentleman of good fame and name, majestical, in 'pparel comely, in gait portly. Let
not therefore your gentle heart be so hard as to despise a proper tall young man of a
handsome life, and by despising him, not only but also, to kill him. Thus expecting
time and tide, I bid you farewell.

Your Servant, Signior Strumbo.'

O wit, O pate, O memory, O hand, O ink, O paper! Well, now I will send it away.—
Trompart, Trompart, what a villain is this? Why sirrah, come when your master
calls you. Trompart!

Trompart entering saith

[TROMPART]   Anon, sir.

STRUMBO   Thou knowest, my pretty boy, what a good master I have been to thee
ever since I took thee into my service.

TROMPART   Ay, sir.

STRUMBO   And how I have cherished thee always, as if you had been the fruit of my
loins, flesh of my flesh, and bone of my bone.

TROMPART   Ay, sir.

STRUMBO   Then show thyself herein a trusty servant, and carry this letter to Mistress
Dorothy, and tell her—   *Speaking in his ear. Exit Trompart*
Nay, masters, you shall see a marriage by and by. But here she comes. Now must I
frame my amorous passions.

9 desperate producing despair/dangerous   Cuprit i.e. Cupid, punning on 'culprit'; Cupid was the blind god of love, those struck by his arrows fell in love with the first creature they saw   vengible vengeful   bird-bolts blunt-headed arrows for shooting birds   unto as far as   10 so … phrase Strumbo is parodying the flowery language and antithetical style of Euphuism   11 Dina … Tom presumably a reference to the story of Diana and Actaeon   13 bale evil, ruin   17 pate head, Strumbo is talking to himself and perhaps scratches or gestures to his head at this point   dite compose   aliquant i.e. eloquent, with a play on 'alicant', a red wine from Alicante in Spain   love-pistle love letter; pistle (from 'epistle' meaning letter) is a bawdy pun on 'pizzle' (penis)   18 scripture writing   presently immediately   19 naught naughty/useless; Strumbo is playing on the bawdy sense of pen as 'penis'   gentlemen … knife as before, Strumbo addresses the audience directly; his goose-quill pen would need regular sharpening   l … speed 'more haste less speed' is proverbial and carries a bawdy implication here   20 speed success   23 ere before   pleasant … fountain referring to her vagina and vaginal secretions   25 'pparel comely decent, suitable, handsome clothes   gait bearing, way of walking   portly handsome, dignified/bulky, corpulent   26 proper fine, elegant/suitable   tall decent/handsome/brave, as well as usual sense   29 Signior term of respect (Italian), equivalent to 'sir', 'Master'   31 Trompart Strumbo's servant, named after Braggadochio's man in Spenser's *The Faerie Queene*, from 'trompant': cheating, deceiving, and 'trump': to deceive   sirrah term of address used to men or boys, expresses contempt   33 Anon at once   43 frame prepare/compose/discipline/get on with

Enter Dorothy and Trompart

DOROTHY   Signior Strumbo, well met! I received your letters by your man here, who
45   told me a pitiful story of your anguish, and so understanding your passions were so
great, I came hither speedily.

STRUMBO   O, my sweet and pigsney, the fecundity of my ingenie is not so great, that
may declare unto you the sorrowful sobs and broken sleeps that I suffered for your
sake: and therefore I desire you to receive me into your familiarity.

50   For your love doth lie,
             As near and as nigh
             Unto my heart within
             As mine eye to my nose,
             My leg unto my hose
55   And my flesh unto my skin.

DOROTHY   Truly, Master Strumbo, you speak too learnedly for me to understand the
drift of your mind and, therefore, tell your tale in plain terms and leave off your
dark riddles.

STRUMBO   Alas, Mistress Dorothy, this is my luck, that when I most would, I cannot
60   be understood so that my great learning is an inconvenience unto me. But to speak
in plain terms, I love you, Mistress Dorothy, if you like to accept me into your
familiarity.

DOROTHY   If this be all, I am content.

STRUMBO   Say'st thou so, sweet wench, let me lick thy toes. Farewell, mistress.
                                                          Turning to the people
65   If any of you be in love, provide ye a cap-case full of new-coined words, and then
shall you soon have the *succado de labres* and something else.   *Exeunt*

Act 1 Scene 4

Enter Locrine, Gwendolyn, Camber, Albanact, Corineus, Assaracus, Debon, Thrasimachus

LOCRINE   Uncle and princes of brave Brittany,
          Since that our noble father is entombed,
          As best beseemed so brave a prince as he,
          If so you please, this day my love and I,
5   Within the Temple of Concordia,
          Will solemnize our royal marriage.

THRASIMACHUS   Right noble lord, your subjects every one,
          Must needs obey your highness at command,
          Especially in such a cause as this,
10   That much concerns your highness' great content.

LOCRINE   Then frolic, lordings, to fair Concord's walls,
          Where we will pass the day in knightly sports,

---

47 **pigsney** term of endearment to a woman, 'sweetheart', 'beloved'   **ingenie** malapropism suggesting 'ingenuity/genius'   49 **familiarity** close
acquaintance, with implications of 'sexual intimacy'   55 **flesh** slang for 'genitals'   65 **cap-case** wallet/receptacle of any kind; plays on 'case', slang for
'vagina'   66 *succado de labres* corruption of the Italian for 'sweetness of lips', i.e. a kiss, with implied bawdy innuendo as the rest of the line makes
clear   *succado* fruit syrup   **1.4**   1 **Brittany** Britain   3 **beseemed** fitted   **so brave a** such a brave   11 **frolic** make merry

The night in dancing and in figured masks,

And offer to god Risus all our sports.   *Exeunt*

Act 2 Scene 1

Enter Até as before, after a little lightning and thundering, let there come forth this show:
Perseus and Andromeda, hand in hand, and Cepheus also with swords and targets. Then
let there come out of another door Phineus, all black in armour, with Ethiopians after him,
driving in Perseus, and having taken away Andromeda, let them depart. Até remaining,
saying:

ATÉ   *Regit omnia numen.*

When Perseus married fair Andromeda,

The only daughter of King Cepheus,

He thought he had established well his crown,

5   And that his kingdom should for aye endure.

But lo, proud Phineus with a band of men,

Contrived of sunburned Ethiopians,

By force of arms the bride he took from him,

And turned their joy into a flood of tears.

10   So fares it with young Locrine and his love;

He thinks this marriage tendeth to his weal

But this foul day, this foul accursèd day,

Is the beginning of his miseries.

Behold where Humber and his Scythians

15   Approacheth nigh with all his warlike train,

I need not, I, the sequel shall declare,

What tragic chances fell out in this war.   *Exeunt*

Act 2 Scene 2

Enter Humber, Hubba, Estrild, Segar and their soldiers

HUMBER   At length the snail doth climb the highest tops,

Ascending up the stately castle walls;

At length the water with continual drops

Doth penetrate the hardest marble stone;

5   At length we are arrived in Albion.

Nor could the barbarous Dacian sovereign,

Nor yet the ruler of brave Belgia

---

13 figured masks patterned or symbolic masks, but playing on the sense of 'pretence, a front, an outward show intended to deceive'   **14 Risus** god of laughter   **2.1**   As before, the dumb show is explained by Até   ***Perseus and Andromeda*** in Greek mythology Andromeda, the daughter of Cepheus, was to be sacrificed to a sea monster sent by Poseidon to punish her mother's arrogance in claiming she was more beautiful than the Nereids or sea nymphs; she was rescued by Perseus and they were married, despite having previously been promised to her uncle Phineus who interrupted the wedding celebrations and carried her off; in Ovid's version, Perseus turned his enemies to stone using the Gorgon's head   ***targets*** round, light shields   **1 *Regit omnia numen*** 'The divine will rules all' (Latin)   **5 aye** ever   **6 lo** behold   **7 Contrived** composed   **11 weal** well-being, happiness, prosperity   **14 Scythians** historic inhabitants of Scythia, a region to the north of the Black Sea with a reputation for cruelty   **15 nigh** near   **2.2**   **6 Dacian** of Dacia, ancient region of central Europe, comparable to modern Romania   **7 Belgia** Belgium

Stay us from cutting over to this isle:
Whereas I hear a troop of Phrygians,
10   Under the conduct of Posthumius' son,
Have pitched up lordly pavilions,
And hope to prosper in this lovely isle.
But I will frustrate all their foolish hope,
And teach them that the Scythian emperor
15   Leads Fortune tied in a chain of gold,
Constraining her to yield unto his will
And grace him with their regal diadem,
Which I will have, maugre their treble hosts,
And all the power their petty kings can make.
20   HUBBA   If she that rules fair Rhamnus' golden gate,
Grant us the honour of the victory,
As hitherto she always favoured us,
Right noble father, we will rule the land,
Enthronized in seats of topaz stones,
25   That Locrine and his brethren all may know,
None must be king but Humber and his son.
HUMBER   Courage my son, fortune shall favour us,
And yield to us the coronet of bay,
That decketh none but noble conquerors.
30   But what saith Estrild to these regions?
How liketh she the temperature thereof?
Are they not pleasant in her gracious eyes?
ESTRILD   The plains, my lord, garnished with Flora's wealth,
And overspread with particoloured flowers,
35   Do yield sweet contentation to my mind,
The airy hills enclosed with shady groves,
The groves replenished with sweet chirping birds,
The birds' resounding heavenly melody,
Are equal to the groves of Thessaly,
40   Where Phoebus with the learnèd ladies nine
Delight themselves with music harmony,
And from the moisture of the mountain tops
The silent springs dance down with murmuring streams
And water all the ground with crystal waves;
45   The gentle blasts of Eurus' modest wind,

---

8 cutting crossing   9 Phrygians Trojans; the historical region of Phrygia comprised much of modern Turkey   10 Posthumius' son i.e. Brutus
15 Fortune the goddess Fortuna, personification of luck   17 diadem crown   18 maugre in spite of   20 Rhamnus' golden gate Nemesis, the Greek
goddess of vengeful fate, had a temple at Rhamnus   28 coronet of bay i.e. laurel wreath, symbol of military victory   33 Flora's Flora was the goddess of
flowers and season of spring   34 particoloured varied, mixed   35 contentation contentment, satisfaction   36 The ... melody these three lines in which
the key word of one becomes the subject of the next is known in rhetoric as the 'marching figure' or 'climax' (from the Greek for 'ladder')   39 Thessaly
area of northern Greece   40 Phoebus alternative name for Apollo, god of music and poetry   learnèd ladies nine i.e. the Muses, the goddesses or spirits
who inspire the creative arts   45 Eurus' Eurus was the Greek god of the east wind

Moving the pittering leaves of Sylvan's woods,
Do equal it with Tempe's paradise.
And thus comforted, all to one effect,
Do make me think these are the happy isles,
50 Most fortunate, if Humber may them win.
HUBBA   Madam, where resolution leads the way
And courage follows with emboldened pace,
Fortune can never use her tyranny,
For valiantness is like unto a rock
55 That standeth on the waves of Ocëan,
Which though the billows beat on every side,
And Boreas fell with his tempestuous storms,
Bloweth upon it with a hideous clamour,
Yet it remaineth still unmovable.
60 HUMBER   Kingly resolved, thou glory of thy sire.
But, worthy Segar, what uncouth novelties
Bring'st thou unto our royal majesty?
SEGAR   My lord, the youngest of all Brutus' sons,
Stout Albanact, with millions of men,
65 Approacheth nigh and meaneth ere the morn,
To try your force by dint of fatal sword.
HUMBER   Tut, let him come with millions of hosts,
He shall find entertainment good enough.
Yea fit for those that are our enemies,
70 For we'll receive them at the lances' points,
And massacre their bodies with our blades:
Yea though they were in number infinite,
More than the mighty Babylonian queen,
Semiramis the ruler of the west,
75 Brought gainst the Emperor of the Scythians,
Yet would we not start back one foot from them,
That they might know we are invincible.
HUBBA   Now by great Jove, the supreme king of heaven,
And the immortal gods that live therein,
80 Whenas the morning shows his cheerful face
And Lucifer mounted upon his steed
Brings in the chariot of the golden sun,
I'll meet young Albanact in the open field
And crack my lance upon his burgonet,
85 To try the valour of his boyish strength.

46 pittering making a succession of light tapping sounds   Sylvan's of the spirit of the woods   47 Tempe's the vale of Tempe, a valley in Thessaly
57 Boreas the north wind   fell fierce, dangerous   61 uncouth novelties strange, unpleasant news   64 millions countless   65 meaneth intends
ere before   66 dint ... sword force of arms   68 entertainment treatment/reception   74 Semiramis legendary Assyrian queen who led her army to
victory after her husband Ninus' death   75 gainst against   80 Whenas when   81 Lucifer in classical mythology, the morning star, herald of the dawn;
Christians later thought of Lucifer as the name of Satan before the fall   84 burgonet light helmet or steel cap

There will I show such ruthful spectacles
And cause so great effusion of blood,
That all his boys shall wonder at my strength:
As when the warlike queen of Amazon,
90   Penthesilea, armèd with her lance,
Girt with a corselet of bright shining steel,
Cooped up the faint-heart Grecians in the camp.

HUMBER   Spoke like a warlike knight, my noble son,
Nay, like a prince that seeks his father's joy.
95   Therefore tomorrow ere fair Titan shine,
And bashful Eos messenger of light,
Expels the liquid sleep from out men's eyes,
Thou shalt conduct the right wing of the host,
The left wing shall be under Segar's charge,
100   The rearward shall be under me myself.
And lovely Estrild fair and gracious,
// If Fortune favour me in mine attempts, //
// Thou shalt be queen of lovely Albion. //
Fortune shall favour me in mine attempts,
105   And make thee queen of lovely Albion.
Come let us in and muster up our train
And furnish up our lusty soldiers,
That they may be a bulwark to our state,
And bring our wishèd joys to perfect end.   *Exeunt*

Act 2 Scene 3

Enter Strumbo, Dorothy, Trompart [and Captain], cobbling shoes and singing

TROMPART	We cobblers lead a merry life:
ALL	Dan, dan, dan, dan.
STRUMBO	Void of all envy and of strife:
ALL	Dan diddle dan.
5 DOROTHY	Our ease is great, our labour small:
ALL	Dan, dan, dan, dan.
STRUMBO	And yet our gains be much withal:
ALL	Dan diddle dan.
DOROTHY	With this art so fine and fair:
10 ALL	Dan, dan, dan, dan.

---

86 ruthful pitiful, exciting compassion   **90 Penthesilea** leader of the tribe of Amazons, or warrior women, who fought with the Trojans against the Greeks in the Trojan war; she was killed by Achilles   **95 Titan** the sun   **96 Eos** Greek goddess of the dawn, Roman Aurora   **102 If … Albion** lines 102–3 are enclosed within solidi because although they appear in the printed texts, they seem to be Shakespeare's first draft of the lines that follow   **106 muster** assemble in preparation for a battle   **train** retinue/followers and vehicles   **107 furnish up** equip   **108 bulwark** defence/fortification   **2.3   1 We … dan** a worksong, such as were commonly sung in workshops – compare the 'two merry three-man's songs' in Thomas Dekker's *The Shoemaker's Holiday* – the nonsensical refrain helps the workers keep time. 'We Cobblers Lead a Merry Life' has been set to music for alto, tenor and bass by Greenhill, published by Leonard Gould and Bolttler   **7 withal** as well

TROMPART	No occupation may compare:
ALL	Dan diddle dan.
STRUMBO	For merry pastime and joyful glee:
[ALL]	Dan, dan, dan, dan.
15 DOROTHY	Most happy men we cobblers be:
[ALL]	Dan diddle dan.
TROMPART	The can stands full of nappy ale:
[ALL]	Dan, dan, dan, dan.
STRUMBO	In our shop still withouten fail:
20 [ALL]	Dan diddle dan.
DOROTHY	This is our meat, this is our food:
[ALL]	Dan, dan, dan, dan.
TROMPART	This brings us to a merry mood:
[ALL]	Dan diddle dan.
25 STRUMBO	This makes us work for company:
[ALL]	Dan, dan, dan, dan.
DOROTHY	To pull the tankards cheerfully:
[ALL]	Dan diddle dan.
TROMPART	Drink to thy husband, Dorothy,
30 [ALL]	Dan, dan, dan, dan.
DOROTHY	Why then, my Strumbo, there's to thee:
[ALL]	Dan diddle dan.
STRUMBO	Drink thou the rest Trompart amain:
[ALL]	Dan, dan, dan, dan.
35 DOROTHY	When that is gone, we'll fill't again:
[ALL]	Dan diddle dan.

CAPTAIN   The poorest state is farthest from annoy,   *Aside*
> How merrily he sitteth on his stool:
> But when he sees that needs he must be pressed,
40 He'll turn his note and sing another tune—
> Ho, by your leave, master cobbler.

STRUMBO   You are welcome, gentleman. What will you any old shoes or buskins, or will you have your shoes clouted? I will do them as well as any cobbler in Caithness whatsoever.   *Captain showing him press money*

45 [CAPTAIN]   O, master cobbler, you are far deceived in me, for don't you see this? I come not to buy any shoes but to buy yourself. Come, sir, you must be a soldier in the king's cause.

STRUMBO   Why, but hear you, sir, has your king any commission to take any man against his will? I promise you, I can scant believe it, or did he give you 50 commission?

---

17 nappy heady, strong   **19 withouten** without, the extra syllable of the archaic form is retained for rhythm   **21 meat … food** since drinking water was unsafe at this time, fermented drinks such as ale or beer were preferred and represented an important part of the diet; some estimates put average consumption at a gallon a day   **33 amain** at once   **37 The … annoy** i.e. 'the poorest people are the happiest'   **39 pressed** forced to enlist for military service; a frequent occurrence when the play was written   **40 turn his note** change his ideas   **42 buskins** boots reaching to the calf or knee   **43 clouted** mended, patched   **Caithness** i.e. the land beyond the Humber   *press money* money paid to a soldier or sailor on enlisting; acceptance was considered legally binding

CAPTAIN   O, sir, ye need not care for that, I need no commission: hold here, I command you in the name of our King Albanact, to appear tomorrow in the town-house of Caithness.

STRUMBO   King Nactaball? I cry God mercy! What have we to do with him, or he with us? But you, sir, Master Capontail, draw your pasteboard, or else I promise you, I'll give you a canvasado with a bastinado over your shoulders, and teach you to come hither with your implements.

CAPTAIN   I pray thee, good fellow, be content: I do the king's command.

STRUMBO   Put me out of your book then.

CAPTAIN   I may not.   *Strumbo snatching up a staff*

[STRUMBO]   No, will! Come, sir, will your stomach serve you? By gog's blue hood and halidom, I will have a bout with you.   *Fight both*

Enter Thrasimachus

THRASIMACHUS   How now, what noise, what sudden clamour's this?

How now, my captain and the cobbler so hard at it?

Sirs, what is your quarrel?

CAPTAIN   Nothing, sir, but that he will not take press money.

THRASIMACHUS   Here, good fellow, take it at my command,

Unless you mean to be stretched.

STRUMBO   Truly, master gentleman, I lack no money: if you please I will resign it to one of these poor fellows.

THRASIMACHUS   No such matter,

Look you be at the common house tomorrow. *Exit Thrasimachus and the Captain*

STRUMBO   O, wife, I have spun a fair thread. If I had been quiet, I had not been pressed, and therefore well may I wayment. But come sirrah, shut up, for we must to the wars.   *Exeunt*

Act 2 Scene 4

Enter Albanact, Debon, Thrasimachus and the lords

ALBANACT   Brave cavaliers, princes of Albany,

Whose trenchant blades with our deceasèd sire,

Passing the frontiers of brave Grecia,

Were bathèd in our enemies' lukewarm blood,

Now is the time to manifest your wills,

Your haughty minds and resolutions.

Now opportunity is offered

52 town-house municipal building containing public offices, equivalent to the modern Town Hall   54 Nactaball comic perversion of Albanact; perhaps playing on 'knack', sexual organ, and 'ball', testicle   55 Capontail insulting malapropism for 'captain'; a 'capon' is a castrated cockrel/eunuch and 'tail' was slang for 'penis'   draw withdraw   pasteboard stiff but pliable material made by pasting three or more sheets of paper together and compressing and rolling them, presumably the book (line 59) in which he enters the names of those pressed for service   56 canvasado sudden attack, shaking up   bastinado beating, cudgelling   57 implements i.e. (legal) instruments   61 No, will! syntax is unclear, presumably means 'No, but you will' or 'Will you not?'   will … you i.e. have you got the stomach for a fight?   gog's euphemism for 'God's'   blue hood perhaps a reference to the blue-cap formerly worn by tradesmen or to the blue-bonnets of the Scots, hence a Scot   62 halidom holiness/holy relic   bout match, round at fighting   68 stretched hanged or perhaps tortured by stretching on a rack   72 common house place where the council meet, the Town Hall   73 spun … thread been my own worst enemy (proverbial)   had not been would not have been   74 wayment lament, wail   shut up i.e. the workshop   2.4   1 cavaliers knights/gallants   2 trenchant sharp, cutting

To try your courage and your earnest zeal,

Which you always protest to Albanact.

10 For at this time, yea at this present time,

Stout fugitives, come from the Scythians' bounds,

Have pestered every place with mutinies.

But trust me, lordings, I will never cease

To persecute the rascal runagates,

15 Till all the rivers stainèd with their blood,

Shall fully show their fatal overthrow.

DEBON   So shall your highness merit great renown,

And imitate your agèd father's steps.

ALBANACT   But tell me, cousin, cam'st thou through the plains?

20 And saw'st thou there the faint-heart fugitives

Mustering their weather-beaten soldiers?

What order keep they in their marshalling?

THRASIMACHUS   After we passed the groves of Caledon,

Where murmuring rivers slide with silent streams,

25 We did behold the straggling Scythian's camp,

Replete with men, stored with munition.

There might we see the valiant-minded knights

Fetching careers along the spacious plains,

Humber and Hubba armed in azure blue,

30 Mounted upon their coursers white as snow,

Went to behold the pleasant flow'ring fields:

Hector and Troilus, Priam's lovely sons,

Chasing the Grecians over Simoïs,

Were not to be compared to these two knights.

35 ALBANACT   Well hast thou painted out in eloquence

The portraiture of Humber and his son:

As fortunate as was Polycrates,

Yet should they not escape our conquering swords

Or boast of aught but of our clemency.

Enter Strumbo and Trompart crying often

40 [STRUMBO *and* TROMPART]   Wild-fire and pitch, wild-fire and pitch, etc.

THRASIMACHUS   What, sirs, what mean you by these clamours made,

These outcries raisèd in our stately court?

STRUMBO   Wild-fire and pitch, wild-fire and pitch!

THRASIMACHUS   Villains, I say, tell us the cause hereof?

45 STRUMBO   Wild-fire and pitch, etc.

---

11 bounds territories, borderlands   **14 runagates** vagabonds, fugitives/renegades   **23 Caledon** Scotland (Caledonia)   **26 Replete** filled   **28 Fetching** making, performing   **careers** short gallops at full speed (on horseback)   **32 Hector and Troilus** sons of King Priam of Troy and chief warriors of the Trojan army   **33 Simoïs** river of Troy   **37 Polycrates** in Greek mythology, a tyrant of Samos, renowned for his good fortune; in order to avert the jealousy of the gods, he was advised to throw away something he held precious. He threw away a valuable ring but a few days later it was returned to him in the belly of a fish   **39 aught** anything   **40 Wild-fire** furious, destructive fire, often caused by lightning/composition of inflammable substances used in warfare and difficult to extinguish   **43 pitch** sticky, black, tar-like substance   **44 Villains** scornful term of addressing implying 'low-born, base-minded'

THRASIMACHUS Tell me, you villains, why you make this noise,

Or with my lance I will prick your bowels out.

ALBANACT   Where are your houses, where's your dwelling place?

STRUMBO   Place! Ha, ha, ha, laugh a month and a day at him. Place! I cry God
50 mercy? Why do you think that such poor honest men as we be hold our habitacles
in king's palaces? Ha, ha, ha! But because you seem to be an abominable chieftain,
I will tell you our state:

From the top to the toe,

From the head to the shoe:

55 From the beginning to the ending.

From the building to the burning.

This honest fellow and I had our mansion-cottage in the suburbs of this city,
hard by the Temple of Mercury. And by the common soldiers of the Shittens, the
Scythians — what do you call them? Withal the suburbs were burned to the ground,
60 and the ashes are left there for the country wives to wash bucks withal. And that
which grieves me most, my loving wife, O cruel strife, the wicked flames did roast.

And therefore, Captain Crust,

We will continually cry,

Except you seek a remedy,

65 Our houses to re-edify,

Which now are burnt to dust.

BOTH (cry)   Wild-fire and pitch! Wild-fire and pitch!

ALBANACT   Well, we must remedy these outrages

And throw revenge upon their hateful heads,

70 And you, good fellows, for your houses burned

We will remunerate you store of gold

And build your houses by our palace gate.

STRUMBO   Gate! O, petty treason to my person, nowhere else but by your backside.
Gate! O, how I am vexed in my choler. Gate! I cry God mercy! Do you hear, Master
75 King? If you mean to gratify such poor men as we be, you must build our houses by
the tavern.

ALBANACT   It shall be done, sir.

STRUMBO   Near the tavern, ay! By'r lady, sir, it was spoken like a good fellow. Do you
hear, sir? When our house is builded, if you do chance to pass or repass that way, we
80 will bestow a quart of the best wine upon you.   *Exit*

ALBANACT   It grieves me, lordings, that my subjects' goods

Should thus be spoilèd by the Scythians,

Who as you see with lightfoot foragers,

Depopulate the places where they come,

---

50 habitacles habitations, dwelling places   51 abominable loathsome; presumably he means 'admirable'   57 mansion-cottage dwelling, the
implication is of a humble residence which was a palace to them   suburbs areas outside the city walls and thus outside the control of the city authorities,
notoriously licentious   58 hard by near   Temple of Mercury perhaps the name of a tavern (or a brothel); Mercury was the patron god of thieves and
cheating   Shittens comic version of Scythians   59 Withal moreover   60 bucks quantities of clothes for washing; ashes were used in the production
of 'buck' or 'lye' for bleaching   withal with   62 Captain Crust familiar form of address; Strumbo may mean 'curst'   65 re-edify rebuild   73 backside
backyard/privy   74 choler bile; one of the four humours of early physiology affecting temperament and character, it produced anger   78 By'r lady by our
lady, i.e. the Virgin Mary   80 quart quarter of a gallon, i.e. two pints   83 lightfoot nimble, active   foragers ravagers

85 But cursèd Humber thou shalt rue the day
That e'er thou cam'st unto Caithnesia.   *Exeunt*

Act 2 Scene 5

Enter Humber, Hubba, Segar, Trussier, and their soldiers

HUMBER   Hubba, go take a coronet of our horse,
As many lancers, and light-armèd knights,
As may suffice for such an enterprise,
And place them in the grove of Caledon.
5 With these whenas the skirmish doth increase,
Retire thou from the shelters of the wood
And set upon the weakened Trojans' backs:
For policy joinèd with chivalry,
Can never be put back from victory.   *Exeunt*

Enter Albanact, clowns with him

10 ALBANACT   Thou base-born Hun, how durst thou be so bold
As once to menace warlike Albanact,
The great commander of these regions?
But thou shalt buy thy rashness with thy death
And rue too late thy over-bold attempts:
15 For with this sword, this instrument of death,
That hath been drenchèd in my foemen's blood,
I'll separate thy body from thy head
And set that coward blood of thine abroach.

STRUMBO   Nay, with this staff, great Strumbo's instrument,
20 I'll crack thy cockscomb, paltry Scythian.

Humber and his soldiers run in

HUMBER   Nor reck I of thy threats, thou princox boy,
Nor do I fear thy foolish insolence:
And but thou better use thy bragging blade
Than thou dost rule thy overflowing tongue,
25 Superbious Briton, thou shalt know too soon
The force of Humber and his Scythians.   *Let them fight*

STRUMBO   O, horrible, terrible!   *[Exeunt]*

Act 2 Scene 6

Sound the alarm. Enter Humber and his soldiers

HUMBER   How bravely this young Briton, Albanact,

2.5   *Location: the battlefield*   **1 coronet** cornet, a company of cavalry or **horse**   **4 grove** small wood   **5 whenas** when   **6 Retire** return, come back
8 policy skill, prudence/cunning, trickery   **9 put back** set aside, renounced   **10 Hun** one of an Asiatic race of warlike nomads   **durst** dare   **16 foemen's**
enemies'   **18 abroach** flowing freely   **20 cockscomb** jester's cap/head, literally a 'cock's crest or comb'; the play on 'staff' and 'instrument' suggests
a bawdy subtext   **21 Nor … Scythians** this speech is addressed to Albanact rather than Strumbo   **reck I of** do I care about   **princox** saucy, insolent
23 but thou unless you can   **25 superbious** proud, overbearing, insolent   **2.6**   *alarm* call to arms

Darteth abroad the thunderbolts of war,

Beating down millions with his furious mood

And in his glory triumphs over all,

5 Moving the massy squadrants of the ground,

Heap hills on hills, to scale the starry sky:

As when Briareus armed with an hundred hands,

Flung forth an hundred mountains at great Jove,

And when the monstrous giant Monichus

10 Hurled mount Olympus at great Mars his targe,

And shot huge cedars at Minerva's shield.

How doth he overlook with haughty front

My fleeting hosts, and lifts his lofty face

Against us all that now do fear his force,

15 Like as we see the wrathful sea from far,

In a great mountain heaped with hideous noise,

With thousand billows beat against the ships,

And toss them in the waves like tennis balls.   *Sound the alarm*

Ay me, I fear my Hubba is surprised.   *Sound again*

Enter Albanact

20 ALBANACT   Follow me, soldiers, follow Albanact!

Pursue the Scythians flying through the field!

Let none of them escape with victory,

That they may know the Britons' force is more

Than all the power of the trembling Huns.

25 THRASIMACHUS Forward, brave soldiers, forward, keep the chase,

He that takes captive Humber or his son

Shall be rewarded with a crown of gold.

Sound alarm, then let them fight, Humber give back, Hubba enter at their backs, and kill

Debon; let Strumbo fall down, Albanact run in, and afterwards enter wounded

ALBANACT   Injurious Fortune, hast thou crossed me thus?

Thus in the morning of my victories,

30 Thus in the prime of my felicity,

To cut me off by such hard overthrow!

Hadst thou no time thy rancour to declare,

But in the spring of all my dignities?

Hadst thou no place to spit thy venom out

35 But on the person of young Albanact?

I that erewhile did scare mine enemies,

And drove them almost to a shameful flight:

I that erewhile full lion-like did fare

Amongst the dangers of the thick-thronged pikes,

---

2 Darteth shoots   **abroad** in many separate places   **3 millions** a great many   **5 massy** solid, weighty   **squadrants** heavy square pieces, presumably refers to artillery   **7 Briareus** a hundred-handed giant in Greek mythology; some stories have him fighting against whilst others have him fighting with Zeus/Jove   **9 Monichus** one of the centaurs   **10 Mars his** i.e. Mars'   **targe** a light shield   **11 Minerva's** belonging to the Roman goddess of warriors and wisdom   **12 front** appearance/face   **18 tennis balls** playing on the sense of Fortune as a game of tennis   **27 crown** a gold coin   *give back* retreat   **36 erewhile** a while before, formerly

40   Must now depart most lamentably slain
     By Humber's treacheries and Fortune's spites.
     Cursed be her charms, damned be her cursèd charms
     That doth delude the wayward hearts of men,
     Of men that trust unto her fickle wheel,
45   Which never leaveth turning upside down.
     O gods, O heavens, allot me but the place
     Where I may find her hateful mansion.
     I'll pass the Alps to wat'ry Meroë,
     Where fiery Phoebus in his chariot,
50   The wheels whereof are decked with emeralds,
     Cast such a heat, yea such a scorching heat,
     And spoileth Flora of her chequered grass.
     I'll overrun the mountain Caucasus,
     Where fell Chimera in her triple shape,
55   Rolleth hot flames from out her monstrous paunch,
     Scaring the beasts with issue of her gorge.
     I'll pass the frozen zone where icy flakes
     Stopping the passage of the fleeting ships
     Do lie, like mountains in the congealed sea,
60   Where, if I find that hateful house of hers,
     I'll pull the fickle wheel from out her hands,
     And tie herself in everlasting bands.
     But all in vain I breathe these threatnings,
     The day is lost, the Huns are conquerors,
65   Debon is slain, my men are done to death,
     The currents swift swim violently with blood,
     And last, O that this last night so long last,
     Myself with wounds past all recovery
     Must leave my crown for Humber to possess.
70   STRUMBO Lord, have mercy upon us! Masters, I think this is a holiday, every man
     lies sleeping in the fields, but God knows full sore against their wills.
     THRASIMACHUS Fly, noble Albanact , and save thyself,
     The Scythians follow with great celerity,
     And there's no way but flight, or speedy death,
75   Fly, noble Albanact, and save thyself.   *Sound the alarm*
     ALBANACT Nay, let them fly that fear to die the death,
     That tremble at the name of fatal Mors,
     Ne'er shall proud Humber boast or brag himself,
     That he hath put young Albanact to flight
80   And lest he should triumph at my decay,

44 fickle wheel in medieval and ancient philosophy, the lives of individuals were determined by the random spinning of Fortune's wheel; a person could be at the top at one moment and at the bottom the next   **48 Meroë** an island in the river Nile   **49 Phoebus** the sun god   **52 spoileth ... grass** i.e. the sun is so hot there that Flora is unable to produce the variety of plants associated with the spring   **53 Caucasus** in Greek mythology, one of the pillars supporting the world   **54 Chimera ... gorge** in Greek mythology, a monstrous fire-breathing creature with a lioness' body, a goat's head in the middle of her back and a tail which culminated in a snake's head   **fell** fierce   **gorge** throat, gullet   **71 full sore** very bitterly, grievously   **73 celerity** swiftness

This sword shall reave his master of his life,
That oft hath saved his master's doubtful life.
But, oh my brethren, if you care for me,
Revenge my death upon his traitorous head.

85   *Et vos queis domus est nigrantis regia ditis,*
Qui regitis rigido stigios moderamine lucos:
Nox cæci regina poli furialis Erinnis,
Diique deæque omnes Albanum tollite regem,
Tollite flumineis undis rigidaque palude
90   *Nunc me fata vocant, hoc condam pectore ferrum.*

Thrust himself through

Enter Trompart

[TROMPART]   O what hath he done? His nose bleeds: but, O, I smell a fox, Look where my master lies, master, master!

STRUMBO   Let me alone, I tell thee, for I am dead.

TROMPART   Yet one word, good, master.

95   STRUMBO   I will not speak, for I am dead I tell thee.

TROMPART   And is my master dead?
             O sticks and stones, brickbats
                 and bones, and is my master dead?
             O you cockatrices, and you bablatrices,
100   that in the woods dwell:
             You briers and brambles, you cookshops and shambles,
                 come howl and yell.
             With howling and screeking, with wailing and weeping,
                 come you to lament.
105   O colliers of Croydon, and rustics of Roydon,
                 and fishers of Kent.
             For Strumbo the cobbler, the fine merry cobbler
                 of Caithness town:
             At this same stour, at this very hour
110   lies dead on the ground.—
             O master, thieves, thieves, thieves!

STRUMBO   Where be they? Cox me tunny, bobekin, let me be rising, begone, we shall be robbed by and by.

Exeunt

---

81 reave rob, bereave   **82 doubtful** i.e. when his life was threatened   **85 Et ... ferrum** 'And you whose home is the palace of black hell / Who rule the Stygian groves with harsh control: / Night, queen of the black heavens, raging Erinnis / And all you gods and goddesses, destroy Albany's king / Destroy him in surging rivers and thick swamps. / Now the fates call me, I will plunge this sword into my breast' (Latin)   **91 smell a fox** am suspicious   **96 And ... ground** Trompart's speech is a comic parody of Albanact's lament, using the same rhetorical figures   **97 brickbats** pieces of brick   **99 cockatrices** serpents identified with the mythical 'basilisk' which could kill with a glance and was hatched from a cock's egg   **bablatrices** a 'nonce-word', used nowhere else, suggested meaning 'female babblers'   **101 shambles** meat stalls or markets   **103 screaking** uttering a shrill cry or grating sound   **105 Croydon** a town south of London which was the centre of the London coal and charcoal industry, hence **colliers**: there was an early seventeenth-century anonymous play of *Grim the Collier of Croyden; or, The Devil and his Dame: with the Devil and Saint Dunston*   **Roydon** name of a small town in Essex and two in Norfolk   **109 stour** armed conflict/occasion, place   **111 O ... thieves** having concluded his lament, Trompart uses this speech to make Strumbo get up   **112 Cox me tunny** an oath, the exact meaning is unclear; 'Cox' was a euphemism for 'God', 'tunny' may refer to the fish   **bobekin** possibly a variant of the common oath 'bodikin' for 'God's dear body'   **begone** get away

Act 2 Scene [7]

Enter Humber, Hubba, Segar, Thrassier, Estrild and the soldiers

HUMBER   Thus from the dreadful shocks of furious Mars,
　　　Thundering alarms, and Rhamnusia's drum
　　　We are retired with joyful victory.
　　　The slaughtered Trojans squelt'ring in their blood,
5　　　Infect the air with their carcasses
　　　And are a prey for every ravenous bird.

ESTRILD   So perish they that are our enemies.
　　　So perish they that love not Humber's weal.
　　　And mighty Jove, commander of the world,
10　　　Protect my love from all false treacheries.

HUMBER   Thanks, lovely Estrild, solace to my soul.
　　　But, valiant Hubba, for thy chivalry
　　　Declared against the men of Albany,
　　　Lo, here a flowering garland wreathed of bay,
15　　　As a reward for this thy forward mind.　　　　　　*Set it on his head*

HUBBA   This unexpected honour, noble sire,
　　　Will prick my courage unto braver deeds,
　　　And cause me to attempt such hard exploits,
　　　That all the world shall sound of Hubba's name.

20　HUMBER   And now, brave soldiers, for this good success,
　　　Carouse whole cups of Amazonian wine,
　　　Sweeter than nectar or ambrosia,
　　　And cast away the clods of cursèd care,
　　　With goblets crowned with Semeleius' gifts,
25　　　Now let us march to Abis' silver streams,
　　　That clearly glide along the champaign fields,
　　　And moist the grassy meads with humid drops.
　　　Sound drums and trumpets, sound up cheerfully,
　　　Sith we return with joy and victory.　　　　　　*Exeunt*

Act 3 Scene 1

Enter Até as before. The dumb show: a crocodile sitting on a river's bank, and a little snake stinging it. Then let both of them fall into the water

ATÉ   　*Scelera in authorem cadunt.*
　　　High on a bank by Nilus' boist'rous streams,
　　　Fearfully sat th'Egyptian crocodile,

2.[7]　**2 Rhamnusia's** Rhamnusia was a surname of Nemesis, Greek goddess of retribution, who had a temple at Rhamnus　**4 squelt'ring** sweltering/ wallowing　**5 air** should be bi-syllabic for metre　**8 weal** well-being, happiness　**13 Declared** made plain　**14 garland … bay** a token of victory　**15 forward** prompt, eager/showing maturity　**21 Carouse** drink off, drain　**Amazonian** perhaps from the near East, the lands traditionally inhabited by these female warriors　**22 nectar or ambrosia** in Greek mythology the drink and food of the gods, respectively　**23 clods** lumps, masses　**24 Semeleius'** Semele was the mother of Dionysus (Greek)/Bacchus (Roman), the god of wine　**25 Abis'** 'Abus' was the earlier name for the river Humber　**26 champaign** flat, open countryside　**29 Sith** since　**3.1**　The third dumb show; Até explains the emblem of the crocodile and the snake in terms of Humber and Locrine; casting Locrine as a snake is suggestive　**1 *Scelera … cadunt*** 'Crimes redound on their author' (Latin)

Dreadfully grinding in his sharp long teeth,
5   The broken bowels of a silly fish.
His back was armed against the dint of spear,
With shields of brass that shined like burnished gold,
And as he stretchèd forth his cruel paws,
A subtle adder creeping closely near,
10   Thrusting his forkèd sting into his claws,
Privily shed his poison through his bones,
Which made him swell that there his bowels burst,
That did so much in his own greatness trust.
So Humber having conquered Albanact,
15   Doth yield his glory unto Locrine's sword.
Mark what ensues, and you may easily see
That all our life is but a tragedy.   [*Exit*]

Act 3 Scene 2

Enter Locrine, Gwendolyn, Corineus, Assaracus, Thrasimachus, Camber

LOCRINE   And is this true, is Albanactus slain?
Hath cursèd Humber with his straggling host,
With that his army made of mongrel curs,
Brought our redoubted brother to his end?
5   O that I had the Thracian Orpheus' harp,
For to awake out of the infernal shade
Those ugly devils of black Erebus
That might torment the damnèd traitor's soul:
O that I had Amphion's instrument,
10   To quicken with his vital notes and tunes
The flinty joints of every stony rock
By which the Scythians might be punishèd:
For, by the lightning of almighty Jove,
The Hun shall die had he ten thousand lives.
15   And would to God he had ten thousand lives,
That I might with the arm-strong Hercules
Crop off so vile an Hydra's hissing heads.
But say me, cousin, for I long to hear
How Albanact came by untimely death?
20   THRASIMACHUS   After the trait'rous host of Scythians
Entered the field with martial equipage,

6 dint stroke, blow   11 Privily secretly, craftily   12 that so that   3.2   4 redoubted feared, respected, distinguished   5 Thracian ... Erebus see note to 1.2.242 which recounts the story of Orpheus' journey to the Underworld to rescue his wife Eurydice; Orpheus was originally from Thrace, historically the region covering a large area of modern Greece, Turkey, Bulgaria and Macedonia   Erebus darkness, a region of the Underworld   9 Amphion's instrument the lyre (harp-like instrument); so great was his skill he charmed the stones to build the city of Thebes   10 quicken bring alive   16 Hercules ... heads one of the twelve labours of the Greek mythical hero was to kill the Lernean hydra, a serpent-like monster with nine heads, who guarded the entrance to the Underworld   18 say me tell me

Young Albanact, impatient of delay,
Led forth his army gainst the straggling mates,
Whose multitude did daunt our soldiers' minds,
25 Yet nothing could dismay the forward prince:
But with a courage most heroical,
Like to a lion 'mongst a flock of lambs,
Made havoc of the faint-heart fugitives,
Hewing a passage through them with his sword.
30 Yea, we had almost given them the repulse,
When suddenly from out the silent wood
Hubba with twenty thousand soldiers,
Cowardly came upon our weakened backs,
And murdered all with fatal massacre:
35 Amongst the which old Debon, martial knight,
With many wounds was brought unto the death:
And Albanact oppressed with multitude,
Whilst valiantly he felled his enemies,
Yielded his life and honour to the dust.
40 He being dead, the soldiers fled amain,
And I alone escapèd them by flight,
To bring you tidings of these accidents.
LOCRINE Not agèd Priam, king of stately Troy,
Grand emperor of barbarous Asia,
45 When he beheld his noble-minded sons
Slain traiterously by all the Myrmidons,
Lamented more than I for Albanact.
GWENDOLYN Not Hecuba the Queen of Ilium,
When she beheld the town of Pergamus,
50 Her palace burnt, with all-devouring flames,
Her fifty sons and daughters fresh of hue,
Murdered by wicked Pyrrhus' bloody sword,
Shed such sad tears as I for Albanact.
CAMBER The grief of Niobë, fair Athens' queen,
55 For her seven sons magnanimous in field,
For her seven daughters fairer than the fairest,
Is not to be compared with my laments.
CORINEUS In vain you sorrow for the slaughtered prince,
In vain you sorrow for his overthrow.
60 He loves not most that doth lament the most,

---

23 **mates** creatures, fellows (depreciative) 25 **forward** eager 30 **repulse** act of driving back, repelling an assault 37 **oppressed with multitude** overcome by a host 40 **amain** straightaway/with full speed 42 **accidents** events, misfortunes 43 **Priam … Myrmidons** a reference to the Trojan war in which many of King Priam's fifty sons were killed by the Greeks; the **Myrmidons** were a Greek tribe, loyal to Achilles, the term later became synonymous with 'hired ruffians' 48 **Hecuba … Ilium** Hecuba was wife to Priam and queen of Troy (**Ilium**) 49 **Pergamus** citadel of Troy 52 **Pyrrhus' bloody sword** Pyrrhus was the alternative name for Neoptolemus, son of Achilles who avenged his father's death, hiding in the Trojan horse and killing Priam 54 **Niobë** in Greek mythology, the wife of Amphion, King of Thebes (not Athens), who boasted of her seven sons and daughters; the jealous gods punished her by killing them and, in her grief, Niobe fled to Mount Sipylus and was turned to stone, still weeping unceasingly

But he that seeks to venge the injury.

Think you to quell the enemy's warlike train

With childish sobs and womanish laments?

Unsheath your swords! Unsheath your conquering sword

65   And seek revenge, the comfort for this sore!

In Cornwall, where I hold my regiment,

Even just ten thousand valiant men at arms

// Hath Corineus ready at command. //

All these and more, if need shall more require,

70   Hath Corineus ready at command.

CAMBER   And in the fields of martial Cambria,

Close by the boisterous Iscan's silver streams,

Where lightfoot fairies skip from bank to bank,

Full twenty thousand brave courageous knights

75   Well exercised in feats of chivalry,

In manly manner most invincible,

Young Camber hath with gold and victual.

All these and more, if need shall more require,

I offer up to venge my brother's death.

80   LOCRINE   Thanks, loving uncle, and good brother too,

For this revenge, for this sweet word revenge

Must ease and cease my wrongful injuries:

And by the sword of bloody Mars I swear,

Ne'er shall sweet quiet enter this my front,

85   Till I be vengèd on his traitorous head

That slew my noble brother, Albanact.

Sound drums and trumpets, muster up the camp,

For we will straight march to Albania.   *Exeunt*

Act 3 Scene 3

Enter Humber, Estrild, Hubba, [Segar,] Trussier and the soldiers

HUMBER   Thus are we come, victorious conquerors,

Unto the flowing current's silver streams

Which, in memorial of our victory,

Shall be agnominated by our name,

5   And talked of by our posterity:

For sure I hope before the golden sun

Posteth his horses to fair Thetis' plains,

To see the waters turnèd into blood,

---

66 regiment rule   **67 Even just** exactly   **68 Hath … command** appears to be a first draft of line 70   **71 Cambria** Wales   **72 Iscan's** Isca was the Roman name for the river Usk in south Wales   **77 victual** supplies of food   **84 front** face/bearing, demeanour   **88 Albania** Scotland   **3.3** *Location: by the river Humber*   **1 Thus … name** they have arrived at the river Humber which is to be renamed (**agnominated**) in Humber's honour   **5 posterity** descendants   **7 Thetis' plains** the sea, Thetis was a goddess of the sea; Humber means before the sun sets and appears to go down into the sea

And change his bluish hue to rueful red,

10   By reason of the fatal massacre,

Which shall be made upon the virent plains.

Enter the Ghost of Albanact [unseen]

[GHOST]   See how the traitor doth presage his harm,

See how he glories at his own decay:

See how he triumphs at his proper loss.

15   O, fortune vile, unstable, fickle, frail!

HUMBER   Methinks I see both armies in the field,

The broken lances climb the crystal skies,

Some headless lie, some breathless on the ground,

And every place is strewed with carcasses.

20   Behold the grass hath lost his pleasant green,

The sweetest sight that ever might be seen.

GHOST   Ay, traitorous Humber, thou shalt find it so,

Yea, to thy cost thou shalt the same behold

With anguish, sorrow, and with sad laments.

25   The grassy plains, that now do please thine eyes,

Shall ere the night be coloured all with blood,

The shady groves which now enclose thy camp,

And yield sweet savours to thy damnèd corpse,

Shall ere the night be figured all with blood:

30   The profound stream that passeth by thy tents,

And with his moisture serveth all thy camp,

Shall ere the night converted be to blood.

Yea, with the blood of those thy straggling boys:

For now revenge shall ease my lingering grief,

35   And now revenge shall glut my longing soul.

HUBBA   Let come what will, I mean to bear it out,

And either live with glorious victory,

Or die with fame renowned for chivalry.

He is not worthy of the honeycomb

40   That shuns the hives because the bees have stings:

That likes me best that is not got with ease,

Which thousand dangers do accompany:

For nothing can dismay our regal mind

Which aims at nothing but a golden crown,

45   The only upshot of mine enterprises.

Were they enchanted in grim Pluto's court,

And kept for treasure 'mongst his hellish crew,

I would either quell the triple Cerberus

---

11 virent verdant   **12 presage** foretell   **14 proper** personal/fitting   **28 corpse** body (not necessarily a dead one)   **29 figured** patterned   **30 profound** deep   **34 For … soul** expressing the classical belief that the ghosts of the dead cannot rest until they're avenged   **41 That … best** impersonal construction for 'I am best pleased by/I prefer'   **44 golden … enterprises** compare Tamburlaine in Marlowe's play: '… the ripest fruit of all, / That perfect bliss and sole felicity, / The sweet fruition of an earthly crown' (2.7.27–9)   **upshot** final shot in an archery competition/mark or end aimed for   **48 triple Cerberus** three-headed dog guarding the gates of Hades

And all the army of his hateful hags,
50   Or roll the stone with wretched Sisyphus.

HUMBER   Right martial be thy thoughts, my noble son,
And all thy words savour of chivalry.
But, warlike Segar, what strange accidents
Makes you to leave the warding of the camp?

55 SEGAR   To arms, my lord, to honourable arms!
Take helm and targe in hand, the Britons come
With greater multitude than erst the Greeks
Brought to the ports of Phrygian Tenedos.

HUMBER   But what saith Segar to these accidents?
60   What counsel gives he in extremities?

SEGAR   Why this, my lord, experience teacheth us,
That resolution is a sole help at need.
And this, my lord, our honour teacheth us,
That we be bold in every enterprise:
65   Then since there is no way but fight or die,
Be resolute, my lord, for victory.

HUMBER   And resolute, Segar, I mean to be,
Perhaps some blissful star will favour us,
And comfort bring to our perplexèd state.
70   Come, let us in and fortify our camp,
So to withstand their strong invasion.   *Exeunt*

Act 3 Scene 4

Enter Strumbo, Trompart, Oliver and his son William following them

STRUMBO   Nay, neighbour Oliver, if you be so hot, come prepare yourself, you shall
find two as stout fellows of us, as any in all the north.

OLIVER   No by my dorth, neighbour Strumbo, ich zee dat you are a man of small
zideration, dat will zeek to injure your old vreends, one of your vamiliar guests, and
5 derefore zeeing your pinion is to deal withouten reason, ich and my zon William
will take dat course, dat shall be fardest vrom reason: how zay you, will you have
my daughter or no?

STRUMBO   A very hard question, neighbour, but I will solve it as I may. What reason
have you to demand it of me?

10 WILLIAM   Marry, sir, what reason had you when my sister was in the barn to tumble
her upon the hay and to fish her belly?

50 **Sisyphus** in classical mythology, he was condemned to an eternity of rolling a stone uphill only for it to continually roll back down again   54 **warding** guarding 56 **helm and targe** helmet and shield 57 **erst** once upon a time 58 **Tenedos** the island in the Aegean near Troy where the Greeks hid their fleet to convince the Trojans that they had admitted defeat and departed, leaving the wooden horse behind 59 **accidents** events **3.4** **1 neighbour** polite form of address, with rustic overtones **hot** angry, excited **prepare yourself** i.e. to fight **3 No … dorth** by my troth; Oliver's speech is characterized as a rustic English west country accent used for comic effect and represented phonetically with 'd' for 't', 'z' for 's', 'v' for 'f', and so on; for example, 'ich zee dat' I see that **10 Marry** by the Virgin Mary **tumble** throw/have sex with **11 fish her belly** penetrate her sexually

STRUMBO   Mass thou say'st true: well, but would you have me marry her therefore? No, I scorn her, and you, and you. Ay, I scorn you all.

OLIVER   You will not have her then?

15   STRUMBO   No, as I am a true gentleman.

WILLIAM   Then will we school you, ere you and we part hence.

Enter Margery and snatch the staff out of her brother's hand as he is fighting

STRUMBO   Ay, you come in pudding time, or else I had dressed them.

MARGERY   You master saucebox, lobcock, coxcomb, you slopsauce, lick-fingers, will you not hear?

20   STRUMBO   Who speak you to? Me?

MARGERY   Ay, sir, to you, John Lackhonesty, little wit, is it you that will have none of me?

STRUMBO   No, by my troth, Mistress Nicebice, how fine you can nickname me: I think you were brought up in the university of Bridewell, you have your rhetoric

25   so ready at your tongue's end, as if you were never well warned when you were young.

MARGERY   Why then, Goodman Codshead, if you will have none of me, farewell.

STRUMBO   If you be so plain, Mistress Driggle-draggle, fare you well.

MARGERY   Nay, Master Strumbo, ere you go from hence we must have more words!

30   You will have none of me?   *They both fight*

STRUMBO   O, my head, my head, leave, leave, leave, I will, I will, I will.

MARGERY   Upon that condition, I let thee alone.

OLIVER   How now, Master Strumbo, hath my daughter taught you a new lesson?

STRUMBO   Ay, but hear you, Goodman Oliver? It will not be for my ease to have my

35   head broken every day, therefore remedy this, and we shall agree.

OLIVER   Well, zon, well, for you are my zon now, all shall be remedied. Daughter be friends with him.   *Shake hands*

STRUMBO   You are a sweet nut, the devil crack you. Masters, I think it be my luck, my first wife was a loving quiet wench, but this I think would weary the devil. I

40   would she might be burnt as my other wife was: if not, I must run to the halter for help. O codpiece, thou hast done thy master: this it is to be meddling with warm plackets.   *Exeunt*

Act 3 Scene 5

Enter Locrine, Camber, Corineus, Thrasimachus, Assaracus

LOCRINE   Now am I guarded with an host of men,
          Whose haughty courage is invincible:

12 Mass by the Mass (sacrament of the Eucharist)   **15 true gentleman** ironic   **16 hence** from here   **17 pudding time** at an opportune moment, i.e. when puddings were to be had   **dressed** treated them properly, i.e. thrashed (ironic)   **18 saucebox** one who habitually makes saucy, insolent remarks   **lobcock** country bumpkin   **23 Nicebice** probably a corruption of 'nicebecetur', a fine, dainty or fashionable woman   **24 Bridewell** house of correction for disorderly women or whores   **25 warned** restrained/forbidden (to speak out)   **27 Goodman Codshead** Goodman, a respectful form of address used ironically here with **Codshead** meaning 'stupid-head, blockhead'   **28 Mistress Driggle-draggle** Strumbo replies in kind since Mistress is a respectful term but 'driggle-draggle' means 'slut' or 'drab'   **38 nut** alluding to the vulva which is opened to get at the sexual kernel   **devil crack** crack signified loss of virginity or sexual reputation; 'hell' the 'devil's crack' was slang for 'vagina'   **40 halter** gallows (for hanging)   **41 codpiece** penis/bag worn over the front of the male genitals   **done** done for, ruined, playing on sexual sense   **42 plackets** petticoats/vaginas

Now am I hemmed with troops of soldiers,

Such as might force Bellona to retire,

5   And make her tremble at their puissance:

Now sit I like the mighty god of war,

When, armèd with his coat of adamant,

Mounted his chariot drawn with mighty bulls,

He drove the Argives over Xanthus' streams.

10   Now, cursèd Humber, doth thy end draw nigh,

Down goes the glory of his victories,

And all his fame, and all his high renown,

Shall in a moment yield to Locrine's sword:

Thy bragging banners crossed with argent streams,

15   The ornaments of thy pavilions,

Shall all be captivated with this hand,

And thou thyself at Albanactus' tomb

Shalt offered be, in satisfaction

Of all the wrongs thou didst him when he lived.

20   But canst thou tell me, brave Thrasimachus,

How far we are distant from Humber's camp?

THRASIMACHUS   My lord, within yon foul accursèd grove

That bears the tokens of our overthrow,

This Humber hath entrenched his damnèd camp.

25   March on, my lord, because I long to see

The treacherous Scythians squelt'ring in their gore.

LOCRINE   Sweet Fortune, favour Locrine with a smile,

That I may venge my noble brother's death,

And in the midst of stately Troynovant

30   I'll build a temple to thy deity

Of perfect marble and of jacinth stones,

That it shall pass the high pyramidës,

Which with their top surmount the firmament.

CAMBER   The arm-strong offspring of the doubted knight,

35   Stout Hercules, Alcmena's mighty son,

That tamed the monsters of the threefold world,

And rid the oppressèd from the tyrants' yokes,

Did never show such valiantness in fight,

As I will now for noble Albanact.

40   CORINEUS   Full fourscore years hath Corineus lived,

3.5   **4 Bellona** Roman war goddess   **5 puissance** power   **6 god of war** Mars (Roman), Ares (Greek)   **7 adamant** poetical name for the embodiment of surpassing hardness, originally a rock   **8 Mounted … streams** reference to the Trojan war when Ares drove the Greeks over the river at Troy   **9 Argives** Greeks   **Xanthus** the great river of Troy   **14 argent streams** silver lines or streaks   **22 yon** that over there   **24 entrenched** fortified, dug in   **26 squelt'ring** wallowing   **gore** filth, slime, dung   **29 Troynovant** new Troy, i.e. London   **31 jacinth** originally a blue gem   **32 pyramidës** should be pronounced with four syllables for metre   **33 firmament** the vault of heaven overhead; in old astronomy: the sphere containing the fixed stars; the eighth heaven of the Ptolemaic system   **34 doubted** feared, dreaded, redouted   **35 Hercules … son** Hercules' father was Zeus who seduced his mother Alcmena by impersonating her husband   **36 threefold world** earth, sea and sky; in his twelve labours Hercules rid the world of oppressive monsters who terrorised the people   **40 fourscore** eighty

Sometime in war, sometime in quiet peace,
And yet I feel myself to be as strong
As erst I was in summer of mine age,
Able to toss this great unwieldy club,
45 Which hath been painted with my foemen's brains;
And with this club I'll break the strong array
Of Humber and his straggling soldiers
Or lose my life amongst the thickest press
And die with honour in my latest days.
50 Yet ere I die they all shall understand,
What force lies in stout Corineus' hand.

THRASIMACHUS And if Thrasimachus detract the fight,
Either for weakness or for cowardice,
Let him not boast that Brutus was his eme,
55 Or that brave Corineus was his sire.

LOCRINE Then courage, soldiers, first for your safety,
Next for your peace, last for your victory. *Exeunt/Sound the Alarm*

Enter Hubba and Segar at one door, and Corineus at the other

CORINEUS Art thou that Humber, prince of fugitives,
That by thy treason slew'st young Albanact?
60 HUBBA I am his son that slew young Albanact,
And if thou take not heed proud Phrygian,
I'll send thy soul unto the Stygian lake,
There to complain of Humber's injuries.

CORINEUS You triumph, sir, before the victory,
65 For Corineus is not so soon slain.
But, cursèd Scythians, you shall rue the day,
That e'er you came into Albania.
So perish they that envy Britain's wealth,
So let them die with endless infamy,
70 And he that seeks his sovereign's overthrow,
Would this my club might aggravate his woe.
Strikes them both down with his club

Enter Humber

HUMBER Where may I find some desert wilderness,
Where I may breathe out curses as I would,
And scare the earth with my condemning voice,
75 Where every echo's repercussion
May help me to bewail mine overthrow,
And aid me in my sorrowful laments?
Where may I find some hollow uncouth rock,
Where I may damn, condemn, and ban my fill

---

43 **erst** once   48 **press** crush in battle   49 **latest** last, final   52 **detract** withdraw from   54 **eme** uncle   62 **Stygian lake** from the river Styx in the infernal regions of classical mythology   63 **injuries** wrongs, sufferings   69 **infamy** shame, disgrace   78 **uncouth** unknown, foreign   79 **ban** curse

80   The heavens, the hell, the earth, the air, the fire,
      And utter curses to the concave sky,
      Which may infect the airy regions
      And light upon the Briton Locrine's head?
      You ugly sprites that in Cocytus mourn
85   And gnash your teeth with dolorous laments,
      You fearful dogs that in black Lethe howl,
      And scare the ghosts with your wide open throats,
      You ugly ghosts that flying from these dogs,
      Do plunge yourselves in Puryflegiton,
90   Come all of you, and with your shrieking notes
      Accompany the Briton's conquering host.
      Come fierce Erynnis, horrible with snakes,
      Come ugly Furies, armèd with your whips,
      You threefold judges of black Tartarus,
95   And all the army of you hellish fiends,
      With new found torments rack proud Locrine's bones.
      O gods and stars, damned be the gods and stars,
      That did not drown me in fair Thetis' plains.
      Cursed be the sea that with outrageous waves,
100   With surging billows did not rive my ships
      Against the rocks of high Ceraunia,
      Or swallowed me into her wat'ry gulf.
      Would God we had arrived upon the shore
      Where Polyphemus and the Cyclops dwell,
105   Or where the bloody Anthropophagi
      With greedy jaws devours the wandering wights,

      Enter the Ghost of Albanact

      But why comes Albanact's bloody ghost,
      To bring a corsive to our miseries?
      Is't not enough to suffer shameful flight,
110   But we must be tormented now with ghosts,
      With apparitions fearful to behold?

GHOST   Revenge, revenge for blood.

HUMBER   So nought will satisfy your wand'ring ghost
         But dire revenge, nothing but Humber's fall,
115   Because he conquered you in Albany.
         Now, by my soul, Humber would be condemned

---

84 **Cocytus** one of five rivers in the Underworld, Cocytus was the river of wailing   86 **Lethe** another river in the Underworld whose waters caused forgetfulness   89 **Puryflegiton** Phlegethon, a river of the Underworld that continually burns   92 **Erinnys** goddess of vengeance, one of the **Furies** who were imaged as ugly, winged women armed with **whips**; their hair, arms and waists were entwined with **snakes**   94 **threefold … Tartarus** Tartarus was the gloomy region below the Underworld where sinners were sent to be punished; the three **judges** of the dead were Rhadamanth, Aeacus and Minos   98 **Thetis'** belonging to the goddess of the sea   100 **rive** tear apart   101 **Ceraunia** a range of mountains in the eastern Caucasus/island containing the cave of Medea   104 **Polyphemus** was one of the **Cyclops**, a cannibal race of one-eyed giants; he was blinded by Odysseus   105 **Anthropophagi** cannibals (Greek for 'man-eaters')   106 **wights** living creatures/human beings   108 **corsive** corrosive/grief, annoyance

To Tantal's hunger, or Ixion's wheel,

Or to the vulture of Prometheus,

Rather than that this murder were undone.

120 Whenas I die I'll drag thy cursèd ghost

Through all the rivers of foul Erebus,

Through burning sulphur of the limbo-lake,

To allay the burning fury of that heat,

That rageth in mine everlasting soul.

125 GHOST   *Vindicta, vindicta!*   *Exeunt*

Act 4 Scene 1

Enter Até as before, then let there follow Omphale daughter to the King of Lydia, having a club in her hand, and a lion's skin on her back, Hercules following with a distaff. Then let Omphale turn about, and taking off her pantofle, strike Hercules on the head; then let them depart, Até remaining, saying:

ATÉ   *Quem non Argolici mandata severa Tyranni,*

        Non potuit Juno vincere, vicit amor.

        Stout Hercules the mirror of the world,

        Son to Alcmena and great Jupiter,

5   After so many conquests won in field,

        After so many monsters quelled by force,

        Yielded his valiant heart to Omphale,

        A fearful woman void of manly strength;

        She took the club, and wore the lion's skin,

10   He took the wheel, and maidenly 'gan spin.

        So martial Locrine cheered with victory,

        Falleth in love with Humber's concubine

        And so forgetteth peerless Gwendolyn.

        His uncle Corineus storms at this,

15   And forceth Locrine for his grace to sue.

        Lo here the sum: the process doth ensue.   *Exit*

Act 4 Scene 2

Enter Locrine, Camber, Corineus, Assaracus, Thrasimachus and the soldiers

LOCRINE   Thus from the fury of Bellona's broils,

        With sound of drum and trumpets' melody,

        The Briton king returns triumphantly,

117 **Tantal's … Prometheus** characters from Greek mythology doomed to eternal punishment for their crimes on earth; **Tantalus** (see note to 1.2.250) to stand in a lake which drains as he tries to drink with fruit dangling before his eyes which was whisked away when he reached out for it; **Ixion** was crucified on a revolving fiery wheel; **Prometheus** was bound to a pillar and had his liver eaten by an eagle by day which was renewed by night   **120 Whenas** when   **121 Erebus** gloomy region of the Underworld   **122 limbo-lake** the pit of hell   **125 *Vindicta*** 'revenge' (Latin)   **4.1** The fourth dumb show represents the story of the Greek mythical hero, Hercules, overcome by his love for Omphale   *pantofle* slipper, loose shoe   **1 *Quem … amor*** 'He whom the harsh commands of the Argolic tyrant could not conquer, nor Juno herself, love conquers' (Latin)   **10 wheel** spinning wheel   **12 concubine** mistress   **4.2**   **1 Bellona's broils** war, quarrels of the Roman goddess of war

The Scythians slain with great occision
5   Do equalize the grass in multitude,
And with their blood have stained the streaming brooks,
Offering their bodies and their dearest blood
As sacrifice to Albanactus' ghost.
Now cursèd Humber hast thou paid thy due
10   For thy deceits and crafty treacheries,
For all thy guises, and damned stratagems,
With loss of life, and ever-during shame.
Where are thy horses trapped with burnished gold,
Thy trampling coursers ruled with foaming bits?
15   Where are thy soldiers strong and numberless,
Thy valiant captains, and thy noble peers?
Even as the country clowns with sharpest scythes,
Do mow the withered grass from off the earth,
Or as the ploughman with his piercing share
20   Renteth the bowels of the fertile fields
And rippeth up the roots with razors keen.
So Locrine with his mighty curtal-axe,
Hath cropped off the heads of all thy Huns,
So Locrine's peers have daunted all thy peers,
25   And drove thine host unto confusion,
That thou may'st suffer penance for thy fault,
And die for murd'ring valiant Albanact.
CORINEUS   And thus, yea thus, shall all the rest be served,
That seek to enter Albion gainst our wills.
30   If the brave nation of the Troglodytes,
If all the coal-black Ethiopians,
If all the forces of the Amazons,
If all the hosts of the barbarian lands,
Should dare to enter this our little world,
35   Soon should they rue their overbold attempts,
That after us our progeny may say,
'There lie the beasts that sought to usurp our land.'
LOCRINE   Ay, they are beasts that seek to usurp our land,
And like to brutish beasts they shall be served.
40   For mighty Jove, the supreme king of heaven,
That guides the concourse of the meteors,
And rules the motion of the azure sky,
Fights always for the Britons' safety.

---

4 occision carnage, slaughter   **5 equalize … multitude** the number of dead Scythians equals the number of blades of grass   **9 due** debt   **11 guises** pretences, disguises   **12 ever-during** everlasting   **13 trapped** protected or adorned with trappings, ornamented cloths spread over the harness or saddle **14 trampling coursers** stamping war-horses   **ruled … bits** horses are controlled by metal bits which go between the mouth and is hence flecked with foaming saliva   **19 share** ploughshare, the iron blade of a plough   **20 Renteth** rends, tears   **21 razors keen** sharp blades   **22 curtal-axe** short, broad cutting sword   **24 daunted** vanquished, overcome   **25 host** forces, army   **30 Troglodytes** cave-dwellers   **36 progeny** offspring, descendants

But stay, methinks I hear some shrieking noise,

45 That draweth near to our pavilion.

Enter the Soldiers leading in Estrild

ESTRILD What prince soe'er adorned with golden [crown],

Doth sway the regal sceptre in his hand

And thinks no chance can ever throw him down

Or that his state shall everlasting stand,

50 Let him behold poor Estrild in this plight,

The perfect platform of a troubled wight.

Once was I guarded with Mavortial bands,

Compassed with princes of the noble blood,

Now am I fallen into my foemen's hands

55 And with my death must pacify their mood.

O life, the harbour of calamities!

O death, the haven of all miseries!

I could compare my sorrows to thy woe,

Thou wretched queen of wretched Pergamus,

60 But that thou viewd'st thy enemies' overthrow,

Nigh to the rock of high Caphareus,

Thou saw'st their death, and then departed'st thence.

I must abide the victor's insolence.

The gods that pitied thy continual grief,

65 Transformed thy corpse, and with thy corpse thy care,

Poor Estrild lives despairing of relief,

For friends in trouble are but few and rare.

What said I few? Ay, few or none at all,

For cruel death made havoc of them all.

70 Thrice happy they whose fortune was so good

To end their lives, and with their lives their woes,

Thrice hapless I, whom fortune so withstood,

That cruelly she gave me to my foes.

O soldiers, is there any misery,

75 To be compared to fortune's treachery?

LOCRINE Camber, this same should be the Scythian queen.

CAMBER So may we judge by her lamenting words.

LOCRINE So fair a dame mine eyes did never see,   *Aside*

With floods of woes she seems o'erwhelmed to be.

80 CAMBER O Locrine, hath she not a cause for to be sad?   *Locrine at one side*

[LOCRINE] If she have cause to weep for Humber's death,   *of the stage*   *Aside*

And shed salt tears for her overthrow:

Locrine may well bewail his proper grief,

Locrine may move his own peculiar woe;

46 **What prince soe'er** whatever prince   51 **platform** pattern, model   **wight** creature   52 **Mavortial** warlike, martial   53 **Compassed** encircled
59 **Thou … Pergamus** i.e. Hecuba, queen of Troy; in revenge for the death of her son, Polydorus, she blinded Polymestor and killed his children; the gods
then turned her into a dog (**Transformed thy corpse,** i.e. 'body' line **66**) allowing her to escape   60 **But** except   61 **Caphareus** cape at the south-eastern
corner of Euboea island   83 **proper** personal   84 **peculiar** particular

85   He being conquered died a speedy death

    And felt not long his lamentable smart;

    I, being conqueror, live a ling'ring life

    And feel the force of Cupid's sudden stroke.

    I gave him cause to die a speedy death;

90   He left me cause to wish a speedy death.

    Oh, that sweet face painted with nature's dye,

    Those roseal cheeks mixed with a snowy white,

    That decent neck surpassing ivory,

    Those comely breasts, which Venus well might spite,

95   Are like to snares which wily fowlers wrought,

    Wherein my yielding heart is prisoner caught.

    The golden tresses of her dainty hair,

    Which shine like rubies glittering with the sun,

    Have so entrapped poor Locrine's lovesick heart,

100   That from the same no way it can be won.

    How true is that which oft I heard declared,

    One dram of joy must have a pound of care.

ESTRILD   Hard is their fall, who from a golden crown

    Are cast into a sea of wretchedness.

105 LOCRINE   Hard is their thrall, who by Cupid's frown   *Aside*

    Are wrapped in waves of endless carefulness.

ESTRILD   O kingdom, object to all miseries.

LOCRINE   O love, the extrem'st of all extremities.   *Aside*

                      Let him [*Locrine*] *go into his chair*

[FIRST] SOLDIER   My lord, in ransacking the Scythian tents,

110   I found this lady, and to manifest

    That earnest zeal I bear unto your grace,

    I here present her to your majesty.

[SECOND] SOLDIER   He lies, my lord, I found the lady first,

    And here present her to your majesty.

115 FIRST SOLDIER   Presumptuous villain, wilt thou take my prize?

SECOND SOLDIER   Nay rather thou depriv'st me of my right.

FIRST SOLDIER   Resign thy title, caitiff, unto me,

    Or with my sword I'll pierce thy coward's loins.

SECOND SOLDIER   Soft words, good sir, 'tis not enough to speak:

120   A barking dog doth seldom strangers bite.

LOCRINE   Unreverent villains, strive you in our sight?

    Take them hence jailor to the dungeon:

    There let them lie and try their quarrel out.

---

85 **He** i.e. Humber   88 **Cupid's sudden stroke** the arrows of Cupid the Roman boy-god of love caused those struck to fall in love with the first creature they saw   92 **roseal** rose-coloured   93 **decent** handsome   94 **Venus** goddess of love, mother of Cupid   95 **snares** devices for capturing birds or small animals   **wrought** made   100 **won** regained, redeemed   102 **One ... care** proverbial   **dram** one-sixteenth of an ounce in weight   105 **thrall** bondage, servitude   106 **carefulness** anxiety, concern   117 **title** legal claim   **caitiff** wretch   123 **try ... out** sort out the rights of their argument

But thou, fair princess, be no whit dismayed,

125   But rather joy that Locrine favours thee.

ESTRILD   How can he favour me that slew my spouse?

LOCRINE   The chance of war, my love, took him from thee.

ESTRILD   But Locrine was the causer of his death.

LOCRINE   He was an enemy to Locrine's state,

130   And slew my noble brother Albanact.

ESTRILD   But he was linked to me in marriage bond,

And would you have me love his slaughterer?

LOCRINE   Better to love, than not to live at all.

ESTRILD   Better to die renowned for chastity

135   Than live with shame and endless infamy.

What would the common sort report of me,

If I forget my love, and cleave to thee?

LOCRINE   Kings need not fear the vulgar sentences.

ESTRILD   But ladies must regard their honest name.

140   LOCRINE   Is it a shame to live in marriage bonds?

ESTRILD   No, but to be a strumpet to a king.

LOCRINE   If thou wilt yield to Locrine's burning love,

Thou shalt be queen of fair Albania.

ESTRILD   But Gwendolyn will undermine my state.

145   LOCRINE   Upon mine honour, thou shalt have no harm.

ESTRILD   Then, lo, brave Locrine, Estrild yields to thee,

And by the gods, whom thou dost invocate,

By the dread ghost of thy deceasèd sire,

By thy right hand, and by thy burning love,

150   Take pity on poor Estrild's wretched thrall.

CORINEUS   Hath Locrine then forgot his Gwendolyn,

That thus he courts the Scythian's paramour?

What, are the words of Brute so soon forgot?

Are my deserts so quickly out of mind?

155   Have I been faithful to thy sire now dead,

Have I protected thee from Humber's hands,

And dost thou quite me with ingratitude?

Is this the guerdon for my grievous wounds?

Is this the honour for my labours past?

160   Now by my sword, Locrine, I swear to thee,

This injury of thine shall be repaid.

LOCRINE   Uncle, scorn you your royal sovereign,

As if we stood for ciphers in the court?

Upbraid you me with those your benefits?

165   Why, it was a subject's duty so to do.

---

124 whit particle, jot   **136 common sort** ordinary people   **137 cleave** cling, attach oneself   **138 vulgar sentences** judgements of the crowd, i.e. public opinion   **141 strumpet** whore   **152 paramour** mistress   **157 quite** repay   **158 guerdon** reward, recompense   **163 ciphers** nonentities, mere-nothings   **164 Upbraid** reproach, censure

What you have done for our deceasèd sire,

We know, and all know you have your reward.

CORINEUS   Avaunt, proud princox! Brav'st thou me withal?

Assure thyself, though thou be emperor,

170   Thou ne'er shalt carry this unpunishèd.

CAMBER   Pardon my brother, noble Corineus,

Pardon this once, and it shall be amended.

ASSARACUS   Cousin, remember Brutus' latest words,

How he desirèd you to cherish them:

175   Let not this fault so much incense your mind,

Which is not yet past all remedy.

CORINEUS   Then, Locrine, lo I reconcile myself

But as thou lov'st thy life, so love thy wife:

But if thou violate those promises,

180   Blood and revenge shall light upon thy head.

Come, let us back to stately Troynovant,

Where all these matters shall be settlèd.

[LOCRINE]   Millions of devils wait upon thy soul!   *To himself*

Legions of spirits vex thy impious ghost:

185   Ten thousand torments rack thy cursèd bones.

Let everything that hath the use of breath,

Be instruments and workers of thy death.   *Exeunt*

Act 4 Scene 3

Enter Humber alone, his hair hanging over his shoulders, his arms all bloody, and a dart in one hand

HUMBER   What basilisk hath hatchèd in this place,

Where everything consumèd is to nought?

What fearful Fury haunts these cursèd groves,

Where not a root is left for Humber's meat?

5   Hath fell Alecto with envenomed blasts,

Breathed forth poison in these tender plains?

Hath triple Cerberus with contagious foam,

Sowed aconitum 'mongst these withered herbs?

Hath dreadful Famës with her charming rods

10   Brought barrenness on every fruitful tree?

What not a root, no fruit, no beast, no bird,

To nourish Humber in this wilderness?

What would you more, you fiends of Erebus?

---

168 Avaunt begone, away   **proud princox** arrogant, insolent boy   **Brav'st** defy/threaten   **172 amended** repaired   **184 impious ghost** wicked spirit, lacking in dutifulness; Locrine is cursing Corineus who as a subject he believes owes him obedience   **4.3** *Humber* Humber's appearance represents emblematically the image of 'Despair'   *dart* light spear   **1 basilisk** fabulous reptile whose glance could kill, alleged to be **hatched** by a serpent from a cock's egg   **4 meat** food   **5 Alecto** one of the Furies, goddesses of vengeance and the anger of the dead   **7 triple Cerberus** three-headed dog who guarded the gates of the Underworld   **contagious foam** poisonous saliva   **8 aconitum** yellow-flowered spring plant (aconite) with poisonous roots   **9 Famës** personification of hunger (famine), pronounced with two syllables   **charming rods** magic wands for casting spells

My very entrails burn for want of drink,

15   My bowels cry, 'Humber, give us some meat!'

But wretched Humber can give you no meat,

These foul accursèd groves afford no meat:

This fruitless soil, this ground brings forth no meat.

The gods, hard-hearted gods, yield me no meat.

20   Then how can Humber give you any meat?

Enter Strumbo with a pitchfork, and a Scotch cap

[STRUMBO]   How do you, masters, how do you? How have you scaped hanging this
long time? I'faith I have scaped many a scouring this year, but I thank God I have
passed them all with a good coraggio, coraggio, and my wife and I are in great love
and charity now, I thank my manhood and my strength. For I will tell you, masters,

25   upon a certain day at night I came home, to say the very truth, with my stomach
full of wine, and ran up into the chamber, where my wife soberly sat rocking my
little baby, leaning her back against the bed, singing lullaby. Now when she saw me
come with my nose foremost, thinking that I been drunk, as I was indeed, snatched
up a faggot-stick in her hand, and came furiously marching towards me with a big

30   face, as though she would have eaten me at a bit: thundering out these words unto
me, 'Thou, drunken knave, where hast thou been so long? I shall teach thee how to
benight me another time!' and so she began to play knaves trumps. Now although I
trembled fearing she would set her ten commandments in my face, ran within her,
and taking her lustily by the middle, I carried her valiantly to the bed, and flinging

35   her upon it, flung myself upon her, and there I delighted her so with the sport I
made, that ever after she would call me 'sweet husband', and so banished brawling
forever: and to see the good will of the wench; she bought with her portion a yard
of land, and by that I am now become one of the richest men in our parish. Well,
masters, what's a clock? It is now breakfast time, you shall see what meat I have

40   here for my breakfast.   *Let him sit down and pull out his victuals*

HUMBER   Was ever land so fruitless as this land?

Was ever grove so graceless as this grove?

Was ever soil so barren as this soil?

O, no: the land where hungry Famës dwelt,

45   May no wise equalize this cursèd land:

No, even the climate of the torrid zone

Brings forth more fruit than this accursèd grove.

Ne'er came sweet Ceres, ne'er came Venus here:

Triptolemus, the god of husbandmen,

50   Ne'er sowed his seed in this foul wilderness.

The hunger-bitten dogs of Acheron,

---

14 entrails guts   **15 My … any meat** example of the rhetorical figure of 'antistrophe' or 'counterturn' where the same word is used at the end of
several lines in succession   **17 afford** yield, supply   *Scotch cap* man's head-dress made of woollen cloth, without a brim, and decorated with two
tails or streamers   **21 masters** Strumbo again addresses the audience directly   **22 scouring** beating   **23 coraggio** courage (Italian)
30 at a bit at one bite   **32 benight** blind/disappoint, darken one's life   **knaves trumps** beat Strumbo (the knave) with her faggot-stick (the trump
card)   **33 ten commandments** ten fingernails (proverbial)   **37 portion** marriage portion, dowry   **yard of land** moderate sized piece of enclosed land
for cultivation   **46 torrid zone** region of the earth between the tropics   **48 Ceres** Roman goddess of agriculture   **49 Triptolemus** Greek demi-god of
agriculture and milling of corn   **51 Acheron** river of pain in the Underworld

Chased from the nine-fold Puryflegiton,

Have set their footsteps in this damnèd ground.

The iron-hearted Furies armed with snakes

55   Scattered huge hydras over all the plains,

Which have consumed the grass, the herbs, the trees,

Which have drunk up the flowing water springs.

Strumbo hearing his voice shall start up, and put [his] meat in his pocket, seeking to hide himself

Thou great commander of the starry sky,

That guid'st the life of every mortal wight

60   From the enclosures of the fleeting clouds,

Rain down some food, or else I faint and die:

Pour down some drink, or else I faint and die.

O Jupiter, hast thou sent Mercury

In clownish shape to minister some food?

65   Some meat, some meat, some meat!

STRUMBO   O, alas, sir, ye are deceived, I am not Mercury,

I am Strumbo.

HUMBER   Give me some meat, villain, give me some meat,

Or gainst this rock, I'll dash thy cursèd brains,

70   And rend thy bowels with my bloody hands.

Give me some meat, villain, give me some meat.

STRUMBO   By the faith of my body, good fellow, I had rather give an whole ox, than that thou should'st serve me in that sort. Dash out my brains? O, horrible, terrible!— I think I have a quarry of stones in my pocket.   *Aside*

Let him make as though he would give him some, and as he putteth out his hand, enter the Ghost of Albanact, and strike him on the hand, and so Strumbo runs out, Humber following him

Exit [Strumbo and Humber]

75   GHOST   Lo, here the gift of fell ambition

Of usurpation and of treachery.

Lo, here the harms that wait upon all those

That do intrude themselves in others' lands,

Which are not under their dominion.   *Exit*

Act 4 Scene 4

Enter Locrine alone

LOCRINE   Seven years hath agèd Corineus lived

To Locrine's grief, and fair Estrilda's woe,

And seven years more he hopeth yet to live:

Oh supreme Jove, annihilate this thought.

---

52 **nine-fold Puryflegiton** Phlegethon, river of fire in the Underworld; **nine-fold** in Greek mythology it's the river Styx not Phlegethon which circles the Underworld nine times   55 **hydras** fabulous many-headed snakes in Greek mythology   58 **Thou ... sky** i.e. Jupiter   63 **Mercury** the messenger of the gods   70 **rend** tear

5 Should he enjoy the air's fruition?

Should he enjoy the benefit of life?

Should he contemplate the radiant sun

That makes my life equal to dreadful death?

Venus convey this monster from the earth,

10 That disobeyeth thus thy sacred hests.

Cupid convey this monster to dark hell,

That disannuls thy mother's sugared laws.

Mars with thy target all beset with flames,

With murdering blade bereave him of his life,

15 That hindreth Locrine in his sweetest joys.

And yet for all his diligent aspect,

His wrathful eyes piercing like Lynceus' eyes,

Well have I overmatched his subtlety.

Nigh Durolitum by the pleasant Lee,

20 Where brackish Thamis slides with silver streams,

Making a breach into the grassy downs,

A curious arch of costly marble fraught,

Hath Locrine framed underneath the ground,

The walls whereof, garnished with diamonds,

25 With ophirs, rubies, glistering emeralds,

And interlaced with sun-bright carbuncles,

Lighten the room with artificial day,

And from the Lee with water-flowing pipes

The moisture is derived into this arch,

30 Where I have placed fair Estrild secretly.

Thither eftsoons accompanied with my page,

I covertly visit my heart's desire,

Without suspicion of the meanest eye,

For love aboundeth still with policy,

35 And thither still means Locrine to repair,

Till Atropos cut off mine uncle's life.   *Exit*

Act 4 Scene 5

Enter Humber alone, saying:

HUMBER *O vita misero longa, foelici brevis!*

Eheu malorum fames extremum malum.

Long have I livèd in this desert cave

4.4 **10 hests** commands **12 disannuls** cancels **thy mother's** Venus' **13 target** shield **17 Lynceus** in Greek mythology, renowned for his keen eyesight **19 Nigh** near **Durolitum** a Roman settlement on the road between London and Chelmsford, near to modern Romford in Essex **Lee** river (also spelled Lea) which rises in the Chiltern hills and flows south-east to join the Thames (**Thamis**) **21 breach** gap **22 fraught** laden, filled **25 ophirs** pieces of gold; from Ophir, in Old Testament times it was exported to Judah (Job 22:24) **26 carbuncles** large precious stones of fiery red **31 eftsoons** afterwards/occasionally/repeatedly **33 meanest** most inferior in perception/those of the lowest social class **34 aboundeth** exists **policy** cunning **35 repair** go **36 Atropos** Greek goddess of fate responsible for cutting off the thread of human life with her shears **4.5** *Location: by the river Humber* **1 O ... malum** 'O life, long to the wretched, brief to the happy! / Alas, hunger is the greatest of all evils' (Latin)

With eating haws and miserable roots,
5   Devouring leaves and beastly excrements.
Caves were my beds, and stones my pillow-beres,
Fear was my sleep, and horror was my dream:
For still me thought at every boisterous blast,
Now Locrine comes, now, Humber, thou must die,
10   So that for fear and hunger, Humber's mind
Can never rest, but always trembling stands.
O what Danubius now may quench my thirst?
What Euphrates, what light-foot Euripus
May now allay the fury of that heat,
15   Which raging in my entrails eats me up?
You ghastly devils of the nine-fold Styx,
You damnèd ghosts of joyless Acheron,
You mournful souls, vexed in Abyssus' vaults,
You coal-black devils of Avernus' pond.
20   Come with your flesh-hooks, rend my famished arms,
These arms that have sustained their master's life:
Come with your razors, rip my bowels up,
With your sharp fire-forks crack my starvèd bones:
Use me as you will, so Humber may not live.
25   Accursèd gods that rule the starry poles,
Accursèd Jove, king of the cursèd gods,
Cast down your lightning on poor Humber's head,
That I may leave this deathlike life of mine:
What hear you not? And shall not Humber die?
30   Nay I will die though all the gods say nay.
And gentle Aby take my troubled corpse,
Take it and keep it from all mortal eyes,
That none may say when I have lost my breath,
'The very floods conspired gainst Humber's death.'   *Fling himself into the river*
Enter the Ghost of Albanact
35   [GHOST]   *En caedem sequitur, caedes in caede quiesco.*
Humber is dead! Joy heavens, leap earth, dance trees:
Now may'st thou reach thy apples Tantalus,
And with them feed thy hunger-bitten limbs:
Now, Sisyphus, leave tumbling of thy rock,
40   And rest thy restless bones upon the same:
Unbind Ixion, cruel Rhadamanth,

6 **pillow-beres** pillowcases   8 **still** always, continually   12 **Danubius** river Danube of central and eastern Europe   13 **Euphrates** river of Middle East in modern-day Iraq   **Euripus** the narrow channel of water separating the Greek island of Euboea in the Aegean Sea from Boeotia on mainland Greece   16 **nine-fold Styx** river of Greek mythology which circles the Underworld nine times   17 **Acheron** river of pain in the Underworld   18 **Abyssus'** of the great deep infernal pit below the earth   19 **Avernus' pond** the lake believed to be the gateway to the Underworld   20 **flesh-hooks** hooks for removing meat from the pot   23 **fire-forks** fork-shaped instruments for stirring up the fire, putting on fuel, etc.   31 **Aby** river Humber (from the Latin name *Abus*)   35 ***En … quiesco*** 'Lo, he pursues blood. Blood, in blood I find peace' (Latin)   37 **Tantalus** his punishment was to be eternally 'tantalized' with food and drink   39 **Sisyphus** was doomed to roll a stone uphill which continually rolled down again   41 **Ixion … wheel** the ghost is appealing to Rhadamanth, one of the judges of the dead, to replace the body of Ixion, a murderer who lusted after Zeus' wife and was punished for all eternity by being stretched out on a fiery spinning-wheel, with Humber

And lay proud Humber on the whirling wheel.

Back will I post to hell mouth Taenarus

And pass Cocytus, to the Elysian fields

45   And tell my father Brutus of these news.   *Exit*

Act 5 Scene 1

Enter Até as before. Jason leading Creon's daughter; Medea following hath a garland in her hand, and putting it on Creon's daughter's head, sets it on fire, and then killing Jason and her, departs

ATÉ   *Non tam Trinacriis exaestuat Aetna cavernis,*

Laesae furtivo quam cor mulieris amore.

Medea seeing Jason leave her love,

And choose the daughter of the Theban king,

5   Went to her devilish charms to work revenge:

And raising up the triple Hecate,

With all the rout of the condemnèd fiends,

Framed a garland by her magic skill,

With which she wrought Jason and Creon's ill.

10   So Gwendolyn seeing herself misused

And Humber's paramour possess her place,

Flies to the dukedom of Cornubia,

And with her brother, stout Thrasimachus,

Gathering a power of Cornish soldiers,

15   Gives battle to her husband and his host,

Nigh to the river of great Mercia:

The chances of this dismal massacre,

That which ensueth shortly will unfold.   *Exit*

Act 5 Scene 2

Enter Locrine, Camber, Assaracus, Thrasimachas

ASSARACUS   But tell me, cousin, died my brother so?

Now who is left to helpless Albion,

That as a pillar might uphold our state,

That might strike terror to our daring foes?

43 post hasten   **Taenarus** a cave, the gateway to the Underworld   **44 Cocytus** Underworld river of wailing   **Elysian fields** section of the Underworld, the final resting place of the heroic and the virtuous   **5.1**   The fifth dumb show mimes the story of Medea and Jason. In Greek mythology, Medea was the daughter of Aeëtes the King of Colchis, niece of Circe and granddaughter of Helios, the sun god. In order to claim his inheritance, Jason had to obtain the Golden Fleece, which he did with Medea's help. They married and had two children but Jason later fell in love with the daughter of Creon, the King of Corinth, and in her fury Medea killed Creon and his daughter by presenting her with a poisoned robe, in this version a garland. In Euripides' play she then killed her own children.   **1 Non ... amore** 'Etna does not burn so fiercely in her Sicilian caves / As the heart of a woman wounded by a secret love' (Latin)   **6 triple Hecate** Greek goddess, originally associated with good fortune but who came to be regarded as a witch and associated with ghosts; she was often represented in **triple** form, sometimes with three heads, a dog, a serpent and a horse although the phrase may relate to her three incarnations as Hecate, Luna, and Diana   **12 Cornubia** Cornwall (from Corineus)   **16 Mercia** one of largest of the seven Anglo-Saxon kingdoms of Britain, covering roughly the whole of the English Midlands

5   Now who is left to hapless Brittany,
         That might defend her from the barbarous hands
         Of those that still desire her ruinous fall,
         And seek to work her downfall and decay.
CAMBER   Ay, uncle, death is our common enemy,
10   And none but death can match our matchless power,
         Witness the fall of Albioneus' crew,
         Witness the fall of Humber and his Huns,
         And this foul death hath now increased our woe
         By taking Corineus from this life,
15   And in his room leaving us worlds of care.
THRASIMACHUS   But none may more bewail his mournful hearse
         Than I that am the issue of his loins:
         Now foul befall that cursèd Humber's throat,
         That was the causer of his ling'ring wound.
20 LOCRINE   Tears cannot raise him from the dead again,
         But where's my lady, Mistress Gwendolyn?
THRASIMACHUS   In Cornwall, Locrine, is my sister now,
         Providing for my father's funeral.
LOCRINE   And let her there provide her mourning weeds,
25   And mourn forever her own widowhood:
         Ne'er shall she come within our palace gate,
         To countercheck brave Locrine in his love.
         Go, boy, to Durolitum, down the Lee,
         Unto the arch where lovely Estrild lies,
30   Bring her and Sabren straight unto the court;
         She shall be queen in Gwendolyna's room.
         Let others wail for Corineus' death,
         I mean not so to macerate my mind,
         For him that barred me from my heart's desire.
35 THRASIMACHUS   Hath Locrine then forsook his Gwendolyn?
         Is Corineus' death so soon forgot?
         If there be gods in heaven, as sure there be,
         If there be fiends in hell, as needs there must,
         They will revenge this, thy notorious wrong,
40   And pour their plagues upon thy cursèd head.
LOCRINE   What, prat'st thou, peasant, to thy sovereign?
         Or art thou stricken in some ecstasy?
         Dost thou not tremble at our royal looks?
         Dost thou not quake when mighty Locrine frowns?
45   Thou, beardless boy, were't not that Locrine scorns

5.2   5 Brittany i.e. Britain   **11 Albioneus' crew** the race of giants who inhabited Britain before the arrival of Brutus   **16 hearse** framework of iron or wood fixed over a tomb or used to support the pall over the body at funerals, covered with rich cloth and lighted tapers   **27 countercheck** rebuke, reprove/ oppose   **31 room** place   **33 macerate** waste away/vex   **41 prat'st** i.e. 'pratest', speak foolishly, boastfully   **42 stricken … ecstasy** thrown into a frenzy of astonishment or passion   **45 beardless boy** Thrasimachus was not represented as very young earlier in the play which has led to speculation that two separate characters may have been combined in the play's revision

To vex his mind with such a heartless child,
With the sharp point of this my battle-axe,
I'd send thy soul to Puryflegiton.

THRASIMACHUS   Though I be young and of a tender age,
50   Yet will I cope with Locrine when he dares.
My noble father, with his conquering sword,
Slew the two giants, kings of Aquitaine.
Thrasimachus is not so degenerate
That he should fear and tremble at the looks
55   Or taunting words of a Venerian squire.

LOCRINE   Menacest thou thy royal sovereign?
Uncivil, not beseeming such as you,
Injurious traitor, for he is no less
That at defiance standeth with his king:
60   Leave these thy taunts, leave these thy bragging words,
Unless thou mean to leave thy wretched life.

THRASIMACHUS   If princes stain their glorious dignity
With ugly spots of monstrous infamy,
They leese their former estimation
65   And throw themselves into a hell of hate.

LOCRINE   Wilt thou abuse my gentle patience
As though thou did'st our high displeasure scorn?
Proud boy, that thou may'st know thy prince is moved,
Yea, greatly moved at this thy swelling pride,
70   We banish thee forever from our court.

THRASIMACHUS   Then, losel Locrine, look unto thyself,
Thrasimachus will venge this injury.   *Exit*

LOCRINE   Farewell, proud boy, and learn to use thy tongue.

ASSARACUS   Alas, my lord, you should have called to mind
75   The latest words that Brutus spake to you:
How he desired you, by the obedience
That children ought to bear their sire,
To love and favour Lady Gwendolyn.
Consider this, that if the injury
80   Do move her mind, as certainly it will,
War and dissension follows speedily.
What though her power be not so great as yours?
Have you not seen a mighty elephant
Slain by the biting of a silly mouse?
85   Even so the chance of war inconstant is.

LOCRINE   Peace, uncle, peace, and cease to talk hereof,
For he that seeks by whispering this or that

---

48 Puryflegiton hell   **50 cope** strike, come to blows   **52 giants … Aquitaine** these two kings were not giants in the original story   **55 Venerian squire** servant of Venus, inclined to wantonness   **64 leese** lose   **71 losel** scoundrel/worthless   **82 power** army

To trouble Locrine in his sweetest life,

Let him persuade himself to die the death.

Enter the Page, with Estrild and Sabren

90 ESTRILD   O, say me, page, tell me, where is the king?

Wherefore doth he send for me to the court?

Is it to die? Is it to end my life?

Say me, sweet boy, tell me and do not feign.

PAGE   No, trust me, madam, if you will credit the little honesty that is yet left me,

95 there is no such danger as you fear, but prepare yourself, yonder's the king.

ESTRILD   Then, Estrild, lift thy dazzled spirits up,

And bless that blessèd time, that day, that hour,

That warlike Locrine first did favour thee.

Peace to the king of Brittany, my love,   *Kneeling*

100 Peace to all those that love and favour him.   *Locrine taking her up*

[LOCRINE]   Doth Estrild fall with such submission

Before her servant king of Albion?

Arise, fair lady, leave this lowly cheer,

Lift up those looks that cherish Locrine's heart

105 That I may freely view that roseal face,

Which so entangled hath my love-sick breast.

Now to the court, where we will court it out,

And pass the night and day in Venus' sports.

Frolic, brave peers, be joyful with your king.   *Exeunt*

Act 5 Scene 3

Enter Gwendolyn, Thrasimachus, Madan and soldiers

GWENDOLYN   You gentle winds that with your modest blasts

Pass through the circuit of the heavenly vault,

Enter the clouds unto the throne of Jove,

And bear my prayers to his all-hearing ears,

5 For Locrine hath forsaken Gwendolyn,

And learned to love proud Humber's concubine.

You happy sprites that in the concave sky

With pleasant joy, enjoy your sweetest love,

Shed forth those tears with me, which then you shed,

10 When first you wooed your ladies to your wills:

Those tears are fittest for my woeful case,

Since Locrine shuns my nothing-pleasant face.

Blush heavens, blush sun, and hide thy shining beams,

Shadow thy radiant locks in gloomy clouds,

15 Deny thy cheerful light unto the world

---

93 feign contrive to deceive   **105 roseal** rose-coloured   **107 court it out** i.e. to the full   **5.3   10 wills** desires   **12 nothing-pleasant** in no way attractive

Where nothing reigns but falsehood and deceit.
What said I, falsehood? Ay, that filthy crime,
For Locrine hath forsaken Gwendolyn.
Behold the heavens do wail for Gwendolyn:
20 The shining sun doth blush for Gwendolyn:
The liquid air doth weep for Gwendolyn:
The very ground doth groan for Gwendolyn.
Ay, they are milder than the Briton king,
For he rejecteth luckless Gwendolyn.

25 THRASIMACHUS　Sister, complaints are bootless in this cause,
This open wrong must have an open plague:
This plague must be repaid with grievous war;
This war must finish with Locrinus' death.
His death will soon extinguish our complaints!

30 GWENDOLYN　O, no, his death will more augment my woes;
He was my husband, brave Thrasimacus,
More dear to me than the apple of mine eye
Nor can I find in heart to work his scathe.

THRASIMACHUS　Madam, if not your proper injuries,
35 Nor my exile can move you to revenge,
Think on our father Corineus' words:
His words to us stand always for a law.
Should Locrine live that caused my father's death?
Should Locrine live that now divorceth you?
40 The heavens, the earth, the air, the fire reclaims:
And then why should all we deny the same?

GWENDOLYN　Then henceforth, farewell womanish complaints,
All childish pity henceforth then farewell!
But cursèd Locrine look unto thyself,
45 For Nemesis, the mistress of revenge,
Sits armed at all points on our dismal blades
And cursèd Estrild that inflamed his heart,
Shall if I live, die a reproachful death.

MADAN　Mother, though nature makes me to lament
50 My luckless father's froward lechery:
Yet for he wrongs my lady mother thus,
I, if I could, myself would work his death.

THRASIMACHUS　See, madam, see, the desire of revenge
Is in the children of a tender age.
55 Forward, brave soldiers, into Mercia,
Where we shall brave the coward to his face.　　　*Exeunt*

---

18 For ... luckless Gwendolyn another example of 'antistrophe' or 'counterturn' when the lines all conclude with the same word　**25 bootless** unprofitable, useless　**26 This ... complaints** rhetorical figure known as 'anadiplosis' when the last word of one line or phrase becomes the first in the next　**plague** blow, smiting　**33 scathe** harm　**34 proper** personal　**40 reclaims** put right, remedy – the singular form of the verb could be used with a plural subject　**48 reproachful** shameful　**50 froward** perverse, ungovernable

Act 5 Scene 4

Enter Locrine, Estrild, Sabren, Assaracus and the soldiers

LOCRINE   Tell me, Assaracus, are the Cornish chuffs
In such great number come to Mercia,
And have they pitchèd there their petty host,
So close unto our royal mansion?

5   ASSARACUS   They are, my lord, and mean incontinent
To bid defiance to your majesty.

LOCRINE   It makes me laugh, to think that Gwendolyn
Should have the heart to come in arms gainst me.

ESTRILD   Alas, my lord, the horse will run amain

10   Whenas the spur doth gall him to the bone.
Jealousy, Locrine, hath a wicked sting.

LOCRINE   Say'st thou so, Estrild, beauty's paragon?
Well, we will try her choler to the proof
And make her know, Locrine can brook no braves.

15   March on, Assaracus, thou must lead the way
And bring us to their proud pavilion.   *Exeunt*

Act 5 Scene 5

Enter the Ghost of Corineus, with thunder and lightning

GHOST   Behold, the circuit of the azure sky
Throws forth sad throbs and grievous suspires,
Prejudicating Locrine's overthrow:
The fire casteth forth sharp darts of flames,

5   The great foundation of the triple world
Trembleth and quaketh with a mighty noise,
Presaging bloody massacres at hand.
The wand'ring birds that flutter in the dark,
When hellish night in cloudy chariot seated

10   Casteth her mists on shady Tellus' face
With sable mantles covering all the earth,
Now flies abroad amid the cheerful day,
Foretelling some unwonted misery.
The snarling curs of darkened Tartarus,

15   Sent from Avernus' ponds by Rhadamanth,

5.4 *Location: near the river Severn which formed the border between Mercia and Wales* **Sabren** the 1595 Quarto calls her 'Habren' which is similar to 'Hafren' the Celtic name for the river Severn **1 chuffs** rustics, clowns, punning on 'chough' the red-legged crow, the national emblem of Cornwall where they are common and form part of the Cornish coat of arms **4 mansion** palace, dwelling **5 incontinent** immediately **9 amain** at full speed **10 Whenas** when **gall** chafe, rub **13 try ... proof** put her anger to the test **14 brook no braves** not tolerate bullies/boastful threats
5.5 **2 suspires** sighs **3 Prejudicating** presaging **5 triple world** Europe, Asia and Africa **8 birds** referring to birds of ill-omen such as owls and ravens **10 Tellus' face** the earth; Tellus was a name for the Roman earth mother goddess **11 sable** black **mantles** cloaks, blankets **12 abroad** over a wide area **13 unwonted** uncommon **14 Tartarus** region where sinners were punished beneath the Underworld in classical mythology, equivalent to hell **15 Avernus' ... Rhadamanth** Lake Avernus was believed to be the gateway to the Underworld where Rhadamanthus was one of the judges of the dead

With howling ditties pester every wood:

The wat'ry ladies and the lightfoot fawns,

And all the rabble of the woody nymphs,

All trembling hide themselves in shady groves,

20 And shroud themselves in hideous hollow pits.

The boisterous Boreas thund'reth forth revenge.

The stony rocks cry out on sharp revenge:

The thorny bush pronounceth dire revenge.   *Sound the alarm*

Now Corineus stay and see revenge,

25 And feed thy soul with Locrine's overthrow.

Behold they come, the trumpets call them forth:

The roaring drums summon the soldiers.

Lo, where their army glistereth on the plains.

Throw forth thy lightning, mighty Jupiter,

30 And pour thy plagues on cursèd Locrine's head.   *Stand aside*

Enter Locrine, Estrild, Assaracus, Sabren and their soldiers at one door; Thrasimachus, Gwendolyn, Madan and their followers at another

LOCRINE   What is the tiger started from his cave?

Is Gwendolyn come from Cornubia,

That thus she braveth Locrine to the teeth?

And hast thou found thine armour, pretty boy,

35 Accompanied with these thy straggling mates?

Believe me but this enterprise was bold

And well deserveth commendation.

GWENDOLYN   Ay, Locrine, traiterous Locrine, we are come,

With full pretence to seek thine overthrow:

40 What have I done that thou should'st scorn me thus?

What have I said that thou should'st me reject?

Have I been disobedient to thy words?

Have I bewrayed thy arcane secrecy?

Have I dishonourèd thy marriage bed

45 With filthy crimes, or with lascivious lusts?

Nay, it is thou that hast dishonoured it,

Thy filthy mind, o'ercome with filthy lusts,

Yieldeth unto affection's filthy darts.

Unkind, thou wrong'st thy first and truest fere,

50 Unkind, thou wrong'st thy best and dearest friend:

Unkind, thou scorn'st all skilful Brutus' laws,

Forgetting father, uncle, and thyself.

ESTRILD   Believe me, Locrine, but the girl is wise

And well would seem to make a vestal nun.

55 How finely frames she her oration!

16 **ditties** songs   17 **wat'ry ladies** Naiads, water nymphs   18 **rabble** boisterous throng   **woody nymphs** Dryads   21 **Boreas** (god of) the north wind   35 **mates** fellows, used depreciatively   39 **pretence** intention/excuse/assertion of a right   43 **bewrayed** revealed, divulged   **arcane** hidden, concealed   48 **affection's** passion's   49 **fere** partner, companion/spouse   54 **vestal** chaste, pure (from the virgin priestesses who tended the sacred fire in the Temple of Vesta in Rome)

THRASIMACHUS   Locrine, we came not here to fight with words,

    Words that can never win the victory,

    But for you are so merry in your frumps,

    Unsheathe your swords and try it out by force,

60   That we may see who hath the better hand.

LOCRINE   Think'st thou to dare me, bold Thrasimacus?

    Think'st thou to fear me with thy taunting braves

    Or do we seem too weak to cope with thee?

    Soon shall I show thee my fine cutting blade

65   And with my sword, the messenger of death,

    Seal thee an acquittance for thy bold attempts.

                                    Exeunt
                                  Sound the alarm

Enter Locrine, Assaracus, and a soldier at one door, Gwendolyn, Thrasimachus, at another, Locrine and his followers driven back. Then let Locrine and Estrild enter again in amaze

LOCRINE   O, fair Estrilda, we have lost the field.

    Thrasimachus hath won the victory

    And we are left to be a laughing-stock,

70   Scoffed at by those that are our enemies.

    Ten thousand soldiers armed with sword and shield

    Prevail against an hundred thousand men:

    Thrasimachus incensed with fuming ire

    Rageth amongst the faint-heart soldiers

75   Like to grim Mars, when covered with his targe

    He fought with Diomedes in the field,

    Close by the banks of silver Simoïs.   *Sound the alarm*

    O, lovely Estrild, now the chase begins,

    Ne'er shall we see the stately Troynovant

80   Mounted on the coursers garnished all with pearls:

    Ne'er shall we view the fair Concordia

    Unless as captives we be thither brought.

    Shall Locrine then be taken prisoner

    By such a youngling as Thrasimachus?

85   Shall Gwendolyna captivate my love?

    Ne'er shall mine eyes behold that dismal hour,

    Ne'er will I view that ruthful spectacle,

    For with my sword, this sharp curtal-axe,

    I'll cut in sunder my accursèd heart.

90   But O, you judges of the ninefold Styx,

    Which with incessant torments rack the ghosts

    Within the bottomless Abyssus' pits,

    You gods, commanders of the heavenly spheres,

    Whose will and laws irrevocable stands,

---

58 for because   **frumps** jeers, mocking speech   **62 fear** frighten   **braves** bullies/boasting speeches   **66 acquittance** settlement/discharge, release (for his audacity)   *amaze* state of mental confusion   **75 Like … Simoïs** the reference is to Homer's *Iliad* when Mars fought on the Trojan side; the **Simoïs** is the main river of Troy   **targe** light shield   **85 captivate my love** capture my beloved (Estrild)   **87 ruthful** pitiful

95 Forgive, forgive, this foul accursèd sin,
    Forget, O gods, this foul condemnèd fault.
    And now, my sword, that in so many fights   *Kiss his sword*
    Hast saved the life of Brutus and his son,
    End now his life that wisheth still for death;
100 Work now his death that wisheth still for death,
    Work now his death that hateth still his life.
    Farewell, fair Estrild, beauty's paragon,
    Framed in the front of forlorn miseries,
    Ne'er shall mine eyes behold thy sunshine eyes
105 But when we meet in the Elysian fields:
    Thither I go before with hastened pace.
    Farewell, vain world, and thy enticing snares.
    Farewell, foul sin, and thy enticing pleasures.
    And welcome death, the end of mortal smart,
110 Welcome to Locrine's overburdened heart.
                              Thrusts himself through with his sword

ESTRILD Break, heart, with sobs and grievous suspires,
    Stream forth, you tears, from forth my wat'ry eyes,
    Help me to mourn for warlike Locrine's death,
    Pour down your tears, you wat'ry regions,
115 For mighty Locrine is bereft of life.
    O fickle fortune! O unstable world!
    What else are all things that this globe contains
    But a confusèd chaos of mishaps?
    Wherein as in a glass we plainly see
120 That all our life is but as a tragedy.
    Since mighty kings are subject to mishap—
    Ay, mighty kings are subject to mishap—
    Since martial Locrine is bereft of life.
    Shall Estrild live then after Locrine's death?
125 Shall love of life bar her from Locrine's sword?
    O no, this sword that hath bereft his life
    Shall now deprive me of my fleeting soul:
    Strengthen these hands, O mighty Jupiter,
    That I may end my woeful misery.
130 Locrine, I come, Locrine, I follow thee!   *Kills herself*
                                                       Sound the alarm

    Enter Sabren
SABREN What doleful sight, what ruthful spectacle
    Hath fortune offered to my hapless heart?
    My father slain with such a fatal sword,
    My mother murdered by a mortal wound!

---

102 paragon outstanding example, model   **105 But** except   **109 mortal smart** human pain/suffering   **111 suspires** sighs   **131 doleful** sorrowful, full of grief

135   What Thracian dog, what barbarous Myrmidon,
        Would not relent at such a ruthful case?
        What fierce Achilles, what hard stony flint
        Would not bemoan this mournful tragedy?
        Locrine, the map of magnanimity,
140   Lies slaughtered in this foul accursèd cave;
        Estrild, the perfect pattern of renown,
        Nature's sole wonder, in whose beauteous breasts
        All heavenly grace and virtue was enshrined,
        Both massacred are dead within this cave
145   And with them dies fair Pallas and sweet love.
        Here lies a sword and Sabren hath a heart,
        This blessèd sword shall cut my cursèd heart
        And bring my soul unto my parents' ghosts
        That they that live and view our tragedy
150   May mourn our case with mournful plaudites.   *Let her offer to kill herself*
        Ay me, my virgin's hands are too too weak
        To penetrate the bulwark of my breast.
        My fingers, used to tune the amorous lute,
        Are not of force to hold this steely glaive,
155   So I am left to wail my parents' death
        Not able for to work my proper death.
        Ah, Locrine, honoured for thy nobleness,
        Ah, Estrild, famous for thy constancy,
        Ill may they fare that wrought your mortal ends!
   Enter Gwendolyn, Thrasimachus, Madan, and the soldiers
160   GWENDOLYN   Search, soldiers, search! Find Locrine and his love,
        Find the proud strumpet, Humber's concubine,
        That I may change those her so pleasing looks
        To pale and ignominious aspect.
        Find me the issue of their cursèd love,
165   Find me young Sabren, Locrine's only joy,
        That I may glut my mind with lukewarm blood,
        Swiftly distilling from the bastard's breast.
        My father's ghost still haunts me for revenge,
        Crying, 'Revenge my over-hastened death!'
170   My brother's exile and mine own divorce
        Banish remorse clean from my brazen heart,
        All mercy from mine adamantine breasts.
  THRASIMACHUS   Nor doth thy husband, lovely Gwendolyn,
        That wonted was to guide our stayless steps,
175   Enjoy this light: see where he murdered lies

---

135 Thracian tribe that fought on the Trojan side in the *Iliad*   **Myrmidon** tribe that fought on the Greek side   **139 map** image, embodiment
145 Pallas Greek goddess of wisdom   **150 plaudites** rounds of applause; it should be pronounced as three syllables here for the sake of the metre
152 bulwark defensive fortification   **154 steely glaive** sword or spear of steel   **156 proper** personal/fitting, appropriate   **161 strumpet** whore
163 ignominious shameful   **172 adamantine** hard/immovable   **174 wonted** accustomed   **stayless** ever-moving, unceasing

By luckless lot and froward frowning fate,
And by him lies his lovely paramour
Fair Estrild gorèd with a dismal sword,
And as it seems both murdered by themselves,
180   Clasping each other in their feebled arms,
With loving zeal as if for company:
Their uncontented corpse' were yet content
To pass foul Styx in Charon's ferry-boat.

GWENDOLYN   And hath proud Estrild then prevented me?
185   Hath she escaped Gwendolyna's wrath
Violently by cutting off her life?
Would God she had the monstrous Hydra's lives
That every hour she might have died a death
Worse than the swing of old Ixion's wheel
190   And every hour revive to die again,
As Tityus, bound to houseless Caucasus,
Doth feed the substance of his own mishap,
And every day for want of food doth die
And every night doth live again to die.
195   But stay, methinks I hear some fainting voice,
Mournfully weeping for their luckless death.

SABREN   You, mountain nymphs which in these deserts reign,
Cease off your hasty chase of savage beasts,
Prepare to see a heart oppressed with care,
200   Address your ears to hear a mournful style:
No human strength, no work can work my weal,
Care in my heart so tyrant-like doth deal.
You Dryads and light-foot Satyri,
You gracious fairies which, at evening tide,
205   Your closets leave with heavenly beauty stored,
And on your shoulders spread your golden locks:
You savage bears in caves and darkened dens,
Come wail with me the martial Locrine's death:
Come mourn with me, for beauteous Estrild's death.
210   Ah, loving parents, little do you know,
What sorrow Sabren suffers for your thrall.

GWENDOLYN   But may this be, and is it possible,
Lives Sabren yet to expiate my wrath?
Fortune, I thank thee for this courtesy
215   And let me never see one prosperous hour
If Sabren die not a reproachful death.

---

176 **lot** destiny   **froward** evilly-disposed   182 **corpse'** i.e. 'corpses' but the metre requires that it be pronounced as one syllable only; until 1750 singular and plural had the same spelling, 'corps'   183 **Styx … ferry-boat** Charon was the ferryman of Hades who carried the souls of the dead across the river Styx that divided the Underworld from the land of the living   187 **Would … to die** Gwendolyn lists characters from mythology suffering eternal torment in Tartarus for their sins   203 **Satyri** Satyrs, half-man and half-goat   205 **closets** hidden, secret places   211 **thrall** trouble, oppression
216 **reproachful** shameful

SABREN   Hard-hearted death, that when the wretched call
　　　　Art furthest off and seldom hear'st at all,
　　　　But in the midst of fortune's good success,
220　　Uncallèd comes, and sheers our life in twain:
　　　　When will that hour, that blessèd hour draw nigh,
　　　　When poor distressèd Sabren may be gone?
　　　　Sweet Atropos, cut off my fatal thread!
　　　　What art thou, Death, shall not poor Sabren die?

　　　　　　　　　　　　　Gwendolyn taking her by the chin, shall say thus:

225　GWENDOLYN   Yes, damsel, yes! Sabren shall surely die,
　　　　Though all the world should seek to save her life,
　　　　And not a common death shall Sabren die,
　　　　But after strange and grievous punishments
　　　　Shortly inflicted upon thy bastard's head.
230　　Thou shalt be cast into the cursèd streams
　　　　And feed the fishes with thy tender flesh.

SABREN   And think'st thou then, thou cruel homicide,
　　　　That these thy deeds shall be unpunishèd?
　　　　No, traitor, no, the gods will venge these wrongs;
235　　The fiends of hell will mark these injuries.
　　　　Never shall these blood-sucking masty curs,
　　　　Bring wretched Sabren to her latest home,
　　　　For I myself, in spite of thee and thine,
　　　　Mean to abridge my former destinies,
240　　And that which Locrine's sword could not perform,
　　　　This pleasant stream shall present bring to pass.　　　　　　*She drowns herself*

GWENDOLYN   One mischief followes another's neck,
　　　　Who would have thought so young a maid as she
　　　　With such a courage would have sought her death.
245　　And for because this river was the place
　　　　Where little Sabren resolutely died,
　　　　Sabren forever shall this same be called.
　　　　And as for Locrine, our deceasèd spouse,
　　　　Because he was the son of mighty Brute
250　　To whom we owe our country, lives and goods,
　　　　He shall be buried in a stately tomb,
　　　　Close by his agèd father Brutus' bones,
　　　　With such great pomp and great solemnity
　　　　As well beseems so brave a prince as he.
255　　Let Estrild lie without the shallow vaults,
　　　　Without the honour due unto the dead,
　　　　Because she was the author of this war.

---

223 Atropos the oldest of the three Fates who cut off the thread of human life with her shears   **236 masty** burly, big-bodied   **239 abridge** cut short   **242 One … neck** misfortunes never come singly (proverbial); **followes** the metre requires that this should have three syllables   **247 Sabren** Sabrina was the Latin name for the river Severn   **255 without** outside

Retire brave followers unto Troynovant,

Where we will celebrate these exequies,

260 And place young Locrine in his father's tomb. *Exeunt omnes*

[Epilogue]

[*Enter Até*]

ATÉ   Lo! Here the end of lawless treachery,

Of usurpation and ambitious pride,

And they that for their private amours dare

Turmoil our land, and set their broils abroach,

5   Let them be warnèd by these premises.

And as a woman was the only cause

That civil discord was then stirrèd up,

So let us pray for that renownèd maid,

That eight and thirty years the sceptre swayed

10   In quiet peace and sweet felicity;

And every wight that seeks her grace's smart,

Would that this sword were piercèd in his heart. *Exit*

FINIS

Textual Notes

Q = Quarto text of 1595

Ed = a correction introduced by a later editor

SD = stage direction

SH = speech heading (i.e. speaker's name)

List of parts = Ed

1.1.4 scaring = Ed. Q = scarring

1.2.3 Ocëan = Ed. Q = th'Ocean   **29 struggle** = Ed. Q = strangle   **52 Aurora** = Ed. Q = Ancora   **55 world** = Ed. Q = word   **66 not** = Ed. *Not in* Q   **67 God** = Ed. Q = Cod   **108 Illyrian** = Ed. Q = Illician   **116 stronds** = Ed. Q = strons   **166 SH BRUTUS** = Ed. *Not in* Q   **237 SH [CORINEUS]** = Ed. *Speech assigned to Locrine in* Q   **Aeacus** = Ed. Q = Lacus   **246 Erebus** = Ed. Q = Crebus   **252 Tithonus** = Ed. Q = Fleithonus   **263 corpse** *spelled* coarse *in* Q

1.3.4 arseward *spelled* asward *in* Q

2.3.45 SH [CAPTAIN] = Ed. *Not in* Q   **61 SH [STRUMBO]** = Ed. *Not in* Q

2.4.28 careers = Ed. Q = carriers   **40 SH [STRUMBO *and* TROMPART]** = Ed. *Not in* Q

259 exequies funeral rites   [Epilogue]   4 Turmoil disturb, throw into confusion   broils abroach quarrels afoot   5 premises foregoing events, i.e. the play   8 renownèd maid Queen Elizabeth I, the virgin Queen   9 eight ... swayed who has ruled for thirty-eight years; Elizabeth came to the throne in 1558 which suggests that the date of performance was 1596, a year after publication of the play   11 wight person   her grace's smart her majesty's harm; 'grace' was formerly used as a courtesy title to the sovereign   12 this ... heart suggesting a dramatic gesture to conclude the performance

2.6.7 As = Ed. *Not in* Q   **44 her** = Ed. Q = their   **74 flight** = Ed. Q = fight   **91 SH [TROMPART]** = Ed. *Not in* Q   **94 word** = Ed. Q = good

3.1.4 his = Ed. Q = her

3.2.82 my = Ed. Q = thy

3.3.12 SH [GHOST] = Ed. *Not in* Q

3.4.1 hot = Ed. Q = whot

3.5.22 yon = Ed. Q = your   **68 they that** = Ed. Q = that they

4.2.46 [crown] = Ed. *Not in* Q   **133 love** = Ed. Q = liue   **148 dread** = Ed. Q = dead   **183 SH [LOCRINE]** = Ed. *Not in* Q

4.3.1 hath = Ed. Q = was

4.5.35 SH [GHOST] = Ed. *Not in* Q

5.2.1 my = Ed. Q = by   **101 SH [LOCRINE]** = Ed. *Not in* Q

5.5.66 acquittance = Ed. Q = acquita-ce

[Epilogue] SD *Enter Até* = Ed. *Not in* Q

Edward III feels like a Shakespearean history play. The opening scene is dominated by a discussion of who owns the right to the throne of France and in particular of the validity of the Salic law whereby inheritance cannot pass through the female line. A French messenger then arrives, demanding that the English king pays fealty. He is rebuffed by Prince Edward, son and heir of King Edward III: 'Defiance, Frenchman? We rebound it back, / Even to the bottom of thy master's throat.' Later in the play, on the fields of France, young Edward, dubbed the Black Prince, will prove a hero, winning a battle despite being heavily outnumbered. When he is surrounded and all seems lost, heralds come from the French with first an offer an mercy and then a horse on which to flee. He returns defiance in their face and sends back the horse, every bit in the manner of Shakespeare's warrior king bouncing back the tennis balls in *Henry V.*

Again as in Shakespeare, the French war is fought whilst there is internal strife within Britain. An Earl of Warwick advises Shakespeare's Henry IV to busy giddy minds with foreign wars as a distraction from civil war at home – back in *Henry IV Part 1* Scottish Douglas and Welsh Glendower had joined forces with English rebels. So too in *Edward III*, King David of Scotland, son of Robert Bruce, is knocking at the door of the north even as the English king is preparing to take his army to France.

One sometimes feels that no Elizabethan history play would be complete without an Earl of Warwick playing the role of a senior counsellor to the king. A curious feature of *Edward III* is that the name of Warwick is missing from the roll-call of courtiers in the opening entry direction, yet in the middle of the first scene the king turns to Warwick and asks him about his daughter, the Countess of Salisbury. We learn that she is besieged by the Scots in her castle at Roxburgh. The absence of Warwick from the entry suggestion is a clue that his character was introduced at a late stage in the writing, so as to pave the way for the Countess of Salisbury sequence.

The action cuts north to Roxburgh. The Countess appears in the above space, as if looking out from her battlements. And the texture of the language changes remarkably. The brisk and workmanlike verse of the opening scene gives way to intensely honed, sometimes showy poetry. The Countess stacks up her adjectives, speaking of the Scots' 'vile uncivil skipping jigs' and of the 'barren, bleak and fruitless air'. Clever rhetorical doubling devices abound. 'Bray forth their conquest and our overthrow' is the figure known as zeugma whereby one verb serves two nouns, while 'the bare report and name of arms' is the answering figure of hendiadys whereby two words connected by a conjunction are used to express a single notion that would normally be expressed by an adjective and a noun. Equally rich are the words tumbling from the mouth of King David as he imagines his troops on horseback with their 'light-borne snaffles', their 'nimble spurs', 'their jacks of gimmaled mail', 'their staves of grainèd Scottish ash', 'their buttoned tawny leathern belts' and their 'biting whinyards'. There is an ease in the deployment of a specific technical vocabulary, in this case military horsemanship, and a relish in the very sound of words. Then, suddenly, a tiny human detail as the Scottish Douglas cries 'Jemmy, my man, saddle my bonny black'. In that one line, both groom and horse, though not even on stage, come vividly to life. And in all this, one can see why the great eighteenth-century editor and scholar Edward Capell became convinced that in the Countess of Salisbury sequence we find ourselves in the face of eight hundred lines of superb and unadulterated Shakespearean verse and characterization.

The main action of the play is based on the chronicles of Froissart, whereas Shakespeare always seems to have begun his history plays from those of Hall or Holinshed. This distinction, along with the very clear stylistic differences between the Countess of Salisbury scenes and most of the military and political ones, gives good reason for the supposition that *Edward III* is a collaborative play, for which Shakespeare was brought in to provide a romance element. Froissart's account of the reign of Edward III was dominated by French and Scottish wars, with a relatively brief excursion regarding the king's amorous life. One plausible writing scenario would have a first draft, or even a stage version, focusing almost exclusively on the exploits of the Black Prince at Crécy and Poitiers, celebrating his glorious name as the old anonymous play *The Famous Victories of Henry V* had celebrated King Harry's. But then somewhere along the creative journey someone had the bright idea of working up the attempted seduction of the Countess of Salisbury, so as to provide a contrast between the lust of King Edward III and the purity of his illustrious son.

Shakespeare had staged a scene of the necessary kind in the encounter of Edward IV and Lady Elizabeth Grey in the play that we now call *Henry VI Part 3*. Furthermore, his involvement with *Edward III* coincides exactly with the time when the archetypal attempted seduction story from classical antiquity – Tarquin and Lucrece – was at the fore of his mind: his narrative poem *The Rape of Lucrece* was published in 1594. He was the obvious man for the job. He had access to William Painter's *Palace of Pleasure*, a popular Elizabethan collection of short novels, mostly from Italian sources (including the tale that Shakespeare would later dramatize as *All's Well that Ends Well*). Painter happened to include a much more detailed imagining of the encounter between Edward and the Countess than the outline version in Froissart. This gave Shakespeare all the raw material he needed.

After some initial sparring, the dialogue between the king and the Countess shifts into rhyming couplets, a traditional medium for the poetry of courtship. Before long, the king is enthralled – 'What needs a tongue to such a speaking eye, / That more persuades than winning oratory?', he says to himself and the audience. The whole exchange reads like a dry run for the electrically charged dialogue between desiring Angelo and chaste Isabella in *Measure for Measure*.

In Painter's novella, there is a secretary who acts as an intermediary for the king's love-letter to the Countess. Shakespeare took this hint and created the character of Lodowick, who enters in the second scene in the sequence. Noting that Lodowick is 'well read in poetry', the king commissions him to write verse that will impress the Countess. Lodowick thus plays the part of a court poet, a role familiar in real life to Shakespeare and his fellow-writers. In some sense, Lodowick thus becomes a representative of Shakespeare himself – for all we know, Shakespeare could have acted the part.

The ingenious poetic language is very close to that of *Lucrece* and several of the plays that Shakespeare was writing in this phase of his career. 'His eye in her eye lost'; the ear drinking the 'sweet tongue's utterance'; 'changing passion, like inconstant clouds / That rack upon the carriage of the winds'; the woman blushing and the man looking pale; a vein of imagery involving the clipping or counterfeiting of coins ('To stamp his image in forbidden metal'); the conjunction of opposites ('poison shows worst in a golden cup', 'Dark night seems darker by the lightning flash', 'Lilies that fester smell far worse than weeds'); a sudden change of tone into a joke about praising a woman as if she were a horse. Such devices all have the authentically Shakespearean hallmark. The exact repetition of the lilies and weeds line in Sonnet 94 is but symptom of a wider concordance.

Then there is the invocation of the poet's 'enchanted pen':

> And when thou writ'st of tears, encouch the word
> Before and after with such sweet laments
> That it may raise drops in a Tartar's eye
> And make a flint-heart Scythian pitiful,
> For so much moving hath a poet's pen.
> Then if thou be a poet move thou so
> And be enrichèd by thy sovereign's love:
> For if the touch of sweet concordant strings
> Could force attendance in the ears of hell,
> How much more shall the strains of poets' wit,
> Beguile and ravish soft and human minds?

The climactic reference is to Orpheus and his lyre, an allusion that Shakespeare uses on several key occasions when referring self-consciously to the power of poetry. These lines truly stand beside some of his greatest set-pieces on his own creative art, such as the 'poet's pen' passage in *A Midsummer Night's Dream*.

In the final scene of the sequence, the king is on the brink of a Tarquin-like rape of the Countess when he is morally corrected by the appearance of his son. He sees his wife's face in his child and his desire is checked – one almost thinks of Lady Macbeth's 'Had he not resembled my father as he slept, I had done it'. The sight of the young Edward readied for battle turns the older Edward back to his proper royal course and he is 'awakèd from his idle dream', just as Shakespeare's Prince Hal will be awakened from the dream of idle dissipation on his coronation at the end of *Henry IV Part 2* ('But being awake, I do despise my dream', he says in rejecting Falstaff). The closure of the sequence gives Shakespeare the opportunity to sign off his contribution with a little nod to his own *Lucrece*:

> Arise true English lady whom our isle
> May better boast of than ever Roman might
> Of her whose ransacked treasury hath tasked
> The vain endeavour of so many pens.
> Arise and be my fault thy honour's fame,
> Which after ages shall enrich thee with.

But did Shakespeare write more than the Countess scenes? When we follow the English army to France, the clunkier poetic style of the co-author returns. The long description of the naval victory off Sluys at the beginning of the third act is clearly influenced by reports of the defeat of the Spanish Armada. This not only helps us in the dating of the play, but also suggests that the history plays of the early 1590s were readily regarded as patriotic works, contributions to national morale at a time of war and frequent internal political crisis. But there is a labour to the poetry, what with 'An earnest-penny of a further wrack' and 'The crannied cleftures of the through-shot planks'.

The movement from the victory at Crécy to the siege of Calais to the reversals on the field of Poitiers, together with the cross-cutting between English and French camps, undoubtedly gave Shakespeare structural hints for the writing of *Henry V*, but there is none of his range of characterization or variety of mood in the war plot, no equivalent of King Henry's doubts and disguise on the night before Agincourt or the banter between the lower-ranking soldiers.

One scene, however, is written at greater intensity. Act 4 scene 4 takes liberties with history and the sources in order to bring about a dramatic transformation. It looks as though the Black Prince is surrounded and doomed, but he takes strength from the courageous example of old Lord Audley – a reincarnation of brave Talbot in *Henry VI Part 1* – and spurs himself on to a heroic victory against all the odds. Once again, the audience can hear a shift of gear in the writing: 'banners, bannerets, / And new-replenished pendants cuff the air / And beat the winds that for their gaudiness / Struggles to kiss them'; the hills are 'proudly royalized' (conversion of an adjective or a noun to a verb is a typically Shakespearean energizing device). From 'a nimble-jointed jennet' and a scornful reference to a 'cap'ring boy' to forceful images of strategems 'texted in thine honourable face' and words that buckle armour on the back, the whole scene carries the smell of Shakespeare and, for us, creates anticipation of the great history plays to come.

KEY FACTS

AUTHORSHIP: Most scholars now agree that Shakespeare collaborated on this play, which was published anonymously. The suggestion was first made by Edward Capell in 1760, and it is now included by several publishers alongside the canonical works. Shakespeare seems to have contributed the 'Countess' scenes (1.2, 2.1, 2.2), and many scholars believe he also wrote 4.4. A very few scholars (notably Eric Sams) have argued that he wrote the whole play; but, while most scholars now accept there are two hands in the play, there is no consensus on the identity of his collaborator. The most common candidates are Peele, Marlowe (championed by Thomas Merriam) and Kyd, for whom Brian Vickers has recently argued strongly, but none of these attributions has yet gained widespread acceptance.

PLOT: King Edward III is assured of his right to the throne of France, and counters defiance from the French court by vowing to subdue the country. John of France is in league with King David of Scotland, who attempts to divide Edward's forces by besieging the Countess of Salisbury in her castle at Roxburgh. The Scots flee at the approach of the English army, but Edward falls in love with the chaste Countess who, after resisting the king, eventually brings him to his senses by threatening to commit suicide. He rewards her faith. The scene shifts to the French wars, and the French navy is defeated at sea. The Black Prince Edward distinguishes himself in battle and is knighted by his father, and the French retreat in confusion as the English press their advantage. Edward dispenses mercy and justice among the conquered. Meanwhile, the Earl of Salisbury and his prisoner Villiers form a bond of trust and honour that impresses the French. In a later battle, Prince Edward and his comrade Audley are beset by overwhelming forces, and the French anticipate a counter-victory. However, against all odds, the Prince prevails. Salisbury is captured; but Prince Charles petitions his father to uphold the vow of safe passage granted earlier. The French king and prince are subsequently captured by the Black Prince and taken to King Edward to swear fealty.

MAJOR PARTS: King Edward III (29%/130/8), King John II (11%/38/8), Prince Edward (11%/30/8), Countess of Salisbury (8%/37/3), Warwick (5%/16/4), Audley (4%/22/8), Salisbury

▷

(4%/10/3), Charles of Normandy (3%/22/6), Mariner (3%/3/1), Derby (2%/18/6), Lodowick (2%/18/2), Artois (2%/11/7), Prince Philip (1%/9/5), Villiers (1%/9/2), King David II (1%/9/2), Lorraine (1%/8/5), First Citizen (1%/6/1), Queen Philippa (1%/4/1).

LINGUISTIC MEDIUM: 100% verse.

DATE: c.1593–94. The only firm evidence for dating is the play's entry in the Stationers' Register in 1595. If the play was written for Derby's Men then a date of 1593–94 appears most likely; however, arguments taking into account the relatively small casting requirements and modest stage resources may suggest that the play was written slightly earlier for Pembroke's Men for touring performance during the plague year of 1593.

SOURCES: Key sources for the plot include Holinshed's *Chronicles of England, Scotland and Ireland*, in the second edition of which Holinshed inserts a note regarding the Countess of Salisbury. The Countess episodes appear in Jean Froissart's *Chroniques* (translated into English 1523–25), but further details were drawn from William Painter's *The Palace of Pleasure* (1567). The play freely adapts and compresses its sources, and also draws heavily on stage traditions of the time, particularly Marlowe's *Tamburlaine* plays.

TEXT: 1596 Quarto. This text is of variable quality, with particular confusion in speech headings, and is set from a manuscript that appears to be a stage removed from authorial or theatrical papers. A slightly revised reprint followed in 1599, making some corrections but introducing new errors.

THE REIGN OF KING EDWARD THE THIRD: as it Hath Been Sundry Times Played About the City of London

KING EDWARD III of England

QUEEN Philippa, his wife

PRINCE EDWARD, their son, the Prince of Wales

Earl of WARWICK

COUNTESS of Salisbury, his daughter

Earl of SALISBURY, her husband

Sir William MONTAGUE, her nephew

LODOWICK, King Edward's secretary

Earl of DERBY

Lord AUDLEY

Lord PERCY

John COPLAND, an English esquire

Two ESQUIRES

A HERALD

Robert, Count of ARTOIS, Earl of Richmond }

Lord MOUNTFORD, Duke of Brittany }

GOBIN DE GRACE, a French prisoner }

} Frenchmen supporting Edward

KING JOHN II of France

Prince CHARLES, the Duke of Normandy, his eldest son (the dauphin)

Prince PHILIP, his younger son

Duke of LORRAINE

VILLIERS, a Norman Lord

The CAPTAIN of Calais

Another CAPTAIN

A MARINER

FRENCHMEN

WOMAN with 2 children

CITIZENS

Three French HERALDS

KING OF BOHEMIA

POLONIAN CAPTAIN

KING DAVID II of Scotland

Earl of DOUGLAS, a Scot

Two MESSENGERS

[Act 1 Scene 1]

Enter King Edward, Derby, Prince Edward, Audley and Artois [with Warwick]

KING EDWARD   Robert of Artois, banished though thou be,
From France thy native country, yet with us,
Thou shalt retain as great a seigniory:
For we create thee Earl of Richmond here.
5   And now go forwards with our pedigree:
Who next succeeded Philip le Beau?

[1.1]   *Location: England*   **1 Artois** former province of northern France   **3 seigniory** lordship, domain   **5 pedigree** ancestral line   **6 Philip le Beau** Philip IV of France (1285–1314)

ARTOIS   Three sons of his, which all successfully
Did sit upon their father's regal throne,
Yet died and left no issue of their loins.

10 KING EDWARD   But was my mother sister unto those?

ARTOIS   She was, my lord, and only Isabel
Was all the daughters that this Philip had
Whom afterward your father took to wife:
And, from the fragrant garden of her womb,
15 Your gracious self, the flower of Europe's hope,
Derivèd is, inheritor to France.
But note the rancour of rebellious minds:
When thus the lineage of le Beau was out,
The French obscured your mother's privilege
20 And, though she were the next of blood, proclaimed
John of the house of Valois now their king.
The reason was, they say the realm of France,
Replete with princes of great parentage,
Ought not admit a governor to rule
25 Except he be descended of the male.
And that's the special ground of their contempt
Wherewith they study to exclude your grace.

[KING EDWARD]   But they shall find that forgèd ground of theirs
To be but dusty heaps of brittle sand.

30 ARTOIS   Perhaps it will be thought a heinous thing
That I, a Frenchman, should discover this,
But heaven I call to record of my vows:
It is not hate nor any private wrong,
But love unto my country and the right
35 Provokes my tongue thus lavish in report.
You are the lineal watchman of our peace
And John of Valois indirectly climbs.
What then should subjects but embrace their king?
Ah, wherein may our duty more be seen
40 Than striving to rebate a tyrant's pride,

---

9 **issue … loins** children; Philip IV was succeeded by his sons, Louis X, Philip V, Charles IV, who died childless or were only survived by daughters **11 only Isabel** Isabel alone **16 inheritor to France** legitimate heir to France and the French crown **17 rancour** resentment, animosity **19 obscured** concealed **privilege** right **20 next of blood** nearest in the direct line of inheritance **21 John … Valois** John was historically the son of Philip who reigned as Philip VI of France from 1328 to 1350; the two kings have been elided here for dramatic purposes and to simplify the narrative; the house of Valois were cousins to the Capetian Philip IV **23 Replete** filled, stocked **25 Except … male** French jurists later resurrected the long defunct Salic law, one of whose tenets was that succession could not pass to a female, in order to justify the exclusion of Edward from the French crown; the same argument recurs at the opening of Shakespeare's *Henry V* **26 special ground** particular reason, motive **28 forgèd ground** invented, spurious reason; Edward's response puns on **ground** meaning earth/soil and contains a reference to Christ's parable of the wise and foolish builders – the foolish builder built his house upon **sand** (Matthew 7:24) **30 heinous** hateful, wicked **31 discover** reveal, disclose **32 to record** as witness **33 private wrong** personal injury/ grievance **35 lavish in report** free, unrestrained of speech **36 lineal** in direct line of descent **watchman** guardian **37 indirectly** not in a direct line/ deviously **38 should subjects** i.e. should subjects do **40 rebate** repress/lessen

And place the true shepherd of our commonwealth?

KING EDWARD   This counsel, Artois, like to fruitful showers,
　　Hath added growth unto my dignity,
　　And by the fiery vigour of thy words
45　Hot courage is engendered in my breast,
　　Which heretofore was racked in ignorance,
　　But now doth mount with golden wings of fame
　　And will approve fair Isabel's descent,
　　Able to yoke their stubborn necks with steel,
50　That spurn against my sovereignty in France.　　　　　*Sound a horn*
　　A messenger, Lord Audley, know from whence.
Enter a messenger [from the Duke of] Lorraine

AUDLEY　　The Duke of Lorraine, having crossed the seas,
　　Entreats he may have conference with your highness.

KING EDWARD　Admit him, lords, that we may hear the news.
[Enter Lorraine]
55　Say, Duke of Lorraine, wherefore art thou come?

LORRAINE　　The most renownèd prince, King John of France,
　　Doth greet thee Edward, and by me commands
　　That for so much as by his liberal gift,
　　The Guyenne dukedom is entailed to thee,
60　Thou do him lowly homage for the same.
　　And for that purpose here I summon thee:
　　Repair to France within these forty days,
　　That there, according as the custom is,
　　Thou mayst be sworn true liegeman to our king,
65　Or else thy title in that province dies,
　　And he himself will repossess the place.

KING EDWARD　See how occasion laughs me in the face:
　　No sooner minded to prepare for France,
　　But straight I am invited, nay, with threats,
70　Upon a penalty enjoined to come:
　　'Twere but a childish part to say him nay.
　　Lorraine, return this answer to thy lord:
　　I mean to visit him as he requests.
　　But how? Not servilely disposed to bend,
75　But like a conqueror to make him bow.
　　His lame unpolished shifts are come to light,

---

41 **place** put in place, position   **commonwealth** general good/body politic   43 **dignity** merit/rank   46 **racked** tormented, i.e. tortured on the rack   48 **approve** confirm/make good/put to the test   49 **yoke** subdue/engage in battle; from the contrivance by which animals were coupled together to draw a plough or other vehicle which consisted of a curved or hollowed piece of wood passed round the animals' necks   50 **spurn** kick/treat with contempt   51 **know from whence** find out where from   52 **Lorraine** region of north-eastern France   53 **Entreats** begs   54 **Admit him** permit him to enter   55 **wherefore art thou** why have you   58 **liberal** free/generous   59 **Guyenne** archaic name for Aquitaine, region of south-west France   **entailed** given, bestowed as an inalienable possession   60 **lowly homage** humble acknowledgement of allegiance   **for the same** in return, i.e. Edward must recognize King John's legitimacy in return for the gift of Aquitaine/Guyenne   62 **Repair** go, make your way   64 **liegeman** sworn vassal/faithful follower   65 **title** legal right   **dies** expires   70 **enjoined** commanded   74 **bend** i.e. place himself in a lower position/bend the knee   76 **lame** weak, unsatisfactory   **unpolished** crude, unsophisticated   **shifts** schemes, devices/devious substitutions, i.e. of people, places and titles

And truth hath pulled the vizard from his face
That set a glass upon his arrogance.
Dare he command a fealty in me?
80   Tell him the crown that he usurps is mine,
And where he sets his foot he ought to kneel;
'Tis not a petty dukedom that I claim
But all the whole dominions of the realm,
Which, if with grudging he refuse to yield,
85   I'll take away those borrowed plumes of his
And send him naked to the wilderness.

LORRAINE   Then, Edward, here in spite of all thy lords,
I do pronounce defiance to thy face.

PRINCE EDWARD   Defiance, Frenchman? We rebound it back,
90   Even to the bottom of thy master's throat,
And, be it spoke with reverence of the king,
My gracious father, and these other lords,
I hold thy message but as scurrilous,
And him that sent thee like the lazy drone
95   Crept up by stealth unto the eagle's nest,
From whence we'll shake him with so rough a storm,
As others shall be warnèd by his harm.

WARWICK   Bid him leave off the lion's case he wears,
Lest meeting with the lion in the field,
100   He chance to tear him piecemeal for his pride.

ARTOIS   The soundest counsel I can give his grace
Is to surrender ere he be constrained.
A voluntary mischief hath less scorn
Than when reproach with violence is borne.

105 LORRAINE   Regenerate traitor, viper to the place
Where thou was fostered in thine infancy:
Bearest thou a part in this conspiracy?   *He draws his sword*

KING EDWARD   Lorraine, behold the sharpness of this steel.   *Draws his sword*
Fervent desire that sits against my heart
110   Is far more thorny pricking than this blade,
That with the nightingale I shall be scarred,
As oft as I dispose myself to rest,
Until my colours be displayed in France.
This is thy final answer, so be gone.

---

77 vizard mask   **78 glass** mirror, looking-glass   **79 fealty** obligation of feudal loyalty to a lord   **89 rebound** return, cast (with force)   **93 scurrilous** coarse, indecent   **94 drone** idler, non-worker (after the male honey bee)   **95 Crept … nest** The image of the **lazy drone** derived from Virgil's *Georgics* (Book IV); in *Euphues* and *Endymion* John Lyly has the parasitic drone creeping to the eagle's nest and Shakespeare picks up on the image in *Henry V* and *2 Henry VI*   **98 case** skin, hide/covering; the English royal coat of arms features a **lion** rampant and is thus a symbol of English royalty; the reference is to Aesop's fable of the ass in the lion's skin betrayed by his braying   **100 pride** arrogance, puns on the collective term for lions, a **pride** of lions   **102 ere** before   **constrained** forced   **103 mischief** misfortune   **104 reproach** source of disgrace or shame   **105 viper … infancy** Lorraine likens Artois, who was raised in France, to the viper in Aesop's fable of the farmer and the frozen viper which he found and placed in his bosom; as soon as it was warm the venomous snake turned and bit him   **111 nightingale … scarred** from the belief that the nightingale stayed awake all night by pressing its breast against a thorn   **112 dispose** prepare/feel inclined   **113 colours** flag/heraldic insignia

115 LORRAINE It is not that, nor any English brave
           Afflicts me so, as doth his poisoned view:
           That is most false should most of all be true.   [*Exit*]

    KING EDWARD Now, lords, our fleeting bark is under sail:
           Our gage is thrown, and war is soon begun,
120   But not so quickly brought unto an end.

    Enter Montague

           But wherefore comes Sir William Montague?
           How stands the league between the Scot and us?

    MONTAGUE Cracked and dissevered, my renownèd lord:
           The treacherous king no sooner was informed
125   Of your withdrawing of your army back,
           But straight, forgetting of his former oath,
           He made invasion on the bordering towns:
           Berwick is won, Newcastle spoiled and lost,
           And now the tyrant hath begirt with siege
130   The castle of Roxburgh, where enclosed,
           The Countess Salisbury is like to perish.

    KING EDWARD That is thy daughter, Warwick, is it not,
           Whose husband hath in Brittany served so long,
           About the planting of Lord Mountford there?

135 WARWICK It is, my lord.

    KING EDWARD Ignoble David hast thou none to grieve,
           But silly ladies with thy threat'ning arms?
           But I will make you shrink your snaily horns!
           First therefore, Audley, this shall be thy charge:
140   Go levy footmen for our wars in France;
           And, Ned, take muster of our men at arms.
           In every shire elect a several band,
           Let them be soldiers of a lusty spirit
           Such as dread nothing but dishonour's blot.
145   Be wary, therefore, since we do commence
           A famous war and with so mighty a nation.
           Derby, be thou ambassador for us,
           Unto our father-in-law, the Earl of Hainault:
           Make him acquainted with our enterprise,
150   And likewise will him, with our own allies
           That are in Flanders, to solicit, too

---

115 **brave** bravado, boastful, threatening behaviour/bully, hired assassin   117 **That** i.e. that man, Robert of Artois   118 **fleeting** fast-moving, plays on sense of 'fleet' as a group of ships but also ironically means 'fickle, inconstant'   **bark** small ship   119 **gage** pledge/challenge; a glove thrown down as a challenge to fight   122 **the Scot** i.e. King David II of Scotland   123 **dissevered** disunited, divided   128 **Berwick** Berwick-upon-Tweed, the most northerly town in England on the English-Scottish border   **Newcastle** Newcastle upon Tyne, a town in the north-east of England   **spoiled** ravaged, pillaged   129 **begirt** surrounded   130 **Roxburgh** important town in the Scottish lowlands   133 **Brittany** region of north-western France, formerly an independent duchy and kingdom   134 **planting** installing   136 **grieve** trouble, oppress, harm   137 **silly** helpless, defenceless   138 **shrink** retract   **snaily** snail-like, i.e. having horns like a snail's tentacles   140 **levy footmen** raise or muster foot soldiers   141 **Ned** Edward, the Black Prince   **take muster** assemble and count   142 **several** separate, distinctive   143 **lusty** courageous, valiant   144 **blot** stain, disgrace   146 **so mighty a** such a great   148 **Hainault** Belgian province, formerly a region of France; Edward's wife was Philippa of Hainault   150 **will** ask, enjoin

The Emperor of Almaine in our name.

Myself, whilst you are jointly thus employed,

Will, with these forces that I have at hand,

155   March and once more repulse the traitorous Scot.

But, sirs, be resolute, we shall have wars

On every side, and, Ned, thou must begin

Now to forget thy study and thy books,

And ure thy shoulders to an armour's weight.

160   PRINCE EDWARD   As cheerful sounding to my youthful spleen,

This tumult is of war's increasing broils,

As at the coronation of a king,

The joyful clamours of the people are,

When *Ave Caesar* they pronounce aloud.

165   Within this school of honour I shall learn,

Either to sacrifice my foes to death,

Or in a rightful quarrel spend my breath.

Then cheerfully forward each a several way,

In great affairs 'tis naught to use delay.   *Exeunt*

[Act 1 Scene 2]

Enter the Countess

COUNTESS   Alas, how much in vain my poor eyes gaze,

For succour that my sovereign should send!

Ah, Cousin Montague, I fear thou want'st

The lively spirit sharply to solicit,

5   With vehement suit the king in my behalf:

Thou dost not tell him what a grief it is

To be the scornful captive to a Scot,

Either to be wooed with broad untunèd oaths,

Or forced by rough insulting barbarism:

10   Thou dost not tell him if he here prevail,

How much they will deride us in the north,

And in their vile uncivil skipping jigs

Bray forth their conquest and our overthrow,

Even in the barren, bleak and fruitless air.

Enter David, Douglas and Lorraine

15   I must withdraw, the everlasting foe   *Aside*

---

152 **Almaine** Germany, from the French 'Allemagne'   159 **ure** inure, accustom   160 **spleen** hot or proud temper, courage; from the bodily organ regarded as the seat of passions   161 **broils** quarrels, disturbances   164 *Ave Caesar* 'Hail Caesar' (Latin), traditional greeting of new Roman emperor   168 **several** separate   169 **naught** evil/pointless   **use** practise   **[1.2]** *Location: Roxburgh Castle; the Countess is within looking out over the walls*   2 **succour** aid   3 **Cousin** kinsman; a term used of a relative other than a parent or sibling or to a close friend; Montague is the Countess' nephew   **thou want'st** you lack   4 **solicit** entreat, petition   5 **vehement** powerful, capable of producing conviction   7 **scornful** contemptible, regarded with scorn   8 **broad** coarse, vulgar/indecent   **untunèd** disordered/lacking harmony   10 **him if he** i.e. King Edward if King David   12 **skipping jigs** lively dances sung to mocking, often scurrilous, ballads   13 **Bray** cry harshly

Comes to the wall. I'll closely step aside
And list their babble blunt and full of pride.

KING DAVID My lord of Lorraine, to our brother of France
Commend us, as the man in Christendom

20   That we most reverence and entirely love.
Touching your embassage, return and say,
That we with England will not enter parley,
Nor never make fair weather or take truce,
But burn their neighbour towns and so persist

25   With eager rods beyond their city, York.
And never shall our bonny riders rest,
Nor rusting canker have the time to eat
Their light-borne snaffles, nor their nimble spurs,
Nor lay aside their jacks of gimmaled mail,

30   Nor hang their staves of grainèd Scottish ash
In peaceful wise upon their city walls,
Nor from their buttoned tawny leathern belts,
Dismiss their biting whinyards, till your king
Cry out 'Enough, spare England now for pity!'

35   Farewell, and tell him that you leave us here,
Before this castle. Say you came from us
Even when we had that yielded to our hands.

LORRAINE I take my leave and fairly will return
Your acceptable greeting to my king.   *Exit Lorraine*

40   KING DAVID Now, Douglas, to our former task again,
For the division of this certain spoil.

DOUGLAS My liege, I crave the lady and no more.

KING DAVID Nay, soft ye, sir! First, I must make my choice,
And first I do bespeak her for myself.

45   DOUGLAS Why then, my liege, let me enjoy her jewels.

KING DAVID Those are her own still liable to her,
And who inherits her hath those withal.

Enter a Scot in haste

MESSENGER My liege, as we were pricking on the hills,
To fetch in booty, marching hitherward,

50   We might descry a mighty host of men,
The sun reflecting on the armour showed
A field of plate, a wood of picks advanced.

---

16 **closely** secretly   17 **list** listen to   **babble** idle, foolish, inarticulate speech   19 **Commend** mention as worthy   **us** i.e. me; King David is using the royal plural pronoun   21 **Touching** with regard to   **embassage** mission   22 **parley** conference with an enemy to discuss terms, negotiation   23 **make fair weather** pretend friendship   **take truce** ask to suspend hostilities   25 **rods** paths, roads (obsolete Scots dialect) but puns on sense of sticks/shafts of spears   26 **bonny** fine/large   27 **rusting canker** corrosion caused by rust   28 **snaffles** horses' bridle bits   29 **jacks** jackets   **gimmaled** linked   30 **ash** tough, close-grained wood, commonly used for spears   31 **wise** manner   33 **whinyards** short swords   36 **Before** in front of   37 **that** i.e. that castle   41 **certain** inevitable/particular   **spoil** prize, booty   44 **bespeak** ask for/promise   46 **liable** legally belonging   47 **withal** along with the rest   48 **pricking** galloping   50 **might descry** were able to make out   52 **field of plate** plain of metal   **wood of picks** forest of pikes or spears

Bethink your highness speedily herein:

An easy march within four hours will bring

55 The hindmost rank unto this place, my liege.

KING DAVID Dislodge, dislodge: it is the King of England.

DOUGLAS Jemmy, my man, saddle my bonny black.

KING DAVID Mean'st thou to fight, Douglas? We are too weak.

DOUGLAS I know it well, my liege, and therefore fly.

60 **COUNTESS** My lords of Scotland, will ye stay and drink?   *Coming forward*

KING DAVID She mocks at us, Douglas: I cannot endure it.

COUNTESS Say, good my lord, which is he must have the lady

And which her jewels? I am sure, my lords,

Ye will not hence till you have shared the spoils.

65 **KING DAVID** She heard the messenger and heard our talk,

And now that comfort makes her scorn at us.

[Enter] another Messenger

SECOND MESSENGER Arm, my good lord, O, we are all surprised!

[COUNTESS] After the French ambassador, my liege,

And tell him that you dare not ride to York:

70 Excuse it that your bonny horse is lame.

KING DAVID She heard that too, intolerable grief.

Woman, farewell, although I do not stay!   *Exeunt Scots*

COUNTESS 'Tis not for fear, and yet you run away —

O happy comfort, welcome to our house!

75 The confident and boist'rous boasting Scot

That swore before my walls they would not back

For all the armèd power of this land,

With faceless fear that ever turns his back,

Turned hence again the blasting north-east wind

80 Upon the bare report and name of arms.

Enter Montague

MONTAGUE O summer's day, see where my cousin comes!

How fares my aunt? We are not Scots,

Why do you shut your gates against your friends?

COUNTESS Well may I give a welcome, cousin, to thee,

85 For thou com'st well to chase my foes from hence.

MONTAGUE The king himself is come in person hither:

Dear aunt, descend and gratulate his highness.

COUNTESS How may I entertain his majesty

To show my duty and his dignity?

Enter King Edward, Warwick, Artois, with others

90 **KING EDWARD** What, are the stealing foxes fled and gone

Before we could uncouple at their heels?

---

53 herein in this case **55 hindmost** furthest in the rear **56 Dislodge** leave a place of encampment **76 back** withdraw, retire **79 again** facing, i.e. he turned northwards **80 bare report** mere mention **81 summer's day** happy circumstance **cousin** kinswoman **87 gratulate** welcome **91 uncouple** release hunting dogs, fastened together in couples, for the chase

WARWICK   They are, my liege, but with a cheerful cry
Hot hounds and hardy chase them at the heels.

KING EDWARD   This is the Countess Warwick, is it not?

95   WARWICK   Even she, liege, whose beauty tyrants' fear,
As a May blossom with pernicious winds,
Hath sullied, withered, overcast and done.

KING EDWARD   Hath she been fairer Warwick than she is?

WARWICK   My gracious king, fair is she not at all,

100   If that herself were by to stain herself,
As I have seen her when she was herself.

KING EDWARD   What strange enchantment lurked in those her eyes
When they excelled this excellence they have,
That now her dim decline hath power to draw

105   My subject eyes from piercing majesty
To gaze on her with doting admiration?

COUNTESS   In duty lower than the ground I kneel,   *Kneels*
And for my dull knees bow my feeling heart
To witness my obedience to your highness

110   With many millions of a subject's thanks
For this your royal presence whose approach
Hath driven war and danger from my gate.

KING EDWARD   Lady, stand up. I come to bring thee peace
However, thereby I have purchased war.

115   COUNTESS   No war to you my liege: the Scots are gone
And gallop home toward Scotland with their hate.

[KING EDWARD]   Lest, yielding here, I pine in shameful love
Come, we'll pursue the Scots.— Artois away!

COUNTESS   A little while, my gracious sovereign, stay

120   And let the power of a mighty king
Honour our roof: my husband in the wars,
When he shall hear it will triumph for joy.
Then, dear my liege, now niggard not thy state,
Being at the wall, enter our homely gate.

125   KING EDWARD   Pardon me, Countess, I will come no near,
I dreamed tonight of treason and I fear.

COUNTESS   Far from this place let ugly treason lie.

KING EDWARD   No farther off than her conspiring eye,   *Aside*
Which shoots infected poison in my heart,

130   Beyond repulse of wit or cure of art.
Now, in the sun alone it doth not lie

---

95 whose ... done fear of tyrants has diminished her beauty as rough winds destroy May blossom   **99 fair ... herself** her present self cannot compare with and would appear stained by her true self's beauty   **102 What ... admiration?** The king is reflecting on the quality of her beauty which even in its decline has the power to turn his majesty, which should have the power of penetration, into a subject   **doting** foolish, infatuated (often relating to old age)   **108 for** in place of   **dull** insensate, without feeling   **117 Lest** just in case   **pine** endure, suffer   **shameful** scandalous, degrading – because the Countess is married and his subject   **123 niggard ... state** do not be mean or grudging with your royal presence   **125 near** nearer, closer   **130 repulse of wit** the power of reason to drive back

With light to take light from a mortal eye:
For here two day-stars that mine eyes would see,
More than the sun steals mine own light from me:
135 Contemplative desire, desire to be
In contemplation, that may master thee.
Warwick, Artois, to horse and let's away!

COUNTESS What might I speak to make my sovereign stay?

KING EDWARD What needs a tongue to such a speaking eye,   *Aside*
140 That more persuades than winning oratory?

COUNTESS Let not thy presence like the April sun
Flatter our earth and suddenly be done:
More happy do not make our outward wall
Than thou wilt grace our inner house withal.
145 Our house, my liege, is like a country swain
Whose habit rude and manners blunt and plain,
Presageth nought, yet inly beautified
With bounty's riches and fair hidden pride.
For where the golden ore doth buried lie,
150 The ground, undecked with nature's tapestry,
Seems barren, sere, unfertile, fruitless, dry;
And where the upper turf of earth doth boast
His pride, perfumes and particoloured cost,
Delve there and find this issue and their pride
155 To spring from ordure and corruption's side.
But to make up my all too long compare,
These ragged walls no testimony are
What is within, but like a cloak doth hide
From weather's waste, the under-garnished pride:
160 More gracious than my terms can let thee be,
Entreat thyself to stay awhile with me.

KING EDWARD As wise as fair, what fond fit can be heard,   *Aside?*
When wisdom keeps the gate as beauty's guard?
Countess, albeit my business urgeth me,   *To her*
165 It shall attend, while I attend on thee:
Come on my lords, here will I host tonight.   *Exeunt*

133 **two day-stars** i.e. the Countess' eyes   135 **Contemplative ... thee** Edward turns to Platonic theory in the belief it may help him translate his physical desire into a spiritual contemplation of the idea of beauty   138 **might I speak** can I say   141 **Let ... done** don't be like the sun in April which comes, making us believe we will have fine weather, and then rapidly disappears again   145 **swain** fellow of low birth   146 **habit rude** inelegant dress/rough customary manner   147 **Presageth** foretells, promises   **nought** nothing   **inly** inwardly   148 **bounty's** of excellence, virtue   **pride** self-respect, sense of self-worth/splendour   150 **undecked ... tapestry** not decorated with nature's colourful covering (of vegetation)   151 **sere** dry, withered   153 **particoloured** variegated   **cost** manner, way/character/expensive appearance   155 **ordure** excrement, dung   156 **all ... compare** overlong comparison   159 **weather's waste** destruction caused by the weather   **under-garnished pride** splendour underneath   165 **It ... thee** my business can wait while I direct my mind to look after/wait upon you; the play of meaning here suggests the ambiguity of Edward's motives   166 **host** lodge/encamp

[Act 2 Scene 1]

[Enter Lodowick]

LODOWICK   I might perceive his eye in her eye lost,
His ear to drink her sweet tongue's utterance,
And changing passion, like inconstant clouds
That rack upon the carriage of the winds,
5   Increase and die in his disturbèd cheeks.
Lo, when she blushed, even then did he look pale,
As if her cheeks by some enchanted power
Attracted had the cherry blood from his.
Anon, with reverent fear when she grew pale
10   His cheek put on their scarlet ornaments,
But no more like her oriental red
Than brick to coral, or live things to dead.
Why did he then thus counterfeit her looks?
If she did blush 'twas tender modest shame,
15   Being in the sacred presence of a king:
If he did blush 'twas red immodest shame,
To vail his eyes amiss, being a king.
If she looked pale 'twas silly woman's fear,
To bear herself in presence of a king:
20   If he looked pale it was with guilty fear,
To dote amiss being a mighty king.
Then Scottish wars farewell! I fear 'twill prove
A ling'ring English siege of peevish love:
Here comes his highness walking all alone.   *He stands aside*

Enter King Edward

25   KING EDWARD   She is grown more fairer far since I came thither,
Her voice more silver every word than other,
Her wit more fluent: what a strange discourse
Unfolded she of David and his Scots!
'Even thus', quoth she, 'he spake', and then spoke broad
30   With epithets and accents of the Scot—
But somewhat better than the Scot could speak—
'And thus', quoth she, and answered then herself—
For who could speak like her? But she herself
Breathes from the wall an angel's note from heaven
35   Of sweet defiance to her barbarous foes.
When she would talk of peace methinks her tongue

[2.1]   *Location: inside Roxburgh castle*   **3 And ... cheeks** passions come and go rapidly in his cheeks, like racing clouds driven by the winds   **6 even then** at once   **9 Anon** immediately   **reverent** deeply respectful   **10 His ... ornaments** i.e. he blushed   **11 oriental** orient; a term used to describe precious stones, especially pearls, meaning 'superior in brilliancy or lustre'   **17 vail** lower in submission, puns on sense of 'have power or might'   **amiss** wrongly   **18 silly** simple/deserving of compassion/weak, helpless   **21 dote** love to excess, be infatuated   **23 peevish** perverse/foolish/mad/harmful/ distasteful/irritable, querulous   **26 every ... other** each one more than the next   **29 quoth** said   **broad** in dialect   **30 epithets** terms, phrases   **34 wall** i.e. the castle wall as she spoke to the besiegers

Commanded war to prison: when of war,

It wakened Caesar from his Roman grave

To hear war beautified by her discourse.

40 Wisdom is foolishness but in her tongue,

Beauty a slander but in her fair face,

There is no summer but in her cheerful looks,

Nor frosty winter but in her disdain.

I cannot blame the Scots that did besiege her,

45 For she is all the treasure of our land:

But call them cowards that they ran away,

Having so rich and fair a cause to stay.—

Art thou there, Lodowick? Give me ink and paper.

LODOWICK I will, my liege.   *Coming forward*

50 KING EDWARD And bid the lords hold on their play at chess,

For we will walk and meditate alone.

LODOWICK I will, my sovereign.   *[Exit]*

KING EDWARD This fellow is well read in poetry,

And hath a lusty and persuasive spirit:

55 I will acquaint him with my passion,

Which he shall shadow with a veil of lawn,

Through which the queen of beauty's queen shall see

Herself the ground of my infirmity.

Enter Lodowick

KING EDWARD Hast thou pen, ink and paper ready, Lodowick?

60 LODOWICK Ready, my liege.

KING EDWARD Then in the summer arbour sit by me,

Make it our council-house or cabinet:

Since green our thoughts, green be the conventicle,

Where we will ease us by disburd'ning them.

65 Now, Lodowick, invocate some golden muse,

To bring thee hither an enchanted pen

That may for sighs set down true sighs indeed:

Talking of grief, to make thee ready groan,

And when thou writ'st of tears, encouch the word

70 Before and after with such sweet laments

That it may raise drops in a Tartar's eye

And make a flint-heart Scythian pitiful,

For so much moving hath a poet's pen.

Then if thou be a poet move thou so

---

40 but except   **43 disdain** scorn, contempt   **50 hold on** continue   **54 lusty** cheerful, lively   **56 shadow** depict   **lawn** kind of fine linen
57 queen ... queen i.e. the Countess who is so beautiful she is Venus' (the queen of beauty's) queen   **58 ground** cause/basis   **61 arbour** garden, bower
62 council-house building for holding meetings   **cabinet** small chamber or room   **63 green** youthful, concerned with life   **conventicle** meeting
place/meeting with a clandestine, irregular or sinister purpose   **65 invocate** invoke/call in prayer   **muse** inspiring goddess; there were nine in classical
mythology, the daughters of Zeus and Mnesomyne (Memory)   **68 ready** inclined, disposed to   **69 encouch** set down in writing, frame/embroider with
golden thread/cause to lie down/bring down/hide, conceal; the play of meaning is suggestive   **71 Tartar's** of an inhabitant of Tartary in central Asia,
renowned for savagery – Genghis Khan is perhaps glanced at here; **Tartar** was also a slang name for a vagabond or thief   **72 Scythian** member of another
harsh, nomadic tribe; Tamburlaine was the most famous Scythian

75   And be enrichèd by thy sovereign's love:
        For if the touch of sweet concordant strings
        Could force attendance in the ears of hell,
        How much more shall the strains of poets' wit,
        Beguile and ravish soft and human minds?

80 LODOWICK To whom, my lord, shall I direct my style?

    KING EDWARD To one that shames the fair and sots the wise,
        Whose body is an abstract or a brief,
        Contains each general virtue in the world.
        'Better than beautiful' thou must begin;
85   Devise for fair a fairer word than fair,
        And every ornament that thou wouldst praise
        Fly it a pitch above the soar of praise.
        For flattery fear thou not to be convicted,
        For were thy admiration ten times more,
90   Ten times ten thousand more the worth exceeds
        Of that thou art to praise, thy praise's worth.
        Begin! I will to contemplate the while:
        Forget not to set down how passionate,
        How heart-sick and how full of languishment
95   Her beauty makes me.

    LODOWICK Write I to a woman?

    KING EDWARD What beauty else could triumph on me
        Or who but women do our love-lays greet?
        What, think'st thou I did bid thee praise a horse?

100 LODOWICK Of what condition or estate she is
        'Twere requisite that I should know, my lord.

    KING EDWARD Of such estate that hers is as a throne
        And my estate the footstool where she treads:
        Then mayst thou judge what her condition is
105   By the proportion of her mightiness.
        Write on while I peruse her in my thoughts:
        Her voice to music or the nightingale?
        To music every summer-leaping swain
        Compares his sunburnt lover when she speaks.
110   And why should I speak of the nightingale?
        The nightingale sings of adulterate wrong,
        And that compared is too satirical,

---

76 **concordant** harmonious   79 **Beguile** charm, amuse/deceive   **human** human/humane, kindly, as well as usual meaning   80 **style** literary composition/stylus, i.e. pen   81 **sots** makes foolish, besots   82 **abstract ... brief** both mean 'summary, epitome'   87 **pitch** highest point, especially of a bird of prey as it soars before swooping down   **soar** range of upward flight   98 **love-lays** love songs   100 **condition** nature/social position   **estate** state, constitution/social status   107 **Her ... nightingale?** i.e. should I liken her voice to music or the nightingale?   108 **summer-leaping** dancing, skipping/ sexually sportive, during summer   **swain** youth/country bumpkin/lover   109 **sunburnt** considered undesirable and unattractive, a mark of the lower classes   111 **nightingale ... wrong** in classical mythology, Philomel was raped by her brother-in-law, Tereus, King of Thrace, who cut out her tongue to prevent her telling of his misdeeds. Philomel, however, embroidered the story in a tapestry and revealed the truth to her sister, Procne, who killed her son Itys in revenge and fed him to his father. When Philomel brought Itys' head in on a platter, Tereus understood what had happened and drew his sword to kill the sisters but all three were instantly turned into birds by the gods: Philomel into the nightingale who now sings her sad story

For sin though sin would not be so esteemed,
But rather virtue sin, sin virtue deemed.
115 Her hair far softer than the silkworm's twist,
Like to a flattering glass doth make more fair
The yellow amber – 'like a flattering glass'
Comes in too soon! For writing of her eyes,
I'll say that like a glass they catch the sun
120 And thence the hot reflection doth rebound
Against my breast and burns my heart within.
Ah, what a world of descant makes my soul
Upon this voluntary ground of love!
Come, Lodowick, hast thou turned thy ink to gold?
125 If not, write but in letters capital my mistress' name
And it will gild thy paper. Read, lord, read!
Fill thou the empty hollows of mine ears
With the sweet hearing of thy poetry.

LODOWICK I have not to a period brought her praise.

130 KING EDWARD Her praise is as my love, both infinite,
Which apprehend such violent extremes
That they disdain an ending period.
Her beauty hath no match but my affection:
Hers more than most, mine most and more than more,
135 Hers more to praise than tell the sea by drops,
Nay, more than drop, the massy earth by sands,
And sand by sand print them in memory;
Then wherefore talk'st thou of a period
To that which craves unended admiration?
140 Read, let us hear!

LODOWICK More fair and chaste than is the queen of shades—

KING EDWARD That love hath two faults gross and palpable;
Comparest thou her to the pale queen of night
Who, being set in dark, seems therefore light?
145 What is she when the sun lifts up his head,
But like a fading taper dim and dead?
My love shall brave the eye of heaven at noon
And being unmasked outshine the golden sun!

LODOWICK What is the other fault, my sovereign lord?

150 KING EDWARD Read o'er the line again.

LODOWICK More fair and chaste—

---

113 **would not be** does not want to be   **esteemed** thought, considered   114 **deemed** judged/thought   115 **silkworm's twist** i.e. silk   **twist** thread   116 **glass** mirror, looking-glass   117 **amber** an alloy of four parts gold to one part silver   **'like ... soon!** Edward is mentally composing his love lyric, rejecting this version   122 **descant** melodious accompaniment/amplification of a theme (musical term)   123 **voluntary** free, unconstrained/ self-inflicted   126 **gild** cover with gold/turn into money   129 **period** conclusion/high point   132 **disdain** scorn   135 **tell** count   136 **massy** solid   141 **queen of shades** here referring to Diana, goddess of the moon, hunting and chastity, rather than Persephone/Proserpina, wife of Hades/ Pluto   142 **gross** glaring, monstrous/striking/coarse, ignorant   **palpable** manifest, plainly observable   143 **queen of night** the moon   146 **taper** candle, long wick coated in wax and lit, giving a weak light   147 **brave** challenge/adorn

KING EDWARD I did not bid thee talk of chastity,
    To ransack so the treasure of her mind,
    For I had rather have her chased than chaste.
155   Out with the moon line — I will none of it —
    And let me have her likened to the sun.
    Say she hath thrice more splendour than the sun,
    That her perfections emulates the sun,
    That she breeds sweets as plenteous as the sun,
160   That she doth thaw cold winter like the sun,
    That she doth cheer fresh summer like the sun,
    That she doth dazzle gazers like the sun,
    And in this application to the sun,
    Bid her be free and general as the sun,
165   Who smiles upon the basest weed that grows
    As lovingly as on the fragrant rose.
    Let's see what follows that same moonlight line?
LODOWICK More fair and chaste than is the lover of shades,
    More bold in constancy—
170 KING EDWARD In constancy than who?
LODOWICK Than Judith was—
KING EDWARD O monstrous line! Put in the next a sword
    And I shall woo her to cut off my head
    Blot, blot, good Lodowick! Let us hear the next.
175 LODOWICK There's all that yet is done.
KING EDWARD I thank thee then thou hast done little ill,
    But what is done is passing passing ill.
    No, let the captain talk of boist'rous war,
    The prisoner of immured dark constraint,
180   The sick man best sets down the pangs of death,
    The man that starves the sweetness of a feast,
    The frozen soul the benefit of fire,
    And every grief his happy opposite;
    Love cannot sound well but in lovers' tongues.
185   Give me the pen and paper: I will write.
Enter Countess
    But soft, here comes the treasurer of my spirit.
    Lodowick, thou knowst not how to draw a battle;
    These wings, these flankers, and these squadrons
    Argue in thee defective discipline.
190   Thou shouldst have placed this here, this other here.
COUNTESS Pardon my boldness, my thrice-gracious lords,

---

171 Judith a widow who never remarried; in the Bible Judith saved the Israelites by ingratiating herself with Holofernes, the enemy general, and decapitated him in his sleep **177 passing passing ill** extremely bad **186 soft** be quiet **188 These … discipline** Edward pretends that he is discussing military strategy with Lodowick **wings** divisions of an army **flankers** cannons posted to defend a position **squadrons** bodies, detachments of soldiers (drawn up in the formation of a square)

Let my intrusion here be called my duty
That comes to see my sovereign how he fares.

KING EDWARD Go draw the same I tell thee in what form.

195   LODOWICK I go.   [*Exit*]

COUNTESS Sorry I am to see my liege so sad:
What may thy subject do to drive from thee
Thy gloomy consort, solemn melancholy?

KING EDWARD Ah, lady, I am blunt and cannot straw

200   The flowers of solace in a ground of shame;
Since I came hither, Countess, I am wronged.

COUNTESS Now God forbid that any in my house
Should think my sovereign wrong, thrice-gentle king;
Acquaint me with their cause of discontent.

205   [KING EDWARD] How near then shall I be to remedy?

COUNTESS As near, my liege, as all my woman's power
Can pawn itself to buy thy remedy.

KING EDWARD If thou speak'st true then have I my redress;
Engage thy power to redeem my joys,

210   And I am joyful, Countess; else I die.

COUNTESS I will, my liege.

KING EDWARD Swear, Countess, that thou wilt.

COUNTESS By heaven I will.

KING EDWARD Then take thyself a little way aside,

215   And tell thyself a king doth dote on thee.
Say that within thy power doth lie
To make him happy, and that thou hast sworn
To give him all the joy within thy power.
Do this and tell me when I shall be happy.

220   COUNTESS All this is done, my thrice-dread sovereign.
That power of love that I have power to give
Thou hast with all devout obedience;
Employ me how thou wilt in proof thereof.

KING EDWARD Thou hear'st me say that I do dote on thee?

225   COUNTESS If on my beauty take it if thou canst,
Though little I do prize it ten times less:
If on my virtue take it if thou canst,
For virtue's store by giving doth augment.
Be it on what it will that I can give,

230   And thou canst take away, inherit it.

KING EDWARD It is thy beauty that I would enjoy.

COUNTESS O, were it painted I would wipe it off
And dispose myself to give it thee.

---

198 **consort** companion   199 **straw** (strew) conceal, cover the ground with rushes etc.   200 **ground** cause, punning on 'earth', 'soil'   203 **thrice-gentle** extremely gentle, playing ironically on all its meanings: kind/noble/courteous   210 **else** otherwise   220 **thrice-dread** extremely revered/feared/terrible   223 **Employ ... thereof** ask me to prove it in whatever way you like   230 **inherit** receive

But, sovereign, it is soldered to my life:
235   Take one and both, for like an humble shadow
It haunts the sunshine of my summer's life.

[KING EDWARD]   But thou mayst leave it me to sport withal.

COUNTESS   As easy may my intellectual soul
Be lent away and yet my body live
240   As lend my body, palace to my soul,
Away from her and yet retain my soul;
My body is her bower, her court, her abbey,
And she an angel pure divine unspotted.
If I should leave her house, my lord, to thee,
245   I kill my poor soul and my poor soul me.

KING EDWARD   Didst thou not swear to give me what I would?

COUNTESS   I did, my liege, so what you would I could.

KING EDWARD   I wish no more of thee than thou mayst give,
Nor beg I do not but I rather buy,
250   That is thy love, and for that love of thine,
In rich exchange I tender to thee mine.

COUNTESS   But that your lips were sacred, my lord,
You would profane the holy name of love.
That love you offer me you cannot give,
255   For Caesar owes that tribute to his queen.
That love you beg of me I cannot give,
For Sarah owes that duty to her lord.
He that doth clip or counterfeit your stamp
Shall die, my lord; and will your sacred self
260   Commit high treason against the king of heaven
To stamp his image in forbidden metal,
Forgetting your allegiance and your oath?
In violating marriage' sacred law,
You break a greater honour than yourself.
265   To be a king is of a younger house
Than to be married; your progenitor,
Sole-reigning Adam, on the universe
By God was honoured for a married man
But not by him anointed for a king.
270   It is a penalty to break your statutes,
Though not enacted with your highness' hand,
How much more to infringe the holy act
Made by the mouth of God, sealed with his hand?

---

234 **soldered** united, welded   235 **shadow** the idea of beauty as a mere shadow, an external, is Platonic in origin   237 **sport withal** play, amuse myself with however   243 **she** i.e. her soul   246 **would** wanted   251 **tender** offer   252 **But that** were it not for the fact that (as an anointed king)   255 **Caesar** surname of the first Roman emperor, hence emperor, monarch   257 **Sarah ... lord** in the book of Genesis, Sarah was noted for her submission to her husband, Abraham   258 **clip** mutilate (current coin) by paring the edges   **stamp** imprint (on a coin)   263 **In ... yourself** breaking the law of marriage is a greater sacrilege than breaking an oath to yourself since it is made to one worthier than you, i.e. God   266 **progenitor** ancestor, forefather

I know my sovereign in my husband's love,

275 Who now doth loyal service in his wars,

Doth but to try the wife of Salisbury,

Whether she will hear a wanton's tale or no.

Lest being therein guilty by my stay,

From that, not from my liege, I turn away.   *Exit*

280 KING EDWARD Whether is her beauty by her words divine

Or are her words sweet chaplains to her beauty?

Like as the wind doth beautify a sail

And as a sail becomes the unseen wind,

So do her words her beauty's, beauty, words.

285 O, that I were a honey-gathering bee

To bear the comb of virtue from his flower,

And not a poison-sucking envious spider,

To turn the vice I take to deadly venom!

Religion is austere and beauty gentle:

290 Too strict a guardian for so fair a ward.

O, that she were as is the air to me!

Why so she is, for when I would embrace her,

This do I, and catch nothing but myself.   *Embraces the air*

I must enjoy her, for I cannot beat

295 With reason and reproof fond love away.

Enter Warwick

Here comes her father: I will work with him

To bear my colours in this field of love.

WARWICK How is it that my sovereign is so sad?

May I, with pardon, know your highness' grief,

300 And that my old endeavour will remove it,

It shall not cumber long your majesty?

KING EDWARD A kind and voluntary gift thou profferest,

That I was forward to have begged of thee.

But, O thou world, great nurse of flattery,

305 Why dost thou tip men's tongues with golden words

And peise their deeds with weight of heavy lead,

That fair performance cannot follow promise?

O, that a man might hold the heart's close book

And choke the lavish tongue when it doth utter

310 The breath of falsehood not corrected there!

WARWICK Far be it from the honour of my age

That I should owe bright gold and render lead;

Age is a cynic, not a flatterer.

---

274 in ... love for love of my husband   **276 Doth ... try** is doing this only to test   **277 wanton's** lewd, unchaste person's   **278 Lest** in case   **280 Whether is** is it the case that   **283 becomes** graces, befits/gives existence to   **287 poison-sucking envious spider** spiders were proverbially but erroneously believed to be poisonous from sucking poison   **300 And** if   **old endeavour** i.e. my efforts as an old man   **301 cumber** trouble, distress/embarrass, hinder   **302 profferest** offer/propose   **303 forward** ready, eager/presumptuous, immodest   **305 tip** adorn, plays on sense of 'overthrow'   **306 peise** weigh down

I say again, that if I knew your grief,
315   And that by me it may be lessenèd,
My proper harm should buy your highness good.
[KING EDWARD]   These are the vulgar tenders of false men
That never pay the duty of their words.
Thou wilt not stick to swear what thou hast said
320   But, when thou know'st my grief's condition,
This rash disgorgèd vomit of thy word
Thou wilt eat up again and leave me helpless.
WARWICK   By heaven I will not, though your majesty
Did bid me run upon your sword and die.
325   [KING EDWARD]   Say that my grief is no way med'cinable
But by the loss and bruising of thine honour?
WARWICK   If nothing but that loss may vantage you
I would account that loss my vantage too.
KING EDWARD   Thinkst that thou canst unswear thy oath again?
330   WARWICK   I cannot nor I would not if I could.
KING EDWARD   But if thou dost what shall I say to thee?
WARWICK   What may be said to any perjured villain
That break the sacred warrant of an oath.
KING EDWARD   What wilt thou say to one that breaks an oath?
335   WARWICK   That he hath broke his faith with God and man,
And from them both stands excommunicate.
KING EDWARD   What office were it to suggest a man
To break a lawful and religious vow?
WARWICK   An office for the devil not for man.
340   KING EDWARD   That devil's office must thou do for me,
Or break thy oath or cancel all the bonds
Of love and duty twixt thyself and me;
And therefore, Warwick, if thou art thyself,
The lord and master of thy word and oath,
345   Go to thy daughter and, in my behalf,
Command her, woo her, win her any ways,
To be my mistress and my secret love.
I will not stand to hear thee make reply,
Thy oath break hers or let thy sovereign die.   *Exit*
350   [WARWICK]   O doting king! O detestable office!
Well may I tempt myself to wrong myself
When he hath sworn me by the name of God,
To break a vow made by the name of God.
What if I swear by this right hand of mine,

---

316 **proper** real/personal   317 **vulgar tenders** common, customary offers   320 **But ... again** refers to the proverb of the dog returning to its vomit (Proverbs 26:11)   321 **rash disgorgèd** quickly thrown-up   325 **medicinable** curable   326 **But** except   336 **excommunicate** cut off, excluded (especially from the religious community)   337 **office** task, duty   **a man To** that a man should   342 **twixt** between   353 **break a vow** i.e. the Countess' marriage vow

355 To cut this right hand off? The better way
Were to profane the idol than confound it,
But neither will I do; I'll keep mine oath,
And to my daughter make a recantation
Of all the virtue I have preached to her.

360 I'll say she must forget her husband, Salisbury,
If she remember to embrace the king;
I'll say an oath may easily be broken,
But not so easily pardoned being broken.
I'll say it is true charity to love,

365 But not true love to be so charitable;
I'll say his greatness may bear out the shame,
But not his kingdom can buy out the sin.
I'll say it is my duty to persuade,
But not her honesty to give consent.

Enter Countess

370 See where she comes, was never father had
Against his child, an embassage so bad.

COUNTESS My lord and father, I have sought for you:
My mother and the peers importune you
To keep in presence of his majesty

375 And do your best to make his highness merry.

WARWICK How shall I enter in this graceless errand?   *Aside*
I must not call her child, for where's the father
That will in such a suit seduce his child?
Then, 'wife of Salisbury', shall I so begin?

380 No he's my friend, and where is found the friend
That will do friendship such endamagement?
Neither my daughter nor my dear friend's wife: *To the Countess*
I am not Warwick as thou thinkst I am,
But an attorney from the court of hell

385 That thus have housed my spirit in his form
To do a message to thee from the king.
The mighty King of England dotes on thee:
He, that hath power to take away thy life,
Hath power to take thy honour, then consent

390 To pawn thine honour rather than thy life.
Honour is often lost and got again,
But life once gone, hath no recovery.
The sun that withers hay doth nourish grass:
The king that would distain thee will advance thee.

356 profane abuse/treat with irreverence   **idol** adored person or thing/false image   **confound** destroy, overthrow   **358 recantation** retraction/rehearsal   **366 bear out** endure/sustain   **367 not … out** his whole kingdom cannot compensate for   **371 embassage** mission, office   **373 peers** lords **importune** urge   **376 graceless** wicked, ungodly   **381 endamagement** injury, loss   **384 attorney** agent/advocate/law officer   **385 housed … form** have taken on Warwick's outward appearance   **386 message** errand/communication   **390 pawn** give or deposit as a pledge   **394 distain** defile, dishonour

395   The poets write that great Achilles' spear
       Could heal the wound it made: the moral is,
       What mighty men misdo, they can amend.
       The lion doth become his bloody jaws,
       And grace his foragement by being mild
400   When vassal fear lies trembling at his feet.
       The king will in his glory hide thy shame,
       And those that gaze on him to find out thee,
       Will lose their eye-sight looking in the sun.
       What can one drop of poison harm the sea,
405   Whose hugy vastures can digest the ill
       And make it lose his operation?
       The king's great name will temper thy misdeeds
       And give the bitter portion of reproach
       A sugared, sweet, and most delicious taste.
410   Besides it is no harm to do the thing
       Which, without shame, could not be left undone.
       Thus have I, in his majesty's behalf,
       Apparelled sin in virtuous sentences,
       And dwell upon thy answer in his suit.
415   COUNTESS Unnatural besiege, woe me unhappy,
       To have escaped the danger of my foes
       And to be ten times worse envired by friends!
       Hath he no means to stain my honest blood,
       But to corrupt the author of my blood
420   To be his scandalous and vile solicitor?
       No marvel though the branches be then infected
       When poison hath encompassèd the root.
       No marvel though the leprous infant die,
       When the stern dame envenometh the dug:
425   Why then, give sin a passport to offend
       And youth the dangerous reign of liberty:
       Blot out the strict forbidding of the law,
       And cancel every canon that prescribes
       A shame for shame, or penance for offence.
430   No! Let me die if his too boisterous will
       Will have it so, before I will consent

---

395 **Achilles' … made** refers to Telephus in classical mythology who was cured by scraping the rust from the spear of Achilles which had wounded him   398 **become** grace, befit   399 **And … feet** refers to the belief that lions will not attack weak or submissive prey   **foragement** hunting for food   **vassal** subject   401 **glory** exalted position/magnificence/boastful spirit   402 **those … sun** plays on the king/sun metaphor and the idea that looking at the sun can cause blindness; hence those who try to scrutinize the king to discover the Countess' infidelity will be injured by his power   405 **hugy vastures** huge vastnesses   406 **operation** poisonous power   407 **temper** mitigate, assuage   408 **portion of reproach** fate/share of shame, disgrace   410 **Besides … undone** excuse on the basis of expediency; you can't be blamed for what you're forced to do in this situation   413 **Apparelled** clothed, dressed up   414 **dwell upon** wait for/consider, reflect on   417 **envired** beset, surrounded   419 **author … blood** i.e. my father   423 **leprous** afflicted with leprosy; in this instance perhaps simply poisoned by the teat which has been treated to hasten the weaning process   424 **stern dame** harsh nurse   **envenometh** poisons, i.e. paints with substance such as wormwood to make the nipple taste unpleasant   **dug** teat, nipple   428 **canon** rule, law   430 **boisterous** violent, savage

To be an actor in his graceless lust.

WARWICK   Why now thou speakst as I would have thee speak:

And mark how I unsay my words again.

435   An honorable grave is more esteemed

Than the polluted closet of a king.

The greater man, the greater is the thing,

Be it good or bad that he shall undertake;

An unreputed mote flying in the sun

440   Presents a greater substance than it is;

The freshest summer's day doth soonest taint

The loathèd carrion that it seems to kiss;

Deep are the blows made with a mighty axe;

That sin doth ten times aggravate itself

445   That is committed in a holy place.

An evil deed done by authority

Is sin and subornation: deck an ape

In tissue and the beauty of the robe

Adds but the greater scorn unto the beast.

450   A spacious field of reasons could I urge

Between his glory, daughter, and thy shame:

That poison shows worst in a golden cup;

Dark night seems darker by the lightning flash;

Lilies that fester smell far worse than weeds;

455   And every glory that inclines to sin,

The shame is treble by the opposite.

So leave I with my blessing in thy bosom

Which then convert to a most heavy curse,

When thou convertest from honour's golden name,

460   To the black faction of bed-blotting shame.

COUNTESS   I'll follow thee, and when my mind turns so,

My body sink my soul in endless woe.   *Exeunt*

[Act 2 Scene 2]

Enter at one door Derby from France, at another door, Audley with a Drum

DERBY   Thrice-noble Audley, well encountered here.

How is it with our sovereign and his peers?

AUDLEY   'Tis full a fortnight since I saw his highness,

What time he sent me forth to muster men,

5   Which I accordingly have done and bring them hither,

---

432 **actor** participant/performer   **436 closet** private apartment, plays on the obsolete sense of 'sewer'   **439 unreputed** unconsidered/unregarded   **mote** particle (of dust)/fault   **442 carrion** corpse/dead meat   **447 subornation** procurement of a crime   **deck** dress, adorn   **448 tissue** rich cloth, interwoven with gold or silver   **454 Lilies ... weeds** this line is identical with the last line of Shakespeare's Sonnet 94; the idea was proverbial   **460 faction** manner of acting/class of persons   **bed-blotting** i.e. adultery that stains the marriage bed   **[2.2]** *Location: Roxburgh castle*   *Drum* drummer/small party sent to carry a message or parley with the enemy   **4 What time** when, at which time

In fair array before his majesty.

What news, my lord of Derby, from the emperor?

DERBY   As good as we desire: the emperor

Hath yielded to his highness friendly aid,

10 And makes our king lieutenant-general

In all his lands and large dominions,

Then *via* for the spacious bounds of France.

AUDLEY   What, doth his highness leap to hear these news?

DERBY   I have not yet found time to open them;

15 The king is in his closet malcontent,

For what I know not, but he gave in charge

Till after dinner, none should interrupt him.

The Countess Salisbury and her father Warwick,

Artois and all look underneath the brows.

20 AUDLEY   Undoubtedly, then, something is amiss.   *Trumpets sound*

Enter the King

DERBY   The trumpets sound, the king is now abroad.

AUDLEY   Here comes his highness.

DERBY   Befall, my sovereign, all my sovereign's wish.

KING EDWARD   Ah, that thou wert a witch to make it so!   *Aside*

25 DERBY   The emperor greeteth you.

KING EDWARD   Would it were the Countess.   *Aside*

DERBY   And hath accorded to your highness' suit.

KING EDWARD   Thou liest she hath not, but I would she had.   *Aside*

AUDLEY   All love and duty to my lord the king.

30 KING EDWARD   Well all but one is none!— What news with you?   *Aside*

AUDLEY   I have, my liege, levied those horse and foot

According as your charge and brought them hither.

KING EDWARD   Then let those foot trudge hence upon those horse

According to our discharge and be gone.

35 Derby, I'll look upon the Countess' mind anon.

DERBY   The Countess' mind, my liege?

KING EDWARD   I mean the emperor; leave me alone.

AUDLEY   What is his mind?

DERBY   Let's leave him to his humour.   *Exeunt [Derby and Audley]*

40 KING EDWARD   Thus from the heart's abundance speaks the tongue:

Countess for emperor, and indeed why not?

She is as imperator over me, and I to her

Am as a kneeling vassal that observes

The pleasure or displeasure of her eye.

---

6 **fair array** good order   7 **emperor** i.e. the Emperor of Almaine, Germany   10 **lieutenant-general** one who has command over a wide area   12 *via*
onward, let's go (Italian)   **bounds** borderlands/territories   15 **closet** private chamber   **malcontent** discontented   16 **gave in charge** ordered
19 **underneath the brows** i.e. with downcast eyes   21 **abroad** about   23 **Befall** may it come about for   24 **that thou wert** if only you were   **witch**
magician   27 **accorded** agreed   31 **horse and foot** cavalry and infantry soldiers   33 **trudge hence** march heavily away, back   35 **anon** at once
40 **abundance** overflowing state   42 **imperator** 'commander' (Latin), hence emperor   43 **vassal** servant, subordinate

Enter Lodowick

45   KING EDWARD   What says the more than Cleopatra's match

To Caesar now?

LODOWICK   That yet, my liege, ere night,

She will resolve your majesty.   *Drum sounds*

KING EDWARD   What drum is this that thunders forth this march,

50   To start the tender Cupid in my bosom?

Poor sheepskin how it brawls with him that beateth it!

Go break the thund'ring parchment bottom out

And I will teach it to conduct sweet lines

Unto the bosom of a heavenly nymph:

55   For I will use it as my writing paper,

And so reduce him from a scolding drum,

To be the herald and dear counsel-bearer,

Betwixt a goddess, and a mighty king.

Go bid the drummer learn to touch the lute

60   Or hang him in the braces of his drum;

For now we think it an uncivil thing,

To trouble heaven with such harsh resounds. Away!   *Exit [Lodowick]*

The quarrel that I have requires no arms

But these of mine and these shall meet my foe

65   In a deep march of penetrable groans.

My eyes shall be my arrows and my sighs

Shall serve me, as the vantage of the wind,

To whirl away my sweetest artillery.

Ah, but alas she wins the sun of me,

70   For that is she herself, and thence it comes

That poets term the wanton warrior blind.

But love hath eyes as judgement to his steps,

Till too much lovèd glory dazzles them—

Enter Lodowick

How now?

75   LODOWICK   My liege, the drum that stroke the lusty march,

Stands with Prince Edward, your thrice-valiant son.   *[Exit Lodowick]*

Enter Prince Edward

KING EDWARD   I see the boy.— O, how his mother's face,   *Aside*

45 Cleopatra's ... Caesar As the Roman Julius Caesar was in love with the Egyptian queen, Edward suggests that he has even more reason to be in love with the Countess who is Cleopatra's superior   **47 ere** before   **48 resolve** answer/satisfy/join with another's opinion/advise of a decision, inform/convince, but ironically the term also means 'cause to melt/disintegrate'   **50 start** startle, awake suddenly   **tender ... bosom** his love for the Countess   **Cupid** the god of love, Venus' son   **51 Poor ... it!** Edward suggests it sounds as though the drummer is quarrelling with his drum; the membrane covering the drum was made of **sheepskin**   **52 parchment bottom** sheepskin covering the base of the drum; sheepskin could also be used for writing, hence **writing paper** (line 55)   **53 conduct** compose   **54 nymph** in classical mythology, a semi-divine spirit in the form of a beautiful maiden but could also mean 'prostitute, woman used for sexual gratification'   **56 him** either the instrument personified or the drummer   **57 counsel-bearer** go-between   **59 touch** play   **lute** stringed instrument associated with love   **60 braces** straps   **62 resounds** reverberations   **63 arms ... foe** Edward imagines his wooing of the Countess as a battle of single combat; such metaphorical play on the relationship between love and war was a poetic commonplace   **65 deep ... groans** sexual intercourse, culminating in penetration and the sounds of orgasm   **67 vantage** advantage, position of superiority/opportunity, perhaps playing on 'ventage' (from 'vent', French for 'wind'), means of escape for air   **68 sweetest artillery** most loving looks   **69 wins ... of** steals the sun from   **70 thence ... blind** that's why poets call Cupid/the lover blind; Cupid was depicted blindfold carrying a bow and arrow   **72 as judgement** presiding over   **75 drum ... march** the drummer who was playing the lively march

Modelled in his, corrects my strayed desire

And rates my heart and chides my thievish eye,

80   Who being rich enough in seeing her,

Yet seek elsewhere; and basest theft is that

Which cannot cloak itself on poverty.—

Now boy, what news?

PRINCE EDWARD   I have assembled, my dear lord and father,

85   The choicest buds of all our English blood,

For our affairs to France, and here we come,

To take direction from your majesty.

KING EDWARD   Still do I see in him delineate,   *Aside*

His mother's visage: those his eyes are hers,

90   Who, looking wistly on me, make me blush;

For faults against themselves give evidence:

Lust as a fire, and me like lanterns show

Light lust within themselves, even through themselves.

Away loose silks of wavering vanity!

95   Shall the large limit of fair Brittany

By me be overthrown, and shall I not

Master this little mansion of myself?

Give me an armour of eternal steel!

I go to conquer kings; and shall I not then

100   Subdue myself and be my enemy's friend?

It must not be.— Come boy, forward, advance,

Let's with our colours sweet the air of France.

Enter Lodowick

LODOWICK   My liege, the Countess with a smiling cheer

Desires access unto your majesty.

105   KING EDWARD   Why there it goes, that very smile of hers,

Hath ransomed captive France, and set the king,

The dauphin and the peers at liberty.

Go leave me, Ned, and revel with thy friends.   *Exit Prince*

Thy mother is but black, and thou like her

110   Dost put it in my mind how foul she is.

Go: fetch the Countess hither in thy hand,   *Exit Lodowick*

And let her chase away these winter clouds,

For she gives beauty both to heaven and earth.

The sin is more to hack and hew poor men

115   Than to embrace in an unlawful bed

---

78 **Modelled** patterned   79 **rates** berates, scolds   82 **cloak ... poverty** claim poverty as an excuse to justify itself   85 **buds** young persons (a term of endearment)   88 **delineate** delineated, traced out   89 **visage** face   90 **wistly** with close attention, intently   92 **Lust ... themselves** a difficult line but the general sense is that both he and lust reveal themselves through the light that shines through them   **lanterns** ('lanthorns') transparent cases of horn or glass containing and protecting light   94 **silks** soft, light, indoor clothing   **wavering** inconstant   102 **sweet** sweeten   103 **cheer** countenance   107 **dauphin** (French), the French heir apparent   109 **black** dark, brunette, considered both unattractive physically and associated morally with evil

The register of all rarities

Since leathern Adam till this youngest hour.

Enter Countess [with Lodowick]

KING EDWARD Go, Lodowick, put thy hand into thy purse,

Play, spend, give, riot, waste, do what thou wilt,

120 So thou wilt hence awhile and leave me here.   *[Exit Lodowick]*

Now, my soul's playfellow, art thou come

To speak the more than heavenly word of 'yea',

To my objection in thy beauteous love?

COUNTESS My father on his blessing hath commanded.

125 KING EDWARD That thou shalt yield to me?

COUNTESS Ay, dear my liege, your due.

KING EDWARD And that, my dearest love, can be no less

Than right for right, and render love for love.

COUNTESS Than wrong for wrong, and endless hate for hate.

130 But sith I see your majesty so bent,

That my unwillingness, my husband's love,

Your high estate, nor no respect respected,

Can be my help, but that your mightiness

Will overbear and awe these dear regards,

135 I bind my discontent to my content

And, what I would not, I'll compel I will,

Provided that yourself remove those lets,

That stand between your highness' love and mine.

KING EDWARD Name them, fair Countess, and by heaven I will.

140 COUNTESS It is their lives that stand between our love

That I would have choked up, my sovereign.

KING EDWARD Whose lives, my lady?

COUNTESS My thrice-loving liege,

Your queen, and Salisbury my wedded husband,

145 Who living have that title in our love,

That we cannot bestow but by their death.

KING EDWARD Thy opposition is beyond our law.

COUNTESS So is your desire; if the law

Can hinder you to execute the one,

150 Let it forbid you to attempt the other.

I cannot think you love me as you say,

Unless you do make good what you have sworn.

[KING EDWARD] No more, thy husband and the queen shall die.

Fairer thou art by far, than Hero was,

---

116 **register ... rarities** catalogue of all excellences, i.e. the Countess 117 **Since ... hour** from the beginning of the world till now **leathern** skin-clad 118 **purse** slang for 'scrotum'; in the following two lines, Edward invites Lodowick to go away and masturbate 123 **objection** object of succeeding 126 **due** what you deserve 130 **sith** since **bent** determined 136 **what ... will** I'll make myself do what I do not wish 137 **lets** hindrances 145 **living** as long as they're alive **title** legal claim, right 146 **bestow** grant 154 **Hero ... lies** Edward is alluding to the story of **Hero** and **Leander**; in classical mythology, Leander was from Abydos and Hero a priestess in the temple of the goddess Aphrodite (Roman Venus) at **Sestos**; Leander died one night while swimming the **Hellespont** (now the Dardanelles), the body of water which divided the lovers; the best-known version is Christopher Marlowe's poem (1598)

155   Beardless Leander not so strong as I:

He swam an easy current for his love,

But I will through a Hellespont of blood,

To arrive at Sestos where my Hero lies.

COUNTESS Nay, you'll do more, you'll make the river too

160   With their heart bloods, that keep our love asunder,

Of which my husband and your wife are twain.

KING EDWARD Thy beauty makes them guilty of their death,

And gives in evidence that they shall die,

Upon which verdict, I, their judge, condemn them.

165 COUNTESS O, perjured beauty, more corrupted judge:

When to the great Star-chamber o'er our heads,

The universal sessions calls to count

This packing evil, we both shall tremble for it.

KING EDWARD What says my fair love, is she resolute?

170 COUNTESS Resolute to be dissolute, and therefore this.

Keep but thy word great king, and I am thine.

Stand where thou dost — I'll part a little from thee —   *Standing aside*

And see how I will yield me to thy hands;

Here by my side doth hang my wedding knives,

175   Take thou the one and with it kill thy queen

And learn by me to find her where she lies,

And with this other I'll dispatch my love,

Which now lies fast asleep within my heart.

When they are gone, then I'll consent to love.

180   Stir not, lascivious king, to hinder me;

My resolution is more nimbler far

Than thy prevention can be in my rescue,

And if thou stir, I strike, therefore stand still

And hear the choice that I will put thee to:

185   Either swear to leave thy most unholy suit,

And never henceforth to solicit me,

Or else by heaven, this sharp pointed knife

Shall stain thy earth with that which thou would stain,

My poor chaste blood. Swear, Edward, swear,

190   Or I will strike and die before thee here.

KING EDWARD Even by that power I swear that gives me now

The power to be ashamèd of myself.

I never mean to part my lips again

In any words that tends to such a suit.

195   Arise true English lady whom our isle

---

160 asunder apart   **161 twain** two elements   **165 perjured** false, deceitful/that has broken an oath   **166 Star-chamber** court of the king's council, here used to signify God's court in heaven   **167 sessions** legal sittings, i.e. Judgement Day   **count** reckon/consider   **168 packing** fraudulent, underhand **174 wedding knives** a pair of knives worn at the girdle by the bride   **176 learn ... heart** the Countess is suggesting in fact that they each kill themselves **180 Stir not** do not move   **lascivious** lewd, wanton   **hinder** prevent

May better boast of than ever Roman might
Of her whose ransacked treasury hath tasked
The vain endeavour of so many pens.
Arise and be my fault thy honour's fame,
200   Which after ages shall enrich thee with:
I am awakèd from this idle dream.
Warwick, my son, Derby, Artois and Audley,
Brave warriors all, where are you all this while?
          Enter all [Warwick, Prince Edward, Derby, Artois and Audley]
Warwick, I make thee Warden of the North,
205   Thou Prince of Wales, and Audley straight to sea,
Scour to Newhaven, some there stay for me.
Myself, Artois and Derby will through Flanders
To greet our friends there, and to crave their aid.
This night will scarce suffice me to discover
210   My folly's siege against a faithful lover,
For ere the sun shall gild the eastern sky,
We'll wake him with our martial harmony.   *Exeunt*

[Act 3 Scene 1]

Enter King John of France, his two sons, Charles of Normandy and Philip, and the Duke of Lorraine

KING JOHN   Here, till our navy of a thousand sail
Have made a breakfast to our foe by sea,
Let us encamp to wait their happy speed.
Lorraine, what readiness is Edward in?
5   How hast thou heard that he provided is
Of martial furniture for this exploit?
LORRAINE   To lay aside unnecessary soothing,
And not to spend the time in circumstance,
'Tis bruited for a certainty, my lord,
10   That he's exceeding strongly fortified;
His subjects flock as willingly to war
As if unto a triumph they were led.
CHARLES   England was wont to harbour malcontents,
Bloodthirsty, and seditious Catilines,

196 **Roman … pens** a reference to Roman Lucrece who was raped by King Tarquin and then killed herself; Shakespeare's poem *The Rape of Lucrece* (1594) is the most famous version   199 **be … fame** may your fame live in after times because of my moral defect   206 **Scour** hasten, go rapidly   **Newhaven** English south-coast port convenient for the journey to Flanders   209 **suffice** be enough for   **discover** reveal   211 **ere** before   212 **martial harmony** military music/agreement to fight together   [3.1]   *Location: near the Flanders' coast*   *Charles of Normandy* Prince Charles, King John's older son, was Duke of Normandy and the dauphin or heir apparent to the French crown   1 **sail** i.e. ships   2 **made … to** swallowed up/destroyed   3 **speed** success   6 **martial furniture** military equipment/provisions   **exploit** military or naval expedition   7 **soothing** maintaining a lie as being true/ encouragement/flattery   8 **circumstance** going over the details   9 **bruited** reported, rumoured   12 **triumph** solemn procession granted to a victorious commander to enter Rome   13 **malcontents** discontented, disaffected persons inclined to rebellion   14 **Catilines** members of the Catiline conspiracy in ancient Rome designed to overthrow the republic

15   Spendthrifts, and such as gape for nothing else
        But changing and alteration of the state.
        And is it possible
        That they are now so loyal in themselves?

LORRAINE   All but the Scot, who solemnly protests,
20   As heretofore I have informed his grace
        Never to sheathe his sword, or take a truce.

KING JOHN   Ah, that's the anch'rage of some better hope!
        But on the other side, to think what friends
        King Edward hath retained in Netherlands,
25   Among those ever-bibbing epicures,
        Those frothy Dutchmen puffed with double beer,
        That drink and swill in every place they come,
        Doth not a little aggravate mine ire.
        Besides we hear the emperor conjoins,
30   And stalls him in his own authority.
        But all the mightier that their number is
        The greater glory reaps the victory,
        Some friends have we beside domestic power,
        The stern Polonian and the warlike Dane:
35   The King of Bohemia, and of Sicily.
        Are all become confederates with us
        And, as I think, are marching hither apace.
        But soft, I hear the music of their drums,   *Drums sound*
        By which I guess that their approach is near.

*Enter the King of Bohemia with Danes, and a Polonian Captain with other soldiers
another way*

40 KING OF BOHEMIA   King John of France, as league and neighbourhood,
        Requires when friends are any way distressed,
        I come to aid thee with my country's force.

POLONIAN CAPTAIN   And from great Moscow, fearful to the Turk,
        And lofty Poland, nurse of hardy men,
45   I bring these servitors to fight for thee
        Who willingly will venture in thy cause.

KING JOHN   Welcome, Bohemian king, and welcome all!
        This, your great kindness, I will not forget.
        Besides your plentiful rewards in crowns
50   That from our treasury ye shall receive,
        There comes a hare-brained nation decked in pride,

---

15 gape eagerly desire/shout   **19 Scot** i.e. King David   **20 heretofore** formerly   **his grace** i.e. King John; Lorraine is responding to Charles'
question   **22 anch'rage** (anchorage) something on which to depend   **25 ever-bibbing** constantly drinking   **epicures** those given up to sensual
indulgence/unbelievers in divine government; followers of the Greek philosopher Epicurus   **26 Those ... beer** the Dutch had a reputation as heavy drinkers
of strong (**double**) beer, hence **frothy** from the foam on beer   **28 ire** anger   **29 conjoins** unites with him   **30 stalls** installs, establishes in a position of rule
or dignity   **33 domestic power** i.e. French troops   **34 stern Polonian** native of Poland, reputed to be grim and resolute in battle   **35 Bohemia** kingdom
in central Europe, now part of the Czech Republic   **37 apace** with speed   **38 soft** hush   **45 servitors** soldiers   **49 crowns** gold coins, issued by Philip of
Valois with a large crown on the obverse side   **51 hare-brained** rash, reckless   **decked** adorned, embellished

The spoil of whom will be a treble gain.

And now my hope is full, my joy complete:

At sea we are as puissant as the force

55 Of Agamemnon in the haven of Troy:

By land with Xerxes we compare of strength,

Whose soldiers drank up rivers in their thirst:

Then Bayard-like, blind overweening Ned,

To reach at our imperial diadem,

60 Is either to be swallowed of the waves,

Or hacked a-pieces when thou com'st ashore.

Enter [Mariner]

MARINER   Near to the coast I have descried, my lord,

As I was busy in my watchful charge,

The proud armado of King Edward's ships,

65 Which at the first far off when I did ken,

Seemed as it were a grove of withered pines,

But drawing near, their glorious bright aspect,

Their streaming ensigns wrought of coloured silk,

Like to a meadow full of sundry flowers,

70 Adorns the naked bosom of the earth.

Majestical the order of their course,

Figuring the hornèd circle of the moon,

And on the top gallant of the admiral

And likewise all the handmaids of his train,

75 The arms of England and of France unite

Are quartered equally by herald's art.

Thus titely carried with a merry gale

They plough the ocean hitherward amain:

[KING JOHN]   Dare he already crop the flower-de-luce?

80 I hope the honey being gathered thence,

He with the spider afterward approached

Shall suck forth deadly venom from the leaves.

But where's our navy? How are they prepared

To wing themselves against this flight of ravens?

85 MARINER   They, having knowledge brought them by the scouts,

Did break from anchor straight, and puffed with rage,

---

52 **spoil** booty, plunder/destruction   **treble gain** (1) the French king's gratitude, (2) the crowns, (3) sharing the spoils   54 **puissant** mighty, powerful
55 **Agamemnon … Troy** a reference to the Trojan war; **Agamemnon** was leader of the Greeks who sailed to the harbour (**haven**) and besieged Troy
56 **Xerxes** Xerxes the Great, king of the mighty Persian empire who conquered Greece in the fifth century BC   58 **Bayard-like** characterized by the
blindness and self-confidence of ignorance; from Bayard, the magic horse given by Charlemagne to Rinaldo in medieval romance   **overweening** arrogant,
self-opinionated   **Ned** Edward   59 **diadem** crown   61 **a-pieces** to pieces   62 **descried** observed   64 **armado** fleet of warships   65 **ken** catch sight
of   66 **withered pines** pine trees without branches   68 **ensigns** flags   **wrought** made   69 **sundry** various different   72 **Figuring** in the shape of
73 **top gallant** highest flag flown from the mizzen-mast, i.e. the mast aft or behind the mainmast of a ship   **admiral** the flagship which carries the naval
commander   74 **likewise … train** all the ships under his command did the same   75 **arms … art** the English fleet are flying flags on which the herald,
responsible for recording the names and pedigrees of those entitled to bear arms, has combined the English and French coats of arms thereby officially
recognizing Edward's claim to the French crown   **unite** united   77 **titely** quickly, speedily   78 **amain** at full speed   79 **flower-de-luce** *fleur-de-lis*
(French); the heraldic lily, symbol of the French monarchy   81 **spider … venom** another reference to the belief that spiders sucked up poison and hence were
poisonous   86 **Did … straight** instantly drew up their anchors and set sail

No otherwise than were their sails with wind
Made forth, as when the empty eagle flies
To satisfy his hungry griping maw.

90   KING JOHN   There's for thy news. Return unto thy bark,   *Gives money*
And if thou scape the bloody stroke of war
And do survive the conflict, come again,
And let us hear the manner of the fight.   *Exit [Mariner]*
Mean space, my lords, 'tis best we be dispersed
95   To several places lest they chance to land.
First you, my lord, with your Bohemian troops,
Shall pitch your battles on the lower hand;
My eldest son, the Duke of Normandy,
Together with this aid of Muscovites,
100   Shall climb the higher ground another way:
Here in the middle cost betwixt you both,
Philip, my youngest boy, and I will lodge.
So, lords, begone, and look unto your charge,   *Exeunt [all but King*
You stand for France, an empire fair and large.   *John and Philip]*
105   Now tell me, Philip, what is thy conceit
Touching the challenge that the English make?
PHILIP   I say, my lord, claim Edward what he can
And bring he ne'er so plain a pedigree,
'Tis you are in possession of the crown
110   And that's the surest point of all the law:
But were it not, yet ere he should prevail,
I'll make a conduit of my dearest blood
Or chase those straggling upstarts home again.
KING JOHN   Well said, young Philip, call for bread and wine,
115   That we may cheer our stomachs with repast,   *The battle heard afar off*
To look our foes more sternly in the face.
Now is begun the heavy day at sea;
Fight Frenchmen, fight, be like the field of bears
When they defend their younglings in their caves.
120   Steer, angry Nemesis, the happy helm
That with the sulphur battles of your rage,
The English fleet may be dispersed and sunk.
PHILIP   O, father! How this echoing cannon shot   *Shot [is heard]*
Like sweet harmony digests my cates.
125   [KING JOHN]   Now, boy, thou hear'st what thund'ring terror 'tis

---

89 griping maw painful, spasmodically constricting crop or craw of a bird   **90 bark** ship   **91 scape** escape   **94 Mean space** meanwhile   **97 battles** battalions, bodies or lines of troops   **101 cost** way, disposition   **105 thy conceit** your conception, understanding   **106 Touching** concerning **108 bring ... pedigree** however pure an ancestral line he is able to produce   **109 'Tis ... law** proverbial: 'Possession is nine tenths of the law'   **111 But ... prevail** even if that wasn't the case, still before he was able to succeed   **112 conduit** channel/fountain   **113 upstarts** arrogant, presumptuous persons   **115 repast** food, a meal   **118 field of bears** bears or the place where they fight; bear-baiting was a popular, bloody form of entertainment   **120 Nemesis** in classical mythology, the goddess of retribution who punishes presumption or wrongdoing   **121 sulphur** applied to thunder and lightning/gun powder **124 Like ... digests** referring to the belief that music was an aid to digestion   **cates** foods, delicacies

To buckle for a kingdom's sovereignty:
The earth with giddy trembling when it shakes
Or when the exhalations of the air
Breaks in extremity of lightning flash,
130 Affrights not more than kings when they dispose
To show the rancour of their high swoll'n hearts.
Retreat is sounded, one side hath the worse—   *Retreat [is heard]*
O, if it be the French, sweet fortune turn
And in thy turning change the froward winds,
135 That with advantage of a favouring sky,
Our men may vanquish and th'other fly.
    Enter Mariner
My heart misgives: say, mirror of pale death,
To whom belongs the honour of this day?
Relate I pray thee, if thy breath will serve,
140 The sad discourse of this discomfiture.
    MARINER   I will, my lord.
My gracious sovereign, France hath ta'en the foil,
And boasting Edward triumphs with success.
These iron-hearted navies,
145 When last I was reporter to your grace,
Both full of angry spleen of hope and fear,
Hasting to meet each other in the face,
At last conjoined, and by their admiral,
Our admiral encountered many shot.
150 By this, the other, that beheld these twain
Give earnest-penny of a further wrack,
Like fiery dragons took their haughty flight,
And, likewise meeting, from their smoky wombs
Sent many grim ambassadors of death.
155 Then 'gan the day to turn to gloomy night
And darkness did as well enclose the quick,
As those that were but newly reft of life.
No leisure served for friends to bid farewell
And if it had, the hideous noise was such
160 As each to other seemèd deaf and dumb.
Purple the sea whose channel filled as fast
With streaming gore that from the maimèd fell,
As did her gushing moisture break into

---

126 **buckle** grapple, engage with an enemy   **sovereignty** power   128 **exhalations** what is breathed forth/vapours   130 **Affrights not more** is not more terrifying   **dispose** make preparation/decide   131 **rancour** resentment, animosity   134 **froward** perverse, refractory/ungovernable   137 **misgives** is filled with apprehension, foreboding   **mirror ... death** the Mariner, who appears deadly pale   140 **discourse** tale, history   **discomfiture** overthrow, defeat in battle   142 **foil** repulse, defeat   146 **spleen** temper, courage/eagerness, impetuosity   147 **in the face** head on   148 **conjoined** came together **by their admiral** from their flagship   149 **shot** cannonballs   150 **By this** by this time   **the other** the rest, others   151 **earnest-penny** down-payment, a small sum of money paid as an instalment to secure a bargain   **wrack** disaster   153 **meeting** i.e. in battle   **wombs** entrails   154 **grim ambassadors** fierce, stern messengers/representatives   156 **quick** living   157 **newly ... life** recently killed   162 **gore** blood

The crannied cleftures of the through-shot planks.
165 Here flew a head dissevered from the trunk,
There mangled arms and legs were tossed aloft
As when a whirlwind takes the summer dust,
And scatters it in middle of the air.
Then might ye see the reeling vessels split
170 And tottering sink into the ruthless flood,
Until their lofty tops were seen no more.
All shifts were tried both for defence and hurt,
And now th'effect of valour and of force,
Of resolution and of a cowardice
175 Were lively pictured, how the one for fame
The other by compulsion laid about:
Much did the *Nonpareille*, that brave ship,
So did the *Black Snake of Boulogne*, than which
A bonnier vessel never yet spread sail,
180 But all in vain, both sun, the wind and tide,
Revolted all unto our foemen's side,
That we perforce were fain to give them way,
And they are landed. Thus my tale is done;
We have untimely lost, and they have won.
185 KING JOHN   Then rests there nothing but with present speed
To join our several forces all in one,
And bid them battle ere they range too far.
Come, gentle Philip, let us hence depart;
This soldier's words have pierced thy father's heart.   *Exeunt*

[Act 3 Scene 2]

Enter two Frenchmen, a Woman and two little children, meet them and other Citizens

FIRST CITIZEN   Well met, my masters! How now, what's the news?
And wherefore are ye laden thus with stuff?
What is it quarter day that you remove,
And carry bag and baggage too?
5 SECOND CITIZEN   Quarter day? Ay, and quartering day I fear!
Have we not heard the news that flies abroad?
FIRST CITIZEN   What news?
THIRD CITIZEN   How the French navy is destroyed at sea

---

164 **crannied cleftures** chinks, small holes   **through-shot** shot through   165 **dissevered** broken off   166 **aloft** upwards   172 **shifts** measures, devices/ strategies   **hurt** attack   176 **by compulsion** because they were forced (to fight)   177 **Nonpareille** name of a ship, meaning 'peerless' (French) 178 **Black Snake of Boulogne** name of a ship   182 **perforce** by constraint/unavoidably   **fain** necessitated, obliged   184 **untimely** inopportunely, at a bad time   187 **bid** invite/command/challenge   **range** roam, wander   188 **gentle** noble   [3.2] *Location: the coast of Normandy*   1 **masters** polite term of address   3 **quarter day** each of four fixed days throughout the year on which tenancies begin and end, payments fall due etc.   5 **quartering** being cut into quarters, i.e. from the treatment expected from the English troops: being 'hung, drawn and quartered'

And that the English army is arrived.

10   FIRST CITIZEN   What then?

SECOND CITIZEN   'What then', quoth you? Why is't not time to fly

When envy and destruction is so nigh?

FIRST CITIZEN   Content thee, man, they are far enough from hence,

And will be met, I warrant ye, to their cost

15   Before they break so far into the realm.

SECOND CITIZEN   Ay, so the grasshopper doth spend the time,

In mirthful jollity till winter come,

And then too late he would redeem his time,

When frozen cold hath nipped his careless head.

20   He that no sooner will provide a cloak

Than when he sees it doth begin to rain

May peradventure for his negligence,

Be throughly washed when he suspects it not.

We that have charge and such a train as this

25   Must look in time to look for them and us,

Lest when we would, we cannot be relieved.

FIRST CITIZEN   Belike you then despair of ill success

And think your country will be subjugate.

THIRD CITIZEN   We cannot tell; 'tis good to fear the worst.

30   FIRST CITIZEN   Yet rather fight, than like unnatural sons,

Forsake your loving parents in distress.

SECOND CITIZEN   Tush, they that have already taken arms,

Are many fearful millions in respect

Of that small handful of our enemies;

35   But 'tis a rightful quarrel must prevail,

Edward is son unto our late king's sister,

Where John Valois, is three degrees removed.

WOMAN   Besides, there goes a prophecy abroad,

Published by one that was a friar once,

40   Whose oracles have many times proved true:

And now he says the time will shortly come,

Whenas a lion rousèd in the west

Shall carry hence the flower-de-luce of France.

These I can tell ye and suchlike surmises,

45   Strike many Frenchmen cold unto the heart.

Enter a Frenchman

[FRENCHMAN]   Fly, countrymen and citizens of France,

Sweet flow'ring peace, the root of happy life,

Is quite abandoned and expulsed the land,

---

16 grasshopper ... head a reference to Aesop's fable of the ant and the grasshopper; the grasshopper sings all summer long and then freezes when winter comes, while the industrious ant works hard to make provision for the forthcoming cold   **22 peradventure** perhaps   **23 throughly** completely, thoroughly   **24 charge** responsibility   **train** number of dependants   **25 look ... look for** be alert in good time to look after   **27 Belike** perhaps   **28 subjugate** conquered   **37 three degrees removed** a cousin, not a direct descendant of Philip IV   **42 Whenas** when   **44 surmises** conjectures   **48 expulsed** expelled from

Instead of whom ransack-constraining war
50   Sits like to ravens upon your houses' tops.
Slaughter and mischief walk within your streets
And unrestrained make havoc as they pass,
The form whereof even now myself beheld:
Upon this fair mountain whence I came,
55   For so far off as I directed mine eyes,
I might perceive five cities all on fire,
Cornfields and vineyards burning like an oven,
And, as the leaking vapour in the wind
Turned but aside, I likewise might discern
60   The poor inhabitants escaped the flame,
Fall numberless upon the soldiers' pikes.
Three ways these dreadful ministers of wrath
Do tread the measures of their tragic march:
Upon the right hand comes the conquering king,
65   Upon the left his hot unbridled son,
And in the midst our nation's glittering host,
All which though distant yet conspire in one
To leave a desolation where they come.
Fly, therefore, citizens if you be wise,
70   Seek out some habitation further off.
Here if you stay your wives will be abused,
Your treasure shared before your weeping eyes.
Shelter you yourselves for now the storm doth rise;
Away, away, methinks I hear their drums,
75   Ah, wretched France, I greatly fear thy fall,
Thy glory shaketh like a tottering wall.   [*Exeunt*]

[Act 3 Scene 3]

Enter King Edward and the Earl of Derby with soldiers, and Gobin de Grace

KING EDWARD Where's the Frenchman by whose cunning guide
We found the shallow of this River Somme,
And had direction how to pass the sea?

GOBIN DE GRACE Here, my good lord.

5   KING EDWARD How art thou called? Tell me thy name.

GOBIN DE GRACE Gobin de Grace, if please, your excellence.

KING EDWARD Then, Gobin, for the service thou hast done,
We here enlarge and give thee liberty

---

49 **ransack-constraining war** war which forces theft, plunder and pillage   50 **ravens** birds of ill omen   63 **tread the measures** usually applied to dancing, so here ironic, poetic, describing the battle formation   67 **All ... come** makes the point that all three groups of soldiers, friend and foe alike, are equally destructive of the poor people's livelihoods and the lands they march across   71 **abused** raped   [3.3] *Location: Picardy in northern France, near the river Somme*   3 **sea** river estuary   8 **enlarge** set at large, free

And for recompense beside this good,

10 Thou shalt receive five hundred marks in gold.

I know not how we should have met our son,

Whom now in heart I wish I might behold.

Enter Artois

[ARTOIS]   Good news, my lord, the prince is hard at hand,

And with him comes Lord Audley and the rest,

15 Whom since our landing we could never meet.

Enter Prince Edward, Lord Audley and soldiers

KING EDWARD   Welcome, fair prince, how hast thou sped, my son,

Since thy arrival on the coast of France?

PRINCE EDWARD   Successfully I thank the gracious heavens.

Some of their strongest cities we have won,

20 As Barfleur, Lô, Crotoy and Carentan,

And others wasted, leaving at our heels

A wide apparent field and beaten path

For solitariness to progress in.

Yet those that would submit we kindly pardoned;

25 For who in scorn refused our proffered peace

Endured the penalty of sharp revenge.

KING EDWARD   Ah France, why shouldst thou be this obstinate

Against the kind embracement of thy friends?

How gently had we thought to touch thy breast

30 And set our foot upon thy tender mould,

But that in froward and disdainful pride

Thou like a skittish and untamèd colt,

Dost start aside and strike us with thy heels.

But tell me, Ned, in all thy warlike course,

35 Hast thou not seen th'usurping King of France?

PRINCE EDWARD   Yes, my good lord, and not two hours ago,

With full a hundred thousand fighting men,

Upon the one side with the river's bank,

And on the other both his multitudes.

40 I feared he would have cropped our smaller power,

But happily perceiving your approach,

He hath withdrawn himself to Crécy plains,

Where, as it seemeth by his good array,

He means to bid us battle presently.

45 KING EDWARD   He shall be welcome: that's the thing we crave.

Enter King John, Dukes of Normandy and Lorraine, King of Bohemia, young Philip, and
soldiers

---

10 marks money; a mark was originally a weight or measure; it had the monetary value of roughly two thirds of a pound sterling   **16 sped** succeeded, prospered   **20 Barfleur** coastal town in Normandy   **Lô** Saint Lô, forty-seven miles to the south of Barfleur   **Crotoy** le Crotoy, port north of the Somme estuary   **Carentan** town on the Normandy coast between Barfleur and Saint Lô   **21 others wasted** the English used a scorched earth policy of destroying everything in their wake   **22 wide ... in** a deserted wasteland, devoid of people   **25 who** those who   **26 penalty ... revenge** death   **30 mould** earth/land considered as a possession/body   **31 froward** perverse, ungovernable   **39 multitudes** large numbers (of troops)   **43 array** martial order

KING JOHN Edward, know that John, the true King of France,
>Musing thou shouldst encroach upon his land
>And in thy tyrannous proceeding slay
>His faithful subjects and subvert his towns,
50>Spits in thy face, and in this manner following,
>Upbraids thee with thine arrogant intrusion.
>First, I condemn thee for a fugitive,
>A thievish pirate, and a needy mate,
>One that hath either no abiding place,
55>Or else inhabiting some barren soil
>Where neither herb or fruitful grain is had,
>Dost altogether live by pilfering;
>Next, insomuch thou hast infringed thy faith,
>Broke league and solemn covenant made with me,
60>I hold thee for a false pernicious wretch;
>And last of all, although I scorn to cope
>With one such inferior to myself,
>Yet in respect thy thirst is all for gold,
>Thy labour rather to be feared than loved,
65>To satisfy thy lust in either part
>Here am I come and with me have I brought
>Exceeding store of treasure, pearl, and coin.
>Leave therefore now to persecute the weak
>And, armèd ent'ring conflict with the armed,
70>Let it be seen 'mongst other petty thefts
>How thou canst win this pillage manfully.

KING EDWARD If gall or wormwood have a pleasant taste,
>Then is thy salutation honey-sweet,
>But as the one hath no such property,
75>So is the other most satirical.
>Yet wot how I regard thy worthless taunts,
>If thou have uttered them to foil my fame
>Or dim the reputation of my birth,
>Know that thy wolfish barking cannot hurt;
80>If slyly to insinuate with the world
>And with a strumpet's artificial line
>To paint thy vicious and deformèd cause,
>Be well assured the counterfeit will fade
>And in the end thy foul defects be seen;

---

47 **Musing** wondering that   **encroach** intrude usurpingly   49 **subvert** overthrow, raze to the ground   51 **Upbraids** adduces, alleges grounds for censure   52 **fugitive** vagabond/one given to running away, hence coward   53 **needy mate** poor creature   54 **no abiding place** no home, nowhere to live   57 **pilfering** petty theft   58 **insomuch** to such an extent   **infringed** not observed/wronged   59 **league** alliance/agreement   **covenant** agreement   60 **false pernicious wretch** lying, evil/dangerous/reprehensible creature   61 **cope** deal/encounter/fight   63 **in respect** given that   65 **either part** both respects, i.e. gold and creating fear   69 **armèd ... armed** fighting only those who are armed   71 **pillage** loot, booty   72 **gall** poison, venom   **wormwood** absinthe, notoriously bitter   74 **property** quality, characteristic   75 **satirical** sarcastic   76 **wot** know   77 **foil** dishonour **fame** reputation   81 **strumpet's** harlot's, prostitute's   **artificial line** i.e. produced by use of cosmetics

85   But if thou didst it to provoke me on,
     As who should say I were but timorous,
     Or coldly negligent did need a spur,
     Bethink thyself how slack I was at sea.
     Now since my landing I have won no towns,
90   Entered no further but upon the coast,
     And there have ever since securely slept.
     But if I have been otherwise employed,
     Imagine, Valois, whether I intend
     To skirmish, not for pillage, but for the crown
95   Which thou dost wear and that I vow to have,
     Or one of us shall fall into this grave.

PRINCE EDWARD   Look not for cross invectives at our hands,
     Or railing execrations of despite:
     Let creeping serpents hid in hollow banks,
100 Sting with their tongues; we have remorseless swords,
     And they shall plead for us and our affairs.
     Yet thus much briefly, by my father's leave:
     As all the immodest poison of thy throat
     Is scandalous and most notorious lies,
105 And our pretended quarrel is truly just,
     So end the battle when we meet today;
     May either of us prosper and prevail,
     Or, luckless curst, receive eternal shame.

KING EDWARD   That needs no further question and I know
110 His conscience witnesseth it is my right.
     Therefore, Valois, say, wilt thou yet resign,
     Before the sickle's thrust into the corn,
     Or that enkindled fury turn to flame?

KING JOHN   Edward, I know what right thou hast in France,
115 And ere I basely will resign my crown,
     This champion field shall be a pool of blood,
     And all our prospect as a slaughterhouse.

PRINCE EDWARD   Ay, that approves thee, tyrant, what thou art:
     No father, king, or shepherd of thy realm,
120 But one that tears her entrails with thy hands,
     And like a thirsty tiger suckst her blood.

AUDLEY   You peers of France, why do you follow him,
     That is so prodigal to spend your lives?

CHARLES   Whom should they follow, agèd impotent,

---

87 spur something to urge me on   **88 Bethink thyself** call to your mind, recollect   **slack** idle, remiss   **91 slept** quietly rested   **93 Valois** i.e. King John
94 skirmish engage in small encounters or battles   **97 cross invectives** angry abuse, violent language   **98 railing ... despite** ranting and uttering scornful,
defiant curses   **100 remorseless** cruel, pitiless   **105 pretended** intended, proposed   **108 luckless curst** ill-starred, heinously wicked   **109 question**
debate   **112 sickle's ... corn** agricultural metaphor for the cutting down of men in battle   **116 champion** flat, level, open country   **117 prospect** view,
outlook   **118 approves** demonstrates, proves to be true   **123 prodigal** reckless   **spend** waste, destroy   **124 agèd impotent** is addressed to Audley

125   But he that is their true-born sovereign?

KING EDWARD Upbraidst thou him because within his face

          Time hath engraved deep characters of age?

          Know that these grave scholars of experience,

          Like stiff grown oaks, will stand immovable,

130   When whirlwind quickly turns up younger trees.

DERBY   Was ever any of thy father's house

          King, but thyself, before this present time?

          Edward's great lineage by the mother's side

          Five hundred years hath held the sceptre up;

135   Judge then, conspirators, by this descent,

          Which is the true-born sovereign, this, or that?

PHILIP   Father, range your battles, prate no more,

          These English fain would spend the time in words

          That night approaching, they might escape unfought.

140 KING JOHN Lords and my loving subjects, now's the time

          That your intended force must bide the touch;

          Therefore, my friends, consider this in brief:

          He that you fight for is your natural king,

          He against whom you fight a foreigner:

145   He that you fight for rules in clemency,

          And reigns you with a mild and gentle bit.

          He against whom you fight, if he prevail,

          Will straight enthrone himself in tyranny,

          Make slaves of you and with a heavy hand

150   Curtail and curb your sweetest liberty.

          Then to protect your country and your king,

          Let but the haughty courage of your hearts

          Answer the number of your able hands

          And we shall quickly chase these fugitives;

155   For what's this Edward but a belly-god,

          A tender and lascivious wantonness,

          That th'other day was almost dead for love?

          And what, I pray you, is his goodly guard?

          Such as but scant them of their chines of beef

160   And take away their downy featherbeds,

          And presently they are as resty-stiff,

          As 'twere a many overridden jades.

---

134 **sceptre** ornamental rod, a symbol of royal authority   137 **range your battles** set out your battalions   **prate** talk idly, to little purpose   138 **fain would** would rather   139 **unfought** without having to fight   141 **intended** extended, strained   **bide** endure, undergo   **touch** trial, test of quality (as in the testing of gold or silver by rubbing it on a touchstone)/knock, blow   145 **clemency** gentleness of temper/mercy   146 **bit** mouthpiece of a horse's bridle, giving a play on **reigns/reins**   147 **prevail** wins, is victorious   150 **Curtail and curb** cut short and restrain, control   152 **Let but** just let   **haughty** proud   153 **Answer** undertake responsibility for/justify/satisfy   154 **fugitives** vagabonds   155 **belly-god** glutton, one who makes a god of his belly   156 **wantonness** character of a vice in the morality plays signifying lewdness, extravagance, indulgence   157 **That ... love?** a reference to his earlier infatuation with the Countess of Salisbury   159 **Such ... them** the sort of men who if you deprive or ration them   **chines** joints consisting of part of the back (ribs or sirloin)   161 **resty-stiff** lazy, disinclined for action or exertion (from resting too much which has made them stiff)   162 **overridden jades** worthless horses, worn out with too much riding

Then, Frenchmen, scorn that such should be your lords
And rather bind ye them in captive bands.

165 ALL FRENCH *Vive le roi*! God save King John of France!

KING JOHN Now on this plain of Crécy spread yourselves
And, Edward, when thou dar'st, begin the fight.

[*Exeunt King John, King of Bohemia*

KING EDWARD We presently will meet thee, John of France, *and all the French*]
And, English lords, let us resolve the day:

170 Either to clear us of that scandalous crime,
Or be entombèd in our innocence.
And, Ned, because this battle is the first
That ever yet thou foughtest in pitched field,
As ancient custom is of martialists

175 To dub thee with the type of chivalry:
In solemn manner we will give thee arms,
Come therefore, heralds, orderly bring forth,
A strong attirement for the prince my son.

Enter four Heralds bringing in a coat-armour, a helmet, a lance and a shield

KING EDWARD Edward Plantagenet, in the name of God,

180 As with this armour I impall thy breast,
So be thy noble unrelenting heart
Walled in with flint of matchless fortitude,
That never base affections enter there.
Fight and be valiant, conquer where thou com'st,

185 Now, follow, lords, and do him honour too.

DERBY Edward Plantagenet, Prince of Wales,
As I do set this helmet on thy head,
Wherewith the chamber of this brain is fenced,
So may thy temples with Bellona's hand

190 Be still adorned with laurel victory.
Fight and be valiant, conquer where thou com'st!

AUDLEY Edward Plantagenet, Prince of Wales,
Receive this lance into thy manly hand:
Use it in fashion of a brazen pen

195 To draw forth bloody stratagems in France
And print thy valiant deeds in honour's book.
Fight and be valiant, vanquish where thou com'st!

ARTOIS Edward Plantagenet, Prince of Wales,
Hold, take this target, wear it on thy arm,

---

164 **captive bands** prisoners' shackles   165 *Vive le roi*! Long live the king! (French)   169 **resolve** conclude/determine   170 **scandalous crime** libellous accusation   173 **pitched field** military encounter on a battlefield at a predetermined time and place involving large numbers   174 **martialists** warriors, those born under the influence of Mars, the Roman god of war   175 **dub** invest with a dignity or title   **type** symbol   178 **attirement** outfit   *coat-armour* a vest of rich material embroidered with heraldic devices, worn as a distinction by knights over their armour   179 **Plantagenet** the surname of the English monarchy   180 **impall** enfold   186 **Prince of Wales** traditional title of the heir apparent   189 **Bellona's** of Bellona, the Roman goddess of war   190 **laurel** the bay tree, *Laurus nobilis*, traditional symbol of victory (or distinction in poetry)   194 **brazen** made of brass, strong, punning on sense of 'shameless'   195 **draw forth** produce   **stratagems** acts of generalship   199 **target** round shield

200   And may the view thereof like Perseus' shield,

Astonish and transform thy gazing foes

To senseless images of meagre death.

Fight and be valiant, conquer where thou com'st!

KING EDWARD   Now wants there nought but knighthood, which deferred

205   We leave till thou hast won it in the field.

[PRINCE EDWARD]   My gracious father and ye forward peers,

This honour you have done me animates

And cheers my green yet scarce appearing strength

With comfortable good-presaging signs,

210   No otherwise than did old Jacob's words

Whenas he breathed his blessings on his sons;

These hallowed gifts of yours when I profane

Or use them not to glory of my God,

To patronage the fatherless and poor,

215   Or for the benefit of England's peace,

Benumb my joints, wax feeble both mine arms,

Wither my heart that like a sapless tree,

I may remain the map of infamy.

KING EDWARD   Then thus our steelèd battles shall be ranged,

220   The leading of the vaward, Ned, is thine,

To dignify whose lusty spirit the more

We temper it with Audley's gravity,

That courage and experience joined in one,

Your manage may be second unto none.

225   For the main battles I will guide myself,

And Derby in the rearward march behind.

That orderly disposed and set in ray,

Let us to horse and God grant us the day.   *Exeunt*

[Act 3 Scene 4]

Alarum. Enter a many Frenchmen flying. After them Prince Edward running
Then enter King John and Duke of Lorraine

KING JOHN   O, Lorraine, say, what mean our men to fly?

Our number is far greater than our foes.

LORRAINE   The garrison of Genoese, my lord,

---

200 **Perseus' ... death** according to classical mythology, the hero Perseus was equipped by the gods with a sword, helmet (of invisibility) and a shield which he used to defeat the monster Medusa, one of the Gorgons. Her look turned humans to stone but by viewing her through his polished shield Perseus was able to defeat her and cut off her head with which he afterwards defeated his enemies by turning the Gorgon's gaze on them   **meagre** lean   **204 wants there nought** all that is lacking is   **206 forward** principal, foremost/eager, ready for action   **208 green** youthful, immature, untried   **209 comfortable** encouraging/morally and spiritually supportive   **good-presaging** that promise or foretell good   **210 Jacob's** i.e. of Jacob, the biblical patriarch who blessed his three sons and prophesied their return to the land of their fathers (Genesis: 48–49)   **211 Whenas** on the occasion when   **214 patronage** uphold, protect   **216 wax** grow, become   **218 map** epitome, incarnation   **219 steelèd battles** armed battalions   **220 vaward** vanguard   **221 lusty** youthful, lively   **222 temper** mix/dilute   **224 manage** management, conduct of affairs   **227 ray** arrangement of soldiers in a line or ranks   **[3.4]** *Location: the battlefield of Crécy (one of the most important battles in the so-called Hundred Years' War between England and France)*   3 **Genoese** i.e. the crossbowmen from Genoa

That came from Paris, weary with their march,

5   Grudging to be suddenly employed,

No sooner in the forefront took their place

But straight retiring so dismayed the rest,

As likewise they betook themselves to flight

In which for haste to make a safe escape,

10   More in the clustering throng are pressed to death

Than by the enemy a thousandfold.

KING JOHN   O hapless fortune! Let us yet assay

If we can counsel some of them to stay.   [*Exeunt*]

Enter King Edward and Audley

KING EDWARD   Lord Audley, whiles our son is in the chase,

15   Withdraw our powers unto this little hill,

And here a season let us breathe ourselves.

AUDLEY   I will, my lord.   *Exit. Sound retreat*

KING EDWARD   Just-dooming heaven, whose secret providence,

To our gross judgement is inscrutable,

20   How are we bound to praise thy wondrous works,

That hast this day given way unto the right,

And made the wicked stumble at themselves!

Enter Artois

[ARTOIS]   Rescue, King Edward, rescue, for thy son!

KING EDWARD   Rescue, Artois? What is he prisoner?

25   Or by violence fell beside his horse?

ARTOIS   Neither, my lord, but narrowly beset,

With turning Frenchmen whom he did pursue

As 'tis impossible that he should scape,

Except your highness presently descend.

30   KING EDWARD   Tut, let him fight! We gave him arms today,

And he is labouring for a knighthood, man.

Enter Derby

DERBY   The prince, my lord, the prince! O, succour him!

He's close encompassed with a world of odds.

KING EDWARD   Then will he win a world of honour too,

35   If he by valour can redeem him thence.

If not, what remedy? We have more sons

Than one to comfort our declining age.

Enter Audley

AUDLEY   Renownèd Edward, give me leave I pray,

To lead my soldiers where I may relieve

40   Your grace's son in danger to be slain.

---

5 **grudging** unwilling, resentful   **suddenly** without warning, unexpectedly   7 **straight retiring** immediately withdrawing/retreating   10 **throng** crowd/danger   **pressed** crushed   12 **hapless** luckless   **assay** judge/attempt   16 **a season** at a favourable opportunity   **breathe ourselves** catch our breaths   18 **Just-dooming** justly judging   19 **gross** earthly/ignorant   26 **beset** set upon/surrounded by   27 **turning** i.e. who were retreating but have now rallied and turned to attack   28 **As 'tis** so that it is   29 **descend** make an attack/fall violently upon   32 **succour** aid/furnish with military assistance   33 **encompassed** surrounded   **with ... odds** and heavily outnumbered

The snares of French, like emmets on a bank,

Muster about him whilst he lion-like,

Entangled in the net of their assaults,

Frantic'lly rends and bites the woven toil,

45   But all in vain, he cannot free himself.

KING EDWARD Audley, content, I will not have a man,

On pain of death sent forth to succour him:

This is the day, ordained by destiny,

To season his courage with those grievous thoughts,

50   That if he breaketh out, Nestor's years on earth

Will make him savour still of this exploit.

DERBY   Ah, but he shall not live to see those days.

KING EDWARD Why then his epitaph is lasting praise.

AUDLEY   Yet, good my lord, 'tis too much wilfulness,

55   To let his blood be spilt that may be saved.

KING EDWARD Exclaim no more, for none of you can tell

Whether a borrowed aid will serve or no.

Perhaps he is already slain or ta'en:

And dare a falcon when she's in her flight

60   And ever after she'll be haggard-like:

Let Edward be delivered by our hands,

And still in danger he'll expect the like,

But if himself, himself redeem from thence,

He will have vanquished cheerful death and fear,

65   And ever after dread their force no more

Than if they were but babes or captive slaves.

AUDLEY   O cruel father! Farewell, Edward, then.

DERBY   Farewell, sweet prince, the hope of chivalry!

ARTOIS   O, would my life might ransom him from death!

70   KING EDWARD But soft, methinks I hear,

The dismal charge of trumpets' loud retreat:

All are not slain I hope that went with him,

Some will return with tidings good or bad.

Enter Prince Edward in triumph, bearing in his hand his shivered lance, and the King of
Bohemia, borne before, wrapped in the colours: they run and embrace him

AUDLEY   O, joyful sight! Victorious Edward lives.

75   DERBY   Welcome, brave prince!

KING EDWARD Welcome, Plantagenet.

PRINCE EDWARD First having done my duty as beseemed,   *Kneels and kisses*
his father's hand

---

41 **emmets ... bank** ants in an anthill   42 **Muster** assemble   44 **rends** tears   **toil** trap or snare for wild animals   49 **season** ripen, bring to maturity
50 **if ... exploit** if he escapes he'll remember and relish for three lifetimes   **Nestor** was King of Troy and features in Homer's *Iliad* as a wise, elder statesman;
according to legend he lived for three generations of men   53 **epitaph** memorial/insciption on a tomb   54 **wilfulness** stubbornness   57 **borrowed** i.e. someone
else's   59 **dare** daze or paralyse (a bird) with the sight of something in order to catch it   60 **haggard-like** like a wild hawk, not to be captured   62 **still** always,
invariably   **like** same treatment   64 **cheerful** cheerfully   *shivered* broken, shattered   *colours* patriotic flag   77 **beseemed** was fitting

Lords, I regreet you all with hearty thanks.
And now behold, after my winter's toil,
80 My painful voyage on the boist'rous sea
Of war's devouring gulfs and steely rocks,
I bring my fraught unto the wishèd port,
My summer's hope, my travel's sweet reward.
And here with humble duty I present
85 This sacrifice, this first fruit of my sword
Cropped and cut down even at the gate of death:
The King of Bohemia, father, whom I slew,
Whose thousands had entrenched me round about
And lay as thick upon my battered crest
90 As on an anvil with their ponderous glaives.
Yet marble courage still did underprop,
And when my weary arms with often blows,
Like the continual labouring woodman's axe
That is enjoined to fell a load of oaks,
95 Began to falter straight I would recover.
My gifts you gave me, and my zealous vow,
And then new courage made me fresh again,
That in despite I carved my passage forth,
And put the multitude to speedy flight.   *His sword borne by a soldier*
100 Lo, thus hath Edward's hand filled your request,
And done I hope the duty of a knight.
KING EDWARD Ay, well thou hast deserved a knighthood, Ned,
And therefore with thy sword, yet reeking, warm   *Knights him*
With blood of those that fought to be thy bane.
105 Arise Prince Edward, trusty knight at arms:
This day thou hast confounded me with joy,
And proved thyself fit heir unto a king.
PRINCE EDWARD Here is a note, my gracious lord, of those
That in this conflict of our foes were slain:
110 Eleven princes of esteem, fourscore barons,
A hundred and twenty knights, and thirty thousand
Common soldiers, and of our men a thousand.
[KING EDWARD] Our God be praised! Now, John of France, I hope,
Thou know'st King Edward for no wantonness,
115 No lovesick cockney, nor his soldiers' jades.
But which way is the fearful king escaped?
PRINCE EDWARD Towards Poitiers, noble father, and his sons.
KING EDWARD Ned, thou and Audley shall pursue them still.

78 **regreet** return and greet   82 **fraught** cargo, freight   88 **entrenched** surrounded   89 **lay** beat/assaulted/did violence to   90 **glaives** spears/
swords/halberts, weapons with a blade fastened to a long handle   91 **marble** i.e. hard, stony and of fine quality   **underprop** support, sustain   92 **often**
frequent   94 **enjoined** ordered   95 **straight** immediately   96 **zealous** passionate, ardent   100 **filled** fulfilled   103 **reeking** smoking (from the heat
of battle)/smeared with blood   104 **bane** death, destruction/ruin   106 **confounded** silenced/surprised   110 **esteem** worth, respect   **fourscore**
eighty   115 **cockney** milksop/one born in a town, hence 'weakling'   117 **Poitiers** French town over three hundred miles from Crécy; the historical
inaccuracy serves to compress time and the dramatic events in the play

Myself and Derby will to Calais straight
120 And there begirt that haven town with siege:
Now lies it on an upshot, therefore strike,
And wistly follow whiles the game's on foot.
What picture's this?

PRINCE EDWARD   A pelican, my lord,
125 Wounding her bosom with her crooked beak,
That so her nest of young ones might be fed
With drops of blood that issue from her heart,
The motto *Sic et vos*: 'And so should you'.   *Exeunt*

[Act 4 Scene 1]

Enter Lord Mountford with a coronet in his hand, with him the Earl of Salisbury

MOUNTFORD   My lord of Salisbury, since by your aid
Mine enemy, Sir Charles of Blois, is slain
And I again am quietly possessed
In Britt'ny's dukedom, know that I resolve
5 For this kind furtherance of your king and you
To swear allegiance to his majesty.
In sign whereof receive this coronet.
Bear it unto him and withal mine oath
Never to be but Edward's faithful friend.

10 SALISBURY   I take it, Mountford. Thus I hope ere long,
The whole dominions of the realm of France
Will be surrendered to his conquering hand.   *Exit [Mountford]*
Now if I knew but safely how to pass,
I would at Calais gladly meet his grace,
15 Whither I am by letters certified
That he intends to have his host removed.
It shall be so, this policy will serve,
Ho, whose within? Bring Villiers to me.

Enter Villiers

Villiers, thou know'st thou art my prisoner,
20 And that I might for ransom if I would,
Require of thee a hundred thousand francs,
Or else retain and keep thee captive still.

---

120 begirt surround   **haven** harbour/place of refuge   **121 lies ... upshot** it depends on the final stroke/draws to a conclusion   **upshot** the last, deciding stroke of an archery competition   **122 wistly** intently, with close attention   **the ... foot** the prey is roused (hunting expression)   **124 pelican ... you** the final five lines of this scene are regarded as an interpolation; they refer to the pelican considered as an emblem of self-sacrifice who wounded herself in order to feed her young. Historically this may relate to the addition to the arms of the Pelham family in 1356 when Sir William Pelham was reputed to have captured King John at Poitiers, although this event is not recorded in the play's main sources   ***Sic et vos*** 'And so should you' (Latin)   **[4.1]** *Location: Brittany*   **4 Britt'ny's** i.e. Brittany's   **7 In sign whereof** as a token of which   **coronet** small crown   **8 withal** in addition   **9 but** anything other than   **10 ere** before   **15 certified** assured   **16 to ... removed** to move his army to   **17 policy** plan   **21 francs** French coins

But so it is that for a smaller charge

Thou mayst be quit, and if thou wilt thyself.

25 And this it is, procure me but a passport

Of Charles, the Duke of Normandy, that I

Without restraint may have recourse to Calais,

Through all the countries where he hath to do,

Which thou mayst easily obtain, I think,

30 By reason I have often heard thee say,

He and thou were students once together

And then thou shalt be set at liberty.

How sayst thou, wilt thou undertake to do it?

VILLIERS   I will, my lord, but I must speak with him.

35 SALISBURY   Why so thou shalt, take horse and post from hence.

Only before thou goest, swear by thy faith

That if thou canst not compass my desire,

Thou wilt return my prisoner back again

And that shall be sufficient warrant for me.

40 VILLIERS   To that condition I agree, my lord,

And will unfeignèdly perform the same.   *Exit*

SALISBURY   Farewell, Villiers.

Thus once I mean to try a Frenchman's faith.   *Exit*

[Act 4 Scene 2]

Enter King Edward and Derby with soldiers

KING EDWARD   Since they refuse our proffered league, my lord,

And will not ope their gates and let us in,

We will entrench ourselves on every side,

That neither victuals nor supply of men

5   May come to succour this accursèd town:

Famine shall combat where our swords are stopped.

Enter six poor Frenchmen

DERBY   The promised aid that made them stand aloof

Is now retired and gone another way,

It will repent them of their stubborn will.

10   But what are these poor ragged slaves, my lord?

KING EDWARD   Ask what they are: it seems they come from Calais.

DERBY   You wretched patterns of despair and woe,

What are you, living men or gliding ghosts

Crept from your graves to walk upon the earth?

---

24 **and ... thyself** if you yourself are willing   25 **procure ... hath** obtain on my behalf an official document from Charles that I may freely travel to Calais through all the lands under his control   **countries** lands   37 **compass** achieve, accomplish   39 **warrant** guarantee   41 **unfeignèdly** sincerely, honestly   **[4.2]** *Location: outside the walls of Calais*   1 **proffered** proposed   2 **ope** open   3 **entrench ourselves** position ourselves within trenches   4 **victuals** food, supplies   **supply of men** reinforcements/supplies   5 **succour** relieve/assist   6 **stopped** obstructed   9 **repent them** make them regret   12 **patterns** pictures   13 **gliding** softly moving

15 FIRST FRENCHMAN   No ghosts, my lord, but men that breathe a life
   Far worse than is the quiet sleep of death:
   We are distressèd poor inhabitants,
   That long have been diseasèd, sick and lame,
   And now because we are not fit to serve,
20   The captain of the town hath thrust us forth
   That so expense of victuals may be saved.

KING EDWARD   A charitable deed no doubt, and worthy praise:
   But how do you imagine then to speed?
   We are your enemies: in such a case
25   We can no less but put ye to the sword
   Since, when we proffered truce, it was refused.

SECOND FRENCHMAN   And if your grace no otherwise vouchsafe,
   As welcome death is unto us as life.

KING EDWARD   Poor silly men, much wronged, and more distressed:
30   Go, Derby, go and see they be relieved.
   Command that victuals be appointed them
   And give to every one five crowns apiece:
   The lion scorns to touch the yielding prey,
   And Edward's sword must fresh itself in such
35   As wilful stubbornness hath made perverse.

Enter Lord Percy

KING EDWARD   Lord Percy, welcome. What's the news in England?

PERCY   The queen, my lord, comes here to your grace,
   And from her highness and the lord vicegerent,
   I bring this happy tidings of success:
40   David of Scotland, lately up in arms,
   Thinking belike he soonest should prevail,
   Your highness being absent from the realm,
   Is, by the fruitful service of your peers,
   And painful travail of the queen herself,
45   That, big with child, was every day in arms,
   Vanquished, subdued, and taken prisoner.

KING EDWARD   Thanks, Percy, for thy news with all my heart.
   What was he took him prisoner in the field?

PERCY   A squire, my lord; John Copland is his name,
50   Who since, entreated by her majesty,
   Denies to make surrender of his prize
   To any but unto your grace alone:
   Whereat the queen is grievously displeased.

---

19 And ... saved i.e. the poor and needy were sent away to save food for those able to fight; there is historical warrant for this episode   **23 speed** prosper   **27 no otherwise vouchsafe** can bestow no other benefit   **29 silly** simple, defenceless   **31 victuals ... them** they are fed   **32 crowns** gold coins **apiece** each   **34 fresh** refresh   **35 perverse** evil/obstinate   **38 lord vicegerent** one appointed to exercise rule on behalf of the king **41 Thinking ... prevail** believing most likely he would more easily overcome   **belike** most likely   **44 painful travail** painstaking efforts/exertions, plays on **travail** meaning 'labour in childbirth' and also 'travel' (journey), an alternative spelling   **45 big with child** heavily pregnant   **49 squire** young man attendant upon a knight/one ranking next to a knight in the feudal system   **51 Denies** refuses

KING EDWARD Well, then we'll have a pursuivant dispatch

55 To summon Copland hither out of hand,

And with him he shall bring his prisoner king.

PERCY The queen's, my lord, herself by this at sea

And purposeth, as soon as wind will serve,

To land at Calais and to visit you.

60 KING EDWARD She shall be welcome, and to wait her coming,

I'll pitch my tent near to the sandy shore.

Enter a Captain

[CAPTAIN] The burgesses of Calais, mighty king,

Have by a council willingly decreed

To yield the town and castle to your hands,

65 Upon condition it will please your grace

To grant them benefit of life and goods.

KING EDWARD They will so? Then belike they may command,

Dispose, elect, and govern as they list.

No, sirrah, tell them since they did refuse

70 Our princely clemency at first proclaimed,

They shall not have it now although they would.

I will accept of nought but fire and sword,

Except, within these two days, six of them

That are the wealthiest merchants in the town

75 Come naked all, but for their linen shirts,

With each a halter hanged about his neck

And prostrate yield themselves upon their knees,

To be afflicted, hanged, or what I please,

And so you may inform their masterships.   *Exeunt [all but the Captain]*

80 CAPTAIN Why this it is to trust a broken staff!

Had we not been persuaded John, our king,

Would with his army have relieved the town,

We had not stood upon defiance so:

But now 'tis past that no man can recall,

85 And better some do go to wrack than all.   *Exit*

[Act 4 Scene 3]

Enter Charles of Normandy and Villiers

CHARLES I wonder, Villiers, thou shouldst importune me

For one that is our deadly enemy.

VILLIERS Not for his sake, my gracious lord, so much

---

54 pursuivant royal or state messenger **dispatch** quickly send off **55 out of hand** immediately **57 this** this time **58 purposeth** intends
62 burgesses elected representatives/freemen of a town **68 list** choose, like **71 although they would** even if they want it now **77 prostrate** lying
face down in token of submission and humility **84 recall** call it back, undo it **[4.3]** *Location: Poitiers (site of the second important battle of the*
Hundred Years' War) **1 importune** pester, annoy/solicit

Am I become an earnest advocate

5   As that thereby my ransom will be quit.

CHARLES   Thy ransom man: why need'st thou talk of that?

Art thou not free? And are not all occasions

That happen for advantage of our foes,

To be accepted of and stood upon?

10   VILLIERS   No, good my lord, except the same be just:

For profit must with honour be commixed

Or else our actions are but scandalous.

But letting pass these intricate objections,

Will't please your highness to subscribe or no?

15   CHARLES   Villiers, I will not, nor I cannot do it.

Salisbury shall not have his will so much

To claim a passport how it pleaseth himself.

VILLIERS   Why then, I know the extremity, my lord,

I must return to prison whence I came.

20   CHARLES   Return, I hope thou wilt not.

What bird that hath escaped the fowler's gin

Will not beware how she's ensnared again?

Or what is he so senseless and secure

That, having hardly passed a dangerous gulf,

25   Will put himself in peril there again?

VILLIERS   Ah, but it is mine oath, my gracious lord,

Which I in conscience may not violate,

Or else a kingdom should not draw me hence.

CHARLES   Thine oath! Why that doth bind thee to abide!

30   Hast thou not sworn obedience to thy prince?

VILLIERS   In all things that uprightly he commands:

But either to persuade or threaten me

Not to perform the covenant of my word

Is lawless, and I need not to obey.

35   CHARLES   Why, is it lawful for a man to kill

And not to break a promise with his foe?

VILLIERS   To kill, my lord, when war is once proclaimed,

So that our quarrel be for wrongs received,

No doubt is lawfully permitted us.

40   But in an oath we must be well advised

How we do swear and, when we once have sworn,

Not to infringe it though we die therefore;

Therefore, my lord, as willing I return,

As if I were to fly to paradise.

45   CHARLES   Stay, my Villiers, thine honourable mind,

---

5 quit paid, cleared   **8 advantage ... foes** give us an advantage over our enemies   **9 stood upon** made the most of   **11 commixed** mixed together
12 scandalous infamous, disgraceful   **14 subscribe** sign   **17 how** just as   **18 extremity** conclusion/utmost penalty   **21 gin** snare   **23 secure**
complacent   **31 uprightly** lawfully   **33 covenant** pledge, agreement   **42 infringe** break, contravene

Deserves to be eternally admired,

Thy suit shall be no longer thus deferred.

Give me the paper, I'll subscribe to it,

And wheretofore I lovèd thee as Villiers,

50   Hereafter I'll embrace thee as myself.

Stay and be still in favour with thy lord.

VILLIERS   I humbly thank your grace. I must dispatch

And send this passport first unto the earl,

And then I will attend your highness' pleasure.

55   CHARLES   Do so, Villiers, and, Charles, when he hath need

Be such his soldiers, howsoe'er he speed.   *Exit Villiers*

Enter King John

KING JOHN   Come, Charles, and arm thee. Edward is entrapped,

The Prince of Wales is fallen into our hands

And we have compassed him; he cannot scape.

60   CHARLES   But will your highness fight today?

KING JOHN   What else, my son? He's scarce eight thousand strong

And we are threescore thousand at the least.

CHARLES   I have a prophecy, my gracious lord,

Wherein is written what success is like

65   To happen us in this outrageous war.

It was delivered me at Crécy's field,

By one that is an agèd hermit there:

'When feathered fowl shall make thine army tremble,   *Reads*

And flintstones rise and break the battle ray,

70   Then think on him that doth not now dissemble

For that shall be the hapless dreadful day.

Yet in the end thy foot thou shalt advance,

As far in England as thy foe in France.'

KING JOHN   By this it seems we shall be fortunate:

75   For as it is impossible that stones

Should ever rise and break the battle ray,

Or airy fowl make men in arms to quake,

So is it like we shall not be subdued:

Or say this might be true, yet in the end

80   Since he doth promise we shall drive him hence,

And forage their country as they have done ours,

By this revenge, that loss will seem the less.

But all are frivolous fancies, toys and dreams:

Once we are sure we have ensnared the son,

85   Catch we the father after how we can.   *Exeunt*

---

48 subscribe to sign   **49 wheretofore** whereas up to now   **52 dispatch** make haste   **55 Charles ... speed** speaking to himself of himself in the third person, the prince asks that 'his own soldiers behave honourably in this way when he has need, whatever his fortune'   **57 Edward** i.e. Prince Edward **59 compassed** surrounded; not in fact historically accurate   **62 threescore** sixty   **65 happen** befall   **outrageous** wicked/excessively violent **69 flintstones** stones of flint, a kind of hard stone with the property of giving off sparks when struck   **ray** arrangement of soldiers in line or ranks **70 dissemble** feign, pretend/put on a false appearance/disperse   **71 hapless** unlucky   **81 forage** overrun in order to obtain supplies, plunder   **83 toys** foolish, idle fancies   **85 how we can** in whatever way we are able

[Act 4 Scene 4]

Enter Prince Edward, Audley and others

PRINCE EDWARD   Audley, the arms of death embrace us round,
And comfort have we none, save that to die
We pay sour earnest for a sweeter life.
At Crécy field our clouds of warlike smoke
5   Choked up those French mouths and dissevered them,
But now their multitudes of millions hide,
Masking, as 'twere, the beauteous burning sun,
Leaving no hope to us but sullen dark,
And eyeless terror of all-ending night.

10   AUDLEY   This sudden, mighty, and expedient head,
That they have made, fair prince, is wonderful.
Before us in the valley lies the king,
Vantaged with all that heaven and earth can yield,
His party stronger battled than our whole:
15   His son, the braving Duke of Normandy,
Hath trimmed the mountain on our right hand up
In shining plate, that now the aspiring hill
Shows like a silver quarry, or an orb
Aloft the which the banners, bannerets,
20   And new-replenished pendants cuff the air
And beat the winds, that for their gaudiness,
Struggles to kiss them. On our left hand lies
Philip, the younger issue of the king,
Coating the other hill in such array
25   That all his gilded upright pikes do seem
Straight trees of gold, the pendant leaves,
And their device of antique heraldry,
Quartered in colours seeming sundry fruits,
Makes it the orchard of the Hesperides.
30   Behind us two the hill doth bear his height,
For like a half-moon opening but one way
It rounds us in: there at our backs are lodged,
The fatal crossbows, and the battle there

[4.4] *Location: the battlefield at Poitiers* **3 sour earnest** a bitter pledge   **sweeter life** i.e. in heaven   **5 dissevered** divided, separated   **9 eyeless** blind   **10 expedient head** rapid progress   **13 Vantaged with** with all the advantages   **14 His ... whole** i.e. King John alone has more troops under his personal command than we have in total   **15 braving** boastful, defiant   **16 trimmed** arranged, strengthened, punning on sense of 'decorated' **17 shining plate** metal armour   **aspiring** ambitious, rising   **18 quarry** site for the extraction of precious metals/prey, object of a hunt/intended victim **orb** circle/earth/celestial sphere   **19 Aloft the which** above which   **bannerets** flags of knights entitled to bring a company of vassals into the field under their own banner   **20 new-replenished pendants** newly-restored streamers   **cuff** strike, beat   **21 gaudiness** showiness   **25 pikes** spears **26 pendant leaves** i.e. flags hanging like leaves   **27 device** design   **28 Quartered in colours** Philip's troops are arranged like a heraldic shield which was traditionally divided into quarters; each section denoted by their distinct   **colours,** i.e. badges or insignia   **sundry** various   **29 orchard ... Hesperides** in classical mythology the goddess Hera's orchard containing an apple tree (or in some versions a grove of such trees) with golden apples which conferred immortality   **33 fatal crossbows** deadly crossbowmen; **crossbows** were dangerous weapons, more powerful and requiring less practice than the English longbow   **battle** troops, body of soldiers

Is governed by the rough Chatillion.

35 Then thus it stands, the valley for our flight
The king binds in, the hills on either hand
Are proudly royalized by his sons,
And on the hill behind stands certain death,
In pay and service with Chatillion.

40 PRINCE EDWARD Death's name is much more mighty than his deeds,
Thy parcelling this power hath made it more;
As many sands as these my hands can hold
Are but my handful of so many sands.
Then all the world, and call it but a power,

45 Easily ta'en up and quickly thrown away;
But if I stand to count them sand by sand
The number would confound my memory
And make a thousand millions of a task,
Which briefly is no more indeed than one.

50 These quarters, squadrons, and these regiments,
Before, behind us, and on either hand,
Are but a power. When we name a man,
His hand, his foot, his head hath several strengths,
And being all but one self instant strength.

55 Why all this many, Audley, is but one
And we can call it all but one man's strength.
He that hath far to go, tells it by miles,
If he should tell the steps, it kills his heart:
The drops are infinite that make a flood,

60 And yet thou know'st we call it but a rain.
There is but one France, one King of France,
That France hath no more kings, and that same king
Hath but the puissant legion of one king?
And we have one, then apprehend no odds,

65 For one to one, is fair equality.

Enter an Herald from King John

PRINCE EDWARD What tidings, messenger? Be plain and brief.

HERALD The King of France, my sovereign lord and master,
Greets by me his foe, the Prince of Wales:
If thou call forth a hundred men of name

70 Of lords, knights, esquires and English gentlemen,
And with thyself and those kneel at his feet,
He straight will fold his bloody colours up,

---

34 rough brutal, violent   **35 Then ... Chatillion** Audley is summarizing the disposition of the French troops in which, as both he and King John have noted, Prince Edward is surrounded by the French   **41 parcelling this power** dividing up of the French army   **42 As ... sands** whatever the number of grains of sand I can hold in my hand, they still only add up to one handful of sand   **44 Then** in the same way   **45 Easily ... away** i.e. like a handful of sand   **47 confound** defeat   **50 quarters** parts of an army   **54 one ... strength** all these various strengths add up to one and the self-same single strength   **57 tells** counts   **63 puissant** mighty, powerful   **legion** body of men, host   **64 apprehend no odds** don't consider the disparity of numbers   **69 name** reputation, especially nobles   **72 He ... up** King John is offering Prince Edward the opportunity to surrender without a fight

And ransom shall redeem lives forfeited:

If not, this day shall drink more English blood,

75   Than ere was buried in our British earth.

What is the answer to his proffered mercy?

PRINCE EDWARD   This heaven that covers France contains the mercy

That draws from me submissive orisons,

That such base breath should vanish from my lips

80   To urge the plea of mercy to a man,

The Lord forbid: return and tell the king,

My tongue is made of steel and it shall beg

My mercy on his coward burgonet.

Tell him my colours are as red as his,

85   My men as bold, our English arms as strong,

Return him my defiance in his face.

HERALD   I go.   [Exit]

Enter another [Herald]

PRINCE EDWARD   What news with thee?

SECOND HERALD   The Duke of Normandy, my lord and master,

90   Pitying thy youth is so engirt with peril,

By me hath sent a nimble-jointed jennet,

As swift as ever yet thou didst bestride,

And therewithal he counsels thee to fly,

Else death himself hath sworn that thou shalt die.

95   PRINCE EDWARD   Back with the beast unto the beast that sent him.

Tell him I cannot sit a coward's horse,

Bid him today bestride the jade himself,

For I will stain my horse quite o'er with blood,

And double gild my spurs, but I will catch him:

100   So tell the cap'ring boy, and get thee gone.   [Exit]

Enter another [Herald]

THIRD HERALD   Edward of Wales, Philip, the second son

To the most mighty Christian King of France,

Seeing thy body's living date expired,

All full of charity and Christian love,

105   Commends this book full fraught with prayers,   *Offers prayerbook*

To thy fair hand, and for thy hour of life

Entreats thee that thou meditate therein,

And arm thy soul for her long journey towards.

Thus have I done his bidding, and return.

110   PRINCE EDWARD   Herald of Philip, greet thy lord from me.

All good that he can send I can receive,

---

75 British Breton   **76 proffered** offered, proposed   **78 orisons** prayers   **83 burgonet** helmet   **90 engirt** surrounded   **91 jennet** small Spanish horse   **97 jade** worthless, broken-down horse   **99 double ... spurs** completely cover my spurs with blood, i.e. from kicking, urging on his horse in battle   **spurs** metal spikes attached to rider's heel   **100 cap'ring** capering, playful, leaping   **103 body's ... expired** i.e. life is over   **105 fraught** stored, supplied   **107 Entreats** begs   **108 towards** at hand

But thinkst thou not the unadvisèd boy
Hath wronged himself in this far tend'ring me?
Haply he cannot pray without the book —
115　　I think him no divine extemporal —,
Then render back this commonplace of prayer,
To do himself good in adversity;
Besides he knows not my sins' quality
And therefore knows no prayers for my avail.
120　　Ere night his prayer may be to pray to God,
To put it in my heart to hear his prayer:
So tell the courtly wanton, and begone.

[THIRD] HERALD   I go.   [Exit]

PRINCE EDWARD   How confident their strength and number makes them!
125　　Now, Audley, sound those silver wings of thine
And let those milk-white messengers of time
Show thy time's learning in this dangerous time.
Thyself art busy and bit with many broils
And stratagems forepast with iron pens
130　　Are texted in thine honourable face.
Thou art a married man in this distress
But danger woos me as a blushing maid:
Teach me an answer to this perilous time.

AUDLEY   To die is all as common as to live:
135　　The one enchased, the other holds in chase:
For from the instant we begin to live,
We do pursue and hunt the time to die.
First bud we, then we blow, and after seed,
Then presently we fall, and as a shade
140　　Follows the body, so we follow death.
If then we hunt for death, why do we fear it?
If we fear it, why do we follow it?
If we do fear, how can we shun it?
If we do fear, with fear we do but aid
145　　The thing we fear to seize on us the sooner.
If we fear not, then no resolvèd proffer
Can overthrow the limit of our fate:
For whether ripe or rotten, drop we shall,

---

112 **unadvisèd** rash, heedless   113 **in ... me** by making me such an offer/treating me with such pity   114 **Haply** perhaps, it may be that   115 **divine extemporal** theologian able to offer up unstudied prayers   116 **render** give   **commonplace** commonplace book, handbook   118 **quality** nature, specific character   119 **avail** assistance, benefit   122 **wanton** spoiled child/lewd, lascivious person   125 **Now ... time** Audley, as the older, more experienced soldier is asked for his advice   **sound** express in words/proclaim/search into, make trial of   **silver wings** eloquent words   **those milk-white ... of time** white hairs of age   128 **busy** engaged in   **bit** wounded   **broils** quarrels, battles   129 **stratagems ... face** the marks of your past military exploits are written on your noble face, i.e. his face is scarred from previous battles   131 **married ... maid** Audley is a man already wedded to war whereas Prince Edward is a virgin soldier   135 **The ... chase** whoever engages in the chase is chased in turn by another   138 **First ... death** the passage of life as a botanical metaphor   **shade** ghost, shadow   141 **If then ... sooner** employs the rhetorical figure of *gradatio* in which the argument is built up stepwise as the last word of one clause begins the next   146 **resolvèd proffer** determined challenge or intention   147 **limit ... fate** destiny

As we do draw the lottery of our doom.

150   PRINCE EDWARD Ah, good old man, a thousand thousand armours,

These words of thine have buckled on my back.

Ah, what an idiot hast thou made of life,

To seek the thing it fears, and how disgraced,

The imperial victory of murd'ring death,

155   Since all the lives his conquering arrows strike

Seek him, and he not them, to shame his glory.

I will not give a penny for a life,

Nor half a halfpenny to shun grim death,

Since for to live is but to seek to die,

160   And dying but beginning of new life.

Let come the hour when he that rules it will:

To live or die I hold indifferent.   *Exeunt*

[Act 4 Scene 5]

Enter King John and [Prince] Charles

KING JOHN A sudden darkness hath defaced the sky,

The winds are crept into their caves for fear,

The leaves move not, the world is hushed and still,

The birds cease singing, and the wand'ring brooks

5   Murmur no wonted greeting to their shores:

Silence attends some wonder, and expecteth

That heaven should pronounce some prophecy.

Where or from whom proceeds this silence, Charles?

CHARLES   Our men with open mouths and staring eyes,

10   Look on each other, as they did attend

Each other's words, and yet no creature speaks;

A tongue-tied fear hath made a midnight hour,

And speeches sleep through all the waking regions.

KING JOHN But now the pompous sun in all his pride

15   Looked through his golden coach upon the world,

And on a sudden hath he hid himself

That now the under-earth is as a grave,

Dark, deadly, silent, and uncomfortable.   *A clamour of ravens*

Hark, what a deadly outcry do I hear?

20   CHARLES   Here comes my brother Philip.

[*Enter Philip*]

KING JOHN All dismayed!

---

149 doom final fate   **159 Since ... life** the passage combines Stoic and Christian philosophy: the notion that human life is a preparation for a good death and that death is the entrance to everlasting life   **Since for** since the reason   **161 when ... will** i.e. whenever God wishes   **162 indifferent** equal **[4.5]** *Location: the battlefield at Poitiers* **1 defaced** spoiled the appearance of/obliterated   **5 wonted** customary   **6 attends** awaits/accompanies **10 as** as if   **attend** await/listen to   **14 But now** a moment ago   **pompous** glorious   **pride** splendour   **16 on a sudden** all at once   **17 under-earth** earth beneath the sky   **18 uncomfortable** disquieting, inconsolable/comfortless   *clamour* loud crying   **21 All dismayed!** Completely terrified!

What fearful words are those thy looks presage?

PHILIP A flight, a flight!

KING JOHN Coward, what flight? Thou liest: there needs no flight.

25 PHILIP A flight—

KING JOHN Awake thy craven powers, and tell on

The substance of that very fear indeed

Which is so ghastly printed in thy face.

What is the matter?

30 PHILIP A flight of ugly ravens

Do croak and hover o'er our soldiers' heads

And keep in triangles and cornered squares,

Right as our forces are embattlèd.

With their approach there came this sudden fog

35 Which now hath hid the airy floor of heaven,

And made at noon a night unnatural

Upon the quaking and dismayèd world.

In brief, our soldiers have let fall their arms,

And stand like metamorphosed images,

40 Bloodless and pale, one gazing on another.

KING JOHN Ay, now I call to mind the prophecy,

But I must give no entrance to a fear.

Return and hearten up these yielding souls,

Tell them the ravens seeing them in arms,

45 So many fair against a famished few,

Come but to dine upon their handiwork,

And prey upon the carrion that they kill.

For when we see a horse laid down to die,

Although not dead, the ravenous birds

50 Sit watching the departure of his life,

Even so these ravens for the carcasses

Of those poor English that are marked to die,

Hover about, and if they cry to us,

'Tis but for meat that we must kill for them.

55 Away, and comfort up my soldiers

And sound the trumpets, and at once dispatch

This little business of a silly fraud.   *Exit Prince [Philip]*

Another noise, Salisbury brought in by a French Captain

CAPTAIN Behold, my liege, this knight and forty more

Of whom the better part are slain and fled,

60 With all endeavour sought to break our ranks

And make their way to the encompassed prince;

---

26 **Awake ... powers** pull yourself together   **craven** cowardly   **tell on** continue to explain   28 **ghastly** horribly   30 **ugly ravens** large black birds of the crow family, regarded as ill-omens foreboding death, probably because, as King John goes on to explain, they followed armies in the expectation of feeding on the corpses   32 **keep ... embattlèd** immediately overhead in the same formation as our troops   35 **floor of heaven** sky   39 **metamorphosed images** shapes turned to stone, like statues   57 **silly fraud** foolish/simple trick or deception

Dispose of him as please your majesty.

KING JOHN Go, and the next bough, soldier, that thou seest,

Disgrace it with his body presently,

65   For I do hold a tree in France too good,

To be the gallows of an English thief.

SALISBURY My lord of Normandy, I have your pass,

And warrant for my safety through this land.

CHARLES   Villiers procured it for thee, did he not?

70   SALISBURY He did.

CHARLES   And it is current, thou shalt freely pass.

KING JOHN Ay, freely to the gallows to be hanged,

Without denial or impediment.

Away with him!

75   [CHARLES] I hope your highness will not so disgrace me,

And dash the virtue of my seal at arms.

He hath my never-broken name to show,

Charact'red with this princely hand of mine,

And rather let me leave to be a prince,

80   Than break the stable verdict of a prince.

I do beseech you let him pass in quiet.

KING JOHN Thou and thy word lie both in my command,

What canst thou promise that I cannot break?

Which of these twain is greater infamy,

85   To disobey thy father or thyself?

Thy word nor no man's may exceed his power,

Nor that same man doth never break his word,

That keeps it to the utmost of his power.

The breach of faith dwells in the soul's consent

90   Which if thyself without consent do break,

Thou art not chargèd with the breach of faith.

Go hang him, for thy licence lies in me,

And my constraint stands the excuse for thee.

CHARLES   What am I not a soldier in my word?

95   Then arms adieu, and let them fight that list.

Shall I not give my girdle from my waist

But with a guardian I shall be controlled,

To say I may not give my things away?

Upon my soul, had Edward Prince of Wales

100   Engaged his word, writ down his noble hand,

For all your knights to pass his father's land,

The royal king, to grace his warlike son,

Would not alone safe conduct give to them

---

64 **Disgrace ... presently** hang him immediately   71 **And** if   76 **dash ... arms** destroy the moral authority of the seal featuring his coat of arms attached to the passport   77 **never-broken name** signature/reputation for honesty   78 **Charact'red** written   79 **leave to be** stop being   80 **stable verdict** trustworthy judgement   93 **constraint ... thee** my coercion can be your excuse   95 **adieu** farewell (French)   **that list** who wish   102 **grace** please/honour   103 **alone** only

But with all bounty feasted them and theirs.

105 KING JOHN Dwell'st thou on precedents? Then be it so.
Say, Englishman, of what degree thou art?

SALISBURY An earl in England, though a prisoner here,
And those that know me call me Salisbury.

KING JOHN Then, Salisbury, say whither thou art bound?

110 SALISBURY To Calais where my liege King Edward is.

KING JOHN To Calais, Salisbury? Then to Calais pack,
And bid the king prepare a noble grave,
To put his princely son Black Edward in;
And as thou travell'st westward from this place,

115 Some two leagues hence there is a lofty hill,
Whose top seems topless, for th'embracing sky
Doth hide his high head in her azure bosom,
Upon whose tall top when thy foot attains,
Look back upon the humble vale beneath—

120 Humble of late, but now made proud with arms—
And thence behold the wretched Prince of Wales,
Hooped with a bond of iron round about.
After which sight to Calais spur amain,
And say the prince was smothered and not slain,

125 And tell the king this is not all his ill,
For I will greet him ere he thinks I will.
Away, begone, the smoke but of our shot
Will choke our foes, though bullets hit them not.   *Exeunt*

[Act 4 Scene 6]

Alarum. Enter Prince Edward and Artois

ARTOIS How fares your grace? Are you not shot, my lord?

PRINCE EDWARD No, dear Artois, but choked with dust and smoke,
And stepped aside for breath and fresher air.

ARTOIS Breathe then, and to it again. The amazèd French

5 Are quite distract with gazing on the crows
And were our quivers full of shafts again,
Your grace should see a glorious day of this.
O, for more arrows, lord, that's our want.

PRINCE EDWARD Courage, Artois, a fig for feathered shafts,

---

104 **bounty** liberality, generosity   105 **Dwell'st ... precedents?** are you insisting on exemplary models/the rules (of chivalry)?   111 **pack** depart   113 **Black Edward** Edward is known to history as 'The Black Prince' perhaps from the black cuirass he wore; King John's appellation is derogatory here   115 **two leagues hence** six miles from here; a **league** was about three miles   117 **azure** bright blue   118 **attains** reaches it   119 **humble** low-lying/unpretentious; the latter sense is picked up on in the next line, **Humble** in contrast to **proud**   **vale** wide, flat valley   120 **of late** before   122 **bond** chain, band   123 **amain** at full speed   124 **smothered** choked, stifled   127 **but** alone   **shot** cannonfire   [4.6]   *Location: the battlefield at Poitiers*   **Alarum** a stage direction to signify fighting, skirmishes; primarily a signal calling soldiers to arms   5 **distract** driven mad, distracted/divided, scattered   6 **quivers** portable cases for carrying arrows   **shafts** arrows   8 **our want** what we need

10 When feathered fowls do bandy on our side,

What need we fight and sweat and keep a coil,

When railing crows outscold our adversaries?

Up, up, Artois! The ground itself is armed,

With fire-containing flint: command our bows

15 To hurl away their pretty-coloured yew,

And to it with stones. Away, Artois, away!

My soul doth prophesy we win the day.   *Exeunt. Alarum*

Enter King John

KING JOHN Our multitudes are in themselves confounded,

Dismayèd, and distraught; swift-starting fear

20 Hath buzzed a cold dismay through all our army,

And every petty disadvantage prompts

The fear-possessèd abject soul to fly.

Myself, whose spirit is steel to their dull lead,

What with recalling of the prophecy,

25 And that our native stones from English arms

Rebel against us, find myself attainted

With strong surprise of weak and yielding fear.

Enter Charles

[CHARLES] Fly, father, fly! The French do kill the French:

Some that would stand let drive at some that fly,

30 Our drums strike nothing but discouragement,

Our trumpets sound dishonour, and retire.

The spirit of fear, that feareth nought but death,

Cowardly works confusion on itself.

Enter Philip

[PHILIP] Pluck out your eyes, and see not this day's shame.

35 An arm hath beat an army; one poor David

Hath with a stone foiled twenty stout Goliaths:

Some twenty naked starvelings with small flints

Hath driven back a puissant host of men,

Arrayed and fenced in all accomplements.

40 KING JOHN *Mort Dieu*! They quoit at us, and kill us up.

No less than forty thousand wicked elders

Have forty lean slaves this day stoned to death.

CHARLES O, that I were some other countryman!

This day hath set derision on the French,

---

10 feathered fowls birds   **bandy** fight/band together   **11 keep a coil** make a fuss   **12 railing** noisily complaining   **outscold** outdo in quarrelling
14 fire-containing flint containing stones of hard flint which produce sparks when struck   **bows** bowmen, archers   **15 pretty-coloured yew** longbows
were made from yew wood and polished red, orange or brown   **18 confounded** confused, disordered   **19 swift-starting** fast flying   **22 abject** despicable,
servile   **25 that** the fact that   **26 attainted** affected/corrupted   **29 would stand** choose to stay and fight   **let drive at** constrain/pursue/shoot
35 David ... Goliaths referring to the biblical tale in which the shepherd boy, David, defeated the giant Goliath with a single stone from his sling (1 Samuel 17)
37 starvelings weak, wretched, underfed creatures   **38 puissant** powerful, mighty   **39 fenced** protected   **accomplements** equipment, trappings
40 *Mort Dieu*! God's death! (French oath)   **quoit** throw (as in the game of quoits)   **kill us up** extinguish us completely   **41 wicked elders** i.e. the
French, senior in rank and age but cowardly   **42 lean slaves** ill-provided, servile creatures

45   And all the world will blurt and scorn at us.

KING JOHN   What! Is there no hope left?

PRINCE PHILIP   No hope but death to bury up our shame.

KING JOHN   Make up once more with me: the twentieth part

           Of those that live, are men enough to quail

50   The feeble handful on the adverse part.

CHARLES   Then charge again, if heaven be not opposed

           We cannot lose the day.

KING JOHN   On, away!   *Exeunt*

Enter Audley wounded, and rescued by two [E]squires

ESQUIRE   How fares my lord?

55   AUDLEY   Even as a man may do

           That dines at such a bloody feast as this.

ESQUIRE   I hope, my lord, that is no mortal scar?

AUDLEY   No matter if it be: the count is cast,

           And in the worst ends but a mortal man.

60   Good friends, convey me to the princely Edward

           That in the crimson bravery of my blood,

           I may become him with saluting him.

           I'll smile and tell him that this open scar,

           Doth end the harvest of his Audley's war.   *Exeunt*

[Act 4 Scene 7]

Enter Prince Edward, King John, Charles, and all with ensigns spread. Retreat sounded

PRINCE EDWARD   Now, John in France, and lately John of France,

           Thy bloody ensigns are my captive colours,

           And you, high-vaunting Charles of Normandy,

           That once today sent me a horse to fly,

5   Are now the subjects of my clemency.

           Fie, lords, is it not a shame that English boys,

           Whose early days are yet not worth a beard,

           Should in the bosom of your kingdom thus,

           One against twenty beat you up together?

10   KING JOHN   Thy fortune, not thy force hath conquered us.

PRINCE EDWARD   An argument that heaven aids the right.

           See, see, Artois doth bring with him along

           The late good counsel given to my soul.

           Welcome, Artois, and welcome, Philip, too:

15   Who now of you or I have need to pray?

---

45 blurt treat contemptuously, literally make a contemptuous puffing gesture with the lips   **48 Make up** get together a force/fight/repair   **49 quail** daunt, discourage/overpower, destroy   **50 adverse part** opposing side   **57 mortal scar** fatal wound   **58 count is cast** account, reckoning is made up
61 bravery finery   **[4.7]** *Location: field of battle at Poitiers*   **2 bloody ensigns** blood-soaked flags, banners   **colours** badges, insignia   **3 high-vaunting** boastful   **7 early** youthful

Now is the proverb verified in you:

Too bright a morning breeds a louring day.   *Sound Trumpets*

Enter Audley

But say, what grim discouragement comes here?

Alas, what thousand armèd men of France

20   Have writ that note of death in Audley's face?

Speak, thou that woo'st death with thy careless smile

And lookst so merrily upon thy grave

As if thou wert enamoured on thine end,

What hungry sword hath so bereaved thy face

25   And lopped a true friend from my loving soul?

AUDLEY   O, prince, thy sweet bemoaning speech to me

Is as a mournful knell to one dead sick.

PRINCE EDWARD   Dear Audley, if my tongue ring out thy end,

My arms shall be thy grave. What may I do

30   To win thy life or to revenge thy death?

If thou wilt drink the blood of captive kings,

Or that it were restorative, command

A health of king's blood and I'll drink to thee.

If honour may dispense for thee with death,

35   The never-dying honour of this day

Share wholly, Audley, to thyself and live.

AUDLEY   Victorious prince, that thou art so, behold

A Caesar's fame in kings' captivity;

If I could hold dim death but at a bay,

40   Till I did see my liege, thy loyal father,

My soul should yield this castle of my flesh,

This mangled tribute, with all willingness

To darkness, consummation, dust and worms.

PRINCE EDWARD   Cheerily, bold man, thy soul is all too proud

45   To yield her city for one little breach,

Should be divorcèd from her earthly spouse,

By the soft temper of a Frenchman's sword.

Lo, to repair thy life, I give to thee,

Three thousand marks a year in English land.

50   AUDLEY   I take thy gift to pay the debts I owe:

These two poor esquires redeemed me from the French

With lusty and dear hazard of their lives;

What thou hast given me I give to them,

---

17 louring gloomy, threatening   **25 lopped** cut off   **26 bemoaning** lamenting, pitying   **27 knell** funeral bell   **28 if … end** if I must speak of your death   **31 wilt** wish to   **32 restorative** capable of restoring health   **33 health** toast drunk in a person's honour   **34 If … death** If honour were able to pay off the debt you owe to death   **37 Victorious … captivity** the proof of your victory is that, like Caesar, you have captured kings   **39 at a bay** hunting term, describing the point when the pack finally had the quarry cornered but held off from the kill   **41 castle … flesh** the body, the house of the soul   **45 breach** violation/wound   **46 her earthly spouse** the soul was imagined as female and hence her **earthly spouse**, her physical husband, the body, as male   **47 soft temper** weak, yielding, nature; plays on the process of 'tempering' in which swords were strengthened by being heated then plunged into cold water   **49 Three … land** land, the income from which was valued at three thousand **marks** a year; a mark was worth roughly two thirds of a pound sterling   **51 esquires** young men of noble birth, immediately below the level of knight in chivalry

And as thou lovest me, prince, lay thy consent
55   To this bequeath in my last testament.
PRINCE EDWARD Renownèd Audley, live and have from me
This gift twice doubled to these esquires and thee:
But live or die, what thou hast given away,
To these and theirs shall lasting freedom stay.
60   Come, gentlemen, I will see my friend bestowed
Within an easy litter, then we'll march
Proudly toward Calais with triumphant pace,
Unto my royal father, and there bring,
The tribute of my wars, fair France his king.   *Exeunt*

[Act 5 Scene 1]

Enter six Citizens in their shirts, barefoot, with halters about their necks.
Enter King Edward, Queen [Philippa], Derby, soldiers
KING EDWARD No more, Queen Philippa, pacify yourself,
Copland, except he can excuse his fault,
Shall find displeasure written in our looks.
And now unto this proud resisting town:
5   Soldiers' assault I will no longer stay,
To be deluded by their false delays;
Put all to sword and make the spoil your own.
ALL   Mercy, king Edward, mercy, gracious lord.
KING EDWARD Contemptuous villains, call ye now for truce?
10   Mine ears are stopped against your bootless cries.
Sound drums alarum, draw threat'ning swords!
FIRST CITIZEN Ah, noble prince, take pity on this town,
And hear us, mighty king.
We claim the promise that your highness made:
15   The two days' respite is not yet expired
And we are come with willingness to bear
What torturing death or punishment you please,
So that the trembling multitude be saved.
KING EDWARD My promise? Well I do confess as much,
20   But I require the chiefest citizens
And men of most account that should submit.
You peradventure are but servile grooms,
Or some felonious robbers on the sea,
Whom apprehended law would execute,

---

60 **bestowed** placed safely   61 **easy** comfortable   **litter** frame supporting a bed for carrying the sick or wounded   **[5.1]**   5 **stay** hold back   7 **Put ... sword** kill   **spoil** booty, plunder   9 **villains** low-born, base-minded rustics   10 **bootless** unavailing, unprofitable   11 **alarum** a call to arms   22 **peradventure** perhaps, possibly   **servile grooms** poor servants, low-born fellows   23 **felonious ... sea** pirates   **felonious** criminal   24 **Whom ... us** sentenced by the law to capital punishment, even if we were disposed to exercise clemency

25   Albeit severity lay dead in us.
            No, no ye cannot overreach us thus.
        SECOND CITIZEN The sun, dread lord, that in the western fall
            Beholds us now low brought through misery,
            Did in the orient purple of the morn
30   Salute our coming forth when we were known,
            Or may our portion be with damnèd fiends.
        KING EDWARD If it be so, then let our covenant stand.
            We take possession of the town in peace
            But for yourselves look you for no remorse
35   But, as imperial justice hath decreed,
            Your bodies shall be dragged about these walls,
            And after feel the stroke of quartering steel:
            This is your doom. Go, soldiers, see it done.
        QUEEN   Ah, be more mild unto these yielding men.
40   It is a glorious thing to stablish peace,
            And kings approach the nearest unto God,
            By giving life and safety unto men.
            As thou intendest to be King of France,
            So let her people live to call thee king,
45   For what the sword cuts down or fire hath spoiled
            Is held in reputation none of ours.
        KING EDWARD Although experience teach us this is true,
            That peaceful quietness brings most delight,
            When most of all abuses are controlled,
50   Yet insomuch it shall be known that we
            As well can master our affections
            As conquer other by the dint of sword,
            Philippa prevail. We yield to thy request:
            These men shall live to boast of clemency,
55   And tyranny strike terror to thyself.
        ALL CITIZENS Long live, your highness! Happy be your reign!
        KING EDWARD Go get you hence, return unto the town,
            And if this kindness hath deserved your love,
            Learn then to reverence Edward as your king.   *Exeunt* [*Citizens*]
60   Now might we hear of our affairs abroad,
            We would till gloomy winter were o'erspent,
            Dispose our men in garrison awhile.
            But who comes here?
        Enter Copland and King David
        DERBY   Copland, my lord, and David King of Scots.

---

26 overreach outwit/overcome   **29 orient ... morn** sunrise in the east   **31 Or ... fiends** if we're not telling the truth may we be damned and go to hell   **34 remorse** compunction/feeling of regret   **37 quartering steel** being cut into quarters with swords   **38 doom** fate/judgement   **40 stablish** establish   **46 Is ... ours** is not considered as belonging to us   **51 affections** passions   **52 dint of sword** force of arms   **61 o'erspent** completely over   **62 garrison** defensive quarters

65   **KING EDWARD**   Is this the proud presumptuous esquire of the north

           That would not yield his prisoner to my queen?

          COPLAND   I am, my liege, a northern esquire indeed,

           But neither proud nor insolent, I trust.

          KING EDWARD   What moved thee then to be so obstinate,

70   To contradict our royal queen's desire?

          COPLAND   No wilful disobedience, mighty lord,

           But my desert and public law at arms.

           I took the king myself in single fight

           And like a soldier would be loath to lose

75   The least pre-eminence that I had won;

           And Copland straight upon your highness' charge

           Is come to France, and with a lowly mind

           Doth vail the bonnet of his victory.

           Receive, dread lord, the custom of my fraught,

80   The wealthy tribute of my labouring hands,

           Which should long since have been surrendered up

           Had but your gracious self been there in place.

          QUEEN   But, Copland, thou didst scorn the king's command

           Neglecting our commission in his name.

85   **COPLAND**   His name I reverence but his person more.

           His name shall keep me in allegiance still,

           But to his person I will bend my knee.

          KING EDWARD   I pray thee, Philippa, let displeasure pass.

           This man doth please me and I like his words,

90   For what is he that will attempt great deeds

           And lose the glory that ensues the fame?

           All rivers have recourse unto the sea

           And Copland's faith relation to his king.

           Kneel, therefore, down! Now rise, King Edward's knight: *Copland kneels, is knighted, and rises*

95   And to maintain thy state I freely give

           Five hundred marks a year to thee and thine.

         Enter Salisbury

           Welcome, Lord Salisbury. What news from Brittany?

         SALISBURY   This, mighty king: the country we have won

           And Charles de Mountford, regent of that place,

100   Presents your highness with this coronet   *Presenting a coronet*

           Protesting true allegiance to your grace.

          KING EDWARD   We thank thee for thy service, valiant earl,

           Challenge our favour for we owe it thee.

---

72 public ... arms existing code of war   **74 loath** reluctant   **75 pre-eminence** privilege/distinction   **76 charge** order   **77 lowly** humble
78 Doth ... bonnet remove his head covering as a mark of respect   **vail** lower   **bonnet** common, soft head-covering especially in the north, distinguished from a hat by the lack of a brim   **79 dread** revered, held in awe/feared   **custom** tribute (paid to a lord or ruler in feudal service)   **fraught** cargo, freight, i.e. King David   **84 commission** order   **91 ensues** follows   **92 recourse** a flowing back, return   **93 faith** loyalty   **relation ... king** i.e. Copland's loyalty to his king bears the same relationship as a river to the sea, it will always flow towards him   **103 Challenge** demand as a right

SALISBURY But now, my lord, as this is joyful news,

105   So must my voice be tragical again

And I must sing of doleful accidents.

KING EDWARD   What have our men the overthrow at Poitiers?

Or is our son beset with too much odds?

SALISBURY He was, my lord, and as my worthless self

110   With forty other serviceable knights,

Under safe-conduct of the dauphin's seal,

Did travel that way, finding him distressed,

A troop of lances met us on the way,

Surprised and brought us prisoners to the king

115   Who proud of this and eager of revenge

Commanded straight to cut off all our heads.

And surely we had died but that the duke,

More full of honour than his angry sire,

Procured our quick deliverance from thence.

120   But ere we went, 'Salute your king', quoth he,

'Bid him provide a funeral for his son.

Today our sword shall cut his thread of life

And sooner than he thinks we'll be with him

To quittance those displeasures he hath done.'

125   This said, we passed, not daring to reply.

Our hearts were dead, our looks diffused and wan:

Wand'ring, at last we climbed unto a hill

From whence, although our grief were much before,

Yet now to see the occasion with our eyes

130   Did thrice so much increase our heaviness,

For there, my lord, oh there we did descry

Down in a valley how both armies lay.

The French had cast their trenches like a ring

And every barricado's open front

135   Was thick embossed with brazen ordinance.

Here stood a battle of ten thousand horse,

There twice as many pikes in quadrant-wise,

Here crossbows and deadly-wounding darts,

And in the midst like to a slender point

140   Within the compass of the horizon,

As 'twere a rising bubble in the sea,

---

106 **doleful accidents** distressing events   107 **the overthrow** been defeated   108 **too much odds** too great a disparity of numbers against him
110 **serviceable** active, diligent in service   113 **lances** lancers, cavalry soldiers armed with lances   118 **sire** father   119 **deliverance** release   120 **ere**
before   122 **cut ... life** a common image for death deriving from classical mythology in which the Fates were represented as three old women whose spinning
controlled human destiny: Klotho held the distaff, Lachesis drew off the thread and Atropos cut it short   124 **quittance** repay   126 **diffused** confused,
distracted   **wan** pale   127 **Wandr'ing** turning aside from our direct route   130 **thrice so much** three times as much   **heaviness** sadness, grief
131 **descry** discover, catch sight of (especially as a scout from a distance)   133 **cast** arranged, disposed   134 **barricado's** barricade's: of a hastily formed
rampart thrown up to obstruct an enemy advance   135 **thick embossed** thickly studded or decorated   **brazen ordinance** military equipment made of
brass, punning on 'ordnance' but playing on sense of 'shameless scheming'   136 **battle** body of troops, battalion   137 **pikes in quadrant-wise** footsoldiers
armed with pikes arranged in square formation   138 **darts** spears   140 **compass** circle

A hazel wand amidst a wood of pines,
Or as a bear fast-chained unto a stake,
Stood famous Edward still expecting when
145 Those dogs of France would fasten on his flesh.
Anon the death-procuring knell begins,
Off go the cannons that with trembling noise
Did shake the very mountain where they stood,
Then sound the trumpets' clangour in the air;
150 The battles join, and when we could no more
Discern the difference twixt the friend and foe—
So intricate the dark confusion was—
Away we turned our wat'ry eyes with sighs
As black as powder fuming into smoke.
155 And thus I fear, unhappy have I told,
The most untimely tale of Edward's fall.
QUEEN   Ah me, is this my welcome into France?
Is this the comfort that I looked to have,
When I should meet with my beloved son?
160 Sweet Ned, I would thy mother in the sea
Had been prevented of this mortal grief.
KING EDWARD   Content thee, Philippa, 'tis not tears will serve,
To call him back if he be taken hence.
Comfort thyself as I do, gentle queen,
165 With hope of sharp unheard of dire revenge.
He bids me to provide his funeral
And so I will, but all the peers in France
Shall mourners be and weep out bloody tears
Until their empty veins be dry and sere.
170 The pillars of his hearse shall be their bones,
The mould that covers him, their city ashes,
His knell the groaning cries of dying men,
And in the stead of tapers on his tomb,
An hundred fifty towers shall burning blaze,
175 While we bewail our valiant son's decease.
After a flourish sounded within, enter a Herald
HERALD   Rejoice, my lord, ascend the imperial throne!
The mighty and redoubted Prince of Wales,
Great servitor to bloody Mars in arms,
The Frenchman's terror and his country's fame,
180 Triumphant rideth like a Roman peer,

---

143 **bear ... flesh** the final image of Edward surrounded by the French troops is from bear-baiting, a popular sport in Tudor times   **expecting** waiting for the moment   146 **Anon** at once   **death-procuring** fatal   **knell** funeral bell   150 **battles** armies   151 **twixt** between   152 **intricate** entangled, obscure   154 **black** gloomy   **powder** gunpowder   **fuming** rising in fumes   156 **untimely** premature, unseasonable; the adjective is used to qualify 'fall' which is what Salisbury intends and King Edward understands but in fact its position next to 'tale' makes it ironically ambiguous and the audience know that Prince Edward was not in fact defeated   161 **prevented** spared/anticipated, i.e. by her own death from drowning   169 **sere** withered   171 **mould** earth   173 **stead** place   178 **servitor** servant/military attendant   **Mars** the Roman god of war

And lowly at his stirrup comes afoot
King John of France, together with his son,
In captive bonds, whose diadem he brings
To crown thee with and to proclaim thee king.

185 KING EDWARD Away with mourning, Philippa, wipe thine eyes!
Sound trumpets! Welcome in Plantagenet.

Enter Prince Edward, King John, [Prince] Philip, Audley, Artois

KING EDWARD As things long lost when they are found again,
So doth my son rejoice his father's heart,
For whom even now my soul was much perplexed.

190 QUEEN   Be this a token to express my joy,   *Kisses him*
For inward passions will not let me speak!

PRINCE EDWARD My gracious father, here receive the gift,
This wreath of conquest, and reward of war,
Got with as mickle peril of our lives
195 As ere was thing of price before this day.
Install your highness in your proper right,
And here withal I render to your hands
These prisoners, chief occasion of our strife.

KING EDWARD So, John of France, I see you keep your word:
200 You promised to be sooner with ourself
Than we did think for, and 'tis so indeed,
But had you done at first as now you do,
How many civil towns had stood untouched,
That now are turned to ragged heaps of stones?
205 How many people's lives mightst thou have saved,
That are untimely sunk into their graves?

KING JOHN Edward, recount not things irrevocable,
Tell me what ransom thou requir'st to have?

KING EDWARD Thy ransom, John, hereafter shall be known.
210 But first to England thou must cross the seas
To see what entertainment it affords:
Howe'er it falls, it cannot be so bad
As ours hath been since we arrived in France.

KING JOHN Accursèd man, of this I was foretold,
215 But did misconster what the prophet told.

PRINCE EDWARD Now, father, this petition Edward makes
To thee, whose grace hath been his strongest shield,
That as thy pleasure chose me for the man
To be the instrument to show thy power,
220 So thou wilt grant that many princes more,

---

181 afoot on foot   **183 diadem** crown   **187 As ... again** echoes the phrases of Christ's parable of the lost sheep (Matthew 18:12–14, Luke 15:3–7)
189 even now just now, a moment ago   **perplexed** afflicted, distressed   **194 mickle** much   **197 withal** in addition   **198 occasion** cause   **203 civil**
well-ordered/civilian   **206 untimely** prematurely   **207 irrevocable** irreversible, that cannot be called back   **212 Howe'er it falls** whatever it's like
215 misconster misconstrue, wrongly interpret

Bred and brought up within that little isle

May still be famous for like victories.

And for my part, the bloody scars I bear,

The weary nights that I have watched in field,

225   The dangerous conflicts I have often had,

The fearful menaces were proffered me,

The heat and cold, and what else might displease,

I wish were now redoubled twenty fold,

So that hereafter ages when they read

230   The painful traffic of my tender youth

Might thereby be inflamed with such resolve,

As not the territories of France alone,

But likewise Spain, Turkey, and what countries else

That justly would provoke fair England's ire,

235   Might at their presence tremble and retire.

KING EDWARD   Here, English lords, we do proclaim a rest,

An intercession of our painful arms:

Sheathe up your swords, refresh your weary limbs,

Peruse your spoils, and after we have breathed

240   A day or two within this haven town,

God willing then for England we'll be shipped,

Where in a happy hour I trust we shall

Arrive three kings, two princes, and a queen.   [*Exeunt*]

FINIS

Textual Notes

Q = Quarto text of 1596

Q2 = Quarto text of 1599

Ed = a correction introduced by a later editor

SD = stage direction

SH = speech heading (i.e. speaker's name)

List of parts = Ed

1.1.1 Artois *spelled* Artoys *in* Q   **6 le Beau** = Ed. Q = of Bew   **17 note** = Ed. Q = not   **21 Valois** = Ed. Q = Valoys   **28 SH [KING EDWARD]** = Ed. *Not in* Q *(continuation of Artois' speech)*   **36 watchman** = Ed. Q = watch men   **42 showers** = Ed. Q = shewers   **51 Audley** *spelled* Awdley *in* Q   **99 Lest** = Ed. Q = Least   **111 scarred** = Ed. Q = scard   **118 lords** = Ed. Q = lord   **121 Montague** = Ed. Q = Mountague   **128 Berwick** = Ed. Q = Barwicke   **130 Roxburgh** *spelled* Rocksborough *in* Q   **134 Mountford** = Ed. Q = Mouneford   **148 Hainault** = Ed. Q = Henalt   **152 Almaine** = Ed. Q = Almaigne

1.2.3 want'st = Ed. Q = wants   **12 jigs** *spelled* gigs *in* Q   **20 most** = Q2. Q = must   **27 rusting** = Ed. Q = rust in   **28 spurs** = Ed. Q = spu   **29 gimmaled** *spelled* Gymould *in* Q   **38 I** = Ed. *Not in* Q

230 traffic dealings, business   **232 As not** so that neither   **234 ire** anger   **237 intercession** suspension

65 **shared** *spelled* shard *in* Q   71 **She** = Ed. Q = He   102 **lurked** = Ed. Q = lurke   133 **two** = Ed. Q = to   157 **testimony** = Ed. Q = testomie   158 **waste** = Ed. Q = West

2.1.11 **oriental** = Ed. Q = oryent   15 **presence** = Ed. Q = present   17 **vail** = Ed. Q = waile   **amiss** = Ed. Q = amisle   36 **tongue** *spelled* tong *in* Q   71 **Tartar's** = Ed. Q = Torters   75 **sovereign's** = Q2 Q = soueraigne   79 **Beguile** = Ed. Q = Beguild   90 **the** = Q2. Q = thy   91 **thy** = Ed. Q = their   137 **sand by sand** = Ed. Q = said, by said   153 **treasure** = Ed. Q = treason   277 **Whether** = Ed. Q = Whither   290 **Too strict** = Q2. Q = To stricke   **ward** = Ed. Q = weed   301 **cumber** = Ed. Q = comber   314 **if** = Ed. Q = I if   328 **account** = Q2. Q = accomplish   329 **unswear** = Ed. Q = answere   341 **bonds** = Ed. Q = bonde   374 **presence** = Q2. Q = promise   376 **errand** = Ed. Q = arrant   393 **doth** = Ed. Q = goth   407 **thy** = Ed. Q = their   417 **envired** = Ed. Q = inuierd   451 **glory** = Ed. Q = gloomie   461 **I'll** = Ed. Q = Ils

2.2.40 **abundance** = Ed. Q = aboundant   51 **brawls** = Ed. Q = brauls   73 **too** = Ed. Q = two   157 **through** = Ed. Q = throng   **Hellespont** = Ed. Q = hellie spout   211 **gild** = Ed. Q = guide   212 **martial** *spelled* marshall *in* Q

3.1.6 **martial** *spelled* marchiall *in* Q   33 **domestic** = Ed. Q = drum stricke   52 **gain** = Q2. Q = game   62 **descried** = Q2. Q = discribde   83 **our** = Ed. Q = out   90 **There's** = Q2. Q = these   105 **thy conceit** = Q2. Q = their concept   120 **Steer** = Ed. Q = Stir   134 **froward** = Q2. Q = forward   136 **th'other** = Q2. Q = thither   164 **crannied** = Ed. Q = cranny   175 **Were** = Ed. Q = We   177 *Nonpareille* = Ed. Q = Nom per illa   178 *Boulogne* = Ed. Q = Bullen   180 **wind** = Q2. Q = wine

3.2.5 **day =** Q2. Q = pay   49 **ransack** = Ed. Q = ransackt   59 **Turned** = Ed. Q = I tourned   65 **his** = Ed. Q = is

3.3.0 SD *Grace* = Ed. Q = Graie   2 **Somme** = Ed. Q = Sone   20 **Barfleur** = Ed. Q = Harflen   **Lô** = Ed. Q = Lie   **Crotoy** = Ed. Q = Crotag   **Carentan** = Ed. Q = Carentigne   51 **Upbraids** = Ed. Q = Obraids   64 **Thy** = Q2. Q = they   99 **hid** = Q2. Q = hide   126 **Upbraidst** = Ed. Q = Obraidst   140 **now's** = Ed. Q = knows   165 **SH ALL FRENCH** Q = 'All. Fra.'   219 **thus** = Q2. Q = this   220 **vaward** = Ed. Q = vorwarde

3.4.60 **haggard** = Q2. Q = huggard   88 **Whose thousands** = Ed. Q = Whom you sayd   99 **carved** = Q2. Q = craud   100 **thus** = Q2. Q = this   108 **proved** = Ed. Q = proude

4.1.1 **your** = Q2. Q = our   14 **at** = Ed. Q = to   15 **Whither** = Q2. Q = Whether   16 **That** = Ed. Q = Yet

4.2.13 **or** = Ed. Q = er   44 **travail** *spelled* trauell *in* Q   57 **queen's** = Q2. Q = queene   62 **SH [CAPTAIN]** = Q2. *Not in* Q   72 **I will** = Q2. Q = Will

4.3.81 **done** = Ed. Q = don

4.4.45 **ta'en** = Ed. Q = tane   103 **body's** = Ed. Q = bodies   114 **Haply** = Q2. Q Happily   123 **SH [THIRD] HERALD** = Ed. Q = Herald   135 **enchased** = Ed. Q = in choice

4.5.20 SD *[Enter Philip]* = Ed. *Not in* Q   35 **floor** = Ed. Q = flower   58 **more** = Ed. Q = mo   75 **SH [CHARLES]** = Ed. Q = Vil.   105 **precedents** *spelled* presidents *in* Q   109 **whither** = Ed. Q = whether

4.6.14 **With** = Ed. *Not in* Q   40 *Mort Dieu!* = Ed. Q = Mordiu!   **quoit** = Ed. Q = quait   45 **will** = Q2. Q = wilt

4.7.13 **given** = Ed. Q = giuer   29 **thy** = Q2. Q = the   33 **health** = Ed. Q = heath

5.1.1 **Philippa** = Ed. Q = Phillip

5.1.12 **SH FIRST CITIZEN** = Ed. Q = All.   38 **doom** = Ed. Q = dome   53 **Philippa** = Ed. Q = Phillip   56 **SH ALL CITIZENS** = Ed. Q = Two: **lose** = Ed. Q = loose   78 **vail** = Ed. Q = vale   88 **Philippa** = Ed. Q = Phillip   112 **travel** *spelled* trauaile *in* Q   162 **Philippa** = Ed. Q = Phillip   169 **their** = Ed. Q = his   185 **Philippa** = Ed. Q = Phillip

THE SPANISH TRAGEDY
(with Additions)

Among the prefatory items published in the First Folio of Shakespeare's plays in 1623 was a poem of praise by his friend and rival Ben Jonson. Shakespeare's works, writes Jonson, outshone those of the peers who preceded him: *'And tell, how far thou didst our* Lyly *outshine, / Or sporting* Kyd *or* Marlowe's *mighty line.'* The name of Christopher Marlowe remains familiar to modern playgoers, those of Lyly and Kyd less so. Lyly was the pioneer of Elizabethan comedy, but in the high art of tragedy there is no doubt that the plays which set the standard were Marlowe's mighty *Tamburlaine the Great* and Thomas Kyd's *The Spanish Tragedy.* To the Elizabethan theatre aficionado, the name of its protagonist, Hieronimo, was synonymous with the barnstorming performance of grief, anger, madness and revenge. The part was high on the list of signature roles of the two most celebrated tragic actors of the age, first Edward Alleyn and then Shakespeare's friend Richard Burbage. Neither the anguished soliloquies of Hamlet nor the precipitation into madness of King Lear would have been possible without the prior example of Kyd's Hieronimo.

There is also a broader sense in which the play sets the pattern for all Shakespeare's work. Not only did *The Spanish Tragedy* create a taste for revenge drama that would set Shakespeare on the road from *Titus Andronicus* to *Hamlet* and beyond. It also raised theatrical self-consciousness to a new level of sophistication, thus showing Shakespeare that one of the most effective things you can do in a play is to play with the idea of a play. Kyd was the first to deploy the device of the 'frame' – an induction, chorus or series of prologues surrounding the action – to its full potential of multivalency and irony. Hieronimo's masque of English conquests is the first surviving instance of a character playing the role of Master of the Revels, and his play in sundry languages is the seminal example of revenge performed through dramatic performance. In this sense, Titus orchestrating his bloody banquet, Peter Quince directing 'Pyramus and Thisbe', Hamlet staging 'The Mousetrap', and Prospero conjuring up the wedding masque in *The Tempest* are all children of Hieronimo.

To create the framing device – we are to imagine the whole action as a performance summoned by Revenge for the edification of the Ghost of Don Andrea – Kyd skilfully combined two techniques from the repertoire of his classical model, the Roman tragedian Seneca: the 'Chorus' who divides the acts with a commentary on the action and the figure from beyond the grave who initiates the action (most relevantly, the Ghost of Tantalus driven on by a Fury at the beginning of Seneca's *Thyestes*). As spectators, Revenge and the Ghost must in some sense function as representatives of the theatre audience. They are not, however, the 'ideal spectators' that the influential nineteenth-century critic A. W. von Schlegel took the chorus of Greek tragedy to be, for they embody the ethic of revenge which the play investigates critically. The audience goes to the theatre having been taught by church and law that revenge is wrong, yet the first encounter they witness is one in which not merely the ethos but the person of Revenge is in charge. By the end of the play, revenge now performed, the two members of the onstage (or above-stage) audience are well satisfied. Their more numerous counterparts in the auditorium will, however, be less certain.

From his debate with himself in Act 3 scene 13 (book in hand, to revenge or not to revenge, that is the question) to his final acts (foreclosures of communication and revelation – tongue bitten out, penknife used to bring death, not to facilitate writing), Hieronimo is a figure who presents the audience with questions, not answers. Even after the full details of his plot have been explained, he insists that something is being held back: 'But never shalt thou force me to reveal / The thing which I have vowed inviolate'. As with Iago's 'Demand me nothing. What you know, you know. / From this time forth I never will speak word' (*Othello*, 5.2.309–10), there is an uncomfortable sense that the end has not revealed all. Andrea is confident that Hieronimo is off to the Elysian Fields, the happy hunting ground of departed virtue in classical myth, but the offstage audience may not be so sure: one may very well imagine his arrival in Avernus being greeted by precisely the kind of disputation about his disposal between the three judges of the Underworld as that concerning Don Andrea with which the play began. The frame sets up a value-structure that is complicated and questioned by the protagonist's anguished quest for justice in the main action.

When Hieronimo stages the tragedy of Soliman and Perseda, he uses the extraordinary device of having it performed with one character speaking in Latin, another in Greek, a third in Italian, and the fourth in French. He deliberately rejects the languages of both his onstage audience (who are Spanish and Portuguese) and his offstage one (the English men and women in the theatre). By writing in a language that no one understands, Kyd makes room for complete concentration on the *action*. Such concentration is needed because of the dazzling complexity of layers of illusion: in playing the murderer Hieronimo actually commits the murder; stage-daggers actually take the lives of Lorenzo, Balthazar and Bel-imperia. But the moment one says this, one recognizes that that is how it looks to the onstage audience, whereas the offstage audience knows perfectly well that Hieronimo, or rather Ed Alleyn or Dick Burbage or whoever is taking the lead, is only playing the murderer. Then again, since the offstage audience is in a similar position to the onstage audience, insofar as it is baffled by the play of sundry languages, perhaps the knowledge that it is only a play has become an *im*perfect knowledge. As with Hermione's statue in Shakespeare's *The Winter's Tale*, but far more troublingly, the interplay of art and life has become blurred.

That blurring is all-important because it forces the critical gaze to turn from art to life. Hieronimo's playing, central to which is his assumption of the role of madman, has created a kind of total theatre, in which every object, word, and action becomes potentially illusory. 'See here my show, look on this spectacle', he says: mirror on mirror mirrored is all the show. Attention is drawn to the tools of the poetic dramatist's craft – tongue, pen, penknife – but then they are instantly transformed from instruments for the creation of art to instruments for the destruction of life. Earlier, proleptically, there has been a tearing of paper, the artist's other instrument. But the papers in question have been not plays but legal documents presented to Hieronimo in his capacity as Knight Marshall: a declaration of debt, an 'action of the case' requiring a special writ, and an '*ejectione firmae* by a lease'. In Kyd's total theatre, the law becomes a text, something as vulnerable as an author's foul papers. As Hieronimo the artist self-destructs by means of his own instruments, so the law is deconstructed by being reduced to a series of props that are displayed and then evacuated of meaningful content. At one moment there is an onstage execution, but at another the law's final instrument, the Hangman's rope, appears not on the gallows but in Hieronimo's hand, from which it is then flung away. As for the law's most merciful instrument, the pardon, it is apparently kept ceremoniously in a box. But the box is never opened and, besides, we know it is empty.

Hieronimo, the man of law, fulfils his role as bringer of justice not in legislation or litigation but when he knocks up a curtain. The public drama progressed by means of bold experimentation and self-conscious play acting of this kind. It is because of their dazzling theatricality as well as their psychological acuity that Marlowe, Shakespeare and a handful of their successors have endured for so long in the repertoire of stage tragedy. For this, they, and we, owe a debt of thanks to *The Spanish Tragedy*.

The enormous influence of *The Spanish Tragedy* is not in itself sufficient to justify its inclusion in a volume of collaborative plays by Shakespeare and others. The text that we have edited is not the first edition, published in 1592, but the revision of 1602, 'Newly corrected, and amended, and enlarged with new additions of the Painter's part, and others, as it hath of late been diverse times acted'. Our text indicates these additions by printing them in a different font from the rest of the play.

There is good reason to doubt the scholarly opinion that the revisions are synonymous with certain 'new adicyons for Jeronymo' for which the theatrical impresario Philip Henslowe paid Ben Jonson around the same time. The exchange between Hieronimo and the Painter is written in a distinct literary style that is not Jonson's. A number of fine critics and scholars over the last two hundred years have judged that this particular very striking enlargement of *The Spanish Tragedy* may well have been contributed by Shakespeare.

His closest colleague Burbage was remembered for playing the part of Hieronimo. And, although it was originally commissioned by Henslowe, a version of *The Spanish Tragedy* seems to have been in the repertoire of the Lord Chamberlain's Men in the late 1590s (this may be inferred from three separate allusions: one in a Cambridge University student play, another in a parody by the dramatist John Marston, the third in John Webster's induction to Marston's *The Malcontent*, which actually features Shakespeare's actors playing themselves). Furthermore, around this time Shakespeare updated his revenge tragedy of *Titus Andronicus* with an additional mad scene – the one where Titus stabs a fly at a dinner party, then mourns its death. Both structurally and stylistically, the new scene for *The Spanish Tragedy* with 'the Painter's part' bears a strong resemblance to this. The circumstantial evidence pointing towards Shakespeare's authorship is thus intriguingly strong.

The first addition develops the intensity of Hieronimo's grief and incipient madness on his discovery of the hanged body of his son Horatio. The essential dramatic device is that of a man talking to himself under the intense pressure of emotion. The second addition is a brief but pointed intervention, its key lines being

> In troth, my lord, it is a thing of nothing,
> The murder of a son, or so:
> A thing of nothing, my lord.

Complexity of feeling is compacted into great simplicity of diction, yet with sophistication of style: look at the way the repetition works, with 'A thing of nothing' repeated after and then before 'my lord'; consider the weight of emotion in the seemingly casual 'or so' that sounds as if it is evoking some little thing precisely because the murder of a son is the biggest thing. This has the aura of the Shakespeare of Macduff's ostensibly muted but utterly devastated reaction to the appalling news of his wife and children's murder in *Macbeth*.

The third addition is a lengthy monologue in which Hieronimo plays down the force of paternal love ('My son! And what's a son? A thing begot / Within a pair of minutes — thereabout') in order to play up the extremity of his grief, which he then wills into the desire for revenge ('Well, heaven is heaven still! / And there is Nemesis and Furies, / And things called whips'). Talking to yourself is sometimes said to be the first sign of madness. But it is also the great innovation of the late Elizabethan stage. Kyd and Marlowe inaugurated, and Shakespeare perfected, the technique of a tragic character discovering his own deepest thoughts and feelings by talking about them out aloud on stage, alone and not alone – not alone, because sometimes there is a silent witness and because always the soliloquy is also a conversation with the audience, whom the actor sees because there is no blinding spotlight, no barrier of a proscenium arch as he stands on a platform thrust out into the surrounding open-air auditorium.

But it is the fourth addition that is a coup of theatrical genius. Hieronimo seems to become Hamlet or Lear before our very eyes, at once mad and not mad. Then a Painter appears, seeking for justice on behalf of his murdered son. The device is a kind of cross between the scene in Shakespeare's *Titus Andronicus* where the Clown's quest for justice gives Titus the opportunity to rail against the injustice of the world, and that in *King Lear* when Gloucester and Lear share the experience of parental loss. But the added twist is the implied debate between the power of painting and that of poetry, something to which Shakespeare will return in *Timon of Athens*. Is it possible to *draw* a murderer? To *paint* madness, grief and death? Perhaps, but never so powerfully on paper or canvas as on a stage with words of poetry and the actions of a great performer.

KEY FACTS

AUTHORSHIP: The play is universally attributed to Thomas Kyd on the basis of contemporary allusions, although all extant editions are anonymous. Some ambiguity surrounds the Additions penned for a later edition. These are usually attributed to Ben Jonson on the basis of payment records made by Philip Henslowe; however, Hugh Craig and Arthur F. Kinney are the latest to argue that Jonson's Additions could not be the same as those published in the same year. This edition suggests that the extant *Spanish Tragedy* may be a different play from Henslowe's. We know that the Chamberlain's Men had a play referred to as 'Hieronimo' and that Burbage was famous in the role, and this may be the *Spanish Tragedy* that survived in an original and revised form. Stylistic analysis by Craig and Kinney, Warren Stevenson and others has tentatively supported the attribution of the Additions to Shakespeare.

PLOT: A Spanish nobleman, Andrea, has been killed during a Portuguese rebellion against Spain, and he and the personification of Revenge begin watching the aftermath of the conflict. Lorenzo, son of the King of Spain, and his companion Horatio have captured Balthazar, Andrea's killer. The King of Spain gives Lorenzo the custody of Balthazar, while Horatio comforts Andrea's bereaved paramour, Bel-imperia. The two fall in love. Balthazar, in love with Bel-imperia, and Lorenzo, jealous of Horatio, conspire to kill him, and leave him hanged.

The body is discovered by Hieronimo, Horatio's father, and his wife Isabella. The two grieve publicly. Bel-imperia is imprisoned by Lorenzo, but secretly sends Hieronimo a letter with the identity of the murderers. Lorenzo covers his tracks by arranging for his associates to be murdered. Hieronimo's appeals for justice are ignored, and he is treated as mad by the courtiers. Isabella commits suicide, and Hieronimo and Bel-imperia join forces, asking Lorenzo and Balthazar to join them in an entertainment for the King and Viceroy of Portugal. During the play, Lorenzo and Balthazar are stabbed and Bel-imperia commits suicide. Under compulsion, Hieronimo bites out his tongue and kills himself. The Ghost of Andrea is able to rest, planning torments for his enemies.

▷

MAJOR PARTS: Hieronimo (33%/145/13), Lorenzo (11%/99/12), King of Spain (8%/55/6), Bel-imperia (7%/60/8), Balthazar (6%/65/11), Viceroy (5%/36/4), Ghost of Andrea (5%/10/5), Pedringano (3%/47/6), Duke of Castile (3%/33/5), Horatio (3%/29/4), Isabella (3%/17/4), General (3%/7/1), Ambassador (2%/14/4).

LINGUISTIC MEDIUM: 98% verse, 2% prose.

DATE: The original play belongs to the late 1580s, perhaps 1587 but potentially as late as 1590. The additions were first published in the 1602 edition and are tentatively dated to c.1597–98.

SOURCES: There are no known direct sources for *The Spanish Tragedy*, but it participates in (and was heavily influential on) the fashion for Senecan revenge tragedy on the Elizabethan stage. The Additions are all original. The plot of Hieronimo's play, during which the final revenge takes place, is that of another play by Thomas Kyd, *Soliman and Perseda*, first printed 1592.

TEXT: The main text of the 1602 Quarto, printed by Thomas Pavier (later responsible for *The Yorkshire Tragedy* and a reprint of *Sir John Oldcastle Part 1* as Shakespeare's) is slavishly reprinted from the careful First Quarto, usually dated to 1592. The Additions themselves are metrically awkward but otherwise well printed. **They are indicated in our text by being printed in a different font from the rest of the play.**

THE SPANISH TRAGEDY

containing the lamentable end of
Don Horatio and Bel-imperia:
with the pitiful death of old Hieronimo.
Newly corrected, amended, and enlarged
with new additions of the Painter's part,
and others, as it hath of late been
diverse times acted

REVENGE ⎫
GHOST OF ANDREA ⎭ Chorus

KING of Spain

Cyprian, Duke of CASTILE, his brother

LORENZO, the duke's son

BEL-IMPERIA, Lorenzo's sister

VICEROY of Portugal

BALTHAZAR, his son

DON PEDRO, the Viceroy's brother

HIERONIMO, Marshal of Spain

ISABELLA, his wife

HORATIO, their son

Spanish GENERAL

DEPUTY

Don Bazulto, an OLD MAN

Three CITIZENS

Portuguese AMBASSADOR

ALEXANDRO ⎫
VILLUPPO ⎭ Portuguese noblemen

PEDRINGANO, Bel-imperia's servant

CHRISTOPHIL, Bel-imperia's custodian

Lorenzo's PAGE

SERBERINE, Balthazar's servant

Isabella's MAID

Messenger

Hangman

Three Kings and three Knights in the first dumb
   show

Hymen and two torchbearers in the second

Bazardo, a PAINTER

PEDRO and JAQUES, Hieronimo's servants

Army. Banquet Royal suites. Noblemen.
   Halberdiers.

Officers. Three Watchmen. Trumpets. Servants, etc.

[Act 1 Scene 1]

Enter the Ghost of Andrea, and with him Revenge

GHOST OF ANDREA   When this eternal substance of my soul
    Did live imprisoned in my wanton flesh,
    Each in their function serving other's need,
    I was a courtier in the Spanish court:
5   My name was Don Andrea; my descent,

[1.1] *Enter* perhaps via the stage trapdoor to suggest the Underworld   **2 wanton** rebellious, undisciplined   **5 Don** Spanish title denoting a
gentleman

Though not ignoble, yet inferior far
To gracious fortunes of my tender youth.
For there, in prime and pride of all my years,
By duteous service and deserving love,
10   In secret I possessed a worthy dame,
Which hight sweet Bel-imperia by name.
But, in the harvest of my summer joys,
Death's winter nipped the blossoms of my bliss,
Forcing divorce betwixt my love and me.
15   For in the late conflict with Portingale
My valour drew me into danger's mouth,
Till life to death made passage through my wounds.
When I was slain, my soul descended straight
To pass the flowing stream of Acheron;
20   But churlish Charon, only boatman there,
Said that, my rites of burial not performed,
I might not sit amongst his passengers.
Ere Sol had slept three nights in Thetis' lap,
And slaked his smoking chariot in her flood,
25   By Don Horatio, our Knight Marshal's son,
My funerals and obsequies were done.
Then was the ferryman of hell content
To pass me over to the slimy strond,
That leads to fell Avernus' ugly waves.
30   There, pleasing Cerberus with honeyed speech,
I passed the perils of the foremost porch.
Not far from hence, amidst ten thousand souls,
Sat Minos, Aeacus, and Rhadamanth,
To whom no sooner 'gan I make approach,
35   To crave a passport for my wand'ring ghost,
But Minos, in graven leaves of lottery,
Drew forth the manner of my life and death.
'This knight', quoth he, 'both lived and died in love,
And for his love tried fortune of the wars,
40   And by war's fortune lost both love and life.'
'Why then,' said Aeacus, 'convey him hence,
To walk with lovers in our fields of love,
And spend the course of everlasting time

8 **prime and pride** earliest and best   11 **Which hight** who was called   14 **divorce** separation   15 **late** recent   **Portingale** Portugal   19 **Acheron** the
river of pain in Greek mythology, one of five Underworld rivers   20 **Charon** the ferryman who carried the souls of the newly dead to the Underworld
22 **might not** would not be allowed to   23 **Ere…flood** before the sun passes over the ocean, i.e. within three days; the image is of the sun god (**Sol**) driving
his chariot into the sea   **Ere** before   **Thetis** a nereid or sea nymph   **slaked** quenched   25 **Knight Marshal** a royal official responsible (in England) for
maintaining order within a twelve-mile radius of the court   26 **obsequies** funeral ceremonies   28 **strond** shore   29 **fell** cruel, terrible   **Avernus** lake
in southern Italy believed to be the entrance to the Underworld   30 **Cerberus** in classical mythology, the many-headed dog guarding the entrance to the
Underworld   31 **porch** entrance   33 **Minos…Rhadamanth** the three judges of the Underworld, selected for their honesty   34 **'gan I** did I begin to
35 **passport** letter of authorization   36 **graven…lottery** slip on which Andrea's life has been engraved

Under green myrtle trees and cypress shades.'
45 'No, no,' said Rhadamanth, 'it were not well,
With loving souls to place a martialist:
He died in war, and must to martial fields,
Where wounded Hector lives in lasting pain,
And Achilles' Myrmidons do scour the plain.'
50 Then Minos, mildest censor of the three,
Made this device to end the difference:
'Send him', quoth he, 'to our infernal king,
To doom him as best seems his majesty.'
To this effect my passport straight was drawn.
55 In keeping on my way to Pluto's court,
Through dreadful shades of ever-glooming night,
I saw more sights than thousand tongues can tell,
Or pens can write, or mortal hearts can think.
Three ways there were: that on the right-hand side
60 Was ready way unto the foresaid fields,
Where lovers live and bloody martialists,
But either sort contained within his bounds.
The left-hand path, declining fearfully,
Was ready downfall to the deepest hell,
65 Where bloody Furies shakes their whips of steel,
And poor Ixion turns an endless wheel;
Where usurers are choked with melting gold,
And wantons are embraced with ugly snakes,
And murd'rers groan with never-killing wounds,
70 And perjured wights scalded in boiling lead,
And all foul sins with torments overwhelmed.
'Twixt these two ways I trod the middle path,
Which brought me to the fair Elysian green,
In midst whereof there stands a stately tower,
75 The walls of brass, the gates of adamant:
Here finding Pluto with his Proserpine,
I showed my passport, humbled on my knee;
Whereat fair Proserpine began to smile,
And begged that only she might give my doom:
80 Pluto was pleased, and sealed it with a kiss.

44 **myrtle** evergreen shrub sacred to Venus, goddess of love　**cypress** coniferous tree, regarded as a symbol of mourning　46 **martialist** warrior
48 **Hector...plain** the Trojan hero (**Hector**) was killed by the **Myrmidons**, the followers of the Greek hero **Achilles** on the **plain** outside Troy
50 **censor** judge　51 **device** arrangement　52 **infernal king** Pluto, god of the Underworld　53 **doom** pronounce judgement on　54 **straight** immediately
56 **ever-glooming** perpetually melancholy/growing darker　60 **fields** i.e. the Elysian fields where the heroic and virtuous went after death　62 **either**
each　**bounds** allotted places　63 **declining fearfully** going steeply down　64 **ready downfall** direct precipice　**deepest hell** Tartarus　65 **Furies**
avenging goddesses　66 **Ixion...wheel** his punishment for offending Zeus by seeking Hera's love　67 **usurers** moneylenders　68 **wantons** lewd or
lascivious persons　70 **perjured wights** liars　72 **middle path** in the *Aeneid* (VI, 540-43) Virgil specifies only two; a third may suggest Andrea's lost,
homeless state　73 **fair Elysian green** where the virtuous go after death　75 **adamant** hard stone, diamond　76 **Proserpine** Pluto's wife, queen of the
Underworld　77 **humbled...knee** i.e. kneeling respectfully　79 **doom** judgement, sentence

Forthwith, Revenge, she rounded thee in th'ear,
And bade thee lead me through the gates of horn,
Where dreams have passage in the silent night.
No sooner had she spoke, but we were here —
85   I wot not how — in twinkling of an eye.

REVENGE   Then know, Andrea, that thou art arrived
Where thou shalt see the author of thy death,
Don Balthazar, the prince of Portingale,
Deprived of life by Bel-imperia.
90   Here sit we down to see the mystery,
And serve for Chorus in this tragedy.

[Act 1 Scene 2]

Enter Spanish King, General, Castile, Hieronimo

KING   Now say, lord General, how fares our camp?

GENERAL   All well, my sovereign liege, except some few
That are deceased by fortune of the war.

KING   But what portends thy cheerful countenance,
5   And posting to our presence thus in haste?
Speak, man, hath fortune given us victory?

GENERAL   Victory, my liege, and that with little loss.

KING   Our Portingales will pay us tribute then?

GENERAL   Tribute and wonted homage therewithal.

10 KING   Then blessed be heaven and guider of the heavens,
From whose fair influence such justice flows.

CASTILE   *O multum dilecte Deo, tibi militat aether,*
Et conjuratae curvato poplite gentes
Succumbunt: recti soror est victoria juris.

15 KING   Thanks to my loving brother of Castile.
But, General, unfold in brief discourse
Your form of battle and your war's success,
That, adding all the pleasure of thy news
Unto the height of former happiness,
20   With deeper wage and greater dignity
We may reward thy blissful chivalry.

GENERAL   Where Spain and Portingale do jointly knit
Their frontiers, leaning on each other's bound,

---

81 **rounded thee** whispered to you   82 **bade** asked, entreated   **gates of horn** according to Virgil (*Aeneid*, VI, 893–6) they lead to true dreams or visions   85 **wot** know   90 **mystery** hidden, secret events   [1.2]   1 **camp** army   2 **liege** lord   5 **posting** travelling via relays of horses   8 **tribute** payment in recognition of their victory   9 **wonted** customary   **therewithal** in addition   12 *O…juris* 'O, one greatly beloved of God, the heavens do battle on your behalf, and the united peoples surrender on bended knee: victory is the true sister of right' (Latin) from the Roman poet Claudian, *De Tertio Consulatio Honorii*, ll: 96–8   16 **unfold** explain   20 **deeper wage** greater reward   **dignity** rank, title   21 **blissful chivalry** wonderful skill in battle   23 **bound** border

There met our armies in their proud array:
25   Both furnished well, both full of hope and fear,
Both menacing alike with daring shows,
Both vaunting sundry colours of device,
Both cheerly sounding trumpets, drums, and fifes,
Both raising dreadful clamours to the sky,
30   That valleys, hills, and rivers made rebound,
And heav'n itself was frighted with the sound.
Our battles both were pitched in squadron form,
Each corner strongly fenced with wings of shot;
But ere we joined and came to push of pike,
35   I brought a squadron of our readiest shot
From out our rearward, to begin the fight:
They brought another wing t'encounter us.
Meanwhile, our ordnance played on either side,
And captains strove to have their valours tried.
40   Don Pedro, their chief horsemen's colonel,
Did with his cornet bravely make attempt
To break the order of our battle ranks:
But Don Rogero, worthy man of war,
Marched forth against him with our musketeers,
45   And stopped the malice of his fell approach.
While they maintain hot skirmish to and fro,
Both battles join, and fall to handy-blows,
Their violent shot resembling th'ocean's rage,
When, roaring loud, and with a swelling tide,
50   It beats upon the rampiers of huge rocks,
And gapes to swallow neighbour-bounding lands.
Now while Bellona rageth here and there,
Thick storms of bullets ran like winter's hail,
And shivered lances darked the troubled air.
55   *Pede pes et cuspide cuspis;*
Arma sonant armis, vir petiturque viro.
On every side drop captains to the ground,
And soldiers, some lie maimed, some slain outright:
Here falls a body sundered from his head,
60   There legs and arms lie bleeding on the grass,
Mingled with weapons and unbowelled steeds,

---

61 unbowelled disembowelled   **24 array** martial order   **25 furnished** equipped   **27 vaunting** showing off   **colours of device** heraldic banners or emblems   **28 cheerly** cheerily   **fifes** small flute-like instruments   **30 rebound** echo   **32 battles** battalions/armies   **squadron form** square formation   **33 fenced** fortified   **wings of shot** soldiers on the wings armed with muskets or other firearms   **34 ere** before   **push of pike** fighting at close quarters   **35 readiest shot** most skilled marksmen   **38 ordnance** cannons, heavy guns   **played** fired   **41 cornet** company of cavalry, so called after the standard or pennon carried at its head   **44 musketeers** soldiers equipped with muskets (long-barrelled infantry guns)   **45 malice** harmful effect   **fell** fierce, ruthless   **47 handy-blows** hand-to-hand fighting   **48 shot** attack/shooting   **50 rampiers** ramparts/dams, barriers   **51 neighbour-bounding** nearby, neighbouring   **52 Bellona** Roman goddess of war   **54 shivered** broken, shattered   **darked** darkened   **55 *Pede ... viro*** 'Foot against foot and spear against spear; arms sound against arms and man is attacked by man' (Latin)   **59 sundered** severed

That scatt'ring overspread the purple plain.
In all this turmoil, three long hours and more,
The victory to neither part inclined;
65 Till Don Andrea, with his brave lanciers,
In their main battle made so great a breach,
That, half dismayed, the multitude retired:
But Bathazar, the Portingales' young prince,
Brought rescue, and encouraged them to stay.
70 Here-hence the fight was eagerly renewed,
And in that conflict was Andrea slain:
Brave man-at-arms, but weak to Balthazar.
Yet while the prince, insulting over him,
Breathed out proud vaunts, sounding to our reproach,
75 Friendship and hardy valour, joined in one,
Pricked forth Horatio, our Knight Marshal's son,
To challenge forth that prince to single fight.
Not long between these twain the fight endured,
But straight the prince was beaten from his horse,
80 And forced to yield him prisoner to his foe.
When he was taken, all the rest they fled,
And our carbines pursued them to the death,
Till, Phoebus waning to the western deep,
Our trumpeters were charged to sound retreat.

85 KING   Thanks, good lord General, for these good news;
And for some argument of more to come,
Take this and wear it for thy sovereign's sake.   *Gives him his chain*
But tell me now, hast thou confirmed a peace?

GENERAL   No peace, my liege, but peace conditional,
90 That if with homage tribute be well paid,
The fury of your forces will be stayed:
And to this peace their Viceroy hath subscribed,   *Gives the King a paper*
And made a solemn vow that, during life,
His tribute shall be truly paid to Spain.

95 KING   These words, these deeds, become thy person well.
But now, Knight Marshal, frolic with thy king,
For 'tis thy son that wins this battle's prize.

HIERONIMO   Long may he live to serve my sovereign liege,
And soon decay, unless he serve my liege.

100 KING   Nor thou, nor he, shall die without reward.   *A trumpet afar off*
What means the warning of this trumpet's sound?

---

62 **purple** i.e. bloodstained   65 **lanciers** lancers   70 **Here-hence** as a result of this/from this point onwards   72 **man-at-arms** heavily armed soldier on horseback   73 **insulting** exulting arrogantly   74 **vaunts** boasts   **sounding...reproach** insulting to us   76 **Pricked forth** spurred on   78 **twain** two   79 **straight** straight away, immediately   80 **him** himself, i.e. the prince   82 **carbines** soldiers armed with these medium-sized firearms   83 **Phoebus** the sun   **waning...deep** setting (in the sea)   86 **argument** token, evidence   89 **but peace conditional** only a conditional peace   91 **stayed** halted/restrained   92 **viceroy** local governor authorized to act in the name of a supreme ruler   **subscribed** consented/signed his name   96 **frolic** celebrate, make merry   99 **decay** decline/fail in health or fortune   100 **Nor** neither

GENERAL   This tells me that your grace's men of war,
Such as war's fortune hath reserved from death,
Come marching on towards your royal seat,
105   To show themselves before your majesty:
For so I gave in charge at my depart.
Whereby by demonstration shall appear,
That all, except three hundred or few more,
Are safe returned, and by their foes enriched.

The Army enters. Balthazar, between Lorenzo and Horatio, captive

110   KING   A gladsome sight: I long to see them here.   *They enter and pass by*
Was that the warlike prince of Portingale,
That by our nephew was in triumph led?

GENERAL   It was, my liege, the prince of Portingale.

KING   But what was he that on the other side
115   Held him by th'arm, as partner of the prize?

HIERONIMO   That was my son, my gracious sovereign;
Of whom though from his tender infancy
My loving thoughts did never hope but well,
He never pleased his father's eyes till now,
120   Nor filled my heart with over-cloying joys.

KING   Go, let them march once more about these walls,
That, staying them, we may confer and talk
With our brave prisoner and his double guard.
Hieronimo, it greatly pleaseth us
125   That in our victory thou have a share,
By virtue of thy worthy son's exploit.

Enter [the Army] again

Bring hither the young prince of Portingale;
The rest march on; but, ere they be dismissed,
We will bestow on every soldier
130   Two ducats and on every leader ten,
That they may know our largess welcomes them.   *Exeunt all but Balthazar,*
Welcome, Don Balthazar! Welcome, nephew!   *Lorenzo, Horatio*
And thou, Horatio, thou art welcome too.
Young prince, although thy father's hard misdeeds,
135   In keeping back the tribute that he owes,
Deserve but evil measure at our hands,
Yet shalt thou know that Spain is honourable.

BALTHAZAR   The trespass that my father made in peace
Is now controlled by fortune of the wars;
140   And cards once dealt, it boots not ask why so.

---

103 Such as those who   **reserved** preserved, saved   **106 gave…depart** ordered when I left   **112 our nephew** i.e. Balthazar   **triumph** victorious procession   **114 what** who   **120 over-cloying** excessively sentimental   **122 staying** stopping   **130 ducats** gold coins of variable value   **131 largess** generosity/sovereign's gift bestowed in celebration   **134 hard misdeeds** obdurate/stingy offences   **136 measure** treatment/return   **138 trespass** offence, breach of duty   **139 controlled** called to account   **140 boots not** does not serve to

His men are slain, a weak'ning to his realm;
His colours seized, a blot unto his name;
His son distressed, a corsive to his heart:
These punishments may clear his late offence.

145 KING   Ay, Balthazar, if he observes this truce,
Our peace will grow the stronger for these wars.
Meanwhile live thou, though not in liberty,
Yet free from bearing any servile yoke;
For in our hearing thy deserts were great,
150 And in our sight thyself art gracious.

BALTHAZAR   And I shall study to deserve this grace.

KING   But tell me — for their holding makes me doubt —
To which of these twain art thou prisoner?

LORENZO   To me, my liege.

155 HORATIO   To me, my sovereign.

LORENZO   This hand first took his courser by the reins.

HORATIO   But first my lance did put him from his horse.

LORENZO   I seized his weapon, and enjoyed it first.

HORATIO   But first I forced him lay his weapons down.

160 KING   Let go his arm, upon our privilege.   [*They*] *let him go*
Say, worthy prince, to whether did'st thou yield?

BALTHAZAR   To him in courtesy, to this perforce:
He spake me fair, this other gave me strokes;
He promised life, this other threatened death;
165 He won my love, this other conquered me,
And, truth to say, I yield myself to both.

HIERONIMO   But that I know your grace for just and wise,
And might seem partial in this difference,
Enforced by nature and by law of arms
170 My tongue should plead for young Horatio's right:
He hunted well that was a lion's death,
Not he that in a garment wore his skin;
So hares may pull dead lions by the beard.

KING   Content thee, Marshal, thou shalt have no wrong;
175 And, for thy sake, thy son shall want no right.
Will both abide the censure of my doom?

LORENZO   I crave no better than your grace awards.

HORATIO   Nor I, although I sit beside my right.

KING   Then, by my judgement, thus your strife shall end:
180 You both deserve, and both shall have reward.

---

142 **colours** army's standards   143 **corsive** corrosive   156 **courser** war horse   158 **enjoyed** took possession of   160 **privilege** royal prerogative   161 **whether** which of these two   162 **To…perforce** i.e. to Horatio for his courteous behaviour/nobility, to Lorenzo through his threat of physical force/necessity   167 **But** were it not for the fact   168 **partial** biased (because Lorenzo is his nephew while Horatio is Hieronomo's son)   171 **He…skin** the one responsible for the lion's death was valiant rather than he who took its skin to wear – the reference is to the fable of the ass who put on the skin of a dead lion   173 **So…beard** in the same way a small, timid creature, such as a hare, can triumph over dead lions by plucking at their beards – also proverbial   176 **censure…doom** declaration of my judgement   178 **sit beside** rest on/forgo, resign – the ambiguity may be deliberate

Nephew, thou took'st his weapon and his horse:

His weapons and his horse are thy reward.

Horatio, thou did'st force him first to yield:

His ransom therefore is thy valour's fee;

185   Appoint the sum, as you shall both agree.

But, nephew, thou shalt have the prince in guard,

For thine estate best fitteth such a guest:

Horatio's house were small for all his train.

Yet, in regard thy substance passeth his,

190   And that just guerdon may befall desert,

To him we yield the armour of the prince.

How likes Don Balthazar of this device?

BALTHAZAR   Right well, my liege, if this proviso were,

That Don Horatio bear us company,

195   Whom I admire and love for chivalry.

KING   Horatio, leave him not that loves thee so.—

Now let us hence to see our soldiers paid,

And feast our prisoner as our friendly guest.   *Exeunt*

[Act 1 Scene 3]

Enter Viceroy, Alexandro, Villuppo [and Attendants]

VICEROY   Is our ambassador despatched for Spain?

ALEXANDRO   Two days, my liege, are passed since his depart.

VICEROY   And tribute-payment gone along with him?

ALEXANDRO   Ay, my good lord.

5   VICEROY   Then rest we here awhile in our unrest,

And feed our sorrows with some inward sighs;

For deepest cares break never into tears.

But wherefore sit I in a regal throne?

This better fits a wretch's endless moan.   *Falls to the ground*

10   Yet this is higher than my fortunes reach,

And therefore better than my state deserves.

Ay, ay, this earth, image of melancholy,

Seeks him whom fates adjudged to misery.

Here let me lie; now am I at the lowest.

15   *Qui jacet in terra, non habet unde cadat.*

In me consumpsit vires fortuna nocendo:

181 Nephew…of the prince the social distinction between Horatio and Lorenzo is emphasized as Lorenzo is awarded Balthazar's weapon and horse and he is judged best suited to guard the prince while Horatio is awarded the cash sum they decide upon to be paid by his family for Balthazar's return plus the prince's armour, in recognition of his merit   188 train retinue   189 substance wealth, estate   190 guerdon reward   desert merit, deserving   192 device arrangement/division   193 if…were given this condition   [1.3]   2 depart departure   11 state present condition   12 earth…melancholy in the classical doctrine of the humours, melancholy corresponds to the element earth and thus the melancholic Viceroy is drawn downwards to the earth   15 *Qui…magis* 'He who lies on the ground, can fall no further. Fortune has used up her power to harm men on me: there is nothing further that can harm me' (Latin)

Nil superest ut jam possit obesse magis.
Yes, Fortune may bereave me of my crown:
Here, take it now. Let Fortune do her worst,
20   She will not rob me of this sable weed:
O, no, she envies none but pleasant things.
Such is the folly of despiteful chance!
Fortune is blind, and sees not my deserts;
So is she deaf, and hears not my laments;
25   And could she hear, yet is she wilful-mad,
And therefore will not pity my distress.
Suppose that she could pity me, what then?
What help can be expected at her hands
Whose foot is standing on a rolling stone,
30   And mind more mutable than fickle winds?
Why wail I then, where's hope of no redress?
O, yes, complaining makes my grief seem less.
My late ambition hath distained my faith;
My breach of faith occasioned bloody wars;
35   Those bloody wars have spent my treasure;
And with my treasure my people's blood;
And with their blood, my joy and best beloved,
My best beloved, my sweet and only son.
O, wherefore went I not to war myself?
40   The cause was mine, I might have died for both:
My years were mellow, his but young and green;
My death were natural, but his was forced.

ALEXANDRO   No doubt, my liege, but still the prince survives.
VICEROY   Survives! Ay, where?
45   ALEXANDRO   In Spain — a prisoner by mischance of war.
VICEROY   Then they have slain him for his father's fault.
ALEXANDRO   That were a breach to common law of arms.
VICEROY   They reck no laws that meditate revenge.
ALEXANDRO   His ransom's worth will stay from foul revenge.
50   VICEROY   No: if he lived, the news would soon be here.
ALEXANDRO   Nay, evil news fly faster still than good.
VICEROY   Tell me no more of news; for he is dead.
VILLUPPO   My sovereign, pardon the author of ill news,
And I'll bewray the fortune of thy son.
55   VICEROY   Speak on, I'll guerdon thee, whate'er it be:

---

20 sable weed black clothing worn as a sign of mourning/clothing made from or trimmed with costly sable fur (from the small carnivorous animal *Mustela zibellina*) associated with royalty   **22 despiteful** cruel, malicious   **23 Fortune is blind** in traditional iconography, the Roman goddess Fortuna was pictured as veiled or blind   **25 could she** even if she could   **wilful-mad** deliberately unreasonable   **29 rolling stone** as well as being blind, Fortuna was thought of as **mutable** (changeable) and pictured on a revolving sphere or wheel   **33 late** past   **distained** sullied   **34 breach of faith** i.e. failing to pay tribute to Spain   **37 my...beloved** i.e. his son Balthazar   **42 forced** too soon (continuing the horticultural metaphor)   **48 reck** take care or thought for   **49 stay from** prevent   **54 bewray** reveal   **55 guerdon** reward

Mine ear is ready to receive ill news;

Mine heart grown hard gainst mischief's battery.

Stand up, I say, and tell thy tale at large.

VILLUPPO   Then hear the truth which these mine eyes have seen:

60   When both the armies were in battle joined,

Don Balthazar, amidst the thickest troops,

To win renown did wondrous feats of arms.

Amongst the rest I saw him, hand to hand,

In single fight with their Lord-General;

65   Till Alexandro, that here counterfeits,

Under the colour of a duteous friend,

Discharged his pistol at the prince's back,

As though he would have slain their general:

But therewithal Don Balthazar fell down,

70   And when he fell, then began we to fly:

But, had he lived, the day had sure been ours.

ALEXANDRO   O, wicked forgery! O, traitorous miscreant!

VICEROY   Hold thou thy peace! But now, Villuppo, say,

Where then became the carcase of my son?

75 VILLUPPO   I saw them drag it to the Spanish tents.

VICEROY   Ay, ay, my nightly dreams have told me this.—

Thou false, unkind, unthankful, traitorous beast,

Wherein had Balthazar offended thee

That thou shouldst thus betray him to our foes?

80   Was't Spanish gold that bleared so thine eyes

That thou couldst see no part of our deserts?

Perchance, because thou art Terceira's lord,

Thou hadst some hope to wear this diadem,

If first my son and then myself were slain;

85   But thy ambitious thought shall break thy neck.

Ay, this was it that made thee spill his blood: *Takes the crown and*

But I'll now wear it till thy blood be spilt.   *puts it on again*

ALEXANDRO   Vouchsafe, dread sovereign, to hear me speak.

VICEROY   Away with him; his sight is second hell.

90   Keep him till we determine of his death.   *[Exit Alexandro, with Attendants]*

If Balthazar be dead, he shall not live.

Villuppo, follow us for thy reward.   *Exit Viceroy*

VILLUPPO   Thus have I with an envious, forged tale

Deceived the king, betrayed mine enemy,

95   And hope for guerdon of my villainy.   *Exit*

---

57 **mischief's** misfortune's/evil's **battery** assault 58 **at large** in full 66 **colour** appearance 69 **therewithal** with that 71 **the…ours** we would certainly have won 72 **forgery** lie **miscreant** villain 74 **carcase** body 80 **bleared** blinded 82 **Terceira's lord** commander of the island of Terceira, one of the largest of the Azores with, perhaps, despotic powers 83 **diadem** crown 88 **Vouchsafe** give permission 93 **envious** malicious/actuated by envy

[Act 1 Scene 4]

Enter Horatio and Bel-imperia

BEL-IMPERIA Signior Horatio, this is the place and hour,
      Wherein I must entreat thee to relate
      The circumstance of Don Andrea's death,
      Who, living, was my garland's sweetest flower,
5   And in his death hath buried my delights.
HORATIO   For love of him and service to yourself,
      I nill refuse this heavy doleful charge;
      Yet tears and sighs, I fear, will hinder me.
      When both our armies were enjoined in fight,
10   Your worthy chevalier amidst the thickest,
      For glorious cause still aiming at the fairest,
      Was at the last by young Don Balthazar
      Encountered hand to hand: their fight was long,
      Their hearts were great, their clamours menacing,
15   Their strength alike, their strokes both dangerous.
      But wrathful Nemesis, that wicked power,
      Envying at Andrea's praise and worth,
      Cut short his life, to end his praise and worth.
      She, she herself, disguised in armour's mask —
20   As Pallas was before proud Pergamus —
      Brought in a fresh supply of halberdiers,
      Which paunched his horse, and dinged him to the ground.
      Then young Don Balthazar with ruthless rage,
      Taking advantage of his foe's distress,
25   Did finish what his halberdiers begun,
      And left not till Andrea's life was done.
      Then, though too late, incensed with just remorse,
      I with my band set forth against the prince,
      And brought him prisoner from his halberdiers.
30 BEL-IMPERIA Would thou hadst slain him that so slew my love!
      But then was Don Andrea's carcase lost?
HORATIO   No, that was it for which I chiefly strove,
      Nor stepped I back till I recovered him:
      I took him up, and wound him in mine arms;
35   And welding him unto my private tent,
      There laid him down, and dewed him with my tears,
      And sighed and sorrowed as became a friend.

[1.4] *Bel-imperia* her name literally means 'beautiful empire' and perhaps glances at a political reading of the play **4 garland's sweetest flower** i.e. most beloved **7 nill** will not **10 chevalier** knight **11 For...fairest** fought nobly inspired always by your beauty **16 Nemesis** Greek goddess of divine retribution **17 Envying at** jealous of **20 Pallas...Pergamus** in the same way that **Pallas** Athena (Greek goddess of war) did before **Pergamus** (Troy) as recounted by Virgil (*Aeneid* II: 615–16) although it was actually Juno who was 'girt with steel' (II: 613) **21 halberdiers** soldiers with halberds (long-handled weapons) **22 paunched** wounded in the belly **dinged** knocked **27 just remorse** righteous pity/regret/revenge **29 brought** took **31 lost** destroyed/forgotten/not kept **34 wound** lifted/wrapped **35 welding** carrying

But neither friendly sorrow, sighs, nor tears
Could win pale Death from his usurpèd right.
40 Yet this I did, and less I could not do:
I saw him honoured with due funeral.
This scarf I plucked from off his lifeless arm,
And wear it in remembrance of my friend.

BEL-IMPERIA I know the scarf: would he had kept it still,
45 For had he lived, he would have kept it still,
And worn it for his Bel-imperia's sake:
For 'twas my favour at his last depart.
But now wear thou it both for him and me,
For after him thou hast deserved it best.
50 But, for thy kindness in his life and death,
Be sure, while Bel-imperia's life endures,
She will be Don Horatio's thankful friend.

HORATIO   And, madam, Don Horatio will not slack
Humbly to serve fair Bel-imperia.
55 But now, if your good liking stand thereto,
I'll crave your pardon to go seek the prince,
For so the duke, your father, gave me charge.   *Exit*

BEL-IMPERIA Ay, go, Horatio, leave me here alone,
For solitude best fits my cheerless mood.
60 Yet what avails to wail Andrea's death,
From whence Horatio proves my second love?
Had he not loved Andrea as he did,
He could not sit in Bel-imperia's thoughts.
But how can love find harbour in my breast,
65 Till I revenge the death of my beloved?
Yes, second love shall further my revenge!
I'll love Horatio, my Andrea's friend,
The more to spite the prince that wrought his end.
And where Don Balthazar, that slew my love,
70 Himself now pleads for favour at my hands,
He shall, in rigour of my just disdain,
Reap long repentance for his murd'rous deed.
For what was't else but murd'rous cowardice,
So many to oppress one valiant knight,
75 Without respect of honour in the fight?
And here he comes that murdered my delight

Enter Lorenzo and Balthazar

LORENZO   Sister, what means this melancholy walk?

---

47 **favour** token of affection given by a lady to her knight; by accepting it Horatio agrees to be her new champion   55 **your…thereto** you're happy for me to   60 **avails** is the use/profit   68 **wrought** brought about   71 **in…disdain** as a requirement of my justifiable scorn/anger/dislike   74 **oppress** attack/overwhelm   77 **Sister…miracles** the following rapid one-line exchanges are an example of stichomythia, typically employed in classical Greek drama in sharp disputations   **melancholy** sad/pensive

	BEL-IMPERIA	That for a while I wish no company.
	LORENZO	But here the prince is come to visit you.
80	BEL-IMPERIA	That argues that he lives in liberty.
	BALTHAZAR	No, madam, but in pleasing servitude.
	BEL-IMPERIA	Your prison then, belike, is your conceit.
	BALTHAZAR	Ay, by conceit my freedom is enthralled.
	BEL-IMPERIA	Then with conceit enlarge yourself again.
85	BALTHAZAR	What if conceit have laid my heart to gage?
	BEL-IMPERIA	Pay that you borrowed, and recover it.
	BALTHAZAR	I die, if it return from whence it lies.
	BEL-IMPERIA	A heartless man and lives? A miracle!
	BALTHAZAR	Ay, lady, love can work such miracles.
90	LORENZO	Tush, tush, my lord let go these ambages,

And in plain terms acquaint her with your love.

BEL-IMPERIA What boots complaint, when there's no remedy?

BALTHAZAR Yes, to your gracious self must I complain
In whose fair answer lies my remedy,
95   On whose perfection all my thoughts attend,
On whose aspect mine eyes find beauty's bower,
In whose translucent breast my heart is lodged.

BEL-IMPERIA Alas, my lord, these are but words of course,
And but devised to drive me from this place.

She, in going in, lets fall her glove, which Horatio, coming out, takes up

100 HORATIO Madam, your glove.

BEL-IMPERIA Thanks, good Horatio, take it for thy pains.

BALTHAZAR Signior Horatio stooped in happy time!

HORATIO I reaped more grace than I deserved or hoped.

LORENZO My lord, be not dismayed for what is past:
105   You know that women oft are humorous,
These clouds will overblow with little wind:
Let me alone, I'll scatter them myself.
Meanwhile, let us devise to spend the time
In some delightful sports and revelling.

110 HORATIO The king, my lords, is coming hither straight,
To feast the Portingale ambassador;
Things were in readiness before I came.

BALTHAZAR Then here it fits us to attend the king,
To welcome hither our ambassador,
115   And learn my father and my country's health.

Enter the Banquet, Trumpets, the King and Ambassador

KING See, lord Ambassador, how Spain entreats

---

82 **belike** perhaps   **conceit** fancy, imagination (sarcastic)   83 **enthralled** captivated, enslaved   85 **laid...gage** pawned my heart   90 **Tush** exclamation of impatient contempt   **ambages** ambiguous language/roundabout ways of speaking   92 **boots** profits/is the point of   98 **words of course** conventional phrases   99 **but...place** just a trick to get me to leave/just a trick to get me to change my mind   105 **humorous** temperamental, capricious: affected by the four bodily humours believed to control mood (and health)   113 **fits** befits, is proper for   116 **entreats** treats

Their prisoner Balthazar, thy Viceroy's son:

We pleasure more in kindness than in wars.

AMBASSADOR   Sad is our king, and Portingale laments,

120   Supposing that Don Balthazar is slain.

BALTHAZAR   So am I slain by beauty's tyranny.   *Aside*

You see, my lord, how Balthazar is slain: *To him*

I frolic with the Duke of Castile's son,

Wrapped every hour in pleasures of the court,

125   And graced with favours of his majesty.

KING   Put off your greetings till our feast be done;

Now come and sit with us and taste our cheer.   *Sit to the banquet*

Sit down, young prince, you are our second guest;

Brother, sit down, and, nephew, take your place.

130   Signior Horatio, wait thou upon our cup,

For well thou hast deserved to be honoured.

Now, lordings, fall to; Spain is Portugal,

And Portugal is Spain: we both are friends;

Tribute is paid, and we enjoy our right.

135   But where is old Hieronimo, our Marshal?

He promised us, in honour of our guest,

To grace our banquet with some pompous jest.

Enter Hieronimo with a drum, three Knights, each [with] his scutcheon; then he fetches
three kings, they [the Knights] take their crowns and them captive

Hieronimo, this masque contents mine eye,

Although I sound not well the mystery.

140   HIERONIMO   The first armed knight, that hung his scutcheon up,   *He takes the*

Was English Robert, Earl of Gloucester,   *scutcheon and gives*

Who, when King Stephen bore sway in Albion,   *it to the King*

Arrived with five and twenty thousand men

In Portingale, and by success of war

145   Enforced the king, then but a Saracen,

To bear the yoke of the English monarchy.

KING   My lord of Portingale, by this you see

That which may comfort both your king and you,

And make your late discomfort seem the less.

150   But say, Hieronimo, what was the next?

HIERONIMO   The second knight, that hung his scutcheon up,   *He doth as he did before*

Was Edmond, Earl of Kent in Albion,

---

118 **pleasure** take pleasure   127 **cheer** hospitality/feast   128 **second guest** second in the place of honour   130 **wait…honoured** wait for the toast to be drunk in your honour/you have deserved the honour of waiting on us at table   137 **pompous jest** magnificent entertainment   *scutcheon* i.e. escutcheon, a shield with a coat of arms   138 **masque** courtly entertainment   139 **sound not well** don't fully understand   **mystery** hidden meaning   141 **Robert…monarchy** there are no historical sources for this campaign   142 **bore sway** ruled   **Albion** England   145 **Saracen** Muslim, Arab: the Iberian peninsula was under Moorish/Islamic control for much of the Middle Ages   146 **yoke** subjection (from the wooden collar-like device used to fasten oxen together for ploughing)   152 **Edmond** he actually fought on the Portuguese side against Spain in 1381–82

> When English Richard wore the diadem.
> He came likewise, and razèd Lisbon walls,
155 And took the King of Portingale in fight;
> For which and other suchlike service done
> He after was created Duke of York.

KING   This is another special argument,
> That Portingale may deign to bear our yoke,
160 When it by little England hath been yoked.
> But now, Hieronimo, what were the last?

HIERONIMO   The third and last, not least, in our account,   *Doing as before*
> Was, as the rest, a valiant Englishman,
> Brave John of Gaunt, the Duke of Lancaster,
165 As by his scutcheon plainly may appear.
> He with a puissant army came to Spain,
> And took our King of Castile prisoner.

AMBASSADOR   This is an argument for our Viceroy
> That Spain may not insult for her success,
170 Since English warriors likewise conquered Spain,
> And made them bow their knees to Albion.

KING   Hieronimo, I drink to thee for this device,
> Which hath pleased both the ambassador and me:
> Pledge me, Hieronimo, if thou love thy king.   *Takes the cup of Horatio*
175 My lord, I fear we sit but over-long,
> Unless our dainties were more delicate:
> But welcome are you to the best we have.
> Now let us in, that you may be despatched:
> I think our council is already set.   *Exeunt omnes*

[Act 1 Scene 5]

[*Enter Ghost of Andrea and Revenge*]

GHOST OF ANDREA   Come we for this from depth of underground,
> To see him feast that gave me my death's wound?
> These pleasant sights are sorrow to my soul:
> Nothing but league, and love, and banqueting?
5 REVENGE   Be still, Andrea; ere we go from hence,
> I'll turn their friendship into fell despite,
> Their love to mortal hate, their day to night,
> Their hope into despair, their peace to war,
> Their joys to pain, their bliss to misery.

---

154 **razèd** tore down, levelled   159 **deign** condescend   166 **puissant** powerful   168 **argument** theme   169 **insult for** boast of   172 **device** masque, entertainment   174 **Pledge** toast   [1.5]   5 **ere** before   6 **fell despite** fierce enmity

[Act 2 Scene 1]

Enter Lorenzo and Balthazar

LORENZO   My lord, though Bel-imperia seem thus coy,
Let reason hold you in your wonted joy:
In time the savage bull sustains the yoke,
In time all haggard hawks will stoop to lure,
5   In time small wedges cleave the hardest oak,
In time the flint is pierced with softest shower,
And she, in time will fall from her disdain,
And rue the sufferance of your friendly pain.

BALTHAZAR   No, she is wilder, and more hard withal,
10   Than beast, or bird, or tree, or stony wall.
But wherefore blot I Bel-imperia's name?
It is my fault, not she, that merits blame.
My feature is not to content her sight,
My words are rude, and work her no delight.
15   The lines I send her are but harsh and ill,
Such as do drop from Pan and Marsyas' quill.
My presents are not of sufficient cost,
And being worthless, all my labour's lost.
Yet might she love me for my valiancy;
20   Ay, but that's slandered by captivity.
Yet might she love me to content her sire:
Ay, but her reason masters his desire.
Yet might she love me as her brother's friend:
Ay, but her hopes aim at some other end.
25   Yet might she love me to uprear her state:
Ay, but perhaps she hopes some nobler mate.
Yet might she love me as her beauty's thrall:
Ay, but I fear she cannot love at all.

LORENZO   My lord, for my sake leave these ecstasies,
30   And doubt not but we'll find some remedy.
Some cause there is that lets you not be loved;
First that must needs be known, and then removed.
What if my sister love some other knight?

BALTHAZAR   My summer's day will turn to winter's night.

35   LORENZO   I have already found a stratagem,
To sound the bottom of this doubtful theme.
My lord, for once you shall be ruled by me;

[2.1] **1 coy** distant, reserved   **2 wonted** accustomed   **3 In…wall** lines modelled on Thomas Watson's *Hecatompathia* (1582) Sonnet XLVII   **4 haggard** wild, untamed   **lure** bait   **5 wedges** tapering tools used to split wood   **8 rue** regret   **sufferance** suffering/patient endurance   **friendly** i.e. caused by your love   **9 withal** besides, moreover   **11 blot** tarnish   **13 feature** form, appearance   **14 rude** unskilled/inexperienced/unrefined   **16 Pan and Marsyas** god of shepherds and a satyr, famous for challenging Apollo unsuccessfully to a flute-playing contest   **quill** musical pipe/pen   **19 valiancy** courage, valour   **20 slandered** discredited   **21 sire** father   **25 uprear** raise   **state** status, social position/wealth   **27 thrall** slave   **29 ecstasies** emotional outbursts   **36 sound** measure, ascertain   **doubtful** uncertain

Hinder me not, whate'er you hear or see.

By force or fair means will I cast about

40   To find the truth of all this question out.

Ho, Pedringano!

PEDRINGANO   Signior!   *Calls from within*

LORENZO   *Vien qui presto.*

Enter Pedringano

PEDRINGANO   Hath your lordship any service to command me?

45   LORENZO   Ay, Pedringano, service of import;

And — not to spend the time in trifling words —

Thus stands the case: it is not long, thou know'st,

Since I did shield thee from my father's wrath,

For thy conveyance in Andrea's love,

50   For which thou wert adjudged to punishment:

I stood betwixt thee and thy punishment,

And since, thou know'st how I have favoured thee.

Now to these favours will I add reward,

Not with fair words, but store of golden coin,

55   And lands and livings joined with dignities,

If thou but satisfy my just demand:

Tell truth, and have me for thy lasting friend.

PEDRINGANO   Whate'er it be your lordship shall demand,

My bounden duty bids me tell the truth,

60   If case it lie in me to tell the truth.

LORENZO   Then, Pedringano, this is my demand:

Whom loves my sister Bel-imperia?

For she reposeth all her trust in thee.

Speak, man, and gain both friendship and reward:

65   I mean, whom loves she in Andrea's place?

PEDRINGANO   Alas, my lord, since Don Andrea's death

I have no credit with her as before;

And therefore know not if she love or no.

LORENZO   Nay, if thou dally, then I am thy foe,   *Draws his sword*

70   And fear shall force what friendship cannot win:

Thy death shall bury what thy life conceals;

Thou diest for more esteeming her than me.

PEDRINGANO   O, stay, my lord.

LORENZO   Yet speak the truth, and I will guerdon thee,

75   And shield thee from whatever can ensue,

And will conceal whate'er proceeds from thee.

But if thou dally once again, thou diest.

PEDRINGANO   If madam Bel-imperia be in love—

---

43 *Vien qui presto* 'come here quickly' (Italian)   **45 import** importance/significance   **49 conveyance** conduct/secret contrivance/carrying of messages   **54 store** abundant supply   **55 livings** estates, possessions   **dignities** honours, titles   **60 If…me** if it is in my power   **67 credit** personal influence/confidence   **69 dally** make a fool of me   **72 esteeming** valuing   **74 guerdon** reward

LORENZO   What, villain, ifs and ands?   *Offers to kill him*

80 PEDRINGANO   O, stay, my lord, she loves Horatio.   *Balthazar starts back*

LORENZO   What, Don Horatio, our Knight Marshal's son?

PEDRINGANO   Even him, my lord.

LORENZO   Now say, but how know'st thou he is her love?

And thou shalt find me kind and liberal:

85   Stand up, I say, and fearless tell the truth.

PEDRINGANO   She sent him letters, which myself perused,

Full-fraught with lines and arguments of love,

Preferring him before Prince Balthazar.

LORENZO   Swear on this cross that what thou say'st is true,

90   And that thou wilt conceal what thou hast told.

PEDRINGANO   I swear to both, by him that made us all.

LORENZO   In hope thine oath is true, here's thy reward: *Gives purse*

But if I prove thee perjured and unjust,

This very sword whereon thou took'st thine oath,

95   Shall be the worker of thy tragedy.

PEDRINGANO   What I have said is true, and shall for me

Be still concealed from Bel-imperia.

Besides, your honour's liberality

Deserves my duteous service, ev'n till death.

100 LORENZO   Let this be all that thou shalt do for me:

Be watchful, when and where these lovers meet,

And give me notice in some secret sort.

PEDRINGANO   I will, my lord.

LORENZO   Then shalt thou find that I am liberal.

105   Thou know'st that I can more advance thy state

Than she, be therefore wise and fail me not.

Go and attend her, as thy custom is,

Lest absence make her think thou dost amiss.   *Exit Pedringano*

Why so: *tam armis quam ingenio*:

110   Where words prevail not, violence prevails;

But gold doth more than either of them both.

How likes Prince Balthazar this stratagem?

BALTHAZAR   Both well and ill; it makes me glad and sad:

Glad, that I know the hinderer of my love;

115   Sad, that I fear she hates me whom I love.

Glad, that I know on whom to be revenged;

Sad, that she'll fly me, if I take revenge.

Yet must I take revenge, or die myself,

For love resisted grows impatient.

120   I think Horatio be my destined plague:

---

80 stay stop   **82 Even** no one but   **87 Full-fraught** filled   **89 cross** i.e. the sword hilt referred to in line 94   **93 unjust** dishonest   **95 worker** instrument   **102 sort** way, manner   **105 state** position   **108 Lest** in case   **amiss** wrong, out of order   **109** *tam...ingenio* 'as much through force as skill' (Latin)

First, in his hand he brandishèd a sword,
And with that sword he fiercely wagèd war,
And in that war he gave me dangerous wounds,
And by those wounds he forcèd me to yield,
125   And by my yielding I became his slave.
Now in his mouth he carries pleasing words,
Which pleasing words do harbour sweet conceits,
Which sweet conceits are limed with sly deceits,
Which sly deceits smooth Bel-imperia's ears,
130   And through her ears dive down into her heart,
And in her heart set him, where I should stand.
Thus hath he ta'en my body by his force,
And now by sleight would captivate my soul:
But in his fall I'll tempt the Destinies,
135   And either lose my life, or win my love.
LORENZO   Let's go, my lord; your staying stays revenge.
Do you but follow me, and gain your love:
Her favour must be won by his remove.   *Exeunt*

[Act 2 Scene 2]

Enter Horatio and Bel-imperia

HORATIO   Now, madam, since by favour of your love
Our hidden smoke is turned to open flame,
And that with looks and words we feed our thoughts
(Two chief contents, where more cannot be had):
5   Thus, in the midst of love's fair blandishments,
Why show you sign of inward languishments?
Pedringano showeth all to the Prince [Balthazar] and Lorenzo, placing them in secret
[above]
BEL-IMPERIA   My heart, sweet friend, is like a ship at sea:
She wisheth port, where riding all at ease,
She may repair what stormy times have worn,
10   And, leaning on the shore, may sing with joy
That pleasure follow pain, and bliss annoy.
Possession of thy love is th'only port,
Wherein my heart, with fears and hopes long tossed,
Each hour doth wish and long to make resort,
15   There to repair the joys that it hath lost,

---

125 **slave** captive/servant (since Balthazar is obliged to Horatio for his life)   127 **sweet conceits** persuasive/enticing notions   128 **limed** literally smeared with birdlime in order to entrap   129 **smooth** flatter   134 **Destinies** the three classical goddesses of fate   136 **stays** delays   138 **remove** removal, i.e. death   **[2.2]**   2 **smoke** sign of their love   **open flame** acknowledged passion   4 **contents** pleasures   5 **blandishments** attractions/ pleasing speeches   6 **languishments** sorrows/sufferings   9 **repair** mend/restore to good condition   11 **bliss annoy** gladness follows trouble   14 **resort** a place of safety to escape to   15 **repair** replace

And, sitting safe, to sing in Cupid's choir

That sweetest bliss is crown of love's desire.   *Balthazar above*

BALTHAZAR   O, sleep, mine eyes, see not my love profaned;

Be deaf, my ears, hear not my discontent;

20   Die, heart: another joys what thou deserv'st.

LORENZO   Watch still, mine eyes, to see this love disjoined;

Hear still, mine ears, to hear them both lament;

Live, heart, to joy at fond Horatio's fall.

BEL-IMPERIA   Why stands Horatio speechless all this while?

25   HORATIO   The less I speak, the more I meditate.

BEL-IMPERIA   But whereon dost thou chiefly meditate?

HORATIO   On dangers past, and pleasures to ensue.

BALTHAZAR   On pleasures past, and dangers to ensue.   *Above*

BEL-IMPERIA   What dangers and what pleasures dost thou mean?

30   HORATIO   Dangers of war, and pleasures of our love.

LORENZO   Dangers of death, but pleasures none at all.   *Above*

BEL-IMPERIA   Let dangers go, thy war shall be with me:

But such a war, as breaks no bond of peace.

Spake thou fair words, I'll cross them with fair words;

35   Send thou sweet looks, I'll meet them with sweet looks;

Write loving lines, I'll answer loving lines;

Give me a kiss, I'll countercheck thy kiss:

Be this our warring peace, or peaceful war.

HORATIO   But, gracious madam, then appoint the field,

40   Where trial of this war shall first be made.

BALTHAZAR   Ambitious villain, how his boldness grows!   *Above*

BEL-IMPERIA   Then be thy father's pleasant bower the field,

Where first we vowed a mutual amity;

The court were dangerous, that place is safe.

45   Our hour shall be when Vesper 'gins to rise,

That summons home distressful travellers:

There none shall hear us but the harmless birds:

Haply the gentle nightingale

Shall carol us asleep ere we be ware,

50   And, singing with the prickle at her breast,

Tell our delight and mirthful dalliance:

Till then each hour will seem a year and more.

HORATIO   But, honey-sweet and honourable love,

Return we now into your father's sight:

---

16 Cupid Roman god of love   **20 joys** enjoys   **21 disjoined** separated   **23 fond** foolish/doting/eager   **34 Spake thou** should you speak   **cross** encounter/oppose   **37 countercheck** oppose   **39 field** place, battlefield   **41 villain** low-born rustic/scoundrel   **42 bower** shady garden retreat **43 amity** love, friendship   **44 were** is (subjunctive)   **45 Vesper** the evening star   **'gins** begins (signifying the arrival of dusk)   **46 distressful** weary/ suffering   **48 Haply** perhaps, by happy chance   **49 ere…ware** before we realize   **50 prickle…breast** the nightingale with her breast resting against a thorn represented the pain of love in traditional iconography; in Greek mythology, Philomel had been raped and her tongue cut out by her brother-in-law Tereus. She turned into a nightingale to escape his wrath and has sung of her sorrows ever since (Ovid, *Metamorphoses*, VI)   **51 dalliance** talk/sport/ flirtation

55 Dangerous suspicion waits on our delight.

LORENZO   Ay, danger mixèd with jealous despite   *Above*

Shall send thy soul into eternal night.   *Exeunt*

[Act 2 Scene 3]

Enter King of Spain, Portingale Ambassador, Don Cyprian [*Castile*], *etc.*

KING   Brother of Castile, to the prince's love

What says your daughter Bel-imperia?

CASTILE   Although she coy it, as becomes her kind,

And yet dissemble that she loves the prince,

5   I doubt not, I, but she will stoop in time.

And were she froward, which she will not be,

Yet herein shall she follow my advice,

Which is to love him, or forgo my love.

KING   Then, lord Ambassador of Portingale,

10   Advise thy king to make this marriage up,

For strength'ning of our late-confirmèd league;

I know no better means to make us friends.

Her dowry shall be large and liberal:

Besides that she is daughter and half-heir

15   Unto our brother here, Don Cyprian,

And shall enjoy the moiety of his land.

I'll grace her marriage with an uncle's gift,

And this it is — in case the match go forward —:

The tribute which you pay shall be released;

20   And if by Balthazar she have a son,

He shall enjoy the kingdom after us.

AMBASSADOR   I'll make the motion to our sovereign liege,

And work it, if my counsel may prevail.

KING   Do so, my lord, and if he give consent,

25   I hope his presence here will honour us,

In celebration of the nuptial day;

And let himself determine of the time.

AMBASSADOR   Will't please your grace command me aught beside?

KING   Commend me to the king, and so farewell.

30   But where's Prince Balthazar to take his leave?

AMBASSADOR   That is performed already, my good lord.

KING   Amongst the rest of what you have in charge,

The prince's ransom must not be forgot:

[2.3]   **3 coy** behaves coyly, i.e. in a reserved manner   **kind** birth/nature   **4 yet** continues to   **dissemble** disguise, conceal   **5 stoop** submit   **6 froward** perverse, difficult   **7 herein** in this matter   **8 forgo** lose, forfeit   **10 make…up** organize this marriage   **11 league** alliance   **13 dowry** the money or property the wife brought her husband on marriage   **16 moiety** half-share   **19 released** revoked, cancelled   **21 enjoy** i.e. inherit   **22 make the motion** put forward your proposal   **23 work** accomplish   **25 his…day** i.e. he will come to the wedding in person   **27 determine…time** name the wedding day   **28 aught** anything else

That's none of mine but his that took him prisoner;

35   And well his forwardness deserves reward:

It was Horatio, our Knight Marshal's son.

AMBASSADOR   Between us there's a price already pitched,

And shall be sent with all convenient speed.

KING   Then once again farewell, my lord.

40   AMBASSADOR   Farewell, my Lord of Castile, and the rest.   *Exit*

KING   Now, brother, you must take some little pain

To win fair Bel-imperia from her will:

Young virgins must be rulèd by their friends.

The prince is amiable, and loves her well;

45   If she neglect him and forgo his love,

She both will wrong her own estate and ours.

Therefore, whiles I do entertain the prince

With greatest pleasures that our court affords,

Endeavour you to win your daughter's thoughts:

50   If she give back, all this will come to nought.   *Exeunt*

[Act 2 Scene 4]

Enter Horatio, Bel-imperia and Pedringano

HORATIO   Now that the night begins with sable wings

To overcloud the brightness of the sun,

And that in darkness pleasures may be done,

Come, Bel-imperia, let us to the bower,

5   And there in safety pass a pleasant hour.

BEL-IMPERIA I follow thee, my love, and will not back,

Although my fainting heart controls my soul.

HORATIO   Why, make you doubt of Pedringano's faith?

BEL-IMPERIA No, he is as trusty as my second self.

10   Go, Pedringano, watch without the gate,

And let us know if any make approach.

PEDRINGANO   Instead of watching, I'll deserve more gold   *Aside*

By fetching Don Lorenzo to this match.   *Exit Pedringano*

HORATIO   What means my love?

15   BEL-IMPERIA I know not what myself:

And yet my heart foretells me some mischance.

HORATIO   Sweet, say not so; fair fortune is our friend,

And heav'ns have shut up day to pleasure us.

The stars, thou see'st, hold back their twinkling shine,

---

34 none of mine doesn't belong to me   35 forwardness zeal/boldness   37 pitched determined, agreed upon   42 will wish, desire, inclination/intention, determination/wilfulness   46 estate status, position   ours yours and mine/mine as king (using the royal plural)   48 affords can supply   49 win discover   50 give back retreats   [2.4]   1 Now...night invocations to night are usually omens of misfortune   sable black   7 controls restrains/overpowers/overrules   10 without outside   13 match lover/rival/lively session/pair/prospective partnership   16 mischance disaster/evil fate

20   And Luna hides herself to pleasure us.

BEL-IMPERIA Thou hast prevailed; I'll conquer my misdoubt,
        And in thy love and counsel drown my fear.
        I fear no more; love now is all my thoughts.
        Why sit we not? For pleasure asketh ease.

25   HORATIO   The more thou sit'st within these leafy bowers,
        The more will Flora deck it with her flowers.

BEL-IMPERIA Ay, but if Flora spy Horatio here,
        Her jealous eye will think I sit too near.

HORATIO   Hark, madam, how the birds record by night,
30   For joy that Bel-imperia sits in sight.

BEL-IMPERIA No, Cupid counterfeits the nightingale,
        To frame sweet music to Horatio's tale.

HORATIO   If Cupid sing, then Venus is not far:
        Ay, thou art Venus, or some fairer star.

35   BEL-IMPERIA If I be Venus, thou must needs be Mars,
        And where Mars reigneth, there must needs be wars.

HORATIO   Then thus begin our wars: put forth thy hand,
        That it may combat with my ruder hand.

BEL-IMPERIA Set forth thy foot to try the push of mine.

40   HORATIO   But first my looks shall combat against thine.

BEL-IMPERIA Then ward thyself: I dart this kiss at thee.

HORATIO   Thus I retort the dart thou threw'st at me.

BEL-IMPERIA Nay, then to gain the glory of the field,
        My twining arms shall yoke and make thee yield.

45   HORATIO   Nay, then my arms are large and strong withal:
        Thus elms by vines are compassed, till they fall.

BEL-IMPERIA O, let me go, for in my troubled eyes
        Now may'st thou read that life in passion dies.

HORATIO   O, stay awhile, and I will die with thee;
50   So shalt thou yield, and yet have conquered me.

BEL-IMPERIA Who's there, Pedringano? We are betrayed!

Enter Lorenzo, Balthazar, Serberine, Pedringano disguised

LORENZO   My lord, away with her, take her aside.—
        O, sir, forbear: your valour is already tried.
        Quickly despatch, my masters.   *They hang him in the arbour*

55   HORATIO   What, will you murder me?

LORENZO   Ay, thus, and thus: these are the fruits of love.   *They stab him*

BEL-IMPERIA O, save his life and let me die for him!
        O, save him, brother; save him, Balthazar:

20 **Luna** the moon   21 **misdoubt** apprehension of evil, fear   24 **asketh** demands, requires   26 **Flora** Roman goddess of flowers   29 **record** quietly rehearse   31 **Cupid** Roman god of love   32 **frame** offer/create   33 **Venus** goddess of beauty and love, and mother of Cupid; the morning and evening **star** was named after her, hence Horatio's reference in the next line   34 **Ay** yes, indeed   35 **Mars** Roman god of war with whom Venus had an adulterous love affair   38 **combat** engage with   **ruder** rougher/humbler   41 **ward** defend, protect   42 **retort** return in kind   44 **yoke** join together (around the neck)/ subjugate   46 **compassed** encircled; **vines** (emblematic of Venus) would usually be thought to hold large trees such as **elms** up rather than cause them to fall as Horatio suggests here   49 **die** puns on the meaning 'achieve sexual orgasm'   53 **forbear** submit, desist   **tried** tested (in battle)   54 **despatch** kill   **my masters** sirs, gentlemen (ironic)

I loved Horatio but he loved not me.

60   BALTHAZAR   But Balthazar loves Bel-imperia.

LORENZO   Although his life were still ambitious-proud,

Yet is he at the highest now he is dead.

BEL-IMPERIA   Murder! Murder! Help, Hieronimo, help!

LORENZO   Come, stop her mouth, away with her.   *Exeunt*

[Act 2 Scene 5]

Enter Hieronimo in his shirt

HIERONIMO   What outcry calls me from my naked bed,

And chill my throbbing heart with trembling fear,

Which never danger yet could daunt before?

Who calls Hieronimo? Speak, here I am.

5   I did not slumber; therefore 'twas no dream.

No, no, it was some woman cried for help,

And here within this garden did she cry,

And in this garden must I rescue her.—

But stay, what murd'rous spectacle is this?

10   A man hanged up and all the murd'rers gone,

And in my bower, to lay the guilt on me.

This place was made for pleasure, not for death.   *He cuts him down*

Those garments that he wears I oft have seen.

Alas, it is Horatio, my sweet son!

15   O, no, but he that whilom was my son!

O, was it thou that call'd'st me from my bed?

O, speak, if any spark of life remain:

I am thy father; who hath slain my son?

What savage monster, not of human kind,

20   Here hath been glutted with thy harmless blood,

And left thy bloody corpse dishonoured here,

For me, amidst this dark and deathful shades,

To drown thee with an ocean of my tears?

O heavens, why made you night to cover sin?

25   By day this deed of darkness had not been.

O earth, why didst thou not in time devour

The vile profaner of this sacred bower?

O poor Horatio, what hadst thou misdone,

To leese thy life ere life was new begun?

---

61 **still** always/secretly   **ambitious-proud** self-seeking and full of pride   62 **highest…dead** a sardonic reference to Horatio's body hanging from a high tree   **[2.5]**   1 **naked bed** common phrase derived from the practice of sleeping naked   9 **stay** wait, hold on   15 **whilom** once upon a time   20 **glutted** gratified/saturated   21 **dishonoured** disgraced/defiled   22 **this** used here in plural sense   **shades** darkness of night/of the Underworld   25 **deed of darkness** a pun on the usual meaning of 'sexual intercourse'   28 **misdone** done wrong   29 **leese** lose, be deprived of   **ere…begun** when your life had scarcely started

30   O wicked butcher, whatsoe'er thou wert,

           How could thou strangle virtue and desert?

           Ay me, most wretched, that have lost my joy,

           In leesing my Horatio, my sweet boy!

Enter Isabella

ISABELLA   My husband's absence makes my heart to throb:—

35   Hieronimo!

HIERONIMO   Here, Isabella, help me to lament,

           For sighs are stopped, and all my tears are spent.

ISABELLA   What world of grief! My son Horatio!

           O, where's the author of this endless woe?

40   HIERONIMO   To know the author were some ease of grief,

           For in revenge my heart would find relief.

ISABELLA   Then is he gone? And is my son gone too?

           O, gush out tears, fountains, and floods of tears,

           Blow sighs, and raise an everlasting storm,

45   For outrage fits our cursèd wretchedness.

           Ay me, Hieronimo, sweet husband, speak!

HIERONIMO   He supped with us tonight, frolic and merry,

           And said he would go visit Balthazar

           At the duke's palace; there the prince doth lodge.

50   He had no custom to stay out so late:

           He may be in his chamber; some go see.

           Roderigo, ho!

Enter Pedro and Jaques

ISABELLA   Ay me, he raves, sweet Hieronimo.

HIERONIMO   True, all Spain takes note of it.

55   Besides, he is so generally beloved,

           His majesty the other day did grace him

           With waiting on his cup: these be favours,

           Which do assure me cannot be short-lived.

ISABELLA   Sweet Hieronimo!

60   HIERONIMO   I wonder how this fellow got his clothes!—

           Sirrah, sirrah, I'll know the truth of all:

           Jaques, run to the Duke of Castile presently,

           And bid my son Horatio to come home:

           I and his mother have had strange dreams tonight.

65   Do ye hear me, sir?

JAQUES   Ay, sir.

HIERONIMO   Well, sir, be gone.

           Pedro, come hither; know'st thou who this is?

---

30 **whatsoe'er thou wert** whatever you might have been   **31 desert** merit   **33 leesing** losing   **39 author** creator, one responsible   **45 outrage** overwhelming passion/indignation   **47 frolic** joyous   **51 some** someone   **56 grace** favour   **57 waiting...cup** a reference back to Act 1 scene 4 lines 130–1 where Horatio was given the honour of waiting on the king at table   **61 Sirrah** term of address to men or boys   **62 presently** at once   **63 bid** tell

PEDRO   Too well, sir.

70 HIERONIMO Too well! Who, who is it? Peace, Isabella!

Nay, blush not, man.

PEDRO   It is my Lord Horatio.

HIERONIMO Ha, ha, Saint James! But this doth make me laugh,

That there are more deluded than myself.

75 PEDRO   Deluded?

HIERONIMO Ay:

I would have sworn myself, within this hour,

That this had been my son Horatio,

His garments are so like.

80   Ha! Are they not great persuasions?

ISABELLA   O, would to God it were not so!

HIERONIMO Were not, Isabella? Dost thou dream it is?

Can thy soft bosom entertain a thought,

That such a black deed of mischief should be done

85   On one so pure and spotless as our son?

Away, I am ashamed.

ISABELLA   Dear Hieronimo,

Cast a more serious eye upon thy grief:

Weak apprehension gives but weak belief.

90 HIERONIMO It was a man, sure, that was hanged up here;

A youth, as I remember: I cut him down.

If it should prove my son now after all—

Say you? Say you?— Light! Lend me a taper,

Let me look again.— O, God!

95   Confusion, mischief, torment, death and hell,

Drop all your stings at once in my cold bosom,

That now is stiff with horror: kill me quickly!

Be gracious to me, thou infective night,

And drop this deed of murder down on me;

100   Gird in my waste of grief with thy large darkness,

And let me not survive to see the light

May put me in the mind I had a son.

ISABELLA   O, sweet Horatio! O, my dearest son!

HIERONIMO How strangely had I lost my way to grief!

105   Sweet lovely rose, ill-plucked before thy time,

Fair worthy son, not conquered but betrayed;

I'll kiss thee now, for words with tears are stayed.

ISABELLA   And I'll close up the glasses of his sight,

For once these eyes were only my delight.

---

71 **blush not** do not be ashamed (to speak the truth)   73 **Saint James** patron saint of Spain   98 **infective** tainted, contaminating   99 **drop...me** allow me to make sense of the reality of this murder little by little   100 **Gird in** encircle, confine   **waste** wilderness/useless expense/devastation; punning on 'waist'   **large** great/generous/capacious   101 **light May** daylight that has the power to   105 **ill-plucked** wickedly killed   107 **stayed** stopped, held back   108 **glasses...sight** eyes   109 **only my delight** my only delight/my delight alone

110 HIERONIMO   See'st thou this handkercher besmeared with blood?

It shall not from me, till I take revenge.

See'st thou those wounds that yet are bleeding fresh?

I'll not entomb them, till I have revenge.

Then will I joy amidst my discontent;

115 Till then my sorrow never shall be spent.

ISABELLA   The heavens are just; murder cannot be hid:

Time is the author both of truth and right,

And time will bring this treachery to light.

HIERONIMO   Meanwhile, good Isabella, cease thy plaints,

120 Or, at the least, dissemble them awhile:

So shall we sooner find the practice out,

And learn by whom all this was brought about.

Come, Isabella, now let's take him up,   *They take him up*

And bear him in from out this cursèd place.

125 I'll say his dirge: singing fits not this case.

O aliquis mihi quas pulchrum ver educet herbas,   *Hieronimo sets his breast*

Misceat, et nostro detur medicina dolori;   *unto his sword*

Aut, si qui faciunt animis oblivia, succos

Praebeat; ipse metam magnum quaecunque per orbem

130 *Gramina Sol pulchras effert in luminis oras;*

Ipse bibam quicquid meditatur saga veneni,

Quicquid et herbarum vi caeca nenia nectit:

Omnia perpetiar, letum quoque, dum semel omnis

Noster in extincto moriatur pectore sensus.—

135 *Ergo tuos oculos nunquam, mea vita, videbo,*

Et tua perpetuus sepelivit lumina somnus?

Emoriar tecum: sic, sic juvat ire sub umbras.—

At tamen absistam properato cedere leto,

Ne mortem vindicta tuam tam nulla sequatur.

                              Here he throws it [the sword] from him
                                        and bears the body away

[Act 2 Scene 6]

[Enter] Ghost of Andrea, Revenge

GHOST OF ANDREA   Brought'st thou me hither to increase my pain?

I looked that Balthazar should have been slain:

---

110 **handkercher** handkerchief/small cloth   111 **It...me** It will stay with me   113 **entomb** bury   114 **discontent** grief/anger   119 **plaints** complaints/ lamentations   120 **dissemble** disguise, conceal   121 **So...about** in this way we shall more quickly learn what happened and who was responsible for this deed   **practice** deed/plot/trick, treachery   125 **dirge** lament, normally a song of mourning   126 *O...sequatur* 'O, someone mix herbs for me that lovely spring brings forth, and may some medicine be given for our sorrows or may he proffer juices if they exist that will bring oblivion to our minds; I, myself, will gather whatever herbs there be throughout the world that the sun brings forth within the bounds of the world; myself will drink that poison the wise woman devises, that her spell creates by its secret power: I will patiently endure all things even death, until all feeling finally dies in my dead breast. So will I never see your eyes, my life, and has perpetual sleep overcome your light? I shall die with you, and thus, thus it is a pleasure to pass to the shadows below. Nevertheless, I shall not depart hastily lest there should be no revenge following your death' (Latin)   **[2.6]**   1 **hither** to this place   2 **looked** expected, anticipated

But 'tis my friend Horatio that is slain,

And they abuse fair Bel-imperia,

5   On whom I doted more than all the world,

Because she loved me more than all the world.

REVENGE   Thou talk'st of harvest, when the corn is green:

The end is crown of every work well done;

The sickle comes not, till the corn be ripe.

10   Be still, and ere I lead thee from this place,

I'll show thee Balthazar in heavy case.

[Act 3 Scene 1]

Enter Viceroy of Portingale, Nobles, Villuppo

VICEROY   Infortunate condition of kings,

Seated amidst so many helpless doubts!

First we are placed upon extremest height,

And oft supplanted with exceeding hate,

5   But ever subject to the wheel of chance;

And at our highest never joy we so,

As we both doubt and dread our overthrow.

So striveth not the waves with sundry winds,

As fortune toileth in th'affairs of kings,

10   That would be feared, yet fear to be beloved,

Sith fear or love to kings is flattery.

For instance, lordings, look upon your king,

By hate deprivèd of his dearest son,

The only hope of our successive line.

15 FIRST NOBLEMAN   I had not thought that Alexandro's heart

Had been envenomed with such extreme hate;

But now I see that words have several works,

And there's no credit in the countenance.

VILLUPPO   No: for, my lord, had you beheld the train,

20   That feignèd love had coloured in his looks,

When he in camp consorted Balthazar,

Far more inconstant had you thought the sun,

That hourly coasts the centre of the earth,

Than Alexandro's purpose to the prince.

25 VICEROY   No more, Villuppo, thou hast said enough,

And with thy words thou slay'st our wounded thoughts.

---

9 **sickle** sharp-bladed reaping hook for harvesting; a traditional emblem of death   11 **heavy case** difficult situation/mourning clothes   **[3.1]**   1 **Infortunate** unlucky/malevolent   2 **Seated...doubts** placed in the middle of so many insoluble fears/problems   5 **chance** human fate was supposedly determined by the ever-turning Wheel of Fortune   7 **doubt** fear/suspect   8 **sundry** various   10 **would** wish to   11 **Sith** since   12 **lordings** gentlemen   14 **successive line** direct line of succession   17 **several works** mean different things and produce different outcomes   18 **credit...countenance** way of telling from the face   19 **train** treachery, deceit   20 **coloured** counterfeited   21 **consorted** kept company with   23 **hourly coasts** continually goes round; in geocentric cosmology the sun's orbit was an emblem of constancy and reliability   24 **purpose** intention

Nor shall I longer dally with the world,

Procrastinating Alexandro's death:

Go some of you, and fetch the traitor forth,

30   That, as he is condemnèd, he may die.

Enter Alexandro, with a Nobleman and Halberts

SECOND NOBLEMAN   In such extremes will nought but patience serve.

ALEXANDRO But in extremes what patience shall I use?

Nor discontents it me to leave the world,

With whom there nothing can prevail but wrong.

35   SECOND NOBLEMAN   Yet hope the best.

ALEXANDRO 'Tis heaven is my hope:

As for the earth, it is too much infect

To yield me hope of any of her mould.

VICEROY   Why linger ye? Bring forth that daring fiend,

40   And let him die for his accursèd deed.

ALEXANDRO Not that I fear the extremity of death

(For nobles cannot stoop to servile fear)

Do I, O, king, thus discontented live.

But this, O, this, torments my labouring soul,

45   That thus I die suspected of a sin,

Whereof, as heavens have known my secret thoughts,

So am I free from this suggestion.

VICEROY   No more, I say! To the tortures! When?

Bind him, and burn his body in those flames,   *They bind him to the stake*

50   That shall prefigure those unquenchèd fires

Of Phlegethon preparèd for his soul.

ALEXANDRO My guiltless death will be avenged on thee,

On thee, Villuppo, that hath maliced thus,

Or for thy meed hast falsely me accused.

55   VILLUPPO   Nay, Alexandro, if thou menace me,

I'll lend a hand to send thee to the lake,

Where those thy words shall perish with thy works:

Injurious traitor! Monstrous homicide!

Enter Ambassador

[AMBASSADOR]   Stay, hold a while;

60   And here — with pardon of his majesty —

Lay hands upon Villuppo.

VICEROY   Ambassador,

What news hath urged this sudden entrance?

AMBASSADOR   Know, sovereign lord, that Balthazar doth live.

65   VICEROY   What say'st thou? Liveth Balthazar our son?

Halberts halberdiers, soldiers armed with halberts (long weapons: part spear, part battle-axe)   **31 In…serve** in such desperate cases, only patience is of any use   **34 With…wrong** where evil alone is victorious   **37 infect** infected   **38 mould** soil/constitution, shape, pattern of men; puns on sense of 'rot', 'mildew'   **44 labouring** struggling   **47 suggestion** accusation   **51 Phlegethon** river of fire in the Underworld   **53 maliced** maligned, sought to injure   **54 meed** corrupt gain/advantage   **56 lake** Acheron into which Phlegethon flows   **63 urged** prompted

AMBASSADOR   Your highness' son, Lord Balthazar, doth live;

And, well entreated in the court of Spain,

Humbly commends him to your majesty.

These eyes beheld — and these my followers —;

70   With these, the letters of the king's commends,   *Gives him letters*

Are happy witnesses of his highness' health.   *The King looks on*

VICEROY   'Thy son doth live, your tribute is received;   *the letters, and proceeds*

Thy peace is made, and we are satisfied.

The rest resolve upon as things proposed

75   For both our honours and thy benefit.'

AMBASSADOR   These are his highness' farther articles.   *He gives him more letters*

VICEROY   Accursèd wretch, to intimate these ills

Against the life and reputation

Of noble Alexandro! Come, my lord, unbind him:

80   Let him unbind thee, that is bound to death,

To make a quittal for thy discontent.   *They unbind him*

ALEXANDRO   Dread lord, in kindness you could do no less,

Upon report of such a damnèd fact;

But thus we see our innocence hath saved

85   The hopeless life which thou, Villuppo, sought

By thy suggestions to have massacred.

VICEROY   Say, false Villuppo, wherefore didst thou thus

Falsely betray Lord Alexandro's life?

Him, whom thou know'st that no unkindness else,

90   But even the slaughter of our dearest son,

Could once have moved us to have misconceived.

ALEXANDRO   Say, treacherous Villuppo, tell the king:

Wherein hath Alexandro used thee ill?

VILLUPPO   Rent with remembrance of so foul a deed,

95   My guilty soul submits me to thy doom:

For not for Alexandro's injuries,

But for reward and hope to be preferred.

Thus have I shamelessly hazarded his life.

VICEROY   Which, villain, shall be ransomed with thy death—

100   And not so mean a torment as we here

Devised for him who, thou said'st, slew our son,

But with the bitterest torments and extremes

That may be yet invented for thine end.   *Alexandro seems to entreat*

Entreat me not; go, take the traitor hence: *Exit Villuppo [guarded by the Halberts]*

105   And, Alexandro, let us honour thee

With public notice of thy loyalty.—

---

67 entreated treated   **70 commends** greetings   **74 rest resolve upon** remaining issues can be defined   **76 articles** terms, conditions   **77 intimate** declare, announce   **81 quittal** repayment, requital   **discontent** grievance   **89 thou…misconceived** you know that no injury except the death of my **dearest son** could ever have led me to suspect   **93 Wherein** in what way   **94 Rent** torn   **96 injuries** wrongful acts   **97 preferred** promoted **98 hazarded** endangered   **99 ransomed** redeemed/paid for   **100 mean** temperate, moderate

To end those things articulated here
By our great lord, the mighty King of Spain,
We with our council will deliberate.

110   Come, Alexandro, keep us company.   *Exeunt*

[Act 3 Scene 2]

Enter Hieronimo

HIERONIMO   O eyes! No eyes, but fountains fraught with tears;
O life! No life, but lively form of death:
O world! No world, but mass of public wrongs,
Confused and filled with murder and misdeeds!

5   O sacred heavens! If this unhallowed deed,
If this inhuman and barbarous attempt,
If this incomparable murder thus
Of mine, but now no more my son,
Shall unrevealed and unrevenged pass,

10   How should we term your dealings to be just,
If you unjustly deal with those that in your justice trust?
The night, sad secretary to my moans,
With direful visions wake my vexèd soul,
And with the wounds of my distressful son

15   Solicit me for notice of his death.
The ugly fiends do sally forth of hell,
And frame my steps to unfrequentèd paths,
And fear my heart with fierce inflamèd thoughts.
The cloudy day my discontents records,

20   Early begins to register my dreams,
And drive me forth to seek the murderer.
Eyes, life, world, heavens, hell, night, and day,
See, search, show, send some man, some mean, that may—   *A letter falleth*
What's here? A letter? Tush! It is not so!

25   A letter written to Hieronimo!   *Red ink*
'For want of ink, receive this bloody writ:
Me hath my hapless brother hid from thee;
Revenge thyself on Balthazar and him,
For these were they that murderèd thy son.

30   Hieronimo, revenge Horatio's death,
And better fare than Bel-imperia doth.'

---

107 **articulated here** set out in the King of Spain's letters   [3.2]   1 **fraught** filled   2 **form** image, likeness   3 **mass** created universe/quantity/solid bulk   4 **Confused** bewildered/disordered   5 **unhallowed** impious, wicked   12 **secretary** confidant   13 **direful** terrible   **wake** wakes   14 **distressful** suffering/causing distress   15 **Solicit** troubles, disturbs   18 **fear** put fear into   19 **cloudy** gloomy, darkened by misfortune, as well as literal meaning   24 **Tush** exclamation of impatience/disbelief   *Red ink* the author's note to use red ink for the letter/book-keeper's reminder to self/just conceivably words spoken aloud by Hieronimo before he learns that the letter's written in blood   26 **bloody writ** written in blood, playing on sense of 'written order demanding the shedding of blood'   27 **hapless** unfortunate

What means this unexpected miracle?
My son slain by Lorenzo and the prince!
What cause had they Horatio to malign?
35 Or what might move thee, Bel-imperia,
To accuse thy brother, had he been the mean?
Hieronimo, beware! — Thou art betrayed,
And to entrap thy life this train is laid.
Advise thee therefore, be not credulous:
40 This is devisèd to endanger thee,
That thou, by this, Lorenzo shouldst accuse,
And he, for thy dishonour done, should draw
Thy life in question and thy name in hate.
Dear was the life of my belovèd son,
45 And of his death behoves me be revenged:
Then hazard not thine own, Hieronimo,
But live t'effect thy resolution.
I therefore will by circumstances try,
What I can gather to confirm this writ,
50 And, heark'ning near the Duke of Castile's house,
Close if I can with Bel-imperia,
To listen more, but nothing to bewray.

Enter Pedringano

Now, Pedringano!

PEDRINGANO   Now, Hieronimo!

55 HIERONIMO   Where's thy lady?

PEDRINGANO   I know not; here's my lord.

Enter Lorenzo

LORENZO   How now, who's this? Hieronimo?

HIERONIMO   My lord—

PEDRINGANO   He asketh for my lady Bel-imperia.

60 LORENZO   What to do, Hieronimo? The duke my father hath,
Upon some disgrace, awhile removed her hence,
But if it be aught I may inform her of,
Tell me, Hieronimo, and I'll let her know it.

HIERONIMO   Nay, nay, my lord, I thank you; it shall not need.
65 I had a suit unto her, but too late,
And her disgrace makes me unfortunate.

LORENZO   Why so, Hieronimo? Use me.

HIERONIMO Who? You my lord?
I reserve your favour for a greater honour,

---

34 **malign** injure, wrong   36 **mean** agent, instrument   37 **betrayed** deceived/exposed   38 **train** plot   39 **Advise thee** reflect, consider   40 **This…hate** this is a plan so that you will accuse Lorenzo, and thus, as payment for your accusation, make yourself hated and put your own life in danger   45 **behoves me** I am morally required to   47 **resolution** determination (to revenge Horatio's death); puns on secondary meaning, 'death'   48 **circumstances** circumstantial details   50 **heark'ning** listening/inquiring   51 **close** meet/unite/come to an agreement   52 **bewray** reveal/accuse   62 **aught** anything   64 **need** be necessary   65 **suit** request, playing on the sense of 'redress of a wrong'

70 This is a very toy, my lord, a toy.

LORENZO All's one, Hieronimo, acquaint me with it.

HIERONIMO I'faith, my lord, 'tis an idle thing I must confess,

I ha'been too slack, too tardy, too remiss unto your honour.

LORENZO How now, Hieronimo?

75 HIERONIMO In troth, my lord, it is a thing of nothing,

The murder of a son, or so:

A thing of nothing, my lord.

LORENZO Why then, farewell.

HIERONIMO My grief no heart, my thoughts no tongue can tell.   *Exit*

80 LORENZO Come hither, Pedringano, see'st thou this?

PEDRINGANO My lord, I see it, and suspect it too.

LORENZO This is that damnèd villain Serberine,

That hath, I fear, revealed Horatio's death.

PEDRINGANO My lord, he could not, 'twas so lately done;

85 And since he hath not left my company.

LORENZO Admit he have not, his condition's such,

As fear or flattering words may make him false.

I know his humour, and therewith repent

That e'er I used him in this enterprise.

90 But, Pedringano, to prevent the worst,

And 'cause I know thee secret as my soul,

Here, for thy further satisfaction, take thou this   *Gives him more gold*

And hearken to me — thus it is devised:

This night thou must (and, prithee, so resolve)

95 Meet Serberine at Saint Luigi's Park —

Thou know'st 'tis here hard by behind the house —

There take thy stand, and see thou strike him sure:

For die he must, if we do mean to live.

PEDRINGANO But how shall Serberine be there, my lord?

100 LORENZO Let me alone, I'll send to him to meet

The prince and me, where thou must do this deed.

PEDRINGANO It shall be done, my lord, it shall be done,

And I'll go arm myself to meet him there.

LORENZO When things shall alter, as I hope they will,

105 Then shalt thou mount for this; thou know'st my mind.   *Exit Pedringano*

Che le Ieron!

Enter Page

PAGE My lord?

LORENZO Go, sirrah,

To Serberine, and bid him forthwith meet

---

70 **very toy** nothing but a piece of nonsense   71 **All's one** it's all the same, i.e. it doesn't matter   73 **slack** careless, idle/moderate   **tardy** dilatory/ reluctant   **remiss** negligent/lenient   75 **In troth** indeed, truly   85 **since** i.e. since then   86 **condition's** nature/position is   87 **As** that   88 **humour** disposition/character   93 **devised** planned   94 **prithee** please   **resolve** be sure   96 **hard** close   97 **sure** without fail   100 **Let me alone** leave that to me   105 **mount** be promoted/rise socially/climb the scaffold in order to be hanged   106 *Che le Ieron!* meaning is unclear; perhaps 'Who's there?' (Italian) plus the page's name or possibly an abbreviation for Hieronimo

110   The prince and me at Saint Luigi's Park,

         Behind the house, this evening, boy!

PAGE   I go, my lord.

LORENZO   But, sirrah, let the hour be eight o'clock:

         Bid him not fail.

115 PAGE   I fly, my lord.   *Exit*

LORENZO   Now to confirm the complot thou hast cast

         Of all these practices, I'll spread the watch,

         Upon precise commandment from the king,

         Strongly to guard the place where Pedringano

120   This night shall murder hapless Serberine.

         Thus must we work that will avoid distrust;

         Thus must we practise to prevent mishap,

         And thus one ill another must expulse.

         This sly enquiry of Hieronimo

125   For Bel-imperia breeds suspicion,

         And this suspicion bodes a further ill.

         As for myself, I know my secret fault,

         And so do they, but I have dealt for them:

         They that for coin their souls endangerèd,

130   To save my life, for coin shall venture theirs;

         And better 'tis that base companions die,

         Than by their life to hazard our good haps.

         Nor shall they live, for me to fear their faith:

         I'll trust myself, myself shall be my friend;

135   For die they shall, slaves are ordained to no other end.   *Exit*

[Act 3 Scene 3]

Enter Pedringano with a pistol

PEDRINGANO   Now, Pedringano, bid thy pistol hold,

         And hold on, Fortune! Once more favour me,

         Give but success to mine attempting spirit,

         And let me shift for taking of mine aim.

5   Here is the gold, this is the gold proposed;

         It is no dream that I adventure for,

         But Pedringano is possessed thereof!

         And he that would not strain his conscience

         For him that thus his liberal purse hath stretched,

---

116 **complot** conspiracy   **cast** contrived, arranged   117 **practices** plots, schemes   **spread the watch** place the nightwatchmen   118 **Upon** as though on   120 **hapless** unfortunate   121 **that** in such a way that   123 **expulse** expel   124 **sly** knowing/cunning   129 **coin** money   130 **venture** risk, hazard   131 **base** low-born, inferior   **companions** fellows/associates   132 **by…haps** risking our lives by letting them live   133 **faith** trustworthiness   135 **slaves** servile, worthless fellows   **ordained** destined/appointed   **[3.3] 1 hold** function   **2 hold on** continue, carry on   **3 attempting** enterprising   **4 shift** manage/get on with/be responsible for   **8 strain** restrain, control   **9 liberal** generous, open

10   Unworthy such a favour, may he fail,

               And, wishing, want, when such as I prevail.

               As for the fear of apprehension,

               I know, if need should be, my noble lord

               Will stand between me and ensuing harms;

15   Besides, this place is free from all suspect:

               Here therefore will I stay and take my stand.

Enter the Watch [behind]

FIRST WATCH I wonder much to what intent it is

               That we are thus expressly charged to watch.

SECOND WATCH 'Tis by commandment in the king's own name.

20   THIRD WATCH But we were never wont to watch nor ward

               So near the duke, his brother's, house before.

SECOND WATCH Content yourself, stand close, there's somewhat in't.

Enter Serberine

SERBERINE Here, Serberine, attend and stay thy pace,

               For here did Don Lorenzo's page appoint

25   That thou by his command shouldst meet with him.

               How fit a place—if one were so disposed—

               Methinks this corner is to close with one.

PEDRINGANO Here comes the bird that I must seize upon:

               Now, Pedringano, or never, play the man!

30   SERBERINE I wonder that his lordship stays so long,

               Or wherefore should he send for me so late?

PEDRINGANO For this, Serberine! — And thou shalt ha't.   *Shoots the dag*

               So, there he lies; my promise is performed.   *The Watch [come forward]*

FIRST WATCH Hark, gentlemen, this is a pistol shot.

35   SECOND WATCH And here's one slain; — stay the murderer.

PEDRINGANO Now by the sorrows of the souls in hell,   *He strives with the Watch*

               Who first lays hand on me, I'll be his priest.

THIRD WATCH Sirrah, confess, and therein play the priest,

               Why hast thou thus unkindly killed the man?

40   PEDRINGANO Why? Because he walked abroad so late.

THIRD WATCH Come, sir, you had been better kept your bed,

               Than have committed this misdeed so late.

SECOND WATCH Come, to the marshal's with the murderer!

FIRST WATCH On to Hieronimo's! Help me here

45   To bring the murdered body with us too.

PEDRINGANO Hieronimo? Carry me before whom you will:

               Whate'er he be, I'll answer him and you,

               And do your worst, for I defy you all.   *Exeunt*

---

10 fail disappoint/not succeed/be reduced to poverty   **11 want** be absent/destitute   **12 apprehension** being caught/arrested   **15 suspect** suspicion   *Watch* group of watchmen who patrolled and guarded the streets at night   **20 wont** accustomed   **watch nor ward** maintain surveillance   **22 close** near/ out of sight   **23 attend** wait/listen carefully   **stay thy pace** slow down/stop   **26 fit** appropriate   **27 close** fight at close quarters   *dag* hand gun   **35 stay** stop, hold   **37 be his priest** i.e. prepare him for death   **40 abroad** out and about   **41 kept** stayed in   **46 whom you will** whoever you like

[Act 3 Scene 4]

Enter Lorenzo and Balthazar

BALTHAZAR   How now, my lord, what makes you rise so soon?

LORENZO   Fear of preventing our mishaps too late.

BALTHAZAR   What mischief is it that we not mistrust?

LORENZO   Our greatest ills we least mistrust, my lord,

5   And inexpected harms do hurt us most.

BALTHAZAR   Why, tell me, Don Lorenzo, tell me, man,

            If aught concerns our honour and your own.

LORENZO   Not you, nor me, my lord, but both in one:

            For I suspect — and the presumption's great —

10   That by those base confederates in our fault

            Touching the death of Don Horatio,

            We are betrayed to old Hieronimo.

BALTHAZAR   Betrayed, Lorenzo? Tush, it cannot be.

LORENZO   A guilty conscience, urgèd with the thought

15   Of former evils, easily cannot err:

            I am persuaded — and dissuade me not —

            That all's revealed to Hieronimo.

            And therefore know that I have cast it thus:—

[Enter Page]

            But here's the page. How now? What news with thee?

20   PAGE   My lord, Serberine is slain.

BALTHAZAR   Who? Serberine, my man?

PAGE   Your highness' man, my lord.

LORENZO   Speak, page, who murdered him?

PAGE   He that is apprehended for the fact.

25   LORENZO   Who?

PAGE   Pedringano.

BALTHAZAR   Is Serberine slain, that loved his lord so well?

            Injurious villain, murderer of his friend!

LORENZO   Hath Pedringano murdered Serberine?

30   My lord, let me entreat you to take the pains

            To exasperate and hasten his revenge

            With your complaints unto my lord the king.

            This their dissension breeds a greater doubt.

BALTHAZAR   Assure thee, Don Lorenzo, he shall die,

35   Or else his highness hardly shall deny.

            Meanwhile I'll haste the marshal-sessions:

[3.4]   **2 preventing** failing to put a stop to   **mishaps** unlucky accidents   **3 mischief** source of harm   **mistrust** doubt/suspect   **5 inexpected** unexpected, unlooked-for   **7 aught concerns** there's anything touching   **9 presumption's** grounds for belief are   **10 confederates…fault** partners in our crime   **18 cast it thus** devised this scheme   **24 fact** deed   **31 exasperate** magnify, exaggerate/make harsher   **33 their…doubt** violent quarrel of theirs creates more suspicion   **35 hardly shall deny** can hardly refuse/would be being harsh if he did refuse (the death penalty)   **36 haste** hasten, speed-up   **marshall-sessions** court of the Knight Marshall or Marshalsea (in England)

For die he shall for this his damnèd deed.   *Exit Balthazar*

LORENZO   Why so, this fits our former policy,

And thus experience bids the wise to deal.

40   I lay the plot: he prosecutes the point;

I set the trap: he breaks the worthless twigs,

And sees not that wherewith the bird was limed.

Thus hopeful men, that mean to hold their own,

Must look like fowlers to their dearest friends.

45   He runs to kill whom I have holp to catch,

And no man knows it was my reaching fatch.

'Tis hard to trust unto a multitude,

Or anyone, in mine opinion,

When men themselves their secrets will reveal.

Enter a Messenger with a letter

50   Boy—

PAGE   My lord?

LORENZO   What's he?

MESSENGER I have a letter to your lordship.

LORENZO   From whence?

55   **MESSENGER** From Pedringano that's imprisoned.

LORENZO   So he is imprisoned then?

MESSENGER Ay, my good lord.

LORENZO   What would he with us? He writes us here: *Reads*

'To stand good lord, and help him in distress etc.'

60   Tell him I have his letters, know his mind,

And what we may, let him assure him of.

Fellow, begone: my boy shall follow thee.—   *Exit Messenger*

This works like wax, yet once more try thy wits.—

Boy, go, convey this purse to Pedringano;

65   Thou know'st the prison, closely give it him,

And be advised that none be there about:

Bid him be merry still, but secret,

And though the marshal-sessions be today,

Bid him not doubt of his delivery.

70   Tell him his pardon is already signed,

And thereon bid him boldly be resolved:

For, were he ready to be turnèd off —

As 'tis my will the uttermost be tried —

Thou with his pardon shalt attend him still.

75   Show him this box, tell him his pardon's in't,

But open't not, and if thou lov'st thy life;

---

38 policy strategy   **40 prosecutes the point** pursues the objective   **42 that wherewith** the one with which   **limed** caught (by being smeared with birdlime)   **43 hold their own** keep what belongs to them   **44 look like fowlers** appear cunning   **45 holp** helped   **46 reaching** deep/far-sighted   **fatch** i.e. 'fetch', far-reaching trick   **61 may** can do (on his behalf)   **63 like wax** very easily   **65 closely** secretly   **66 be advised** make sure   **none** no one else   **67 secret** discreet   **69 delivery** rescue, release   **71 boldly be resolved** be confidently satisfied   **72 turnèd off** hanged   **73 'tis…tried** I shall do my best to bring about   **74 still** secretly   **76 and if** if

But let him wisely keep his hopes unknown:
He shall not want while Don Lorenzo lives.
Away!

80 PAGE   I go, my lord, I run.

LORENZO   But, sirrah, see that this be cleanly done.   *Exit Page*

Now stands our fortune on a tickle point,
And now or never ends Lorenzo's doubts.
One only thing is uneffected yet,

85   And that's to see the executioner.
But to what end? I list not trust the air
With utterance of our pretence therein,
For fear the privy whispering of the wind
Convey our words amongst unfriendly ears,

90   That lie too open to advantages.
E quel che voglio io, nessun lo sa;
Intendo io: quel mi basterà.   *Exit*

[Act 3 Scene 5]

Enter Boy [Page] with the box

PAGE   My master hath forbidden me to look in this box, and, by my troth, 'tis likely, if he had not warned me, I should not have had so much idle time, for we men's-kind, in our minority, are like women in their uncertainty: that they are most forbidden, they will soonest attempt: so I now. — By my bare honesty, here's

5   nothing but the bare empty box: were it not sin against secrecy, I would say it were a piece of gentlemanlike knavery. I must go to Pedringano, and tell him his pardon is in this box: nay, I would have sworn it, had I not seen the contrary. — I cannot choose but smile to think how the villain will flout the gallows, scorn the audience, and descant on the hangman, and all presuming of his pardon from hence. Will't

10   not be an odd jest for me to stand and grace every jest he makes, pointing my finger at this box as who sould say: 'Mock on, here's thy warrant.' Is't not a scurvy jest that a man should jest himself to death? Alas, poor Pedringano, I am in a sort sorry for thee, but if I should be hanged with thee, I cannot weep.   *Exit*

77 **unknown** a secret   81 **cleanly** adroitly   82 **tickle** delicate/tricky/dangerous/uncertain   83 **doubts** fears/difficulties/dangers   84 **uneffected** not done   86 **list not** do not wish   88 **privy** secret/private   90 **advantages** circumstances/favourable opportunities for someone   91 *E...basterà* 'And what I want, no one knows; I understand, which is enough for me' (Italian)   **[3.5]**   1 **by my troth** on my honour   2 **had...time** bothered   3 **minority** youth   **uncertainty** hesitation, lack of confidence   **that...attempt** whatever they're especially told not to do is the first thing they'll try   4 **bare** simple   6 **knavery** villainy, dishonesty   8 **flout** mock, express contempt for   **gallows** apparatus for the punishment of death by hanging   **audience** those who have come to watch; public executions were the norm   9 **descant** make remarks   10 **grace** embellish   11 **scurvy** poor, shabby   12 **a sort** some way   13 **if** even if

[Act 3 Scene 6]

Enter Hieronimo and the Deputy

HIERONIMO   Thus must we toil in other men's extremes,
That know not how to remedy our own,
And do them justice, when unjustly we,
For all our wrongs, can compass no redress.

5   But shall I never live to see the day
That I may come by justice of the heavens,
To know the cause that may my cares allay?
This toils my body, this consumeth age,
That only I to all men just must be,

10   And neither gods nor men be just to me.

DEPUTY   Worthy Hieronimo, your office asks
A care to punish such as do transgress.

HIERONIMO   So is't my duty to regard his death
Who, when he lived, deserved my dearest blood.

15   But come, for that we came for: let's begin,
For here lies that which bids me to be gone.

Enter Officers, Boy, and Pedringano with a letter in his hand, bound

DEPUTY   Bring forth the prisoner, for the court is set.

PEDRINGANO   Gramercy, boy, but it was time to come,   *Aside*
For I had written to my lord anew

20   A nearer matter that concerneth him,
For fear his lordship had forgotten me.
But sith he hath remembered me so well—
Come, come, come on, when shall we to this gear?

HIERONIMO   Stand forth, thou monster, murderer of men,

25   And here, for satisfaction of the world,
Confess thy folly and repent thy fault,
For there's thy place of execution.   *Indicating the gallows*

PEDRINGANO   This is short work! Well, to your marshalship:
First, I confess — nor fear I death therefore —

30   I am the man: 'twas I slew Serberine.
But, sir, then you think this shall be the place,
Where we shall satisfy you for this gear?

DEPUTY   Ay, Pedringano.

PEDRINGANO   Now I think not so.

35   HIERONIMO   Peace, impudent, for thou shalt find it so:
For blood with blood shall, while I sit as judge,

[3.6] *Deputy* Knight Marshall's official assistant   **1 extremes** hardships   **4 compass** contrive/obtain   **7 allay** calm   **8 toils** wearies   **consumeth age** wears old age away   **9 only I** I alone   **12 care** duty   **14 deserved...blood** merited my deepest passion/was worthy of me giving my own precious blood in revenge – an allusion to Genesis 9:6   **16 here lies that** Hieronimo may touch the concealed bloody handkerchief at this point   **17 set** seated/ready   **18 Gramercy** thanks   **19 anew** once more about   **22 sith** since   **23 gear** business; possibly playing sardonically on sense of 'apparatus' referring to the **gallows**   **28 marshalship** a facetious use of Hieronimo's title   **32 gear** affair

Be satisfied, and the law discharged.—

And though myself cannot receive the like,   *Aside?*

Yet will I see that others have their right.—

40   Despatch: the fault's approved and confessed,

And by our law he is condemned to die.

HANGMAN   Come on, sir, are you ready?

PEDRINGANO   To do what, my fine officious knave?

HANGMAN   To go to this gear.

45   **PEDRINGANO**   O sir, you are too forward:

Thou wouldst fain furnish me with a halter,

To disfurnish me of my habit.

So I should go out of this gear, my raiment,

Into that gear, the rope,

50   But, hangman, now I spy your knavery,

I'll not change without boot, that's flat.

HANGMAN   Come, sir.

PEDRINGANO   So then, I must up?

HANGMAN   No remedy.

55   **PEDRINGANO**   Yes, but there shall be for my coming down.

HANGMAN   Indeed, here's a remedy for that.

PEDRINGANO   How? Be turned off?

HANGMAN   Ay, truly, come, are you ready? I pray you, sir, despatch: the day goes

away.

60   **PEDRINGANO**   What, do you hang by the hour? If you do, I may chance to break your

old custom.

HANGMAN   Faith, you have no reason, for I am like to break your young neck.

PEDRINGANO   Dost thou mock me, hangman? Pray God, I be not preserved to break

your knave's pate for this.

65   **HANGMAN**   Alas, sir! You are a foot too low to reach it, and I hope you will never

grow so high while I am in the office.

PEDRINGANO   Sirrah, dost see yonder boy with the box in his hand?

HANGMAN   What, he that points to it with his finger?

PEDRINGANO   Ay, that companion.

70   **HANGMAN**   I know him not, but what of him?

PEDRINGANO   Dost thou think to live till his old doublet will make thee a new truss?

HANGMAN   Ay, and many a fair year after, to truss up many an honester man than

either thou or he.

PEDRINGANO   What hath he in his box, as thou thinkest?

75   **HANGMAN**   Faith, I cannot tell, nor I care not greatly; methinks you should rather

hearken to your soul's health.

---

45 O … flat (lines 45–51) this speech is set as loose verse, but was probably written as prose   **forward** eager/presumptuous   **46 fain … halter** like to put a
noose (**halter**) around my neck   **47 disfurnish … habit** remove my clothes (**habit**), which were the hangman's perquisite   **50 knavery** trick/villainy
51 boot profit, punning on sense of 'with no boots'   **flat** definite   **57 turned off** thrust off the ladder up to the gallows, i.e. be hanged   **58 dispatch** hurry
up   **goes away** is passing   **60 by the hour** at an appointed time   **64 pate** head   **69 companion** fellow   **71 doublet** close-fitting jacket   **truss** close-
fitting jacket; the hangman plays in the line below on the meaning 'tie up'   **76 hearken** concern yourself with

PEDRINGANO   Why, sirrah hangman, I take it that that is good for the body is likewise good for the soul, and it may be, in that box is balm for both.

HANGMAN   Well, thou art even the merriest piece of man's flesh that e'er groaned at
80 my office door!

PEDRINGANO   Is your roguery become an office with a knave's name?

HANGMAN   Ay, and that shall all they witness that see you seal it with a thief's name.

PEDRINGANO   I prithee, request this good company to pray with me.

85 HANGMAN   Ay, marry, sir, this is a good motion: my masters, you see here's a good fellow.

PEDRINGANO   Nay, nay, now I remember me, let them alone till some other time, for now I have no great need.

HIERONIMO   I have not seen a wretch so impudent.
90   O monstrous times, where murder's set so light,
         And where the soul, that should be shrined in heaven,
         Solely delights in interdicted things,
         Still wand'ring in the thorny passages,
         That intercepts itself of happiness.
95   Murder! O bloody monster! God forbid
         A fault so foul should scape unpunishèd
         Dispatch, and see this execution done!—
         This makes me to remember thee, my son.   *Exit Hieronimo*

PEDRINGANO   Nay, soft, no haste.

100 DEPUTY   Why, wherefore stay you? Have you hope of life?

PEDRINGANO   Why, ay!

HANGMAN   As how?

PEDRINGANO   Why, rascal, by my pardon from the king.

HANGMAN   Stand you on that? Then you shall off with this.   *He turns him off*

105 DEPUTY   So, executioner, convey him hence,
         But let his body be unburied:
         Let not the earth be chokèd or infect
         With that which heaven contemns, and men neglect.   *Exeunt*

[Act 3 Scene 7]

Enter Hieronimo

HIERONIMO   Where shall I run to breathe abroad my woes,
         My woes, whose weight hath wearièd the earth?
         Or mine exclaims, that have surcharged the air

---

78 balm soothing ointment; ironically it can also refer to 'a preparation for embalming the dead'   **81 roguery** facetious title   **office** official title/duty
85 marry indeed, literally 'by the Virgin Mary'   **motion** move/show/suggestion   **90 set so light** taken so lightly   **91 shrined** canonized/embraced/
enshrined   **92 interdicted** forbidden, prohibited   **94 intercepts itself of** hinders/cuts itself off from   **97 Dispatch** hurry/kill   **99 soft** slowly   **104 Stand
you** do you insist/are you building your hopes; the hangman plays on both literal and metaphorical senses   *turns him off* pushes the support away from
under him   **105 convey him hence** take him away   **107 infect** infected   **108 contemns** scorns, treats with contempt   **[3.7]   1 breathe abroad** spread
news of   **3 exclaims** exclamations, outcries   **surcharged** overloaded

With ceaseless plaints for my deceasèd son?

5   The blust'ring winds, conspiring with my words,

At my lament have moved the leafless trees,

Disrobed the meadows of their flowered green,

Made mountains marsh with spring-tide of my tears,

And broken through the brazen gates of hell.

10   Yet still tormented is my tortured soul

With broken sighs and restless passions,

That wingèd mount, and, hov'ring in the air

Beat at the windows of the brightest heavens,

Soliciting for justice and revenge:

15   But they are placed in those empyreal heights,

Where, countermured with walls of diamond,

I find the place impregnable, and they

Resist my woes, and give my words no way.

Enter Hangman with a letter

HANGMAN   O, lord, sir! God bless you, sir! The man, sir, Petergade, sir, he that was so

20   full of merry conceits—

HIERONIMO   Well, what of him?

HANGMAN   O, lord, sir, he went the wrong way; the fellow had a fair commission to the contrary. Sir, here is his passport; I pray you, sir, we have done him wrong.

25   **HIERONIMO**   I warrant thee, give it me.

HANGMAN   You will stand between the gallows and me?

HIERONIMO   Ay, ay.

HANGMAN   I thank your lord worship.   *Exit Hangman*

HIERONIMO   And yet, though somewhat nearer me concerns,

30   I will, to ease the grief that I sustain,

Take truce with sorrow while I read on this.

'My lord, I write, as my extremes required,

That you would labour my delivery:

If you neglect, my life is desperate,

35   And in my death I shall reveal the truth.

You know, my lord, I slew him for your sake,

And was confederate with the prince and you;

Won by rewards and hopeful promises,

I holp to murder Don Horatio too.' —

40   Holp he to murder mine Horatio?

And actors in th'accursèd tragedy

---

8 **spring-tide** the copious flow   11 **passions** sufferings, afflictions/overpowering emotions   14 **Soliciting** petitioning, entreating   15 **empyreal** celestial, of highest heaven   16 **countermured** fortified by one wall inside another   19 **Petergade** comic mispronunication of Pedringano   20 **conceits** fanciful notions/tricks, playing on sense of 'personal vanities'   22 **went…way** i.e. was wrongfully hanged   **fair commission** legitimate order   23 **passport** official document   25 **warrant** protect/vouch for   26 **stand…me** i.e. protect me from the law   29 **somewhat…concerns** I am more troubled by personal concerns   32 **extremes** desperate circumstances/last moments of life   33 **labour my delivery** work hard to achieve my release   38 **Won** persuaded   39 **holp** helped

Wast thou, Lorenzo, Balthazar and thou,
Of whom my son, my son deserved so well?
What have I heard, what have mine eyes beheld?
45   O sacred heavens, may it come to pass
That such a monstrous and detestèd deed,
So closely smothered, and so long concealed,
Shall thus by this be vengèd or revealed?
Now see I what I durst not then suspect,
50   That Bel-imperia's letter was not feigned.
Nor feignèd she, though falsely they have wronged
Both her, myself, Horatio, and themselves.
Now may I make compare 'twixt hers and this,
Of every accident I ne'er could find
55   Till now, and now I feelingly perceive
They did what heaven unpunished would not leave.
O, false Lorenzo, are these thy flatt'ring looks?
Is this the honour that thou didst my son?
And Balthazar — bane to thy soul and me!
60   Was this the ransom he reserved thee for?
Woe to the cause of these constrainèd wars!
Woe to thy baseness and captivity,
Woe to thy birth, thy body and thy soul,
Thy cursèd father, and thy conquered self!
65   And banned with bitter execrations be
The day and place where he did pity thee!
But wherefore waste I mine unfruitful words,
When naught but blood will satisfy my woes?
I will go plain me to my lord the king,
70   And cry aloud for justice through the court,
Wearing the flints with these my withered feet,
And either purchase justice by entreats,
Or tire them all with my revenging threats.   *Exit*

[Act 3 Scene 8]

Enter Isabella and her Maid

ISABELLA   So that, you say, this herb, will purge the eye,
And this, the head? —
Ah! — But none of them will purge the heart!

---

47 **closely smothered** privately hushed up   49 **durst** dared   50 **feigned** fictitiously invented/contrived for deception   53 **make…this** i.e. compare Bel-imperia's letter with Pedringano's   54 **accident** circumstance/incident   **find** discover/make sense of   56 **leave** allow   59 **bane** murderer/poison/ruin   60 **reserved** saved, preserved   61 **constrainèd** unnatural/unnecessary   65 **banned** cursed   **execrations** cursings   66 **pity thee** show you mercy (by sparing your life in battle)   68 **blood** bloodshed/revenge   69 **plain** make a formal complaint   70 **through the court** throughout the royal court/via the law   71 **Wearing the flints** wearing down the stones   72 **entreats** entreaties   **[3.8]**   1 **purge** cleanse/heal

No, there's no medicine left for my disease,
5   Nor any physic to recure the dead.
Horatio! O, where's Horatio?   *She runs lunatic*

MAID   Good madam, affright not thus yourself
With outrage for your son Horatio:
He sleeps in quiet in the Elysian fields.

10   ISABELLA   Why, did I not give you gowns and goodly things,
Bought you a whistle and a whipstalk too,
To be revengèd on their villainies?

MAID   Madam, these humours do torment my soul.

ISABELLA   My soul? Poor soul, thou talks of things,
15   Thou know'st not what: my soul hath silver wings,
That mounts me up unto the highest heavens.
To heaven, ay, there sits my Horatio,
Backed with a troop of fiery Cherubins,
Dancing about his newly-healèd wounds,
20   Singing sweet hymns and chanting heavenly notes:
Rare harmony to greet his innocence,
That died, ay died, a mirror in our days.
But say, where shall I find the men, the murderers,
That slew Horatio? Whither shall I run
25   To find them out that murderèd my son?   *Exeunt*

[Act 3 Scene 9]

Bel-imperia at a window

BEL-IMPERIA   What means this outrage that is offered me?
Why am I thus sequestered from the court?
No notice! Shall I not know the cause
Of this my secret and suspicious ills?
5   Accursèd brother, unkind murderer,
Why bends thou thus thy mind to martyr me?
Hieronimo, why write I of thy wrongs,
Or why art thou so slack in thy revenge?
Andrea, O Andrea! That thou saw'st
10   Me for thy friend Horatio handled thus,
And him for me thus causeless murdered! —

5 physic medicine   recure restore to health   *lunatic* mad, presumably indicating certain conventional stage business   8 outrage excitement, violent outcry   9 Elysian fields where the blessed went after death in Greek mythology   11 whipstalk whip handle   18 troop...Cherubins company of angels; the second order of angels, reputed to excel in knowledge and often coloured red (hence fiery)   22 mirror paragon, model of excellence   [3.9] 1 outrage gross indignity   2 sequestered cut off, separated   3 notice information/response   4 this these   5 unkind unnatural   6 bends thou do you constrain/ pervert/aim   8 slack slow/remiss   10 for on account of

Well, force perforce, I must constrain myself
To patience, and apply me to the time,
Till heav'n, as I have hoped, shall set me free.

Enter Christophil

15 CHRISTOPHIL Come, madam Bel-imperia, this may not be.　　　　　　*Exeunt*

[Act 3 Scene 10]

Enter Lorenzo, Balthazar and the Page

LORENZO Boy, talk no further; thus far things go well.
Thou art assured that thou saw'st him dead?

PAGE Or else, my lord, I live not.

LORENZO That's enough.

5 As for his resolution in his end,
Leave that to him with whom he sojourns now.—
Here, take my ring and give it Christophil,　　　　　　*Hands over ring*
And bid him let my sister be enlarged,
And bring her hither straight—　　　　　　*Exit Page*

10 This that I did was for a policy,
To smooth and keep the murder secret,
Which, as a nine-days' wonder, being o'erblown,
My gentle sister will I now enlarge.

BALTHAZAR And time, Lorenzo, for my lord the duke,

15 You heard, enquirèd for her yesternight.

LORENZO Why, and my lord, I hope you heard me say
Sufficient reason why she kept away;
But that's all one. My lord, you love her?

BALTHAZAR Ay.

20 LORENZO Then in your love beware, deal cunningly,
Salve all suspicions, only soothe me up;
And if she hap to stand on terms with us
As for her sweetheart and concealment so,
Jest with her gently: under feignèd jest

25 Are things concealed that else would breed unrest.—
But here she comes.

Enter Bel-imperia

Now, sister?

BEL-IMPERIA Sister? No!

12 **force perforce** under compulsion/of necessity　**constrain** compel　13 **apply me** submit/adapt myself　[3.10]　2 **him** i.e. Pedringano　5 **resolution** determination/explanation　6 **him** i.e. God or the devil　**sojourns** resides　8 **enlarged** set free　10 **policy** prudence　11 **smooth** hush up　12 **o'erblown** blown over, forgotten about　13 **gentle** noble, excellent　14 **time** not before time　15 **yesternight** last night　18 **all one** not important　20 **beware** be careful　**deal cunningly** act wisely　21 **Salve** smooth over, allay　**soothe** back　22 **hap** happens　**stand on terms** insist upon conditions/stand on her dignity　23 **As for** because of　**concealment** suppression of the truth/shutting her away　25 **else** otherwise　**breed unrest** cause trouble

Thou art no brother, but an enemy,

30 Else wouldst thou not have used thy sister so:
First, to affright me with thy weapons drawn,
And with extremes abuse my company;
And then to hurry me, like whirlwind's rage,
Amidst a crew of thy confederates,

35 And clap me up, where none might come at me,
Nor I at any, to reveal my wrongs.
What madding fury did possess thy wits?
Or wherein is't that I offended thee?

LORENZO   Advise you better, Bel-imperia,

40 For I have done you no disparagement;
Unless, by more discretion than deserved,
I sought to save your honour and mine own.

BEL-IMPERIA Mine honour? Why, Lorenzo, wherein is't
That I neglect my reputation so,

45 As you, or any, need to rescue it?

LORENZO   His highness and my father were resolved
To come confer with old Hieronimo,
Concerning certain matters of estate,
That by the Viceroy was determined.

50 BEL-IMPERIA And wherein was mine honour touched in that?

BALTHAZAR Have patience, Bel-imperia, hear the rest.

LORENZO   Me, next in sight, as messenger they sent,
To give him notice that they were so nigh:
Now when I came, consorted with the prince,

55 And unexpected, in an arbour there,
Found Bel-imperia with Horatio—

BEL-IMPERIA How then?

LORENZO   Why, then, remembering that old disgrace,
Which you for Don Andrea had endured,

60 And now were likely longer to sustain,
By being found so meanly accompanied,
Thought rather, for I knew no readier mean,
To thrust Horatio forth my father's way.

BALTHAZAR And carry you obscurely somewhere else,

65 Lest that his highness should have found you there.

BEL-IMPERIA Even so, my lord? And you are witness
That this is true which he entreateth of?
You, gentle brother, forged this for my sake,

---

32 **extremes** violent actions   **company** guest, i.e. Horatio   35 **clap me up** imprison me unceremoniously   37 **madding** crazy   39 **Advise you better** consider more carefully   40 **disparagement** dishonour, playing on the primary meaning of 'marriage to one of inferior rank'   47 **come confer** come in order to confer   48 **estate** state/property   52 **next in sight** first person they saw   53 **nigh** near   54 **consorted with** accompanied by   58 **old disgrace** i.e. of loving Don Andrea, a social inferior; 'In secret I possessed' (1.1.10)   61 **so meanly accompanied** i.e. by a social inferior   62 **mean** method, means   63 **forth** out of   66 **even so** really   67 **entreateth of** is talking about/pleading by persuasion   68 **forged this** did this deed/made up this story; the ambiguity is perhaps deliberate on Bel-imperia's part

And you, my lord, were made his instrument?

70   A work of worth, worthy the noting too!

But what's the cause that you concealed me since?

LORENZO   Your melancholy, sister, since the news

Of your first favourite Don Andrea's death,

My father's old wrath hath exasperate.

75   BALTHAZAR   And better was't for you, being in disgrace,

To absent yourself, and give his fury place.

BEL-IMPERIA   But why had I no notice of his ire?

LORENZO   That were to add more fuel to the fire,

Who burnt like Etna for Andrea's loss.

80   BEL-IMPERIA   Hath not my father then enquired for me?

LORENZO   Sister, he hath, and thus excused I thee.

But, Bel-imperia, see the gentle prince;   *He whispereth in her ear*

Look on thy love, behold young Balthazar,

Whose passions by thy presence are increased,

85   And in whose melancholy thou mayst see

Thy hate, his love: thy flight, his following thee.

BEL-IMPERIA   Brother, you are become an orator—

I know not, I, by what experience,

Too politic for me, past all compare—

90   Since last I saw you, but content yourself:

The prince is meditating higher things.

BALTHAZAR   'Tis of thy beauty then that conquers kings:

Of those thy tresses, Ariadne's twines,

Wherewith my liberty thou hast surprised;

95   Of that thine ivory front, my sorrow's map,

Wherein I see no haven to rest my hope.

BEL-IMPERIA   To love and fear, and both at once, my lord,

In my conceit, are things of more import

Than women's wits are to be busied with.

100   BALTHAZAR   'Tis I that love.

BEL-IMPERIA   Whom?

BALTHAZAR   Bel-imperia.

BEL-IMPERIA   But I that fear.

BALTHAZAR   Whom?

105   BEL-IMPERIA   Bel-imperia.

LORENZO   Fear yourself?

BEL-IMPERIA   Ay, brother.

LORENZO   How?

BEL-IMPERIA   As those

---

69 **instrument** agent, means   74 **exasperate** intensified   76 **place** room   77 **ire** anger   79 **Who** which   **Etna** active Sicilian volcano   89 **politic** skilful/cunning   93 **Ariadne's twines** Ariadne, daughter of King Minos of Crete, used thread to guide Theseus through the Minotaur's labyrinth, but Kyd is perhaps confusing her with Arachne, the mortal weaver, who triumphed over Athena in a weaving contest and was turned into a spider; the implication is that Bel-imperia has caught Balthazar in her hair like a spider in its web   94 **surprised** captured by sudden attack   95 **front** forehead   98 **conceit** opinion   **import** consequence, significance

110   That what they love are loath and fear to lose.

BALTHAZAR   Then, fair, let Balthazar your keeper be.

BEL-IMPERIA   No, Balthazar doth fear as well as we:

        Et tremulo me tui pavidum junxere timorem,

        Est vanum stolidae proditionis opus.   *Exit*

115   LORENZO   Nay, and you argue things so cunningly,

        We'll go continue this discourse at court.

BALTHAZAR   Led by the loadstar of her heavenly looks,

        Wends poor, oppressèd Balthazar,

        As o'er the mountains walks the wanderer,

120   Incertain to effect his pilgrimage.   *Exeunt*

[Act 3 Scene 11]

Enter two Portingales, and Hieronimo meets them

FIRST PORTINGALE   By your leave, sir.

HIERONIMO   'Tis neither as you think, nor as you think,

        Nor as you think: you're wide all.

        These slippers are not mine — they were my son Horatio's.

5   My son! And what's a son? A thing begot

        Within a pair of minutes — thereabout:

        A lump bred up in darkness, and doth serve

        To ballast these light creatures we call women;

        And, at nine month's end, creeps forth to light.

10   What is there yet in a son,

        To make a father dote, rave, or run mad?

        Being born, it pouts, cries, and breeds teeth.

        What is there yet in a son? He must be fed,

        Be taught to go, and speak. Ay, or yet

15   Why might not a man love a calf as well?

        Or melt in passion o'er a frisking kid,

        As for a son? Methinks a young bacon,

        Or a fine little smooth horse colt,

        Should move a man as much as doth a son:

20   For one of these, in very little time,

        Will grow to some good use; whereas a son,

        The more he grows in stature and in years,

        The more unsquared, unbevelled he appears,

        Reckons his parents among the rank of fools,

25   Strikes care upon their heads with his mad riots;

---

110 **loath** angry/unpleasant/unwilling   113 *Est...opus* 'It is useless to join your quaking fear with mine and an act of stupid treachery' (Latin)
115 **and** if   **cunningly** cleverly/artfully   117 **loadstar** guiding star   118 **Wends** turns   120 **Incertain** uncertain   **[3.11]**   1 **By your leave** with your permission   3 **wide all** all wide of the mark, wrong/loose, immoral   5 **begot** procreated   8 **light** puns on senses of 'immoral'/'delivered of a child'
17 **bacon** pig   23 **unsquared** unfinished/unsmooth   **unbevelled** incorrectly put together, from 'bevel', originally a heraldic term signifying 'a line broken so as to have two equal acute alternate angles'; the overall sense suggests a 'gangly, ill-made youth'

Makes them look old, before they meet with age.

This is a son! — And what a loss were this,

Considered truly? — O, but my Horatio

Grew out of reach of these insatiate humours:

30 He loved his loving parents;

He was my comfort, and his mother's joy,

The very arm that did hold up our house:

Our hopes were stored up in him,

None but a damned murderer could hate him.

35 He had not seen the back of nineteen year,

When his strong arm unhorsed

The proud Prince Balthazar, and his great mind,

Too full of honour, took him unto mercy —

That valiant, but ignoble Portingale!

40 Well, heaven is heaven still!

And there is Nemesis, and Furies,

And things called whips,

And they sometimes do meet with murderers:

They do not always scape, that's some comfort.

45 Ay, ay, ay; and then time steals on,

And steals, and steals, till violence leaps forth

Like thunder wrapped in a ball of fire,

And so doth bring confusion to them all.

Good leave have you: nay, I pray you go,

50 For I'll leave you, if you can leave me so.

SECOND PORTINGALE Pray you, which is the next way to my lord the duke's?

HIERONIMO The next way from me.

FIRST PORTINGALE To his house, we mean.

HIERONIMO O, hard by: 'tis yon house that ye see.

55 SECOND PORTINGALE You could not tell us if his son were there?

HIERONIMO Who, my Lord Lorenzo?

FIRST PORTINGALE Ay, sir.   *He goes in at one door and*

HIERONIMO O, forbear!   *comes out at another*

For other talk for us far fitter were.

60 But if you be importunate to know

The way to him, and where to find him out,

Then list to me, and I'll resolve your doubt.

There is a path upon your left-hand side,

That leadeth from a guilty conscience

---

29 out of reach beyond, out of   **insatiate** insatiable   **humours** moods/tendencies   **35 back…year** i.e. not yet twenty   **41 Nemesis** in classical mythology, the goddess of retribution   **Furies** avenging goddesses with snakes in their hair   **44 scape** escape   **49 Good…you** Hieronimo's response to the First Portingale's request for permission to leave in the first line of the scene before the 1602 additions   **51 next** nearest   **54 hard** close   **yon** the one just over there   **He … another** this and Hieronimo's following words suggest increasing mental derangement   **58 forbear** have patience/desist   **60 importunate** determined   **62 list** listen   **63 path…side** which leads to hell, as Andrea explains in 1.1.63–4

65   Unto a forest of distrust and fear —
        A darksome place, and dangerous to pass:
        There shall you meet with melancholy thoughts,
        Whose baleful humours if you but uphold,
        It will conduct you to despair and death —
70   Whose rocky cliffs when you have once beheld,
        Within a hugy dale of lasting night,
        That, kindled with the world's iniquities,
        Doth cast up filthy and detested fumes.
        Not far from thence, where murderers have built
75   A habitation for their cursèd souls:
        There, in a brazen cauldron fixed by Jove
        In his fell wrath upon a sulphur flame,
        Yourselves shall find Lorenzo bathing him
        In boiling lead and blood of innocents.
80   FIRST PORTINGALE   Ha, ha, ha!
     HIERONIMO   Ha, ha, ha!
        Why, ha, ha, ha! Farewell, good ha, ha, ha!   *Exit*
     SECOND PORTINGALE   Doubtless this man is passing lunatic,
        Or imperfection of his age doth make him dote.
85   Come, let's away to seek my lord the duke.   *Exeunt*

[Act 3 Scene 12]

Enter Hieronimo with a poniard in one hand and a rope in the other

     HIERONIMO   Now, sir, perhaps I come and see the king;
        The king sees me, and fain would hear my suit:
        Why, is not this a strange and seld-seen thing,
        That standers-by with toys should strike me mute?—
5   Go to, I see their shifts, and say no more.
        Hieronimo, 'tis time for thee to trudge:
        Down by the dale that flows with purple gore,
        Standeth a fiery tower: there sits a judge
        Upon a seat of steel and molten brass,
10   And 'twixt his teeth he holds a fire-brand,
        That leads unto the lake where hell doth stand.
        Away, Hieronimo! To him be gone:
        He'll do thee justice for Horatio's death.
        Turn down this path: thou shalt be with him straight,
15   Or this, and then thou need'st not take thy breath.

---

68 **baleful humours** destructive tendencies/noxious vapours   **uphold** endure/support   71 **hugy** huge, deep   **lasting** everlasting   76 **brazen** brass
77 **fell** savage, terrible   78 **him** himself   83 **passing lunatic** completely mad   84 **dote** act or talk foolishly   [3.12] *poniard* small, slim dagger   2 **fain**
gladly   **suit** petition/case   3 **seld-seen** rare   4 **toys** trivialities   5 **shifts** tricks, devices   6 **trudge** get on my way   7 **gore** blood   10 **fire-brand** piece
of flaming wood

This way or that way? Soft and fair, not so:
For if I hang or kill myself, let's know
Who will revenge Horatio's murder then?
No, no! Fie, no! Pardon me, I'll none of that. *He flings away the dagger and halter*
20 This way I'll take, and this way comes the king: *He takes them up again*
And here I'll have a fling at him, that's flat.
And, Balthazar, I'll be with thee to bring,
And thee, Lorenzo— Here's the king— nay, stay —
And here, ay here— there goes the hare away.
Enter King, Ambassador, Castile and Lorenzo

25 KING   Now show, Ambassador, what our Viceroy saith:
Hath he received the articles we sent?

HIERONIMO   Justice, O, justice to Hieronimo.

LORENZO   Back! See'st thou not the king is busy?

HIERONIMO   O, is he so?

30 KING   Who is he that interrupts our business?

HIERONIMO   Not I.— Hieronimo, beware! Go by, go by!

AMBASSADOR   Renownèd King, he hath received and read
Thy kingly proffers, and thy promised league,
And, as a man extremely overjoyed
35 To hear his son so princely entertained,
Whose death he had so solemnly bewailed,
This, for thy further satisfaction
And kingly love, he kindly lets thee know:
First, for the marriage of his princely son
40 With Bel-imperia, thy belovèd niece,
The news are more delightful to his soul
Than myrrh or incense to the offended heavens.
In person, therefore, will he come himself
To see the marriage rites solemnized,
45 And, in the presence of the court of Spain,
To knit a sure inexplicable band
Of kingly love and everlasting league
Betwixt the crowns of Spain and Portingale.
There will he give his crown to Balthazar,
50 And make a queen of Bel-imperia.

KING   Brother, how like you this our Viceroy's love?

CASTILE   No doubt, my lord, it is an argument
Of honourable care to keep his friend,
And wondrous zeal to Balthazar his son;
55 Nor am I least indebted to his grace,

---

16 Soft and fair gently   **21 fling** attempt/attack   **flat** definite   **22 bring** fetch/lay a charge against you   **23 Here's…stay** the king enters but fails to see Hieronimo   **24 there…away** there the matter ends   **31 Go…by** let it pass   **33 proffers** proposals   **league** political alliance   **35 so princely entertained** entertained in such a princely manner   **36 bewailed** mourned/lamented   **42 myrrh** aromatic resin used as soothing balm   **46 inexplicable** inextricable, that can't be broken   **band** bond   **52 argument** token, proof

That bends his liking to my daughter thus.

AMBASSADOR   Now last, dread lord, here hath his highness sent

(Although he send not that his son return)

His ransom due to Don Horatio.

60   HIERONIMO   Horatio! Who calls Horatio?

KING   And well remembered: thank his majesty—

Here, see it given to Horatio.   *Gives purse*

HIERONIMO   Justice, O, justice, justice, gentle king!

KING   Who is that? Hieronimo?

65   HIERONIMO   Justice, O, justice! O my son, my son!

My son, whom nought can ransom or redeem!

LORENZO   Hieronimo, you are not well-advised.

HIERONIMO   Away, Lorenzo, hinder me no more,

For thou hast made me bankrupt of my bliss.

70   Give me my son! You shall not ransom him!

Away! I'll rip the bowels of the earth,   *He diggeth with his dagger*

And ferry over to th'Elysian plains,

And bring my son to show his deadly wounds.

Stand from about me!

75   I'll make a pickaxe of my poniard

And here surrender up my marshalship:

For I'll go marshal up the fiends in hell,

To be avengèd on you all for this.

KING   What means this outrage?

80   Will none of you restrain his fury?

HIERONIMO   Nay, soft and fair! You shall not need to strive:

Needs must he go that the devils drive.   *Exit*

KING   What accident hath happed to Hieronimo?

I have not seen him to demean him so.

85   LORENZO   My gracious lord, he is with extreme pride

Conceived of young Horatio his son,

And, covetous of having to himself

The ransom of the young prince Balthazar,

Distract, and in a manner lunatic.

90   KING   Believe me, nephew, we are sorry for it:

This is the love that fathers bear their sons.

But, gentle brother, go give to him this gold,

The prince's ransom: let him have his due.

For what he hath, Horatio shall not want,

95   Haply Hieronimo hath need thereof.

LORENZO   But if he be thus haplessly distract,

57 **dread** revered   58 **send...return** does not ask for his son's return/does not ask that the ransom be returned to his son   67 **well-advised** prudent/in your right mind   69 **bankrupt** bereft   72 **th'Elysian plains** where the blessed go after death in classical mythology   74 **from about** away from   79 **outrage** violent outburst   83 **accident** unforeseen event/disaster   **happed to** befallen   84 **demean him** conduct himself   85 **extreme .. of** filled with the utmost pride for   95 **Haply** probably   96 **haplessly** unfortunately   **distract** mentally deranged

'Tis requisite his office be resigned,

And given to one of more discretion.

KING   We shall increase his melancholy so.

100   'Tis best that we see further in it first,

Till when ourself will exempt the place.

And, brother, now bring in th'Ambassador,

That he may be a witness of the match

'Twixt Balthazar and Bel-imperia,

105   And that we may prefix a certain time,

Wherein the marriage shall be solemnized,

That we may have thy lord, the Viceroy, here.

AMBASSADOR   Therein your highness highly shall content

His majesty that longs to hear from hence.

110   KING   On, then, and hear you, lord Ambassador.   *Exeunt*

[Act 3 Scene 13]

Enter Jaques and Pedro

JAQUES   I wonder, Pedro, why our master thus

At midnight sends us with our torches light,

When man and bird and beast are all at rest,

Save those that watch for rape and bloody murder?

5   PEDRO   O, Jaques, know thou that our master's mind

Is much distraught since his Horatio died,

And, now his agèd years should sleep in rest,

His heart in quiet, like a desperate man,

Grows lunatic and childish for his son.

10   Sometimes as he doth at his table sit,

He speaks as if Horatio stood by him,

Then starting in a rage, falls on the earth,

Cries out 'Horatio, where is my Horatio?'

So that with extreme grief and cutting sorrow

15   There is not left in him one inch of man:

See, where he comes.

Enter Hieronimo

HIERONIMO   I pry through every crevice of each wall,

Look on each tree, and search through every brake,

Beat at the bushes, stamp our grandam earth,

20   Dive in the water, and stare up to heaven,

Yet cannot I behold my son Horatio.

How now, who's there? Spirits, spirits?

PEDRO   We are your servants that attend you, sir.

---

100 **see…it** investigate the matter further   101 **ourself** I, using the royal plural pronoun   **exempt** relieve him of   105 **prefix** set in advance
[3.13]   4 **Save** except   18 **brake** clump of bushes, thicket   19 **grandam** grandmother

HIERONIMO What make you with your torches in the dark?

25 PEDRO   You bid us light them and attend you here.

HIERONIMO No, no, you are deceived! Not I! You are deceived!

Was I so mad to bid you light your torches now?

Light me your torches at the mid of noon,

Whenas the sun god rides in all his glory;

30   Light me your torches then.

PEDRO   Then we burn daylight.

HIERONIMO Let it be burnt! Night is a murderous slut

That would not have her treasons to be seen,

And yonder pale-faced He-cat there, the moon,

35   Doth give consent to that is done in darkness;

And all those stars that gaze upon her face,

Are aglets on her sleeve, pins on her train;

And those that should be powerful and divine,

Do sleep in darkness, when they most should shine.

40 PEDRO   Provoke them not, fair sir, with tempting words:

The heavens are gracious, and your miseries

And sorrow makes you speak, you know not what.

HIERONIMO Villain, thou liest! And thou dost naught

But tell me I am mad: thou liest, I am not mad!

45   I know thee to be Pedro, and he Jaques.

I'll prove it to thee, and were I mad, how could I?

Where was she that same night when my Horatio

Was murdered? She should have shone: search thou the book.

Had the moon shone in my boy's face there was

50   A kind of grace: that I know — nay,

I do know — had the murderer seen him,

His weapon would have fall'n and cut the earth,

Had he been framed of naught but blood and death.

Alack! When mischief doth it knows not what,

55   What shall we say to mischief?

Enter Isabella

ISABELLA   Dear Hieronimo, come in adoors;

O, seek not means so to increase thy sorrow.

HIERONIMO Indeed, Isabella, we do nothing here;

I do not cry: ask Pedro, and ask Jaques;

60   Not I indeed: we are very merry, very merry.

ISABELLA   How? Be merry here, be merry here?

Is not this the place, and this the very tree,

Where my Horatio died, where he was murdered?

HIERONIMO Was—do not say what: let her weep it out.

---

24 **make you** are you doing   25 **attend** await   29 **Whenas** when   34 **He-cat** Hecate, goddess associated with the moon and also the Underworld, spelt 'Hee-cat' in Q4, with feline play   35 **that** that which   37 **aglets** ornamental studs/tags attached to the end of laces to make threading easier   **pins** decorative, pin-shaped fasteners   **train** elongated back of a formal robe   53 **framed** created   56 **adoors** at the doors

65   This was the tree — I set it of a kernel —

And when our hot Spain could not let it grow,

But that the infant and the human sap

Began to wither, duly twice a-morning

Would I be sprinkling it with fountain-water.

70   At last it grew and grew, and bore and bore,

Till at the length it grew a gallows,

And did bear our son: it bore thy fruit and mine—

O wicked, wicked plant!   *One knocks within at the door*

      See, who knock there.

PEDRO   It is a painter, sir.

75   **HIERONIMO**   Bid him come in, and paint some comfort.

For surely there's none lives but painted comfort,

Let him come in!— One knows not what may chance —

God's will that I should set this tree!— But even so

Masters ungrateful servants rear from naught,

80   And then they hate them that did bring them up.

Enter the Painter

PAINTER   God bless you, sir.

HIERONIMO   Wherefore, why, thou scornful villain,

How, where, or by what means should I be blessed?

ISABELLA   What wouldst thou have, good fellow?

85   **PAINTER**   Justice, madam.

HIERONIMO   O, ambitious beggar!

Wouldst thou have that that lives not in the world?

Why, all the undelved mines cannot buy

An ounce of justice, 'tis a jewel so inestimable:

90   I tell thee, God hath engrossed all justice in his hands,

And there is none but what comes from him.

PAINTER   O, then I see

That God must right me for my murdered son.

HIERONIMO   How, was thy son murdered?

95   **PAINTER**   Ay, sir, no man did hold a son so dear.

HIERONIMO   What, not as thine? That's a lie,

As massy as the earth: I had a son,

Whose least unvalued hair did weigh

A thousand of thy sons and he was murdered.

100   **PAINTER**   Alas, sir, I had no more but he.

HIERONIMO   Nor I, nor I: but this same one of mine

Was worth a legion. But all is one.

Pedro, Jaques, go in adoors; Isabella, go,

---

65 **set…kernel** planted it from seed   68 **a-morning** in the morning   76 **painted** pretended   78 **even…naught** in the same way masters bring up servants from nothing who then show them no gratitude   88 **undelved** undug, hence full of treasure   90 **engrossed** concentrated, amassed   97 **massy** great, gross

And this good fellow here and I

105   Will range this hideous orchard up and down,

Like to two lions reavèd of their young.

Go in adoors, I say.   *Exeunt* [*Pedro, Jaques and Isabella*]

                                        The Painter and he [*Hieronimo*] *sits down*

Come, let's talk wisely now.

Was thy son murdered?

110   PAINTER   Ay, sir.

HIERONIMO   So was mine.

How dost take it? Art thou not sometimes mad?

Is there no tricks that comes before thine eyes?

PAINTER   O Lord, yes, sir.

115   HIERONIMO   Art a painter? Canst paint me a tear, or a wound,

A groan, or a sigh? Canst paint me such a tree as this?

PAINTER   Sir, I am sure you have heard of my painting: my name's Bazardo.

HIERONIMO   Bazardo! Afore God, an excellent fellow. Look you, sir,

Do you see, I'd have you paint me for my gallery

120   In your oil-colours matted, and draw me

Five years younger than I am —

Do ye see, sir, let five years go,

Let them go — like the Marshal of Spain,

My wife Isabella standing by me,

125   With a speaking look to my son Horatio,

Which should intend to this, or some such-like purpose:

'God bless thee, my sweet son',

And my hand leaning upon his head thus, sir;

Do you see? May it be done?

130   PAINTER   Very well, sir.

HIERONIMO   Nay, I pray, mark me, sir.

Then, sir, would I have you paint me this tree,

This very tree! Canst paint a doleful cry?

PAINTER   Seemingly, sir.

135   HIERONIMO   Nay, it should cry; but all is one. Well, sir,

Paint me a youth run through and through with villains' swords,

Hanging upon this tree. Canst thou draw a murderer?

PAINTER   I'll warrant you, sir; I have the pattern of the most notorious villains that

ever lived in all Spain.

140   HIERONIMO   O, let them be worse, worse: stretch thine art,

And let their beards be of Judas his own colour;

And let their eyebrows jutty over;

In any case observe that. Then, sir,

---

105 range wander   **106 reaved** robbed   **113 tricks** illusions, phantoms   **119 gallery** apartment devoted to the exhibition of works of art/covered space for walking   **120 matted** covered   **125 speaking** highly expressive   **126 intend to** convey the sense of   **131 mark** pay attention to   **133 doleful** sorrowful   **134 Seemingly** so as to appear real   **135 all is one** it doesn't matter   **138 warrant** guarantee   **pattern** example/design   **141 Judas...colour** Judas Iscariot, who betrayed Christ, was believed to be red-haired   **142 jutty over** overhang, stick out over (the eyes)

After some violent noise, bring me forth in my shirt,
145   And my gown under mine arm, with my torch in my hand,
And my sword reared up thus — and with these words:
'What noise is this; who calls Hieronimo?'
May it be done?

PAINTER   Yea, sir.

150 [HIERONIMO]   Well, sir;
Then bring me forth, bring me thorough alley and alley,
Still with a distracted countenance going along,
And let my hair heave up my night-cap.
Let the clouds scowl, make the moon dark, the stars extinct,
155   The winds blowing, the bells tolling, the owls shrieking,
The toads croaking, the minutes jarring,
And the clock striking twelve: and then at last,
Sir, starting, behold a man hanging,
And tottering and tottering,
160   As you know the wind will weave a man,
And I with a trice to cut him down.
And looking upon him by the advantage of my torch,
Find it to be my son Horatio.
There you may show a passion: there you may show a passion!
165   Draw me like old Priam of Troy, crying:
'The house is afire! The house is afire, as the torch over my head!'
Make me curse, make me rave, make me cry, make me mad,
Make me well again, make me curse hell, invocate heaven,
And in the end leave me in a trance — and so forth.

170 PAINTER   And is this the end?

HIERONIMO   O, no, there is no end: the end is death and madness!
As I am never better than when I am mad:
Then methinks I am a brave fellow;
Then I do wonders, but reason abuseth me,
175   And there's the torment, there's the hell.
At the last, sir, bring me to one of the murderers:
Were he as strong as Hector, thus would I tear
And drag him up and down.

He beats the Painter in, then comes out again, with a book in his hand

180 HIERONIMO   *Vindicta mihi!*
Ay, heaven will be revenged of every ill,
Nor will they suffer murder unrepaid.

---

144 **shirt** nightshirt, as in Act 2 scene 5 when he discovers Horatio's body   153 **heave** lift: presumably to give the impression that his hair's standing on end   156 **jarring** discordant, grating upon the ear   158 **starting** as though experiencing a sudden shock   159 **tottering** reeling, staggering   160 **weave** toss to and fro, make the body sway from side to side   161 **with a trice** without delay, at a single pull   165 **Priam** last king of **Troy** at the time of the Trojan war when the city was overrun and burned by the Greeks   168 **invocate** invoke, call upon   173 **brave** fine/excellent/courageous   174 **abuseth** deceives, cheats (him of the illusion)   177 **Hector** son of Priam and leading Trojan warrior   *book* generally assumed to be Seneca from whom he later quotes   180 *Vindicta mihi!* 'Vengeance is mine!' (Latin); biblical injunction against earthly revenge (Romans 12:19)

Then stay, Hieronimo, attend their will,

For mortal men may not appoint their time:

Per scelus semper tutum est sceleribus iter.

185   Strike, and strike home, where wrong is offered thee:

For evils unto ills conductors be,

And death's the worst of resolution.

For he that thinks with patience to contend

To quiet life, his life shall easily end. —

190   *Fata si miseros juvant, habes salutem;*

Fata si vitam negant, habes sepulchrum:

If destiny thy miseries do ease,

Then hast thou health, and happy shalt thou be;

If destiny deny thee life, Hieronimo,

195   Yet shalt thou be assurèd of a tomb —:

If neither, yet let this thy comfort be,

Heaven covereth him that hath no burial.

And to conclude, I will revenge his death!

But how? Not as the vulgar wits of men,

200   With open but inevitable ills,

As by a secret, yet a certain mean,

Which under kindship will be cloakèd best.

Wise men will take their opportunity

Closely and safely, fitting things to time, —

205   But in extremes advantage hath no time,

And therefore all times fit not for revenge.

Thus therefore will I rest me in unrest,

Dissembling quiet in unquietness,

Not seeming that I know their villainies,

210   That my simplicity may make them think,

That ignorantly I will let it slip:

For ignorance, I wot, and well they know,

Remedium malorum iners est.

Nor aught avails it me to menace them

215   Who, as a wintry storm upon a plain,

Will bear me down with their nobility.

No, no, Hieronimo, thou must enjoin

Thine eyes to observation, and thy tongue

To milder speeches than thy spirit afford,

220   Thy heart to patience, and thy hands to rest,

---

184 *Per…iter* 'Crime is always the safest way for crime' (Latin), an inexact quotation from Seneca's *Agamemnon*, 115   **186 evils…be** evils are leaders towards ills   **187 resolution** ending   **188 contend** strive earnestly   **190 *Fata…sepulchrum*** loose quotation from Seneca's *Troades*, lines 510–12, which are Englished by Kyd in the four lines following   **196 neither** i.e. health nor tomb   **199 vulgar** common, customary   **200 open** obvious, straightforward   **inevitable ills** unavoidable evils   **201 As** but rather   **mean** method   **202 cloakèd** disguised   **204 Closely** secretly   **207 rest…unrest** keep myself in a state of alertness/activity   **212 wot** know   **213 *Remedium…est*** (ignorance) 'is an idle remedy for evils' (Latin)   **214 aught…me** does it profit me in any way   **216 nobility** social superiority/power   **217 enjoin** urge, task   **219 afford** provides

Thy cap to courtesy, and thy knee to bow,

Till to revenge thou know, when, where and how.   *A noise within*

How now, what noise? What coil is that you keep?

Enter a Servant

SERVANT   Here are a sort of poor petitioners,

225   That are importunate, and it shall please you, sir,

That you should plead their cases to the king.

HIERONIMO   That I should plead their several actions?

Why, let them enter, and let me see them.

Enter three Citizens and an Old Man

FIRST CITIZEN   So,

230   I tell you this: for learning and for law,

There is not any advocate in Spain

That can prevail, or will take half the pain

That he will, in pursuit of equity.

HIERONIMO   Come near, you men, that thus importune me.—

235   Now must I bear a face of gravity,   *Aside*

For thus I used, before my marshalship,

To plead in causes as corregidor.—

Come on, sirs, what's the matter?

SECOND CITIZEN   Sir, an action.

240   HIERONIMO   Of battery?

FIRST CITIZEN   Mine of debt.

HIERONIMO   Give place.

SECOND CITIZEN   No, sir, mine is an action of the case.

THIRD CITIZEN   Mine an *ejectione firmae* by a lease.

245   HIERONIMO   Content you, sirs; are you determinèd

That I should plead your several actions?

FIRST CITIZEN   Ay, sir, and here's my declaration.

SECOND CITIZEN   And here is my band.

THIRD CITIZEN   And here is my lease.   *They give him papers*

250   HIERONIMO   But wherefore stand you, silly man, so mute,

With mournful eyes and hands to heaven upreared?

Come hither, father, let me know thy cause.

OLD MAN   O, worthy sir, my cause but slightly known

May move the hearts of warlike Myrmidons,

255   And melt the Corsic rocks with ruthful tears.

HIERONIMO   Say, father, tell me what's thy suit?

OLD MAN   No, sir, could my woes

Give way unto my most distressful words,

---

221 **cap to courtesy** i.e. remove your hat as a mark of respect   223 **coil…keep?** is that fuss you're making?   224 **sort** assortment   225 **importunate** persistent in requesting   **and** if   226 **plead** argue/present   227 **several** various/separate   233 **equity** fairness, impartiality   234 **importune** solicit/pester   237 **corregidor** Spanish magistrate   239 **action** lawsuit   240 **battery** unlawful attack causing injury   242 **Give place** make room   243 **action…case** i.e. needing a special writ   244 *ejectione firmae* writ to remove a tenant before the expiry of his **lease**   248 **band** bond   250 **silly** deserving of pity/frail/simple/humble   251 **upreared** raised   254 **Myrmidons** followers of Achilles, foremost Greek warrior of the Trojan war   255 **Corsic** Corsican   **ruthful** compassionate

Then should I not in paper, as you see,
260 With ink bewray what blood began in me.

HIERONIMO   What's here? 'The humble supplication
Of Don Bazulto for his murdered son.'

OLD MAN   Ay, sir.

HIERONIMO   No, sir, it was my murdered son:
265 O, my son, my son, O, my son Horatio!
But mine, or thine, Bazulto, be content.
Here, take my handkercher and wipe thine eyes,
Whiles wretched I in thy mishaps may see
The lively portrait of my dying self.   *He draweth out a bloody napkin*
270 O no, not this, Horatio, this was thine,
And when I dyed it in thy dearest blood,
This was a token 'twixt thy soul and me,
That of thy death revengèd I should be.
But here, take this, and this— what, my purse?   *Gives napkin, then purse*
275 Ay, this, and that, and all of them are thine,
For all as one are our extremities.

FIRST CITIZEN   O, see the kindness of Hieronimo!

[SECOND CITIZEN]   This gentleness shows him a gentleman.

HIERONIMO   See, see, O, see thy shame, Hieronimo,
280 See here a loving father to his son!
Behold the sorrows and the sad laments
That he delivered for his son's decease!
If love's effects so strive in lesser things,
If love enforce such moods in meaner wits,
285 If love express such power in poor estates,
Hieronimo, whenas a raging sea,
Tossed with the wind and tide o'erturnest, then
The upper billows' course of waves to keep,
Whilst lesser waters labour in the deep:
290 Then sham'st thou not, Hieronimo, to neglect
The swift revenge of thy Horatio?
Though on this earth justice will not be found,
I'll down to hell and in this passion
Knock at the dismal gates of Pluto's court,
295 Getting by force, as once Alcides did,
A troop of Furies and tormenting hags
To torture Don Lorenzo and the rest.
Yet lest the triple-headed porter should

---

260 **bewray** reveal, disclose   **blood** the shedding of blood/family ties/anger   267 **handkercher** handkerchief/small cloth   269 **lively** living
276 **extremities** extreme hardships   284 **meaner** more common/less educated/weaker/humbler   286 **whenas...Horatio** Hieronimo uses the image
of a storm and the relative positions of the waves metaphorically to suggest that he should present Horatio's claim for justice as lesser men do   **whenas**
when   287 **o'erturnest** upsets, capsizes   294 **Pluto's court** the underworld of which Pluto was king   295 **Alcides** Hercules; the last of his twelve
labours was to conquer Cerberus, the three-headed dog who guarded the entrance to the Underworld   296 **Furies** avenging goddesses   298 **triple-
headed porter** i.e. Cerberus, see note above to **Alcides**

	Deny my passage to the slimy strond,	
300	The Thracian poet thou shalt counterfeit:	

> Deny my passage to the slimy strond,
>
> 300 The Thracian poet thou shalt counterfeit:
>
> Come on, old father, be my Orpheus,
>
> And if thou canst no notes upon the harp,
>
> Then sound the burden of the sore heart's grief,
>
> Till we do gain that Proserpine may grant,
>
> 305 Revenge on them that murderèd my son.
>
> Then will I rent and tear them, thus and thus,
>
> Shivering their limbs in pieces with my teeth.   *Tears the papers*

FIRST CITIZEN   O, sir, my declaration!   *Exit Hieronimo, and they after*

SECOND CITIZEN   Save my bond!

310 *Enter Hieronimo*

SECOND CITIZEN   Save my bond!

THIRD CITIZEN   Alas, my lease! It cost me ten pound,

> And you my lord, have torn the same.

HIERONIMO   That cannot be, I gave it never a wound!

> Show me one drop of blood fall from the same:
>
> 315 How is it possible I should slay it then?
>
> Tush, no! Run after, catch me if you can.   *Exeunt all but the Old Man*

Bazulto remains till Hieronimo enters again, who, staring him in the face, speaks

HIERONIMO   And art thou come, Horatio, from the depth,

> To ask for justice in this upper earth,
>
> To tell thy father thou art unrevenged,
>
> 320 To wring more tears from Isabella's eyes,
>
> Whose lights are dimmed with overlong laments?
>
> Go back, my son, complain to Aeacus,
>
> For here's no justice; gentle boy, be gone,
>
> For justice is exited from the earth:
>
> 325 Hieronimo will bear thee company.
>
> Thy mother cries on righteous Rhadamanth
>
> For just revenge against the murderers.

OLD MAN   Alas, my lord, whence springs this troubled speech?

HIERONIMO   But let me look on my Horatio.

> 330 Sweet boy, how art thou changed in death's black shade!
>
> Had Proserpine no pity on thy youth,
>
> But suffered thy fair crimson-coloured spring
>
> With withered winter to be blasted thus?
>
> Horatio, thou art older than thy father:
>
> 335 Ah, ruthless fate, that favour thus transforms!

OLD MAN   Ah, my good lord, I am not your young son.

---

299 **slimy** slippery/disgusting, morally objectionable   **strond** shore   300 **Thracian poet** i.e. **Orpheus**, a legendary poet and musician of classical mythology   302 **canst no** cannot play any   303 **burden** weight (of grief), playing on the sense of the 'chorus' or 'refrain' of a song   304 **Proserpine** queen of the Underworld who allowed **Orpheus** to enter Hades (the Underworld) to bring his wife, Eurydice, back from death   306 **rent…teeth** an allusion to the Maenads or Bacchantes who killed **Orpheus** by tearing him limb from limb in their violent frenzy: interpreted as symbolizing the divorce of life and art   322 **Aeacus** a mortal king renowned for justice and wisdom who was appointed one of the three judges of the Underworld after his death, the others being **Minos** and **Rhadamanthus**   330 **shade** darkness, shadow   332 **suffered** allowed   333 **blasted** blighted, cursed   335 **favour** beauty/appearance

HIERONIMO   What, not my son? Thou then a Fury art,
                   Sent from the empty kingdom of black night
                   To summon me to make appearance
340   Before grim Minos and just Rhadamanth,
                   To plague Hieronimo that is remiss,
                   And seeks not vengeance for Horatio's death.
OLD MAN   I am a grievèd man, and not a ghost,
                   That came for justice for my murdered son.
345   HIERONIMO   Ay, now I know thee, now thou nam'st my son:
                   Thou art the lively image of my grief:
                   Within thy face, my sorrows I may see.
                   Thy eyes are gummed with tears, thy cheeks are wan,
                   Thy forehead troubled, and thy muttering lips
350   Murmur sad words abruptly broken off;
                   By force of windy sighs thy spirit breathes,
                   And all this sorrow riseth for thy son:
                   And selfsame sorrow feel I for my son.
                   Come in, old man, thou shalt to Isabel;
355   Lean on my arm: I thee, thou me, shalt stay.
                   And thou, and I, and she will sing a song,
                   Three parts in one, but all of discords framed—:
                   Talk not of chords, but let us now be gone,
                   For with a cord Horatio was slain.   *Exeunt*

[Act 3 Scene 14]

Enter King of Spain, the Duke, Viceroy, and Lorenzo, Balthazar, Don Pedro and
Bel-imperia

KING   Go, brother, 'tis the Duke of Castile's cause;
                   Salute the Viceroy in our name.
CASTILE   I go.
VICEROY   Go forth, Don Pedro, for thy nephew's sake,
5   And greet the Duke of Castile.
[DON] PEDRO   It shall be so.
KING   And now to meet the Portuguese:
                   For as we now are, so sometimes were these,
                   Kings and commanders of the western Indies.
10   Welcome, brave Viceroy, to the court of Spain,
                   And welcome all his honourable train!
                   'Tis not unknown to us for why you come,

---

337 **Fury** avenging deity   340 **Minos…Rhadamanth** judges of the underworld, see note above on **Aeacus**   346 **lively** living/lifelike   348 **gummed** bleary   355 **stay** support   356 **song** i.e. a song of mourning or dirge for Horatio   **[3.14]**   1 **cause** affair, concern   8 **sometimes** previously   9 **western Indies** Portugal never officially colonized the West Indies, although they landed in Barbados; the reference may be to Brazil which came under Spanish rule for a period in the late sixteenth century   10 **brave** worthy, excellent   11 **train** retinue

Or have so kingly crossed the seas:

Sufficeth it, in this we note the troth

15   And more than common love you lend to us.

So is it that mine honourable niece

(For it beseems us now that it be known)

Already is betrothed to Balthazar,

And, by appointment and our condescent,

20   Tomorrow are they to be married.

To this intent we entertain thyself,

Thy followers, their pleasure, and our peace.

Speak, men of Portingale, shall it be so?

If ay, say so; if not, say flatly no.

25   VICEROY   Renownèd king, I come not, as thou think'st,

With doubtful followers, unresolvèd men,

But such as have upon thine articles

Confirmed thy motion and contented me.

Know, sovereign, I come to solemnize

30   The marriage of thy beloved niece,

Fair Bel-imperia, with my Balthazar,

With thee, my son, whom sith I live to see,

Here take my crown, I give it her and thee:

And let me live a solitary life,

35   In ceaseless prayers,

To think how strangely heaven hath thee preserved.

   KING   See, brother, see, how nature strives in him!

Come, worthy Viceroy, and accompany

Thy friend with thine extremities:

40   A place more private fits this princely mood.

   VICEROY   Or here, or where your highness thinks it good.   *Exeunt all but*

   CASTILE   Nay, stay, Lorenzo, let me talk with you.   *Castile and Lorenzo*

See'st thou this entertainment of these kings?

   LORENZO   I do, my lord, and joy to see the same.

45   CASTILE   And know'st thou why this meeting is?

   LORENZO   For her, my lord, whom Balthazar doth love,

And to confirm their promised marriage.

   CASTILE   She is thy sister?

   LORENZO   Who, Bel-imperia? Ay,

50   My gracious lord, and this is the day,

That I have longed so happily to see.

   CASTILE   Thou wouldst be loath that any fault of thine

Should intercept her in her happiness?

---

13 **crossed the seas** only necessary or possible if the Spanish court was in Seville at the time   14 **troth** loyalty/pledge   17 **it beseems us** I understand   19 **condescent** consent/condescension   26 **doubtful** apprehensive/undecided   28 **motion** proposition   32 **sith** since   34 **solitary** secluded, retired   36 **strangely** wonderfully   37 **nature…him** he is overcome with emotion   39 **extremities** intense emotions   43 **entertainment** reception/social behaviour   52 **loath** displeased   53 **intercept** hinder, prevent

LORENZO   Heavens will not let Lorenzo err so much.

55 CASTILE   Why then, Lorenzo, listen to my words:
It is suspected, and reported too,
That thou, Lorenzo, wrongst Hieronimo,
And in his suits towards his majesty
Still keeps him back, and seeks to cross his suit.

60 LORENZO   That I, my lord—?

CASTILE   I tell thee, son, myself have heard it said,
When (to my sorrow) I have been ashamed
To answer for thee, though thou art my son.
Lorenzo, know'st thou not the common love

65 And kindness that Hieronimo hath won
By his deserts within the court of Spain?
Or see'st thou not the king my brother's care
In his behalf, and to procure his health?
Lorenzo, shouldst thou thwart his passions,

70 And he exclaim against thee to the king,
What honour were't in this assembly,
Or what a scandal were't among the kings
To hear Hieronimo exclaim on thee?
Tell me — and look thou tell me truly too —

75 Whence grows the ground of this report in court?

LORENZO   My lord, it lies not in Lorenzo's power
To stop the vulgar, liberal of their tongues:
A small advantage makes a water-breach,
And no man lives that long contenteth all.

80 CASTILE   Myself have seen thee busy to keep back
Him and his supplications from the king.

LORENZO   Yourself, my lord, hath seen his passions,
That ill-beseemed the presence of a king:
And for I pitied him in his distress,

85 I held him thence with kind and courteous words,
As free from malice to Hieronimo
As to my soul, my lord.

CASTILE   Hieronimo, my son, mistakes thee then.

LORENZO   My gracious father, believe me, so he doth.

90 But what's a silly man, distract in mind
To think upon the murder of his son?
Alas! How easy is it for him to err!
But for his satisfaction and the world's,
'Twere good, my lord, that Hieronimo and I

---

59 **cross** thwart/obstruct   64 **common** public, general   66 **deserts** merits   69 **thwart** frustrate   70 **exclaim against** blame/accuse loudly   77 **vulgar** common people   **liberal...tongues** speaking freely   78 **advantage** opportunity   **water-breach** leak, i.e. for gossip in this case   80 **busy** anxious/determined   83 **ill-beseemed** were inappropriate for   84 **for** because   85 **thence** back from there   90 **silly** simple/humble/foolish   **distract** confused/deranged

95   Were reconciled, if he misconster me.

CASTILE   Lorenzo, thou hast said: it shall be so.
        Go one of you, and call Hieronimo.

Enter Balthazar and Bel-imperia

BALTHAZAR   Come, Bel-imperia, Balthazar's content,
        My sorrow's ease and sovereign of my bliss,
100   Sith heaven hath ordained thee to be mine:
        Disperse those clouds and melancholy looks,
        And clear them up with those thy sun-bright eyes,
        Wherein my hope and heaven's fair beauty lies.

BEL-IMPERIA   My looks, my lord, are fitting for my love,
105   Which, new-begun, can show no brighter yet.

BALTHAZAR   New-kindled flames should burn as morning sun.

BEL-IMPERIA   But not too fast, lest heat and all be done.
        I see my lord my father.

BALTHAZAR   Truce, my love: I will go salute him.

110   CASTILE   Welcome, Balthazar,
        Welcome, brave prince, the pledge of Castile's peace!
        And welcome, Bel-imperia!— How now, girl?
        Why com'st thou sadly to salute us thus?
        Content thyself, for I am satisfied:
115   It is not now as when Andrea lived;
        We have forgotten and forgiven that,
        And thou art gracèd with a happier love.
        But, Balthazar, here comes Hieronimo;
        I'll have a word with him.

Enter Hieronimo and a Servant

120   HIERONIMO   And where's the duke?

SERVANT   Yonder.

HIERONIMO   Even so.—
        What new device have they devisèd, trow?
        Pocas palabras! Mild as the lamb!
125   Is't I will be revenged? No, I am not the man.—

CASTILE   Welcome, Hieronimo.

LORENZO   Welcome, Hieronimo.

BALTHAZAR   Welcome, Hieronimo.

HIERONIMO   My lords, I thank you for Horatio.

130   CASTILE   Hieronimo, the reason that I sent
        To speak with you is this.

HIERONIMO   What, so short?
        Then I'll be gone, I thank you for't.

CASTILE   Nay, stay, Hieronimo!— Go call him, son.

---

95 misconster misinterprets   **101 clouds** troubles, afflictions   **107 done** used up   **112 How now** what's the matter?   **113 sadly** gravely   **salute** greet
122 Even so so he is   **123 device** trick/plan   **trow** do you think   **124 *Pocas palabras!*** 'Few words!' (Spanish)

135	LORENZO	Hieronimo, my father craves a word with you.
	HIERONIMO	With me, sir? Why, my lord, I thought you had done.
	LORENZO	No.— Would he had!

Aside

CASTILE   Hieronimo, I hear

You find yourself aggrievèd at my son,

140   Because you have not access unto th'king,

And say 'tis he that intercepts your suits.

HIERONIMO   Why, is not this a miserable thing, my lord?

CASTILE   Hieronimo, I hope you have no cause,

And would be loath that one of your deserts

145   Should once have reason to suspect my son,

Considering how I think of you myself.

HIERONIMO   Your son Lorenzo! Whom, my noble lord?

The hope of Spain, mine honourable friend?

Grant me the combat of them, if they dare: *Draws out his sword*

150   I'll meet him face to face, to tell me so!

These be the scandalous reports of such

As love not me, and hate my lord too much:

Should I suspect Lorenzo would prevent

Or cross my suit, that loved my son so well?

155   My lord, I am ashamed it should be said.

LORENZO   Hieronimo, I never gave you cause.

HIERONIMO   My good lord, I know you did not.

CASTILE   There then pause,

And for the satisfaction of the world,

160   Hieronimo, frequent my homely house,

The Duke of Castile, Cyprian's ancient seat,

And when thou wilt, use me, my son, and it:

But here, before Prince Balthazar and me,

Embrace each other, and be perfect friends.

165   HIERONIMO   Ay, marry, my lord, and shall.   *Embrace*

Friends, quoth he? See, I'll be friends with you all:

Especially with you, my lovely lord;

For divers causes it is fit for us

That we be friends: the world is suspicious,

170   And men may think what we imagine not.

BALTHAZAR   Why, this is friendly done, Hieronimo.

LORENZO   And that I hope: old grudges are forgot.

HIERONIMO   What else? It were a shame it should not be so.

CASTILE   Come on, Hieronimo, at my request,

175   Let us entreat your company today.   *Exeunt [all but Hieronimo]*

HIERONIMO   Your lordship's to command.— Pha! Keep your way:

---

149 **combat of them** opportunity to meet them in a duel   154 **cross** obstruct   160 **frequent** visit   **homely** hospitable   161 **ancient seat** historical family residence   162 **use** make use of   166 **quoth** says   168 **divers** various   175 **entreat** earnestly request   176 **Pha!** Exclamation of disgust/contempt

Chimi fa più carezze che non suole,

Tradito mi ha, o tradir mi vuole.   *Exit*

[Act 3 Scene 15]

Enter Ghost and Revenge

GHOST OF ANDREA   Awake, Erichtho! Cerberus, awake!

Solicit Pluto, gentle Proserpine!

To combat, Acheron and Erebus!

For ne'er, by Styx and Phlegethon in hell,

5   Nor ferried Charon to the fiery lakes

Such fearful sights, as poor Andrea sees.

Revenge, awake!

REVENGE   Awake? For why?

GHOST OF ANDREA   Awake, Revenge, for thou art ill-advised

10   To sleep away! What, thou art warned to watch!

REVENGE   Content thyself and do not trouble me.

GHOST OF ANDREA   Awake, Revenge, if love — as love hath had —

Have yet the power or prevalence in hell!

Hieronimo with Lorenzo is joined in league,

15   And intercepts our passage to revenge:

Awake, Revenge, or we are woebegone!

REVENGE   Thus worldlings ground what they have dreamed upon.

Content thyself, Andrea: though I sleep,

Yet is my mood soliciting their souls.

20   Sufficeth thee that poor Hieronimo

Cannot forget his son Horatio.

Nor dies Revenge, although he sleep awhile,

For in unquiet quietness is feigned,

And slumb'ring is a common worldly wile.—

25   Behold, Andrea, for an instance, how

Revenge hath slept, and then imagine thou,

What 'tis to be subject to destiny.

Enter a Dumb Show

GHOST OF ANDREA   Awake, Revenge: reveal this mystery.

REVENGE   The two first the nuptial torches bore

30   As bright-burning as the midday's sun,

But after them doth Hymen hie as fast,

---

177 Chi...vuole 'He who treats me with more affection than usual has either betrayed me or plans to do so' (Italian)   **[3.15]   1 Erichtho** legendary Thessalian witch who descended to hell to bring back a spirit (Dante, *Divine Comedy*, *Inferno*, IX:23)   **Cerberus** three-headed dog guarding the gates to the Underworld   **2 Pluto** king of the Underworld   **Proserpine** Pluto's queen   **3 Acheron** river of pain in the Underworld   **Erebus** the personification of darkness   **4 Styx and Phlegethon** two more Underworld rivers   **5 Charon** the ferryman of the newly-dead to the Underworld   **15 intercepts** prevents/hinders   **16 woebegone** oppressed with misery   **17 ground** base   **19 soliciting** troubling/inciting (to an act of lawlessness)   **24 wile** trick/device   **Dumb Show** a common dramatic device of silent mimed actions derived from medieval theatre   **28 reveal** explain   **29 nuptial** marriage   **31 Hymen** god of marriage   **hie** hurry

Clothèd in sable and a saffron robe,

And blows them out, and quencheth them with blood,

As discontent that things continue so.

35 GHOST OF ANDREA Sufficeth me, thy meaning's understood,

And thanks to thee and those infernal powers,

That will not tolerate a lover's woe.—

Rest thee, for I will sit to see the rest.

REVENGE Then argue not, for thou hast thy request. *Exeunt*

[Act 4 Scene 1]

Enter Bel-imperia and Hieronimo

BEL-IMPERIA Is this the love thou bear'st Horatio?

Is this the kindness that thou counterfeits?

Are these the fruits of thine incessant tears?

Hieronimo, are these thy passions,

5 Thy protestations and thy deep laments,

That thou wert wont to weary men withal?

O unkind father! O deceitful world!

With what dishonour and the hate of men:

From this dishonour and the hate of men,

10 Thus to neglect the life and loss of him

Whom both my letters and thine own belief

Assures thee to be causeless slaughtered!

Hieronimo, for shame, Hieronimo,

Be not a history to aftertimes

15 Of such ingratitude unto thy son:

Unhappy mothers of such children then,

But monstrous fathers to forget so soon

The death of those, whom they with care and cost

Have tendered so, thus careless should be lost.

20 Myself, a stranger in respect of thee,

So loved his life, as still I wish their deaths.

Nor shall his death be unrevenged by me,

Although I bear it out for fashion's sake:

For here I swear, in sight of heaven and earth,

25 Shouldst thou neglect the love thou shouldst retain,

And give it over, and devise no more,

Myself should send their hateful souls to hell,

---

32 **sable…saffron** traditionally worn by **Hymen**, saffron robes were dyed with the orange-red stigma of the *Crocus sativas* plant; their covering of **sable** or black is an ominous sign   34 **discontent** dissatisfaction, displeasure   35 **Sufficeth me** I'm satisfied   **[4.1]**   2 **counterfeits** simulates   6 **wert wont** were accustomed   **withal** in addition   8 **With…men** there may be a compositorial error at this point or a line missing   14 **history** record/exemplary tale   **aftertimes** posterity   19 **tendered** cherished/nurtured   20 **respect of** comparison with   23 **bear it out** endure it   **fashion's** appearances'   26 **devise** plot (revenge)

That wrought his downfall with extremest death.

HIERONIMO   But may it be that Bel-imperia

30   Vows such revenge as she hath deigned to say?

Why, then I see that heaven applies our drift,

And all the saints do sit soliciting

For vengeance on those cursèd murderers.

Madam, 'tis true, and now I find it so:

35   I found a letter written in your name,

And in that letter how Horatio died.

Pardon, O pardon, Bel-imperia,

My fear and care in not believing it,

Nor think I thoughtless think upon a mean

40   To let his death be unrevenged at full.

And here I vow — so you but give consent,

And will conceal my resolution —

I will ere long determine of their deaths

That causeless thus have murderèd my son.

45   BEL-IMPERIA   Hieronimo, I will consent, conceal,

And aught that may effect for thine avail,

Join with thee to revenge Horatio's death.

HIERONIMO   On, then, and whatsoever I devise,

Let me entreat you, grace my practices,

50   For why the plot's already in mine head.

Here they are.

Enter Balthazar and Lorenzo

BALTHAZAR   How now, Hieronimo?

What, courting Bel-imperia?

HIERONIMO   Ay, my lord;

55   Such courting as, I promise you,

She hath my heart, but you, my lord, have hers.

LORENZO   But now, Hieronimo, or never,

We are to entreat your help.

HIERONIMO   My help?

60   Why, my good lords, assure yourselves of me,

For you have given me cause—:

Ay, by my faith have you!

BALTHAZAR   It pleased you,

At the entertainment of the ambassador,

65   To grace the king so much as with a show.

Now, were your study so well furnished,

As for the passing of the first night's sport

---

28 **wrought** fashioned, prepared   **extremest** the most violent   30 **deigned** condescended/graciously acknowledged   31 **applies** brings together/ administers   **drift** impulse/purpose   39 **thoughtless** without consideration   **mean** method   41 **so** as long as   46 **aught** anything   **avail** benefit, advantage   49 **grace** countenance/add grace to   50 **For why** because   65 **grace** favour/honour   **so...with** to the extent that you put on   66 **study** affection, inclination/learning, literary composition/private room   **furnished** provided   67 **sport** entertainment

To entertain my father with the like,

Or any such-like pleasing motion,

70   Assure yourself, it would content them well.

HIERONIMO   Is this all?

BALTHAZAR   Ay, this is all.

HIERONIMO   Why then, I'll fit you; say no more.

When I was young, I gave my mind

75   And plied myself to fruitless poetry,

Which though it profit the professor naught,

Yet is it passing pleasing to the world.

LORENZO   And how for that?

HIERONIMO   Marry, my good lord, thus:—

80   And yet, methinks, you are too quick with us—   *Aside*

When in Toledo there I studied,

It was my chance to write a tragedy:

See here, my lords —   *He shows them a book*

Which, long forgot, I found this other day.

85   Now would your lordships favour me so much

As but to grace me with your acting it —

I mean each one of you to play a part —

Assure you it will prove most passing strange,

And wondrous plausible to that assembly.

90   BALTHAZAR   What, would you have us play a tragedy?

HIERONIMO   Why, Nero thought it no disparagement,

And kings and emperors have ta'en delight

To make experience of their wits in plays.

LORENZO   Nay, be not angry, good Hieronimo;

95   The prince but asked a question.

BALTHAZAR   In faith, Hieronimo, and you be in earnest,

I'll make one.

LORENZO   And I another.

HIERONIMO   Now, my good lord, could you entreat

100   Your sister Bel-imperia to make one?

For what's a play without a woman in't?

BEL-IMPERIA   Little entreaty shall serve me, Hieronimo,

For I must needs be employed in your play.

HIERONIMO   Why, this is well: I tell you, lordings,

105   It was determined to have been acted,

By gentlemen and scholars too,

Such as could tell what to speak.

---

69 **motion** show, entertainment   73 **fit** accommodate, punning on secondary meaning 'punish'   76 **professor** practitioner   77 **passing** more than   81 **Toledo** ancient university city of central Spain, famed for steel-making and weaponry   **there** where   82 **chance** good fortune   86 **grace** honour   88 **passing strange** exceptional, remarkable   91 **Nero** Roman emperor who promoted and performed in theatrical entertainments   93 **experience** trial/demonstration   96 **and** if   97 **make one** i.e. of the performers   101 **woman** an ironic, meta-theatrical comment given that while women performed on the Spanish stage at this period, in England female parts were performed by young male actors   105 **determined** designed/planned

BALTHAZAR And now
    It shall be played by princes and courtiers,
110   Such as can tell how to speak:
    If, as it is our country manner,
    You will but let us know the argument.
HIERONIMO That shall I roundly. The chronicles of Spain
    Record this written of a knight of Rhodes:
115   He was betrothed, and wedded at the length,
    To one Perseda, an Italian dame,
    Whose beauty ravished all that her beheld,
    Especially the soul of Soliman,
    Who at the marriage was the chiefest guest.
120   By sundry means sought Soliman to win
    Perseda's love, and could not gain the same.
    Then 'gan he break his passions to a friend,
    One of his bashaws, whom he held full dear;
    Her had this bashaw long solicited,
125   And saw she was not otherwise to be won
    But by her husband's death, this knight of Rhodes,
    Whom presently by treachery he slew.
    She, stirred with an exceeding hate therefore,
    As cause of this slew Soliman,
130   And, to escape the bashaw's tyranny,
    Did stab herself: and this the tragedy.
LORENZO O, excellent!
BEL-IMPERIA But say, Hieronimo, what then became
    Of him that was the bashaw?
135 HIERONIMO Marry, thus:
    Moved with remorse of his misdeeds,
    Ran to a mountain-top, and hung himself.
BALTHAZAR But which of us is to perform that part?
HIERONIMO O, that will I, my lords, make no doubt of it:
140   I'll play the murderer, I warrant you,
    For I already have conceited that.
BALTHAZAR And what shall I?
HIERONIMO Great Soliman, the Turkish emperor.
LORENZO And I?
145 HIERONIMO Erastus, the knight of Rhodes.
BEL-IMPERIA And I?
HIERONIMO Perseda, chaste and resolute.—
    And here, my lords, are several abstracts drawn,

111 **country** national/rustic 112 **argument** subject matter/plot 113 **roundly** in full/directly/promptly **chronicles…Rhodes** Hieronimo seems to be offering a loose summary of Kyd's play *Soliman and Perseda* written two years later; the Greek island of **Rhodes** was under Ottoman rule during this period 120 **sundry** various 122 **'gan he break** he began to confide 123 **bashaws** i.e. pashas, high-ranking Turkish military commanders 126 **But** except 141 **conceited** thought of/planned 148 **abstracts drawn** extracts/parts written out

For each of you to note your parts,
150   And act it, as occasion's offered you.
      You must provide a Turkish cap,
      A black mustachio and a falchion;   *Gives a paper to Balthazar*
      You with a cross, like to a knight of Rhodes;   *Gives another to Lorenzo*
      And, madam, you must attire yourself   *He gives Bel-imperia another*
155   Like Phoebe, Flora, or the huntress,
      Which to your discretion shall seem best.
      And as for me, my lords, I'll look to one,
      And with the ransom that the Viceroy sent,
      So furnish and perform this tragedy,
160   As all the world shall say, Hieronimo
      Was liberal in gracing of it so.
BALTHAZAR   Hieronimo, methinks a comedy were better.
HIERONIMO   A comedy?
      Fie! Comedies are fit for common wits,
165   But to present a kingly troop withal,
      Give me a stately-written tragedy,
      Tragedia cothurnata, fitting kings,
      Containing matter and not common things.
      My lords, all this must be performed,
170   As fitting for the first night's revelling.
      The Italian tragedians were so sharp of wit,
      That in one hour's meditation
      They would perform anything in action.
LORENZO   And well it may; for I have seen the like
175   In Paris 'mongst the French tragedians.
HIERONIMO   In Paris? Mass! And well rememberèd!
      There's one thing more that rests for us to do.
BALTHAZAR   What's that, Hieronimo? Forget not anything.
HIERONIMO   Each one of us
180   Must act his part in unknown languages,
      That it may breed the more variety:
      As you, my lord, in Latin, I in Greek,
      You in Italian, and for because I know
      That Bel-imperia hath practised the French,
185   In courtly French shall all her phrases be.
BEL-IMPERIA   You mean to try my cunning then, Hieronimo?
BALTHAZAR   But this will be a mere confusion,
      And hardly shall we all be understood.
HIERONIMO   It must be so, for the conclusion

---

151 **Turkish cap** fez 152 **falchion** curved sword 155 **Phoebe** goddess of the moon **Flora** goddess of flowers **huntress** Diana, goddess of hunting and virginity 161 **liberal** generous **gracing** honouring/giving pleasure 165 **kingly troop** royal company of actors/party, audience 167 *Tragedia cothurnata* the most serious of Greek tragedies in which the actors wore thick-soled boots or buskins (**cothurnata**) 168 **matter** substance 171 **Italian tragedians** the improvising actors of the *commedia dell'arte* 176 **Mass!** by the mass or Eucharist, a common oath 177 **rests** remains 186 **cunning** knowledge, skill

190 Shall prove the invention and all was good:
    And I myself in an oration,
    And with a strange and wondrous show besides,
    That I will have there behind a curtain,
    Assure yourself, shall make the matter known:
195 And all shall be concluded in one scene,
    For there's no pleasure ta'en in tediousness.

BALTHAZAR How like you this?   *Aside to Lorenzo*

LORENZO Why, thus my lord:
    We must resolve to soothe his humours up.

200 BALTHAZAR On then, Hieronimo: farewell till soon.

HIERONIMO You'll ply this gear?

LORENZO I warrant you.   *Exeunt all but Hieronimo*

HIERONIMO Ay, why so:
    Now shall I see the fall of Babylon,
205 Wrought by the heavens in this confusion.
    And if the world like not this tragedy,
    Hard is the hap of old Hieronimo.   *Exit*

[Act 4 Scene 2]

Enter Isabella with a weapon

ISABELLA   Tell me no more! — O monstrous homicides!
    Since neither piety nor pity moves
    The king to justice or compassion,
    I will revenge myself upon this place,
5   Where thus they murdered my belovèd son.   *She cuts down the arbour*
    Down with those branches and these loathsome boughs
    Of this unfortunate and fatal pine:
    Down with them, Isabella, rent them up,
    And burn the roots from whence the rest is sprung.
10 I will not leave a root, a stalk, a tree,
    A bough, a branch, a blossom, nor a leaf,
    No, not an herb within this garden-plot:
    Accursèd complot of my misery!
    Fruitless forever may this garden be,
15 Barren the earth, and blissless whosoe'er
    Imagines not to keep it unmanured!
    An eastern wind, commixed with noisome airs,

190 **invention** original idea/literary composition   191 **oration** prayer to God/formal discourse   192 **strange…show** i.e. Horatio's body   199 **resolve…up** indulge his whims   201 **ply** agree/apply yourself to   **gear** business   202 **warrant** promise   203 **why so** so then in this way   204 **Babylon** perhaps an error for Babel renowned in the book of Genesis for its confusion of tongues/the wicked city punished by God (Isaiah 13, Jeremiah 2)/signifying Rome, centre of Roman Catholicism and seat of the Pope   207 **hap** luck, fortune   **[4.2]**   7 **unfortunate** unlucky   8 **rent** tear   13 **complot** conspiracy   15 **blissless** miserable   16 **unmanured** uncultivated   17 **commixed** mixed together   **noisome** unpleasant/noxious

Shall blast the plants and the young saplings;
The earth with serpents shall be pesterèd,
20 And passengers, for fear to be infect,
Shall stand aloof, and, looking at it, tell
'There, murdered, died the son of Isabel.'
Ay, here he died, and here I him embrace:
See, where his ghost solicits with his wounds,
25 Revenge on her that should revenge his death.
Hieronimo, make haste to see thy son,
For sorrow and despair hath cited me
To hear Horatio plead with Rhadamanth:
Make haste, Hieronimo, to hold excused
30 Thy negligence in pursuit of their deaths,
Whose hateful wrath bereaved him of his breath.—
Ah, nay, thou dost delay their deaths,
Forgives the murderers of thy noble son,
And none but I bestir me — to no end!
35 And as I curse this tree from further fruit,
So shall my womb be cursèd for his sake,
And with this weapon will I wound the breast,
The hapless breast, that gave Horatio suck.   *She stabs herself [and exits]*

[Act 4 Scene 3]

Enter Hieronimo; he knocks up the curtain
Enter the Duke of Castile

CASTILE   How now, Hieronimo, where's your fellows,
That you take all this pain?
HIERONIMO   O, sir, it is for the author's credit
To look that all things may go well.
5   But, good my lord, let me entreat your grace,
To give the king the copy of the play:
This is the argument of what we show.
CASTILE   I will, Hieronimo.
HIERONIMO   One thing more, my good lord.
10 CASTILE   What's that?
HIERONIMO   Let me entreat your grace
That, when the train are passed into the gallery,
You would vouchsafe to throw me down the key.
CASTILE   I will, Hieronimo.   *Exit Castile*

---

18 **blast** destroy   19 **pesterèd** infested, plagued   20 **passengers** travellers, passers-by   **infect** infected   27 **cited** summoned   [4.3] *knocks* fastens by knocking (with a hammer or similar)   1 **fellows** fellow actors   2 **you…pain** you're doing everything yourself   7 **argument** synopsis, with cast list   12 **train** the whole party   **gallery** hall   13 **vouchsafe** condescend

15   HIERONIMO   What, are you ready, Balthazar?
             Bring a chair and a cushion for the king.
             Enter Balthazar with a chair
             Well done, Balthazar, hang up the title:
             Our scene is Rhodes— what, is your beard on?
      BALTHAZAR   Half on, the other is in my hand.
20   HIERONIMO   Dispatch for shame, are you so long?   *Exit Balthazar*
             Bethink thyself, Hieronimo,
             Recall thy wits, recount thy former wrongs
             Thou hast received by murder of thy son,
             And lastly—not least—how Isabel,
25   Once his mother and thy dearest wife,
             All woe-begone for him, hath slain herself.
             Behoves thee then, Hieronimo, to be revenged!
             The plot is laid of dire revenge:
             On, then, Hieronimo, pursue revenge,
30   For nothing wants but acting of revenge!   *Exit Hieronimo*

[Act 4 Scene 4]

             Enter Spanish King, Viceroy, the Duke of Castile and their train
      KING   Now, Viceroy, shall we see the tragedy
             Of Soliman, the Turkish emperor,
             Performed — of pleasure — by your son the prince,
             My nephew Don Lorenzo, and my niece.
5   VICEROY   Who? Bel-imperia?
      KING   Ay, and Hieronimo, our Marshal,
             At whose request they deign to do't themselves:
             These be our pastimes in the court of Spain.
             Here, brother, you shall be the book-keeper:
10   This is the argument of that they show.   *He giveth him a book*
             Gentlemen, this play of Hieronimo in sundry languages was thought good to be set down in
             English more largely for the easier understanding to every public reader.
             Enter Balthazar, Bel-imperia and Hieronimo
      BALTHAZAR [AS SOLIMAN]   Bashaw, that Rhodes is ours, yield heavens the honour,
             And holy Mahomet, our sacred prophet!
             And be thou graced with every excellence
             That Soliman can give, or thou desire.
15   But thy desert in conquering Rhodes is less
             Than in reserving this fair Christian nymph
             Perseda, blissful lamp of excellence,

---

17 **title** placard giving the name   20 **Dispatch** hurry up   27 **Behoves thee** you are morally obliged   28 **dire** terrible   30 **wants** is lacking   [4.4]   7 **deign** condescend   9 **book-keeper** prompter, holder in the Elizabethan theatre of the single copy of the play text   *Gentlemen...reader* the note seems to suggest translation of the stage original   16 **reserving** saving

Whose eyes compel, like powerful adamant
The warlike heart of Soliman to wait.

20   KING   See, Viceroy, that is Balthazar, your son,
That represents the emperor Soliman:
How well he acts his amorous passion!

VICEROY   Ay, Bel-imperia hath taught him that.

CASTILE   That's because his mind runs all on Bel-imperia.

25   HIERONIMO [AS BASHAW]   Whatever joy earth yields, betide your majesty.

BALTHAZAR [AS SOLIMAN]   Earth yields no joy without Perseda's love.

HIERONIMO [AS BASHAW]   Then let Perseda on your grace attend.

BALTHAZAR [AS SOLIMAN]   She shall not wait on me, but I on her:
Drawn by the influence of her lights, I yield.

30   But let my friend, the Rhodian knight, come forth,
Erasto, dearer than my life to me,
That he may see Perseda, my beloved.

Enter [Lorenzo as] Erasto

KING   Here comes Lorenzo: look upon the plot,
And tell me, brother, what part plays he?

35   BEL-IMPERIA [AS PERSEDA]   Ah, my Erasto, welcome to Perseda.

LORENZO [AS ERASTO]   Thrice happy is Erasto that thou liv'st;
Rhodes' loss is nothing to Erasto's joy:
Sith his Perseda lives, his life survives.

BALTHAZAR [AS SOLIMAN]   Ah, Bashaw, here is love between Erasto

40   And fair Perseda, sovereign of my soul.

HIERONIMO [AS BASHAW]   Remove Erasto, mighty Soliman,
And then Perseda will be quickly won.

BALTHAZAR [AS SOLIMAN]   Erasto is my friend, and while he lives,
Perseda never will remove her love.

45   HIERONIMO [AS BASHAW]   Let not Erasto live to grieve great Soliman.

BALTHAZAR [AS SOLIMAN]   Dear is Erasto in our princely eye.

HIERONIMO [AS BASHAW]   But if he be your rival, let him die.

BALTHAZAR [AS SOLIMAN]   Why, let him die!— So love commandeth me.
Yet grieve I that Erasto should so die.

50   HIERONIMO [AS BASHAW]   Erasto, Soliman saluteth thee,
And lets thee wit by me his highness' will,
Which is thou shouldst be thus employed.   *Stabs him*

BEL-IMPERIA [AS PERSEDA]   Ay me!
Erasto! See, Soliman, Erasto's slain!

55   BALTHAZAR [AS SOLIMAN]   Yet liveth Soliman to comfort thee.
Fair queen of beauty, let not favour die,
But with a gracious eye behold his grief,
That with Perseda's beauty is increased,
If by Perseda his grief be not released.

---

18 adamant lodestone/diamond, originally exceptionally hard mineral   **25 betide** befall   **29 lights** eyes/excellent qualities   **33 plot** i.e. the argument with cast list   **38 Sith** since   **51 wit** know

| 60 | BEL-IMPERIA [AS PERSEDA] | Tyrant, desist soliciting vain suits, |

60   BEL-IMPERIA [AS PERSEDA]   Tyrant, desist soliciting vain suits,
          Relentless are mine ears to thy laments,
          As thy butcher is pitiless and base,
          Which seized on my Erasto, harmless knight.
          Yet by thy power thou thinkest to command,
65   And to thy power Perseda doth obey:
          But, were she able, thus she would revenge
          Thy treacheries on thee, ignoble prince: *Let her stab him*
          And on herself she would be thus revenged.   *Stabs herself*
     KING   Well said!— Old Marshal, this was bravely done!
70   HIERONIMO   But Bel-imperia plays Perseda well!
     VICEROY   Were this in earnest, Bel-imperia,
          You would be better to my son than so.
     KING   But now what follows for Hieronimo?
     HIERONIMO   Marry, this follows for Hieronimo:
75   Here break we off our sundry languages,
          And thus conclude I in our vulgar tongue.
          Haply you think — but bootless be your thoughts —
          That this is fabulously counterfeit,
          And that we do as all tragedians do:
80   To die today, for fashioning our scene,
          The death of Ajax or some Roman peer,
          And in a minute starting up again,
          Revive to please tomorrow's audience.
          No, princes: know I am Hieronimo,
85   The hopeless father of a hapless son,
          Whose tongue is tuned to tell his latest tale,
          Not to excuse gross errors in the play.
          I see your looks urge instance of these words,
          Behold the reason urging me to this: *He shows his dead son*
90   See here my show, look on this spectacle:
          Here lay my hope, and here my hope hath end;
          Here lay my heart, and here my heart was slain;
          Here lay my treasure, here my treasure lost;
          Here lay my bliss, and here my bliss bereft:
95   But hope, heart, treasure, joy, and bliss,
          All fled, failed, died, yea, all decayed with this.
          From forth these wounds came breath that gave me life
          They murdered me that made these fatal marks.
          The cause was love, whence grew this mortal hate,
100   The hate: Lorenzo and young Balthazar,
          The love: my son to Bel-imperia.

---

69 bravely splendidly   **76 vulgar** common, vernacular   **77 Haply** perhaps   **bootless** pointless   **78 fabulously counterfeit** fictitiously represented **80 fashioning our scene** creating our play   **81 Ajax** Greek hero of the Trojan war who fell on his sword after Odysseus was awarded the armour of Achilles which he claimed   **82 starting** jumping   **86 latest tale** the story of his death   **88 instance** evidence

But night, the coverer of accursèd crimes,
With pitchy silence hushed these traitors' harms,
And lent them leave, for they had sorted leisure
105   To take advantage in my garden-plot
Upon my son, my dear Horatio.
There merciless they butchered up my boy,
In black, dark night, to pale, dim, cruel death.
He shrieks: I heard, and yet methinks I hear,
110   His dismal outcry echo in the air.
With soonest speed I hasted to the noise,
Where hanging on a tree I found my son,
Through-girt with wounds, and slaughtered as you see.
And grieved I, think you, at this spectacle?
115   Speak, Portuguese, whose loss resembles mine:
If thou canst weep upon thy Balthazar,
'Tis like I wailed for my Horatio.—
And you, my lord, whose reconcilèd son
Marched in a net, and thought himself unseen,
120   And rated me for brainsick lunacy,
With 'God amend that mad Hieronimo!'
How can you brook our play's catastrophe?
And here behold this bloody handkercher,
Which at Horatio's death I weeping dipped
125   Within the river of his bleeding wounds:
It, as propitious see, I have reserved,
And never hath it left my bloody heart,
Soliciting remembrance of my vow
With these, O, these accursèd murderers,
130   Which now performed my heart is satisfied.
And to this end the bashaw I became
That might revenge me on Lorenzo's life,
Who therefore was appointed to the part,
And was to represent the knight of Rhodes,
135   That I might kill him more conveniently.—
So, Viceroy, was this Balthazar, thy son,
That Soliman which Bel-imperia,
In person of Perseda, murdered,
Solely appointed to that tragic part
140   That she might slay him that offended her.
Poor Bel-imperia missed her part in this:
For though the story saith she should have died,

---

103 **pitchy** pitch-black/morally wicked   **harms** evil deeds   104 **sorted** arranged   109 **yet** still   113 **Through-girt** cut through   115 **Portuguese** i.e. the Viceroy   117 **like** likely, probable   118 **reconcilèd son** i.e. Lorenzo   119 **Marched…net** was exposed while thinking himself concealed (proverbial, although 'danced' was the more usual verb   120 **rated** rebuked   122 **brook** bear, endure   **catastrophe** dramatic conclusion/disastrous ending   126 **propitious** auspicious, a good omen   **reserved** kept

Yet I of kindness, and of care to her,

Did otherwise determine of her end,

145 But love of him whom they did hate too much

Did urge her resolution to be such.—

And, princes, now behold Hieronimo,

Author and actor in this tragedy,

Bearing his latest fortune in his fist,

150 And will as resolute conclude his part,

As any of the actors gone before.

And, gentles, thus I end my play;

Urge no more words: I have no more to say.   *He runs to hang himself*

KING   O, hearken, Viceroy! Hold, Hieronimo!

155 Brother, my nephew and thy son are slain!

VICEROY   We are betrayed: my Balthazar is slain!

Break ope the doors; run, save Hieronimo.   *They break in and hold Hieronimo*

Hieronimo,

Do but inform the king of these events;

160 Upon mine honour, thou shalt have no harm.

HIERONIMO   Viceroy, I will not trust thee with my life,

Which I this day have offered to my son.

Accursèd wretch!

Why stay'st thou him that was resolved to die?

165 KING   Speak, traitor! Damned, bloody murderer, speak!

For now I have thee, I will make thee speak.

Why hast thou done this undeserving deed?

VICEROY   Why hast thou murderèd my Balthazar?

CASTILE   Why hast thou butchered both my children thus?

170 HIERONIMO   But are you sure they are dead?

CASTILE   Ay, slave, too sure.

HIERONIMO   What, and yours too.

VICEROY   Ay, all are dead: not one of them survive.

HIERONIMO   Nay, then I care not: come and we shall be friends;

175 Let us lay our heads together:

See here's a goodly noose will hold them all.

VICEROY   O damnèd devil, how secure he is!

HIERONIMO   Secure? Why, dost thou wonder at it?

I tell thee, Viceroy, this day I have seen revenge,

180 And in that sight am grown a prouder monarch,

Than ever sat under the crown of Spain.

Had I as many lives as there be stars,

As many heavens to go to, as those lives,

I'd give them all, ay, and my soul to boot,

---

146 resolution death   152 gentles nobles   157 ope open   171 slave used as a term of contempt   177 secure sure of himself   184 to boot in addition

185   But I would see thee ride in this red pool.

CASTILE   Speak, who were thy confederates in this?

VICEROY   That was thy daughter, Bel-imperia,

For by her hand my Balthazar was slain:

I saw her stab him.

190   HIERONIMO   O, good words:

As dear to me was my Horatio,

As yours, or yours, or yours, my lord, to you.

My guiltless son was by Lorenzo slain,

And by Lorenzo and that Balthazar,

195   Am I at last revengèd thoroughly,

Upon whose souls may heavens be yet revenged

With greater far than these afflictions.

Methinks since I grew inward with revenge,

I cannot look with scorn enough on death.

200   KING   What, dost thou mock us, slave? Bring tortures forth.

HIERONIMO   Do, do, do, and meantime I'll torture you.

You had a son, as I take it: and your son   *Addressed to Viceroy*

Should ha' been married to your daughter: *Addressed to Castile*

Ha, was't not so? You had a son too,

205   He was my liege's nephew. He was proud,

And politic. Had he lived, he might ha' come

To wear the crown of Spain, I think 'twas so.

'Twas I that killed him. Look you, this same hand,   *Addressed to Viceroy*

'Twas it that stabbed his heart — do you see this hand? —

210   For one Horatio, if you ever knew him, a youth,

One that they hanged up in his father's garden,

One that did force your valiant son to yield,

While your more valiant son did take him prisoner.   *Addressed to Castile*

VICEROY   Be deaf my senses, I can hear no more.

215   KING   Fall, heaven, and cover us with thy sad ruins.

CASTILE   Roll all the world within thy pitchy cloud.

HIERONIMO   Now do I applaud what I have acted

Nunc iners cadat manus.

Now to express the rupture of my part,

220   First take my tongue, and afterwards my heart.   *He bites out his tongue*

KING   O, monstrous resolution of a wretch!

See, Viceroy, he hath bitten forth his tongue,

Rather than to reveal what we required.

CASTILE   Yet can he write.

225   KING   And if in this he satisfy us not,

We will devise th'extremest kind of death

---

198 grew inward turned in upon myself   **206 politic** shrewd/cunning   **216 pitchy** pitch-black/wicked   **218 *Nunc…manus*** 'Now may my hand fall idle'
(Latin)   **219 rupture** breaking   **221 resolution** determination/confidence/disintegration/death   **226 th'extremest** the most violent

That ever was invented for a wretch.   *He [Hieronimo] makes signs*

CASTILE   O, he would have a knife to mend his pen.   *for a knife to mend his pen*

VICEROY   Here, and advise thee that thou write the troth.—

He [Hieronimo] with the knife

230   Look to my brother! Save Hieronimo!   *stabs the Duke and himself*

KING   What age hath ever heard such monstrous deeds?

My brother and the whole succeeding hope

That Spain expected after my decease!

Go: bear his body hence, that we may mourn

235   The loss of our belovèd brother's death,

That he may be entombed: whate'er befall,

I am the next, the nearest, last of all.

VICEROY   And thou, Don Pedro, do the like for us:

Take up our hapless son, untimely slain,

240   Set me with him, and he with woeful me,

Upon the mainmast of a ship unmanned,

And let the wind and tide haul me along

To Scylla's barking and untamèd gulf,

Or to the loathsome pool of Acheron,

245   To weep my want for my sweet Balthazar:

Spain hath no refuge for a Portingale.

The trumpets sound a dead march; the King of Spain mourning after his brother's body, and
the [Viceroy] of Portingale bearing the body of his son

[Act 4 Scene 5]

Enter Ghost and Revenge

GHOST OF ANDREA   Ay, now my hopes have end in their effects,

When blood and sorrow finish my desires:

Horatio murdered in his father's bower;

Vile Serberine by Pedringano slain;

5   False Pedringano hanged by quaint device;

Fair Isabella by herself misdone;

Prince Balthazar by Bel-imperia stabbed;

The Duke of Castile and his wicked son

Both done to death by old Hieronimo;

10   My Bel-imperia fall'n, as Dido fell,

And good Hieronimo slain by himself:

Ay, these were spectacles to please my soul!

Now will I beg at lovely Proserpine

That by the virtue of her princely doom,

---

229 troth truth   **241 mainmast** principal mast of a ship   **243 Scylla's** belonging to the mythical sea monster identified with a treacherous rock in the
Strait of Messina between Sicily and mainland Italy   **barking** noisily aggressive   **gulf** chasm, abyss   **244 Acheron** the river of pain in the Underworld
[4.5]   1 have end are concluded

15   I may consort my friends in pleasing sort,
       And on my foes work just and sharp revenge.
       I'll lead my friend Horatio through those fields,
       Where never-dying wars are still inured;
       I'll lead fair Isabella to that train,
20   Where pity weeps, but never feeleth pain;
       I'll lead my Bel-imperia to those joys,
       That vestal virgins and fair queens possess;
       I'll lead Hieronimo where Orpheus plays,
       Adding sweet pleasure to eternal days.
25   But say, Revenge — for thou must help or none —
       Against the rest how shall my hate be shown?
REVENGE   This hand shall hale them down to deepest hell,
       Where none but Furies, bugs and tortures dwell.
GHOST OF ANDREA   Then, sweet Revenge, do this at my request:
30   Let me be judge, and doom them to unrest.
       Let loose poor Tityus from the vulture's gripe,
       And let Don Cyprian supply his room;
       Place Don Lorenzo on Ixion's wheel,
       And let the lover's endless pains surcease:
35   Juno forgets old wrath, and grants him ease.
       Hang Balthazar about Chimera's neck,
       And let him there bewail his bloody love,
       Repining at our joys that are above;
       Let Serberine go roll the fatal stone,
40   And take from Sisyphus his endless moan;
       False Pedringano, for his treachery,
       Let him be dragged through boiling Acheron,
       And there live, dying still in endless flames,
       Blaspheming gods and all their holy names.
45   REVENGE   Then haste we down to meet thy friends and foes:
       To place thy friends in ease, the rest in woes,
       For here though death hath end their misery,
       I'll there begin their endless tragedy.   *Exeunt*

FINIS

---

15 **consort** accompany   **sort** manner/group   18 **inured** rendered habitual   19 **train** company   22 **vestal virgins** pure maidens, originally priestesses tending the sacred fire in the temple of Vesta   25 **none** no one   27 **hale** drag   31 **Tityus** a giant who assaulted the goddess Leto and was punished in the Underworld by being held down as vultures fed on his regenerating liver   **gripe** grip   32 **Don Cyprian** i.e. Castile   33 **Ixion's wheel** being perpetually bound to a fiery spinning wheel was Ixion's punishment for slaying his father-in-law and then attempting to violate Hera, Zeus' queen   36 **Chimera's** of the fire-breathing monster of mythology, part lion, part serpent, part goat   40 **Sisyphus…moan** the mythical Greek king was punished for his deceitfulness by being forced to roll a huge **stone** up a hill only to see it roll back down again in perpetuity   42 **Acheron** the river of pain in the Underworld

Original Q1 version of 4.4.190–220

HIERONIMO   O, good words!
    As dear to me was my Horatio,
    As yours, or yours, or yours, my lord, to you.
    My guiltless son was by Lorenzo slain,
    And by Lorenzo and that Balthazar
    Upon whose souls may heav'ns be yet avenged
    With greater far than these afflictions.
CASTILE   But who were thy confederates in this?
VICEROY   That was thy daughter Bel-imperia;
    For by her hand my Balthazar was slain:
    I saw her stab him.
KING   Why speak'st thou not?
HIERONIMO   What lesser liberty can kings afford
    Than harmless silence? then afford it me.

Sufficeth, I may not, nor I will not tell thee.
KING   Fetch forth the tortures: traitor as thou art,
    I'll make thee tell.
HIERONIMO   Indeed,
    Thou may'st torment me, as his wretched son
    Hath done in murd'ring my Horatio:
    But never shalt thou force me to reveal
    The thing which I have vowed inviolate.
    And therefore, in despite of all thy threats,
    Pleased with their deaths, and eased with their
      revenge,
    First take my tongue, and afterwards my heart.
                [*He bites out his tongue*]

Textual Notes

Q1 = First Quarto of 1592 (?)

Q4 = Fourth Quarto of 1602 *(the first to include the additional passages perhaps written by Shakespeare, and thus the copy-text for this edition)*

Ed = a correction introduced by a later editor

List of parts = Ed

1.1.69 groan with never-killing = Q1. Q4 = greeue with euerkilling   **82 horn** = Ed. Q4 = horror

1.2.56 *Arma sonant armis* = Ed. Q4 = *Anni sonant annis*   **58 lie maimed** = Q4. Q1 = ill-maimed   **61 unbowelled** = Q1. Q4 = vnbowed   **77 to** = Q4. Q1 = in   **147 though ... liberty** = Q1. Q4 = as though in liberty   **148 free** = Q1. *Not in Q4*

1.3.8 a = Q1. *Not in Q4*   **57 Mine** = Q4. Q1 = My

1.4.42 I = Q1. *Not in Q4*   **72 for** = Q1. Q4 = of   **174 thy** = Ed. Q1, Q4 = the

2.1.27 beauty's = Ed. Q4 = beauteous   **45 import** = Q1. Q4 = impart   **110 prevail** = Q1. Q4 = peuailes

2.2.15 There to = Q1. Q4 = Thereon   **28 pleasures** = Q1. Q4 = pleasure   **31 at** = Q1. *Not in Q4*   **33 war** = Ed. Q4 = warring

2.3.28 grace command = Q1. Q4 = grace to command

2.4.11 approach = Q1. Q4 = reproach   **36 wars** = Ed. Q4 = warre   **61 still** = Q1. *Not in Q4*

2.5.1 outcry calls = Q4. Q1 = outcries pluck   **85 pure** = Ed. Q4 = poore   **107 stayed** = Ed. Q4 = staind

2.6.8 crown = Q1. Q4 = grown

3.1.33 world = Q1. Q4 = words   **39 fiend** = Q1. Q4 = friend   **95 guilty** = Q1. Q4 = guiltless

3.2.93 devised = Q1. Q4 = disguised

3.3.20 nor = Q4. Q1 = and   **21 brother's** = Q1. *Not in Q4*

3.4.91 *E quel ... sa* = Ed. Q4 = *Et quel que voglio Il nessun le sa*   **92 *basterà*** = Ed. Q4 = *bassara*

3.6.55 my = Q1. *Not in Q4*

3.7.13 Beat = Q1. Q4 = But

3.8.22 That died = Q1. Q4 = That liude

3.10.112 No = Q1. *Not in Q4*

3.11.38 unto = Ed. Q4 = vs to   **51 next** = Q1. *Not in Q4*   **76 souls** = Q1. Q4 = soule

3.12.83 happed = Q1. Q4 = hapt to   **110 you** = Q1. Q4 = your

3.13.37 aglets = Ed. Q4 = aggots   **156 jarring** = Ed. Q4 = iering   **164 show** [*first occurrence*] = Ed. *Not in* Q4   **190, 191 *Fata*** = Q1. Q4 = *Futa*   **205 advantage** = Q1. Q4 = vantage   **250 stand you** = Q4. Q1   **283 love's…strive** = Q1. Q4 = love…striues   **295 did** = Q1. *Not in* Q4   **301 on** = Q1. *Not in* Q4   **335 fate** = Ed. Q4 = father

3.14.6 so = Q1. Q4 = sir   **177–8 *Chi…vuole*** = Ed. Q4 = *Mi chi mi fa? Pui Correzza che non sule / Tradito niba otrade vule*

3.15.3 Erebus = Ed. Q4 = Ericbus   **4 ne'er** = Ed. Q4 = neerd   **in hell** = Ed. *Placed at end of line 3 in* Q1, Q4

4.1.16 mothers = Q1. Q4 = mother   **109 played** = Q1. Q4 = said   **145 Erastus** = Q1. Q4 = Erasto   **153 to** = Q1. *Not in* Q4

4.2.5 thus = Q1. *Not in* Q4   **32 nay** = Q1. Q4 = ha

4.4.59 his = Q1. *Not in* Q4   **179 revenge** = Ed. Q4 = reveng'd   **218 *Nunc…manus*** = Ed. Q4 = *Nunck mers cadœ manus*   **243 gulf** = Ed. Q4 = griefe

THOMAS LORD CROMWELL

The figure of King Henry VIII towered over the Elizabethans. He was the father of their queen. His break from Rome had reformed the practices and doctrines of the Church which gave shape to the lives of every parish in the land – from baptisms, marriages and funerals to the weekly forms of worship and the moral and political homilies delivered from the pulpits. And the names of his chief ministers were legendary. 'O, what a dangerous time is this we live in!' says Bishop Stephen Gardiner in the pivotal fourth act of *Thomas Lord Cromwell*:

> There's Thomas Wolsey, he's already gone,
> And Thomas More, he followed after him:
> Another Thomas yet there doth remain.

King Henry's three Thomases were remembered by almost everyone as embodiments of the vicissitudes of power-politics and the precarious status of every royal favourite. As the character of Sir Christopher Hales, another real-life lawyer and politician, puts it when speaking of Wolsey's fall a little earlier in the play:

> O how uncertain is the wheel of state!
> Who lately greater than the cardinal,
> For fear, and love? And now who lower lies?
> Gay honours are but Fortune's flatteries,
> And whom this day pride and promotion swells,
> Tomorrow envy and ambition quells.

Thomas Wolsey, Thomas More, Thomas Cromwell: each of the three put in a number of appearances on the London stage in the final years of Queen Elizabeth's reign. The office of the Lord Chamberlain, which controlled the censorship of the public theatre, would not have looked favourably upon a stage representation of the queen's father himself, but the story of his reign and his reformation of the Church could be told by way of the lives and deaths of his ministers.

In 1601–02 Philip Henslowe, proprietor of the Rose Theatre and manager of the Admiral's Men, principal rivals to Shakespeare's Chamberlain's Men, paid for the writing and staging of *Cardinal Wolsey* in two parts. To judge from the large sum of £35 he disbursed for the costumes and 'divers things' required for the first part alone, it must have been a notably spectacular show. A butcher's son from Ipswich becoming a cardinal of the Roman Catholic Church and then Lord Chancellor of England, with more genuine power at his command that any previous politician in the nation's history: it was the ultimate rags-to-riches story. But one with the inevitable twist in its tale: when Wolsey failed to secure Henry's divorce from Katherine of Aragon to enable the king to marry Anne Boleyn, his fall was as dramatic as his rise.

The likeliest scenario for the writing of *Thomas Lord Cromwell* is that it was commissioned by the Lord Chamberlain's Men in response to the success of Henslowe's Wolsey plays. It certainly reads like a somewhat rushed job, brisk in pace but exceptionally thin in poetic texture. No reputable scholar thinks there is a remote possibility of it actually being by Shakespeare, but there is no reason to doubt the attribution to his company, so it stands as an exemplar of the kind of journeyman theatre in which he and his fellow-actors were participating at precisely the time when, at the height of his powers, he was producing for them such plays as *Julius Caesar*, *Hamlet* and *Twelfth Night*.

The acts are very irregular in length and there is a strong contrast between the first three acts, which follow Thomas Cromwell from his father's smithy in Putney to his continental travels, and the last two, which race through his political rise and fall. It is possible that the published text is a stripped down amalgamation of a two-part play into one, but more likely that the contrast between the two halves is a purposeful juxtaposition whereby the first three acts portray the education of a politician in the wider world and the second half brings the chickens home to roost. Thus there is a neat symmetry whereby the various plot lines of the first three acts are pulled together in the fourth, as Cromwell brings together acquaintances from all periods of his life for a celebratory dinner, thanking his various benefactors. The core moral message of the play ('Do unto others ...') is rehearsed in a number of scenarios, particularly among the reciprocal acts of kindness of Friskiball and the Banisters.*

The principal influence on the play's structure was Christopher Marlowe's hugely successful *Dr Faustus*, which was revived in 1602 with new additions by the dramatist Samuel Rowley. The *Cromwell* author follows Marlowe's movement from student in his study to traveller around Europe getting involved in a good deal of knockabout humour, through to a climax in which the central character, having aspired higher than he could ever have imagined, comes to face his own end. And, as in *Faustus*, there is a low-life sub-plot, written in prose, with a series of parallel adventures that entertain the audience and universalize the experience. But there the similarities end: Marlowe's play is great for the glory of its poetry, the depth of the interior life of Faustus's soliloquies, the dramatic intensity of the relationship between Faustus and the devil Mephistopheles, and the boldness whereby the hero is brought to damnation. Despite a promising start in which young Cromwell complains that the noise from the family blacksmith shop below is disturbing his studies, the central character has very little internal life. There are no memorable soliloquies and, though he goes to his death with dignity, the audience is given pious sentiments rather than human emotions.

In dramatic terms, the only really strong relationship is the antagonistic one between Cromwell and Bishop Gardiner, who represents the voice of Catholicism. Cromwell versus Gardiner is the play's equivalent of Faustus versus Mephistopheles, played out at the level of sectarian accusation as opposed to psychological warfare:

> GARDINER   Have I not reason, when religion is wronged?
>   You had no colour for what you have done.
> CROMWELL   Yes: the abolishing of antichrist,
>   And of this popish order from our realm:
>   I am no enemy to religion,
>   But what is done, it is for England's good.
>   What did they serve for but to feed a sort
>   Of lazy abbots and of full-fed friars?
>   They neither plough, nor sow, and yet they reap

---

* This point is owed to Peter Kirwan.

> The fat of all the land, and suck the poor:
> Look, what was theirs, is in King Henry's hands;
> His wealth before lay in the abbey lands.
> GARDINER   Indeed these things you have alleged, my lord,
> When God doth know the infant yet unborn
> Will curse the time the abbeys were pulled down.
> I pray, now where is hospitality?
> Where now may poor distressèd people go
> For to relieve their need, or rest their bones,
> When weary travel doth oppress their limbs?

For the audience at the Globe, the most attractive aspect of the play would have been its representation of ordinary people. Like Shakespeare's recent *Julius Caesar*, it begins with the voice of the workers. There is an aspirational quality of a kind that would have been understood by Shakespeare – son of a provincial tradesman who rose to gain the privilege of hearing his words spoken before the court. As a young man above his father's business premises in Stratford-upon-Avon, one could imagine young Will saying, like the young Thomas Cromwell, 'My books is all the wealth I do possess / And unto them I have engaged my heart.' Equally, one could imagine Shakespeare just as well as Marlowe or his Faustus saying with Cromwell, 'Why should my birth keep down my mounting spirit?' And old John Shakespeare might perhaps have complained,

> Why, knave, I say, have I thus carked and cared
> And all to keep thee like a gentleman?
> And dost thou let my servants at their work,
> That sweat for thee, knave, labour thus for thee?

The trope of the son not wanting to follow his father into the family business became a familiar one in the drama of the age. Ben Jonson's *Poetaster* has the father of Ovid complaining about his boy wanting to enter the disreputable trade of poetry. For young men, the act of going to the public theatre – in the afternoon, when you really should have been working – was itself a kind of rebellion and an opportunity to dream of a better life. Though Cromwell ends with a severed head, the story of his travels and his rise to power carries the moral that if you work hard, keep your integrity and behave well towards those you meet along the way, then you might get on in life. The bourgeois Protestant work ethic emerged via sentiments of this kind.

Shakespeare was not a gentleman. Rank mattered in Elizabethan times. There was even a strictly enforceable dress code, known as sumptuary law, based on social status. If you were wearing cloth of gold, or tissue or fur of sables, that meant you must be a duchess or a countess. If there was tinselled satin on your partlet you had to be a baroness. Wearing velvet embroidery told us you were a Lady of the Privy Chamber or a Maid of Honour. Unless you were of the rank of knight, your fur had to be of grey genet, bodge or wolf.

And we know that status mattered to Shakespeare himself. When he first made his name in the London theatre world, there were mutterings from established dramatists, educated at Oxford or Cambridge (whose degrees automatically conferred genteel status upon the recipient), that an 'upstart crow', a 'rude groom' from the shires, a mere actor with no degree to his name, was getting above his station by presuming to write for the theatre. Once he had begun to make some serious money out of his plays and his share in the acting company of the Lord Chamberlain's Men, he applied on behalf of his family for a coat of arms. Once it was granted, he was able to call himself a gentleman – though one of the heralds in the College of Arms complained about such honours being dished out to vulgar men such as 'Shakespeare the player'. The spat in the heralds' office occurred in the very year when *Thomas Lord Cromwell* was published (and not long after Ben Jonson seems to have mocked Shakespeare's armorial ambitions in his comedy *Every Man out of his Humour*). None of this has any bearing on the question of how much or how little Shakespeare was involved – as commissioner, script overseer, director, marketer or actor – in the bringing of *Thomas Lord Cromwell* to the stage, but all of it provides context for this particular play's appearance with the initials 'W. S.' on the title page.

The identity of the playwright will probably never be known. There are few stylistic matches with those theatre-writers whose works survive in a sufficiently large corpus for the evidence to be reliable. *Thomas Lord Cromwell* is, however, recognizable as an example of what might be called the drama of everyday life and death in Shakespeare's England. Consider, for example, a playbook published just a year before, under the title *Two Lamentable Tragedies: The One, of the Murder of Master Beech, a Chandler in Thames Street, and his boy, done by Thomas Merry. The Other, of a Young Child Murdered in a Wood by Two Ruffians, with the Consent of his Uncle*. Attributed to a certain Robert Yarington, of whom we know nothing else, this lively double-header shares several characteristics with *Thomas Lord Cromwell*: a high instance of the auxiliary 'do' verb formation, such rare words as 'cark' and 'cog', a 'chorus' technique of presentation (the play is presented by a figure called Homicide), a stage filled with ordinary people, London street scenes, banter brought on by drink.

This is not to suggest that Yarington was the author of *Cromwell*, but rather that the play is an interesting example of Shakespeare's acting company yoking together two distinct genres. In one respect, it is an anticipation of *Henry VIII*, Shakespeare's collaboration with Fletcher at the end of his career, in which the rise and fall of the great politicians of the English Reformation – Wolsey, Gardiner and Cromwell – is played out more fully. In another, it is history from the ground up, often close in tone to other distinctly uncourtly plays with which Shakespeare's name would soon be associated: *The London Prodigal*, *A Yorkshire Tragedy* and *The Puritan or the Widow of Watling Street*. And, most intriguingly, this dual aspect, with its cross-cutting between London streets and Henry's royal court, is also a feature of the play of that other Thomas, *Sir Thomas More*, to which Shakespeare seems to have contributed one great scene just around this time.

KEY FACTS

AUTHORSHIP: The title page attributes the play to 'W. S.' By 1602, Shakespeare had a substantial print presence in London, so the initials may deliberately attempt to capitalize on this. Scholars have conjectured that a number of other candidates, including Wentworth Smith and William Smith, may be the intended reference; however, in the absence of any extant work by these writers, such attributions can only be conjectural. The Shakespeare attribution has been universally rejected on grounds of style, and it has been suggested that the fact of the play belonging to the Lord Chamberlain's/King's Men may have caused confusion. Some critics have suggested the play may contain multiple hands, but this is perhaps an impression borne of textual confusion.

▷

PLOT: From humble beginnings, Thomas Cromwell, a smith's son, rises to power and prominence in Tudor England. The self-educated Cromwell's industry and integrity see him promoted to the post of clerk in Antwerp, where he helps foil the villainous attempts of a broker, Bagot, to ruin the merchant Banister. Travelling in Europe with his servant, Hodge, he is robbed by bandits but relieved by the good-hearted Friskiball, and then advances himself by securing the freedom of the Earl of Bedford, who is imprisoned in Bologna. Back in London, Cardinal Wolsey takes an interest in the young man and employs him. Following the deaths of Wolsey and Thomas More, Cromwell is appointed Keeper of the Privy Seal, in which position he is able to reward those who have previously helped him. The jealous Gardiner, however, secures Cromwell's downfall on false charges of treason, despite Bedford's attempts to help him. Cromwell is arrested, imprisoned and executed, to the absent king's regret.

MAJOR PARTS: Thomas Cromwell (28%/103/13), Gardiner, Bishop of Winchester (9%/36/6), Hodge (7%/34/6), Bedford (6%/33/7), Friskiball (6%/21/4), Bagot (6%/19/3), Hales (4%/11/2), Norfolk (3%/22/5), Mistress Banister (3%/15/4), Bowser (3%/11/2), Old Cromwell (3%/12/3), Banister (2%/14/3), Governor (2%/12/1), Wolsey (2%/9/1), Chorus (2%/3/3).

LINGUISTIC MEDIUM: 95% verse, 5% prose.

DATE: The play is usually dated to c.1599–1602. It is one of the earlier contributions to a group of plays concerned with Tudor history that marked the transition in monarch, and was followed by Rowley's *When You See Me, You Know Me* and Heywood's *If You Know Not Me, You Know Nobody*, among others. Henry VIII does not appear, suggesting that the play was written while Elizabeth was still on the throne (he took the leading role in the Jacobean *When You See Me, You Know Me*, performed once the queen could no longer take offence).

SOURCES: The primary source is John Foxe's *Book of Martyrs*, which contains a section 'The History concerning the Life, Acts and Death of the famous and worthy Councillor, Lord Thomas Cromwell'. Foxe adapted the sub-plot of Friskiball from one of Bandello's novels (Part II, no. 27). The play may also have borne some relation to the two-part *Cardinal Wolsey* plays performed by Henslowe's company, now lost.

TEXT: The play was first published in a 1602 Quarto, reprinted in 1613. The text is generally good, but increasingly shows indications of compression in the second half, which has led some critics to suggest that the extant text may be an abbreviated version of a longer or even two-part play.

THE TRUE CHRONICLE HISTORY OF THE WHOLE LIFE AND DEATH OF THOMAS LORD CROMWELL. As it hath been sundry times publicly acted by the Right Honourable the Lord Chamberlain his Servants. Written by W. S.

OLD CROMWELL, a blacksmith at Putney

Young Thomas Lord CROMWELL, his son

Harry Cromwell, Thomas' SON

HODGE, Will, and Tom, old Cromwell's men

Earl of BEDFORD

Duke of NORFOLK

Duke of SUFFOLK

Sir Christopher HALES

Cardinal WOLSEY

Sir Thomas MORE

Stephen GARDINER, Bishop of Winchester

Sir Ralph SADLER

Master BOWSER, a Merchant

BANISTER, a broken Merchant

MISTRESS BANISTER, his wife

BAGOT, a cruel covetous broker

FRISKIBALL, a Florentine merchant

The GOVERNOR of the English house at Antwerp

BOLOGNAN GOVERNOR with States and Officers

Goodman SEELY and his WIFE Joan

HOST

A POST

MESSENGERS

USHERS and SERVANTS

LIEUTENANT of the Tower

Two CITIZENS

Two MERCHANTS

A HANGMAN

Two WITNESSES

Three SMITHS

SERGEANT-at arms

CHORUS

[Act 1 Scene 1]

Enter three smiths, Hodge and two other[s], old Cromwell's men

HODGE   Come, masters, I think it be past five o'clock;

    Is it not time we were at work?

    My old master he'll be stirring anon.

FIRST SMITH   I cannot tell whether my old master

5   Will be stirring or no but I am sure

    I can hardly take my afternoon's nap

    For my young Master Thomas:

    He keeps such a coil in his study,

    With the sun, and the moon, and the seven stars,

[1.1] *Location: Putney, the entrance of Old Cromwell's smith's shop* **smiths** workers in iron or other metals **Hodge** familiar by-form and abbreviation of the name *Roger*; used as a typical name for the English agricultural labourer or rustic **1 masters** polite form of address, suggesting the men are skilled craftsmen **five o'clock** in the morning; it was customary to rise with the sun and start work early **3 anon** straight away **8 coil** bustle/confused din/fuss **9 seven stars** either the Pleiades (a prominent cluster of stars in the constellation Taurus, also known as the seven sisters), the constellation of the Great Bear or perhaps the seven planets then known; the suggestion is that Cromwell is addicted to the study of astronomy/astrology which were not then differentiated

10   That I do verily think he'll read out his wits.

HODGE   He, skill of the stars? There's goodman Carr of Fulham,
        He that carried us to the strong ale, where goody Trundell
        Had her maid got with child. O, he knows the stars:
        He'll tickle you Charles' Wain in nine degrees.

15   That same man will tell you goody Trundell
        When her ale shall miscarry, only by the stars.

SECOND SMITH   Ay, that's a great virtue; indeed I think Thomas
        Be nobody in comparison to him.

FIRST SMITH   Well, masters, come, shall we to our hammers?

20 HODGE   Ay, content; first let's take our morning's draught,
        And then to work roundly!

SECOND SMITH   Ay, agreed. Go in, Hodge.   *Exeunt omnes*

[Act 1 Scene 2]

Enter young Cromwell

CROMWELL   Good morrow, morn, I do salute thy brightness.
        The night seems tedious to my troubled soul,
        Whose black obscurity binds in my mind
        A thousand sundry cogitations:

5   And now Aurora, with a lively dye,
        Adds comfort to my spirit that mounts on high —
        Too high indeed, my state being so mean!
        My study, like a mineral of gold,
        Makes my heart proud, wherein my hope's enrolled:

10   My books is all the wealth I do possess   *Here within they must*
        And unto them I have engaged my heart.   *beat with their hammers*
        O learning, how divine thou seems to me,
        Within whose arms is all felicity.—
        Peace with your hammers! Leave your knocking there:

15   You do disturb my study and my rest.
        Leave off, I say, you mad me with the noise.

Enter Hodge and the two men

HODGE   Why, how now, Master Thomas, how now?
        Will you not let us work for you?

CROMWELL   You fret my heart with making of this noise.

20 HODGE   How, fret your heart? Ay, but, Thomas, you'll fret

---

11 goodman title of respect used for those under the rank of gentleman   **Fulham** area of West London between Putney and Chelsea   **12 goody** goodwife: equivalent female title implying a married woman and used with her husband's surname   **13 Had ... child** perhaps suggesting she was used for surrogacy, although we never learn more of this teasing hint   **14 tickle ... degrees** an obscure reference to his astrological skill, perhaps with bawdy implication   **Charles' Wain** The Plough, a group of seven stars in the constellation *Ursa Major* (the great bear)   **Wain** wagon   **16 miscarry** fail   **20 draught** drink, commonly of ale or small beer since the water was too contaminated to drink   **[1.2]** *Location: the same*   **1 Good morrow, morn** hello/welcome morning   **4 sundry cogitations** various reflections   **5 Aurora** Roman goddess of the dawn   **7 mean** poor/humble   **10 books is** not uncommon to use a plural subject with a singular verb   **17 how now** what's up

Your father's purse if you let us from working.

SECOND SMITH   Ay, this 'tis, for him to make him a gentleman!

Shall we leave work for your musing? That's well, i'faith!

But here comes my old master now.

Enter Old Cromwell

25 **OLD CROMWELL**   You idle knaves, what, are you loitering now?

No hammers walking and my work to do!

What, not a heat among your work today?

HODGE   Marry, sir, your son Thomas will not let us work at all.

OLD CROMWELL   Why, knave, I say, have I thus carked and cared

30 And all to keep thee like a gentleman?

And dost thou let my servants at their work,

That sweat for thee, knave, labour thus for thee?

CROMWELL   Father, their hammers do offend my study.

OLD CROMWELL   Out of my doors, knave, if thou lik'st it not.

35 I cry you mercy! Is your ears so fine?

I tell thee, knave, these get when I do sleep:

I will not have my anvil stand for thee.

CROMWELL   There's money, father, I will pay your men.   *He throws money*

OLD CROMWELL   Have I thus brought thee up unto my cost,   *among them*

40 In hope that one day thou wouldst relieve my age,

And art thou now so lavish of thy coin

To scatter it among these idle knaves?

CROMWELL   Father, be patient, and content yourself.

The time will come I shall hold gold as trash:

45 And here I speak with a presaging soul,

To build a palace where now this cottage stands,

As fine as is King Henry's house at Sheen.

OLD CROMWELL   You build a house! You knave, you'll be a beggar.

Now, afore God, all is but cast away,

50 That is bestowed upon this thriftless lad.

Well, had I bound him to some honest trade,

This had not been, but it was his mother's doing,

To send him to the university.

How? Build a house where now this cottage stands,

55 As fair as that at Sheen!— He shall not hear me.   *Aside*

A good boy Tom! I can thee thank, Tom!

Well said, Tom! Gramercies, Tom!—

Into your work, knaves; hence, you saucy boy!   *Exit all but young Cromwell*

CROMWELL   Why should my birth keep down my mounting spirit?

60 Are not all creatures subject unto time?

---

21 let liberate/prevent   **26 walking** moving, i.e. at work   **28 Marry** by the virgin Mary   **29 carked** fretted, worried   **35 cry you mercy** implore, beg you   **fine** refined   **36 get** make a profit   **37 stand** i.e. stand idle   **39 unto** at   **47 King…Sheen** i.e. Richmond Palace, one of the principal royal residences   **48 You…house!** Cromwell did build a house on the site of the Augustinian monastery, Launde Abbey, in Leicestershire but did not live to take up residence there   **51 bound him** i.e. as an apprentice   **57 Gramercies** thanks

To time, who doth abuse the world,
And fills it full of hodge-podge bastardy?
There's legions now of beggars on the earth,
That their original did spring from kings:
65   And many monarchs now whose fathers were
The riff-raff of their age: for time and fortune
Wears out a noble train to beggary,
And from the dunghill minions do advance
To state and mark in this admiring world.
70   This is but course, which in the name of fate
Is seen as often as it whirls about:
The river Thames that by our door doth pass,
His first beginning is but small and shallow,
Yet keeping on his course grows to a sea.
75   And likewise Wolsey, the wonder of our age,
His birth as mean as mine, a butcher's son:
Now who within this land a greater man?
Then, Cromwell, cheer thee up, and tell thy soul
That thou mayst live to flourish and control.

Enter Old Cromwell

80   OLD CROMWELL   Tom Cromwell! What, Tom, I say!

CROMWELL   Do you call, sir?

OLD CROMWELL   Here is Master Bowser, come to know if you have dispatched his petition for the lords of the council or no.

CROMWELL   Father, I have; please you to call him in.

85   OLD CROMWELL   That's well said, Tom: a good lad, Tom!

Enter Master Bowser

BOWSER   Now, Master Cromwell, have you dispatched this petition?

CROMWELL   I have, sir. Here it is: please you peruse it.

BOWSER   It shall not need; we'll read it as we go by water:
And, Master Cromwell, I have made a motion
90   May do you good, and if you like of it.
Our secretary at Antwerp, sir, is dead,
And the merchants there hath sent to me
For to provide a man fit for the place:
Now I do know none fitter than yourself,
95   If with your liking it stand, Master Cromwell.

CROMWELL   With all my heart, sir, and I much am bound
In love and duty for your kindness shown.

---

62 **hodge-podge** clumsy mixed   67 **train** following/line (of descendants)   68 **minions** hangers-on/servile underlings   69 **state and mark** status and distinction   70 **but course** only the natural course of things   75 **Wolsey** Cardinal Wolsey rose from his reportedly humble beginnings as the son of a butcher to become Lord Chancellor and one of Henry VIII's most influential advisers until his failure to achieve the annulment of Henry's marriage to Katherine of Aragon led to his downfall; in fact his father, Robert Wolsey, seems to have been a wealthy cloth merchant. Cromwell became his most faithful, trusted follower   82 **Bowser** his surname means 'treasurer, bursar'   83 **lords...council** i.e. the Privy Council, the monarch's closest advisers
88 **It...need** it's not necessary   91 **Antwerp** this Belgian town was the leading commercial centre of western Europe with trading houses established for a number of countries including England

OLD CROMWELL   Body of me! Tom, make haste, lest somebody

 Get between thee and home, Tom. I thank you,

100 Good Master Bowser, I thank you for my boy,

 I thank you always, I thank you most heartily, sir.

 Ho, a cup of beer there for Master Bowser.

BOWSER   It shall not need, sir. Master Cromwell, will you go?

CROMWELL   I will attend you, sir.

105 OLD CROMWELL   Farewell, Tom; God bless thee, Tom;

 God speed thee, good Tom.   *Exeunt omnes*

[Act 1 Scene 3]

Enter Bagot, a broker, solus

BAGOT   I hope this day is fatal unto some,

 And by their loss must Bagot seek to gain.

 This is the lodging of Master Friskiball,

 A liberal merchant, and a Florentine,

5 To whom Banister owes a thousand pound,

 A merchant bankrupt, whose father was my master.

 What do I care for pity or regard?

 He once was wealthy, but he now is fallen,

 And this morning have I got him arrested,

10 At the suit of Master Friskiball,

 And by this means shall I be sure of coin,

 For doing this same good to him unknown:

 And in good time, see where the merchant comes.

Enter Friskiball

 Good morrow to kind Master Friskiball.

15 FRISKIBALL   Good morrow to yourself, good Master Bagot.

 And what's the news, you are so early stirring:

 It is for gain, I make no doubt of that.

BAGOT   It is for the love, sir, that I bear to you.

 When did you see your debtor Banister?

20 FRISKIBALL   I promise you, I have not seen the man

 This two month's day: his poverty is such,

 As I do think he shames to see his friends.

BAGOT   Why then, assure yourself to see him straight,

 For at your suit I have arrested him,

25 And here they will be with him presently.

FRISKIBALL   Arrest him at my suit? You were to blame.

 I know the man's misfortunes to be such,

98 Body of me! a common oath **104 attend** follow/accompany **[1.3]** *Location: London, a street before Friskiball's house* **broker** commercial middle-man, the term often carried negative connotations *solus* 'alone' (Latin) **3 Friskiball** English rendering of the Italian surname 'Frescobaldi', a prominent Florentine family of merchant bankers **10 suit** lawsuit, legal prosecution to enforce a claim

As he's not able for to pay the debt,

And were it known to some he were undone—

30 BAGOT   This is your pitiful heart to think it so,

But you are much deceived in Banister.

Why such as he will break for fashion sake,

And unto those they owe a thousand pound,

Pay scarce an hundred. O, sir, beware of him.

35 The man is lewdly given to dice and drabs,

Spends all he hath in harlots' companies:

It is no mercy for to pity him.

I speak the truth of him, for nothing else

But for the kindness that I bear to you.

40 FRISKIBALL   If it be so, he hath deceived me much,

And to deal strictly with such a one as he —

Better severe than too much lenity.

But here is Master Banister himself,

And with him, as I take, the officers.

Enter Banister, his wife, and two Officers

45 BANISTER   O, Master Friskiball, you have undone me.

My state was well nigh overthrown before,

Now altogether downcast by your means.

MISTRESS BANISTER   O, Master Friskiball, pity my husband's case.

He is a man hath lived as well as any,

50 Till envious fortune and the ravenous sea

Did rob, disrobe, and spoil us of our own.

FRISKIBALL   Mistress Banister, I envy not your husband,

Nor willingly would I have used him thus,

But that I hear he is so lewdly given,

55 Haunts wicked company, and hath enough

To pay his debts, yet will not be known thereof.

BANISTER   This is that damned broker, that same Bagot,

Whom I have often from my trencher fed:

Ingrateful villain for to use me thus!

60 BAGOT   What I have said to him is nought but truth.

MISTRESS BANISTER   What thou hast said springs from an envious heart:

A cannibal that doth eat men alive!

But here upon my knee, believe me, sir,   *She kneels*

And what I speak, so help me God, is true:

65 We scarce have meat to feed our little babes.

Most of our plate is in that broker's hand,

Which, had we money to defray our debt,

---

32 break go bust/become bankrupt **fashion** pretence/mere form, i.e. a fraudulent commercial practice **33 thousand...hundred** and only pay ten per cent of their debts **35 lewdly** wickedly/lasciviously **dice and drabs** gambling and loose women **38 nothing else** no other reason **45 undone** ruined **58 trencher** platter on which meat was cut and served **59 Ingrateful** ungrateful **66 plate** tableware, originally but not necessarily of silver **67 defray** discharge

O think! We would not bide that penury.

Be merciful, kind Master Friskiball.

70 My husband, children, and myself will eat

But one meal a day, the other will we keep and sell

As part to pay the debt we owe to you:

If ever tears did pierce a tender mind,

Be pitiful, let me some favour find.

75 BAGOT   Be not you so mad, sir, to believe her tears.

FRISKIBALL   Go to, I see thou art an envious man.

Good Mistress Banister, kneel not to me,

I pray rise up: you shall have your desire.—   *She rises*

Hold officers, be gone, there's for your pains.—

80 You know you owe to me a thousand pound,

Here, take my hand: if e'er God make you able,

And place you in your former state again,

Pay me: but if still your fortune frown,

Upon my faith I'll never ask you crown:

85 I never yet did wrong to men in thrall,

For God doth know what to myself may fall.

BANISTER   This unexpected favour, undeserved,

Doth make my heart bleed inwardly with joy.

Ne'er may aught prosper with me is my own,

90 If I forget this kindness you have shown.

MISTRESS BANISTER   My children in their prayers, both night and day,

For your good fortune and success shall pray.

FRISKIBALL   I thank you both; I pray, go dine with me.

Within these three days, if God give me leave,

95 I will to Florence, to my native home.

Bagot, hold; there's a portague to drink,

Although you ill deserved it by your merit:

Give not such cruel scope unto your heart,

Be sure the ill you do will be requited.

100 Remember what I say, Bagot, farewell.

Come, Master Banister; you shall with me.

My fare is but simple, but welcome heartily.   *Exit all but Bagot*

BAGOT   A plague go with you! Would you had eat your last!

Is this the thanks I have for all my pains?

105 Confusion light upon you all for me!

Where he had wont to give a score of crowns,

Doth he now foist me with a portague!

Well, I will be revenged upon this Banister.

I'll to his creditors, buy all the debt he owes,

---

68 bide endure, remain in   **76 Go to** phrase expressing disapprobation, compare for example 'Come, come'   **84 crown** for a crown, a coin worth five shillings, one quarter of a pound   **85 thrall** bondage, captivity   **89 aught** anything   **96 portague** Portuguese gold coin   **98 scope** reach/opportunity or liberty to act   **99 requited** repaid   **106 wont** custom, habit   **score of crowns** twenty five shilling pieces, i.e. five pounds   **107 foist me** fob me off

110 As seeming that I do it for good will.
I am sure to have them at an easy rate,
And when 'tis done, in Christendom he stays not,
But I'll make his heart to ache with sorrow,
And if that Banister become my debtor,
115 By heaven and earth I'll make his plague the greater.   *Exit Bagot*

[Act 2]

Enter Chorus

CHORUS   Now, gentlemen, imagine that young Cromwell is
In Antwerp ledger for the English merchants:
And Banister, to shun this Bagot's hate,
Hearing that he hath got some of his debts,
5 Is fled to Antwerp with his wife and children,
Which Bagot hearing is gone after them
And thither sends his bills of debt before,
To be revenged on wretched Banister.
What doth fall out, with patience sit and see:
10 A just requital of false treachery!   *Exit*

[Act 2 Scene 1]

Cromwell in his study with bags of money before him casting of account

CROMWELL   Thus far my reckoning doth go straight and even,
But, Cromwell, this same plodding fits not thee:
Thy mind is altogether set on travel,
And not to live thus cloistered like a nun.
5 It is not this same trash that I regard:
Experience is the jewel of my heart.

Enter a Post

POST   I pray, sir, are you ready to dispatch me?
CROMWELL   Yes; here's those sums of money you must carry;
You go so far as Frankfurt, do you not?
10 POST   I do, sir.
CROMWELL   Well, prithee make all the haste thou canst,
For there be certain English gentlemen
Are bound for Venice, and may haply want,
And if that you should linger by the way:
15 But in hope that you'll make good speed,

[2] **2 ledger** agent or commissioner   [2.1] *Location: Antwerp* **2 plodding** slow, laborious working   **4 cloistered** shut up, confined   **5 trash** i.e. money   *Post* courier, post-rider   **7 dispatch me** send me off   **11 prithee** pray thee, please   **13 haply** perhaps   **want** be in need

There's two angels to buy you spurs and wands.

POST   I thank you, sir; this will add wings indeed.   [*Exit*]

CROMWELL   Gold is of power would make an eagle's speed!

Enter Mistress Banister

What gentlewoman is this that grieves so much?

20   It seems she doth address herself to me.

MISTRESS BANISTER   God save you, sir. Pray, is your name Master Cromwell?

CROMWELL   My name is Thomas Cromwell, gentlewoman.

MISTRESS BANISTER   Know you not one Bagot, sir, that's come to Antwerp?

CROMWELL   No, trust me, I never saw the man,

25   But here are bills of debt I have received,

Against one Banister, a merchant fallen into decay.

MISTRESS BANISTER   Into decay, indeed, long of that wretch.

I am the wife to woeful Banister

And by that bloody villain am pursued

30   From London here to Antwerp.

My husband he is in the governor's hands,

And God of heaven knows how he'll deal with him.

Now, sir, your heart is framed of milder temper,

Be merciful to a distressèd soul

35   And God no doubt will treble-bless your gain.

CROMWELL   Good Mistress Banister, what I can, I will,

In anything that lies within my power.

MISTRESS BANISTER   O speak to Bagot, that same wicked wretch,

An angel's voice may move a damnèd devil.

40   CROMWELL   Why, is he come to Antwerp as you hear?

MISTRESS BANISTER   I heard he landed some two hours since.

CROMWELL   Well, Mistress Banister, assure yourself,

I'll speak to Bagot in your own behalf

And win him to all the pity that I can.

45   Meantime, to comfort you in your distress,

Receive these angels to relieve your need,

And be assured that what I can effect

To do you good, no way I will neglect.

MISTRESS BANISTER   That mighty God, that knows each mortal's heart,

50   Keep you from trouble, sorrow, grief, and smart.   *Exit Mistress Banister*

CROMWELL   Thanks, courteous woman, for thy hearty prayer.

It grieves my soul to see her misery,

But we that live under the work of fate,

May hope the best, yet knows not to what state

55   Our stars and destinies hath us assigned:

Fickle is Fortune and her face is blind.   [*Exit*]

---

16 angels old English gold coins depicting the Archangel Michael; their value varied between a third and a half of one pound sterling   **wands** sticks to encourage his horse to go faster   **27 long of** all because of   **56 Fortune…blind** Fortuna, the Roman goddess of destiny was imaged as veiled and blind, suggesting her capriciousness

[Act 2 Scene 2]

Enter Bagot solus

BAGOT   So all goes well: it is as I would have it!
Banister, he is with the governor
And shortly shall have gyves upon his heels.
It glads my heart to think upon the slave;
5   I hope to have his body rot in prison,
And after here, his wife to hang herself
And all his children die for want of food.
The jewels that I have brought to Antwerp
Are reckoned to be worth five thousand pound,
10   Which scarcely stood me in three hundred pound.
I bought them at an easy kind of rate:
I care not which way they came by them
That sold them me: it comes not near my heart.
And lest they should be stolen — as sure they are —
15   I thought it meet to sell them here in Antwerp,
And so have left them in the governor's hand,
Who offers me within two hundred pound
Of all my price. But now no more of that!
I must go see and if my bills be safe,
20   The which I sent to Master Cromwell,
That if the wind should keep me on the sea,
He might arrest him here before I came:
[Enter Cromwell]
And in good time, see where he is. God save you, sir.

CROMWELL   And you: pray pardon me, I know you not.

25   BAGOT   It may be so, sir, but my name is Bagot,
The man that sent to you the bills of debt.

CROMWELL   O, the man that pursues Banister.
Here are the bills of debt you sent to me:
As for the man, you know best where he is.
30   It is reported you have a flinty heart,
A mind that will not stoop to any pity,
An eye that knows not how to shed a tear,
A hand that's always open for reward;
But, Master Bagot, would you be ruled by me,
35   You should turn all these to the contrary.
Your heart should still have feeling of remorse,
Your mind according to your state be liberal
To those that stand in need and in distress,
Your hand to help them that do stand in want,

[2.2]   *Location: A street in Antwerp*   **3 gyves** leg shackles, fetters   **10 stood** cost   **14 lest** in case   **15 meet** appropriate (because it was out of England and they would be likely to fetch the best price there)   **30 flinty** made of flintstone, i.e. very hard   **34 would you** if you would   **36 still** always, continually

40   Rather than with your poise to hold them down;
      For every ill turn show yourself more kind;
      Thus should I do: pardon, I speak my mind.

BAGOT   Ay, sir, you speak to hear what I would say,
      But you must live, I know, as well as I.
45   I know this place to be extortion,
      And 'tis not for a man to keep him,
      But he must lie, cog with his dearest friend,
      And, as for pity, scorn it: hate all conscience.
      But yet I do commend your wit in this,
50   To make a show of what I hope you are not.
      But I commend you and 'tis well done:
      This is the only way to bring your gain.

CROMWELL   My gain! I had rather chain me to an oar,
      And like a slave there toil out all my life,
55   Before I'd live so base a slave as thou:
      Ay, like an hypocrite to make a show
      Of seeming virtue and a devil within!
      No, Bagot, would thy conscience were as clear:
      Poor Banister ne'er had been troubled here.

60   BAGOT   Nay, good Master Cromwell, be not angry, sir.
      I know full well you are no such man,
      But if your conscience were as white as snow,
      It will be thought that you are otherwise.

CROMWELL   Will it be thought that I am otherwise?
65   Let them that think so know they are deceived.
      Shall Cromwell live to have his faith misconstered?
      Antwerp, for all the wealth within thy town,
      I will not stay here not two hours longer.
      As good luck serves, my accounts are all made even,
70   Therefore I'll straight unto the treasurer.
      Bagot, I know you'll to the governor:
      Commend me to him, say I am bound to travel,
      To see the fruitful parts of Italy,
      And as you ever bore a Christian mind,
75   Let Banister some favour of you find.

BAGOT   For your sake, sir, I'll help him all I can—
      To starve his heart out ere he gets a groat.   *Aside*
      So, Master Cromwell, do I take my leave,
      For I must straight unto the governor.   *Exit Bagot*

---

40 poise weight/burdensomeness   **43 to … say** i.e. merely to test me   **45 this place** i.e. the trading house at Antwerp   **46 'tis … him** it's impossible for a man to make a living   **47 cog** employ fraud or deceit, cheat (a dicing term)   **53 chain … life** he would rather be a galley slave, condemned to work the oar in a galley, a flat seagoing vessel propelled by boat and oars, usually manned by criminals or slaves, common in the Mediterranean   **66 misconstered** misconstrued, wrongly interpreted   **69 made even** reconciled and correct   **72 travel** puns on 'travail', to suffer   **77 groat** coin worth four old pence, a small sum

80 CROMWELL   Farewell, sir; pray you remember what I said.

No, Cromwell, no: thy heart was ne'er so base,

To live by falsehood or by brokery!

But't falls out well, I little it repent;

Hereafter, time in travel shall be spent.

Enter Hodge, his father's man

85 HODGE   Your son Thomas, quoth you: I have been Thomased! I had thought it had been no such matter to 'a gone by water: for at Putney I'll go you to Parish-garden for two pence, sit as still as may be, without any wagging or jolting in my guts, in a little boat too: here we were scarce four mile in the great green water, but I — thinking to go to my afternoon's nuncheons, as 'twas my manner at home — 90 but I felt a kind of rising in my guts. At last one o' the sailors spying of me, 'Be o' good cheer,' says he, 'set down thy victuals, and up with it, thou hast nothing but an eel in thy belly!' Well to't went I, to my victuals went the sailors, and thinking I to be a man of better experience than any in the ship, asked me what wood the ship was made of. They all swore I told them as right as if I had been acquainted 95 with the carpenter that made it. At last we grew near land, and I grew villainous hungry, went to my bag: the devil a bit there was. The sailors had tickled me; yet I cannot blame them: it was a part of kindness, for I in kindness told them what wood the ship was made of, and they in kindness eat up my victuals, as indeed one good turn asketh another. Well, would I, could I, find my Master Thomas in this Dutch 100 town — he might put some English beer into my belly.

CROMWELL   What, Hodge, my father's man? By my hand, welcome!

How doth my father? What's the news at home?

HODGE   Master Thomas, O, good Master Thomas: your hand, glove and all! This is to give you to understanding that your father is in health, and Alice Downing 105 here hath sent you a nutmeg, and Bess Makewater a race of ginger: my fellow Will and Tom hath between them sent you a dozen of points, and goodman Tolle of the Goat a pair of mittens, myself came in person: and this is all the news.

CROMWELL   Gramercy, good Hodge, and thou art welcome to me,

But in as ill a time thou com'st as may be,

110 For I am travelling into Italy.

What say'st thou, Hodge? Wilt thou bear me company?

HODGE   Will I bear thee company, Tom? What tell'st me of Italy? Were it to the furthest part of Flanders, I would go with thee, Tom. I am thine in all weal and woe, thy own to command. What, Tom! I have passed the rigorous waves of Neptune's 115 blasts; I tell you, Thomas, I have been in the danger of the floods; and when I have

86 **'a gone** have travelled   **Parish-garden** Paris Garden was the usual name for the Beargarden, where bear-baiting, bull-baiting and other animal 'sports' were carried on; it was located in Bankside on the south bank of the Thames, near the Globe Theatre and was a similar three-storey round or polygonal building; it would be logical for Hodge to travel there by boat from Putney Bridge   **87 two pence** pronounced 'tuppence', a small sum of money   **89 nuncheons** snacks, light refreshment, generally taken in the afternoon   **91 victuals** food, provisions   **up with it** throw up, vomit   **92 eel…belly** describing the sensation of sea-sickness   **96 bit** bite, i.e. there was nothing left   **tickled** teased/caught (a method used to catch trout)   **99 Dutch** technically Antwerp is in Belgium but Hodge is either confused or using the term loosely to cover all the 'low countries'   **105 race** root; spices such as nutmeg and ginger were expensive luxury items   **106 points** tagged pieces of ribbon or cord used for lacing, fastening clothes, before the use of buttons   **113 Flanders** province of the low countries, technically that part where the Flemings live, then a county; the joke is that Hodge doesn't realize how much further away Italy is   **weal** prosperity, well-being   **114 Neptune's** of the Roman god of water and the sea

seen Boreas begin to play the ruffin with us, then would I down of my knees and
call upon Vulcan.

CROMWELL   And why upon him?

HODGE   Because, as this same fellow Neptune is god of the seas, so Vulcan is lord
120   over the smiths, and therefore, I, being a smith, thought his godhead would have
some care yet of me.

CROMWELL   A good conceit! But tell, hast thou dined yet?

HODGE   Thomas, to speak the truth: not a bit yet, I.

CROMWELL   Come, go with me; thou shalt have cheer good store.

125   And farewell, Antwerp, if I come no more.

HODGE   I follow thee, sweet Tom, I follow thee.   *Exeunt omnes*

[Act 2 Scene 3]

Enter the Governor of the English house, Bagot, Banister, his wife, and two Officers

GOVERNOR   Is Cromwell gone then, say you, Master Bagot?
            What dislike, I pray? What was the cause?

BAGOT   To tell you true, a wild brain of his own —
            Such youth as they cannot see when they are well:
5   He is all bent to travel, that's his reason,
            And doth not love to eat his bread at home.

GOVERNOR   Well, good fortune with him, if the man be gone.
            We hardly shall find such a one as he
            To fit our turns, his dealings were so honest.
10   But now, sir, for your jewels that I have,
            What do you say? Will you take my price?

BAGOT   O, sir, you offer too much underfoot.

GOVERNOR   'Tis but two hundred pound between us, man:
            What's that in payment of five thousand pound?

15   BAGOT   Two hundred pound! By'r'lady, sir, 'tis great!
            Before I got so much, it made me sweat.

GOVERNOR   Well, Master Bagot, I'll proffer you fairly.
            You see this merchant, Master Banister,
            Is going now to prison at your suit:
20   His substance all is gone, what would you have?
            Yet in regard I knew the man of wealth —
            Never dishonest dealing, but such mishaps
            Hath fallen on him, may light on me or you —
            There is two hundred pound between us,
25   We will divide the same: I'll give you one
            On that condition you will set him free.

---

116 **Boreas** Greek god of the north wind   **ruffin** name of a fiend, the devil, later 'ruffian'   117 **Vulcan** Roman god of fire, he became associated with the
Greek smith-god Hephaestus   124 **cheer** cheerful, hospitable   **[2.3]** *Location: Antwerp*   12 **too much underfoot** far too low a price   15 **By'r'lady**
i.e. by the Virgin Mary   16 **Before…sweat** before I was wealthy, I had to work hard to earn two hundred pounds   17 **proffer** propose (a course of
action)   20 **His…have?** since his wealth is all gone, what benefit is it to you?   23 **light** descend

His state is nothing, that you see yourself,

And where nought is, the king must lose his right.

BAGOT   Sir, sir, you speak out of your love,

30   'Tis foolish love, sir, sure, to pity him:

Therefore, content yourself; this is my mind:

To do him good I will not bate a penny.

BANISTER   This is my comfort: though thou dost no good,

A mighty ebb follows a mighty flood.

35   MISTRESS BANISTER   O thou base wretch, whom we have fosterèd

Even as a serpent for to poison us,

If God did ever right a woman's wrong,

To that same God I bend and bow my heart,

To let his heavy wrath fall on thy head,

40   By whom my hopes and joys are butcherèd.

BAGOT   Alas, fond woman, I pray thee, pray thy worst:

The fox fares better still when he is curst.

Enter Master Bowser, a merchant

GOVERNOR   Master Bowser! You're welcome, sir, from England.

What's the best news? How doth all our friends?

45   BOWSER   They are all well and do commend them to you:

There's letters from your brother and your son.

So fare you well, sir, I must take my leave:

My haste and business doth require such.

GOVERNOR   Before you dine, sir? What, go you out of town?

50   BOWSER   Ay, faith, unless I hear some news in town,

I must away: there is no remedy.

GOVERNOR   Master Bowser, what is your business? May I know it?

BOWSER   You may, sir, and so shall all the city.

The king of late hath had his treasury robbed,

55   And of the choicest jewels that he had:

The value of them was some seven thousand pound.

The fellow that did steal these jewels, he is hanged,

And did confess that for three hundred pound

He sold them to one Bagot dwelling in London.

60   Now Bagot's fled, and, as we hear, to Antwerp,

And hither am I come to seek him out,

And they that first can tell me of his news

Shall have a hundred pound for their reward.

BANISTER   How just is God to right the innocent!

65   GOVERNOR   Master Bowser, you come in happy time:

Here is the villain Bagot that you seek,

And all those jewels have I in my hands.

---

28 king…right since he has nothing the king cannot collect the taxes he is legally due   **32 bate** reduce the amount by/subtract   **34 mighty ebb…flood** a very high tide is always followed by a low tide, i.e. in the course of things you'll be brought low and get your just deserts   **35 fosterèd…us** a reference to the fable of the viper revived and reared in the farmer's bosom who then bit him, i.e. to befriend a person who proves treacherous   **41 fond** foolish

  Officers, look to him, hold him fast.   *Officers seize Bagot*

BAGOT The devil ought me a shame, and now hath paid it.

70 BOWSER Is this that Bagot? Fellows, bear him hence.

  We will not now stand for his reply.

  Lade him with irons; we will have him tried

  In England, where his villainies are known.

BAGOT Mischief, confusion, light upon you all!

75 O hang me, drown me, let me kill myself!

  Let go my arms; let me run quick to hell.

BOWSER Away, bear him away; stop the slave's mouth. *They carry him away*

MISTRESS BANISTER Thy works are infinite, great God of heaven!

GOVERNOR I heard this Bagot was a wealthy fellow.

80 BOWSER He was indeed, for when his goods were seized,

  Of jewels, coin, and plate within his house,

  Was found the value of five thousand pound:

  His furniture fully worth half so much,

  Which being all strained for, for the king,

85 He frankly gave it to the Antwerp merchants,

  And they again, out of their bounteous mind,

  Hath to a brother of their company,

  A man decayed by fortune of the seas,

  Given Bagot's wealth, to set him up again

90 And keep it for him: his name is Banister.

GOVERNOR Master Bowser, with this happy news

  You have revived two from the gates of death:

  This is that Banister, and this his wife.

BOWSER Sir, I am glad my fortune is so good,

95 To bring such tidings as may comfort you.

BANISTER You have given life unto a man deemed dead,

  For by these news, my life is newly bred.

MISTRESS BANISTER Thanks to my God, next to my sovereign king,

  And last to you that these good hopes doth bring.

100 GOVERNOR The hundred pound I must receive as due

  For finding Bagot, I freely give to you.

BOWSER And, Master Banister, if so you please,

  I'll bear you company, when you cross the seas.

BANISTER If it please you, sir, my company is but mean,

105 Stands with your liking, I'll wait on you.

GOVERNOR I am glad that all things do accord so well:

  Come, Master Bowser, let us into dinner:

  And, Mistress Banister, be merry, woman!

  Come, after sorrow now let's cheer your spirit:

110 Knaves have their due, and you but what you merit.   *Exeunt omnes*

---

69 ought owed **72 Lade** load, burden **84 strained for** compelled, seized **85 frankly** freely

[Act 2 Scene 4]

Enter Cromwell and Hodge in their shirts, and without hats

HODGE   Call ye this seeing of fashions?

Marry, would I had stayed at Putney still.

O, Master Thomas, we are spoiled! We are gone!

CROMWELL   Content thee, man, this is but fortune.

5   HODGE   Fortune; a plague of this fortune makes me go wet-shod; the rogues would not leave me a shoe to my feet. For my hose, they scorned them with their heels, but for my doublet and hat, O lord, they embraced me, and unlaced me, and took away my clothes, and so disgraced me.

CROMWELL   Well, Hodge, what remedy? What shift shall we make now?

10   HODGE   Nay, I know not. For begging I am nought, for stealing worse: by my troth, I must even fall to my old trade, to the hammer and the horse heels again: but now the worst is, I am not acquainted with the humour of the horses in this country, whether they are not coltish, given much to kicking, or no, for when I have one leg in my hand, if he should up and lay t'other of my chops, I were gone: there

15   lay I, there lay Hodge.

CROMWELL   Hodge, I believe thou must work for us both.

HODGE   O, Master Thomas, have not I told you of this? Have not I many a time and often said, Tom, or Master Thomas, learn to make a horse-shoe, it will be your own another day: this was not regarded. Hark you, Thomas, what do you call the

20   fellows that robbed us?

CROMWELL   The Bandetto.

HODGE   The Bandetto, do you call them? I know not what they are called here, but I am sure we call them plain thieves in England. O, Thomas, that we were now at Putney, at the ale there!

25   CROMWELL   Content thee, man; here set up these two bills,

And let us keep our standing on the bridge:

The fashion of this country is such,

If any stranger be oppressed with want,

To write the manner of his misery,

30   And such as are disposed to succour him,

Will do it. What, hast thou set them up?

HODGE   Ay, they're up; God send some to read them,

And not only to read them, but also to look on us;

And not altogether to look on us,   *One stands at one end, and one at t'other*

35   But to relieve us. O cold, cold, cold!

Enter Friskiball, the merchant, and reads the bills

FRISKIBALL   What's here? Two Englishmen robbed by the Bandetto!

One of them seems to be a gentleman.

[2.4]   *Location: The principal bridge at Florence*   **5 wet-shod** having wet feet   **6 hose** leggings, stockings   **scorned…heels** the thieves rejected them, the implication being they were too disreputable   **7 doublet** a close-fitting jacket   **9 shift** device, contrivance   **10 by my troth** indeed, upon my word   **11 troth** good faith, honesty   **even** just/directly   **hammer…heels** i.e. as a smith or farrier and make horseshoes   **12 humour** temper, mood   **13 coltish** wild, frisky, untrained   **14 chops** jaws, sides of the face   **21 Bandetto** outlaws, gangs of bandits, especially in Italy, Sicily and southern Europe   **30 succour** aid

'Tis pity that his fortune was so hard,
To fall into the desperate hands of thieves:

40   I'll question him of what estate he is.—
God save you, sir, are you an Englishman?

CROMWELL   I am, sir, a distressèd Englishman.

FRISKIBALL   And what are you, my friend?

HODGE   Who, I, sir? By my troth, I do not know myself what I am now, but, sir, I

45 was a smith, sir, a poor farrier of Putney. That's my master, sir, yonder. I was robbed
for his sake, sir.

FRISKIBALL   I see you have been met by the Bandetto,
And therefore need not ask how you came thus.—
But, Friskiball, why dost thou question them

50   Of their estate and not relieve their need?—
Sir, the coin I have about me is not much:
There's sixteen ducats for to clothe yourselves,
There's sixteen more to buy your diet with,
And there's sixteen to pay for your horse hire:

55   'Tis all the wealth, you see, my purse possesses,
But if you please for to enquire me out,
You shall not want for aught that I can do.
My name is Friskiball, a Florence merchant,
A man that always loved your nation.

60 CROMWELL   This unexpected favour at your hands,
Which God doth know if ever I shall requite it,
Necessity makes me to take your bounty,
And for your gold can yield you nought but thanks.
Your charity hath helped me from despair:

65   Your name shall still be in my hearty prayer.

FRISKIBALL   It is not worth such thanks. Come to my house:
Your want shall better be relieved than thus.

CROMWELL   I pray, excuse me; this shall well suffice
To bear my charges to Bologna,

70   Whereas a noble earl is much distressed:
An Englishman, Russell, the earl of Bedford,
Is by the French king sold unto his death.
It may fall out that I may do him good:
To save his life, I'll hazard my heart blood.

75   Therefore, kind sir, thanks for your liberal gift:
I must be gone to aid him: there's no shift.

FRISKIBALL   I'll be no hinderer to so good an act.
Heaven prosper you in that you go about!
If Fortune bring you this way back again,

---

40 estate state, condition/rank, status/class   **45 yonder** over there   **52 ducats** gold or silver coins of varying value; the Italian ducat was worth 3s 6d, that is roughly six to the pound   **57 aught** anything   **61 requite** repay   **69 bear my charges** pay my expenses   **Bologna** the Italian town was known as 'Bononia'; spelling modernized here, but needs to be pronounced as four syllables   **70 Whereas** where

80   Pray let me see you: so I take my leave:

    All good a man can wish, I do bequeath.   *Exit Friskiball*

CROMWELL   All good that God doth send, light on your head:

    There's few such men within our climate bred.

    How say you now, Hodge? Is not this good fortune?

85   **HODGE**   How say you? I'll tell you what, Master Thomas,

    If all men be of this gentleman's mind,

    Let's keep our standings upon this bridge:

    We shall get more here with begging in one day,

    Than I shall with making horseshoes in a whole year.

90   **CROMWELL**   No Hodge, we must be gone unto Bologna,

    There to relieve the noble Earl of Bedford:

    Where, if I fail not in my policy,

    I shall deceive their subtle treachery.

  HODGE   Nay, I'll follow you. God bless us from the thieving bandettoes again!

          Exeunt omnes

[Act 2 Scene 5]

Enter Bedford and his Host

BEDFORD   Am I betrayed? Was Bedford born to die

    By such base slaves in such a place as this?

    Have I escaped so many times in France,

    So many battles have I overpassed,

5   And made the French stir when they heard my name;

    And am I now betrayed unto my death?

    Some of their hearts' blood first shall pay for it.

  HOST   They do desire, my lord, to speak with you.

  BEDFORD   The traitors do desire to have my blood,

10   But by my birth, my honour, and my name,

    By all my hopes, my life shall cost them dear.

    Open the door: I'll venture out upon them,

    And if I must die, then I'll die with honour.

  HOST   Alas, my lord, that is a desperate course;

15   They have begirt you round about the house:

    Their meaning is to take you prisoner

    And so to send your body unto France.

  BEDFORD   First shall the ocean be as dry as sand,

    Before alive they send me unto France:

20   I'll have my body first bored like a sieve

---

92 policy plan   **[2.5]**   *Location: Bologna, a room in an hotel*   **4 overpassed** passed through; John Russell, first Earl of Bedford, fought in the Italian Wars (1494–1559), a series of conflicts which involved most of western Europe as well as the Ottoman Empire and were essentially a struggle for power and territory between the participants   **15 begirt** enclosed, surrounded   **20 bored...sieve** i.e. full of wounds

And die as Hector gainst the Myrmidons,

Ere France shall boast Bedford's their prisoner.

Treacherous France, that, gainst the law of arms,

Hath here betrayed thy enemy to death.

25 But be assured, my blood shall be revenged

Upon the best lives that remains in France.—

Enter a Servant

Stand back, or else thou run'st upon thy death.

MESSENGER Pardon, my lord; I come to tell your honour,

That they have hired a Neapolitan,

30 Who by his oratory hath promised them,

Without the shedding of one drop of blood,

Into their hands safe to deliver you,

And therefore craves none but himself may enter

And a poor swain that attends on him.

35 BEDFORD   A Neapolitan? Bid him come in.   *Exit Servant*

Were he as cunning in his eloquence

As Cicero, the famous man of Rome,

His words would be as chaff against the wind:

Sweet-tongued Ulysses that made Ajax mad,

40 Were he and his tongue in this speaker's head,

Alive he wins me not: then, 'tis no conquest dead.

Enter Cromwell like a Neapolitan, and Hodge with him

CROMWELL Sir, are you the master of the house?

HOST   I am, sir.

CROMWELL By this same token you must leave this place,

45 And leave none but the earl and I together,

And this, my peasant here, to tend on us.

HOST   With all my heart! God grant, you do some good.   *Exit Host. Cromwell*

BEDFORD   Now, sir, what's your will with me?   *shuts the door*

CROMWELL Intends your honour not to yield yourself?

50 BEDFORD   No, goodman goose, not while my sword doth last.

Is this your eloquence for to persuade me?

CROMWELL My lord, my eloquence is for to save you.

I am not, as you judge, a Neapolitan,

But Cromwell, your servant, and an Englishman!

55 BEDFORD   How? Cromwell? Not my farrier's son?

CROMWELL The same, sir, and am come to succour you.

HODGE   Yes, faith, sir; and I am Hodge, your poor smith.

---

21 **Hector…Myrmidons** a reference to the Trojan war, from Homer's *Iliad*, in which **Hector**, the most famous Trojan hero, was ultimately killed by the Greek Achilles and his followers the **Myrmidons**, who desecrated Hector's body   22 **Ere** before   23 **law of arms** accepted military code of behaviour   29 **Neapolitan** one from the southern Italian city of Naples   34 **swain** male servant/rustic fellow   37 **Cicero** Marcus Tullius Cicero (106–43 BC), famous Roman statesman and orator, was widely read and studied in the Renaissance as a model of **eloquence**   38 **chaff** lightweight refuse, literally the husks left after winnowing or threshing of corn   39 **Sweet-tongued…mad** another reference to the Trojan war; after the death of Achilles, **Ulysses** (the Greek Odysseus) and **Ajax** quarrelled over who should inherit Achilles' armour. The other generals awarded it to **Ulysses**, persuaded by his superior oratory and **Ajax** subsequently went mad   50 **goodman goose** foolish man

Many a time and oft have I shoed your dapper grey.

BEDFORD   And what avails it me that thou art here?

60   CROMWELL   It may avail, if you'll be ruled by me.

My lord, you know the men of Mantua

And these Bolognans are at deadly strife,

And they, my lord, both love and honour you.

Could you but get out of the Mantua port,

65   Then were you safe despite of all their force.

BEDFORD   Tut, man, thou talk'st of things impossible!

Dost thou not see that we are round beset?

How, then, is it possible we should escape?

CROMWELL   By force we cannot, but by policy.

70   Put on the apparel here that Hodge doth wear,

And give him yours — the States, they know you not,

For, as I think, they never saw your face —

And at a watchword must I call them in,

And will desire, that we safe may pass

75   To Mantua, where I'll say my business lies.

How doth your honour like of this devise?

BEDFORD   O wondrous good! But wilt thou venture, Hodge?

HODGE   Will I? O noble lord,

I do accord in anything I can,

80   And do agree to set thee free, do Fortune what she can.

BEDFORD   Come, then, let's change our apparel straight.

CROMWELL   Go, Hodge, make haste, lest they chance to call.

HODGE   I warrant you I'll fit him with a suit.   *Exit Earl and Hodge*

CROMWELL   Heavens grant this policy doth take success,

85   And that the earl may safely scape away.

And yet it grieves me for this simple wretch,

For fear they should offer him violence:

But of two evils, 'tis best to shun the greatest,

And better is it that he lives in thrall,

90   Than such a noble earl as he should fall.

Their stubborn hearts, it may be, will relent,

Since he is gone to whom their hate is bent.—

My lord, have you dispatched?

Enter Bedford like the Clown, and Hodge in his cloak and his hat

BEDFORD   How dost thou like us, Cromwell? Is it well?

95   CROMWELL   O, my lord, excellent: Hodge, how dost feel thyself?

HODGE   How do I feel myself? Why, as a nobleman should do.

O, how I feel honour come creeping on!

---

58 **dapper grey** neat, trim, grey horse; perhaps he means 'dapple-grey', i.e. where the colour is marked with patches and blotches   59 **avails** profits, benefits   61 **Mantua** Italian city, capital of the province of Lombardy   64 **port** gate; Bologna was an inland medieval city protected by walls and ports or gates; the **Mantua** gate would probably be the San Vitale which led north-eastward out of Bologna toward Mantua, eighty-six kilometres/fifty-three miles away   71 **States** ruling body of the city   73 **watchword** password   76 **devise** scheme, device   77 **venture** take the risk   79 **accord** give consent   89 **thrall** captivity

My nobility is wonderful melancholy:

Is it not most gentleman-like to be melancholy?

100 CROMWELL Yes, Hodge; now go sit down in his study,

And take state upon thee.

HODGE I warrant you, my lord; let me alone to take state upon me: but hark you, my lord, do you feel nothing bite about you?

BEDFORD No, trust me, Hodge.

105 HODGE Ay, they know they want their pasture; it's a strange thing of this vermin, they dare not meddle with nobility.

CROMWELL Go, take thy place, Hodge; I'll call them in.— *Hodge sits in the study,*

All is done, enter and if you please. *and Cromwell calls in the States*

Enter the States and Officers, with Halberts

BOLOGNAN GOVERNOR What, have you won him? Will he yield himself?

110 CROMWELL I have, an't please you, and the quiet earl

Doth yield himself to be disposed by you.

BOLOGNAN GOVERNOR Give him the money that we promised him:

So let him go, whither it please himself.

CROMWELL My business, sir, lies unto Mantua,

115 Please you to give me safe conduct thither.

BOLOGNAN GOVERNOR Go and conduct him to the Mantua port,

And see him safe delivered presently. *Exit Cromwell and Bedford*

Go draw the curtains, let us see the earl.—

O, he is writing; stand apart awhile.

120 HODGE [*reads*] 'Fellow William, I am not as I have been: I went from you a smith, I write to you as a lord. I am, at this present writing, among the Bolognan sausages. I do commend my lordship to Raphe and to Roger, to Bridget and to Dority, and so to all the youth of Putney.'

BOLOGNAN GOVERNOR Sure, these are the names of English noblemen,

125 Some of his special friends, to whom he writes:

But stay, he doth address himself to sing.

Here he sings a song

My lord, I am glad you are so frolic and so blithe:

Believe me, noble lord, if you know all,

You'd change your merry vein to sudden sorrow.

130 HODGE I change my merry vein? No, thou Bolognan, no!

I am a lord — and therefore let me go —

And do defy thee and thy sausages:

Therefore stand off, and come not near my honour!

BOLOGNAN GOVERNOR My lord, this jesting cannot serve your turn.

135 HODGE Dost think, thou black Bolognan beast,

---

98 **nobility ... melancholy** a satirical comment on the aristocratic fashion for adopting a melancholic pose   101 **state** high rank, greatness
106 **they ... nobility** Hodge is asking the earl if he's been bitten by fleas now that they've exchanged clothes; he suggests that the **vermin** (fleas) know better than to bite a member of the aristocracy   *States* rulers of the city   *Halberts* soldiers carrying halberds, a military weapon which was a combination of spear and battle-axe   110 **an't please you** if you please   121 **Bolognan sausages** Bologna was famous for its large seasoned smoked sausages, from where we get the word 'baloney' meaning 'nonsense'; Hodge may be referring disparagingly to the city's inhabitants, and in the Quarto text he uses the comic pronunciation 'Polonian Casiges'

That I do flout, do gibe, or jest?

No, no, thou beer-pot, know that I,

A noble earl, a lord pardie—   *A trumpet sounds*

BOLOGNAN GOVERNOR   What means this trumpet's sound?

Enter a Messenger

140   CITIZEN   One come from the States of Mantua.

BOLOGNAN GOVERNOR   What would you with us? Speak, thou man of Mantua.

MESSENGER   Men of Bologna, this my message is:

To let you know the noble earl of Bedford

Is safe within the town of Mantua,

145   And wills you send the peasant that you have,

Who hath deceived your expectation,

Or else the States of Mantua have vowed

They will recall the truce that they have made,

And not a man shall stir from forth your town,

150   That shall return, unless you send him back.

BOLOGNAN GOVERNOR   O this misfortune, how it mads my heart!

The Neapolitan hath beguiled us all.

Hence with this fool! What shall we do with him,

The earl being gone? A plague upon it all!

155   HODGE   No, I'll assure you, I am no earl, but a smith, sir,

One Hodge, a smith at Putney, sir:

One that hath gulled you, that hath bored you, sir.

BOLOGNAN GOVERNOR   Away with him! Take hence the fool you came for.

HODGE   Ay, sir, and I'll leave the greater fool with you.

160   MESSENGER   Farewell, Bolognans! Come, friend, along with me.

HODGE   My friend afore; my lordship will follow thee.   *Exit*

BOLOGNAN GOVERNOR   Well, Mantua, since by thee the earl is lost,

Within few days I hope to see thee crossed.   *Exit omnes*

[Act 3]

Enter Chorus

CHORUS   Thus far you see how Cromwell's fortune passed.

The Earl of Bedford, being safe in Mantua,

Desires Cromwell's company into France,

To make requital for his courtesy:

5   But Cromwell doth deny the earl his suit,

And tells him that those parts he meant to see,

He had not yet set footing on the land,

And so directly takes his way to Spain:

The earl to France, and so they both do part.

---

136 **flout** mock, jeer, insult   **gibe** taunt   138 **pardie** indeed, without a doubt (from the French *par dieu!*, 'by God!')   151 **mads** angers   157 **gulled** fooled,
deceived   **bored** tricked, made a fool of   161 **afore** in front   163 **crossed** thwarted, opposed   [3]   4 **requital** repayment

10   Now let your thoughts, as swift as is the wind,
      Skip some few years that Cromwell spent in travel,
      And now imagine him to be in England,
      Servant unto the Master of the Rolls,
      Where in short time there he began to flourish.
15   An hour shall show you what few years did cherish.   *Exit*

[Act 3 Scene 1]

The music plays, they bring out the banquet. Enter Sir Christopher Hales,
and Cromwell, and two servants

HALES   Come, sirs, be careful of your master's credit,
      And as our bounty now exceeds the figure
      Of common entertainment, so do you
      With looks as free as is your master's soul,
5   Give formal welcome to the throngèd tables,
      That shall receive the Cardinal's followers
      And the attendants of the Lord Chancellor.
      But all my care, Cromwell, depends on thee.
      Thou art a man differing from vulgar form,
10   And by how much thy spirit is ranked 'bove these
      In rules of art, by so much it shines brighter
      By travel, whose observance pleads his merit,
      In a most learnèd, yet unaffecting spirit.
      Good Cromwell, cast an eye of fair regard
15   'Bout all my house, and what this ruder flesh,
      Through ignorance, or wine, do miscreate,
      Salve thou with courtesy: if welcome want,
      Full bowls and ample banquets will seem scant.
CROMWELL   Sir, whatsoever lies in me,
20   Assure I will show my utmost duty.   *Exit Cromwell*
HALES   About it, then; the lords will straight be here.—
      Cromwell, thou hast those parts would rather suit
      The service of the state than of my house.
      I look upon thee with a loving eye,
25   That one day will prefer thy destiny.
Enter Messenger
MESSENGER   Sir, the lords be at hand.

13 **Master of the Rolls** originally the title of the keeper of records (**rolls**) of the Lord Chancellor, now a senior judge   **[3.1]**   *Location: London, a room in Sir Christopher Hales's house*   **banquet** a sumptuous feast/course of sweetmeats, fruit and wine, served either as a separate entertainment, or as a continuation of the principal meal   **1 credit** reputation, in personal and financial senses   **2 figure** form appearance/sum, amount   **5 throngèd** crowded/filled   **6 Cardinal's…Chancellor** Cardinal Wolsey (1471–1530) was Henry VIII's Lord Chancellor from 1515 till 1529, the year before his death   **9 vulgar form** the common sort   **11 rules of art** understanding of the skilful application of learning, aesthetic and organizational principles   **12 observance** attentive care/dutiful service/observation   **13 unaffecting** free from affectation   **14 fair regard** honest judgement/observant attention   **15 'Bout** around   **ruder** less educated or knowledgeable   **16 miscreate** does wrongly or improperly   **17 Salve…courtesy** will you remedy through your courtesy and good manners   **if…scant** if the manner of greeting guests is inadequate, lots of food and drink won't make up for it   **22 parts** natural gifts   **25 prefer** promote   **26 be at hand** are nearby

| HALES | They are welcome: bid Cromwell straight attend us, |

HALES   They are welcome: bid Cromwell straight attend us,
           And look you all things be in perfect readiness.   [*Exit Messenger*]

The music plays. Enter Cardinal Wolsey, Sir Thomas More and Gardiner [*and Cromwell, separately*]

WOLSEY   O, sir Christopher,
30   You are too liberal! What, a banquet too?
HALES   My lords, if words could show the ample welcome,
           That my free heart affords you, I could then
           Become a prater, but I now must deal
           Like a feast-politician with your lordships,
35   Defer your welcome till the banquet end,
           That it may then salve our defect of fare:
           Yet welcome now and all that tend on you!
WOLSEY   Thanks to the kind Master of the Rolls.
           Come and sit down; sit down, Sir Thomas More.
40   'Tis strange, how that we and the Spaniard differ:
           Their dinner is our banquet after dinner,
           And they are men of active disposition.
           This I gather: that by their sparing meat
           Their body is more fitter for the wars,
45   And if that famine chance to pinch their maws,
           Being used to fast it breeds less pain.
HALES   Fill me some wine: I'll answer Cardinal Wolsey.
           My lord, we English are of more freer souls
           Than hunger-starved and ill-complexioned Spaniards;
50   They that are rich in Spain spare belly-food
           To deck their backs with an Italian hood
           And silks of Seville, and the poorest snake,
           That feeds on lemons, pilchards, and ne'er heated
           His palate with sweet flesh, will bear a case
55   More fat and gallant than his starvèd face.
           Pride, the Inquisition, and this belly-evil,
           Are, in my judgement, Spain's three-headed devil!
MORE   Indeed it is a plague unto their nation,
           Who stagger after in blind imitation.
60 HALES My lords, with welcome, I present your lordships
           A solemn health!
MORE   I love health well, but when healths do bring
           Pain to the head and bodies surfeiting,
           Then cease I healths.— Nay, spill not, friend,

---

33 prater boaster, idle talker   **34 feast-politician** a nonce word which seems to mean 'one who organizes a feast with a politician's skill in order to gain maximum personal advantage'   **41 banquet after dinner** refers in this instance to a course of sweetmeats, fruit and wine, served as a continuation of the principal meal   **45 maws** stomachs   **50 spare belly-food** eat little   **52 snake** poor, needy, humble person/drudge (a contemptuous term) **54 case** skin, i.e. clothes   **55 fat** rich   **gallant** gorgeous, showy in appearance   **56 Inquisition** Roman Catholic ecclesiastical tribunal for the suppression of heresy and punishment of heretics; the Spanish Inquisition was notorious for its severity   **59 blind imitation** follow this example without considering the matter   **61 health** toast

65   For though the drops be small,
        Yet have they force to force men to the wall.

WOLSEY   Sir Christopher, is that your man?

HALES   An't like your grace, he is a scholar and
          A linguist, one that hath travelled many parts
70   Of Christendom, my lord.

WOLSEY   My friend, come nearer: have you been a traveller?

CROMWELL My lord, I have added to my knowledge the low countries,
          France, Spain, Germany, and Italy:
          And though small gain, of profit I did find,
75   Yet did it please my eye, content my mind.

WOLSEY   What do you think of the several states
          And princes' courts as you have travellèd?

CROMWELL My lord, no court with England may compare,
          Neither for state nor civil government:
80   Lust dwells in France, in Italy, and Spain,
          From the poor peasant to the prince's train:
          In Germany and Holland riot serves,
          And he that most can drink, most he deserves:
          England I praise not, for I here was born,
85   But that she laugh'th the others unto scorn.

WOLSEY   My lord, there dwells within that spirit
          More than can be discerned by outward eye.
          Sir Christopher, will you part with your man?

HALES   I have sought to proffer him to your lordship,
90   And now I see he hath preferred himself.

WOLSEY   What is thy name?

CROMWELL Cromwell, my lord.

WOLSEY   Then, Cromwell, here we make thee solicitor of our causes,
          And nearest next ourself.
95   Gardiner give you kind welcome to the man.   *Gardiner embraces him*

MORE   My lord, you are a royal winner,
          Have got a man besides your bounteous dinner.
          Well, knight, pray we come no more,
          If we come often, or shut up thy door.

100 WOLSEY   Sir Christopher, hadst thou given me
          Half thy lands, thou couldst not have pleased me
          So much as with this man of thine.
          My infant thoughts do spell:
          Shortly his fortune shall be lifted higher:
105   True industry doth kindle honour's fire.
          And so, kind Master of the Rolls, farewell.

---

66 **force…wall** cause men to fail in life; More is putting the case for moderation in the use of alcohol   93 **solicitor…causes** Cromwell was appointed Wolsey's legal secretary in 1520   94 **ourself** Wolsey is using the royal plural pronoun of himself, suggesting arrogance and self-importance   97 **besides** as well as   103 **infant** early   **spell** suggest, make out by close observation

HALES   Cromwell, farewell.

CROMWELL   Cromwell takes his leave of you,

    That ne'er will leave to love and honour you.

                                      Exeunt omnes

                          The music plays as they go in

[Act 4]

Enter Chorus

CHORUS   Now Cromwell's highest fortunes doth begin.

    Wolsey, that loved him as he did his life,

    Committed all his treasure to his hands.

    Wolsey is dead, and Gardiner, his man,

5   Is now created Bishop of Winchester:

    Pardon if we omit all Wolsey's life,

    Because our play depends on Cromwell's death.

    Now sit and see his highest state of all:

    His height of rising and his sudden fall.

10   Pardon the errors is already past,

    And live in hope the best doth come at last:

    My hope upon your favour doth depend,

    And look to have your liking ere the end.   *Exit*

[Act 4 Scene 1]

Enter Gardiner Bishop of Winchester, the Dukes of Norfolk and of Suffolk, Sir Thomas More, Sir Christopher Hales, and Cromwell

NORFOLK   Master Cromwell, since Cardinal Wolsey's death,

    His majesty is given to understand

    There's certain bills and writings in your hand,

    That much concerns the state of England.

5   My lord of Winchester, is it not so?

GARDINER   My lord of Norfolk, we two were whilom fellows

    And, Master Cromwell, though our master's love

    Did bind us while his love was to the king,

    It is not boot now to deny these things,

10   Which may be prejudicial to the state:

    And though that God hath raised my fortune higher

    Than any way I looked for or deserved,

    Yet my life no longer with me dwell

    Than I prove true unto my sovereign:

15   What say you, Master Cromwell? Have you those writings?

    Ay, or no?

109 leave cease, leave off   **[4.1]**   *Location: London, a public walk*   **6 whilom** sometime, previously   **9 boot** of any advantage or profit

CROMWELL   Here are the writings, and upon my knees,
I give them up unto the worthy dukes
Of Suffolk and of Norfolk: he was my master,
20   And each virtuous part,
That lived in him, I tendered with my heart,
But what his head complotted gainst the state
My country's love commands me that to hate.
His sudden death I grieve for, not his fall,
25   Because he sought to work my country's thrall.

SUFFOLK   Cromwell, the king shall hear of this thy duty,
Whom I assure myself will well reward thee.
My lord, let's go unto his majesty,
And show these writings which he longs to see.   *Exit Norfolk and Suffolk*

Enter Bedford hastily

30   BEDFORD   How now, who's this?
Cromwell, by my soul! Welcome to England:
Thou once didst save my life, didst not Cromwell?

CROMWELL   If I did so, 'tis greater glory for me,
That you remember it, than of myself
35   Vainly to report it.

BEDFORD   Well, Cromwell, now is the time,
I shall commend thee to my sovereign:
Cheer up thyself, for I will raise thy state.
A Russell yet was never found ingrate.   *Exit*

40   HALES   O how uncertain is the wheel of state!
Who lately greater than the cardinal,
For fear, and love? And now who lower lies?
Gay honours are but Fortune's flatteries,
And whom this day pride and promotion swells,
45   Tomorrow envy and ambition quells.

MORE   Who sees the cobweb entangle the poor fly,
May boldly say the wretch's death is nigh.

GARDINER   I know his state and proud ambition
Was too too violent to last overlong.

50   HALES   Who soars too near the sun with golden wings
Melts them, to ruin his own fortune brings.

Enter the Duke of Suffolk

SUFFOLK   Cromwell, kneel down in King Henry's name.—
Arise Sir Thomas Cromwell; thus begins thy fame.

Enter the Duke of Norfolk

---

21 tendered cherished, held dear/offered in payment   **22 complotted** plotted with others   **gainst** against   **25 thrall** bondage, captivity; Wolsey was falsely accused of treason and urging the Pope to excommunicate Henry and take the throne for himself. He fell ill and died on his way to the Tower of London   **35 Vainly** to satisfy my vanity/pointlessly   **38 state** position, status   **40 wheel of state** change, mutability of position or governance/the endless cycle of events   **44 swells** enlarges, puffs up   **45 quells** strikes down   **47 nigh** near   **50 Who…wings** a reference to the mythological story of Icarus, which was interpreted as a moral of overweening ambition; his father Daedalus made him a pair of wings of wax in order to escape from Crete, but despite his father's warning Icarus flew too close to the sun, his wings melted and he fell into the sea

NORFOLK   Cromwell, the majesty of England,

55   For the good liking he conceives of thee,

        Makes thee Master of the Jewel House,

        Chief Secretary to himself, and withal,

        Creates thee one of his highness' Privy Council.

Enter the Earl of Bedford

BEDFORD   Where is Sir Thomas Cromwell? Is he knighted?

60   SUFFOLK   He is, my lord.

BEDFORD   Then to add honour to his name,

        The king creates him Lord Keeper of

        His Privy Seal and Master of the Rolls,

        Which you Sir Christopher do now enjoy:

65   The king determines higher place for you.

CROMWELL   My lords,

        These honours are too high for my desert.

MORE   O content thee, man! Who would not choose it?

        Yet thou art wise in seeming to refuse it.

70   GARDINER   Here's honours, titles, and promotions:

        I fear this climbing will have a sudden fall.

NORFOLK   Then come, my lords; let's altogether bring

        This new-made councillor to England's king.   *Exeunt all but Gardiner*

GARDINER   But Gardiner means his glory shall be dimmed.

75   Shall Cromwell live a greater man than I?

        My envy with his honour now is bred:

        I hope to shorten Cromwell by the head.   *Exit*

[Act 4 Scene 2]

Enter Friskiball very poor

FRISKIBALL   O Friskiball, what shall become of thee?

        Where shalt thou go, or which way shalt thou turn?

        Fortune, that turns her too unconstant wheel,

        Hath turned thy wealth and riches in the sea.

5   All parts abroad wherever I have been

        Grows weary of me, and denies me succour;

        My debtors, they that should relieve my want,

        Forswears my money, says they owe me none:

        They know my state too mean to bear out law,

---

55 good liking despite his closeness and loyalty to Wolsey, Cromwell was able to survive his fall from favour and rise under Henry for a further ten years   **56 Master...House** a position in the British royal household with the responsibility of running the Jewel Office which holds the sovereign's jewels – Cromwell held this post from 1532 to 1533; the well-known portrait of Cromwell by Hans Holbein was inscribed 'Master of the Jewel House' and is presumed therefore to have been painted while he held this office   **57 withal** in addition   **62 Lord...Rolls** two of the great offices of state; historically Cromwell was appointed **Master of the Rolls** from 1534 to 1536 (i.e. before rather than after **Sir Christopher** Hales) and **Lord Privy Seal** from 1536 to 1540   **63 Privy Seal** the monarch's private seal (as opposed to the great seal of state) impressed into melted wax to signify authorization of letters or documents   **[4.2]** *Location: London, a street before Cromwell's house Friskiball very poor* an instant illustration of the mutability of individual fortune **8 Forswears** deny me **9 They...law** they know I'm too poor to take them to court to prove my case against them

10   And here in London, where I oft have been,

And have done good to many a wretched man,

Am now most wretched here, despised myself.

In vain it is, more of their hearts to try:

Be patient, therefore, lay thee down and die.   *He lies down*

Enter goodman Seely, and his wife Joan

15   SEELY   Come, Joan, come; let's see what he'll do for us now. Iwis we have done for him, when many a time and often he might have gone a-hungry to bed.

WIFE   Alas, man, now he is made a lord, he'll never look upon us; he'll fulfil the old proverb: 'Set beggars a-horseback and they'll ride.'— Ah welladay for my cow! Such as he hath made us come behindhand: we had never pawned our cow else to

20   pay our rent.

SEELY   Well, Joan, he'll come this way: and by God's dickers, I'll tell him roundly of it, and if he were ten lords: a shall know that I had not my cheese and my bacon for nothing.

WIFE   Do you remember, husband, how he would mouch up my cheesecakes?

25   He hath forgot this now, but we'll remember him.

SEELY   Ay, we shall have now three flaps with a foxtail; but, i'faith, I'll gibber a joint but I'll tell him his own. Stay, who comes here? O stand up! Here he comes: stand up!

Enter Hodge very fine with a tipstaff, Cromwell, the mace carried before him, Norfolk, and Suffolk, and attendants

HODGE   Come, away with these beggars here; rise up, sirrah!—

30   Come out the good people: run afore there, ho!

Friskiball rises, and stands afar off

SEELY   Ay, we are kicked away, now we come for our own; the time hath been he would 'a looked more friendly upon us. And you, Hodge, we know you well enough, though you are so fine.

CROMWELL   Come hither, sirrah!— Stay, what men are these?

35   My honest host of Hounslow and his wife!

I owe thee money, father, do I not?

SEELY   Ay, by the body of me, dost thou. Would thou wouldst pay me: good four pound it is, I have a' the post at home.

CROMWELL   I know 'tis true.— Sirrah, give him ten angels—

40   And look your wife and you do stay to dinner:

And while you live, I freely give to you

Four pound a year, for the four pound I ought you.

SEELY   Art not changed, art old Tom still?

Seely a surname meaning 'pious, good/innocent, harmless/defenceless, deserving of sympathy/foolish, simple'   *Joan* a generic name for a female rustic   **15 Iwis** truly   **18 'Set…ride'** the usual saying was: 'Set a beggar on horseback, and he'll ride to the Devil'; the implication is that once someone is rich they become proud and don't want to acknowledge their previous companions   **welladay** alas! An exclamation of regret   **19 Such…behindhand** people like him (who don't pay us what they owe) are the reason that we have got behind with the rent and hence have had to **pawn our cow   21 God's dickers** a mild oath of uncertain meaning; **dicker** referred to the number ten and was the customary unit of exchange for items such as hides or skins, i.e. a package of ten hides, hence it was used for a 'lot' or 'heap'   **22 a** he   **24 mouch** eat up greedily   **25 remember** remind   **26 three…foxtail** be treated like fools/be dismissed contemptuously; a **foxtail** was one of the badges of the fool or jester   **flaps** light blows or strokes   **27 tell…own** i.e. tell him a few home-truths   *tipstaff* staff with a metal tip borne as a badge of office   *mace* sceptre or staff of office   **35 Hounslow** a town ten miles to the south-west of London, now a London suburb   **36 father** a respectful title given to an old and venerable man   **38 I…home** i.e. I've kept a tally or record of the account   **post** doorpost on which the reckoning at a tavern was kept; (hence) a record of the account or score   **39 ten angels** i.e. eighty shillings or four pounds   **42 ought** owed

Now God bless the good lord Tom!

45 Home, Joan, home; I'll dine with my lord Tom today,

And thou shalt come next week.

Fetch my cow; home, Joan, home!

WIFE   Now God bless thee, my good lord Tom:

I'll fetch my cow presently.   *Exit Wife*

Enter Gardiner

50 **CROMWELL**   Sirrah, go to yon stranger: tell him I desire him   *Indicates Friskiball*

Stay at dinner. I must speak with him.

GARDINER   My lord of Norfolk, see you this same bubble,

That same puff? But mark the end, my lord,

Mark the end.

55 **NORFOLK**   I promise you, I like not something he hath done,

But let that pass; the king doth love him well.

CROMWELL   Good morrow to my lord of Winchester:

I know you bear me hard about the abbey lands.

GARDINER   Have I not reason, when religion is wronged?

60 You had no colour for what you have done.

CROMWELL   Yes: the abolishing of antichrist,

And of this popish order from our realm:

I am no enemy to religion,

But what is done, it is for England's good.

65 What did they serve for but to feed a sort

Of lazy abbots and of full-fed friars?

They neither plough, nor sow, and yet they reap

The fat of all the land, and suck the poor:

Look, what was theirs, is in King Henry's hands;

70 His wealth before lay in the abbey lands.

GARDINER   Indeed these things you have alleged, my lord,

When God doth know the infant yet unborn

Will curse the time the abbeys were pulled down.

I pray, now where is hospitality?

75 Where now may poor distressèd people go

For to relieve their need, or rest their bones,

When weary travel doth oppress their limbs?

And where religious men should take them in,

Shall now be kept back with a mastiff dog

---

49 **presently** immediately   52 **bubble** empty, deceptive show; Cromwell was well-known for rewarding his friends and allies generously   53 **puff** pride, vanity/showy self-advertisement   55 **something...done** Norfolk, a staunch Catholic, is alluding to Cromwell's instrumental part in the break with Rome and the dissolution of the monasteries   58 **bear...lands** dislike me for my part in the dissolution of the monasteries and appropriation and sale of abbey lands to raise money for the king   60 **colour** pretext, cloak to give the appearance of justice for your actions   61 **antichrist** enemy or opponent of Christ, often applied to the Pope   62 **popish...realm** when the Pope refused to grant the annulment of Henry's marriage to his first wife, Katherine of Aragon, it was Cromwell who encouraged Henry to declare himself head of the English Church and hence no longer subject to the Pope's authority so that he could divorce Katherine and marry Anne Bullen (or Boleyn)   65 **What...poor** What use were the monastic orders except to look after themselves and their own interests, living a lazy life and getting rich and fat at the expense of the poor? The charge of such abuses were commonplace   74 **hospitality?...limbs** religious houses such as abbeys and monasteries were originally set up as charitable institutions with the Christian duty of caring for the poor, sick and weary   78 **religious...dog** whereas before, the monks would take such people in, now the lands and houses have been sold off and the new owners feel no such moral duty of care or hospitality and keep folk out with a fierce guard dog

80   And thousand thousand—

NORFOLK O, my lord, no more: things past redress

   'Tis bootless to complain!

CROMWELL What, shall we to the convocation house?

NORFOLK We'll follow you, my lord; pray, lead the way.

Enter Old Cromwell like a farmer

85 OLD CROMWELL How? One Cromwell made Lord Keeper since I left Putney

   And dwelt in Yorkshire. I never heard better news:

   I'll see that Cromwell, or it shall go hard.

CROMWELL My agèd father! State set aside,

   Father, on my knee I crave your blessing:

90   One of my servants go and have him in;

   At better leisure will we talk with him.

OLD CROMWELL Now if I die, how happy were the day!

   To see this comfort rains forth showers of joy.   *Exit Old Cromwell*

NORFOLK This duty in him shows a kind of grace.

95 CROMWELL Go on before, for time draws on apace.   *Exeunt all but Friskiball*

FRISKIBALL I wonder what this lord would have with me.

   His man so strictly gave me charge to stay:

   I never did offend him to my knowledge.

   Well, good or bad, I mean to bide it all;

100   Worse than I am now never can befall.

Enter Banister and his wife

BANISTER Come, wife, I take it be almost dinner time,

   For Master Newton, and Master Crosby sent

   To me last night, they would come dine with me,

   And take their bond in: I pray thee, hie thee home,

105   And see that all things be in readiness.

MISTRESS BANISTER They shall be welcome, husband: I'll go before.—

   But is not that man Master Friskiball?   *She runs and embraces him*

BANISTER O heavens, it is kind Master Friskiball!

   Say sir, what hap hath brought you to this pass?

110 FRISKIBALL The same that brought you to your misery.

BANISTER Why would you not acquaint me with your state?

   Is Banister your poor friend quite forgot,

   Whose goods, whose love, whose life and all is yours?

FRISKIBALL I thought your usage would be as the rest,

115   That had more kindness at my hands than you,

   Yet looked askance, whenas they saw me poor.

MISTRESS BANISTER If Banister should bear so base a heart,

---

81 past redress which can't be altered **82 bootless** pointless **complain** bemoan, complain about **83 convocation house** place where a gathering of clergy meet to discuss ecclesiastical matters ***Old…farmer*** Thomas Cromwell's father, Walter, followed a number of different trades, working as a brewer and fuller as well as a smith; he was by all accounts of a vicious and turbulent disposition, and was perpetually being fined for drunkenness and evading his taxes, and on at least one occasion for assault **86 Yorkshire** there does not seem to be any historical evidence for this **99 bide** await **104 take…in** i.e. collect their bond having repaid what they owed **hie** hurry **109 hap** fortune, accident, event **pass** position **116 askance** sideways, with mistrust **whenas** at the time when

I never would look my husband in the face,

But hate him as I would a cockatrice.

120 BANISTER   And well thou mightst, should Banister deal so.

Since that I saw you, sir, my state is mended:

And for the thousand pound I owe to you,

I have it ready for you, sir, at home;

And though I grieve your fortune is so bad,

125 Yet that my hap's to help you makes me glad.

And now, sir, will it please you walk with me?

FRISKIBALL   Not yet I cannot, for the Lord Chancellor

Hath here commanded me to wait on him,

For what I know not: pray God 'tis for my good.

130 BANISTER   Never make doubt of that: I'll warrant you,

He is as kind a noble gentleman

As ever did possess the place he hath.

MISTRESS BANISTER   Sir, my brother is his steward: if you please,

We'll go along and bear you company:

135 I know we shall not want for welcome there.

FRISKIBALL   With all my heart: but what's become of Bagot?

BANISTER   He is hanged, for buying jewels of the king's.

FRISKIBALL   A just reward for one so impious.

The time draws on, sir; will you go along?

140 BANISTER   I'll follow you, kind Master Friskiball.   *Exeunt Omnes*

[Act 4 Scene 3]

Enter two Merchants

FIRST MERCHANT   Now, Master Crosby, I see you have a care,

To keep your word, in payment of your money.

SECOND MERCHANT   By my faith, I have reason upon a bond:

Three thousand pound is too much to forfeit,

5 Yet I doubt not Master Banister.

FIRST MERCHANT   By my faith, your sum is more than mine,

And yet I am not much behind you too,

Considering that today I paid at court.

SECOND MERCHANT   Mass, and well remembered:

10 What's the reason the Lord Cromwell's men

Wear such long skirts upon their coats?

They reach almost down to their very ham.

FIRST MERCHANT   I will resolve you, sir, and thus it is:

The Bishop of Winchester, that loves not Cromwell —

15 As great men are envied as well as less —

---

119 **cockatrice** fabulous serpent or monster that could kill with one glance   [4.3] *Location: a London street*   9 **Mass** by the Mass, the liturgical celebration of the Eucharist   11 **skirts** bottom, lower portions or tails of a coat   12 **ham** the back of the knee   13 **resolve** explain to

A while ago there was a jar between them,

And it was brought to my lord Cromwell's ear,

That bishop Gardiner would sit on his skirt,

Upon which word, he made his men long blue coats,

20 And in the court wore one of them himself,

And meeting with the bishop, quoth he, 'My lord,

Here's skirt enough now for your grace to sit on',

Which vexed the bishop to the very heart.

This is the reason why they wear long coats.

25 SECOND MERCHANT   'Tis always seen, and mark it for a rule,

That one great man will envy still another:

But 'tis a thing that nothing concerns me.

What, shall we now to Master Banister's?

FIRST MERCHANT   Ay, come, we'll pay him royally for our dinner.   *Exeunt*

[Act 4 Scene 4]

Enter the Usher and the Sewer, the meat goes over the stage

USHER   Uncover there, gentlemen.

Enter Cromwell, Bedford, Suffolk, Old Cromwell, Friskiball, goodman Seely, and attendants

CROMWELL   My noble lords of Suffolk and of Bedford,

Your honours' welcome to poor Cromwell's house.

Where is my father? Nay, be covered, father.

5 Although that duty to these noblemen

Doth challenge it, yet I'll make bold with them.

Your head doth bear the calendar of care.

What, Cromwell covered and his father bare!

It must not be.— Now, sir, to you. Is not

10 Your name Friskiball and a Florentine?

FRISKIBALL   My name was Friskiball, till cruel fate

Did rob me of my name and of my state.

CROMWELL   What fortune brought you to this country now?

FRISKIBALL   All other parts hath left me succourless,

15 Save only this because of debts I have:

I hope to gain for to relieve my want.

CROMWELL   Did you not once, upon your Florence bridge,

Help two distressed men, robbed by the Bandetto?

His name was Cromwell.

16 jar disagreement, quarrel   **18 sit…skirt** punish severely, press hard upon, deal heavily with   **[4.4]**   *Location: London, a room in Cromwell's house*   **Usher** officer at court or in a dignitary's household whose duty it was to walk before one of high rank, also a chamberlain or steward, an officer charged with the management of a noble household   **Sewer** household officer who superintended the arrangement of the table, seating of guests, tasting and serving of dishes   **meat** i.e. food   **1 Uncover** remove your hats from your heads (as a mark of respect)   **4 be covered** put your hat back on, implying that his age exonerated him from the need to remove his hat in the presence of nobles, although a negative interpretation might be that Cromwell was arrogantly suggesting that his father was now their social equal   **7 calendar** record/outward sign, index   **15 Save only this** except this one (England)   **16 for** in order

20   FRISKIBALL   I never made my brain a calendar of any good I did:

I always loved this nation with my heart.

CROMWELL   I am that Cromwell that you there relieved.

Sixteen ducats you gave me for to clothe me,

Sixteen to bear my charges by the way,

25   And sixteen more I had for my horse-hire:

There be those several sums justly returned,   *Gives money to Friskiball*

Yet with injustice, serving at my need,

And to repay them without interest:

Therefore receive of me these four several bags,   *Gives four bags to Friskiball*

30   In each of them there is four hundred mark,

And bring me the names of all your debitors,

And if they will not see you paid, I will.

O, God forbid that I should see him fall,

That helped me in my greatest need of all.

35   Here stands my father that first gave me life,

Alas, what duty is too much for him?

This man in time of need did save my life,

And therefore cannot do too much for him;

By this old man I oftentimes was fed,   *Indicating Seely*

40   Else might I have gone supperless to bed.

Such kindness have I had of these three men,

That Cromwell no way can repay again.

Now in to dinner, for we stay too long,

And to good stomachs is no greater wrong.   *Exeunt omnes*

[Act 4 Scene 5]

Enter Gardiner in his study, and his man

GARDINER   Sirrah, where be those men I caused to stay?

SERVANT   They do attend your pleasure, sir, within.

GARDINER   Bid them come hither, and stay you without —

For by those men, the fox of this same land,

5   That makes a goose of better than himself,

We'll worry him unto his latest home,

Or Gardiner will fail in his intent.

As for the Dukes of Suffolk and of Norfolk,

Whom I have sent for to come speak with me,

10   Howsoever, outwardly they shadow it,

---

30 mark originally a measure of weight of gold or silver; the monetary equivalent was roughly two thirds of one pound sterling, so that the total of Cromwell's gift is over one thousand pounds, a huge sum and a generous return on the original sum   **31 your debitors** debtors, those who owe you money   **[4.5]**   *Location: London, a room in the Bishop of Winchester's house*   **1 stay** remain   **4 fox** i.e. Cromwell; foxes were considered vermin and renowned for cunning   **same land** England, as opposed to foreign foxes such as Ferdinand of Aragon, father of Katherine of Aragon and Henry VIII's father-in-law, praised by Machiavelli as the 'cunning fox'   **5 goose** fool   **6 worry...home** harass him to his final den or resting place, i.e. to death   **10 shadow it** cover it up

Yet in their hearts I know they love him not:
As for the Earl of Bedford, he is but one,
And dares not gainsay what we do set down.

Enter the two witnesses

Now, my friends, you know I saved your lives,
When by the law you had deservèd death,   15
And then you promised me upon your oaths,
To venture both your lives to do me good.

BOTH WITNESSES   We swore no more than that we will perform.

GARDINER   I take your words: and that which you must do
Is service for your God and for your king   20
To root a rebel from this flourishing land,
One that's an enemy unto the church:
And therefore must you take your solemn oaths,
That you heard Cromwell, the Lord Chancellor,
Did wish a dagger at King Henry's heart.   25
Fear not to swear it, for I heard him speak it:
Therefore we'll shield you from ensuing harms.

SECOND WITNESS   If you will warrant us the deed is good,
We'll undertake it.

GARDINER   Kneel down, and I will here absolve you both.   30
This crucifix I lay upon your head,
And sprinkle holy-water on your brows.
The deed is meritorious that you do,
And by it shall you purchase grace from heaven.

FIRST WITNESS   Now, sir, we'll undertake it, by our souls.   35

SECOND WITNESS   For Cromwell never loved none of our sort.

GARDINER   I know he doth not, and for both of you,
I will prefer you to some place of worth:
Now get you in, until I call for you,
For presently the dukes means to be here.   *Exit witnesses*   40
Cromwell, sit fast, thy time's not long to reign.
The abbeys that were pulled down by thy means
Is now a mean for me to pull thee down;
Thy pride also thy own head lights upon,
For thou art he hath changed religion —   45
But now no more, for here the dukes are come.

Enter Suffolk, Norfolk, and the Earl of Bedford

SUFFOLK   Goode'en to my lord Bishop.

NORFOLK   How fares my lord? What, are you all alone?

GARDINER   No, not alone. My lords, my mind is troubled:
I know your honours muse wherefore I sent   50
And in such haste. What, came you from the king?

---

13 **gainsay** contradict, deny   30 **absolve** set you free from guilt or blame   50 **wherefore I sent** why I sent for you

NORFOLK   We did, and left none but Lord Cromwell with him.

GARDINER   O, what a dangerous time is this we live in!

There's Thomas Wolsey, he's already gone,

55   And Thomas More, he followed after him:

Another Thomas yet there doth remain,

That is far worse than either of those twain,

And if with speed, my lords, we not pursue it,

I fear the king and all the land will rue it.

60   BEDFORD   Another Thomas! Pray God it be not Cromwell.

GARDINER   My lord of Bedford, it is that traitor Cromwell.

BEDFORD   Is Cromwell false? My heart will never think it.

SUFFOLK   My lord of Winchester, what likelihood,

Or proof have you of this his treachery?

65   GARDINER   My lord, too much.— Call in the men within.   *Enter witnesses*

These men, my lord, upon their oaths affirm

That they did hear Lord Cromwell in his garden,

Wished a dagger sticking at the heart

Of our King Henry. What is this but treason?

70   BEDFORD   If it be so, my heart doth bleed with sorrow.

SUFFOLK   How say you friends? What, did you hear these words?

FIRST WITNESS   We did, an't like your grace.

NORFOLK   In what place was Lord Cromwell when he spake them?

SECOND WITNESS   In his garden, where we did attend a suit,

75   Which we had waited for two year and more.

SUFFOLK   How long is't since you heard him speak these words?

SECOND WITNESS   Some half-year since.

BEDFORD   How chance that you concealed it all this time?

FIRST WITNESS   His greatness made us fear, that was the cause.

80   GARDINER   Ay, ay, his greatness, that's the cause indeed:

And to make his treason here more manifest,

He calls his servants to him round about,

Tells them of Wolsey's life and of his fall,

Says that himself hath many enemies,

85   And gives to some of them a park or manor,

To others leases, lands to othersome:

What need he do thus in his prime of life,

And if he were not fearful of his death?

SUFFOLK   My lord, these likelihoods are very great.

90   BEDFORD   Pardon me, lords, for I must needs depart:

Their proofs are great, but greater is my heart.   *Exit Bedford*

NORFOLK   My friends, take heed of that which you have said.

Your souls must answer what your tongues reports:

Therefore take heed, be wary what you do.

57 **twain** two   72 **an't like** if it please   74 **suit** lawsuit; lengthy delay in reaching judgements was common   86 **othersome** some others

95 SECOND WITNESS   My lord, we speak no more but truth.

NORFOLK   Let them depart.

My lord of Winchester, let these men

Be close kept until the day of trial.

GARDINER   They shall, my lord.— Ho, take in these two men.—   *Exit witnesses*

100 My lords, if Cromwell have a public trial,

That which we do is void by his denial:

You know the king will credit none but him.

NORFOLK   'Tis true, he rules the king even as he pleases.

SUFFOLK   How shall we do for to attach him, then?

105 GARDINER   Marry, my lords, thus: by an act he made himself,

With an intent to entrap some of our lives,

And this it is: if any councillor

Be convicted of high treason, he shall

Be executed without a public trial.

110 This act, my lords, he caused the king to make.

SUFFOLK   A did indeed, and I remember it,

And now it is like to fall upon himself.

NORFOLK   Let us not slack it, 'tis for England's good.

We must be wary, else he'll go beyond us.

115 GARDINER   Well hath your grace said, my lord of Norfolk:

Therefore let us presently to Lambeth.

Thither comes Cromwell from the court tonight:

Let us arrest him, send him to the Tower,

And in the morning cut off the traitor's head.

120 NORFOLK   Come, then, about it, let us guard the town.

This is the day that Cromwell must go down.

GARDINER   Along, my lords.— Well, Cromwell is half dead: *Aside*

He shaked my heart, but I will shave his head.   *Exeunt*

[Act 5 Scene 1]

Enter Bedford solus

BEDFORD   My soul is like a water troublèd,

And Gardiner is the man that makes it so.

O, Cromwell, I do fear thy end is near:

Yet I'll prevent their malice if I can.

5 And in good time, see where the man doth come,

Who little knows how nears his day of doom.

Enter Cromwell with his train. Bedford makes as though he would speak to him: he goes on

CROMWELL   You're well encountered, my good lord of Bedford.

98 **close** safely/secretly   102 **credit** believe, give credence to   104 **attach** arrest, indict   111 **A** he   113 **slack** it be remiss, leave anything undone
114 **go beyond** get round, circumvent   116 **Lambeth** ancient settlement on the south bank of the river Thames; Lambeth Palace is still the chief residence
of the Archbishop of Canterbury   118 **Tower** the Tower of London where traitors were held prisoner prior to their execution   **[5.1]**   *Location: A street in*
London   6 **day of doom** judgement day, i.e. his death, when in Christian theology he will come before God to be judged

I see your honour is addressed to talk:

Pray pardon me, I am sent for to the king,

10   And do not know the business yet myself.

So fare you well, for I must needs be gone.   *Exit all the train*

BEDFORD   You must: well, what remedy?

I fear too soon you must be gone indeed.

The king hath business, but little dost thou know,

15   Who's busy for thy life: thou thinks not so.

Enter Cromwell and the train again

CROMWELL   The second time well met, my lord of Bedford,

I am very sorry that my haste is such:

Lord Marquis Dorset being sick to death,

I must receive of him the privy seal.

20   At Lambeth, soon, my lord, we'll talk our fill.   *Exit the train*

BEDFORD   How smooth and easy is the way to death!

Enter a servant

MESSENGER   My lord, the Dukes of Norfolk and of Suffolk,

Accompanied with the Bishop of Winchester,

Entreats you to come presently to Lambeth,

25   On earnest matters that concerns the state.

BEDFORD   To Lambeth? So! Go fetch me pen and ink.

I and Lord Cromwell there shall talk enough:

Ay, and our last, I fear, and if he come.   *He writes a letter*

Here, take this letter, and bear it to Lord Cromwell.

30   Bid him read it; say it concerns him near:

Away, begone, make all the haste you can.

To Lambeth do I go a woeful man.   *Exit*

[Act 5 Scene 2]

Enter Cromwell and his train

CROMWELL   Is the barge ready? I will straight to Lambeth,

And if this one day's business once were past,

I'd take my ease tomorrow after trouble.—

[Enter Messenger]

How now, my friend, wouldst thou speak with me?

The Messenger brings him the letter; he puts it in his pocket

5   MESSENGER   Sir, here's a letter from my lord of Bedford.

CROMWELL   O, good my friend, commend me to thy lord.

Hold, take those angels; drink them for thy pains.

---

8 addressed prepared, made ready   **18 Lord Marquis Dorset** Thomas Grey, second Marquis of Dorset, was a soldier and favourite courtier of Henry VIII; he died on 10 October 1530. He was not Lord Privy Seal, however, so it is unclear why Cromwell would need to receive the seal from him – it may be authorial error or a simple plot device; the Lord Privy Seal prior to Cromwell was Thomas Bullen (or Boleyn), Earl of Wiltshire, who was removed from office by Henry in 1536 after the downfall of his daughter Anne, Henry's second wife   **30 near** closely   **[5.2]** *Location: A street near the Thames*   **6 good my friend** my good friend   **commend** remember me kindly   **7 angels** coins   **pains** efforts

MESSENGER He doth desire your grace to read it,

    Because he says it doth concern you near.

10   CROMWELL Bid him assure himself of that. Farewell.

    Tomorrow, tell him, shall he hear from me.—

    Set on before there, and away to Lambeth.   *Exeunt omnes*

[Act 5 Scene 3]

Enter Winchester, Suffolk, Norfolk, Bedford, Sergeant-at-arms, the Herald, and Halberts

GARDINER Halberts, stand close unto the waterside:

    Sergeant-at-arms, be bold in your office:

    Herald, deliver your proclamation!

HERALD This is to give notice to all the king's subjects: *Reads*

5   'The late Lord Cromwell, Lord Chancellor of England, vicar general over the realm,

    him to hold and esteem as a traitor against the crown and dignity of England: so

    God save the king.'

GARDINER Amen.

BEDFORD Amen: and root thee from the land,

10   For whilst thou liv'st truth cannot stand.

NORFOLK Make a lane there, the traitor's at hand.

    Keep back Cromwell's men:

    Drown them if they come on.— Sergeant, your office.

Enter Cromwell, they make a lane with their halberds

15   CROMWELL What means my lord of Norfolk by these words?

    Sirs, come along.

GARDINER Kill them, if they come on.

SERGEANT Lord Cromwell, in King Henry's name,

    I do arrest your honour of high treason.

CROMWELL Sergeant, me of treason?   *Cromwell's men offer to draw*

20   SUFFOLK Kill them, if they draw a sword.

CROMWELL Hold: I charge you, as you love me, draw not a sword.

    Who dares accuse Cromwell of treason now?

GARDINER This is no place to reckon up your crime:

    Your dove-like looks were viewed with serpent's eyes.

25   CROMWELL With serpent's eyes, indeed, by thine they were!

    But, Gardiner, do thy worst, I fear thee not.

    My faith, compared with thine, as much shall pass

    As doth the diamond excel the glass.

    Attached of treason, no accusers by!

30   Indeed, what tongue dares speak so foul a lie?

[5.3] *Location: Lambeth* **Halberts** soldiers bearing halberds, a long weapon which was a combination of spear and battle-axe **5 vicar general** despite not being a clergyman, Cromwell had been appointed to this post of deputy to a bishop or archbishop in 1535 **9 root thee** root you out, remove you **29 Attached of** arrested for

NORFOLK   My lord, my lord, matters are too well known,
And it is time the king had note thereof.

CROMWELL   The king! Let me go to him face to face:
No better trial I desire than that.

35   Let him but say that Cromwell's faith was feigned,
Then let my honour and my name be stained.
If ever my heart against my king was set,
O let my soul in judgement answer it:
Then, if my faith's confirmed with his reason,

40   Gainst whom hath Cromwell, then, committed treason?

SUFFOLK   My lord, your matter shall be tried;
Meantime, with patience content yourself.

CROMWELL   Perforce I must with patience be content.
O, dear friend Bedford, dost thou stand so near?

45   Cromwell rejoiceth one friend sheds a tear.
And whither is't? Which way must Cromwell now?

GARDINER   My lord, you must unto the Tower.
Lieutenant, take him to your charge.

CROMWELL   Well, where you please; yet before I part,

50   Let me confer a little with my men.

GARDINER   As you go by water, so you shall.

CROMWELL   I have some business present to impart.

NORFOLK   You may not stay. Lieutenant, take your charge.

CROMWELL   Well, well, my lord, you second Gardiner's text.

55   Norfolk, farewell: thy turn will be the next.   *Exit Cromwell and the*

GARDINER   His guilty conscience makes him rave, my lord.   *Lieutenant*

NORFOLK   Ay, let him talk; his time is short enough.

GARDINER   My lord of Bedford, come; you weep for him,
That would not shed half a tear for you.

60   BEDFORD   It grieves me for to see his sudden fall.

GARDINER   Such success wish I to traitors still.   *Exeunt*

[Act 5 Scene 4]

Enter two Citizens

FIRST CITIZEN   Why, can this news be true? Is't possible?
The great Lord Cromwell arrested upon treason!
I hardly will believe it can be so.

SECOND CITIZEN   It is too true, sir; would it were otherwise,

---

43 Perforce by the threat of force/of necessity   **54 second** echo   **55 Norfolk...next** Thomas Howard, third Duke of Norfolk, was the uncle of both Anne Bullen and Catherine Howard; after Catherine's execution he was arrested and imprisoned in the Tower of London but Henry died the day before he was to be executed. His sentence was commuted and he was eventually released and his dukedom restored by Queen Mary I   *Lieutenant* the Quarto exit direction presumably refers to the character called 'Sergeant-at-arms' earlier in the scene, but may indicate that this is the same character as the Lieutenant of the Tower in Act 5 scene 5   **61 still** on every occasion/secretly   **[5.4]**   *Location: a London street*

5   Condition I spent half the wealth I had.

I was at Lambeth, saw him there arrested,

And afterward committed to the Tower.

FIRST CITIZEN What, was't for treason that he was committed?

SECOND CITIZEN Kind, noble gentleman! I may rue the time.

10   All that I have, I did enjoy by him,

And if he die, then all my state is gone.

FIRST CITIZEN It may be doubted that he shall not die,

Because the king did favour him so much.

SECOND CITIZEN O sir, you are deceived in thinking so.

15   The grace and favour he had with the king

Hath caused him have so many enemies:

He that in court secure will keep himself,

Must not be great, for then he is envied at.

The shrub is safe, whenas the cedar shakes;

20   For where the king doth love above compare,

Of others they as much more envied are.

FIRST CITIZEN 'Tis pity that this noble man should fall,

He did so many charitable deeds.

SECOND CITIZEN 'Tis true, and yet you see in each estate,

25   There's none so good, but someone doth him hate.

And they before would smile him in the face,

Will be the foremost to do him disgrace:

What, will you go along unto the court?

FIRST CITIZEN I care not if I do, and hear the news,

30   How men will judge what shall become of him.

SECOND CITIZEN Some will speak hardly, some will speak in pity.

Go you to the court, I'll unto the city:

There I am sure to hear more news than you.

FIRST CITIZEN Why, then, soon will we meet again.   *Exeunt*

[Act 5 Scene 5]

Enter Cromwell in the Tower

CROMWELL Now, Cromwell, hast thou time to meditate,

And think upon thy state, and of the time.

Thy honours came unsought, Ay, and unlooked for:

Thy fall as sudden, and unlooked for too.

5   What glory was in England that I had not?

Who in this land commanded more than Cromwell?

Except the king who greater than myself?

But now I see, what after ages shall:

9 rue regret   **19 whenas** when/whereas   **cedar** a tall, stately tree; an unimportant person is like a **shrub** that will survive a storm when a tall tree like a cedar is destroyed   **31 hardly** harshly   **[5.5]** *Location: a room in the Tower of London*

The greater man, more sudden is their fall.

10 And now do I remember the Earl of Bedford

Was very desirous for to speak to me,

And afterward sent to me a letter,

The which I think I have still in my pocket.

Now may I read it, for I now have leisure,

15 And this I take it is: *He reads the letter*

'My lord, come not this night to Lambeth,

For if you do, your state is overthrown,

And much I doubt your life, and if you come;

Then if you love yourself, stay where you are.'

20 O God! Had I but read this letter,

Then had I been free from the lion's paw:

Deferring this to read until tomorrow,

I spurned at joy, and did embrace my sorrow.

Enter the Lieutenant of the Tower and Officers [including executioner]

Now, master Lieutenant, when's this day of death?

25 LIEUTENANT   Alas, my lord, would I might never see it.

Here are the Dukes of Suffolk and of Norfolk,

Winchester, Bedford, and Sir Richard Ratcliffe,

With others, but why they come I know not.

CROMWELL   No matter wherefore, Cromwell is prepared:

30 For Gardiner has my state and life ensnared.

Bid them come in, or you shall do them wrong,

For here stands he, whom some thinks lives too long.

Learning kills learning, and instead of ink

To dip his pen, Cromwell's heart blood doth drink.

Enter all the nobles

35 NORFOLK   Good morrow, Cromwell. What, alone, so sad?

CROMWELL   One good among you, none of you are bad:

For my part, it best fits me be alone,

Sadness with me, not I with anyone.

What, is the king acquainted with my cause?

40 NORFOLK   We have, and he hath answered us, my lord.

CROMWELL   How, shall I come to speak with him myself?

GARDINER   The king is so advertised of your guilt,

He will by no means admit you to his presence.

CROMWELL   No way admit me? Am I so soon forgot?

45 Did he but yesterday embrace my neck,

And said that Cromwell was even half himself,

And is his princely ears so much bewitched

With scandalous ignomy, and slanderous speeches,

---

18 much I doubt I greatly fear   **21 lion's paw** lion's foot used to catch and kill its prey; the **lion** was a traditional symbol of royalty   **23 spurned at** treated with contempt/rejected   **29 wherefore** why   **33 Learning kills learning** educated men (such as Gardiner) are responsible for the deaths of other educated men/true knowledge   **42 advertised** well aware/warned   **48 ignomy** shortened form of 'ignominy' meaning 'dishonour, disgrace'

That now he doth deny to look on me?

50 Well, my lord of Winchester, no doubt but you

Are much in favour with his majesty:

Will you bear a letter from me to his grace?

GARDINER   Pardon me, I'll bear no traitor's letters.

CROMWELL   Ha! Will you do this kindness then? Tell him

55 By word of mouth, what I shall say to you?

GARDINER   That will I.

CROMWELL   But, on your honour, will you?

GARDINER   Ay, on my honour.

CROMWELL   Bear witness, lords.—

60 Tell him when he hath known you,

And tried your faith but half so much as mine,

He'll find you to be the falsest-hearted man

In England. Pray, tell him this.

BEDFORD   Be patient, good my lord, in these extremes.

65 CROMWELL   My kind and honourable lord of Bedford,

I know your honour always loved me well:

But, pardon me, this still shall be my theme;

Gardiner is the cause makes Cromwell so extreme.

Sir Ralph Sadler, pray, a word with you:

70 You were my man, and all that you possess

Came by my means: to requite all this,

Will you take this letter here of me,

And give it with your own hands to the king?

SADLER   I kiss your hand, and never will I rest,

75 Ere to the king this will be delivered.   *Exit Sadler*

CROMWELL   Why yet Cromwell hath one friend in store.

GARDINER   But all the haste he makes shall be but vain.—

Here's a discharge for your prisoner,

To see him executed presently.—

80 My lord, you hear the tenor of your life.

CROMWELL   I do embrace it, welcome my last date,

And of this glistering world I take last leave:

And, noble lords, I take my leave of you –

As willingly I go to meet with death,

85 As Gardiner did pronounce it with his breath:

From treason is my heart as white as snow,

My death only procurèd by my foe.

I pray, commend me to my sovereign king,

And tell him in what sort his Cromwell died,

90 To lose his head before his cause were tried.

But let his grace, when he shall hear my name,

---

64 extremes dire straits   **75 Ere** before   **78 discharge** release from custody or perhaps exoneration from blame for the Lieutenant   **79 presently**
immediately   **80 tenor** meaning, effect   **82 glistering** glittering, brilliant

Say only this: Gardiner procured the same.

Enter young Cromwell

LIEUTENANT   Here is your son, come to take his leave.

CROMWELL   To take his leave! Come hither, Harry Cromwell.

95   Mark, boy, the last words that I speak to thee.

Flatter not fortune, neither fawn upon her;

Gape not for state, yet lose no spark of honour;

Ambition, like the plague see thou eschew it;

I die for treason, boy, and never knew it.

100   Yet let thy faith as spotless be as mine,

And Cromwell's virtues in thy face shall shine.

Come, go along and see me leave my breath,

And I'll leave thee upon the flower of death.

SON   O, father, I shall die to see that wound:

105   Your blood being spilt will make my heart to sound.

CROMWELL   How, boy, not look upon the axe!

How shall I do then to have my head stroke off?

Come on, my child, and see the end of all,

And after say that Gardiner was my fall.

110 GARDINER   My lord, you speak it of an envious heart;

I have done no more than law and equity.

BEDFORD   O, good my lord of Winchester, forbear:

It would 'a better seemed you to been absent,

Than with your words disturb a dying man.

115 CROMWELL   Who me, my lord? No, he disturbs not me.

My mind he stirs not, though his mighty shock

Hath brought mo' peers' heads down to the block.

Farewell, my boy! All Cromwell can bequeath,

My hearty blessing: so I take my leave.

120 HANGMAN   I am your death's man: pray, my lord, forgive me.

CROMWELL   Even with my soul. Why, man, thou art my doctor,

And brings me precious physic for my soul.—

My lord of Bedford, I desire of you

Before my death, a corporal embrace.   *Bedford comes to him,*

125   Farewell, great lord, my love I do commend: *Cromwell embraces him*

My heart to you, my soul to heaven I send.

This is my joy that, ere my body fleet,

Your honoured arms is my true winding-sheet.

Farewell, dear Bedford, my peace is made in heaven.

---

94 Harry Cromwell Thomas Cromwell's son was in fact called Gregory, calling him Harry suggests a compliment to the king; Gregory Cromwell was married to Elizabeth Seymour, sister of Queen Jane Seymour and thus a cousin of Edward VI: he became first Baron Cromwell   **97 Gape not** do not be eager to obtain   **98 eschew** avoid   **99 never knew it** was never acquainted with it, i.e. I'm completely innocent   **111 equity** fairness, impartiality **112 forbear** desist, refrain (from speaking)   **113 It…you** it would have been more becoming on your part   **116 shock** opposition   **117 mo'** more **120 HANGMAN** Cromwell was in fact beheaded on Tower Hill; 'Hangman' was sometimes used to mean 'executioner'   **I…me** it was customary for the executioner to ask pardon   **122 physic** medicine   **127 ere** before   **fleet** passes away/vanishes   **128 winding-sheet** sheet in which a corpse is wrapped for burial, shroud

130	Thus falls great Cromwell a poor ell in length,
	To rise to unmeasured height, winged with new strength,
	The land of worms which dying men discover,
	My soul is shrined with heaven's celestial cover.

Exit Cromwell and the
Officers, and others

BEDFORD   Well, farewell, Cromwell, the truest friend,

135   That ever Bedford shall possess again.—
Well, lords, I fear, when this man is dead,
You'll wish in vain that Cromwell had a head.

Enter one with Cromwell's head

OFFICER   Here is the head of the deceased Cromwell.

BEDFORD   Pray thee, go hence, and bear his head away

140   Unto his body: inter them both in clay.

Enter Sir Ralph Sadler

SADLER   How now, my lords: what, is Lord Cromwell dead?

BEDFORD   Lord Cromwell's body now doth want a head.

SADLER   O God! A little speed had saved his life.
Here is a kind reprieve come from the king,

145   To bring him straight unto his majesty.

SUFFOLK   Ay, ay, Sir Ralph, reprieves comes now too late.

GARDINER   My conscience now tells me this deed was ill:
Would Christ that Cromwell were alive again.

NORFOLK   Come, let us to the king, whom well I know,

150   Will grieve for Cromwell that his death was so.

Exeunt omnes

FINIS

Textual Notes

Q = Quarto of 1602

Ed = a correction introduced by a later editor

List of parts = Ed

1.1.8 coil = Ed. Q = quile

1.2.26 walking = Q. Ed = talking   **56 can** = Ed. Q = con

Act 2 Chorus 1 is = Ed. *Not in* Q

2.1.9 Frankfurt *spelled* Frankford *in* Q   **13 haply** *spelled* hapilie *in* Q

2.2.72 travel *spelled* travaile *in* Q   **83 But't** = Ed. Q = But   **89 nuncheons** = Ed. Q = unchines
103 good = Ed. Q = God

2.3.15 By'r'lady *spelled* birladie *in* Q   **53 SH BOWSER** = Ed. *Speech continued by the Governor in* Q
57 these jewels = Ed. Q = the solewels   **80 seized** *spelled* zeased *in* Q

---

130 poor ell mere measuring rod; an **ell** was a measure of length, in England of forty-five inches, i.e. just under four feet, which would be rather short for a man's body even without the head   **133 shrined** containing a shrine   **140 inter…clay** bury them (head and torso) together in the earth; in fact Cromwell's head was boiled and then set upon a spike on London Bridge (the usual custom with traitors)   **143 had** would have   **144 kind reprieve** dramatic device rather than historical fact; Henry was indeed said to have regretted the loss of one of his most able and faithful servants but not until about eight months later

2.5.110 an't = Ed. Q = ante   **113 whither** *spelled* whether *in* Q

Act 3 Chorus 14 there = Ed. Q = where

3.1.5 formal = Ed. Q = former   **30, 35 banquet** *spelled* banket *in* Q   **48 English** = Ed. Q = Spaniards
   68 An't = Ed. Q = And   **96 winner** *spelled* winer *in* Q   **109 ne'er** *spelled* neare *in* Q

4.3.19 blue *spelled* blew *in* Q

4.5.20 your = Ed. Q = you   **44 also** = Ed. Q = upon   **72 an't** = Ed. Q = and

SIR THOMAS MORE

It begins on the street, nastily. An immigrant has got his hands on an English woman. Trouble is brewing. Then there is a dispute about money, involving a 'Lombard' – the identification originally applied to immigrants from Lombardy in northern Italy, famous for its banking, but it had gradually become a term of abuse for all foreigners engaged in trade or banking, a word bandied around in the same way as 'Jew'. Doll, the lusty London woman who has been hauled by the arm, sums up the popular sentiment of the day: 'I am ashamed that freeborn Englishmen, having beaten strangers within their own homes, should thus be braved and abused by them at home.' In other words: we won the war overseas, but now the foreigners ('strangers') are coming over here, taking our jobs and our women.

Before long, London is burning. Order has broken down and the people have taken the law into their own hands. The mob mentality calls it rough justice. The ringleader is one John Lincoln:

> Then, gallant bloods, you whose free souls do scorn
> To bear th'enforcèd wrongs of aliens,
> Add rage to resolution, fire the houses
> Of these audacious strangers. This is St Martin's,
> And yonder dwells Mutas, a wealthy Picard,
> At the Green Gate,
> De Bard, Peter Van Hollocke, Adrian Martine,
> With many more outlandish fugitives.
> Shall these enjoy more privilege than we
> In our own country? Let's, then, become their slaves.
> Since justice keeps not them in greater awe,
> We'll be ourselves rough ministers at law.

The scene can be as readily imagined in the early sixteenth century, when the play is set, the early seventeenth, when it seems to have been written and rewritten, and the early twenty-first, in which it has been re-edited, revived on stage and justly admired.

On May Day 1517 London witnessed the worst race riot of the age. A mob of over a thousand angry young men and women gathered near St Paul's and tore through the City, destroying property and assaulting anyone who stood in their path. Most were poor labourers or apprentices. They broke into Newgate Prison, freeing inmates who had been detained for attacking foreigners. The riot was brought to a temporary halt when the charismatic Under-sheriff of London, Sir Thomas More, confronted the crowd. But soon they went on the rampage again, trashing foreign-owned small businesses and demanding the deportation of immigrants.

In the final years of Queen Elizabeth's reign, Shakespeare dramatized the encounter between More and the crowd as his contribution to this multi-authored comi-tragedy, which has a complicated history of collaboration and revision (discussed at length in our essay on 'Authorship and Attribution'). He gave More a powerful speech asking the crowd to put themselves into the position of the outsider, to imagine what it would be like to be 'the wretched strangers, / Their babies at their backs, with their poor luggage / Plodding to th'ports and coasts for transportation'. But even with More's subsequent lines about the king as God's representative on earth and the need for the people to show absolute obedience, the subject matter was too hot to handle.

The play had already been refused permission for staging, unless major revisions were undertaken: 'Leave out the insurrection wholly', wrote Master of the Revels Edmund Tilney on the manuscript, 'with the cause thereof, and begin with Sir Thomas More at the Mayor's sessions with a report afterwards of his good service done, being Sheriff of London, upon a mutiny against the Lombards only by a short report and not otherwise, at your own peril.' As far as we know, even with the revisions, the play was never staged. Shakespeare's scene remained unknown for two centuries. By good fortune, the prompter's master-copy – known as the 'book' – was preserved and later rediscovered. The inserted scene, in the original holograph that scholars call 'Hand D', is the only surviving example of a working manuscript in Shakespeare's hand. Now held in the British Library in London, these three pages are among the most precious literary documents in the world.

One can readily understand why Shakespeareans often look at the scene in isolation (we transcribed and edited it in our *RSC Complete Works* edition). But in approaching Shakespeare as collaborator, we must place it in context. For one thing, it fits seamlessly into the play. For another, it is probably not Shakespeare's only intervention in the script. And besides, taken as a whole, the play is a riveting piece of theatre, as has been seen in a number of modern revivals – at the Nottingham Playhouse in 1964 with a young Ian McKellen in the title role, in Bristol and London in 1980 by a company called the Poor Players directed by future RSC Artistic Director Gregory Doran, and in 2005 on the stage of the Swan theatre in Stratford-upon-Avon.

The role of More, six times the length of the second-biggest part, is one of the largest in the entire repertoire of Elizabethan and Jacobean drama. It calls for an actor of great versatility: we see him commanding both a crowd and a council chamber, meditating in soliloquy and taking rapid action, philosophizing and philanthropizing. He is a prankster, a Christian and a voice of reason, truly the wisest fool in Christendom (though it is disappointing that his encounter with his great fellow-philosopher and wit, Erasmus of Rotterdam, comes to so little). If, as seems likely, the Shakespearean intervention in the script was intended for a production by the Lord Chamberlain's Men, then one can see why they wanted to stage the play: it would have been a magnificent showcase for their lead tragedian and Shakespeare's intimate friend Richard Burbage.

As a tragedy, *Sir Thomas More* belongs beside the Chamberlain's Men's *Thomas Lord Cromwell* and Shakespeare and Fletcher's *Henry VIII* as the story of the rise and fall of a royal counsellor in the turbulent time of the English Reformation. More ascends from Sheriff of London to Lord Chancellor, but falls from the king's favour when he refuses to participate in the process of enacting the break from Rome. It's a satisfying arc: we get a full ascendancy, a brief period of power and favour, and then a slow descent to the execution. The moments of More's career chosen to illustrate this movement are well chosen, oscillating between his most public appearances (the May Day riots, his execution) and private ones (his conversation with Erasmus, his defence of his position to his family). In balancing character and plot, the dramatists create a coherent portrait that, ultimately, goes to show the fickleness of favour and the cost of piety. In the closing scenes, we see him preparing for death with dignity and grace. Whereas the usual scenario in such dramas places the condemned man alone in his cell, sometimes in conversation with his keeper, here we also witness More's farewell to his family. He is seen as a husband and parent, not just a holy man and a politician.

As in *Thomas Lord Cromwell*, Henry VIII is kept resolutely offstage. Since we do not see the king, we do not hear his point of view. The power of the state is represented not in the monarch but in the figure of Downes, who only opens his mouth to announce More's arrest. We therefore identify much more with More's Catholic integrity than the official Reformation line. One key difference from *Cromwell*, apart from the fact that More remained loyal to his Roman faith whereas Cromwell was the chief architect of the new Protestantism, is that the action proceeds without a strong antagonist working against the hero: there is no equivalent of *Cromwell*'s Bishop Gardiner.

It may partly have been because the role of More is so demanding that the dramatists introduced a play-within-the-play halfway through, allowing him to rest a little and become a passive spectator instead of a continually active player. At the same time, *The Marriage of Wit and Wisdom* serves as an enactment of More's own virtues: he was revered for precisely this combination of qualities. Every bit as much as 'Pyramus and Thisbe' in *A Midsummer Night's Dream*, 'The Mousetrap' in *Hamlet* and Hieronimo's production of 'Soliman and Perseda' in *The Spanish Tragedy*, this interlude provides fascinating insights into the stagecraft of early touring players. Luggins has run to get a beard, one boy-actor is down to play three parts, and Wit is required to improvise to match More's interruptions. In a very Shakespearean way, the inclusion of a play-within-the-play is a reminder that we are all players on this great stage of the world. As More puts it in the very final scene, 'my offence to his highness makes me of a state pleader a stage player (though I am old, and have a bad voice) to act this last scene of my tragedy'.

As well as creating a genuine tragic hero out of Sir Thomas More, the play presents history from the ground up. The ordinary citizens are more fully realized and individualized than in most Elizabethan dramas of this kind. Doll Williamson is as good a part as Doll Tearsheet in *Henry IV Part 2*. There are touches of uniquely Shakespearean genius in his contribution: Lincoln manages to turn even vegetables into a form of racial abuse ('They bring in strange roots, which is merely to the undoing of poor prentices, for what's a sorry parsnip to a good heart?'), while Doll gives an instantaneous back-story to the people's affection for More by recalling that 'a keeps a plentiful shrievalty, and a made my brother Arthur Watchins sergeant Safe's yeoman'. But in Munday's original script the bit parts such as Faulkner, Randall and Lifter are also sympathetically drawn. Even the nameless Warders and Woman of the final act are surprisingly fleshed out.

Equally, even before Shakespeare's intervention, the riot scenes of the first two acts are a source of genuine excitement. Picking up on similar scenes in Shakespeare's *Henry VI Part 2* (the Jack Cade sequence) and the anonymous play of *Jack Straw*, they allow rioting citizens to both air their grievances and condemn themselves with their foolishness. Lincoln is a complicated anti-hero, seemingly noble at first, then succumbing to more base demands, before being allowed a fine gallows speech. The bustle of these scenes is expertly drawn and this gives all the more impact to More's great oration, with its balance between empathy for the outsider and the need to respect the rule of law.*

The language of More's address to the crowd towers over the play. As suggested in our general introduction, no one but Shakespeare could have invented such images as 'in ruff of your opinions clothed', a metaphor that is utterly characteristic in itself clothing an abstract idea in material dress, or 'For other ruffians ... / Would shark on you, and men like ravenous fishes / Would feed on one another', with its – again, deeply characteristic – device of creating poetic energy by turning a noun into a verb. But there is some beautiful poetry elsewhere in the play, particularly in More's reflections on his own rise and fall. The soliloquy at the pivotal point in the third act ('It is in heaven

---

* Several points in this overview of the play's qualities are owed to Peter Kirwan.

that I am thus and thus'), though written in the hand of the playhouse scribe, has all the hallmarks of a further Shakespearean addition, probably written in for the sake of strengthening Burbage's part still further. 'Prerogative and tithe of knees' and 'the smooth and dexter way' are fine examples of Shakespeare's favoured doubling device known in rhetoric as hendiadysis, while a phrase such as 'humble bench of birth', together with images of blood turned to corruption and of 'serpents' natures', has the feel of mature Shakespeare, as does the climactic image-cluster that winds together several terms out of the language of weaving ('thread ... spun ... / A bottom greatly wound up greatly undone' – a 'bottom' is a ball of thread or the clew on which the thread is wound, from which Shakespeare got the name for Bottom the weaver in *A Midsummer Night's Dream*).

The exact circumstances in which Shakespeare made his contribution to *Sir Thomas More* will never be known, though scholars now lean strongly to the view that he did so when at the height of his powers in the early 1600s, not in a prior stage of his career, as was once supposed. But, whatever the date and context, an overwhelming body of internal evidence, in the form of unique marks of orthography, spelling, vocabulary and literary technique, attests that the so-called 'Hand D' in the manuscript is truly his. This is Shakespeare in the act of composition, writing rapidly, occasionally changing a word or scratching out a line, mining his capacious imagination and minting his incomparable poetic imagery. But it is also Shakespeare the collaborator, building on the work of other dramatists and contributing to a magnificent team effort.

KEY FACTS

AUTHORSHIP: The presence of seven hands has been identified in the manuscript. The original version appears to have been written by Anthony Munday (Hand S), while scholarly consensus suggests that the additions are by Henry Chettle (Hand A), Thomas Heywood (Hand B), a playhouse scribe (Hand C), William Shakespeare (Hand D) and Thomas Dekker (Hand E). The final hand is that of Edmund Tilney, Master of the Revels, who requests several changes to the plot. The identification of Shakespeare with Hand D was first made in 1871 by Richard Simpson and was enthusiastically embraced in the early twentieth century. It has been recently questioned by scholars including Ward Elliott and Robert J. Valenza, but is popularly accepted as the only remaining fragment of dramatic writing in Shakespeare's own hand.

PLOT: Thomas More, a Sheriff of London, is called upon to quell the May Day riots, in which a group of working men and apprentices have taken up arms in protest against the liberties taken by French immigrants with their money and women. More calms the riot, and is promoted to the post of Lord High Chancellor. The pious and witty More demonstrates his justice, generosity and hospitality on a number of occasions, particularly in his charity to the poor and hospitality towards the great, including the famous Erasmus. However, More refuses to sign certain papers passed down from King Henry VIII, as a result of which More is stripped of his position and imprisoned in the Tower of London. Refusing to recant, and maintaining his witty piety to the end, he is executed, to the protests of the common people.

MAJOR PARTS: Thomas More (38%/170/12), The Earl of Surrey (6%/35/10), Doll Williamson (4%/31/4), The Earl of Shrewsbury (4%/27/8), John Lincoln (4%/25/4), Lady More (3%/33/4), Inclination (3%/21/1), Suresby (3%/19/1), Faulkner (3%/31/1), Sheriff (2%/21/4), Lord Mayor (2%/19/4), Clown (2%/18/4), Roper (2%/17/4), Lifter (2%/17/1), Wit (2%/14/1), Palmer (2%/13/3).

▷

LINGUISTIC MEDIUM: 83% verse, 17% prose.

DATE: Both the date of the original version of the play and the revised version with Additions have been hotly contested. While a longstanding school of thought dated the original to 1592, coinciding with the May Day riots of the previous year, this edition follows more recent studies (particularly those of John Jowett) in arguing that the original text was part of a group of plays about Henry VIII's chief counsellors written c.1600 (of which *Thomas Lord Cromwell* is another). On stylistic grounds, the Additions were likely written c.1604.

SOURCES: The play draws on multiple sources for its episodic presentation of the well-known true story of More. Holinshed's *Chronicles* (1587) provides the basis for the May Day riots. John Foxe's *Acts and Monuments* contributes several episodes, including that of the long-haired ruffian, and Nicholas Harpsfield's *Life* was a primary biographical source, drawing on materials including the biography written by More's son-in-law (and character in the play), Roper.

TEXT: *The Booke of Sir Thomas More* survives only in manuscript, now held at the British Library. It provides one of the most fascinating examples of a working dramatic document, with several pieces of paper pasted together in a rough semblance of order, and copious revisions, deletions and insertions.

THE BOOK OF SIR THOMAS MORE [by Anthony Munday and Henry Chettle, revised by Henry Chettle, Thomas Dekker, Thomas Heywood and William Shakespeare]

Thomas MORE, Sheriff of London, later Sir Thomas, Lord Chancellor
LADY MORE, his wife
Master ROPER, More's son-in-law
ROPER'S WIFE, More's elder daughter
More's younger DAUGHTER

GOUGH
CATESBY
RANDALL
Ned BUTLER
Robin BREWER   } members of More's household
Giles PORTER
Ralph HORSEKEEPER
SERVINGMAN

Earl of SHREWSBURY
Earl of SURREY
Sir Thomas PALMER
Sir Roger CHOLMLEY
Dr John Fisher, Bishop of ROCHESTER
SIR JOHN Munday, an alderman
DOWNES, a Sergeant-at-Arms
CROFTS, the king's messenger

ERASMUS of Rotterdam, scholar and friend of More

LORD MAYOR of London
LADY MAYORESS, his wife
SURESBY, a Justice
ANOTHER JUSTICE
RECORDER
LIFTER, a cutpurse

Smart, plaintiff against him
TWO SHERIFFS of London
OFFICERS
MESSENGERS
CLERK of the Privy Council

John LINCOLN, a broker, leader of the rebels

GEORGE Betts
Ralph Betts, the CLOWN, his brother
WILLIAMSON, a carpenter
DOLL, his wife
SHERWIN, a goldsmith
Francis DE BARD, a Lombard
CAVALER, another Lombard
HARRY, ROBIN, KIT and other Apprentices
MORRIS, secretary to the Bishop of Winchester
Jack FAULKNER, his servant
A poor WOMAN

PLAYER
INCLINATION
PROLOGUE   } Lord Cardinal's Players
WIT
LADY VANITY
LUGGINS

LIEUTENANT of the Tower
THREE WARDERS of the Tower
GENTLEMAN PORTER of the Tower
HANGMAN

Lords, Gentlemen, Guard, Attendants

[Act 1 Scene 1]

Enter, at one end, John Lincoln, with the two Bettses [George and Ralph, the Clown]
together. At the other end enters Francis de [Bard and Doll,] a lusty woman, he haling her
by the arm

DOLL   Whither wilt thou hale me?

BARD   Whither I please: thou art my prize and I plead purchase of thee.

DOLL   Purchase of me? Away, ye rascal! I am an honest plain carpenter's wife
and though I have no beauty to like a husband, yet whatsoever is mine scorns to
5   stoop to a stranger. Hand off, then, when I bid thee!

BARD   Go with me quietly, or I'll compel thee.

DOLL   Compel me, ye dog's face! Thou think'st thou hast the goldsmith's wife
in hand, whom thou enticed'st from her husband with all his plate, and when thou
turned'st her home to him again, mad'st him, like an ass, pay for his wife's board.

10   BARD   So will I make thy husband too, if please me.

Enter Cavaler with a pair of doves, Williamson the carpenter and Sherwin following him

DOLL   Here he comes himself; tell him so, if thou dar'st.

CAVALER   Follow me no further; I say thou shalt not have them.

WILLIAMSON   I bought them in Cheapside, and paid my money for them.

SHERWIN   He did, sir, indeed, and you offer him wrong, both to take them from him,
15   and not restore him his money neither.

CAVALER   If he paid for them, let it suffice that I possess them: beef and brewis may
serve such hinds. Are pigeons meat for a coarse carpenter?

LINCOLN   It is hard when Englishmen's patience must be thus jetted on by strangers,
and they not dare to revenge their own wrongs.

20   GEORGE   Lincoln, let's beat them down, and bear no more of these abuses.

LINCOLN   We may not, Betts: be patient, and hear more.

DOLL   How now, husband? What, one stranger take thy food from thee, and
another thy wife! By our Lady, flesh and blood, I think, can hardly brook that.

LINCOLN   Will this gear never be otherwise? Must these wrongs be thus endured?

25   GEORGE   Let us step in, and help to revenge their injury.

BARD   What art thou that talk'st of revenge? My lord ambassador shall once
more make your Mayor have a check, if he punish thee for this saucy presumption.

WILLIAMSON   Indeed, my Lord Mayor, on the ambassador's complaint, sent me to
Newgate one day, because (against my will) I took the wall of a stranger. You may do
30   anything; the goldsmith's wife and mine now must be at your commandment.

GEORGE   The more patient fools are ye both to suffer it.

[1.1] *Original Text (Munday). Location: A London Street, the week before Easter 1517* **lusty** strong, vigorous   **haling** dragging, pulling
2 purchase of thee you as booty/I've bought you   **3 plain** common, ordinary/straightforward/blunt, outspoken/not beautiful; perhaps punning on 'plane',
a tool of her husband's trade as carpenter   **4 like** please   **5 Hand off** take your hand off me – the singular was possible   **7 goldsmith's...board** an incident
reported in Holinshed's chronicle, although neither the name nor the husband's trade is given   **8 plate** tableware, especially of gold or silver   **10 if please
me** if I want; omission of 'it' was grammatically possible but may be designed to suggest he's foreign   *Cavaler* the name suggests 'a quibbling disputant'
(caviller) and is derived from the Italian Cavallari or Cavalieri, named simply as a merchant from Lucca in Holinshed in which the incident concerned a
Frenchman not a Lombard   **13 Cheapside** the City of London's main food market   **14 offer** do   **16 brewis** broth   **17 hinds** servants/peasants   **meat**
food, punning on 'meet' appropriate; **pigeons,** originally bred for the table, were considered a delicacy   **coarse** base, common   **18 jetted on** walked all
over   **22 stranger** foreigner   **23 our Lady** i.e. the Virgin Mary   **brook** tolerate, put up with   **24 gear** business/manners, doings/rubbish   **27 Mayor** i.e.
the Lord Mayor of London   **check** rebuke, reprimand   **29 Newgate** a London prison, built on the site of one of the gates in the Roman London Wall   **took
the wall** took precedence and hence showed disrespect by walking on the inner side of the path next to the wall

BARD   Suffer it! Mend it thou or he, if ye can or dare. I tell thee, fellow, an she were the Mayor of London's wife, had I her once in my possession, I would keep her in spite of him that durst say nay.

35   GEORGE   I tell thee, Lombard, these words should cost thy best cap, were I not curbed by duty and obedience: the Mayor of London's wife! O God, shall it be thus?

DOLL   Why, Betts, am not I as dear to my husband as my Lord Mayor's wife to him? And wilt thou so neglectly suffer thine own shame?— Hands off, proud stranger or, by him that bought me, if men's milky hearts dare not strike a stranger,

40   yet women beat them down, ere they bear these abuses.

BARD   Mistress, I say you shall along with me.

DOLL   Touch not Doll Williamson, lest she lay thee along on God's dear earth.— (*To Cavaler*) And you, sir, that allow such coarse cates to carpenters, whilst pigeons, which they pay for, must serve your dainty appetite, deliver them back to my

45   husband again, or I'll call so many women to mine assistance as will not leave one inch untorn of thee: if our husbands must be bridled by law, and forced to bear your wrongs, their wives will be a little lawless, and soundly beat ye.

CAVALER   Come away, De Bard, and let us go complain to my lord ambassador.

Exeunt ambo

DOLL   Ay, go, and send him among us, and we'll give him his welcome too. I

50   am ashamed that freeborn Englishmen, having beaten strangers within their own homes, should thus be braved and abused by them at home.

SHERWIN   It is not our lack of courage in the cause, but the strict obedience that we are bound to. I am the goldsmith whose wrongs you talked of, but how to redress yours or mine own is a matter beyond our abilities.

55   LINCOLN   Not so, not so, my good friends: I, though a mean man, a broker by profession, and named John Lincoln, have long time winked at these vile enormities with mighty impatience, and, as these two brethren here (Betts by name) can witness, with loss of mine own life would gladly remedy them.

GEORGE   And he is in a good forwardness, I tell ye, if all hit right.

60   DOLL   As how, I prithee? Tell it to Doll Williamson.

LINCOLN   You know the Spital sermons begin the next week: I have drawn a bill of our wrongs and the strangers' insolences.

GEORGE   Which he means the preachers shall there openly publish in the pulpit.

WILLIAMSON   O, but that they would! I'faith, it would tickle our strangers thoroughly.

65   DOLL   Ay, and if you men durst not undertake it, before God, we women would. Take an honest woman from her husband! Why, it is intolerable.

SHERWIN   But how find ye the preachers affected to our proceeding?

LINCOLN   Master Doctor Standish hath answered that it becomes not him to move any such thing in his sermon, and tells us we must move the Mayor and aldermen to

32 an if   35 Lombard native of Lombardy in northern Italy, often engaged in finance, hence banker, money-changer, pawnbroker   cap head/masculine headdress: Milan in Lombardy was noted for hat-making, hence 'millinery'   38 neglectly carelessly, negligently   39 him...me Christ whose suffering redeemed the world   milky weak, timorous   40 ere before   43 cates foods, victuals   *ambo* both (Latin), i.e. De Bard and Cavaler   49 I...home a reference to the English victories in France in the Hundred Years' War (1337–1453)   55 broker middleman, agent, retailer/pimp   56 winked at closed my eyes to   57 brethren brothers   59 forwardness state of readiness/boldness/presumptuous self-confidence   hit succeeds, comes off   60 I prithee please, literally 'I pray thee'   61 Spital sermons preached at the Pulpit Cross in the precincts of the church of St Mary Spital, i.e. St Mary of the Hospital, during Easter week (20–25 April in 1517)   64 but that if only   tickle vex/provoke/chastise   68 Doctor Standish Henry Standish (c.1475–1535), a Franciscan monk, Bishop of St Asaph from 1518 and court preacher from 1515 to 1530; he was an opponent of Erasmus and humanism

70 reform it, and doubts not but happy success will ensue on statement of our wrongs. You shall perceive there's no hurt in the bill: here's a copy of it; I pray ye, hear it.

ALL   With all our hearts, for God's sake, read it.

LINCOLN   'To you all, the worshipful lords and masters of this city, that will take *Reads*

75 compassion over the poor people your neighbours, and also of the great importable hurts, losses, and hindrances, whereof proceedeth extreme poverty to all the king's subjects that inhabit within this city and suburbs of the same. For so it is that aliens and strangers eat the bread from the fatherless children, and take the living from all the artificers and the intercourse from all the merchants, whereby poverty is so much increased, that every man bewaileth the misery of other, for craftsmen

80 be brought to beggary, and merchants to neediness. Wherefore, the premises considered, the redress must be of the commons, knit and united to one part, and as the hurt and damage grieveth all men, so must all men see to their willing power for remedy, and not suffer the said aliens in their wealth, and the natural born men of this region to come to confusion.'

85 DOLL   Before God, 'tis excellent, and I'll maintain the suit to be honest.

SHERWIN   Well, say 'tis read, what is your further meaning in the matter?

GEORGE   What! Marry, list to me. No doubt but this will store us with friends enough, whose names we will closely keep in writing; and on May Day next in the morning we'll go forth a-Maying, but make it the worst May Day for the strangers

90 that ever they saw. How say ye? Do ye subscribe, or are ye faint-hearted revolters?

DOLL   Hold thee, George Betts, there's my hand and my heart. By the lord, I'll make a captain among ye, and do somewhat to be talk of forever after.

WILLIAMSON   My masters, ere we part, let's friendly go and drink together, and swear true secrecy upon our lives.

95 GEORGE   There spake an angel! Come, let us along, then.   *Exeunt*

[Act 1 Scene 2]

An arras is drawn and behind it, as in sessions, sit the Lord Mayor, Justice Suresby, and other Justices [and the Recorder], Sheriff More and the other Sheriff sitting by. Smart is the plaintiff, Lifter the prisoner at the bar

LORD MAYOR   Having dispatched our weightier businesses,

We may give ear to petty felonies.

Master Sheriff More, what is this fellow?

MORE   My lord, he stands indicted for a purse.

5 He hath been tried; the jury is together.

LORD MAYOR   Who sent him in?

SURESBY   That did I, my lord:

Had he had right, he had been hanged ere this,

73 **masters** licensed members of the trade guilds/employers/male heads of households   74 **importable** unbearable   78 **artificers** craftsmen   **intercourse** trade, business   79 **other** i.e. the others   82 **willing** wishful/ready to be of service   84 **confusion** ruin   87 **Marry** by the Virgin Mary   88 **May Day** 1 May, traditionally the first day of summer   89 **a-Maying** traditional celebrations involving going into the woods and fields to gather flowers and branches   91 **Hold** hang on, wait/take my hand   92 **somewhat** something   **talk of** a topic of conversation, talked about   **[1.2]** *Original Text (Munday). Location: London, the Court of Sessions in the Guildhall*   **arras** tapestry wall hanging   **Smart** an ironic name for a silent character   **Lifter** his name means 'thief'   2 **petty felonies** minor offences   4 **indicted...purse** charged with stealing a purse   5 **together** considering its verdict   8 **right** what he deserves, justice   **he...this** he would have been hanged before now

The only captain of the cutpurse crew.

10   LORD MAYOR   What is his name?

  SURESBY   As his profession is, Lifter, my lord,

One that can lift a purse right cunningly.

  LORD MAYOR   And is that he accuses him?

  SURESBY   The same, my lord, whom, by your honour's leave,

15   I must say somewhat too, because I find

In some respects he is well worthy blame.

  LORD MAYOR   Good Master Justice Suresby, speak your mind;

We are well pleased to give you audience.

  SURESBY   Hear me, Smart; thou art a foolish fellow,

20   If Lifter be convicted by the law,

As I see not how the jury can acquit him,

I'll stand to't thou art guilty of his death.

  MORE   My lord, that's worthy the hearing.

  LORD MAYOR   Listen, then, good Master More.

25   SURESBY   I tell thee plain, it is a shame for thee   *To Smart*

With such a sum to tempt necessity:

No less than ten pounds, sir, will serve your turn,

To carry in your purse about with ye,

To crack and brag in taverns of your money.

30   I promise ye, a man that goes abroad

With an intent of truth, meeting such a booty,

May be provoked to that he never meant.

What makes so many pilferers and felons

But such fond baits that foolish people lay

35   To tempt the needy, miserable wretch?

Ten pounds, odd money: this is a pretty sum

To bear about, which were more safe at home.

'Fore God, 'twere well to fine ye as much more   *Lord Mayor and More whisper*

To the relief of the poor prisoners,

40   To teach ye be more careful of your own.

In sooth, I say ye were but rightly served,

If ye had lost as much as twice ten pounds.

  MORE   Good my lord, soothe a point or two for once,

Only to try conclusions in this case.

45   LORD MAYOR   Content, good Master More: we'll rise awhile,

And, till the jury can return their verdict,

Walk in the garden.— How say ye, Justices?

  ALL   We like it well, my lord; we'll follow ye.   *Exeunt Lord Mayor and Justices*

  MORE   Nay, plaintiff, go you too;— and officers,   *Exit Smart*

50   Stand you aside, and leave the prisoner

---

12 right very   **26 necessity** the poor and needy   **27 serve your turn** do for you   **29 crack** boast, talk big   **31 meeting** coming across   **booty** prize   **34 fond** foolish   **36 odd money** plus small change   **41 In sooth** truly   **ye…served** you would have got your just deserts   **43 soothe** demonstrate/corroborate

To me awhile.— Lifter, come hither.   [*Exeunt all but More and Lifter*]

LIFTER   What is your worship's pleasure?

MORE   Sirrah, you know that you are known to me,

And I have often saved ye from this place,

55   Since first I came in office. Thou see'st beside,

That Justice Suresby is thy heavy friend,

By all the blame that he pretends to Smart

For tempting thee with such a sum of money.

I tell thee what; devise me but a means

60   To pick or cut his purse and on my credit

And as I am a Christian and a man,

I will procure thy pardon for that jest.

LIFTER   Good Master Shrieve, seek not my overthrow:

You know, sir, I have many heavy friends

65   And more indictments like to come upon me.

You are too deep for me to deal withal:

You are known to be one of the wisest men

That is in England: I pray ye, Master Sheriff,

Go not about to undermine my life.

70   MORE   Lifter, I am true subject to my king.

Thou much mistak'st me, and for thou shalt not think

I mean by this to hurt thy life at all,

I will maintain the act when thou hast done it.

Thou know'st there are such matters in my hands

75   As, if I pleased to give them to the jury,

I should not need this way to circumvent thee.

All that I aim at is a merry jest:

Perform it, Lifter, and expect my best.

LIFTER   I thank your worship: God preserve your life!

80   But Master Justice Suresby is gone in,

I know not how to come near where he is.

MORE   Let me alone for that, I'll be thy setter;

I'll send him hither to thee presently,

Under the colour of thine own request

85   Of private matters to acquaint him with.

LIFTER   If ye do so, sir, then let me alone:

Forty to one but then his purse is gone.

MORE   Well said, but see that thou diminish not

One penny of the money, but give it me:

90   It is the cunning act that credits thee.

LIFTER   I will, good Master Sheriff, I assure ye.   *Exit More*

---

53 **Sirrah** term of address to men or boys, expressing superiority on the part of the speaker   56 **heavy friend** enemy   63 **Shrieve** variant of 'sheriff', derived from 'shire-reeve' (county magistrate)   66 **withal** furthermore   71 **for** so that   73 **maintain** stand by, defend   76 **circumvent** use to trap   77 **merry jest** More was famous for liking practical jokes and wrote *A Merry Jest how a Sergeant would Learn to Play the Frere* (1516) in his youth   82 **setter** decoy employed by criminals to set up their victim   84 **Under the colour** on the pretext   86 **let me alone** leave it to me   87 **Forty to one** betting odds on his success

I see the purpose of this gentleman
Is but to check the folly of the justice
For blaming others in a desperate case

95   Wherein himself may fall as soon as any.
To save my life, it is a good adventure:
Silence there, ho! Now doth the Justice enter.

Enter Justice Suresby

SURESBY   Now, sirrah, now, what is your will with me?
Wilt thou discharge thy conscience like an honest man?

100   What say'st to me, sirrah? Be brief, be brief.

LIFTER   As brief, sir, as I can.—
If ye stand fair, I will be brief anon.   *Aside*

SURESBY   Speak out and mumble not, what say'st thou, sirrah?

LIFTER   Sir, I am charged, as God shall be my comfort,

105   With more than's true.

SURESBY   Sir, sir, ye are indeed, with more than's true,
For you are flatly charged with felony;
You're charged with more than truth, and that is theft;
More than a true man should be charged withal;

110   Thou art a varlet, that's no more than true.
Trifle not with me; do not, do not, sirrah;
Confess but what thou know'st, I ask no more.

LIFTER   There be, sir, there be, if't shall please your worship—

SURESBY   There be, varlet! What be there? Tell me what there be.

115   Come off or on: there be! What be there, knave?

LIFTER   There be, sir, diverse very cunning fellows,
That, while you stand and look them in the face,
Will have your purse.

SURESBY   Th'art an honest knave:

120   Tell me what are they? Where they may be caught?
Ay, those are they I look for.

LIFTER   You talk of me, sir:
Alas, I am a puny! There's one indeed
Goes by my name, he puts down all for purses

125   He'll steal your worship's purse under your nose.

SURESBY   Ha, ha! Art thou so sure, varlet?
Well, well,
Be as familiar as thou wilt, my knave,
'Tis this I long to know.

130   LIFTER   And you shall have your longing ere ye go.—
This fellow, sir, perhaps will meet ye thus,
Or thus, or thus, and in kind compliment   *Action*

---

93 check rebuke   **96 adventure** chance, opportunity   **97 Silence there, ho!** a direction addressed directly to the audience   **102 stand…anon** If you stand in the right place, I'll soon be finished   **110 varlet** rogue, rascal   **115 Come…on** get on with it   **123 puny** novice, beginner   **124 puts…purses** he's the best for stealing purses   ***Action*** meaning 'stage business' – presumably Lifter embraces Suresby or shakes his hand at this point and may even steal his purse

> Pretend acquaintance, somewhat doubtfully,
> And these embraces serve—

135 SURESBY Ay, marry, Lifter, wherefore serve they?   *Shrugging gladly*

LIFTER Only to feel
> Whether you go full under sail or no,
> Or that your lading be aboard your bark.

SURESBY In plainer English, Lifter, if my purse
140 Be stored or no?

LIFTER Ye have it, sir.

SURESBY Excellent, excellent.

LIFTER Then, sir, you cannot but for manners' sake
> Walk on with him, for he will walk your way,
145 Alleging either you have much forgot him,
> Or he mistakes you.

SURESBY But in this time has he my purse or no?

LIFTER Not yet, sir, fie!
> No, nor I have not yours.—   *Aside, as he takes Suresby's purse?*

Enter Lord Mayor, etc.

150 But now we must forbear; my lords return.

SURESBY A murrain on't! Lifter, we'll more anon:
> Ay, thou say'st true, there are shrewd knaves indeed.   *He sits down*
> But let them gull me, widgeon me, rook me, fop me!
> I'faith, i'faith, they are too short for me.
155 Knaves and fools meet when purses go:
> Wise men look to their purses well enow.

MORE Lifter, is it done?   *Aside*

LIFTER Done, Master Shrieve, and there it is.   *Aside*   **Gives purse**

MORE Then build upon my word; I'll save thy life.   *Aside*   **to More**

160 RECORDER Lifter, stand to the bar. The jury have returned thee guilty; thou must
die according to the custom.— Look to it, Master Shrieve.

LORD MAYOR Then, gentlemen, as you are wont to do,
> Because as yet we have no burial place,
> What charity your meaning's to bestow
165 Toward burial of the prisoners now condemned,
> Let it be given. There is first for me.

RECORDER And there's for me.

ANOTHER JUSTICE And me.

SURESBY Body of me, my purse is gone!

Shrugging gladly suggests he complacently shakes Lifter's embrace off   **136 Only…bark** i.e. to see whether the victim is carrying a full purse; the language is nautical   **137 full under sail** when all a ship's sails are set and it's ready to go   **138 lading** cargo, i.e. purse   **bark** ship, i.e. body   **141 Ye have it** you've got the idea   **148 fie** exclamation of indignant reproach   **149 No … yours** unclear whether Lifter is telling the truth; this may also be the signal for taking the purse (compare line 132)   **151 murrain** plague, curse; from the infectious disease of cattle   **152 shrewd** wicked/cunning   **153 gull…fop** all four verbs mean 'dupe, deceive, take in'; gull, widgeon and rook are bird names; a fop is a 'fool'   **154 short** inferior, weak   **156 enow** enough, alternative form, to rhyme with 'go' in the line above   **159 build** depend   **160 RECORDER** senior magistrate who kept a record of court proceedings   **162 wont** accustomed   **164 charity…burial** contribution toward the cost of burial   **169 Body of me** a common oath equivalent to 'on my life'

170	MORE	Gone, sir! What, here! How can that be?
	LORD MAYOR	Against all reason, sitting on the bench.
	SURESBY	Lifter, I talked with you; you have not lifted me? Ha!
	LIFTER	Suspect ye me, sir? O, what a world is this!
	MORE	But hear ye, Master Suresby, are ye sure

170 MORE   Gone, sir! What, here! How can that be?
LORD MAYOR   Against all reason, sitting on the bench.
SURESBY   Lifter, I talked with you; you have not lifted me? Ha!
LIFTER   Suspect ye me, sir? O, what a world is this!
MORE   But hear ye, Master Suresby, are ye sure
175   Ye had a purse about ye?
SURESBY   Sure, Master Shrieve! As sure as you are there,
    And in it seven pounds odd money on my faith.
MORE   Seven pounds odd money! What, were you so mad,
    Being a wise man and a magistrate,
180   To trust your purse with such a liberal sum?
    Seven pounds odd money! 'Fore God, it is a shame,
    With such a sum to tempt necessity:
    I promise ye, a man that goes abroad
    With an intent of truth, meeting such a booty,
185   May be provoked to that he never thought.
    What makes so many pilferers and felons
    But these fond baits that foolish people lay
    To tempt the needy miserable wretch?
    Should he be taken now that has your purse,
190   I'd stand to't, you are guilty of his death,
    For questionless he would be cast by law.
    'Twere a good deed to fine ye as much more,
    To the relief of the poor prisoners,
    To teach ye lock your money up at home.
195   SURESBY   Well, Master More, you are a merry man;
    I find ye, sir, I find ye well enough.
MORE   Nay, ye shall see, sir, trusting thus your money,
    And Lifter here in trial for like case,
    But that the poor man is a prisoner
200   It would be now suspected that he had it.
    Thus may ye see what mischief often comes
    By the fond carriage of such needless sums.
LORD MAYOR   Believe me, Master Suresby, this is strange,
    You, being a man so settled in assurance,
205   Will fall in that which you condemned in other.
MORE   Well, Master Suresby, there's your purse again,
    And all your money; fear nothing of More:
    Wisdom still keeps the mean and locks the door.   [*Exeunt*]

172 **lifted** robbed   177 **odd money** plus small change   180 **liberal** large   181 **'Fore...home** More repeats Suresby's speech above (1.2.25–42) almost word for word   191 **questionless** without any question   **cast by law** convicted and condemned   196 **I find ye** I understand what you're doing   202 **fond carriage** foolish carrying   204 **settled in assurance** full of conviction/sure of yourself   208 **keeps the mean** follows the middle way

[Act 1 Scene 3]

Enter the Earls of Shrewsbury and Surrey, Sir Thomas Palmer and Sir Roger Cholmley

SHREWSBURY My lord of Surrey, and Sir Thomas Palmer
    Might I with patience tempt your grave advice?
    I tell ye true, that in these dangerous times
    I do not like this frowning vulgar brow.
5   My searching eye did never entertain
    A more distracted countenance of grief
    Than I have late observed
    In the displeasèd commons of the city.
SURREY 'Tis strange that from his princely clemency,
10   So well a tempered mercy and a grace,
    To all the aliens in this fruitful land,
    That this high-crested insolence should spring
    From them that breathe from his majestic bounty,
    That, fattened with the traffic of our country,
15   Already leap into his subjects' face.
PALMER Yet Sherwin, hindered to commence his suit
    Against De Bard by the ambassador,
    By supplication made unto the king,
    Who having first enticed away his wife,
20   And got his plate, near worth four hundred pound,
    To grieve some wrongèd citizens that found
    This vile disgrace oft cast into their teeth,
    Of late sues Sherwin, and arrested him
    For money for the boarding of his wife.
25 SURREY The more knave Bard, that, using Sherwin's goods,
    Doth ask him interest for the occupation.
    I like not that, my lord of Shrewsbury:
    He's ill bested that lends a well-paced horse
    Unto a man that will not find him meat.
30 CHOLMLEY My lord of Surrey will be pleasant still.
PALMER Ay, being then employed by your honours
    To stay the broil that fell about the same,
    Where by persuasion I enforced the wrongs
    And urged the grief of the displeasèd city.
35   He answered me, and with a solemn oath,
    That, if he had the Mayor of London's wife,

[1.3] *Original Text (Munday). Location: London, a state apartment* **Surrey** the poet Henry Howard is confused with the historical earl, his father **Sir Roger Cholmley** pronounced 'Chumley', was Lieutenant of the Tower of London from 1513 to 1520 **4 frowning vulgar brow** popular discontent, the metaphor suggests a crowd communally frowning **6 distracted countenance** troubled, agitated appearance/conduct **9 princely clemency** i.e. the king's gentle behaviour in allowing foreign merchants royal privilege **10 well a tempered** good-natured **12 high-crested** proud, arrogant **14 traffic** trade **15 leap … face** abuse his (the king's) subjects by confrontations **16 Yet … wife** refers to the case discussed in Act 1 scene 1 in which De Bard took Sherwin's wife and silver and then sued Sherwin for his wife's board; the syntax is very confused though **28 ill bested** badly placed/ in a difficult situation **well-paced** one that goes well, with obvious sexual innuendo **29 find** provide with **30 pleasant** joking **32 stay the broil** stop the quarrel **fell** occurred **33 enforced** emphasized, argued forcibly **34 urged** made a strong argument about

He would keep her in despite of any English.

SURREY 'Tis good, Sir Thomas, then, for you and me,

Your wife is dead and I a bachelor:

40   If no man can possess his wife alone,

I am glad, Sir Thomas Palmer, I have none.

CHOLMLEY If a take my wife, a shall find her meat.

SURREY And reason good, Sir Roger Cholmley, too.

If these hot Frenchmen needsly will have sport,

45   They should in kindness yet defray the charge:

'Tis hard when men possess our wives in quiet,

And yet leave us in to discharge their diet.

SHREWSBURY My lord, our caters shall not use the market

For our provision but some stranger now

50   Will take the victuals from him he hath bought.

A carpenter, as I was late informed,

Who having bought a pair of doves in Cheap,

Immediately a Frenchman took them from him

And beat the poor man for resisting him,

55   And when the fellow did complain his wrongs,

He was severely punished for his labour.

SURREY But if the English blood be once but up,

As I perceive their hearts already full,

I fear me much, before their spleens be cold,

60   Some of these saucy aliens for their pride

Will pay for't soundly, wheresoe'er it lights.

This tide of rage that with the eddy strives,

I fear me much, will drown too many lives.

CHOLMLEY Now, afore God, your honours pardon me,

65   Men of your place and greatness are to blame,

I tell ye true, my lords, in that his majesty

Is not informèd of this base abuse,

And daily wrongs are offered to his subjects.

For, if he were, I know his gracious wisdom

70   Would soon redress it.

Enter a Messenger

SHREWSBURY Sirrah, what news?

CHOLMLEY None good, I fear.

MESSENGER My lord, ill news, and worse I fear will follow

If speedily it be not looked unto.

---

42 **a** he, a common colloquialism   43 **reason good** you're right, i.e. for a good reason   44 **hot** passionate, lustful   **Frenchmen** De Bard was in fact French but in this play he's supposed to be from Lombardy   **needsly** necessarily, to satisfy their needs   45 **defray the charge** pay the bill   46 **in quiet** on the quiet, secretly   47 **leave us in** allow us access (as their husbands), probably with sexual connotations   **discharge** pay for, but the word also has connotations of 'ejaculate'   **diet** food/dry food as part of the treatment for venereal disease   48 **caters** buyers of provisions, caterers   50 **victuals** food, provisions   51 **late** lately   52 **Cheap** Cheapside, the market   57 **blood...up** once their tempers are aroused   59 **spleens** passions; the spleen was regarded as a bodily organ responsible for the emotions   61 **lights** lands, falls   62 **eddy** small whirlpool   **strives** struggles   70 **redress** rectify/compensate/reform

75   The city is in an uproar and the Mayor

Is threatened if he come out of his house.

A number poor artificers are up

In arms and threaten to avenge their wrongs.

CHOLMLEY   We feared what this would come unto:

80   This follows on the doctor's publishing

The bill of wrongs in public at the Spital.

SHREWSBURY   That Doctor Beale may chance beshrew himself

For reading of the bill.

PALMER   Let us go gather forces to the Mayor,

85   For quick suppressing this rebellious rout.

SURREY   Now I bethink myself of Master More,

One of the sheriffs, a wise and learnèd gentleman,

And in especial favour with the people.

He, backed with other grave and sober men,

90   May by his gentle and persuasive speech

Perhaps prevail more than we can with power.

SHREWSBURY   Believe me, but your honour well advises:

Let us make haste for I do greatly fear

Some of their graves this morning's work will bear.   *Exeunt*

[Act 2 Scene 1]

Enter three or four Prentices of trades, with a pair of cudgels

HARRY   Come, lay down the cudgels. Ho, Robin, you met us well at Bunhill, to have you with us a-Maying this morning.

ROBIN   Faith, Harry, the head drawer at the Mitre by the Great Conduit called me up, and we went to breakfast into St Anne's Lane. But come, who begins? In good

5 faith, I am clean out of practice. When was't at Garret's school, Harry?

HARRY   Not this great while, never since I break his usher's head, when he played his scholar's prize at the Star in Bread Street. I use all to George Philpot's at Dowgate: he's the best backsword man in England.

KIT   Bate me an ace of that, quoth Bolton.

10 HARRY   I'll not bate ye a pin on't, sir, for by this cudgel, 'tis true.

KIT   I will cudgel that opinion out of ye: did you break an usher's head, sir?

HARRY   Ay, marry, did I, sir.

KIT   I am very glad on't: you shall break mine too, an ye can.

HARRY   Sirrah, I prithee, what art thou?

---

77 **number** i.e. number of   81 **bill of wrongs** as read out by Lincoln at 1.1.73–84   82 **beshrew** curse   85 **rout** company/gathering/riot   **[2.1]** *Original Text (Munday). Location: London, Cheapside*   **Prentices** apprentices   **cudgels** short thick sticks used for fencing with small shields (bucklers)   **1 Bunhill** Bone Hill, elevation to the north of the City of London used as a burial site from early times but most likely deriving its name from the piles of bones brought there in 1549 (historically after More's time) when St Paul's charnel house was cleared out to make room for fresh burials; Bunhill Fields were used for archery and other military **practice**   **3 drawer** tapster, one who draws beer or ale in a tavern   **Mitre** a well-known tavern   **Great Conduit** man-made underground channel which piped drinking water from the Tyburn to Cheapside   **5 clean** completely   **Garret's school** fencing academy   **6 usher's** assistant master's   **7 scholar's prize** won the fencing competition at his school   **Star** another tavern   **use all** only use/usually patronize   **George Philpot's** either another fencing school or a joke name for a tapster, 'fill pots'   **Dowgate** a ward in the City of London   **8 backsword man** at fencing with a backsword, i.e. a sword with only one cutting edge   **9 Bate...Bolton** expression of incredulity, i.e. that can't be true   **Bate** deduct   **ace** the lowest number in cards or dice   **quoth** said   **Bolton** either a generic term for everyone or John Bolton, a courtier of Henry VIII's who was said to have flattered the king by asking for some advantage when they played   **11 cudgel** knock   **13 an** if

15   KIT   Why, I am a prentice as thou art, see'st thou now? I'll play with thee at blunt here in Cheapside and when thou hast done, if thou be'st angry, I'll fight with thee at sharp in Moorfields. I have a sword to serve my turn in a favour. […] come July, to serve […]   *[Exeunt]*

[Act 2 Scene 2]

[Enter Lincoln, two Bettses, Williamson, Sherwin and other[s], armed; Doll in a shirt of mail, a headpiece, sword and buckler; a crew attending]

CLOWN   Come, come; we'll tickle their turnips, we'll butter their boxes. Shall strangers rule the roost? Yes, but we'll baste the roast. Come, come, aflaunt, aflaunt!

GEORGE   Brother, give place and hear John Lincoln speak.

5   CLOWN   Ay, Lincoln my leader,
And Doll my true breeder,
With the rest of our crew,
Shall ran tan tarra ran,
Do all they what they can.
10   Shall we be bobbed, braved? No.
Shall we be held under? No.
We are freeborn
And do take scorn
To be used so.

15   DOLL   Peace there, I say! Hear captain Lincoln speak;
Keep silence, till we know his mind at large.

CLOWN   Then largely deliver; speak, bully, and he that presumes to interrupt thee in thy oration, this for him!   *Makes an obscene gesture*

LINCOLN   Then, gallant bloods, you whose free souls do scorn
20   To bear th'enforcèd wrongs of aliens,
Add rage to resolution, fire the houses
Of these audacious strangers. This is St Martin's,
And yonder dwells Mutas, a wealthy Picard,
At the Green Gate,
25   De Bard, Peter Van Hollocke, Adrian Martine,
With many more outlandish fugitives.
Shall these enjoy more privilege than we

---

16 **blunt** using a blunt sword   **thou be'st** you are (dialectical)   17 **sharp** using a sharp sword, fight a duel   **Moorfields** open land within the city used for recreation   **come July** when July comes   18 **to serve…** the end of the scene cannot be satisfactorily deciphered from the manuscript   **[2.2]** *Addition II (Heywood?).* **Location:** St Martin's-le-Grand, a main thoroughfare in Aldersgate   **buckler** small round shield   1 **tickle their turnips** beat their backsides, punning on turn-up (the rear end) but also playing on the root vegetable which had recently been imported from France   **butter their boxes** a similar threat, punning on 'butter-box' (slang for a Dutchman)   2 **rule the roost** be in charge   **roost** hen-house   **baste the roast** make it hot for them, punning on 'baste', to moisten roasting meat by spooning melted fat over it/beat, thrash; **roast** plays on **roost** in previous sentence   **aflaunt** proudly/in a flaunting manner, waving our weapons as banners   4 **give place** make way for   6 **true breeder** loyal wife, mother   8 **ran…ran** noisily make the sound of a drum   10 **bobbed** cheated, made fools of/beaten   **braved** challenged, defied/threatened   15 **captain** leader   16 **at large** fully   17 **bully** friend, a term of endearment and familiarity   19 **gallant bloods** brave fellows   22 **St Martin's** thoroughfare named after the church that used to stand on the site   23 **Mutas** John Meautis, French secretary to Henry VIII   **Picard** native of Picardy in northern France   25 **Van…Martine** neither is mentioned in Holinshed   26 **outlandish** foreign, alien   **fugitives** exiles, refugees/outlaws; many were in fact fleeing religious or political persecution

In our own country? Let's, then, become their slaves.

Since justice keeps not them in greater awe,

30   We'll be ourselves rough ministers at law.

CLOWN   Use no more swords,

Nor no more words,

But fire the houses!

Brave captain courageous,

35   Fire me their houses!

DOLL   Ay, for we may as well make bonfires on May Day as at midsummer: we'll alter the day in the calendar, and set it down in flaming letters.

SHERWIN   Stay!

No, that would much endanger the whole city

40   Whereto I would not the least prejudice.

DOLL   No, nor I neither, so may mine own house be burned for company. I'll tell ye what: we'll drag the strangers into Moorfields, and there bombast them till they stink again.

CLOWN   And that's soon done, for they smell for fear already.

45   **GEORGE**   Let some of us enter the strangers' houses,

And, if we find them there, then bring them forth.

DOLL   But if ye bring them forth ere ye find them, I'll ne'er allow of that.

CLOWN   Now, Mars, for thy honour,

Dutch or French,

50   So it be a wench,

I'll upon her.   *[Exeunt some and Sherwin]*

WILLIAMSON   Now, lads, sure shall we labour in our safety.

I hear the Mayor hath gathered men in arms,

And that Shrieve More an hour ago received

55   Some of the Privy Council in at Ludgate:

Force now must make our peace or else we fall:

'Twill soon be known we are the principal.

DOLL   And what of that? If thou be'st afraid, husband, go home again, and hide thy head, for, by the lord, I'll have a little sport, now we are at it.

60   **GEORGE**   Let's stand upon our swords, and if they come

Receive them as they were our enemies.

[Enter Sherwin and the rest]

CLOWN   A purchase, a purchase! We have found, we ha' found—

DOLL   What?

CLOWN   Nothing! Not a French Fleming nor a Fleming French to be found, but all

65   fled in plain English.

---

28 **Let's…slaves** if that's the case we might as well be their slaves   29 **awe** fear/restraint   36 **midsummer** 24 June, traditionally celebrated with bonfires   37 **flaming letters** saints' days were traditionally printed in red in Roman Catholic calendars; criminals were also branded with red **letters** on the forehead   40 **Whereto…prejudice** towards which I feel no hostility/would not wish any harm   41 **so…company** since my own house may burn down as well   42 **bombast** fill, stuff (with blows)/perhaps more likely 'thrash' from 'bumbaste'   43 **stink again** the implication is that they will soil themselves from fear   48 **Mars** Roman god of war   55 **Privy Council** the monarch's closest advisers   57 **principal** the ringleaders   60 **swords** originally read 'guard', a less threatening proposition   62 **purchase** prize   64 **French Fleming** French-speaking inhabitant of Flanders, a geographical region covering parts of modern-day Belgium, France and the Netherlands   **Fleming French** Frenchman from Flanders, playing on 'flaming' in the derogatory sense of 'bloody'

LINCOLN   How now! Have you found any?

SHERWIN   No, not one, they're all fled.

LINCOLN   Then fire the houses that the Mayor being busy

    About the quenching of them, we may 'scape.

70   Burn down their kennels, let us, straight away,

    Lest this day prove to us an ill May Day.   *[Exeunt,] the Clown remains*

CLOWN   Fire, fire! I'll be the first:

    If hanging come, 'tis welcome, that's the worst.   *[Exit]*

[Act 2 Scene 3]

Enter at one door Sir Thomas More and Lord Mayor; at another door Sir John Munday, hurt

LORD MAYOR   What, Sir John Munday, are you hurt?

SIR JOHN   A little knock, my lord. There was even now

    A sort of prentices playing at cudgels.

    I did command them to their masters' houses,

5   But one of them, backed by the other crew,

    Wounded me in the forehead with his cudgel.

    And now, I fear me, they are gone to join

    With Lincoln, Sherwin and their dangerous train.

MORE   The captains of this insurrection

10   Have ta'en themselves to arms, and came but now

    To both the Counters, where they have released

    Sundry indebted prisoners and from thence

    I hear that they are gone into St Martin's,

    Where they intend to offer violence

15   To the amazed Lombards; therefore, my lord,

    If we expect the safety of the city,

    'Tis time that force or parley do encounter

    With these displeasèd men.

Enter a Messenger

LORD MAYOR   How now! What news?

20 MESSENGER   My lord, the rebels have broke open Newgate,

    From whence they have delivered many prisoners,

    Both felons and notorious murderers,

    That desperately cleave to their lawless train.

LORD MAYOR   Up with the drawbridge, gather some forces

25   To Cornhill and Cheapside: and, gentlemen,

---

70 kennels houses, usually shelters for dogs   **73 worst** i.e. the worst thing that can happen to us   **[2.3]**   *Addition II continued (Playhouse Scribe, attributed to Chettle). Location: London, the Guildhall*   **3 sort** particular kind   **8 train** followers   **9 captains** leaders   **10 ta'en** taken   **but now** only a short while ago   **11 Counters** debtors' prisons attached to a city court; there were two in London at this time, the first in Bread Street, the other in Wood Street, Cheapside   **12 Sundry** various   **indebted prisoners** those imprisoned for debt   **15 amazed** bewildered/terrified   **18 displeasèd** angry, discontented   **20 Newgate** the prison   **23 cleave** hang on, attach themselves   **24 Up...drawbridge** put up the defences   **drawbridge** hinged bridge which could be raised at one end to prevent access, normally associated with a castle surrounded by a moat

If diligence be weighed on every side,

A quiet ebb will follow this rough tide.   *[Exit Messenger]*

Enter Shrewsbury, Surrey, Palmer and Cholmley

SHREWSBURY   Lord Mayor, his majesty, receiving notice

Of this most dangerous insurrection,

30   Hath sent my lord of Surrey and myself,

Sir Thomas Palmer and our followers

To add unto your forces our best means

For pacifying of this mutiny.

In God's name, then, set on with happy speed:

35   The king laments if one true subject bleed.

SURREY   I hear they mean to fire the Lombards' houses.

O power, what art thou in a madman's eyes:

Thou mak'st the plodding idiot bloody-wise.

MORE   My lords, I doubt not but we shall appease

40   With a calm breath this flux of discontent.

PALMER   To call them to a parley questionless

May fall out good: 'tis well said, Master More.

MORE   Let's to these simple men, for many sweat

Under this act that knows not the law's debt

45   Which hangs upon their lives. For silly men

Plod on they know not how, like a fool's pen

That, ending, shows not any sentence writ,

Linked but to common reason or slightest wit,

These follow for no harm, but yet incur

50   Self penalty with those that raised this stir.

A God's name, on, to calm our private foes

With breath of gravity, not dangerous blows!   *Exeunt*

[Act 2 Scene 4]

Enter Lincoln, Doll, Clown, George Betts, Williamson, others

LINCOLN   Peace, hear me: he that will not see a red herring at a Harry groat, butter
at eleven pence a pound, meal at nine shillings a bushel, and beef at four nobles a
stone, list to me.

GEORGE   It will come to that pass, if strangers be suffered. Mark him.

5   LINCOLN   Our country is a great eating country, *ergo*, they eat more in our country
than they do in their own.

26 **If…tide** if everyone does their duty, we should bring about a peaceful end   **ebb** decline, literally return of tidewater to the sea   **34 set…speed**
let's go with good fortune/power/success   **37 O…bloody-wise** power goes to fools' heads causing them to behave in a rash violent way   **40 flux** flow
of blood/discharge   **43 simple** harmless, innocent/humble, common   **many…lives** many don't realize they will incur the death penalty (hanging) for
their actions   **45 silly** deserving of pity/helpless/poor, weak/ignorant, foolish   **50 Self penalty** the same penalty (hanging) or 'self-penalty' meaning
as a result of their own actions   **stir** riot, public disorder   **51 A** in   **52 breath of gravity** calm, authoritative words   **[2.4]** *Lines 1–148 Addition II*
continued (Shakespeare); 149–243 Original Text (Munday). Location: St Martin's Gate   **1 he…me** those of you who don't want to see these inflated
prices for staple foods, listen to me   **Harry groat** coin worth four old pence dating from Henry VIII's time   **2 meal**
flour   **bushel** measure for dry goods such as corn   **nobles** gold coins worth one third of a pound sterling   **3 stone** fourteen pounds in weight   **4 pass**
critical situation   **suffered** allowed to remain/tolerated   **5 great eating country** England had a reputation for gluttony   **ergo** 'therefore' (Latin)

CLOWN   By a halfpenny loaf a day troy weight.

LINCOLN   They bring in strange roots, which is merely to the undoing of poor prentices, for what's a sorry parsnip to a good heart?

10   WILLIAMSON   Trash, trash! They breed sore eyes and 'tis enough to infect the city with the palsy.

LINCOLN   Nay, it has infected it with the palsy, for these bastards of dung, as you know they grow in dung, have infected us, and it is our infection will make the city shake, which partly comes through the eating of parsnips.

15   CLOWN   True, and pumpkins together.

Enter [Downes, the Sergeant-at-arms]

DOWNES   What say ye to the mercy of the king?
    Do ye refuse it?

LINCOLN   You would have us upon th'hip, would you? No, marry, do we not; we accept of the king's mercy, but we will show no mercy upon the strangers.

20   DOWNES   You are the simplest things that ever stood
    In such a question.

LINCOLN   How say ye now, prentices? Prentices simple! Down with him!

ALL   Prentices simple! Prentices simple!

Enter the Lord Mayor, Surrey, Shrewsbury [and More]

LORD MAYOR   Hold! In the king's name, hold!

25   SURREY   Friends, masters, countrymen—

LORD MAYOR   Peace, ho, peace! I charge you, keep the peace!

SHREWSBURY   My masters, countrymen—

WILLIAMSON   The noble earl of Shrewsbury, let's hear him.

GEORGE   We'll hear the Earl of Surrey.

30   LINCOLN   The Earl of Shrewsbury.

GEORGE   We'll hear both.

ALL   Both, both, both, both!

LINCOLN   Peace, I say, peace! Are you men of wisdom or what are you?

SURREY   What you will have them, but not men of wisdom.

35   ALL   We'll not hear my lord of Surrey: no, no, no, no, no! Shrewsbury, Shrewsbury!

MORE   Whiles they are o'er the bank of their obedience,
    Thus will they bear down all things.

LINCOLN   Sheriff More speaks; shall we hear Sheriff More speak?

40   DOLL   Let's hear him: a keeps a plentiful shrievalty, and a made my brother Arthur Watchins sergeant Safe's yeoman. Let's hear Shrieve More.

ALL   Shrieve More, More, More, Shrieve More!

---

7 **troy weight** the standard system of weights used for precious metals and formerly also for bread   8 **strange roots** foreign vegetables, considered very poor fare   **undoing** ruin   9 **sorry** wretched   **good heart** courageous spirit   11 **palsy** weakness, paralysis   12 **bastards of dung** illegitimately produced by manuring   13 **our infection** perhaps a reference to the plague; the theatres in London were closed in 1603 due to a severe outbreak   18 **upon th'hip** at a disadvantage, because off balance (a wrestling term)   20 **simplest** most foolish, unsophisticated, gullible   25 **Friends, masters, countrymen** an echo of Mark Antony's speech in Shakespeare's *Julius Caesar*, 'Friends, Romans, countrymen' (3.2.70)   37 **Whiles…things** they'll destroy everything in their wake while their passions overflow; the image is of a river in flood bursting its banks   40 **a keeps…shrievalty** he's a generous patron as sheriff   41 **yeoman** assistant

MORE   Even by the rule you have among yourselves,
        Command still audience.

45   ALL   Surrey, Surrey! More, More!

LINCOLN *and* GEORGE   Peace, peace, silence, peace!

MORE   You that have voice and credit with the number
        Command them to a stillness.

LINCOLN   A plague on them, they will not hold their peace,

50   The devil cannot rule them!

MORE   Then what a rough and riotous charge have you,
        To lead those that the devil cannot rule!—
        Good masters, hear me speak.

DOLL   Ay, by th'mass, will we, More: th'art a good housekeeper and I thank thy
55 good worship for my brother Arthur Watchins.

ALL   Peace, peace!

MORE   Look, what you do offend you cry upon,
        That is, the peace: not one of you here present,
        Had there such fellows lived when you were babes,
60   That could have topped the peace, as now you would,
        The peace wherein you have till now grown up
        Had been ta'en from you, and the bloody times
        Could not have brought you to the state of men.
        Alas, poor things, what is it you have got,
65   Although we grant you get the thing you seek?

GEORGE   Marry, the removing of the strangers, which cannot choose but much
advantage the poor handicrafts of the city.

MORE   Grant them removed, and grant that this your noise
        Hath chid down all the majesty of England.
70   Imagine that you see the wretched strangers,
        Their babies at their backs, with their poor luggage
        Plodding to th'ports and coasts for transportation,
        And that you sit as kings in your desires,
        Authority quite silenced by your brawl,
75   And you in ruff of your opinions clothed:
        What had you got? I'll tell you: you had taught
        How insolence and strong hand should prevail,
        How order should be quelled, and by this pattern
        Not one of you should live an agèd man,
80   For other ruffians, as their fancies wrought,

---

43 Even…audience More appeals to the crowd's self-discipline for calm   47 voice…number More asks those able to make themselves heard, with authority with the crowd to appeal for calm   51 charge burden/responsibility (of care for those entrusted to your care)/source of trouble, inconvenience   54 by th'mass an oath referring to the celebration of the Eucharist in Roman Catholicism   good housekeeper generous host/ competent official   55 for on behalf of   57 what…peace you call for peace but are destroying it at the same time   60 topped lopped the head off, hence destroyed   63 not…men none of you would have been here today if others like yourselves had been around when you were young to destroy the peace as you wish to do   state of men manhood, adulthood   64 what…seek? what will you really have gained even if we grant what you ask?   67 handicrafts workmen, artisans   68 Grant them let's agree they are   69 chid down forced into submission by your angry scolding   majesty greatness, dignity/ sovereign power   74 brawl noisy row, fuss   75 ruff…clothed wrapped up to the fullest degree in your own pride; plays on ruff the elaborate, starched, fluted neckwear of the upper classes   78 quelled crushed, overcome   pattern model, example   79 live i.e. live long enough to become   80 ruffians violent brutes, again playing on ruff   fancies wrought whims took them

With selfsame hand, self-reasons, and self-right,
Would shark on you, and men like ravenous fishes
Would feed on one another.

DOL   Before God, that's as true as the gospel.

85 GEORGE   Nay, this a sound fellow, I tell you: let's mark him.

MORE   Let me set up before your thoughts, good friends,
One supposition, which if you will mark,
You shall perceive how horrible a shape
Your innovation bears: first, 'tis a sin
90 Which oft th'apostle did forewarn us of,
Urging obedience to authority,
And 'twere no error if I told you all
You were in arms gainst your God himself.

ALL   Marry, God forbid that!

95 MORE   Nay certainly you are,
For to the king God hath his office lent
Of dread, of justice, power and command,
Hath bid him rule, and willed you to obey;
And, to add ampler majesty to this,
100 He hath not only lent the king his figure,
His throne and sword, but given him his own name,
Calls him a god on earth. What do you then,
Rising gainst him that God himself installs,
But rise gainst God? What do you to your souls
105 In doing this? O, desperate as you are,
Wash your foul minds with tears, and those same hands,
That you like rebels lift against the peace,
Lift up for peace, and your unreverent knees,
Make them your feet. To kneel to be forgiven
110 Is safer wars than ever you can make
Whose discipline is riot.
In, in, to your obedience! Why, even your hurly
Cannot proceed but by obedience.
Tell me but this: what rebel captain,
115 As mutinies are incident, by his name
Can still the rout? Who will obey a traitor?
Or how can well that proclamation sound
When there is no addition but a rebel
To qualify a rebel? You'll put down strangers,
120 Kill them, cut their throats, possess their houses,
And lead the majesty of law in lyam,
To slip him like a hound. Say now the king,

---

81 **selfsame** very same, identical   **self-reasons** same reasons   **self-right** same sense of right   82 **shark on** victimize, oppress   85 **this** i.e. this is, a common construction   89 **innovation** rebellion, political revolution   90 **th'apostle** St Paul (Romans 13:1–7)   96 **office** authority   97 **dread** deep awe, reverence   106 **foul** corrupt, loathsome, tainted   108 **unreverent** irreverent, disrespectful   115 **incident** liable to occur   116 **still the rout** calm the disorderly crowd   118 **addition** title or thing to distinguish him by   119 **qualify** characterize, designate/invest with qualities of   121 **in lyam** on a leash (for hounds, a hunting term)   122 **slip…hound** let him loose like a dog (as in hunting), playing on negative senses of **slip** neglect/sin/ lose hold of

As he is clement if th'offender mourn,

Should so much come too short of your great trespass

125 As but to banish you, whither would you go?

What country, by the nature of your error,

Should give you harbour? Go you to France or Flanders,

To any German province, to Spain or Portugal,

Nay, anywhere that not adheres to England,

130 Why, you must needs be strangers. Would you be pleased

To find a nation of such barbarous temper

That, breaking out in hideous violence,

Would not afford you an abode on earth,

Whet their detested knives against your throats,

135 Spurn you like dogs, and like as if that God

Owed not nor made not you, nor that the elements

Were not all appropriate to your comforts,

But chartered unto them? What would you think

To be thus used? This is the strangers' case,

140 And this your mountainish inhumanity.

ALL   Faith, a says true: let's do as we may be done to.

LINCOLN   We'll be ruled by you, Master More, if you'll stand our friend to procure

our pardon.

MORE   Submit you to these noble gentlemen,

145 Entreat their mediation to the king,

Give up yourself to form, obey the magistrate,

And there's no doubt but mercy may be found,

If you so seek it.

To persist in it is present death: but, if you

150 Yield yourselves, no doubt what punishment

You in simplicity have incurred, his highness

In mercy will most graciously pardon.

ALL   We yield, and desire his highness' mercy.   *They lay by their weapons*

MORE   No doubt his majesty will grant it you:

155 But you must yield to go to several prisons,

Till that his highness' will be further known.

ALL   Most willingly, whither you will have us.

SHREWSBURY   Lord Mayor, let them be sent to several prisons,

And there, in any case, be well entreated.—

160 My lord of Surrey, please you to take horse

And ride to Cheapside, where the aldermen

Are with their several companies in arms.

Will them to go unto their several wards,

Both for the stay of further mutiny,

165 And for the apprehending of such persons

---

123 clement lenient, merciful   **mourn** expresses regret   **124 trespass** offence, sin, breach of law or duty   **125 but** only   **126 by** given   **127 harbour** shelter   **129 adheres to** maintains, follows the practices of   **133 abode** dwelling place   **134 Whet** sharpen   **135 Spurn** kick/treat with contempt   **like as...you** as though God neither created nor acknowledged you as his own   **136 Owed** owned/acknowledged   **137 appropriate** suitable   **138 chartered unto** bestowed on/thrust upon   **139 used** treated   **140 mountainish** monstrous   **141 a** he (colloquial)   **let's...to** Christian sentiment derived from the Sermon on the Mount, Matthew 7:12 and Luke 6:31   **146 form** formal procedure (legal phrase)/appropriate behaviour   **155 several** various, separate   **157 whither** wherever   **159 entreated** treated   **163 Will** desire, request   **164 stay** control, restraint

As shall contend.

SURREY   I go, my noble lord.   *Exit Surrey*

SHREWSBURY   We'll straight go tell his highness these good news.

Withal, Shrieve More, I'll tell him how your breath

170   Hath ransomed many a subject from sad death.   *Exit Shrewsbury*

LORD MAYOR   Lincoln and Sherwin, you shall both to Newgate,

The rest unto the Counters.

PALMER   Go guard them hence: a little breath well spent

Cheats expectation in his fairest event.

175   DOLL   Well, Sheriff More, thou hast done more with thy good words than all they

could with their weapons: give me thy hand, keep thy promise now for the king's

pardon, or, by the lord, I'll call thee a plain cony-catcher.

LINCOLN   Farewell, Shrieve More, and as we yield by thee,

So make our peace, then thou deal'st honestly.

180   CLOWN   Ay, and save us from the gallows, else a deals double honestly!   *They are*

LORD MAYOR   Master Shrieve More, you have preserved the city   *led away*

From a most dangerous fierce commotion,

For if this limb of riot here in St Martin's

Had joined with other branches of the city

185   That did begin to kindle, 'twould have bred

Great rage, that rage much murder would have fed.

PALMER   Not steel, but eloquence hath wrought this good:

You have redeemed us from much threatened blood.

MORE   My lord and brethren, what I here have spoke,

190   My country's love, and next the city's care

Enjoined me to, which since it thus prevails

Think God hath made weak More his instrument

To thwart sedition's violent intent.

I think 'twere best, my lord, some two hours hence

195   We meet at the Guildhall, and there determine

That thorough every ward the watch be clad

In armour, but especially provide

That at the city gates selected men,

Substantial citizens, do ward tonight

200   For fear of further mischief.

LORD MAYOR   It shall be so:

But yond methinks my lord of Shrewsbury.

Enter Shrewsbury

SHREWSBURY   My lord, his majesty sends loving thanks

To you, your brethren, and his faithful subjects,

---

166 **contend** dispute, fight   169 **Withal** in addition   170 **ransomed** preserved   171 **Newgate** London prison on the corner of Newgate Street and the Old Bailey court   172 **Counters** smaller borough prisons   173 **little … event** a good speech such as More's can avert anticipated disaster   177 **cony-catcher** cheat, con-man   **cony** dupe, gull (literally rabbit)   180 **Ay** yes   **else … honestly** otherwise he's a real double dealer (ironic)   183 **limb** part, section   185 **kindle** catch light   187 **steel** i.e. swords   **wrought** created, produced   196 **thorough** throughout   **watch** town guard, a body of citizens appointed to act as watchmen in towns from sunset to sunrise, before the introduction of police   199 **Substantial citizens** persons of worth, reliability and reputation   **ward** guard

205	Your careful citizens.— But, Master More, to you
	A rougher, yet as kind, a salutation:
	Your name is yet too short. Nay, you must kneel.
	A knight's creation is this knightly steel.
	Rise up, Sir Thomas More.

More kneels and is knighted

MORE 　I thank his highness for thus honouring me.　　　　　　*Rising*

SHREWSBURY 　This is but first taste of his princely favour,

For it hath pleased his high majesty,

Noting your wisdom and deserving merit,

To put this staff of honour in your hand,

For he hath chose you of his Privy Council.

MORE 　My lord, for to deny my sovereign's bounty

Were to drop precious stones into the heaps

Whence first they came, from whence they'd ne'er return;

To urge my imperfections in excuse,

Were all as stale as custom. No, my lord,

My service is my king's, good reason why,

Since life or death hangs on our sovereign's eye.

LORD MAYOR 　His majesty hath honoured much the city

In this his princely choice.

MORE 　My lord and brethren,

Though I depart for court my love shall rest

With you, as heretofore, a faithful guest.

I now must sleep in court: sound sleeps forbear,

The chamberlain to state is public care,

Yet, in this rising of my private blood,

My studious thoughts shall tend the city's good.

Enter Crofts

SHREWSBURY 　How now, Crofts! What news?

CROFTS 　My lord, his highness sends express command

That a record be entered of this riot,

And that the chief and capital offenders

Be thereon straight arraigned, for himself intends

To sit in person on the rest tomorrow

At Westminster.

SHREWSBURY 　Lord Mayor, you hear your charge.—

Come, good Sir Thomas More, to court let's hie,

You are th'appeaser of this mutiny.

MORE 　My lord, farewell, new days begets new tides:

Life whirls 'bout fate then to a grave it slides.　　　　　　*Exeunt severally*

---

206 **rougher** since being dubbed a knight requires him to kneel and receive a blow on the shoulder with the flat of a sword　**salutation** greeting
214 **staff of honour** rod or wand of wood or ivory, the badge of office for certain officers of the crown　215 **you…Council** to become one of his **Privy Council**, the monarch's closest confidential advisers　216 **for…return** gifts or benefits once refused are lost forever　**deny** refuse　**bounty** liberality, generosity　217 **Were to drop** would be like dropping　219 **To…custom** drawing attention to my own unworthiness as an excuse would just be for the sake of form, a meaningless habit　**urge** draw attention to　221 **good reason why** and for a very good reason　225 **brethren** brothers, i.e. fellow sheriffs　227 **heretofore** up to this point　228 **sound…care** sound sleep must be given up since concern for the welfare of the public is a constant attendant on those in authority　**chamberlain** personal attendant of a sovereign or nobleman　230 **private blood** humble, non-aristocratic family
236 **arraigned** indicted on criminal charges　240 **hie** hasten　*severally* separately

[Act 3 Scene 1]

Enter Master Sheriff, and meet a Messenger

SHERIFF   Messenger, what news?

MESSENGER Is execution yet performed?

SHERIFF   Not yet, the carts stand ready at the stairs,

And they shall presently away to Tyburn.

5   MESSENGER Stay, Master Shrieve; it is the council's pleasure,

For more example in so bad a case,

A gibbet be erected in Cheapside,

Hard by the Standard, whither you must bring

Lincoln and those that were the chief with him,

Enter Officers

10   To suffer death, and that immediately.

SHERIFF   It shall be done, sir.—   *Exit Messenger*

Officers, be speedy,

Call for a gibbet, see it be erected;

Others make haste to Newgate, bid them bring

15   The prisoners hither, for they here must die.

Away I say, and see no time be slacked.

OFFICERS   We go, sir.   *Exeunt some severally.*

SHERIFF   That's well said, fellows; now you do your duty.   *Others set up the gibbet*

God for his pity help these troublous times!

20   The street's stopped up with gazing multitudes:

Command our armed officers with halberds

Make way for entrance of the prisoners.

Let proclamation once again be made

That every householder, on pain of death,

25   Keep in his prentices, and every man

Stand with a weapon ready at his door,

As he will answer to the contrary.

OFFICER   I'll see it done, sir.   *Exit*

Enter another Officer

SHERIFF   Bring them away to execution.

30   The writ is come above two hours since:

The city will be fined for this neglect.

OFFICER   There's such a press and multitude at Newgate,

They cannot bring the carts unto the stairs

To take the prisoners in.

[3.1] *Original Text (Munday); lines 45, 75–6 and 86–91 insertions by Hand B (Heywood?). Location: the Standard in Cheapside; fountain and rallying point in Cheapside where previously criminals had been executed*   **4 Tyburn** place of public execution; the gallows erected at the site of London's present-day Marble Arch   **7 gibbet** gallows, apparatus used to hang criminals   **8 Hard** close, right   **16 slacked** lost   **18 well said** i.e. well done   **19 troublous** turbulent, unquiet, sad   **20 stopped up** full of/blocked by   **21 halberds** military weapons consisting of a spear and axe-head mounted on a long pole   **27 As…contrary** or he will have to explain if he fails to do so   **30 writ** written order for their execution   **above…since** more than two hours ago   **31 neglect** failure to comply (with the order)   **32 press** throng, crowd of people   **33 unto** right up to

35   SHERIFF   Then let them come on foot:

      We may not dally time with great command.

  OFFICER   Some of the Bench, sir, think it very fit

      That stay be made, and give it out abroad

      The execution is deferred till morning,

40   And, when the streets shall be a little cleared,

      To chain them up and suddenly dispatch it.

  SHERIFF   Stay, in meantime methinks they come along:

      See, they are coming. So, 'tis very well:

The prisoners are brought in [Lincoln, Doll, Williamson, Clown, Sherwin], well-guarded [and Hangman]

      Bring Lincoln there the first unto the tree.

45   CLOWN   Ay, for I cry lag, sir.

  LINCOLN   I knew the first, sir, did belong to me:

      This the old proverb now complete doth make,

      That Lincoln should be hanged for London's sake.   *He goes up*

      A God's name let's to work. Fellow, dispatch: *To Hangman*

50   I was the foremost man in this rebellion,

      And I the foremost that must die for it.

  DOLL   Bravely, John Lincoln, let thy death express

      That as thou lived'st a man, thou died'st no less.

  LINCOLN   Doll Williamson, thine eyes shall witness it.—

55   Then to all you that come to view mine end

      I must confess I had no ill intent,

      But against such as wronged us overmuch,

      And now I can perceive it was not fit

      That private men should carve out their redress,

60   Which way they list. No, learn it now by me,

      Obedience is the best in each degree,

      And asking mercy meekly of my king,

      I patiently submit me to the law.

      But God forgive them that were cause of it,

65   And, as a Christian, truly from my heart

      I likewise crave they would forgive me too,

      As freely as I do forgive their wrong,

      That others by example of the same

      Henceforth be warned to attempt the like

70   Gainst any alien that repaireth hither.

      Fare ye well, all: the next time that we meet,

      I trust in heaven we shall each other greet.   *He leaps off*

  DOLL   Farewell, John Lincoln: say all what they can,

      Thou lived'st a good fellow, and died'st an honest man.

---

36 dally...command delay or treat it lightly in view of the order's authority   **37 Bench** collective name for judges or magistrates, specifically the King's Bench, a court originally presided over by the sovereign   **fit** appropriate   **38 stay** a halt or delay   **give...abroad** publicly announced   **41 them** i.e. the streets, which could be closed off with chains in emergencies   **dispatch it** carry it out, i.e. the execution   **42 Stay** wait   **44 tree** gallows   **45 lag** the last or hindmost person in a race or game   **48 Lincoln...sake** punning on the proverb: 'Lincoln was, London is, and York shall be' referring to the supposed rise of London at the expense of Lincoln, the Roman capital   **49 to work** get on with it   **60 list** please, choose   **61 degree** rank, station in life   **70 Gainst** against   **alien...hither** foreigner who comes here

| 75 | CLOWN | Would I were so far on my journey! The first stretch is the worst |

75   **CLOWN**   Would I were so far on my journey! The first stretch is the worst
methinks.

    SHERIFF   Bring Williamson there forward.

    DOLL   Good Master Shrieve, I have an earnest suit,

        And, as you are a man, deny't me not.

80   **SHERIFF**   Woman, what is it? Be it in my power,

        Thou shalt obtain it.

    DOLL   Let me die next, sir, that is all I crave:

        You know not what a comfort you shall bring

        To my poor heart to die before my husband.

85   **SHERIFF**   Bring her to death: she shall have her desire.

    CLOWN   Sir, and I have a suit to you too.

    SHERIFF   What is it?

    CLOWN   That, as you have hanged Lincoln first, and will hang her next, so you will
not hang me at all.

90   **SHERIFF**   Nay, you set ope the Counter gates, and you must hang chiefly.

    CLOWN   Well, then, so much for it!

    DOLL   Sir, your free bounty much contents my mind.

        Commend me to that good shrieve Master More,

        And tell him, had't not been for his persuasion,

95   John Lincoln had not hung here as he does:

        We would first have locked us up in Leadenhall,

        And there been burnt to ashes with the roof.

    SHERIFF   Woman, what Master More did was a subject's duty,

        And hath so pleased our gracious lord the king,

100   That he is hence removed to higher place,

        And made of council to his majesty.

    DOLL   Well is he worthy of it, by my troth,

        An honest, wise, well-spoken gentleman,

        Yet would I praise his honesty much more

105   If he had kept his word and saved our lives.

        But let that pass: men are but men, and so

        Words are but words and pays not what men owe.—

        You, husband, since perhaps the world may say

        That through my means thou com'st thus to thy end,

110   Here I begin this cup of death to thee,

        Because thou shalt be sure to taste no worse

        Than I have taken that must go before thee.

---

75 stretch deviation from principle/physical pull of the hangman's noose around the neck   **78 earnest suit** important request   **84 die** there may be sexual innuendo in the references to **die** (achieve orgasm), **crave** (desire) and **desire**   **90 ope** open   **Counter** one of the prisons broken into by the rebels   **96 us** ourselves   **Leadenhall** London food market set around a manor house with a lead roof and donated in 1445 by Simon Eyre, the then Lord Mayor of London; the events of Eyre's life are recorded in Thomas Dekker's popular play, *The Shoemaker's Holiday* (1599)   **101 made…majesty** been appointed to the Privy Council   **103 well-spoken** eloquent/courteous and refined in speech   **106 let that pass** let's not go into that; the catchphrase of Eyre's wife, Margery, in Dekker's play   **110 cup of death** imaged as a loving-cup which was passed round from hand to hand

What though I be a woman, that's no matter,

I do owe God a death, and I must pay him.

115   Husband, give me thy hand, be not dismayed,

This chore being chored, then all our debt is paid.

Only two little babes we leave behind us,

And all I can bequeath them at this time

Is but the love of some good honest friend

120   To bring them up in charitable sort.

What, masters, he goes upright that never halts,

And they may live to mend their parents' faults.

WILLIAMSON   Why, well said, wife; i'faith, thou cheer'st my heart:

Give me thy hand; let's kiss, and so let's part.   *He kisses her on the ladder*

125   **DOLL**   The next kiss, Williamson, shall be in heaven.—

Now cheerly, lads, George Betts, a hand with thee,

And thine too, Ralph, and thine, good honest Sherwin.

Now let me tell the women of this town,

No stranger yet brought Doll to lying down:

130   So long as I an Englishman can see,

Nor French nor Dutch shall get a kiss of me,

And when that I am dead, for me yet say

I died in scorn to be a stranger's prey.

              A great shout and noise, [shouts] within 'Pardon, pardon,

              pardon, pardon! Room for the Earl of Surrey, room there, room!'

Enter Surrey

   SURREY   Save the man's life, if it be possible.

135   **SHERIFF**   It is too late, my lord, he's dead already.

   SURREY   I tell ye, Master Sheriff, you are too forward,

To make such haste with men unto their death.

I think your pains will merit little thanks,

Since that his highness is so merciful

140   As not to spill the blood of any subject.

   SHERIFF   My noble lord, would we so much had known!

The Council's warrant hastened our dispatch;

It had not else been done so suddenly.

   SURREY   Sir Thomas More humbly upon his knee

145   Did beg the lives of all, since on his word

They did so gently yield: the king hath granted it,

And made him Lord High Chancellor of England,

According as he worthily deserves.

Since Lincoln's life cannot be had again,

150   Then for the rest, from my dread sovereign's lips

I here pronounce free pardon for them all.

114 owe...death proverbial   **116 chore being chored** job being done   **debt** i.e. to nature   **120 sort** character, disposition/destiny, fate   **121 halts** walks unsteadily, limps (proverbial)   **126 cheerly** cheerfully/with a will   **129 to lying down** i.e. for sex   **143 had not else** would not otherwise have   **147 Lord High Chancellor** senior and most important government functionary, at this time also head of the judiciary; historically More was promoted to this role twelve years after these events in October 1529 but his career has been telescoped within the play's action for dramatic effect

ALL   God save the king! God save the king!
             My good Lord Chancellor, and the Earl of Surrey!   *Flinging up caps*

DOLL   And Doll desires it from her very heart,
155   More's name may live for this right noble part;
             And whensoe'er we talk of ill May Day,
             Praise More whose [...] falls [...].

SURREY   In hope his highness' clemency and mercy,
             Which in the arms of mild and meek compassion
160   Would rather clip you, as the loving nurse
             Oft doth the wayward infant, than to leave you
             To the sharp rod of justice, so to draw you
             To shun such lewd assemblies as beget
             Unlawful riots and such traitorous acts
165   That, striking with the hand of private hate,
             Maim your dear country with a public wound.
             O God, that Mercy, whose majestic brow
             Should be unwrinkled, and that awful Justice,
             Which looketh through a veil of sufferance
170   Upon the frailty of the multitude,
             Should with the clamours of outrageous wrongs
             Be stirred and wakened thus to punishment!
             But your deservèd death he doth forgive:
             Who gives you life, pray all he long may live.
175 ALL   God save the king, God save the king!
             My good Lord Chancellor and the Earl of Surrey!   *Exeunt*

[Act 3 Scene 2]

A table being covered with a green carpet, a state cushion on it, and the purse and mace lying thereon. Enter Sir Thomas More

MORE   It is in heaven that I am thus and thus,
             And that which we profanely term our fortunes
             Is the provision of the power above,
             Fitted and shaped just to that strength of nature
5   Which we are born withal. Good God, good God,
             That I from such an humble bench of birth
             Should step as 'twere up to my country's head
             And give the law out there! I, in my father's life,

---

caps normal headgear for men and boys   157 **[...]** there is a lacuna in the manuscript at this point   160 **clip** embrace   163 **lewd** wicked, unprincipled   **assemblies** gatherings   166 **Maim** injure   169 **sufferance** patient endurance/toleration   **[3.2]** *Lines 1–21 Addition III (Playhouse Scribe, attributed to Shakespeare); 22–239 Addition IV (Playhouse Scribe, attributed to Dekker; 'I am ipse' at line 221 in Dekker's hand); 240–66 Addition IV continued (Dekker).* **Location:** Chelsea: a room in More's house, although the opening stage directions suggest a more formal setting, perhaps in the chancery state rooms   **carpet** cloth   **purse and mace** the insignia of the Lord Chancellor, the purse contained the Great Seal, used to symbolize the monarch's approval of state documents, and the mace his staff of office   2 **profanely** blasphemously, impiously   5 **withal** with   6 **humble...birth** lowly origins, playing on **bench** meaning legal profession; in fact More's father was a judge of the King's Bench from 1520   8 **I** the pronoun 'I' and the interjection 'ay' sounded the same and were frequently indistinguishable in Elizabethan spelling, hence rather than referring to himself here, More might mean 'ay' (indeed)

        To take prerogative and tithe of knees

10   From elder kinsmen, and him bind by my place

        To give the smooth and dexter way to me

        That owe it him by nature! Sure, these things,

        Not physicked by respect, might turn our blood

        To much corruption: but, More, the more thou hast,

15   Either of honour, office, wealth and calling,

        Which might accite thee to embrace and hug them,

        The more do thou in serpents' natures think them;

        Fear their gay skins with thought of their sharp state

        And let this be thy maxim: to be great

20   Is when the thread of heyday is once spun,

        A bottom great wound up greatly undone.—

        Come on, sir, are you ready?

Enter his man Randall attired like him

RANDALL   Yes, my lord, I stand but on a few points; I shall have done presently. Before God, I have practised your lordship's shift so well that I think I shall grow proud,

25   my lord.

MORE   'Tis fit thou shouldst wax proud, or else thou'lt ne'er

        Be near allied to greatness. Observe me, sirrah:

        The learned clerk Erasmus is arrived

        Within our English court: last night I hear

30   He feasted with our honoured English poet,

        The Earl of Surrey and I learned today

        The famous clerk of Rotterdam will visit

        Sir Thomas More. Therefore, sir, take my seat:

        You are Lord Chancellor. Dress your behaviour

35   According to my carriage, but beware

        You talk not over much, for 'twill betray thee:

        Who prates not much seems wise, his wit few scan

        While the tongue blabs tales of the imperfect man.

        I'll see if great Erasmus can distinguish

40   Merit and outward ceremony.

RANDALL   If I do not deserve a share for playing of your lordship well, let me be yeoman usher to your sumpter, and be banished from wearing of a gold chain forever.

---

9 **To…nature** More is reflecting on the paradox that his new position means that he automatically takes precedence over older male relatives, notably his father, and against what he perceives as the natural order   **prerogative** right   **tithe** tenth part of annual produce of the land due as payment to the church, hence 'tribute'   **tithe of knees** tribute of reverent bows   **11 smooth** even   **dexter** right   **13 physicked** treated, alleviated   **14 More, the more** usual pun on his name   **16 accite** arouse   **17 serpents' natures** like serpents by nature   **18 skins** outsides, external attractions   **sharp state** dangerous inner reality   **19 to…undone** great worldly achievement is liable to great failure; the metaphor used is a ball of thread which increases in size and then unravels, inspired perhaps by the classical notion of the individual life as a thread spun, measured and then cut by the goddesses of Destiny   **heyday** state of exaltation or excitement   **21 bottom** nucleus of a ball of thread/foundation, lowest part   **undone** ruined/unravelled   **23 stand…points** there are just a few remaining details to be settled; punning on **points** features, characteristics/laces or ribbons used (before buttons) to attach hose or breeches/legal principles   **24 shift** movement/jest, entertaining or humorous device/subterfuge/change of clothing   **26 wax** grow   **28 Erasmus** well-known humanist scholar   **34 Dress** prepare   **35 carriage** conduct/bearing   **37 prates** chatters, talks idly or boastfully   **wit few scan** few accurately assess his intelligence   **38 tongue…man** the talk of the foolish chatterbox says everything about him   **39 I'll…ceremony** the test set up for Erasmus is unhistorical but based on the story of Erasmus' failure to recognize More when they first met   **41 share** commercial stake in a company of actors   **42 yeoman usher** superior, gentleman servant   **sumpter** packhorse driver, a lower servant   **gold chain** worn by superior servants but here playing on More's badge of office as Lord Chancellor

MORE   Well, sir, I'll hide our motion: act my part

45   With a firm boldness, and thou winn'st my heart.

Enter the Sheriff with Faulkner (a ruffian) and Officers

How now! What's the matter?

FAULKNER   Tug me not, I'm no bear. 'Sblood, if all the dogs in Paris Garden hung at my tail, I'd shake 'em off with this, that I'll appear before no king christened but my good Lord Chancellor.

50   SHERIFF   We'll christen you, sirrah.— Bring him forward.

MORE   How now! What tumults make you?

FAULKNER   The azured heavens protect my noble Lord Chancellor!

MORE   What fellow's this?

SHERIFF   A ruffian, my lord, that hath set half the city in an uproar.

55   FAULKNER   My lord—

SHERIFF   There was a fray in Paternoster Row, and because they would not be parted, the street was choked up with carts.

FAULKNER   My noble lord, Panyer Alley's throat was open.

MORE   Sirrah, hold your peace.

60   FAULKNER   I'll prove the street was not choked but is as well as ever it was since it was a street.

SHERIFF   This fellow was a principal broacher of the broil.

FAULKNER   'Sblood, I broached none; it was broached and half run out before I had a lick at it.

65   SHERIFF   And would be brought before no justice but your honour.

FAULKNER   I am haled, my noble lord.

MORE   No ear to choose for every trivial noise

But mine, and in so full a time! Away!

You wrong me, Master Shrieve: dispose of him

70   At your own pleasure; send the knave to Newgate.

FAULKNER   To Newgate! 'Sblood, Sir Thomas More, I appeal, I appeal from Newgate to any of the two worshipful Counters.

MORE   Fellow, whose man are you that are thus lusty?

FAULKNER   My name's Jack Faulkner. I serve, next under God and my prince, Master

75   Morris, secretary to my Lord of Winchester.

MORE   A fellow of your hair is very fit

To be a secretary's follower!

FAULKNER   I hope so, my lord. The fray was between the bishops' men of Ely and Winchester and I could not in honour but part them. I thought it stood not with my

---

44 motion entertainment, puppet-show   **act my part** impersonate me   **47 'Sblood** by God's/Christ's blood   **Paris Garden** main bear-garden (arena for fights between a **bear** and **dogs**) in London; it was situated on the south bank of the Thames at Southwark   **48 christened** Christian   **51 tumults** commotion, disturbance   **52 azured** blue   **56 fray** affray, disturbance, noisy brawl   **Paternoster Row** London street running along the side of St Paul's Cathedral where the clergy walked chanting the Lord's Prayer (*pater noster*) and later religious books were sold   **58 Panyer Alley's throat** the entrance to Panyer Alley, London's main bread market   **62 broacher…broil** instigator of the quarrel   **63 broached** incited; Faulkner then shifts to literal sense of 'pierced or tapped in order to draw off liquor'   **64 lick** taste   **66 haled** dragged by force   **68 full** busy   **70 knave** rogue   **71 Newgate…Counters** Faulkner objects to being sent to **Newgate**, the prison for criminal offenders whereas the **Counters** were mainly for less serious offences or debtors, hence **worshipful** (honourable, respectable)   **73 whose…you** who is your master?   **lusty** insolent, arrogant   **75 Lord of Winchester** i.e. the Bishop of Winchester   **76 hair** More is commenting on Faulkner's long hair and punning on the meaning 'stamp', 'character'   **77 secretary's follower** perhaps because its length made keeping secrets easy   **79 stood not** was not compatible with

80 reputation and degree to come to my questions and answers before a city justice.
I knew I should to the pot.

MORE Thou hast been there, it seems, too late already.

FAULKNER I know your honour is wise and so forth and I desire to be only catechized
or examined by you, my noble Lord Chancellor.

85 MORE Sirrah, sirrah, you are a busy dangerous ruffian.

FAULKNER Ruffian!

MORE How long have you worn this hair?

FAULKNER I have worn this hair ever since I was born.

MORE You know that's not my question, but how long
90 Hath this shag fleece hung dangling on they head?

FAULKNER How long, my lord? Why, sometimes thus long, sometimes lower, as the
Fates and humours please.

MORE So quick, sir, with me, ha? I see, good fellow,
Thou lov'st plain dealing. Sirrah, tell me now,
95 When were you last at barber's? How long time
Have you upon your head worn this shag hair?

FAULKNER My lord, Jack Faulkner tells no Aesop's fables:
Troth, I was not at barber's this three years;
I have not been cut nor will not be cut,
100 Upon a foolish vow which, as the Destinies shall direct,
I am sworn to keep.

MORE When comes that vow out?

FAULKNER Why, when the humours are purged, not these three years.

MORE Vows are recorded in the court of heaven,
105 For they are holy acts. Young man, I charge thee
And do advise thee, start not from that vow:
And for I will be sure thou shalt not shear
Besides, because it is an odious sight
To see a man thus hairy, thou shalt lie
110 In Newgate till thy vow and thy three years
Be full expired.— Away with him!

FAULKNER My lord—

MORE Cut off this fleece, and lie there but a month.

FAULKNER I'll not lose a hair to be Lord Chancellor of Europe.

115 MORE To Newgate, then. Sirrah, great sins are bred
In all that body where there's a foul head.—
Away with him! *Exeunt [all except Randall]*

Enter Surrey, Erasmus and Attendants

80 degree social station   81 to the pot be ruined; in the next line More puns on pot as a drinking vessel, implying Faulkner has been drinking
83 catechized questioned/instructed; the catechism is an elementary treatise of Christian instruction in a question-and-answer format   85 busy
interfering, meddlesome   90 shag fleece long, rough, shaggy mass of hair   92 Fates classical goddesses of destiny supposed to determine the course
of human life; the Destinies (3.2.100)   humours moods, dependent on the relative balance of the four bodily fluids thought to determine temperament/
whims   93 quick sharp, caustic   97 Aesop's fables popular, well-known collection of stories which had been recently translated from Greek   98 Troth
in truth   102 comes...out? will the vow be completed?   vow a solemn promise made to God/undertaking to achieve something   106 start not do not
withdraw/deviate   115 great...head proverbial; the saying is often used with a political implication

SURREY   Now, great Erasmus, you approach the presence

Of a most worthy learned gentleman:

120   This little isle holds not a truer friend

Unto the arts, nor doth his greatness add

A feignèd flourish to his worthy parts:

He's great in study, that's the statist's grace

That gains more reverence than the outward place.

125   ERASMUS   Report, my lord, hath crossed the narrow seas

And to the several parts of Christendom,

Hath borne the fame of your lord chancellor:

I long to see him whom with loving thoughts

I in my study oft have visited.

130   Is that Sir Thomas More?

SURREY   It is, Erasmus:

Now shall you view the honourablest scholar,

The most religious politician,

The worthiest counsellor that tends our state.

135   That study is the general watch of England:

In it the prince's safety and the peace

That shines upon our commonwealth are forged

By loyal industry.

ERASMUS   I doubt him not

140   To be as near the life of excellence

As you proclaim him, when his meanest servants

Are of some weight. You saw, my lord, his porter

Give entertainment to us at the gate

In Latin good phrase: what's the master then,

145   When such good parts shine in his meanest men?

SURREY   His lordship hath some weighty business,

For, see, yet he takes no notice of us.

ERASMUS   I think 'twere best I did my duty to him

In a short Latin speech.—   *Takes off his hat*

150   *Qui in celiberrima patria natus est et gloriosa, plus habet negotii ut in lucem veniat quam*

qui—

RANDALL   I prithee, good Erasmus, be covered. I have forsworn speaking of Latin,

else, as I am true counsellor I'd tickle you with a speech. Nay, sit, Erasmus. Sit, good

my lord of Surrey. I'll make my lady come to you anon, if she will, and give you

155   entertainment.

ERASMUS   Is this Sir Thomas More?

SURREY   O, good Erasmus, you must conceive his vein:

---

122 feignèd fictitiously invented, fabled   flourish perfection, vigour/ostentatious embellishment, varnish   parts qualities, talents, perhaps playing on the theatrical sense   123 statist's statesman's, politician's   124 outward place official position, i.e. the chancellorship   127 borne carried   134 tends serves/takes care of   135 study...watch the phrasing is ambiguous: 'More's study (office) is the place from which vigil is kept over the realm'/'Everyone is studying and watching what More does or thinks'   140 life of excellence living perfection   141 meanest humblest, of lowest social status   142 weight impressiveness   150 *Qui...qui–* 'He who was born in a most famous, glorious country has more trouble shining than he who–' (Latin)   152 be covered put your hat back on; removing one's hat was a mark of respect   forsworn renounced   153 tickle please, amuse/provoke   154 anon presently   157 conceive understand   vein character, way of behaving

He's ever furnished with these conceits.

RANDALL   Yes, faith, my learned poet doth not lie for that matter: I am neither more
160   nor less than merry Sir Thomas always. Wilt sup with me? By God, I love a parlous
wise fellow that smells of a politician better than a long progress.

Enter Sir Thomas More

SURREY   We are deluded, this is not his lordship.

RANDALL   I pray you, Erasmus, how long will the Holland cheese in your country
keep without maggots?

165   MORE   Fool, painted barbarism, retire thyself
Into thy first creation!   *[Exit Randall]*

Thus you see,
My loving learnèd friends, how far respect
Waits often on the ceremonious train
Of base illiterate wealth, whilst men of schools,
170   Shrouded in poverty, are counted fools.
Pardon, thou reverend German, I have mixed
So slight a jest to the fair entertainment
Of thy most worthy self; for know, Erasmus,
Mirth wrinkles up my face and I still crave
175   When that forsakes me I may hug my grave.

ERASMUS   Your honour's merry humour is best physic
Unto your able body; for we learn
Where melancholy chokes the passages
Of blood and breath, the erected spirit still
180   Lengthens our days with sportful exercise.
Study should be the saddest time of life,
The rest a sport exempt from thought of strife.

MORE   Erasmus preacheth gospel against physic.
My noble poet—

185   SURREY   O, my lord, you tax me
In that word poet of much idleness;
It is a study that makes poor our fate:
Poets were ever thought unfit for state.

MORE   O, give not up fair poesy, sweet lord,
190   To such contempt! That I may speak my heart,

---

158 **ever furnished with** always full of   **conceits** ideas, devices/fanciful, witty notions/tricks   160 **Wilt sup** will you dine   **parlous** shrewd, wonderful/
desperate, dangerous   161 **progress** official journey, visit by a monarch; it was reported that Henry VIII took More with him on visits to Oxford and
Cambridge to respond on his behalf to the orations they addressed to him   165 **painted** coloured so as to deceive, artificial   **barbarism** ignorance,
uncivilized rudeness   **retire...creation** go back to that for which you were first created, i.e. being a servant   168 **train** following, entourage   169 **men
of schools** (university) educated men   170 **Shrouded** clothed/hidden, concealed   **counted** considered/treated as   171 **reverend** worthy of great
respect   **German** Erasmus was in fact from the Netherlands but Dutch and German were used almost interchangeably   174 **still** continually   **crave**
earnestly desire   175 **hug** embrace   176 **best physic** the best medicine   177 **Unto...body** to keep your body fit   178 **melancholy...breath** according to
the doctrine of the humours, **melancholy** (black bile) could obstruct the passage of **blood** and air to the vital organs   179 **erected** noble, aspiring   **spirit**
vital principle/soul/impulse/character, disposition/intellect   180 **sportful** light-hearted, playful   181 **saddest** most serious, truest   183 **Erasmus...
physic** perhaps a reference to Erasmus' *Moriae Encomium* (1511), a satire on folly, *The Praise of Folly* but which, punning on his name, could also be
translated as *In Praise of More*, to whom it was dedicated   185 **tax** accuse, charge   187 **poor** wretched, unfortunate   188 **Poets...state** ironically both
Surrey and More were executed   189 **poesy** poetic composition

It is the sweetest heraldry of art

That sets a difference 'tween the tough sharp holly

And tender bay tree.

SURREY   Yet, my lord,

195   It is become the very lag number

To all mechanic sciences.

MORE   Why, I'll show the reason.

This is no age for poets: they should sing

To the loud canon *heroica facta*:

200   *Qui faciunt reges heroica carmina laudant*:

And, as great subjects of their pen decay,

Even so unphysicked they do melt away.

Enter Master Morris

Come, will your lordship in?— My dear Erasmus—

I'll hear you, Master Morris, presently.—

205   My lord, I make you master of my house:

We'll banquet here with fresh and staid delights,

The Muses' music here shall cheer our sprites;

The cates must be but mean where scholars sit,

For they're made all with courses of neat wit.   [*Exeunt Surrey,*

210   How now, Master Morris?   *Erasmus and Attendants*]

MORRIS   I am a suitor to your lordship in behalf of a servant of mine.

MORE   The fellow with long hair? Good Master Morris,

Come to me three years hence and then I'll hear you.

MORRIS   I understand your honour, but the foolish knave has submitted himself to

215   the mercy of a barber, and is without, ready to make a new vow before your lordship,

hereafter to live civil.

MORE   Nay, then, let's talk with him. Pray, call him in.

Enter Faulkner and Officers

FAULKNER   Bless your honour, a new man, my lord.

MORE   Why, sure, this is not he.

220   FAULKNER   An your lordship will, the barber shall give you a sample of my head:

I am he in faith, my lord, I am *ipse*.

MORE   Why, now thy face is like an honest man's:

Thou hast played well at this new cut and won.

FAULKNER   No, my lord, lost all that ever God sent me.

225   MORE   God sent thee into the world as thou art now,

With a short hair. How quickly are three years

Run out of Newgate!

FAULKNER   I think so, my lord, for there was but a hair's length between my going

thither and so long time.

191 **heraldry** symbolic practice, regulation   192 **holly** prickly evergreen tree symbolizing the harshness of politics   193 **tender bay tree** a wreath of Sweet Bay or *Laurus nobilis* was traditionally awarded to poets or conquerors   195 **lag number** last category   196 **mechanic sciences** fields of learning involving manual labour or skill, as opposed to the liberal arts   199 **canon** musical composition in parts, playing on the sense of a military 'cannon'   ***heroica facta*** 'heroic deeds' (Latin)   200 ***Qui...laudant*** 'epic poems praise what kings do' (Latin)   201 **great...away** poets decline without heroic subjects to write about   202 **unphysicked** untreated   206 **banquet** enjoy a light repast consisting of sweetmeats, fruit and wine   **staid** sober   207 **Muses** nine classical goddesses regarded as presiding over and inspiring the arts   **sprites** spirits   208 **cates** provisions, food, delicacies   209 **neat** elegant/pure   211 **suitor** petitioner   215 **without** outside   216 **civil** as befits a citizen   220 **An** if   **will** wishes   221 ***ipse*** 'himself' (Latin)   223 **cut** haircut/chance (as in the drawing of lots)   228 **hair's length** playing on the phrase a 'hair's breadth'

230 MORE   Because I see some grace in thee, go free.—

Discharge him, fellows.— Farewell, Master Morris.—   *[Exeunt Officers]*

Thy head is for thy shoulders now more fit:

Thou hast less hair upon it but more wit.   *[Exit]*

MORRIS   Did not I tell thee always of these locks?

235 FAULKNER   An the locks were on again, all the goldsmiths in Cheapside should not pick them open. 'S'heart, if my hair stand not on end when I look for my face in a glass, I am a polecat. Here's a lousy jest! But, if I notch not that rogue Tom Barber, that makes me look thus like a Brownist, hang me! I'll be worse to the nittical knave than ten tooth drawings. Here's a head with a pox!

240 MORRIS   What ail'st thou? Art thou mad now?

FAULKNER   Mad now? 'Nails, if loss of hair cannot mad a man, what can? I am deposed: my crown is taken from me. More had been better 'a scoured Moorditch than 'a notched me thus: does he begin sheep-shearing with Jack Faulkner?

MORRIS   Nay, 'an you feed this vein, sir, fare you well.

245 FAULKNER   Why, farewell frost. I'll go hang myself out for the poll head. Make a Saracen of Jack?

MORRIS   Thou desperate knave! For that I see the devil

Wholly gets hold of thee—

FAULKNER   The devil's a damned rascal.

250 MORRIS   I charge thee, wait on me no more: no more

Call me thy master.

FAULKNER   Why, then, a word, Master Morris.

MORRIS   I'll hear no words, sir, fare you well.

FAULKNER   'Sblood, farewell.

255 MORRIS   Why dost thou follow me?

FAULKNER   Because I'm an ass. Do you set your shavers upon me, and then cast me off? Must I condole? Have the Fates played the fools? Am I their cut? Now the poor sconce is taken, must Jack march with bag and baggage?   *Weeps*

MORRIS   You coxcomb!

260 FAULKNER   Nay, you ha' poached me; you ha' given me a hair, it's here, here.   *Indicating his head*

MORRIS   Away, you kind ass, come, sir, dry your eyes:

Keep you old place and mend these fooleries.

FAULKNER   I care not to be turned off, an 'twere a ladder, so it be in my humour or the Fates beckon to me. Nay, pray, sir, if the Destinies spin me a fine thread, Faulkner

---

233 **less…wit** playing on the common proverb, 'more hair than wit' 235 **An** if 236 **'S'heart** i.e. God's heart, an exclamation denoting surprise 237 **glass** looking-glass, mirror **polecat** small carnivorous animal noted for its smell, a common term of abuse **notch** crop/cut the hair unevenly/ mark 238 **Brownist** member of a banned dissenting sect, followers of Robert Brown, distinguished by their short hair; historically after More's time **nittical** infested with nits 239 **tooth drawings** taking out of teeth, another part of a barber's trade **head…pox** baldness was thought to be caused by the **pox** (venereal disease), playing on the common curse, 'pox on you' 241 **'Nails** by the nails on Christ's cross 242 **crown** encircling ornament for the head/wreath awarded as a sign of distinction/symbol of sovereignty/top of the head **'a scoured Moorditch** to have cleared out **Moorditch**, part of the moat around London which had become an open sewer and needed constant cleansing 243 **'a notched me** to have cut my hair 244 **an…vein** if you go on like this 245 **farewell frost** goodbye nothing; part of the saying, 'Farewell frost, nothing got nor nothing lost' **hang…head** Faulkner is playing on the idea of his shaven head being used as an inn sign, like the **Saracen**'s Head near Newgate 246 **Saracen** heathen, non-Christian/Turk's head for tilting at 250 **wait on** serve 256 **shavers** barbers/razors/swindlers/jokers 257 **condole** suffer, grieve **cut** chance victim drawn by lot/hack-horse (common term of abuse) 258 **sconce** crown of the head 259 **coxcomb** fool, from the 'cock's comb' shaped cap worn by professional fools 260 **poached** cooked like an egg, without its shell/shoved, thrust out/trampled **you…here** meaning unclear, perhaps 'you've given me something of very small value' or 'a cause of annoyance'; Faulkner's play on 'hair' and 'here', suggests indicative action of some kind 261 **kind ass** natural fool 262 **place** position 263 **turned off** dismissed; Faulkner shifts sense to allude to the hanged man who was said to be **'turned off** the ladder' at the moment of execution 264 **Fates/Destinies** alternative names for the classical deities responsible for an individual's life, imaged as a **thread** which was spun, measured out and finally cut

265   flies another pitch, and to avoid the headache hereafter, before I'll be a hair-monger
         I'll be a whoremonger.   *Exeunt*

[Act 3 Scene 3]

Enter [Sir Thomas More, Attendants and] a Messenger to More

MESSENGER   My honourable lord, the Mayor of London,
         Accompanied with his lady and her train,
         Are coming hither, and are hard at hand,
         To feast with you: a sergeant's come before,
5   To tell your lordship of their near approach.   *[Exit]*
     MORE   Why, this is cheerful news! Friends go and come:
         Reverend Erasmus, whose delicious words
         Express the very soul and life of wit,
         Newly took sad leave of me, and with tears
10   Troubled the silver channel of the Thames,
         Which, glad of such a burden, proudly swelled
         And on her bosom bore him toward the sea.
         He's gone to Rotterdam: peace go with him,
         He left me heavy when he went from hence,
15   But this recomforts me: the kind Lord Mayor,
         His brethren aldermen with their fair wives,
         Will feast this night with us. Why, so't should be:
         More's merry heart lives by good company.
         Good gentlemen, be careful; give great charge
20   Our diet be made dainty for the taste,
         For of all people that the earth affords,
         The Londoners fare richest at their boards.   *[Exeunt]*

[Act 4 Scene 1]

Enter Sir Thomas More, Master Roper and Servingmen setting stools

     MORE   Come, my good fellows, stir, be diligent,
         Sloth is an idle fellow, leave him now;
         The time requires your expeditious service.
         Place me here stools, to set the ladies on.—

---

265 pitch high point/height to which a bird of prey (or falcon) soars before swooping down on its quarry; Faulkner is punning on his own name **hair-monger** one who sells hair (for making wigs) **266 whoremonger** fornicator, lecher/pimp **[3.3]** *Addition V (Playhouse Scribe; possibly Shakespeare, revised by Heywood?). Location: an antechamber in More's house in the city of London* **2 train** retinue **3 hard** close **4 sergeant's** servingman, attendant **9 Newly** very lately **14 heavy** sad **15 recomforts** consoles **16 brethren** fellow, literally 'brothers' **19 gentlemen** addressed to the Attendants or senior members of More's household **be careful** take good care, pay attention to **give great charge** take a lot of trouble/spend as much as necessary **20 diet…taste** our food is delicious **22 fare…boards** have the most delicious/expensive foods at their tables **[4.1]** *Lines 1–275 Original Text (Munday); 276–323 Addition VI (Heywood?). Location: a room in More's house* **3 expeditious** speedy **4 me** the ethic dative is used for emphasis

5   Son Roper, you have given order for the banquet?

ROPER   I have, my lord, and everything is ready.

Enter Lady [More]

MORE   O, welcome, wife! Give you direction

How women should be placed, you know it best.

For my Lord Mayor, his brethren, and the rest,

10   Let me alone: men best can order men.

LADY MORE   I warrant ye, my lord, all shall be well.

There's one without that stays to speak with ye,

And bade me tell ye that he is a player.

MORE   A player, wife! One of ye bid him come in.   *Exit one*

15   Nay, stir there, fellows; fie, ye are too slow!

See that your lights be in a readiness:

The banquet shall be here. God's me, madam,

Leave my Lady Mayoress! Both of us from the board!

And my son Roper too! What may our guests think?

20   LADY MORE   My lord, they are risen and sitting by the fire.

MORE   Why, yet go you and keep them company,

It is not meet we should be absent both.   *Exit Lady*

Enter Player

Welcome, good friend, what is your will with me?

PLAYER   My lord, my fellows and myself

25   Are come to tender ye our willing service,

So please you to command us.

MORE   What, for a play, you mean?

Whom do ye serve?

PLAYER   My Lord Cardinal's grace.

30   MORE   My Lord Cardinal's players! Now, trust me, welcome.

You happen hither in a lucky time,

To pleasure me, and benefit yourselves.

The Mayor of London and some aldermen,

His lady and their wives, are my kind guests

35   This night at supper: now, to have a play

Before the banquet will be excellent.—

How think you, son Roper?

ROPER   'Twill do well, my lord,

And be right pleasing pastime to your guests.

40   MORE   I prithee, tell me, what plays have ye?

PLAYER   Divers, my lord: *The Cradle of Security*,

Hit Nail o'th'Head, *Impatient Poverty*,

---

5 banquet dessert course   **11 LADY MORE** More had married his first wife Jane Colt in 1505 and they had four children; after her death in 1511, he remarried a wealthy widow, Alice Middleton   **warrant** assure   **12 one…stays** someone outside waiting   **13 bade me** requested me to   **player** actor   **15 fie** exclamation of impatience   **16 lights** torches   **17 God's me** God bless/save me   **18 from the board** away from the table, i.e. leaving our guests   **20 they are risen** they've finished eating and left the table   **22 meet** fit, proper   **29 Lord Cardinal's grace** all acting companies were legally obliged to be under the protection of some nobleman; this non-historical episode was probably suggested by More's reputed acting ability when a page in Cardinal Morton's household   **34 kind** courteous, agreeable   **40 prithee** ask you   **41 Divers** various   ***The…Security*** now lost; R. Willis gives an account of a performance he attended around 1572 in *Mount Tabor, or Private Exercises of a Penitent Sinner*   **42 *Hit Nail o'th'Head*** perhaps an invented title   ***Impatient Poverty*** anonymous play printed in 1560

The Play of Four P's, Dives and Lazarus,

Lusty Juventus, and *The Marriage of Wit and Wisdom.*

45   MORE   *The Marriage of Wit and Wisdom!* That, my lads,

I'll none but that; the theme is very good,

And may maintain a liberal argument.

To marry wit to wisdom asks some cunning:

Many have wit that may come short of wisdom.

50   We'll see how master poet plays his part,

And whether wit or wisdom grace his art.—

Go, make him drink, and all his fellows too.—   *To Servingman*

How many are ye?

PLAYER   Four men and a boy, sir.

55   MORE   But one boy?

Then I see there's but few women in the play.

PLAYER   Three, my lord; Dame Science, Lady Vanity,

And Wisdom, she herself.

MORE   And one boy play them all? By our lady, he's laden!

60   Well, my good fellow, get ye straight together,

And make ye ready with what haste ye may.—

Provide their supper gainst the play be done,

Else shall we stay our guests here overlong.—

Make haste, I pray ye.

65   PLAYER   We will, my lord.   *Exeunt Servingmen and Player*

MORE   Where are the waits? Go, bid them play,

To spend the time awhile.

Enter Lady [*More*]

How now, madam?

LADY MORE   My lord, they're coming hither.

70   MORE   They're welcome. Wife, I'll tell ye one thing:

One sport is somewhat mended, we shall have

A play tonight, *The Marriage of Wit and Wisdom,*

And acted by my good Lord Cardinal's players.

How like ye that, wife?

75   LADY MORE   My lord, I like it well.

See, they are coming.   *The waits play hautboys*

Enter Lord Mayor, so many Aldermen as may, the Lady Mayoress in scarlet, with other

Ladies and Sir Thomas More's daughters, Servants carrying lighted torches by them

---

43 The Play...P's an interlude involving a debate between a Pardoner, a Palmer, an (a)Pothecary (one who kept a store or shop of non-perishable commodities, spices, drugs, comfits, preserves, etc.), and a Pedlar **Dives and Lazarus** based on the biblical story in Luke 16:19–31 **44 Lusty Juventus** popular anti-Catholic interlude by R. Wever on the follies of youth **The...Wisdom** interlude by Francis Marbury; this is not the same as the play performed here which is a pastiche mainly based on *Lusty Juventus* but with elements from *The Trial of Treasure, The Disobedient Child* and other interludes of the time **47 liberal** intellectual, suitable to persons of superior social station **48 cunning** learning/intelligence/skill **50 master poet** the playwright **54 boy...women** women's parts were played by boys **57 Science** knowledge; as in all morality plays, characters represent abstract qualities **59 laden** burdened, got a lot to do **62 gainst...done** for the end of the performance **63 Else...overlong** otherwise (if they eat beforehand) our guests will be kept waiting too long **66 waits** the town band, who played wind instruments and were maintained at public charge to entertain the citizens **67 spend... awhile** pass the short time while we wait *hautboys* wind instruments, forerunners of the oboe *as may* as there are actors available *in scarlet* refers to all the entrants, not just the Mayoress, as was customary on ceremonial occasions

MORE	Once again, welcome, welcome, my good Lord Mayor,
	And brethren all, for once I was your brother
	And so I am still in heart: it is not state

80
That can our love from London separate.
True, upstart fools, by sudden fortune tried,
Regard their former mates with naught but pride,
But they that cast an eye still whence they came,
Know how they rose, and how to use the same.

85 LORD MAYOR My lord, you set a gloss on London's fame
And make it happy ever by your name.
Needs must we say, when we remember More,
'Twas he that drove rebellion from our door
With grave discretions mild and gentle breath
90
Shielding a many subjects' lives from death.
O, how our city is by you renowned,
And with your virtues our endeavours crowned!

MORE   No more, my good Lord Mayor, but thanks to all
That on so short a summons you would come
95
To visit him that holds your kindness dear.—
Madam, you are not merry with my Lady Mayoress
And these fair ladies: pray ye, seat them all,
And here, my lord, let me appoint your place,
The rest to seat themselves. Nay, I'll weary ye,
100
You will not long in haste to visit me.

LADY MORE   Good madam, sit, in sooth you shall sit here.

LADY MAYORESS   Good madam, pardon me, it may not be.

LADY MORE   In troth, I'll have it so, I'll sit here by ye.—
Good ladies, sit.— More stools here, ho!

105 LADY MAYORESS   It is your favour, madam, makes me thus
Presume above my merit.

LADY MORE   When we come to you,
Then shall you rule us as we rule you here.
Now must I tell ye, madam, we have a play
110
To welcome ye withal; how good soe'er,
That know not I; my lord will have it so.

MORE   Wife, hope the best. I am sure they'll do their best: *Aside to her*
They that would better comes not at their feast.—
My good Lord Cardinal's players, I thank them for it,
115
Play us a play to lengthen out your welcome:
They say it is *The Marriage of Wit and Wisdom*,
A theme of some import, howe'er it prove,
But if art fail, we'll inch it out with love.

[*Enter a Servant*]

---

79 **state** social position, rank/riches, possessions   83 **still** constantly   84 **use** accustom themselves to   **the same** i.e. their fortune   89 **breath** words   99 **rest...themselves** may sit where they like   100 **You...me** you won't be so ready to visit me next time   101 **sooth** truth   103 **troth** truth, deed   110 **withal** in addition   **soe'er** it may be   113 **They...feast** those who are hard to please are never satisfied   117 **howe'er it prove** whatever the quality of the performance   118 **inch it out** eke it out, increase by small amounts

What, are they ready?

120 SERVANT   My lord, one of the players craves to speak with you.

MORE   With me? Where is he?

Enter [the actor playing] Inclination, the Vice, ready

INCLINATION   Here, my lord.

MORE   How now! What's the matter?

INCLINATION   We would desire your honour but to stay a little; one of my fellows is but
125 run to Ogle's for a long beard for young Wit, and he'll be here presently.

MORE   A long beard for young Wit! Why, man, he may be without a beard till he
come to marriage, for wit goes not all by the hair. When comes Wit in?

INCLINATION   In the second scene, next to the Prologue, my lord.

MORE   Why, play on till that scene come and by that time Wit's beard will be
130 grown, or else the fellow returned with it. And what part play'st thou?

INCLINATION   Inclination the Vice, my lord.

MORE   Gramercies, now I may take the vice if I list; and wherefore hast thou that
bridle in thy hand?

INCLINATION   I must be bridled anon, my lord.

135 MORE   An thou be'st not saddled too, it makes no matter, for then Wit's inclination
may gallop so fast that he will outstrip wisdom and fall to folly.

INCLINATION   Indeed, so he does to Lady Vanity; but we have no folly in our play.

MORE   Then there's no wit in't, I'll be sworn: folly waits on wit as the shadow on
the body, and where wit is ripest there folly still is readiest. But begin, I prithee, we'll
140 rather allow a beardless Wit, than wit all beard to have no brain.

INCLINATION   Nay, he has his apparel on too, my lord, and therefore he is the readier
to enter.

MORE   Then, good Inclination, begin at a venture.—   *Exit*
My Lord Mayor,   [*the actor playing Inclination*]
145 Wit lacks a beard, or else they would begin:
I'd lend him mine, but that it is too thin.
Silence, they come.   *The trumpet sounds*

Enter the Prologue

PROLOGUE   Now, for as much as in these latter days,
Throughout the whole world in every land,
150 Vice doth increase and virtue decays,
Iniquity having the upper hand,
We therefore intend, good gentle audience,
A pretty short interlude to play at this present,
Desiring your leave and quiet silence,
155 To show the same as is meet and expedient.

Vice comic character in a morality play representing one of the vices   *ready* in stage costume   **125 Ogle's** John Ogle's shop, the best-known theatrical
wig-maker of the period   **presently** soon   **127 wit...hair** another reference to the saying 'more wit than hair'; perhaps with a sexual innuendo on **wit**
meaning genitals   **132 Gramercies** many thanks (from French *grand merci*)   **134 bridled anon** in the anonymous *The Trial of Treasure* (1567), Inclination
the Vice is bridled by Just and Patience   **135 An...folly** as long as you don't ride wit as well, it doesn't matter, since wit may get carried away with itself and
become foolish   **saddled** ridden, straddled   **139 folly...readiest** perhaps an allusion to Erasmus' *Praise of Folly*, or to More's own well-known ready wit
140 allow...brain having the actor with the wit to play Wit without a beard is preferable to having one with a beard but without a brain   **141 apparel**
costume   **143 at a venture** right away   *The trumpet sounds* the usual way of announcing a performance   **148 Now...expedient** the first eight lines of
the prologue are from Thomas Ingelend's *The Disobedient Child*

It is called *The Marriage of Wit and Wisdom*,
A matter right pithy and pleasing to hear,
Whereof in brief we will show the whole sum,
But I must be gone, for Wit doth appear.   *Exit*

Enter Wit ruffling, and Inclination the Vice

160 WIT   In an arbour green, asleep whereas I lay,   *Sings*
                The birds sang sweetly in the midst of the day,
                I dreamed fast of mirth and play.
                In youth is pleasure, in youth is pleasure.
                Methought I walked still to and fro,
165   And from her company I could not go,
                But when I waked, it was not so.
                In youth is pleasure, in youth is pleasure.
                Therefore my heart is surely plight,
                Of her alone to have a sight,
170   Which is my joy and heart's delight.
                In youth is pleasure, in youth is pleasure.

MORE   Mark ye, my lord, this is Wit without a beard: what will he be by that time
he comes to the commodity of a beard?   *Aside to Lord Mayor*

INCLINATION   O, sir, the ground is the better on which she doth go,
175   For she will make better cheer with a little she can get,
                Than many a one can with a great banquet of meat.

WIT   And is her name Wisdom?

INCLINATION   Ay, sir, a wife most fit
                For you, my good master, my dainty sweet Wit.

180 WIT   To be in her company my heart it is set:
                Therefore I prithee to let us be gone,
                For unto Wisdom Wit hath inclination.

INCLINATION   O, sir, she will come herself even anon,
                For I told her before where we would stand,
185   And then she said she would beck us with her hand.
                Back with those boys and saucy great knaves!   *Flourishing his dagger*
                What, stand ye here so big in your braves?
                My dagger about your coxcombs shall walk
                If I may but so much as hear ye chat or talk.

190 WIT   But will she take pains to come for us hither?

INCLINATION   I warrant ye, therefore you must be familiar with her;
                When she cometh in place,
                You must her embrace
                Somewhat handsomely,
195   Lest she think it danger,

---

ruffling swaggering, arroganity   **160 arbour** bower of trees and shrubs   *Sings* Wit's song is from *Lusty Juventus*   **162 fast** immediately/fixedly
164 still continually   **168 plight** pledged   **173 commodity** advantage/gain, addition   **175 cheer** food, provision/entertainment   **176 banquet** feast
178 fit suitable   **181 prithee** beg you   **183 even anon** just now   **185 beck** beckon, gesture to   **187 braves** bravado, boastful or threatening behaviour
188 coxcombs heads   **191 warrant ye** guarantee you   **192 cometh in place** arrives in person

Because you are a stranger,

To come in your company.

WIT   I warrant thee, Inclination, I will be busy:

O, how Wit longs to be in Wisdom's company!

Enter Lady Vanity singing, and beckoning with her hand

200   VANITY   Come hither, come hither, come hither, come:

Such cheer as I have, thou shalt have some.

MORE   This is Lady Vanity, I'll hold my life:

Beware, good Wit, you take not her to wife.

INCLINATION   What, Unknown Honesty, a word in your ear.   *She offers to depart*

205   You shall not be gone as yet, I swear:

Here's none but friends, you need not to fray,

This young gentleman loves ye, therefore you must stay.

WIT   I trust in me she will think no danger,

For I love well the company of fair women,

210   And though to you I am a stranger,

Yet Wit may pleasure you now and then.

VANITY   Who, you? Nay, you are such a holy man,

That to touch on you dare not be bold;

I think you would not kiss a young woman,

215   If one would give ye twenty pound in gold.

WIT   Yes, in good sadness, lady, that I would,

I could find in my heart to kiss you in your smock.

VANITY   My back is broad enough to bear that mock,

For it hath been told me many a time

220   That you would be seen in no such company as mine.

WIT   Not Wit in the company of Lady Wisdom?

O Jove, for what do I hither come?

INCLINATION   Sir, she did this nothing else but to prove

Whether a little thing would you move

225   To be angry and fret:

What, and if one said so,

Let such trifling matters go

And with a kind kiss come out of her debt.—

Is Luggins come yet with the beard?

Enter another Player

230   PLAYER   No, faith, he is not come: alas, what shall we do?

INCLINATION   Forsooth, we can go no further till our fellow Luggins come, for he   *To More*

plays Good Counsel, and now he should enter, to admonish Wit that this is Lady

Vanity, and not Lady Wisdom.

MORE   Nay, and it be no more but so, ye shall not tarry at a stand for that; we'll

235   not have our play marred for lack of a little good counsel: till your fellow come,

---

201 **cheer** food   202 **hold** offer as a wager, bet   204 **Unknown Honesty** a character from *Lusty Juventus*   206 **fray** be afraid   216 **good sadness**
all seriousness   217 **smock** shift, undergarment   222 **Jove** chief Roman god   226 **and** even   231 **Forsooth** truly, indeed   232 **admonish** inform/
warn   234 **tarry** wait, delay   **stand** stop, pause/state of being unable to proceed

I'll give him the best counsel that I can.— Pardon me, my Lord Mayor, I love to be
merry.—

    O, Wit, thou art now on the bow-hand,   *Playing Good Counsel*

    And blindly in thine own opinion dost stand.

240   I tell thee, this naughty lewd Inclination

    Does lead thee amiss in a very strange fashion:

    This is not Wisdom, but Lady Vanity,

    Therefore list to Good Counsel, and be ruled by me.

INCLINATION In troth, my lord, it is as right to Luggins's part as can be.— Speak, Wit.

245   MORE   Nay, we will not have our audience disappointed, if I can help it.

    WIT   Art thou Good Counsel, and will tell me so?

    Wouldst thou have Wit from Lady Wisdom to go?

    Thou art some deceiver, I tell thee verily,

    In saying that this is Lady Vanity.

250   MORE   Wit, judge not things by the outward show,

    The eye oft mistakes, right well you do know:

    Good Counsel assures thee upon his honesty,

    That this is not Wisdom, but Lady Vanity.

Enter Luggins, with the beard

INCLINATION O, my lord, he is come, now we shall go forward.

255   MORE   Art thou come? Well, fellow, I have holp to save thine honesty a little.
Now, if thou canst give Wit any better counsel than I have done, spare not: there I
leave him to thy mercy.

    But by this time, I am sure our banquet's ready:

    My lord and ladies, we will taste that first

260   And then they shall begin the play again,

    Which, through the fellow's absence, and by me,

    Instead of helping, hath been hindered.—

    Prepare against we come.— Lights there, I say!—

    Thus fools oft times do help to mar the play.   *Exeunt all but players*

265   WIT   Fie, fellow Luggins, you serve us handsomely; do ye not, think ye?

    LUGGINS   Why, Ogle was not within and his wife would not let me have the beard,
and, by my troth, I ran so fast that I sweat again.

INCLINATION Do ye hear, fellows? Would not my lord make a rare player? O, he would
uphold a company beyond all hope, better than Mason among the king's players! Did

270   ye mark how extemprically he fell to the matter, and spake Luggins's part almost as
it is in the very book set down?

    WIT   Peace, do ye know what ye say? My lord a player! Let us not meddle with
any such matters: yet I may be a little proud that my lord hath answered me in my
part. But come, let us go, and be ready to begin the play again.

---

238 **bow-hand** hand which holds the bow in archery, i.e. the left hand; hence, wide of the mark, 'out'   239 **blindly…stand** you're deceived in your own
opinion   240 **lewd** wicked, unprincipled/lascivious, unchaste   243 **list** listen   248 **verily** truly   250 **outward show** external appearance; proverbial,
from John, 7:24   255 **holp** helped   263 **against we come** for our return from the banquet   264 **mar** hinder/spoil   265 **handsomely** in fine style
(ironic)   266 **within** at his shop   268 **rare player** fine actor   269 **uphold** succeed in   **Mason…players** there is no record of any actor of this name,
nor was there a company of king's players in Henry VIII's time   270 **extemprically** extempore, without rehearsal; the word may be a malapropism for
'extemporarily'   **spake** spoke   271 **very…down** as it's written in the company's own promptbook   272 **My…player!** an unthinkable idea for such a
humble profession   273 **answered…part** given me my cue

275   LUGGINS   Ay, that's the best, for now we lack nothing.

Enter a Servingman to the players with a reward

SERVINGMAN   Where be these players?

ALL   Here, sir.

SERVINGMAN   My lord is sent for to the court,

And all the guests do after supper part,

280   And, for he will not trouble you again,

By me for your reward a sends eight angels,

With many thanks. But sup before you go:

It is his will you should be fairly entreated:

Follow, I pray ye.   [*Exit*]

285   WIT   This, Luggins, is your negligence:

Wanting Wit's beard brought things into dislike,

For otherwise the play had been all seen,

Where now some curious citizen disgraced it,

And discommending it, all is dismissed.

290   INCLINATION   'Fore God, a says true. But hear ye, sirs, eight angels, ha! My lord would never give's eight angels, more or less for twelvepence. Either it should be three pounds, five pounds or ten pounds. There's twenty shillings wanting, sure.

WIT   Twenty to one, 'tis so. I have a trick: my lord comes, stand aside.

Enter More with Attendants, with purse and mace

MORE   In haste to council! What's the business now

295   That all so late his highness sends for me?—

What seek'st thou, fellow?

WIT   Nay, nothing:

Your lordship sent eight angels by your man,

And I have lost two of them in the rushes.

300   MORE   Wit, look to that: eight angels? I did send them ten.— Who gave it them?

SERVINGMAN   I, my lord, I had no more about me,

But by and by they shall receive the rest.

MORE   Well, Wit, 'twas wisely done: thou play'st Wit well indeed,

Not to be thus deceived of thy right.

305   Am I a man by office truly ordained

Equally to decide true right his own,

And shall I have deceivers in my house?

Then what avails my bounty, when such servants

Deceive the poor of what the master gives?

310   Go on, and pull his coat over his ears.

There are too many such. Give them their right.

Wit, let thy fellows thank thee: 'twas well done:

---

281 **a** he   **angels** English gold coins, worth approximately eight shillings in Henry VIII's time   283 **entreated** treated/entertained   288 **curious** difficult to satisfy, fastidious   **disgraced** disparaged, reviled   289 **discommending** finding fault with   **all is** all of us are   291 **more...twelvepence** the sense seems to be that he wouldn't quibble over a small sum   **twelvepence** one shilling   292 **twenty shillings** worth one pound sterling   **wanting** missing   299 **rushes** used for strewing on floors   304 **deceived** cheated   305 **office...own** whose position and training is to ensure that everyone is awarded what they truly deserve   **ordained** appointed   307 **deceivers** cheats, liars   308 **avails my bounty** is the value of my generosity   310 **pull... ears** remove his livery coat, the symbol of his employment, hence 'dismiss him'   311 **their right** the money owed them

Thou now deserv'st to match with Lady Wisdom.   [*Exit More, with Attendants*]

INCLINATION   God 'a mercy, Wit!— Sir, you had a master Sir Thomas More more, but
315   now we shall have more.

LUGGINS   God bless him! I would there were more of his mind! A loves our quality,
and yet he's a learned man and knows what the world is.

INCLINATION   Well, a kind man, and more loving than many other, but I think we
ha' met with the first—

320   LUGGINS   First served his man that had our angels, and he may chance dine with
Duke Humphrey tomorrow, being turned away today. Come, let's go!

INCLINATION   And many such rewards would make us all ride, and horse us with the
best nags in Smithfield.   [*Exeunt*]

[Act 4 Scene 2]

Enter the Earls of Shrewsbury [and] Surrey, [the] Bishop of Rochester, and other lords,
severally, doing courtesy to each other, [the] Clerk of the Council waiting bareheaded

SURREY   Good morrow to my lord of Shrewsbury.

SHREWSBURY   The like unto the honoured Earl of Surrey.
Yond comes my lord of Rochester.

ROCHESTER   Good morrow, my good lords.

5   SURREY   Clerk of the Council, what time is't of day?

CLERK   Past eight o'clock, my lord.

SHREWSBURY   I wonder that my good Lord Chancellor
Doth stay so long, considering there's matters
Of high importance to be scanned upon.

10   SURREY   Clerk of the Council, certify his lordship
The lords expect him here.

ROCHESTER   It shall not need:
Yond comes his lordship.

Enter Sir Thomas More, with purse and mace borne before him

MORE   Good morrow to this fair assembly.

15   Come, my good lords, let's sit. O serious square,   *They sit*
Upon this little board is daily scanned
The health and preservation of the land;

---

313 **match with** be married to   314 **God 'a mercy** God have mercy on us   **Sir, … more** addressed to the dismissed servant, the phrase is awkward but seems to mean, 'You, fellow, had a master, Sir Thomas More, who was more than a master but now we shall have more than you'   316 **mind** judgement, way of thinking   **quality** profession/people of the same profession, especially actors   318 **loving** affectionate, good-natured   320 **served** gave him what he deserved, i.e. dismissed him   **dine … Humphrey** go without dinner; Duke Humphrey's tomb in St Paul's cathedral was where the poor and masterless men would gather in the hope of finding a friend to invite them to dine or a new employer   321 **turned away** dismissed   322 **horse … Smithfield** provide us all with broken down horses   **Smithfield** London's main livestock market, notorious for rogue horse dealing   [4.2]   *Original Text (Munday).* *Location: Whitehall: the Council chamber; the scene conflates events and manipulates time for dramatic purposes*   **Surrey** Thomas Howard was created third Duke of Norfolk in 1524 and a member of the Privy Council   *severally* separately/through separate entrances   *doing courtesy* bowing   1 **morrow** morning; the time is **eight o'clock** in the morning not, as the previous scene implies, the evening   3 **lord of Rochester** Dr John Fisher, Bishop of Rochester from 1504 and Chancellor of the University of Cambridge; he was executed in 1535 for refusing to recognize Henry VIII as head of the Church of England   8 **stay** delay   9 **scanned upon** examined, passed judgement on   10 **certify** clearly inform   13 **Yond** yonder, at some distance but within sight   15 **square** council table/guiding principle, example, playing on the sense of a carpenter's square, used to determine perfect right angles

We the physicians that effect this good,

Now by choice diet, anon by letting blood.

20   Our toil and careful watching brings the king

In league with slumbers, to which peace doth sing.—

Avoid the room there!—   *[Exeunt Attendants]*

What business, lords, today?

SHREWSBURY   This, my good lord,

25   About the entertainment of the emperor

Gainst the perfidious French into our pay.

SURREY   My lords, as 'tis the custom in this place

The youngest should speak first, so, if I chance

In this case to speak youngly, pardon me.

30   I will agree, France now hath her full strength,

As having new recovered the pale blood

Which war sluiced forth, and I consent to this,

That the conjunction of our English forces

With arms of Germany may sooner bring

35   This prize of conquest in, but then, my lords,

As in the moral hunting 'twixt the lion

And other beasts, force joined with greed

Frighted the weaker sharers from their parts.

So, if the empire's sovereign chance to put

40   His plea of partnership into war's court,

Swords should decide the difference and our blood

In private tears lament his entertainment.

SHREWSBURY   To doubt the worst is still the wise man's shield

That arms him safely; but the world knows this:

45   The emperor is a man of royal faith.

His love unto our sovereign brings him down

From his imperial seat to march in pay

Under our English flag and wear the cross,

Like some high order, on his manly breast.

50   Thus serving, he's not master of himself,

But, like a colonel commanding other,

Is by the general overawed himself.

ROCHESTER   Yet, my good lord—

---

19 choice diet carefully chosen foodstuffs, i.e. judicious deeds   **anon** then, at other times   **letting blood** bloodletting or phlebotomy was a standard medical procedure of the time; in terms of the medico-political metaphor employed here, capital punishment   **20 Our…sing** our hard work and vigilance allow the king to sleep peacefully to the sound of lullabies   **22 Avoid** clear, i.e. of non-Privy Council members   **25 entertainment** employment   **emperor…pay** Maximilian I of Habsburg supported the English against France; he was Holy Roman Emperor from 1508 to 1519 when he was succeeded by his grandson, Charles V   **29 youngly** youthfully, immaturely; reveals further confusion between the youthful Henry Howard and his father   **32 sluiced forth** caused to flow, as in the releasing of a sluice gate   **36 moral…beasts** based on Aesop's fable on hunting in which the lion defrauds an ass out of its share of the spoils; a later version includes a cow, sheep and goat   **38 sharers…parts** perhaps a reference to the practice in acting companies at the time, in which the leading actors received the lion's share of the profits   **39 empire…entertainment** Surrey warns against an alliance with the Holy Roman Emperor on the grounds that his superior military power may prove a threat to his allies   **43 To…safely** fearing the worst is a safeguard against danger   **doubt** fear   **48 cross** the red cross of St George   **49 high order** noble insignia   **51 other** others   **52 overawed** restrained, controlled by respect tinged with fear

SHREWSBURY Let me conclude my speech.

55   As subjects share no portion in the conquest

    Of their true sovereign, other than the merit

    That from the sovereign guerdons the true subject,

    So the good emperor, in a friendly league

    Of amity with England, will not soil

60   His honour with the theft of English spoil.

MORE   There is no question but this entertainment

    Will be most honourable, most commodious.

    I have oft heard good captains wish to have

    Rich soldiers to attend them, such as would fight

65   Both for their lives and livings: such a one

    Is the good emperor — I would to God

    We had ten thousand of such able men.

    Ha, then there would appear no court, no city,

    But where the wars were, they would pay themselves.

70   Then, to prevent in French wars England's loss,

    Let German flags wave with our English cross.

Enter Sir Thomas Palmer

PALMER   My lords, his majesty hath sent by me

    These articles enclosed, first to be viewed

    And then to be subscribed to: I tender them

75   In that due reverence which befits this place.   *With great reverence*

MORE   Subscribe these articles? Stay, let us pause:

    Our conscience first shall parley with our laws.

    My lord of Rochester, view you the paper.

ROCHESTER Subscribe to these! Now, good Sir Thomas Palmer,

80   Beseech the king that he will pardon me.

    My heart will check my hand whilst I do write:

    Subscribing so, I were an hypocrite.

PALMER   Do you refuse it, then, my lord?

ROCHESTER I do, Sir Thomas.

85 PALMER   Then here I summon you forthwith t'appear

    Before his majesty, to answer there

    This capital contempt.

ROCHESTER   I rise and part,

    In lieu of this, to tender him my heart.   *He riseth*

---

57 **guerdons** rewards 60 **spoil** booty 62 **commodious** advantageous, profitable 65 **livings** estates, possessions 68 **then...themselves** precise meaning obscure but the general sense is 'in that case there would be no need for any state since each landowner would bring in enough plunder to self-fund the war' 73 **articles** presumably the *Articles Devised by the Whole Consent of the King's Council* (1533); they are identified here with the later Oath of Supremacy and Act of Succession 74 **subscribed** signed *With great reverence* employing a gesture of respect such as a deep bow or bended knee 77 **parley** come to terms with 80 **Beseech** earnestly beg **pardon** excuse/forgive 81 **check** stop, restrain/rebuke 87 **capital contempt** open disrespect of the king, a capital offence punishable by death 89 **lieu** place **this** i.e. his signature on the document **tender** offer (in discharge of a debt), a legal term; Fisher had in fact already resigned at this point

90 PALMER   Wilt please your honour to subscribe, my lord?

    MORE   Sir, tell his highness, I entreat

             Some time for to bethink me of this task:

             In the meanwhile I do resign mine office

             Into my sovereign's hands.

95 PALMER   Then, my lord,

             Hear the prepared order from the king:

             On your refusal, you shall straight depart

             Unto your house at Chelsea, till you know

             Our sovereign's further pleasure.

100 MORE   Most willingly I go.—

             My lords, if you will visit me at Chelsea,

             We'll go a-fishing, and with a cunning net,

             Not like weak film, we'll catch none but the great.

             Farewell, my noble lords. Why, this is right:

105   Good morrow to the sun, to state good night!   *Exit*

    PALMER   Will you subscribe, my lords?

    SURREY   Instantly, good Sir Thomas,

             We'll bring the writing unto our sovereign.   *They write*

    PALMER   My lord of Rochester,

110   You must with me, to answer this contempt.

    ROCHESTER   This is the worst,

             Who's freed from life is from all care exempt.   *Exeunt Rochester and Palmer*

    SURREY   Now let us hasten to our sovereign.

             'Tis strange that my Lord Chancellor should refuse

115   The duty that the law of God bequeaths

             Unto the king.

    SHREWSBURY   Come, let us in. No doubt

             His mind will alter, and the bishop's too:

             Error in learnèd heads hath much to do.   *[Exeunt]*

[Act 4 Scene 3]

Enter the Lady More, her two daughters, and Master Roper, as walking

    ROPER   Madam, what ails ye for to look so sad?

    LADY MORE   Troth, son, I know not what; I am not sick,

             And yet I am not well. I would be merry,

             But somewhat lies so heavy on heart,

5   I cannot choose but sigh. You are a scholar:

             I pray ye, tell me, may one credit dreams?

    ROPER   Why ask you that, dear madam?

---

91 **entreat** beg   93 **mine office** his post as Lord Chancellor; More resigned in 1532 and retired to his house in Chelsea   102 **cunning** skilful, ingenious
103 **weak film** fine gossamer thread   112 **Who's** whoever is   **exempt** free, removed   114 **'Tis…king** More's disobedience to the king is **strange** because
in quelling the riot (in Act 2) he employed the argument that subjects were bound to obey their king, as God's representative on earth   119 **Error…do**
there is a lot of scope for an educated person to fall into error   **[4.3]**   *Original Text (Munday). Location: Chelsea*   2 **Troth** indeed, truly   4 **somewhat**
there's something   6 **credit** believe

LADY MORE　Because tonight I had the strangest dream

That e'er my sleep was troubled with. Methought 'twas night,

10　And that the king and queen went on the Thames

In barges to hear music, my lord and I

Were in a little boat methought — Lord, Lord,

What strange things live in slumbers! – and being near,

We grappled to the barge that bare the king.

15　But after many pleasing voices spent

In that still moving music house, methought

The violence of the stream did sever us

Quite from the golden fleet, and hurried us

Unto the bridge, which with unusèd horror

20　We entered at full tide; thence some slight shoot

Being carried by the waves, our boat stood still

Just opposite the Tower, and there it turned

And turned about, as when a whirlpool sucks

The circled waters: methought that we both cried,

25　Till that we sunk, where arm in arm we died.

ROPER　Give no respect, dear madam, to fond dreams:

They are but slight illusions of the blood.

LADY MORE　Tell me not all are so, for often dreams

Are true diviners, either of good or ill.

30　I cannot be in quiet till I hear

How my lord fares.

ROPER　(*Aside*) Nor I.— Come hither, wife,

I will not fright thy mother, to interpret

The nature of a dream, but trust me, sweet,

35　This night I have been troubled with thy father

Beyond all thought.

ROPER'S WIFE　Truly, and so have I:

Methought I saw him here in Chelsea church,

Standing upon the rood-loft, now defaced,

40　And whilst he kneeled and prayed before the image,

It fell with him into the upper choir,

Where my poor father lay all stained in blood.

ROPER　Our dreams all meet in one conclusion,

Fatal, I fear.

45　LADY MORE　What's that you talk? I pray ye, let me know it.

ROPER'S WIFE　Nothing, good mother.

LADY MORE　This is your fashion still, I must know nothing.

Call Master Catesby; he shall straight to court,

---

14 grappled fastened with grappling irons, perhaps playing on the sense of 'fought at close quarters'　**bare** bore　**15 pleasing voices** i.e. of singing and conversation　**16 still** continually　**music house** a barge with musicians on the Thames, a popular royal entertainment　**17 sever us Quite** completely cut us off　**19 unusèd** unaccustomed　**20 slight shoot** small but sudden rush of water　**22 Tower** Tower of London; traitors were taken by river through Traitors' Gate　**24 circled** circling　**26 Give no respect** pay no attention　**fond** foolish　**27 slight illusions** weak fancies　**38 Chelsea church** where More spent much of his time praying during these events　**39 rood-loft** gallery above the nave of a church, with a screen of richly carved stone or wood and bearing the figure of Christ on the cross　**now defaced** referring to the Protestant destruction of such images that took place after More's death　**41 choir** part of the church reserved for the choir to sing

And see how my lord does: I shall not rest

50   Until my heart leave panting on his breast.

Enter Sir Thomas More merrily, Servants attending

DAUGHTER   See where my father comes, joyful and merry.

MORE   As seamen, having passed a troubled storm,

Dance on the pleasant shore, so I — O, I could speak

Now like a poet! Now, afore God, I am passing light—

55   Wife, give me kind welcome: thou wast wont to blame

My kissing when my beard was in the stubble,

But I have been trimmed of late: I have had

A smooth court shaving, in good faith I have.   *Daughters kneel*

God bless ye! Son Roper, give me your hand.

60   ROPER   Your honour's welcome home.

MORE   Honour! Ha ha!— And how dost, wife?

ROPER   He bears himself most strangely.

LADY MORE   Will your lordship in?

MORE   Lordship? No, wife, that's gone:

65   The ground was slight that we did lean upon.

LADY MORE   Lord, that your honour ne'er will leave these jests!

In faith, it ill becomes ye.

MORE   O, good wife,

Honour and jests are both together fled:

70   The merriest councillor of England's dead.

LADY MORE   Who's that, my lord?

MORE   Still lord! The Lord Chancellor, wife.

LADY MORE   That's you.

MORE   Certain, but I have changed my life.

75   Am I not leaner than I was before?

The fat is gone: my title's only More.

Contented with one style, I'll live at rest:

They that have many names are not still best.

I have resigned mine office: count'st me not wise?

80   LADY MORE   O God!

MORE   Come, breed not female children in your eyes:

The king will have it so.

LADY MORE   What's the offence?

MORE   Tush, let that pass; we'll talk of that anon.

85   The king seems a physician to my fate,

---

50 leave panting ceases breathing heavily, which may mean 'until I die'; other editors have conjectured that it should read 'lean panting' meaning that Lady More will not rest until she rests her head on More's chest and knows that he's alive   **54 passing light** extremely cheerful/relieved of a great weight/ of small account, no longer commanding social respect, perhaps playing on further senses of 'clean', 'pure', 'luminous'   **55 thou...shaving** you used to complain about **kissing** me when I had **stubble** on my chin but now the **court** has given me a very close shave; this is ironic in view of More's earlier treatment of Faulkner   **62 bears himself** is behaving   **65 ground...upon** the foundation on which our social rise was based was flimsy   **77 style** name/ way of living   **81 female children** womanish tears   **84 Tush** exclamation of impatience   **anon** later   **85 king...state** Henry wishes to improve More's condition by encouraging him to resume his duties

His princely mind would train me back to state.

ROPER   Then be his patient, my most honoured father.

MORE   O, son Roper,

Ubi turpis est medicina, sanari piget!—

90   No, wife, be merry, and be merry, all:

You smiled at rising, weep not at my fall.

Let's in, and hear joy like to private friends,

Since days of pleasure have repentant ends:

The light of greatness is with triumph born,

95   It sets at midday oft with public scorn.   *Exeunt*

[Act 4 Scene 4]

Enter the Bishop of Rochester, Surrey, Shrewsbury, Lieutenant of the Tower and Warders
with weapons

ROCHESTER   Your kind persuasions, honourable lords,

I can but thank ye for, but in this breast

There lives a soul that aims at higher things

Than temporary pleasing earthly kings.

5   God bless his highness even with all my heart,

We shall meet one day, though that now we part.

SURREY   We not misdoubt your wisdom can discern

What best befits it, yet in love and zeal

We could entreat it might be otherwise.

10   SHREWSBURY   No doubt your fatherhood will by yourself

Consider better of the present case,

And grow as great in favour as before.

ROCHESTER   For that, as pleaseth God, in my restraint

From worldly causes, I shall better see

15   Into myself than at proud liberty:

The Tower and I will privately confer

Of things, wherein at freedom I may err.

But I am troublesome unto your honours,

And hold ye longer than becomes my duty.

20   Master Lieutenant, I am now your charge,

And though you keep my body, yet my love

Waits on my king and you, while Fisher lives.

SURREY   Farewell, my lord of Rochester, we'll pray

For your release, and labour't as we may.

---

89 *Ubi...piget* When the medicine is repulsive, one is reluctant to be cured (Latin) from Seneca's *Oedipus*, l. 517   94 **light...scorn** earthly triumph is
likened to the sun; it frequently ends in failure when success is at its high point   **[4.4]**   *Original Text (Munday).* **Location:** *The Tower of London*
6 **meet one day** i.e. in heaven after death   7 **not misdoubt** do not doubt   8 **zeal** fervent devotion   13 **For...liberty** as for reconsidering my position, it will
be easier to do this in prison where I am free from worldly cares   19 **hold ye** detain you   **becomes my duty** I should do   20 **charge** responsibility
22 **Waits on** is at the service of/observes   24 **labour't...may** do what we can to bring it about

25 SHREWSBURY Thereof assure yourself; so do we leave ye,

And to your happy private thoughts bequeath ye.   *Exeunt Lords*

ROCHESTER Now, Master Lieutenant, on, a God's name, go!

And with as glad a mind go I with you

As ever truant bade the school adieu.   *Exeunt*

[Act 4 Scene 5]

Enter Sir Thomas More, his Lady, Daughters, Master Roper, Gentlemen, and Servants
[including Catesby and Gough], as in his house at Chelsea. Low stools [are brought in]

MORE   Good morrow, good son Roper.

Sit, good madam,

Upon an humble seat: the time so craves.

Rest your good heart on earth, the roof of graves.

5   You see the floor of greatness is uneven,

The cricket and high throne alike near heaven.

Now, daughters, you that like to branches spread

And give best shadow to a private house,

Be comforted, my girls; your hopes stand fair:

10   Virtue breeds gentry, she makes the best heir.

BOTH DAUGHTERS Good morrow to your honour.

MORE   Nay, goodnight rather:

Your honour's crest-fall'n with your happy father.

ROPER   O, what formality, what square observance,

15   Lives in a little room! Here public care

Gags not the eyes of slumber; here fierce riot

Ruffles not proudly in a coat of trust,

Whilst, like a pawn at chess, he keeps in rank

With kings and mighty fellows; yet indeed

20   Those men that stand on tiptoe smile to see

Him pawn his fortunes.

MORE   True, son, here [...]

Nor does the wanton tongue here screw itself

Into the ear, that like a vice drinks up

25   The iron instrument.

LADY MORE We are here at peace.

MORE   Then peace, good wife.

---

26 **bequeath ye** deliver you, hand you over   27 **on** move on   **a** in   29 **bade** wished   **adieu** 'farewell' (French)   [4.5] *Lines 1–59, 131–214 Original Text (Munday); 60–130 Addition I (Chettle). Location: Chelsea: a room in More's house*   3 **craves** demands   6 **cricket** low wooden stool   10 **Virtue breeds gentry** virtue is the true nobility   13 **Your...father** the title 'your honour' is no longer applicable to your father which makes him happy   **crest-fall'n** humbled, cast-down   14 **formality** decorum, propriety (of behaviour)   **square observance** honest care/adherence to duty   15 **a little room** i.e. More's humble house   16 **Gags not** does not prop open/deprive   17 **Ruffles not** does not swagger   **in...trust** while wearing the livery of greatness (which gives impunity)   18 **Whilst...fellows** he mingles with kings, knights and bishops, as a pawn does in the game of chess   20 **Those...tiptoe** the ambitious, who are anxious to raise themselves as high as possible   21 **pawn** risk, stake, playing on the sense of 'minion', 'person of little value'   22 **[...]** there is a gap or lacuna in the manuscript at this point, but the sense suggests a negative as More continues comparing the superficiality of the court with the honest simplicity of his home   23 **wanton** undisciplined/ill-mannered/lascivious   **tongue...instrument** the image is of the tongue as a metal screw which penetrates the ear which then grips it tightly   27 **peace** let's have peace/don't say any more

LADY MORE For keeping still in compass, a strange point

In time's new navigation, we have sailed

30 Beyond our course.

MORE Have done.

LADY MORE We are exiled the court.

MORE Still thou harp'st on that:

'Tis sin for to deserve that banishment,

35 But he that ne'er knew court courts sweet content.

LADY MORE O, but dear husband—

MORE I will not hear thee, wife;

The winding labyrinth of thy strange discourse

Will ne'er have end. Sit still and, my good wife,

40 Entreat thy tongue be still, or credit me,

Thou shalt not understand a word we speak,

We'll talk in Latin:

Humida vallis raros patitur fulminis ictus.

More rest enjoys the subject meanly bred

45 Than he that bears the kingdom in his head.

Great men are still musicians, else the world lies,

They learn low strains after the notes that rise.

ROPER Good sir, be still yourself, and but remember

How in this general court of short-lived pleasure,

50 The world, creation is the ample food

That is digested in the maw of time.

If man himself be subject to such ruin,

How shall his garment then or the loose points

That tie respect unto his awful place,

55 Avoid destruction? Most honoured father-in-law,

The blood you have bequeathed these several hearts

To nourish your posterity, stands firm,

And, as with joy you led us first to rise,

So with like hearts we'll lock preferment's eyes.

60 MORE Now will I speak like More in melancholy;

For if grief's power could with her sharpest darts

Pierce my firm bosom, here's sufficient cause

To take my farewell of mirth's hurtless laws.

Poor humbled lady, thou that wert of late

---

28 **keeping…course** a nautical metaphor: maintaining their course, an odd destination in these times, they have lost their way and gone too far **compass** instrument for determining a ship's course at sea/the bounds of moderation 43 *Humida…ictus* the low, damp valley is rarely struck by thunderbolts (Latin), from Seneca's *Hippolytus*, ll:1132–3; in fact More's second wife knew some Latin 44 **meanly bred** of humble birth and upbringing 46 **Great…rise** great men survive (play music), if the world is right, by learning from those who overreach themselves (singing high notes) 50 **creation** all living things **ample** abundant 51 **maw** jaws, mouth 53 **garment** outer covering, i.e. earthly riches and honours **loose points** loosely tied laces which fasten the doublet to the hose 54 **awful** commanding fear, respect 56 **these several** each and every one of these various 57 **nourish your posterity** nurture your descendants/inheritance 59 **So…eyes** we will with similarly joyful hearts close our eyes to social advancement/high office 60 **in melancholy** as affected by the disease caused, according to medical thinking at the time, by an excess of black bile 62 **here's** probably referring to his wife 63 **hurtless** harmless 64 **Poor…earthly thing** this passage of text (lines 64–77) was deleted by Chettle in the MS, possibly for its subversive depiction of the king as complicit in courtly corruption; cf. lines 85–90 **wert** were (old verb form, second-person singular, past tense)

65   Placed with the noblest women of the land,
     Invited to their angel companies,
     Seeming a bright star in the courtly sphere:
     Why shouldst thou like a widow sit thus low
     And all thy fair consorts move from the clouds
70   That overdrip thy beauty and thy worth?
     I'll tell thee the true cause: the court like heaven
     Examines not the anger of the prince,
     And being more frail-composed of gilded earth
     Shines upon them on whom the king doth shine;
75   Smiles if he smile; decline if he decline;
     Yet, seeing both are mortal, court and king,
     Shed not one tear for any earthly thing.
     For, so God pardon me, in my saddest hour
     Thou hast no more occasion to lament,
80   Nor these, nor those, my exile from the court –
     No, nor this body's torture, were't imposed,
     As commonly disgraces of great men
     Are the forewarnings of a hasty death –
     Than to behold me after many a toil
85   Honoured with endless rest. Perchance the king,
     Seeing the court is full of vanity,
     Has pity lest our souls should be misled
     And sends us to a life contemplative.
     O happy banishment from worldly pride
90   When souls by private life are sanctified!

LADY MORE   O but I fear some plot against your life.

MORE   Why then, 'tis thus: the king, of his high grace,
     Seeing my faithful service to his state
     Intends to send me to the king of heaven
95   For a rich present; where my soul shall prove
     A true rememb'rer of his majesty.
     Come, prithee, mourn not; the worst chance is death,
     And that brings endless joy for fickle breath.

LADY MORE   Ah, but your children.

100 MORE   Tush, let them alone.

65 **Placed with** ranked alongside   67 **sphere** region of the heavens in ancient astrology   68 **thus low** i.e. the *Low stools* mentioned in the entrance direction, signs of humble domesticity   69 **consorts** companions   **move from** move away from; the sense is of false friends deserting in times of trouble   70 **overdrip** i.e. rain on; the literal sense of her falling tears may add to the metaphor (cf. line 77)   71 **the court…not** i.e. the court does not examine like heaven does   72 **Examines** questions/scrutinizes   77 **Shed…tear** he is telling Lady More not to cry   **for** over   78 **so** as   79 **occasion** reason   80 **Nor…those** 'these' and 'those' refer to his onstage family and servants respectively; he is saying that neither she (Lady More) nor either faction have any more cause to grieve at the circumstances of his impending death (exile and execution) than they would if he were to die peacefully and naturally after a long life   81 **were't imposed** if it (torture) were carried out   82 **disgraces** falls from favour   84 **Than to** than if you were to; carries on from 'no more occasion' at line 79   **toil** labour, effort/difficulty   85 **Perchance…contemplative** perhaps More is mollifying his wife in reaction to her sorrow at talk of his death, exploring the possibility that he is to be exiled only, along with his family (see next note); however, '**life contemplative**' supports both the sense of the secluded life of a monk/hermit and life eternal after death; perhaps '**private life**' at line 90 supports the former, though More may have both senses in mind, as his next speech suggests   88 **us** our family/me (royal we)   90 **sanctified** purified from sin   92 **the…present** continuing the link between the king and God; hard to judge the balance between sincerity and irony here; cf. *Richard III* 1.1.121–3   **of** in   95 **For** as   97 **prithee** please, literally 'I pray thee'   **chance** outcome, possibility   98 **for** in exchange for   **fickle breath** uncertain, inconstant life ('breath')   100 **Tush** common exclamation of impatience   **let them alone** never mind about them

Say they be stripped from this poor painted cloth,

This outside of the earth, left houseless, bare;

They have minds instructed how to gather more.

There's no man that's ingenious can be poor;

105   And therefore do not weep, my little ones,

Though you lose all the earth. Keep your souls even

And you shall find inheritance in heaven.

But for my servants: there's my chiefest care.

Come hither, faithful steward; be not grieved   *To Catesby*

110   That in thy person I discharge both thee

And all thy other fellow officers,

For my great master hath dischargèd me.

If thou by serving me hast suffered loss

Then benefit thyself by leaving me.

115   I hope thou hast not, for such times as these

Bring gain to officers, whoever leese.

Great lords have only name, but in the fall

Lord Spend-All's steward's Master Gather-All.

But I suspect not thee. Admit thou hast:

120   It's good the servants save when masters waste.

But you, poor gentlemen, that had no place

T'enrich yourselves but by loathed bribery,

Which I abhorred, and never found you loved:

Think, when an oak falls, underwood shrinks down,

125   And yet may live, though bruised. I pray ye strive

To shun my ruin; for the axe is set

Even at my root, to fell me to the ground.

The best I can do to prefer you all

With my mean store expect; for heaven can tell

130   The More loves his followers more than well.

Enter a Servant

[SERVANT]   My lord, there are new-lighted at the gate

The Earls of Surrey and of Shrewsbury,

And they expect you in the inner court.

MORE   Entreat their lordships come into the hall.   [*Exit Servant*]

135   LADY MORE   O God, what news with them?

MORE   Why, how now, wife?

101 from of   painted cloth referring to wall hangings, tapestries, symbolic both of worldly goods and superficial outward appearances   102 earth i.e. earthly, material values   104 ingenious bright, resourceful   106 Though even if you   even steady, unwavering/straightforward, direct/level   108 for as for   there's...care that's my chief concern   109 steward controller of a household's domestic affairs   110 in...officers i.e. in discharging his head servant he is effectively discharging all under him   111 officers household servants   113 If thou...waste this passage of text (lines 113–20) was deleted by Chettle and replaced with a second draft (lines 121–30); John Jowett suggests the word 'steward' – spelled 'Stuart' in the MS – near 'Spend-All' may have sounded riskily like a criticism of James I's profligacy, hence the cut   116 leese lose, is the loser   118 Lord...Gather-All i.e. the steward of a spendthrift lord gathers the squandered wealth; may also mean that a servant can always find employment after his master loses everything   119 Admit even if you were to admit   121 place position of influence, office   122 but by only by i.e. they had no position whereby they could exploit the culture of bribery   124 when...down a rigid oak falling in a storm while supple reeds remain standing was proverbial (the oak and the reed was one of Aesop's fables)   underwood small trees and shrubs that grow beneath taller trees   shrinks down is beaten down   125 bruised battered, blown about   126 shun get clear of, look to escape   set directed, pointed   128 prefer promote, advantage, recommend   129 mean store humble, poor resources   can tell knows   130 more than well puns on More's name   131 new-lighted newly-arrived   136 how now what's the matter

They are but come to visit their old friend.

LADY MORE   O God, I fear, I fear!

MORE   What shouldst thou fear, fond woman?

140   *Iustum, si fractus illabatur orbis, inpavidum ferient ruinae.*

Here let me live estranged from great men's looks,

They are like golden flies on leaden hooks.

Enter the Earls [of Surrey and Shrewsbury], Downes with his mace, and Attendants

SHREWSBURY   Good morrow, good Sir Thomas.

SURREY   Good day, good madam.   *Kind salutations*

145   MORE   Welcome, my good lords.

What ails your lordships look so melancholy?

O, I know: you live in court and the court diet

Is only friend to physic.

SURREY   O, Sir Thomas,

150   Our words are now the king's, and our sad looks

The interest of your love! We are sent to you

From our mild sovereign, once more to demand

If you'll subscribe unto those articles

He sent ye th'other day. Be well advised,

155   For on mine honour, lord, grave Doctor Fisher

Bishop of Rochester, at the selfsame instant

Attached with you, is sent unto the Tower

For the like obstinacy; his majesty

Hath only sent you prisoner to your house,

160   But if you now refuse for to subscribe,

A stricter course will follow.

LADY MORE   O, dear husband!

BOTH DAUGHTERS   Dear father!   *Kneeling and weeping*

MORE   See, my lords,

165   This partner and these subjects to my flesh

Prove rebels to my conscience! But, my good lords,

If I refuse, must I unto the Tower?

SHREWSBURY   You must, my lord; here is an officer

Ready for to arrest you of high treason.

170   LADY MORE *and* DAUGHTERS   O, God! O, God!

ROPER   Be patient, good madam.

MORE   Ay, Downes, is't thou? I once did save thy life,

When else by cruel riotous assault

Thou hadst been torn in pieces: thou art reserved

175   To be my summ'ner to yond spiritual court.

137 **but** only   139 **fond** foolish/loving   140 *Iustum...ruinae* 'the just man, if the world is shattered and broken, will face the ruins undaunted' (Latin), from Horace, *Odes*, 3:3   142 **golden...hooks** a fishing metaphor in which gold/prestige is used as political bait   *Downes* sergeant-at-arms   *mace* sceptre or staff of office   146 **ails** troubles/is wrong with you   147 **court...physic** the rich food/gluttony at court is only good for medicine   151 **interest of** what we have earned from/concern for   153 **articles** i.e. the Oath of Supremacy and Act of Succession   157 **Attached** arrested/accused   158 **like** same   161 **course** method of proceeding   165 **This partner** my wife   **subjects...flesh** daughters of mine   166 **Prove...conscience** rebel against the dictate of my conscience   172 **thou...pieces** on 'Ill May Day' (Act 2)   175 **summ'ner** summoner; petty legal officer who cites and warns people to appear in court   **yond spiritual court** i.e. the court of heaven

Give me thy hand, good fellow, smooth thy face:
The diet that thou drink'st is spiced with mace
And I could ne'er abide it: 'twill not disgest,
'Twill lie too heavily, man, on my weak breast.

180 SHREWSBURY Be brief, my lord, for we are limited
Unto an hour.

MORE   Unto an hour! 'Tis well:
The bell (earth's thunder) soon shall toll my knell.

LADY MORE Dear loving husband, if you respect not me,

185   Yet think upon your daughters.   *Kneeling*

MORE   Wife, stand up. I have bethought me,
And I'll now satisfy the king's good pleasure.   *Pondering to himself*

BOTH DAUGHTERS O, happy alteration!

SHREWSBURY Come then, subscribe, my lord.

190 SURREY   I am right glad of this your fair conversion.

MORE   O, pardon me,
I will subscribe to go unto the Tower
With all submissive willingness, and thereto add
My bones to strengthen the foundation

195   Of Julius Caesar's palace. Now, my lord,
I'll satisfy the king, even with my blood,
Nor will I wrong your patience.— Friend, do thine office.

DOWNES   Sir Thomas More, Lord Chancellor of England,
I arrest you in the king's name of high treason.

200 MORE   Gramercies, friend.
To a great prison, to discharge the strife
Commenced 'twixt conscience and my frailer life,
More now must march. Chelsea, adieu, adieu!
Strange farewell, thou shalt ne'er more see More true,

205   For I shall ne'er see thee more.—Servants, farewell.—
Wife, mar not thine indifferent face, be wise:
More's widow's husband, he must make thee rise.—
Daughters [...] what's here, what's here?
Mine eye had almost parted with a tear.—

210   Dear son, possess my virtue, that I ne'er gave.—
Grave More thus lightly walks to a quick grave.

ROPER   *Curae leves loquuntur, ingentes stupent.*

MORE   You that way in, mind you my course in prayer:
By water I to prison, to heaven through air.   *Exeunt*

---

177 mace heavy club or staff/his staff of office/aromatic spice (the outer covering of the nutmeg)   **178 abide** wait for/withstand/submit to/endure/ tolerate/atone for   **disgest** be digested   **183 toll my knell** ring my funeral bell   **186 bethought me** considered this   **195 Julius Caesar's palace** Julius Caesar was popularly believed to have built the original Tower of London; it was rumoured that the bones of the young princes, supposedly murdered by Richard III of whom More had written a critical biography, had been found there   **197 Friend** addressed to Downes   **office** duty   **199 high treason** violation of the monarch; in More's case his refusal to recognize the king as supreme head of the Church   **200 Gramercies** thanks   **206 indifferent** impartial/average   **210 son** son-in-law, Roper   **possess...gave** perhaps 'be virtuous in the way that I was unable to pass on to you'   **211 quick** rapid/ living   **grave** tomb, playing on the senses of 'weighty', 'authoritative', 'serious'   **212 *Curae...stupent*** 'light cares can speak, great ones are struck dumb' (Latin)   **213 mind...prayer** pray for me on my journey

[Act 5 Scene 1]

Enter the Warders of the Tower, with halberds

FIRST WARDER   Ho, make a guard there!

SECOND WARDER   Master Lieutenant gives a straight command,
    The people be avoided from the bridge.

THIRD WARDER   From whence is he committed, who can tell?

5   FIRST WARDER   From Durham House, I hear.

SECOND WARDER   The guard were waiting there are hour ago.

THIRD WARDER   If he stay long, he'll not get near the wharf,
    There's such a crowd of boats upon the Thames.

SECOND WARDER   Well, be it spoken without offence to any,

10   A wiser or more virtuous gentleman
    Was never bred in England.

THIRD WARDER   I think the poor will bury him in tears:
    I never heard a man, since I was born,
    So generally bewailed of everyone.

Enter a Poor Woman

15   What means this woman? — Whither dost thou press?

FIRST WARDER   This woman will be trod to death anon.

SECOND WARDER   What mak'st thou here?

WOMAN   To speak with that good man, Sir Thomas More.

SECOND WARDER   To speak with him! He's not Lord Chancellor.

20   WOMAN   The more's the pity, sir, if it pleased God.

SECOND WARDER   Therefore, if thou hast a petition to deliver,
    Thou mayst keep it now, for anything I know.

WOMAN   I am a poor woman, and have had, God knows,
    A suit this two year in the Chancery,

25   And he hath all the evidence I have
    Which should I lose, I am utterly undone.

SECOND WARDER   Faith, and I fear thou'lt hardly come by 'em now;
    I am sorry for thee even with all my heart.

Enter the Lords with Sir Thomas More and Attendants, and enter Lieutenant and
Gentleman Porter

    Woman, stand back, you must avoid this place:

30   The lords must pass this way into the Tower.

MORE   I thank your lordships for your pains thus far
    To my strong house.

WOMAN   Now, good Sir Thomas More, for Christ's dear sake,
    Deliver me my writings back again

[5.1]   *Original Text (Munday). Location: The Tower Gate   halberds* long spears with axe-heads   **3 avoided** cleared from   **5 Durham House**
residence of the Bishops of Durham in the Strand; More was actually taken to the Tower from the Abbot of Westminster's   **15 Whither…press?** Where are
you pushing/hurrying forward to?   **17 mak'st thou** are you doing   **24 Chancery** Lord Chancellor's court   **25 evidence** documents relating to the case
27 come by 'em get hold of them, i.e. the documents   **29 avoid** leave   **31 pains thus far** the trouble you've taken in accompanying me so far on my
way   **32 strong house** fortified house, castle, i.e. the Tower   **34 writings** documents

35   That do concern my title.

MORE   What, my old client, are thou got hither too?

Poor silly wretch, I must confess indeed

I had such writings as concern thee near

But the king has ta'en the matter into his own hand:

40   He has all I had; then, woman, sue to him,

I cannot help thee: thou must bear with me.

WOMAN   Ah, gentle heart, my soul for thee is sad:

Farewell the best friend that the poor e'er had.   *Exit Woman*

GENTLEMAN PORTER   Before you enter through the Tower gate,

45   Your upper garment, sir, belongs to me.

MORE   Sir, you shall have it; there it is.   *He gives him his cap*

GENTLEMAN PORTER   The upmost on your back, sir, you mistake me.

MORE   Sir, now I understand ye very well;   ***He gives him his cloak***

But that you name my back

50   Sure else my cap had been the uppermost.

SHREWSBURY   Farewell, kind lord, God send us merry meeting!

MORE   Amen, my lord.

SURREY   Farewell, dear friend, I hope your safe return.

MORE   My lord, and my dear fellow in the Muses,

55   Farewell, farewell, most noble poet.

LIEUTENANT   Adieu, most honoured lords.   *Exeunt Lords*

MORE   Fair prison, welcome; yet, methinks,

For thy fair building 'tis too foul a name.

Many a guilty soul, and many an innocent,

60   Have breathed their farewell to thy hollow rooms.

I oft have entered into thee this way,

Yet, I thank God, ne'er with a clearer conscience

Than at this hour.

This is my comfort yet, how hard soe'er

65   My lodging prove, the cry of the poor suitor,

Fatherless orphan or distressed widow,

Shall not disturb me in my quiet sleep.

On, then, a God's name, to our close abode:

God is as strong here as he is abroad.   *Exeunt*

[Act 5 Scene 2]

Enter Butler, Brewer, Porter and Horsekeeper several ways

BUTLER   Robin Brewer, how now, man! What cheer, what cheer?

---

35 title legal right to possession of a property   **37 silly** simple/helpless, deserving pity   **40 sue** appeal, petition   **45 upper garment** outer clothes, given to the jailer as a security measure   **47 upmost** uppermost, outermost   **49 But** except   **50 else** otherwise   **54 fellow...Muses** fellow poet, lover of the arts   **64 how hard soe'er** however hard   **68 close** near/enclosed   **abode** dwelling   **69 abroad** outdoors   **[5.2]** *Original Text (Munday).* **Location:** *More's house* **Butler...Horsekeeper** servants in charge of the pantry, cellar, doors and stables, respectively   *several ways* from various/different directions   **1 What cheer** how are you?

BREWER   Faith, Ned Butler, sick of thy disease; and these our other fellows here, Ralph Horsekeeper and Giles Porter, sad, sad: they say my lord goes to his trial today.

5   HORSEKEEPER   To it, man! Why, he is now at it, God send him well to speed!

PORTER   Amen: even as I wish to mine own soul, so speed it with my honourable lord and master, Sir Thomas More.

BUTLER   I cannot tell, I have nothing to do with matters above my capacity, but as God judge me, if I might speak my mind, I think there lives not a more harmless

10   gentleman in the universal world.

BREWER   Nor a wiser, nor a merrier, nor an honester: go to, I'll put that in upon mine own knowledge.

PORTER   Nay, and ye bate him his due of his housekeeping, hang ye all! Ye have many lord chancellors comes in debt at the year's end, and for very housekeeping.

15   HORSEKEEPER   Well, he was too good a lord for us, and therefore, I fear, God himself will take him: but I'll be hanged, if ever I have such another service.

BREWER   Soft, man, we are not discharged yet: my lord may come home again and all will be well.

BUTLER   I much mistrust it; when they go to 'raigning once, there's ever foul

20   weather for a great while after. But soft, here comes Master Gough and Master Catesby: now we shall hear more.

Enter Gough and Catesby, with a paper

HORSEKEEPER   Before God, they are very sad; I doubt my lord is condemned.

PORTER   God bless his soul, and a fig then for all worldly condemnation.

GOUGH   Well said, Giles Porter, I commend thee for it,
25   'Twas spoken like a well affected servant
Of him that was a kind lord to us all.

CATESBY   Which now no more he shall be, for, dear fellows,
Now we are masterless, though he may live
So long as please the king: but law hath made him
30   A dead man to the world, and given the axe his head,
But his sweet soul to live among the saints.

GOUGH   Let us entreat ye to go call together
The rest of your sad fellows (by the roll
You're just seven score), and tell them what ye hear
35   A virtuous honourable lord hath done
Even for the meanest follower that he had.
This writing found my lady in his study
This instant morning, wherein is set down
Each servant's name, according to his place

---

2 **sick...disease** as ill/fed up as you are   5 **God...speed** May God help him succeed   6 **speed it** may it prosper   8 **capacity** mental power   11 **go to** exhortation, 'get on with you!'   **I'll...in** I can vouch for that   13 **and...housekeeping** if you omit to mention his management of household affairs/keeping a good table/hospitality   16 **service** position (as servant)   17 **Soft** quietly   19 **'raigning** arraigning, accusing, examining; with a pun on 'raining'   22 **doubt** fear   23 **fig then for** expression of contempt   **fig** something small and valueless   25 **well affected** well-disposed, devoted   28 **though...head** More has been found guilty and stripped of all worldly position and condemned to execution at a time of the king's choosing   31 **soul...saints** More was eventually canonised 400 years later in 1935   33 **by the roll** according to the register, housekeeping book   34 **seven score** one hundred and forty, a large number for the household of a Lord Chancellor   36 **meanest** humblest   38 **instant** same, very   39 **place** position

40 And office in the house: on every man

He frankly hath bestown twenty nobles,

The best and worst together, all alike,

Which Master Catesby here forth will pay ye.

CATESBY   Take it as it is meant, a kind remembrance

45 Of a far kinder lord, with whose sad fall

He gives up house, and farewell to us all.

Thus the fair spreading oak falls not alone,

But all the neighbour plants and under-trees

Are crushed down with his weight. No more of this:

50 Come, and receive your due, and after go

Fellow-like hence, co-partners of one woe.   *Exeunt*

[Act 5 Scene 3]

Enter Sir Thomas More, the Lieutenant, and a Servant attending, as in his chamber in the Tower

MORE   Master Lieutenant, is the warrant come?

If it be so, a God's name, let us know it.

LIEUTENANT   My lord, it is.

MORE   'Tis welcome, sir, to me with all my heart;

5 His blessèd will be done!

LIEUTENANT   Your wisdom, sir, hath been so well approved,

And your fair patience in imprisonment

Hath ever shown such constancy of mind

And Christian resolution in all troubles,

10 As warrants us you are not unprepared.

MORE   No, Master Lieutenant;

I thank my God I have peace of conscience,

Though the world and I are at a little odds,

But we'll be even now, I hope, ere long.

15 When is the execution of your warrant?

LIEUTENANT   Tomorrow morning.

MORE   So, sir, I thank ye:

I have not lived so ill, I fear to die.

Master Lieutenant,

20 I have had a sore fit of the stone tonight

---

40 **office** duty   41 **frankly** freely/generously   **bestown** bestowed, given   **twenty nobles** sum of money worth between seven and ten pounds sterling, roughly half a year's average wage   **nobles** gold coins of variable value, at this time worth between a third and a half of one pound   42 **best…together** with no distinction between highest and lowest   51 **Fellow-like hence** from here as friends, colleagues   **co-partners** companions   [5.3] *Original Text (Munday). Location: The Tower of London*   1 **warrant** death warrant, the order for his execution   6 **approved** tested/established by experience   10 **warrants** assures, guarantees, playing on 'warrant' in More's opening question   13 **at…odds** rather in conflict/unequal; in the following line, More plays on **even**   14 **ere** before   18 **ill** wickedly   20 **sore fit** bad attack   **stone** painful disease of the kidney in which crystals are separated out from the urine to form stone-like concretions which are then excreted with difficulty

But the king hath sent me such a rare receipt,

I thank him, as I shall not need to fear it much.

LIEUTENANT   In life and death still merry Sir Thomas More.

MORE   Sirrah fellow, reach me the urinal: [*The Servant*] *gives it him*

25   Ha! Let me see there's gravel in the water;

And yet I see no grave danger in that

The man were likely to live long enough,

So pleased the king.— Here, fellow, take it.

SERVANT   Shall I go with it to the doctor, sir?

30   MORE   No, save thy labour; we'll cozen him of a fee.

Thou shalt see me take a dram tomorrow morning,

Shall cure the stone, I warrant, doubt it not.—

Master Lieutenant, what news of my lord of Rochester?

LIEUTENANT   Yesterday morning was he put to death.

35   MORE   The peace of soul sleep with him!

He was a learnèd and a reverend prelate,

And a rich man, believe me.

LIEUTENANT   If he were rich, what is Sir Thomas More,

That all this while hath been Lord Chancellor?

40   MORE   Say ye so, Master Lieutenant? What do ye think

A man, that with my time had held my place,

Might purchase?

LIEUTENANT   Perhaps, my lord, two thousand pound a year.

MORE   Master Lieutenant, I protest to you

45   I never had the means in all my life

To purchase one poor hundred pound a year:

I think I am the poorest chancellor

That ever was in England, though I could wish,

For credit of the place, that my estate were better.

50   LIEUTENANT   It's very strange.

MORE   It will be found as true.

I think, sir, that with most part of my coin

I have purchased as strange commodities

As ever you heard tell of in your life.

55   LIEUTENANT   Commodities, my lord!

Might I, without offence, enquire of them?

MORE   Crutches, Master Lieutenant, and bare cloaks,

For halting soldiers and poor needy scholars

Have had my gettings in the Chancery:

60   To think but what acheat the crown shall have

---

21 **receipt** prescription   25 **gravel** small urinary stones   26 **And...that** the manuscript is damaged at this point, hence the line is conjectural   28 **So...king** if the king wished him to   30 **cozen** cheat   31 **dram** dose of medicine   32 **warrant** guarantee   33 **Rochester?...death** in fact Fisher was executed two weeks rather than two days before More, on 22 June 1535   36 **reverend prelate** respected bishop   37 **rich** More means in spiritual terms but in his response the Lieutenant takes him to mean financially   42 **purchase** gain, amass   49 **credit...place** reputation of the office   **estate** condition, fortune   53 **commodities** goods   57 **bare** simple   58 **halting** lame, limping   59 **gettings...Chancery** what I have earned through my work as Lord Chancellor   60 **acheat** punning on 'escheat: the crown's confiscation of property under feudal law' and 'a cheat' because More has so little the king will be cheated

By my attainder!

I prithee, if thou be'st a gentleman,

Get but a copy of my inventory.

That part of poet that was given me

65 Made me a very unthrift:

For this is the disease attends us all,

Poets were never thrifty, never shall.

Enter Lady More mourning, Daughters, Master Roper

LIEUTENANT   O, noble More!—

My lord, your wife, your son-in-law, and daughters.

70 MORE   Son Roper, welcome! Welcome, wife, and girls.

Why do you weep? Because I live at ease?

Did you not see, when I was chancellor,

I was so cloyed with suitors every hour,

I could not sleep, nor dine, nor sup in quiet?

75 Here's none of this; here I can sit and talk

With my honest keeper half a day together,

Laugh and be merry: why, then, should you weep?

ROPER   These tears, my lord, for this your long restraint

Hope had dried up with comfort that we yet,

80 Although imprisoned, might have had your life.

MORE   To live in prison, what a life were that!

The king (I thank him) loves me more than so.

Tomorrow I shall be at liberty

To go even whither I can,

85 After I have dispatched my business.

LADY MORE   Ah, husband, husband, yet submit yourself:

Have care of your poor wife and children.

MORE   Wife, so I have, and I do leave you all

To his protection hath the power to keep you

90 Safer than I can:

The father of the widow and the orphans.

ROPER   The world, my lord, hath ever held you wise,

And't shall be no distaste unto your wisdom,

To yield to the opinion of the state.

95 MORE   I have deceived myself, I must acknowledge,

And, as you say, son Roper, to confess the same,

It will be no disparagement at all.

LADY MORE   His highness shall be certified thereof immediately.   *Offering to depart*

MORE   Nay, hear me, wife; first let me tell ye how:

100 I thought to have had a barber for my beard,

Now I remember, that were labour lost,

61 **attainder** forfeiture of a felon's estate   65 **very unthrift** real spendthrift, prodigal   73 **cloyed with suitors** wearied/encumbered by followers/
petitioners   76 **together** at a time   78 **These…life** these tears would have been dried if hope had allowed us to believe that your life might have been
spared, despite your long imprisonment   **long restraint** More was imprisoned in the Tower from April 1534 to July 1535   83 **at liberty** free, i.e.
dead   84 **even whither** to wherever   91 **father…orphans** God   93 **distaste** offence   97 **disparagement** disgrace, dishonour

The headsman now shall cut off head and all.

ROPER'S WIFE   Father, his majesty, upon your meek submission

Will yet, they say, receive you to his grace

105   In as great credit as you were before.

MORE   [...] wench. Faith, my lord the king

Has appointed me to do a little business.

If that were past, my girl, thou then shouldst see

What I would say to him about that matter,

110   But I shall be so busy until then,

I shall not tend it.

DAUGHTER   Ah, my dear father!

LADY MORE   Dear lord and husband!

MORE   Be comforted, good wife, to live and love my children,

115   For with thee leave I all my care of them.

Son Roper, for my sake that have loved thee well,

And for her virtue's sake, cherish my child.

Girl, be not proud, but of thy husband's love.

Ever retain thy virtuous modesty.

120   That modesty is such a comely garment

As it is never out of fashion, sits as fair

Upon the meaner woman as the empress;

No stuff that gold can buy is half so rich,

Nor ornament that so becomes a woman.

125   Live all and love together, and thereby

You give your father a rich obsequy.

BOTH DAUGHTERS   Your blessing, dear father.

MORE   I must be gone — God bless you —

To talk with God, who now doth call.

130   LADY MORE   Ah, my dear husband.

MORE   Sweet wife, goodnight, goodnight:

God send us all his everlasting light.

ROPER   I think, before this hour,

More heavy hearts ne'er parted in the Tower.   *Exeunt*

[Act 5 Scene 4]

Enter the Sheriffs of London and their Officers at one door, the Warders with their halberds at another

SECOND SHERIFF   Officers, what time of day is't?

OFFICER   Almost eight o'clock.

SECOND SHERIFF   We must make haste then, lest we stay too long.

SECOND WARDER   Good morrow, Master Shrieves of London; Master Lieutenant

102 **headsman** executioner   104 **yet** once more   105 **credit** estimation, honour   106 [...] there is a lacuna in the manuscript at this point   111 **tend** turn my mind to   121 **sits...Upon** fits, suits equally well   122 **meaner** humbler   125 **together** each other   126 **obsequy** service/act of compliance/ funeral ceremony   **[5.4]**   *Original Text (Munday). Location: Tower Hill*

5   Wills ye repair to the limits of the Tower,

There to receive your prisoner.

FIRST SHERIFF   Go back, and tell his worship we are ready.

SECOND SHERIFF   Go bid the officers make clear the way,

There may be passage for the prisoner.

Enter Lieutenant and his Guard, with More

10   MORE   Yet, God be thanked, here's a fair day toward

To take our journey in. Master Lieutenant,

It were fair walking on the Tower leads.

LIEUTENANT   And so it might have liked my sovereign lord,

I would to God you might have walked there still!   *He weeps*

15   MORE   Sir, we are walking to a better place.

O, sir, your kind and loving tears

Are like sweet odours to embalm your friend.

Thank your good lady, since I was your guest

She has made me a very wanton, in good sooth.

20   LIEUTENANT   O, I had hoped we should not yet have parted!

MORE   But I must leave ye for a little while.

Within an hour or two you may look for me,

But there will be so many come to see me

That I shall be so proud I will not speak,

25   And, sure, my memory is grown so ill,

I fear I shall forget my head behind me.

LIEUTENANT   God and his blessèd angels be about ye!—

Here, Master Shrieves, receive your prisoner.

MORE   Good morrow, Master Shrieves of London, to ye both:

30   I thank ye that ye will vouchsafe to meet me.

I see by this you have not quite forgot

That I was in times past, as you are now,

A Sheriff of London.

SECOND SHERIFF   Sir, then you know our duty doth require it.

35   MORE   I know it well, sir, else I would have been glad

You might have saved a labour at this time.

Ah, Master sheriff,

You and I have been of old acquaintance!

You were a patient auditor of mine,

40   When I read the divinity lecture at St Lawrence's.

SECOND SHERIFF   Sir Thomas More, I have heard you oft,

As many other did, to our great comfort.

MORE   Pray God, you may so now, with all my heart!

And, as I call to mind,

---

5 repair go   **limits** boundary   **9 There** so that there   **10 toward** coming   **12 leads** paths   **14 still** always, forever   **17 embalm** preserve/anoint **19 made…wanton** spoiled me (like a child)   **in good sooth** indeed, truly   **30 vouchsafe** graciously agree, condescend   **39 auditor** listener, member of the audience

45   When I studied the law in Lincoln's Inn,

            I was of council with ye in a cause.

    SECOND SHERIFF   I was about to say so, good Sir Thomas.

            [...]

    MORE   O, is this the place?

50   I promise ye, it is a goodly scaffold:

            In sooth, I am come about a headless errand,

            For I have not much to say, now I am here.

            Well, let's ascend, a God's name:

            In troth, methinks, your stair is somewhat weak;

55   I prithee, honest friend, lend me thy hand

            To help me up: as for my coming down,

            Let me alone, I'll look to that myself.

As he is going up the stairs, enters the Earls of Surrey and Shrewsbury

My lords of Surrey and Shrewsbury, give me your hands yet before we part. Ye see, though it pleaseth the king to raise me thus high yet I am not proud, for the higher

60   I mount the better I can see my friends about me. I am now on a far voyage and this strange wooden horse must bear me thither; yet I perceive by your looks you like my bargain so ill that there's not one of ye all dare venture with me. Truly, here's a most sweet gallery. (*Walking*) I like the air of it better than my garden at Chelsea. By your patience, good people, that have pressed thus into my bedchamber, if you'll not

65   trouble me, I'll take a sound sleep here.

    SHREWSBURY   My lord, 'twere good you'd publish to the world

            Your great offence unto his majesty.

    MORE   My lord, I'll bequeath this legacy to the hangman,   (*Gives him his gown*) and do it instantly. I confess his majesty hath been ever good to me, and my offence

70   to his highness makes me of a state pleader a stage player (though I am old, and have a bad voice) to act this last scene of my tragedy. I'll send him, for my trespass, a reverent head, somewhat bald, for it is not requisite any head should stand covered to so high majesty. If that content him not, because I think my body will then do me small pleasure, let him but bury it, and take it.

75   SURREY   My lord, my lord, hold conference with your soul:

            You see, my lord, the time of life is short.

    MORE   I see it, my good lord, I dispatched that business the last night. I come hither only to be let blood; my doctor here tells me it is good for the headache.

    HANGMAN   I beseech thee, my lord, forgive me.

80   MORE   Forgive thee, honest fellow! Why?

    HANGMAN For your death, my lord.

---

45 **Lincoln's Inn** one of the Inns of Court in London, where young men studied the law   46 **I...cause** you and I defended a case together   48 **[...]** the missing line is indecipherable   51 **headless** mindless, playing on sense of 'without a head'   53 **a** in   61 **wooden horse** the scaffold   62 **bargain** deal, business agreement   **venture** take the risk of going   63 **gallery** covered space for walking/raised playing space in the theatre   64 **pressed** crowded   **bedchamber** i.e. the place where I shall go to sleep/die   66 **publish** make public acknowledgement of your crimes, part of the execution ritual   68 **bequeath...hangman** the clothes of the condemned were a perquisite of the job; in fact More's sentence was commuted by the king to execution by decapitation, so that the character is in fact the 'headsman'   70 **state pleader** legal advocate on behalf of the state   71 **trespass** offence   72 **reverent** deeply respectful   **stand covered** it was customary to remove headgear as a sign of respect   78 **let blood** joke about bloodletting as a common medical procedure

MORE   O, my death? I had rather it were in thy power to forgive me, for thou hast the sharpest action against me. The law, my honest friend, lies in thy hands now: here's thy fee (*His purse*) and, my good fellow, let my suit be dispatched presently; for

85   'tis all one pain to die a lingering death and to live in the continual mill of a lawsuit. But I can tell thee, my neck is so short, that, if thou shouldst behead an hundred noblemen like myself, thou wouldst ne'er get credit by it. Therefore, look ye, sir, do it handsomely, or of my word, thou shalt never deal with me hereafter.

HANGMAN   I'll take an order for that, my lord.

90   MORE   One thing more, take heed thou cut'st not off my beard. O, I forgot, execution passed upon that last night, and the body of it lies buried in the Tower.— Stay, is't not possible to make a scape from all this strong guard? It is.

There is a thing within me, that will raise

And elevate my better part 'bove sight

95   Of these same weaker eyes; and, Master Shrieves,

For all this troop of steel that tends my death,

I shall break from you and fly up to heaven.

Let's seek the means for this.

HANGMAN   My lord, I pray ye, put off your doublet.

100   MORE   Speak not so coldly to me, I am hoarse already,

I would be loath, good fellow, to take more.

Point me the block, I ne'er was here before.

HANGMAN   To the east side, my lord.

MORE   Then to the east

105   We go to sigh, that o'er, to sleep in rest.

Here More forsakes all mirth, good reason why:

The fool of flesh must with her frail life die.

No eye salute my trunk with a sad tear;

Our birth to heaven should be thus, void of fear.   *Exit* [*with Hangman*]

110   SURREY   A very learned worthy gentleman

Seals error with his blood. Come, we'll to court.

Let's sadly hence to perfect unknown fates,

Whilst he tends progress to the state of states.   [*Exit*]

FINIS

---

83 **sharpest action** most severe legal suit; playing on the action of cutting off his head with an axe   *His purse* which he gives to his executioner
85 **continual mill** slow grinding action of the law; playing on the 'suit of mill', which obliged the tenant to grind his corn at a mill of his landlord's choosing   87 **credit** honour, a good reputation   88 **handsomely** properly, skilfully/elegantly, in fine style   **of** on   90 **take…that** follow your instructions to the letter   93 **scape** escape   96 **tends** accompanies/takes care of/awaits   99 **put** take   **doublet** close-fitting garment for the upper body   100 **coldly** calmly, plays on the sense of making me cold, by having me remove my garments/making me catch a cold   101 **loath** reluctant
104 **east** the place of Christ's crucifixion; Christian churches were traditionally aligned from east to west, with the altar aligned to the east
105 **sigh** expire/lament   107 **fool of flesh** humanity/More himself   **her** flesh's (personified as feminine)   108 **trunk** body/headless body   109 **birth to heaven** rebirth into eternal life   111 **error** the phrase is ambiguous since it isn't clear whose is the error   112 **perfect** complete   **unknown fates** the original audiences would have been aware of the irony of Surrey having himself been charged with high treason and beheaded in 1547   114 **progress** advancement to a higher stage/official tour   **state of states** highest possible state, i.e. the kingdom of heaven

Textual Notes

MS = unique manuscript of *The Booke of Sir Thomas More (readings in the original MS are distinguished here from those in the revised MS)*

Ed = a correction introduced by a later editor

List of Parts = Ed

1.1.16 brewis = Ed. MS = brews   **22 thy** = Ed. MS = they   **28 Mayor** = Ed. MS = major   **32 an** = Ed. MS = and   **37 to my** = Ed. MS = t m   **39 by** = Ed. *Not in* MS   **42 lest** *spelled* least *in* MS   **51 homes** = Ed. MS = boun   **56 vile** = Ed. MS = wild   **61 bill** = Ed. *Not in* MS   **65 would** = Ed. *Not in* MS   **66 Take** = Ed. *Not in* MS   **67 our proceeding** = Ed. *Not in* MS   **68–9 hath…aldermen to** = Ed *(based on the relevant passage in Holinshed's* Chronicles*) Not in* MS   **70 on statement of** = Ed. *Not in* MS   **71 copy** = Ed. MS = couple

1.2.29 crack *spelled* crake *in* MS   **39 poor prisoners** = Ed. MS *damaged* = po soners   **40 more careful of** = Ed. *Not in* MS   **41 In…but** = Ed. *Not in* MS   **42 If…pounds** = Ed. *Not in* MS   **43 point or two** = Ed. *Not in* MS.   **57 By** = Ed. *Not in* MS   **71 mistak'st** = Ed. MS = mistake   **shalt** = Ed. MS = shall   **125–8 He'll…Be** = Ed. *Not in* MS   **151 murrain** = Ed. MS = murren   **208 keeps…locks** = Ed. *Not in* MS

1.3.50 victuals *spelled* vittailes *in* MS   **77–9 artificers…We** = Ed. MS *damaged*

2.1 *The scene may be marked for omission in the revised ; 2.1 appears in original MS after the material replaced by added scene 2.2*   **17 sharp** = Ed. *Not in* MS

2.2.2 roast *spelled* roste *in* MS   **20 th'enforcèd** = Ed. MS = inforced   **30 We'll** = Ed. MS = We   **54 received** = Ed. MS = rised   **59 thy** = Ed. MS = they   **60 swords** = *revised* MS. *Original* MS = guards

2.4.18 th'hip *spelled* thipp *in* MS   **50 devil** *spelled* deule *in* MS   **74 silenced** = Ed. MS = silent   **87 One** = Ed. MS = On   **93 God himself** = Ed. *Not in* MS   **110–12 Is…obedience** *marked for omission in* MS   **121 lyam** = Ed. MS = liom   **140 mountainish** = Ed. MS = montanish *or* momtanish   **148 seek it** = Ed. MS = seek y   **149–52 To…pardon** *marked for omission in* MS   **164 further** = Ed. MS = furth   **180 Ay…honestly** = Ed. MS = clo. I and saues vs fro [ ] the gallowes then […] a dob […] dibile   **218 from…return** *marked for omission in* MS   **226 court** = Ed. *Not in* MS   **227 With…guest** = Ed. *Not in* MS

3.1.18–31 That's…neglect *marked for omission by the censor*   **45 lag** = Ed. MS = lug   **67 As…wrong** = Ed. MS *damaged*   **116 chore** *spelled* chare *in* MS   **157 falls** = Ed. MS *damaged*

3.2.5 withal = Ed. *Not in* MS   **20 heyday** = Ed. MS = hazard   **41 deserve** = Ed. MS = serve   **83 catechized** *spelled* cathecized *in* MS   **103 these** = Ed. MS = theis   **107 shear** = Ed. MS = shreve   **127 fame** = *original* MS. *Revised* MS = same   **153 else** = Ed. *Not in* MS

3.3.7 whose = Ed. MS = who   **17 so't** *spelled* soet *in* MS

4.1.81–2 True…with = Ed. *Not in* MS   **143 venture** = Ed. MS = venter   **257 thy** = Ed. MS = they   **291 Either** = Ed. MS = ether   **299 rushes** = Ed. MS = rishes   **302 receive** = Ed. MS = rescue

4.2.37 with greed = Ed. *Not in* MS   **113 hasten** = Ed. *Not in* MS

4.5.46–7 Great…rise *Marked for omission in* MS   **58 And** = Ed. MS = As   **104 ingenious** = Ed. MS = ingenuous   **118 Lord…Gather-All** = Ed. MS = Lord Spend-alls Stuart's master gathers all   **183 The…knell** *marked for omission in* MS

5.1.62 clearer = Ed. MS = clear   **64 soe'er** = Ed. MS = sore

5.3.10 warrants = Ed. MS = warrant   **25 there's** = Ed. *Not in* MS   **26 And…that** = Ed. *Not in* MS

5.4.3 haste = Ed. *Not in* MS   **58 part** = Ed. *Not in* MS   **113 progress** *spelled* prograce *in* MS

THE LONDON PRODIGAL

The London Prodigal offers a lively snapshot of city life in the early seventeenth century. A spendthrift youth, a father who wants to marry his daughter into a fortune, a set of three sisters (the clever one, the shallow one, the pretty and lovable one), a contrast between love and money: these are stock character types and dramatic situations, but in this play they are effectively individualized. The action provides vivid details of the household habits and street encounters of the citizenry who were themselves the primary audience in the public theatres. The drama holds up a mirror to the lives of the spectators: their clothes, their drinking habits, the topography of their city and nascent suburbia (Peckham, Greenwich, Cuckold's Haven). At the same time, the title indicates that this is a quasi-allegorical tale, a modern morality play. One moment we will meet seemingly real-life characters from the backstreets – a pair of swindling 'cony-catchers' called Dick and Rafe – and the next there will be an appearance from a figure labelled simply as a Ruffian or an ancient Citizen.

'On goes he that knows no end of his journey', says the principal character, Master Matthew Flowerdale, as he enters alone at the beginning of the final scene, where all the threads of the plot will be gathered together. The journey is at one and the same time a kind of pilgrim's progress with a clear direction towards penitence, and a tour, or series of detours, through the busy, chaotic ways of a city where people from very different backgrounds are thrown together and nearly everybody is out to make money or somehow better themselves.

'A certain man had two sons', says Jesus to his disciples in the fifteenth book of St Luke's Gospel. One of them asks for his inheritance early, then goes away and squanders it on 'riotous living'. When, as is inevitable, he falls on hard times, he is welcomed home and forgiven by his father. The well-behaved brother is understandably annoyed that the 'fatted calf' has been killed in honour of the prodigal, but the purpose of the parable is to illustrate that there is special joy in Heaven when a sinner converts (in the same chapter Jesus has told of the 'lost sheep' that is found). The Geneva Bible, which Shakespeare and his contemporaries knew well, interpreted the story in a marginal gloss:

> Men by their voluntary falling from God, having spoiled themselves of the benefits which they received of him, cast themselves headlong into infinite calamities; but God of his singular goodness, offering himself freely to them, whom he called to repentance, through the greatness of their misery wherewith they were tamed, doeth not only gently receive them, but also enricheth them with far greater gifts, and blesseth them with the chiefest bliss. (1599 edition, note to Luke 15.11)

In early modern Protestant culture a new and particular importance attached to the idea of repentance and the possibility of instant Salvation. A Roman Catholic who lived a bad life and then asked for forgiveness on their deathbed would still have to serve time in Purgatory. But the Reformation abolished Purgatory: a Protestant who truly repented could, thanks to God's infinite mercy, gain immediate access to the Kingdom of Heaven, however debauched their earlier life.

The promise of a great reward for a fresh start was an immensely powerful idea for ordinary men and women in Shakespeare's England. And the notion of a life-journey with a U-turn from reckless extravagance to the path of righteousness had an inherent dramatic force. The transformation of the prodigal was accordingly a popular plot device in the fiction and theatre of the age.

The progress of the prodigal Flowerdale is charted through both his monologues and his dialogues – not to mention his reading ('By my troth, gentlemen, I have been / A-reading over Nick Machiavel: / I find him good to be known, not to be followed'). He gets worse before he gets better: 'Even grown a master in the school of vice, / One that doth nothing but invent deceit'. His waywardness is dramatized principally through the conflict between him and his father, which reaches its height after the interrupted wedding reception in the ninth scene. 'My father was an ass, an old ass', says Flowerdale, which is not the kind of thing anyone should say in a society where respect and obedience for one's elders was a prime consideration ('Honour thy father and thy mother' was a biblical Commandment engrained upon every child). The insult is especially unfortunate since, unknown to Matthew, the servant to whom he speaks these words is really that very father in disguise. 'Thy father? Proud licentious villain! / What, are you at your foils? I'll foil with you.' Weapons are drawn and bloodshed is only prevented by the intervention of good girl Luce (whose name means 'light'), whom Flowerdale has married for money rather than love. This being a comedy, it is Luce who eventually brings Flowerdale to a moment of penitence:

> LUCE   O, Master Flowerdale, if too much grief
> Have not stopped up the organs of your voice,
> Then speak to her that is thy faithful wife,
> Or doth contempt of me thus tie thy tongue?
> Turn not away, I am no Ethiope,
> No wanton Cressid, nor a changing Helen,
> But rather one made wretched by thy loss.
> What, turn'st thou still from me? O, then,
> I guess thee woefull'st among hapless men.
> FLOWERDALE   I am indeed, wife, wonder among wives!
> Thy chastity and virtue hath infused
> Another soul in me, red with defame,
> For in my blushing cheeks is seen my shame.

The dramatist has skilfully combined the prodigal son narrative with the archetypal character of Patient Griselda, familiar from Chaucer and portrayed in a play by Thomas Dekker and others around this time. Luce is another Griselda, a wife who remains loyal and faithful whatever happens – the kind of woman who is the opposite of 'wanton Cressid' or fickle Helen of Troy.

Young Matthew Flowerdale is a *London* prodigal. Where his biblical prototype goes travelling, in this play it is the father who ventures abroad, leaving his son to the temptations of the city. This allows the dramatist to combine the prodigal motif with another favoured device, that of the 'disguised ruler'. The action begins with Flowerdale Senior returning from Venice in disguise in order to 'prove the humours' of his son. The play was published in 1605 and probably first performed early in the reign of King James I, when there was a vogue for such stories. The most famous example is Shakespeare's *Measure for Measure* – a dark city-comedy in which Vienna stands in for London – where the duke goes away with the specific purpose of testing the virtue of the deputy whom he leaves in charge and whose (very questionable) performance he watches over when he returns disguised as a friar. Thomas Middleton, one of the many candidates for authorship of *The London Prodigal*, worked with a similar scheme in *The Phoenix* (performed at court early in 1604), a city comedy in which a prince, as part of his education for future rule, goes in various disguises in order to uncover abuses within the law, the various ranks of society and the state of matrimony.

As with the many varieties of disguise in Elizabethan and Jacobean comedy, feigned identity has multiple dramatic possibilities. Quite apart from the intrinsic pleasure an audience takes in witnessing characters mistake whom it is they are talking to, with the resultant unintended confessions and revelations, a well-to-do merchant taking on the role of servant to his own son raises questions about both rank and familial relationship. Later in the play, the device is neatly repeated in female form, when Luce, with Old Flowerdale's assistance, disguises herself as a Dutch maid.

Among the most popular late Elizabethan comedies was Thomas Dekker's *The Shoemaker's Holiday* (published 1600), in which an aristocrat called Rowland Lacy falls in love with a middle-ranking girl called Rose Oatley. Their fathers refuse to approve the match because of the class difference and Rowland's spendthrift lifestyle. Rowland is told to redeem himself by joining the army fighting in France. To avoid the draft, he disguises himself as a Dutch shoemaker called Hans. This enables him to be reunited with Rose and secretly marry her. The king blesses the marriage, saying that 'love respects no blood, / Cares not for difference of birth or state'. A drama of social mobility is combined with laughter at the expense of the pseudo-Dutchman's funny accent and verbal mistakes. *The Shoemaker's Holiday* seems to have inaugurated a vogue for stage Dutch, and the author of *The London Prodigal* duly obliged with Luce as Tannakin ('Vat is your vill wit me?').

London was a cultural melting pot. One of the great attractions of the genre of city comedy was the bringing together of characters from different geographical as well as different social origins. The city was indeed home to hundreds of Dutch migrants, typically either traders or refugees from the wars in the Low Countries, many of whom became highly successful in the skilled crafts that were supplying a new demand for consumer goods in the burgeoning urban economy. There was money to be made in the capital, and people came from the provinces as well as overseas. The naive country gentleman being gulled by fortune-hunters as soon as he arrives in town would eventually become a stock type on the English stage. *The London Prodigal* includes a wealthy clothier from Devon whom Luce's father wants her to marry for his money. His presence gives the dramatist the opportunity to play with a West Country dialect, creating jokes and puns along the lines of 'And whore is the gentlewoman thy wife, mezel? / Whore is she, zirrah, ha?'

A good play makes a seemingly simple story more morally complicated than it first looks. Is Old Flowerdale the father really any better than his spendthrift son? He hardly shows himself to be a paragon of paternal love and moral integrity when he hatches a plan to win wealthy Sir Lancelot Spurcock's daughter for his son by means of a faked will. He mentions in passing to his brother that he was a bit of a prodigal in his own youth. With his plot to have his son publicly humiliated by being arrested for debt on his wedding day, he shows himself to be more of a trickster and a showman than a stern moral arbiter. While the father–son relationship is complicated in this way, the end of the play asks questions about the convention that all comedies must end with a wedding and a bedding. The final female word goes to the clever sister Delia, who vows that she will never marry and put herself through the pain of childbirth. To which the rich man from Devon replies, 'Che zet not a vig by a wife, if a wife zet not a vig by me.' A fig for marriage: it is not how you expect such a comedy to end.

The language of *The London Prodigal* is sometimes rudimentary: 'As for this wench I not regard a pin, / It is her gold must bring my pleasures in.' But there is ample verbal invention to compensate, and not just in the weird and wonderful Devon and Dutch dialects. For the investigator into questions of authorship and attribution, it is frustrating that the rare words which sometimes crop up cannot be used as markers to reveal the style of a specific known playwright. Thus 'arbalester' also occurs in Dekker and Webster, 'trenchmore' in Marston and Fletcher, 'carcanet' in Dekker and Shakespeare, 'ruddocks' in Webster and the multi-authored *Sir John Oldcastle*, 'clap him up' in Fletcher, Middleton and Webster, 'dogged' as a verb in Shakespeare and Fletcher, 'rattle baby' in Heywood, and 'snick up' in Beaumont, Chapman, Heywood, Porter and Shakespeare. Which just about gives a complete run of possible authorship contenders. 'Greasy chuff', 'greedy gnat', 'I'll father-in-law you', 'rerages' and 'by the mouse-foot' appear to be unique, but may well have occurred somewhere among the hundreds of lost plays from the period.

The smart attribution money is on either Dekker (though would he have sought to pull off the same Dutch disguise trick a second time?) or Fletcher (though it would be very early Fletcher). We know that they both excelled in the genre and that they both wrote for Shakespeare's company. And it does seem that their work was sometimes passed off as being Shakespeare's – witness the appearance of the collaborative *Henry VIII* in the Shakespeare First Folio without any acknowledgement of Fletcher's part in it, and, in Dekker's case, the claim, in a Cambridge student drama, that Shakespeare 'administered a purge' to Ben Jonson, something that actually happens in a play called *Satiromastix* that was written not by Shakespeare but by Dekker for Shakespeare's company.

But whoever the author, *The London Prodigal* is well worth reading and staging. It is almost certainly not by Shakespeare, but it represents the closest that Shakespeare's name came to an explicitly London-located city comedy, one of the most enjoyable and successful dramatic genres of the age.

KEY FACTS

AUTHORSHIP: The play was attributed unambiguously on its first and all subsequent publications to William Shakespeare, an attribution supported by the play's ascription to the King's Men and the date, which places it alongside related plays such as *All's Well that Ends Well* and *Measure for Measure*. Only the play's exclusion from the Folio provides external evidence against the attribution. This attribution has been hotly disputed and most contemporary dramatists have been suggested at various times. Stylometric work most strongly favours John Fletcher, though the play's date would be unusually early for this author.

PLOT: The merchant Old Flowerdale (the Father), recently returned from abroad, wishes to investigate the prodigal behaviour of his spendthrift son, and thus engages himself in disguise as Young Flowerdale's servant. Meanwhile the wealthy Sir Lancelot Spurcock plans the futures of his daughters: the clever Delia, who refuses all suitors, the shallow Franck, who marries the rich, foolish Civet, and Luce, who is courted by Flowerdale, the Devonshire clothier Oliver (her father's choice) and her preferred lover, Sir Arthur Greenshield. Flowerdale's Father helps his son's cause by contriving a duel between Oliver and Flowerdale, and sends Lancelot a fake

▷

will bequeathing Luce Flowerdale's wealth. Impressed, Lancelot stops the duel and offers Luce to Flowerdale. However, Flowerdale has no love for Luce and so, as a test, the Father arranges for him to be arrested on his wedding day. Publicly exposed as a bankrupt, Flowerdale pleads for bail and is denied. Lancelot instructs Luce to forsake her new husband, but she refuses and is herself subsequently disowned. Luce pleads for relief for Flowerdale, and is successful; but Flowerdale repays her by abandoning her and going off to resume his prodigal lifestyle. The Father helps Luce to a disguise as a Dutch maid at Civet's house. Bankrupt again, Flowerdale turns pickpocket and beggar. He pleads to the disguised Luce for succour and offers to run away with her if she can steal Civet's plate, claiming his wife is dead. Lancelot arrives and orders Flowerdale's arrest on charges of murder, but Luce reveals herself, and Flowerdale is shamed by her loyalty. The Father reveals his identity, and all are reconciled. Oliver proposes to Delia, but she turns him down, preferring unmarried life.

MAJOR PARTS: Flowerdale (21%/135/7), Lancelot (20%/138/8), Father (14%/91/8), Oliver (7%/64/6), Luce (7%/54/7), Uncle (6%/60/4), Weathercock (5%/47/8), Civet (4%/40/6), Delia (4%/29/6), Arthur (4%/28/6), Franck (2%/26/7), Artichoke (2%/23/7), Daffodil (2%/17/3).

LINGUISTIC MEDIUM: 85% verse, 15% prose.

DATE: c.1604. The play's subject matter relates it closely to other King's Men's plays of this period, and the motif of the disguised authority figure was particularly common in the years immediately following James's accession to the English throne, in keeping with the King's political theories.

SOURCES: The plot is original. The play draws on several current theatrical trends, including the humours comedy pioneered by George Chapman and Ben Jonson, and the stock types of the prodigal husband and patient wife (based on the old story of Patient Grissel). These types would be stretched to the limit in the company's *A Yorkshire Tragedy*, which followed shortly after.

TEXT: The Quarto of 1605 is a passable text that poses few significant problems. It shows a clear awareness of practical performance, so may be derived directly from the theatre. A distinctive feature is the use of cod-Dutch for the disguised Luce and the Devonshire dialect of Oliver, the accents of which are both evoked in phonetic spelling of their dialogue.

THE LONDON PRODIGAL, as it was played by the King's Majesty's Servants. By William Shakespeare.

Mat FLOWERDALE

Old Flowerdale, his FATHER, disguised throughout

UNCLE to Mat Flowerdale

Sir LANCELOT Spurcock

FRANCK ⎫
LUCE ⎬ His daughters
DELIA ⎭

Sir ARTHUR Greenshield, a military
    officer in love with Luce

Master Tom CIVET, in love with
    Franck

Master WEATHERCOCK

OLIVER, a Devonshire clothier, in
    love with Luce

⎱ Their Suitors

ARTICHOKE ⎫ Servants to
DAFFODIL ⎭ Sir Lancelot Spurcock

DICK ⎫ Mat Flowerdale's
RAFE ⎭ associates

A DRAWER at the George Inn

A RUFFIAN

A SOLDIER

An ancient CITIZEN

A CITIZEN'S WIFE

Alexander, her torchbearer

Soldiers, lieutenant, sheriff and officers

[Scene 1]

Enter Old Flowerdale and his brother

FATHER   Brother, from Venice, being thus disguised,
    I come to prove the humours of my son:
    How hath he borne himself since my departure,
    I leaving you his patron and his guide?

5   UNCLE   I'faith, brother, so as you will grieve to hear,
    And I almost ashamed to report it.

FATHER   Why, how is't, brother? What doth he spend beyond the allowance I left him?

UNCLE   How! Beyond that and far more: why, your exhibition is nothing. He
10   hath spent that, and since hath borrowed, protested with oaths, alleged kindred to
    wring money from me, by the love I bore his father, by the fortunes might fall upon
    himself, to furnish his wants. That done, I have had since his bond, his friend, and

FLOWERDALE suggests 'flower of youth'/'the froth on the top of beer' (flowered ale) Sir LANCELOT Spurcock 'Lancelot' alludes to the adulterous knight of the Round Table; 'cock' slang for 'penis' FRANCK common diminutive of 'Frances' – a well-known name for a whore, and a stock character in the Commedia dell'Arte; her name means 'free' and also suggests 'pig-sty' LUCE meaning 'light' (Latin) Greenshield suggesting raw and inexperienced CIVET substance with a strong musky smell, obtained from the anal glands of the African Civet cat, used in the production of perfume; its use was regarded as a sign of decadence WEATHERCOCK weathervane/fantastical person OLIVER from the olive tree, a symbol of peace, used ironically given his quarrelsome disposition ARTICHOKE referring either to the globe artichoke, a well-known aphrodisiac, or the Jerusalem artichoke, a root vegetable with a knobbly, irregular appearance DRAWER a tapster in a tavern [Scene 1] *Location: London, Flowerdale's uncle's residence* 1 Venice Independent Italian city-state associated with trade, luxury and prostitution; also the name of a house of ill-fame in Whitefriars, London 2 prove test/establish humours inclinations, dispositions; the four humours: blood, bile, phlegm and black bile were thought to determine physical and mental disposition 3 borne conducted, behaved 4 patron example, model deserving imitation 5 so in such a way as 9 exhibition financial allowance 10 protested vowed, promised alleged kindred so-called relatives 11 fortunes...himself expectations of inheritance 12 his...bond the text may be corrupted at this point since the uncle would seem to imply 'his friend's and his friend's friend's bond' bond deed promising future payment friend's bond although I know that he spends is yours, yet it grieves me to see the unbridled wildness that reigns over him.

15   FATHER   Brother, what is the manner of his life? How is the name of his offences? If they do not relish altogether of damnation, his youth may privilege his wantonness: I myself ran an unbridled course till thirty, nay almost till forty; well, you see how I am: for vice once looked into with the eyes of discretion, and well balanced with the weights of reason, the course past seems so abominable that the landlord of

20   himself, which is the heart of his body, will rather entomb himself in the earth, or seek a new tenant to remain in him, which once settled, how much better are they that in their youth have known all these vices and left it, than those that knew little and in their age runs into it? Believe me, brother, they that die most virtuous hath in their youth lived most vicious, and none knows the danger of the fire more

25   than he that falls into it. But say, how is the course of his life? Let's hear his particulars.

UNCLE   Why, I'll tell you, brother. He is a continual swearer, and a breaker of his oaths, which is bad.

[FATHER]   I grant indeed to swear is bad, but not keeping those oaths is better, for

30   who will set by a bad thing? Nay, by my faith, I hold this rather a virtue than a vice. Well, I pray, proceed.

UNCLE   He is a mighty brawler and comes commonly by the worst.

FATHER   By my faith, this is none of the worst neither, for if he brawl and be beaten for it, it will in time make him shun it: for what brings man or child more to virtue

35   than correction? What reigns over him else?

UNCLE   He is a great drinker, and one that will forget himself.

FATHER   O, best of all, vice should be forgotten:
        Let him drink on, so he drink not churches.
        Nay, an this be the worst, I hold it rather a happiness in him

40   Than any iniquity. Hath he any more attendants?

UNCLE   Brother, he is one that will borrow of any man.

FATHER   Why, you see, so doth the sea; it borrows of all the small currents in the world to increase himself.

UNCLE   Ay, but the sea pays it again, and so will never your son.

45   FATHER   No more would the sea neither, if it were as dry as my son.

UNCLE   Then, brother, I see you rather like these vices in your son than any way condemn them.

FATHER   Nay, mistake me not, brother, for though I slur them over now,
        As things slight and nothing, his crimes being in the bud,

50   It would gall my heart they should ever reign in him.

---

13 **that** that which   14 **unbridled** uncontrolled, i.e. without a 'bridle' – the head-stall, bit and reins which control a horse   **reigns** rules, playing on 'rains'/'reins'   16 **relish** smack, savour   **privilege** authorize, license   **wantonness** sexual incontinence/unruliness/effeminacy/arrogance/caprice   17 **I myself…it** (lines 17–25) Old Flowerdale confesses to his own prodigal youth and argues that age and reason will bring discretion and reform of character in his son, since only those acquainted with vice understand the true meaning of virtue   26 **particulars** details   27 **swearer** taker of oaths/blasphemer   30 **set by** esteem, regard/establish by agreement   32 **brawler** quarrelsome, noisy fellow   **comes…worst** usually comes off worst, is defeated   38 **Let…churches** the sense is unclear and could refer to: the money put aside in someone's inheritance to build churches. Old Flowerdale doesn't object to his son's drinking habits, so long as he doesn't dry up that part of his own inheritance/the quantity of drink, since churches were the largest buildings in communities/church ales, which were made and sold to raise money for church fabric and equipment   39 **an** if   40 **attendants** accompanying vices/companions   48 **slur them over** pass over them lightly   50 **they should** i.e. if they should

FLOWERDALE   Ho! Who's within? Ho!   *Flowerdale knocks within*

UNCLE   That's your son: he is come to borrow more money.

FATHER   For God's sake, give it out I am dead, see how he'll take it;

Say I have brought you news from his father.

55   I have here drawn a formal will, as it were

From myself, which I'll deliver him.

UNCLE   Go to, brother, no more: I will.

FLOWERDALE   Uncle, where are you, uncle?   *Within*

UNCLE   Let my cousin in there.

60   FATHER   I am a sailor come from Venice and my name is Christopher.

Enter Flowerdale

FLOWERDALE   By the Lord, in truth, uncle.

UNCLE   'In truth' would ha' served, cousin, without the 'Lord'.

FLOWERDALE   By your leave, uncle, the Lord is the Lord of truth.

A couple of rascals at the gate set upon me for my purse.

65   UNCLE   You never come but you bring a brawl in your mouth.

FLOWERDALE   By my truth, uncle, you must needs lend me ten pound.

UNCLE   Give my cousin some small beer here.

FLOWERDALE   Nay, look you, you turn it to a jest now.

By this light, I should ride to Croydon Fair

70   To meet Sir Lancelot Spurcock.

I should have his daughter Luce, and for scurvy ten pound,

A man shall lose nine hundred threescore and odd pounds,

And a daily friend beside, by this hand,

Uncle, 'tis true.

75   UNCLE   Why, anything is true, for aught I know.

FLOWERDALE   To see now: why, you shall have my bond, uncle, or Tom White's,

James Brock's, or Nick Hall's — as good rapier and dagger men as any be in

England. Let's be damned if we do not pay you: the worst of us all will not damn

ourselves for ten pound. A pox of ten pound!

80   UNCLE   Cousin, this is not the first time I have believed you.

FLOWERDALE   Why, trust me now, you know not what may fall.

If one thing were but true, I would not greatly care,

I should not need ten pound, but when a man

Cannot be believed, there's it.

85   UNCLE   Why, what is it, cousin?

FLOWERDALE Marry, this, uncle. Can you tell me if the Katernhugh be come home or no?

UNCLE Ay, marry, is't.

FLOWERDALE By God, I thank you for that news. What, is't in the Pool, can you tell?

90 **UNCLE** It is. What of that?

FLOWERDALE What? Why then I have six pieces of velvet sent me.

I'll give you a piece, uncle, for thus said the letter:

'A piece of ash-colour, a three-piled black,

A colour-de-roy, a crimson, a sad green,

95 And a purple': yes, i'faith.

UNCLE From whom should you receive this?

FLOWERDALE From who? Why, from my father! With commendations to you, uncle, and thus he writes: 'I know', saith he, 'thou hast much troubled thy kind uncle whom, God willing, at my return, I will see amply satisfied.' 'Amply', I remember,

100 was the very word, so God help me.

UNCLE Have you the letter here?

FLOWERDALE Yes, I have the letter here; here is the letter: no, yes, no! Let me see, what breeches wore I o'Saturday? Let me see, o'Tuesday my calamanco, o'Wednesday my peach-colour satin, o'Thursday my velour, o'Friday my

105 calamanco again, o'Saturday, let me see, o'Saturday — for in those breeches I wore o'Saturday is the letter: O, my riding breeches, uncle, those that you thought had been velvet. In those very breeches is the letter.

UNCLE When should it be dated?

FLOWERDALE Marry, *duodecimo tertios septembris*, no, no, *tredecimo tertio octobris*.

110 Ay, *octobris*, so it is.

UNCLE *Duodecimo tertios octobris*: and here receive I a letter that your father died in June. How say you, Kester?

FATHER Yes, truly, sir, your father is dead: these hands of mine holp to wind him.

FLOWERDALE Dead?

115 **FATHER** Ay, sir, dead.

FLOWERDALE 'Sblood, how should my father come dead?

FATHER I'faith, sir, according to the old proverb:

'The child was born and cried,

Became man, after, fell sick, and died.'

120 **UNCLE** Nay, cousin, do not take it so heavily.

FLOWERDALE Nay, I cannot weep you extempore. Marry, some two or three days hence, I shall weep without any stintance. But I hope he died in good memory.

---

86 Katernhugh contracted, familiar name for the ship later referred to as the *Katherine and Hugh*   **88 marry** by the Virgin Mary   **89 the Pool** part of the river Thames between London Bridge and Limehouse (or Cuckold's) Point   **91 velvet** extravagant and luxurious cloth which according to Sumptuary Law (repealed 1604) was only to be worn by those above the rank of knight   **93 three-piled black** the richest and most costly kind of velvet in the most expensive dye   **94 colour-de-roy** i.e. the king's colour (French): originally purple, later a lion-like orange-brown   **sad** dark   **103 calamanco** shiny, checked cloth of silk or satin   **104 velour** velvet   **105 breeches** trousers which come just below the knee   **106 riding** used for horseriding, punning on slang meaning, 'for having sex'   **109 *duodecimo tertios septembris*** probably '12 September' (Latin) with *tertios* a repeated mistake for *mensis* (month)   ***tredecimo...octobris*** 13 October (Latin)   **111 *Duodecimo tertios octobris*** the correct Latin would be *duodecimo [mensis] octobris* 12 October; the errors may be part of a joke at Flowerdale's expense   **112 Kester** familiar, diminutive of Christopher   **113 holp** helped   **wind** wrap him in his shroud or winding-sheet for burial   **116 'Sblood** by God's blood   **121 extempore** on the instant, without premeditation   **122 stintance** pause, limit

FATHER   Very well, sir, and set down everything in good order.

And the *Katherine and Hugh* you talked of, I came over in,

125   And I saw all the bills of lading, and the velvet

That you talked of, there is no such aboard.

FLOWERDALE   By God, I assure you, then there is knavery abroad.

FATHER   I'll be sworn of that: there's knavery abroad,

Although there were never a piece of velvet in Venice.

130   FLOWERDALE   I hope he died in good estate.

FATHER   To the report of the world he did, and made his will,

Of which I am an unworthy bearer.

FLOWERDALE   His will? Have you his will?

FATHER   Yes, sir, and in the presence of your uncle,

135   I was willed to deliver it.   *Delivering the will*

UNCLE   I hope, cousin, now God hath blessed you with wealth, you will not be
unmindful of me.

FLOWERDALE   I'll do reason, uncle; yet, i'faith, I take the denial of this ten pound
very hardly.

140   UNCLE   Nay, I denied you not.

FLOWERDALE   By God, you denied me directly.

UNCLE   I'll be judged by this good fellow.

FATHER   Not directly, sir.

FLOWERDALE   Why, he said he would lend me none, and that had wont to be a

145   direct denial, if the old phrase hold. Well, uncle, come, we'll fall to the legacies.

'In the name of God, Amen. Item: I bequeath to my brother Flowerdale three   *Reads*

hundred pounds to pay such trivial debts as I owe in London. Item: to my son, Mat

Flowerdale, I bequeath two bale of false dice, videlicet, high men and low men,

fulhams, stop cater-treys, and other bones of function.' 'Sblood, what doth he mean

150   by this?

UNCLE   Proceed, cousin.

FLOWERDALE   'These precepts I leave him. Let him borrow of his oath,

For of his word nobody will trust him.

Let him by no means marry an honest woman,

155   For the other will keep herself.

Let him steal as much as he can, that a guilty conscience

May bring him to his destinate repentance.'

---

124 *Katherine and Hugh* i.e. the ship   125 **bills of lading** itemized lists of cargo   127 **knavery** trickery, dishonest dealing   **abroad** about, at large;
his father puns on the sense of 'overseas' in the next line   129 **piece of velvet** puns on **piece** slang for 'genitals' and **velvet** as an allusion to the pox or
venereal disease   130 **estate** plays ambiguously on moral and worldly senses, i.e. condition/fortune   138 **denial** refusal   139 **hardly** badly   144 **wont**
customary usage   145 **old phrase** it's not clear what 'old phrase' is referred to here   **fall to** get on with   148 **bale** set of dice, playing on sense of 'evil,
malign influence'   **videlicet** 'that is to say' (Latin)   **high...men** two kinds of false dice made to turn up high and low numbers respectively   149 **fulhams**
loaded dice   **stop cater-treys** dice loaded to stop on three and four   **bones** dice (which were usually made from bone)   152 **precepts** rules for moral
conduct   **borrow...oath** meaning he must swear an oath each time he borrows money   154 **Let...herself** meaning either, 'if he were to marry a chaste,
respectable woman she would be unable to rely on him and have to fend for herself'/'let him marry a whore who is able to keep herself (by prostitution)'
157 **destinate** predestined, inevitable   **repentance** remorse, contrition for past action

I think he means hanging. An this were his last will and testament, the devil stood laughing at his bed's feet while he made it. 'Sblood, what, doth he think to fob off his
160   posterity with paradoxes?

FATHER   This he made, sir, with his own hands.

FLOWERDALE   Ay, well. Nay, come, good uncle, let me have this ten pound. Imagine you have lost it, or robbed of it, or misreckoned yourself so much — any way to make it come easily off, good uncle.

165   **UNCLE**   Not a penny.

FATHER   I'faith, lend it him, sir. I myself have an estate in the city worth twenty pound: all that I'll engage for him; he saith it concerns him in a marriage.

FLOWERDALE   Ay, marry, doth it; this is a fellow of some sense, this. Come, good uncle.

170   **UNCLE**   Will you give your word for it, Kester?

FATHER   I will, sir, willingly.

UNCLE   Well, cousin, come to me some hour hence, you shall have it ready.

FLOWERDALE   Shall I not fail?

UNCLE   You shall not: come, or send.

175   **FLOWERDALE**   Nay, I'll come myself.

FATHER   By my troth, would I were your worship's man.

FLOWERDALE   What, wouldst thou serve?

FATHER   Very willingly, sir.

FLOWERDALE   Why, I'll tell thee what thou shalt do. Thou saith thou hast twenty
180   pound; go into Birchin Lane, put thyself into clothes; thou shalt ride with me to Croydon Fair.

FATHER   I thank you, sir, I will attend you.

FLOWERDALE   Well, uncle, you will not fail me an hour hence?

UNCLE   I will not, cousin.

185   **FLOWERDALE**   What's thy name — Kester?

FATHER   Ay, sir.

FLOWERDALE   Well, provide thyself. Uncle, farewell till anon.   *Exit*

UNCLE   Brother, how do you like your son?

FATHER   I'faith, brother, like a mad unbridled colt,
190   Or as a hawk, that never stooped to lure:
The one must be tamed with an iron bit,
The other must be watched, or still she is wild —
Such is my son. Awhile let him be so,
For counsel still is folly's deadly foe.

---

158 hanging as punishment for his crimes, alluding to the proverb: 'Better be half hanged than ill wed'   **devil…it** implying that the devil must have watched, amused, as the will was written; perhaps an allusion to the proverb: 'every man before he dies shall see the devil'   **159 fob off** make a fool of, cheat   **160 posterity** descendants   **paradoxes** absurd or fantastic statements which contradict received opinion   **163 robbed of** carried off, stolen   **misreckoned** miscalculated   **164 make…off** as long as you part with it easily   **167 engage** pledge/pawn/mortgage   **168 marry** by the Virgin Mary, punning on 'marriage'   **173 Shall…fail?** i.e. 'Shall I be sure to receive the £10?'   **176 By my troth** truly, on my honour   **man** servant   **180 Birchin Lane** London street, running north from Lombard Street to Cornhill, occupied by drapers and second-hand clothes dealers   **182 attend** serve/await   **187 till anon** for a little while   **189 colt** young horse/lascivious, wanton fellow   **190 hawk…lure** bird of prey which has not been trained   **lure** apparatus used by falconers to recall their hawks; it is attached to a long cord or thong and is the place from which the hawk is fed   **191 The one…watched** whilst young horses were trained and controlled by an iron bit in the mouth, hawks were kept awake and deprived of sleep   **192 she** i.e. the hawk – the larger female birds were preferred in falconry   **194 counsel…foe** folly hates advice   **still** always

195   I'll serve his youth, for youth must have his course,

For being restrained, it makes him ten times worse.

His pride, his riot, all that may be named,

Time may recall, and all his madness tamed.   *Exeunt*

Scene 2

Enter Sir Lancelot, Master Weathercock, Daffodil, Artichoke, Luce and Franck

LANCELOT   Sirrah Artichoke, get you home before,

And, as you proved yourself a calf in buying,

Drive home your fellow calves that you have bought.

ARTICHOKE   Yes, forsooth. Shall not my fellow Daffodil go along with me?

5   LANCELOT   No, sir, no: I must have one to wait on me.

ARTICHOKE   Daffodil, farewell, good fellow Daffodil.

You may see, mistress, I am set up by the halves:

Instead of waiting on you, I am sent to drive home calves.   *Exit*

LANCELOT   I'faith, Franck, I must turn away this Daffodil,

10   He's grown a very foolish, saucy fellow.

FRANCK   Indeed la, father, he was so since I had him:

Before, he was wise enough for a foolish serving-man.

WEATHERCOCK   But what say you to me, Sir Lancelot?

LANCELOT   O, about my daughters, well, I will go forward,

15   Here's two of them, God save them, but the third,

O, she's a stranger in her course of life;

She hath refused you, Master Weathercock.

WEATHERCOCK   Ay, by the rood, Sir Lancelot, that she hath,

But had she tried me, she should ha' found a man of me indeed.

20   LANCELOT   Nay, be not angry, sir, at her denial;

She hath refused seven of the worshipfullest,

And worthiest, housekeepers this day in Kent:

Indeed, she will not marry, I suppose.

WEATHERCOCK   The more fool she!

25   LANCELOT   What, is it folly to love charity?

WEATHERCOCK   No, mistake me not, Sir Lancelot,

But 'tis an old proverb, and you know it well,

That women, dying maids, lead apes in hell.

LANCELOT   That's a foolish proverb and a false.

30   WEATHERCOCK   By the mass, I think it be, and therefore let it go.

But who shall marry with Mistress Frances?

---

195 **youth...course** proverbial   198 **recall** undo, revoke, annul   **Scene 2** *Location: Croydon Fair, later the George Inn*   1 **Sirrah** term of address used to men or boys expressing contempt, reprimand or the speaker's assumption of authority   **before** in advance   2 **calf in buying** obscure: perhaps related to the phrase, 'his purse hath cast her calf', implying that all the money has gone leaving only the leather; the general sense is that he is a poor servant   7 **I...halves** I am divided in my duties   10 **saucy** insolent, presumptuous   11 **la** emphatic exclamation, 'so'   14 **go forward** proceed   15 **third...life** Delia, who is not behaving in a manner appropriate to her situation   18 **rood** holy cross/crucifix   21 **worshipfullest** most worshipful, i.e. worthiest, most distinguished   22 **housekeepers** householders   28 **women...hell** to lead apes in hell was the proverbial punishment for old maids

FRANCK   By my troth, they are talking of marrying me, sister.

LUCE   Peace, let them talk:

Fools may have leave to prattle as they walk.

35   DAFFODIL   Sentences still, sweet mistress?

You have a wit, and it were your arbalester.

LUCE   I'faith, and thy tongue trips trenchmore.

LANCELOT   No, of my knighthood, not a suitor yet:

Alas, God help her, silly girl, a fool, a very fool:

40   But there's the other black-brows, a shrewd girl,

She hath wit at will and suitors two or three:

Sir Arthur Greenshield one, a gallant knight,

A valiant soldier, but his power but poor.

Then there's young Oliver, the Devonshire lad,

45   A wary fellow, marry, full of wit,

And rich, by the rood; but there's a third all air,

Light as a feather, changing as the wind: young Flowerdale.

WEATHERCOCK   O, he, sir, he's a desperate Dick indeed.

Bar him your house!

50   LANCELOT   Fie, not so: he's of good parentage.

WEATHERCOCK   By my fay, and so he is, and a proper man.

LANCELOT   Ay, proper enough, had he good qualities.

WEATHERCOCK   Ay, marry, there's the point, Sir Lancelot,

For there's an old saying:

55   'Be he rich, or be he poor,

Be he high, or be he low,

Be he born in barn, or hall,

'Tis manners makes the man and all.'

LANCELOT   You are in the right, Master Weathercock.

Enter Monsieur Civet

60   CIVET   Soul, I think I am sure crossed, or witched with an owl.   *Aside*

I have haunted them: inn after inn, booth after booth, yet cannot find them. Ha,

yonder they are! That's she, I hope to God 'tis she; nay, I know 'tis she now, for she

treads her shoe a little awry.

LANCELOT   Where is this inn? We are past it, Daffodil.

65   DAFFODIL   The good sign is here, sir, but the back gate is before.

CIVET   Save you, sir. I pray, may I borrow a piece of a word with you?   *To Daffodil*

---

35 Sentences judgements/maxims, aphorisms   **36 wit** vagina (slang)   **arbalestar** a crossbow, consisting of a steel bow fitted to a wooden shaft used for the discharge of arrows, emphasizing her sharp wit   **37 trenchmore** in a frisky, lively, or boisterous manner, from the old English country dance of that name   **38 knighthood** signifier of chivalry and rank but any freeholder worth £40 a year could become a knight on the occasion of a coronation, or marriage of a king's daughter   **40 black-brows** referring to Luce's dark eyes and brows, or general colouring; not conventionally regarded as attractive features   **shrewd** sharp tongued/keen-witted/mischievous   **43 power** mental strength, energy/personal or social influence/capacity to act/regiment   **45 wary** careful, cautious/thrifty   **46 air** impetuosity/outward show   **48 desperate Dick** reckless/hopeless fellow   **51 fay** faith   **proper** honest, worthy/handsome, elegant   **58 manners...man** proverbial, the motto of Winchester school: 'Manners make a man'   ***Monsieur Civet*** the French designation suggests affectation   **60 Soul** a common expletive   **crossed** thwarted, opposed   **witched...owl** bewitched by (or in the same way as) an **owl**, a small nocturnal bird of prey regarded as an ill-omen/familiar spirit of witches   **61 booth** fairground tent   **63 treads...awry** proverbial for 'producing a lapse from virtue' (through adultery)   **65 good...before** i.e. they're at the back of the inn   **66 Save you** God save you, a common greeting

DAFFODIL   No pieces, sir.

CIVET   Why, then the whole.

I pray, sir, what may yonder gentlewomen be?

70   DAFFODIL   They may be ladies, sir, if the destinies and mortality work.

CIVET   What's her name, sir?

DAFFODIL   Mistress Frances Spurcock, Sir Lancelot Spurcock's daughter.

CIVET   Is she a maid, sir?

DAFFODIL   You may ask Pluto and Dame Proserpine that:

75   I would be loath to be riddled, sir.

CIVET   Is she married, I mean, sir?

DAFFODIL   The Fates knows not yet what shoemaker shall make her wedding shoes.

CIVET   I pray, where inn you, sir? I would be very glad to bestow the wine of that

80   gentlewoman.

DAFFODIL   At the George, sir.

CIVET   God save you, sir.

DAFFODIL   I pray your name, sir?

CIVET   My name is Master Civet, sir.

85   DAFFODIL   A sweet name; God be with you, good Master Civet.   *Exit Civet*

[*Enter a drawer*]

LANCELOT   Ah, have we spied you, stout St George?

For all your dragon, you had best sell's good wine —

That needs no ivy bush. Well, we'll not sit by it,

As you do on your horse: this room shall serve.

90   Drawer, let me have sack for us old men:

For these girls and knaves, small wines are best.

A pint of sack, no more.

DRAWER   A quart of sack in the Three Tuns.   [*Exit*]

LANCELOT   A pint, draw but a pint!

95   Daffodil, call for wine to make yourselves drink.

FRANCK   And a cup of small beer, and a cake, good Daffodil.   *Daffodil brings some drink and food*

Enter Young Flowerdale [and Old Flowerdale as his servant]

FLOWERDALE   How now! Fie, sit in the open room?

Now, good Sir Lancelot, and my kind friend, worshipful Master Weathercock,

What, at your pint? A quart, for shame!

100   LANCELOT   Nay, roister, by your leave we will away.

FLOWERDALE   Come, give's some music, we'll go dance.

Begone, Sir Lancelot? What, and fair day, too?

[LUCE]   'Twere foully done to dance within the fair!

---

67 **pieces** punning on sense of 'casks of wine'   74 **Pluto…Proserpine** the classical god of the Underworld and his queen, regarded as fairies   75 **riddled** questioned/sifted   77 **Fates** classical goddesses controlling human destiny   79 **where inn you** where do you lodge?   85 **sweet** puns on the use of 'Civet' in the manufacture of perfume   86 **stout** proud/valiant   **George?…dragon** referring to the story of St George and the dragon, commonly represented on inn signs thrusting his lance deep into the dragon's throat   87 **sell's** sell us   88 **ivy bush** used on signs to signify the sale of wine: proverbial, 'Good wine needs no bush'   89 **you…horse** Sir Lancelot seems to be addressing the inn sign at this point   90 **sack** white wine from Spain or the Canary Isles   91 **small wines** i.e. of low alcoholic content, cf. 'small beer' (line 96)   92 **pint…quart** the Drawer has doubled the order since a **pint** is half a **quart**   93 **Three Tuns** the name of the room; naming individual inn rooms was common practice   **Tuns** large casks or barrels; three large casks made up the arms of the Vintner's Company   94 **pint** Sir Lancelot's insistence suggests either abstemiousness, inability to hold his drink or meanness   97 **How now!** What's this?   **Fie** exclamation of shock or disgust   **open** i.e. public, as opposed to hiring a private room   100 **roister** riotous fellow/swaggerer/noisy reveller   103 **foully** disgracefully, shamefully

FLOWERDALE   Nay, if you say so, fairest of all fairs,

105   Then I'll not dance. A pox upon my tailor,

He hath spoiled me a peach-colour satin suit,

Cut upon cloth of silver. But if ever the rascal serve me such another trick, I'll give him leave, i'faith, to put me in the calendar of fools: and you, and you, Sir Lancelot, and Master Weathercock. My goldsmith, too, on t'other side, I bespoke thee, Luce,

110   a carcanet of gold, and thought thou shouldst ha' had it for a fairing, and the rogue puts me in rerages for orient pearl, but thou shalt have it by Sunday night, wench.

Enter the drawer

DRAWER   Sir, here is one hath sent you a pottle of Rhenish wine brewed with rose-water.

115   FLOWERDALE   To me?

DRAWER   No, sir, to the knight, and desires his more acquaintance.

LANCELOT   To me? What's he that proves so kind?

DAFFODIL   I have a trick to know his name, sir,

He hath a month's mind here to Mistress Frances:

120   His name is Master Civet.

LANCELOT   Call him in, Daffodil.

FLOWERDALE   O, I know him, sir, he is a fool, but reasonable rich. His father was one of these lease-mongers, these corn-mongers, these money-mongers, but he never had the wit to be a whore-monger.

Enter Master Civet

125   LANCELOT   I promise you, sir, you are at too much charge.

CIVET   The charge is small charge, sir. I thank God my father left me wherewithal. If it please you, sir, I have a great mind to this gentlewoman here in the way of marriage.

LANCELOT   I thank you, sir. Please you come to Lewisham

130   To my poor house, you shall be kindly welcome —

I knew your father, he was a wary husband —

To pay here, drawer!

DRAWER   All is paid, sir. This gentleman hath paid all.

LANCELOT   I'faith, you do us wrong,

135   But we shall live to make amends ere long.

Master Flowerdale, is that your man?

FLOWERDALE   Yes, faith, a good old knave.

LANCELOT   Nay, then, I think

You will turn wise now you take such a servant.

---

106 spoiled damaged   **108 calendar** list, register   **110 carcanet** ornamental collar or necklace   **fairing** gift bought from a fair   **111 rerages** arrears of payment   **112 wench** familiar form of address to a young woman   **113 pottle** pot containing two quarts, half a gallon (2.3 litres)   **Rhenish** from the Rhine region   **114 rose-water** water distilled from roses, used as a perfume   **118 trick** knack, art   **119 month's mind** fancy, inclination, liking   **123 lease-mongers…whore-monger** dealers in various goods   **money-mongers** money-lenders, usurers, with connotations of underhand dealings   **124 whore-monger** pimp   **125 you…charge** you have gone to too much expense/put yourself to too much trouble   **126 wherewithal** financial resources   **127 great mind** strong inclination, desire   **129 Lewisham** then a village in Kent six miles south-east of London, of which it is now a borough   **130 poor** conventionally modest or apologetic reference to one's estate   **131 wary husband** prudent manager   **132 To pay here** Sir Lancelot is asking for his bill   **135 ere** before   **137 knave** servant, not a respectful term   **139 You…servant** perhaps an allusion to 'A wise servant shall have rule over a lewd son' (Proverbs 17:2)

140   Come: you'll ride with us to Lewisham? Let's away:

      'Tis scarce two hours to the end of day.   *Exeunt*

Scene 3

Enter Sir Arthur Greenshield, Oliver, Lieutenant and soldiers

ARTHUR   Lieutenant, lead your soldiers to the ships.

      There let them have their coats; at their arrival,

      They shall have pay. Farewell, look to your charge.

SOLDIER   Ay, we are now sent away and cannot so much as speak with our

5   friends.

OLIVER   No, man! What, ere you used 'o zutch a fashion thick you cannot take

leave of your vreens?

ARTHUR   Fellow, no more. Lieutenant, lead them off.

SOLDIER   Well, if I have not my pay and my clothes,

10   I'll venture a running away, though I hang for't.

ARTHUR   Away, sirrah, charm your tongue.   *Exeunt soldiers*

OLIVER   Bean't you a presser, sir?

ARTHUR   I am a commander, sir, under the king.

OLIVER   'Sfoot man, an you be ne'er zutch a commander,

15   Should a' spoke with my vreens before ich'ud a' gone, zo should.

ARTHUR   Content yourself, man. My authority will stretch to press so good a man

as you.

OLIVER   Press me? I devy ye. Press scoundrels and thy mezels. Press me? 'Che

scorns thee, i'faith. For, see'st thee, here's a worshipful knight knows 'cham not to

20   be pressed by thee.

Enter Sir Lancelot, Weathercock, Young Flowerdale, Old Flowerdale, Luce, [and] Franck

LANCELOT   Sir Arthur,

      Welcome to Lewisham, welcome, by my troth.

      What's the matter, man, why are you vexed?

OLIVER   Why, man, he would press me.

25 LANCELOT   O fie, Sir Arthur, press him? He is a man of reckoning.

WEATHERCOCK   Ay, that he is, Sir Arthur. He hath the nobles,

      The golden ruddocks, he!

ARTHUR   The fitter for the wars: and, were he not

      In favour with your worships, he should see

30   That I have power to press so good as he.

OLIVER   'Ch'ill stand to the trial, so 'ch'ill.

Scene 3 *Location: Lewisham, near Sir Lancelot's house*   **2 coats** uniforms   **6 What…vreens?** Oliver's Devon dialect is rendered phonetically: this sentence means 'What, are you used to [being treated in] such a fashion that you cannot take leave of your friends?'   **11 charm your tongue** hold your tongue; keep silent   **12 Bean't…presser** aren't you a presser   **presser** one commissioned to press (force) men into military service   **14 'Sfoot…should** Heavens man, even if you were such a commander, I'd have spoken with my friends before I'd have gone, so I should   **18 Press me? I…thee** Press me? I defy you. Press scoundrels and wretches (**mezels**). Press me? I scorn thee   **25 reckoning** estimation, distinction, worth/expectation/calculation   **26 nobles** gold coins   **27 ruddocks** gold coins (slang)   **31 'Ch'ill…'ch'ill** I'll put it to the test so I will

FLOWERDALE   Ay, marry, shall he — press-cloth and kersey,
White-pot and drowsen broth — tut, tut, he cannot.

OLIVER   Well, sir, though you see vlauten cloth and kersey, 'che a' zeen zutch a
35   kersey coat wear out the town sick a zilken jacket as thick-a one you wear.

FLOWERDALE   Well said, vlittan vlattan.

OLIVER   Ah, and well said, cocknell and Bow-bell, too: what, dost think 'cham
aveard of thy zilken coat? No vear vor thee.

LANCELOT   Nay, come, no more. Be all lovers and friends.

40   WEATHERCOCK   Ay, 'tis best so, good Master Oliver.

FLOWERDALE   Is your name Master Oliver, I pray you?

OLIVER   What, tit an be, tit an grieve you?

FLOWERDALE   No, but I'd gladly know if a man might not have a foolish plot out of
Master Oliver to work upon.

45   OLIVER   Work thy plots upon me? Stand aside! Work thy foolish plots upon me?
'Ch'ill zo use thee, thou wert never zo used since thy dame bound thy head — work
upon me?

FLOWERDALE   Let him come, let him come!

OLIVER   Zirrah, zirrah, if it were not vor shame, 'che would a' given thee zutch a
50   whister poop under the ear, 'che would a' made thee a' vanged another at my feet.
Stand aside, let me loose, 'cham all of a vlaming fire-brand. Stand aside!

FLOWERDALE   Well, I forbear you, for your friends' sake.

OLIVER   A vig for all my vreens! Dost thou tell me of my vreens?

LANCELOT   No more, good Master Oliver, no more,

55   Sir Arthur. And maiden, here in the sight
Of all your suitors, every man of worth,
I'll tell you whom I fainest would prefer
To the hard bargain of your marriage bed:
Shall I be plain among you, gentlemen?

60   ARTHUR   Ay, sir, 'tis best.

LANCELOT   Then, sir, first to you:
I do confess you a most gallant knight,
A worthy soldier, and an honest man:
But honesty maintains not a French hood,
65   Goes very seldom in a chain of gold,
Keeps a small train of servants, hath few friends.

---

32 Ay…cannot Flowerdale is mocking Oliver's rusticity: **press-cloth** woollen-cloth pressed and folded ready for sale   **kersey** coarse narrow cloth, woven from long wool and usually ribbed   **White-pot** a kind of custard or milk pudding   **drowsen broth** oatmeal pottage/beverage of grounds of beer boiled up with herbs   **34 Well … you wear** Well, sir, although you see me dressed in **vlauten** (homespun) cloth, I have seen a **kersey** coat like mine last longer in the town than such a silken coat, like this one you wear   **36 vlittan vlattan** nonsensical mocking of Oliver's pronunciation of 'f's as 'v's   **37 cocknell** cockney, i.e. milksop/townie   **Bow-bell** cockneys traditionally were supposed to be born within the sound of the bells of the church of St Mary-le-Bow   **what…thee** what, do you think I'm afraid of your silken coat? No fear of you   **39 lovers** well-wishers   **42 What…you?** What if it is, does it hurt you?   **43 but…upon** while the general sense seems designed to insult and provoke Oliver, the specific sense is much less clear offering a wide play of possible meanings   **foolish** befitting a fool/amusing/poor, mean   **plot** piece of land/scab, stain/plan, scheme/storyline   **44 work upon** perform, practise/construct, fashion/compose, write/influence, urge   **46 since…head** proverbial, 'Since you were a child'   **dame** mother   **49 Zirrah…aside** Sirrah, sirrah, if it weren't for shame, I would have given you such a clout under the ear, I would have made you take another one from my feet. Stand aside, let me go, I'm like a flaming fire-brand all over   **52 forbear** tolerate, put up with   **53 A…vreens** A fig for all my friends! Do you talk to me about my friends?   **vig** (fig) anything small, valueless, contemptible   **57 fainest** rather/most gladly, most willingly   **64 French hood** elaborate head-dress worn by women in the sixteenth and seventeenth centuries, also by women when punished for unchastity   **66 train** retinue

And for this wild oats here, young Flowerdale,

I will not judge. God can work miracles,

But he were better make a hundred new,

70   Than thee a thrifty and an honest one.

WEATHERCOCK   Believe me, he hath bit you there.

He hath touched you to the quick, that hath he.

FLOWERDALE   Woodcock o' my side. Why, Master Weathercock,

You know I am honest, howsoever thriftless.

75   WEATHERCOCK   Now, by my troth, I know no otherwise.

O, your old mother was a dame indeed!

Heaven hath her soul, and my wife's, too, I trust:

And your good father, honest gentleman,

He is gone a journey, as I hear, far hence.

80   FLOWERDALE   Ay, God be praised, he is far enough.

He is gone a pilgrimage to paradise,

And left me to cut a caper against care.

Luce, look on me that am as light as air.

LUCE   I'faith, I like not shadows, bubbles, breath,

85   I hate a light o'love, as I hate death.

LANCELOT   Girl, hold thee there. Look on this Devonshire lad:

Fat, fair, and lovely, both in purse and person.

OLIVER   Well, sir, 'cham as the lord hath made me. You know me well, y-vind.

'Che have three-score pack o' kersey at Blackem Hall, and chief credit beside, and

90   my fortunes may be zo good as another's, zo it may.

[LUCE]   'Tis you I love, whatsoever others say.   *Aside to Sir Arthur*

ARTHUR   Thanks, fairest.

FLOWERDALE   What, wouldst thou have me quarrel with him?

FATHER   Do but say he shall hear from you.

95   LANCELOT   Yet, gentlemen, howsoever I prefer

This Devonshire suitor, I'll enforce no love.

My daughter shall have liberty to choose

Whom she likes best. In your love suit, proceed:

Not all of you, but only one must speed.

100   WEATHERCOCK   You have said well: indeed, right well.

Enter Artichoke

ARTICHOKE   Mistress, here's one would speak with you. My fellow Daffodil hath him

in the cellar already: he knows him — he met him at Croydon Fair.

LANCELOT   O, I remember, a little man.

ARTICHOKE   Ay, a very little man.

---

67 **wild oats** dissolute young man, with implication of sexual immorality   68 **God ... one** God can work miracles, and it would be better for him to make a hundred new suitors, than to make you a thrifty and an honest one   71 **bit** spoken sharply and injuriously against   73 **Woodcock** fool, simpleton – from the bird of the same name which was notoriously easy to catch   74 **howsoever** however/albeit   81 **paradise** heaven   82 **cut a caper** dance lightly/ act fantastically   85 **light o'love** one who is inconstant in love/harlot   88 **Well ... may** Well, sir, I am as the lord hath made me. You know me well, I find. I have sixty (**three-score**) packs of kersey cloth at Blackwell Hall, and excellent credit besides, and my fortune may be as good as any man's, so it may   **Blackem Hall** Blackwell or Bakewell Hall on the west side and almost at the south end of Basinghall Street, London, passed into the Bakewell family in the reign of Edward III, later sold to the City for £50 and turned into a cloth exchange, a weekly market place for woollen cloth   94 **Do ... you** i.e. challenge him to a duel   99 **speed** succeed, obtain his desire

| 105 | LANCELOT | And yet a proper man. |

LANCELOT   And yet a proper man.

ARTICHOKE   A very proper, very little, man.

LANCELOT   His name is Monsieur Civet.

ARTICHOKE   The same, sir.

LANCELOT   Come, gentlemen. If other suitors come,

110   My foolish daughter will be fitted, too.

But Delia, my saint, no man dare move.

Exeunt all but Young Flowerdale, Oliver, and Old Flowerdale

FLOWERDALE   Hark you, sir, a word.

OLIVER   What ha'an you to say to me now?

FLOWERDALE   Ye shall hear from me, and that very shortly.

115   OLIVER   Is that all? Vare thee well, 'che vear thee not a vig.   *Exit Oliver*

FLOWERDALE   What if should come more? I am fairly dressed.

FATHER   I do not mean that you shall meet with him.

But presently we'll go and draw a will,

Where we'll set down land that we never saw,

120   And we will have it of so large a sum,

Sir Lancelot shall entreat you take his daughter:

This being formed, give it Master Weathercock,

And make Sir Lancelot's daughter heir of all,

And make him swear never to show the will

125   To anyone, until that you be dead.

This done, the foolish changing Weathercock

Will straight discourse unto Sir Lancelot

The form and tenor of your testament;

Nor stand to pause of it, be ruled by me:

130   What will ensue, that shall you quickly see.

FLOWERDALE   Come, let's about it: if that a will, sweet Kit,

Can get the wench, I shall renown thy wit.   *Exeunt*

Scene 4

Enter Daffodil [and Luce]

DAFFODIL   Mistress, still froward?

No kind looks unto your Daffodil now, by the gods.

LUCE   Away, you foolish knave, let my hand go.

DAFFODIL   There is your hand, but this shall go with me:

5   My heart is thine; this is my true love's fee.   *Takes off her bracelet*

LUCE   I'll have your coat stripped o'er your ears for this,

You saucy rascal!

---

110 **fitted** provided for/suitably matched – a bawdy, slang meaning implies 'sexually enjoyed'   113 **ha'an** have   115 **Vare ... vig** Fare thee well, I fear thee not a fig   116 **fairly dressed** wearing my good clothes   118 **presently** immediately   121 **entreat** beg   127 **discourse** relate it   128 **tenor** meaning, substance   129 **Nor ... it** do not delay in this   131 **Kit** familiar diminutive of Kester/Christopher   132 **renown** make famous   **Scene 4** *Location: Lewisham, Sir Lancelot's residence*   1 **froward** perverse   6 **coat ... ears** proverbial: 'To pull one's coat over his ears', i.e. to dismiss   **coat** servant's livery coat

Enter Lancelot and Weathercock

LANCELOT   How now, maid, what is the news with you?

LUCE   Your man is something saucy.   *Exit Luce*

10   LANCELOT   Go to, sirrah, I'll talk with you anon.

DAFFODIL   Sir, I am a man to be talked withal,

I am no horse, I trow:

I know my strength, then, no more than so.

WEATHERCOCK   Ah, by the mackins,

15   Good Sir Lancelot, I saw him the other day

Hold up the bucklers like an Hercules.

I'faith, God ha' mercy, lad, I like thee well.

LANCELOT   Ay, I like him well. Go, sirrah, fetch me a cup of wine,

That ere I part with Master Weathercock,

20   We may drink down our farewell in French wine.

WEATHERCOCK   I thank you, sir, I thank you, friendly knight.

I'll come and visit you, by the mouse-foot, I will:

In the meantime, take heed of cutting Flowerdale,

He is a desperate Dick, I warrant you.

25   LANCELOT   He is, he is. Fill, Daffodil, fill me some wine.—

[*Aside*] Ha, what wears he on his arm?

My daughter Luce's bracelet? Ay, 'tis the same.—

Ha, to you, Master Weathercock.

WEATHERCOCK   I thank you, sir. Here, Daffodil, an honest fellow and a tall thou art.

30   Well, I'll take my leave, good knight, and hope to have you and all your daughters,

at my poor house, in good sooth I must.

LANCELOT   Thanks, Master Weathercock. I shall be bold to trouble you, be sure.

WEATHERCOCK   And welcome; heartily farewell.   *Exit Weathercock*

LANCELOT   Sirrah, I saw my daughter's wrong and, withal, her bracelet on your

35   arm. Off with it! And with my livery, too! Have I care to see my daughter matched

with men of worship, and are you grown so bold? Go, sirrah, from my house, or I'll

whip you hence.

DAFFODIL   I'll not be whipped, sir, there's your livery.

This is a serving-man's reward! What care I?

40   I have means to trust to: I scorn service, I.   *Exit Daffodil*

LANCELOT   Ay, a lusty knave, but I must let him go:

Our servants must be taught what they should know.   [*Exit*]

---

9 **something** somewhat/rather too   10 **anon** shortly   11 **withal** with/in spite of all   12 **trow** trust, believe   14 **by the mackins** by the Mass/ by the Matins (early morning religious service)   16 **Hold…bucklers** perform well (in a mock-combat)   **bucklers** small round shields with central spike   **Hercules** classical hero, proverbial for strength and sexual prowess   22 **by the mouse-foot** an old oath, perhaps relating to the transmigration of souls (the belief that the soul would transform into an animal when leaving the body), thus it may refer to the point of death   23 **cutting** swaggering blade (young fellow)   29 **tall** goodly, handsome/brave, bold   31 **in good sooth** truly, indeed   34 **wrong** injury/transgression/mischief   **withal** furthermore   35 **livery** badge or collar or other token of an employer   40 **means** resources

Scene 5

Enter Sir Arthur and Luce

LUCE   Sir, as I am a maid, I do affect
           You above any suitor that I have,
           Although that soldiers scarce knows how to love.

ARTHUR   I am a soldier, and a gentleman,
5   Knows what belongs to war, what to a lady:
           What man offends me, that my sword shall right:
           What woman loves me, I am her faithful knight.

LUCE   I neither doubt your valour, nor your love,
           But there be some that bears a soldier's form,
10   That swears by him they never think upon,
           Goes swaggering up and down from house to house
           Crying, 'God pays! and—

ARTHUR   I'faith, lady, I'll descry you such a man:
           Of them there be many, which you have spoke of,
15   That bear the name and shape of soldiers —
           Yet, God knows, very seldom saw the war —
           That haunt your taverns and your ordinaries,
           Your ale-houses, sometimes, for all a-like
           To uphold the brutish humour of their minds,
20   Being marked down for the bondmen of despair.
           Their mirth begins in wine, but ends in blood,
           Their drink is clear, but their conceits are mud.

LUCE   Yet these are great gentlemen soldiers.

ARTHUR   No, they are wretched slaves,
25   Whose desperate lives doth bring them timeless graves.

LUCE   Both for yourself, and for your form of life,
           If I may choose, I'll be a soldier's wife.   [*Exeunt*]

Scene 6

Enter Sir Lancelot and Oliver

OLIVER   And tit trust to it, so then.

LANCELOT Assure yourself,
           You shall be married with all speed we may:
           One day shall serve for Frances and for Luce.

Scene 5   *Location: unspecified, most likely Sir Lancelot's residence*   **1 maid** virgin   **affect** like, love   **3 Although** despite the fact   **knows** a singular verb and plural subject is not uncommon   **6 What** whatever   **10 him…upon** i.e. God   **12 'God pays!'** 'God is responsible for all!'   **13 descry** proclaim, denounce   **17 ordinaries** eating houses where meals were provided at a fixed price   **18 a-like** enjoy: the 'a-' prefix helps the line scan; alternatively it may be a compositor error which should read: 'for all alike / Uphold'   **20 bondmen** serfs, slaves   **22 conceits** fancies, whims   **mud** slimy, dirty, impure   **23 gentlemen soldiers** i.e. deriving from the gentry (or those who bore coats of arms), such as Sir Arthur   **Scene 6**   *Location: imprecise, perhaps Sir Lancelot's residence*   **1 And…then** If you can trust to it, truly then

5   OLIVER   Why, 'che would vain know the time for providing wedding raiments.

LANCELOT   Why, no more but this, first get your assurance made

Touching my daughter's jointure. That dispatched,

We will in two days make provision.

OLIVER   Why, man, 'ch'ill have the writings made by tomorrow.

10 LANCELOT   Tomorrow be it, then. Let's meet at the King's Head in Fish Street.

OLIVER   No, fie, man, no! Let's meet at the Rose at Temple Bar,

That will be nearer your counsellor and mine.

LANCELOT   At the Rose be it then, the hour nine,

He that comes last forfeits a pint of wine.

15 OLIVER   A pint is no payment: let it be a whole quart or nothing.

Enter Artichoke

ARTICHOKE   Master, here is a man would speak with Master Oliver. He comes from young Master Flowerdale.

OLIVER   Why, 'ch'ill speak with him, 'ch'ill speak with him.   [*Exit Artichoke*]

LANCELOT   Nay, son Oliver. I'll surely see,

20 What young Flowerdale hath sent to you.

I pray God it be no quarrel.

OLIVER   Why, man, if he quarrel with me, 'ch'ill give him his hands full.

Enter Old Flowerdale

FATHER   God save you, good Sir Lancelot.

LANCELOT   Welcome, honest friend.

25 FATHER   To you and yours my master wisheth health,—

But unto you, sir, this and this he sends: *To Oliver*

There is the length, sir, of his rapier,

And in that paper shall you know his mind.   *Delivers a letter*

OLIVER   Here 'ch'ill meet him, my vreend, 'ch'ill meet him.

30 LANCELOT   Meet him? You shall not meet the ruffian, fie.

OLIVER   An I do not meet him, 'ch'ill give you leave to call

Me cut. Where is't, sirrah? Where is't? Where is't?

FATHER   The letter shows both the time and place,

And if you be a man, then keep your word.

35 LANCELOT   Sir, he shall not keep his word. He shall not meet.

FATHER   Why, let him choose, he'll be the better known

For a base rascal and reputed so.

OLIVER   Zirrah, zirrah, an 'twere not an old fellow, and sent after an arrant,

'ch'ud give thee something, but 'ch'ud be no money. But hold thee, for I see thou art

---

5 Why…raiments Why, I would gladly know how long I have to get wedding clothes   7 Touching concerning   jointure settlement of property or land in case of widowhood/dowry   9 'ch'ill I'll   writings paperwork, legal documentation   10 King's Head a common tavern sign in London; there was a King's Head in New Fish Street   Fish Street running south from East Cheap to London Thames Street, it was the main thoroughfare to London Bridge   11 Rose tavern at the corner of Thanet Place outside Temple Bar, one of the Inns of Court   12 counsellor counsellor-at-law, barrister or advocate   29 Here…him Here I'll meet him, friend, I'll meet him, i.e. fight him in a duel   32 cut castrated, a term of abuse   36 better known more widely proclaimed   38 Zirrah…vor' thee Sirrah, sirrah, if you were not an old fellow sent after a knave, I'd give you something, but it wouldn't be money. But wait, I see you're a little down on your luck. Look, there's forty shillings for you. Bring your master a-field, and I'll give you forty more. Make sure you bring him, now. I'll maul him, tell him, I'll mar his dancing legs. I'll use him – he was never so used since his dame bound his head. I'll do him from capering anymore, I warn you   arrant good-for-nothing, thief, vagabond

40 somewhat testern, hold thee, there's vorty shillings. Bring thy master avield, 'ch'ill give thee vorty more. Look thou bring him. 'Ch'ill maul him, tell him, 'ch'ill mar his dancing trestles. 'Ch'ill use him — he was ne'er so used since his dam bound his head. 'Ch'ill make him for capering any more, 'che vor' thee.

FATHER   You seem a man stout and resolute,

45   And I will so report, whate'er befall.

LANCELOT   An't fall out ill, assure thy master this,
    I'll make him fly the land, or use him worse.

FATHER   My master, sir, deserves not this of you,
    And that you'll shortly find.

50 LANCELOT   Thy master is an unthrift, you a knave,
    And I'll attach you first, next clap him up,
    Or have him bound unto his good behaviour.

OLIVER   I would you were a sprite, if you do him any harm for this. An you do, 'ch'ill ne'er zee you, nor any of yours, while 'ch'ill have eyes open. What, do you

55 think 'ch'ill be a-baffled up and down the town for a mezel and a scoundrel? No, 'che vor' you.— Zirrah, 'ch'ill come. Zay no more, 'ch'ill come tell him.   *To Father*

FATHER   Well, sir, my master deserves not this of you,
    And that you'll shortly find.   *Exit*

OLIVER   No matter. He's an unthrift, I devy him.

60 LANCELOT   Now, gentle son, let me know the place.

OLIVER   No, 'che vor' you.

LANCELOT   Let me see the note.

OLIVER   Nay, 'ch'ill watch you for zutch a trick. But if 'che meet him, zo; if not, zo: 'ch'ill make him know me, or 'ch'ill know why I shall not, 'ch'ill vare the worse.

65 LANCELOT   What, will you then neglect my daughter's love?
    Venture your state, and hers, for a loose brawl?

OLIVER   Why, man, 'ch'ill not kill him. Marry, 'ch'ill veeze him, to and again. An zo, God be with you, vather. What, man, we shall met tomorrow.   *Exit [Oliver]*

LANCELOT   Who would ha' thought he had been so desperate?

70   Come forth, my honest servant Artichoke.

Enter Artichoke

ARTICHOKE   Now, what's the matter? Some brawl toward, I warrant you.

LANCELOT   Go, get me thy sword bright scoured, thy buckler mended.— O, for that knave, that villain Daffodil would have done good service.— But, to thee.

ARTICHOKE   Ay, this is the tricks of all you gentlemen when you stand in need of a

75   good fellow. 'O, for that Daffodil! O, where is he?' But if you be angry, an it be but for the wagging of a straw, then, 'Out o' doors with the knave, turn the coat over his ears.' This is the humour of you all.

---

40 **testern** obscure but seems to imply he looks down on his luck; **tester** was slang for a sixpence   42 **dancing trestles** legs, from **trestles** as 'support'; to dance was also to fornicate   45 **whate'er befall** whatever happens   46 **An't…ill** if it ends badly, i.e. if Oliver dies   47 **fly the land** flee the country   50 **unthrift** prodigal, spendthrift   51 **attach** arrest, seize   **clap him up** imprison, confine him   52 **bound…behaviour** legally forced to behave better   53 **I…him** I would you were a spirit, if you do him any harm over this. If you do, I'll never see you, nor any of yours, while I have my eyes open. What, do you think I'll be **a-baffled** (disgraced) up and down the town for a **mezel** (wretch) and a scoundrel? No, I warrant you. Sirrah, I'll come. Say no more, I'll come tell him   59 **devy** defy   61 **'che vor'** I warn   63 **Nay…worse** Nay, I've got my eye on you for such a trick. If I meet him, so; if not, so. I'll make him know me, or I'll know why I can't, and so fare the worst   66 **Venture** risk   67 **Why…tomorrow** Why, man, I'll not kill him. By the Virgin Mary, I'll beat him, to and again. And so, God be with you, father. What man, we shall [be] met tomorrow   **'ch'ill veeze him** i.e. I'll do for him   **veeze** (feeze) drive off, frighten   69 **desperate** reckless, infuriated   71 **toward** coming, impending   **warrant** guarantee   72 **scoured** cleaned, polished   73 **But, to thee** anyway, to return to you   74 **tricks** particular habits, characteristics   76 **wagging…straw** proverbial: to 'be angry at the wagging of a straw', a possibly bawdy allusion to penis (**straw**)

LANCELOT   Oh, for that knave, that lusty Daffodil!

ARTICHOKE   Why, there 'tis now: our year's wages and our vails will scarce pay
for broken swords and bucklers that we use in your quarrels. But I'll not fight if
Daffodil be o' t'other side, that's flat.

LANCELOT   'Tis no such matter, man. Get weapons ready and be at London ere the
break of day. Watch near the lodging of the Devonshire youth, but be unseen. And,
as he goes out, as he will go out, and that very early without doubt—

ARTICHOKE   What, would you have me draw upon him as he goes in the street?

LANCELOT   Not for a world, man,
> Into the fields. For to the field he goes,
> There to meet the desperate Flowerdale;
> Take thou the part of Oliver my son,
> For he shall be my son, and marry Luce:
> Dost thou understand me, knave?

ARTICHOKE   Ay, sir, I do understand you, but my young mistress might be better
provided in matching with my fellow Daffodil.

LANCELOT   No more! Daffodil is a knave:
> That Daffodil is a most notorious knave.   *Exit [Artichoke]*

Enter Weathercock
> Master Weathercock, you come in happy time.
> The desperate Flowerdale hath writ a challenge,
> And who think you must answer it,
> But the Devonshire man, my son Oliver?

WEATHERCOCK   Marry, I am sorry for it, good Sir Lancelot.
> But, if you will be ruled by me, we'll stay the fury.

LANCELOT   As how, I pray?

WEATHERCOCK   Marry, I'll tell you, by promising young Flowerdale the red-lipped Luce.

LANCELOT   I'll rather follow her unto her grave.

WEATHERCOCK   Ay, Sir Lancelot, I would have thought so, too,
> But you and I have been deceived in him:
> Come, read this will, or deed, or what you call it,
> I know not. Come, come, your spectacles, I pray.   *Gives him the will*

LANCELOT   Nay, I thank God, I see very well.

WEATHERCOCK   Marry, God bless your eyes: mine hath been dim almost this thirty
years.

LANCELOT   Ha? What is this? What is this?

WEATHERCOCK   Nay, there is true love indeed.
> He gave it to me but this very morn,
> And bid me keep it unseen from anyone.
> Good youth, to see how men may be deceived.

LANCELOT   Passion of me! What a wretch am I
> To hate this loving youth. He hath made me,

---

79 vails tips, gratuities   **87 fields** could refer to Finsbury Fields, north of Cripplegate and Moorgate; Tuttle Fields in Westminster; or, more likely, St George's Fields, south of the Thames between Southwark and Lambeth: all were likely places for duels   **101 stay** stop, halt the course of   **fury** violent fellow
110 mine...years suggesting Weathercock is not a young man

Together with my Luce he loves so dear,

120   Executors of all his wealth.

WEATHERCOCK   All, all, good man, he hath given you all.

LANCELOT   Three ships, now in the straits, and homeward bound,

Two lordships, of two hundred pound a year:

The one in Wales, the other in Gloucestershire:

125   Debts and accounts are thirty thousand pound,

Plate, money, jewels, sixteen thousand more,

Two housen furnished well in Coleman Street,

Beside whatsoever his uncle leaves to him,

Being of great demesnes and wealth at Peckham.

130   WEATHERCOCK   How like you this, good knight? How like you this?

LANCELOT   I have done him wrong, but now I'll make amends.

The Devonshire man shall whistle for a wife.

He marry Luce? Luce shall be Flowerdale's.

WEATHERCOCK   Why, that is friendly said.

135   Let's ride to London and prevent their match,

By promising your daughter to that lovely lad.

LANCELOT   We'll ride to London, or it shall not need,

We'll cross to Deptford Strand and take a boat:

Where be these knaves? What, Artichoke, what, fop?

Enter Artichoke

140   ARTICHOKE   Here be the very knaves, but not the merry knaves.

LANCELOT   Here, take my cloak, I'll have a walk to Deptford.

ARTICHOKE   Sir, we have been scouring of our swords and bucklers for your defence.

LANCELOT   Defence me no defence, let your swords rust,

I'll have no fighting: ay, let blows alone.

145   Bid Delia see all things be in readiness

Against the wedding: we'll have two at once,

And that will save charges, Master Weathercock.

ARTICHOKE   Well, we will do it, sir.   *Exeunt*

Scene 7

Enter Civet, Franck and Delia

CIVET   By my truth, this is good luck; I thank God for this. In good sooth, I have
even my heart's desire. Sister Delia, now I may boldly call you so, for your father
hath frank and freely given me his daughter, Franck.

---

122 **straits** perhaps of Gibraltar   126 **Plate** generic term for household items originally silver but later pewter, copper or brass   127 **housen** archaic plural of
'houses'   **Coleman Street** a fine street running north from the east end of Gresham Street to Fore Street, frequented ironically by Puritans   129 **demesnes**
lands, estates   **Peckham** then a village in Surrey about three miles south of St Paul's, now part of the London borough of Southwark   132 **whistle for** expect
in vain, go without   138 **Deptford Strand** on the south bank of the Thames four miles east of London, a main crossing-point into the city   139 **fop** fool
146 **Against** with respect to   147 **charges** expenses   **Scene 7**   *Location: Lewisham, Sir Lancelot's residence*   2 **even** exactly, precisely   3 **frank** without
restraint/generously, punning on her name

FRANCK   Ay, by my troth, Tom, thou hast my good will too, for, I thank God, I longed
5   for a husband, and would I might never stir for one whose name was Tom.

DELIA   Why, sister, now you have your wish.

CIVET   You say very true, sister Delia, and I prithee call me nothing but Tom,
and I'll call thee sweetheart, and Franck: will it not do well, sister Delia?

DELIA   It will do very well with both of you.

10   FRANCK   But, Tom, must I go as I do now when I am married?

CIVET   No, Franck. I'll have thee go like a citizen,
            In a guarded gown and a French hood.

FRANCK   By my troth, that will be excellent indeed.

DELIA   Brother, maintain your wife to your estate,
15   Apparel you yourself like to your father,
            And let her go like to your ancient mother.
            He sparing got his wealth, left it to you.
            Brother, take heed of pride, some bids thrift adieu.

CIVET   So, as my father and my mother went — that's a jest indeed. Why, she
20   went in a fringed gown, a single ruff, and a white cap. And my father in a mockado
coat, a pair of red satin sleeves, and a canvas back.

DELIA   And yet his wealth was all as much as yours.

CIVET   My estate, my estate, I thank God, is forty pound a year in good leases
and tenements, besides twenty mark a year at Cuckold's Haven, and that comes to
25   us all by inheritance.

DELIA   That may indeed, 'tis very fitly plied:
            I know not how it comes, but so it falls out
            That those whose fathers have died wondrous rich,
            And took no pleasure but to gather wealth,
30   Thinking of little that they leave behind:
            For them they hope will be of their like mind.
            But falls out contrary: forty years' sparing
            Is scarce three seven years' spending, never caring
            What will ensue, when all their coin is gone,
35   And all too late, then thrift is thought upon:
            Oft have I heard that pride and riot kissed,
            And then repentance cries, 'For had-I-wist'.

---

5 stir move, be active, with a presumably unconscious bawdy meaning of 'have sex'   **10 go** dress, again with a bawdy meaning of 'participate actively in sex'   **11 citizen** freeman (or woman) of the city with certain rights and privileges; citizens' wives were notorious for fine clothes and often represented as sexually lax   **12 guarded gown** ornamented or trimmed with lace, braid or velvet   **French hood** elaborate female head-dress, also worn by women when punished for unchastity   **15 Apparel** dress   **16 ancient** past, former/elderly/venerable   **17 sparing** being economical, saving   **18 some** i.e. even a small amount of pride   **thrift** prosperity   **adieu** 'goodbye' (French)   **19 Why…back** Civet is mocking his parents' cheap clothing   **went** used to dress, go about   **fringed gown** bordered with a fringe – no longer fashionable by 1603–05   **single ruff** article of neck wear, consisting of starched linen muslin arranged in horizontal flutings and standing out all around the neck; these could be very elaborate but a **single** one would be cheaper and less ostentatious   **white cap** probably a simple coif (a small cap covering the back and sides of the head, worn as an indoor head-dress)   **mockado** inferior material, often worn by those unable to afford velvet   **21 satin** not as luxurious as silk, being glossy only on one side; Civet's father could only afford it for the sleeves of his shirt   **canvas back** back of a garment made of canvas, used mainly for domestic linen   **23 forty pound** the average income at this time was £15 a year   **24 tenements** property holdings   **mark** originally a weight of gold or silver, the monetary equivalent to two thirds of a pound sterling   **Cuckold's Haven** on the south side of the Thames at the entrance of Limehouse Reach, below Rotherhithe Chapel: the legend goes that the miller of Charlton, having discovered King John kissing his wife, demanded compensation and was granted all the land he could see from his door, thereafter called Cuckold's point, on condition that he walk every 18 October to the point with a pair of buck's horns (signifying he was a cuckold) on his head   **that…inheritance** the implication is that it refers not only to the lands but the condition of being a **cuckold**, i.e. a married man with an unfaithful wife   **26 fitly** appropriately   **plied** offered frequently   **27 falls out** happens, occurs   **28 wondrous** wonderfully   **31 For…mind** since they expect their children to think in the same way as they do   **33 three seven years'** twenty-one years'   **36 pride…kissed** vanity and extravagance go together   **37 had-I-wist** if I'd known

CIVET   You say well, sister Delia, you say well. But I mean to live within my bounds: for, look you, I have set down my rest thus far, but to maintain my wife in her
40   French hood, and her coach, keep a couple of geldings, and a brace of greyhounds, and this is all I'll do.

DELIA   And you'll do this with forty pound a year?

CIVET   Ay, and a better penny, sister.

FRANCK   Sister, you forget that at Cuckold's Haven.

45   CIVET   By my troth, well remembered, Franck.
         I'll give thee that to buy thee pins.

DELIA   Keep you the rest for points. Alas the day,
         Fools shall have wealth, though all the world say nay.
         Come, brother, will you in? Dinner stays for us.

50   CIVET   Ay, good sister, with all my heart.

FRANCK   Ay, by my troth, Tom, for I have a good stomach.

CIVET   And I the like, sweet Franck.— No, sister,
         Do not think I'll go beyond my bounds.

DELIA   God grant you may not!   *Exeunt*

Scene 8

Enter Young Flowerdale and his Father with foils in their hands

FLOWERDALE   Sirrah Kit, tarry thou there. I have spied Sir Lancelot and old Weathercock coming this way; they are hard at hand. I will by no means be spoken withal.

FATHER   I'll warrant you. Go, get you in!   [*Exit Flowerdale*]

Enter Lancelot and Weathercock

5   LANCELOT   Now, my honest friend, thou dost belong to Master Flowerdale?

FATHER   I do, sir.

LANCELOT   Is he within, my good fellow?

FATHER   No, sir, he is not within.

LANCELOT   I prithee, if he be within, let me speak with him.

10   FATHER   Sir, to tell you true, my master is within but indeed would not be spoke withal. There be some terms that stands upon his reputation, therefore he will not admit any conference till he hath shook them off.

LANCELOT   I prithee, tell him his very good friend, Sir Lancelot Spurcock, entreats to speak with him.

15   FATHER   By my troth, sir, if you come to take up the matter between my master and the Devonshire man, you do but beguile your hopes and lose your labour.

---

39 bounds financial limits   **set...rest** made up my mind, determined   **40 geldings** castrated horses for riding   **brace** couple; **greyhounds** racing was a popular coursing sport   **42 And...year?** Delia is right to be sceptical that Civet's income will go so far   **43 better penny** proverbial, cf. 'pretty penny'   **44 that** the money   **46 buy thee pins** for pin money: annual clothing allowance given to a woman/a trivial sum of money, with a play on the bawdy sense of pin as 'penis'   **47 points** tagged laces used for fastening where buttons are now used/another bawdy pun on 'penis'   **49 Dinner** the main meal of the day generally served between 11 a.m. and 12 noon   **stays** awaits   **51 good stomach** healthy appetite (for food/sex)   **52 the like** likewise, similarly   **53 bounds** financial/moral limits   **Scene 8**   *Location: Flowerdale's residence*   **foils** light weapons used in fencing   **1 tarry** wait   **2 hard at hand** very near   **3 withal** with   **4 warrant you** keep you safe (from them)   **9 prithee** beg you, literally 'pray thee'   **11 terms** circumstances, conditions/words   **stands upon** concern, have to do with   **12 conference** conversation, communication   **15 matter** i.e. disagreement, duel   **16 beguile** flatter/deceive/disappoint

LANCELOT   Honest friend, I have not any such thing to him. I come to speak with him about other matters.

FATHER   For my master, sir, hath set down his resolution:

20   Either to redeem his honour, or leave his life behind him.

LANCELOT   My friend, I do not know any quarrel touching thy master or any other person. My business is of a different nature to him, and I prithee so tell him.

FATHER   For howsoever the Devonshire man is,

My master's mind is bloody, that's a round O.

25   And therefore, sir, entreaty is but vain.

LANCELOT   I have no such thing to tell him, I tell thee once again.

FATHER   I will then so signify to him.   *Exit Father*

LANCELOT   Ah, sirrah, I see this matter is hotly carried,

But I'll labour to dissuade him from it.

Enter Flowerdale [and his Father]

30   Good morrow, Master Flowerdale.

FLOWERDALE   Good morrow, good Sir Lancelot. Good morrow, Master Weathercock.

By my troth, gentlemen, I have been

A-reading over Nick Machiavel:

I find him good to be known, not to be followed:

35   A pestilent humane fellow — I have made

Certain annotations of him, such as they be.

And how is't, Sir Lancelot? Ha? How is't?

A mad world, men cannot live quiet in it.

LANCELOT   Master Flowerdale, I do understand there is some jar

40   Between the Devonshire man and you.

FATHER   They, sir? They are good friends as can be.

FLOWERDALE   Who, Master Oliver and I? As good friends as can be!

LANCELOT   It is a kind of safety in you to deny it,

And a generous silence, which too few are endued withal:

45   But, sir, such a thing I hear, and I could wish it otherwise.

FLOWERDALE   No such thing, Sir Lancelot, o' my reputation,

As I am an honest man.

LANCELOT   Now I do believe you, then,

If you do engage your reputation, there is none.

50   FLOWERDALE   Nay, I do not engage my reputation there is not.

You shall not bind me to any condition of hardness:

But if there be anything between us, then there is.

If there be not, then there is not: be or be not, all is one.

LANCELOT   I do perceive by this that there is something between you, and I am very

55   sorry for it.

---

20 **redeem** regain, recover   24 **bloody** looking towards bloodshed   **round O** obscure: round lie/complete negative/absolute truth   28 **hotly carried** conducted with anger   33 **Nick Machiavel** Niccolò Machiavelli (1469–1527): Florentine civil servant and political theorist whose most famous work, *The Prince*, made him a byword for scheming and ruthless political practice   35 **humane** kind, benevolent; Flowerdale may be teasing his guests or using the term to mean 'humanist', relating to study of the humanities   36 **annotations** explanatory notes   39 **jar** dispute   44 **generous** honourable, noble-minded   **endued** brought up in   **withal** furthermore   45 **such a thing** i.e . the 'jar'   49 **none** i.e. no quarrel   51 **condition of hardness** inflexible contract   53 **all is one** it's all the same

FLOWERDALE   You may be deceived, Sir Lancelot. The Italian

Hath a pretty saying, '*Questo* —' I have forgot it, too.

'Tis out of my head, but in my translation,

If't hold, thus, 'Thou hast a friend, keep him, if a foe, trip him.'

60   LANCELOT   Come, I do see by this there is somewhat between you,

And before God I could wish it otherwise.

FLOWERDALE   Well, what is between us can hardly be altered.

Sir Lancelot, I am to ride forth tomorrow:

That way which I must ride, no man must deny me the sun;

65   I would not by any particular man

Be denied common and general passage.

If anyone saith, 'Flowerdale, thou passest not this way',

My answer is, 'I must either on, or return',

But 'return' is not my word, I must 'on':

70   If I cannot then make my way, nature

Hath done the last for me, and there's the fine.

LANCELOT   Master Flowerdale, every man hath one tongue,

And two ears: nature in her building

Is a most curious work-master.

75   FLOWERDALE   That is as much to say, a man should hear more than he should speak.

LANCELOT   You say true and, indeed, I have heard more, than at this time I will speak.

FLOWERDALE   You say well.

LANCELOT   Slanders are more common than truths, Master Flowerdale, but proof is

80   the rule for both.

FLOWERDALE   You say true. What-do-you-call-him hath it there in his third canton.

LANCELOT   I have heard you have been wild: I have believed it.

FLOWERDALE   'Twas fit, 'twas necessary.

85   LANCELOT   But I have seen somewhat of late in you,

That hath confirmed in me an opinion of goodness toward you.

FLOWERDALE   I'faith, sir, I am sure I never did you harm.

Some good I have done, either to you or yours,

I am sure you know not, neither is it my will you should.

90   LANCELOT   Ay, your will, sir.

FLOWERDALE   Ay, my will sir. 'Sfoot, do you know aught of my will?

By God, an you do, sir, I am abused.

LANCELOT   Go, Master Flowerdale, what I know, I know,

And know you thus much out of my knowledge,

95   That I truly love you. For my daughter,

She's yours. And, if you like a marriage better

---

56 The Italian Machiavelli   **57 *Questo*** 'This' (Italian)   **71 fine** end, conclusion   **81 What-do-you-call-him...canton** perhaps Book 1, canto 3 of Edmund Spenser's *The Faerie Queene*, in which Abessa slanders Una or chapter 3 of Machiavelli's *The Prince*, 'troubles can be detected when they are just beginning and effective measures can be taken quickly. But if one does not, the troubles are encountered when they have grown, and nothing can be done about them'   **82 canton** part, chapter   **89 will** wish, desire, also a reminder of the purpose of the visit   **91 aught of** anything about   **92 an** if   **abused** imposed upon, deceived

Than a brawl, all quirks of reputation

Set aside, go with me presently:

And, where you should fight a bloody battle,

100   You shall be married to a lovely lady.

FLOWERDALE   Nay, but Sir Lancelot—

LANCELOT   If you will not embrace

My offer, yet assure yourself thus much,

I will have order to hinder your encounter.

105   FLOWERDALE   Nay, but hear me, Sir Lancelot—

LANCELOT   Nay,

Stand not you upon imputative honour:

'Tis merely unsound, unprofitable, and idle inferences.

Your business is to wed my daughter,

110   Therefore, give me your present word to do it.

I'll go and provide the maid; therefore,

Give me your present resolution either now, or never.

FLOWERDALE   Will you so put me to it?

[LANCELOT]   Ay, afore God,

115   Either take me now, or take me never, else what

I thought should be our match, shall be our parting.

So fare you well forever.

FLOWERDALE   Stay:

Fall out what may fall, my love is above all:

120   I will come.

LANCELOT   I expect you, and so fare you well.

Exeunt Sir Lancelot [and Weathercock]

FATHER   Now, sir, how shall we do for wedding apparel?

FLOWERDALE   By the mass, that's true. Now help, Kit,

The marriage ended, we'll make amends for all.

125   FATHER   Well, no more; prepare you for your bride:

We will not want for clothes whatsoe'er betide.

FLOWERDALE   And thou shalt see, when once I have my dower,

In mirth we'll spend full many a merry hour.

As for this wench I not regard a pin,

130   It is her gold must bring my pleasures in.   *[Exit]*

FATHER   Is't possible he hath his second living,

Forsaking God, himself to the devil giving?

But that I knew his mother firm and chaste,

My heart would say my head she had disgraced:

135   Else would I swear he never was my son,

But her fair mind so foul a deed did shun.

97 quirks subtle arguments/preoccupations/irregularities   **104 hinder** prevent   **107 imputative** so-called   **108 unsound** not based on reason   **idle inferences** foolish conclusions   **111 provide** supply/prepare/equip   **the maid** i.e. Luce   **112 resolution** decision   **124 ended** completed, with an ironic play on its usual meaning   **127 dower** dowry, the money or property a wife brings her husband on marriage   **129 wench** young woman, term of address expressing anything from tenderness to contempt   **regard a pin** don't care about her   **131 his second living** another to match him in depravity/new lease of life (with Luce's money to spend)   **133 But** if it weren't for the fact   **134 head…disgraced** by planting the horns of the cuckold on his forehead   **136 so…deed** i.e. adultery   **shun** scorn, reject, avoid

Enter Uncle

UNCLE   How now, brother, how do you find your son?

FATHER   O, brother, heedless as a libertine,

Even grown a master in the school of vice,

140   One that doth nothing but invent deceit:

For all the day he humours up and down,

How he the next day might deceive his friend.

He thinks of nothing but the present time:

For one groat ready down, he'll pay a shilling,

145   But then the lender must needs stay for it.

When I was young I had the scope of youth,

Both wild and wanton, careless and desperate,

But such mad strains as he's possessed withal,

I thought it wonder for to dream upon.

150   UNCLE   I told you so, but you would not believe it.

FATHER   Well, I have found it, but one thing comforts me,

Brother, tomorrow he's to be married

To beauteous Luce, Sir Lancelot Spurcock's daughter.

UNCLE   Is't possible?

155   FATHER   'Tis true, and thus I mean to curb him.

This day, brother, I will you shall arrest him:

If anything will tame him, it must be that,

For he is rank in mischief, chained to a life

That will increase his shame and kill his wife.

160   UNCLE   What, arrest him on his wedding day?

That were unchristian and an unhumane part.

How many couple, even for that very day,

Hath purchased seven years' sorrow afterward?

Forbear him then today, do it tomorrow,

165   And this day mingle not his joy with sorrow.

FATHER   Brother, I'll have it done this very day,

And in the view of all as he comes from church,

Do but observe the course that he will take.

Upon my life, he will forswear the debt,

170   And for we'll have the sum shall not be slight,

Say that he owes you near three thousand pound:

Good brother, let be done immediately.

UNCLE   Well, seeing you will have it so,

Brother, I'll do't and straight provide the sheriff.

---

138 heedless careless, negligent   **libertine** one who leads a dissolute, immoral life (especially with regard to their treatment of women)   **141 humours...down** goes around devising scams   **144 For...it** He'll borrow at an exorbitant rate of interest because he's so desperate for cash but then he can't repay it   **groat** coin worth four old pence   **ready down** cash/guaranteed, already laid in gambling   **shilling** coin worth twelve old pence, an average day's wages   **145 stay** wait, tarry   **146 scope** liberty, licence   **148 strains** tendencies, characteristics   **149 I...upon** it would have seemed astonishing/terrible even to dream of   **155 curb** bend/restrain   **158 rank** full of/violent/headstrong   **161 unhumane** inhuman, inhumane, cruel   **164 Forbear** bear with, put up with   **169 forswear** deny, swear falsely on oath   **170 for we'll have** since we'll make sure   **slight** insignificant   **171 near...pound** almost three thousand pounds (a huge sum of money)   **174 sheriff** law officer

175 FATHER   So, brother, by this means shall we perceive
             What Sir Lancelot in this pinch will do:
             And how his wife doth stand affected to him.
             Her love will then be tried to the uttermost:
             And all the rest of them. Brother, what I will do,
180   Shall harm him much, and much avail him, too.   [*Exeunt*]

Scene 9

             [*Enter Oliver*]
      OLIVER   'Cham assured thick be the place that the scoundrel
             Appointed to meet me. If a come, zo: if a come not, zo.
             An 'che war avise he should make a coistrel an us,
             'Ch'ud veeze him and 'che vang him in hand. 'Che would
5   Hoist him and give it him, to and again, zo 'ch'ud.
             [*Enter Sir Arthur*]
             Who bin a-there? Sir Arthur! 'Ch'ill stay aside.
      ARTHUR   I have dogged the Devonshire man into the field,
             For fear of any harm that should befall him:
             I had an inkling of it yesternight,
10   That Flowerdale and he should meet this morning.
             Though, of my soul, Oliver fears him not,
             Yet for I'd see fair play on either side
             Made me to come, to see their valours tried.
             Good morrow to Master Oliver.
15   OLIVER   God and good morrow.
      ARTHUR   What, Master Oliver, are you angry?
      OLIVER   Why, an it be, tit an grieven you?
      ARTHUR   Not me at all, sir, but I imagine,
             By your being here thus armed, you stay for some
20   That you should fight withal.
      OLIVER   Why, an he do,
             'Che would not desire you to take his part.
      ARTHUR   No, by my troth, I think you need it not,
             For he you look for I think means not to come.
25   OLIVER   No: an 'che war assure o' that, 'ch'ud a' veeze him in another place.
             Enter Daffodil
      DAFFODIL   O, Sir Arthur! Master Oliver, ay me!
             Your love, and yours, and mine, sweet mistress Luce,

---

176 **pinch** critical point, tight spot   177 **stand affected** feel disposed/remain loving   179 **And…them** likewise everyone will be tested   180 **avail** benefit, profit   **Scene 9**   *Location: London, duelling fields*   1 **'Cham…zo 'ch'ud** I'm sure this is the place that the scoundrel appointed to meet me. If he comes, right, if he doesn't, right. If I thought he'd treat me like a knave (**coistrel**) I'd do for him (**veeze**) and strike him out of hand. I'd hoist him and give it to him too, so I would   6 **Who bin a-there?** Who's that there?   **'Ch'ill stay** I'll stand   7 **dogged** followed closely   9 **inkling** hint   **yesternight** last night   12 **for** because   13 **tried** put to the test   17 **an it…you?** So what if I am, does it hurt you?   19 **some** someone   21 **an** if   22 **'Che** I   25 **No…place** No, if I were sure of that I'd strike him in another place

This morn is married to young Flowerdale.

ARTHUR   Married to Flowerdale! 'Tis impossible!

30   OLIVER   Married, man? 'Che hope thou dost but jest,

To maken a vloutin' merriment of it.

DAFFODIL   O, 'tis too true. Here comes his uncle.

Enter [Uncle], Sheriff and Officers

UNCLE   Good morrow, Sir Arthur. Good morrow, Master Oliver.

OLIVER   God and good morn, Master Flowerdale. I pray you

35   Tellen us, is your scoundrel kinsman married?

ARTHUR   Master Oliver, call him what you will,

But he is married to Sir Lancelot's daughter here.

UNCLE   Sir Arthur, unto her!

OLIVER   Ay, ha' the old yellow zarved me thick trick?

40   Why, man, he was a' promise 'ch'ill 'ch'ud a' had her:

Is a zutch a vox? 'Ch'ill look to his water, 'che vor' him.

UNCLE   The music plays, they are coming from the church.

Sheriff do your office. Fellows, stand stoutly to it.

Enter all to the wedding: [Flowerdale, Luce, Sir Lancelot, Master Weathercock, Old
Flowerdale, Franck, Civet, Delia and Artichoke]

OLIVER   God give you joy, as the old zaid proverb is, and some zorrow among. You

45   met us well, did you not?

LANCELOT   Nay, be not angry, sir. The fault is in me. I have done all the wrong, kept
him from coming to the field to you, as I might sir, for I am a justice and sworn to
keep the peace.

WEATHERCOCK   Ay, marry is he, sir, a very justice and sworn to keep the peace. You

50   must not disturb the weddings.

LANCELOT   Nay, never frown nor storm, sir. If you do,

I'll have an order taken for you.

OLIVER   Well, well, 'ch'ill be quiet.

WEATHERCOCK   Master Flowerdale, Sir Lancelot, look you who here is? Master

55   Flowerdale.

LANCELOT   Master Flowerdale, welcome with all my heart.   *To Uncle*

FLOWERDALE   Uncle, this is she, i'faith.— Master Under-sheriff,

Arrest me? At whose suit? Draw, Kit!

UNCLE   At my suit, sir.

60   LANCELOT   Why, what's the matter, Master Flowerdale?

UNCLE   This is the matter, sir. This unthrift here

Hath cozened you, and hath had of me,

In several sums, three thousand pound.

FLOWERDALE   Why, uncle, uncle!

65   UNCLE   Cousin, cousin, you have uncled me,

---

31 **vloutin' merriment** flouting (mocking) joke   39 **Ay ... him** Yes, has the old fellow served me this trick? Why, man, he promised me I'd have had her: is he
such a fox? I'll have a look at his water, I warn him, i.e. check his urine to see if he's ill   47 **justice** magistrate appointed to keep the peace   58 **suit** charge,
instigation   **Draw** i.e. your sword   62 **cozened** tricked, conned   63 **several** separate   65 **uncled** called me uncle/cheated, swindled

And if you be not stayed, you'll prove

A cozener unto all that know you.

LANCELOT　Why, sir, suppose he be to you in debt

Ten thousand pound: his state to me appear

70　To be at least three thousand by the year?

UNCLE　O sir, I was too late informèd of that plot,

How that he went about to cozen you,

And formed a will, and sent it

To your good friend there, Master Weathercock,

75　In which was nothing true, but brags and lies.

LANCELOT　Ha? Hath he not such lordships, lands, and ships?

UNCLE　Not worth a groat, not worth a halfpenny, he!

LANCELOT　I pray, tell us true: be plain, young Flowerdale.

FLOWERDALE　My uncle here's mad, and disposed to do me wrong,

80　But here's my man, an honest fellow, by the lord,

And of good credit, knows all is true.

FATHER　Not I, sir, I am too old to lie. I rather know

You forged a will, where every line you writ,

You studied where to quote your lands might lie.

85　WEATHERCOCK　And, I prithee, where be they, honest friend?

FATHER　I'faith, nowhere, sir, for he hath none at all.

WEATHERCOCK　*Benedicite*! We are o'er-wretchèd, I believe.

LANCELOT　I am cozened and my hopefull'st child undone.

FLOWERDALE　You are not cozened, nor is she undone:

90　They slander me! By this light, they slander me!

Look you, my uncle here's an usurer,

And would undo me, but I'll stand in law.

Do you but bail me, you shall do no more.

You, brother Civet, and Master Weathercock, do but

95　Bail me and let me have my marriage money paid me,

And we'll ride down, and there your own eyes shall see

How my poor tenants there will welcome me.

You shall but bail me, you shall do no more,

And you, greedy gnat, their bail will serve?

100　UNCLE　Ay, sir, I'll ask no better bail.

LANCELOT　No, sir, you shall not take my bail, nor his,

Nor my son Civet's: I'll not be cheated, I.

Shrieve, take your prisoner; I'll not deal with him.

Let's uncle make false dice with his false bones.

105　I will not have to do with him: mocked, gulled, and wronged.

Come, girl, though it be late, it falls out well,

---

66 stayed stopped, prevented　**67 cozener** cheat, punning on 'cousin'　**68 Why...year?** So what if he owes you even ten thousand pounds since his annual income seems to be three thousand pounds a year?　**75 but brags** nothing except loud noises, i.e. meaningless boasts　**79 disposed** inclined　**87** *Benedicite*! 'Bless us!' (Latin)　**o'er-wretchèd** completely miserable/degraded　**88 hopefull'st** most promising/optimistic　**undone** ruined　**92 stand** remain firm **93 Do...more** If you will just stand bail for me, you don't have to do anything else　**103 Shrieve** sheriff　**104 Let's** Let his　**105 gulled** cheated　**106 falls out** has turned out

Thou shalt not live with him in beggars' hell.

LUCE   He is my husband, and high heaven doth know,

With what unwillingness I went to church,

110   But you enforced me, you compelled me to it!

The holy churchman pronounced these words but now:

I must not leave my husband in distress.

Now I must comfort him, not go with you.

LANCELOT   Comfort a cozener? On my curse, forsake him.

115   LUCE   This day you caused me on your curse to take him:

Do not, I pray, my grievèd soul oppress.

God knows my heart doth bleed at his distress.

LANCELOT   O, Master Weathercock,

I must confess I forced her to this match,

120   Led with opinion his false will was true.

WEATHERCOCK   Ah, he hath over-reached me, too.

LANCELOT   She might have lived

Like Delia, in a happy virgin's state.

DELIA   Father, be patient, sorrow comes too late.

125   LANCELOT   And on her knees she begged and did entreat,

If she must needs taste a sad marriage life,

She craved to be Sir Arthur Greenshield's wife.

ARTHUR   You have done her and me the greater wrong.

LANCELOT   O, take her yet.

130   ARTHUR   Not I.

LANCELOT   Or Master Oliver?

Accept my child and half my wealth is yours.

OLIVER   No, sir, 'ch'ill break no laws.

LUCE   Never fear, she will not trouble you.

135   DELIA   Yet, sister, in this passion,

Do not run headlong to confusion.

You may affect him, though not follow him.

FRANCK   Do, sister, hang him, let him go!

WEATHERCOCK   Do, 'faith, Mistress Luce, leave him.

140   LUCE   You are three gross fools. Let me alone:

I swear I'll live with him in all moan.

OLIVER   But an he have his legs at liberty,

'Cham aveard he will never live with you.

ARTHUR   Ay, but he is now in hucksters' handling for running away.

145   LANCELOT   Hussy, you hear how you and I am wronged,

And if you will redress it, yet you may:

But, if you stand on terms to follow him,

Never come near my sight nor look on me,

---

107 beggars' hell place/condition suffered by beggars   **121 over-reached** got the better of/cheated   **137 affect** care for, love   **138 hang him** a common curse   **140 gross** great/monstrous/complete/vulgar/stupid, ignorant   **141 moan** grief, sorrow   **143 'Cham aveard** I'm afraid   **144 hucksters' handling** a difficult position/beyond the likelihood of recovery   **huckster** unscrupulous dealer   **145 Hussy** pert, worthless girl or woman   **146 redress** make amends   **yet you may** you still can   **147 stand on terms** are determined

Call me not father, look not for a groat,

150   For all thy portion I will this day give

Unto thy sister Frances.

FRANCK   How say you to that, Tom? I shall have a good deal.

Besides, I'll be a good wife, and a good wife

Is a good thing, I can tell.

155   CIVET   Peace, Franck, I would be sorry to see thy sister

Cast away, as I am a gentleman.

LANCELOT   What, are you yet resolved?

LUCE   Yes, I am resolved.

LANCELOT   Come then, away: or now or never come.

160   LUCE   This way I turn. Go you unto your feast,

And I to weep that am with grief oppressed.

LANCELOT   Forever fly my sight! Come, gentlemen,

Let's in I'll help you to far better wives than her.

Delia, upon my blessing, talk not to her —

165   Base baggage, in such haste to beggary!

UNCLE   Sheriff, take your prisoner to your charge.

FLOWERDALE   Uncle, by God you have used me very hardly,

By my troth, upon my wedding day.   *Exeunt all but Young Flowerdale,*

his Father, Uncle, [Luce,] Sheriff and Officers

LUCE   O, Master Flowerdale, but hear me speak—

170   Stay but a little while, good master sheriff,

If not for him, for my sake pity him—

Good sir, stop not your ears at my complaint,   *Kneels*

My voice grows weak, for women's words are faint.

FLOWERDALE   Look you, uncle, she kneels to you.

175   UNCLE   Fair maid — for you, I love you with my heart,

And grieve, sweet soul, thy fortune is so bad,

That thou shouldst match with such a graceless youth —

Go to thy father, think not upon him,

Whom hell hath marked to be the son of shame.

180   LUCE   Impute his wildness, sir, unto his youth,

And think that now is the time he doth repent.

Alas, what good or gain can you receive

To imprison him that nothing hath to pay?

And where nought is, the king doth lose his due.

185   O, pity him, as God shall pity you.

UNCLE   Lady, I know his humours all too well,

And nothing in the world can do him good,

But misery itself to chain him with.

LUCE   Say that your debts were paid, then is he free?

---

150 **portion** dowry/inheritance   159 **or now … come** either come now or never come   167 **hardly** harshly   170 **Stay** delay, wait   184 **where … due** proverbial: where no money can be paid, even the king must lose that which is owed to him   186 **humours** moods/constitution of his character   188 **misery … with** only by being made wretched will he begin to understand his folly and benefit from a moral lesson

190	UNCLE	Ay, virgin, that being answered, I have done
		But to him that is all as impossible
		As I to scale the high pyramidies.
		Sheriff, take your prisoner. Maiden, fare thee well.
	LUCE	O, go not yet, good Master Flowerdale:
195		Take my word for the debt, my word, my bond.
	FLOWERDALE	Ay, by God, uncle, and my bond, too.
	LUCE	Alas, I ne'er owed nothing but I paid it,
		And I can work; alas, he can do nothing:
		I have some friends perhaps will pity me,
200		His chiefest friends do seek his misery.
		All that I can or beg, get, or receive,
		Shall be for you: O, do not turn away,
		Methinks within a face so reverend,
		So well experienced in this tottering world,
205		Should have some feeling of a maiden's grief.
		For my sake, his father's and your brother's sake,
		Ay, for your soul's sake, that doth hope for joy,
		Pity my state: do not two souls destroy.
	UNCLE	Fair maid, stand up: not in regard of him,
210		But in pity of thy hapless choice,
		I do release him. Master sheriff, I thank you:
		And, officers, there is for you to drink.

He gives them a tip and they leave

		Here, maid, take this money, there is a hundred angels,
		And for I will be sure he shall not have it,
215		Here, Kester, take it you and use it sparingly,
		But let not her have any want at all.
		Dry your eyes, niece. Do not too much lament
		For him, whose life hath been in riot spent:
		If well he useth thee, he gets him friends,
220		If ill, a shameful end on him depends.

Exit Uncle

	FLOWERDALE	A plague go with you for an old fornicator.
		Come, Kit, the money; come, honest Kit!
	FATHER	Nay, by my faith, sir, you shall pardon me.
	FLOWERDALE	And why, sir, pardon you? Give me the money,
225		You old rascal, or I shall make you.
	LUCE	Pray, hold your hands. Give it him, honest friend.
	FATHER	If you be so content, with all my heart.
	FLOWERDALE	Content, sir? 'Sblood,
		She shall be content, whether she will or no!
230		A rattle baby come to follow me:

---

192 scale climb, get to the top of   **pyramidies** pyramids   **195 Take...bond** Luce offers her own name as Flowerdale's credit for the debt to his uncle   **196 bond** physical bond holding him under arrest/marriage bond he has just entered into   **201 or** either   **203 Methinks** it seems to me   **reverend** worthy of respect (on account of age or character)   **204 tottering** wavering, unstable   **210 hapless** unfortunate   **213 angels** gold coins depicting the archangel Michael, worth approximately half a pound sterling   **217 niece** wife of his nephew   **228 'Sblood** God's blood, a common oath   **230 rattle baby** rattling doll/child

Go, get you gone to the greasy chuff your father,

Bring me your dowry, or never look on me.

FATHER   Sir, she hath forsook her father and all her friends for you.

FLOWERDALE   Hang thee, her friends, and father altogether!

235   FATHER   Yet part with something to provide her lodging.

FLOWERDALE   Yes, I mean to part with her and you,

But if I part with one angel, hang me at a post.

I'll rather throw them at a cast at dice,

As I have done a thousand of their fellows.

240   FATHER   Nay, then I will be plain: degenerate boy,

Thou hadst a father would have been ashamed.

FLOWERDALE   My father was an ass, an old ass.

FATHER   Thy father? Proud licentious villain!

What, are you at your foils? I'll foil with you.   *Flowerdale starts to draw*

245   LUCE   Good sir, forbear him.   *Holds father's arm*

FATHER   Did not this whining woman hang on me,

I'd teach thee what it was to abuse thy father:

Go, hang, beg, starve, dice, game, that when all is gone

Thou may'st after despair and hang thyself.

250   LUCE   O, do not curse him.

FATHER   I do not curse him, and to pray for him were vain.

It grieves me that he bears his father's name.

FLOWERDALE   Well, you old rascal, I shall meet with you.

Sirrah, get you gone. I will not strip the livery

255   Over your ears, because you paid for it:

But do not use my name, sirrah, do you hear?

Look you do not use my name, you were best.

FATHER   Pay me the twenty pound, then, that I lent you,

Or give me security when I may have it.

260   FLOWERDALE   I'll pay thee not a penny,

And for security, I'll give thee none.

Minikin, look you do not follow me,

Look you do not.

If you do, beggar, I shall slit your nose.

265   LUCE   Alas, what shall I do?

FLOWERDALE   Why, turn whore, that's a good trade:

And so, perhaps, I'll see thee now and then.   *Exit Flowerdale*

LUCE   Alas the day that ever I was born!

FATHER   Sweet mistress, do not weep, I'll stick to you.

270   LUCE   Alas, my friend, I know not what to do.

My father and my friends they have despised me:

---

231 **greasy chuff** fat churl/miser/clown, with a pun on 'chough', a bird of the crow family renowned for talking, hence 'chatterbox'   237 **at a post** with express speed/from a nearby beam   244 **foils** rapiers   **foil** thrust at with a foil/defeat, overthrow   245 **forbear** be patient with   246 **whining** crying   253 **meet with you** fight you in a duel   256 **use my name** servants could use their master's name for security – ironic under the circumstances   262 **Minikin** affectionate name for a young woman

And I, a wretched maid, thus cast away,

Knows neither where to go, nor what to say.

FATHER   It grieves me at the soul to see her tears   *Aside*

275   Thus stain the crimson roses of her cheeks—

Lady, take comfort, do not mourn in vain,

I have a little living in this town,

The which I think comes to a hundred pound,

All that and more shall be at your dispose.

280   I'll straight go help you to some strange disguise,

And place you in a service in this town,

Where you shall know all, yet yourself unknown:

Come, grieve no more, where no help can be had;

Weep not for him that is worse than bad.

285 LUCE   I thank you, sir.   [*Exeunt*]

Scene 10

Enter Sir Lancelot, Master Weathercock, and [to] them [Oliver, Civet, Franck, Delia and Sir Arthur]

OLIVER   Well, 'che a' bin zerved many a sluttish trick,

But such a lerripoop as thick, ich was ne'er a' zarved.

LANCELOT   Son Civet, daughter Frances, bear with me:

You see how I am pressed down with inward grief

5   About that luckless girl, your sister Luce:

But 'tis fallen out with me, as with many families beside,

They are most unhappy that are most beloved.

CIVET   Father 'tis so, 'tis even fallen out so,

But what remedy? Set hand to your heart

10   And let it pass. Here is your daughter, Frances, and I,

And we'll not say we'll bring forth as witty children,

But as pretty children, as ever she was,

Though she had the prick and praise for a pretty wench.

But father, dun is the mouse: you'll come?

15 LANCELOT   Ay, son Civet, I'll come.

CIVET   And you, Master Oliver?

OLIVER   Ay, for 'che a' vexed out this veast, 'ch'ill see if a gan

Make a better veast there.

CIVET   And you, Sir Arthur?

20 ARTHUR   Ay, sir, although my heart be full,

---

277 little living small property/income   **280 strange** unfamiliar   **281 service** position as a servant   **Scene 10**   *Location: unspecified, most likely Sir Lancelot's residence*   **1 Well…zarved** Well, I've been served many a lowdown (**sluttish**) trick but such a fine to-do (**lerripoop**) as this, I was never caught by   **4 pressed down** oppressed, burdened   **11 witty** intelligent   **13 prick and praise** proverbial: the praise of excellence or success   **prick** acme, highest point/end, objective   **14 dun…mouse** proverbial, i.e. 'what's done is done' playing on the mouse's (**dun**) colour which can't be changed   **17 Ay…there** Yes, since I've been vexed out of enjoying this feast, I'll see if I can make a better feast there   **20 full** overcharged with emotion

I'll be a partner at your wedding feast.

CIVET   And welcome all indeed, and welcome. Come, Franck, are you ready?

FRANCK   Jesu, how hasty these husbands are!

I pray, father, pray to God to bless me.

25 LANCELOT   God bless thee, and I do. God make thee wise,

Send you both joy, I wish it with wet eyes.

FRANCK   But, father, shall not my sister Delia go along with us?

She is excellent good at cookery and such things.

LANCELOT   Yes, marry, shall she: Delia, make you ready.

30 DELIA   I am ready, sir. I will first go to Greenwich,

From thence to my cousin Chesterfield's, and so to London.

CIVET   It shall suffice, good sister Delia, it shall suffice.

But fail us not, good sister; give order to cooks and others,

For I would not have my sweet Franck

35   To soil her fingers.

FRANCK   No, by my troth, not I: a gentlewoman,

And a married gentlewoman, too,

To be companions to cooks and kitchen boys?

Not I, i'faith, I scorn that.

40 CIVET   Why, I do not mean thou shalt, sweetheart.

Thou see'st I do not go about it. Well, farewell, to you.

God's pity, Master Weathercock, we shall have your company, too?

WEATHERCOCK   With all my heart, for I love good cheer.

CIVET   Well, God be with you all. Come, Franck.

45 FRANCK   God be with you, father, God be with you, Sir Arthur, Master Oliver, and

Master Weathercock. Sister, God be with you all. God be with you father: God be

with you, everyone.   [*Exeunt Civet and Franck*]

WEATHERCOCK   Why, how now, Sir Arthur? All amort? Master Oliver, how now

man?

50   Cheerily, Sir Lancelot, and merrily say,

Who can hold that will away?

LANCELOT   Ay, she is gone indeed, poor girl, undone,

But, when they'll be self-willed, children must smart.

ARTHUR   But, sir, that she is wronged, you are the chiefest cause.

55   Therefore 'tis reason you redress her wrong.

WEATHERCOCK   Indeed you must, Sir Lancelot, you must.

LANCELOT   Must? Who can compel me, Master Weathercock?

I hope I may do what I list.

WEATHERCOCK   I grant you may: you may do what you list.

60 OLIVER   Nay, but an you be well avisen; it were not good,

---

26 **wet eyes** tears   30 **Greenwich** then a town in Kent on the south bank of the Thames, site of an ancient royal palace; now a London borough   35 **soil** sully, dirty (with work)   36 **gentlewoman** woman of gentle (good) birth   48 **Arthur? All amort?** Pun on Malory's *Morte d'Arthur*   **amort** as though dead   51 **that will** that which desires to be   53 **smart** suffer   58 **list** wish, desire   60 **Nay ... Civet's** (lines 60–8) No, but if you will be well advised, it's not right through this bad temper (**vrampoldness**) and perverseness (**vrowardness**) to reject (**cast away**) as pretty a sweetheart (**Dowsabel**) as you could chance to see on a summer's day. I'll tell you what I shall do; I'll go spy up and down the town, and see if I can hear any tale or tidings (news) of her, and take her away from this villain for I'm assured, he'll bring her to ruin (**the spoil**). And so fare you well, we shall meet at your son (in-law) Civet's

By this vrampoldness and vrowardness, to cast away

As pretty a Dowsabel as one 'ch'ould chance to see

In a summer's day. 'Ch'ill tell you what 'ch'all do:

'Ch'ill go spy up and down the town, and see if I

65   Can hear any tale or didings of her,

And take her away from thick-a mezel, vor 'cham

Assured he'll but bring her to the spoil.

And so, vare you well, we shall meet at your son Civet's.

LANCELOT   I thank you, sir, I take it very kindly.

70   ARTHUR   To find her out I'll spend my dearest blood,

So well I loved her, to effect her good.   *Exeunt [Sir Arthur and Oliver]*

LANCELOT   O, Master Weathercock, what hap had I to force my daughter

From Master Oliver and this good knight,

To one that hath no goodness in his thought?

75   WEATHERCOCK   Ill luck, but what remedy?

LANCELOT   Yes, I have almost devised a remedy:

Young Flowerdale is sure a prisoner?

WEATHERCOCK   Sure? Nothing more sure.

LANCELOT   And yet, perhaps, his uncle hath released him.

80   WEATHERCOCK   It may be, very like, no doubt he hath.

LANCELOT   Well, if he be in prison, I'll have warrants

To 'tach my daughter till the law be tried,

For I will sue him upon cozenage.

WEATHERCOCK   Marry, may you, and overthrow him, too.

85   LANCELOT   Nay, that's not so, I may chance be scoffed,

And sentence passed with him.

WEATHERCOCK   Believe me, so he may, therefore take heed.

LANCELOT   Well, howsoever, yet I will have warrants,

In prison or at liberty, all's one.

90   You will help to serve them, Master Weathercock?   *Exeunt*

Scene 11

Enter Flowerdale

FLOWERDALE   A plague of the devil: the devil take the dice!

The dice and the devil and his dam go together:

Of all my hundred golden angels,

I have not left me one denier:

5   A pox of 'come a five', what shall I do?

---

70 **spend** use up, consume/allow to be spilt   71 **effect** bring about   72 **hap** fortune   82 **'tach** seize, arrest   83 **upon cozenage** on the grounds of fraud; error in condition, or misrepresentation of social status, provided grounds for annulment: ironically, so did forced marriage   85 **scoffed** mocked, ridiculed   89 **In...one** It makes no difference whether Flowerdale is free or not   **all's one** it's all the same   **Scene 11** *Location: the road to Greenwich*   2 **the devil...dam** proverbial   **dam** mother   4 **denier** small copper coin, one tenth of an old English penny   5 **'come a five'** gaming cry for a number five to be thrown

I can borrow no more of my credit,

There's not any of my acquaintance, man nor boy,

But I have borrowed more or less of.

I would I knew where to take a good purse,

10   And go clear away, by this light, I'll venture for it;

God's lid, my sister Delia, I'll rob her, by this hand.

Enter Delia and Aritchoke

DELIA   I prithee, Artichoke, go not so fast,

The weather is hot and I am something weary.

ARTICHOKE   Nay, I warrant you, Mistress Delia, I'll not tire you with leading.

15   We'll go an extreme moderate pace.

FLOWERDALE   Stand! Deliver your purse!

ARTICHOKE   O, lord! Thieves! Thieves!   *Exit Artichoke*

FLOWERDALE   Come, come, your purse, lady, your purse.

DELIA   That voice I have heard often before this time.

20   What, brother Flowerdale, become a thief?

FLOWERDALE   Ay, a plague on't, I thank your father.

But, sister, come, your money, come:

What, the world must find me; I am born to live.

'Tis not a sin to steal when none will give.

25   DELIA   O, God, is all grace banished from thy heart?

Think of the shame that doth attend this fact.

FLOWERDALE   Shame me no shames! Come, give me your purse!

I'll bind you, sister, lest I fare the worse.

DELIA   No, bind me not: hold, there is all I have,

30   And would that money would redeem thy shame.

Enter Oliver, Sir Arthur, and Artichoke

ARTICHOKE   Thieves! Thieves! Thieves!

OLIVER   Thieves? Where, man? Why, how now, Mistress Delia?

Ha' you a' liked to bin a' robbed?

DELIA   No, Master Oliver, 'tis Master Flowerdale: he did but jest with me.

35   OLIVER   How, Flowerdale, that scoundrel? Sirrah, you meten us well.

Vang thee that!   *Strikes him*

FLOWERDALE   Well, sir, I'll not meddle with you, because I have a charge.

DELIA   Here, brother Flowerdale, I'll lend you this same money.

FLOWERDALE   I thank you, sister.

40   OLIVER   I wad you were y-split an you let the mezel have a penny.

But since you cannot keep it, 'ch'ill keep it myself.

ARTHUR   'Tis pity to relieve him in this sort,

Who makes a trompant life his daily sport.

---

9 **take** steal   10 **venture** attempt/take the risk   11 **God's lid** by God's eyelid   13 **something** somewhat, rather   16 **Stand! Deliver** traditional command of the highwayman   23 **What...live** the world must provide for me since I have to live   24 **'Tis...give** perhaps an allusion to Proverbs 6:30: 'men do not despise a thief, when he steals to satisfy his soul, because he is hungry'   35 **meten** meet   36 **Vang** receive, take   37 **charge** duty, responsibility   40 **I...myself** I'll wish you were nothing to do with each other if you let this wretch (**mezel**) have a penny. But since you can't keep it, I'll keep it myself   **y-split** torn asunder (by shipwreck)   42 **'Tis...sort** it's charitable/a shame to provide for him in this way   43 **trompant** cheating, dishonest

DELIA   Brother, you see how all men censure you:

45   Farewell, and I pray God amend your life.

OLIVER   Come, 'ch'ill bring you along, and keep you safe enough,

From twenty such scoundrels as thick-a one is.

Farewell and be hanged, zirrah, as I think,

So thou wilt be shortly. Come, Sir Arthur.   *Exeunt all but Flowerdale*

50   FLOWERDALE   A plague go with you for a kersey rascal!

This Devonshire man, I think, is made all of pork,

His hands made only for to heave up packs,

His heart as fat and big as is his face,

As differing far from all brave gallant minds

55   As I to serve the hogs and drink with hinds,

As I am very near now: well, what remedy,

When money, means, and friends do grow so small,

Then farewell life, and there's an end of all.   *Exit*

Scene 12

Enter Father, Luce like a Dutch Frow, Civet and his wife, Mistress Frances

CIVET   By my troth, God-a-mercy for this, good Christopher;

I thank thee for my maid. I like her very well.

How dost thou like her, Frances?

FRANCK   In good sadness, Tom, very well, excellent well,

5   She speaks so prettily. I pray, what's your name?

LUCE   My name, forsooth, be callèd Tannakin.

FRANCK   By my troth, a fine name. O, Tannakin, you are excellent for dressing
one's head a new fashion.

LUCE   Me sall do everyting about da head.

10   CIVET   What countrywoman is she, Kester?

FATHER   A Dutchwoman, sir.

CIVET   Why, then, she is outlandish, is she not?

FATHER   Ay, sir, she is.

FRANCK   O, then thou canst tell how to help me to cheeks and ears.

15   LUCE   Yes, mistress, very vell.

FATHER   Cheeks and ears? Why, Mistress Frances, want you cheeks and ears?
Methinks you have very fair ones.

FRANCK   Thou art a fool indeed.— Tom, thou knowest what I mean.

44 censure criticize, judge   **50 kersey** woollen cloth   **51 made...pork** resembles a pig, referring to his size   **53 heart...big** although Flowerdale intends
it as an insult, he is ironically accurate since Oliver is indeed generous-hearted   **55 serve the hogs** look after pigs (an explicit allusion to the parable of the
prodigal son who became a swineherd)   **hinds** farm servants/female deer   **Scene 12**   *Location: Civet's residence*   **Father...Frow** Flowerdale's father
and Luce have found employment as servants in the Civets' household, with Luce disguised as a Dutchwoman   *Frow* Dutchwoman, from *vrouw*, 'woman'
(Dutch)   **4 good sadness** all seriousness, proverbial   **6 Tannakin** diminutive pet-form of Ann or Anna, used for a German or Dutch girl; Anna means
'grace'   **9 Me...head** 'I shall do everything to look after your head', phonetically rendered with a Dutch accent   **11 Dutchwoman** i.e. from the Netherlands/
slang for a 'whore'   **12 outlandish** strange, foreign/bizarre   **14 cheeks and ears** kind of head-dress: a coif, embroidered in coloured silks, the sides made to
curve forwards over the ears

CIVET   Ay, ay, Kester, 'tis such as they wear o'their heads.

20   I prithee, Kit, have her in and show her my house.

FATHER   I will, sir. Come, Tannakin.

FRANCK   O, Tom, you have not bussed me today, Tom.

CIVET   No, Frances: we must not kiss afore folks, God save me, Franck.

Enter Delia and Artichoke

    See, yonder my sister Delia is come: welcome, good sister.

25   FRANCK   Welcome, good sister. How do you like the tire of my head?

DELIA   Very well, sister.

CIVET   I am glad you're come, sister Delia, to give order for supper: they will be here soon.

ARTICHOKE   Ay, but if good luck had not served, she had not been here now.

30   Filching Flowerdale had like to peppered us,

    But for Master Oliver, we had been robbed.

DELIA   Peace, sirrah, no more.

FATHER   Robbed! By whom?

ARTICHOKE   Marry, by none but by Flowerdale, he is turned thief.

35   CIVET   By my faith, but that is not well, but God be praised

    For your escape; will you draw near, sister?

FATHER   Sirrah, come hither; would Flowerdale, he that was my master, ha' robbed you? I prithee, tell me true.

ARTICHOKE   Yes, i'faith, even that Flowerdale that was thy master.

40   FATHER   Hold thee. There is a French crown, and speak no more of this.

ARTICHOKE   Not I, not a word.— Now do I smell knavery: *Aside*

    In every purse Flowerdale takes he is half

    And gives me this to keep counsel.— No, not a word, I.

FATHER   Why, God-a-mercy!

45   FRANCK   Sister, look here, I have a new Dutch maid,

    And she speaks so fine, it would do your heart good.

CIVET   How do you like her, sister?

DELIA   I like your maid well.

CIVET   Well, dear sister, will you draw near and give directions for supper?

50   Guests will be here presently.

DELIA   Yes, brother, lead the way, I'll follow you.   *Exeunt all*

    Hark you, Dutch frow, a word.   *but Delia and Luce*

LUCE   Vat is your vill wit me?

DELIA   Sister Luce, 'tis not your broken language,

55   Nor this same habit, can disguise your face

    From I that know you: pray, tell me, what means this?

LUCE   Sister, I see you know me, yet be secret:

    This borrowed shape that I have ta'en upon me

    Is but to keep myself a space unknown,

---

22 bussed kissed   **23 afore** in front of   **25 tire** head dress   **30 Filching** pilfering   **peppered** inflicted severe punishment on   **40 French crown** the 'écu', roughly equivalent in value to the English crown, a quarter of a pound sterling   **41 Now…counsel** Artichoke believes that Flowerdale's father (**Christopher**) is in league with Flowerdale and gets half of everything he makes, and that the French crown is to buy his silence   **55 habit** outfit   **59 space** short period of time

60   Both from my father and my nearest friends,

Until I see how time will bring to pass

The desperate course of Master Flowerdale.

DELIA   O, he is worse than bad, I prithee leave him,

And let not once thy heart to think on him.

65 LUCE   Do not persuade me once to such a thought;

Imagine yet that he is worse than nought,

Yet one hour's time may all that ill undo,

That all his former life did run into.

Therefore, kind sister, do not disclose my estate,

70   If e'er his heart doth turn, 'tis ne'er too late.

DELIA   Well, seeing no counsel can remove your mind,

I'll not disclose you that art wilful blind.

LUCE   Delia, I thank you. I now must please her eyes,

My sister Frances, neither fair nor wise.   *Exeunt*

Scene 13

Enter Flowerdale, solus

FLOWERDALE   On goes he that knows no end of his journey.

I have passed the very utmost bounds of shifting.

I have no course now but to hang myself:

I have lived since yesterday, two o'clock, of a

5   Spice-cake I had at a burial, and for drink,

I got it at an alehouse among porters such as

Will bear out a man if he have no money indeed,

I mean out of their companies, for they are men

Of good carriage. Who comes here?

10   The two cony-catchers that won all my money of me:

I'll try if they'll lend me any.

Enter Dick and Rafe

What, Master Richard, how do you?

How dost thou, Rafe? By God, gentlemen, the world

Grows bare with me: will you do as much as lend

15   Me an angel between you both, you know

You won a hundred of me the other day?

RAFE   How? An angel? God damn us if we lost not every penny

Within an hour after thou wert gone.

FLOWERDALE   I prithee,

---

66 **nought** nothing/evil   69 **estate** condition, i.e. her disguise   70 **ne'er too late** repentance never comes too late, proverbial   71 **remove** change, alter   72 **wilful** wilfully, determined to be   **Scene 13** *Location: solus* 'alone' (Latin)   2 **utmost** furthest   **shifting** devising expedients   3 **course** method of proceeding/way out   5 **Spice-cake** rich spiced fruit cake, given to the mourners while poorer ones were distributed to the populace   6 **porters** door keepers   7 **bear out** support, back up   8 **I...carriage** Flowerdale's pun suggests he was treated well not thrown out by them since they are men who know how to behave properly   10 **cony-catchers** cheats, swindlers; literally 'rabbit-catchers'   14 **bare** empty/desolate   15 **angel** about half a pound sterling

20   Lend me so much as will pay for my supper;

I'll pay you again, as I am a gentleman.

RAFE   I'faith, we have not a farthing, not a mite:

I wonder at it, Master Flowerdale,

You will so carelessly undo yourself.

25   Why, you will lose more money in an hour

Than any honest man spends in a year:

For shame, betake you to some honest trade,

And live not thus so like a vagabond.   *Exeunt [Dick and Rafe]*

FLOWERDALE   A vagabond indeed! More villains you!

30   They gave me counsel that first cozened me:

Those devils first brought me to this I am,

And, being thus, the first that do me wrong.

Well, yet I have one friend left in store:

Not far from hence, there dwells a cockatrice,

35   One that I first put in a satin gown,

And not a tooth that dwell within her head,

But stands me at the least in twenty pound.

Her will I visit, now my coin is gone,

And, as I take it, here dwells the gentlewoman.

40   What ho, is Mistress Apricock within?

Enter Ruffian

RUFFIAN   What saucy rascal is that which knocks so bold?

O, is it you, old spendthrift, are you here?

One that is turned cozener about the town.

My mistress saw you, and sends this word by me,

45   Either be packing quickly from the door,

Or you shall have such a greeting sent you straight,

As you will little like on: you had best be gone.   [*Exit Ruffian*]

FLOWERDALE   Why so, this is as it should be, being poor:

Thus art thou served by a vile, painted whore.

50   Well, since thy damnèd crew do so abuse thee,

I'll try of honest men, how they will use me.

Enter an ancient Citizen

Sir, I beseech you to take compassion

Of a man, one whose fortunes have been better

Than at this instant they seem to be. But,

55   If I might crave of you so much little portion

As would bring me to my friends, I should rest

---

22 **farthing** one quarter of an old penny   **mite** small unit of money, possibly one sixteenth of a farthing, an ironic allusion to the gospel story of the widow's mite in Mark 12:41–4 and Luke 21:1–4   24 **undo** ruin   27 **betake you** turn your course   28 **vagabond** homeless vagrant/idle loafer, regarded by law as a potential social threat   34 **cockatrice** prostitute, whore/a fabulous monster of classical mythology   40 **Apricock** early version of 'apricot', her name, with a bawdy pun on 'après-cock'   ***Ruffian*** bawd, pimp   42 **spendthrift** careless, extravagant money-waster/moral reprobate   45 **be packing** take yourself off   49 **vile** mean/morally depraved   **painted** one who uses cosmetics   50 **thy damnèd crew** your own wretched gang   **damnèd** wretched/destined for hell   55 **so…portion** any help however small

    Thankful until I had requited so great a courtesy.

CITIZEN Fie, fie, young man, this course is very bad.

    Too many such have we about this city,

60   Yet, for I have not seen you in this sort,

    Nor noted you to be a common beggar,

    Hold, there's an angel to bear your charges down.

    Go to your friends: do not on this depend,

    Such bad beginnings oft have worser ends.   *Exit Citizen*

65 **FLOWERDALE** Worser ends? Nay, if it fall out no worse

    Than in old angels, I care not. Nay, now

    I have had such a fortunate beginning,

    I'll not let a sixpenny purse escape me.

    By the mass, here comes another.

Enter a Citizen's Wife with a torch[bearer] before her

70 God bless you, fair mistress. Now would it please you, gentlewoman, to look into the wants of a poor gentleman, a younger brother? I doubt not but God will treble restore it back again, one that never before this time demanded penny, halfpenny, nor farthing.

CITIZEN'S WIFE [*To her torchbearer*] Stay, Alexander, now, by my troth, a very proper

75 man, and 'tis great pity: hold, my friend, there's all the money I have about me, a couple of shillings, and God bless thee.

FLOWERDALE Now God thank you, sweet lady. If you have any screen, or garden house, where you may employ a poor gentleman as your friend, I am yours to command in all secret service.

80 **CITIZEN'S WIFE** I thank you, good friend. I prithee, let me see that again I gave thee: there is one of them a brass shilling. Give me them, and here is half a crown in gold.   *He gives it her*

  Now, out upon thee, rascal! Secret service: what dost thou make of me? It were a good deed to have thee whipped: now I have my money again, I'll see thee hanged

85 before I give thee a penny. Secret service! On, good Alexander!

    Exeunt [Citizen's Wife and torchbearer]

FLOWERDALE This is villainous luck: I perceive dishonesty

    Will not thrive: here comes more. God forgive me,

    Sir Arthur and Master Oliver! Afore God, I'll speak to them.

    God save you, Sir Arthur. God save you, Master Oliver.

Enter Sir Arthur and Oliver

90 **OLIVER** Bin you there, zirrah?

    Come, will you y-taken yourself to your tools, coistrel?

FLOWERDALE Nay, Master Oliver, I'll not fight with you.

    Alas, sir, you know it was not my doings,

    It was only a plot to get Sir Lancelot's daughter:

---

57 requited repaid **courtesy** a possible allusion to a sexual favour **60 sort** fortune, destiny **62 your charges down** your fare home **66 old angels** had a higher gold content, and would thus have been worth more **68 sixpenny purse** i.e. one containing a total of sixpence, the fee charged by a whore or a barber for the treatment of venereal disease **71 younger brother** i.e. without the prospect of an inheritance, thus allying him with the biblical prodigal son **78 friend** lover, paramour **79 secret service** illicit activity, especially sexual **81 brass shilling** coin of little worth **90 Bin...coistrel?** Are you there, sirrah? Come, will you take up your weapons (**tools**), villain?

95   By God, I never meant you harm.

OLIVER   And whore is the gentlewoman thy wife, mezel?

Whore is she, zirrah, ha?

FLOWERDALE   By my troth, Master Oliver, sick, very sick;

And God is my judge, I know not what means to make for her, good gentlewoman.

100   OLIVER   Tell me true, is she sick? Tell me true, ich 'vise thee.

FLOWERDALE   Yes, faith, I tell you true. Master Oliver, if you would do me the small

kindness but to lend me forty shillings, so God help me, I will pay you so soon as my

ability shall make me able, as I am a gentleman.

OLIVER   Well, thou zay'st thy wife is zick: hold, there's vorty shillings. Give it to

105   thy wife, look thou give it her, or I shall zo veeze thee, thou wert not so veezed this

zeven year; look to it!

ARTHUR   I'faith, Master Oliver, it is in vain,

To give to him that never thinks of her.

OLIVER   Well, would 'che could y-vind it.

110   FLOWERDALE   I tell you true, Sir Arthur, as I am a gentleman.

OLIVER   Well, fare you well, zirrah. Come, Sir Arthur.   *Exeunt*

FLOWERDALE   By the lord, this is excellent.   [*Oliver and Sir Arthur*]

Five golden angels compassed in an hour:

If this trade hold, I'll never seek a new.

115   Welcome, sweet gold, and beggary, adieu.

Enter Uncle and [*Father*]

UNCLE   See, Kester, if you can find the house.

FLOWERDALE   Who's here? My uncle and my man Kester?

By the mass, 'tis they!

How do you, uncle? How dost thou, Kester?

120   By my troth, uncle, you must needs lend me

Some money: the poor gentlewoman,

My wife, so God help me, is very sick.

I was robbed of the hundred angels you gave me:

They are gone.

125   UNCLE   Ay, they are gone indeed. Come, Kester, away.

FLOWERDALE   Nay, uncle. Do you hear? Good uncle.

UNCLE   Out, hypocrite, I will not hear thee speak.

Come, leave him, Kester.

FLOWERDALE   Kester, honest Kester.

130   FATHER   Sir, I have nought to say to you.—

Open the door, Tannakin: thou hadst best   *Calling*

Lock't fast, for there's a false knave without.

FLOWERDALE   You are an old lying rascal, so you are.

Exeunt [*Uncle and Father*]

Enter Luce, [*disguised as before*]

---

96 whore presumably 'where' in Oliver's dialect but with an uncomfortable play on its usual meaning   **100 ich 'vise thee** I advise you   **105 this zeven year** these seven years, proverbial meaning 'for a long time'   **109 Well ... it** Well, I would I could find that myself   **113 compassed** obtained/cunningly contrived

LUCE	Vat is de matter? Vat be you, younker?	
135 FLOWERDALE	By this light, a Dutch frow, they say they are called kind:	*Aside*

LUCE Vat is de matter? Vat be you, younker?

135 FLOWERDALE By this light, a Dutch frow, they say they are called kind: *Aside*
by this light, I'll try her.

LUCE Vat bin you, younker? Why do you not speak?

FLOWERDALE By my troth, sweetheart, a poor gentleman that would desire of you, if
it stand with your liking, the bounty of your purse.

Enter [Father]

140 LUCE O, Heer God, so young an armine.

FLOWERDALE Armine, sweet heart? I know not what you mean by that, but I am
almost a beggar.

LUCE Are you not a married man? Vere bin your vife?
Here is all I have, take dis. *Giving him money*

145 FLOWERDALE What, gold, young frow? This is brave.

FATHER If he have any grace, he'll now repent. *Aside*

LUCE Why speak you not? Were be your vife?

FLOWERDALE Dead, dead, she's dead. 'Tis she hath undone me,
Spent me all I had, and kept rascals under mine nose to brave me.

150 LUCE Did you use her vell?

FLOWERDALE Use her? There's never a gentlewoman in England could be better used
than I did her. I could but coach her, her diet stood me in forty pound a month, but
she is dead, and in her grave my cares are buried.

LUCE Indeed, dat vas not schoon.

155 FATHER He is turned more devil than he was before. *Aside*

FLOWERDALE Thou dost belong to Master Civet, here, dost thou not?

LUCE Yes, me do.

FLOWERDALE Why, there's it: there's not a handful of plate
But belongs to me, God's my judge:
160 If I had but such a wench as thou art,
There's never a man in England would make more of her
Than I would do, so she had any stock.

They call within: 'O, why, Tannakin!'

LUCE Stay, one doth call; I shall come by and by again. *Exit*

FLOWERDALE By this hand, this Dutch wench is in love with me.
165 Were it not admirable to make her steal
All Civet's plate and run away?

FATHER 'Twere beastly. O, Master Flowerdale,
Have you no fear of God, nor conscience?
What do you mean by this vile course you take?

170 FLOWERDALE What do I mean? Why, to live, that I mean.

FATHER To live in this sort? Fie upon the course!
Your life doth show you are a very coward.

134 **Vat...younker?** What's the matter? Who are you, young sir?   **younker** gay, fashionable young man/prodigal/greenhorn/younger son, from Middle Dutch meaning 'young lord'   135 **kind** gentle, sympathetic/sexually obliging   139 **bounty** liberality, generosity   140 **Heer** Lord (Dutch)   **armine** poor, unhappy man from *arminc* (Dutch)   145 **brave** capital, excellent   150 **vell** well   152 **could but coach** had to provide her with a coach   154 **schoon** 'nice' (Dutch)   158 **there's it** i.e. the thing is that   **there's not...me** Civet and Franck were given all Luce's dowry   162 **stock** money set aside/dowry/pedigree, i.e. family with connections   171 **sort** way, manner

FLOWERDALE   A coward, I pray, in what?

FATHER   Why, you will borrow sixpence of a boy.

175 FLOWERDALE   'Snails! Is there such cowardice in that?

I dare borrow it of a man, ay,

And of the tallest man in England, if he will lend it me.

Let me borrow it how I can,

And let them come by it how they dare.

180 And it is well known I might ha' rid out

A hundred times if I would, so I might.

FATHER   It was not want of will, but cowardice.

There is none that lends to you, but know they gain,

And what is that but only stealth in you?

185 Delia might hang you now, did not her heart

Take pity of you, for her sister's sake.

Go, get you hence, lest lingering here you stay,

You fall into their hands you look not for.

FLOWERDALE   I'll tarry here till the Dutch frow comes,

190 If all the devils in hell were here.   *Exit Father*

Enter Sir Lancelot, Master Weathercock and Artichoke

LANCELOT   Where is the door? Are we not past it, Artichoke?

ARTICHOKE   By th' mass, here's one, I'll ask him. Do you hear, sir?

What, are you so proud? Do you hear? Which is the way

To Master Civet's house? What, will you not speak?

195 O me, this is filching Flowerdale!

LANCELOT   O, wonderful, is this lewd villain here?

O, you cheating rogue, you cut-purse cony-catcher!

What ditch, you villain, is my daughter's grave?

A cozening rascal, that must make a will,

200 Take on him that strict habit, very that,

When he should turn to angel, a dying grace.

I'll father-in-law you, sir, I'll make a will!

Speak, villain, where's my daughter?

Poisoned, I warrant you, or knocked o' the head:

205 And to abuse good Master Weathercock

With his forged will — and, Master Weathercock —

To mock my grounded resolution,

Then to abuse the Devonshire gentleman:

Go, away with him to prison!

210 FLOWERDALE   Wherefore to prison? Sir, I will not go.

Enter Master Civet, his wife [Franck], Oliver, Sir Arthur, Father, Uncle and Delia

---

174 **Why … boy** i.e. rob a child   175 **'Snails!** By God's nails!   177 **tallest** most valiant   180 **ha' rid out** have ridden out (as a highwayman)   184 **stealth** theft, stealing   187 **here you** here where you   195 **filching** thieving   196 **lewd** bad, vile, worthless   197 **cut-purse** pickpocket, thief   **cony-catcher** swindler   199 **cozening … grace** Lancelot is recalling the way in which Flowerdale tricked him by appearing honest and serious in making his will when he should have had his mind on his soul and reformation   204 **warrant** assure, guarantee   207 **grounded** firmly fixed, or established   **resolution** decision, verdict

LANCELOT   O, here's his uncle. Welcome, gentlemen, welcome all.

Such a cozener, gentlemen, a murderer, too,

For anything I know. My daughter is missing:

Hath been looked for, cannot be found. A vild upon thee!

215   UNCLE   He is my kinsman, although his life be vile,

Therefore, in God's name, do with him what you will.

LANCELOT   Marry, to prison.

FLOWERDALE   Wherefore to prison? Snick up, I owe you nothing.

LANCELOT   Bring forth my daughter, then. Away with him!

220   FLOWERDALE   Go, seek your daughter: what do you lay to my charge?

LANCELOT   Suspicion of murder. Go! Away with him!

FLOWERDALE   Murder, you dogs? I murder your daughter?

Come, Uncle, I know you'll bail me.

UNCLE   Not I, were there no more than I

225   The jailer, thou the prisoner.

LANCELOT   Go, away with him.

Enter Luce, [disguised, as before], like a [Dutch] frow

LUCE   O'my life here, where will you ha' de man?

Vat ha de younker done?

WEATHERCOCK   Woman, he hath killed his wife.

230   LUCE   His vife? Dat is not good, dat is not schoon.

LANCELOT   Hang not upon him, huswife, if you do, I'll lay you by him.

LUCE   Have me no ander way dan you have him:

He tell me dat he love me heartily.

FRANCK   Lead away my maid to prison? Why, Tom, will you suffer that?

235   CIVET   No, by your leave, Father, she is no vagrant:

She is my wife's chambermaid, and as true as the skin between any man's

brows here.

LANCELOT   Go to, you're both fools:

Son Civet, of my life this is a plot,

240   Some straggling counterfeit preferred to you,

No doubt to rob you of your plate and jewels —

I'll have you led away to prison, trull.

LUCE   I am no trull, neither outlandish frow,

Nor he, nor I, shall to the prison go: *Revealing herself*

245   Know you me now? Nay, never stand amazed.

Father, I know I have offended you,

And though that duty wills me bend my knees

To you in duty and obedience,

Yet this ways do I turn, and to him yield   *Kneels to Flowerdale*

250   My love, my duty and my humbleness.

LANCELOT   Bastard in nature, kneel to such a slave?

---

214 **vild upon thee** a curse, despicable creature   218 **Snick up** go hang   230 **schoon** good   232 **Have…him** treat me the same way you treat him
236 **as true…brows** proverbial   240 **straggling** vagabond-like, vagrant   **counterfeit** pretender, impostor   **preferred** recommended/placed   242 **trull**
strumpet, trollop   251 **Bastard in nature** untrue to your family/your duty   **slave** wretch

LUCE   O, Master Flowerdale, if too much grief
            Have not stopped up the organs of your voice,
            Then speak to her that is thy faithful wife,
255   Or doth contempt of me thus tie thy tongue?
            Turn not away, I am no Ethiope,
            No wanton Cressid, nor a changing Helen,
            But rather one made wretched by thy loss.
            What, turn'st thou still from me? O, then,
260   I guess thee woefull'st among hapless men.
FLOWERDALE   I am indeed, wife, wonder among wives!
            Thy chastity and virtue hath infused
            Another soul in me, red with defame,
            For in my blushing cheeks is seen my shame.
265 LANCELOT   Out, hypocrite! I charge thee, trust him not.
LUCE   Not trust him? By my hopes of after-bliss,
            I know no sorrow can be compared to his.
LANCELOT   Well, since thou wert ordained to beggary,
            Follow thy fortune. I defy thee, aye.
270 OLIVER   I would 'che were zo well y-doused as was ever white cloth in a
            tucking-mill, and 'che a' not made me weep.
FATHER   If he hath any grace, he'll now repent.
ARTHUR   It moves my heart.
WEATHERCOCK   By my troth, I must weep: I cannot choose.
275 UNCLE   None but a beast would such a maid misuse.
FLOWERDALE   Content thyself. I hope to win his favour,
            And to redeem my reputation lost.
            And gentlemen, believe me, I beseech you,
            I hope your eyes shall behold such change,
280   As shall deceive your expectation.
OLIVER   I would 'che were y-split now, but 'che believe him.
LANCELOT   How, believe him?
WEATHERCOCK   By the mackins, I do.
LANCELOT   What, do you think that e'er he will have grace?
285 WEATHERCOCK   By my faith, it will go hard.
OLIVER   Well, 'che vor' ye, he is changed and, Master Flowerdale, in hope you
            been zo, hold, there's vorty pound toward your zetting up: what, be not ashamed,
            vang it, man, vang it: be a good husband, loven your wife and you shall not want
            for vorty more, ich vor' thee.
290 ARTHUR   My means are little, but if you'll follow me,

---

256 **Ethiope** Ethiopian, relating to her physical appearance   257 **wanton Cressid** whore, false mistress: a reference to the story of Troilus and Cressida, set against the Trojan war, in which Cressida betrays the Trojan prince Troilus with the Greek Diomedes   **changing Helen** Helen of Troy, the most beautiful woman in the world; she was either seduced or abducted by the Trojan prince Paris and left her husband Menelaus, and was thus the cause of the ten-year-long Trojan war celebrated in Homer's *Iliad*   260 **woefull'st** the most distressed   **hapless** unfortunate   262 **chastity** constancy, virtuosity   **infused** imparted by divine influence   263 **defame** disgrace, dishonour   266 **after-bliss** joy in heaven   268 **ordained** destined, appointed   270 **I...weep** I wish I were as well drenched as white cloth is in the ducking mill, and that you had not made me weep   **y-doused** plunged vigorously in water   **white cloth** which would probably have required the most dressing   **tucking-mill** west English term; **tucking** part of the process of cleaning and thickening cloth   276 **his** presumably referring to his uncle's   281 **y-split** broken apart   283 **By the mackins** an oath expressing confirmation, probably from 'Mass' or 'matins'   287 **vorty pound** forty pounds, equalling Civet's annual estate income   288 **vang** accept, take

I will instruct you in my ablest power:

But to your wife I give this diamond,

And prove true diamond, fair in all your life.

FLOWERDALE   Thanks, good Sir Arthur. Master Oliver,

295   You being my enemy, and grown so kind,

Binds me in all endeavour to restore.

OLIVER   What? Restore me no restorings man:

I have vorty pound more for Luce. Here, vang it:

Zooth, 'ch'ill devy London else. What, do not think me

300   A mezel or a scoundrel to throw away my money!

'Che have a hundred pound more to purchase of any good 'spectation:

I hope your vader and your uncle here will vollow my zamples.

UNCLE   You have guessed right of me. If he leave off this course of life, he shall be

mine heir.

305   LANCELOT   But he shall never get a groat of me:

A cozener, a deceiver, one that killed

His painful father, honest gentleman,

That passed the fearful danger of the sea,

To get him living and maintain him brave.

310   WEATHERCOCK   What, hath he killed his father?

LANCELOT   Ay, sir, with conceit of his vile courses.

FATHER   Sir, you are misinformed.

LANCELOT   Why, thou old knave, thou told'st me so thyself.

FATHER   I wronged him then; and, toward my master's stock,

315   There's twenty nobles for to make amends.

FLOWERDALE   No, Kester, I have troubled thee and wrong thee more,

What thou in love gives, I in love restore.

FRANCK   Ha, ha, sister, there you played bo-peep with:

Tom, what shall I give her toward household?

320   Sister Delia, shall I give her my fan?

DELIA   You were best ask your husband.

FRANCK   Shall I, Tom?

CIVET   Ay, do, Franck: I'll buy thee a new one with a longer handle.

FRANCK   A russet one, Tom.

325   CIVET   Ay, with russet feathers.

FRANCK   Here, sister, there's my fan toward household, to keep you warm.

LUCE   I thank you, sister.

---

296 Binds…restore obliges me to make every effort to pay it back   **299 Zooth** by God's tooth   **'ch'ill devy** I'll defy   **301 'spectation** expectation, prospect/observation, inspection   **305 groat** coin worth four old pence   **307 painful** painstaking, diligent   **309 brave** in fine style   **311 conceit** thought, knowledge   **314 stock** fund, store; playing on sense of 'family', 'kindred'   **315 twenty nobles** about seven pounds sterling   **318 bo-peep** children's game of concealing and revealing the face   **320 fan** introduced to Elizabeth's court from Italy, fans were often ornate and made from precious feathers, embroidered silk, or velvet/an instrument for blowing a fire, which seems more appropriate for Franck's suggestion that it is '**to keep you warm**' (line 326)   **323 longer handle** the handle was usually the most expensive part of the fan, and was often inlaid with precious stones, or metals   **324 russet** made of woollen cloth/reddish brown coloured

WEATHERCOCK   Why, this is well, and toward fair Luce's stock, here's forty shillings:
and forty good shillings more I'll give her, marry. Come, Sir Lancelot, I must have
330   you friends.

LANCELOT   Not I. All this is counterfeit,
     He will consume it, were it a million.

FATHER   Sir, what is your daughter's dower worth?

LANCELOT   Had she been married to an honest man,
335   It had been better than a thousand pound.

FATHER   Pay it him and I'll give you my bond,
     To make her jointure better worth than three.

LANCELOT   Your bond, sir, why, what are you?

FATHER   One whose word in London, though I say it,
340   Will pass there for as much as yours.

LANCELOT   Wert not thou late that unthrift's servingman?

FATHER   Look on me better, now my scar is off.   *Revealing himself*
     Ne'er muse, man, at this metamorphosis.

LANCELOT   Master Flowerdale!

345   FLOWERDALE   My father! O, I shame to look on him.
     Pardon, dear father, the follies that are past.

FATHER   Son, son, I do, and joy at this thy change,
     And applaud thy fortune in this virtuous maid,
     Whom heaven hath sent to thee to save thy soul.

350   LUCE   This addeth joy to joy: high heaven be praised!

WEATHERCOCK   Master Flowerdale, welcome from death, good Master Flowerdale.
     'Twas said so here, 'twas said so here, good faith.

FATHER   I caused that rumour to be spread myself,
     Because I'd see the humours of my son,
355   Which to relate the circumstance is needless.
     And, sirrah, see you run no more into that same disease,
     For he that's once cured of that malady,
     Of riot, swearing, drunkenness, and pride,
     And falls again into the like distress,
360   That fever is deadly, doth till death endure:
     Such men die mad as of a calenture.

FLOWERDALE   Heaven helping me, I'll hate the course as hell.

UNCLE   Say it and do it, cousin, all is well.

LANCELOT   Well, being in hope you'll prove an honest man,
365   I take you to my favour. Brother Flowerdale,
     Welcome with all my heart: I see your care
     Hath brought these acts to this conclusion,
     And I am glad of it; come, let's in and feast.

OLIVER   Nay, zoft you a while, you promised to make

---

333 dower dowry, the money a wife brings to her husband on marriage   **335 better** worth more   **336 bond** sworn deed, agreement   **337 jointure** financial
settlement, especially for widows   **361 calenture** fever, delirium

370   Sir Arthur and me amends. Here is your wisest daughter:

See which on's she'll have.

LANCELOT   O' God's name, you have my good will — get hers.

OLIVER   How say you then, damsel, tit on's have?

DELIA   I, sir, am yours.

375 **OLIVER**   Why, then send for a vicar and 'ch'ill have it

Dispatched in a trice, so 'ch'ill.

DELIA   Pardon me, sir. I mean I am yours,

In love, in duty, and affection,

But not to love as wife; shall ne'er be said,

380   Delia was buried married, but a maid.

ARTHUR   Do not condemn yourself forever,

Virtuous fair, you were born to love.

OLIVER   Why, you say true, Sir Arthur, she was y-bere to it

So well as her mother, but, I pray you, show us

385   Some zamples or reasons why you will not marry?

DELIA   Not that I do condemn a married life,

For 'tis no doubt a sanctimonious thing,

But for the care and crosses of a wife,

The trouble in this world that children bring,

390   My vow is in heaven in earth to live alone.

Husbands, howsoever good, I will have none.

OLIVER   Why then, 'ch'ill live bachelor, too.

'Che zet not a vig by a wife, if a wife zet not a vig by me. Come, shall's go to dinner?

FATHER   Tomorrow I crave your companies in Mark Lane:

395   Tonight we'll frolic in Master Civet's house,

And to each health drink down a full carouse.   *[Exeunt]*

FINIS

Textual Notes

Q = Quarto text of 1605

F3 = a correction introduced in the Third Folio text of 1663

Ed = a correction introduced by a later editor

SD = stage direction

SH = speech heading (i.e. speaker's name)

List of parts = Ed. *Not in* Q

1.14 reigns = Ed. Q = raines   **19 weights** = Ed. Q = waites   **29 not keeping** = Ed. Q = not in keeping   **35 reigns** = Ed. Q = raignes   **103 calamanco** = Ed. Q = calymanka   **105 calamanco** = Ed. Q = callymanka

373 damsel young unmarried lady of noble or gentle birth   **tit on's have?** which of us will you have?   **383 y-bere** born   **387 sanctimonious** sacred   **393 'Che...me** I set not a fig by a wife if a wife sets not a fig by me   **394 Mark Lane** London street, running south from Fenchurch Street to Great Tower Street; the name is a corruption of the mart or market that used to be held there   **395 frolic** make merry   **396 health** toast drunk in someone's honour   **carouse** cupful of liquor

109 *duodecimo tertios* = Ed. Q = Didicimo tersios   *tredecimo tertios* = Ed. Q = trydisimo tersios   **111** *Duodecimo tertios* = Ed. Q = dicditomo tersios   **121 cannot** = Ed. Q = cannon **149 fulhams** = Ed. Q = fullomes   **159 fob** = Ed. Q = fop

2.35 Sentences = Ed. Q = sentesses   **36 arbalester** = Ed. Q = alabaster   **38 suitor** = Ed. Q = shuter **40 shrewd** = Ed. Q = shroad   **61 haunted** = Ed. Q = hanted   **87 sell's** = F3, Q = selles   **106 suit** = Ed. Q = shute

3.12 Bean't = Ed. Q = Bin and   **18 devy ye** = Ed. Q = deuye   **25 a** = Ed. *Not in* Q   **38 vear vor** = Ed. Q = fer vere   **56 suitors** = Ed. Q = shuters   **64 not** = Ed. *Not in* Q   **74 thriftless** = Ed. Q = triffles **84 breath** = Ed. Q = broath   **130 ensue** = Ed. Q = enshue

4.14 mackins = Ed. Q = matkins

6.60 Now = Ed. Q = No   **61 No** = Ed. Q = Now   **80 your** = Ed. Q = our   **91 thou** = Ed. *Not in* Q

7.5 whose = Ed. Q = his

8.33 Machiavel = Ed. Q = Matchiuill   **44 endued** = Ed. Q = inducd

9.31 maken a vloutin' = Ed. Q = make an a volowten   **41 zutch** = Ed. Q = zitch   **84 quote** = Ed. Q = coate   **85 they, honest friend** = Ed. Q = thy honest friends   **132 Accept** = Ed. Q = except **144 SH ARTHUR** = Q *(catchword on previous page; the line itself is mistakenly assigned to Artichoke)* **145 Hussy** *spelled* Huswife *in* Q   **197 owed** = Ed. Q = ought   **262 Minikin** = Ed. Q = Minckins

10.62 one = Ed. Q = am

11.43 trompant = Ed. Q = triumphant   **44 censure** = Ed. Q = consure   **46 Keep** = Ed. *Not in* Q **53 is** = Ed. Not in Q

12.50 Guests = Ed. Q = guesse   **67 hour's** = Ed. Q = louers

13.77 screen = Ed. Q = friend   **131 Tannakin** = Ed. Q = to my kin   **154 schoon** = Ed. Q = scone **165 admirable** = Ed. Q = admiral   **207 mock** = Ed. Q = make   **223 you** = Ed. Q = your   **231 schoon** = Ed. Q = seene   **233 no...dan** = Ed. Q = no and or way do   **266 my** = Ed. *Not in* Q   **of** = Ed. Q = *Not in* Q   **301 purchase** = Ed. Q = pace   **'spectation** = Ed. Q = spotation   **302 vader** = Ed. Q = vnder   **324 Tom** = Ed. Q = Franke   **342 scar** = Q. Ed. = scarf   **373 tit on's have** = Ed. Q = tyters hate

A YORKSHIRE TRAGEDY

A man racks up debts and mortgages. He gambles and drinks, stays out late and womanizes. He beats up his wife. He has a filthy temper and is always swearing. He borrows money from his studious brother, who can ill afford it. When a well-meaning neighbour dares to criticize him for calling his wife a whore, they get into a fight and the wife is falsely accused of having an affair – with the result that she is in for more verbal abuse and another beating when he gets home. Inevitably, the children are also shouted at and assaulted.

It is an unchanging story, as familiar today as in Shakespeare's time, the stuff of gritty realism in both stage-play and soap opera. Sometimes, a case becomes extreme. Something snaps and the violence is stepped up. A routine of daily abuse gives way to a rampage, a killing spree, a tragedy that will make the news headlines.

So it was in Yorkshire in 1605. A squire named Walter Calverley had been orphaned as a child. He had gone to university in Cambridge, but soon dropped out. Back home in Yorkshire, he had become engaged to the daughter of a well-to-do neighbour. But on visiting London, he had been forced to submit to the will of his guardian, who had connections high in the aristocracy. Calverley was matched to an upper-class girl, a granddaughter of Lord Cobham (who was for a brief time Lord Chamberlain and thus patron of Shakespeare's acting company). Calverley didn't like his wife. But he took her back to the family home of Calverley Hall. He drank, he gambled, he ran through all his money. In April 1605 news was brought to him that a relative, a student at Cambridge, had been arrested for a debt for which he was himself responsible. In a drunken frenzy, he rushed at his two eldest children, William and Walter, the former four years old and the latter eighteenth months, and killed them both. At the same time he stabbed his wife, but not fatally. He then rode off to a neighbouring village where a third infant son, Henry, was out at nurse. His intention was to complete a trio of murders, but he was overtaken on the road and brought before the local magistrate, who committed him to prison at Wakefield. After some delay, he was brought to trial at York. He declined to plead and was pressed to death in York Castle on 5 August 1605.

His story became national news: a pamphlet about the murders was published in June, before the trial, and an account of his execution appeared within weeks of it taking place. A dramatization of the story – new, 'lamentable' and true – was acted by the King's Men, His Majesty's Players, at the Globe. It was published in 1608 with a title page claiming that it was 'Written by W. Shakespeare'.

Another play based on the story, but with names changed and a lighter mood, was penned by George Wilkins, Shakespeare's collaborator on the contemporaneous *Pericles*. The Wilkins play was called *The Miseries of Enforced Marriage*, its point being that a ward had no choice but to marry the wife of his guardian's choosing – the implication was that if Calverley had been allowed to marry the girl next door, whom he loved, as opposed to his being used as a pawn in an aristocratic game of estate consolidation and alliance building, the murders would not have taken place.

A Yorkshire Tragedy is only seven hundred lines long and, if the published text is to be believed, was one of a sequence of four short dramas performed 'in one'. There were precedents for this: one of the surviving plot outlines in the papers of theatrical producer Philip Henslowe is *The Second Part of the Seven Deadly Sins*, a series of linked playlets illustrating different vices. Equally, Robert

Yarington's *Two Lamentable Tragedies*, published in 1601, is a pair of murder stories dramatized from pamphlets or broadsheets describing lurid real-life killings. One could readily imagine *A Yorkshire Tragedy* forming part of a murder quartet alongside similar material to that in the two Yarington plays, one of which concerns a woodland child murder and the other of which features a tradesman beating his neighbour to death with fifteen blows of a hammer (both these murders also seem to have been dramatized by Henslowe's company). Four such plays in one would have formed a gory but entertaining afternoon at the Globe, in which audience members would have seen stage-characters much closer to their own lives than the monarchs, dukes and courtiers of the King's Men's more standard tragic fare. Perhaps we could fantasize that Shakespeare himself wrote the fourth piece and that somewhere there is a lost manuscript of a one-act domestic murder story in his hand. After all, this was precisely the moment in his career when he wrote a short, vivid and horrific scene of child-killing: the murder of Macduff's children in *Macbeth*.

The killing of the children in *A Yorkshire Tragedy* is very much in the cruelly witty and utterly savage vein that makes the comparable scene in *Macbeth* so terribly memorable.

> SON   O, what will you do, father? I am your white boy.
> HUSBAND   Thou shalt be my red boy: take that.   *Strikes him*

Here, though, it is 'Son' and 'Husband', not the family of a full-realized character such as Macduff. The characters in *A Yorkshire Tragedy* are not individualized or even named. For that matter, the dialogue never mentions Yorkshire: perhaps the association of Calverley with the acting company's sometime patron Cobham led them to be cautious, especially as they had not long before got into trouble with his family over the name of Sir John Oldcastle (the fat knight in *Henry IV* had to be rechristened Falstaff because the historical Oldcastle was a Cobham ancestor).

The lack of local colour has the advantage of giving the story a universal quality. This could be any abusive Husband, any long-suffering Wife. There is a deep truth to life that goes with the simplicity of language and plotting:

> WIFE   Good sir, by all our vows I do beseech you,
>   Show me the true cause of your discontent.
> HUSBAND   Money, money, money, and thou must supply me.

Money, and in particular a Husband's squandering of it, thus bringing misery to a marriage: it is both one of the oldest and the most modern stories.

The abusive language of the Husband, constantly calling his Wife 'filth' and 'whore' and 'strumpet'; his screaming at her, 'Where's the money? Let's see the money … the money, where is't?'; his jealousy of his brother for sticking with his studies ('University— That long word runs through me'); his recognition that he has thrown away what his family has built up through the years ('I am mad to think that moon was mine, mine and my father's, and my forefathers' generations, generations. Down goes the house of us, down, down it sinks. Now is the name a beggar, begs in me! That name, which hundreds of years has made this shire famous, in me and my posterity runs out'); the point at which the Husband snaps (the guilt induced by the news brought by the Master of his brother's college); the sense that once the rampage has begun, it must be completed. All these details, these moments, these reactions, ring true. And, although the characters are not named, several of them are economically brought to life. There is, for instance, the Servant who dares to stand up to his master, inevitably to find himself bruised and trampled for his pains. This is a cameo as forcefully rendered as that of the Servant who challenges Cornwall during the scene in *King Lear*, another contemporaneous play, when Gloucester is blinded.

Strong stylistic evidence now attributes the bulk of the play to Thomas Middleton, despite the unequivocal naming of Shakespeare on the original title page. The first scene is, however, rather different from the rest, and some scholars see Shakespeare's composing, guiding or revising hand within it. Here, the story is viewed askance, through the eyes of the household of the woman who was engaged to Calverley, and who has been waiting for him for years, not knowing that he has married someone else, had two or three children and become a wife-beater. Honest Sam the servant, returning home to the country with news from London, recognizes that his mistress has had a lucky escape, but that does not stop her from pining – she is a background presence somewhat akin to Mariana at the moated grange in *Measure for Measure*, though never seen.

This opening sequence is functional, in that it sets up the back story and prepares us for the appalling behaviour of the Husband, but it has a different kind of realism from that of the spare, stripped-down, pacey subsequent action:

> RALPH *and* OLIVER   Honest fellow Sam, welcome, i'faith! What tricks hast thou brought from London?
>
> SAM   You see I am hanged after the truest fashion: three hats and two glasses bobbing upon them, two rebato wires upon my breast, a cap-case by my side, a brush at my back, an almanac in my pocket, and three ballads in my codpiece: nay, I am the true picture of a common servingman.

Whereas the unnamed characters in the main body of the play become archetypal figures, here we have that intense individualization and humanization that – even if the scene is not by Shakespeare – is so characteristic of Shakespeare. One thinks, for example, of the Carriers in the inn-yard at Rochester in *Henry IV Part 1*, or indeed the figures in the crowd in Shakespeare's scene for *Sir Thomas More*. Whatever Shakespeare's involvement, or lack of involvement, in the writing and stage-realization of the scene, to the first audiences of *A Yorkshire Tragedy* at the Globe, and for the first readers of the Quarto published under his name, this opening provided a very Shakespearean beginning to a very memorable short play.

KEY FACTS

AUTHORSHIP: The entire play is now almost universally attributed to Thomas Middleton, following the pioneering studies of R. V. Holdsworth, David Lake and MacDonald P. Jackson. The play was attributed to 'W. Shakespere' on first publication and in all subsequent printings, and it has a longstanding connection to the author. Part of 'four plays in one', it has been suggested that Shakespeare may have been responsible for the overall design of the sequence, or for other plays within it. The title page attributes the play to the King's Men, suggesting that Shakespeare's involvement could be operating at a different level. The first scene is markedly

▷

different to the rest of the play, with named characters and a comic tone, but Jackson has argued persuasively for the play's integrity.

PLOT: An anonymous nobleman has fallen into debt and shame on account of his prodigal lifestyle, which has resulted in the imprisonment of his brother. The Husband is visited by several wellwishers, including the Master of his brother's college and assorted Gentlemen. The Husband becomes convinced that his Wife is having an affair and his children are not his, and grows increasingly violent, but is beaten by one of the Gentlemen. Running mad, he kills his son and babe-in-arms, as well as a maid, and stabs his Wife, then overthrows a servant who attempts to intervene. The Husband flees to find his final child, but his horse throws him. The Master and Gentlemen bring officers and arrest the unrepentant Husband, who is arraigned and sentenced to death. On his way to execution, he passes his house and has a final conversation with his injured Wife, who forgives him.

MAJOR PARTS: Husband (37%/76/7), Wife (24%/39/4), Master (8%/19/5), 4 Gentleman (7%/13/1), 1 Servant (5%/15/3), Sam (5%/12/1), Oliver (3%/14/1), Knight (3%/8/1), Ralph (2%/8/1), 1 Gentleman (1%/2/4), Son (1%/5/2), Maid (1%/2/1).

LINGUISTIC MEDIUM: 91% verse, 9% prose.

DATE: 1605. The uncertainty of the play's ending, which assumes but does not state execution for the Husband, along with the close dependence on the play's source of the same year, has led some critics to suggest that the play was written at speed and performed before the trial on which it was based had taken place.

SOURCES: The play (from scene 2 onwards) is very closely based on the sensational pamphlet *Two most vnnaturall and bloodie Murthers* (1605), making extensive verbal borrowings that have led some critics to suggest that Middleton may have authored both. The most noticeable difference is that all names and places are expunged from the text; there are no references to Calverley or even to Yorkshire, save in the title, and this may reflect a necessary anonymity in the original performances in order to avoid censure. The play is closely related to George Wilkins' *The Miseries of Enforced Marriage* (printed 1607), also based on the Calverley story but suddenly diverting into a happy ending.

TEXT: The 1608 Quarto, printed by Thomas Pavier, shows some signs of being composed at haste, including metrical irregularities and mislineation. It is most likely set from authorial 'foul papers', and its most distinctive feature is its extreme brevity at only 700 lines long. While the title page gives the title as *A Yorkshire Tragedy*, the inner title page reintroduces the text as *ALL's ONE, OR, One of the four Plays in one, called A Yorkshire Tragedy*, which may suggest the play had multiple titles depending on its relationship to the other plays associated with it.

A YORKSHIRE TRAGEDY.
Not so New as Lamentable and True. Acted by His Majesty's Players at the Globe. Written by W. Shakespeare

ALL'S ONE, OR, One of the four Plays in one, called
A Yorkshire Tragedy: as it was played by the King's Majesty's Players

HUSBAND

WIFE

SON of the Husband and Wife

MAID with their second child

MASTER of the College

KNIGHT

OLIVER
RALPH } servingmen
SAM

5 GENTLEMEN

3 SERVANTS

OFFICER

[Scene 1]

Enter Oliver and Ralph, two servingmen

OLIVER   Sirrah Ralph, my young mistress is in such a pitiful passionate humour for the long absence of her love—

RALPH   Why, can you blame her? Why, apples hanging longer on the tree than when they are ripe makes so many fallings: viz., mad wenches, because they are not

5   gathered in time, are fain to drop of themselves, and then 'tis common you know for every man to take them up.

OLIVER   Mass, thou say'st true, 'tis common indeed: but, sirrah, is neither our young master returned, nor our fellow Sam come from London?

A Yorkshire Tragedy was based on the true story of Walter Calverley who murdered two of his sons and stabbed his wife at his ancestral home, Calverley Hall in Yorkshire, on 23 April 1605   **ALL'S ONE** appears to be an alternative title to this play and means 'It's all the same'. It was performed as one in a quartet of **four Plays in one** by the King's Men, the company with which William Shakespeare was associated; the other three plays are now lost. It has been argued that in structure and mood this is reminiscent of the mystery play cycles – the York Cycle being one of the best known   **[Scene 1]** *Location: a house in the country, the home of the young woman previously contracted to the Husband; the servants offer a detached commentary on the events in the play*   *Ralph* was generally pronounced 'Rafe'   **1 Sirrah** a term of address used to young men or boys, often from a superior to an inferior **my young mistress** refers to the young woman to whom the Husband was formerly contracted, rather than the Wife of the play **2 for** on account of **4 makes** causes; the subject is the phrase '**apples...ripe**', hence the singular verb **fallings** windfalls/moral failures **viz.** namely, abbreviated form of *videlicet* (Latin) **mad...up** this spells out the analogy implied in the previous phrase; young women go mad if they do not find a lover when they are ripe for sexual relations and subsequently become promiscuous **5 fain** inclined, apt **7 Mass** by the mass **thou** familiar form of 'you' used between equals or to social inferiors

RALPH   Neither of either, as the Puritan bawd says. 'Slid, I hear Sam. Sam's come —

10   here's — tarry, come, i'faith, now my nose itches for news.

OLIVER   And so does mine elbow.

SAM *(calls within)* Where are you there? Boy, look you walk my horse with discretion: I have rid him simply. I warrant his skin sticks to his back with very heat: if 'a should catch cold and get the cough of the lungs I were well served,

15   were I not?

[*Enter Sam*] *furnished with things from London*

   What? Ralph and Oliver!

RALPH *and* OLIVER   Honest fellow Sam, welcome, i'faith! What tricks hast thou brought from London?

SAM   You see I am hanged after the truest fashion: three hats and two glasses

20   bobbing upon them, two rebato wires upon my breast, a cap-case by my side, a brush at my back, an almanac in my pocket, and three ballads in my codpiece: nay, I am the true picture of a common servingman.

OLIVER   I'll swear thou art. Thou mayst set up when thou wilt. There's many a one begins with less, I can tell thee, that proves a rich man ere he dies. But what's

25   the news from London, Sam?

RALPH   Ay, that's well said: what's the news from London, sirrah? My young mistress keeps such a puling for her love.

SAM   Why, the more fool she! Ay, the more ninnyhammer she.

OLIVER   Why, Sam, why?

30   SAM   Why, he's married to another long ago.

RALPH *and* OLIVER   I'faith, ye jest!

SAM   Why, did you not know that till now? Why, he's married, beats his wife, and has two or three children by her: for you must note that any woman bears the more when she is beaten.

35   RALPH   Ay, that's true, for she bears the blows.

OLIVER   Sirrah Sam, I would not for two years' wages my young mistress knew so much: she'd run upon the left hand of her wit, and ne'er be her own woman again.

SAM   And I think she was blessed in her cradle that he never came in her bed:

40   why, he has consumed all, pawned his lands, and made his university brother stand in wax for him — there's a fine phrase for a scrivener! Puh, he owes more than his skin's worth.

OLIVER   Is't possible?

9 Neither of either neither one thing nor the other   Puritan bawd a contradiction in terms since puritans were of strict moral virtue whereas **bawd** signifies a pimp or procuress   'Slid by God's eyelid   10 here's here he is   tarry wait, hang on   i'faith in faith, truly   nose…elbow popularly believed to signify the arrival of news   13 simply foolishly, recklessly   warrant guarantee   14 'a he, referring to the horse   cough…lungs a chronic cough known as 'heaves' or 'broken wind'   I…served i.e. it would serve me right   17 tricks trinkets, knick-knacks/pranks/clever devices/habits   19 hanged decorated   glasses mirrors, sometimes worn as decoration for heads or hats   20 rebato wires wire frames used to support the stiff collars or ruffs (rebatos) fashionable in the period   cap-case travelling case, bag   21 almanac annual book of tables containing meteorological and astrological forecasts   ballads popular songs which could be romantic but frequently related to celebrated events or persons, often of a scurrilous nature; indeed a ballad based on this case was entered in the Stationers' Register on 3June 1605   codpiece cloth attachment hung in front of hose or breeches by men to cover the genitals from c. fifteenth century to c. seventeenth century; these could be padded and highly decorated   23 Thou…up set yourself up in business independently   when thou wilt whenever you like   24 ere before   27 puling whining, crying/pining, wasting away   28 ninnyhammer fool, blockhead   33 any…beaten proverbial   37 run…wit go mad   be…again recover her sanity   41 stand in wax enter into a bond which would have been sealed with wax   scrivener scribe or notary authorized to draw up bills; Sam may be playing on a later meaning, 'author', referring to his pleasure at coining an apt new phrase

SAM   Nay, I'll tell you moreover, he calls his wife whore as familiarly as one
45   would call Moll and Doll, and his children bastards as naturally as can be.— But
what have we here? I thought 'twas somewhat pulled down my breeches: I quite
forgot my two poting sticks. These came from London: now anything is good here
that comes from London.

OLIVER   Ay, far-fetched you know.

50   SAM   But speak in your conscience, i'faith, have not we as good poting sticks
i'the country as need to be put i'th'fire. The mind of a thing is all. The mind of a
thing's all and as thou said'st e'en now, 'far-fetched is the best things for ladies'.

OLIVER   Ay, and for waiting-gentlewomen too.

SAM   But, Ralph, what, is our beer sour this thunder?

55   OLIVER   No, no, it holds countenance yet.

SAM   Why, then, follow me: I'll teach you the finest humour to be drunk in, I
learned it at London last week.

RALPH *and* OLIVER   I'faith, let's hear it, let's hear it.

SAM   The bravest humour, 'twould do a man good to be drunk in't. They call it
60   'knighting' in London, when they drink upon their knees.

RALPH *and* OLIVER   Faith, that's excellent!

SAM   Come, follow me: I'll give you all the degrees on't in order.   *Exeunt*

[Scene 2]

Enter Wife

WIFE   What will become of us? All will away.
My husband never ceases in expense
Both to consume his credit and his house:
And 'tis set down by heaven's just decree
5   That riot's child must needs be beggary.
Are these the virtues that his youth did promise:
Dice, and voluptuous meetings, midnight revels,
Taking his bed with surfeits ill-beseeming
The ancient honour of his house and name?
10   And this not all, but that which kills me most,
When he recounts his losses and false fortunes,
The weakness of his state so much dejected,
Not as a man repentant, but half mad,

---

45 Moll and Doll common names for prostitutes; pet names for 'Mary' and 'Dorothy'   **47 poting sticks** tools for crimping linen (such as ruffs); Sam plays on their potential for bawdy innuendo in his next speech   **49 far-fetched** brought from far/strained, unlikely   **53 waiting-gentlewomen** women of good birth who attended upon ladies of rank; puns on the situation of the 'young mistress' with obvious sexual implication   **54 beer...thunder** referring to the popular belief that hot, thundery weather turned beer sour   **55 holds countenance** looks good still   **59 bravest** most excellent, daring   **60 'knighting'...knees** refers to the practice of drinking toasts while on the knees   **62 degrees** all the degrees of drunkenness   **[Scene 2]**   *Location: the Husband's ancestral home*   **1 All will away** everything will be lost   **3 Both to consume** which consumes both   **credit** good name, reputation   **5 riot's...beggary** poverty is the inevitable outcome of   **riot** (loose living, debauchery, extravagance)   **8 Taking** taking to   **surfeits** illnesses brought on by his over-indulgence   **ill-beseeming** not suitable to or appropriate to   **9 house and name** family and lineage   **10 this** this is   **12 dejected** humbled, cast down

His fortunes cannot answer his expense.

15   He sits and sullenly locks up his arms,
Forgetting heaven looks downward, which makes him
Appear so dreadful that he frights my heart,
Walks heavily as if his soul were earth,
Not penitent for those his sins are past,
20   But vexed, his money cannot make them last:
A fearful, melancholy, ungodly sorrow!
O, yonder he comes, now in despite of ills
I'll speak to him, and I will hear him speak
And do my best to drive it from his heart.

Enter Husband

25   HUSBAND   Pox o'th'last throw! It made
Five hundred angels vanish from my sight.
I'm damned! I'm damned! The angels have forsook me.
Nay, 'tis certainly true: for he that has
No coin is damned in this world. He's gone, he's gone!

30   WIFE   Dear husband!

HUSBAND   O! Most punishment of all, I have a wife.

WIFE   I do entreat you, as you love your soul,
Tell me the cause of this your discontent.

HUSBAND   A vengeance strip thee naked! Thou art cause,
35   Effect, quality, property, thou, thou, thou!   *Exit*

WIFE   Bad turned to worse! Both beggary of the soul
As of the body and so much unlike
Himself at first, as if some vexed spirit
Had got his form upon him—

Enter Husband again

40   He comes again.
He says I am the cause: I never yet
Spoke less than words of duty and of love.

HUSBAND   If marriage be honourable, then cuckolds are honourable, for they cannot
be made without marriage. Fool! What, meant I to marry to get beggars? Now must
45   my eldest son be a knave or nothing: he cannot live upo'th'soil for he will have no
land to maintain him: that mortgage sits like a snaffle upon mine inheritance and
makes me chaw upon iron. My second son must be a promoter, and my third a thief
or an underputter, a slave pander. O beggary, beggary! To what base uses dost thou
put a man! I think the devil scorns to be a bawd. He bears himself more proudly, has
50   more care on's credit.

14 answer meet the charge of   **25 Pox o'th'** exclamation of impatience   **pox** from diseases characterized by pustules, such as chickenpox or smallpox but often confused with syphilis known as 'the French pox'   **throw** i.e. of the dice   **26 angels** gold coins with the image of the Archangel Michael, worth approximately ten shillings (half a pound sterling); the following line puns on the religious sense   **27 forsook** forsaken, abandoned   **34 vengeance** a curse, i.e. may an act of vengeance   **35 quality** character, nature   **property** tool, instrument   **38 vexed…him** tormented soul inhabited his outward shape; there are hints throughout the play that the Husband's change of personality is due to demonic possession   **43 cuckolds** men with unfaithful wives   **44 get** beget   **45 knave** servant/rogue   **live upo'th'soil** make a living from the produce of the earth   **46 snaffle** restraint, literally a horse's bridle-bit   **47 chaw** chew, champ   **promoter** professional informer   **48 underputter** pimp, sexual procurer   **slave pander** servile, contemptible pimp   **49 bawd** pimp   **50 on's credit** of his reputation

Base, slavish, abject, filthy poverty!

WIFE   Good sir, by all our vows I do beseech you,
Show me the true cause of your discontent.

HUSBAND   Money, money, money, and thou must supply me.

55   WIFE   Alas, I am the least cause of your discontent,
Yet what is mine, either in rings or jewels,
Use to your own desire, but I beseech you,
As you're a gentleman by many bloods,
Though I myself be out of your respect,
60   Think on the state of these three lovely boys
You have been father to.

HUSBAND   Puh! Bastards, bastards, bastards: begot in tricks, begot in tricks.

WIFE   Heaven knows how those words wrong me: but I may
Endure these griefs among a thousand more.
65   O, call to mind your lands already mortgaged,
Yourself wound into debts, your hopeful brother
At the university in bonds for you,
Like to be seized upon: And—

HUSBAND   Ha' done, thou harlot,
70   Whom, though for fashion sake I married,
I never could abide. Think'st thou thy words
Shall kill my pleasures? Fall off to thy friends,
Thou and thy bastards beg: I will not bate
A whit in humour! Midnight, still I love you
75   And revel in your company. Curbed in?
Shall it be said in all societies
That I broke custom, that I flagged in money?
No, those thy jewels I will play as freely
As when my state was fullest.

80   WIFE   Be it so.

HUSBAND   Nay I protest, and take that for an earnest,   *Spurns her*
I will forever hold thee in contempt
And never touch the sheets that cover thee,
But be divorced in bed till thou consent
85   Thy dowry shall be sold to give new life
Unto those pleasures which I most affect.

WIFE   Sir, do but turn a gentle eye on me,
And what the law shall give me leave to do
You shall command.

---

52 **vows** i.e. marriage vows   58 **bloods** noble ancestors   59 **respect** favour/esteem/rank, standing/consideration   62 **begot** conceived   **tricks** deceit, fraud/lechery   66 **wound** driven/having followed a devious route   **hopeful** promising   67 **in bonds** indebted, legally bound   68 **Like…upon** likely to be arrested   69 **Ha' done** that's enough   70 **for fashion sake** in outward show or ceremony/in accordance with prevailing custom   72 **Fall off** go away   73 **bate…humour** moderate or soften my temper at all   75 **revel** make merry   **Curbed in?** Shall I be restrained?   76 **societies** groups, companies   77 **flagged in money** was slow in paying/hard pressed financially   78 **those…play** I'll gamble with those jewels of yours   79 **State was fullest** situation was most prosperous   81 **earnest** instalment   *Spurns* kicks   84 **divorced in bed** refrain from sexual contact   85 **dowry** the property she brought to her husband on marriage   86 **affect** enjoy

90 HUSBAND   Look it be done: shall I want dust and like a slave

Wear nothing in my pockets but my hands,

To fill them up with nails?   *Holding his hands in his pockets*

O, much against my blood! Let it be done.

I was never made to be a looker-on,

95   A bawd to dice: I'll shake the drabs myself

And make them yield. I say, look it be done.

WIFE   I take my leave: it shall.   *Exit*

HUSBAND   Speedily, speedily!

I hate the very hour I chose a wife:

100   A trouble, trouble!

Three children like three evils hang upon me.

Fie, fie, fie!

Strumpet and bastards, strumpet and bastards!

Enter three Gentlemen hearing him

1 GENTLEMAN   Still do those loathsome thoughts jar on your tongue,

105   Yourself to stain the honour of your wife,

Nobly descended? Those whom men call mad

Endanger others, but he's more than mad

That wounds himself, whose own words do proclaim

Scandals unjust to soil his better name!

110   It is not fit: I pray, forsake it.

2 GENTLEMAN   Good sir, let modesty reprove you.

3 GENTLEMAN   Let honest kindness sway so much with you.

HUSBAND   Good e'en, I thank you, sir, how do you? Adieu!

I'm glad to see you. Farewell instructions, admonitions!   *Exeunt Gentlemen*

Enter a Servant

115 HUSBAND   How now, sirrah: what would you?

1 SERVANT   Only to certify you, sir, that my mistress was met by the way by they who were sent for her up to London by her honourable uncle, your worship's late guardian.

HUSBAND   So, sir, then she is gone and so may you be: but let her look that the thing
120 be done she wots of or hell will stand more pleasant than her house at home.

[*Exit 1 Servant*]

Enter a Gentleman

4 GENTLEMAN   Well or ill met, I care not.

HUSBAND   No, nor I.

4 GENTLEMAN   I am come with confidence to chide you.

HUSBAND   Who? me?

---

90 Look...done make sure you do it   dust money, cash (slang)   92 nails fingernails, i.e. something worthless   93 blood family/temper   95 bawd to dice go-between who procures others to gamble   drabs harlots, i.e. the dice   103 Strumpet prostitute   113 Good e'en good evening, used any time after noon   Adieu! Goodbye! (French)   114 admonitions warnings, reproofs   115 what would you? What do you want?   116 certify inform, assure   mistress...uncle the mistress has been met by those her honourable uncle sent to take her to London   118 guardian the historical Walter Calverley, whose family were Catholic recusants (those who refused to acknowledge the authority of the Church of England), had been made a ward of court at the age of seventeen after his father's death and forced to marry a woman selected by his guardian   120 wots of knows about, i.e. the sale of land from her dowry to provide him with money   121 Well...met whether you're pleased to see me or not; this suggests that he may be one of the 'Gentlemen' previously dismissed

125   Chide me? Do't finely then: let it not move me,
         For if thou chid'st me angry, I shall strike.

   4 GENTLEMAN   Strike thine own follies, for it is they deserve
         To be well beaten. We are now in private:
         There's none but thou and I. Thou'rt fond and peevish,
130   An unclean rioter: thy lands and credit
         Lie now both sick of a consumption.
         I am sorry for thee: that man spends with shame
         That with his riches does consume his name:
         And such art thou.

135   HUSBAND   Peace!

   4 GENTLEMAN   No! Thou shalt hear me further.
         Thy father's and forefathers' worthy honours,
         Which were our country monuments, our grace,
         Follies in thee begin now to deface.
140   The springtime of thy youth did fairly promise
         Such a most fruitful summer to thy friends
         It scarce can enter into men's beliefs
         Such dearth should hang on thee. We that see it,
         Are sorry to believe it: in thy change,
145   This voice into all places will be hurled.
         Thou and the devil has deceived the world.

   HUSBAND   I'll not endure thee.

   4 GENTLEMAN   But of all the worst:
         Thy virtuous wife, right honourably allied,
150   Thou hast proclaimed a strumpet.

   HUSBAND   Nay, then, I know thee.
         Thou art her champion, thou, her private friend,
         The party you wot on.

   4 GENTLEMAN   O ignoble thought.
155   I am past my patient blood: shall I stand idle
         And see my reputation touched to death?

   HUSBAND   'T'as galled you, this, has it?

   4 GENTLEMAN   No, monster, I will prove
         My thoughts did only tend to virtuous love.

160   [HUSBAND]   Love of her virtues? There it goes.

   4 GENTLEMAN   Base spirit,
         To lay thy hate upon the fruitful honour
         Of thine own bed.   *They fight and the Husband's hurt*

   HUSBAND   O!

---

125 finely subtly, delicately   **move me** i.e. to anger   **126 chid'st me angry** anger me with your rebukes, criticisms   **129 fond** foolish, mad   **peevish** perverse, spiteful   **130 unclean rioter** morally impure reveller or debauched person   **131 consumption** wasting disease, i.e. his dissolute, extravagant lifestyle   **138 country** local   **monuments** memorable examples of distinction, often a tomb or sepulchre   **143 dearth** failure (to come to harvest), deficiency   **145 voice** report, judgement   **149 right honourably allied** very nobly connected; Walter Calverley's wife, Philippa Brooke, was the granddaughter of Lord Cobham and niece of the wife of Sir Robert Cecil, Earl of Salisbury and one of King James I's chief ministers   **150 strumpet** whore   **152 private friend** secret lover   **153 party...on** individual or side in a dispute/member of a conspiracy you know about   **wot** know   **155 past...blood** furious, beyond all patience   **156 touched to death** damaged, destroyed   **157 'T'as galled** it has vexed, irritated   **160 There it goes** you would say that!   **162 To...bed** i.e. to impugn your wife's honour and proclaim your children illegitimate

165   4 GENTLEMAN   Would thou yield it yet?

       HUSBAND   Sir, sir, I have not done with you.

       4 GENTLEMAN   I hope nor ne'er shall do.   *Fight again*

       HUSBAND   Have you got tricks? Are you in cunning with me?

       4 GENTLEMAN   No, plain and right.

170   He needs no cunning that for truth doth fight.   *Husband falls down*

       HUSBAND   Hard fortune, am I levelled with the ground?

       4 GENTLEMAN   Now, sir, you lie at mercy.

       HUSBAND   Ay, you slave.

       4 GENTLEMAN   Alas, that hate should bring us to our grave!

175   You see my sword's not thirsty for your life,

      I am sorrier for your wound than yourself.

      You're of a virtuous house, show virtuous deeds!

      'Tis not your honour, 'tis your folly bleeds.

      Much good has been expected in your life,

180   Cancel not all men's hopes: you have a wife,

      Kind and obedient, heap not wrongful shame

      On her and your posterity. Let only sin be sore

      And by this fall, rise never to fall more.

      And so I leave you.   *Exit*

185   HUSBAND   Has the dog left me then,

      After his tooth hath left me? O, my heart

      Would fain leap after him. Revenge, I say,

      I'm mad to be revenged. My strumpet wife,

      It is thy quarrel that rips thus my flesh

190   And makes my breast spit blood, but thou shalt bleed.

      Vanquished? Got down? Unable e'en to speak?

      Surely 'tis want of money makes men weak.

      Ay, 'twas that o'erthrew me: I'd ne'er been down else.   *Exit*

[Scene 3]

Enter Wife in a riding-suit with a Servingman

    1 SERVANT   Faith, mistress, if it might not be presumption

      In me to tell you so, for his excuse

      You had small reason, knowing his abuse—

    WIFE   I grant I had: but, alas,

5   Why should our faults at home be spread abroad?

      'Tis grief enough within doors! At first sight

      Mine uncle could run o'er his prodigal life

---

165 yield it confess the truth/admit defeat   **168 in cunning** using underhand devices/magic   **178 'Tis...bleeds** it's your own stupidity not your honour which has caused you to be wounded   **186 tooth** i.e. sword   **187 fain** gladly, willingly   **193 else** otherwise   **[Scene 3]** *Location: the Husband's ancestral home*   **riding-suit** signifying she has just returned from a journey   **2 his excuse** excusing his behaviour (to her uncle)   **3 abuse** ill-usage **6 within doors** in private (without making it common knowledge)   **At...follies** (lines 6–9) as soon as he set eyes on me my uncle knew all about my husband's behaviour

As perfectly as if his serious eye
Had numbered all his follies,
10   Knew of his mortgaged lands, his friends in bonds,
Himself withered with debts and in that minute
Had I added his usage and unkindness,
'Twould have confounded every thought of good
Where now, fathering his riots on his youth,
15   Which time and tame experience will shake off,
Guessing his kindness to me (as I smoothed him
With all the skill I had) though his deserts
Are in form uglier than an unshaped bear,
He's ready to prefer him to some office
20   And place at court: a good and sure relief
To all his stooping fortunes. 'Twill be a means, I hope,
To make new league between us and redeem
His virtues with his lands.

1 SERVANT   I should think so, mistress. If he should not now be kind to you and love
25   you, and cherish you up, I should think the devil himself kept open house in him.

WIFE   I doubt not but he will now. Prithee, leave me: I think I hear him
coming.

1 SERVANT   I am gone.   *Exit*

WIFE   By this good means I shall preserve my lands
30   And free my husband out of usurer's hands.
Now there is no need of sale: my uncle's kind,
I hope if aught, this will content his mind.
Here comes my husband.

Enter Husband

HUSBAND   Now, are you come? Where's the money? Let's see the money.
35   Is the rubbish sold, those wiseacres your lands? Why, when?
The money, where is't? Pour't down, down with it, down with it:
I say pour't o'the ground! Let's see't, let's see't!

WIFE   Good sir, keep but in patience and I hope
My words shall like you well: I bring you better
40   Comfort than the sale of my dowry.

HUSBAND   Ha, what's that?

WIFE   Pray, do not fright me, sir, but vouchsafe me hearing: my uncle, glad of
your kindness to me and mild usage, for so I made it to him, has in pity of your
declining fortunes, provided a place for you at court of worth and credit, which so
45   much overjoyed me—

HUSBAND   Out on thee, filth! Over and over-joyed, when I'm in torments? Thou
politic whore, subtler than nine devils. Was this thy journey to nunc, to set down

---

8 eye sight, understanding   **13 confounded** destroyed   **14 Where** whereas   **fathering…youth** blaming his dissolute behaviour on his youth   **16 smoothed him** excused him, glossed over his faults   **17 deserts** merits   **18 unshaped bear** from the popular notion that the mother bear licked her newly-born cubs into shape (see Sir Thomas Browne, *Pseudoxia Epidemica*, 1646, sig. P2v)   **19 prefer** advance, recommend   **office** post, duty   **21 stooping** declining   **26 Prithee** please, literally 'I pray thee'   **32 aught** anything (will)   **35 wiseacres** fools who think themselves clever; the husband applies the term sarcastically to her lands   **39 like you well** please you   **42 vouchsafe** grant   **43 made…him** pretended that was the case   **47 politic** cunning, devious   **nunc** uncle (contemptuous)

the history of me, of my state and fortunes? Shall I, that dedicated myself to
pleasure, be now confined in service to crouch and stand like an old man i'th'hams,
50 my hat off? I that never could abide to uncover my head i'th'church! Base slut!
This fruit bears thy complaints.   *Spurns her*

WIFE   O, heaven knows
That my complaints were praises, and best words
Of you and your estate: only my friends
55 Knew of our mortgaged lands, and were possessed
Of every accident before I came.
If thou suspect it but a plot in me
To keep my dowry, or for mine own good
Or my poor children's — though it suits a mother
60 To show a natural care in their reliefs —
Yet I'll forget myself to calm your blood.
Consume it as your pleasure counsels you
And all I wish e'en clemency affords;
Give me but comely looks and modest words.
65 HUSBAND   Money, whore, money, or I'll—   *Draws his dagger*
Enters a Servant very hastily
(*To his manservant in a fear*) What the devil? How now? Thy hasty news?
2 SERVANT   May it please you, sir—
HUSBAND   What? May I not look upon my dagger? Speak villain, or I will execute the
point on thee: quick, short.
70 2 SERVANT   Why, sir, a gentleman from the university stays below to speak with you.
HUSBAND   From the university? So! University—
That long word runs through me.   [*Exeunt Husband and*
WIFE   Was ever wife so wretchedly beset?   *2 Servant leaving the*] *Wife alone*
Had not this news stepped in between, the point
75 Had offered violence unto my breast.
That which some women call great misery
Would show but little here, would scarce be seen
Amongst my miseries. I may compare
For wretched fortunes with all wives that are!
80 Nothing will please him, until all be nothing.
He calls it slavery to be preferred,
A place of credit a base servitude.
What shall become of me and my poor children,
Two here and one at nurse, my pretty beggars?

---

49 **confined in service** restricted like a servant by duty   **stand...i'th'hams** obsequiously with bent knees   50 **my hat off** as a sign of respect
51 **This...complaints** this is what your complaints have produced   *Spurns* kicks   54 **estate** situation, condition   **only...came** it's just that my relatives
already knew all the details before I arrived   **friends** could also be applied to relatives, kinsfolk   56 **accident** incident   58 **or** either   62 **it** i.e. her
dowry   63 **e'en clemency affords** nothing else but gentleness of temper has the power to give   64 **comely** decent, sober/pleasant   **modest** avoiding
extremes of behaviour, not harsh or domineering   70 **university** at this period there were only two universities in England: Oxford and Cambridge   **stays** is
waiting   73 **beset** bestowed in marriage/assailed/trapped by circumstance   74 **point** of his dagger   77 **seen** noticed   79 **all...are** any woman alive
80 **all be nothing** all we have is lost   81 **preferred** advanced   82 **place of credit** prestigious position   84 **one at nurse** aristocratic mothers commonly
sent their infants to a wet nurse until they were weaned   **beggars** poor things – can be used as a term of endearment

85   I see how ruin with a palsy hand

Begins to shake the ancient seat to dust:

The heavy weight of sorrow draws my lids

Over my dankish eyes: I can scarce see.

Thus grief will last: it wakes and sleeps with me.   [*Exit*]

[Scene 4]

Enter the Husband with the Master of the College

HUSBAND   Please you draw near, sir, you're exceeding welcome.

MASTER   That's my doubt: I fear I come not to be welcome.

HUSBAND   Yes, howsoever.

MASTER   'Tis not my fashion, sir, to dwell in long circumstance, but to be plain,
5   and effectual. Therefore, to the purpose: the cause of my setting forth was piteous
and lamentable. That hopeful young gentleman, your brother, whose virtues we all
love dearly, through your default and unnatural negligence, lies in bond executed
for your debt, a prisoner, all his studies amazed, his hope struck dead, and the pride
of his youth muffled in these dark clouds of oppression.

10   **HUSBAND**   Hum, um, um.

MASTER   O, you have killed the towardest hope of all our university: wherefore,
without repentance and amends, expect ponderous and sudden judgements to fall
grievously upon you. Your brother, a man who profited in his divine employments,
might have made ten thousand souls fit for heaven. Now, by your careless courses
15   cast in prison, which you must answer for, and assure your spirit it will come home
at length.

HUSBAND   O God! O!

MASTER   Wise men think ill of you, others speak ill of you, no man loves you, nay,
even those whom honesty condemns, condemn you. And take this from the virtuous
20   affection I bear your brother: never look for prosperous hour, good thought, quiet
sleeps, contented walks, nor anything that makes man perfect till you redeem him.
What is your answer? How will you bestow him: upon desperate misery, or better
hopes? I suffer, till I have your answer.

HUSBAND   Sir, you have much wrought with me. I feel you in my soul: you are your
25   art's master. I never had sense till now: your syllables have cleft me. Both for your
words and pains I thank you: I cannot but acknowledge grievous wrongs done to
my brother, mighty, mighty, mighty wrongs.— Within there!

Enter a Servingman

[2 SERVANT]   Sir?

---

85 palsy weak, trembling brought about by disease, terror or other extreme emotion; here the 'gentleman's palsy' referred to by the Husband brought on by shaking the dice at 2.95   **86 ancient seat** ancestral house and lands   **88 dankish** wet, moist   **[Scene 4]**   *Location: the Husband's ancestral home*   **3 howsoever** nevertheless   **4 dwell...circumstance** waste time going all round a subject   **5 effectual** to the point/earnest/diligent   **7 default** failure in duty (to honour the terms of your bond)   **lies...debt** is imprisoned due to your failure to honour your bond (and repay the money you owe)   **8 amazed** thrown into confusion   **11 towardest** most promising   **13 divine employments** religious duties   **14 might...heaven** (who) might have saved ten thousand souls (by his preaching)   **careless courses** reckless behaviour   **16 come home** be felt and understood/be revenged   **21 perfect** virtuous/contented   **redeem him** repay the debt and release him   **22 bestow** dispose of   **24 wrought** affected/agitated; from the literal sense of metal beaten or shaped with a hammer   **25 art's master** proficient as a master of persuasive rhetoric, playing on his title, 'master of arts'   **cleft** struck/split

HUSBAND   Fill me a bowl of wine. Alas, poor brother,

30   Bruised with an execution for my sake.   *Exit Servant for wine*

MASTER   A bruise indeed makes many a mortal sore

Till the grave cure them.

Enter [Servant] with wine

HUSBAND   Sir, I begin to you, you've chid your welcome.

MASTER   I could have wished it better for your sake.

35   I pledge you, sir, to the kind man in prison.

HUSBAND   Let it be so.   *Drink both*

Now, sir, if you so please to spend but a few minutes in a walk about my grounds
below, my man here shall attend you. I doubt not but by that time to be furnished of
a sufficient answer and therein my brother fully satisfied.

40   MASTER   Good sir, in that the angels would be pleased

And the world's murmurs calmed, and I should say

I set forth then upon a lucky day.   *Exeunt [with Servant]*

HUSBAND   O, thou confused man! Thy pleasant sins have undone thee: thy damnation
has beggared thee! That heaven should say we must not sin, and yet made women,
45   gives our senses way to find pleasure, which being found confounds us. Why should
we know those things so much misuse us? — O, would virtue had been forbidden!
We should then have proved all virtuous, for 'tis our blood to love what we are
forbidden. Had not drunkenness been forbidden, what man would have been fool
to a beast and zany to a swine, to show tricks in the mire? What is there in three
50   dice to make a man draw thrice three thousand acres into the compass of a round
little table, and with the gentleman's palsy in the hand shake out his posterity
thieves or beggars? 'Tis done! I ha' done't, i'faith: terrible, horrible misery. How well
was I left! Very well, very well! My lands showed like a full moon about me, but
now the moon's i'the last quarter, waning, waning. And I am mad to think that
55   moon was mine, mine and my father's, and my forefathers' generations, generations.
Down goes the house of us, down, down it sinks. Now is the name a beggar, begs
in me! That name, which hundreds of years has made this shire famous, in me and
my posterity runs out. In my seed five are made miserable besides myself: my riot is
now my brother's jailer, my wife's sighing, my three boys' penury, and mine own
60   confusion.

Tears his hair

Why sit my hairs upon my cursèd head?

Will not this poison scatter them? O my brother's

In execution among devils that

---

30 execution seizure of person (or goods) of a debtor in default of payment   **31 mortal sore** fatal wound/person suffer pain; debtors frequently died in prison
33 begin i.e. to propose a toast   **chid** argued, scolded by way of/expressed displeasure at   **35 pledge you** give you a toast/make you a promise   **kind** related
by kinship/well-bred/generous/good-natured   **38 below** suggesting that the scene takes place in an upper room   **furnished of** provided with   **39 sufficient**
satisfactory   **fully satisfied** with his debt repaid in full   **45 confounds** ruins   **46 things** vices/pleasures/women (which)   **misuse** abuse   **47 blood** natural
desire   **49 to** in comparison with   **zany** comic imitator/attendant on   **50 compass** circle/cunning device   **51 table** i.e. gaming table   **gentleman's palsy**
ruin from gambling, see 3.85   **posterity** descendants   **53 left** provided for by my inheritance   **like…moon** i.e. they surrounded him   **54 now…waning** his
property is dwindling steadily; Calverley had sold off his lands piecemeal to maintain his extravagant lifestyle   **55 generations** descendants   **56 house of us**
our family line   **57 me** my own person   **which** i.e. which (for)   **60 confusion** ruin/putting to shame/mental agitation/disorder   **62 poison** referring to his
present situation and the notion that certain poisons caused the hair to fall out   **63 execution** the debtors' prison for defaulting on payment of a debt   **devils**
wicked people, i.e. his jailers

Stretch him and make him give. And I in want,

65　Not able for to live, nor to redeem him.

Divines and dying men may talk of hell

But in my heart her several torments dwell.

Slavery and misery! Who in this case

Would not take up money upon his soul,

70　Pawn his salvation, live at interest?

I, that did ever in abundance dwell,

For me to want exceeds the throes of hell.

Enter his little Son with a top and a scourge

SON　　What, ail you, father? Are you not well? I cannot scourge my top as long as you stand so: you take up all the room with your wide legs. Puh, you cannot

75　make me afeard with this: I fear no vizards nor bugbears.

Husband takes up the child by the skirts of his long coat in one hand and draws his dagger with the other

HUSBAND　Up, sir, for here thou hast no inheritance left.

SON　　O, what will you do, father? I am your white boy.

HUSBAND　Thou shalt be my red boy: take that.　　　　*Strikes him*

SON　　O, you hurt me, father!

80　HUSBAND　My eldest beggar! Thou shalt not live to ask an usurer bread, to cry at a great man's gate, or follow, 'good your honour', by a couch: no, nor your brother: 'tis charity to brain you.

SON　　How shall I learn now my head's broke?

HUSBAND　Bleed, bleed rather than beg, beg!　　　　*Stabs him*

85　Be not thy name's disgrace:

Spurn thou thy fortunes first if they be base:

Come view thy second brother.— Fates, my children's blood

Shall spin into your faces, you shall see

How confidently we scorn beggary!　　　　*Exit with his son*

[Scene 5]

Enter a Maid with a child in her arms, the mother by her asleep

MAID　　Sleep, sweet babe: sorrow makes thy mother sleep.

It bodes small good when heaviness falls so deep.

Hush, pretty boy, thy hopes might have been better:

'Tis lost at dice what ancient honour won —

---

64 **Stretch…give** sense is unclear but suggests he was tortured on the rack and forced to give money or information; there is no historical evidence to support this   66 **Divines…dwell** a commonplace first found in Thomas Nashe's *Pierce Penniless* (1592)   67 **several** various   68 **case** position, plight   69 **take…upon** pawn or pledge (offering his soul as security)   70 **at interest** on the money lent as interest on his soul   72 **throes** agonies   *scourge* whip   73 **ail you** are you ill   75 **vizards** masks, disguises/faces like masks/ghosts – the exact sense is unclear but the general sense seems to be that the Husband is so disturbed his expression is frightening   **bugbears** hobgoblins, imaginary terrors (used to frighten children)   77 **white boy** pet, favourite   80 **usurer** moneylender (for)   **cry** beg   81 **'good your honour'** please sir, typical phrase used by beggars   **couch** an allowance for the night   82 **brain you** dash your brains out   86 **Spurn…first** reject/strike against your fortunes before resorting to begging   88 **spin** gush, spurt   **[Scene 5]**   *Location: a bedroom in the Husband's ancestral home*   2 **It…deep** such deep sleep promises little good

5   Hard when the father plays away the son!

Nothing but misery serves in this house.

Ruin and desolation, O!

Enter Husband with the Boy bleeding

HUSBAND	Whore, give me that boy.	*Strives with her for the child*
MAID	O, help, help! Out alas, murder, murder!	

10   HUSBAND   Are you gossiping, prating, sturdy quean?

I'll break your clamour with your neck: downstairs!

Tumble, tumble, headlong!   *Throws her down*

So! The surest way to charm a woman's tongue

Is break her neck: a politician did it.

15 SON	Mother, mother: I am killed, mother!	*Wife wakes*
[WIFE]	Ha, whose that cried? O me, my children!	
	Both, both, both: bloody, bloody!	*Catches up the youngest*
HUSBAND	Strumpet, let go the boy, let go the beggar.	
WIFE	O, my sweet husband!	
20 HUSBAND	Filth, harlot!	
WIFE	O, what will you do, dear husband?	
HUSBAND	Give me the bastard.	
WIFE	Your own sweet boy!	
HUSBAND	There are too many beggars.	
25 WIFE	Good my husband—	
HUSBAND	Dost thou prevent me still?	
WIFE	O God!	
HUSBAND	Have at his heart!	*Stabs at the child in her arms*
WIFE	O, my dear boy!	*Gets it from her*
30 HUSBAND	Brat, thou shalt not live to shame thy house!	
WIFE	O, heaven!	*She's hurt and sinks down*
HUSBAND	And perish! Now begone:	

There's whores enough and want would make thee one.

Enter a lusty Servant

1 SERVANT	O, sir, what deeds are these?
35 HUSBAND	Base slave, my vassal:

Com'st thou between my fury to question me?

1 SERVANT	Were you the devil, I would hold you, sir.
HUSBAND	Hold me? Presumption! I'll undo thee for't.
1 SERVANT	'Sblood, you have undone us all, sir.
40 HUSBAND	Tug at thy master?
1 SERVANT	Tug at a monster!
HUSBAND	Have I no power? Shall my slave fetter me?

---

5 **plays…son** gambles away the son's inheritance   *Strives* struggles   10 **sturdy quean** violent whore   *Throws her down* i.e. downstairs
14 **break…politician** a reference to the suspicious death of Amy Robsart, wife of Robert Dudley, Earl of Leicester, who died after falling downstairs in 1560. It was rumoured that he had ordered her death to leave the way open for him to marry Elizabeth I   **politician** schemer   23 **own sweet boy** i.e. legitimate son, not a bastard   28 **Have at** let me strike   33 **want** poverty; i.e. prostitution would be your only means of supporting yourself   *lusty* strong, courageous   35 **vassal** servant; in the feudal system one owing duty and allegiance   38 **undo** destroy   39 **'Sblood** by God's blood   42 **fetter** restrain

1 SERVANT   Nay, then, the devil wrestles, I am thrown.

HUSBAND   O, villain, now I'll tug thee,   *Overcomes him*

45   Now I'll tear thee:

Set quick spurs to my vassal, bruise him, trample him.   *Kicking him*

So! I think thou wilt not follow me in haste.

My horse stands ready saddled. Away, away:

Now to my brat at nurse, my sucking beggar.

50   Fates, I'll not leave you one to trample on.

The Master meets him

MASTER   How is't with you, sir? Methinks you look

Of a distracted colour.

HUSBAND   Who? I, sir? 'Tis but your fancy.

Please you walk in, sir, and I'll soon resolve you.

55   I want one small part to make up the sum

And then my brother shall rest satisfied.

MASTER   I shall be glad to see it: sir, I'll attend you.

Exeunt [Husband and Master]

1 SERVANT   O, I am scarce able to heave up myself:

He's so bruised me with his devilish weight

60   And torn my flesh with his blood-hasty spur.

A man before of easy constitution

Till now hell's power supplied to his soul's wrong.

O, how damnation can make weak men strong!

Enter Master and two servants

1 SERVANT   O, the most piteous deed, sir, since you came.

65   MASTER   A deadly greeting! Has he summed up these

To satisfy his brother? Here's another:

And by the bleeding infants, the dead mother.

WIFE   O, O!

MASTER   Surgeons, surgeons! She recovers life.

70   One of his men all faint and bloodied.

1 SERVANT   Follow, our murderous master has took horse

To kill his child at nurse: O, follow quickly.

MASTER   I am the readiest: it shall be my charge

To raise the town upon him.   *Exeunt Master and servants*

75   1 SERVANT   Good sir, do follow him.

WIFE   O, my children!

1 SERVANT   How is it with my most afflicted mistress?

WIFE   Why do I now recover? Why half live?

To see my children bleed before mine eyes?

80   A sight able to kill a mother's breast

Without an executioner! What, art thou

---

49 **at nurse** with the wet nurse   **sucking** unweaned   54 **walk in** suggesting that this takes place outside   **resolve** satisfy   55 **sum** i.e. of money owing   57 **attend** accompany/wait for   60 **blood-hasty** rash, bloodthirsty   61 **easy constitution** gentle nature   62 **hell's** hell has; another reference to his supposed demonic possession

Mangled too?

1 SERVANT   Ay, thinking to prevent what his quick mischiefs

Had so soon acted, came and rushed upon him.

85   We struggled, but a fouler strength than his

O'erthrew me with his arms: then did he bruise me

And rent my flesh, and robbed me of my hair,

Like a man mad in execution:

Made me unfit to rise and follow him.

90   WIFE   What is it has beguiled him of all grace

And stole away humanity from his breast,

To slay his children, purpose to kill his wife,

And spoil his servants?

Enter two Servants

BOTH SERVANTS   Please you leave this most accursèd place,

95   A surgeon waits within.

WIFE   Willing to leave it!

'Tis guilty of sweet blood, innocent blood:

Murder has took this chamber with full hands

And will ne'er out as long as the house stands.   *Exeunt*

[Scene 6]

Enter Husband as being thrown off his horse, and falls

HUSBAND   O stumbling jade, the spavin overtake thee,

The fifty diseases stop thee!

O, I am sorely bruised: plague founder thee:

Thou runn'st at ease and pleasure. Heart, of chance

5   To throw me now within a flight o'th'town,

In such plain even ground! 'Sfoot, a man

May dice up on't and throw away the meadows.

Filthy beast!   *Cry within, 'Follow, follow, follow!'*

Ha! I hear sounds of men, like hue and cry.

10   Up, up, and struggle to thy horse, make on:

Dispatch that little beggar and all's done.   [*Cry within,*]

At my back? O,   '*Here, this way, this way!'*

What fate have I? My limbs deny me go,

My will is bated; beggary claims a part.

15   O, could I here reach to the infant's heart!

---

83 **mischiefs** injuries   88 **execution** action/purpose/passion   92 **purpose** plan/try   93 **spoil** injure   98 **Murder...stands** Murder is here personified and imagined as having taken the room over, alluding to the belief that blood shed in such a way can never be eradicated   **[Scene 6]**   *Location: the highway near the Husband's ancestral home*   1 **jade** contemptuous name for a horse   **spavin** painful tumour in a horse's leg   2 **fifty diseases** a reference to Gervase Markham's, *The Fifty Diseases of a Horse*   3 **founder** make you lame   4 **Heart** God's heart!   6 **plain even** flat level; considered a bad omen to stumble on even ground   **'Sfoot** by God's foot!   7 **throw** gamble   9 **hue and cry** outcry following the pursuit of a felon   10 **make on** go forward/ hurry   11 **Dispatch** kill   **that little beggar** the nursling residing with the wet nurse   13 **deny** refuse to let   14 **bated** diminished, lessened   **claims a part** is partly responsible

Enter Master of the College, Three Gentlemen, and others with halberds [who] find him

ALL   Here, here: yonder, yonder!

MASTER   Unnatural, flinty, more than barbarous:

The Scythians in their marble-hearted feats

Could not have acted more remorseless deeds

20   In their relentless natures than these of thine.

Was this the answer I long waited on,

.The satisfaction for thy prisoned brother?

HUSBAND   Why, he can have no more on's than our skins,

And some of 'em want but flaying.

25   1 GENTLEMAN   Great sins have made him impudent.

MASTER   He's shed so much blood that he cannot blush.

2 GENTLEMAN   Away with him, bear him along to the Justices.

A gentleman of worship dwells at hand:

There shall his deeds be blazed.

30   HUSBAND   Why, all the better.

My glory 'tis to have my action known:

I grieve for nothing, but I missed of one.

MASTER   There's little of a father in that grief:

Bear him away.   *Exeunt*

[Scene 7]

Enter a Knight with two or three Gentlemen

KNIGHT   Endangered so his wife? Murdered his children?

5 GENTLEMAN   So the cry comes.

KNIGHT   I am sorry I e'er knew him,

That ever he took life and natural being

5   From such an honoured stock, and fair descent:

Till this black minute without stain or blemish.

5 GENTLEMAN   Here come the men.

Enter the Master of the College and the rest, with the [Husband as] prisoner

KNIGHT   The serpent of his house! I'm sorry

For this time that I am in place of justice.

10   MASTER   Please you, sir—

KNIGHT   Do not repeat it twice: I know too much.

Would it had ne'er been thought on:

Sir, I bleed for you.   *To Husband*

---

halberds military weapons, a cross between a spear and a battleaxe   **17 flinty** unfeeling, hard-hearted   **18 Scythians** ancient nomadic tribe noted for their cruelty; Tamburlaine was a Scythian   **21 long waited on** was kept waiting for so long   **23 he...skins** (proverbial)   **on's** of us   **24 flaying** stripping, peeling off (the skin)   **25 impudent** shameless   **28 worship** repute/standing   **29 blazed** made known   **32 of one** one of them, i.e. the baby   **[Scene 7]** *Location: the Knight's residence*   **2 cry comes** rumour proclaims it   **5 honoured stock** worthy family   **fair descent** noble lineage (who were)   **6 stain or blemish** moral blot or disgrace   **8 serpent** a symbol of malice with biblical connotations of the devil   **9 For...justice** that on this occasion I have to fulfil the office of justice (as the local magistrate)   **12 thought on** considered

5 GENTLEMAN   Your father's sorrows are alive in me:

15   What made you show such monstrous cruelty?

HUSBAND   In a word, sir, I have consumèd all,

Played away long-acre, and I thought it

The charitablest deed I could do,

To cozen beggary and knock my house o'th'head.

20   KNIGHT   O, in a cooler blood you will repent it.

HUSBAND   I repent now, that one's left unkilled,

My brat at nurse. O, I would full fain have weaned him.

KNIGHT   Well, I do not think but in tomorrow's judgement,

The terror will sit closer to your soul,

25   When the dread thought of death remembers you:

To further which, take this sad voice from me:

Never was act played more unnaturally.

HUSBAND   I thank you, sir.

KNIGHT   Go, lead him to the jail:

30   Where justice claims all, there must pity fail.

HUSBAND   Come, come, away with me.   *Exit prisoner*

MASTER   Sir, you deserve the worship of your place.

Would all did so: in you the law is grace.

KNIGHT   It is my wish it should be so. Ruinous man,

35   The desolation of his house, the blot

Upon his predecessors' honoured name:

That man is nearest shame that is past shame.   *Exeunt*

[Scene 8]

Enter Husband with the officers, the Master and Gentlemen, as going by his house

HUSBAND   I am right against my house, seat of my ancestors:

I hear my wife's alive: but much endangered.

Let me entreat to speak with her

Before the prison gripe me.

Enter his Wife, brought in a chair

5   5 GENTLEMAN   See: here she comes of herself.

WIFE   O, my sweet husband, my dear distressed husband,

Now in the hands of unrelenting laws!

My greatest sorrow, my extremest bleeding,

Now my soul bleeds.

10   HUSBAND   How now? Kind to me?

Did I not wound thee, left thee for dead?

---

14 father's sorrows i.e. the grief your father would have felt   17 long-acre one's estate or patrimony; literally the usual name for a long narrow field containing an acre   19 cozen cheat   knock…o'th'head put an end to my family line   22 full fain dearly liked to   25 remembers is called to mind   26 sad voice tragic opinion   32 deserve…place you are worthy of the honour of your position   37 nearest…past shame is most shameful who is unable to feel shame   [Scene 8] *Location: in front of the Husband's ancestral home*   1 seat place of residence   4 gripe seizes, takes possession of   chair i.e. an invalid chair   5 of herself of her own accord

WIFE   Tut, far greater wounds did my breast feel:
Unkindness strikes a deeper wound than steel:
You have been still unkind to me.

15   HUSBAND   Faith, and so I think I have:
I did my murders roughly, out of hand,
Desperate and sudden, but thou hast devised
A fine way now to kill me: thou hast given mine eyes
Seven wounds a-piece. Now glides the devil from me,

20   Departs at every joint, heaves up my nails.
O, catch him new torments, that were near invented,
Bind him one thousand more, you blessed angels,
In that pit bottomless: let him not rise
To make men act unnatural tragedies,

25   To spread into a father, and in fury,
Make him his children's executioners,
Murder his wife, his servants, and who not:
For that man's dark, where heaven is quite forgot.

WIFE   O, my repentant husband!

30   HUSBAND   My dear soul, whom I too much have wronged,
For death I die, and for this have I longed.

WIFE   Thou shouldst not, be assured, for these faults die
If the law could forgive as soon as I.

HUSBAND   What sight is yonder?   *Children laid out*

35   WIFE   O, our two bleeding boys
Laid forth upon the threshold.

HUSBAND   Here's weight enough to make a heart-string crack.
O, were it lawful that your pretty souls
Might look from heaven into your father's eyes,

40   Then should you see the penitent glasses melt
And both your murders shoot upon my cheeks:
But you are playing in the angels' laps
And will not look on me,
Who, void of grace, killed you in beggary.

45   O, that I might my wishes now attain,
I should then wish you living were again,
Though I did beg with you, which thing I feared,
O, 'twas the enemy my eyes so bleared.
O, would you could pray heaven me to forgive,

50   That will unto my end repentant live.

---

14 **still** continually   19 **Seven wounds** recalling the seven wounds Christ suffered during Holy Week (Matthew 26:67, John 18:22) as distinct from the five wounds on the Cross   **a-piece** each   **Now…me** suggesting that his demonic possession is over   20 **heaves** lifts   21 **near** recently   22 **one thousand more** would seem to refer to **torments** but may be a printer's error; in *The Collected Works of Thomas Middleton* (Oxford, 2007), it is suggested that '"more" may be an error for "year"', p. 465n   23 **pit bottomless** i.e. hell   24 **act** enact, perform   27 **who not** whoever else (compare 'what not')   *Children laid out* the dead sons are presumably brought on stage at this point   35 **bleeding** perhaps referring to the popular superstition that dead bodies bleed in the presence of their murderer   40 **glasses** eyes, literally mirrors into which you look and see yourselves   **melt** with his tears   41 **shoot upon** gush across   48 **enemy** devil   **bleared** blinded   50 **That…live** who will repent of what he has done as long as he lives

WIFE   It makes me e'en forget all other sorrows
        And leave part with this.

[OFFICER]   Come, will you go?

HUSBAND   I'll kiss the blood I spilt and then I go:

55   My soul is bloodied, well may my lips be so.
        Farewell, dear wife, now thou and I must part,
        I of thy wrongs repent me with my heart.

WIFE   O stay, thou shalt not go.

HUSBAND   That's but in vain, you see it must be so.

60   Farewell, ye bloody ashes of my boys!
        My punishments are their eternal joys.
        Let every father look into my deeds,
        And then their heirs may prosper, while mine bleeds.

WIFE   More wretched am I now in this distress,   *Exeunt Husband*

65   Than former sorrows made me.   *with Halberds*

MASTER   O kind wife,
        Be comforted. One joy is yet unmurderèd:
        You have a boy at nurse: your joy's in him.

WIFE   Dearer than all is my poor husband's life:

70   Heaven give my body strength, which yet is faint
        With much expense of blood, and I will kneel,
        Sue for his life, number up all my friends
        To plead for pardon for my dear husband's life.

MASTER   Was it in man to wound so kind a creature?

75   I'll ever praise a woman for thy sake.
        I must return with grief, my answer's set:
        I shall bring news weighs heavier than the debt.
        Two brothers: one in bond lies overthrown,
        This on a deadlier execution.   [*Exeunt*]

FINIS

52 leave part i.e. forget part of my own sorrows to share in yours   60 ashes remains   61 My…joys his earthly execution and the pains he will endure in hell for his deeds are the same events that will ensure his sons' eternal bliss in heaven   *Halberds* officers armed with halberds   75 woman womankind/the Virgin Mary   76 set imposed (by law)   77 weighs…debt more serious than the debt (for which his brother has been imprisoned) 78 in…overthrown is ruined by being imprisoned   79 This…execution whereas this one must undergo capital punishment; Walter Calverley refused to enter a plea and was pressed to death on 5 August. If a defendant refused to plead the trial could not proceed but it meant that his remaining son would inherit his estate   execution arrest for debt/capital punishment

Textual Notes

Q = Quarto text of 1608

Ed = a correction introduced by a later editor

SD = stage direction

SH = speech heading (i.e. speaker's name)

List of parts = Ed

1.17 SH RALPH *and* **OLIVER** = Ed. Q = *Am. (Latin 'Ambo' meaning both)*   **21 ballads** *spelled* ballats *in* Q   **62 SH SAM** = Ed. Q = *Am.*

2.45 upo'th'soil = Ed. Q = vppot'h foole   **68 seized** = Ed. Q = ceald   **113 Good e'en** *spelled* God den *in* Q   **127 follies** = Ed. Q = follie   **160 SH [HUSBAND]** = Ed. Q = *Gent.*   **165 would** = Ed. Q = woult   **182 her and your** = Ed. Q = her your

4.28 SH [2 SERVANT] = Ed., *Not in Q*   **81 couch** = Q. Ed. = crouch

5.50 on = Ed. Q = one

6 SD [*Cry within,*] = Ed. Q = *Kni. (mistakenly assigning the line to a Knight who is not onstage)*   **18 feats** = Ed. Q = fates   **24 flaying** = Ed. Q = fleaing

8.53 SH [OFFICER] = Ed. *Not in Q*

MUCEDORUS

Mucedorus was the most popular drama of the age. It was reprinted almost twice as often as any other play (joint runners-up in this regard were *Henry IV Part 1*, *Richard III* and *The Spanish Tragedy*). Here, then, is a snapshot of theatrical taste in Shakespeare's time. Among the play's features are a prince disguised as a shepherd, a beautiful princess who challenges her father's will, a hapless but lovable clown, adventures and mistakings in a pastoral world including an encounter with a wild man of the woods, the stage direction '*pursued with a bear*', and a festive mood in which, despite some very dark moments, there is always the expectation, duly fulfilled, that all will end well.

Originally produced in the 1590s, it was revived by Shakespeare's acting company and played before King James I in his palace at Whitehall during the Shrovetide (eve of Lent) festivities in 1610 or 1611. That is precisely the time when Shakespeare himself was writing such plays as *The Winter's Tale*, which shares most of the features just noted, and *The Tempest*, which has its own wild man named Caliban. Like these plays, *Mucedorus* was formally classified as a 'comedy', but they are works best understood as stage-offshoots of the literary tradition of 'romance', in which extraordinary events, heroic deeds and amorous pursuits are played out in an exotic setting remote from the everyday world of the reader or the spectator.

Sir Philip Sidney's *Arcadia*, published in 1590, was the most famous Elizabethan example in prose, Edmund Spenser's *The Faerie Queene* (1590–96) in verse, while in the late 1580s the dramatist Robert Greene turned out a succession of very popular (and less long-winded) romances with such titles as *Pandosto* and *Menaphon*. In the *Arcadia* the prince disguised as a shepherd (who rescues his beloved from danger) is called Musidorus, so early spectators of a play with that name might have expected it to dramatize a particular incident in Sidney, which it does not. Its world and its tone are, however, shaped by the *Arcadia*. In the case of Shakespeare's *Winter's Tale*, the play actually is a dramatization of Greene's *Pandosto* (with some vital changes), which was republished in 1607 just as the London acting companies were taking fresh interest in stage romance. The revised *Mucedorus* and the turn to romance in late Shakespeare should be seen in the context of this revival.

The play is full of details that will remind the reader of Shakespeare's pastoral world. There is banter like that between Jaques and Corin in *As You Like It*:

> **MESSENGER** All hail, worthy shepherd.
> **MOUSE** All rain, lousy shepherd.

There is a lovely mix of lyricism, comedy and grotesquerie when Bremo the Wild Man is tamed by Amadine's beauty and offers to feed her with quails and partridges, blackbirds, larks, thrushes and nightingales, give her goat's milk and spring water, as she is attended by satyrs and wood-nymphs and invited to walk on violets, cowslips and sweet marigolds, every bit in the manner of the treats that fairy queen Titania proposes for Bottom the ass in *A Midsummer Night's Dream*. And, as in so many of Shakespeare's comedies, there are layers of disguise and revelation: the hermit's disguise is removed to reveal the shepherd and then the shepherd's to reveal the prince.

Our edition follows the 1610 text, which incorporates the King's Men revisions. This also has a new Prologue addressed to King James I and an updated version of the actors' doubling chart that had prefaced the original edition. The latter gives a rare glimpse into both the typecasting and the versatility of the players in Shakespeare's company. Thus one of the adult actors would have been tasked to bring what was known as a choleric (angry) humour to the three aggressive parts of Envy in the Induction, Tremelio the soldier and Bremo the wild man. One of the boy-actors, by contrast, would have had to shift from Comedy in the Induction to a boy, an old woman and a maid. The four lead players, meanwhile, would have stuck to single roles: the hero Mucedorus (presumably Burbage), Mouse (almost certainly the company clown Robert Armin), Segasto the anti-hero (perhaps Henry Condell), and Amadine the heroine (the company's best boy).

The Induction is one of those characteristic Elizabethan-Jacobean pieces of 'meta-theatre' or dramatic self-reflection in which Comedy vies with Tragedy, the latter in the guise of 'Envy' (which could mean malignancy, enmity and the desire to spoil). The debate readies the audience for those moments of violence and potential tragedy that will occur within the comedy.

In the King's Men's version of the play, the action itself begins with the parting of courtly friends, the donning of disguise and the hero setting off on a quest. Then we enter a pastoral but by no means idyllic world. As in Shakespeare's *Winter's Tale*, the shift of location from court to country is indicated by a clown and a bear-chase:

> *Enter Mouse with a bottle of hay*
>
> MOUSE   O, horrible, terrible! Was ever poor gentleman so scared out of
> his seven senses? A bear? Nay, sure it cannot be a bear, but some devil
> in a bear's doublet: for a bear could never have had that agility to have
> frighted me. ... But soft: this way she followed me, therefore I'll take the
> other path and because I'll be sure to have an eye on her, I will take
> hands with some foolish creditor and make every step backward.
>
> > *As he goes backwards, the bear comes in, and he tumbles over her,*
> > *and runs away, and leaves his bottle of hay behind him*
> *Enter Segasto running and Amadine after him, being pursued with a bear*

This double-bear business nicely captures the duality of comedy and tragedy: Clown trips over Bear is Comedy, whereas Heroine pursued and potentially eaten by Bear is Tragedy, though with a further comic twist in that a Cowardly Knight is running away even faster than the damsel in distress. The conventional romance trope of Hero killing Monstrous Beast and thus winning the heart of Heroine will come a moment later.

But the business must have been difficult to stage. Its complexity is the consequence of the King's Men's alterations: the original play *began* (after the Induction) with the stage direction '*Enter Segasto running and Amadine after him, being pursued with a bear*'. Mouse, his bottle of hay and the trip over the bear are new bits of comedy introduced by the King's Men. Theatre manager Philip Henslowe had a bear costume in his wardrobe at the Rose and there can be little doubt that the original staging of *Mucedorus* featured an actor 'in a bear's doublet'. It is made clear from some later lines of Mouse, which appear in both editions, that this is a *white* bear. White bears were signifiers of romance as opposed to realism: Aragon and Valencia in Spain, where the play is set, are not notable for snow-covered landscapes of the kind where real white bears roam. In another romance play of the early 1590s, George Peele's *Old Wives' Tale*, there is a reference to a mythical 'White Bear of

England'. While brown bears were familiar from baitings and menageries, white ones were more like legendary creatures of the imagination.

Given this, it would have been an amazing theatrical coup – inspiring in the audience simultaneous wonder and mirth, the two emotions that the play keeps seeking to conjure up – if in the King's Men's revision of the play Mouse were to have tripped over a real white bear. Henslowe, who ran the Bear Garden in Southwark as well as the Rose Theatre, had obtained the royal office of Master of the Bulls, Bears, and Mastiff Dogs. In 1609, he was entrusted with the care of two polar bear cubs that had been captured in the Arctic and presented to King James. On New Year's Day 1611, Ben Jonson's masque entitled *Oberon, the Fairy Prince* was performed at court. This included a triumphal entry for the king's son, Prince Henry, who played the lead role: *'at the further end of all, OBERON, in a chariot, which, to a loud triumphant music, began to move forward, drawn by two white bears, and on either side guarded by three Sylvans, with one going in front'*. It is almost certain that those two closely-guarded white creatures are the young polar bears. Could one of them also have been borrowed by the King's Men for *Mucedorus*, perhaps held under restraint in the 'discovery space' at the back of the stage? Theatre historians debate as to whether or not Mouse's bear was real. One possible solution to the problem created by the jamming together of old and new stage directions in the revised text would have been for Mouse to tumble over the real polar bear in the discovery space, the curtains to close and an actor 'in a bear's doublet' to pursue Segasto and Amadine across the stage.

The contrast between Segasto the cowardly gentleman and Mucedorus the brave shepherd calls class prejudices into question. Noble behaviour was expected of the nobly born. One of the key differences between the original text and the King's Men's revision is the new opening scene, in which Mucedorus dons his disguise. In the original, no one else in the play knows that he is really a prince and not a shepherd. Not even the theatre audience knows, unless they guess the fact from his name, with its allusion to the disguised prince in Sidney's famous *Arcadia*. The King's Men's version is, in a sense, more politically orthodox: no one here is allowed to imagine that a princess might *really* marry a shepherd. *The Winter's Tale*, of course, goes even further in this direction: there, the audience knows that neither Florizel nor Perdita is of common blood.

A word of warning is required with regard to the text printed here. We have worked from the edition of 1610 because that is the version that reflects the additions introduced by Shakespeare's company. The printers must have had manuscript copy for the additions, but for the original form of the play they relied on the 1606 edition, which had itself introduced some minor changes (including a new Epilogue, reflecting the fact that there was now a king on the throne). Some of the 1606 changes are probably printing errors, but the compositors of the 1610 edition would not have known that they were mistakes. So, for example, at the threatening moment when Amadine refuses to return Bremo's love, he says:

> See how she flings away from me!
> I will follow and give attend to her:
> Deny my love! Ah, worm of beauty,
> I will chastise thee. Come, come!
> Prepare thy head upon the block.

'Attend to her' could mean 'deal with her', so this makes sense but it is weaker than the original text's 'give a rend to her'. 'Rend' as a noun was a new and rare word meaning tear, split or rupture – here powerfully suggestive of rape – which the 1606 printer failed to recognize. 'Give a rend' should probably be restored in performance, though in our text we have respected the integrity of the 1610 edition.

We do not know how many authors were involved in revising the play for its King's Men's revival. Several different tasks were necessary. We can well imagine the new Prologue for the king being entrusted to Ben Jonson, expert in the poetry of praise (lines such as 'For from your beams Europe shall borrow light' bear his stamp). The enhancement of Mouse's role could have been left to Robert Armin, the company clown, who was also writing plays of his own by this time. But what about the new scenes set in Mucedorus' home court of Valencia? Scene 10 in particular is clearly a rewrite of the opening of *Twelfth Night*:

> Enough of music, it but adds to torment:
> Delights to vexèd spirits are as dates
> Set to a sickly man, which rather cloy than comfort.
> Let me entreat you to entreat no more.

More than one phrase in the scene is unique to Shakespeare – 'worthless trunk' (*Henry V*), 'high extolment' (*Hamlet*) – while many others are typical of him: 'former dolours', 'young-fed humour / Nursed within the brain', 'Makes my tongue blab what my breast vowed, concealment'. Either this scene is Shakespeare or it is someone else – Armin, perhaps, or Jonson or Fletcher – writing as if they were Shakespeare.

KEY FACTS

AUTHORSHIP: No author has been convincingly proposed for the original version of *Mucedorus*. It has been associated with Robert Greene, writer of other romances of the mid-1580s, but this is little more than conjectural. More interest has been paid to the Additions first printed in 1610. While these are too short for confident analysis, MacDonald Jackson has argued that they are by Shakespeare, in preparation for a court revival, which would be in keeping with his presumed responsibilities as resident dramatist for the King's Men.

PLOT: In an Induction, Comedy and Envy battle for supremacy over the stage. In their play, Mucedorus, Prince of Valencia, disguises himself as a shepherd and travels to Aragon in order to woo the Princess Amadine. He kills a bear that is pursuing her and her cowardly suitor Segasto, and is honoured at the King of Aragon's court. Segasto entertains a comic servant, Mouse, and plots to have Mucedorus murdered, but after Mucedorus kills the assassin, Segasto procures his banishment. Amadine flees with Mucedorus to the woods, but they are separated and Amadine is captured by Bremo, a wild and cannibalistic wood-dweller, who takes her to be his queen. Mucedorus, now disguised as a hermit, talks his way into Bremo's favour, then tricks him into handing over his weapon, with which he dispatches the wild man. Mucedorus reveals his true identity, Segasto gives up his claim to Amadine, and the Kings of Aragon and Valencia bless the marriage. Comedy claims victory before the monarch.

▷

MAJOR PARTS: Mucedorus (23%/97/9), Mouse (15%/133/11), Segasto (13%/105/9), Amadine (13%/79/8), Bremo (10%/38/4), King Androstus (7%/30/3), Comedy (6%/12/2), Envy (5%/12/2), Anselmo (2%/12/3), King of Valencia (2%/7/2), Collin (1%/6/2), Tremelio (1%/5/2).

LINGUISTIC MEDIUM: 76% verse, 24% prose.

DATE: Although the play was not published until 1598, *Mucedorus* is usually dated to the late 1580s or early 1590s, when romance was a dominant genre, and possibly followed the publication of Philip Sidney's *Arcadia* in 1590, leading this edition to propose a date of 1590–1. There is evidence of a revival early in King James' reign, as the 1606 edition adjusts the gender of the monarch addressed in the epilogue. New Additions were added in 1610, most likely for another revival, and it has been conjectured that it may have been performed alongside *The Winter's Tale* to take advantage of the availability of a real polar bear cub. Performances of the play continued throughout the seventeenth century, including at Witney in Oxfordshire in 1652, a performance which ended in the collapse of the venue.

SOURCES: The primary source is Sidney's *Arcadia*, which had been circulating for some years before its 1590 publication, although this provides only a bare outline for the play. It draws on a number of stock romance motifs – the magical forest, the wild man, the disguised prince, the comic squire – and, to the disdain of many modern critics, panders to a popular audience with its nostalgic pastoral atmosphere and sensational sequences. The popularity of the play in print following 1610 is perhaps indicative of the play's influence on later tragicomic romance, including Shakespeare's final plays.

TEXT: *Mucedorus* is the most printed of all early modern plays, appearing in seventeen known editions between 1598 and 1668. Minor changes were made to the Second Quarto of 1606 to reflect the change in monarch, and an enlarged version with several additional passages was published in 1610. **This edition breaks new ground in printing the additional passages in a different typeface,** allowing readers to see at a glance the differences between the old version and the new. Most of the changes are designed to stress Mucedorus' real identity as a prince – in the original version, there is no explicit indication of his true rank until the play's final scene. The text is usually considered to derive from theatrical performance and, unusually, includes a doubling chart, which may suggest that it was deliberately encouraging amateur performances.

A MOST PLEASANT COMEDY OF MUCEDORUS THE KING'S SON OF VALENCIA, AND AMADINE, THE KING'S DAUGHTER OF ARAGON, WITH THE MERRY CONCEITS OF MOUSE.

Amplified with new additions, as it was acted before the King's Majesty at Whitehall on Shrove-Sunday night by his Highness' Servants usually playing at the Globe: very delectable and full of conceited mirth

COMEDY

ENVY

King of VALENCIA

MUCEDORUS, Prince of Valencia, his son

ANSELMO, friend to Mucedorus

RODRIGO, a nobleman of Valencia

Androstus, KING of Aragon

AMADINE, his daughter

SEGASTO, a nobleman, her betrothed

RUMBELO, his servant

TREMELIO, a Captain in Androstus' army

COLLIN, a Counsellor of Androstus

Prince

Barachius

MOUSE, a Clown, later Segasto's man

BREMO, a wild man

MESSENGER

ARIENA, Amadine's maid

Boy

OLD WOMAN, Mother Nip

Bear

The Prologue

> Most sacred majesty, whose great deserts
> Thy subject England, nay, the world admires,
> Which heaven grant still increase: O may your praise,
> Multiplying with your hours, your fame still raise,

MUCEDORUS the name of the play's eponymous hero was most probably inspired by Musidorus, one of the heroes of Sir Philip Sidney's pastoral romance, *The Countess of Pembroke's Arcadia*, who also disguised himself as a shepherd and rescued his beloved   VALENCIA province of south-eastern Spain, then a separate kingdom   ARAGON province of north-eastern Spain, also a separate kingdom   new additions refers to the six additional passages that first appear in the third quarto of 1610   King's Majesty i.e. James I of England (who was also James VI of Scotland)   Whitehall the Palace of Whitehall was the principal London residence of English monarchs from 1530 to 1698   Shrove-Sunday the Sunday of Shrovetide, i.e. the period immediately preceding Lent in the Christian calendar   his Highness' servants the King's Men, the theatrical company to which Shakespeare belonged   Globe the Globe theatre on the south bank of the River Thames had been built by the Lord Chamberlain's Men (who later became the King's Men) in 1599; after 1608 the company also used the indoor Blackfriars theatre   conceited clever, ingenious   The Prologue which is addressed to the king was written for performance before King James I and was added in the 1610 Quarto

5 Embrace your Council, love with faith them guide
That both, as one bench by each other's side,
So may your life pass on and run so even
That your firm zeal plant you a throne in heaven,
Where smiling angels shall your guardians be
10 From blemished traitors stained with perjury.
And, as the night's inferior to the day,
So be all earthly regions to your sway:
Be as the sun to day, the day to night,
For from your beams Europe shall borrow light:
15 Mirth drown your bosom, fair delight your mind
And may our pastime your contentment find.   *Exit*

Ten persons may easily play it

The King and Rumbelo	}	for one
King Valencia	}	for one
Mucedorus the Prince of Valencia	}	for one
Anselmo	}	for one
Amadine, the king's daughter of Aragon	}	for one
Segasto, a nobleman	}	for one
Envy, Tremelio a Captain, Bremo a wild man	}	for one
Comedy, a Boy, an old Woman, Ariena, Amadine's maid	}	for one
Collin a Counsellor, a Messenger	}	for one
Mouse the Clown	}	for one

A most pleasant Comedy of Mucedorus, the King's son of Valencia, and Amadine, the King's daughter of Aragon

[Induction]

Enter Comedy joyfully with a garland of bays on her head

COMEDY   Why so? Thus do I hope to please!
Music revives and mirth is tolerable:
Comedy, play thy part and please,

---

10 blemished traitors a reference to those who carried out the Gunpowder Plot which attempted to blow up the Houses of Parliament and assassinate King James in 1605   **13 sun** a traditional emblem of royalty   **15 drown** fill, overwhelm   **16 pastime** amusement, entertainment   **Ten...it** giving the possibilities for doubling roles, ten actors can perform the play   **[Induction]** a common dramatic device in Elizabethan plays, an introductory passage which frames the play and sets out the main subject   **Comedy** a feminine personification of the abstract quality   **garland of bays** laurel wreath, traditionally awarded as a token of victory or sign of excellence in poetry   **1 Why so?** Why do I appear before you in this way?

Make merry them that comes to joy with thee:

5   Joy then, good gentles, I hope to make you laugh.

Sound forth Bellona's silver tunèd strings.

Time fits us well, the day and place is ours.

Enter Envy, his arms naked, besmeared with blood

ENVY   Nay stay, minion, there lies a block:

What all on mirth? I'll interrupt your tale

10   And mix your music with a tragic end.

COMEDY   What monstrous ugly hag is this,

That dares control the pleasures of our will?

Vaunt, churlish cur, besmeared with gory blood

That seem'st to check the blossom of delight

15   And stiff the sound of sweet Bellona's breath.

Blush, monster, blush, and post away with shame,

That seek'st disturbance of a goddess' deeds.

ENVY   Post hence thyself, thou counterchecking trull,

I will possess this habit spite of thee

20   And gain the glory of thy wishèd port.

I'll thunder music shall appal the nymphs

And make them shiver their clattering strings,

Flying for succour to their dankish caves.

                          Sound drums within and cry, 'Stab, stab!'

Hearken, thou shalt hear a noise

25   Shall fill the air with a shrilling sound,

And thunder music to the gods above:

Mars shall himself breathe down

A peerless crown upon brave Envy's head,

And raise his chival with a lasting fame.

30   In this brave music Envy takes delight,

Where I may see them wallow in their blood

To spurn at arms and legs quite shivered off,

And hear the cries of many thousand slain.

How lik'st thou this, my trull? This sport alone for me.

35   COMEDY   Vaunt, bloody cur, nursed up with tiger's sap,

That so dost seek to quail a woman's mind.

Comedy is mild, gentle, willing for to please

And seeks to gain the love of all estates,

---

5 gentles ladies and gentlemen; a flattering form of address to the audience   **6 Bellona's…strings** Bellona was the Roman goddess of war and is associated with the trumpet rather than stringed instruments; the poet seems to be confusing her with a more benign goddess, perhaps one of the Muses   *Envy* personified as masculine   **8 minion** servile hanger-on   **block** blockhead, a stupid, senseless person   **13 Vaunt** boast, be proud, vainglorious   **churlish** vulgar, common/surly, niggardly   **cur** ill-bred, cowardly fellow, literally 'dog'   **gory** bloody, clotted with blood   **16 post** hurry   **18 counterchecking** taunting/rebuking as an expression of opposition/preventing by counteracting   **trull** term of abuse applied to a female, trollop   **19 habit** habitation, abode/ behaviour, bearing   **20 port** harbour, refuge/destination/bearing, behaviour/rank, status   **21 appal** dismay, shock, terrify, literally 'make pale'   **nymphs** semi-divine female spirits of classical mythology associated with natural features such as rivers, mountains, woods, trees and the sea   **22 shiver** break, shatter   **clattering** rattling, babbling   **strings** stringed musical instruments   **23 succour** shelter, protection   **dankish** unpleasantly wet, damp   **24 Hearken** attend, listen   **25 Shall** that will   **27 Mars** Roman god of war   **29 chival** horse   **30 brave** fine, excellent   **32 spurn** kick   **shivered** broken, splintered   **34 trull** trollop   **35 sap** juice or fluid of any kind, hence 'milk' or 'blood'   **36 quail** daunt, intimidate/destroy   **38 estates** sorts of people, i.e. in terms of status, rank, dignity

Delighting in mirth, mixed all with lovely tales,
40 And bringeth things with treble joy to pass.
Thou, bloody, envious disdainer of men's joys,
Whose name is fraught with bloody stratagems,
Delights in nothing but in spoil and death,
Where thou mayst trample in their lukewarm blood
45 And grasp their hearts within thy cursèd paws.
Yet vail thy mind, revenge thou not on me;
A silly woman begs it at thy hands,
Give me the leave to utter out my play,
Forbear this place, I humbly crave thee hence,
50 And mix not death 'mongst pleasing comedies,
That treats nought else but pleasure and delight.
If any spark of human rests in thee,
Forbear, begone, tender the suit of me.

ENVY   Why, so I will: forbearance shall be such
55 As treble death shall cross thee with despite
And make thee mourn where most thou joyest,
Turning thy mirth into a deadly dole,
Whirling thy pleasures with a peal of death,
And drench thy methods in a sea of blood.
60 This will I do! Thus shall I bear with thee,
And more, to vex thee with a deeper spite,
I will with threats of blood begin thy play,
Favouring thee with envy and with hate.

COMEDY   Then, ugly monster, do thy worst!
65 I will defend them in despite of thee
And though thou think'st with tragic fumes
To brave my play unto my deep disgrace,
I force it not: I scorn what thou canst do.
I'll grace it so, thyself shall it confess
70 From tragic stuff to be a pleasant comedy.

ENVY   Why then, Comedy, send thy actors forth
And I will cross the first steps of their trade:
Making them fear the very dart of death.

COMEDY   And I'll defend them maugre all thy spite
75 So, ugly fiend, farewell, till time shall serve
That we may meet to parley for the best.

ENVY   Content, Comedy, I'll go spread my branch,
And scattered blossoms from mine envious tree
Shall prove two monsters, spoiling of their joys.   *Exeunt*

---

39 **lovely** beautiful/amorous   41 **disdainer** scorner, despiser   42 **fraught** filled   46 **vail** humble, submit   47 **silly** defenceless   48 **Give…leave** allow   49 **Forbear** avoid, keep away from   51 **nought** nothing   53 **tender the suit** accede to the request   57 **dole** portion   59 **methods** designs, plans/procedures/arrangement of ideas   67 **brave** challenge, threaten/adorn   72 **cross** thwart   74 **maugre** in spite of, notwithstanding   76 **parley** discuss terms   79 **prove** turn out to be

[Scene 1]

Sound. Enter Mucedorus and Anselmo, his friend

MUCEDORUS Anselmo?

ANSELMO   My lord and friend.

MUCEDORUS True, my Anselmo, both thy lord and friend,
    Whose dear affections bosom with my heart

5   And keep their domination in one orb.

ANSELMO   Whence ne'er disloyalty shall root it forth,
    But faith plant firmer in your choice respect.

MUCEDORUS Much blame were mine if I should other deem,
    Nor can coy fortune contrary allow.

10   But, my Anselmo, loath I am to say,
    I must estrange that friendship —
    Misconster not, 'tis from the realm, not thee:
    Though lands part bodies, hearts keep company.
    Thou know'st that I imparted often have

15   Private relations with my royal sire,
    Had as concerning beauteous Amadine,
    Rich Aragon's bright jewel, whose face — some say —
    That blooming lilies never shone so gay,
    Excelling not excelled: yet lest report

20   Does mangle verity, boasting of what is not,
    Winged with desire, thither I'll straight repair,
    And be my fortunes as my thoughts are, fair.

ANSELMO   Will you forsake Valencia, leave the court,
    Absent you from the eye of sovereignty?

25   Do not, sweet prince, adventure on that task,
    Since danger lurks each-where: be won from it.

MUCEDORUS Desist dissuasion:
    My resolution brooks no battery,
    Therefore, if thou retain thy wonted form,

30   Assist what I intend.

ANSELMO   Your miss will breed a blemish in the court,
    And throw a frosty dew upon that beard
    Whose front Valencia stoops to.

MUCEDORUS If thou my welfare tender, then, no more!

35   Let love's strong magic charm thy trivial phrase,
    Wasted as vainly as to gripe the sun.
    Augment not then more answers: lock thy lips,

[Scene 1] *Location: Valencia* **12 Misconster not** do not misconstrue it/misunderstand **15 relations** discussions **royal sire** i.e. his father, the king **17 face...excelled** the beauty of her face, according to some, was greater than lilies in flower which were less lovely **19 lest** in case **21 thither** i.e. to Aragon **repair** go **26 each-where** everywhere **won from it** prevailed upon not to go **28 brooks** tolerates **battery** assault, attempt on it **29 wonted** customary **form** nature, character **31 miss** absence, loss **32 throw...dew** i.e. will turn the hair grey **33 front** forehead, face **Valencia stoops to** i.e. the ruler of Valencia, whose people lower their heads as a sign of respect in the king's presence **34 tender** value, hold dear **36 Wasted...sun** as useless as trying to catch hold of the sun **gripe** catch hold of/come close to

Unless thy wisdom suit me with disguise
According to my purpose.

40 ANSELMO   That action craves no counsel,
Since what you rightly are will more command
Than best usurpèd shape.

MUCEDORUS   Thou still art opposite in disposition,
A more obscure, servile habiliment
45 Beseems this enterprise.

ANSELMO   Then like a Florentine or mountebank?

MUCEDORUS   'Tis much too tedious, I dislike thy judgement,
My mind is grafted on an humbler stock.

ANSELMO   Within my closet does there hang a cassock,
50 Though base the weed is: 'twas a shepherd's
Which I presented in Lord Julio's masque.

MUCEDORUS   That, my Anselmo, and none else but that
Mask Mucedorus from the vulgar view.
That habit suits my mind: fetch me that weed.   *Exit Anselmo*
55 Better than kings have not disdained that state,
And much inferior to obtain their mate.

Enter Anselmo with a shepherd's coat

So, let our respect command thy secrecy:
At once a brief farewell,
Delay to lovers is a second hell.   *Exit Mucedorus*

60 ANSELMO   Prosperity forerun thee, awkward chance
Never be neighbour to thy wish's venture:
Content and fame advance thee, ever thrive
And glory thy mortality survive.   *Exit [Anselmo]*

[Scene 2]

Enter Mouse with a bottle of hay

MOUSE   O, horrible, terrible! Was ever poor gentleman so scared out of his seven
senses? A bear? Nay, sure it cannot be a bear, but some devil in a bear's doublet:
for a bear could never have had that agility to have frighted me. Well, I'll see my
father hanged before I'll serve his horse any more. Well, I'll carry home my bottle of
5 hay, and for once make my father's horse turn puritan and observe fasting days, for

38 suit me with is agreeable to/provides me with suitable clothing   **41 rightly** truly, in reality   **42 best usurpèd shape** the most brilliant disguise
43 opposite in disposition taking the opposite view to what I've planned   **44 habiliment** outfit   **45 Beseems** is appropriate to   **46 Florentine** a native
of Florence, then an Italian city-state   **mountebank** itinerant charlatan   **48 grafted…stock** fixed on a lower social group, playing on the horticultural
sense of creating a new plant by grafting, i.e. inserting a shoot from one tree (**stock**) into another   **49 cassock** loose coat or gown worn by rustics,
shepherds and sailors among others   **50 base** lowly   **weed** garment   **51 masque** courtly dramatic entertainment   **52 none** nothing   **53 Mask** shall
mask or disguise   **vulgar** common, of the crowd   **54 habit** garment, outfit/outward appearance/mental disposition   **57 respect** relationship   **[Scene
2]   *Location: Aragon*   *Mouse*** the name of a small rodent or a quiet retiring person, which does not describe this character, however the term also refers
to 'any of various parts of meat rich in muscle tissue' which is perhaps what is hinted at in the name since the character is obsessed with food   ***bottle***
bundle   **1 seven senses** the usual five – sight, taste, touch, smell and hearing – plus vitality and feeling   **2 doublet** suit   **5 puritan** member of a strict
Christian religious sect   **fasting days** days in the religious calendar when meat was not supposed to be consumed

he gets not a bit. But soft: this way she followed me, therefore I'll take the other path and because I'll be sure to have an eye on her, I will take hands with some foolish creditor and make every step backward.

> *As he goes backwards, the bear comes in, and he tumbles over her, and runs away, and leaves his bottle of hay behind him*

Enter Segasto running and Amadine after him, being pursued with a bear

SEGASTO   O, fly, madam, fly or else we are but dead.

10   AMADINE   Help, Segasto, help! Help, sweet Segasto, or else I die!

SEGASTO   Alas, madam, there is no way but flight,

Then haste and save yourself.   *Segasto runs away*

AMADINE   Why then I die. Ah, help me in distress!

Enter Mucedorus like a shepherd with a sword drawn and a bear's head in his hand

MUCEDORUS Stay, lady, stay, and be no more dismayed.

15   That cruel beast most merciless and fell,

Which have bereaved thousands of their lives,

Affrighted many with his hard pursues,

Prying from place to place to find his prey,

Prolonging thus his life by others' death,

20   His carcass now lies headless, void of breath.

AMADINE   That foul deformèd monster, is he dead?

MUCEDORUS Assure yourself thereof, behold his head:

Which if it please you, lady, to accept,

With willing heart I yield it to your majesty.

25   AMADINE   Thanks, worthy shepherd, thanks a thousand times

This gift assure thyself contents me more,

Than greatest bounty of a mighty prince,

Although he were the monarch of the world.

MUCEDORUS Most gracious goddess, more than mortal wight —

30   Your heavenly hue of right imports no less —

Most glad am I, in that it was my chance

To undertake this enterprise in hand,

Which doth so greatly glad your princely mind.

AMADINE   No goddess, shepherd, but a mortal wight —

35   A mortal wight distressèd as thou see'st.

My father here is king of Aragon:

I, Amadine, his only daughter am

And after him sole heir unto the crown.

Now whereas it is my father's will

40   To marry me unto Segasto,

---

8 **backward** unfavourably, in a lowly manner; in the Italian *commedia dell'arte* it was a traditional *lazzo* or comic turn for the Clown to enter backwards **bear** it has been suggested that this may have been a real (young) polar bear; the stage direction reminds us of Shakespeare's famous exit line in *The Winter's Tale* which it probably inspired 9 **but** as good as 15 **fell** fierce, savage 17 **hard** harsh/determined/difficult to deal with **pursues** pursuits/attacks 18 **Prying** searching 27 **bounty** gift bestowed by a sovereign/gracious liberality, munificence 29 **mortal wight** human being 30 **Your...less** truly the ethereal quality of your colour can mean nothing less (than that you are a goddess) 33 **glad** gladden, please

On whose wealth through father's former usury
Is known to be no less than wonderful.
We both of custom oftentimes did use —
Leaving the court — to walk within the fields
45 For recreation especially the spring,
In that it yields great store of rare delights,
And passing further than our wonted walks,
Scarce entered were within these luckless woods,
But right before us down a steep-fall hill
50 A monstrous ugly bear did hie him fast
To meet us both — I faint to tell the rest,
Good shepherd, but suppose the ghastly looks,
The hideous fears, the thousand hundred woes,
Which at this instant Amadine sustained.

55 MUCEDORUS   Yet, worthy princess, let thy sorrow cease,
And let this sight your former joys revive.

AMADINE   Believe me, shepherd, so it doth no less.

MUCEDORUS   Long may they last unto your heart's content.
But tell me, lady what is become of him,
60 Segasto called, what is become of him?

AMADINE   I know not, I: that know the powers divine:
But God grant this, that sweet Segasto live.

MUCEDORUS   Yet hard-hearted he in such a case,
So cowardly to save himself by flight
65 And leave so brave a princess to the spoil.

A MADINE   Well, shepherd, for thy worthy valour tried,
Endangering thyself to set me free,
Unrecompensed sure thou shalt not be.
In court thy courage shall be plainly known:
70 Throughout the kingdom will I spread thy name,
To thy renown and never-dying fame:
And that thy courage may be better known,
Bear thou the head of this most monstrous beast
In open sight to every courtier's view:
75 So will the king my father thee reward.
Come let's away, and guard me to the court.

MUCEDORUS   With all my heart!   *Exeunt*

Enter Segasto solus

SEGASTO   When heaps of harms do hover overhead,
'Tis time as then, some say, to look about
80 And of ensuing harms to choose the least:
But hard, yea hapless, is that wretch's chance,

41 through…usury gained by his father's former money-lending activities; the taking of interest on loans was against Christian teaching although in practice Elizabethan commerce could not function without it   43 did use were in the habit of   47 wonted customary   49 steep-fall steep   50 hie strive, exert himself/hasten   52 suppose imagine   ghastly horrible, frightening   72 that in order that   *solus* 'alone' (Latin)

Luckless his lot and caitiff-like accursed,
At whose proceedings Fortune ever frowns:
Myself I mean, most subject unto thrall,
85 For I, the more I seek to shun the worst,
The more by proof I find myself accursed.
Erewhiles assaulted with an ugly bear —
Fair Amadine in company all alone —
Forthwith by flight I thought to save myself,
90 Leaving my Amadine unto her shifts,
For death it was for to resist the bear
And death no less of Amadine's harms to hear.
Accursèd I in ling'ring life thus long!
In living thus each minute of an hour
95 Doth pierce my heart with darts of thousand deaths:
If she by flight her fury do escape,
What will she think?
Will she not say, yea, flatly to my face,
Accusing me of mere disloyalty,
100 'A trusty friend is tried in time of need'?
But I, when she in danger was of death,
And needed me and cried, 'Segasto, help!'
I turned my back and quickly ran away.
Unworthy I to bear this vital breath!
105 But what, what needs these plaints?
If Amadine do live then happy I,
She will in time forgive and so forget:
Amadine is merciful, not Juno-like
In harmful heart to harbour hatred long.

Enter Mouse, the Clown, running crying 'Clubs!'

110 MOUSE   Clubs, prongs, pitchforks, bills, O, help! A bear, a bear, a bear!

SEGASTO   Still bears, and nothing else but bears! Tell me, sirrah, where she is.

MOUSE   O sir, she is run down the woods: I saw her white head and her white belly.

SEGASTO   Thou talkest of wonders, to tell me of white bears. But, sirrah, didst thou ever see any such?

115 MOUSE   No faith, I never saw any such but I remember my father's words: he bade me take heed I was not caught with a white bear.

SEGASTO   A lamentable tale no doubt!

---

82 **caitiff-like** like a poor wretch, one in a piteous case   **accursed** doomed to misery   84 **thrall** bondage/oppression, misery   86 **by proof** as events prove or turn out   87 **Erewhiles** a while ago   89 **Forthwith** immediately   90 **shifts** own devices, to help herself   93 **ling'ring** clinging on to/slowly suffering   96 **fury** avenging spirit, i.e. the bear   99 **mere** infamous/pure, unalloyed   105 **plaints** complaints/laments   108 **Juno-like** Juno was the wife of Jupiter, the chief of the Roman gods in classical mythology, and was renowned for spite and ill temper   *'Clubs!'* the cry used to summon the Watch when brawls took place in London; literally 'thick sticks used as weapons'   110 **prongs** weapons, stakes or implements with a sharp point   **pitchforks** long-handled forks with two sharp prongs for shifting hay etc.   **bills** obsolete military weapons of varying design, consisting of a blade or axehead on a long handle   111 **sirrah** term of address to an inferior   115 **faith** i.e. by my faith, indeed   116 **bade** commanded/threatened/begged, past tense of the verb 'to bid'   **heed** care   **bear** regarded as a symbol of unchastity; Mouse's speech plays across sexual allusion and innuendo   117 **tale** story, playing on 'tail' genitals

MOUSE   I tell you what, sir, as I was going a-field to serve my father's great horse, and carried a bottle of hay upon my head, now do you see, sir, I, fast hoodwinked,

120   that I could see nothing. I, perceiving the bear coming, I threw my hay into the hedge and ran away.

SEGASTO   What, from nothing?

MOUSE   I warrant you, yes. I saw something, for there was two load of thorns besides my bottle of hay, and that made three.

125   SEGASTO   But tell me, sirrah, the bear that thou didst see, did she not bear a bucket on her arm?

MOUSE   Ha ha, ha! I never saw bear go a-milking in all my life. But hark you, sir, I did not look so high as her arm: I saw nothing but her white head and her white belly.

130   SEGASTO   But tell me, sirrah, where dost thou dwell?

MOUSE   Why, do you not know me?

SEGASTO   Why no! How should I know thee?

MOUSE   Why then you know nobody and you know not me. I tell you, sir, I am the goodman rat's son of the next parish over the hill.

135   SEGASTO   Goodman Ratson! Why, what's thy name?

MOUSE   Why, I am very near kin unto him.

SEGASTO   I think so, but what's thy name?

MOUSE   My name? I have very pretty name. I'll tell you what my name is: my name is Mouse.

140   SEGASTO   What, plain Mouse?

MOUSE   Ay, plain mouse without either welt or guard. But do you hear, sir, I am but a very young mouse, for my tail is scarce grown out yet: look you here else.

SEGASTO   But I pray thee, who gave thee that name?

145   MOUSE   Faith, sir, I know not that, but if you would fain know, ask my father's great horse, for he hath been half a year longer with my father than I have.

SEGASTO   This seems to be a merry fellow,   *Aside*

I care not if I take him home with me:

Mirth is a comfort to a troubled mind,

150   A merry man, a merry master makes!

How say'st thou, sirrah, wilt thou dwell with me?

MOUSE   Nay soft, sir, two words to a bargain: pray you what occupation are you?

SEGASTO   No occupation: I live upon my lands.

MOUSE   Your lands? Away! You are no master for me, why do you think that I

155   am so mad to go seek my living in the lands amongst the stones, briars and bushes, and tear my holiday apparel? Not I, by your leave.

SEGASTO   Why, I do not mean thou shalt.

MOUSE   How then?

---

119 fast hoodwinked securely blindfolded   **133 and…me** if you don't know me   **and if**   **134 goodman** title of respect used to one under the rank of a gentleman, sometimes used ironically as it is here   **141 welt** frill, fringe or trimming (usually a narrow strip of material on the edge of a garment)   **guard** ornamental border or trimming on a garment   **142 tail…out** playing on slang for 'penis'; according to contemporary anatomical theory derived from the ancients, such as Galen, men and women had the same genital structure but women's was inside whereas men's was outside, hence Mouse is only just a man   **145 fain** like to   **148 care not** should not mind

SEGASTO	Why thou shalt be my man and wait upon me at the court.
160 MOUSE	What's that?
SEGASTO	Where the king lies.
MOUSE	What's that same king, a man or woman?
SEGASTO	A man as thou art.
MOUSE	As I am? Hark you, sir, pray you: what kin is he to Goodman King of
165	our parish, the churchwarden?
SEGASTO	No kin to him, he is the king of the whole land.
MOUSE	King of the land, I never see him.
SEGASTO	If thou wilt dwell with me, thou shalt see him every day.
MOUSE	Shall I go home again to be torn in pieces with bears? No not I: I will go
170	home and put on a clean shirt, and then go drown myself.
SEGASTO	Thou shalt not need: if thou wilt dwell with me, thou shalt want
	nothing.
MOUSE	Shall I not? Then here's my hand, I'll dwell with you, and hark you, sir,
	now you have entertained me, I will tell you what I can do: I can keep my tongue
175	from picking and stealing, and my hands from lying and slandering, I warrant you,
	as well as ever you had man in all your life. ·
SEGASTO	Now will I to court with sorrowful heart, rounded with doubts. If
	Amadine do live, then happy I: yea, happy I if Amadine do live. [*Exeunt*]

[Scene 3]

Enter the King with a young prince prisoner, Amadine, Tremelio with Collin [, Segasto, Mouse] and counsellors

KING	Now, brave lords, our wars are brought to end,
	Our foes the foil and we in safety rest.
	It us behoves to use such clemency
	In peace as valour in the wars.
5	It is as great honour to be bountiful at home,
	As to be conquerors in the field.
	Therefore, my lords, the more to my content
	Your liking and your country's safeguard,
	We are disposed in marriage for to give
10	Our daughter to Lord Segasto here,
	Who shall succeed the diadem after me:
	And reign hereafter as I tofore have done
	Your sole and lawful King of Aragon:
	What say you, lordings, like you of my advice?

---

167 **never see** have never seen   175 **picking** pilfering; a quotation from the catechism in the Book of Common Prayer, 'to keep my hands from picking and stealing' **warrant** assure, guarantee   177 **rounded with** surrounded by   [Scene 3] *Location: the court of Aragon* 2 **Our...foil** defeated our enemies   3 **It us behoves** we are morally obliged   **clemency** mercy, leniency   11 **diadem** crown, as symbol of royal dignity   12 **tofore** before, previously   14 **lordings** sirs, gentlemen

15 COLLIN   An't please your majesty, we do not only allow of your highness'
pleasure but also vow faithfully, in what we may, to further it.

   KING   Thanks, good my lords, if long Androstus live
   He will at full requite your courtesies.
   Tremelio, in recompense of thy late valour done,
20   Take unto thee the Catalan, a prince,
   Lately our prisoner taken in the wars.
   Be thou his keeper, his ransom shall be thine,
   We'll think of it when leisure shall afford:
   Meanwhile do use him well, his father is a king.

25 TREMELIO   Thanks to your majesty: his usage shall be such,
   As he thereat shall think no cause to grudge.

                                        Exeunt [all but King and Collin]

   KING   Then march we on to court and rest our wearied limbs.
   But Collin, I have a tale in secret kept for thee:
   When thou shalt hear a watchword from thy king,
30   Think then some weighty matter is at hand
   That highly shall concern our state.
   Then Collin look thou be not far from me,
   And for thy service thou tofore hast done,
   Thy truth and valour proved in every point,
35   I shall with bounties thee enlarge therefore:
   So guard us to the court.

   COLLIN   What so my sovereign doth command me do,
   With willing mind I gladly yield consent.   *Exeunt*

[Scene 4]

   Enter Segasto and the Clown [Mouse], with weapons about him

   SEGASTO   Tell me, sirrah, how do you like your weapons?

   MOUSE   O, very well, very well: they keep my sides warm.

   SEGASTO   They keep the dogs from your shins very well, do they not?

   MOUSE   How, keep the dogs from my shins? I would scorn but my shins should
5 keep the dogs from them.

   SEGASTO   Well, sirrah, leaving idle talk, tell me: dost thou know Captain Tremelio's
   chamber?

   MOUSE   Ay, very well, it hath a door.

   SEGASTO   I think so, for so hath every chamber. But dost thou know the man?

10 MOUSE   Ay, forsooth: he hath a nose on his face.

---

15 **An't** if it   16 **what we may** whatever we can   18 **requite** repay   20 **Catalan** a native of Catalonia in north-eastern Spain which was part of the crown of Aragon; it is not clear which wars are referred to in the play   22 **ransom** aristocratic prisoners were customarily returned to their home for a sum of money   26 **grudge** complain   29 **watchword** word or short phrase used as a password   30 **weighty matter** no further reference is made to this, suggesting a possible sub-plot which was not developed   37 **What so** whatever   **[Scene 4]** *Location: Aragon*   10 **nose...know** (lines 10–12) Mouse's apparently illogical response is a reference to the destruction of the nasal bridge and flattening of the nose which was one among a number of symptoms of syphilis

SEGASTO	Why, so hath everyone.
MOUSE	That's more than I know.
SEGASTO	But dost thou remember the captain, that was here with the king even now, that brought the young prince prisoner?

15

MOUSE	O, very well.
SEGASTO	Go unto him and bid him come to me. Tell him I have a matter in secret to impart to him.
MOUSE	I will, master. Master, what's his name?
SEGASTO	Why, Captain Tremelio.

20

MOUSE	O, the mealman, I know him very well. He brings meal every Saturday: but, hark you, master, must I bid him come to you or must you come to him?
SEGASTO	No, sirrah, he must come to me.
MOUSE	Hark you, master, how if he be not at home, what shall I do then?
SEGASTO	Why, then leave word with some of his folks.

25

MOUSE	O, master, if there be nobody within, I will leave word with his dog.
SEGASTO	Why, can his dog speak?
MOUSE	I cannot tell, wherefore doth he keep his chamber else?
SEGASTO	To keep out such knaves as thou art!
MOUSE	Nay, by Lady, then go yourself.

30

SEGASTO	You will go, sir, will you not?
MOUSE	Yes, marry, will I. O 'tis come to my head, and a be not within, I'll bring his chamber to you.
SEGASTO	What wilt thou pluck down the king's house?
MOUSE	Nay, by lady, I'll know the price of it first. Master, it is such a hard name

35 I have forgotten it again. I pray you tell me his name.

SEGASTO	I tell thee, Captain Tremelio.
MOUSE	O, Captain Treble Knave, Captain Treble Knave!

Enter Tremelio

TREMELIO	How now, sirrah, dost thou call me?
MOUSE	You must come to my master, Captain Treble Knave.

40

TREMELIO	My Lord Segasto, did you send for me?
SEGASTO	I did, Tremelio.— Sirrah, about your business!	*To Mouse*
MOUSE	Ay, marry, what's that? Can you tell?
SEGASTO	No, not well.
MOUSE	Marry, then I can: straight to the kitchen dresser to John the cook

45 and get me a good piece of beef and brewis, and then to the buttery-hatch to Thomas the butler for a jack of beer, and there for an hour I'll so belabour myself, and therefore I pray you call me not till you think I have done, I pray you good master. *Exit*

---

14 even now just now, a moment ago   **20 mealman** one who deals in meal or flour; Mouse's confusion suggests how **Tremelio** should be pronounced   **27 wherefore…else?** why does he stay in his room otherwise?   **28 knaves** rogues   **29 by Lady** by the Virgin Mary   **31 marry** indeed, 'by the Virgin Mary   **a be not** he is not; **a** is an abbreviation for 'he' here   **32 chamber** Mouse shifts the sense from 'private apartment' to an abbreviation for 'chamber-pot' while Segasto puns on another sense of 'military materials, ammunition'   **45 brewis** broth in which beef and vegetables have been boiled   **buttery-hatch** the half-door over which provisions are served from the **buttery**, where food and drink are stored   **46 butler** servant in charge of the wine cellar who dispenses liquor   **jack** leather jug or tankard for liquor   **belabour** exert

SEGASTO   Well, sir, away. Tremelio, this it is. Thou knowest the valour of Segasto,
50   spread through all the kingdom of Aragon and such as have found triumph and
favours, never-daunted at any time; but now is a shepherd admirèd at in court for
worthiness and Segasto's honour laid aside. My will therefore is this, that thou dost
find some means to work the shepherd's death. I know thy strength sufficient to
perform my desire and thy love no otherwise than to revenge my injuries.

55   TREMELIO   It is not the frowns of a shepherd that Tremelio fears. Therefore, account
it accomplished what I take in hand.

SEGASTO   Thanks, good Tremelio, and assure thyself,
What I promise that will I perform.

TREMELIO   Thanks, my good lord, and in good time.
60   See where he cometh, stand by awhile
And you shall see me put in practice your intended drift.
Have at thee, swain, if that I hit thee right!   *Draws his sword*

Enter Mucedorus

MUCEDORUS   Vile coward, so without cause to strike a man.
Turn, coward, turn; now strike and do thy worst!   *Mucedorus kills him*

65   SEGASTO   Hold, shepherd, hold, spare him! Kill him not!
Accursèd villain, tell me what hast thou done.
Ah, Tremelio, trusty Tremelio, I sorrow for thy death,
And since that thou living, didst prove faithful
To Segasto, so Segasto, now living, will honour
70   The dead corpse of Tremelio with revenge.
Bloodthirsty villain, born and bred to merciless murder,
Tell me how durst thou be so bold
As once to lay thy hands upon the least of mine?
Assure thyself, thou shalt be used according to the law.

75   MUCEDORUS   Segasto, cease. These threats are needless.
Accuse me not of murder, that have done nothing
But in mine own defence.

SEGASTO   Nay, shepherd, reason not with me.
I'll manifest thy fact unto the king,
80   Whose doom will be thy death as thou deserv'st,
What ho, Mouse, come away.

Enter Mouse

MOUSE   Why how now, what's the matter? I thought you would be calling before
I had done.

SEGASTO   Come, help, away with my friend.

85   MOUSE   Why is he drunk? Cannot he stand on his feet?

SEGASTO   No, he is not drunk, he is slain.

MOUSE   Slain, no! By lady, he is not slain.

SEGASTO   He's killed I tell thee.

---

51 **admirèd** marvelled   61 **drift** plan   62 **Have at thee** here's for you   **swain** peasant   79 **manifest** reveal   **fact** deed   80 **doom** sentence

	MOUSE	What, do you use to kill your friends? I will serve you no longer.
90	SEGASTO	I tell thee the shepherd killed him.
	MOUSE	O, did a so? But master, I will have all his apparel if I carry him away.
	SEGASTO	Why so thou shalt.
	MOUSE	Come then, I will help. Mass, master, I think his mother sung

'looby' to him, he is so heavy.

Exeunt [Segasto with Mouse bearing Tremelio's body]

95   MUCEDORUS   Behold the fickle state of man, always mutable,

Never at one: sometimes we feed on fancies

With the sweet of our desires, sometimes again

We feel the heat of extreme miseries.

Now am I in favour about the court and country:

100   Tomorrow those favours will turn to frowns,

Today I live revengèd on my foe,

Tomorrow I die, my foe revenged on me.   *Exit*

[Scene 5]

Enter Bremo, a wild man

BREMO   No passenger this morning? What not one?

A chance that seldom doth befall!

What not one? Then lie thou there   *Puts down cudgel*

And rest thyself till I have further need:

5   Now, Bremo, sith thy leisure so affords.

A needless thing, who knows not Bremo's strength   *Pointing to cudgel*

Who like a king commands within these woods?

The bear, the boar, dares not abide my sight,

But haste away to save themselves by flight:

10   The crystal waters in the bubbling brooks,

When I come by, doth swiftly slide away

And clap themselves in closets under banks,

Afraid to look bold Bremo in the face.

The agèd oaks at Bremo's breath do bow,

15   And all things else are still at my command.

Else what would I?

Rend them in pieces and pluck them from the earth,

And each way else I would revenge myself.

Why, who comes here with whom I dare not fight?

20   Who fights with me and doth not die the death? Not one!

What favour shows this sturdy stick to those

---

89 do you use are you accustomed   **91 O…so?** Oh, did he indeed?   **93 Mass** by the mass, i.e. the Christian sacrament of the Eucharist   **94 'looby'** lullaby/ lazy, hulking fellow   **95 mutable** liable to change or alteration   **[Scene 5]** *Location: the woods in Aragon*   **5 sith** since   **affords** allows   **12 clap** shut   **closets** dens or lairs of wild beasts   **16 Else…I?** What would I do otherwise (if they weren't subservient)?   **18 each way else** in every other way

That here within these woods are combatants with me?

Why death and nothing else but present death!

With restless rage I wander through these woods,

25 No creature here but feareth Bremo's force,

Man, woman, child, beast and bird,

And everything that doth approach my sight,

Are forced to fall if Bremo once do frown.

Come, cudgel, come, my partner in my spoils,   *Picks up cudgel*

30 For here I see this day it will not be,

But when it falls that I encounter any,

One pat sufficeth for to work my will.

What comes not one? Then let's be gone,

A time will serve when we shall better speed.   *Exit*

[Scene 6]

Enter the King, Segasto, the Shepherd [Mucedorus] and the Clown [Mouse] with others

KING   Shepherd, thou hast heard thine accusers:

Murder is laid to thy charge,

What canst thou say? Thou hast deserved death.

MUCEDORUS Dread sovereign, I must needs confess,

5   I slew this captain in mine own defence,

Not of any malice but by chance,

But mine accuser hath a further meaning.

SEGASTO   Words will not here prevail,

I seek for justice, and justice craves his death.

10 KING   Shepherd, thine own confession hath condemned thee. Sirrah, take him away and do him to execution straight.

MOUSE   So he shall I warrant him, but do you hear, master King, he is kin to a monkey, his neck is bigger than his head.

SEGASTO   Come, sirrah, away with him, and hang him about the middle.

15 MOUSE   Yes, forsooth I warrant you: come on, sirrah,

Ah, so like a sheep-biter a looks.

Enter Amadine and a Boy with a bear's head

AMADINE   Dread sovereign and well belovèd sire,

On bended knee I crave the life of this

Condemnèd shepherd, which heretofore preserved

20 The life of thy sometime distressed daughter.

KING   Preserved the life of my sometime distressed daughter?

---

32 pat blow   34 speed succeed   [Scene 6]   *Location: the court of Aragon*   4 Dread revered, held in awe   16 sheep-biter a looks he looks like a shifty, sneaking or thievish fellow/whore-monger, woman-hunter, one who runs after 'mutton' (women)   19 heretofore before this time   20 sometime at one time or another

How can that be? I never knew the time
Wherein thou was distressed; I never knew the day
But that I have maintained thy estate
25   As best beseemed the daughter of a king.
I never saw the shepherd until now,
How comes it then that he preserved thy life?

AMADINE   Once walking with Segasto in the woods,
Further than our accustomed manner was,
30   Right before us down a steep-fall hill,
A monstrous ugly bear did hie him fast
To meet us both: now whether this be true,
I refer it to the credit of Segasto.

SEGASTO   Most true, an't like your majesty.

35   KING   How then?

AMADINE   The bear being eager to obtain his prey
Made forward to us with an open mouth,
As if he meant to swallow us both at once,
The sight whereof did make us both to dread,
40   But specially your daughter Amadine,
Who — for I saw no succour incident
But in Segasto's valour — I grew desperate,
And he most coward-like began to fly,
Left me distressed to be devoured of him.
45   How say you, Segasto, is it not true?

KING   His silence verifies it to be true. What then?

AMADINE   Then I amazed, distressèd, all alone,
Did hie me fast to scape that ugly bear,
But all in vain! For why? He reachèd after me,
50   And hardly I did oft escape his paws,
Till at the length this shepherd came,
And brought to me his head.
Come hither, boy.
Lo, here it is, which I present unto your majesty.

55   KING   The slaughter of this bear deserves great fame.

SEGASTO   The slaughter of a man deserves great blame.

KING   Indeed occasion oftentimes so falls out.

SEGASTO   Tremelio in the wars, O king, preservèd thee.

AMADINE   The shepherd in the woods, O king, preservèd me.

60   SEGASTO   Tremelio fought when many men did yield.

AMADINE   So would the shepherd had he been in field.

MOUSE   So would my master had he not run away.   *Aside*

---

22 How…be? It does seem strange that the king has not heard of this or seen Mucedorus before who has been at court long enough for Segasto to become jealous **24 But** other than **estate** state, condition **25 beseemed** became, was appropriate to **30 steep-fall** steep **33 credit** trustworthiness, credibility **34 an't like** if it please **41 for…incident** because I could see no other help at hand **47 amazed** stunned, stupified **54 Lo** behold **55 The…else** (lines 55–65) an example of stichomythia, a technique originally from classical Greek drama, consisting of dialogue in alternate lines, employed in sharp disputation, and characterized by antithesis and rhetorical repetition or taking up of the opponent's words

	SEGASTO	Tremelio's force saved thousands from the foe.
	AMADINE	The shepherd's force have savèd thousands moe.
65	MOUSE	Ay, sheep's ticks, nothing else.

Aside

	KING	Segasto, cease to accuse the shepherd,

His worthiness deserves a recompense:

All we are bound to do the shepherd good.

Shepherd, whereas it was my sentence, thou shouldst die,

70   So shall my sentence stand, for thou shalt die.

SEGASTO   Thanks to your majesty.

KING   But soft, Segasto, not for this offence.

Long mayst thou live and when the Sisters shall decree

To cut in twain the twisted thread of life

75   Then let him die. For this I set thee free

And for thy valour I will honour thee.

MUCEDORUS   Thanks to your majesty.

KING   Come, daughter, let us now depart, to honour the worthy valour of the shepherd with our rewards.   *Exeunt [all but Mouse and Segasto]*

80   MOUSE   O, master, hear you, you have made a fresh hand now! I thought you would beshrew you. What will you do now? You have lost me a good occupation by this means. Faith, master now I cannot hang the shepherd, I pray you let me take the pains to hang you, it is but half an hour's exercise.

SEGASTO   You are still in your knavery: but sith I cannot have his life I will
85   procure his banishment forever. Come on, sirrah.

MOUSE   Yes forsooth, I come. Laugh at him, I pray you.   *Exeunt*

[Scene 7]

Enter Mucedorus solus

MUCEDORUS   From Amadine and from her father's court,

With gold and silver and with rich rewards,

Flowing from the banks of golden treasuries,

More may I boast and say, but I

5   Was never shepherd in such dignity.

Enter the Messenger and the Clown [Mouse]

MESSENGER   All hail, worthy shepherd.

MOUSE   All rain, lousy shepherd.

MUCEDORUS   Welcome, my friends, from whence come you?

MESSENGER   The king and Amadine greet thee well, and after greeting done, bids
10   thee depart the court. Shepherd begone!

---

64 **moe** more   65 **sheep's ticks** parasitic insects which infest sheep   73 **Sisters…life** the Fates of classical mythology who determined the length of human life, envisaged as a **thread** which Clotho spun, Lachesis measured out and Atropos **cut**   75 **For this** referring either to the time or Mucedorus' deed   80 **fresh hand** new situation   81 **beshrew** curse   **good occupation** partly ironic but since the clothes of those he executed were considered the hangman's rightful perquisite it could prove profitable   84 **sith** since   86 **forsooth** truly, indeed   **[Scene 7]**   *Location: the court of Aragon*

MOUSE	Shepherd, take law-legs, fly away, shepherd.
MUCEDORUS	Whose words are these? Came these from Amadine?
MESSENGER	Ay, from Amadine.
MOUSE	Ay, from Amadine.

15 MUCEDORUS Ah, luckless fortune, worse than Phaeton's tale:

My former bliss is now become my bale.

MOUSE   What, wilt thou poison thyself?

MUCEDORUS My former heaven is now become my hell.

MOUSE   The worst alehouse that I ever came in, in all my life!

20 MUCEDORUS What shall I do?

MOUSE   Even go hang thyself half an hour.

MUCEDORUS Can Amadine so churlishly command

To banish the shepherd from her father's court?

MESSENGER What should shepherds do in the court?

25 MOUSE   What should shepherds do amongst us? Have we not lords enough on us in the court?

MUCEDORUS Why, shepherds are men, and kings are no more.

MESSENGER Shepherds are men and masters — over their flock.

MOUSE   That's a lie! Who pays them their wages then?

30 MESSENGER Well, you are always interrupting of me, but you were best to look to him lest you hang for him when he is gone.   *Exit*

The Clown sings

MOUSE   'And you shall hang for company,

For leaving me alone—'

Shepherd, stand forth and hear my sentence: shepherd, begone within three days in

35 pain of my displeasure.

'Shepherd begone, shepherd begone,

Begone, begone, begone,

Shepherd, shepherd, shepherd.'   *Exit [Mouse]*

MUCEDORUS And must I go? And must I needs depart?

40 Ye, goodly groves, partakers of my songs

In time tofore when fortune did not frown,

Pour forth your plaints and wail awhile with me.

And thou, bright sun, my comfort in the cold,

Hide, hide thy face and leave me comfortless.

45 Ye wholesome herbs and sweet-smelling savours,

Yea, each thing else prolonging life of man,

Change, change your wonted course,

That I wanting your aid, in woeful sort may die.

Enter Amadine, and Ariena her maid

AMADINE   Ariena, if anybody ask for me,

---

11 **take law-legs** run away   15 **Phaeton's tale** the story of Phaeton, son of the sun god Helios, who was allowed to drive his father's sun chariot but lost control and was killed   16 **bale** suffering, evil, death   19 **worst alehouse** i.e. hell   41 **tofore** before, previously   42 **plaints** complaints, laments   45 **savours** scents   46 **Yea** yes, indeed   **each** every   47 **wonted** customary   48 **wanting** lacking, in need of   **sort** destiny/mood

50   Make some excuse till I return.

ARIENA   What and Segasto call?

AMADINE   Do thou the like to him, I mean not to stay long.   *Exit* [*Ariena*]

MUCEDORUS   This voice so sweet my pining spirits revives.

AMADINE   Shepherd, well met: tell me how thou dost.

55   MUCEDORUS   I linger life, yet wish for speedy death.

AMADINE   Shepherd, although thy banishment already

Be decreed and all against my will, yet Amadine—

MUCEDORUS   Ah, Amadine, to hear of banishment

Is death, ay, double death to me.

60   But since I must depart, one thing I crave.

AMADINE   Say on with all my heart.

MUCEDORUS   That in my absence, either far or near,

You honour me as servant with your name.

AMADINE   Not so!

65   MUCEDORUS   And why?

AMADINE   I honour thee as sovereign with my heart.

MUCEDORUS   A shepherd and a sovereign nothing like.

AMADINE   Yet like enough where there is no dislike.

MUCEDORUS   Yet great dislike, or else no banishment.

70   AMADINE   Shepherd, it is only Segasto that procures thy banishment.

MUCEDORUS   Unworthy wights are most in jealousy.

AMADINE   Would God they would free thee from banishment,

Or likewise banish me.

MUCEDORUS   Amen, say I, to have your company.

75   AMADINE   Well, shepherd, sith thou suff'rest this for my sake,

With thee in exile also let me live:

On this condition, shepherd, thou canst love.

MUCEDORUS   No longer love, no longer let me live!

AMADINE   Of late I lovèd one indeed, now love I none but only thee.

80   MUCEDORUS   Thanks, worthy princess, I burn likewise,

Yet smother up the blast.

I dare not promise what I may perform.

AMADINE   Well, shepherd, hark what I shall say.

I will return unto my father's court,

85   There for to provide me of such necessaries,

As for our journey I shall think most fit.

This being done I will return to thee.

Do thou, therefore, appoint the place

Where we may meet.

90   MUCEDORUS   Down in the valley where I slew the bear,

And there doth grow a fair broad-branchèd beech,

---

51 and Segasto call if Segasto should call **52 like** same **53 pining** suffering **71 wights** creatures **most** greatest **75 sith** since

That overshades a well, whoso comes first

Let them abide the happy meeting of us both.

How like you this?

95   AMADINE   I like it very well.

MUCEDORUS   Now, if you please, you may appoint the time.

AMADINE   Full three hours hence, God willing, I will return.

MUCEDORUS   The thanks that Paris gave the Grecian queen

The like doth Mucedorus yield.

100   AMADINE   Then, Mucedorus, for three hours farewell.   *Exit*

MUCEDORUS   Your departure lady breeds a privy pain.   *Exit*

[Scene 8]

Enter Segasto solus

SEGASTO   'Tis well Segasto that thou hast thy will,

Should such a shepherd, such a simple swain

As he, eclipse thy credit famous through the court?

No! Ply, Segasto, ply: let it not in Aragon be said,

5   A shepherd hath Segasto's honour won.

Enter Mouse the Clown calling his master

MOUSE   What ho, master, will you come away?

SEGASTO   Will you come hither, I pray you? What's the matter?

MOUSE   Why, is it not past eleven o'clock?

SEGASTO   How then, sir?

10   MOUSE   I pray you come away to dinner.

SEGASTO   I pray you, come hither.

MOUSE   Here's such ado with you! Will you never come?

SEGASTO   I pray you, sir, what news of the message I sent you about?

MOUSE   I tell you all the messes be on the table already. There wants not so

15   much as a mess of mustard half an hour ago.

SEGASTO   Come, sir, your mind is all upon your belly:

You have forgotten what I bid you do.

MOUSE   Faith, I know nothing but you bade me go to breakfast.

SEGASTO   Was that all?

20   MOUSE   Faith, I have forgotten it: the very scent of the meat made me hath forget

it quite.

SEGASTO   You have forgotten the errand I bid you do?

MOUSE   What arrant? An arrant knave or an arrant whore?

SEGASTO   Why, thou knave, did I not bid thee banish the shepherd?

---

92 whoso whichever (of us two)   **93 abide** await   **98 Paris…queen** Paris stole away Helen of Troy, wife of Menelaus, King of Sparta, which event precipitated the Trojan war   **101 privy** secret   **[Scene 8]**   *Location: the court of Aragon*   **2 swain** rustic, peasant/menial/country gallant or lover   **3 credit** honour, reputation   **4 Ply** exert, apply yourself   **10 dinner** the main meal of the day was eaten mid-morning   **14 messe** servings of food   **21 quite** completely   **23 arrant** notorious, downright; Mouse is playing on the similarity between 'errand' and 'errant' (of which 'arrant' is a variant) meaning 'travelling, roaming', as in 'knight errant'. Etymological confusion exists between this word and 'errant' one who errs, usually applied to a thief or knave

25   MOUSE   O, the shepherd's bastard?

    SEGASTO   I tell thee the shepherd's banishment!

    MOUSE   I tell you the shepherd's bastard shall be well kept: I'll look to it myself;
but I pray you come away to dinner.

    SEGASTO   Then you will not tell me whether you have banished him or no?

30   MOUSE   Why I cannot say 'banishment' and you would give me a thousand
pounds to say so.

    SEGASTO   Why, you whoreson slave, have you forgotten that I sent you and
another to drive away the shepherd?

    MOUSE   What an ass are you! Here's a stir indeed: here's 'message', 'arrant',
35   'banishment', and I cannot tell what!

    SEGASTO   I pray you, sir, shall I know whether you have drove him away?

    MOUSE   Faith, I think I have, and you will not believe me, ask my staff.

    SEGASTO   Why, can thy staff tell?

    MOUSE   Why, he was with me too.

40   SEGASTO   Then happy I, that have obtained my will.

    MOUSE   And happier I, if you would go to dinner.

    SEGASTO   Come, sirrah, follow me.

    MOUSE   I warrant you I will not lose an inch of you now you are going to
dinner.—

45   I promise you, I thought seven year before I could get him away.   *Aside to the audience*

Exeunt

[Scene 9]

Enter Amadine solus

    AMADINE   God grant my long delay procures no harm,

    Nor this my tarrying frustrate my pretence!

    My Mucedorus surely stays for me,

    And thinks me overlong: at length I come

5   My present promise to perform.

    Ah, what a thing is firm unfeignèd love,

    What is it which true love dares not attempt?

    My father he may make, but I must match;

    Segasto loves, but Amadine must like:

10   Where likes her best, compulsion is a thrall.

    No, no, the hearty choice is all in all:

    The shepherd's virtue Amadine esteems.

    But what! Methinks my shepherd is not come!

    I muse at that, the hour is at hand,

15   Well here I'll rest till Mucedorus come.   *She sits down*

---

30 and if   45 I thought i.e. I thought it had lasted or it would be   [Scene 9] *Location: the woods of Aragon*   1 procures brings about   2 tarrying delaying   pretence intention, design   4 overlong an excessively long time   11 hearty of the heart

Enter Bremo looking about, hastily takes hold of her

BREMO   A happy prey, now Bremo feed on flesh,

Dainties, Bremo, dainties, thy hungry paunch to fill:

Now glut thy greedy guts with lukewarm blood.

Come fight with me — I long to see thee dead.

20 AMADINE   How can she fight that weapons cannot wield?

BREMO   What canst not fight? Then lie thee down and die.

AMADINE   What, must I die?

BREMO   What needs these words? I thirst to suck thy blood.

AMADINE   Yet pity me, and let me live awhile.

25 BREMO   No pity, I! I'll feed upon thy flesh:

I'll tear thy body piecemeal joint from joint.

AMADINE   Ah, now I want my shepherd's company.

BREMO   I'll crush thy bones betwixt two oaken trees.

AMADINE   Haste, shepherd, haste or else thou com'st too late!

30 BREMO   I'll suck the sweetness from thy marrow-bones.

AMADINE   Ah spare, ah spare to shed my guiltless blood.

BREMO   With this, my bat will I beat out thy brains!

Down, down, I say, prostrate thyself upon the ground.

AMADINE   Then, Mucedorus, farewell, my hopèd joys farewell.

35 Yea, farewell life, and welcome present death   *She kneels*

To thee, O God, I yield my dying ghost.

BREMO   Now, Bremo, play thy part!   *He goes to strike her*

How now, what sudden chance is this?

My limbs do tremble and my sinews shake,

40 My unweakened arms have lost their former force.

Ah, Bremo, Bremo, what a foil hast thou,

That yet at no time ever wast afraid

To dare the greatest gods to fight with thee,   *He strikes*

And now wants strength for one down-driving blow!

45 Ah, how my courage fails when I should strike,

Some new-come spirit abiding in my breast.

Shall I spare her? — Bremo, spare her! Do not kill! —

Saith spare her, which never sparèd any?

To it, Bremo, to it! Say again.

50 I cannot wield my weapons in my hand:

Methinks I should not strike so fair a one.

I think her beauty hath bewitched my force

Or else within me altered nature's course,

Ay, woman, wilt thou live in woods with me?

55 AMADINE   Fain would I live; yet loath to live in woods.

17 **paunch** stomach   21 **Then ... die** Bremo's threat is sexually charged with its instruction to **lie down** and play on **die** meaning 'achieve sexual orgasm'   30 **marrow-bones** those bones (chiefly the long bones such as leg or arm) which contain **marrow**, soft, fatty material from which new cells are produced, hence very rich and nutritious   36 **ghost** spirit   41 **foil** repulse, baffling check   44 **down-driving** hard downward   47 **Shall...again** an example of psychomachia or conflict of the soul, in which a character is torn in different directions; these are sometimes externalized as a good and a bad angel giving contradictory advice

BREMO	Thou shalt not choose, it shall be as I say

And therefore follow me.   *Exeunt*

Enter Mucedorus solus

MUCEDORUS It was my will an hour ago and more,

    As was my promise for to make return,

60   But other business hindered my pretence.

    It is a world to see when man appoints,

    And purposely one certain thing decrees,

    How many things may hinder his intent.

    What one would wish, the same is farthest off.

65   But yet the appointed time cannot be past,

    Nor hath her presence yet prevented me.

    Well here I'll stay, and expect her coming.

They cry within, 'Hold him, hold him!'

MUCEDORUS Someone or other is pursued no doubt,

    Perhaps some search for me: 'tis good to doubt the worst,

70   Therefore I'll be gone.   *Exit*

Cry within 'Hold him, hold him!'

Enter Mouse the Clown with a pot

MOUSE 'Hold him, hold him, hold him!' Here's a stir indeed! Here came hue after the crier, and I was set close at Mother Nip's house, and there I called for three pots of ale, as 'tis the manner of us courtiers. Now, sirrah, I had taken the maidenhead of two of them. Now as I was lifting up the third to my mouth, there came, 'Hold him, hold him!' Now I could not tell whom to catch hold on, but I am sure I caught one: perchance a may be in this pot? Well I'll see: mass, I cannot see him yet. Well, I'll look a little further: mass, he is a little slave if a be here! Why, here's nobody! All this goes well yet: but if the old trot should come for her pot? Ay, marry, there's the matter. But I care not, I'll face her out and call her old rusty, dusty, musty, fusty, crusty firebrand, and worse than all that, and so face her out of her pot: but soft here she comes.

Enter the Old Woman

OLD WOMAN Come, you knave! Where's my pot, you knave?

MOUSE Go look! Your pot? Come not to me for your pot 'twere good for you.

OLD WOMAN Thou liest, thou knave, thou hast my pot!

85 MOUSE You lie and you say it. I, your pot? I know what I'll say—

[OLD WOMAN] Why, what wilt thou say?

MOUSE But say I have him and thou dar'st.

OLD WOMAN Why, thou knave, thou hast not only my pot but my drink unpaid for!

MOUSE You lie like an old— I will not say, whore.

---

58 **will** intention   60 **pretence** purpose, design   64 **What** that which   67 **expect** wait for   71 **stir** commotion   **hue…crier** 'hue and cry' was a legal term for the 'outcry calling for the pursuit of a felon, raised by the party aggrieved, by a constable, etc.'; they are seeking Mucedorus   72 **set close** nearby   **Mother Nip's house** alehouse belonging to Mother Nip who may be the name of the character or a generic name from 'nip' meaning 'pinch, sharp bite/cutting remark/pickpocket, cutpurse'   74 **maidenhead** virginity, i.e. he drank them   76 **perchance…pot** perhaps he's in this pot; another comic routine in which Mouse peers further and further into the tankard, eventually drinking the contents   77 **a be** he is   78 **trot** old woman, hag (contemptuous)   79 **face her out** confront her/brazen it out   80 **fusty** old-fashioned/stale-smelling   **crusty** bad-tempered, harshly spoken   **firebrand** one who deserves to burn in hell   83 **'twere** it were, i.e. if you know what's   85 **and** if

90 OLD WOMAN   Dost thou call me whore? I'll cap thee for my pot.

MOUSE   Cap me and thou darest: search me whether I have it or no.

She searches him, and he drinks over her head and casts down the pot; she stumbles
at it, then they fall together by the ears: she takes up her pot and goes out

Enter Segasto

SEGASTO   How now, sirrah, what's the matter?

MOUSE   O, flies, master, flies.

SEGASTO   Flies, where are they?

95 MOUSE   O, here, master, all about your face.

SEGASTO   Why, thou liest! I think thou art mad.

MOUSE   Why, master, I have killed a dung-cart full at the least.

SEGASTO   Go to, sirrah. Leaving this idle talk, give ear to me.

MOUSE   How, give you one of my ears? Not and you were ten masters.

100 SEGASTO   Why, sir, I bid you give ear to my words.

MOUSE   I tell you I will not be made a curtal for no man's pleasure.

SEGASTO   I tell thee, attend what I say: go thy ways straight and rear the whole town.

MOUSE   How, rear the town? Even go yourself, it is more than I can do. Why do
you think I can rear a town, that can scarce rear a pot of ale to my head? I should
105 rear a town, should I not?

SEGASTO   Go to the constable and make a privy search, for the shepherd is run
away with the king's daughter.

MOUSE   How? Is the shepherd run away with the king's daughter, or is the king's
daughter run away with the shepherd?

110 SEGASTO   I cannot tell, but they are both gone together.

MOUSE   What a fool is she to run away with the shepherd! Why I think I am a
little handsomer man than the shepherd myself. But tell me, master, must I make a
privy search or search in the privy?

SEGASTO   Why, dost thou think they will be there?

115 MOUSE   I cannot tell.

SEGASTO   Well then search everywhere, leave no place unsearched for them.   *Exit*

MOUSE   O, now am I in office: now will I to that old firebrand's house and will
not leave one place unsearched. Nay, I'll to her ale-stand and drink as long as I
can stand, and when I have done I'll let out all the rest to see if he be not hid in the
120 barrel, and I find him not there, I'll to the cupboard. I'll not leave one corner of her
house unsearched, i'faith, ye old crust, I will be with you now!   *Exit*

[Scene 10]

Sound music

Enter the King of Valencia, Anselmo, Roderigo, Lord Barachius, with others

VALENCIA   Enough of music, it but adds to torment:
Delights to vexèd spirits are as dates

90 **cap** arrest/beat   98 **Go to** expression of disbelief, 'come, come' also an exhortation to 'get on with it'   101 **curtal** horse with its tail cut short, from 'curtail'; can apply to shortening by cutting any part   102 **rear** raise, rouse from sleep   106 **privy** private, secret; Mouse then shifts the sense to mean 'lavatory'   117 **in office** an officer   119 **rest** i.e. of the ale in the barrel   [Scene 10] *Location: Valencia, the court*

Set to a sickly man, which rather cloy than comfort.

Let me entreat you to entreat no more.

5   RODERIGO   Let your strings sleep: have done there!   *Let the music cease*

VALENCIA   Mirth, to a soul disturbed, are embers turned,

Which sudden gleam with molestation,

But sooner lose their light for't.

'Tis gold bestowed upon a rioter

10   Which not relieves, but murders him:

'Tis a drug given to the healthful,

Which infects not cures.

How can a father that hath lost his son —

A prince both wise, virtuous and valiant —

15   Take pleasure in the idle acts of time?

No, no: till Mucedorus I shall see again

All joy is comfortless, all pleasures pain.

ANSELMO   Your son, my lord, is well.

VALENCIA   I prithee, speak that thrice.

20   ANSELMO   The prince, your son, is safe.

VALENCIA   O, where, Anselmo? Surfeit me with that.

ANSELMO   In Aragon, my liege,

And at his parture, bound my secrecy,

By his affectious love, not to disclose it.

25   But care of him and pity of your age

Makes my tongue blab what my breast vowed, concealment.

VALENCIA   Thou not deceiv'st me: I ever thought thee

What I find thee now, an upright, loyal man.

But what desire or young-fed humour

30   Nursed within the brain

Drew him so privately to Aragon?

ANSELMO   A forcing adamant:

Love mixed with fear and doubtful jealousy,

Whether report gilded a worthless trunk,

35   Or Amadine deserved her high extolment.

VALENCIA   See our provision be in readiness:

Collect us followers of the comeliest hue

For our chief guardians: we will thither wend.

The crystal eye of heaven shall not thrice wink

40   Nor the green flood six times his shoulders turn,

Till we salute the Aragonian king.

---

6 are…for't are like embers of a fire which when raked over will suddenly gleam with life but disturbing them will cause them to go out more quickly **9 rioter** reveller, a dissolute person given to licentious living; money (**gold**) doesn't help him but exacerbates the problem   **19 prithee** beg you, literally 'pray thee'   **thrice** three times, i.e. 'say that again!'   **21 Surfeit** indulge excessively   **22 liege** lord, one to whom is owed a (feudal) duty of service and loyalty   **23 parture** departure   **24 affectious** earnest   **26 blab** utter, reveal indiscreetly   **29 young-fed** youthful   **humour** mood/whim   **32 forcing adamant** powerful magnet   **34 report…trunk** her fame and reputation was deserved or was merely a gloss (**gilded** of gold leaf) on a worthless pedestal or shaft of a column, punning on the sense of 'body'   **35 extolment** praising, eulogising   **38 thither wend** go there (to Aragon)   **39 crystal…wink** sun shall not close its eyes three times, i.e. within three days   **40 green…turn** the tide of the sea turn six times, another expression meaning 'within three days'   **41 salute** greet

Music speak loudly now, the season's apt,

For former dolours are in pleasure wrapped.   *Exeunt omnes*

[Scene 11]

Enter Mucedorus to disguise himself

MUCEDORUS Now, Mucedorus, whither wilt thou go?

Home to thy father, to thy native soil,

Or try some long abode within these woods?

Well, I will hence depart and hie me home.

5   What, hie me home, said I? That may not be.

In Amadine rests my felicity.

Then, Mucedorus, do as thou didst decree,

Attire thee hermit-like, within these groves,

Walk often to the beech and view the well,

10   Make settles there and seat thyself thereon,

And when thou feel'st thyself to be athirst,

Then drink a hearty draught to Amadine.

No doubt she thinks on thee,

And will one day come pledge thee at this well.

15   Come, habit, thou art fit for me!   *He disguises himself*

No shepherd now, a hermit I must be:

Methinks this fits me very well.

Now must I learn to bear a walking-staff,

And exercise some gravity withal.

Enter the Clown [Mouse]

20   MOUSE   Here's through the woods, and through the woods, to look out a shepherd and a stray king's daughter. But soft, who have we here? What art thou?

MUCEDORUS I am an hermit.

MOUSE   An emmet? I never saw such big emmet in all my life before!

MUCEDORUS I tell you, sir, I am an hermit, one that leads a solitary life within these

25   woods.

MOUSE   O, I know thee now! Thou art her that eats up all the hips and haws: we could not have one piece of fat bacon for thee all this year.

MUCEDORUS Thou dost mistake me. But, I pray thee, tell me what dost thou seek in these woods?

30   MOUSE   What do I seek? For a stray king's daughter run away with a shepherd!

MUCEDORUS A stray king's daughter run away with a shepherd! Wherefore, canst thou tell?

---

42 **season's apt** time is right   43 **dolours** sorrows   *omnes* 'all' (Latin)   **[Scene 11]**   *Location: the woods of Aragon*   3 **abode** stay/residence   4 **hie** hasten   10 **settles** seats   11 **athirst** thirsty/earnestly desirous   14 **pledge** drink to/make a promise to   15 **habit** garment, especially the dress of a religious order   19 **withal** in addition   20 **Here's…woods** Mouse is complaining about the constant search for Mucedorus and Amadine   23 **emmet** ant   26 **hips and haws** hedgerow fruits (from the rose and the hawthorn respectively) which would normally be fed to the pig to produce **fat bacon**   27 **for** because of   31 **Wherefore** for what reason

MOUSE   Yes, that I can. 'Tis this: my master and Amadine walking one day abroad nearer to these woods than they were used — about what I cannot tell —
35   but towards them comes running a great bear; now my master he played the man and ran away, and Amadine crying after him. Now, sir, comes me a shepherd and he strikes off the bear's head. Now whether the bear were dead before or no, I cannot tell, for bring twenty bears before me and bind their hands and feet and I'll kill them all! Now, ever since Amadine hath been in love with the shepherd, and for good will,
40   she's even run away with the shepherd.

MUCEDORUS   What manner of man was he? Canst describe him unto me?

MOUSE   Scribe him? Ay, I warrant you that I can: a was a little low, broad, tall, narrow, big, well-favoured fellow, a jerkin of white cloth and buttons of the same cloth.

45   MUCEDORUS   Thou describest him well, but if I chance to see any such, pray you where shall I find you, or what's your name?

MOUSE   My name is called, Master Mouse.

MUCEDORUS   Oh, Master Mouse, I pray you what office might you bear in the court?

50   MOUSE   Marry, sir, I am a rusher of the stable.

MUCEDORUS   O, usher of the table!

MOUSE   Nay, I say rusher and I'll prove mine office good: for look, sir, when any comes from under the sea or so, and a dog chance to blow his nose backward, then with a whip I give him the good time of the day, and strew rushes presently,
55   therefore I am a rusher, a high office, I promise ye.

MUCEDORUS   But where shall I find you in the court?

MOUSE   Why, where it is best being, either in the kitchen a-eating or in the buttery drinking: but if you come I will provide for thee a piece of beef and brewis knuckle deep in fat. Pray you take pains: remember Master Mouse.   *Exit*

60   MUCEDORUS   Ay, sir, I warrant I will not forget you.
         Ah, Amadine! What should become of thee?
         Whither shouldst thou go so long unknown?
         With watch and ward each passage is beset,
         So that she cannot long escape unknown.
65   Doubtless she hath lost herself within these woods
         And wand'ring to and fro she seeks the well,
         Which yet she cannot find, therefore will I seek her out.   *Exit*

Enter Bremo and Amadine

BREMO   Amadine, how like you Bremo and his woods?

AMADINE   As like the woods as Bremo's cruelty!
70   Though I were dumb and could not answer him,
         The beasts themselves would, with relenting tears,
         Bewail thy savage and inhuman deeds.

---

34 **abroad** far from home   36 **me** now (an exclamatory particle)   43 **jerkin** close-fitting jacket   48 **office** position, post   51 **usher…table** officer at court in charge of the table   53 **blow…backward** make a mess, presumably urinate or defecate   54 **strew** scatter, spread loosely   **rushes** the green stems or stalks of marsh plants; these were traditionally used on floors in place of mats or carpets   63 **watch and ward** surveillance, acting as sentinel (originally a law phrase)   **passage** thoroughfare, road, path   **beset** surrounded

	BREMO	My love, why dost thou murmur to thyself?
		Speak louder, for thy Bremo hears thee not.
75	AMADINE	My Bremo? No the shepherd is my love.
	BREMO	Have I not savèd thee from sudden death,
		Giving thee leave to live that thou mightst love?
		And dost thou whet me on to cruelty?
		Come kiss me, sweet, for all my favours past.
80	AMADINE	I may not, Bremo, and therefore pardon me.
	BREMO	See how she flings away from me!
		I will follow and give attend to her:
		Deny my love! Ah, worm of beauty,
		I will chastise thee. Come, come!
85		Prepare thy head upon the block.
	AMADINE	O, spare me, Bremo: love should limit life,
		Not to be made a murderer of himself.
		If thou wilt glut thy loving heart with blood,
		Encounter with the lion or the bear,
90		And like a wolf, prey not upon a lamb.
	BREMO	Why then dost thou repine at me?
		If thou wilt love me thou shalt be my queen.
		I will crown thee with a chaplet made of ivy,
		And make the rose and lily wait on thee:
95		I'll rend the burly branches from the oak,
		To shadow thee from burning sun.
		The trees shall spread themselves where thou dost go,
		And as they spread, I'll trace along with thee.
	AMADINE	You may, for who but you? *Aside*
100	BREMO	Thou shalt be fed with quails and partridges
		With blackbirds, larks, thrushes and nightingales.
		Thy drink shall be goat's milk and crystal water,
		Distilled from the fountains and the clearest springs.
		And all the dainties that the woods afford
105		I'll freely give thee to obtain thy love.
	AMADINE	You may, for who but you? *Aside*
	BREMO	The day I'll spend to recreate my love,
		With all the pleasures that I can devise,
		And in the night I'll be thy bedfellow,
110		And lovingly embrace thee in mine arms.
	AMADINE	One may, so may not you. *Aside*
	BREMO	The satyrs and the wood-nymphs shall attend on thee
		And lull thee asleep with music's sound:
		And in the morning when thou dost awake

78 **whet** incite   82 **attend** attendance; the 1598 Quarto had 'a rend' meaning 'tear, split or rupture' suggesting 'rape' and intensifying the sexual threat to Amadine   84 **chastise** correct, reform/discipline   91 **repine** complain, feel discontent   93 **chaplet** wreath for the head   95 **rend** tear   **burly** noble/sturdy   98 **trace** walk   99 **You...you?** You can if you like   107 **recreate** cheer, refresh/entertain   112 **satyrs** wood gods or demons of classical mythology who were half human, half animal

115	The lark shall sing good morn to my queen,
	And whilst he sings I'll kiss mine Amadine.

AMADINE   You may, for who but you?   *Aside*

BREMO   When thou art up, the wood lanes shall be strewed

With violets, cowslips and sweet marigolds,

120   For thee to trample and to trace upon;

And I will teach thee how to kill the deer,

To chase the hart and how to rouse the roe,

If thou wilt live to love and honour me.

AMADINE   You may, for who but you?   *Aside*

Enter Mucedorus

125   BREMO   Welcome, sir. An hour ago I looked for such a guest:

Be merry, wench, we'll have a frolic feast:

Here's flesh enough for to suffice us both.

Stay, sirrah, wilt thou fight or dost thou mean to die?

MUCEDORUS   I want a weapon, how can I fight?

130   BREMO   Thou wants a weapon? Why then thou yieldst to die?

MUCEDORUS   I say not so, I do not yield to die.

BREMO   Thou shalt not choose, I long to see thee dead.

AMADINE   Yet spare him, Bremo, spare him!

BREMO   Away, I say, I will not spare him.

135   MUCEDORUS   Yet give me leave to speak.

BREMO   Thou shalt not speak.

AMADINE   Yet give him leave to speak, for my sake.

BREMO   Speak on, but be not overlong.

MUCEDORUS   In time of yore when men like brutish beasts

140   Did lead their lives in loathsome cells and woods

And wholly gave themselves to witless will,

A rude unruly rout: then man to man became

A present prey. Then might prevailed,

The weakest went to walls;

145   Right was unknown, for wrong was all in all.

As men thus lived in this great outrage,

Behold one Orpheus came, as poets tell,

And them from rudeness unto reason brought,

Who led by reason soon forsook the woods.

150   Instead of caves they built them castles strong,

Cities and towns were founded by them then:

Glad were they they found such ease,

---

118 **wood lanes** paths through the woods   122 **hart** male deer after its fifth year   **rouse** to make game come out of its cover or lair (a hunting term)
roe small species of deer   126 **wench** girl/sweetheart   **frolic** merry, joyous   127 **suffice** satisfy   129 **want** lack   139 **time of yore** the past, previously
141 **witless will** unreasoning appetite   142 **rude unruly rout** ignorant, disorderly rabble   143 **might** force, power/bodily strength   144 **went to
walls** succumbed (in the struggle for survival)   146 **outrage** disorder   147 **Orpheus** venerated in classical mythology as chief among poets and
musicians   **poets…brought** the most influential version of this story is in Horace's *Ars Poetica*: 'While men still roamed the forests, they were restrained
from bloodshed and a bestial way of life by Orpheus' (Wilkins, London, 1939)

And in the end they grew to perfect amity.

Weighing their former wickedness,

155 They termed the time wherein they livèd then

A golden age, a goodly golden age.

Now, Bremo, for so I hear thee called,

If men which lived tofore as thou dost now,

Wild in wood, addicted all to spoil,

160 Returnèd were by worthy Orpheus' means.

Let me like Orpheus cause thee to return

From murder, bloodshed and like cruelty:

What, should we fight before we have a cause?

No, let's live and love together faithfully:

165 I'll fight for thee.

BREMO   Fight for me or die: or fight or else thou diest!

AMADINE Hold, Bremo, hold!

BREMO   Away I say, thou troublest me.

AMADINE You promised me to make me your queen.

170 BREMO I did, I mean no less.

AMADINE You promised that I should have my will.

BREMO   I did: I mean no less.

AMADINE Then save this hermit's life, for he may save us both.

BREMO   At thy request I'll spare him, but never any after him.

175 Say, hermit, what canst thou do?

MUCEDORUS I'll wait on thee, sometime upon the queen,

Such service shalt thou shortly have, as Bremo never had.   *Exeunt*

[Scene 12]

Enter Segasto, the Clown [Mouse] and Rumbelo

SEGASTO Come, sirs, what shall I never have you find out Amadine and the shepherd?

MOUSE And I have been through the woods, and through the woods, and could see nothing but an emmet.

5 RUMBELO Why I see a thousand emmets: thou meanest a little one?

MOUSE Nay! That emmet that I saw was bigger than thou art.

RUMBELO Bigger than I? What a fool have you to your man! I pray you, master, turn him away.

SEGASTO But dost thou hear, was he not a man?

10 MOUSE I think he was, for he said he did lead a salt-seller's life about the woods.

SEGASTO Thou wouldst say, a solitary life about the woods?

---

153 amity friendship   **156 golden age** the earliest, most perfect time on earth according to poets such as Hesiod in *Works and Days*, Virgil in *The Georgics* and Ovid in his *Metamorphoses*   **158 tofore** in the past   **159 spoil** plundering, pillaging   **160 Returnèd** bent, turned back   **166 or fight or** either fight or   **167 hold** wait, delay   **[Scene 12]**   *Location: Aragon, the court*   *Rumbelo* the name from 'rumbelow' suggests a blow, stroke/rumbling sound/ meaningless refrain (of a song)   **8 turn him away** dismiss him from your service   **10 salt-seller's life** i.e. itinerant, as salt was an expensive commodity traded along ancient salt roads; Mouse may also be alluding to Mucedorus' white clothing

MOUSE	I think it was so indeed.
RUMBELO	I thought? What a fool thou art!
MOUSE	Thou are a wise man! Why he did nothing but sleep since he went.
15 SEGASTO	But tell me, Mouse, how did he go?
MOUSE	In a white gown and a white hat on his head and a staff in his hand!
SEGASTO	I thought so, it was an hermit that walked a solitary life in the woods.

Well, get you to dinner, and after, never leave seeking till you bring some news of them, or I'll hang you both.   *Exit*

20 MOUSE	How now, Rumbelo, what shall we do now?
RUMBELO	Faith I'll home to dinner, and afterward to sleep.
MOUSE	Why then, thou wilt be hanged!
RUMBELO	Faith, I care not, for I know I shall never find them. Well, I'll once more

abroad, and if I cannot find them, I'll never come home again.

25 MOUSE	I tell thee what, Rumbelo, thou shalt go in at one end of the wood and I

at the other, and we will meet both together in the midst.

RUMBELO	Content, let's away to dinner. *Exeunt*

[Scene 13]

Enter Mucedorus solus

MUCEDORUS   Unknown to any here within these woods,
    With bloody Bremo do I lead my life.
    The monster he doth murder all he meets:
    He spareth none and none doth him escape.
5   Who would continue, who but only I,
    In such a cruel cut-throat's company?
    Yet Amadine is there: how can I choose?
    Ah, silly soul, how oftentimes she sits
    And sighs, and calls, 'Come, shepherd, come!
10   Sweet Mucedorus, come and set me free.'
    When Mucedorus, present stands her by—
    But here she comes.

Enter Amadine

    What news, fair lady as you walk, these woods?

AMADINE	Ah, hermit! None but bad: and such as thou know'st.
15 MUCEDORUS	How do you like your Bremo and his woods?
AMADINE	Not my Bremo, nor his Bremo woods!
MUCEDORUS	And why not yours? Methinks he loves you well.
AMADINE	I like him not: his love to me is nothing worth.
MUCEDORUS	Lady, in this methinks you offer wrong
20	To hate the man that ever loves you best.
AMADINE	Ah, hermit, I take no pleasure in his love.
	Neither doth Bremo like me best.

---

15 **how…go** what did he look like   **[Scene 13]** *Location: the woods of Aragon*   **2 bloody** cruel, bloodthirsty   **8 silly** defenceless

MUCEDORUS Pardon my boldness, fair lady, sith we both
    May safely talk now out of Bremo's sight;
25   Unfold to me, if so you please, the full discourse
    How, when, and why you came into these woods,
    And fell into this bloody butcher's hands.

AMADINE Hermit, I will. Of late a worthy shepherd I did love.

MUCEDORUS A shepherd, lady? Sure, a man unfit to match with you?

30 AMADINE Hermit, this is true, and when we had—

MUCEDORUS Stay there, the wild man comes
    Refer the rest until another time.

Enter Bremo

BREMO What secret tale is this? What whispering have we here?
    Villain, I charge thee tell thy tale again.

35 MUCEDORUS If needs I must, lo, here it is again:
    Whenas we both had lost the sight of thee,
    It grieved us both, but specially thy queen,
    Who in thy absence ever fears the worst,
    Lest some mischance befall your royal grace:
40   'Shall my sweet Bremo wander through the woods,
    Toil to and fro, for to redress my want,
    Hazard his life and all to cherish me?
    I like not this!' quoth she,
    And thereupon craved to know of me
45   If I could teach her handle weapons well.
    My answer was, I had small skill therein,
    But gladsome, mighty king, to learn of thee:
    And this was all.

BREMO Was't so? None can dislike of this.
50   I'll teach you both to fight, but first, my queen, begin.
    Here, take this weapon: see how thou canst use it.

AMADINE This is too big, I cannot wield it in my arm.

BREMO Is't so? We'll have a knotty crab-tree staff for thee:
    But, sirrah, tell me, what say'st thou?

55 MUCEDORUS With all my heart, I willing am to learn.

BREMO Then take my staff and see how thou canst wield it.

MUCEDORUS First teach me how to hold it in my hand.

BREMO Thou hold'st it well. Look how he doth:
    Thou mayst the sooner learn.

60 MUCEDORUS Next tell me how and when 'tis best to strike.

BREMO 'Tis best to strike when time doth serve,
    'Tis best to lose no time.

MUCEDORUS Then now or never is my time to strike.

---

23 sith since   **31 Stay there** stop at this point/say no more   **32 Refer** postpone   **36 Whenas** when   **39 mischance** accident   **41 redress** remedy, relieve   **47 gladsome** filled with gladness   **53 knotty crab-tree staff** gnarled, rugged stick of wood from a crab-apple tree   **61 time doth serve** a favourable opportunity presents itself

BREMO	And when thou strik'st, be sure to hit the head.	
65	MUCEDORUS	The head?
	BREMO	The very head!
	MUCEDORUS	Then have at thine!

He strikes him down dead

So, lie there and die: a death no doubt according to desert:

Or else a worse, as thou deserv'st a worse.

70   AMADINE   It glads my heart this tyrant's death to see.

MUCEDORUS   Now, lady, it remains in you

To end the tale you lately had begun,

Being interrupted by this wicked wight.

You said you loved a shepherd?

75   AMADINE   Ay, so I do, and none but only him

And will do still as long as life shall last.

MUCEDORUS   But tell me, lady, sith I set you free,

What course of life do you intend to take?

AMADINE   I will disguisèd wander through the world

80   Till I have found him out.

MUCEDORUS   How if you find your shepherd in these woods?

AMADINE   Ah, none so happy then as Amadine!

He discloseth himself

MUCEDORUS   In tract of time a man may alter much:

Say, lady, do you know your shepherd well?

85   AMADINE   My Mucedorus, hath he set me free?

MUCEDORUS   He hath set thee free.

AMADINE   And lived so long unknown to Amadine?

MUCEDORUS   Ay, that's a question whereof you may not be resolved.

You know that I am banished from the court?

90   I know likewise each passage is beset,

So that we cannot long escape unknown,

Therefore my will is this, that we return

Right through the thickets to the wild man's cave

And there awhile live on his provision,

95   Until the search and narrow watch be past.

This is my counsel, and I think it best.

AMADINE   I think the very same.

MUCEDORUS   Come let's be gone.

[Enter Mouse] The Clown searches and falls over the wild man [Bremo] and so carries him away

MOUSE   Nay soft, sir, are you here? A bots on you,

100   I was like to be hanged for not finding you!

We would borrow a certain stray king's daughter of you,

A wench, a wench, sir, we would have.

MUCEDORUS   A wench of me! I'll make thee eat my sword.

---

discloseth reveals   **83 tract** passing, course   **93 thickets** dense growth of shrubs   **94 provision** store (of food)   **95 narrow** strict   **99 A…you** may you be afflicted with the **bots**, parasitical worms or maggots affecting cattle and horses

	MOUSE	O, Lord! Nay, and you are so lusty, I'll call a cooling card for you.
105		Ho, master, master! Ay, come away quickly!

Enter Segasto

	SEGASTO	What's the matter?
	MOUSE	Look, master: Amadine and the shepherd: O brave!
	SEGASTO	What, minion, have I found you out?
	MOUSE	Nay, that's a lie, I found her out myself.
110	SEGASTO	Thou gadding housewife, what cause hadst thou to gad abroad,
		Whenas thou knowest our wedding day so nigh?
	AMADINE	Not so, Segasto, no such thing in hand;
		Show your assurance, then I'll answer you.
	SEGASTO	Thy father's promise my assurance is.
115	AMADINE	But what he promised, he hath not performed.
	SEGASTO	It rests in thee for to perform the same.
	AMADINE	Not I!
	SEGASTO	And why?
	AMADINE	So is my will and therefore even so.
120	MOUSE	Master, with a nonny, nonny no!
	SEGASTO	Ah, wicked villain, art thou here?
	MUCEDORUS	What needs these words? We weigh them not?
	SEGASTO	'We weigh them not!' Proud shepherd, I scorn thy company.
	MOUSE	We'll not have a corner of thy company.
125	MUCEDORUS	I scorn not thee, nor yet the least of thine.
	MOUSE	That's a lie, a would have killed me with his pugs-nando.
	SEGASTO	This stoutness, Amadine, contents me not.
	AMADINE	Then seek another that may you better please.
	MUCEDORUS	Well, Amadine, it only rests in thee
130		Without delay to make thy choice of three:
		There stands Segasto, here a shepherd stands,
		There stands the third, now make thy choice.
	MOUSE	A lord at the least I am.
	AMADINE	My choice is made, for I will none but thee.
135	SEGASTO	A worthy mate, no doubt, for such a wife.
	MUCEDORUS	And Amadine, why wilt thou none but me?
		I cannot keep thee as thy father did:
		I have no lands for to maintain thy state,
		Moreover if thou mean to be my wife,
140		Commonly this must be thy use,
		To bed at midnight, up at four,

---

104 **and...lusty** if you are so valiant, vigorous   **and if**   **cooling card** something that cools a person's passion or enthusiasm (the term is assumed to be derived from some unidentified card game)   107 **brave** excellent, capital   108 **minion** mistress, woman kept for sexual favours/slave, underling; a derogatory term which seems to be addressed to Amadine rather than Mucedorus here   110 **gadding housewife** idly wandering hussie (worthless woman)   **gad abroad** wander away from home   111 **Whenas** when   **nigh** near, close   112 **in hand** in process, being carried on   113 **assurance** betrothal, formal engagement   119 **even so** just that   120 **nonny, nonny no!** a nonsense refrain (of a song), the general sense is negative here and plays on 'nonny-no', a mere trifle, 'nonny-nonny' a euphemism for a woman's 'vulva'   122 **weigh** value/consider   124 **corner** even the smallest part   125 **least of thine** most unimportant of your family   126 **a** would he would   **pugs-nando** presumably Mouse's rendering of 'pugnacity' (belligerence) or 'poniardo', a slim dagger   127 **stoutness** arrogance, haughtiness   140 **Commonly** generally, normally   **use** practice

Drudge all day and trudge from place to place,

Whereby our daily victual for to win:

And last of all, which is the worst of all,

145   No princess then but plain a shepherd's wife.

MOUSE   Then, 'God give you good morrow, goody shepherd'.

AMADINE   It shall not need, if Amadine do live,

Thou shalt be crownèd king of Aragon.

MOUSE   O, master, laugh, when he's king then I'll be a queen.

150   MUCEDORUS   Then know that which ne'er tofore was known:

I am no shepherd, no Aragonian I,

But born of royal blood — my father's of Valencia

King, my mother queen — who for thy sacred sake

Took this hard task in hand.

155   AMADINE   Ah, how I joy, my fortune is so good.

SEGASTO   Well now I see, Segasto, shall not speed!

But, Mucedorus, I as much do joy

To see thee here within our court of Aragon

As if a kingdom had befallen me this time.

160   I, with my heart, surrender her to thee   *He gives her to him*

And lose what right to Amadine I have.

MOUSE   What barn's door and born where my father

Was constable! A bots on thee, how dost thee?

MUCEDORUS   Thanks, Segasto, but yet you levelled at the crown.

165   MOUSE   Master, bear this and bear all.

SEGASTO   Why so, sir?

MOUSE   He says you take a goose by the crown.

SEGASTO   Go to, sir! Away, post you to the king,

Whose heart is fraught with careful doubts,

170   Glad him up and tell him these good news,

And we will follow as fast as we may.

MOUSE   I go master, I run master.   *Exeunt*

[Scene 14]

Enter the King and Collin

KING   Break heart and end my pallid woes,

My Amadine — the comfort of my life —

How can I joy except she were in sight?

---

142 **Drudge** work hard performing servile, menial tasks   **trudge** walk wearily   143 **victual** food   **win** earn, gain   146 **'God…shepherd'** 'Good morning, mistress shepherd's wife'; Mouse is parodying the speech of working folk and the way in which Amadine would be addressed if she were to marry a shepherd   **goody** polite form of address to a married woman of the lower classes, from 'goodwife'   156 **speed** be successful   162 **barn's door** i.e. a proverbially large door, applied humorously to something too big to be missed   163 **A…thee** a plague on you – used here in a jovial sense   164 **levelled** aimed   167 **goose…crown** apart from the literal meaning, **goose** was slang for a 'loose woman or prostitute' and **crown** means 'head'   168 **Go to** get on with you   **post** hurry   169 **fraught** full, laden down   **careful doubts** anxious worries   **[Scene 14]   1 pallid** pale, wan (from illness or shock)   3 **except…sight** unless I can see her

Her absence breeds sorrow to my soul

5   And with a thunder breaks my heart in twain.

COLLIN   Forbear those passions, gentle king,

And you shall see t'will turn unto the best,

And bring your soul to quiet and to joy.

KING   Such joy as death, I do assure me that,

10   And nought but death unless of her I hear,

And that with speed, I cannot sigh thus long.

But what a tumult do I hear within?   *They cry within,*

COLLIN   I hear a noise of over-passing joy   *'Joy and happiness!'*

Within the court. My lord, be of good comfort;

15   And here comes one in haste.

Enter the Clown [Mouse] running

MOUSE   A king, a king, a king!

COLLIN   Why how now, sirrah, what's the matter?

MOUSE   O, 'tis news for a king: 'tis worth money.

KING   Why, sirrah, thou shalt have silver and gold, if it be good.

20   MOUSE   O, 'tis good, 'tis good! Amadine!

KING   Oh, what of her? Tell me, and I will make thee a knight.

MOUSE   How a spright? No by lady, I will not be a spright!

Masters, get you away, if I be a spright, I shall be so lean

I shall make you all afraid.

25   COLLIN   Thou sot! The king means to make thee a gentleman.

MOUSE   Why, I shall want 'parrel.

KING   Thou shalt want for nothing.

MOUSE   Then stand away, trick up thyself: here they come.

Enter Segasto, Mucedorus and Amadine

AMADINE   My gracious father, pardon thy disloyal daughter.

30   KING   What, do mine eyes behold my daughter Amadine?

Rise up, dear daughter, and let these, my embracing arms,

Show some token of thy father's joy,

Which ever since thy departure

Hath languishèd in sorrow.

35   MUCEDORUS   Dear father,

Never were your sorrows greater than my griefs:

Never you so desolate as I comfortless,

Yet nevertheless, acknowledging myself

To be the cause of both, on bended knees,

40   I humbly crave your pardon.

KING   I'll pardon thee, dear daughter: but as for him—

AMADINE   Ah, father, what of him?

KING   As sure as I am king, and wear the crown,

I will revenge on that accursèd wretch.

---

22 spright ghost, disembodied spirit   **25 sot** fool/drunkard   **26 'parrel** apparel, clothing   **28 trick up thyself** get yourself dressed up

45	MUCEDORUS	Yet, worthy prince, work not thy will in wrath
		Show favour.
	KING	Ay, such favour as thou deservest.
	MUCEDORUS	I do deserve the daughter of a king.
	KING	O, impudent! A shepherd and so insolent!
50	MUCEDORUS	No shepherd I, but a worthy prince.
	KING	In fair conceit, not princely born.
	MUCEDORUS	Yes, princely born: my father is a king,
		My mother queen, and of Valencia both.
	KING	What, Mucedorus? Welcome to our court!
55		What cause hadst thou to come to me disguised?
	MUCEDORUS	No cause to fear. I causèd no offence
		But this: desiring thy daughter's virtues for to see,
		Disguised myself from out my father's court,
		Unknown to any; in secret I did rest
60		And passèd many troubles near to death.
		So hath your daughter my partaker been,
		As you shall know hereafter more at large:
		Desiring you, you will give her to me,
		Even as mine own and sovereign of my life,
65		Then shall I think my travels are well spent.
	KING	With all my heart: but this.
		Segasto claims my promise made tofore,
		That he should have her as his only wife,
		Before my council when we came from war.
70		Segasto, may I crave thee let it pass
		And give Amadine as wife to Mucedorus?
	SEGASTO	With all my heart, were it a far greater thing,
		And what I may to furnish up their rites,
		With pleasing sports and pastimes you shall see.
75	KING	Thanks, good Segasto: I will think of this.
	MUCEDORUS	Thanks, good my lord, and, while I live
		Account of me in what I can or may.
	AMADINE	And, good Segasto, these great courtesies
		Shall not be forgot.
80	MOUSE	Why hark you, master: bones, what have you done?
		What given away the wench you made me take such pains for! You are wise indeed!
		Mass, and I had known of that I would have had her myself. Faith, master now we
		may go to breakfast with a woodcock pie.
	SEGASTO	Go, sir, you were best leave this knavery.
85	KING	Come on, my lords, let's now to court

---

51 **fair conceit** just capacity/judgement/disposition/personal vanity   62 **at large** in more detail   65 **travels** journeys, playing on 'travails' hardships/ suffering   73 **what...rites** whatever else will serve to facilitate their marriage celebrations   77 **Account...may** count on me to do whatever I am able or permitted   80 **bones** by God's bones   82 **and...myself** i.e. if I'd known you were going to do that I'd have taken her myself, with a bawdy play on **had**   83 **woodcock** game bird/fool, simpleton, one easily caught like the bird

Where we may finish up the joyfullest day

That ever happed to a distressèd king.

Were but thy father, the Valencia lord,

Present in view of this combining knot!   *A shout within*

Enter a Messenger

90   What shout was that?

MESSENGER   My lord, the great Valencia king,

Newly arrived, entreats your presence.

MUCEDORUS   My father?

KING   Prepared welcomes give him entertainment:

95   A happier planet never reigned than that

Which governs at this hour.   *Sound [trumpets]*

Enter the King of Valencia, Anselmo, Rodrigo, Barachius, with others: the king runs

and embraces his son

VALENCIA   Rise, honour of my age, food to my rest.—

Condemn not, mighty king of Aragon,

My rude behaviour, so compelled by nature,

100   That manners stood unacknowledged.

KING   What we have to recite would tedious prove.

By declaration: therefore, in and feast:

Tomorrow the performance shall explain

What words conceal. Till then, drums speak, bells ring,

105   Give plausive welcomes to our brother king.   *Sound drums and trumpets*

                                                           Exeunt omnes

[Epilogue]

Enter Comedy and Envy

COMEDY   How now, Envy, what blushest thou already?

Peep forth, hide not thy head with shame

But with courage praise a woman's deeds.

Thy threats were vain: thou couldst do me no hurt,

5   Although thou seem'st to cross me with despite,

I overwhelmed and turned upside down thy block

And made thyself to stumble at the same.

ENVY   Though stumbled yet not overthrown:

Thou canst not draw my heart to mildness.

10   Yet must I needs confess thou hast done well

And played thy part with mirth and pleasant glee.

Say all this, yet canst thou not conquer me,

Although this time thou hast got

Yet not the conquest neither:

15   A double revenge another time I'll have.

87 **happed** befell, occurred 88 **Were but** if only 89 **combining knot** betrothal or marriage, joining these two together 99 **rude** discourteous (by arriving uninvited) **compelled by nature** forced by natural affection 105 **plausive** deserving of applause **[Epilogue]** 5 **despite** contemptuous treatment/scorn/defiance/malice, hatred 6 **block** obstacle

COMEDY Envy, spit thy gall,

Plot, work, contrive, create new fallacies.

Teem from thy womb each minute a black traitor

Whose blood and thoughts have twin conception.

20 Study to act deeds yet unchronicled,

Cast native monsters in the moulds of men,

Case vicious devils under sancted rochets,

Unhasp the wicket where all perjureds roost

And swarm this ball with treasons. Do thy worst!

25 Thou canst not, hell-hound, cross my star tonight,

Nor blind that glory where I wish delight.

ENVY I can, I will.

COMEDY Nefarious hag, begin,

And let us tug till one the mast'ry win.

30 ENVY Comedy, thou art a shallow goose,

I'll overthrow thee in thine own intent

And make thy fall, by comic merriment.

COMEDY Thy policy wants gravity, thou art too weak:

Speak, fiend, as how?

35 ENVY Why thus:

From my foul study will I hoist a wretch,

A lean and hungry neger cannibal

Whose jaws swell to his eyes, with chawing malice,

And him I'll make a poet.

40 COMEDY What's that to the purpose?

ENVY This scrambling raven with his needy beard

Will I whet on to write a comedy

Wherein shall be composed dark sentences,

Pleasing to factious brains,

45 And every otherwhere place me a jest

Whose high abuse shall more torment than blows.

Then I myself (quicker than lightning)

Will fly me to the puissant magistrate

And, waiting with a trencher at his back,

50 In the midst of jollity rehearse those galls,

With some additions, so lately vented in your theatre.

He, upon this, cannot but make complaint

To your great danger or at least restraint.

COMEDY Ha, ha, ha! I laugh to hear thy folly!

---

16 gall bile/rancour **17 fallacies** tricks, lies **18 Teem** produce, give birth to **19 twin conception** double, deceitful purposes **20 act** perform, carry out **22 Case** cover, clothe **sancted** i.e. sainted, sacred **rochets** white ecclesiastical vestments similar to surplices, usually worn by bishops **23 Unhasp** unfasten **wicket** small door or gate **perjureds** those guilty of lies, false oaths or testimonies **roost** lodge **24 swarm this ball** fill, beset this earth, globe **28 Nefarious hag** wicked demon, evil spirit (usually in female form) **29 tug** contend, strive in opposition **30 goose** fool/whore **37 neger** negro **38 chawing** chewing/ruminating **40 What's … purpose?** What's the point of that? **41 scrambling** shambling, uncouth/ambitious, unscrupulous **raven** one who brings bad news or makes gloomy predictions, literally a bird of the crow family, and feeds on carrion, dead flesh, hence 'scavenger' **needy** poor/under an obligation **42 whet on** incite, encourage **43 dark sentences** difficult problems, enigmas **44 factious** argumentative **45 otherwhere** other place **48 puissant** powerful, influential **49 trencher** knife/platter for serving meat **50 rehearse those galls** repeat those bitter jibes; 'to dip one's pen in **gall**' meant to write with virulence and rancour **51 vented** poured out **52 He** i.e. the poet

55   This is a trap for boys, not men, nor such,

        Especially desertful in their doings,

        Whose staid discretion rules their purposes:

        I and my faction do eschew those vices.

        But see, O, see, the weary sun for rest

60   Hath lain his golden compass to the west

        Where he perpetuall bide, and ever shine

        As David's offspring in this happy clime.

        Stoop, Envy, stoop, bow to the earth with me,

        Let's beg our pardon on our bended knee.   *They kneel*

65   ENVY   My power hath lost her might, Envy's date's expired.

        Yon splendent majesty hath felled my sting

        And I amazèd am.   *Fall down and quake*

        COMEDY   Glorious and wise, arch-Caesar on this earth,

        At whose appearance Envy's strucken dumb

70   And all bad things cease operation.

        Vouchsafe to pardon our unwilling error,

        So late presented to your gracious view,

        And we'll endeavour with excess of pain

        To please your senses in a choicer strain.

75   Thus we commit you to the arms of night

        Whose spangled carcass would for your delight

        Strive to excel the day. Be blessèd then:

        Who other wishes let him never speak.

        ENVY   Amen.

80   To fame and honour we commend your rest,

        Live still more happy, every hour more blessed.

FINIS

The following passage from Q1, which originally followed scene 14 line 87, was replaced by the arrival of the King of Valencia in Q3

Lines are numbered from 1 for ease of reference

        With mirth and joy and great solemnity,
        We'll finish up these Hymen's rites most pleasantly.
        MOUSE   Ho, lords, at the first — I am one too — but hear, master king, by your leave a cast,
        now you have done with them. I pray you begin with me.

55 This…vices (lines 55–8) this passage refers to the companies such as the Queen's Revels who performed satirical works by well-known writers; the company's royal patronage was withdrawn in 1605 after their performance of Jonson, Marston and Chapman's *Eastward Ho* with its satirical reference to the Scots and the subsequent imprisonment of two of the poets   **boys, not men** a reference to the companies of boy players such as the Children of the Queen's Revels   **eschew** avoid, keep clear of   **62 David's** the biblical King David whose offspring were promised eternal reign by God   **clime** region, realm   **66 Yon splendent majesty** i.e. King James   **Yon** over there   **splendent** magnificent   **felled my sting** defeated my capacity to inflict harm   **68 arch-Caesar** pre-eminent ruler (the title is derived from the Roman emperors of that name); James I was flattered by the comparison of himself with Augustus Caesar who had brought peace, the *pax romana*, to the Roman empire   **71 Vouchsafe** grant, graciously bestow   **73 pain** effort   **76 spangled carcass** starry body, i.e. of the person of Night   **78 other wishes** desires otherwise   *Q1 scene 14 passage:*   **2 Hymen's rites** celebrations of marriage; Hymen was the Greek god of marriage   **3 cast** cast-off (clothing)

5	KING	Why what wouldst thou have?
	MOUSE	O, you forgot, now, a little apparel to make's handsome: what should lords go so beggarly as I do?
	KING	What I did promise thee, I will perform: attend on me. Come let's depart.
	ALL	We'll wait on you with all our hearts.
10	MOUSE	And with a piece of my liver too! *Exeunt omnes*

The following is the ending of the play in Q1, written for a court performance before Queen Elizabeth. The Q3 ending was written for a court performance before King James. This extract followed directly on from Epilogue line 15

Lines are numbered from 1 for ease of reference

COMEDY Then caitiff cursed, stoop upon thy knee
Yield to a woman, though not to me,
And pray we both together with our hearts,
That she thrice Nestor's years may with us rest,
5 And from her foes high God defend her still,
That they against her may never work their will.
ENVY Envy, were he never so stout,
Would beck and bow unto her majesty.
Indeed, Comedy, thou hast overrun me now
10 And forced me stoop unto a woman's sway.
God grant her grace amongst us long may reign,
And those that would not have it so,
Would that, by Envy, soon their hearts they might forgo.
COMEDY The council, nobles, and this realm,
15 Lord guide it still with thy most holy hand;
The commons and the subjects grant them grace
Their prince to serve, her to obey and treason to deface.
Long may she reign in joy and great felicity!
Each Christian heart do say 'amen' with me.

FINIS

Textual Notes

Q = Quarto text of 1598

Q1 = Quarto text of 1606

Q3 = Quarto text of 1610

Ed = a correction introduced by a later editor???

List of parts = Ed

Induction 15 breath = Q1. Q3 = bearth **23 dankish** = Ed. Q3 = Danish **36 seek to** =Q1 *Not in Q3*
  54 forbearance = Q1. Q3 = forbeare
1.6 ne'er = Ed. Q3 = neare **19 lest** = Ed. Q3 = least
2.6 her = Ed. Q = him **80 of** = Ed. Q3 = so **116 bade** *spelled* bad *in Q3*

6 **make's** make us; aristocrats frequently gave or sold their unwanted clothes to the acting companies; in the absence of scenery, costume provided necessary onstage spectacle and cost far more than a playtext *Q1 Epilogue ending:* 1 **caitiff cursed** cursed villain, wretch 2 **woman** Queen Elizabeth I, this conclusion relates to an earlier version of the play before 1603 when Elizabeth was on the throne 4 **thrice Nestor's years** Nestor was the wise, elder statesman of the Greeks who reputedly lived for three centuries, so the plea is for Elizabeth to live for 900 years 8 **beck** give a sign of respect or obeisance 13 **forgo** relinquish, resign 16 **commons** common people, the House of Commons in Parliament which represents common people

3.26 grudge = Ed. Q3 = grutch

4.4 should = Q1. Q3 = could   **51 is** = Ed. *Not in* Q3   **59 my good lord** = Q1. Q3 = good my lord

5.6 A needless = Ed. Q3 = An endless   **7 commands** = Ed. Q = commander   **14 do** = Q1. Q3 = doth

6.15 sirrah = Q1. Q3 = sirra   **65 sheep's ticks** = Ed. Q3 = shipsticks   **75 thee** = Q1. Q3 = him   **80 I thought** = Q 1650. *Not in* Q3   **82 this** = Ed. Q3 = the

7.31 lest = Ed. Q3 = least   **66 with** = Q1. Q3 = of   **my** = Ed. *Not in* Q3   **86 our** = Q1. Q3 = my   **92 whoso** = Ed. Q3 = so who

9.78 for = Q1. Q3 = or   **118 her** = Q1. Q3 = the

10.8 light = Ed. Q3 = sight   **24 affectious** = Q3. Ed = affection's

11.16 I must be = Q1. Q3 = must I be   **28 what** = Q1. Q3 = who   **52 I'll** = Q1. Q3 = I   **69 as** = Ed. Q3 = of   **90 like a** = Ed. Q1 = a like   **93 chaplet** = Ed. Q3 = complet   **ivy** = Ed. Q3 = Ivorie   **95 oak** = Q1. Q3 = oxe   **146 this** = Ed. Q1 = his. Q3 = their   **149 soon** = Ed. Q3 = some   **176 the** = Q1. Q3 = thy

12.10 I = Ed. *Not in* Q3

13.11 present = Ed. Q1 = pesent. Q3 = peasant   **25 if so** = Q1. Q3 = so if   **39 Lest** = Ed. Q3 = Least   **120 nonny, nonny** = Ed. Q3 = none, none   **161 lose** = Ed. Q3 = looke   **167 says** = Ed. Q3 = sees

14.28 trick = Q1. Q3 = strike   **87 happed** = Ed. Q3 = hapt   **100 unacknowledged** = Ed. Q3 = unknowledged

Epilogue 62 this = Ed. Q3 = his

Q1 Epilogue 14 nobles = Ed. Q1 = noble

DOUBLE FALSEHOOD or THE DISTRESSED LOVERS

Double Falsehood is the odd play out in this collection. We can say for sure of all the others that they are plays from the Elizabethan and Jacobean period, to which Shakespeare may or may not have contributed. All of them are written in a poetic and prose language that is authentically of the period and recognizable as characteristic of that greatest age of English drama. *Double Falsehood*, by contrast, is, in the form in which it survives, unquestionably a drama that belongs to the early eighteenth century. Precisely what, if any, relationship it bears to a putative lost play by William Shakespeare and John Fletcher remains a matter of fierce debate.

The evidence in the case is laid out in brief in the Key Facts box and at length in the essay on Authorship and Attribution. But it is worth stating the headlines here. We know that at the end of his career Shakespeare collaborated with John Fletcher, a younger dramatist who specialized in tragicomedy and who had perhaps come to Shakespeare's particular attention by virtue of his sequel to *The Taming of the Shrew* called *The Woman's Prize, or the Tamer Tamed*. There is a broad scholarly consensus that *Henry VIII* and *The Two Noble Kinsmen* are collaborations between Shakespeare and Fletcher. Internal stylistic evidence clearly supports this view and indeed scholars have decisively identified which scenes of those plays were Shakespeare's and which were Fletcher's. *The Two Noble Kinsmen* was published in 1634 with a clear attribution to both dramatists. Fletcher continued to write for the King's Men after Shakespeare's death and it is generally assumed that he effectively took over the role of company in-house playwright with the consent of the master. The old idea that Shakespeare renounced the theatre and retired to Stratford-upon-Avon after writing *The Tempest* in 1611 is very questionable. He purchased a gatehouse close to the Blackfriars Theatre in 1613 and there is a sighting of him in London in late 1614, only eighteen months before his death.

Given this, there is an inherent plausibility in an entry in the Stationer's Register for 1653, where a bookseller called Humphrey Moseley registered his right to publish 'The History of Cardenio by Mr Fletcher and Shakespeare'. Many of Moseley's attributions are highly questionable and some of them plain wrong. But, even though the play was never published, he must have had a script that he considered publishing and it is a reasonable inference that what he had bore some relationship to a play called *Cardenna* or *Cardenno*, for which John Hemings, business manager of the King's Men and intimate friend of Shakespeare, received payments for court performances in May and June 1613, exactly the time when a Shakespeare-Fletcher collaboration along the lines of *The Two Noble Kinsmen* could still have been live.

But the manuscript of *Cardenna/Cardenno/Cardenio* has vanished. What we have instead is a play that the eighteenth-century Shakespeare scholar Lewis Theobald *claimed* was 'revised and adapted' from 'the manuscript copy of an original play of William Shakespeare'. It was in 1727 that Theobald, rival to Alexander Pope for the position of Shakespeare's editorial representative on earth, made this startling announcement – akin in the world of incipient Bardolatry to the discovery of the Holy Grail (or at least of the elusive *Love's Labour's Won*). The play was staged to some acclaim and duly published the following year, with a special royal licence giving Theobald exclusive rights to the text.

A lively debate raged in the periodical press and the coffee houses: had Theobald discovered a lost jewel or fabricated a monstrous forgery? A suspicious degree of obfuscation surrounds his various claims about the authenticity of the piece, but the balance of probability suggests that he did possess a manuscript in the handwriting of John Downes, the prompter of the Restoration acting company that inherited much of the Shakespeare and Fletcher repertoire. The trouble is, Restoration acting companies played fast and loose with old plays. Notoriously, Nahum Tate, author of the hymn 'While Shepherds Watched their Flocks by Night', held the stage for a hundred and fifty years with a 1681 version of *King Lear* that has no Fool and a happy ending in which Cordelia marries Edgar. Imagine that the early printed texts of Shakespeare's *Lear* had not survived, and we only had the Tate reworking. That would be the equivalent of the situation with *Cardenio*. Even if Theobald was telling the truth about his manuscript, not perpetrating his own double falsehood, the play is at a double distance from Shakespeare himself: there's Theobald and behind him there was the Restoration adapter, and behind them there seems to have been a lot more Fletcher than Shakespeare.

At worst, Theobald was lying and forging outright, and the play is a pseudo-Shakespearean pastiche. As such, it would be of some interest and is of some accomplishment: it paves the way for numerous later eighteenth-century and Romantic verse dramas that tried to catch the aura of Shakespearean verse as a way of paying homage to his poetic and dramatic genius. At best, we have the shadow or the ghost of a lost play written in late 1612 or early 1613, and performed at court, and almost certainly on the stage of the Blackfriars and/or the Globe, by the King's Men at a time when there was something of a political rapprochement with Spain and a concomitant interest in all matters Spanish.

The plot is based on the love-madness of Cardenio, a character encountered by Don Quixote and Sancho Panza in the immortal novel by Shakespeare's exact contemporary, Miguel de Cervantes. *Don Quixote* had been translated into English for the first time by one Thomas Shelton in that very year of 1612. *Double Falsehood* has some very specific verbal echoes of Shelton, so we can say with certainty that either Theobald or Shakespeare/Fletcher (or all of them) had a copy of the translation to hand. We reproduce the relevant passages from Shelton as an appendix to our script of *Double Falsehood*, thus enabling readers to reconstruct their own lost *Cardenio* in the gap between the source and the adaptation.

One complication comes from the names. Shakespeare often changed the names of the characters in his sources, as when adapting Greene's *Pandosto* into *The Winter's Tale*. Sometimes, though, he retained them, as when he and Fletcher adapted Chaucer's *The Knight's Tale* into *The Two Noble Kinsmen*. Equally, Restoration and early eighteenth-century stage alterations of Shakespeare sometimes changed the names of characters. In this case, since the early references are to 'Cardenio' (or 'Cardenno' or 'Cardenna'), the likelihood is that the changes of name belong to a later stage alteration (either that of the Downes manuscript or that of Theobald). It is hard to imagine a play called *Cardenio* in which Cardenio does not feature because he has become Julio. In imagining the lost *Cardenio* in the context of its source, the reader has to remember that

Theobald's Julio was Cardenio in Shelton's translation of Cervantes.
Theobald's Leonora was Lucinda in Shelton's translation of Cervantes.
Theobald's Henriquez was Fernando in Shelton's translation of Cervantes.
Theobald's Violante was Dorothea in Shelton's translation of Cervantes.

In addition, Theobald's Duke Angelo (who, as it happens, is only named in the *dramatis personae* list and one scene header, never in the dialogue) was Duke Ricardo in Shelton.

It is almost impossible to tell how much of the play is Theobald's invention, how much derives from a possible Restoration adaptation and how much is somehow authentically Fletcherian or Shakespearean. None of the vocabulary is glaringly eighteenth century as opposed to early seventeenth century, but the tone and rhythms of the play have undoubtedly been filtered through an early eighteenth-century sensibility. Most notably, a veil of propriety is drawn over certain aspects of the rape of Violante in a way that would almost certainly have been less modest in the original. There is a taste for feminine endings in the iambic pentameter rhythm, and a certain slackness to the poetic imagery, that has the feel much more of Fletcher than of Shakespeare.

The handling of the source material in *Don Quixote* is an especially Fletcherian feature. The difficulty of dramatizing the story of Cardenio is that in Cervantes it is woven in with the story of Don Quixote himself. *Double Falsehood* resolves the plot simply and elegantly without all the elaborate journeys to inns and the involvement of the Don, the barber and others as interlocutors and interferers. It does so by greatly expanding the role of the virtuous elder brother Roderick (who must originally have been a more Hispanic Roderigo). Unnamed and incidental in Cervantes/Shelton, he becomes a benign fixer. His role is typical of a pattern in many Fletcher plays, where virtuous and vicious foils set each other off: Fletcher, who always wrote with a close eye on the court of King James I, was particularly keen on the idea of royal virtue, so if there was to be a lascivious prince it was necessary to introduce a notably well-intentioned brother by way of contrast.

Some of Theobald's early critics said that the play was much more likely to have been by Fletcher than Shakespeare, and that may be why, after the initial flurry of publicity, Theobald did not overpress his claim in later years. Perhaps he omitted *Double Falsehood* from his subsequent edition of Shakespeare's complete plays not only because he knew it was an adaptation as opposed to an original but because he came to see that the genuine original might have found its true home in an edition of Fletcher. It would have been odd for Theobald to forge Shakespeare in the style of Fletcher rather than Shakespeare, so the general Fletcherian aura rather tells against those who claimed the whole thing was a fabrication.

When Henriquez speaks of his sighs riding 'on the night's chill vapour' and of Violante being 'as fair / As nature's richest mould and skill can make her, / Mended with strong imagination', the language could be Shakespearean but could equally well be pastiche. But for some good critics there is an art beyond the capacity of Theobald or even Fletcher in some of the imagery. One passage in particular seems to sound the authentic late-Shakespearean verse-note:

VIOLANTE   ... Home, my lord,
    What you can say, is most unseasonable; what sing,
    Most absonant and harsh: nay, your perfume,
    Which I smell hither, cheers not my sense
    Like our field-violet's breath.
HENRIQUEZ Why this dismission
    Does more invite my staying.

The delicate pattern of repetition ('what ... say', 'what sing', 'most unseasonable', 'Most ... harsh'); the rare sixteenth-century word 'absonant' (meaning discordant); the specificity of imagination which chooses 'field-violet' rather than plain 'violet': these have the feel not of decorous eighteenth-century imitation but of genuine Shakespearean word-work. Equally, Henriquez is very like the

Angelo of *Measure for Measure* – or for that matter King Edward III trying to seduce the Countess of Salisbury – in the way that the fact of being rebuffed spurs his ardour to win the woman to his sexual will.

There are many obvious parallels with Shakespearean scenes. When 'A gleam of day breaks sudden' from Violante's window and she appears in the 'above' space, we inevitably think of *Romeo and Juliet*. In the pitting of heterosexual desire against bonds of male friendship, there are echoes of both *The Two Gentlemen of Verona* and *The Two Noble Kinsmen*. When Leonora swoons upon being betrothed, then returns many scenes later under a veil, as if coming back from death, there is an obvious similarity to Hero in *Much Ado about Nothing*. When the action moves to the pastoral world, complete with jolly shepherds, we inevitably think of *The Winter's Tale* (especially as there is a character called Camillo). And the cross-dressed adventures of Violante follow in the tracks of Viola as Cesario in *Twelfth Night*, Innogen as Fidele in *Cymbeline* and several more.

Again, however, we simply cannot know whether Shakespeare was imitating himself (which he sometimes did), whether Fletcher was imitating Shakespeare (which he often did, for example in the Ophelia-like character of the Jailer's Daughter in *The Two Noble Kinsmen*), or whether Theobald created the imitation a hundred years later. Whatever the true history, *Double Falsehood/Cardenio*, which has recently been revived in a number of reconstructions, including one by Gregory Doran, Artistic Director of the Royal Shakespeare Company (see his account in 'From Script to Stage'), is a fascinating embodiment of the collaboration that ultimately keeps Shakespeare alive: that between the original theatre-work of his company and the authors, adapters, editors and acting companies who have revivified his work in later generations.

KEY FACTS

AUTHORSHIP: The extant play is avowedly by Lewis Theobald, a claim which is undisputed. Theobald claimed that the play was adapted from a hitherto unknown Shakespearean play, of which he possessed three copies. Scholars continue to debate whether or not Theobald was telling the truth or whether the play was an elaborate forgery. Against him is counted the non-survival of his manuscripts and the unlikelihood of the situation; in his favour, the play follows Cervantes' story of Cardenio which, unknown to Theobald's contemporaries, is the most likely source for a lost play called *Cardenna/Cardenno* attributed to Shakespeare in 1613. Despite the fact that Shakespeare's chronology would not be established until the 1790s, *Double Falsehood* is closely related to the themes and structures of Shakespeare's plays from this period. Further, Theobald claimed that the original was by Shakespeare, yet it contains linguistic features more usually associated with John Fletcher, who was Shakespeare's reported collaborator on the lost play.

The growing consensus, as followed by Gary Taylor, Brean Hammond, David Carnegie, MacDonald Jackson and Richard Proudfoot, is that Shakespeare and Fletcher collaborated on *Cardenna/Cardenno* around 1613, with Shakespeare largely responsible for the first two acts of the play and Fletcher for the final three. A Restoration adaptation has been posited; which, to judge by the treatment accorded to Davenant's adaptation of the similarly collaborative *The Two Noble Kinsmen*, would likely have excised more Shakespeare than Fletcher in accordance with the poetic preferences of the day. Theobald's play, based on this adaptation, retains some Fletcherian and very little Shakespearean dialogue, as evidenced by several authorship

▷

studies, but still contains useful evidence of the original play's plot, structure and concerns. However, since the publication of the play in the Arden Shakespeare series, the case for forgery has been more strongly asserted by several scholars including Tiffany Stern, and the play remains a source of contention.

PLOT: Julio and Leonora are in love, and are awaiting the consent of their respective fathers, Camillo and Don Bernard, to be wed. However, Julio is called away to court in the hope that he can be a calming influence on the Duke's prodigal son, Henriquez. Henriquez lusts after Violante, his social inferior, and he rapes her when she refuses his advances. He then switches his affections to Leonora, and arranges for Julio to be kept at court while he arranges with Don Bernard to force Leonora into marriage. Leonora gets word to Julio, who arrives to disrupt the wedding but is ejected from the ceremony and runs away to the mountains, mad. Leonora flees to a nunnery, and Henriquez sets out to find her; while the ruined Violante disguises herself as a boy and sets out to follow Henriquez. Some time later, Julio is raving in the hillsides near where Violante is living with a group of shepherds. Roderick, the Duke's elder son, arrives seeking his brother and is in time to rescue Violante from another rape attempt by the Master of the Flocks. He meets his brother, and they extract Leonora from the nunnery in an empty coffin. Meanwhile, Julio and Violante meet and recognize each other, and Violante employs Roderick's help to right their wrongs. As the Duke and fathers arrive in the country, it is left to Roderick to enact the reconciliation of lovers, parents and children.

MAJOR PARTS: Julio (16%/78/6), Henriquez (14%/52/7), Leonora (14%/48/6), Violante (13%/64/7), Roderick (11%/66/5), Camillo (9%/69/4), Don Bernard (7%/43/6), Duke Angelo (5%/32/2), Master of the Flocks (2%/19/1), Citizen (1%/12/3), 1 Shepherd (1%/13/1).

LINGUISTIC MEDIUM: 86% verse, 14% prose.

DATE: *Cardenna/Cardenno* was performed in 1613, according to two court accounts which register payment to John Hemings on behalf of the King's Men, and was probably written in 1612, immediately following the publication of Thomas Shelton's translation of the relevant parts of *Don Quixote* in that year. *Double Falsehood* was first performed at Drury Lane in 1727 and published the following year.

SOURCES: The primary source is Miguel de Cervantes' *Don Quixote* Part 3, Chapters 5, 9–10, 14; and Part 4, Chapters 1–2, 9–10. Shelton's English translation (1612) was used by the authors. The original features the Cardenio story in fragments, interspersed among the ongoing adventures of Don Quixote and Sancho Panza. As well as changing all the character names (Cardenio himself becomes Julio), the framing material is removed and the story remoulded into a more conventional tragicomic/romance structure.

TEXT: Two Octavo editions were issued in 1728, both appearing to be reasonably accurate reflections of the text as performed on the eighteenth-century stage, although printed slightly carelessly, particularly in respect of lineation. The second issue was essentially a reprint, but included an extended preface which expressed more reticence about the play's authorship, following disputation by Theobald's peers. Theobald took the unusual step of securing a royal licence for the published version of the play, seemingly conferring more legitimacy on his claims.

[Royal Licence]
George Rex[*]

George the Second, by the grace of God, king of Great Britain, France and Ireland, defender of the faith, etc. to all to whom these presents shall come, greeting. Whereas our trusty, and well-beloved Lewis Theobald,[†] of our city of London, gent.[‡] hath, by his petition, humbly represented to us, that he having, at a considerable expense, purchased the manuscript copy of an original play of William Shakespeare,[§] called, *Double Falsehood or The Distressed Lovers*, and, with great labour and pains, revised, and adapted the same to the stage has humbly besought us to grant him our royal privilege and licence[¶] for the sole printing and publishing thereof, for the term of fourteen years. We, being willing to give all due encouragement to this his undertaking, are graciously pleased to condescend to his request and do therefore, by these presents, so far as may be agreeable to the statute in that behalf made and provided, for us, our heirs, and successors, grant unto him, the said Lewis Theobald, his executors, administrators, and assigns, our royal licence, for the sole printing and publishing the said play, in such size and manner, as he and they shall think fit, for the term of fourteen years, to be computed from the date hereof; strictly forbidding all our subjects within our kingdoms and dominions, to reprint the same, either in the like, or in any other size, or manner whatsoever; or to import, buy, vend, utter or distribute any copies thereof, reprinted beyond the seas, during the aforesaid term of fourteen years, without the consent, or approbation of the said Lewis Theobald, his heirs, executors, and assigns, under his, or their hands and seals first had, and obtained; as they will answer the contrary at their peril: whereof the commissioners, and other officers of our customs, the Master, Warden, and Company of Stationers, are to take notice, that the same may be entered in the register of the said company, and that due obedience be rendered thereunto. Given at our court at St. James's, the fifth day of December, 1727; in the first year of our reign.

By his majesty's command,
Holles Newcastle.^{**}

---

[*] **Rex** 'king' (Latin); George II (1683–1760)

[†] **Lewis Theobald** a distinguished editor of Shakespeare's plays, in 1726 he produced a Shakespeare variorum: *Shakespeare Restored, or a Specimen of the many Errors as well Committed as Unamended by Mr Pope in his late edition of this poet; designed not only to correct the said Edition, but to restore the true Reading of Shakespeare in all the Editions ever published.* Theobald's own edition of Shakespeare's plays (1733) set a new standard of scholarship. He conducted a long-standing, bad-tempered quarrel with Alexander Pope who made him the hero of his satirical poem, *The Dunciad* (1728) in which his name is pronounced 'Tibbald'

[‡] **gent.** gentleman, an indication of social rank

[§] **manuscript…Shakespeare** this manuscript has never been found and both contemporaries such as Pope and some later critics believe the claim to be a fiction and the play a forgery; the modern scholarly consensus however agrees that the play is an eighteenth-century rewriting of the lost Shakespeare play, *Cardenio*

[¶] **licence** the Statute of Anne (1709) gave authors copyright over their material for a fixed term; the 1662 Licensing Act had established a register of published books, a copy to be lodged with the Stationers' Company which protected the rights of the printer rather than the author; the Theatrical Licensing Act of 1737 required that all plays must be submitted to the Lord Chamberlain for approval before performance

^{**} **Holles Newcastle** Thomas Pelham-Holles, Duke of Newcastle, was Lord Chamberlain from 1717 to 1724; an influential Whig politician, he later became Prime Minister

DOUBLE FALSEHOOD or THE DISTRESSED LOVERS. A play as it is acted at the THEATRE-ROYAL in DRURY-LANE.[*] Written Originally by W. SHAKESPEARE; And now Revised and Adapted to the Stage By Mr Theobald, the Author of Shakespeare Restored.

> — *Quod optanti Divûm promittere nemo*
> *Auderet, volvenda Dies, en! attulit ultrò.*[†] Virgil

[Dedication]

To the Right Honourable George Dodington,[‡] Esq;

Sir,

Nothing can more strongly second the pleasure I feel, from the universal applause which crowns this orphan play, than this other which I take in presuming to shelter it under your name. I bear so dear an affection to the writings and memory of Shakespeare, that, as it is my good fortune to retrieve this remnant of his pen from obscurity, so it is my greatest ambition that this piece should be received into the protection of such a patron: and, I hope, future times, when they mean to pay Shakespeare the best compliment, will remember to say, Mr. Dodington was that friend to his remains, which his own Southampton[§] was to his living merit.

It is from the fine discernment of our patrons, that we can generally best promise ourselves the good opinion of the public. You are not only a distinguished friend of the muses, but most intimately allied to them: and from hence it is I flatter myself, that if you shall think fit to pronounce this piece genuine, it will silence the censures of those unbelievers, who think it impossible a manuscript of Shakespeare could so long have lain dormant; and who are blindly paying me a greater compliment than either they design, or I can merit, while they cannot but confess themselves pleased, yet would fain insinuate that they are imposed upon. I should esteem it some sort of virtue, were I able to commit so agreeable a cheat.

---

[*] **Theatre-Royal in Drury-Lane** the oldest London theatre dating back to 1663 when it was one of two Restoration patent theatres

[†] *Quod... ultrò* 'What none of all the gods could grant thy vows, / That, Turnus, this auspicious day bestows', a quotation from Virgil (*Aeneid* 9: 6) in John Dryden's translation frequently quoted in the period in relation to the Restoration of Charles II in 1660

[‡] **George Dodington** first Baron Melcombe, an English politician and friend of the Prince of Wales

[§] **Southampton** Henry Wriothesley, Earl of Southampton, and the dedicatee of Shakespeare's narrative poems, *Venus and Adonis* and *The Rape of Lucrece*; he is sometimes thought of as Shakespeare's patron although there is no direct evidence of his patronage

But pardon me, sir, for a digression that perverts the very rule of dedications. I own, I have my reasons for it. As, sir, your known integrity, and honour engages the warmest wishes of all good men for your prosperity, so your known distinction in polite letters, and your generous encouragement of those who pretend to them, obliges us to consider your advancement, as our own personal interest, and as a good omen, at least, if not as the surest means of the future flourishing condition of those humane arts amongst us, which we profess, and which you adorn. But neither your modesty, nor my inability, will suffer me to enter upon that subject. Permit me therefore, sir, to convert panegyric* into a most ardent wish, that you would look with a tender eye on this dear relic, and that you would believe me, with the most unfeigned zeal and respect,

Sir,
Your most devoted and obedient humble servant,
Great Russell Street,
21st December, 1727.

Lewis Theobald.

Preface of the Editor

The success, which this play has met with from the town in the representation, (to say nothing of the reception it found from those great judges, to whom I have had the honour of communicating it in manuscript;) has almost made the purpose of a preface unnecessary: and therefore what I have to say, is designed rather to wipe out a flying objection or two, than to labour at proving it the production of Shakespeare.

It has been alleged as incredible, that such a curiosity should be stifled and lost to the world for above a century. To this my answer is short; that though it never till now made its appearance on the stage, yet one of the manuscript copies, which I have, is of above sixty years' standing, in the handwriting of Mr. Downes,† the famous old prompter; and, as I am credibly informed, was early in the possession of the celebrated Mr. Betterton,‡ and by him designed to have been ushered into the world. What accident prevented this purpose of his, I do not pretend to know: or through what hands it had successively passed before that period of time. There is a tradition (which I have from the noble person, who supplied me with one of my copies) that this play was given by our author, as a present of value, to a natural§ daughter of his, for whose sake he wrote it, in the time of his retirement from the stage. Two other copies I have, (one of which I was glad to purchase at a very good rate,) which may not, perhaps, be quite so old as the former; but one of them is much more perfect, and has fewer flaws and interruptions in the sense.

Another objection has been started, (which would carry much more weight with it, were it fact;) that the tale of this play, being built upon a novel in *Don Quixote*, chronology is against us, and Shakespeare could not be the author. But it happens, that the first part of *Don Quixote*, which contains the novel upon which the tale of this play seems to be built, was published in the year 1605, and our Shakespeare did not die till April 1616;¶ an interval of no less than eleven years, and more than sufficient for all that we want granted.

---

* **panegyric** public speech or published text of praise
† **Mr. Downes** John Downes (died c.1712) was prompter at the Duke's Company and later the United Company (1660–1700) with Betterton as actor-manager. His theatrical review of the period, *Roscius Anglicanus* (1708), is an invaluable historical source
‡ **Mr. Betterton** Thomas Betterton (1635–1710) was the greatest actor-manager of the age
§ **natural** illegitimate
¶ **1616** Miguel de Cervantes, the author of *Don Quixote* (or *Don Quijote* in modern Spanish) is said to have died on the same day as Shakespeare, 23 April 1616

Others again, to depreciate the affair, as they thought, have been pleased to urge, that though the play may have some resemblances of Shakespeare, yet the colouring, diction, and characters, come nearer to the style and manner of Fletcher.[*] This, I think, is far from deserving any answer, I submit it to the determination of better judgments though my partiality for Shakespeare makes me wish, that everything which is good, or pleasing, in that other great poet, had been owing to his pen. I had once designed a dissertation to prove this play to be of Shakespeare's writing, from some of its remarkable peculiarities in the language, and nature of the thoughts but as I could not be sure that the play might be attacked, I found it advisable, upon second consideration, to reserve that part to my defence. That danger, I think, is now over so I must look out for a better occasion. I am honoured with so many powerful solicitations, pressing me to the prosecution of an attempt, which I have begun with some little success, of restoring Shakespeare from the numerous corruptions of his text that I can neither in gratitude nor good manners longer resist them. I therefore think it not amiss here to promise, that, though private property should so far stand in my way, as to prevent me from putting out an edition of Shakespeare,[†] yet, some way or other, if I live, the public shall receive from my hand his whole works corrected, with my best care and ability. This may furnish an occasion for speaking more at large concerning the present play, for which reason I shall now drop it for another subject.

As to the performance[‡] of the respective actors concerned in this play, my applauding it here would be altogether superfluous. The public has distinguished and given them a praise, much beyond any that can flow from my pen. But I have some particular acknowledgments to make to the managers of this company, for which I am glad to embrace so fair an opportunity.

I came to them at this juncture as an editor, not an author, and have met with so much candour and handsome treatment from them that I am willing to believe the complaint, which has so commonly obtained, of their disregard and ill behaviour to writers, has been more severely urged[§] than it is justly grounded. They must certainly be too good judges of their own interest not to know that a theatre cannot always subsist on old stock, but that the town requires novelty at their hands. On the other hand, they must be so far judges of their own art and profession, as to know that all the compositions which are offered them would never go down with audiences of so nice and delicate a taste as in this age frequent the theatres. It would be very hard upon such a community, where so many interests are concerned and so much merit in their business allowed, if they had not a privilege of refusing some crude pieces, too imperfect for the entertainment of the public. I would not be thought to infer that they have never discouraged what they might, perhaps, afterwards wish they had received. They do not, I believe, set up for such a constant infallibility. But if we do but fairly consider, out of above four thousand plays extant, how small a number will now stand the test; if we do but consider too, how often a raw performance has been extolled[¶] by the partiality of private friendship and what a clamour of injury has been raised from that quarter upon such performance meeting a repulse, we may pretty easily account for the grounds upon which they proceeded in discountenancing some plays, and the harsh things that are thrown out upon their giving a repulse to others.

But I should beg pardon for interfering in this question, in which I am properly neither party nor judge. I am only throwing out a private opinion, without interest or prejudice, and if I am right in the notion, *Valeat quantum valere potest.*[**]

---

[*] **Fletcher** John Fletcher (1579–1625) succeeded Shakespeare as playwright of the King's Men, collaborating with him in the writing of *Henry VIII*, *The Two Noble Kinsmen* and almost certainly *Cardenio*

[†] **edition of Shakespeare** Theobald's scrupulously annotated edition finally appeared in 1733

[‡] **performance** the play had been successfully staged at Drury Lane in 1727

[§] **urged** alleged

[¶] **extolled** elevated/highly praised

[**] *Valeat...potest* 'Let it pass for what it is worth' (Latin)

Dramatis Personae

MEN

Duke Angelo	Mr Corey
Roderick, his Elder Son	Mr Mills
Henriquez, his Younger Son	Mr Wilks
Don Bernard, Father to Leonora	Mr Harper
Camillo, Father to Julio	Mr Griffin
Julio, in Love with Leonora	Mr Booth
Citizen Mr Oates	
Master of the Flocks	Mr Bridgwater
First Shepherd	Mr Norris
Second Shepherd	Mr Ray

WOMEN

Leonora	Mrs Porter
Violante	Mrs Booth

SCENE, the Province of Andalusia in Spain.

Prologue

Written by Philip Frowde Esquire,
And spoken by Mr Wilks

As in some region where indulgent skies
Enrich the soil, a thousand plants arise
Frequent and bold, a thousand landscapes meet
Our ravished view, irregularly sweet:
5 We gaze, divided, now on these, now those,
While all one beauteous wilderness compose.
Such Shakespeare's genius was: let Britons boast
The glorious birth and, eager, strive who most
Shall celebrate his verse, for while we raise
10 Trophies of fame to him, ourselves we praise:
Display the talents of a British mind,
Where all is great, free, open, unconfined.
Be it our pride, to reach his daring flight,
And relish beauties, he alone could write.
15 Most modern authors, fearful to aspire,
With imitation cramp their genial fire,
The well-schemed plan keep strict before their eyes,
Dwell on proportions, trifling decencies,

Prologue   Philip Frowde Esquire (1678/79–1738), a minor poet and playwright, the designation 'Esquire' suggests his status as a gentleman
18 trifling decencies the eighteenth and nineteenth centuries were concerned with politeness and social etiquette, rejecting the bawdy of earlier periods

While noble nature all neglected lies.
20   Nature, that claims precedency of place,
Perfection's basis, and essential grace!
Nature so intimately Shakespeare knew,
From her first springs his sentiments he drew,
Most greatly wild they flow, and, when most wild, yet true.
25   While these, secure in what the critics teach,
Of servile laws still dread the dangerous breach;
His vast, unbounded soul disdained their rule,
Above the precepts of the pedant school!
O, could the Bard, revisiting our light,
30   Receive these honours done his shade tonight,
How would he bless the scene this age displays,
Transcending his Eliza's golden days!
When great Augustus fills the British throne,
And his loved consort makes the muse her own.
35   How would he joy, to see fair merit's claim
Thus answered in his own reviving fame!
How cry with pride, 'Oblivion I forgive,
This my last child to latest times shall live:
Lost to the world, well for the birth it stayed
40   To this auspicious era well delayed.'

Act 1 Scene 1

Scene: A royal palace
[*Enter*] *Duke Angelo, Roderick and Courtiers*

RODERICK   My gracious father, this unwonted strain
Visits my heart with sadness.

DUKE   Why, my son?
Making my death familiar to my tongue
5   Digs not my grave one jot before the date.
I've worn the garland of my honours long,
And would not leave it withered to thy brow,
But flourishing and green, worthy the man,
Who, with my dukedoms, heirs my better glories.

10   RODERICK   This praise, which is my pride, spreads me with blushes.

DUKE   Think not that I can flatter thee, my Roderick,

---

20 precedency precedence, pre-eminence   **30 shade** ghost   **32 Eliza's golden days** the reign of Queen Elizabeth I   **33 Augustus** a flattering reference to George II, whose second name was Augustus, likening him to Caesar Augustus, the Roman Emperor with whom George II's father, George I, had wished to be identified: literature written in Augustus' era by writers such as Virgil and Horace is considered the high point of Latin literature; the literature of the late seventeenth/early eighteenth century with its emphasis on taste and decorum and following of classical models is similarly referred to as Augustan   **34 consort** i.e. Queen Caroline   **38 last child** implying *Cardenio* was Shakespeare's final play   **1.1   1 unwonted strain** unaccustomed characteristic (way of talking)   **4 Making…tongue** talking in a **familiar** way of my death   **9 heirs** inherits

Or let the scale of love o'erpoise my judgement.

Like a fair glass of retrospection, thou

Reflect'st the virtues of my early youth,

15   Making my old blood mend its pace with transport:

While fond Henriquez, thy irregular brother,

Sets the large credit of his name at stake,

A truant to my wishes, and his birth;

His taints of wildness hurt our nicer honour,

20   And call for swift reclaim.

RODERICK   I trust, my brother

Will, by the vantage of his cooler wisdom,

E'er-while redeem the hot escapes of youth,

And court opinion with a golden conduct.

25   DUKE   Be thou a prophet in that kind suggestion!

But I, by fears weighing his unweighed course,

Interpret for the future from the past.

And strange misgivings, why he hath of late

By importunity and strained petition,

30   Wrested our leave of absence from the court,

Awake suspicion. Thou art inward with him

And, haply, from the bosomed trust canst shape

Some formal cause to qualify my doubts.

RODERICK   Why he hath pressed this absence, sir, I know not

35   But have his letters of a modern date,

Wherein by Julio, good Camillo's son,

(Who, as he says, shall follow hard upon

And whom I with the growing hour expect)

He doth solicit the return of gold

40   To purchase certain horse that like him well.

This Julio he encountered first in France,

And lovingly commends him to my favour,

Wishing, I would detain him some few days,

To know the value of his well-placed trust.

45   DUKE   O, do it, Roderick, and assay to mould him

An honest spy upon thy brother's riots.

Make us acquainted when the youth arrives;

---

12 **o'erpoise** weighs down/overbalances   15 **mend** restore, correct   **transport** joy, rapture   16 **fond** foolish, mad   **irregular** lawless, disorderly
17 **Sets…stake** gambles with the great reputation of his family name   18 **truant** one who neglects his duty   19 **taints** touches   **nicer** more
scrupulous   20 **reclaim** improvement, reformation   22 **by the vantage** from the superior position   **cooler** calmer, more composed   23 **E'er-while**
meanwhile   **hot** lustful, licentious/dangerous   **escapes** mistakes/transgressions (especially breaches of chastity)   24 **court opinion** seek to win
esteem   **golden** excellent   25 **Be thou** may you be   **kind** generous, affectionate/agreeable   26 **unweighed** ill-considered, hasty   29 **importunity**
persistent, troublesome requesting   **strained** pushed beyond what is natural or reasonable   **petition** entreaty, request   30 **Wrested** extracted by
force   31 **inward** close, intimate   32 **haply** perhaps   **bosomed** enclosed, hidden (in the bosom)   **trust** confidence   33 **formal cause** reasonable
motive/essential reason   **qualify** moderate, mitigate   **doubts** fears   34 **pressed** insisted upon   35 **modern** recent   36 **Wherein** in which   37 **hard**
upon very shortly   40 **horse** i.e. horses   **like him well** that suit, please him (and hence he wants to buy)   42 **lovingly commends** recommends him
affectionately   44 **know** become acquainted with   45 **assay** try/test whether you can   **mould** make him into   46 **honest** virtuous, having honourable
motives/truthful   **riots** debaucheries   47 **Make us acquainted** let me know

We'll see this Julio, and he shall from us
Receive the secret loan his friend requires.
50   Bring him to court.   *Exeunt*

Act 1 Scene 2

[*Scene:*] *Prospect of a village at a distance*
Enters Camillo with a letter

CAMILLO   How comes the duke to take such notice of my son, that he must needs
have him in court, and I must send him upon the view of his letter? Horsemanship!
What horsemanship has Julio? I think he can no more but gallop a hackney,
unless he practised riding in France. It may be he did so, for he was there a good
5   continuance. But I have not heard him speak much of his horsemanship. That's
no matter: if he be not a good horseman, all's one in such a case, he must bear.
Princes are absolute; they may do what they will in anything, save what they
cannot do.

Enters Julio

O, come on, sir: read this paper: no more ado, but read it: it must not be answered by
10   my hand nor yours but in gross, by your person: your sole person. Read aloud.

JULIO   Please you, to let me first o'erlook it, sir.

CAMILLO   I was this other day in a spleen against your new suits: I do now think,
some fate was the tailor that hath fitted them: for, this hour, they are for the palace
of the duke. Your father's house is too dusty.

15   JULIO   Hem! To court? Which is the better, to serve a mistress, or a duke? I am   *Aside*
sued to be his slave, and I sue to be Leonora's.

CAMILLO   You shall find your horsemanship much praised there; are you so good
a horseman?

JULIO   I have been,

20   Ere now, commended for my seat, or mocked.

CAMILLO   Take one commendation with another, every third's a mock. Affect not
therefore to be praised. Here's a deal of command and entreaty mixed; there's no
denying; you must go, peremptorily he enforces that.

JULIO   What fortune soever my going shall encounter cannot be good fortune;
25   what I part withal unseasons any other goodness.   *Aside*

CAMILLO   You must needs go; he rather conjures than importunes.

JULIO   No moving of my love-suit to him now!   *Aside*

CAMILLO   Great fortunes have grown out of less grounds.

---

49 his friend i.e. Henriquez   **1.2**   *Prospect* view/a pictorial representation: such painted backdrops were a theatrical innovation of the period   **3 hackney**
ordinary riding horse (as opposed to a war horse)   **5 continuance** long time   **6 all's one** it's all the same/it doesn't matter   **bear** suffer, endure   **7 absolute**
autonomous, having unlimited power or authority   **10 in gross** generally/in full, playing on sense of 'in the flesh'   **12 spleen** fit of temper, the 'spleen' was
regarded as an organ generating a variety of passions   **13 fate** agent of destiny   **14 dusty** full of dust/mean, worthless   **16 sued** petitioned, requested
17 there i.e. in the letter   **20 Ere** before   **seat** way of sitting (on horseback)   **21 Affect not** don't aspire to/be fond of   **23 denying** refusing   **peremptorily**
as a positive command/without question   **25 part** leave, forsake   **withal** besides/at the same time   **unseasons** deprives of relish   **26 must needs** are
obliged to   **conjures** charges, constrains by oath   **importunes** requests, urges   **27 moving** advancing, promoting   **love-suit** pursuit of love, playing on
legal sense of 'suit', the prosecution of a cause   **28 grounds** foundations/well-founded reasons

JULIO	What may her father think of me, who expects to be solicited	*Aside*

30 this very night?

CAMILLO   Those scattered pieces of virtue which are in him, the court will solder

together, varnish, and rectify.

JULIO	He will surely think I deal too slightly, or unmannerly, or	*Aside*

foolishly, indeed, nay, dishonestly; to bear him in hand with my father's consent,

35 who yet hath not been touched with so much as a request to it.

CAMILLO   Well, sir, have you read it over?

JULIO   Yes, sir.

CAMILLO   And considered it?

JULIO   As I can.

40 CAMILLO   If you are courted by good fortune, you must go.

JULIO   So it please you, sir.

CAMILLO   By any means, and tomorrow: is it not there the limit of his request?

JULIO   It is, sir.

CAMILLO   I must bethink me of some necessaries without which you might be

45 unfurnished and my supplies shall at all convenience follow you. Come to my closet

by and by; I would there speak with you.   *Exit Camillo*

JULIO   I do not see that fervour in the maid,   *Manet Julio solus*

Which youth and love should kindle. She consents

As 'twere to feed without an appetite,

50 Tells me she is content and plays the coy one,

Like those that subtly make their words their ward,

Keeping address at distance. This affection

Is such a feigned one as will break untouched,

Die frosty ere it can be thawed, while mine,

55 Like to a clime beneath Hyperion's eye,

Burns with one constant heat. I'll straight go to her,

Pray her to regard my honour: but she greets me.

Enter Leonora and Maid

See, how her beauty doth enrich the place!

O, add the music of thy charming tongue,

60 Sweet as the lark that wakens up the morn,

And make me think it paradise indeed.

I was about to seek thee, Leonora,

And chide thy coldness, love.

LEONORA   What says your father?

65 JULIO   I have not moved him yet.

LEONORA   Then do not, Julio.

JULIO   Not move him? Was it not your own command,

29 **solicited** approached, asked (for his daughter's hand in marriage)   31 **solder...rectify** unite, embellish and bring to a proper condition/convert to a particular use   33 **slightly** carelessly/with too little respect   34 **bear...hand** delude   35 **who...it** i.e. whom I have not yet broached the subject with   42 **any** whatever   45 **unfurnished** unprepared, unequipped   **closet** private room   *Manet Julio solus* 'Julio remains alone' (Latin)   51 **ward** guard, watchman   52 **address** courtship   55 **clime** region of the earth   **Hyperion's eye** the sun; in classical mythology Hyperion was one of the Titans, often referred to as *Helios Hyperion*   64 **LEONORA** was originally LEON. in speech headings throughout

That his consent should ratify our loves?

LEONORA   Perhaps, it was: but now I've changed my mind.
70   You purchase at too dear a rate, that puts you
        To woo me and your father too: besides,
        As he, perchance, may say you shall not have me,
        You, who are so obedient, must discharge me
        Out of your fancy: then, you know, 'twill prove
75   My shame and sorrow, meeting such repulse,
        To wear the willow in my prime of youth.

JULIO   O, do not rack me with these ill-placed doubts;
        Nor think, though age has in my father's breast
        Put out love's flame, he therefore has not eyes
80   Or is in judgement blind. You wrong your beauties,
        Venus will frown if you disprize her gifts,
        That have a face would make a frozen hermit
        Leap from his cell, and burn his beads to kiss it,
        Eyes that are nothing but continual births
85   Of new desires in those that view their beams.
        You cannot have a cause to doubt.

LEONORA   Why, Julio?
        When you that dare not choose without your father,
        And, where you love, you dare not vouch it; must not,
90   Though you have eyes, see with 'em; can I, think you,
        Somewhat, perhaps, infected with your suit,
        Sit down content to say, you would, but dare not?

JULIO   Urge not suspicions of what cannot be;
        You deal unkindly, misbecomingly,
95   I'm loath to say: for all that waits on you
        Is graced, and graces. No impediment
        Shall bar my wishes, but such grave delays
        As reason presses patience with, which blunt not
        But rather whet our loves. Be patient, sweet.

100 LEONORA   Patient! What else? My flames are in the flint.
        Haply, to lose a husband I may weep,
        Never to get one: when I cry for bondage,
        Let freedom quit me.

JULIO   From what a spirit comes this?
105   I now perceive too plain you care not for me!
        Duke, I obey thy summons, be its tenor
        Whate'er it will: if war, I come thy soldier,

---

70 **purchase...rate** undertake too great a task   72 **perchance** perhaps   73 **discharge** release/get rid of   74 **fancy** fantasy/imagination/love   75 **repulse** rejection, rebuff   76 **wear the willow** grieve for the loss of a loved one   77 **rack me** tear me apart/torture me (from the instrument of torture used to stretch the victim's joints)   **ill-placed** misplaced, inopportune   **doubts** fears, apprehensions/uncertainties   81 **Venus** Roman goddess of love   **disprize** undervalue, make of small account   82 **frozen** cold-blooded, not subject to sexual desire   83 **beads** rosary beads, used for keeping count of the number of prayers said   89 **vouch** announce/assert/give proof   94 **misbecomingly** unbecomingly, unfittingly   95 **loath** unwilling, reluctant   98 **presses** urges/tries hard to persuade/pushes forward   99 **whet** sharpen   100 **flames...flint** passions are firm, steadfast

Or if to waste my silken hours at court,
The slave of fashion, I with willing soul
110   Embrace the lazy banishment for life,
Since Leonora has pronounced my doom.

LEONORA   What do you mean? Why talk you of the duke?
Wherefore of war, or court, or banishment?

JULIO   How this new note is grown of me, I know not
115   But the duke writes for me. Coming to move
My father in our business, I did find him
Reading this letter whose contents require
My instant service, and repair to court.

LEONORA   Now I perceive the birth of these delays,
120   Why Leonora was not worth your suit.
Repair to court? Ay, there you shall, perhaps,
(Rather, past doubt) behold some choicer beauty,
Rich in her charms, trained to the arts of soothing,
Shall prompt you to a spirit of hardiness,
125   To say, 'So please you, father, I have chosen
This mistress for my own.'

JULIO   Still you mistake me:
Ever your servant I profess myself,
And will not blot me with a change for all
130   That sea and land inherit.

LEONORA   But when go you?

JULIO   Tomorrow, love, so runs the duke's command;
Stinting our farewell-kisses, cutting off
The forms of parting and the interchange
135   Of thousand precious vows with haste too rude.
Lovers have things of moment to debate,
More than a prince or dreaming statesman know:
Such ceremonies wait on Cupid's throne.
Why heaved that sigh?

140   LEONORA   O, Julio, let me whisper
What, but for parting, I should blush to tell thee:
My heart beats thick with fears lest the gay scene,
The splendours of a court, should from thy breast
Banish my image, kill my int'rest in thee,
145   And I be left, the scoff of maids, to drop
A widow's tear for thy departed faith.

JULIO   O, let assurance, strong as words can bind,

---

111 doom fate, judgement   **114 note** circumstance   **grown of me** come into existence on my behalf   **118 repair** going   **122 choicer** more exquisite/
appropriate   **124 hardiness** boldness   **129 blot me** stain, tarnish my reputation   **133 Stinting** cutting short   **135 rude** barbarous/unmannerly
136 moment importance, significance   **138 Cupid's** belonging to Cupid, the Roman god of love, son of Venus   **145 scoff** object of contempt or scorn,
mark for derision

Tell thy pleased soul, I will be wond'rous faithful;
True, as the sun is to his race of light,
150 As shade to darkness, as desire to beauty:
And when I swerve, let wretchedness o'ertake me,
Great as e'er falsehood met, or change can merit.

LEONORA   Enough! I'm satisfied and will remain
Yours, with a firm and untired constancy.
155 Make not your absence long: old men are wav'ring,
And swayed by int'rest more than promise giv'n.
Should some fresh offer start when you're away,
I may be pressed to something which must put
My faith, or my obedience, to the rack.

160 JULIO   Fear not, but I with swiftest wing of time
Will labour my return. And in my absence,
My noble friend, and now our honoured guest,
The Lord Henriquez, will in my behalf
Hang at your father's ear, and with kind hints,
165 Poured from a friendly tongue, secure my claim;
And play the lover for thy absent Julio.

LEONORA   Is there no instance of a friend turned false?
Take heed of that: no love by proxy, Julio.
My father—

Enters Don Bernard

170 DON BERNARD   What, Julio, in public? This wooing is too urgent. Is your father yet
moved in the suit who must be the prime unfolder of this business?

JULIO   I have not yet, indeed, at full possessed
My father, whom it is my service follows,
But only that I have a wife in chase.

175 DON BERNARD   Chase! Let chase alone: no matter for that. You may halt after her,
whom you profess to pursue, and catch her too; marry, not unless your father let
you slip. Briefly, I desire you, (for she tells me, my instructions shall be both eyes
and feet to her) no farther to insist in your requiring, till, as I have formerly said,
Camillo make known to me that his good liking goes along with us, which but
180 once breathed, all is done; till when, the business has no life, and cannot find a
beginning.

JULIO   Sir, I will know his mind, ere I taste sleep:
At morn, you shall be learned in his desire.
I take my leave.— O virtuous Leonora,
185 Repose, sweet as thy beauties, seal thy eyes;

---

148 **pleased** contented   149 **race of light** i.e. to cross the sky   151 **swerve** go astray/am disloyal   156 **int'rest** interest, regard to their own profit
or advantage   158 **must...rack** i.e. which is bound to stretch my faith (in you) and obedience (to my father) to the limit   161 **labour** work to bring
about   168 **by proxy** through a substitute   171 **prime unfolder** main instigator   172 **full...father** put my father in full possession of the facts
173 **service** condition of being a servant (of Love/a lady), derived from the medieval concept of 'courtly love'   174 **have...chase** am in pursuit of a wife
175 **halt** limp, walk unsteadily/waver/play false   176 **profess** vow/claim   **marry** get married to/by the Virgin Mary, exclamation expressing surprise, outrage
177 **slip** loose/escape

Once more, adieu. I have thy promise, love;

Remember, and be faithful.   *Exit Julio*

DON BERNARD   His father is as unsettled, as he is wayward, in his disposition. If I
thought young Julio's temper were not mended by the mettle of his mother, I should

190   be something crazy in giving my consent to this match: and, to tell you true, if my
eyes might be the directors to your mind, I could in this town look upon twenty
men of more delicate choice. I speak not this altogether to unbend your affections
to him: but the meaning of what I say is, that you set such price upon yourself to
him, as many, and much his betters, would buy you at; (and reckon those virtues in

195   you at the rate of their scarcity) to which if he come not up, you remain for a better
mart.

LEONORA   My obedience, sir, is chained to your advice.

DON BERNARD   'Tis well said, and wisely. I fear, your lover is a little folly-tainted;
which, shortly after it proves so, you will repent.

200   LEONORA   Sir, I confess, I approve him of all the men I know; but that approbation
is nothing, till seasoned by your consent.

DON BERNARD   We shall hear soon what his father will do, and so proceed accordingly.
I have no great heart to the business, neither will I with any violence oppose it: but
leave it to that power which rules in these conjunctions, and there's an end. Come;

205   haste we homeward, girl.   *Exeunt*

[Act 1] Scene 3

Enter Henriquez, and Servants with lights

HENRIQUEZ   Bear the lights close: where is the music, sirs?

SERVANT   Coming, my lord.

HENRIQUEZ   Let 'em not come too near. This maid,

For whom my sighs ride on the night's chill vapour

5   Is born most humbly, though she be as fair

As nature's richest mould and skill can make her,

Mended with strong imagination.

But what of that? Th'obscureness of her birth

Cannot eclipse the lustre of her eyes,

10   Which make her all one light.— Strike up, my masters;

But touch the strings with a religious softness;

Teach sound to languish through the night's dull ear,

Till melancholy start from her lazy couch,

And carelessness grow convert to attention.   *Music plays*

15   She drives me into wonder, when I sometimes

---

186 **adieu** 'goodbye' (French)   188 **wayward** self-willed, disobedient   189 **mettle** disposition/courage   192 **delicate** charming/fastidious   194 **reckon**
calculate/measure   196 **mart** market   200 **approve** commend/find by experience   201 **seasoned** perfected/disciplined   **[1.]3   Scene:** *Location not
specified*   7 **Mended** improved   8 **Th'obscureness** the obscurity/inconspicuousness, lack of importance (socially)   13 **melancholy … couch** one of
the medieval or Renaissance humours or temperaments, **melancholy** is here personified and imaged as lazily lying down, to be woken suddenly by the
music   **start** awake or move suddenly   14 **carelessness** indifference, inattention   **grow convert to** is converted into

Hear her discourse; the court, where of report
And guess alone inform her, she will rave at,
As if she there sev'n reigns had slandered time.
Then, when she reasons on her country state,
20 Health, virtue, plainness, and simplicity,
On beauties true in title, scorning art,
Freedom as well to do, as think, what's good;
My heart grows sick of birth and empty rank,
And I become a villager in wish.
25 Play on — she sleeps too sound — be still, and vanish:
A gleam of day breaks sudden from her window:
O taper, graced by that midnight hand!

Violante appears above at her window

VIOLANTE Who is't, that woos at this late hour? What are you?

HENRIQUEZ One, who for your dear sake—

30 VIOLANTE Watches the starless night!
My lord Henriquez, or my ear deceives me.
You've had my answer, and 'tis more than strange
You'll combat these repulses. Good my lord,
Be friend to your own health, and give me leave,
35 Securing my poor fame, nothing to pity
What pangs you swear you suffer. 'Tis impossible
To plant your choice affections in my shade,
At least, for them to grow there.

HENRIQUEZ Why, Violante?

40 VIOLANTE Alas! Sir, there are reasons numberless
To bar your aims. Be warned to hours more wholesome,
For these you watch in vain. I have read stories,
(I fear, too true ones) how young lords, like you,
Have thus besung mean windows, rhymed their sufferings
45 Even to th'abuse of things divine, set up
Plain girls, like me, the idols of their worship,
Then left them to bewail their easy faith,
And stand the world's contempt.

HENRIQUEZ Your memory,

50 Too faithful to the wrongs of few lost maids,
Makes fear too general.

VIOLANTE Let us be homely,
And let us too be chaste, doing you lords no wrong,
But crediting your oaths with such a spirit,

16 whereof...her which she only knows about from what she's heard or guesses   **17 rave at** angrily complain about   **18 sev'n reigns** for the duration of seven monarchs, i.e. a long time   **27 taper** candle   **33 combat** oppose   **repulses** rejections, refusals   **35 Securing...fame** guarding my humble reputation   **nothing** in no way   **37 choice** appropriate, worthy of being chosen   **shade** comparative obscurity/unsubstantial image/ quiet habitation   **41 warned** advised   **42 watch** remain awake, keep vigil   **44 besung** sung to   **mean** humble, of low social status   **47 faith** trust, confidence   **50 lost** ruined, i.e. who have been seduced   **52 Let...homely** allow us (girls) to remain unpolished, unsophisticated at home, but perhaps playing on an ambiguous sense of 'let us two be plain/intimate'

55   As you profess them: so no party trusted
Shall make a losing bargain. Home, my lord,
What you can say, is most unseasonable; what sing,
Most absonant and harsh: nay, your perfume,
Which I smell hither, cheers not my sense
60   Like our field-violet's breath.

HENRIQUEZ   Why this dismission
Does more invite my staying.

VIOLANTE   Men of your temper
Make ev'rything their bramble. But I wrong
65   That which I am preserving, my maid's name,
To hold so long discourse. Your virtues guide you
T'effect some nobler purpose!   *Exit Violante*

HENRIQUEZ   Stay, bright maid!
Come back, and leave me with a fairer hope.
70   She's gone. Who am I that am thus contemned?
The second son to a prince? Yes, well, what then?
Why, your great birth forbids you to descend
To a low alliance; hers is the self-same stuff,
Whereof we dukes are made but clay more pure!
75   And take away my title, which is acquired
Not by myself, but thrown by fortune on me,
Or by the merit of some ancestor
Of singular quality; she doth inherit
Deserts t'outweigh me. I must stoop to gain her;
80   Throw all my gay comparisons aside,
And turn my proud additions out of service,
Rather than keep them to become my masters.
The dignities we wear, are gifts of pride,
And laughed at by the wise, as mere outside.   *Exit*

Act 2 Scene 1

Scene: The prospect of a village

Enter Fabian and Lopez, Henriquez on the opposite side

LOPEZ   Soft, soft you, neighbour, who comes here? Pray you, slink aside.

HENRIQUEZ   Ha! Is it come to this? O, the devil, the devil, the devil!

FABIAN   Lo you now! For want of the discreet ladle of a cool

---

55 no party trusted no honest person/neither person believing the other   **57 What** whatever   **unseasonable** unsuited to the time or occasion
58 absonant discordant, unnatural   **61 dismission** dismissal, sending away/rejection   **64 bramble** perhaps from 'bramble-net', a net for catching
birds   **70 contemned** treated with contempt, despised   **74 more pure** i.e. morally, but playing on the sense of 'in her unmixed blood line'   **78 inherit** derive
from her progenitors naturally   **80 comparisons** mocking or scoffing similitudes, perhaps punning on 'caparisons', dress and ornaments   **81 additions**
titles, marks signifying rank   **2.1**   **1 Soft** go quietly, unobtrusively   **neighbour** form of address   **slink** move quietly/hide oneself/avoid   **3 For...over!** i.e.
he needs something to cool him down

Understanding, will this fellow's brains boil over!

5   HENRIQUEZ   To have enjoyed her, I would have given — what?
     All that at present I could boast my own,
     And the reversion of the world to boot,
     Had the inheritance been mine: and now,
     (Just doom of guilty joys!) I grieve as much
10   That I have rifled all the stores of beauty,
     Those charms of innocence and artless love,
     As just before I was devoured with sorrow,
     That she refused my vows, and shut the door
     Upon my ardent longings!

15   LOPEZ   Love! Love! Downright love! I see by the foolishness of it.

     HENRIQUEZ   Now then to recollection — was't not so? A promise first of marriage — not a promise only, for 'twas bound with surety of a thousand oaths — and those not light ones neither — yet I remember too, those oaths could not prevail; th'unpractised maid trembled to meet my love: by force alone I snatched th'imperfect
20   joy, which now torments my memory. Not love, but brutal violence prevailed, to which the time, and place, and opportunity, were accessories most dishonourable. Shame, shame upon it!

     FABIAN   What a heap of stuff's this? I fancy, this fellow's head would make a good   *To Lopez*
     pedlar's pack, neighbour.

25   HENRIQUEZ   Hold, let me be severe to myself, but not unjust. Was it a rape then? No. Her shrieks, her exclamations then had drove me from her. True, she did not consent; as true, she did resist; but still in silence all. 'Twas but the coyness of a modest bride, not the resentment of a ravished maid. And is the man yet born, who would not risk the guilt, to meet the joy? The guilt! That's true, but then the danger;
30   the tears, the clamours of the ruined maid pursuing me to court. That, that, I fear will (as it already does my conscience) something shatter my honour. What's to be done? But now I have no choice. Fair Leonora reigns confessed the tyrant queen of my revolted heart, and Violante seems a short usurper there. Julio's already by my arts removed.— O friendship, how wilt thou answer that? O, that a man could
35   reason down this fever of the blood, or sooth with words the tumult in his heart! Then, Julio, I might be, indeed, thy friend. They, they only should condemn me, who born devoid of passion ne'er have proved the fierce disputes 'twixt virtue and desire. While they, who have, like me,
     The loose escapes of youthful nature known,
40   Must wink at mine, indulgent to their own.   *Exit Henriquez*

     LOPEZ   This man is certainly mad, and may be mischievous. Prithee, neighbour, let's follow him but at some distance, for fear of the worst.   *Exeunt after Henriquez*

---

5 enjoyed possessed her sexually   **7 reversion** the right of succeeding to   **to boot** into the bargain   **10 rifled** ransacked, plundered   **17 surety** pledge, bond   **26 drove** driven   **31 something** to some extent   **shatter my honour** destroy my reputation, as well as usual moral sense   **33 revolted** rebel, that has changed allegiance   **37 proved** tested   **39 escapes** transgressions, peccadilloes   **41 mischievous** inflict harm or injury   **Prithee** please, literally 'I pray thee'

[Act 2] Scene 2

[Scene:] An apartment

Enters Violante alone

VIOLANTE   Whom shall I look upon without a blush?

There's not a maid, whose eye with virgin gaze

Pierces not to my guilt. What will't avail me,

To say I was not willing;

5   Nothing; but that I publish my dishonour,

And wound my fame anew. O misery,

To seem to all one's neighbours rich, yet know

Oneself necessitous and wretched.

Enter Maid, and afterwards Gerald with a letter

MAID   Madam, here's Gerald, Lord Henriquez's servant; he brings a letter to you.

10   VIOLANTE   A letter to me! How I tremble now!

Your lord's for court, good Gerald, is he not?

GERALD   Not so, lady.

VIOLANTE   O, my presaging heart! When goes he then?

GERALD   His business now steers him some other course.

15   VIOLANTE   Whither, I pray you?— How my fears torment me!

GERALD   Some two months' progress.

VIOLANTE   Whither, whither, sir,

I do beseech you? Good heav'ns, I lose all patience.

Did he deliberate this? Or was the business

20   But then conceived, when it was born?

GERALD   Lady, I know not that; nor is it in the command I have to wait your

answer. For the perusing the letter I commend you to your leisure.   *Exit Gerald*

VIOLANTE   To hearts like mine suspense is misery.

Wax, render up thy trust: be the contents

25   Prosp'rous, or fatal, they are all my due.

Reads   'Our prudence should now teach us to forget,

What our indiscretion has committed. I

Have already made one step towards this

Wisdom, by prevailing on myself to bid you

30   Farewell.'

O, wretched and betrayed! Lost Violante!

Heart-wounded with a thousand perjured vows,

Poisoned with studied language, and bequeathed

To desperation. I am now become

35   The tomb of my own honour: a dark mansion,

For death alone to dwell in. I invite thee,

[2.]2 *apartment* single room of a house   **3 avail** help, profit   **8 necessitous** poor, needy   **13 presaging** foreboding, prophetic (of misfortune)
16 progress journey, travelling   **18 beseech** beg (to know)   **19 deliberate** carefully consider   **24 Wax** grow   **render up** resign, surrender   **33 studied** skilled, practised   **35 tomb...o'erthrow** (lines 35–9) the metaphor of architectural destruction for rape, comparing the body to a temple or mansion, is used in Shakespeare's narrative poem, *The Rape of Lucrece*, see lines 1170–6 for example

Consuming desolation to this temple,
Now fit to be thy spoil: the ruined fabric,
Which cannot be repaired, at once o'erthrow.
40 What must I do? — But that's not worth my thought:
I will commend to hazard all the time
That I shall spend hereafter: farewell, my father,
Whom I'll no more offend: and men, adieu,
Whom I'll no more believe: and maids, adieu,
45 Whom I'll no longer shame. The way I go,
As yet I know not, sorrow be my guide.   *Exit Violante*

[Act 2] Scene 3

[*Scene:*] *Prospect of a village, before Don Bernard's house*

Enters Henriquez

HENRIQUEZ   Where were the eyes, the voice, the various charms,
Each beauteous particle, each nameless grace,
Parents of glowing love? All these in her,
It seems, were not: but a disease in me,
5 That fancied graces in her. Who ne'er beheld
More than a hawthorn, shall have cause to say
The cedar's a tall tree, and scorn the shade
The loved bush once had lent him. Soft! Mine honour
Begins to sicken in this black reflection.
10 How can it be, that with my honour safe
I should pursue Leonora for my wife?
That were accumulating injuries,
To Violante first, and now to Julio;
To her a perjured wretch, to him perfidious,
15 And to myself in strongest terms accused
Of murd'ring honour wilfully, without which
My dog's the creature of the nobler kind.
But pleasure is too strong for reason's curb,
And conscience sinks o'er-powered with beauty's sweets.
20 Come, Leonora, auth'ress of my crime,
Appear, and vindicate thy empire here;
Aid me to drive this ling'ring honour hence,
And I am wholly thine.

Enter to him Don Bernard and Leonora

DON BERNARD   Fie, my good lord; why would you wait without?

---

41 hazard chance   **[2.]3   3 Parents** causes, sources   **12 injuries** wrongful acts/insults/damage   **14 perfidious** deliberately faithless   **18 curb** check, restraint   **21 vindicate** assert or establish possession of/claim as one's rightful property   **24 Fie** exclamation of indignant reproach   **without** outside

25   If you suspect your welcome, I have brought
      My Leonora to assure you of it.   *Henriquez salutes Leonora*

      HENRIQUEZ   O kiss, sweet as the odours of the spring,
      But cold as dews that dwell on morning flow'rs!
      Say, Leonora, has your father conquered?
30   Shall duty then at last obtain the prize
      Which you refused to love? And shall Henriquez
      Owe all his happiness to good Bernardo?
      Ah, no! I read my ruin in your eyes:
      That sorrow, louder than a thousand tongues,
35   Pronounces my despair.

      DON BERNARDO   Come, Leonora,
      You are not now to learn, this noble lord
      (Whom but to name restores my failing age),
      Has with a lover's eye beheld your beauty
40   Through which his heart speaks more than language can;
      It offers joy and happiness to you,
      And honour to our house. Imagine then
      The birth and qualities of him that loves you,
      Which when you know, you cannot rate too dear.

45   LEONORA   My father, on my knees I do beseech you
      To pause one moment on your daughter's ruin.
      I vow, my heart ev'n bleeds, that I must thank you
      For your past tenderness and yet distrust
      That which is yet behind. Consider, sir,
50   Whoe'er's th'occasion of another's fault
      Cannot himself be innocent. O, give not
      The censuring world occasion to reproach
      Your harsh commands; or to my charge lay that
      Which most I fear, the fault of disobedience!

55   DON BERNARD   Prithee, fear neither the one, nor the other: I tell thee, girl, there's
      more fear than danger. For my own part, as soon as thou art married to this noble
      lord, my fears will be over.

      LEONORA   Sir, I should be the vainest of my sex
      Not to esteem myself unworthy far
60   Of this high honour. Once there was a time,
      When to have heard my lord Henriquez's vows,
      Might have subdued my unexperienced heart,
      And made me wholly his. But that's now past:
      And my firm-plighted faith by your consent
65   Was long since given to the injured Julio.

---

25 suspect imagine something wrong with *salutes* greets with a kiss **38 restores…age** makes me young again **44 rate** value/scold, rebuke **dear**
highly, at great cost **49 yet behind** still to come **50 Whoe'er's** whoever is **th'occasion** the cause/pretext **64 firm-plighted faith** certain promise of
marriage

DON BERNARD   Why then, by my consent e'en take it back again. Thou, like a simple wench, hast given thy affections to a fellow that does not care a farthing for them. One, that has left thee for a jaunt to court, as who should say, I'll get a place now, 'tis time enough to marry when I'm turned out of it.

70 **HENRIQUEZ**   So, surely, it should seem, most lovely maid;
Julio, alas, feels nothing of my passion:
His love is but th'amusement of an hour,
A short relief from business or ambition,
The sport of youth and fashion of the age.
75 O, had he known the hopes, the doubts, the ardours,
Or half the fond varieties of passion
That play the tyrant with my tortured soul,
He had not left thee to pursue his fortune:
To practise cringes in a slavish circle,
80 And barter real bliss for unsure honour.

LEONORA   O, the opposing wind
Should'ring the tide makes here a fearful billow:
I needs must perish in it.— O, my lord,
Is it then possible, you can forget
85 What's due to your great name and princely birth,
To friendship's holy law, to faith reposed,
To truth, to honour, and poor injured Julio?
O think, my lord, how much this Julio loves you;
Recall his services, his well-tried faith;
90 Think too, this very hour, where-e'er he be,
Your favour is the envy of the court,
And secret triumph of his grateful heart.—
Poor Julio, how securely thou depend'st
Upon the faith and honour of thy master;
95 Mistaken youth! This very hour he robs thee
Of all thy heart holds dear.— 'Tis so Henriquez
Repays the merits of unhappy Julio.   *Weeps*

HENRIQUEZ   My slumb'ring honour catches the alarm.
I was to blame to parley with her thus:
100 She's shown me to myself. It troubles me.   *Aside*

DON BERNARD   Mad, mad. Stark mad, by this light.

LEONORA   I but begin to be so.— I conjure you,   *To Don Bernard*
By all the tender interests of nature,
By the chaste love 'twixt you and my dear mother,
105 (O, holy heav'n, that she were living now!)
Forgive and pity me.— O, sir, remember,

---

67 wench country girl   **farthing** quarter of an old penny, an insignificant sum   **68 jaunt** excursion taken for pleasure   **75 ardours** passionate desires   **76 fond** infatuated, foolish   **78 He had not** he would not have   **79 cringes** servile obeisance; derisive name for a bow   **slavish circle** servile group of courtiers   **80 unsure** uncertain   **81 O…billow** Leonora compares her situation to being overwhelmed by a great wave which will carry her along   **96 so** thus, in this manner   **103 interests** shares in, claims upon/rights, titles/benefits   **104 chaste** virtuous, innocent

I've heard my mother say a thousand times,

Her father would have forced her virgin choice

But when the conflict was 'twixt love and duty,

110 Which should be first obeyed, my mother quickly

Paid up her vows to love and married you.

You thought this well, and she was praised for this;

For this her name was honoured, disobedience

Was ne'er imputed to her, her firm love

115 Conquered whate'er opposed it, and she prospered

Long time your wife. My case is now the same;

You are the father, which you then condemned;

I, what my mother was; but not so happy—

DON BERNARD Go to, you're a fool. No doubt, you have old stories enough to undo

120 you. What, you can't throw yourself away but by precedent, ha? You will needs be

married to one, that will none of you? You will be happy nobody's way but your own,

forsooth. But, d'ye mark me, spare your tongue for the future (and that's using you

hardly too, to bid you spare what you have a great deal too much of). Go, go your

ways, and d'ye hear, get ready within these two days to be married to a husband

125 you don't deserve. Do it, or, by my dead father's soul, you are no acquaintance of

mine.

HENRIQUEZ She weeps: be gentler to her, good Bernardo.

LEONORA   Then woe the day! I'm circled round with fire;

No way for my escape, but through the flames.

130 O, can I e'er resolve to live without

A father's blessing, or abandon Julio?

With other maids, the choice were not so hard;

Int'rest, that rules the world, has made at last

A merchandise of hearts: and virgins now

135 Choose as they're bid, and wed without esteem.

By nobler springs shall my affections move,

Nor own a master but the man I love.   *Exit Leonora*

DON BERNARD Go thy ways, contradiction!— Follow her, my lord, follow her, in the

very heat. This obstinacy must be combated by importunity as obstinate.

Exit Henriquez after her

140 The girl says right; her mother was just such another. I remember, two of us courted

her at the same time. She loved neither of us, but she chose me purely to spite that

surly old blockhead my father-in-law. Who comes here, Camillo? Now the refusing

part will lie on my side.

Enters Camillo

CAMILLO   My worthy neighbour, I am much in fortune's favour to find you thus

145 alone. I have a suit to you.

---

119 Go to expression of disapprobation   **121 will** wants, will have   **122 forsooth** in truth   **123 hardly** harshly   **go your ways** off you go
125 you…mine I'll no longer acknowledge you as my daughter   **133 Int'rest** self-interest/profit   **134 merchandise** saleable commodity   **137 Nor…love**
nor will my affections acknowledge any master except for the man I love   **139 importunity** continued solicitation   **140 such another** the same   **143 part**
role   **145 suit** request, petition/solicitation for a woman's hand

DON BERNARD   Please to name it, sir.

CAMILLO   Sir, I have long held you in singular esteem and what I shall now say, will be a proof of it. You know, sir, I have but one son.

DON BERNARD   Ay, sir.

150   CAMILLO   And the fortune I am blessed withal, you pretty well know what it is.

DON BERNARD   'Tis a fair one, sir.

CAMILLO   Such as it is, the whole reversion is my son's. He is now engaged in his attendance on our master, the duke. But ere he went, he left with me the secret of his heart, his love for your fair daughter. For your consent, he said, 'twas ready: I took

155   a night, indeed, to think upon it, and now have brought you mine and am come to bind the contract with half my fortune in present, the whole sometime hence, and, in the meanwhile, my hearty blessing. Ha? What say you to't, don Bernard?

DON BERNARD   Why, really, neighbour, I must own, I have heard something of this matter—

160   CAMILLO   Heard something of it? No doubt, you have.

DON BERNARD   Yes, now I recollect it well.

CAMILLO   Was it so long ago then?

DON BERNARD   Very long ago, neighbour, on Tuesday last.

CAMILLO   What, am I mocked in this business, don Bernard?

165   DON BERNARD   Not mocked, good Camillo, not mocked! But in love-matters, you know, there are abundance of changes in half an hour. Time, time, neighbour, plays tricks with all of us.

CAMILLO   Time, sir! What tell you me of time? Come, I see how this goes. Can a little time take a man by the shoulder and shake off his honour? Let me tell you,

170   neighbour, it must either be a strong wind, or a very mellow honesty that drops so easily. Time, quotha?

DON BERNARD   Look'ee, Camillo, will you please to put your indignation in your pocket for half a moment, while I tell you the whole truth of the matter. My daughter, you must know, is such a tender soul she cannot possibly see a duke's younger son

175   without falling desperately in love with him. Now, you know, neighbour, when greatness rides post after a man of my years, 'tis both prudence and good breeding, to let oneself be overtaken by it. And who can help all this? I profess it was not my seeking, neighbour.

CAMILLO   I profess, a fox might earth in the hollowness of your heart, neighbour,

180   and there's an end. If I were to give a bad conscience its true likeness, it should be drawn after a very near neighbour to a certain poor neighbour of yours. Neighbour! With a pox!

DON BERNARD   Nay, you are so nimble with me, you will hear nothing.

CAMILLO   Sir, if I must speak nothing, I will hear nothing. As for what you have

185   to say, if it comes from your heart, 'tis a lie before you speak it. I'll to Leonora and if

---

147 **singular esteem** especially high regard   150 **withal** as well   152 **reversion** right of inheritance   153 **ere** before   156 **in present** immediately   **whole sometime hence** the rest at some point in the future   170 **mellow** soft, pliable   171 **quotha** says he/indeed, used ironically or contemptuously   176 **post** with haste   177 **profess** declare   179 **earth** run and hide himself (in his earth or hole)   182 **With a pox!** exclamation of irritation; **pox**, literally a disease characterized by pocks, often used to mean 'syphilis'   183 **nimble with me** quick-witted, clever at my expense

I find her in the same story, why, I shall believe your wife was true to you, and your daughter is your own. Fare you well.   *Exit, as into Don Bernard's House*

DON BERNARD   Ay, but two words must go to that bargain. It happens, that I am at present of opinion my daughter shall receive no more company today; at least, no

190   such visits as yours.   *Exit Don Bernard, following him*

[Act 2] Scene 4

[Scene:] Changes to another prospect of Don Bernard's house

Leonora, above

LEONORA   How tediously I've waited at the window,
　　　　Yet know not one that passes. Should I trust
　　　　My letter to a stranger, whom I think
　　　　To bear an honest face, (in which sometimes
5　　　We fancy we are wond'rous skilful) then
　　　　I might be much deceived. This late example
　　　　Of base Henriquez, bleeding in me now,
　　　　From each good aspect takes away my trust:
　　　　For his face seemed to promise truth and honour.
10　　Since nature's gifts in noblest forms deceive,
　　　　Be happy you that want 'em! Here comes one;
　　　　I've seen him, though I know him not; he has
　　　　An honest face too — that's no matter. Sir!

Enters Citizen

CITIZEN   To me?

15   LEONORA   As you were of a virtuous matron born,
　　　　(There is no doubt you are) I do conjure you
　　　　Grant me one boon. Say, do you know me, sir?

CITIZEN   Ay, Leonora, and your worthy father.

LEONORA   I have not time to press the suit I've to you
20　　With many words; nay, I should want the words,
　　　　Though I had leisure: but for love of justice,
　　　　And as you pity misery — but I wander
　　　　Wide from my subject. Know you Julio, sir?

CITIZEN   Yes, very well; and love him too, as well.

25   LEONORA   O, there an angel spake! Then I conjure you,
　　　　Convey this paper to him: and believe me,
　　　　You do heav'n service in't, and shall have cause
　　　　Not to repent your pains. I know not what
　　　　Your fortune is — pardon me, gentle sir,
30　　That I am bold to offer this.   *Throws down a purse with money*

[2.]4   *above* i.e. positioned in an upper playing space   **2 Should I** if I were to   **6 late** recent   **7 bleeding** causing suffering   **8 aspect** face, countenance
11 want 'em lack, do not possess them   **16 conjure** implore, solemnly appeal   **17 boon** favour, request   **25 spake** spoke

DON BERNARD (*within*) Leonora!

LEONORA   I trust to you; heav'n put it in your heart
To work me some relief.

CITIZEN   Doubt it not, lady. You have moved me so,

35   That though a thousand dangers barred my way,
I'd dare 'em all to serve you.   *Exit Citizen*

LEONORA   Thanks from a richer hand than mine requite you!

DON BERNARD (*within*) Why, daughter—

LEONORA   I come!— O, Julio, feel but half my grief,

40   And thou wilt out-fly time to bring relief.   *Exit Leonora from the window*

Act 3 Scene 1

Scene: The prospect of a village

Enter Julio with a letter, and Citizen

CITIZEN   When from the window she did bow and call,
Her passions shook her voice, and from her eyes
Mistemper and distraction, with strange wildness,
Bespoke concern above a common sorrow.

5   **JULIO**   Poor Leonora! Treacherous, damned Henriquez!
She bids me fill my memory with her danger;
I do, my Leonora; yes, I fill
The region of my thought with nothing else;
Lower, she tells me here, that this affair

10   Shall yield a testimony of her love
And prays her letter may come safe and sudden.
This prayer the heav'ns have heard, and I beseech 'em,
To hear all prayers she makes.

CITIZEN   Have patience, sir.

15   **JULIO**   O, my good friend, methinks I am too patient.
Is there a treachery, like this in baseness
Recorded anywhere? It is the deepest:
None but itself can be its parallel,
And from a friend professed! Friendship? Why, 'tis

20   A word for ever maimed; in human nature
It was a thing the noblest, and 'mong beasts,
It stood not in mean place: things of fierce nature
Hold amity and concordance. Such a villainy
A writer could not put down in his scene,

---

37 requite repay, reward (for a service)   **3.1   3 Mistemper** discomposure, indisposition   **4 Bespoke** expressed, revealed   **11 sudden** without delay
19 friend professed one who professes (claims) to be a friend   **20 maimed** injured, damaged   **22 mean** inferior/unimportant   **23 amity** friendly relations
concordance agreement, harmony

25   Without taxation of his auditory
                 For fiction most enormous.

CITIZEN   These upbraidings
                 Cool time while they are vented.

JULIO   I am counselled.

30   For you, evermore, thanks. You've done much for us,
                 So gently pressed to't, that I may persuade me
                 You'll do a little more.

CITIZEN   Put me t'employment
                 That's honest, though not safe, with my best spirits

35   I'll give't accomplishment.

JULIO   No more but this;
                 For I must see Leonora, and to appear
                 Like Julio, as I am, might haply spoil
                 Some good event ensuing. Let me crave

40   Th'exchange of habit with you: some disguise
                 May bear me to my love, unmarked and secret.

CITIZEN   You shall not want. Yonder's the house before us:
                 Make haste to reach it.

JULIO   Still I thank you, sir.

45   O Leonora! Stand but this rude shock;
                 Hold out thy faith against the dread assault
                 Of this base lord, the service of my life
                 Shall be devoted to repay thy constancy.   *Exeunt*

[Act 3] Scene 2

[Scene:] Don Bernard's house

Enters Leonora

LEONORA   I've hoped to th'latest minute hope can give:
                 He will not come: he's not received my letter:
                 Maybe some other view has from our home
                 Repealed his changed eye, for what business can

5   Excuse a tardiness thus wilful? None.
                 Well then, it is not business. O, that letter!
                 I say, is not delivered, or he's sick,
                 Or, O, suggestion, wherefore wilt thou fright me?
                 Julio does to Henriquez on mere purpose,

10   On plotted purpose, yield me up, and he

25 **taxation** reproof, censure   **auditory** audience   27 **upbraidings** reproaches, reproofs   28 **Cool** waste by losing   **vented** uttered   29 **counselled** advised   31 **pressed** hired or engaged with partial payment in advance   34 **though not safe** even if it isn't free from danger   35 **give't accomplishment** do it   38 **haply** perhaps   39 **event** outcome   **ensuing** resulting/subsequent   40 **habit** clothing   44 **Still** always   45 **rude** harsh, barbarous   **shock** blow/ mental disturbance caused by pain or grief   46 **dread** dreadful, greatly feared   **[3.]2   3 view** sight, prospect/design, intention/consideration   **4 Repealed** recalled, withdrawn/repelled   **9 mere** infamous/simple, straightforward

Hath chose another mistress. All presumptions
Make pow'rful to this point: his own protraction,
Henriquez left behind — that strain lacked jealousy,
Therefore lacked love so sure as life shall empty

15 Itself in death, this new surmise of mine
Is a bold certainty. 'Tis plain, and obvious,
Henriquez would not, durst not, thus infringe
The law of friendship, thus provoke a man
That bears a sword and wears his flag of youth

20 As fresh as he: he durst not: 'tis contrivance,
Gross-daubing 'twixt them both. But I'm o'erheard.   *Going*

Enters Julio, disguised

JULIO   Stay, Leonora; has this outward veil
Quite lost me to thy knowledge?

LEONORA   O, my Julio!

25 Thy presence ends the stern debate of doubt,
And cures me of a thousand heartsick fears,
Sprung from thy absence yet awakes a train
Of other sleeping terrors. Do you weep?

JULIO   No, Leonora, when I weep, it must be

30 The substance of mine eye. Would I could weep,
For then mine eye would drop upon my heart,
And swage the fire there.

LEONORA   You are full possessed
How things go here. First, welcome heartily;

35 Welcome to th'ending of my last good hour:
Now summer bliss and gaudy-days are gone,
My lease in 'em's expired.

JULIO   Not so, Leonora.

LEONORA   Yes, Julio, yes; an everlasting storm

40 Is come upon me which I can't bear out.
I cannot stay much talk; we have lost leisure;
And thus it is: your absence hath giv'n breeding
To what my letter hath declared, and is
This instant on th'effecting. Hark! The music   *Flourish within*

45 Is now on tuning which must celebrate
This business so discordant. Tell me then,
What you will do?

---

11 **chose** chosen   **presumptions** assumptions, suppositions   12 **Make...point** lead to this conclusion   **protraction** delay   13 **strain** way of behaving   15 **surmise** suspicion/conjecture   16 **bold** daring/sure   19 **flag of youth** his appearance signifying that he is young (and fit)   20 **fresh** blooming, healthy-looking/vigorous, active/clearly, freshly   **durst not** would not dare   **contrivance** a trick, plot   21 **Gross-daubing** obvious putting a false show on   **'twixt them both** between the two of them   22 **outward veil** external disguise   23 **Quite...knowledge** made you completely fail to recognize/forget/acknowledge me   25 **stern** painful, harsh   30 **substance** purpose   **Would** I wish, if only   31 **drop** let fall in drops, i.e. tears   32 **swage** assuage, relieve   33 **full possessed** completely aware of   36 **gaudy-days** days of rejoicing, festivals, gala days   37 **lease...expired** time for enjoying them has run out   40 **bear out** endure   41 **stay** delay, stop for   **leisure** opportunity/time before it is too late   44 **on th'effecting** about to be accomplished   45 **on tuning** about to play   46 **discordant** incongruous, inharmonious

JULIO	I know not what: advise me:	
	I'll kill the traitor.	
50	LEONORA	O, take heed: his death	
	Betters our cause no whit. No killing, Julio,	
JULIO	My blood stands still, and all my faculties	
	Are by enchantment dulled. You gracious pow'rs,	
	The guardians of sworn faith and suff'ring virtue,	
55		Inspire prevention of this dreaded mischief!	
	This moment is our own; let's use it, love,	
	And fly o'th'instant from this house of woe.	
LEONORA	Alas! Impossible: my steps are watched;	
	There's no escape for me. You must stay too.	
60	JULIO	What! Stay, and see thee ravished from my arms?	
	I'll force thy passage. Wear I not a sword?	
	Ne'er on man's thigh rode better. If I suffer	
	The traitor play his part, if I not do	
	Manhood and justice honour let me be deemed	
65		A tame, pale, coward, whom the night-owl's hoot	
	May turn to aspen-leaf: some man take this,	
	Give me a distaff for it.	
LEONORA	Patience, Julio,	
	And trust to me: I have forethought the means	

LEONORA   Patience, Julio,

        And trust to me: I have forethought the means

70   To disappoint these nuptials. Hark! Again!   *Music within*

        These are the bells knoll for us. See, the lights

        Move this way, Julio. Quick, behind yon arras,

        And take thy secret stand. Dispute it not;

        I have my reasons, you anon shall know them:

75   There you may mark the passages of the night.

        Yet, more: I charge you by the dearest ties,

        Whate'er you see, or hear, whate'er shall hap,

        In your concealment rest a silent statue.

        Nay, hide thee straight — or — see, I'm armed and vow   *Shows a dagger*

80   To fall a bleeding sacrifice before thee.   *Thrusts him out to the arras*

        I dare not tell thee of my purpose, Julio,

        Lest it should wrap thee in such agonies,

        Which my love could not look on.

Scene opens to a large hall: an altar prepared with tapers. Enter at one door servants
with lights, Henriquez, Don Bernard and Churchman: at another, attendants to Leonora.
Henriquez runs to her

HENRIQUEZ   Why, Leonora, wilt thou with this gloom

---

51 **Betters…whit** in no way improves our situation   **whit** jot, particle   57 **fly o'th'instant** flee immediately   60 **ravished** carried away, stolen   61 **force thy passage** use violence to prevent your being taken away   62 **rode better** was a better one carried   64 **deemed** judged   66 **aspen-leaf** leaf of a type of poplar tree which quivers and trembles in the slightest breeze, hence the sound of the owl's hooting will make him tremble with fear   **this** i.e. his sword   67 **distaff** stick around which yarn was wound for spinning   70 **disappoint** frustrate, foil   **nuptials** wedding ceremonies   71 **knoll** ring/summon (especially for a funeral)   72 **yon arras** the hanging tapestry screen over there   73 **stand** place to stand and hide   74 **anon** soon   75 **passages** periods of time

85   Darken my triumph, suff'ring discontent,

And wan displeasure to subdue that cheek

Where love should sit enthroned? Behold your slave;

Nay, frown not; for each hour of growing time

Shall task me to thy service, till by merit

90   Of dearest love I blot the lowborn Julio

From thy fair mind.

LEONORA   So I shall make it foul;

This counsel is corrupt.

HENRIQUEZ   Come, you will change—

95   **LEONORA**   Why would you make a wife of such a one

That is so apt to change? This foul proceeding

Still speaks against itself, and vilifies

The purest of your judgement. For your birth's sake

I will not dart my hoarded curses at you,

100   Nor give my meanings language: for the love

Of all good things together, yet take heed,

And spurn the tempter back.

DON BERNARD   I think, you're mad. Perverse, and foolish, wretch!

LEONORA   How may I be obedient, and wise too?

105   Of my obedience, sir, I cannot strip me,

Nor can I then be wise: grace against grace!

Ungracious, if I not obey a father;

Most perjured, if I do. Yet, lord, consider,

Or e'er too late, or e'er that knot be tied,

110   Which may with violence damnable be broken,

No other way dissevered: yet consider,

You wed my body, not my heart, my lord;

No part of my affection. Sounds it well,

That Julio's love is Lord Henriquez's wife?

115   Have you an ear for this harsh sound?

HENRIQUEZ   No shot of reason can come near the place,

Where my love's fortified. The day shall come,

Wherein you'll chide this backwardness and bless

Our fervour in this course.

120   **LEONORA**   No, no, Henriquez,

When you shall find what prophet you are proved,

You'll prophesy no more.

DON BERNARD   Have done this talking,

If you will cleave to your obedience, do't;

125   If not, unbolt the portal and begone;

My blessing stay behind you.

---

85 **suff'ring** patiently enduring **86 wan** sad **89 task** impose a task on **102 spurn** strike with the foot, kick **tempter** devil **109 Or e'er** before ever **knot** i.e. marriage-knot **110 damnable** highly reprehensible/subject to divine condemnation **111 dissevered** separated, divided **124 cleave** cling **125 portal** door, gate **begone** leave, depart

LEONORA   Sir, your pardon:

I will not swerve a hair's-breadth from my duty;

It shall first cost me dear.

130   DON BERNARD   Well then, to th' point:

Give me your hand.— My honoured lord, receive

My daughter of me (nay, no dragging back,

But with my curses), whom I frankly give you,

And wish you joy and honour.

As Don Bernard goes to give Leonora to Henriquez, Julio advances from the arras and steps

between

135   JULIO   Hold, Don Bernard,

Mine is the elder claim.

DON BERNARD   What are you, sir?

JULIO   A wretch, that's almost lost to his own knowledge,

Struck through with injuries.

140   HENRIQUEZ   Ha! Julio? Hear you,

Were you not sent on our commands to court?

Ordered to wait your fair dismission thence?

And have you dared, knowing you are our vassal,

To steal away unprivileged, and leave

145   My business and your duty unaccomplished?

JULIO   Ungen'rous lord! The circumstance of things

Should stop the tongue of question. You have wronged me;

Wronged me so basely, in so dear a point,

As stains the cheek of honour with a blush;

150   Cancels the bonds of service; bids allegiance

Throw to the wind all high respects of birth,

Title, and eminence; and, in their stead,

Fills up the panting heart with just defiance.

If you have sense of shame, or justice, lord,

155   Forgo this bad intent; or with your sword

Answer me like a man, and I shall thank you.

Julio once dead, Leonora may be thine;

But, living, she's a prize too rich to part with.

HENRIQUEZ   Vain man! The present hour is fraught with business

160   Of richer moment. Love shall first be served:

Then, if your courage hold to claim it of me,

I may have leisure to chastise this boldness.

JULIO   Nay, then I'll seize my right.

HENRIQUEZ   What, here, a brawl?

---

128 hair's-breadth the breadth of a hair, i.e. at all   **133 frankly** freely/unconditionally   **142 fair dismission** kind permission to depart   **143 vassal** subject, subordinate; in the feudal system one who owed a duty of allegiance to a lord   **144 steal away** depart quietly, secretly   **unprivileged** without any right   **148 dear** important   **150 bonds of service** the duty that Julio owes to Henriquez as his **vassal**   **155 Forgo** abstain or refrain from/renounce, relinquish   **intent** intention/scheme   **sword…man** i.e. fight me, Julio is challenging Henriquez to a duel   **159 fraught with** full of   **160 moment** importance, significance

165 My servants, turn this boist'rous sworder forth,

And see he come not to disturb our joys.

JULIO   Hold, dogs!— Leonora!— Coward, base, Henriquez!

Julio is seized and dragged out by the servants

HENRIQUEZ   She dies upon me; help!

Leonora swoons; as they endeavour to recover her,
a paper drops from her

DON BERNARD   Throng not about her;

170 But give her air.

HENRIQUEZ   What paper's that? Let's see it.

It is her own handwriting.

DON BERNARD   Bow her head:

'Tis but her fright; she will recover soon.

175 What learn you by that paper, good my lord?

HENRIQUEZ   That she would do the violence to herself,

Which Nature hath anticipated on her.

What dagger means she? Search her well, I pray you.

DON BERNARD   Here is the dagger! O, the stubborn sex,

180 Rash ev'n to madness!

HENRIQUEZ   Bear her to her chamber:

Life flows in her again.— Pray, bear her hence:

And tend her, as you would the world's best treasure.

Women carry Leonora off

Don Bernard, this wild tumult soon will cease,

185 The cause removed and all return to calmness.

Passions in women are as short in working,

As strong in their effect. Let the priest wait:

Come, go we in: my soul is all on fire,

And burns impatient of this forced delay.

Exeunt, and the scene closes

[Act 3] Scene 3

[Scene:] Prospect of a village at a distance

Enters Roderick

RODERICK   Julio's departure thus in secret from me,

With the long doubtful absence of my brother,

(Who cannot suffer but my father feels it)

Have trusted me with strong suspicions,

5 And dreams, that will not let me sleep, nor eat,

---

165 **turn...forth** throw this violent assassin out   **boist'rous** rough/violent/savage   **sworder** one who kills with a sword, assassin, cut-throat
169 **Throng not** do not crowd   176 **That...her** She wished to harm herself in the way that Nature has already done, i.e. kill herself   184 **tumult** agitation of mind, confused and violent emotion   189 **impatient of** unable to endure   [3.]3   2 **doubtful** giving cause for anxiety or alarm   3 **Who...it** who is unable to suffer although my father does on his behalf   4 **trusted** filled

Nor taste those recreations health demands:
But, like a whirlwind, hither have they snatched me,
Perforce, to be resolved. I know my brother
Had Julio's father for his host: from him

10 Enquiry may befriend me.

Enters Camillo

Old sir, I'm glad
To've met you thus: What ails the man? Camillo—

CAMILLO   Ha?

RODERICK   Is't possible, you should forget your friends?

15 CAMILLO   Friends! What are those?

RODERICK   Why, those that love you, sir.

CAMILLO   You're none of those, sure, if you be Lord Roderick.

RODERICK   Yes, I am that Lord Roderick, and I lie not,
If I protest, I love you passing well.

20 CAMILLO   You loved my son too passing well, I take it:
One that believed too suddenly his court-creed.

RODERICK   All is not well—   *Aside*
Good old man, do not rail.

CAMILLO   My lord, my lord, you've dealt dishonourably.

25 RODERICK   Good sir, I am so far from doing wrongs
Of that base strain, I understand you not.

CAMILLO   Indeed! You know not neither, o' my conscience,
How your most virtuous brother, noble Henriquez,
(You look so like him, lord, you are the worse for't;

30 Rots upon such dissemblers!) under colour
Of buying coursers, and I know not what,
Bought my poor boy out of possession
Ev'n of his plighted faith. Was not this honour?
And this a constant friend?

35 RODERICK   I dare not say so.

CAMILLO   Now you have robbed him of his love, take all;
Make up your malice and dispatch his life too.

RODERICK   If you would hear me, sir,—

CAMILLO   Your brave old father

40 Would have been torn in pieces with wild horses,
Ere he had done this treachery. On my conscience,
Had he but dreamt you two durst have committed
This base, unmanly crime—

RODERICK   Why, this is madness—

---

8 Perforce by force/of necessity **10 befriend** assist, favour **12 ails** troubles, afflicts **19 passing** exceedingly **21 court-creed** set of ideas, beliefs belonging to the court **23 rail** complain persistently, rant **26 base strain** degrading conduct or character **30 Rots…dissemblers!** May such hypocritical, deceitful rascals get a rotting, wasting disease **under colour** on the pretext **31 coursers** horses **know not what** don't know what else, i.e. what other pretext he used **32 Bought…faith** meaning either 'Henriquez cheated my poor son Julio even out of his fiancée by employing him to purchase horses on his behalf' or 'Henriquez stole my poor son's fiancée away by paying more for her' **37 Make up** complete the full amount of **dispatch** get rid of (by killing) **41 Ere…done** before he would have committed

45	CAMILLO	I've done; I've eased my heart; now you may talk.
	RODERICK	Then as I am a gentleman, believe me,
		(For I will lie for no man) I'm so far
		From being guilty of the least suspicion
		Of sin that way, that, fearing the long absence
50		Of Julio and my brother might beget
		Something to start at, hither have I travelled
		To know the truth of you.

Enters Violante behind

	VIOLANTE	My servant loiters; sure, he means me well.	
		Camillo, and a stranger? These may give me	
55		Some comfort from their talk. I'll step aside:	
		And hear what fame is stirring.	*Violante retires*
	RODERICK	Why this wond'ring?	
	CAMILLO	Can there be one so near in blood as you are	
		To that Henriquez, and an honest man?	
60	RODERICK	While he was good, I do confess my nearness;	
		But, since his fall from honour, he's to me	
		As a strange face I saw but yesterday,	
		And as soon lost.	
	CAMILLO	I ask your pardon, lord;	
65		I was too rash and bold.	
	RODERICK	No harm done, sir.	
	CAMILLO	But is it possible, you should not hear	
		The passage 'twixt Leonora and your brother?	
	RODERICK	None of all this.	

Enters Citizen

70	CAMILLO	How now?	
	CITIZEN	I bear you tidings, sir, which I could wish	
		Some other tongue delivered.	
	CAMILLO	Whence, I pray you?	
	CITIZEN	From your son, sir.	
75	CAMILLO	Prithee, where is he?	
	CITIZEN	That's more than I know now, sir.	
		But this I can assure you, he has left	
		The city raging mad; heav'n comfort him!	
		He came to that curst marriage: the fiends take it!	
80	CAMILLO	Prithee, be gone, and bid the bell knoll for me:	
		I have had one foot in the grave sometime.	
		Nay, go, good friend; thy news deserve no thanks.	
		How does your lordship?	*Exit Citizen*

---

50 beget produce, give rise to   **51 start at** startle one (from surprise or fright)   **hither** to this place   **52 of** from   **56 fame** rumour, public report   **57 wond'ring** surprise, astonishment/doubt, uncertainty   **58 near in blood** closely related   **62 but** only   **67 hear...'twixt** hear about what has happened between   **70 How now?** How or what is it now?   **78 raging mad** raving in fury/acting violently/out of his mind   **79 curst** detestable/heinously wicked   **80 knoll** toll, ring as for a funeral   **81 sometime** at one time or another

RODERICK   That's well said, old man.

85   I hope all shall be well yet.

CAMILLO   It had need;

For 'tis a crooked world. Farewell, poor boy!

Enters Don Bernard

DON BERNARD   This comes of forcing women where they hate:

It was my own sin, and I am rewarded.

90   Now I am like an agèd oak, alone,

Left for all tempests. I would cry, but cannot:

I'm dried to death almost with these vexations.

Lord! What a heavy load I have within me!

My heart! My heart! My heart!

95   CAMILLO   Has this ill weather

Met with thee too?

DON BERNARD   O, wench, that I were with thee!

CAMILLO   You do not come to mock at me now?

DON BERNARD   Ha?

100   CAMILLO   Do not dissemble; thou may'st find a knave

As bad as thou art to undo thee too:

I hope to see that day before I die yet.

DON BERNARD   It needeth not, Camillo; I am knave

Sufficient to myself. If thou wilt rail,

105   Do it as bitterly as thou canst think of,

For I deserve it. Draw thy sword, and strike me,

And I will thank thee for't. I've lost my daughter;

She's stol'n away, and whither gone, I know not.

CAMILLO   She has a fair blessing in being from you, sir.

110   I was too poor a brother for your greatness;

You must be grafted into noble stocks,

And have your titles raised. My state was laughed at

And my alliance scorned. I've lost a son too,

Which must not be put up, so—   *Offers to draw*

115   RODERICK   Hold! Be counselled.

You've equal losses; urge no farther anger.

Heav'n, pleased now at your love, may bring again,

And, no doubt will, your children to your comforts:

In which adventure my foot shall be foremost.

120   And one more will I add, my honoured father,

Who has a son to grieve for too, though tainted.

Let your joint sorrow be as balm to heal

---

88 forcing compelling, overcoming the resistance of/violating, ravishing   **90 like…tempests** Don Bernard likens himself to an old oak tree that's vulnerable to storms and other catastrophic events   **92 dried to death** perhaps from shedding tears   **100 knave** base and crafty rogue   **101 undo** ruin   **103 It needeth not** that won't be necessary   **knave…myself** I've behaved in such a base, dishonest way that I've brought ruin upon myself **104 rail** rant, persistently complain   **111 grafted…stocks** have your offspring married into the aristocracy, a horticultural metaphor describing how a shoot from one tree is inserted into another   **114 put up** tolerated, patiently endured   **117 love** reconciliation   **121 tainted** morally corrupted   **122 balm** healing, soothing agent, literally 'ointment'

These wounds of adverse fortune.

DON BERNARD Come, Camillo,

125   Do not deny your love, for charity;

I ask it of you. Let this noble lord

Make brothers of us, whom our own cross fates

Could never join. What I have been, forget;

What I intend to be, believe and nourish:

130   I do confess my wrongs; give me your hand.

CAMILLO Heav'n make thee honest — there!   *Gives his hand*

RODERICK 'Tis done like good men.

Now there rests nought but that we part and each

Take sev'ral ways in quest of our lost friends:

135   Some of my train o'er the wild rocks shall wait you.

Our best search ended, here we'll meet again,

And tell the fortunes of our separate travels.   *Exeunt*

Violante comes forward

VIOLANTE I would, your brother had but half your virtue!

Yet there remains a little spark of hope

140   That lights me to some comfort. The match is crossed;

The parties separate, and I again

May come to see this man that has betrayed me,

And wound his conscience for it: home again

I will not go, whatever fortune guides me,

145   Though ev'ry step I went, I trod upon

Dangers as fearful and as pale as death.

No, no, Henriquez; I will follow thee

Where there is day. Time may beget a wonder.

Enters Servant

O, are you come? What news?

150   **SERVANT** None, but the worst. Your father makes mighty offers yonder by a crier,

to anyone can bring you home again.

VIOLANTE Art thou corrupted?

SERVANT No.

VIOLANTE Wilt thou be honest?

155   **SERVANT** I hope you do not fear me.

VIOLANTE Indeed, I do not. Thou hast an honest face,

And such a face, when it deceives, take heed,

Is cursed of all heav'n's creatures.

SERVANT I'll hang first.

160   **VIOLANTE** Heav'n bless thee from that end! I've heard a man

Say more than this, and yet that man was false.

---

127 cross adverse, contrary, opposing   **133 rests** remains   **134 sev'ral** separate, i.e. several – the elision is for metrical reasons   **135 train** retinue, group of followers   **137 tell** recount   **140 match is crossed** wedding between Henriquez and Leonora is thwarted   **150 mighty offers** i.e. a large reward   **crier** one appointed to make public announcements   **158 of** by   **160 bless** sanctify you (usually by making the sign of the cross) as a defence against evil

Thou'lt not be so, I hope.

SERVANT   By my life, mistress,—

VIOLANTE   Swear not; I credit thee. But prithee though,

165   Take heed thou dost not fail: I do not doubt thee:

Yet I have trusted such a serious face,

And been abused too.

SERVANT   If I fail your trust—

VIOLANTE   I do thee wrong to hold thy honesty

170   At distance thus: thou shalt know all my fortunes.

Get me a shepherd's habit.

SERVANT   Well, what else?

VIOLANTE   And wait me in the evening, where I told thee:

There thou shalt know my farther ends. Take heed.

175   **SERVANT**   D'ye fear me still?

VIOLANTE   No; this is only counsel:

My life and death I have put equally

Into thy hand: let not rewards, nor hopes,

Be cast into the scale to turn thy faith.

180   Be honest but for virtue's sake, that's all;

He, that has such a treasure, cannot fall.

Exeunt

Act 4 Scene 1

Scene: A wide plain, with a prospect of mountains at a distance

Enter Master of the flocks, three or four Shepherds and Violante in boy's clothes

1 SHEPHERD   Well, he's as sweet a man — heav'n comfort him! — as ever these eyes looked on.

2 SHEPHERD   If he have a other, I believe, neighbours, she's a woe-woman for him at this hour.

5   **MASTER**   Why should he haunt these wild unpeopled mountains,

Where nothing dwells but hunger and sharp winds?

1 SHEPHERD   His melancholy, sir, that's the main devil does it. Go to, I fear he has had too much foul play offered him.

MASTER   How gets he meat?

10   **2 SHEPHERD**   Why, now and then he takes our victuals from us, though we desire him to eat, and instead of a short grace, beats us well and soundly, and then falls to.

MASTER   Where lies he?

1 SHEPHERD   Ev'n where the night o'ertakes him.

---

164 credit believe/have confidence in   **165 heed** care   **171 habit** clothing, outfit   **174 ends** purposes   **4.1   3 a other** another person, someone else; the use of 'a' for 'an' is presumably to render a country accent   **woe-woman** a woman who brings him woe (a nonce word), perhaps playing on the false etymology of 'woman' as 'woe of man'   **5 unpeopled** uninhabited   **9 meat** food, sustenance   **10 victuals** provisions   **desire** request   **11 falls to** begins to eat   **12 lies he** does he sleep   **13 Ev'n ... him** wherever he happens to be when night falls

2 SHEPHERD Now will I be hanged, an' some fair-snouted skittish woman, or other,
15 be not at the end of this madness.

1 SHEPHERD Well, if he lodged within the sound of us, I knew our music would allure him. How attentively he stood, and how he fixed his eyes, when your boy sung his love-ditty. O, here he comes again.

MASTER Let him alone; he wonders strangely at us.

20 **1 SHEPHERD** Not a word, sirs, to cross him, as you love your shoulders.

2 SHEPHERD He seems much disturbed: I believe the mad fit is upon him.

Enters Julio

JULIO Horsemanship! Hell! Riding shall be abolished!
Turn the barbed steed loose to his native wildness;
It is a beast too noble to be made
25 The property of man's baseness. What a letter
Wrote he to's brother? What a man was I?
Why, Perseus did not know his seat like me!
The Parthian, that rides swift without the rein,
Matched not my grace and firmness. Shall this lord
30 Die when men pray for him? Think you 'tis meet?

1 SHEPHERD I don't know what to say: neither I, nor all the
Confessors in Spain can unriddle this wild stuff.

JULIO I must to court! Be ushered into grace
By a large list of praises ready penned!
35 O devil! What a venomous world is this,
When commendations are the baits to ruin!
All these good words were gyves and fetters, sir,
To keep me bolted there: while the false sender
Played out the game of treach'ry. Hold! Come hither!
40 You have an aspect, sir, of wond'rous wisdom,
And, as it seems, are travelled deep in knowledge;
Have you e'er seen the phoenix of the earth,
The bird of paradise?

2 SHEPHERD In troth, not I, sir.

45 **JULIO** I have, and known her haunts, and where she built
Her spicy nest: till, like a credulous fool,
I showed the treasure to a friend in trust,
And he hath robbed me of her. Trust no friend:
Keep thy heart's counsels close. Hast thou a mistress?

---

14 an' if   fair-snouted having a pretty nose or mouth   **skittish** fickle, inconstant   **15 at the end** the final cause   **16 within…us** near enough to hear us   **23 barbed steed** horse from Barbary or Morocco, noted for speed and endurance   **27 Perseus** mythological hero who rode the winged horse Pegasus in some stories   **28 Parthian** one from the ancient region of Parthia (modern Iran) noted for skill and dexterity in the management of horses   **30 meet** appropriate   **32 unriddle** solve, explain   **33 must** was ordered to go; Julio is rehearsing the course of previous events   **ushered into grace** ceremoniously conducted into favour at court   **36 baits** temptations, enticements   **37 gyves** shackles, especially for the leg   **38 bolted** fastened with a bolt   **40 aspect** look/countenance   **42 phoenix** mythological bird which lived for five or six hundred years before burning itself to ashes on a funeral pyre ignited by the sun and fanned by its own wings, only to rise from its ashes with renewed youth to live through another such cycle   **45 haunts** habits, customs/usual places she visits   **46 spicy** sweet-scented, aromatic   **49 close** secret

50 Give her not out in words; nor let thy pride

Be wanton to display her charms to view;

Love is contagious and a breath of praise,

Or a slight glance has kindled up its flame,

And turned a friend a traitor. 'Tis in proof,

55 And it has hurt my brain.

1 SHEPHERD   Marry, now there is some moral in his madness, and we may profit by it.

MASTER   See, he grows cool, and pensive.

Go towards him, boy, but do not look that way.

VIOLANTE   Alas! I tremble—

60 JULIO   O, my pretty youth!

Come hither, child; did not your song imply

Something of love?

1 SHEPHERD   Ha! Ha! Goes it there? Now if the boy be witty, we shall trace something.

VIOLANTE   Yes, sir, it was the subject.

65 JULIO   Sit here then: come, shake not, good pretty soul,

Nor do not fear me; I'll not do thee wrong.

VIOLANTE   Why do you look so on me?

JULIO   I have reasons.

It puzzles my philosophy to think

70 That the rude blast, hot sun, and dashing rains

Have made no fiercer war upon thy youth,

Nor hurt the bloom of that vermilion cheek.

You weep too, do you not?

VIOLANTE   Sometimes, I do.

75 JULIO   I weep sometimes too. You're extremely young.

VIOLANTE   Indeed, I've seen more sorrows far than years.

JULIO   Yet all these have not broken your complexion.

You have a strong heart, and you are the happier.

I warrant, you're a very loving woman.

80 VIOLANTE   A woman, sir?— I fear, he's found me out.   *Aside*

2 SHEPHERD   He takes the boy for a woman.— Mad, again!

JULIO   You've met some disappointment, some foul play

Has crossed your love.—I read it in your face.

VIOLANTE   You read a truth then.

85 JULIO   Where can lie the fault?

Is't in the man, or some dissembling knave,

He put in trust? Ho! Have I hit the cause?

VIOLANTE   You're not far off.

JULIO   This world is full of coz'ners, very full;

90 Young virgins must be wary in their ways.

---

50 Give…out do not report, publish   51 wanton undisciplined/self-indulgent/insolent, reckless   54 in proof proved, established/witnessed   56 Marry expressing surprise or astonishment, literally 'by the Virgin Mary'   moral practical lesson to be drawn   61 imply involve/hint at   63 witty clever/ cunning/prudent   trace discover, find out   70 rude blast rough gust of wind   72 vermilion red-coloured   76 more sorrows far far more sorrows   77 broken spoiled, ruined   79 warrant guarantee   86 dissembling knave deceiving rogue   89 coz'ners deceivers, i.e. cozeners – the elision is for metrical purposes

I've known a duke's son do as great a knavery.

Will you be ruled by me?

VIOLANTE   Yes.

JULIO   Kill yourself.

95   'Twill be a terror to the villain's conscience,

The longest day he lives.

VIOLANTE   By no means. What?

Commit self-murder!

JULIO   Yes, I'll have it so.

100   1 SHEPHERD   I fear his fit is returning. Take heed of all hands!— Sir, do you want anything?

JULIO   Thou liest; thou can'st not hurt me: I am proof

Gainst farther wrongs.— Steal close behind me, lady.

I will avenge thee.

105   VIOLANTE   Thank the heav'ns, I'm free.

JULIO   O, treach'rous, base Henriquez! Have I caught thee?

Julio seizes on the Shepherd

2 SHEPHERD   Help! Help! Good neighbours; he will kill me else.   *Violante runs out*

JULIO   Here thou shalt pay thy heart-blood for the wrongs

Thou'st heaped upon this head. Faith-breaker! Villain!

110   I'll suck thy life-blood.

1 SHEPHERD   Good sir, have patience; this is no Henriquez.   *They rescue the Shepherd*

JULIO   Well; let him slink to court, and hide a coward;

Not all his father's guards shall shield him there.

Or if he prove too strong for mortal arm,

115   I will solicit ev'ry saint in heav'n

To lend me vengeance. I'll about it straight.

The wrathful elements shall wage this war;

Furies shall haunt him, vultures gnaw his heart

And nature pour forth all her stores of plagues,

120   To join in punishment of trust betrayed.   *Exit Julio*

2 SHEPHERD   Go thy ways, and a vengeance go with thee!— Pray, feel my nose; is it fast, neighbours?

1 SHEPHERD   'Tis as well as may be.

2 SHEPHERD   He pulled at it, as he would have dragged a bullock backward by the tail.

125   An't had been some men's nose that I know, neighbours, who knows where it had been now? He has given me such a devilish dash o'er the mouth, that I feel, I shall never whistle to my sheep again: then they'll make holiday.

1 SHEPHERD   Come, shall we go? For, I fear, if the youth return, our second course will be much more against our stomachs.

130   MASTER   Walk you afore; I will but give my boy

---

92 ruled guided   **100 Take…hands!** Everyone watch out!   **102 proof Gainst** invulnerable, resistant to   **103 Steal** move quietly   **107 else** otherwise   **112 slink** go in a sneaking manner   **116 straight** immediately   **118 Furies** in classical mythology, goddesses with snakes twined in their hair, sent from Tartarus to avenge wrong and punish crime   **121 Go thy ways** be off with you   **vengeance…thee** a curse or malediction, 'may you be punished'   **122 fast** firmly fixed in its place   **125 An't** if it   **126 dash o'er** violent blow across   **127 make holiday** cease from work   **130 afore** in front

Some short instructions, and I'll follow straight.

We'll crash a cup together.

1 SHEPHERD Pray, do not linger.

MASTER   I will not, sirs.— This must not be a boy;

135 His voice, mien, gesture, ev'rything he does,

Savour of soft and female delicacy.

He but puts on this seeming, and his garb

Speaks him of such a rank as well persuades me,

He plays the swain, rather to cloak some purpose

140 Than forced to't by a need: I've waited long

To mark the end he has in his disguise,

But am not perfect in't. The madman's coil

Has driv'n him shaking hence. These fears betray him.

If he prove right, I'm happy. O, he's here.

Enters Violante

145 Come hither, boy; where did you leave the flock, child?

VIOLANTE   Grazing below, sir.— What does he mean, to stroke   *Aside*

one o'the cheek so? I hope, I'm not betrayed.

MASTER   Have you learnt the whistle yet, and when to fold?

And how to make the dog bring in the strayers?

150 **VIOLANTE**   Time, sir, will furnish me with all these rules;

My will is able, but my knowledge weak, sir.

MASTER   That's a good child: why dost thou blush, my boy?

'Tis certainly a woman.— Speak, my boy.   *Aside*

VIOLANTE   Heav'n! How I tremble.— 'Tis unusual to me

155 To find such kindness at a master's hand,

That am a poor boy, ev'ry way unable,

Unless it be in pray'rs to merit it.

Besides, I've often heard old people say,

Too much indulgence makes boys rude and saucy.

160 **MASTER**   Are you so cunning?—

VIOLANTE   How his eyes shake fire,

And measure ev'ry piece of youth about me!   *Aside*

The ewes want water, sir: shall I go drive 'em

Down to the cisterns? Shall I make haste, sir?

165 Would I were five miles from him— how he gripes me!   *Aside*

MASTER   Come, come, all this is not sufficient, child,

To make a fool of me.— This is a fine hand,

A delicate fine hand — never change colour,

You understand me — and a woman's hand.

---

132 crash a cup have a drink (of alcohol)   **134 must not** cannot   **135 mien** look, bearing, manner   **136 Savour** reveal the characteristics of
137 seeming external appearance   **garb** elegance/behaviour, manner/costume   **139 swain** youth/rustic, shepherd   **141 end** purpose   **142 perfect in't**
completely satisfied about it   **coil** noisy fuss   **144 prove right** prospers/turns out to be honest/shows himself to be as I suspect   **148 fold** shut up sheep in
a pen   **149 strayers** stray sheep   **150 furnish** supply, provide   **151 able** strong/ready/obedient   **156 unable** unfit, unqualified/weak   **163 ewes** female
sheep   **164 cisterns** ponds, natural reservoirs   **165 gripes** grasps, clutches   **168 never** do not

170	VIOLANTE	You're strangely out: yet if I were a woman,
		I know, you are so honest and so good,
		That though I wore disguises for some ends,
		You would not wrong me.
	MASTER	Come, you're made for love;
175		Will you comply? I'm madder with this talk.
		There's nothing you can say, can take my edge off.
	VIOLANTE	O, do but quench these foul affections in you,
		That, like base thieves, have robbed you of your reason,
		And I will be a woman, and begin
180		So sad a story, that if there be aught
		Of humane in you, or a soul that's gentle,
		You cannot choose but pity my lost youth.
	MASTER	No stories now—
	VIOLANTE	Kill me directly, sir;
185		As you have any goodness, take my life.

RODERICK   Hoa! Shepherd, will you hear, sir?   *Within*

MASTER   What bawling rogue is that, i'th'devil's name?

VIOLANTE   Blessings upon him, whatsoe'er he be!   *Runs out*

Enters Roderick

RODERICK   Good even, my friend; I thought, you all had been asleep in this country.

190   MASTER   You had lied then; for you were waking, when you thought so.

RODERICK   I thank you, sir.

MASTER   I pray, be covered; 'tis not so much worth, sir.

RODERICK   Was that thy boy ran crying?

MASTER   Yes; what then?

195   RODERICK   Why dost thou beat him so?

MASTER   To make him grow.

RODERICK   A pretty med'cine! Thou can'st not tell me the way to the next nunnery?

MASTER   How do you know that?— Yes, I can tell you, but the question is whether

I will or no; and, indeed, I will not. Fare you well.   *Exit Master*

200	RODERICK	What a brute fellow's this! Are they all thus?
		My brother Henriquez tells me by his letters,
		The mistress of his soul not far from hence
		Hath taken sanctuary: from which he prays
		My aid to bring her back. From what Camillo
205		Hinted, I wear some doubts. Here 'tis appointed
		That we should meet; it must be here; 'tis so.
		He comes.

Enters Henriquez

Now, brother, what's this post-haste business

---

170 out mistaken   **yet** but   **175 comply** yield, do as I wish/consent   **madder** more infatuated/wildly excited/carried away by desire, passion/annoyed, exasperated   **176 take…off** lessen my sexual desire   **177 quench** extinguish   **affections** feelings, emotions/passions   **180 aught** anything whatever   **181 humane** sympathy, compassion   **184 directly** immediately, straight away   **186 Hoa!** exclamation to attract attention   **189 even** evening   **192 be covered** put your hat on; Roderick must have removed his as a mark of respect   **208 post-haste** urgent

    You hurry me about? Some wenching matter—

210 HENRIQUEZ My letter told you, sir.

    RODERICK   'Tis true, it tells me, that you've lost a mistress

    Whom your heart bleeds for; but the means to win her

    From her close life, I take it, is not mentioned.

    You're ever in these troubles—

215 HENRIQUEZ Noble brother,

    I own, I have too freely giv'n a scope

    To youth's intemp'rate heat and rash desires:

    But think not, that I would engage your virtues

    To any cause, wherein my constant heart

220 Attended not my eye. Till now my passions

    Reigned in my blood, ne'er pierced into my mind,

    But I'm a convert grown to purest thoughts:

    And must in anguish spend my days to come,

    If I possess not her: so much I love.

225 RODERICK   The means? She's in a cloister, is she not?

    Within whose walls to enter as we are,

    Will never be: few men, but friars, come there;

    Which we shall never make.

    HENRIQUEZ If that would do it,

230 I would make anything.

    RODERICK   Are you so hot?

    I'll serve him, be it but to save his honour.   *Aside*

    To feign a corpse, by th'mass, it shall be so.

    We must pretend we do transport a body

235 As 'twere to's funeral: and coming late by,

    Crave a night's leave to rest the hearse i'th'convent.

    That be our course; for to such charity

    Strict zeal and custom of the house give way.

    HENRIQUEZ   And, opportune, a vacant hearse passed by

240 From rites but new performed: this for a price

    We'll hire, to put our scheme in act. Ho! Gerald—

Enter Gerald, whom Henriquez whispers, then Gerald goes out

    RODERICK   When we're once lodged, the means of her conveyance,

    By safe and secret force, with ease we'll compass

    But, brother, know my terms. – If that your mistress

245 Will to the world come back, and she appear

    An object worthy in our father's eye,

    Woo her and win her; but if his consent

    Keep not pace with your purpose—

---

209 **wenching** associated with women   213 **close** enclosed (in the nunnery)   216 **own** confess   **giv'n a scope** opportunity or liberty to act
217 **intemp'rate heat** violent, immoderate passion, ardour   220 **Attended not** did not direct or follow/guard/follow closely upon   225 **cloister** place of
religious seclusion, nunnery   227 **but** except   231 **hot** passionate/lustful   235 **coming late by** passing late in the evening   241 **in act** into action
243 **compass** accomplish, achieve (our purpose)

HENRIQUEZ   Doubt it not.

250   I've looked not with a common eye, but chose

A noble virgin, who to make her so,

Has all the gifts of heav'n and earth upon her.

If ever woman yet could be an angel,

She is the nearest.

255   RODERICK   Well, a lover's praise

Feasts not a common ear. Now to our plot;

We shall bring night in with us.   *Exeunt*

[Act 4] Scene 2

Enter Julio, and Two Gentlemen

1 GENTLEMAN   Good sir, compose yourself.

JULIO   O, Leonora,

That heav'n had made thee stronger than a woman,

How happy had I been!

5   1 GENTLEMAN   He's calm again: *To the Second Gentleman*

I'll take this interval to work upon him.—

These wild and solitary places, sir,

But feed your pain, let better reason guide you,

And quit this forlorn state that yields no comfort.

                                        Lute sounds within

10   JULIO   Ha! Hark, a sound from heav'n! Do you hear nothing?

1 GENTLEMAN   Yes, sir; the touch of some sweet instrument:

Here's no inhabitant.

JULIO   No, no, the better.

1 GENTLEMAN   This is a strange place to hear music in.

15   JULIO   I'm often visited with these sweet airs.

The spirit of some hapless man that died,

And left his love hid in a faithless woman,

Sure haunts these mountains.

VIOLANTE   *(sings within)*

Fond echo! Forgo thy light strain,

20   And heedfully hear a lost maid;

Go, tell the false ear of the swain

How deeply his vows have betrayed.

Go, tell him, what sorrows I bear;

See, yet if his heart feel my woe:

25   'Tis now he must heal my despair,

---

257 **night** darkness, literally and metaphorically   **[4.]2**   *Scene: Location not specified*   **3 That heav'n** if only heaven   *Lute* stringed musical instrument   **12 Here's no inhabitant** there's no human being here   **18 Sure** surely   **19 Fond** foolish, infatuated   **Forgo…strain** refrain from your usual light-hearted expression   **20 heedfully** carefully, attentively   **lost maid** ruined virgin (morally and physically)

Or death will make pity too slow.

GENTLEMAN   See, how his soul strives in him! This sad strain
Has searched him to the heart.

JULIO   Excellent sorrow!

30   You never loved?

GENTLEMAN   No.

JULIO   Peace; and learn to grieve then.

VIOLANTE   *(sings within)*
Go, tell him, what sorrows I bear;

35   See, yet if his heart feel my woe:
'Tis now he must heal my despair,
Or death will make pity too slow.

JULIO   Is not this heav'nly?

GENTLEMAN   I never heard the like, sir.

40   JULIO   I'll tell you, my good friends; but pray, say nothing;
I'm strangely touched with this. The heav'nly sound
Diffuses a sweet peace through all my soul.
But yet I wonder what new, sad, companion
Grief has brought hither to outbid my sorrows.

45   Stand off, stand off, stand off — friends, it appears.

Enters Violante

VIOLANTE   How much more grateful are these craggy mountains,
And these wild trees than things of nobler natures;
For these receive my plaints, and mourn again
In many echoes to me. All good people

50   Are fall'n asleep forever. None are left
That have the sense and touch of tenderness
For virtue's sake: no, scarce their memory:
From whom I may expect counsel in fears,
Ease to complainings or redress of wrongs.

55   JULIO   This is a moving sorrow, but say nothing.

VIOLANTE   What dangers have I run, and to what insults
Exposed this ruin of myself? Oh! Mischief
On that soul-spotted hind, my vicious master!
Who would have thought that such poor worms as they,

60   Whose best feed is coarse bread, whose bev'rage, water,
Should have so much rank blood? I shake all over,
And blush to think what had become of me,
If that good man had not relieved me from him.

JULIO   Since she is not Leonora, she is heav'nly.

65   When she speaks next, listen as seriously,
As women do that have their loves at sea,

---

44 outbid outdo, surpass   **46 grateful** welcome, pleasing to the mind or senses   **48 plaints** laments, audible expressions of sorrow   **58 soul-spotted hind** rustic, boor with a morally blemished soul   **59 Who...blood?** Violante is surprised that the lower-class master of the shepherds should have lustful feelings, conventionally associated with the corruption of the court rather than the virtue and simplicity of pastoral   **61 rank** lustful/coarse/insolent **62 what had** what would have

What wind blows ev'ry morning.

VIOLANTE   I cannot get this false man's memory
Out of my mind. You maidens, that shall live
70 To hear my mournful tale, when I am ashes,
Be wise; and to an oath no more give credit,
To tears, to vows, (false both!) or anything
A man shall promise, than to clouds, that now
Bear such a pleasing shape, and now are nothing.
75 For they will cozen (if they may be cozened),
The very gods they worship.— Valour, justice,
Discretion, honesty, and all they covet,
To make them seeming-saints, are but the wiles
By which these sirens lure us to destruction.

80 **JULIO**   Do not you weep now? I could drop myself
Into a fountain for her.

GENTLEMAN   She weeps extremely.

JULIO   Let her weep; 'tis well:
Her heart will break else. Great sorrows live in tears.

85 **VIOLANTE**   O, false Henriquez!

JULIO   Ha!

VIOLANTE   And O, thou fool,
Forsaken Violante, whose belief
And childish love have made thee so — go, die;
90 For there is nothing left thee now to look for
That can bring comfort, but a quiet grave.
There all the miseries I long have felt,
And those to come, shall sweetly sleep together.
Fortune may guide that false Henriquez hither,
95 To weep repentance o'er my pale, dead corpse,
And cheer my wand'ring spirit with those loved obsequies.   *Going*

JULIO   Stay, lady, stay: can it be possible,
That you are Violante?

VIOLANTE   That lost name,
100 Spoken by one, that needs must know my fortunes,
Has taken much fear from me. Who are you, sir?
For, sure, I am that hopeless Violante.

JULIO   And I, as far from any earthly comfort
That I know yet, the much-wronged Julio!

105 **VIOLANTE**   Julio!

JULIO   I once was thought so. If the curst Henriquez
Had pow'r to change you to a boy, why, lady,
Should not that mischief make me anything

---

75 **cozen** cheat, deceive   78 **seeming-saints** saints in appearance only   79 **sirens** fabulous mythological creatures, part woman, part bird, who lured sailors to their death with enchanted singing   96 **obsequies** funeral rites

That have an equal share in all the miseries
110   His crimes have flung upon us?

VIOLANTE   Well I know it:
And pardon me, I could not know your virtues,
Before your griefs. Methought, when last we met,
The accent of your voice struck on my ear
115   Like something I had known, but floods of sorrow
Drowned the remembrance. If you'll please to sit,
(Since I have found a suff'ring true companion),
And give me hearing, I will tell you something
Of Leonora, that may comfort you.

120   JULIO   Blessing upon thee! Henceforth, I protest
Never to leave thee, if heav'n say amen.
But, soft! Let's shift our ground, guide our sad steps
To some remoter gloom, where, undisturbed,
We may compare our woes; dwell on the tale
125   Of mutual injuries, till our eyes run o'er,
And we infect each other with fresh sorrows.
Talked you of comfort? 'Tis the food of fools,
And we will none on't; but indulge despair:
So, worn with griefs, steal to the cave of death,
130   And in a sigh give up our latest breath.   *Exeunt*

Act 5 Scene 1

Scene: The prospect of the mountains continued

Enter Roderick, Leonora veiled, Henriquez, Attendants as Mourners

RODERICK   Rest certain, lady, nothing shall betide you,
But fair, and noble usage. Pardon me,
That hit her to a course of violence
Has snatched you from that seat of contemplation
5   To which you gave your afterlife.

LEONORA   Where am I?

RODERICK   Not in the nunnery; never blush, nor tremble;
Your honour has as fair a guard as when
Within a cloister. Know then, what is done,
10   (Which, I presume, you understand not truly)
Has this use, to preserve the life of one
Dying for love of you: my brother, and your friend:
Under which colour we desired to rest
Our hearse one night within your hallowed walls,

---

112 **know** perceive, recognize 123 **gloom** deeply shaded or darkened place 130 **latest** last, final 5.1 1 **betide** happen befall 3 **hitherto** up to this
point, until now 5 **afterlife** later period of one's life 11 **use** purpose, object 13 **colour** pretext

15   Where we surprised you.

LEONORA   Are you that lord Roderick,

So spoken of for virtue and fair life,

And dare you lose these to be advocate

For such a brother, such a sinful brother,

20   Such an unfaithful, treacherous, brutal brother?

RODERICK   This is a fearful charge.   *Looks at Henriquez*

LEONORA   If you would have me

Think you still bear respect for virtue's name;

As you would wish your daughters, thus distressed,

25   Might find a guard, protect me from Henriquez,

And I am happy.

RODERICK   Come, sir, make your answer;

For as I have a soul, I am ashamed on't.

HENRIQUEZ   O, Leonora, see! Thus self-condemned,

30   I throw me at your feet, and sue for mercy.

If I have erred, impute it to my love;

The tyrant god that bows us to his sway,

Rebellious to the laws of reas'ning men,

That will not have his votaries' actions scanned,

35   But calls it justice, when we most obey him.

He but commanded what your eyes inspired,

Whose sacred beams darted into my soul,

Have purged the mansion from impure desires,

And kindled in my heart a vestal's flame.

40   LEONORA   Rise, rise, my lord; this well-dissembled passion

Has gained you nothing but a deeper hate.

Should I imagine he can truly love me

That, like a villain, murders my desires?

Or should I drink that wine and think it cordial,

45   When I see poison in't?

RODERICK   Draw this way, lady;

I am not perfect in your story yet,

But see you've had some wrongs that want redress.

Only you must have patience to go with us

50   To yon small lodge, which meets the sight from hence,

Where your distress shall find the due respect:

Till when, your griefs shall govern me as much,

As nearness and affection to my brother.

Call my attendants yours and use them freely;

55   For as I am a gentleman, no pow'r,

---

15 surprised seized by force   **32 tyrant god** Cupid, god of love   **bows…sway** Cupid made people fall in love by shooting arrows from his bow at them   **34 votaries' actions scanned** the deeds of his devout followers judged or criticized   **36 eyes…beams** the ancient 'emission theory' of sight believed that the eyes emitted rays that fell onto an object which then became visible   **38 mansion** i.e. the body, the dwelling place of the soul   **39 vestal's flame** a pure, chaste flame, named after the virgin priestesses who tended the sacred fire in the temple of the Roman goddess Vesta   **44 cordial** heartfelt, sincere   **50 yon** that one over there   **meets…hence** is just out of sight

Above your own will, shall come near your person.

As they are going out, Violante enters and plucks Roderick by the sleeve; the rest go out

VIOLANTE   Your ear a moment: scorn not my tender youth.

RODERICK   Look to the lady there. I follow straight.—

What ails this boy? Why dost thou single me?

60   VIOLANTE   The due observance of your noble virtue,

Vowed to this mourning virgin, makes me bold

To give it more employment.

RODERICK   Art not thou

The surly shepherd's boy, that, when I called

65   To know the way, ran crying by me?

VIOLANTE   Yes, sir.

And I thank heav'n and you for helping me.

RODERICK   How did I help thee, boy?

VIOLANTE   I do but seem so, sir; and am indeed

70   A woman; one your brother once has loved;

Or, heav'n forgive him else, he lied extremely.

RODERICK   Weep not, good maid. O, this licentious brother!

But how came you a wand'rer on these mountains?

VIOLANTE   That, as we pass, an't please you, I'll discover.

75   I will assure you, sir, these barren mountains

Hold many wonders of your brother's making.

Here wanders hapless Julio, worthy man!

Besides himself with wrongs—

RODERICK   That once again—

80   VIOLANTE   Sir, I said, Julio.— Sleep weighed down his eyelids,

Oppressed with watching, just as you approached us.

RODERICK   O, brother! We shall sound the depths of falsehood.

If this be true, no more but guide me to him:

I hope a fair end will succeed all yet.

85   If it be he, by your leave, gentle brother,

I'll see him served first.— Maid, you have o'erjoyed me.

Thou shalt have right too: make thy fair appeal

To the good duke, and doubt not but thy tears

Shall be repaid with interest from his justice.

90   Lead me to Julio.   *Exeunt*

[Act 5] Scene 2

[*Scene:*] *An apartment in the lodge*

Enter Duke, Don Bernard and Camillo

---

74 **an't** if it   **discover** reveal   78 **Besides himself** out of his mind   82 **sound the depths** penetrate to the bottom of, a nautical metaphor from the use of a line with a lead weight employed to ascertain the depth of water   84 **succeed** follow, ensue   86 **served** looked after   87 **right** justice

CAMILLO   Ay, then your grace had had a son more; he, a daughter; and I, an heir:
But let it be as 'tis, I cannot mend it; one way or other, I shall rub it over, with
rubbing to my grave, and there's an end on't.

DUKE   Our sorrows cannot help us, gentlemen.

5   CAMILLO   Hang me, sir, if I shed one tear more. By Jove, I've wept so long, I'm as
blind as justice. When I come to see my hawks (which I held a toy next to my son) if
they be but house-high, I must stand aiming at them like a gunner.

DUKE   Why, he mourns like a man. Don Bernard, you
Are still like April, full of show'rs and dews:
10   And yet I blame you not: for I myself
Feel the self-same affections.— Let them go;
They're disobedient children.

DON BERNARD   Ay, my lord;
Yet they may turn again.

15   CAMILLO   Let them e'en have their swing: they're young and wanton; the next
storm we shall have them gallop homeward, whining as pigs do in the wind.

DON BERNARD   Would I had my daughter anyway.

CAMILLO   Would'st thou have her with bairn, man, tell me that?

DON BERNARD   I care not, if an honest father got it.

20   CAMILLO   You might have had her so in this good time,
Had my son had her: now you may go seek
Your fool to stop a gap with.

DUKE   You say, that Rod'rick charged you here should wait him:
He has o'erslipped the time at which his letters
25   Of speed request that I should also meet him.
I fear, some bad event is ushered in
By this delay— how now?

Enters Gentleman

GENTLEMAN   So please your grace,
Lord Rod'rick makes approach.

30   DUKE   I thank thee, fellow,
For thy so timely news: comes he alone?

GENTLEMAN   No, sir, attended well; and in his train
Follows a hearse with all due rites of mourning.   *Exit Gentleman*

DUKE   Heav'n send, Henriquez live!

35   CAMILLO   'Tis my poor Julio.—

Enters Roderick, hastily

DUKE   O welcome, welcome,
Welcome, good Rod'rick! Say, what news?

CAMILLO   Do you bring joy or grief, my lord? For me,

[5.]2   **1 then** in that case   **had…more** would have had another son   **2 rub it over** turn the business over in my mind   **3 rubbing** careful examination/
passing   **5 Hang me** expression of anger or impatience   **Jove** Jupiter, chief of the Roman gods   **6 blind as justice** the Roman goddess Justitia
was imaged carrying scales or a sword and blindfold signifying impartiality   **toy** trifle, thing of little value   **15 swing** fling, freedom to indulge
themselves   **wanton** naughty, unruly   **18 with bairn** pregnant, with child   **20 have…so** i.e. honest, because she would have been married to Julio and
perhaps become pregnant as well   **23 charged…him** ordered you to wait for him here   **24 o'erslipped** mistaken/passed   **32 train** retinue/vehicles
bringing baggage

Come what can come, I'll live a month or two

40 If the gout please; curse my physician once more,

And then—

Under this stone

Lies sev'nty one.

RODERICK   Signor, you do express a manly patience.

45 My noble father, something I have brought

To ease your sorrows: my endeavours have not

Been altogether barren in my journey.

DUKE   It comes at need, boy; but I hoped it from thee.

Enter Leonora veiled, Henriquez behind, and Attendants

RODERICK   The company I bring will bear me witness,

50 The busiest of my time has been employed

On this good task. Don Bernard finds beneath

This veil his daughter: you, my royal father,

Behind that lady find a wand'ring son.

How I met with them, and how brought them hither,

55 More leisure must unfold.

HENRIQUEZ   My father here!

And Julio's! O, confusion! Low as earth

I bow me for your pardon.   *To the Duke*

DON BERNARD   O, my girl!

60 Thou bring'st new life.—   *Embraces Leonora*

DUKE   And you, my son, restore me   *To Roderick*

One comfort here that has been missing long.

I hope, thy follies thou hast left abroad.   *To Henriquez*

CAMILLO   Ay, ay; you've all comforts but I; you have ruined me, killed my poor

65 boy, cheated and ruined him, and I have no comfort.

RODERICK   Be patient, signor; time may guide my hand

To work you comfort too.

CAMILLO   I thank your lordship;

Would grandsire Time had been so kind to've done it;

70 We might have joyed together like good fellows.

But he's so full of business, good old man,

'Tis wonder he could do the good he has done.

DON BERNARD   Nay, child, be comforted. These tears distract me.

DUKE   Hear your good father, lady.

75 LEONORA   Willingly.

DUKE   The voice of parents is the voice of gods:

For to their children they are heav'n's lieutenants:

Made fathers, not for common uses merely

Of procreation, beasts and birds would be

---

42 stone i.e. tombstone, Camillo is referring to his imminent death and the wording of the headstone   **44 Signor** 'sir' (Italian)   **53 wand'ring**
erring, disloyal/restless, wanton   **69 grandsire Time** (Old) Father Time, conventionally represented as an elderly bearded man with a scythe and an
hourglass   **77 lieutenants** substitutes

80	As noble then as we are, but to steer
	The wanton freight of youth through storms and dangers,
	Which with full sails they bear upon, and straighten
	The moral line of life they bend so often.
	For these are we made fathers; and for these,
85	May challenge duty on our children's part.
	Obedience is the sacrifice of angels,
	Whose form you carry.

DON BERNARD   Hear the duke, good wench.

LEONORA   I do most heedfully. My gracious lord,   *To the Duke*

90   Let me be so unmannered to request,
He would not farther press me with persuasions
O'th'instant hour: but have the gentle patience
To bury this keen suit, till I shake hands
With my old sorrows,—

95   **CAMILLO**   Why dost look at me?
Alas! I cannot help thee.

LEONORA   And but weep
A farewell to my murdered Julio—

CAMILLO   Blessing be with thy soul, whene'er it leaves thee!

100   **LEONORA**   For such sad rites must be performed, my lord,
Ere I can love again. Maids, that have loved,
If they be worth that noble testimony,
Wear their loves here, my lord, here in their hearts;
Deep, deep within, not in their eyes, or accents;

105   Such may be slipped away or with two tears
Washed out of all remembrance: mine, no physic,
But time, or death, can cure.

HENRIQUEZ   You make your own conditions, and I seal them
Thus on your virtuous hand.   *Aside*

110   **CAMILLO**   Well, wench, thy equal
Shall not be found in haste; I give thee that:
Thou art a right one, ev'ry inch. Thy father
(For, without doubt, that snuff never begot thee)
Was some choice fellow, some true gentleman;

115   I give thy mother thanks for't – there's no harm done.—
Would I were young again, and had but thee,
A good horse under me, and a good sword,
And thus much for inheritance—   *Makes a dismissive gesture*

Violante offers once or twice to show herself, but goes back

DUKE   What boy's that,

120   Has offered twice or thrice to break upon us?

---

81 freight load, burden   **85 challenge** have a natural right or claim to   **93 bury** abandon, forget   **keen suit** cruel, painful case   **106 remembrance** memory   **physic** medicine   **112 a right one** a direct descendant/an honest girl   **113 snuff** feeble creature (likening Don Bernardo to a candle end)   **begot** produced, fathered   **114 choice** well-chosen, appropriate/excellent

I've noted him, and still he falls back fearful.

RODERICK   A little boy, sir, like a shepherd?

DUKE   Yes.

RODERICK   'Tis your page, brother, one that was so, late.

125 HENRIQUEZ   My page! What page?

RODERICK   Ev'n so he says, your page;

And more, and worse, you stole him from his friends,

And promised him preferment.

HENRIQUEZ   I, preferment!

130 RODERICK   And on some slight occasion let him slip

Here on these mountains, where he had been starved,

Had not my people found him as we travelled.

This was not handsome, brother.

HENRIQUEZ   You are merry.

135 RODERICK   You'll find it sober truth.

DUKE   If so, 'tis ill.

HENRIQUEZ   'Tis fiction all, sir.— Brother, you must please

To look some other fool to put these tricks on,

They are too obvious.— Please, your grace, give leave

140 T'admit the boy; if he know me, and say,

I stole him from his friends and cast him off,

Know me no more.— Brother, pray do not wrong me.

Enters Violante

RODERICK   Here is the boy. If he deny this to you,

Then I have wronged you.

145 DUKE   Hear me: what's thy name, boy?

VIOLANTE   Florio, an't like your grace.

DUKE   A pretty child.

Where wast thou born?

VIOLANTE   On t'other side the mountains.

150 DUKE   What are thy friends?

VIOLANTE   A father, sir, but poor.

DUKE   How cam'st thou hither? How, to leave thy father?

VIOLANTE   That noble gentleman pleased once to like me,   *Pointing to Henriquez*

And, not to lie, so much to dote upon me,

155 That with his promises he won my youth,

And duty, from my father: him I followed.

RODERICK   How say you now, brother?

CAMILLO   Ay, my lord, how say you?

HENRIQUEZ   As I have life and soul, 'tis all a trick, sir.

160 I never saw the boy before.

---

124 page boy employed as a personal attendant to one of high rank   **late** recently   **128 preferment** promotion/advancement by marriage   **130 occasion** pretext, excuse   **let him slip** gave him the slip, playing on sense of 'fall into moral error'   **133 handsome** proper/gracious/generous   **134 merry** joking

VIOLANTE   O, sir,

Call not your soul to witness in a wrong:

And 'tis not noble in you to despise

What you have made thus. If I lie, let justice

165   Turn all her rods upon me.

DUKE   Fie, Henriquez;

There is no trace of cunning in this boy.

CAMILLO   A good boy!— Be not fearful: speak thy mind, child.

Nature, sure, meant thou shouldst have been a wench,

170   And then't had been no marvel he had bobbed thee.

DUKE   Why did he put thee from him?

VIOLANTE   That to me

Is yet unknown, sir; for my faith, he could not;

I never did deceive him: for my service,

175   He had no just cause; what my youth was able,

My will still put in act, to please my master:

I cannot steal; therefore that can be nothing

To my undoing: no, nor lie; my breeding,

Though it be plain, is honest.

180   DUKE   Weep not, child.

CAMILLO   This lord has abused men, women, and children already: what farther

plot he has, the devil knows.

DUKE   If thou can'st bring a witness of thy wrong,

(Else it would be injustice to believe thee,

185   He having sworn against it) thou shalt have,

I bind it with my honour, satisfaction

To thine own wishes.

VIOLANTE   I desire no more, sir.

I have a witness, and a noble one,

190   For truth and honesty.

RODERICK   Go, bring him hither.   *Exit Violante*

HENRIQUEZ   This lying boy will take him to his heels,

And leave me slandered.

RODERICK   No; I'll be his voucher.

195   HENRIQUEZ   Nay then 'tis plain, this is confederacy.

RODERICK   That he has been an agent in your service,

Appears from this. Here is a letter, brother,

Produced, perforce, to give him credit with me,

The writing, yours; the matter, love; for so,

200   He says, he can explain it.

CAMILLO   Then, belike,

---

165 rods sticks for administering punishment   **166 Fie** exclamation of indignant reproach   **170 bobbed** deceived, made a fool of, playing on sense of 'had sex with'   **171 put...him** cast you off/get rid of you   **173 faith** fidelity, loyalty   **178 undoing** ruin   **breeding** parentage/upbringing   **194 voucher** guarantor, one who vouches for or corroborates the truth   **195 confederacy** a conspiracy   **198 perforce** of necessity   **credit** credibility   **201 belike** most likely, probably

A young he-bawd.

HENRIQUEZ This forgery confounds me!

DUKE   Read it, Roderick.

205 **RODERICK** (*Reads*) 'Our prudence should now teach us to forget, what our indiscretion has committed. I have already made one step towards this wisdom—'

HENRIQUEZ Hold, sir.— My very words to Violante!   *Aside*

DUKE   Go on.

HENRIQUEZ My gracious father, give me pardon;

210   I do confess, I some such letter wrote,

The purport all too trivial for your ear,

But how it reached this young dissembler's hands,

Is what I cannot solve; for on my soul,

And by the honours of my birth and house,

215   The minion's face till now I never saw.

RODERICK Run not too far in debt on protestation.

Why should you do a child this wrong?

HENRIQUEZ Go to!

Your friendships past warrant not this abuse:

220   If you provoke me thus, I shall forget

What you are to me. This is a mere practice

And villainy to draw me into scandal.

RODERICK No more; you are a boy.— Here comes a witness,

Shall prove you so. No more.

Enter Julio, disguised, [and] Violante, as a woman

225 **HENRIQUEZ** Another rascal!

DUKE   Hold—

HENRIQUEZ Ha!   *Seeing Violante*

DUKE   What's here?

HENRIQUEZ By all my sins, the injured Violante!   *Aside*

230 **RODERICK** Now, sir, whose practice breaks?

CAMILLO Is this a page?   *To Henriquez*

RODERICK One that has done him service,

And he has paid her for't but broke his covenant.

VIOLANTE My lord, I come not now to wound your spirit.

235   Your pure affection dead, which first betrayed me,

My claim die with it! Only let me not

Shrink to the grave with infamy upon me:

Protect my virtue, though it hurt your faith,

And my last breath shall speak Henriquez noble.

240 **HENRIQUEZ** What a fierce conflict shame and wounded honour,

---

202 **he-bawd** male pimp or sexual procurer 212 **dissembler's** deceiver's, rogue's 215 **minion's** hanger-on's/slave's, the term bore a derogatory implication of homosexuality 216 **Run...protestation** don't increase your legal liability by protesting too much **protestation** legal term relating to pleading: 'an affirmation or denial by a pleader of the truth of an allegation which cannot be directly affirmed or denied without duplicating the plea, and which cannot be passed over in case it should be held to have been tacitly waived or admitted' 219 **Your...abuse** your past kind behaviour did not promise this ill-treatment **warrant** promise, predict 221 **practice** trick 223 **boy** rogue, worthless fellow 233 **covenant** agreement, pledge

Raise in my breast! But honour shall o'ercome.
She looks as beauteous, and as innocent,
As when I wronged her.— Virtuous Violante!
Too good for me! Dare you still love a man
245 So faithless as I am? I know you love me.
Thus, thus, and thus, I print my vowed repentance:
Let all men read it here.— My gracious father,
Forgive, and make me rich with your consent,
This is my wife; no other would I choose,
250 Were she a queen.

CAMILLO Here's a new change. Bernard looks dull upon't.

HENRIQUEZ And fair Leonora, from whose virgin arms
I forced my wronged friend Julio, O forgive me.
Take home your holy vows, and let him have 'em
255 That has deserved them. O that he were here,
That I might own the baseness of my wrong,
And purposed recompense. My Violante,
You must again be widowed: for I vow
A ceaseless pilgrimage, ne'er to know joy,
260 Till I can give it to the injured Julio.

CAMILLO This almost melts me.— But my poor lost boy—

RODERICK I'll stop that voyage, brother.— Gentle lady,
What think you of this honest man?   *Indicating Julio*

LEONORA Alas!
265 My thoughts, my lord, were all employed within!
He has a face makes me remember something
I have thought well of; how he looks upon me!
Poor man, he weeps.— Ha! Stay! It cannot be—
He has his eye, his features, shape, and gesture.—
270 Would he would speak.

JULIO Leonora—   *Throws off his disguise*

LEONORA Yes, 'tis he!
O, ecstasy of joy!   *They embrace*

CAMILLO Now, what's the matter?

275 RODERICK Let 'em alone; they're almost starved for kisses.

CAMILLO Stand forty foot off; no man trouble 'em.
Much good may't do your hearts!— What is he, lord,
What is he?

RODERICK A certain son of yours.

280 CAMILLO The devil he is.

RODERICK If he be the devil, that devil must call you father.

CAMILLO By your leave a little, ho!— Are you my Julio?

JULIO My duty tells me so, sir,

---

251 **dull** downcast, somewhat depressed 262 **voyage** journey

Still on my knees.— But love engrossed me all;

285   O, Leonora, do I once more hold thee?

CAMILLO   Nay, to't again: I will not hinder you a kiss,

'Tis he—   *Leaps*

LEONORA   The righteous pow'rs at length have crowned our loves.

Think, Julio, from the storm that's now o'erblown,

290   Though sour affliction combat hope awhile,

When lovers swear true faith, the list'ning angels

Stand on the golden battlements of heav'n

And waft their vows to the eternal throne.

Such were our vows, and so are they repaid.

295   DUKE   E'en as you are, we'll join your hands together.

A providence above our pow'r rules all.

Ask him forgiveness, boy.   *To Henriquez*

JULIO   He has it, sir:

The fault was love's, not his.

300   HENRIQUEZ   Brave, gen'rous Julio!

I knew thy nobleness of old, and prized it,

Till passion made me blind— once more, my friend,

Share in a heart that ne'er shall wrong thee more.

And, brother,—

305   RODERICK   This embrace cuts off excuses.

DUKE   I must, in part, repair my son's offence:

At your best leisure, Julio, know our court.

And, Violante, (for I know you now)

I have a debt to pay: your good old father,

310   Once, when I chased the boar, preserved my life:

For that good deed, and for your virtue's sake,

Though your descent be low, call me your father.

A match drawn out of honesty, and goodness,

Is pedigree enough.— Are you all pleased?   *Gives her to Henriquez*

315   CAMILLO   All.

HENRIQUEZ *and* DON BERNARD   All, sir.

JULIO   All.

DUKE   And I not least. We'll now return to court:

And that short travel, and your loves completed,

320   Shall, as I trust, for life restrain these wand'rings.

There, the solemnity, and grace, I'll do

Your sev'ral nuptials, shall approve my joy,

And make grieved lovers, that your story read,

Wish, true love's wand'rings may like yours succeed.   *Curtain falls*

FINIS

322 **sev'ral** each and all of   **approve** prove, demonstrate

Epilogue

Written by a friend
Spoken by Mrs Oldfield

Well, heaven defend us from these ancient plays,
These moral bards of good Queen Bess's days!
They write from virtue's laws, and think no further,
But draw a rape as dreadful as a murther.
5 You modern wits, more deeply versed in nature,
Can tip the wink to tell us you know better,
As who should say, ''Tis no such killing matter!'
We've heard old stories told, and yet ne'er wondered,
Of many a prude that has endured a hundred,
10 And Violante grieves, or we're mistaken,
Not, because ravished but because forsaken.
Had this been written to the modern stage,
Her manners had been copied from the age.
Then, though she had been once a little wrong,
15 She still had had the grace t'ave held her tongue,
And after all, with downcast looks, been led
Like any virgin to the bridal bed.
There, if the good man questioned her misdoing,
She'd stop him short, 'Pray, who made you so knowing?
20 What, doubt my virtue! What's your base intention?
Sir, that's a point above your comprehension.'
Well, heav'n be praised, the virtue of our times
Secures us from our gothic grandsires' crimes.
Rapes, magic, new opinions, which before
25 Have filled our chronicles, are now no more
And this reforming age may justly boast,
That dreadful sin polygamy is lost.
So far from multiplying wives, 'tis known
Our husbands find they've work enough with one.
30 Then, as for rapes, those dangerous days are past,
Our dapper sparks are seldom in such haste.
In Shakespeare's age the English youth inspired,
Loved, as they fought, by him and beauty fired.
'Tis yours to crown the Bard, whose magic strain
35 Could charm the heroes of that glorious reign,
Which humbled to the dust the pride of Spain.

Epilogue the defiant tone of this addition suggests defensiveness on the subject of Violante's subsequent marriage to her rapist, a morally repugnant outcome to modern sensibilities but regarded as an acceptable solution according to the 'honour code'   **Mrs Oldfield** Anne Oldfield was the most celebrated actress of the early eighteenth century   **4 murther** i.e. murder   **15 t'ave** to have   **23 gothic** barbarous, uncouth   **31 dapper sparks** elegant young men

CARDENIO: THE SOURCE
Extracts from
The History of the Valorous and Witty Knight-Errant, Don Quixote of the Mancha. Translated out of the Spanish [by Thomas Shelton] London 1612

Miguel de Cervantes' novel, Don Quixote de la Mancha, *was an instant success when the first part was published in 1605. Thomas Shelton's 1612 translation of Part 1 was used as the source for a number of Jacobean plays. The plot of Cardenio comes from an interpolated tale in chapters 23–36. The hero of Cervantes' novel, Alonso Quixano, a middle-aged country gentleman, is so obsessed by books of chivalric romance that he determines to become a knight-errant himself. He dons an old suit of armour and, calling himself 'Don Quixote de la Mancha', sets off on his adventures. In his deluded state he takes inns for castles, farm girls for noble ladies and famously tilts at windmills, mistaking them for fierce giants. His simple neighbour, Sancho Panza, accompanies him as his faithful squire. At this point in the narrative Don Quixote and Sancho have just escaped into the Sierra Morena (a mountain range in southern Spain) to avoid the wrath of the Holy Brotherhood (i.e. the police authorities) after Quixote has misguidedly freed a group of condemned galley-slaves. He only agrees to this after Sancho promises that he will never reveal to any that he fled for fear but agrees that he did so only to satisfy his squire who points out that, 'to retire is not to fly, and to expect is wisdom, when the danger exceedeth all hope'.*

Unfortunately, while they are asleep, one of the freed criminals, Gines de Pasamonte, who has also chosen the Sierra Morena to hide from the authorities, steals Sancho's ass. He is desolate at this loss but greatly comforted when the knight finds 'a saddle-cushion and a portmanteau fast to it'. He is delighted when it turns out to contain clean linen and a quantity of gold. Don Quixote is more concerned, however, with the 'tablet' (bound sheets of stiff writing paper) and the verses and letter it contains:

> 'Or Love of understanding quite is void:
> Or he abounds in cruelty, or my pain
> The occasion equals not; for which I bide
> The torments dire he maketh me sustain.

> 'But if Love be a god, I dare maintain
> He nought ignores; and reason aye decides
> Gods should not cruel be: then who ordains
> This pain I worship, which my heart divides?

'Filis!' I err, if thou I say it is;
For so great ill and good cannot consist.
Nor doth this wrack from Heaven befall, but yet
That shortly I must die can no way miss.
For the evil whose cause is hardly well expressed,
By miracle alone true cure may get.'

'Thy false promise, and my certain misfortune, do carry me to such a place, as from thence thou shalt sooner receive news of my death than reasons of my just complaints. Thou hast disdained me, O ingrate! For one that hath more, but not for one that is worth more than I am; but if virtue were a treasure of estimation, I would not emulate other men's fortunes, nor weep thus for mine own misfortunes. That which thy beauty erected, thy works have overthrown; by it I deemed thee to be an angel, and by these I certainly know thee to be but a woman. Rest in peace, O causer of my war! And let Heaven work so that thy spouse's deceits remain still concealed, to the end thou mayst not repent what thou didst, and I be constrained to take revenge of that I desire not.'

Shortly afterwards they see a young man leaping among the rocks and then meet some goatherds who confirm that the young man is indeed the owner of these items but that he is afflicted with periodic bouts of violent madness.

'Don Quixote rested marvellously admired[†] at the goatherd's tale; and, with greater desire to know who that unfortunate madman was, purposed with himself, as he had already resolved, to search him throughout the mountains, without leaving a corner or cave of it unsought until he had gotten him. But fortune disposed the matter better than he expected; for he appeared in that very instant in a cleft of a rock that answered to the place where they stood speaking; who came towards them, murmuring somewhat to himself, which could not be understood near at hand, and much less afar off. His apparel was such as we have delivered, only differing in this, as Don Quixote perceived when he drew nearer, that he wore on him, although torn, a leather jerkin, perfumed with amber; by which he thoroughly collected that the person which wore such attire was not of the least quality.

'When the young man came to the place where they discoursed, he saluted them with a hoarse voice, but with great courtesy; and Don Quixote returned him his greetings with no less compliment; and, alighting from Rozinante,[‡] he advanced to embrace him with very good carriage and countenance, and held him a good while straitly between his arms, as if he had known him of long time. The other, whom we may call the Unfortunate Knight of the Rock as well as Don Quixote the Knight of the Ill-favoured Face, after he had permitted himself to be embraced a while, did step a little off from our knight, and, laying his hands on his shoulders, began to behold him earnestly, as one desirous to call to mind whether he had ever seen him before; being, perhaps, no less admired to see Don Quixote's figure, proportion, and arms, than Don Quixote was to view him. In resolution, the first that spoke after the embracing was the ragged knight, and said what we will presently recount...

'My name is Cardenio, the place of my birth one of the best cities in Andalusia, my lineage noble, my parents rich, and my misfortunes so great as I think my parents have ere this deplored and my kinsfolk

---

* **Filis** Spanish rendering of 'Phyllis', a generic proper name for heroines of pastoral poetry
† **admired** in admiration/wondering
‡ **Rozinante** Don Quixote's horse; literally 'hack before'

condoled them, being very little able with their wealth to redress them; for the goods of fortune are but of small virtue to remedy the disasters of heaven. There dwelt in the same city a heaven, wherein love had placed all the glory that I could desire; so great is the beauty of Lucinda, a damsel as noble and rich as I, but more fortunate, and less constant than my honourable desires expected. I loved, honoured, and adored this Lucinda almost from my very infancy, and she affected me likewise, with all the integrity and goodwill which with her so young years did accord. Our parents knew our mutual amity, for which they were nothing aggrieved, perceiving very well, that although we continued it, yet could it have none other end but that of matrimony: a thing which the equality of our blood and substance did of itself almost invite us to. Our age and affection increased in such sort, as it seemed fit for Lucinda's father, for certain good respects, to deny me the entrance of his house any longer, imitating in a manner therein Thisbe,* so much solemnised by the poets, her parents; which hindrance served only to add flame to flame, and desire to desire; for, although it set silence to our tongues, yet would they not impose it to our pens, which are wont to express to whom it pleased, the most hidden secrecies of our souls, with more liberty than the tongue; for the presence of the beloved doth often distract, trouble, and strike dumb the boldest tongue and firmest resolution. O heavens! How many letters have I written unto her! What cheerful and honest answers have I received! How many ditties and amorous verses have I composed, wherein my soul declared and published her passions, declined her inflamed desires, entertained her remembrance, and recreated her will! In effect, perceiving myself to be forced, and that my soul consumed with a perpetual desire to behold her, I resolved to put my desires in execution, and finish in an instant that which I deemed most expedient for the better achieving of my desired and deserved reward; which was (as I did indeed), to demand her of her father for my lawful spouse.'

'To which he made answer, that he did gratify the good-will which I showed by honouring him, and desire to honour myself with pawns that were his; but, seeing my father yet lived, the motion of that matter properly most concerned him: for, if it were not done with his good liking and pleasure, Lucinda was not a woman to be taken or given by stealth. I rendered him thanks for his goodwill, his words seeming unto me very reasonable, as that my father should agree unto them as soon as I should explain the matter; and therefore departed presently to acquaint him with my desires: who, at the time which I entered into a chamber wherein he was, stood with a letter open in his hand; and, espying me, ere I could break my mind unto him, gave it me, saying, "By that letter, Cardenio, you may gather the desire that Duke Ricardo bears to do you any pleasure or favour."

'This Duke Ricardo, as I think you know, sirs, already, is a grandee of Spain, whose dukedom is seated in the best part of all Andalusia. I took the letter and read it, which appeared so urgent, as I myself accounted it would be ill done if my father did not accomplish the contents thereof, which were indeed, that he should presently address me to his court, to the end I might be companion (and not servant) to his eldest son; and that he would incharge† himself with the advancing of me to such preferments as might be answerable unto the value and estimation he made of my person. I passed over the whole letter, and was strucken dumb at the reading thereof, but chiefly hearing my father to say, "Cardenio, thou must depart within two days, to accomplish the duke's desire, and omit not to render Almighty God thanks, which doth thus open the way by which thou mayst attain in fine to that which I know thou dost merit." And to these words added certain

---

* **Thisbe** the tragic heroine of Ovid's 'Pyramus and Thisbe' (*Metamorphoses* IV:55–166) in which the lovers are separated by a wall dividing their parents' estates. They communicate through a crack in the wall and arrange to meet the next evening at Ninus' tomb. Thisbe arrives first but flees when she sees a lioness, dropping her veil as she runs. The lioness whose jaws are bloody picks up and tosses the veil. Pyramus arrives, sees the lion's pawprints, finds the bloodied veil and assuming Thisbe is dead, smites himself with his sword. She meanwhile returns only to find her lover dying and in despair kills herself. The story was retold by Giovanni Boccaccio in *On Famous Women* (biography no. 12) and Chaucer in his *Legend of Good Women*. Shakespeare famously parodies the story in the Mechanicals' play-within-a-play in *A Midsummer Night's Dream*

† **incharge** commission, impose as a duty

others of fatherly counsel and direction. The term of my departure arrived, and I spoke to my Lucinda on a certain night, and recounted unto her all that passed, and likewise to her father, entreating them to overslip* a few days, and defer the bestowing of his daughter elsewhere, until I went to understand Duke Ricardo his will; which he promised me, and she confirmed it, with a thousand oaths and promises.

'Finally, I came to Duke Ricardo's court, and was so friendly received and entertained by him, as even then very envy began to exercise her accustomed function, being forthwith emulated by the ancient servitors, persuading themselves that the tokens the duke showed to do me favours could not but turn to their prejudice. But he that rejoiced most at mine arrival was a second son of the duke's, called Fernando, who was young, gallant, very comely, liberal, and amorous; who, within a while after my coming, held me so dearly as every one wondered thereat; and although the elder loved me well, and did me favour, yet was it in no respect comparable to that wherewithal Don Fernando loved and treated me. It therefore befell that, as there is no secrecy amongst friends so great but they will communicate it the one to the other, and the familiarity which I had with Don Fernando was now past the limits of favour and turned into dearest amity, he revealed unto me all his thoughts, but chiefly one of his love, which did not a little molest him; for he was enamoured on a farmer's daughter, that was his father's vassal, whose parents were marvellous rich, and she herself so beautiful, wary, discreet, and honest, as never a one that knew her could absolutely determine wherein or in which of all her perfections she did most excel, or was most accomplished. And those good parts of the beautiful country maid reduced Don Fernando his desires to such an exigent, as he resolved, that he might the better gain her good-will and conquer her integrity, to pass her a promise of marriage; for otherwise he should labour to effect that which was impossible, and but strive against the stream. I, as one bound thereunto by our friendship, did thwart and dissuade him from his purpose; with the best reasons and most efficacious words I might; and, seeing all could not prevail, I determined to acquaint the Duke Ricardo his father wherewithal. But Don Fernando, being very crafty and discreet, suspected and feared as much, because he considered that, in the law of a faithful servant, I was bound not to conceal a thing that would turn so much to the prejudice of the duke, my lord; and therefore, both to divert and deceive me at once, [he said] that he could find no means so good to deface the remembrance of that beauty out of his mind, which held his heart in such subjection, than to absent himself for certain months; and he would likewise have that absence to be this, that both of us should depart together, and come to my father's house, under pretence (as he would inform the duke) that he went to see and cheapen certain great horses that were in the city wherein I was born, a place of breeding the best horses in the world.

'Scarce had I heard him say this, when (borne away by the natural propension each one hath to his country, and my love joined) although his designment had not been so good, yet would I have ratified it, as one of the most expedient that could be imagined, because I saw occasion and opportunity so fairly offered, to return and see again my Lucinda; and therefore, set on by this thought and desire, I approved his opinion, and did quicken his purpose, persuading him to prosecute it with all possible speed; for absence would in the end work her effect in despite of the most forcible and urgent thoughts. And when he said this to me, he had already, under the title of a husband (as it was afterward known), reaped the fruits of his longing desires from his beautiful country maid, and did only await an opportunity to reveal it without his own detriment, fearful of the duke his father's indignation when he should understand his error.

'It afterwards happened that, as love in young men is not for the most part love, but lust, the which (as [that which] it ever proposeth to itself as his last end and period is delight) so soon as it obtaineth the same, it likewise decayeth and maketh forcibly to retire that which was termed love; for it cannot transgress the limits which Nature hath assigned it, which boundings or measures Nature hath in no wise allotted

---

* **overslip** let pass

to true and sincere affection, — I would say that, as soon as Don Fernando had enjoyed his country lass, his desires weakened, and his importunities waxed cold; and if at the first he feigned an excuse to absent himself, that he might with more facility compass them, he did now in very good earnest procure to depart, to the end he might not put them in execution. The duke gave him license to depart, and commanded me to accompany him. We came to my city, where my father entertained him according to his calling. I saw Lucinda, and then again were revived (although, indeed, they were neither dead nor mortified) my desires, and I acquainted Don Fernando (alas! to my total ruin) with them, because I thought it was not lawful, by the law of amity, to keep anything concealed from him. There I dilated to him on the beauty, wit, and discretion of Lucinda, in so ample a manner as my praise stirred in him a desire to view a damsel so greatly adorned, and enriched with so rare endowments. And this his desire I (through my misfortune) satisfied, showing her unto him by the light of a candle, at a window where we two were wont to parley together; where he beheld her to be such as was sufficient to blot out of his memory all the beauties which ever he had viewed before. He stood mute, beside himself, and ravished; and, moreover, rested so greatly enamoured, as you may perceive in the discourse of this my doleful narration. And, to inflame his desires the more (a thing which I fearfully avoided, and only discovered to Heaven), fortune so disposed that he found after me one of her letters, wherein she requested that I would demand her of her father for wife, which was so discreet, honest, and amorously penned, as he said, after reading it, that in Lucinda alone were included all the graces of beauty and understanding jointly, which were divided and separate in all the other women of the world.

'Yet, in good sooth, I will here confess the truth, that although I saw clearly how deservedly Lucinda was thus extolled by Don Fernando, yet did not her praises please me so much pronounced by him; and therefore began to fear and suspect him, because he let no moment overslip us without making some mention of Lucinda, and would still himself begin the discourse, were the occasion never so far-fetched: a thing which roused in me I cannot tell what jealousy; not that I did fear any traverse in Lucinda's loyalty, but yet, for all, my fates made me the very thing which they most assured me. And Don Fernando procured to read all the papers I sent to Lucinda, or she to me, under pretext that he took extraordinary delight to note the witty conceits of us both. It therefore fell out, that Lucinda, having demanded of me a book of chivalry to read, wherein she took marvellous delight, and was that of Amadis de Gaul"—

At this point in Cardenio's narration, he and Don Quixote have a furious argument concerning the nature of the relationship between Master Elisabat the barber and Queen Madasima, one of the heroines of his beloved romances. Cardenio refuses to continue his tale and strikes Quixote with a stone and a general punch-up ensues. The rest of Cardenio's tale is finally told to friends of Don Quixote, the Curate and the Barber, who have disguised themselves – the Barber in a false beard and the Curate by dressing in a gown borrowed from the local innkeeper's wife – and come to rescue him. They hear a voice singing these verses:

> 'Who doth my weal diminish thus and stain?
>   Disdain.
> And say by whom my woes augmented be?
>   By jealousy.
> And who my patience doth by trial wrong?

---

* **Amadis de Gaul** the most famous of Spanish romances concerning star-crossed lovers, knight-errantry and magic, it enjoyed huge popularity, although authorship of the four volumes of Amadis' adventures is disputed

An absence long.
If that be so, then for my grievous wrong,
No remedy at all I may obtain,
Since my best hopes I cruelly find slain
By disdain, jealousy, and absence long.

'Who in my mind those dolours still doth move?
      Dire love.
And who my glory's ebb doth most importune?
      Fortune.
And to my plaints by whom increase is giv'n?
      By Heav'n.
If that be so, then my mistrust jumps ev'n,
That of my wondrous evil I needs must die;
Since in my harm join'd and united be,
Love, wavering fortune, and a rigorous Heaven.

'Who better hap can unto me bequeath?
      Death.
From whom his favours doth not love estrange?
      From change.
And his too serious harms, who cureth wholly?
      Folly.
If that be so, it is no wisdom truly,
To think by human means to cure that care,
Where the only antidotes and med'cines are
Desired death, light change, and endless folly.'

The hour, the time, the solitariness of the place, voice, and art of him that sung, struck wonder and delight in the hearers' minds, which remained still quiet, listening whether they might hear anything else; but, perceiving that the silence continued a pretty while, they agreed to issue and seek out the musician that sung so harmoniously; and being ready to put their resolution in practice, they were again arrested by the same voice, the which touched their ears anew with this sonnet:

A SONNET.
'Holy amity! which, with nimble wings,
Thy semblance leaving here on earth behind,
Among the blessed souls of heaven, up-flings,
To those imperial rooms to cheer thy mind:
And thence to us, is (when thou lik'st) assign'd
Just Peace, whom shady veil so covered brings;
As oft, instead of her, Deceit we find
Clad in weeds of good and virtuous things.
Leave heaven, O amity! do not permit
Foul Fraud thus openly thy robes to invest;

With which, sincere intents destroy does it:
For if thy likeness from it thou dost not wrest,
The world will turn to the first conflict soon,
Of discord, chaos, and confusion.'

The song was concluded with a profound sigh, and both the others lent attentive ear to hear if he would sing any more; but perceiving that the music was converted into throbs and doleful plaints, they resolved to go and learn who was the wretch, as excellent for his voice as dolorous in his sighs. And after they had gone a little, at the doubling of the point of a crag, they perceived one of the very same form the fashion that Sancho had painted unto them when he told them the history of Cardenio; which man espying them likewise, showed no semblance of fear, but stood still with his head hanging on his breast like a malcontent, not once lifting up his eyes to behold them from the first time when they unexpectedly arrived.

The curate, who was a man very well spoken (as one that had already intelligence of his misfortune; for he knew him by his signs), drew nearer to him, and prayed and persuaded him, with short but very forcible reasons, to forsake that miserable life, lest he should there eternally lose it, which of all miseries would prove the most miserable. Cardenio at this season was in his right sense, free from the furious accident that distracted him so often; and therefore, viewing them both attired in so strange and unusual a fashion from that which was used among those deserts,* he rested somewhat admired, but chiefly hearing them speak in his affair, as in a matter known (for so much he gathered out of the curate's speeches); and therefore answered in this manner: 'I perceive well, good sirs (whosoever you be), that Heaven, which hath always care to succour good men; yea, even, and the wicked many times, hath, without any desert, addressed unto me by these deserts and places so remote from the vulgar haunt, persons which, laying before mine eyes with quick and pregnant reasons the little I have to lead this kind of life, do labour to remove me from this place to a better; and by reason they know not as much as I do, and that after escaping this harm I shall fall into a far greater, they account me perhaps for a man of weak discourse, and what is worse, for one wholly devoid of judgment. And were it so, yet is it no marvel; for it seems to me that the force of the imagination of my disasters is too bent and powerful in my destruction, that I, without being able to make it any resistance, do become like a stone, void of all good feeling and knowledge. And I come to know the certainty of this truth when some men do recount and show unto me tokens of the things I have done whilst this terrible accident overrules me; and after I can do no more than be grieved, though in vain, and curse, without benefit, my too froward† fortune, and render as an excuse of my madness the relation of the cause thereof to as many as please to hear it; for wise men perceiving the cause will not wonder at the effects, and though they give me no remedy, yet at least will not condemn me; for it will convert the anger they conceive at my misrules into compassion for my disgraces. And, sirs, if by chance it be so that you come with the same intention that others did, I request you, ere you enlarge further your discreet persuasions, that you will give ear awhile to the relation of my mishaps; for perhaps, when you have understood it, you may save the labour that you would take, comforting an evil wholly incapable of consolation.'

Both of them, which desired nothing so much [as] to understand from his own mouth the occasion of his harms, did entreat him to relate it, promising to do nothing else in his remedy or comfort but what himself pleased. And with this the sorrowful gentleman began his doleful history, with the very same words almost that he had rehearsed it to Don Quixote and the goatherd a few days past, when, by occasion of Master Elisabat and Don Quixote's curiosity in observing the decorum of chivalry, the tale remained imperfect, as

---

* **deserts** wild, deserted places
† **froward** perverse

our history left it above. But now good fortune so disposed things, that his foolish fit came not upon him, but gave him leisure to continue his story to the end; and so arriving to the passage that spoke of the letter Don Fernando found in the book of Amadis de Gaul, Cardenio said that he had it very well in memory, and the sense was this:

'"LUCINDA TO CARDENIO.

'"I discover daily in thee worths that oblige and enforce me to hold thee dear; and therefore, if thou desirest to have me discharge this debt, without serving a writ on my honour, thou mayst easily do it. I have a father that knows thee, and loves me likewise well, who, without forcing my will, will accomplish that which justly thou oughtest to have, if it be so that thou esteemest me as much as thou sayst, and I do believe."

'This letter moved me to demand Lucinda of her father for my wife, as I have already recounted; and by it also Lucinda remained in Don Fernando's opinion crowned for one of the most discreet women of her time. And this billet letter was that which first put him in mind to destroy me ere I could effect my desires. I told to Don Fernando wherein consisted all the difficulty of her father's protracting of the marriage, to wit, in that my father should first demand her; the which I dared not to mention unto him, fearing lest he would not willingly consent thereunto; not for that the quality, bounty, virtue, and beauty of Lucinda were to him unknown, or that she had not parts in her able to ennoble and adorn any other lineage of Spain whatsoever, but because I understood by him, that he desired not to marry me until he had seen what Duke Ricardo would do for me. Finally, I told him that I dared not reveal it to my father, as well for that inconvenience, as for many others that made me so afraid, without knowing what they were, as methought my desires would never take effect.

'To all this Don Fernando made me answer, that he would take upon him to speak to my father, and persuade him to treat of that affair also with Lucinda's. O ambitious Marius!* O cruel Catiline!† O facinorous‡ Sylla!§ O treacherous Galalon!¶ O traitorous Vellido!** O revengeful Julian!†† O covetous Judas!‡‡ Traitor, cruel, revengeful, and cozening, what indeserts did this wench commit, who with such plaints discovered to thee the secrets and delights of her heart? What offence committed I against thee? What words did I speak, or counsel did I give, that were not all addressed to the increasing of thine honour and profit? But on what do I (the worst of all wretches!) complain seeing that when the current of the stars doth bring with it mishaps, by reason they come down precipitately from above, there is no earthly force can withhold, or human industry prevent or evacuate them? Who would have imagined that Don Fernando, a noble gentleman, discreet, obliged by my deserts, and powerful to obtain whatsoever the amorous desire would exact of him, where and whensoever it seized on his heart, would (as they say) become so corrupt as to deprive me of one only sheep, which yet I did not possess? But let these considerations be laid apart as unprofitable, that we may knit up again the broken thread of my unfortunate history. And therefore I say that, Don Fernando believing that my presence was a hindrance to put his treacherous and wicked design in execution, he resolved to send me to his eldest brother, under pretext to get some money of him for to buy six great horses, that he had of purpose, and only to the end I might absent myself, bought the very same

---

* **Marius** Roman general 157–86 BC whose personal ambition was criticised by the Roman historian Sallust
† **Catiline** Roman politician of the first century BC, who attempted to overthrow the Roman Republic and was denounced by political enemies such as Cicero and Sallust who accused him of human sacrifice among other enormities
‡ **facinorous** extremely wicked
§ **Sylla** Roman consul and dictator, notorious for his ruthlessness
¶ **Galalon** i.e. Ganelon, eighth-century knight who betrayed Charlemagne's army to the Muslims
** **Vellido** Vellido Adolfo, treacherous knight who murdered king Sancho II in 1072
†† **Julian** Count of Ceuta, was held responsible by Spanish Christian writers for helping the Muslim conquest of Spain in AD 711
‡‡ **Judas** the disciple Judas Iscariot who betrayed Christ with a kiss for thirty pieces of silver

day that he offered to speak himself to my father, and would have me go for the money, because he might bring his treacherous intent the better to pass. Could I prevent this treason? Or could I perhaps but once imagine it? No, truly; but rather, glad for the good merchandise he had made, did make proffer of myself to depart for the money very willingly. I spoke that night to Lucinda, and acquainted her with the agreement passed between me and Don Fernando, bidding her to hope firmly that our good just desires would sort a wished and happy end. She answered me again (as little suspecting Don Fernando's treason as myself), bidding me to return with all speed, because she believed that the conclusion of our affections should be no longer deferred than my father deferred to speak unto hers. And what was the cause I know not, but as soon as she had said this unto me, her eyes were filled with tears, and somewhat thwarting her throat, hindered her from saying many other things, which methought she strived to speak.

'I rested admired at this new accident,* until that time never seen in her; for always, as many times as my good fortune and diligence granted it, we conversed with all sport and delight, without ever intermeddling in our discourses any tears, sighs, complaints, suspicions, or fears. All my speech was to advance my fortune for having received her from Heaven as my lady and mistress; then would I amplify her beauty, admire her worth, and praise her discretion. She, on the other side, would return me the exchange, extolling in me what she, as one enamoured, accounted worthy of laud and commendation. After this we would recount a hundred thousand toys† and chances befallen our neighbours and acquaintance; and that to which my presumption dared furthest to extend itself, was sometimes to take her beautiful and ivory hands perforce, and kiss them as well as I might, through the rigorous strictness of a niggardly iron grate which divided us. But the precedent night to the day of my sad departure, she wept, sobbed, and sighed, and departed, leaving me full of confusion and inward assaults, amazed to behold such new and doleful tokens of sorrow and feeling in Lucinda. But because I would not murder my hopes, I did attribute all these things to the force of her affection towards me, and to the grief which absence is wont to stir in those that love one another dearly. To be brief, I departed from thence sorrowful and pensive, my soul being full of imaginations and suspicions, and yet knew not what I suspected or imagined: clear tokens, foretelling the sad success and misfortune which attended me. I arrived to the place where I was sent, and delivered my letter to Don Fernando's brother, and was well entertained, but not well despatched; for he commanded me to expect‡ (a thing to me most displeasing) eight days, and that out of the duke his father's presence, because his brother had written unto him to send him certain moneys unknown to his father. And all this was but false Don Fernando's invention; for his brother wanted not money wherewithal to have despatched me presently, had not he written the contrary.

'This was so displeasing a commandment and order, as almost it brought me to terms of disobeying it, because it seemed to me a thing most impossible to sustain my life so many days in the absence of my Lucinda, and specially having left her so sorrowful as I have recounted; yet, notwithstanding, I did obey like a good servant, although I knew it would be with the cost of my health. But on the fourth day after I had arrived, there came a man in my search with a letter, which he delivered unto me, and by the endorsement I knew it to be Lucinda's; for the hand was like hers. I opened it (not without fear and assailment of my senses), knowing that it must have been some serious occasion which could move her to write unto me, being absent, seeing she did it so rarely even when I was present. I demanded of the bearer, before I read, who had delivered it to him, and what time he had spent in the way. He answered me, "that passing by chance at midday through a street of the city, a very beautiful lady did call him from a certain window. Her eyes were all beblubbered with tears, and said unto him very hastily, 'Brother, if thou beest a Christian,

---

* **admired...accident** amazed by this new event
† **toys** fantastic notions
‡ **expect** wait for

as thou appearest to be one, I pray thee, for God's sake, that thou do forthwith address this letter to the place and person that the superscription assigneth (for they be well known), and therein thou shalt do our Lord great service; and because thou mayst not want means to do it, take what thou shalt find wrapped in that handkerchief.' And, saying so, she threw out of the window a handkerchief, wherein were lapped up a hundred reals,* this ring of gold which I carry here, and that letter which I delivered unto you; and presently, without expecting mine answer, she departed, but first saw me take up the handkerchief and letter, and then I made her signs that I would accomplish herein her command. And after, perceiving the pains I might take in bringing you it so well considered, and seeing by the endorsement that you were the man to whom it was addressed, — for, sir, I know you very well, — and also obliged to do it by the tears of that beautiful lady, I determined not to trust any other with it, but to come and bring it you myself in person; and in sixteen hours since it was given unto me, I have travelled the journey you know, which is at least eighteen leagues long." Whilst the thankful new messenger spake thus unto me, I remained in a manner hanging on his words, and my thighs did tremble in such manner as I could very hardly sustain myself on foot; yet, taking courage, at last I opened the letter, whereof these were the contents:

> '"The word that Don Fernando hath passed unto you to speak to your father, that he might speak to mine, he hath accomplished more to his own pleasure than to your profit. For, sir, you shall understand that he hath demanded me for his wife; and my father (borne away by the advantage of worths which he supposes to be in Don Fernando more than in you) hath agreed to his demand in so good earnest, as the espousals shall be celebrated within these two days, and that so secretly and alone as only the heavens and some folk of the house shall be witnesses. How I remain, imagine, and whether it be convenient you should return, you may consider; and the success of this affair shall let you to perceive whether I love you well or no. I beseech Almighty God that this may arrive unto your hands before mine shall be in danger to join itself with his, which keepeth his promised faith so ill."

'These were, in sum, the contents of the letter, and the motives that persuaded me presently to depart, without attending any other answer or other moneys; for then I conceived clearly that it was not the buyal of the horses, but that of his delights, which had moved Don Fernando to send me to his brother. The rage which I conceived against him, joined with the fear to lose the jewel which I had gained by so many years' service and desires, did set wings on me, for I arrived as I had flown next day at mine own city, in the hour and moment fit to go speak to Lucinda. I entered secretly, and left my mule whereon I rode in the honest man's house that had brought me the letter, and my fortune purposing then to be favourable to me, disposed so mine affairs, that I found Lucinda sitting at that iron grate which was the sole witness of our loves. Lucinda knew me straight and I her, but not as we ought to know one another. But who is he in the world that can truly vaunt that he hath penetrated and thoroughly exhausted the confused thoughts and mutable nature of women? Truly none. I say, then, to proceed with my tale, that as soon as Lucinda perceived me, she said, "Cardenio, I am attired with my wedding garments, and in the hall doth wait for me the traitor Don Fernando, and my covetous father, with other witnesses, which shall rather be such of my death than of mine espousals. Be not troubled, dear friend, but procure to be present at this sacrifice, the which if I cannot hinder by my persuasions and reasons, I carry hidden about me a poniard† secretly, which may hinder more resolute forces by giving end to my life, and a beginning to thee, to know certain

---

* **reals** Spanish silver coins
† **poniard** small, slim dagger

the affection which I have ever borne and do bear unto thee." I answered her troubled and hastily, fearing I should not have the leisure to reply unto her, saying, "Sweet lady, let thy works verify thy words; for if thou carriest a poniard to defend thy credit, I do here likewise bear a sword wherewithal I will defend thee, or kill myself, if fortune prove adverse and contrary." I believe that she could not hear all my words, by reason she was called hastily away, as I perceived, for that the bridegroom expected her coming. By this the night of my sorrows did thoroughly fall, and the sun of my gladness was set, and I remained without light in mine eyes or discourse in my understanding. I could not find the way into her house, nor could I move myself to any part; yet, considering at last how important my presence was for that which might befall in that adventure, I animated myself the best I could, and entered into the house; and as one that knew very well all the entries and passages thereof, and specially by reason of the trouble and business that was then in hand, I went in unperceived of any. And thus, without being seen, I had the opportunity to place myself in the hollow room of a window of the same hall, which was covered by the ends of two encountering pieces of tapestry, from whence I could see all that was done in the hall, remaining myself unviewed of any. Who could now describe the assaults and surprisals of my heart while I there abode? the thoughts which encountered my mind? the considerations which I had? which were so many and such, as they can neither be said, nor is it reason they should. Let it suffice you to know that the bridegroom entered into the hall without any ornament, wearing the ordinary array he was wont, and was accompanied by a cousin-german* of Lucinda's, and in all the hall there was no stranger present, nor any other than the household servants. Within a while after, Lucinda came out of the parlour, accompanied by her mother and two waiting-maids of her own, as richly attired and decked as her calling and beauty deserved, and the perfection of courtly pomp and bravery could afford. My distraction and trouble of mind lent me no time to note particularly the apparel she wore, and therefore did only mark the colours, which were carnation and white; and the splendour which the precious stones and jewels of her tires and all the rest of her garments yielded; yet did the singular beauty of her fair and golden tresses surpass them so much, as being in competency with the precious stones, and flame of four links† that lighted in the hall, yet did the splendour thereof seem far more bright and glorious to mine eyes. O memory! the mortal enemy of mine ease, to what end serves it now to represent unto me the incomparable beauty of that my adored enemy? Were it not better, cruel memory! to remember and represent that which she did then, that, being moved by so manifest a wrong, I may at least endeavour to lose my life, since I cannot procure a revenge? Tire not, good sirs, to hear the digressions I make; for my grief is not of that kind that may be rehearsed succinctly and speedily, seeing that in mine opinion every passage of it is worthy of a large discourse.'

To this the curate answered, that not only they were not tired or wearied hearing of him, but rather they received marvellous delight to her him recount each minuity and circumstance, because they were such as deserved not to be passed over in silence, but rather merited as much attention as the principal parts of the history.

'You shall then wit,' quoth Cardenio, 'that as they thus stood in the hall, the curate of the parish entered, and, taking them both by the hand to do that which in such an act is required at the saying of, "Will you, Lady Lucinda, take the Lord Don Fernando, who is here present, for your lawful spouse, according as our holy mother of the Church commands?" I thrust out all my head and neck out of the tapestry, and, with most attentive ears and a troubled mind, settled myself to hear what Lucinda answered, expecting by it the sentence of my death or the confirmation of my life. Oh, if one had dared to sally out at that time, and cry with a loud voice, "O Lucinda! Lucinda! see well what thou doest; consider withal what thou owest me!

* **cousin-german** first cousin
† **links** torches

Behold how thou art mine, and that thou canst not be any other's; Note that thy saying of Yea and the end of my life shall be both in one instant. O traitor, Don Fernando, robber of my glory! death of my life! what is this thou pretendest? what wilt thou do? Consider that thou canst not, Christian-like, achieve thine intention, seeing Lucinda is my spouse, and I am her husband." O foolish man! now that I am absent, and far from the danger, I say what I should have done, and not what I did. Now, after that I have permitted my dear jewel to be robbed, I exclaim on the thief, on whom I might have revenged myself, had I had as much heart to do it as I have to complain. In fine, since I was then a coward and a fool, it is no matter though I now die ashamed, sorry, and frantic. The curate stood expecting Lucinda's answer a good while ere she gave it; and in the end, when I hoped that she would take out the poniard to stab herself, or would unloose her tongue to say some truth, or use some reason or persuasion that might redound to my benefit, I heard her instead thereof answer, with a dismayed and languishing voice, the word "I will." And then Don Fernando said the same; and, giving her the ring, they remained tied with an indissoluble knot. Then the bridegroom coming to kiss his spouse, she set her hand upon her heart, and fell in a trance between her mother's arms.

'Now only remains untold the case wherein I was, seeing in that Yea, which I had heard, my hopes deluded, Lucinda's words and promises falsified, and myself wholly disabled to recover in any time the good which I lost in that instant. I rested void of counsel, abandoned (in mine opinion) by Heaven, proclaimed an enemy to the earth which upheld me, the air denying breath enough for my sighs, and the water humour sufficient to mine eyes; only the fire increased in such manner as I burned thoroughly with rage and jealousy. All the house was in a tumult for this sudden amazement* of Lucinda; and as her mother unclasped her bosom to give her the air, there appeared in it a paper, folded up, which Don Fernando presently seized on, and went aside to read it by the light of a torch; and after he had read it, he sat down in a chair, laying his hands on his cheek, with manifest signs of melancholy discontent, without bethinking himself of the remedies that were applied to his spouse to bring her again to herself. I, seeing all the folk of the house thus in an uproar, did adventure myself to issue, not weighing much whether I were seen or no, bearing withal a resolution (if I were perceived) to play such a rash part, as all the world should understand the just indignation of my breast, by the revenge I would take on false Don Fernando and the mutable and dismayed traitress. But my destiny, which hath reserved me for greater evils (if possibly there be any greater than mine own), ordained that instant my wit should abound, whereof ever since I have so great want; and therefore, without will to take revenge of my greatest enemies (of whom I might have taken it with all facility, by reason they suspected so little my being there), I determined to take it on myself, and execute in myself the pain which they deserved, and that perhaps with more rigour than I would have used toward them if I had slain them at that time, seeing that the sudden death finisheth presently the pain; but that which doth lingeringly torment, kills always, without ending the life.

'To be short, I went out of the house, and came to the other where I had left my mule, which I caused to be saddled; and, without bidding mine host adieu, I mounted on her, and rode out of the city, without daring, like another Lot,† to turn back and behold it; and then, seeing myself alone in the fields, and that the darkness of the night did cover me, and the silence thereof invite me to complain, without respect or fear to be heard or known, I did let slip my voice, and untied my tongue with so many curses of Lucinda and Don Fernando, as if thereby I might satisfy the wrong they had done me. I gave her the title of cruel, ungrateful, false, and scornful, but especially of covetous, seeing the riches of mine enemy had shut up the eyes of her affection, to deprive me thereof, and render it to him with whom fortune had dealt more frankly and liberally; and in the midst of this tune of maledictions and scorns, I did excuse her, saying,

---

* **amazement** loss of wits
† **Lot** nephew of Abraham, warned by the angels to leave Sodom before God's wrath fell on the city but not to turn back; he obeyed the command but his wife looked back and was turned into a pillar of salt (Genesis:11–14, 19)

that it was no marvel that a maiden kept close in her parents' house, made and accustomed always to obey them, should at last condescend to their will, specially seeing they bestowed upon her for husband so noble, so rich, and proper a gentleman, as to refuse him would be reputed in her to proceed either from want of judgment, or from having bestowed her affections elsewhere, which things must of force greatly prejudice her good opinion and renown. Presently would I turn again to say, that though she had told them that I was her spouse, they might easily perceive that in choosing me she had not made so ill an election that she might not be excused, seeing that before Don Fernando offered himself, they themselves could not happen to desire, if their wishes were guided by reason, so fit a match for their daughter as myself; and she might easily have said, before she put herself in that last and forcible pass of giving her hand, that I had already given her mine, which I would come out to confess, and confirm all that she could any way feign in this case; and concluded in the end, that little love, less judgment, much ambition, and desire of greatness caused her to forget the words wherewithal she had deceived, entertained, and sustained me in my firm hopes and honest desires.

'Using these words, and feeling this unquietness in my breast, I travelled all the rest of the night, and struck about dawn into one of the entries of these mountains, through which I travelled three days at random, without following or finding any path or way, until I arrived at last to certain meadows and fields, that lie I know not in which part of these mountains; and finding there certain herds, I demanded of them which way lay the most craggy and inaccessible places of these rocks, and they directed me hither; and presently I travelled towards it, with purpose here to end my life; and, entering in among those deserts, my mule, through weariness and hunger, fell dead under me, or rather, as I may better suppose, to disburden himself of so vile and unprofitable a burden as he carried of me. I remained afoot, overcome by nature, and pierced through and through by hunger, without having any help, or knowing who might succour me, and remained after that manner I know not how long, prostrate on the ground, and then I rose again without any hunger, and I found near unto me certain goatherds, who were those doubtlessly that fed me in my hunger; for they told me in what manner they found me, and how I spake so many foolish and mad words as gave certain argument that I was devoid of judgment; and I have felt in myself since that time that I enjoy not my wits perfectly, but rather perceive them to be so weakened and impaired, as I commit a hundred follies, tearing mine apparel, crying loudly through these deserts, cursing my fates, and idly repeating the abhorred name of mine enemy, without having any other intent or discourse at that time than to endeavour to finish my life ere long; and when I turn to myself, I am so broken and tired as I am scarce able to stir me. My most ordinary mansion-place is in the hollowness of a cork-tree, sufficiently able to cover this wretched carcase. The cowherds and the goatherds that feed their cattle here in these mountains, moved by charity, gave me sustenance, leaving meat for me by the ways and on the rocks which they suppose I frequent, and where they think I may find it; and so, although I do then want the use of reason, yet doth natural necessity induce me to know my meat, and stirreth my appetite to covet, and my will to take it. They tell me, when they meet me in my wits, that I do other times come out to the highways and take it from them violently, even when they themselves do offer it unto me willingly. After this manner do I pass my miserable life, until Heaven shall be pleased to conduct it to the last period, or so change my memory as I may no more remember the beauty and treachery of Lucinda or the injury done by Don Fernando; for, if it do me this favour, without depriving my life, then will I convert my thoughts to better discourses; if not, there is no other remedy but to pray God to receive my soul into His mercy, for I neither find valour nor strength in myself to rid my body out of the straits wherein for my pleasure I did at first willingly intrude it.

'This is, sirs, the bitter relation of my disasters; wherefore judge if it be such as may be celebrated with less feeling and compassion than that which you may by this time have perceived in myself; and do not in vain labour to persuade or counsel me that which reason should afford you may be good for my remedy, for it will work no other effect in me than a medicine prescribed by a skilful physician to a patient that will in no sort receive it. I will have no health without Lucinda; and since she pleaseth to alienate herself, being or seeing she ought to be mine, so do I also take delight to be of the retinue of mishap, although I might be a retainer to good fortune. She hath ordained that her changing shall establish my perdition; and I will labour, by procuring mine own loss, to please and satisfy her will. And it shall be an example to ensuing ages, that I alone wanted that wherewith all other wretches abounded, to whom the impossibility of receiving comfort proved sometimes a cure; but in me it is an occasion of greater feeling and harm, because I am persuaded that my harms cannot end even with very death itself.'

Here Cardenio finished his large discourse and unfortunate and amorous history; and just about the time that the curate was be-thinking himself of some comfortable reasons to answer and persuade him, he was suspended by a voice arrived to his hearing, which with pitiful accents said what shall be recounted in the Fourth Part of this narration; for in this very point the wise and most absolute historiographer, Cid Hamet Benengeli,* finished the Third Book of this history.

The Fourth Book

I. Wherein Is Discoursed the New and Pleasant Adventure That Happened to the Curate and the Barber in Sierra Morena

MOST happy and fortunate were those times wherein the thrice audacious and bold knight, Don Quixote of the Mancha, was bestowed on the world, by whose most honourable resolution to revive and renew in it the already worn-out and well-night deceased exercise of arms, we joy in this our so niggard and scant an age of all pastimes, not only the sweetness of his true history, but also of the other tales and digressions contained therein, which are in some respects no less pleasing, artificial, and true than the very history itself; the which, prosecuting the carded, spun, and self-twined thread of the relation, says that, as the curate began to bethink himself upon some answer that might both comfort and animate Cardenio, he was hindered by a voice which came to his hearing, said very dolefully the words ensuing:

'O God, is it possible that I have yet found out the place which may serve for a hidden sepulchre to the load of this loathsome body that I unwillingly bear so long? Yes, it may be, if the solitariness of these rocks do not illude† me. Ah, unfortunate that I am! How much more grateful companions will these crags and thickets prove to my designs, by affording me leisure to communicate my mishaps to Heaven with plaints, than that of any mortal man living, since there is none upon earth from whom may be expected counsel in doubts, ease in complaints, or in harms remedy?' The curate and his companions heard and understood all the words clearly, and forasmuch as they conjectured (as indeed it was) that those plaints were delivered very near unto them, they did all arise to search out the plaintiff; and, having gone some twenty steps thence, they beheld a young youth behind a rock, sitting under an ash-tree, and attired like a country swain, whom, by reason his face was inclined, as he sat washing of his feet in the clear stream that glided that way, they could not perfectly discern, and therefore approached towards him with so great silence, as they were not descried by him, who only attended to the washing of his feet, which were so white, as they properly resembled two pieces of clear crystal that grew among the other stones of the stream. The whiteness and beauty of the feet amazed them, being not made, as they well conjectured, to tread clods, or measure the steps of lazy oxen, and holding the plough, as the youth's apparel would persuade them; and

---

* **Cid Hemet Benengeli** name of the fictitious Arabic historian, whose work the narrator claims to be relating
† **illude** mock/deceive with false hopes

therefore the curate, who went before the rest, seeing they were not yet spied, made signs to the other two that they should divert a little out of the way, or hide themselves behind some broken cliffs that were near the place, which they did all of them, noting what the youth did with very great attention. He wore a little brown capouch* girt very near to his body with a white towel, also a pair of breeches and gamashoes† of the same coloured cloth, and on his head a clay-coloured cap; his gamashoes were lifted up half the leg, which verily seemed to be white alabaster. Finally, having washed his feet, taking out a linen kerchief from under his cap, he dried them therewithal, and at the taking out of the kerchief he held up his face, and then those which stood gazing on him had leisure to discern an unmatchable beauty, so surpassing great, as Cardenio, rounding the curate in the ear, said, 'This body, since it is not Lucinda, can be no human creature, but a divine.' The youth took off his cap at last, and, shaking his head to the one and other part, did dishevel and discover such beautiful hairs as those of Phoebus might justly emulate them; and thereby they knew the supposed swain to be a delicate woman; yea, and the fairest that ever the first two had seen in their lives, or Cardenio himself, the lovely Lucinda excepted; for, as he after affirmed, no feature save Lucinda's could contend with hers. The long and golden hairs did not only cover her shoulders, but did also hide her round about in such sort as (her feet excepted) no other part of her body appeared, they were so near and long. At this time her hands served her for a comb, which, as her feet seemed pieces of crystal in the water, so did they appear among her hairs like pieces of driven snow. All which circumstances did possess the three which stood gazing at her with great admiration and desire to know what she was, and therefore resolved to show themselves; and with the noise which they made when they arose, the beautiful maiden held up her head, and, removing her hairs from before her eyes with both hands, she espied those that had made it; and presently arising, full of fear and trouble, she laid hand on a packet that was by her, which seemed to be of apparel and thought to fly away without staying to pull on her shoes, or to gather up her hair. But scarce had she gone six paces when her delicate and tender feet, unable to abide the rough encounter of the stones, made her to fall to the earth; which the three perceiving, they came out to her, and the curate arriving first of all, said to her, 'Lady, whatsoever you be, stay and fear nothing; for we which you behold here come only with intention to do you service, and therefore you need not pretend so impertinent a flight, which neither your feet can endure, nor would we permit.'

The poor girl remained so amazed and confounded as she answered not a word; wherefore, the curate and the rest drawing nearer, they took her by the hand, and then he prosecuted his speech, saying, 'What your habit concealed from us, lady, your hairs have bewrayed,‡ being manifest arguments that the causes were of no small moment which have thus bemasked your singular beauty under so unworthy array, and conducted you to this all-abandoned desert, wherein it was a wonderful chance to have met you, if not to remedy your harms, yet at least to give you some comfort, seeing no evil can afflict and vex one so much, and plunge him in so deep extremes (whilst it deprives not the life), that will wholly abhor from listening to the advice that is offered with a good and sincere intention; so that, fair lady, or lord, or what else you shall please to be termed, shake off your affrightment, and rehearse unto us your good or ill fortune; for you shall find in us jointly, or in every one part, companions to help you to deplore your disasters.'

Whilst the curate made this speech, the disguised woman stood as one half asleep, now beholding the one, now the other, without once moving her lip or saying a word; just like a rustical clown, when rare and unseen things to him before are unexpectedly presented to his view.

But the curate insisting, and using other persuasive reasons addressed to that effect, won her at last to make a breach on her tedious silence, and, with a profound sigh, blow open her coral gates, saying somewhat

---

* **capouch** hood
† **gamashoes** leggings
‡ **bewrayed** revealed

to this effect: 'Since the solitariness of these rocks hath not been potent to conceal me, nor the dishevelling of my disordered hairs licensed my tongue to belie my sex, it were in vain for me to feign that anew which, if you believed it, would be more for courtesy's sake than any other respect. Which presupposed, I say, good sirs, that I do gratify you highly for the liberal offers you have made me, which are such as have bound me to satisfy your demand as near as I may, although I fear the relation which I must make to you of my mishaps will breed sorrow at once with compassion in you, by reason you shall not be able to find any salve that may cure, comfort, or beguile them; yet, notwithstanding, to the end my reputation may not hover longer suspended in your opinions, seeing you know me to be a woman, and view me young, alone, and thus attired, being things all of them able, either joined or parted, to overthrow the best credit, I must be enforced to unfold what I could otherwise most willingly conceal.'

All this she, that appeared so comely, spoke without stop or staggering, with so ready delivery, and so sweet a voice, as her discretion admired them no less than her beauty; and, renewing again their compliments and entreaties to her to accomplish speedily her promise, she, setting all coyness apart, drawing on her shoes very modestly, and winding up her hair, sat her down on a stone, and the other three about her, where she used no little violence to smother certain rebellious tears that strove to break forth without her permission, and them, with a reposed and clear voice, she began the history of her life in this manner: 'In this province of Andalusia there is a certain town from whence a duke derives his denomination,* which makes him one of those in Spain are called grandees. He hath two sons — the elder is heir of his states, and likewise, as may be presumed, of his virtues; the younger is heir I know not of what, if he be not of Vellido, his treacheries or Galalon's frauds. My parents are this nobleman's vassals, of humble and low calling, but so rich as, if the goods of nature had equalled those of their fortunes, then should they have had nothing else to desire, nor I feared to see myself in the misfortunes wherein I now am plunged, for perhaps my mishaps proceed from that of theirs, in not being nobly descended. True it is that they are not so base as they should therefore shame their calling, nor so high as may check my conceit, which persuades me that my disasters proceed from their lowness. In conclusion, they are but farmers and plain people, but without any touch or spot of bad blood,† and, as we usually say, old, rusty Christians, yet so rusty and ancient as yet their riches and magnificent port‡ gain them, by little and little, the title of gentility, yea, and of worship also; although the treasure and nobility whereof they made most price and account was to have had me for their daughter; and therefore, as well by reason that they had none other heir than myself, as also because, as affectionate parents, they held me most dear, I was one of the most made of and cherished daughters that ever father brought up. I was the mirror wherein they beheld themselves, the staff of their old age, and the subject to which they addressed all their desires, from which, because they were most virtuous, mine did not stray an inch; and even in the same manner that I was lady of their minds, so was I also of their goods. By me were servants admitted or dismissed; the notice and account of what was sowed or reaped passed through my hands; of the oil-mills, the wine-presses, the number of great and little cattle, the bee-hives — in fine, of all that so rich a farmer as my father was, had, or could have, I kept the account, and was the steward thereof and mistress, with such care of my side, and pleasure of theirs, as I cannot possibly endear it enough. The times of leisure that I had in the day, after I had given what was necessary to the head servants and other labourers, I did entertain in those exercises which were both commendable and requisite for maidens, to wit, in sewing, making of bone lace, and many times handling the distaff; and

---

* **duke…denomination** most likely Osuna
† **bad blood** referring to the Spanish concept of *pureza de sangre* – purity of blood, meaning in practice an unblemished Christian lineage, i.e. no Jewish or Moorish blood, came to be associated with the peasantry as opposed to the upper classes since in an earlier, and we might think nowadays happier period, there had been freedom of relations between Christians, Jews and Moors in Spain and a degree of intermarriage between them so that many families especially of the nobility had mixed ancestry
‡ **port** style of living

if sometimes I left those exercises to recreate my mind a little, I would then take some godly book in hand, or play on the harp; for experience had taught me that music ordereth disordered minds, and doth lighten the passions that afflict the spirit.

'This was the life which I led in my father's house, the recounting whereof so particularly hath not been done for ostentation, nor to give you to understand that I am rich, but to the end you may note how much, without mine own fault, have I fallen from that happy state I have said, unto the unhappy plight into which I am now reduced. The history, therefore, is this, that passing my life in so many occupations, and that with such recollection as might be compared to a religious life, unseen, as I thought, by any other person than those of our house; for when I went to mass it was commonly so early, and so accompanied by my mother and other maid-servants, and I myself so covered and watchful as mine eyes did scarce see the earth whereon I trod; and yet, notwithstanding, those of love, or, as I may better term them, of idleness, to which lynx eyes may not be compared, did represent me to Don Fernando's affection and care; for this is the name of the duke's younger son of whom I spake before.'

Scarce had she named Don Fernando, when Cardenio changed colour, and began to sweat, with such alteration of body and countenance, as the curate and barber which beheld it, feared that the accident of frenzy did assault him, which was wont (as they had heard) to possess him at times. But Cardenio did nothing else than sweat, and stood still, beholding now and then the country girl, imagining straight what she was; who, without taking notice of his alteration, followed on her discourse in this manner:

'And scarce had he seen me, when (as he himself after confessed) he abode greatly surprised by my love, as his actions, did after give evident demonstration. But to conclude soon the relation of those misfortunes which have no conclusion, I will overslip in silence the diligences and practices of Don Fernando, used to declare unto me his affection. He suborned all the folk of the house; he bestowed gifts and favours on my parents. Every day was a holiday and a day of sports in the streets where I dwelt; at night no man could sleep for music. The letters were innumerable that came to my hands, without knowing who brought them farsed* too full of amorous conceits and offers, and containing more promises and protestations, than characters. All which not only could not mollify my mind, but rather hardened it so much as if he were my mortal enemy; and therefore did construe all the endeavours he used to gain my goodwill to be practised to a contrary end; which I did not as accounting Don Fernando ungentle, or that I esteemed him too importunate; for I took a kind of delight to see myself so highly esteemed and beloved of so noble a gentleman; nor was I anything offended to see his papers written in my praise; for, if I be not deceived in this point, be we women ever so foul, we love to hear men call us beautiful. But mine honesty was that which opposed itself unto all these things, and the continual admonitions of my parents, which had by this plainly perceived Don Fernando's pretence, as one that cared not all the world should know it. They would often say unto me that they had deposited their honours and reputation in my virtue alone and discretion, and bade me consider the inequality that was between Don Fernando and me, and that I might collect by it how his thoughts (did he ever so much affirm the contrary) were more addressed to compass his pleasures than my profit; and that if I feared any inconvenience might befall, to the end they might cross it, and cause him to abandon his so unjust a pursuit, they would match me where I most liked, either to the best of that town or any other adjoining, saying, they might easily compass it, both by reason of their great wealth and my good report. I fortified my resolution and integrity with these certain promises and the known truth which they told me, and therefore would never answer to Don Fernando any word that might ever so far off argue the least hope of condescending to his desires. All which cautions of mine, which I think he deemed to be disdains, did inflame more his lascivious appetite (for this is the name wherewithal I entitle

* **farsed** amplified with inserted comments

his affection towards me), which, had it been such as it ought, you had not known it now, for then the cause of revealing it had not befallen me. Finally, Don Fernando, understanding how my parents meant to marry me, to the end they might make void his hope of ever possessing me, or at least set more guards to preserve mine honour, and this news or surmise was an occasion that he did what you shall presently hear.

'For, one night as I sat in my chamber, only attended by a young maiden that served me, I having shut the doors very safe, for fear lest, through my negligence, my honesty might incur any danger, without knowing or imagining how it might happen, notwithstanding all my diligences used and preventions, and amidst the solitude of this silence and recollection, he stood before me in my chamber. At his presence I was so troubled as I lost both sight and speech, and by reason thereof could not cry, nor I think he would not, though I had attempted it, permit me; for he presently ran over to me, and, taking me between his arms (for, as I have said, I was so amazed as I had no power to defend myself), he spake such things to me as I know not how it is possible that so many lies should have ability to feign things resembling in show so much the truth; and the traitor caused tears to give credit to his words, and sighs to give countenance to his intention.

'I, poor soul, being alone amidst my friends, and weakly practised in such affairs, began, I know not how, to account his leasings* for verities, but not in such sort as his tears or sighs might any wise move me to any compassion that were not commendable. And so, the first trouble and amazement of mind being past, I began again to recover my defective spirits, and then said to him, with more courage than I thought I should have had, "If, as I am, my lord between your arms, I were between the paws of a fierce lion, and that I were made certain of my liberty on condition to do or say anything prejudicial to mine honour, it would prove as impossible for me to accept it as for that which once hath been to leave off his essence and being. Wherefore, even as you have engirt my middle with your arms, so likewise have I tied fast my mind with virtuous and forcible desires that are wholly different from yours, as you shall perceive, if, seeking to force me, you presume to pass further with your inordinate design. I am your vassal,† but not your slave; nor hath the nobility of your blood power, nor ought it to harden, to dishonour, stain, or hold in little account the humility of mine; and I do esteem myself, though a country wench and farmer's daughter, as much as you can yourself, though a nobleman and a lord. With me your violence shall not prevail, your riches gain any grace, your words have power to deceive, or your sighs and tears be able to move; yet, if I shall find any of these properties mentioned in him whom my parent shall please to bestow on me for my spouse, I will presently subject my will to his, nor shall it ever vary from his mind a jot; so that, if I might remain with honour, although I rested void of delights, yet would I willingly bestow on you that which you presently labour so much to obtain: all which I do say to divert your straying thought from ever thinking that any one may obtain of me aught who is not my lawful spouse." "If the let‡ only consists therein, most beautiful Dorothea" (for so I am called), answered the disloyal lord, "behold, I give thee here my hand to be thine alone; and let the heavens, from which nothing is concealed, and this image of Our Lady, which thou hast here present, be witnesses of this truth!"'

When Cardenio heard her say that she was called Dorothea, he fell again into his former suspicion, and in the end confirmed his first opinion to be true, but would not interrupt her speech, being desirous to know the success, which he knew wholly almost before, and therefore said only, 'Lady, is it possible that you are named Dorothea? I have heard report of another of that name, which perhaps hath run the like course of your misfortune; but I request you to continue your relation, for a time may come wherein I may recount unto you things of the same kind, which will breed no small admiration.' Dorothea noted Cardenio's words

* **leasings** lies
† **vassal** one who, under the feudal system owes allegiance and duty
‡ **let** impediment

and his uncouth and disastrous attire, and then entreated him very instantly if he knew anything of her affairs he would acquaint her therewithal; for if fortune had left her any good, it was only the courage which she had to bear patiently any disaster that might befall her, being certain in her opinion that no new one could arrive which might increase a whit those she had already.

'Lady, I would not let slip the occasion,' quoth Cardenio, 'to tell you what I think, if that which I imagine were true; and yet there is no commodity left to do it, nor can it avail you much to know it.' 'Let it be what it list,' said Dorothea; 'but that which after befel of my relation was this: That Don Fernando took an image that was in my chamber for witness of our contract, and added withal most forcible words and unusual oaths, promising unto me to become my husband; although I warned him, before he had ended his speech, to see well what he did, and to weigh the wrath of his father when he should see him married to one so base and his vassal, and that therefore he should take heed that my beauty (such as it was) should not blind him, seeing he should not find therein a sufficient excuse for his error, and that if he meant to do me any good, I conjured him, by the love that he bore unto me, to licence my fortunes to rule in their own sphere, according as my quality reached; for such unequal matches do never please long, nor persevere with that delight wherewithal they began.

'All the reasons here rehearsed I said unto him, and many more which now are fallen out of mind, but yet proved of no efficacy to wean him from his obstinate purpose; even like unto one that goeth to buy, with intention never to pay for what he takes, and therefore never considers the price, worth, or defect of the stuff he takes to credit. I at this season made a brief discourse, and said thus to myself, "I may do this, for I am not the first which by matrimony hath ascended from a low degree to a high estate; nor shall Don Fernando be the first whom beauty or blind affection (for that is the most certain) hath induced to make choice of a consort unequal to his greatness. Then, since herein I create to new world nor custom, what error can be committed by embracing the honour wherewithal fortune crowns me, although it so befel that his affection to me endured no longer than till he accomplished his will? for before God I certes* shall still remain his wife. And if I should disdainfully give him the repulse, I see him now in such terms as, perhaps forgetting the duty of a nobleman, he may use violence, and then shall I remain for ever dishonoured, and also without excuse of the imputations of the ignorant, which knew not how much without any fault I have fallen into this inevitable danger; for what reasons may be sufficiently forcible to persuade my father and others that this nobleman did enter into my chamber without my consent?" All these demands and answers did I, in an instant, revolve in mine imagination, and found myself chiefly forced (how I cannot tell) to assent to his petition by the witnesses he invoked, the tears he shed, and finally by his sweet disposition and comely feature, which, accompanied with so many arguments of unfeigned affection, were able to conquer and enthrall any other heart, though it were as free and wary as mine own. Then called I for my waiting-maid, that she might on earth accompany the celestial witnesses.

'And then Don Fernando turned again to reiterate and confirm his oaths, and added to his former other new saints as witnesses, and wished a thousand succeeding maledictions to light on him if he did not accomplish his promise to me. His eyes again waxed moist, his sighs increased, and himself enwreathed me more straitly between his arms, from which he had never once loosed me; and with this, and my maiden's departure, I left to be a maiden, and he began to be a traitor and a disloyal man. The day that succeeded to the night of my mishaps came not, I think, so soon as Don Fernando desired it; for, after a man hath satisfied that which the appetite covets, the greatest delight it can take after is to apart itself from the place where the desire was accomplished. I say this, because Don Fernando did hasten his departure from me: by my maid's industry, who was the very same that had brought him into my chamber, he was got in the

* **certes** certainly

street before dawning. And at his departure from me he said (although not with so great show of affection and vehemency as he had used at his coming) that I might be secure of his faith, and that his oaths were firm and most true; and for a more confirmation of his word, he took a rich ring off his finger and put it on mine. In fine,* he departed, and I remained behind, I cannot well say whether joyful or sad; but this much I know, that I rested confused and pensive, and almost beside myself for the late mischance; yet either I had not the heart, or else I forgot to chide my maid for her treachery committed by shutting up Don Fernando in my chamber; for as yet I could not determine whether that which had befallen me was a good or an evil.

'I said to Don Fernando, at his departure, that he might see me other nights when he pleased, by the same means he had come that night, seeing I was his own, and would rest so, until it pleased him to let the world know that I was his wife. But he never returned again but the next night following, nor could I see him after, for the space of a month, either in the street or church, so as I did but spend time in vain to expect him; although I understood that he was still in town, and rode every other day a-hunting, an exercise to which he was much addicted.

'Those days were, I know, unfortunate and accursed to me, and those hours sorrowful; for in them I began to doubt, nay, rather wholly to discredit Don Fernando's faith; and my maid did then hear loudly the checks I gave unto her for her presumption, ever until then dissembled; and I was, moreover, constrained to watch and keep guard on my tears and countenance, lest I should give occasion to my parents to demand of me the cause of my discontents, and thereby engage me to use ambages† or untruths to cover them. But all this ended in an instant, one moment arriving whereon all these respects stumbled, all honourable discourses ended, patience was lost, and my most hidden secrets issued in public; which was, when there was spread a certain rumour throughout the town, within a few days after, that Don Fernando had married, in a city near adjoining, a damsel of surpassing beauty, and of very noble birth, although not so rich as could deserve, by her preferment or dowry, so worthy a husband; it was also said that she was named Lucinda, with many other things that happened at their espousals worthy of admiration.' Cardenio hearing Lucinda named did nothing else but lift up his shoulders, bite his lip, bend his brows, and after a little while shed from his eyes two floods of tears. But yet for all that Dorothea did not interrupt the file of her history, saying, 'This doleful news came to my hearing; and my heart, instead of freezing thereat, was so inflamed with choler and rage, as I had well-nigh run out to the streets, and with outcries published the deceit and treason that was done to me; but my fury was presently assuaged by the resolution which I made to do what I put in execution the very same night, and then I put on this habit which you see, being given unto me by one of those that among us country-folk are called swains, who was my father's servant; to whom I disclosed all my misfortunes, and requested him to accompany me to the city where I understood my enemy sojourned. He, after he had reprehended my boldness, perceiving me to have an inflexible resolution, made offer to attend on me, as he said, unto the end of the world; and presently after I trussed up in a pillow-bear a woman's attire, some money, and jewels, to prevent necessities that might befall; and in the silence of night, without acquainting my treacherous maid with my purpose, I issued out of my house, accompanied by my servant and many imaginations, and in that manner set on towards the city, and though I went on foot, was yet borne away flying by my desires, to come, if not in time enough to hinder that which was past, yet at least to demand of Don Fernando that he would tell me with what conscience of soul he had done it. I arrived where I wished within two days and a half; and at the entry of the city I demanded where Lucinda her father dwelt; and he of whom I first demanded the question answered me more than I desired to hear.

* **fine** conclusion
† **ambages** roundabout or indirect ways of speaking

He showed me the house, and recounted to me all that befell at the daughter's marriage, being a thing so public and known in the city, as men made meetings of purpose to discourse thereof.

'He said to me that the very night wherein Don Fernando was espoused to Lucinda, after she had given her consent to be his wife, she was instantly assailed by a terrible accident that struck her into a trance, and her spouse approaching to unclasp her bosom that she might take the air; found a paper folded in it, written with Lucinda's own hand, wherein she said and declared that she could not be Don Fernando's wife, because she was already Cardenio's, who was, as the man told me, a very principal gentleman of the same city; and that if she had given her consent to Don Fernando, it was only done because she would not disobey her parents. In conclusion, he told me that the paper made also mention how she had a resolution to kill herself presently after the marriage, and did also lay down therein the motives she had to do it; all which, as they say, was confirmed by a poniard that was found hidden about her in her apparel. Which Don Fernando perceiving, presuming that Lucinda did flout him, and hold him in little account, he set upon her ere she was come to herself, and attempted to kill her with the very same poniard, and had done it, if her father and other friends which were present had not opposed themselves and hindered his determination. Moreover, they reported that presently after Don Fernando absented himself from the city, and that Lucinda turned not out of her agony until the next day, and then recounted to her parents how she was verily spouse to that Cardenio of whom we spake even now. I learned besides that Cardenio, as it is rumoured, was present at the marriage, and that as soon as he saw her married, being a thing he would never have credited, departed out of the city in a desperate mood, but first left behind him a letter, wherein he showed at large the wrong Lucinda had done to him, and that he himself meant to go to some place where people should never after hear of him. All this was notorious, and publicly bruited* throughout the city, and every one spoke thereof, but most of all having very soon after understood that Lucinda was missing from her parent's house and the city, for she could not be found in neither of both; for which her parents were almost beside themselves, not knowing what means to use to find her.

'These news reduced my hopes again to their ranks, and I esteemed it better to find Don Fernando unmarried than married, presuming that yet the gates of my remedy were not wholly shut, I giving myself to understand that Heaven had peradventure set that impediment on the second marriage to make him understand what he ought to the first, and to remember how he was a Christian, and that he was more obliged to his soul than to human respects. I revolved all these things in my mind, and comfortless did yet comfort myself, by feigning large yet languishing hopes, to sustain that life which I now do so much abhor. And whilst I stayed thus in the city, ignorant what I might do, seeing I found not Don Fernando, I heard a crier go about publicly, promising great rewards to any one that could find me out, giving signs of the very age and apparel I wore; and I likewise heard it was bruited abroad that the youth which came with me had carried me away from my father's house — a thing that touched my soul very nearly, to view my credit so greatly wrecked, seeing that it was not sufficient to have lost it by my coming away, without the addition [of] him with whom I departed, being a subject so base and unworthy of my loftier thoughts. Having heard this cry, I departed out of the city with my servant, who even then began to give tokens that he faltered in the fidelity he had promised to me; and both of us, together entered the very same night into the most hidden parts of this mountain, fearing lest we might be found. But, as it is commonly said that one evil calls on another, and that the end of one disaster is the beginning of a greater, so proved it with me; for my good servant, until then faithful and trusty, rather incited by his villainy than my beauty, thought to have taken the benefit of the opportunity which these inhabitable places offered, and solicited me of love, with little shame and less fear of God, or respect of myself; and now seeing that I answered his

* **bruited** reported

impudences with severe and reprehensive words, leaving the entreaties aside wherewithal he thought first to have compassed his will, he began to use his force; but just Heaven, which seldom or never neglects the just man's assistance, did so favour my proceedings, as with my weak forces, and very little labour, I threw him down a steep rock, and there I left him, I know not whether alive or dead; and presently I entered in among these mountains with more swiftness than my fear and weariness required, having therein no other project or design than to hide myself in them, and shun my father and others, which by his entreaty and means sought for me everywhere.

'Some months are past since my first coming here, where I found a herdman, who carried me to a village seated in the midst of these rocks, wherein he dwelt, and entertained me, whom I have served as a shepherd ever since, procuring as much as lay in me to abide still in the field, to cover these hairs which have now so unexpectedly betrayed me; yet all my care and industry availed not, seeing my master came at last to the notice that I was no man, but a woman, which was an occasion that the like evil thought sprung in him as before in my servant; and as fortune gives not always remedy for the difficulties which occur, I found neither rock nor downfall to cool and cure my master's infirmity, as I had done for my man, and therefore I accounted it a less inconvenience to depart thence, and hide myself again among these deserts, than to adventure the trial of my strength or reason with him; therefore, as I say, I turned to imbosk* myself, and search out some place where, without any encumbrance, I might entreat Heaven, with my sighs and tears, to have compassion on my mishap, and lend me industry and favour, either to issue fortunately out of it, or else to die amidst these solitudes, not leaving any memory of a wretch, who hath ministered matter, although not through her own default, that men may speak and murmur of her, both in her own and in other countries.'

II. Which Treats of the Discretion of the Beautiful Dorothea, and the Artificial Manner Used to Dissuade the Amorous Knight from Continuing His Penance; and How He Was Gotten Away; with Many Other Delightful and Pleasant Occurrences

'THIS is, sirs, the true relation of my tragedy; see therefore, now, and judge, whether the sighs you heard, the words to which you listened, and the tears that gushed out at mine eyes, have not sufficient occasion to appear in greater abundance; and, having considered the quality of my disgrace, you shall perceive all comfort to be vain, seeing the remedy thereof is impossible. Only I will request at your hands one favour, which you ought and may easily grant, and is, that you will address me unto some place where I may live secure from the fear and suspicion I have to be found by those which I know do daily travel in my pursuit; for although I am sure that my parents' great affection toward me doth warrant me to be kindly received and entertained by them, yet the shame is so great that possesseth me, only to think that I shall not return to their presence in that state which they expect, as I account it far better to banish myself from their sight for ever, than once to behold their face with the least suspicion that they again would behold mine, divorced from that honesty which whilom† my modest behaviour promised.' Here she ended, and her face, suddenly overrun by a lovely scarlet, perspicuously denoted the feeling and bashfulness of her soul. The audients of her sad story felt great motions both of pity and admiration for her misfortunes; and although the curate thought to comfort and counsel her forthwith, yet was he prevented by Cardenio, who, taking her first by the hand, said at last, 'Lady, thou art the beautiful Dorothea, daughter unto rich Clenardo.' Dorothea rested admired when she heard her father's name, and saw of how little value he seemed who had named him, for we have already recounted how raggedly Cardenio was clothed; and therefore she said unto him, 'And who

* **imbosk** hide, conceal
† **whilom** at a former time

art thou, friend, that knowest so well my father's name? for until this hour (if I have not forgotten myself) I did not once name him throughout the whole discourse of my unfortunate tale.'

'I am,' answered Cardenio, 'the unlucky knight whom Lucinda (as thou saidst) affirmed to be her husband. I am the disastrous Cardenio, whom the wicked proceeding of him that hath also brought thee to those terms wherein thou art, hath conducted me to the state in which I am, and thou mayst behold — ragged, naked, abandoned by all human comfort, and, what is worse, void of sense, seeing I only enjoy it but at some few short times, and that when Heaven pleaseth to lend it me. I am he, Dorothea, that was present at Don Fernando's unreasonable wedding, and that heard the consent which Lucinda gave him to be his wife. I was he that had not the courage to stay and see the end of her trance, or what became of the paper found in her bosom; for my soul had not power or sufferance to behold so many misfortunes at once, and therefore abandoned the place and my patience together, and only left a letter with mine host, whom I entreated to deliver it into Lucinda her own hands, and then came into these deserts, with resolution to end in them my miserable life, which, since that hour, I have hated as my most mortal enemy; but fortune hath not pleased to deprive me of it, thinking it sufficient to have impaired my wit, perhaps reserving me for the good success befallen me now in finding of yourself; for, that being true (as I believe it is) which you have here discoursed, peradventure it may have reserved yet better hap for us both in our disasters than we expect.

'For, presupposing that Lucinda cannot marry with Don Fernando, because she is mine, nor Don Fernando with her, because yours, and that she hath declared so manifestly the same, we may well hope that Heaven hath means to restore to every one that which is his own, seeing it yet consists in being not made away or annihilated. And seeing this comfort remains, not sprung from any very remote hope, nor founded on idle surmises, I request thee, fair lady, to take another resolution in thine honourable thought, seeing I mean to do it in mine, and let us accommodate ourselves to expect better success; for I do vow unto thee, by the faith of a gentleman and Christian, not to forsake thee until I see thee in Don Fernando's possession; and when I shall not, by reasons, be able to induce him to acknowledge how far he rests indebted to thee, then will I use the liberty granted to me as a gentleman, and with just title challenge him to the field in respect of the wrong he hath done unto thee, forgetting wholly mine own injuries, whose revenge I will leave to Heaven, that I may be able to right yours on earth.'

Dorothea rested wonderfully admired, having known and heard Cardenio, and, ignoring what competent thanks she might return him in satisfaction of his large offers, she cast herself down at his feet to have kissed them, which Cardenio would not permit; and the licentiate answered for both, praising greatly Cardenio's discourse, and chiefly entreated, prayed, and counselled them, that they would go with him to his village, where they might fit themselves with such things as they wanted, and also take order how to search out Don Fernando, or carry Dorothea to her father's house, or do else what they deemed most convenient. Cardenio and Dorothea gratified his courtesies, and accepted the favour he preferred. The barber also, who had stood all the while silent and suspended, made them a pretty discourse, with as friendly an offer of himself and his service as master curate, and likewise did briefly relate the occasion of their coming thither with the extravagant kind of madness which Don Quixote had, and how they expected now his squire's return, whom they had sent to search for him. Cardenio having heard him named, remembered presently, as in a dream, the conflict passed between them both, and recounted it unto them, but could not in any wise call to mind the occasion thereof.

Dorothea then offers to help with Don Quixote's cure by counterfeiting the distressed lady herself and with the curate's prompting becomes Princess Micomicona who is seeking the famous Don Quixote in order to release her kingdom from the tyranny of a fierce giant, Pandafilando of the Dusky Sight. They all return

to the inn together where discussion of romances leads to the relation of yet another interpolated tale,
The Curious Impertinent (dramatized most probably by Thomas Middleton and generally known as The
Second Maiden's Tragedy *but at one time attributed to Shakespeare and even called* Cardenio, *owing to its*
proximity to the Cardenio story in Cervantes). Whilst the curate is relating this, Don Quixote in his madness
mistakes the wineskins filled with red wine for the head of the giant Pandafilo and stabs it furiously. He is
calmed by the curate who then finishes the story but concludes that it cannot be true but must be fiction,
a topic which is debated by all those present.

IX. Which Treats of Many Rare Successes Befallen in the Inn

Whilst they discoursed thus, the innkeeper, who stood all the while at the door, said, 'Here comes a fair
troop of guests, and if they will here alight we may sing Gaudeamus.'* 'What folk is it?' quoth Cardenio.
'Four men on horseback,' quoth the host, 'and ride jennet-wise,† with lances and targets,‡ and masks on
their faces; and with them comes likewise a woman apparelled in white, in a side-saddle, and her face
also masked, and two lackeys that run with them a-foot.' 'Are they near?' quoth the curate. 'So near,'
replied the innkeeper, 'as they do now arrive.' Dorothea hearing him say so, covered her face, and Cardenio
entered into Don Quixote's chamber; and scarce had they leisure to do it, when the others of whom the host
spake, entered into the inn, and the four horsemen alighting, which were all of very comely and gallant
disposition, they went to help down the lady that rode in the side-saddle, and one of them taking her down
in his arms, did seat her in a chair that stood at the chamber door, into which Cardenio had entered: and all
this while neither she nor they took off their masks, or spake a word, only the gentlewoman, at her sitting
down in the chair, breathed forth a very deep sigh, and let fall her arms like a sick and dismayed person.
The lackeys carried away their horses to the stable. Master curate seeing and noting all this, and curious
to know what they were that came to the inn in so unwonted an attire, and kept such profound silence
therein, went to the lackeys and demanded of one of them that which he desired to know, who answered,
'In good faith, sir, I cannot tell you what folk this is: only this I know, that they seem to be very noble, but
chiefly he that went and took down the lady in his arms that you see there; and this I say, because all the
others do respect him very much, and nothing is done but what he ordains and commands,' 'And the lady,
what is she?' quoth the curate. 'I can as hardly inform you,' quoth the lackey, 'for I have not once seen her
face in all this journey; yet I have heard her often groan and breathe out so profound sighs, as it seems she
would give up the ghost at every one of them. And it is no marvel that we should know no more than we
have said, for my companion and myself have been in their company but two days; for they encountered
us on the way, and prayed and persuaded us to go with them unto Andalusia, promising that they would
recompense our pains largely.' 'And hast thou heard them name one another?' said the curate. 'No, truly,'
answered the lackey; 'for they all travel with such silence, as it is a wonder; for you shall not hear a word
among, but the sighs and throbs of the poor lady, which do move in us very great compassion. And we do
questionless persuade ourselves that she is forced wheresoever she goes: and as it may be collected by her
attire, she is a nun, or, as is most probable, goes to be one; and perhaps she goeth so sorrowful as it seems
because she hath no desire to become religious.' 'It may very well be so,' quoth the curate. And so leaving
them, he returned to the place where he had left Dorothea; who, hearing the disguised lady to sigh so often,
moved by the native compassion of that sex, drew near her and said, 'What ails you, good madam? I pray
you think if it be any of those inconveniences to which woman be subject, and whereof they may have use

* **Gaudeamus** *gaudeamus igitur,* name of a popular academic song of celebration, literally 'let us rejoice' (Latin)
† **jennet-wise** like Spanish light horsemen
‡ **targets** small round shields

and experience to cure them, I do offer unto you my service, assistance, and good-will to help you, as much as lies in my power.' To all those compliments the doleful lady answered nothing; and although Dorothea made her again larger offers of her service, yet stood she, ever silent, until the bemasked gentleman (whom the lackey said the rest did obey) came over and said to Dorothea, 'Lady, do not trouble yourself to offer anything to that woman, for she is of a most ungrateful nature, and is never wont to gratify any courtesy, nor do you seek her to answer unto your demands, if you would not hear some lie from her mouth.' 'I never said any,' quoth the silent lady, 'but rather because I am so true and sincere, without guiles, I am now drowned here in those misfortunes; and of this I would have thyself bear witness, seeing my pure truth makes thee to be so false and disloyal.'

Cardenio overheard those words very clear and distinctly, as one that stood so near unto her that said them, as only Don Quixote's chamber door stood between them. And instantly when he heard them, he said with a very loud voice, 'Good God! what is this that I hear? What voice is this that hath touched mine ear?' The lady, moved with a sudden passion, turned her head at those outcries, and seeing she could not perceive him that gave them, she got up, and would have entered into the room, which the gentleman espying, withheld her, and would not let her stir out of the place: and with the alteration and sudden motion the mask fell off her face, and she discovered* an incomparable beauty, and an angelical countenance, although it was somewhat wan and pale, and turned here and there with her eyes to every place so earnestly as she seemed to be distracted; which motions, without knowing the reason why they were made, struck Dorothea and the rest that beheld her into very great compassion. The gentleman holding her very strongly fast by the shoulders, the mask he wore on his own face was falling; and he being so busied could not hold it up, but in the end [it] fell wholly. Dorothea, who had likewise embraced the lady, lifting up her eyes by chance, saw that he which did also embrace the lady was her spouse Don Fernando; and scarce had she known him, when, breathing out a long and most pitiful 'Alas!' from the bottom of her heart, she fell backward in a trance; and if the barber had not been by good hap at hand, she would have fallen on the ground with all the weight of her body. The curate presently repaired to take off the veil of her face and cast water thereon: and as soon as he did discover it, Don Fernando, who was he indeed that held fast the other, knew her, and looked like a dead man as soon as he viewed her, but did not all this while let go Lucinda, who was the other whom he held so fast, and that laboured so much to escape out of his hands, Cardenio likewise heard the 'Alas!' that Dorothea said when she fell into a trance, and, believing that it was his Lucinda, issued out of the chamber greatly altered, and the first he espied was Don Fernando, which held Lucinda fast, who forthwith knew him. And all the three — Lucinda, Cardenio, and Dorothea — stood dumb and amazed, as folk that knew not what had befallen unto them. All of them held their peace, and beheld one another; Dorothea looked on Don Fernando, Don Fernando on Cardenio, Cardenio on Lucinda, and Lucinda again on Cardenio; but Lucinda was the first that broke silence, speaking to Don Fernando in this manner: 'Leave me off, Lord Fernando, I conjure thee, by that thou shouldst be; for that which thou art, if thou wilt not do it for any other respect; let me cleave to the wall whose ivy I am; to the supporter from whom neither thy importunity nor threats, promises or gifts, could once deflect me. Note how Heaven, by unusual, unfrequented, and from us concealed ways, hath set my true spouse before mine eyes; and thou dost know well, by a thousand costly experiences, that only death is potent to blot forth his remembrance out of my memory. Let, then, so manifest truths be of power (if thou must do none other) to convert thine affliction into rage, and thy good-will into despite, and therewithal end my life; for if I may render up the ghost in the presence of my dear spouse, I shall account it fortunately lost. Perhaps by my death he will remain satisfied of the faith which I have kept sincere towards him until the last period of my life.' By

---

* **discovered** revealed

this time Dorothea was come to herself, and listened to most of Lucinda's reasons, and by them came to the knowledge of herself. But seeing Don Fernando did not yet let her depart from between his arms, nor answer anything to her words, encouraging herself the best that she might, she arose, and, kneeling at his feet, and shedding a number of crystal and penetrating tears, she spoke to him thus:

'If it be not so, my lord, that the beams of that sun which thou holdest eclipsed between thine arms do darken and deprive those of thine eyes, thou mightest have by this perceived how she that is prostrated at thy feet is the unfortunate (until thou shalt please) and the disastrous Dorothea. I am that poor humble countrywoman whom thou, either through thy bounty, or for thy pleasure, didst deign to raise to that height that she might call thee her own. I am she which, some time immured within the limits of honesty, did lead a most contented life, until it opened the gates of her recollection and wariness to thine importunity, and seeming just and amorous requests, and rendered up to thee the keys of her liberty; a gift by thee so ill recompensed, as the finding myself in so remote a place as this wherein you have met with me, and I seen you, may clearly testify; but yet for all this, I would not have you to imagine that I come here guided by dishonourable steps, being only hitherto conducted by the tracts of dolour and feeling, to see myself thus forgotten by thee. It was thy will that I should be thine own, and thou didst desire it in such a manner, as although now thou wouldst not have it so, yet canst not thou possibly leave off to be mine. Know, my dear lord, that the matchless affections that I do bear towards thee may recompense and be equivalent to her beauty and nobility for whom thou dost abandon me. 'Thou canst not be the beautiful Lucinda's, because thou art mine; nor she thine, forasmuch as she belongs to Cardenio; and it will be more easy, if you will note it well, to reduce thy will to love her that adores thee, than to address hers, that hates thee, to bear thee affection. Thou didst solicit my recklessness, thou prayedst to mine integrity, and wast not ignorant of my quality; thou knowest also very well upon what terms I subjected myself to thy will, so as there remains no place nor colour to term it a fraud or deceit; and all this being so, as in verity it is, and that thou beest as Christian as thou art noble, why dost thou with these so many untoward wreathings* dilate the making of mine end happy, whose commencement thou didst illustrate so much? And if thou wilt not have me for what I am, who am thy true and lawful spouse, yet at least take and admit me for thy slave, for so that I may be in thy possession I will account myself happy and fortunate. Do not permit that by leaving and abandoning me, meetings may be made to discourse of my dishonour. Do not vex thus the declining years of my parents, seeing that the loyal services which they ever have done as vassals to thine deserve not so [dis]honest a recompense. And if thou esteemest that thy blood by meddling with mine shall be stained or embased, consider how few noble houses, or rather none at all, are there in the world which have not run the same way, and that the woman's side is not essentially requisite for the illustrating of noble descents. How much more, seeing that true nobility consists in virtue, which if it shall want in thee, by refusing that which thou owest me so justly, I shall remain with many more degrees of nobility than thou shalt. And in conclusion, that which I will lastly say is, that whether thou wilt or no, I am thy wife; the witnesses are thine own words, which neither should nor ought to lie, if thou dost esteem thyself to have that for the want of which thou despisest me. Witness shall also be thine own handwriting. Witness Heaven, which thou didst invoke to bear witness of that which thou didst promise unto me: and when all this shall fail, thy very conscience shall never fail from using clamours, being silent in thy mirth and turning, for this truth which I have said to thee now shall trouble the greatest pleasure and delight.'

These and many other like reasons did the sweetly grieved Dorothea use with such feeling, as all those that were presents, as well such as accompanied Don Fernando, and all the others that did accompany her,

---

* **untoward wreathings** stubborn, perverse contortions

shed abundance of tears. Don Fernando listened unto her without replying a word, until she had ended her speech, and given beginning to so many sighs and sobs, as the heart that could endure to behold them without moving were harder than brass. Lucinda did also regard her, no less compassionate of her sorrow than admired at her discretion and beauty, and although she would have approached to her, and used some consolatory words, yet was she hindered by Don Fernando's arms, which held her still embraced, who, full of confusion and marvel, after he had stood very attentively beholding Dorothea a good while, opening his arms, and leaving Lucinda free, said, 'Thou hast vanquished, O beautiful Dorothea! thou hast vanquished me; for it is not possible to resist or deny so many united truths.' Lucinda, through her former trance and weakness, as Don Fernando left her, was like to fall, if Cardenio, who stood behind Don Fernando all the while lest he should be known, shaking off all fear and endangering his person, had not started forward to stay her from falling; and, clasping her sweetly between his arms, he said, 'If pitiful Heaven be pleased, and would have thee now at last take some ease, my loyal, constant, and beautiful lady, I presume that thou canst not possess it more securely than between these arms which do now receive thee, as whilom they did when fortune was pleased that I might call thee mine own.' And then Lucinda, first severing her eyelids, beheld Cardenio, and having first taken notice of him by his voice, and confirmed it again by her sight, like one quite distracted, without further regarding modest respects, she cast both her arms about his neck, and, joining her face to his, said, 'Yea, thou indeed art my lord; thou, the true owner of this poor captive, howsoever adverse fortune shall thwart it, or this life, which is only sustained and lives by thine, be ever so much threatened.' This was a marvellous spectacle to Don Fernando, and all the rest of the beholders, which did universally admire at this so unexpected an event. And Dorothea, perceiving Don Fernando to change colour, as one resolving to take revenge on Cardenio, for he had set hand to his sword, which she conjecturing, did with marvellous expedition kneel, and, catching hold on his legs, kissing them, she strained them with so loving embracements as he could not stir out of the place, and then, with her eyes overflown with tears, said unto him, "What meanest thou to do, my only refuge in this unexpected trance? Thou hast here thine own spouse at thy feet, and her whom thou wouldst fain possess is between her own husband's arms. Judge, then, whether it become thee, or is a thing possible, to dissolve that which Heaven hath knit, or whether it be anywise laudable to endeavour to raise and equal to thyself her who, contemning all dangers and inconveniences, and confirmed in faith and constancy, doth in thy presence bathe her eyes with amorous liquor of her true love's face and bosom. I desire thee for God's sake, and by thine own worths I request thee, that this so notorious a verity may not only assuage thy choler, but also diminish it in such sort, as thou mayst quietly and peaceably permit those two lovers to enjoy their desires without any encumbrance all the time that Heaven shall grant it to them; and herein thou shalt show the generosity of thy magnanimous and noble breast, and give the world to understand how reason prevaileth in thee, and domineereth over passion.' All the time that Dorothea spoke thus to Don Fernando, although Cardenio held Lucinda between his arms, yet did he never take his eyes off Don Fernando, with resolution that if he did see him once stir in his prejudice, he would labour both to defend himself and offend his adversary and all those who should join with him to do him any harm, as much as he could, although it were with the rest of his life. But Don Fernando's friends, the curate and barber, that were present and saw all that was passed, repaired in the mean season, without omitting the good Sancho Panza, and all of them together compassed Don Fernando, entreating him to have regard of the beautiful Dorothea's tears, and it being true (as they believed it was) that she had said, he should not permit her to remain defrauded of her so just and lawful hopes, assuring him that it was not by chance, but rather by the particular providence and disposition of the heavens, that they had all met together so unexpectedly; and that he should remember, as master curate said very well, that only death could sever Lucinda from her Cardenio; and that although the edge of a sword might divide and part them asunder, yet in that case they would account their death most happy; and that, in irremediless* events, it was highest prudence, by straining and overcoming himself, to show a generous mind, and that he might conquer his own will, by permitting these two to enjoy that good which Heaven had already granted to them; and that he should turn his eyes to behold the beauty of Dorothea, and he should see that few or none could for feature paragon† with her, and much less excel her; and that he should confer her humility and extreme love which she bore to him with her other endowments: and principally, that if he gloried in the titles of nobility or Christianity, he could not do any other than accomplish the promise that he had passed to her; and that by fulfilling it he should please God and satisfy discreet persons, which know very well how it is a special prerogative of beauty, though it be in an humble and mean subject, if it be consorted with modesty and virtue, to exalt and equal itself to any dignity, without disparagement of him which doth help to raise or unite it to himself. And when the strong laws of delight are accomplished (so that there intercur‡ no sin in the acting thereof), he is not to be condemned which doth follow them. Finally, they added to these reasons others so many and forcible, that the valorous breast of Don Fernando (as commonly all those that are warmed and nourished by noble blood are wont) was mollified, and permitted itself to be vanquished by that truth which he could not deny though he would. And the token that he gave of his being overcome, was to stoop down and embrace Dorothea, saying unto her, 'Arise, lady; for it is not just that she be prostrate at my feet whose image I have erected in my mind. And if I have not hitherto given demonstrations of what I now aver, it hath perhaps befallen through the disposition of Heaven, to the end I might, by noting the constancy and faith wherewithal thou dost affect me, know after how to value and esteem thee according unto thy merits. And that which in recompense thereof I do entreat of thee is, that thou wilt excuse in me mine ill manner of proceeding and exceeding carelessness in repaying thy good-will; for the very occasion and violent passions that made me to accept thee as mine, the very same did also impel me again not to be thine; and for the more verifying of mine assertion, do but once behold the eyes of the now contented Lucinda, and thou mayst read in them a thousand excuses for mine error; and seeing she hath found and obtained her heart's desire, and I have in thee also gotten what is most convenient — for I wish she may live securely and joyfully many and happy years with her Cardenio: for I will pray the same, that it will license me to enjoy my beloved Dorothea.' And saying so, he embraced her again, and joined his face to hers with so lovely motion, as it constrained him to hold watch over his tears, lest violently bursting forth, they should give doubtless arguments of his fervent love and remorse.

Cardenio, Lucinda, and almost all the rest could not do so, for the greater number of them shed so many tears, some for their private contentments, and others for their friends, as it seemed that some grievous and heavy misfortune had betided them all; even very Sancho Panza wept, although he excused it afterward, saying that he wept only because that he saw that Dorothea was not the Queen Micomicona, as he had imagined, of whom he hoped to have received so great gifts and favours. The admiration and tears joined, endured in them all for a pretty space; and presently after, Cardenio and Lucinda went and kneeled to Don Fernando, yielding him thanks for the favour that he had done to them, with so courteous compliments as he knew not what to answer, and therefore lifted them up, and embraced them with very great affection and kindness, and presently after he demanded of Dorothea how she came to that place, so far from her own dwelling. And she recounted unto him all that she had told to Cardenio; whereat Don Fernando and those which came with him took so great delight, as they could have wished that her story had continued a longer time in the telling than it did – so great was Dorothea's grace in setting out her misfortunes. And as soon as she had ended, Don Fernando told all that had befallen him in the city, after that he had found the

---

* **irremediless** beyond all remedy
† **feature paragon** equal for beauty
‡ **intercur** come between

scroll in Lucinda's bosom, wherein she declared Cardenio to be her husband, and that he therefore could not marry her; and also how he attempted to kill her, and would have done it, were it not that her parents hindered him; and that he therefore departed out of the house, full of shame and despite, with resolution to revenge himself more commodiously; and how he understood the next day following, how Lucinda was secretly departed from her father's house, and gone nobody knew where, but that he finally learned within a few months after, that she had entered into a certain monastery, with intention to remain there all the days of her life, if she could not pass them with Cardenio; and that as soon as he had learned that, choosing those three gentlemen for his associates, he came to the place where she was, but would not speak to her, fearing lest that, as soon as they knew of his being there, they would increase the guards of the monastery; and therefore expected until he found on a day the gates of the monastery open, and leaving two of his fellows to keep the door, he with the other entered into the abbey in Lucinda's search, whom they found talking with a nun in the cloister; and, snatching her away ere she could retire herself, they brought her to a certain village, where they disguised themselves in that sort they were; for so it was requisite for to bring her away: all which they did with the more facility, that the monastery was seated abroad in the fields, a good way from any village. He likewise told that, as soon as Lucinda saw herself in his power, she fell into a swoon; and that, after she had returned to herself, she never did any other thing but weep and sigh, without speaking a word; and that in that manner, accompanied with silence and tears, they had arrived to that inn, which was to him as grateful as an arrival to heaven, wherein all earthly mishaps are concluded and finished.

Now reconciled Cardenio, Don Fernando, Lucinda and Dorothea agree to continue the charade and take Don Quixote home to be cured when yet more travellers appear at the inn, a Moorish princess, Zoraida, accompanied by an escaped Spanish captive, who proceeds to tell their tale.

* There is a biographical element to the story since Cervantes was himself captured by Algerian pirates and held captive for five years before being ransomed. The story of Zoraida appears in Mary Shelley's *Frankenstein* (chapter XIII) where she is called 'Safie'.

AUTHORSHIP AND ATTRIBUTION
Will Sharpe

Big, bold claims help sell books, and books seeking to re-evaluate the lives and activities of famous writers are practically obliged to come up with some. The potential big, bold claims about the book you are now holding are clear. Yet even the biggest and boldest of them all, though made in the fervent attempt to raise controversy, would probably raise little more than a collective and somewhat sceptical eyebrow among readers. Not because the idea of Shakespeare having written all these plays is implausible in itself, especially not to those who know little of what broadly constitutes his accepted canon. It is more the pervasive and nagging sense that, when it comes to him, we must have heard it all by now. From the most devout Bardolator to the most recalcitrant heretic – the canon/apocrypha labels are, after all, biblical – few people who pick up a newspaper more than once or twice a week can have failed to notice how often the latest scoop about the world's most famous writer gets an airing in the popular media. Remaking Shakespeare is big business, and the commodity is revelation. We seek busily, continually in the dust for those ever-elusive signs that we imagine will unlock the mystery of his creativity: a new identity, a new sexual orientation, a new religion, a new secret lover, or, perhaps the ultimate prize, the Grail-like prospect of a new work.

The staggering human achievement that we associate with Shakespeare's name has made him, to borrow a phrase used of the comparably revered Mozart, culturally supernatural. Mozart composed over six hundred works in his short life, some merely interesting, most near sublime, yet as an authorial figure he is both fixed and grounded through the many surviving letters in which, alongside serious confessions of personal hardship, he cattily describes people's looks or takes childish delight in the lowest scatological humour. Of course, none of this explains the Requiem (the parts of it he wrote) or the piano concerto in D minor, but equally no one really doubts the provenance of Mozart's work or assumes that there must be more. Shakespeare, on the other hand, is authorial dark matter, absent from his writing and from historical record to an extraordinary degree, opening the door upon a world of strange attempts to draw him in. This finds its most obvious expression in the phenomenon of authorship doubting, the bizarrely widespread belief traceable only as far back as the nineteenth century in a shadowy, ideally aristocratic, figure masked behind the famous Shakespeare mugshot. If genius means closer to God – albeit that any dictionary would define it as a purely natural engine, however extraordinary – the British will naturally seek it among the socially higher up, though it might also be observed that the idea has found robust global support over many years, particularly in the United States and Germany. Roland Emmerich's 2011 film *Anonymous*, championing Edward de Vere, the seventeenth Earl of Oxford, is the most recent high-profile addition to this now unstoppable industry in which some seventy-plus candidates have been touted as the 'real' Shakespeare.[1]

And yet the object of study we will pursue here, the four hundred years' worth of attempts to suggest that we have not yet sounded the full depths of Shakespeare's creativity, is in fact the flip side of the same coin. The authorship question, though fuelled by class prejudice, is nonetheless founded on love, its accusations of fraud intended to elevate, not to condemn, the revered works. And that same love acts as the spur in the quest to attribute new plays and poems to our greatest, most exciting poet: this enterprise has literary-biographical aims, but equally has at its heart the desire to consolidate the true image of the author. Claims of both kinds have been such a consistent feature of the Shakespeare juggernaut that they have become unfairly amalgamated, and anything new, whether a legitimate question or not, tends to get routinely dismissed as yet another entry by the lunatic fringe. What follows here, we hope, is a timely and necessary pursuit of the authorship question. Not one indulging the suggestion that William Shakespeare did not write his own work; rather, one seeking to determine the limits of what he did and did not write.

Adding to the Shakespeare canon can theoretically be achieved in two ways: either by discovering texts that as far as we can currently prove are no longer, or were never, there to be discovered, which has never happened; or, as this book will illustrate, by patiently scouring the lines of texts that do exist, which has proved frequently divisive and always difficult. The question of there really being any more Shakespeare still out there, staring us in the face, has been explored with almost maniacal vigour since the rise of serious scholarly editing and amateur enthusiasm for his work in the eighteenth century. Many of the attempts to answer 'yes' have lacked evidence, sound analysis, or even logic, while many recent studies have been scrupulously exacting and statistically precise. And it is to the careful, often overlooked labours of this latter group of scholars that we owe the stuff really worthy of a reader's attention. Though weakened by a longstanding tradition of wolf-crying around Shakespeare in general, claims regarding his authorship of the plays herein were, it seems, big after all: because some of them, under intense scrutiny, have proved almost certainly to be right. But before expanding on this, it will perhaps be useful to offer a sliding-scale taxonomy of works we believe genuinely likely, or not, to contain Shakespeare's writing, cases for which can be found in the individual essays that follow. The first rank covers roughly the territory from almost certain to very likely; the second might be described as worth considering; the third, highly unlikely to almost impossible:

I. *Sir Thomas More*, *Edward III*, *Arden of Faversham*, *The Spanish Tragedy* (with Additions), *Double Falsehood*
II. *Mucedorus* (with Additions)
III. *A Yorkshire Tragedy*, *The London Prodigal*, *Locrine*, *Thomas Lord Cromwell*

Oddly, perhaps, the strongest claims for Shakespearean authorship in this list have come to attach to three plays that name neither author nor company in their earliest textual states. This may seem counterintuitive considering that the four least likely plays name Shakespeare – suggestively in the case of the latter two – on their title pages, while *Arden of Faversham* and *Edward III* were published as anonymous Quartos in the early 1590s. *Sir Thomas More* exists only in manuscript, actually allowing us to see the different handwritings of its multiple authors, a rare scenario that many imagine as a sort of idealized panacea behind printed texts (the bibliographical scholar Fredson Bowers saw the 'veil of print' as covering the truths that original manuscripts would supposedly reveal).[2] Yet it only offers us a different set of intractable problems. As we have no other samples of Shakespeare's hand save only a few signatures with which to make a comparison, and cannot even be sure which company first performed the play, we are again left with a 'Shakespeare' section that is not a straightforward ascription. Notwithstanding, cases for his presence in *Edward III*, *Arden* and *More*, first advanced in 1760, 1770 and 1871 respectively, have become strong enough to be now considered almost certain among many scholars. Both *More* and *Edward III* have, in fact, been printed in commercial editions of Shakespeare's complete works, as well as in major series of individual plays under the Shakespeare banner. *Arden of Faversham*, an otherwise anonymous historical play from the early 1590s, is based on material found in Raphael Holinshed's *Chronicles*, the book on which Shakespeare drew so heavily for his cycle of English history plays in that decade. Although it has yet to find its way into a major edition of Shakespeare, two important studies within the last ten years claim to have all but confirmed his hand in a small section of the play.

This is instructive about how the authorship debate works both ways. Far from enabling these anonymous plays to pass under the radar, their very authorlessness recommends them for consideration as potential hidden Shakespearean gems, and as much interest has been stirred by his possible authorship of plays that do not bear his name as by those that do. This is not to say that these conclusions have been, and are still, without their detractors. Sir Brian Vickers, one of the world's leading scholarly practitioners of authorship attribution, has recently dismissed Shakespeare claims both old and new relating to *Arden of Faversham*, claiming it solely for the canon of Thomas Kyd, an early contemporary of Shakespeare with one securely acknowledged play to his name, the seminal Elizabethan masterpiece, *The Spanish Tragedy*. He also posits Kyd as Shakespeare's collaborator on *Edward III*, showing how candidacy for authorship of these apocryphal plays is continually in flux, and may always remain so as long as absolute proof is unattainable. The fact is that no piece of hard external evidence has been brought to light to prove once and for all that Shakespeare was involved in any of the plays herein. Jonathan Bate's General Introduction details the external textual evidence behind both the formation of the traditional canon and the attempts to expand it, to which the reader is directed for a wealth of context informing the following analyses. Title-page attributions to Shakespeare of plays excluded from the 1623 First Folio have been mostly deemed – with the exceptions of *Pericles* and *The Two Noble Kinsmen* – little more than mere guesswork or wishful thinking, not worth the paper they were printed on. So if we are not to believe what we read in old books, how then are we to know when or if we are looking at Shakespeare? The most reliable answer, it seems, lies in the notoriously tricky foundations of 'internal evidence'; that is, the evidence of the poetry itself. We must not look at what a book says, in other words; we must listen for how it says it.

'WHAT'S LIKE TO BE THEIR WORDS': THE CASE FOR INTERNAL EVIDENCE

Internal evidence begins with readers, familiar with the plays of Shakespeare, and, ideally, a good deal of other drama from the period, getting a 'feeling' from a piece of dramatic writing; a sense that somehow a scene or passage differs markedly in quality from the play around it. There will be a perception that stylistic features such as its imagery, linguistic richness, style, cadence, or dramatic mood are somehow more sophisticated or impressive – in short, more Shakespearean – than in the parts of the play from which this sense is absent. We may argue that all Elizabethan dramatists have this essential 'fingerprint'; the verse lines in iambic pentameter, filled with deliberate rhetorical contrivances – metaphor, allusion, imagery, rhyme, precise syntactical texture – that strive for emotional affect through poetic effect. So how can we claim, if all writers do this kind of thing, to be in Shakespeare territory? Although we can never definitively answer this there are nonetheless powerful qualities that distinguish Shakespeare's writing which the attribution scholar MacDonald P. Jackson attempts to describe:

> His achievement as a dramatist is inseparable from his achievement as a poet. In his verse words simply *do* more than in the verse of other playwrights. The language, with its kaleidoscopic show of imagery and allusion, is continually extending the range of experience gathered into the play, which becomes much more than a series of dramatized events. The poetry helps to transmit Shakespeare's sense of life and to create the imaginative world through which that sense of life is communicated. Rhythmically, the verse mimics the movements of the speaker's mind and heart. Visual and auditory elements enhance each other, as Shakespeare, writing for the bare Renaissance stage, conducts, by means of speech, a kind of 'movie-making for the mind's eye'.[3]

It would be fair to level the counterargument that it is only in the mind's eye of the beholder that such eulogistic judgements, lacking any empirical foundation, have a place. It is also frequently asserted, most often to discredit said eulogizing, that Shakespeare was not incapable of boring or simply functional passages in his plays, passages which would be difficult to distinguish from those of less accomplished writers. Probably also true. But proponents of this reasoning must acknowledge that it comes with a price. If they are stating that it is possible, routinely possible, in fact, to identify humdrum writing, then it necessarily follows that it is also possible to tell when we are witnessing its opposite. The more ordinary the passage the more potential authors behind it, including Shakespeare, who was also not the only dramatist from the period to do great things with language and dramatic affect. But Shakespearean highs are very high indeed, and there are many plays by more minor dramatists that simply do not fire with that linguistic alchemy both rich and strange, nor allow for such sustained, complex empathy or character interest on the part of the audience, while all of Shakespeare's acknowledged plays achieve this, at least in parts. Thus, if we encounter an anonymous passage which – and again, there can be no objective standard for this – strikes the reader as being both poetically impressive and dramatically compelling, then Shakespeare's body of work earns him the right to be at least shortlisted for candidacy as its author. Statements of this kind will naturally polarize readers, though debates about the deservedness of Shakespeare's cultural reputation notwithstanding, we are simply talking about literary judgement as a reasonable starting point for inquiry. Indeed, Ward Elliott and Robert Valenza, two leading exponents of computer-aided Shakespeare attribution, employ human cognition alongside their data in what they refer to as 'Golden Ear' tests. In this the sensory responses of readers are used as partial supporting evidence for their overall authorial profiling of plays.[4] Yet as they know, we cannot rely only on the sensation that we are in the presence of Shakespeare. Richard Proudfoot summarizes the problem we face:

> The individuality of Shakespeare is apparent to actors and students, to spectators and readers, but it is not easily resolved into transferable formulas which can form the basis of statistical demonstration of what he did or did not write.[5]

And yet it is necessary, however difficult, to try to do precisely this: to supplement our observations with the establishment and employment of a set of identifiable criteria for the ways in which Shakespeare's writing actually works, to see if our profile matches up with the characteristics of an anonymous passage. There is a robust strand of Shakespeare scholarship dedicated entirely to such demonstration, and MacDonald Jackson and others have made enormous leaps to devise methodologies whereby more forensic examinations of the language of Shakespeare and his contemporaries may be used to substantiate theories about authorship. Jackson's methods, devised in the 1970s as a continuation of the work of Cyrus Hoy, who in the 1950s pioneered this work in his attempts to discriminate between different authorial hands in the Beaumont and Fletcher Folio, sought to look beneath the veneer of poetic impression and into the nuts and bolts of language, to trace authors through the kinds of linguistic features that would usually slip under the radar.[6] To this end, more molecular stylistic markers in an author's work are considered, such as:

- **favoured contractions**: some writers prefer *I'll* to *I will*, *on't* to *on it*, *h'as* to *he has*, *'em* to *them*, *i'th* and *o'th* to *in the* and *on/of the*, and *e'en* to *even*, to name a few
- **metrics**: different writers show different habits in their verse patterns; Fletcher, for example, employs a lot of feminine endings – regular iambic pentameter lines with one extra syllable – in his verse, while some writers vary in the predictability of their stress or pause patterns
- **oaths**: some writers have swear words that they use more consistently than others, such as *pox*, *'sblood*, *zounds*, *by the mass*, *God's bread*; many of these proliferate commonly in the writing of the

period, but if a writer shows a particular fondness for one, its relatively high rate of occurrence in a given play/scene may work to suggest that writer's hand

- **prepositions:** some writers will favour *betwixt* over *between*, *whilst* over *while*, *amongst* over *among*, or use *on* instead of *of* ('I think not *on* my father', for example)
- **pronouns:** *you* can predominate over *ye* and vice versa, as with John Fletcher, Shakespeare's collaborator on *Cardenio*, *Henry VIII* and *Kinsmen*, who clearly favours *ye*; other writers favour *thee/thou* to *you*, or vice versa
- **verb forms:** some writers prefer *hath* to *has*, *doth* to *does*, and vice versa, or may, as Jonathan Hope pointed out, use auxiliary verbs more habitually than others (I *do* like, I *do* think, etc.)[7]

This list is by no means exhaustive; many other techniques, some far more advanced, have been employed in the 'stylometric' analysis of drama. Linguistic profiling of this kind relies on the idea that such choices are often merely unconscious; that a writer is betraying himself through stylistic tics that most people would disregard. Profiles for Shakespeare and for many contemporary writers, from the more major figures such as Ben Jonson, Thomas Middleton, John Fletcher and John Ford, to the lowlier likes of Henry Chettle, Thomas Dekker, George Chapman and George Peele, were drawn up by Jackson and David J. Lake, following on from such earlier pioneers as H. Dugdale Sykes, Muriel St Clare Byrne and Cyrus Hoy. Jackson and Lake's studies, although still considered eminent and paradigmatic, were confined to a narrow readership given the small circulation of their publication through academic presses.[8] The discipline was first brought to the attention of a wider audience by Gary Taylor in the *Textual Companion* that accompanied the flagship *Oxford Shakespeare* in 1987, along with detailed accounts of Shakespeare's activities as a co-author within his acknowledged canon. Taylor also detailed many categories of internal evidence useful in determining the chronology of plays and company ownership – of great help in attribution cases – as well as the identity of authors. Summarized briefly they are: theatrical provenance, quotations, verbal echoes, sources for plays (and when they were published), topical allusions, cast sizes, use of rhyme, biographical evidence, rhetorical evidence (an author's rhetorical tropes), vocabulary, linguistic evidence (including colloquialisms), verbal parallels and metrics.[9]

Taylor's work has since been variously tested, contested, bolstered and expanded upon by many others, including Hugh Craig, Marcus Dahl, Ward Elliott, Donald Foster, Jonathan Hope, John Jowett, Arthur F. Kinney, Thomas Merriam, Lene Petersen, Richard Proudfoot, Marina Tarlinskaja, Robert Valenza and Sir Brian Vickers. Remarkably, all early stylometric work was done by hand and eye, but in the last two decades computer databases of early modern drama with sophisticated search functions have made such Herculean labours relatively easy. What must have amounted for Jackson and Lake to years, maybe decades, of searching can now be done in seconds. Jackson continues to push attribution studies forward using innovative search techniques on the database Literature Online (LION), a subscription website containing literally thousands of literary texts that may be searched in a variety of ways. It has allowed for a new technique of collocation searches; that is breaking a passage down into two or three word chunks to see how rare or common they are in the drama of the period. Consider, for example, the following passage:

> Now is the winter of our discontent
> Made glorious summer by this sun of York:
> And all the clouds that loured upon our house
> In the deep bosom of the ocean buried.

As a poetic sample it is clearly interesting and arresting as a complete idea, but there are also standout constituent phrases within it. Database searching allows us to see how many instances there are of 'winter of our discontent', or 'this sun of York', though as Shakespeare's *Richard III* was enormously popular even in its own day we would not expect to find any that were not parodying, or relying on the reader to recognize, the source. But collocations such as 'now is the', 'by this sun', 'and all the', 'all the clouds', 'upon our house', might prove suggestive. Sometimes collocations that seem entirely innocuous can show strong links to an individual author if they appear, say, two or three times in their acknowledged works and nowhere in the works of others. If the passage in which they appear also shows other links to that author, such as the pronoun forms or contractions they favour, the kind of verse habits we might expect from them, as well as parallel images and a 'sense' of their presence, then we can be said to be much closer to certainty than we could ever be by relying on that sense alone. We do not need to carry out such testing on this passage as we know it to be by Shakespeare, but the linguistic data it contains can be applied comparatively to anonymous passages.

We now also have concordance programmes that can process a play as a text file and list its word frequencies in order. Predictably with any work the most hits will be produced by words like *the, a, and, of, that*; these are referred to as 'function words', and were employed by Gary Taylor in his stylometric work. In some cases this more apparently trivial data is very useful for author profiling. If, for example, one author seems prone to use *of* significantly more than another, we could use the frequency of its appearance in a scene (low or high) as partial evidence in suggesting an authorial presence. Yet sometimes even plays we know to be by a certain author will fall outside the 'baseline' statistics of their work (established by averaging the linguistic data from their known canon), showing that it is far from foolproof. More exotic 'lexical' words will appear far less frequently, but some of them can be shown to recur in a writer's work far more than another's, which is something we might not detect through reading alone, though we must always beware of coincidence and plagiarism. Jonathan Hope has pioneered a 'socio-linguistic' study of authorship, analysing uses of language we might expect from an author based on what we know of their regional and social backgrounds. This employs two main criteria for measuring language use: (1) the use of the auxiliary 'do' verb, and (2) 'relative marker' or 'relativization' evidence; that is the ways in which the relative pronouns 'that', 'who' and 'which' were used by writers in relation to personal and non-personal antecedents, for example 'that slave / *Which* told me' ..., or 'the elements / Of *whom* your swords are tempered' (*Coriolanus* 1.6.46–7, *The Tempest* 3.3.72–3). Hope's work has been important to authorship studies generally and to studies of the Shakespeare apocrypha, drawing unique attention as it does to the ways in which language shifted from region to region and from decade to decade in the period of the early theatres, and is referenced in many of the following entries. Marina Tarlinskaja's work looks intensively at the development of authors' habits of forming stress patterns in their lines of verse, and Brian Vickers has recently used anti-plagiarism software to detect authorial 'self-plagiarism' in multiple-word collocations, just some examples of the myriad ways in which we can dust for writers' 'fingerprints'.

Attribution studies then seek to find as many things that can be said to be characteristic of, or more likely to be used by, a particular author, to distinguish as many of these from the habits of other known authors, and to find as good a fit as possible between an author's profile and the features of a given passage or play. And yet as a pseudo-science it is bedevilled by an uncomfortable fact that many practitioners seem reluctant to acknowledge. Poetry is not a naturally occurring phenomenon: it is an artificial product of deliberate and considered work, and words, as units of measurement, never occur in predictable, patterned ways in poetry as nucleotides can be expected to do in a DNA strand. Poetry is at once both able to be broken down into units and stubbornly resistant to non-cognitive measurement. A poetic feat seeks always to distinguish itself, to avoid repetition, to innovate. Shakespeare was a daring and experimental writer, shifting genres, moods and poetic textures and styles throughout his career; his verse habits, for instance, fluctuate and morph surprisingly at different phases of his work. In a metrics test of an anonymous passage it would be necessary to measure it against Shakespeare plays from, or as close as possible to, the year of its composition, if that fact could be known or at least inferred. *Edward III* appeared in 1596, so it would be no good measuring its metrics against those of Shakespeare's late plays, containing as they do many more feminine endings, with crabbed, difficult and inverted stress patterns – seemingly Shakespearean experiments in his mature phase with the potential for verse to depict psychological turmoil through its sheer fractal architecture. The problem is not limited to Shakespeare, and in fact poetic impersonality can be as great an enemy to the statistician as adaptability and change:

> The task is at its most difficult with authors like John Dryden, whose stylistic repertoire exhibits unusual versatility; Edmund Waller, whose work changes radically over a long career; and an occasional hard case like Thomas D'Urfey, whose style is almost too colourless to yield a legible 'signature'. Unexpectedly perhaps, the stylistic repertoire of the man in the street is usually so narrow as to be easily distinguished from other styles.[10]

Adaptability and change, though, are Shakespearean problems. He deployed precisely chosen language and syntax to furnish, develop and exploit the dramatic moods he sought to bestow on different plays; from the crammed, elliptical, constrictive oddities of *Macbeth*'s tortured and unreal mental landscape, to the sonorous, poignant lyricism of *Othello*, the magical, imaginative playground of *A Midsummer Night's Dream*, or the strange, intellectual rigours of *The Tempest*. The thoughtful creation of a poetic texture to fit these moods frequently governs word choice or image patterns in his work: an analysis of *Macbeth*, for example, could give the impression that Shakespeare was particularly prone to use the words *blood*, *sleep*, *milk* and *nature*, while an analysis of *King Lear* on its own might suggest that Shakespeare particularly favoured images relating to eyes, sight and blindness. But these are intellectual concerns specific to these particular plays, and their development in tandem with the narratives in which they appear accounts for the locally high frequencies of related vocabulary. Shakespeare was a writer who tended to repeat himself very rarely, which does not mean that words do not recur throughout his works. But pure linguistic number crunching does not take into account the inventiveness of a word's use within its poetic and semantic contexts. This is critical to bear in mind if we try to dismiss them as evidence on the basis that other writers seem to use them no less frequently than Shakespeare. For example, the word 'cuff', used as a verb, meaning to hit or strike, is often used in literal senses in the drama of the period, found in such phrases as 'I swear I'll cuff you' (in *The Taming of the Shrew*, 2.1.221). Its appearance in *Edward III* though is much more singular and imaginative, figuratively deployed to suggest the threatening majesty of the opposing army's colours flapping in the wind, thoughtfully playing on the sense of the physical violence about to ensue, with a segue into the final arresting idea of the air itself as an abused lover receiving blows for kisses:

> And new-replenished pendants cuff the air
> And beat the winds, that for their gaudiness,
> Struggles to kiss them ...   (4.4.20–2)

It is a rich, evocative phrase put together, for the most part, from words that might seem fairly ordinary when viewed in isolation. This example is not intended to assert Shakespearean authorship of this passage – though it might also be observed that, in addition to the impressiveness of the language, joining a plural subject to a singular verb ('the winds ... Struggles') is a technique Shakespeare frequently used – but to illustrate the fact that statistical data can often fail to inform unless it is supplemented by close reading: considered appreciation of how the poetic language is functioning alongside lists of its individual constituent parts.[11] The appearance or non-appearance of a word within a statistical analysis is only a part of the story;

the mental construct within which that word has a precise function is something only literary analysis can discern. This is but one of the ways in which we slowly build a picture of an authorial profile through the combined 'evidence' of our senses and intellect, and through more scientifically rigorous methods to arrive, hopefully, at a reasonable consensus.

Yet even the best close analysis can only take us towards the realm of that we seek. We can never be more than 99 per cent certain in the absence of reliable external evidence that will finally confirm an author's presence, as seen in some high-profile success stories relating to linguistic forensics in the last twenty years. Ted Kaczynski, the notorious 'Unabomber', was tentatively identified on the strength of verbal parallels and similar phraseology perceived by his brother, David, between the 'Unabomber manifesto' – entitled *Industrial Society and its Future*, published in the *New York Times* and the *Washington Post* in September 1995 – and some of Kaczynski's letters to newspapers from the 1970s on similar themes, still in his brother's possession. The FBI conducted more detailed linguistic analysis between the manifesto and an essay Kaczynski had written in 1971, which established a very strong match, and a subsequent raid on Kaczynski's home in 1996 provided the investigators with all the evidence they needed to complete the conviction. The novel *Primary Colors*, which purported to describe Bill Clinton's 1992 presidential campaign, was published anonymously in 1996, amid a furore of controversy. Its actual author, the columnist Joe Klein, was identified through the stylometric analysis of Donald Foster, a professor at Vassar College, and no stranger to Shakespearean authorship arguments himself. At first Klein denied authoring the book and publicly denounced Foster's findings, though the *Washington Post* later published results from a handwriting analysis of annotation found on an early typescript of the book, and Klein reluctantly acknowledged the book as his. In both these cases the authorial subjects under investigation were living, and had grown up in a world in which comprehensive records are kept of individuals' activities and affiliations, effectively guaranteeing all the external evidence we could wish for when pursuing our modern-day suspects. What we are doing when we analyse early modern literature for the author beneath is essentially the same as we are doing when we perform acts of literary or historical criticism upon it: we are expressing our desire, in Stephen Greenblatt's famous formulation, to speak with the dead. And it is their inability to speak back to us that dictates the irresolvable nature of most early modern attribution cases.

We might draw further cause for despair by acknowledging that the pitfalls do not end with what has already been described, and attribution work must take stock of as many potential hazards as possible if it is to produce meaningful conclusions. To all of the above can be added a host of other objections to apparent discoveries of authorial 'discriminators'. Firstly, attribution work will always be governed partially by the practitioner's interpretation of evidence, or their theories about how co-authorship works, which may be at odds with what is actually happening in the text. In any instance, a writer could be modifying their style to accommodate the abilities or limitations of their co-author, or closely working together with them to make the play feel more of a piece, and not too jarringly schizophrenic in its linguistic and dramatic energies. In any given passage or play we could be witnessing conscious or unconscious imitation of the style of the other writer on the part of the collaborator (which does not only mean the other writer imitating the superior Shakespeare; we must allow for the possibility of this working the other way as well). We could equally be seeing a writer imitating the style of a writer not involved in the collaboration, or subtly plagiarizing little poetic flourishes or images that appealed to them from another writer's plays. One writer could be revising the other's work, or they could both have contributed passages and lines to the same scene as they were composing it, thus commixing and complicating the stylistic data we want or expect to find. If the attribution scholar assumes that the units of individual composition break down as whole scenes or acts then he/she will be blinded to this possibility: we need to consider that both writers may be present within a single scene, or even a single speech.

We also frequently find playwrights varying their favoured forms (*you* for *ye*, for example) within their solo-authored works for reasons that are impossible to explain. Perhaps, if such habits really are unconscious, a writer can be as likely to deviate from a relatively inconsequential norm as to revert to type, though again this is mere conjecture. Another routine feature of the early theatre is the revision and updating of plays for the purposes of revivals, frequently by other authors. When we are analysing any play that we know was revived prior to its printing, we must consider that it may contain material by someone else, perhaps even someone who could not have been involved in the original composition as they would have been too young, or not even born, at the time, so we must be extremely open-minded about the identities of possible other hands in a surviving play text. There is also the possibility of professional scribes, frequently employed to prepare legible copies of plays in the early modern theatre, or even compositors in the printing house, imposing their own habits in seemingly insignificant places. Ralph Crane, a professional scribe who worked for Shakespeare's company, the King's Men, is known to have prepared copies of some of Shakespeare's plays for the Folio including *The Tempest*, into which his spelling and punctuation habits made their way. Added to this are problems in establishing the data we are using; Ward Elliott and Robert Valenza used the appearance of hyphenated compound words such as 'tongue-tied' as an authorial discriminator in their work on *Edward III*, counting thirty-five in the Quarto text but noting, however, that the number went up to sixty-six when they modernized the text, acknowledging that this latter number is also problematic in that it relies on their interpretation of what is a compound versus a two-word combination.[12] Compounds in historical texts could sometimes be the product of printing house style, and this problem extends to all features of punctuation used as discriminators in the stylometric analysis of old-spelling texts. Anthony Graham-White provides a full account of the development of punctuation from the medieval into the early modern period, and identifies the problems surrounding punctuation in the works of playwrights in print:

> In drama of the sixteenth and seventeenth centuries we find a set of practices that changes over time and varies from playwright to playwright. Indeed, given the vagaries of copy transmission from holograph to printed edition, the punctuation in the works of a single playwright might vary from play to play and even from page to page within a single play, if set by more than one compositor.[13]

Printers wanted to eliminate error from their product for the sake of their professional reputations, yet the spelling and punctuation in early modern books still seem highly erratic by modern standards. If the almost entirely unpunctuated Hand D section in *Sir Thomas More* really typifies a Shakespearean manuscript then we can see that features of punctuation in printed texts are of little value as authorial markers when it comes to Shakespeare. The same is true when we look at modern editions of Shakespeare, which differ in hundreds, maybe thousands of localized details of grammatical and syntactical interpretation as different editors attempt the thorny job of modernization. Online databases such as LION simply reproduce in electronic form the old spelling texts that are themselves editions prepared by non-authorial agents, and carry the added potential for transcription errors by those employed to key in thousands of words of text, often in an unfamiliar language (much transcription work on literature databases is outsourced to the Far East).

It might seem then that we are irrecoverably mired, but the situation is not as gloomy as all this might seem to suggest, the problems not as endemic or prohibitive. All of the above examples are possible, and are sensible objections that we might raise, but they do not invalidate the enterprise of attribution studies. When imagining any one of these scenarios we must also allow for its opposite, or any number of alternatives. Going merely by what we can infer from the words that survive in historical documents, the various methods employed by scholars to determine the authorship of the plays that follow have been, albeit imperfect, rigorous, powerfully demonstrative and mutually reinforcing, and the most successful attribution work has been carried out by practitioners who have shown real awareness of all the pitfalls delineated above:

> The introduction of statistical analysis into literary studies merely highlights an ancient truth: with internal evidence we form our conclusions on the balance of probability. And that balance tilts in our favour when several independent tests yield mutually corroborative outcomes at high levels of confidence. That is why we must keep trying out the tests in cases where the truth is known.[14]

Any attribution of an anonymous passage to any writer based on stylistic (literary) and stylometric (statistical) analysis, no matter how sophisticated, must always come with caveats of uncertainty attached, and will always be met with as much scepticism as credulity, as long as absolute proof is absent. Any, all, or a combination of the aforementioned objections could be imagined as muddying the waters of any data we might proffer as evidence, and of course they will always haunt positive pronouncements in favour of Shakespeare or any other writer. It is right that they should give us pause as we approach the bench to deliver a verdict. And yet, if the methods used to arrive at that verdict are transparent, logical, provably effective and repeatable, reinforced by as many other kinds of empirical, impressionistic and biographical evidence as possible, and show us that a piece of writing that feels like Shakespeare also behaves like Shakespeare, we just might be justified in calling it Shakespeare after all.

PLAYS INCLUDED IN THIS EDITION

Arden of Faversham (c.1590)

Whoever wrote *Arden of Faversham* was one of the most innovative and daring talents the Renaissance theatre ever saw, and yet no contemporary record links this watershed work, written in or around 1590, to any author. It was a time when the public stage, and especially the genre of tragedy within it, was in its infancy. Thomas Kyd and Christopher Marlowe's radical overhauling of form was the foundation stone on which English secular tragedy was built; yet no sooner had they put into place dramatic principles that remade classical tragedy in their own image than *Arden of Faversham* appeared, announcing the real English revolution in drama.[15] It wasn't just made in England, it *was* England, bringing action into local places, into the here and now, and giving for the first time a voice to ordinary people in a new kind of domestic setting:

> Tragedy traditionally dealt with the falls of princes, but this play's protagonist is just plain old Master Arden. Tragedies laid their action long ago and far away, but *Arden of Faversham* dramatizes a murder which took place in an English provincial town only forty years earlier...English drama had seen nothing like it ever before...It takes Shakespeare's Cleopatra almost the whole play to realize that, though Queen of Egypt, she is dominated by the same passions as those which drive a milkmaid. That realization, from the other end on, is the conceptual starting point for these domestic tragedies.[16]

The play's mystery author is usually imagined to have come from the professional theatre scene, either one of the major playwrights provably working at the time, or another figure we may or may not know about, be they a dramatist who later rose to prominence, or an actor. Scepticism has largely dogged ascriptions to Shakespeare, Marlowe, and, to a lesser extent, Kyd, though so far no other candidate has emerged strongly or been tested comprehensively.[17] Kyd has been proposed more frequently than any other dramatist, seeming a particularly good fit not only because the time at which the play was written suits the hypothesis, but also because his one securely attributed work, *The Spanish Tragedy*, marks him out as a truly mature stage poet and an originary influence on the genre of revenge tragedy. On the basis of formal generic predisposition *Arden* is thoroughly unlike a Shakespeare tragedy, which always obeyed the rules in being set long ago (*King Lear*, *Macbeth*), far away (*Romeo and Juliet*, *Othello*), or, more typically, both (*Titus Andronicus*, *Julius Caesar*, *Hamlet*, *Timon of Athens*, *Antony and Cleopatra* and *Coriolanus*). If Kyd had already redefined tragedy a mere three years earlier, why might he not be doing it again with *Arden of Faversham*?

Searching for Kyd within *Arden*, however, involves acknowledgement that we have only a very small secure canon against which to test, his other work being second-hand, insecurely attributed or no longer extant. We know he translated Robert Garnier's French neoclassical play, *Cornelia*, in 1594, though fairly brittle evidence is all that links him to two other works with which he is traditionally associated: the anonymous *Soliman and Perseda* (1592), on the basis of perceived similarities to *The Spanish Tragedy*, and the 'Ur-*Hamlet*', a lost play apparently based on the Hamlet story. Thomas Nashe, in the preface to Greene's *Menaphon* (1589), launched an attack on 'a sort of shifting companions' and their uninspired plundering of 'English Seneca' for content, which he mockingly suggests 'will afford you whole Hamlets, I should say handfuls of tragical speeches'. A few lines later he makes a pun on Kyd's name, which many accept as implying Kyd's authorship of a lost Hamlet play, and the debts Shakespeare's *Hamlet* owes *The Spanish Tragedy* are obvious and well discussed.[18] It is perhaps fitting that in addition to initiating the genre of revenge tragedy on the public stage, Kyd may also have written a play that Shakespeare was to rework into its greatest exemplar. But even if we accept Kyd to be the author of a Hamlet play as the follow-up to his one undisputed bequest to English tragedy, *Arden of Faversham*, whichever way we look at it, is an altogether different animal.

The size of Marlowe and Shakespeare's canons means that there is plenty of material available for comparative analysis, and it has proved hard to pin *Arden* on either of them on hunch-driven, stylistic grounds. Nobody has ever seriously proposed Robert Greene or George Peele, though neither has been considered capable of a play of *Arden*'s visionary originality and poetic strength. Sometimes the more we know about a writer's style the more that knowledge can weaken cases for their potential authorship of anonymous works. Conversely, however, Martin Wine observes that although the comparative neglect of the Shakespeare question regarding *Arden* has been a good thing as it has 'tended to focus closer attention upon its merits as a work of dramatic literature', recognition of the play's considerable poetic and dramatic merits has led to the 'unintentional result' of bringing Shakespeare's name 'in again by the back door'.[19] In other words, the better the play, the more likely it is to be Shakespeare. Although many critics have concurred with Kenneth Muir's consideration of *Arden* as the 'best of the apocryphal plays', and while the Shakespeare canon shows us that it is not unreasonable to conceive of Shakespeare as someone likely to write a good play, such judgements will not do as serious criteria for a positive attribution, just as subjective judgements about Greene and Peele's writing will not do for a negative one.[20]

Arden was entered in the Stationers' Register by the bookseller Edward White on 3 April 1592 and printed sometime later that year, probably, on the basis of the appearance of an ornament used at the end of the text, by Edward Allde, to whom the rights in publishing the play were transferred in 1624. A Stationers' Court record of 18 December 1592 shows that White and the printer Abel Jeffes both got into trouble that year for each printing texts that belonged to the other; White paid Allde to print *The Spanish Tragedy*, which belonged to Jeffes, and Jeffes printed *Arden of Faversham*. Jeffes had been imprisoned on 7 August and so his edition is likely to have appeared before that date and to have been a reprint of White's, although no copies of it survive. If they did, we can probably assume they would be as unforthcoming as White's, three copies of which survive, on the subject of authorship. White issued a second edition in 1599, printed by James Roberts, and Allde's widow, Elizabeth, issued a third in 1633. Perhaps the most striking detail to take from all three title pages is not that they do not name an author (this was entirely normal, especially at the beginning of the

1590s), but that they do not name a theatre company. What this means is that there is effectively no evidence for the play having been performed in the early theatres, with the first concrete records of its being acted at all dating from the eighteenth century. The unanswered question of provenance has proved especially significant for *Arden*'s recent editors in their discussions of authorship; if it wasn't owned or performed by a professional theatre company are we then still looking at the work of a professional dramatist? Martin White argues that we are, citing a list of the play's technical, linguistic and dramatic attributes in support of the conclusion that 'whoever wrote this play had direct, practical experience of the theatre'.[21] He reviews some of the arguments that had been made for the play's authorship prior to 1982, when his edition was published, naming all the major suspects of the early 1590s professional theatre – Greene, Peele, Kyd, Marlowe and Shakespeare – and, though adjudging the matter impossible to determine, settling on a professional dramatist:

> The undoubted strengths of the play – the complexity of its characterization, the linking of language and themes, the interweaving of public and private issues, and the constant awareness of the potential of the theatrical experience – demonstrate that the author was a master playwright, but one whose identity must remain (at least on present evidence), tantalisingly unknown.[22]

Martin Wiggins, however, takes an entirely contrary line by pointing to a technical naivety in the play's construction that betrays a writer with no practical experience of the mechanics of staging:

> He was not a theatre professional. He was certainly familiar with the new wave of tragedy which developed in the late 1580s, driven by the innovations of Marlowe and Kyd. He had seen and appreciated *The Spanish Tragedy*, which was still unpublished when *Arden* saw print, for he imitates one of its more memorable lines (4.88). He knew the theatre but he did not really know how it worked: as a practical stage-writer he was immensely inexperienced, even naïve.[23]

The dramaturgical and technical flaws Wiggins identifies can be summarized thus:

- Frequent discontinuities in the action, exemplified by the delivery of Greene's letter by Bradshaw in scene 8, given to him in scene 2, which mentions persons and events that hadn't been introduced when the letter was given.
- The part of Alice, at around 600 lines, places demands on a boy apprentice actor that were not usually made by professional companies. Typically, boys' parts in professional companies of the early 1590s were about 200–300 lines, compared to 600–800 for a leading man.
- The author frequently conjures up locale and travel in his mind's eye, without thinking about how that practically translates to the limited onstage and backstage areas of the theatre.
- The dramatist has not thought through the incident where Shakebag becomes 'bewrayed' with filth when he falls into a ditch. The actor must either (a) have a bucket of mud thrown on him by a stage hand when he falls through the trap, which would create problems of damaging expensive clothes or at least having to clean them after each performance; or (b) change into an already muddied costume, an action for which the dialogue does not offer enough time.
- Key moments of action for which no accompanying, or covering, dialogue is provided: when Arden begins to eat the poisoned broth and later when the murderers take his body out, leaving Alice alone onstage with nothing to say or do. Similar moments in professional plays keep the momentum going with a speech or piece of dialogue during moments in which practical actions, which are likely to take at least 15–30 seconds, are carried out.

So the proof that our writer was not a professional does not only rest in the evidence within the text of his practical inexperience; the very fact that these dramaturgical problems remain agrees with the complete lack of external evidence for performance in suggesting that the play had probably never been put on its feet in 1592. Of course, we are in danger of overstating the case. Other plays that we know were performed abound with inconsistencies of plot (even Shakespeare's), and Shakebag's muddied costume could be explained away as a piece of imaginative stage convention ('Think, when we talk of horses, that you see them'). As for the play's being staged, all we can say for certain is that the copy from which the Quarto was printed was not theatrical in that it lacks the kinds of notation made by theatre personnel relating to practical performance issues – such as props, entrances and sound cues – found in many printed plays of the time. But that does not mean that a professional company never performed *Arden of Faversham*.

Some scholars have claimed that the 1592 text is defective, containing what Alfred Hart termed 'harsh or unmetrical' lines, echoes of other plays, and incoherencies of plot, in attempts to establish that it is the product of a memorial reconstruction. This conclusion has been taken as evidence that it must therefore have been performed, though it would have severe repercussions for stylometric analysis, as Gary Taylor has pointed out. If it is a memorial reconstruction, it is a remarkably good one, as many of the speeches are rich with powerful, precise imagery, strikingly inventive turns of phrase, lacking the logical inconsistencies and narrative lacunae characteristic of some supposedly pirated texts. Wiggins adjudges the reported text claims 'wildly overstated', and argues that the perceived defects are 'equally explicable as marks of authorial inexperience'.[24] He states that the play:

> was certainly not written by a mid-career Marlowe, nor by a Shakespeare making his first tentative move across from acting into script-writing, nor by Kyd, nor Greene, nor Peele, nor any other experienced commercial playwright, nor an enterprising actor...The play's strengths and weaknesses suggest instead the work of an enthusiastic amateur – or, in modern terms, a fan.[25]

Other characteristics Wiggins identifies in *Arden*'s author are that he knew Ovid's *Amores* well enough to play on one of them in one of Arden's speeches from the opening scene, demonstrating a 'broader-than-usual classical education', and that he 'knew north Kent intimately'.[26] Both of these lend themselves circumstantially to an attribution to Marlowe, who translated the *Amores* and who was a native of Canterbury, and yet the play has never really been made to stick to him on any stylistic grounds. Wiggins' views on the matter of the dramatist being an unknown amateur were undeterred by vigorous reappraisals of the play's authorship that had been undertaken in the last decade using detailed stylometric methods, chiefly by MacDonald Jackson, who proposes Shakespeare's hand in the play, and by Brian Vickers, who gives the play in its entirety to Kyd. More recently Arthur F. Kinney has supported Shakespeare's presence in the play. Not only does Wiggins' hypothesis contradict the conclusions of these current stylometric arguments, but much of the entire attribution history of the play, which has for the most part similarly sought either to affirm or to rubbish ascriptions to known dramatists.

Arden of Faversham did not appear in any of the four Folio editions of Shakespeare's plays, though it is likely to have been attributed to Shakespeare in Edward Archer's frequently dubious catalogue of 1656: W. W. Greg argued plausibly that the 'Rich. Bernard' next to the *Arden* entry was in fact mislineated, and it is Shakespeare, whose name appears directly above, Archer intended to nominate as author.[27] Even if this is right, Archer's list contains many wildly inaccurate ascriptions of plays to Shakespeare, so this one cannot be taken as authoritative. His list is essentially an expansion of the one that had appeared in the 1656 edition of Thomas Goffe's *The Careless Shepherdess*, in which no author was named for *Arden*, so where his information came from is difficult to determine. The first scholarly attempt to assert Shakespeare's authorship was made in 1770 by *Arden*'s earliest editor, Edward Jacob, though Tucker Brooke derides Jacob's evidence as 'a scant half-page of parallel phrases' which he dismisses as 'of so general a character as to prove nothing at all, beyond the obvious fact that *Arden of Faversham* and Shakespeare both belong to the Elizabethan period'.[28] Interest in the matter was revived in the nineteenth century, and focussed almost exclusively on Shakespeare, with such luminaries as Charles Knight, Nicholas Delius, G. B. Kuitert, François-Victor Hugo, W. J. Courthope and Algernon Charles Swinburne arguing in favour of the attribution, meeting with resistance from Hermann Ulrici, Henry Tyrrell, A. H. Bullen, Karl Warnke, Ludwig Proescholdt, the Rev. Ronald Bayne, and, at the turn of the century, J. A. Symonds. However, Symonds, Tyrell and Bullen came round to believe that Shakespeare could have been involved as a reviser or corrector. C. F. Tucker Brooke argued against the Shakespeare attribution and adjudged the 'balance of critical opinion' to have largely come to rest on 'the side of respectful incredulity' in his 1908 edition of *The Shakespeare Apocrypha*.[29] And he was largely right; F. G. Fleay's 1891 proposal of Thomas Kyd as the *Arden* dramatist was taken up in the following decade by Charles Crawford and Walter Miksch – Tucker Brooke adjudged the arguments for Kyd to hold 'a considerable degree of plausibility' – and was to dominate the majority of twentieth-century scholarship on the matter up until the late 1960s, finding favour with such scholars as H. Dugdale Sykes, J. M. Robertson, Felix E. Schelling, T. S. Eliot, H. B. Charlton, R. D. Waller, Marion Grubb, Philip Henderson, William Wells, P. V. Rubow and Felix Carrère.[30] Those who proposed Kyd slightly more tentatively included Willard Farnham, Kenneth Muir, Alan S. Downer, A. P. Rossiter, W. Bridges Adams, Wilfred T. Jewkes, José Axelrad and Michelle Willems, while Peter Alexander, F. W. Bateson, Philip Edwards, Zdeněk Stříbrnỳ and Arthur Freeman all expressed varying degrees of doubt about Kyd's involvement.

The other major candidate was Christopher Marlowe, whose great champion was E. H. C. Oliphant, though, as already stated, widespread and lasting belief in the ascription never really took hold. Oliphant first rubbished the claim for Shakespeare in his 1911 article, 'Problems of Authorship in Elizabethan Dramatic Literature', in which he stated: '*Arden*'s claim to rank even among the Shakspere [*sic*] apocrypha is on external evidence absolutely *nil*; nor is it his on the internal evidence'.[31] He aligned himself with the Kyd hypothesis but also stated an equal conviction in Marlowe's presence, adjudging the play 'full of Marlowe parallels' – in spite of A. H. Bullen's statement to the contrary – and proposing 'numerous instances in which lines occurring in Marlowe's plays are found'.[32] Oliphant's position can hardly be considered solid; external evidence for Shakespeare's authorship is very weak for all the 'apocryphal' plays, while his internal analysis is limited solely to verbal parallels, a highly problematic category of evidence which is at the centre of one of the most current debates surrounding *Arden*'s authorship. Oliphant reaffirmed his position a decade later, and within another four years restated it to give the larger portion of the play to Marlowe, with his collaborators possibly having been Kyd and Samuel Rowley. Tucker Brooke countered Oliphant's claims, though Marlowe continued to find limited favour, with Percy Allen and M. B. Smith independently proposing three-way collaboration with Kyd and Shakespeare, and Frederick S. Boas, John Bakeless and Gabriele Baldini all allowing for the possibility that Marlowe had written the play unaided. Other candidates were also sporadically put forward, with Anthony Munday proposed by H. W. Crundell, and George Wilkins tentatively suggested by no less a figure than Kenneth Tynan. Dorothy and Charlton Ogburn made the eccentric claim that Lord Oxford had written it, and A. W. Titherley joined the ranks of authorship conspiracy fantasists when he suggested that responsibility lay with William Stanley, sixth Earl of Derby, who was, of course, the person also responsible for the works of Shakespeare. Felix Sper asserted that the authorship was impossible to determine, though was convinced it was collaborative, while E. K. Chambers similarly ruled that the play must be considered anonymous. Wiggins' conclusions, though not his analyses, were mirrored much earlier in the century, with Louis Gillet ruling in favour of an otherwise unknown contemporary of Shakespeare, and F. S. Boas of someone imitating Kyd's style.

The Shakespeare question resurfaced from time to time, with James Agate, Max J. Wolff, W. W. Greg, Kenneth Tynan and Kenneth Muir all rejecting claims for his authorship, the possibility of which was nonetheless upheld by Clara Longworth, and, in perhaps the first serious stylometric study of the play, by a young MacDonald Jackson in an unpublished B.Litt. thesis undertaken at Oxford in 1963. All of the arguments detailed above, apart from Jackson's, were based on purely impressionistic grounds, either by forming judgements of a writer's style or by drawing verbal parallels between the play and other works from the period. Samuel Schoenbaum, writing in 1966, debunked in large part the methodology and results of parallel passage analysis and noted that: 'The conjecturists seem to have given up on *Arden of Feversham* [*sic*]. This shift may be due in part to changes in sensibility, in part to recognition of the law of diminishing returns'.[33] Over the following twenty years the matter of *Arden*'s authorship was indeed largely abandoned, despite it being edited four times. Martin Wine's 1973 edition is the most thorough, surveying much scholarship up to that date, though he ultimately preferred caution to any conjectural claim, as did T. W. Craik and Martin White. Russell A. Fraser and Norman Rabkin alone among the editors pronounce definitively on the matter, stating 'conclusively' that 'Shakespeare did not write the play'.[34] Keith Sturgess, however, in a review of Wine's edition, expressed the belief that the 'quarrel scene' in the play was Shakespeare's. Alexander Leggatt surveyed many of the play's speeches and ideas and paralleled them with the tone of later works by Shakespeare, Middleton and Webster, not, as he says, to suggest the author's identity, but his influence:

> What the *Arden* playwright has done, I think, is to open a vein of realism in Elizabethan drama to run beside and later enrich the heroics of tragedy and the romantic fantasy of comedy. It is a realism that consists of a hard, tough appraisal of things as they are, and a resistance to conventional formulae.[35]

However, in 1987 Gary Taylor reopened stylometric inquiry into the matter. He performed a detailed statistical function-word analysis, looking specifically at the usage of the words *but, by, for, no, not, so, that, the, to,* and *with* within the Shakespeare core canon, and measuring the rates of deviation in their appearance in twenty-eight provably non-Shakespearean, and three apocryphal, plays, including *Arden*. Of all the plays tested, *Arden* ranked second behind Marlowe's *Edward II* in having the fewest standard deviations from Shakespeare. Of course Shakespearean authorship is not proved; a play by Marlowe is closer to the Shakespeare mean, and both have fewer deviations than *The Two Gentlemen of Verona, King Lear* and the *Sonnets*, highlighting the manifold problems of internal evidence, no matter how rigorously scrutinized. Taylor is right in saying that the play cannot be 'decisively endorsed or vetoed by this particular test', though the closeness of fit is indeed intriguing.[36] MacDonald Jackson returned to the question in 1993 with a highly technical analysis of many facets of the syntactical and linguistic idiosyncrasies of Shakespeare's early poetic language, and how it is mirrored in *Arden*. It was a non computer-aided study, taking place as it did prior to the development of the online corpora that would make possible the testing he subsequently undertook, in a series of articles fortifying his case for Shakespeare's presence.[37] He, along with Jayne Carroll, used Literature Online to search for 'rare links between *Arden of Feversham* and the works of the most prominent playwrights of the 1580s and early 1590s', finding links with the group of early Shakespeare plays used as control 'almost twice as frequent as links with Marlowe, exactly twice as frequent as links with Greene, and over five times more frequent than links with Peele'.[38] Jackson also prepared a list of compound adjectives, some very unusual, in the play and tested them on LION against 'all plays first performed within the period 1580–1600'.[39] The results are indeed striking, with only nine of the more than 130 plays within these limits containing three or more of the *Arden* adjectives, five of them being by Shakespeare, either solo-authored or in collaboration (*Henry VI Part 2, Titus Andronicus, The Comedy of Errors, Henry V* and *Edward III*). Moreover,

Jackson notes: 'Between them the twenty-three Shakespeare plays of the period use fifteen of the *Arden* adjectives, while the more than one hundred other plays use twenty.'[40]

Jackson narrowed this study using the same search limits onto scene 8, or the 'quarrel scene', finding twenty-eight plays that share four or more collocation and rare phrase links with it, eighteen by Shakespeare, with the top eight in terms of numbers of links being also all by Shakespeare. With an aim similar to his 1993 study, Jackson also used LION to analyse some of the 'complex congeries of words, ideas, and images that occur and recur in the Shakespeare canon' as part of a comparative study with the poetry of scene 8. The results delivered an astonishingly close association with Shakespeare's *Rape of Lucrece* (1594), with Jackson noting that 'no non-Shakespearean passage of 250 lines in any work of literature in English shares with the quarrel scene so many images, image subjects, and key vocabulary words'.[41]

Ward Elliott and Robert Valenza's tests ruled out Shakespeare's involvement in *Arden* because of its ten rejections from their Shakespeare baseline: they note 'of twenty-nine plays in our Shakespeare core baseline, only seven have as many as two Shakespeare rejections in forty-eight tests. Of fifty-one plays by Shakespeare claimants, none has fewer than ten Shakespeare rejections (aspects of liguistic profiling which contraindicate Shakespeare).'[42] This, they argue, puts the play well outside the realms of probability for Shakespearean involvement, and yet Jackson notes that *Henry VI Part 1* also has ten rejections in their tests and is therefore left off their baseline, despite it being 'undoubtedly at least partly by Shakespeare', and argues that their tests 'do not rule out the possibility that *Arden* is too'.[43] More recently, Brian Vickers has argued that Thomas Kyd is the play's sole author based on the use of anti-plagiarism software 'devised by the law faculty of Maastricht University to counteract student plagiarists' with which he claimed 'to study self-plagiarism, Elizabethan authors' re-cycling of their own work'.[44] Vickers came up with a large number of Kyd parallels, though the Kyd canon he defined was larger than many scholars allow, including *King Leir* and *Henry VI Part 1*. Jackson published a rebuttal arguing Vickers' methodology was indistinct from early parallel passage attribution, which merely represented a narrow critical prejudice at the expense of wider search limits. Jackson comes up with many alternative examples of 'self-plagiarism', claiming to have found more unique *Arden* matches in *Henry VI Part 2* and *The Taming of the Shrew* than in 'any of Kyd's plays'.[45] Arthur Kinney's recent stylometric analysis takes in the kind of observations so common among sensitive early twentieth-century readers such as Sykes and Oliphant. He points to a complexity of imagery beyond the scope of that encountered in plays by other early 1590s dramatists, to the repeated use of 'an unfolding soliloquy or monologue in which a character's insight develops before us', and to a rich ambiguity characterizing the whole piece, all of which he proffers as Shakespearean traits that bolster the linguistic data.[46] His function and lexical word tests prove to be, he argues, 'mutually reinforcing' in suggesting that the play is co-authored, that Shakespeare is one of the authors, and that 'his part is concentrated in the middle section of the play'.[47] His results also argue strongly against Kyd and Marlowe.

In an article responding to these findings, Jackson furthers the analysis, consolidating the conclusions that Shakespeare is most strongly present in scenes 4–9, broadly speaking the Act 3 section of the play, the equivalent section, incidentally, in which Craig and Kinney's tests yield the strongest evidence for Shakespeare's hand in *Henry VI Part 2*, another early play, which they and others are beginning to now regard as collaborative.[48] Jackson follows Michael Neill's observations about the importance of the vocabulary of social status in *Arden*, and to them adds Craig and Kinney's identifications of some of these words as favoured lexical items in the Shakespeare canon. Indeed, only *Arden*, *A Midsummer Night's Dream* and *Henry V* of all plays dated 1575–1600 call for the assembled 'gentles' to 'pardon' what they have seen in a prologue or epilogue. Not only does Jackson rule out Marlowe and Kyd as collaborators, he also suggests that the beginning and ending sections of the play, although possibly contaminated by faulty textual transmission, are suffused throughout with the ideas and imagery of status favoured by Shakespeare. He suggests it is not inconceivable that they were 'written by Shakespeare at a stage of his career before a style recognizable by the Craig-Kinney tests had been formed', and that if the play was indeed collaborative, the process 'must have been close, with the co-authors sharing the same grim vision, though one enlivened by humour'.[49]

The resultant picture is therefore extremely difficult to determine. Lexical and image analyses have proved very strong in arguments for Shakespeare's authorship of at least one scene, and probably more, in the middle of the play, although these findings are difficult to reconcile with other circumstantial facts and vagaries. *Arden* predates all of Shakespeare's acknowledged tragedies, and so could represent an early, failed Shakespearean experiment (assuming, that is, it was never performed), a youthful collaboration, or a work of revision, though links to Shakespeare could also perhaps be the product of extreme coincidence or plagiarism. If the latter, *Lucrece* was not written in 1592, so Shakespeare could indeed be the borrower, though Jackson's argument is aimed more at suggesting that the same imagination is at work in both texts. Shakespeare elsewhere shows himself a very rare self-plagiarist, though we cannot rule out any possibility. If, as some scholars believe, the play could have been written as early as 1588, then the evident theatrical inexperience could be Shakespeare's. We also cannot state definitively that the play was never performed, though if it was not that might go a long way towards explaining why domestic tragedy took so long to catch on in theatres. Wiggins points out that the prologue to Thomas Heywood's *A Woman Killed With Kindness*, one of the first domestic tragedies to come after *Arden of Faversham*, shows that 'a tragedy without any high politics was still unusual enough to require specific acknowledgement' when it was written, performed and printed in 1603.[50] What we can know and infer from the surviving and lost tragedies recorded in Harbage's *Annals of English Drama* for the years between 1590 and 1603 shows that the genre indeed tended almost exclusively to represent classical subject matter. This makes *Arden* all the more remarkable as a genuinely original dramatic template that it would take the theatres more than a decade to catch up to, the genre only really establishing itself in the Jacobean repertory in plays like *A Yorkshire Tragedy* (1605) and *The Miseries of Enforced Marriage* (1606).[51]

That said, stylometric work on the play has grown in such mutually reinforcing strength that Jackson, although still on the cusp of pushing further to suggest Shakespearean involvement throughout the play, nonetheless deems the probability of his presence 'so high that *Arden of Faversham* seems no less worthy than *Edward III* of inclusion in the canon'.[52] We feel there is sound evidence to suggest strongly Shakespeare's involvement in scene 8 at least, although we still do not know by whom, and under what circumstances, the rest of the play was written, just as we cannot know the circumstances of its textual transmission. But we still offer it to readers of this volume as one of the finest plays that a young Shakespeare, possibly, never wrote.

Locrine (c.1586?, revised c.1591–95)

Locrine was entered to Thomas Creede in the Stationers' Register on 20 July 1594, and printed by him in 1595, the date given on the Quarto's title page. The play's epilogue makes reference to the 'eight and thirty years' of Elizabeth's reign, meaning publication must, as R. B. McKerrow pointed out, have been somewhere between 17 November 1595, when the thirty-seventh anniversary of the accession had been celebrated, and the following 24 March (New Year's Eve in old, Annunciation-style dating). That the thirty-eighth year is meant is likelier than the text being out by one, though the more important thing is that somebody clearly made this alteration prior to publication. Who that was is cryptically identified in the title-page statement:

Newly set foorth, ouerseene and corrected,
By *W. S.*

This has of course given rise to centuries' worth of debate about the identity of 'W. S.' and the nature of his involvement. Certainly the editors of the 1664 Third Folio took the abbreviation to signify Shakespeare, including the play alongside six other apocryphal works, though the Quarto was seemingly the only basis for this judgement. If Shakespeare is implied, it is unusual that it would be another three years before his name first appeared in full on a title page (the 1598 Quarto of *Love's Labour's Lost*). Plays later attributed to him, either suggestively or explicitly, came about when he was a major figure in both the theatrical and publishing worlds, while in 1595 he was still an emergent force as a stage poet in print. He had, however, enjoyed tremendous success with his non-dramatic poems, *Venus and Adonis* and *The Rape of Lucrece* (1593–94), his one deliberate publishing experiment, and was therefore a selling point for a demographic of bookbuyers by the time of *Locrine*'s publication. He had also acquired a strong popular reputation as a dramatist, and we must consider the possibility that it is here being taken on trust that these initials would readily imply him.

We must also decipher what is meant by both 'newly set forth' and 'overseen and corrected'. Are we to read this accreditation as a list, or as two separate statements? If the former, then connotations of authorship, or at least revision of an old play, perhaps rest in 'newly set forth', as Jane Lytton Gooch has argued.[53] Baldwin Maxwell observes that it has also been read as implying another Quarto edition preceded it, which he dismisses on the strength of other title-page claims, such as *Tamburlaine*'s (1590) 'Now first, and newly published'.[54] It would be useful in this case to have a word as unambiguous as 'published': could 'newly set forth' mean recently authored from scratch? If so, 'overseen and corrected' could refer exclusively to printing house activities, and Laurie Maguire gives multiple examples of authorial proofing and correction during the printing process, such as Marston's explanation that his:

> 'enforced absence' from the printing house obliged him to 'rely upon the printer's discretion' in the first quarto of *The Malcontent* (1604).[55]

She also records how:

> The printer of Reginald Scot's *A perfite platforme of a Hoppe Garden* (1574) reveals that 'M Scot could not be present at the printing of this his Booke whereby I might have used his advice in the correction of the same'.[56]

Breaking the title-page information up into two statements, however, are we to infer that this play, whether new or old, was being printed for the first time and that 'W. S.' was simply the one who saw it through the press, as Leonard R. N. Ashley contends:

> But in any case, could we prove that the 'W.S.' of the quarto was William Shakespeare (and I cannot see how this could be done) we would still have a more important question left unanswered: who composed the work that 'W.S.' was preparing for the press? Many of the critics who quote or mention the quarto's title page do not seem to have grasped what it so clearly says: the W.S., whoever that was, was not the author of the play.[57]

Maxwell argues that the Quarto's many errors, as well as the fact that there are no variants within the five copies collated by McKerrow, means that close proofreading by anyone is unlikely to have been undertaken, and that the claim more likely refers to a reworking or revision of the play. Adding to the complexity, Gooch points out that the two statements could be separated elsewhere: 'The question arises whether the phrase

"By W. S." is meant to refer to the whole play or only to the revisions; the more likely case would be that "W. S." is the reviser.' Maybe so, but following this logic the claim could equally be that the play was originally 'By W. S.', and has been revised and corrected by someone else. We might also read it as a play 'By W. S.' which has not been revised, and is simply being printed carefully and diligently for the first time. Gooch, like Maxwell, opts for the interpretation that 'W. S.' is being proffered as the play's reviser. However, Peter Kirwan has argued that the designation 'set forth by' almost always appears on works of translation or anthology, suggesting we are perhaps looking, more simply, at a work that 'W. S.' has prepared rather than authored.[58]

Locrine was in fact several years old in 1595 and the title-page statement seems to anticipate its audience knowing this. Although its provenance is mysterious it is associated with the Queen's Men in its early days, and G. K. Hunter has shown that it was one of a number of plays released for publication in 1594 from companies broken by the long plague closures of 1593–94.[59] It must have seemed an antiquated beast by then, though Hunter speaks of the pragmatism of the Admiral's/Chamberlain's duopoly in mixing the old with the new in their repertories as part of their ever-shifting experiments with audience appeal. The Quarto is unusual in the way it refers to the role 'W. S.' played, though perhaps it speaks to unusual circumstances. If the Chamberlain's Men, of the two companies operating in London in 1595, had acquired the play, then Shakespeare would be their most obvious script doctor. The only change we can confidently identify is the reference to Elizabeth's reign, though Sonia Massai suggests 'W. S.' wrote the Epilogue in its entirety, possibly for a court performance with the Queen's Men, with whom she claims Shakespeare was associated in his early career.[60] She suggests the changing of the date could be the point at which Shakespeare the company man meets Shakespeare the author in print, showing his continued sense of obligation to an ex-patron, though nonetheless urges that it is not the actual but the implied Shakespearean authorship that dominates *Locrine*'s paratexts. Nonetheless, there is no direct evidence that Shakespeare was ever associated with the Queen's Men (see essays on *The Spanish Tragedy* and *Edward III*), and we cannot be sure when and by whom the *Locrine* epilogue was first written. Did 'W. S.' simply 'set forth' the text his company had acquired in having it printed, overseeing the job and supplying minor corrections only?

If we believe that Shakespeare is implied then this seems an attractive explanation, more so because of the good internal and external evidence to suggest that extensive revision was carried out on the play sometime between 1591 and 1594. Scholarship had consistently connected *Locrine* to the late 1580s school of drama by the University Wits, within which Marlowe was the only stage poet of real distinction, alongside such acolytes as Robert Greene and George Peele, who copied his style in such plays as *Alphonsus, King of Aragon* and *The Battle of Alcazar*. Baldwin Maxwell's analysis, however, was concerned with showing that *Locrine* was composed later than previously thought on the strength of its verbal borrowings from Spenser's *Complaints*, not published until 1591. Nonetheless, he gave it to Greene (d.1592) or Peele (d.1596), ignoring the issue of revision and relegating to a dismissive footnote what is probably the strongest external evidence for the play's original authorship. A manuscript note on an extant copy of the 1595 Quarto, apparently in the hand of Sir George Buc, later Master of the Revels, attributes the play to Charles Tilney (cousin of Edmund, Buc's predecessor), and gives the original title of the play as *Estrild*.[61] Buc himself also claims to have supplied dumb shows:

> Char. Tilney wrote< a>
> Tragedy of this mattr <w^{ch}>
> hee named Estrild: <& w^{ch}>
> I think is this. it was l<ost?>
> by his death. & now s<ome?>
> fellow hath published <it.>

I made dūbe shewes for it.

wch I yet haue. G. B<.>⁶²

We do not know when Buc made this note: it could have been any time between 1595 and his death in 1622. Greg states that Buc was 'in an excellent position to ascertain the authorship of contemporary drama', though reminds us that in 1595 he had no connection with the Revels Office, and that he died insane. Still, the note does not seem like the ramblings of madness, and if it was written shortly after the Quarto's publication – as is possibly suggested by the phrase '*now* some fellow hath published it' – Buc's position, or lack of, with the Revels Office is of little account if he had worked on the play himself as a young man some ten years earlier. Buc was also a respected scholar and antiquarian, admired by such figures as William Camden, and exhibited impressive rigour in his historical treatises. He is therefore unlikely, as both an accurate and a principled scholar, to be the victim of faulty memory or the perpetrator of a fabrication, especially in what is apparently a private note to himself. J. P. Collier was the first to draw attention to this evidence in 1865, which did more harm than good on the basis of his controversial reputation as a Shakespeare scholar, who, alongside much useful work, committed many acts of forgery upon early modern documents. However, in 1924 Seymour DeRicci suggested the writing very much resembled Buc's, and Thornton S. Graves the following year argued that this evidence, dismissed for sixty years because of doubt in Collier, was in fact genuine, a view corroborated by E. K. Chambers, W. W. Greg and R. C. Bald between 1930 and 1934.[63]

If Buc is correct, the play can be no later than 1586, when Tilney was executed for his part in the Babington Plot to assassinate Queen Elizabeth. Buc and Tilney were almost exact contemporaries – Buc was born in 1560 and Tilney in 1561 – and while little is known of Tilney except that he had become a gentleman pensioner at court by the time of his death, Buc had entered the Middle Temple from New Inn in 1585. This may be significant in that *Locrine* shares many features with the kind of Senecan Inns of Court tragedies pioneered by Norton and Sackville's *Gorboduc* (1562), even imitating its first scene from its progenitor. It also has Até, the classical figure of chaos, as a chorus between acts, numerous direct borrowings from Seneca, and dumb shows (which Buc may have provided), all entirely redolent of private, academic drama, and all suggesting that *Locrine*'s substrate does indeed predate 1587 and the great innovations of Marlowe and Kyd's tragedies on the public stage. Tucker Brooke also notes how it is entirely in the English-Senecan vein of *Gorboduc* in that it chooses 'gruesome passages from the mythical history of Britain...as an equivalent of the horrors of Greek mythology'.[64] Seneca was a revered figure from classical antiquity to Elizabethans, a Roman dramatist famous for bloody revenge plays. His style was adapted from Greek tragedy – all his surviving plays were in fact reworkings of Greek originals by Sophocles, Euripides and Aeschylus – and bequeathed to Elizabethan drama a five-act structure, an emphasis on heightened, bombastic expression, and the influence of the supernatural (both *The Spanish Tragedy* and *Hamlet*, for example, feature ghosts). Where *Locrine* diverts from *Gorboduc* and others, which may provide further proof of the play's revision, is in its clown character, Strumbo, and in its multiple instances of stage combat. Jonathan Bate has noted that while *Gorboduc* is 'a static work of Senecan debate', *Locrine* contains 'action and spectacle', prerequisites for the public, as opposed to the private, stage.[65] If we accept the Spenser parallels as indicative of revision, then we seem to have a fairly strong case for a c.1586 academic tragedy revised for the public stage between 1591 and 1594. Peter Berek notes an archaic, pre-Marlovian style in the play's neat moralizing about excessive human ambition and its just consequences, married with the definite influence, in the vaunting characterization and rhetoric of Humber and Albanact, of *Tamburlaine* and the vogue for conqueror plays it ushered in.[66] As these elements seem more competing than harmonious within *Locrine*, Berek urges it as another sign of early 1590s revision of an early 1580s play.

But by whom? Of the professional playwrights, it can only have been a writer we know to have been active up to and including 1595: Robert Wilson, Henry Porter, John Lyly, Thomas Kyd, Christopher Marlowe, Robert Greene, George Peele, Thomas Lodge and William Shakespeare. Wilson, Porter and Lyly are all thoroughly unlikely candidates based on their generic predispositions for comedies and morals and on the fact that their known work all predates 1591.[67] Marlowe and Shakespeare are almost impossible candidates based on the stylistic qualities of *Locrine* compared with their acknowledged canons, and Kyd's *The Spanish Tragedy* displays far more sophisticated and innovative dramatic and poetic qualities than *Locrine*. The play has, justly, been likened in tone and style to the bombastic school of Marlovian imitators working around the late 1580s to early 1590s, whose chief proponents were Robert Greene and George Peele:

> *Locrine* is possibly as characteristic an example as can be found of the type of drama developed by Greene and Peele. The usual faults of their school are in this play exaggerated into vices, but the special lyric beauty, the imaginative fervour, and the delicate feeling for natural loveliness are equally prominent; and both in its defects and its merits *Locrine* manifests a close consanguinity with the acknowledged plays of the 'university wits'. No reader can well fail to note the infinity of classical allusion, the craze for mouth-filling but meaningless adjectival epithets, the ranting bombast of the heroic figures, the wearisome lyrical repetition of high-sounding words and phrases, or the childish delight in such freaks of verbiage as 'agnominated' and 'contentation'. No less striking, however, and no less indicative of its authorship are the poetic beauties of *Locrine*, detached, for the most part, and scattered like living springs in the dreary waste of rhetoric and affectation.[68]

So wrote C. F. Tucker Brooke in 1908. He had been inspired by P. A. Daniel's 1898 observation that *Locrine* shared exact verbal parallels with the anonymous Queen's Men play, *Selimus*. Rudolf Brotanek and Charles Crawford expanded on this, the latter claiming that *Locrine* plagiarized *Selimus*, though Emil Koeppel showed that the debt was actually reversed, a view now widely accepted. *Selimus* was printed in 1594 by Thomas Creede, who printed *Alphonsus, King of Aragon* in 1599, attributing it to 'R. G.' – Robert Greene – on the title page, which is itself not a concrete ascription, although largely accepted. This link between *Locrine*, *Selimus* and *Alphonsus* being all printed by Creede, as well as the similarity of *Selimus* to *Alphonsus* as a sub-Marlovian conqueror play, the attribution to Greene on the title page of *Alphonsus* and the direct and undeniable parallels between *Locrine* and *Selimus* have led many critics to the belief that all three point in the direction of Greene. *Selimus* names the Queen's Men as the company which performed it, for whom Greene may also have written *James IV* and *A Looking Glass for London and England* (both 1590). The 1600 anthology *England's Parnassus* attributes excerpts from *Selimus* to Greene, but also attributes to him passages known to be by other authors. Alexander Grosart attributed *Selimus* to Greene, a view contested by J. Churton Collins, who nonetheless felt *Selimus* and *Locrine* were by the same author. Maxwell also argued for mutual authorship, and developed the case for Greene. John W. Cunliffe, however, argued that no Elizabethan writer would repeat himself or self-plagiarize to such an extent, and that the two plays must have different authors. W. S. Gaud published a list of parallels between *Locrine* and the works of Peele in 1904, and J. M. Robertson the following year declared *Locrine* a play by Peele, linking it with *Titus Andronicus*. He wanted to show that Shakespeare had not written *Titus*, and it may be striking to note that modern scholarship now attributes Act 1 of *Titus*, a play that delights in parodying and grotesquely exploiting the fashion for Senecan drama, to Peele.[69] Tucker Brooke argued that *Locrine* was stylistically closer to Greene than Peele in its comedy, its fondness for classical allusion, its sparing use of run-on lines, and the 'over-decoration' of its verse. He rightly saw features indicating it as 'a tragedy of the type of about 1585' (though he made no mention of the Buc evidence), concluding the whole play dates from then, and that *Selimus* is likewise early Greene, 'marking the transition from *Locrine* to *Alphonsus*'.[70] As for the 1595 role of 'W. S.', Brooke felt it stretched no further beyond the updating of the epilogue than 'the crossing of an occasional "t" or the dotting of an "i"'.[71]

Henry Ulrici was in fact the first to link Peele to the play, claiming that Shakespeare had written the comic scenes and Peele the rest. Others agreeing with the Peele attribution include F. G. Fleay, A. W. Ward, Felix E. Schelling, who later recanted, Alden Brooks, who also felt Shakespeare was the co-author, and Leonard R. N. Ashley. Other Greene proponents are J. A. Symonds, Ernest A. Gerrard, who argued Shakespeare revised the play, Arthur Acheson and Irving Ribner, while J. M. Robertson and H. Dugdale Sykes felt the two men had co-authored it. Conversely, F. Eisinger, Elizabeth Holmes, Harold M. Dowling, Marco Mincoff, Hardin Craig, J. C. Maxwell, W. Bridges Adams, Margareta Braun and David Bevington have all expressed doubts in the presence of either author. Shakespeare has never really been considered seriously as the play's author, certainly not in the twentieth century. The play was reprinted in the Fourth Folio, and appeared in Rowe's 1709 edition of Shakespeare. Malone attributed it to Marlowe, and in the nineteenth century Ludwig Tieck, W. G. Simms, Max Moltke, and A. F. Hopkinson allowed for Shakespeare's presence, while Schlegel remained unconvinced. No editor of Shakespeare in the last century has allowed for his authorship of the play. Ward Elliott and Robert Valenza's tests argue strongly against his authorship, and, in a result that perhaps reveals the friable nature of stylometric testing, Jonathan Hope's sociolinguistic analysis suggests the play is probably not collaborative, that Shakespeare, Marlowe, and Dekker all fit the profile, but that their authorship is not seriously expected, in spite of the data.

As for the 'W. S.' named by the Quarto, many critics have suggested an exploitation of Shakespeare's name by Creede, while some have allowed it possible that Shakespeare did in fact see the play through the press. Gooch also suggests:

> The possibility remains that Creede was not trying to deceive anyone ... 'W. S.' may refer to a lesser known poet, playwright *or* actor ... [candidates] include William Smith, the author of a collection of sonnets, *Chloris; or, The Complaint of the Passionate Despised Shepheard* [sic] (1596); William Stanley, Earl of Derby, who supported his own company of actors (1594–1618); and Wentworth Smith, frequently mentioned by Henslowe in the years 1601–1603 as a collaborator in the writing of plays. It is possible but not probable that any of these three men may have had some connection with *Locrine*: William Smith is not known to have written for the stage; William Stanley would probably have produced plays for the Derby's Men, and there is reason to believe that *Locrine* was connected with the Queen's Men; and the dramatic activity of Wentworth Smith is six years later than the date of publication of *Locrine*. Another candidate is William Smyght, one of three players recorded by Henslowe to have witnessed a loan on June 1, 1595 to his nephew, Francis, a member of the Queen's Company. Another actor with the right initials, William Sheppard, is mentioned by Chambers in *The Elizabethan Stage* (II, 339). We cannot assume that either Smyght or Sheppard was involved in writing as well as in acting plays.[72]

It is ultimately impossible to know who is signified by the initials 'W. S.', how he came to be associated with the play, and what was his specific role in the preparation of the text. The identity of the play's reviser must likewise remain mysterious until either more serious stylometric analysis is performed upon it – never a guarantee of concrete proof anyway – or more evidence is uncovered, which seems unlikely. The evidence for Tilney's authorship of the substrate play, on the other hand, seems strong. If Greene revised it then he obviously did so prior to his death in September 1592, whereas Peele remains in the frame any time, presumably, up until the play's 1594 entry in the Stationers' Register. The possibility that we are looking at someone else entirely renders the date somewhat fluid, albeit one phase of revision must begin in 1591 with the publication of Spenser's *Complaints*, and end with the publication of *Selimus* in 1594. The reference to Elizabeth's reign in the epilogue suggests that the text went through at least one stage of correction shortly before its publication in 1595, though we know neither the extent of the changes made at this time nor whether they were supplied for performance or print only. These are important considerations when thinking about Shakespeare as a working writer for his company and the various obligations this might have entailed, if he is indeed the 'W. S.' named by the Quarto. But on the balance of the available external and stylistic evidence, we feel a serious attribution to him of *Locrine*'s authorship, in whole or in significant part, would be badly misplaced.

Edward III (c.1593–94?)

The Elizabethan history play *Edward III* is, along with *Sir Thomas More*, the most likely of all the plays herein to be authentically part-Shakespearean. Arguments for Shakespeare's presence have been prolific and taken very seriously since the late nineteenth century, with the majority of attention centring on the romantic subplot scenes involving the Countess of Salisbury (1.2, 2.1, 2.2), and one scene drawn from the martial main plot (4.4). Although scholarly consensus on either the fact of Shakespeare's involvement or the extent of it is far from unanimous, so much positive stylistic and stylometric inquiry has been directed at the play and at these scenes in particular over the last century that, as the eminent apocrypha scholar Richard Proudfoot rightly observes, both it and *More* 'are more than just "candidates"; they have already attained some measure of canonical acceptance'.[73] And yet there is no external evidence of any kind regarding *Edward III*'s authorship, its date, or the company which first performed it. As Proudfoot notes:

> No contemporary statement attaches it to Shakespeare, or to any other playwright or playwrights. It may be of collaborative authorship, but if so the identity of the other playwright or playwrights remains to be established. It is the only play whose attribution to Shakespeare has been persuasively argued entirely on internal grounds of its congruence, in whole or in part, with what we know of the poetic, metrical, linguistic, thematic and dramatic qualities of Shakespeare's attested plays.[74]

Since this statement was made in 2001, there has been a growing consensus that *Arden of Faversham* is partly Shakespeare's based solely on internal evidence, so *Edward III* no longer stands alone in that regard. Yet apart from this debatable modification, everything else Proudfoot says is true. When it was first printed in 1596, *Edward III* bore no authorial or company attribution on its title page, stating merely that it had been 'sundrie times plaied about the Citie of London'. It was reprinted in 1599, with no additional information. The only antedating possible via external evidence is the 1 December 1595 entry in the Stationers' Register, though the year of composition is usually imagined to be earlier than this. How much earlier is most often determined by attempts to describe the presence of Shakespeare, to whom the first recorded attribution was made in a catalogue appended to the 1656 edition of Thomas Goffe's *The Careless Shepherdess*, published by London booksellers Richard Rogers and William Ley. It should be noted that the catalogue also gave him Marlowe's *Edward II* and Heywood's *Edward IV*, perhaps reflective of a marketing strategy associating Shakespeare, considered the pre-eminent writer of histories thanks to the Folio, with plays about historical monarchs. Nothing is said, however, of the authorship of *Richard II* and *King John*, two plays that he did write. All of his remaining histories are accurately attributed, albeit that the list is likewise silent on the multi-authorship of *Henry VI Part 1* and the issue of Fletcher's hand in *Henry VIII*, and is otherwise interested only in a handful of Shakespeare's other plays, all accurate save *The London Prodigal*. None of this really proves anything beyond the well-known fact that historical documents of this kind tend to behave erratically at best, fraudulently at worst, and not in the ways we want or expect them to in most cases. It is by no means the most inaccurate bookseller's list of the 1650s; surely Edward Archer's catalogue, also of 1656, holds that distinction, so its attribution to Shakespeare of these three 'Edward' plays, two definitely not by him, one possibly, is intriguing. Yet it seems most likely that the connection of his name to *Edward III* here owes more to luck than to judgement or knowledge.

In spite of what seems like a one-off incident of mere marketing fantasy, many subsequent commentators attempted the attribution based on more considered criteria. The eighteenth-century textual scholar, Edward Capell, in his 1760 volume *Prolusions; or Select Pieces of Ancient Poetry*, was the first to edit the play and to propose seriously the notion that Shakespeare had written it, though with admirable restraint:

> That it was indeed written by Shakespeare, it cannot be said with candour that there is any external evidence at all. Something of proof arises from resemblance between the style of his earlier performances and of the work in question; and a more conclusive one yet from consideration of the time it appeared in, in which there was no known writer equal to such a play. The fable of it too is taken from the same books which that author is known to have followed in some other plays; to wit, Holinshed's *Chronicles*, and a book of novels called *The Palace of Pleasure*. But, after all, it must be confessed that its being his work is conjecture only, and matter of opinion; and the reader must form one of his own, guided by what is now before him, and by what he shall meet with in perusal of the piece itself.

Capell's words can be regarded as the first printed scholarly consideration of the question; a carefully reasoned account of the play's similarity of style to parts of Shakespeare's acknowledged canon, supported by a knowledge of the source material Shakespeare used in the composition of his history plays and of his pre-eminence within the genre. Shakespeare's principal sources were Edward Hall's *The Union of the Two Noble and Illustre Families of Lancaster and York* (1548), and Raphael Holinshed's *Chronicles*, the 1587 revised edition of which, as Martin Wiggins has noted, 'was to become the source for more plays of the period than any other book'.[75] Many plays survive from the period which take English history as their theme, and Henslowe's *Diary* shows us many more that are now lost, so *Edward III*'s status as a history play, even one chronologically linked to Shakespeare's second tetralogy, does not make it an automatic candidate for his authorship. It is also based on different source material from the majority of Shakespeare's histories, with the author or authors relying mainly on Lord Berners' 1523 translation of Jean Froissart's *Chronicles*. This does not disprove Shakespeare's hand, as it is likely that *Richard II* owes much to Froissart's moving account of Richard's deposition. Scholars are also undecided on whether the Countess of Salisbury scenes are based on episodes found in William Painter's *Palace of Pleasure*, which Capell mentions, a collection of prose tales from which Shakespeare derived plot outlines for several of his works, including *The Rape of Lucrece* and *Romeo and Juliet* – two works likely to have been written around the same time as *Edward III* – or simply derived from Froissart, who provides brief details. Many who believe that Froissart was the source assert that *Edward III* is more likely to be of single authorship, either solely Shakespeare or solely another. The Countess scenes have conversely engendered the argument that the play must be multi-authored because they seem tangential to the thrust of the French narrative established in the first scene and resumed in Act 3. Whatever the case, Shakespeare's name has been stubbornly linked to them for over a century.

In his other history plays, Shakespeare approached the two halves of the historical narrative sequence in reverse order. The first tetralogy (*Henry VI Parts 1, 2 and 3* and *Richard III*) was composed roughly between 1591 and 1593–94, and the second (*Richard II, Henry IV Parts 1 and 2* and *Henry V*) between 1595 and 1599. *Edward III* dramatizes, among other things, the beginnings of the Hundred Years' War, events that form an historical prelude to the second half of Shakespeare's great cycle, which dealt with the troubled succession of the line of monarchs from Richard II to Henry V, and many believe it was written in between the two. Several structural and thematic parallels with *Henry V* have also been invoked to bolster the Shakespeare attribution: Edward seeking affirmation about the righteousness of his claims to the French throne at the play's opening; the Duc de Lorraine ordering Edward to swear allegiance and being soundly rebuked, in a similar manner to the tennis balls episode in *Henry V*; and Edward overcoming internal revolt before leading his armies to France, again, similar to Henry's quelling of the Cambridge, Scrope and Grey rebellion at the same juncture in Act 2. That Shakespeare at least knew *Edward III* is also seemingly confirmed by the repetition in *Henry V* of a unique historical error, in which the Scottish king, David, is brought as a prisoner to France (he was in fact held at London for the duration of his capture; see 4.2.40–56 and *Henry V*, 1.2.162–4).

Yet for many *Edward III* sits uneasily among Shakespeare's acknowledged histories, which are generally of a far more autumnal and pessimistic strain than the jingoistic flourishes that characterize much of this play. In contrast with many romanticized pseudo-history plays from the 1590s, Shakespeare's are sophisticated dramatic reimaginings of chronicle material, turned by the master playwright into complex psychodramas, where the crown measures only the physical limits of the isolated and imprisoned human mind. They add flesh and bone to familiar stories, past concerns become present, with suffering and the uncertainty of all things immediate and stark realities. One of the most notable features of the second tetralogy in particular is its apparent refusal to corroborate Hall's view of a providential plan underpinning past political events in England. In this we see Shakespeare communing with written historical narratives for plot details, but rejecting their principles in favour of material, human dramas, quite unwilling to sanctify the lives of his subjects or gloss over the psychological and political problems that they faced. Shakespeare shows in them that in the present people struggle to make sense of their own lives, to interpret their relationships with themselves and others, and that what history comes to remember as outcomes of strategy and greatness can be as much due to luck, vanity, foolhardiness and political cynicism. Even fictional characters find that as the years slip away it becomes easier to indulge in falsely amplified memories of youthful transgressions than to face up to the reality of one's past as a steady agglomeration of missed opportunities. Easier to take refuge in the safety of hyperbolic promises made in drink than to take up swords and 'pluck bright honour from the pale-faced moon' (*Henry IV Part 1*, 1.3.205).

This general mood is a consistent feature, despite the fact that Shakespeare found such different ways in to his treatment of history in each play. *Richard II* aims a laser-like spotlight on one man's tragic performance of his own life, while the *Henry IV* plays flit between court and whorehouse, battlefield and bordello, and, in spite of a yeasty humour that gradually yields to sorrow, act as darkly cynical exposés of the fragmentary confusion that both shapes history and is omitted from accounts of it. *Part 2* in particular promises action and consequence only to deliver inertia and infirmity. It builds its picture of history from chaotic offcuts of circumstance, fuelled by rumour, muddied by conjecture, ignorance and fear, manipulated to uncertain ends by calculated rhetoric and ruthlessness, and yet inseparable from completely mundane actions, from memory, hospitality, friendship, everyday conversation, quirks of personality. It takes the time to zoom in on unrecorded little lives lived far away, geographically and experientially, from the great march of political events, and is neither in the business of accusation nor apology when it comes to history as seen in the fabric of ordinary existence. Societal orders change with glacial slowness, personal fortunes wax and wane, bodies age, friends meet, young men dream of owning the future, old men reminisce about their role in the past, the ceaseless movement of news throughout the realm leads nowhere, armies converge for battle and scatter like fallen leaves, people die, time ebbs inexorably away, and the by-product, history, is merely a partial residue of uncertain significance. Even *Henry V*, a play that has suffered much simplistic categorization as a folkloric hymn to French-bashing, which many critics have noted as structurally and thematically similar to *Edward III*, walks a delicate line between heroic fable and coldly mechanistic treatment of the realities of leadership in war. It also ends with a reminder of Henry's premature death and the fact that everything he gained would soon be lost under his weak and ineffectual son, which Shakespeare's audience already well knew thanks to his multi-part dramatization of Henry VI's disastrous reign.

It is worth remembering all this when considering *Edward III* as a play by Shakespeare, as in many of its scenes it seems simply unwilling or unable to trade and traffic in such levels of human detail and historiographical scepticism. Furthermore, we might question its status as an opening chapter, not on the basis of how good it is or whether it 'feels' like Shakespeare, but because of the irregularity of its narrative interests. It has links to the second tetralogy in terms of historical chronology, yet it is principally concerned with English victories against Scotland and France, a subject in which the first three plays of the second half of Shakespeare's saga are almost entirely uninterested. There is nothing unusual about this historically; Richard II was a minor when he ascended the throne, a fact which, combined with continued troubles with Scotland, dramatized in *Edward III*, forced the signing of the Truce of Leulingham in 1389, which lasted until 1415 when Henry V sought to renew the conflict. Henry IV's short reign was blighted by civil struggles, around which the two plays Shakespeare gives us revolve, with only *Part 2* briefly alluding to troubles with the French in the main body of its action (1.3.70–87). Its ending, of course, signals the dawn of a slick, steely political age in which French wars are sought to 'busy giddy minds' at home. In *Henry V*, the matter of the Scots is raised and dismissed in fairly shorthand fashion (1.2.138–85), and Shakespeare is almost at pains to remind us that the French question is old and long-neglected (1.2.105–12).

The first tetralogy similarly eschews interest in the French wars for the most part. It deals almost entirely with the Wars of the Roses, and, except for the somewhat misfit *Henry VI Part 1*, which takes a lengthy sojourn in France and ends with English victory, is otherwise entirely concerned with English factionalism in a darker, ensemble mood, before its surprising culmination in the delicious, breathtaking symbiosis between a master-dramatist and a master-actor that is *Richard III*. The traditional view was that Shakespeare wrote the plays in order, but the weight of contemporary scholarship now views *Part 1* as a collaborative prequel, which post-dates *Part 2* and *Part 3*. We shall probably never know the exact scenario, but the case of *Henry VI Part 1* has massive implications for our placing of *Edward III*. Both, because of their comparative optimism and jingoism, have been explained away as very early plays because few critics, even adherents to the theory that Shakespeare is solely responsible for them, have been able to deny that they lack the more complex, dark, narrative sophistication of Shakespeare's other histories. And yet we are now almost sure that *Part 1* is not the earliest play in the saga, and equally have every reason to believe that *Edward III* is later than we think, suggested in part by the appearance of the line 'Lilies that fester smell far worse than weeds' at 2.1.454, which also ends Sonnet 94. While Shakespeare's *Sonnets* were not printed until 1609, described as being in circulation only 'among his private friends' by Francis Meres in 1598, MacDonald Jackson's stylometric work on them dates numbers 61–103 at c.1594–95. This makes the line's appearance in *Edward III* seem very promising both as proof that Shakespeare is present, and that the play is likely to be later than usually imagined. We may, of course, be witnessing a simple act of plagiarism, either on the part of one of the 'private friends' or of Shakespeare himself, picking someone else's line out for use in his sonnet. However, Michael Dobson notes that the c.1594 dating is strengthened by 'the play's references to Lucrece and to Hero and Leander, its metre, [and] the generally agreed superiority of the King-Countess material to the comparable but less mature scenes between Edward IV and Lady Elizabeth Grey in *3 Henry VI*'.[76] Arguments for Shakespeare's authorship predicated on a very early dating usually push the idea that the play appealed to a patriotic, post-Spanish Armada sensibility, and place it c.1589–90.[77] Yet the linguistic evidence is somewhat incompatible with this view, as Gary Taylor has noted:

Those who favour Shakespeare's authorship generally presume such an early date. Wentersdorf (1960) concludes that the metrical tests independently support such a dating, if we assume Shakespearian authorship; but his conclusions cannot be given much weight, for metrical evidence at the very beginning of the canon is bedevilled by inconsistencies, and by the problems created by possible collaboration. In the colloquialism-in-verse test, *Edward III*'s figure places it closest, among the history plays, to *Richard III*; unless *Contention* [*Henry VI Part 2*] and *Duke of York* [*Henry VI Part 3*] are collaborative plays, by this test *Edward III* belongs after them, not before. Jackson (1965), on the basis of alleged echoes in apparently memorial texts, concludes that the play belonged at some stage to Pembroke's Men. This evidence is weaker than one would desire, and the play's company affiliations remain uncertain.[78]

Following an early date rationale, Richard Proudfoot pursued the Pembroke's Men connection, although Gary Taylor argues:

> The casting pattern would fit the Chamberlain's Men as readily as the pre-1590 Admiral's, or what we conjecture about Pembroke's. Indeed, the size of cast does not resemble any Shakespeare play which we place before June 1592 except *Two Gentlemen*, which cannot be dated with any certainty.[79]

Giorgio Melchiori concluded that *Edward III*'s dating 'cannot be other than late 1592 – early 1593', based on the argument that the casting considerations reflect a knowledge on the dramatists' part that plague was likely to strike and that the play would have to find its audiences on the road, in stripped-down touring productions (the theatres were closed for almost all of 1593, and Melchiori assumes the play is pre-Chamberlain's).[80] Proudfoot took the converse line in arguing for Pembroke's, noting that the play needed 'doubling, by eleven men, three or four boys, and about ten non-speaking extras', as well as use of different stage levels and complex sound effects, all of which suggest a professional company in situ at a London theatre.[81] It is hard to trace Shakespeare's company affiliations prior to the formation of the Chamberlain's/Admiral's duopoly in May 1594, but he has been linked both with Lord Strange's Men, who performed the 'harey vj' listed as new in Henslowe's Diary on 3 March 1592, and Pembroke's Men, identified as the company that performed *Part 3* on the 1595 Octavo title page. Those following the chronological argument have argued that Shakespeare started with Strange's, for whom he wrote *Henry VI Part 1*, before moving on to work with Pembroke's on, at least, *Part 3*. Taking the converse line, if *Part 1* is a prequel, it still does not necessarily mean that Shakespeare went the other way, from Pembroke's to Strange's. Several members of both companies went on to join the Chamberlain's, and we do not know with any certainty whether Shakespeare's plays all came with him, or whether some came with the actors who had performed in them with other companies. We know that in early 1591 the Admiral's and Strange's were both using the Theatre, James Burbage's playhouse in the Shoreditch region north of the city. An argument between Edward Alleyn and Burbage in May that year led to Alleyn joining Strange's and relocating them to the Rose, while the remaining Admiral's cohort left on a provincial tour, leaving the Theatre standing empty. Pembroke's company was formed to become its new tenants, featuring, presumably, Richard Burbage, who would have stayed behind with his father, as a principal actor, and, it has been hypothesized, a young, untried Shakespeare to whom they turned to provide scripts, resulting in the penning of the two-part *Contention* during late 1591 to early 1592.[82]

In a recent lecture Brian Vickers contended that Henslowe's 'harey vj' is, as many scholars have argued, the play we now know as *Henry VI Part 1*, but that it was written originally by Thomas Nashe and Thomas Kyd for Strange's company to compete with Shakespeare's plays (now known as *Part 2* and *Part 3*), which were being performed north of the river by Pembroke's at the same time.[83] Shakespeare later reworked the play and added the scenes now attributed to him when the Chamberlain's company, via members of Derby's who joined them, acquired the manuscript in May 1594 (Ferdinando Stanley, Lord Strange, became the Earl of Derby on 25 September 1593, at which time his troupe became Derby's Men). Other scholars have argued that it was an entirely pre-Chamberlain's play, written quite quickly as a collaboration between Shakespeare, Nashe, and at least one other writer for Strange's as a stop-gap to maintain audience interest in the events of the sequence while the solo-authored and infinitely more well-laboured *Richard III* was under construction. Yet Shakespeare was not with Strange's in 1592. Moreover, Pembroke's Men collapsed in autumn 1593 during the long plague closure of the theatres, at which time a without-patron Shakespeare seems likely to have gone south to join Derby's. Strange's ancestor, Thomas, Lord Stanley (first Earl of Derby), is made much of in *Richard III*, taken by many as a sign that Shakespeare was offering a flattering portrait of his new benefactor's family history. He could therefore have added his portions of *Henry VI Part 1* while still a member of Derby's in late 1593 to early 1594. It seems likelier, however, that this happened after the Chamberlain's had acquired both it and the two *Contention* plays from Pembroke's and the commercial impetus to stage the three together as a sequence arose. The differences between the Quarto and Folio versions of the *Contention* plays seem also to suggest Shakespearean revision of those plays for the Chamberlain's.

We do not know whether the supposed Shakespeare portions of *Edward III* are pre-Chamberlain's, and, if so, which company they were written for. Randall Martin shows that the casting for *Henry VI Part 3* requires fifteen adult and four boy-actors, adding up to numbers similar to those needed for *Edward III*.[84] If it was written for Pembroke's in London then it must date between late 1591 and the beginning of 1593. The company went on tour for most of that year, though Shakespeare was clearly busy with *Venus and Adonis*, which was entered in the Stationers' register on 18 April, for the first four months. Could he have contributed scenes to a play that was written for the touring company in the summer months? This seems the most unlikely. He could also have written them for Derby's Men sometime during the winter of 1593–94, whose *Richard III* requires very similar cast numbers, albeit with more boys, to the *Henry*s and *Edward III*.[85] Martin Wiggins argues this was the case, based on a combination of the facts that the Earl of Derby is a character, and the Earl of Warwick, whom Melchiori argues was a late addition into the play, has lines reassigned to him from Audley's part rather than Derby's; the closest literary connections in the Shakespeare sections are to *Richard III*, the *Sonnets* and *Lucrece*, dating them nearer 1594; and the Henslowe records for 1592–93 do not list it as either an old or a new play.[86] This seems highly plausible, and perhaps also likelier to be pre-Chamberlain's in that Shakespeare, who becomes a very reluctant collaborator for a number of years post-1594, would not have had autonomous control over his writing practices at that time. We also cannot know whether he was already planning his second tetralogy, and, if so, how much of it he envisaged in 1593–94. Yet *Henry VI Part 1* provides a precedent that Shakespeare could and did collaborate – or at least perform revision – at around this time on a history play that has narrative connections to others that he wrote.

Critics of Shakespeare's early histories tend to view them – apart from *Richard III*, in which many see his first ascent to the top tier of his artistic achievement – as apprentice pieces, with Shakespeare on a vertiginous learning curve throughout, usually as a way of trying to explain why *Henry VI Part 1* seems such a comparatively immature work. Could *Edward III* be even later than *Richard III* and be entirely Shakespearean? Its omission from the Folio argues against his sole authorship, though many critics have been undeterred by the fact. As has been noted, Edward Capell made the first serious scholarly claim that Shakespeare wrote the play, which found agreement in the nineteenth century from such scholars as Ludwig Tieck, Ernst Ortlepp, A. F. Hopkinson, J. P. Collier and Alexander Teetgen, while Henry Tyrrell and Max Moltke allowed the attribution more tentatively. Nicolaus Delius, F. J. Furnivall, Charles Knight, J. A.

Symonds, Hermann Ulrici, Karl Warnke and Ludwig Proescholdt adjudged the attribution highly unlikely, and A. C. Swinburne, who roundly snubbed the play, followed suit somewhat dismissively by proposing an anonymous Marlovian imitator as the likely author. The play appeared in C. F. Tucker Brooke's edition of *The Shakespeare Apocrypha*, in which he reasoned it to be of single authorship and, because of its 'inability to grasp strongly the realities of life', judged it 'distinctly un-Shakespearean', proposing George Peele as the most likely author based on perceived similarities of dramatic structure with Peele's other plays.[87] He came to revise his opinion later in life, allowing, thirty years later, that it may be partly Shakespearean after all, and was joined in the notion that the play continually echoes Shakespeare in small ways by the great Shakespearean scholars Muriel Bradbrook and E. H .C. Oliphant. Many other writers were proposed throughout the twentieth century, including minor figures such as Michael Drayton, Robert Greene, Robert Wilson, to more major candidates such as Thomas Kyd and Christopher Marlowe.

The Shakespeare-only attribution continued to find limited favour throughout the twentieth century with scholars such as Frank O'Connor, A. W. Titherley, who proposed in the same article that Shakespeare was the sixth Earl of Derby, D. and C. Ogburn, who favoured the Earl of Oxford as their Shakespeare, E. B. Everitt, Karl P. Wentersdorf, and F. R. Lapides. MacDonald Jackson argued that it was a Pembroke's play, probably by Shakespeare early in his career. Richard Proudfoot, who perhaps knows the play better than any other scholar through his continued labours on it over many years, has vacillated on his position regarding the extent of Shakespeare's involvement, but has held firm on his belief in it. Eliot Slater's epic 1981 study, *The Problem of the Reign of King Edward III: A Statistical Approach*, offered thousands of rare word examples arguing for Shakespeare's sole-authorship, and Proudfoot, who oversaw the work as a thesis, and its publication after the author's death in 1983, felt the case for Shakespeare's sole authorship not proven in the light of Eliot's study, but recommended it as an indispensable platform for future work. Slater's methods were later discredited by M. W. A. Smith, whose stylometric results for the play nevertheless also led him to propose Shakespeare, while the bullish Eric Sams edited the play in 1996 as *Shakespeare's Edward III*, devoting much of his commentary to perceived parallels with Shakespeare's plays, and following up on his belief that *Edmond Ironside* is also solely by Shakespeare and that 'both plays are plainly from the same hand'.[88] His single-mindedness found him few supporters. Jonathan Hope's sociolinguistic analysis of the play concluded that both the relativization and the auxiliary 'do' evidence was compatible with Shakespearean authorship throughout.

Concurrently, many have perceived, based often on gut reactions which have been borne out by stylometric qualification, that there are two hands at work, one being a perceptibly and markedly inferior poet to the other. The prolific Renaissance scholar, F. G. Fleay, whose conclusions are not always the most reliable, was the first to propose co-authorship in 1874, suggesting that Shakespeare had written Acts 1 and 2 and persons unknown the rest, and Brian Vickers has argued:

> Anyone who reads the play attentively will agree that these scenes have many signs of Shakespeare's hand, and that his collaborator was an experienced plotter, a diligent user of historical sources, but only a competent versifier, with little individuality or wit.[89]

Arthur Acheson proposed in 1922 that the play was Marlowe's, revised by Shakespeare in 1593–94, which Thomas Merriam also proposed in 1999. Marina Tarlinskaja has cautiously restated this position after undertaking painstaking metrics testing as recently as 2010. Albert Yang, C. K. Peng and Ary Goldberger, in a co-authored paper of 2004, proposed Marlowe as the sole author of the play, which J. M. Robertson had suggested in 1924, adding that Greene had revised Act 2, with Peele and Kyd also contributing. Most critics who allowed Shakespeare as part-author focused mainly on the Countess scenes, including E. K. Chambers,

Willis B. Dobson, Irving Ribner and C. B. Hobday. Brian Vickers has stated numerous times that Shakespeare was part-author only, and has recently adjudged his collaborator to be Thomas Kyd based on collocation (word sequence) matches between the play, *The Spanish Tragedy* and other works which Vickers claims for the Kyd canon: *Arden of Faversham*, *Soliman and Perseda*, *Fair Em*, *Henry VI Part 1*, *Cornelia*, and *King Leir*, not to be confused with Shakespeare's *King Lear*. His work has been challenged by Thomas Merriam who claims that function word analyses of the text conflict with the Kyd evidence and that 'further work should be done to reconcile the results'.[90] *Edward III* appeared in the Second Edition of the *Riverside Shakespeare* in 1997, the first time it had appeared in any complete works since its inclusion in F.J. Furnivall's *Leopold Shakespeare* in 1877, and was also included in the Second Edition of *The Oxford Shakespeare* in 2005, presented as partly-Shakespearean, as it was in *Riverside*. The Oxford editors excluded it from their original *Complete Works* in 1986, but said in the accompanying *Textual Companion* at the time:

> We have excluded *Edward III* in part because of uncertainties about date, in part because Shakespeare's share of the early plays is itself problematic: for instance, Slater's rare vocabulary test links *Edward III* most closely to *1 Henry VI*, of which Shakespeare only wrote about 20 per cent. The function word test is ambiguous. The stylistic evidence for Shakespeare's authorship of *Edward III* is greater than that for the additions to *Sir Thomas More* (excluding the palaeographical argument); if we attempted a thorough reinvestigation of candidates for inclusion in the early dramatic canon, it would have begun with *Edward III*.[91]

They proposed in their 2005 edition that Shakespeare's contribution in 1.2 begins at Edward's entrance at line 90, and that he is possibly responsible for 4.5 in addition to the other scenes identified at the beginning of this essay: 2.1, 2.2 and 4.4. Ward Elliott and Robert Valenza, thoroughgoing stylometrists and apocrypha sceptics, allowed in 2009 that the putative Shakespeare scenes were possibly his after extensive computer-aided language analysis. Giorgio Melchiori's 1998 edition of the play adjudged it an early Shakespeare collaboration, with his hand evident in many scenes, but his authorship of Act 2 'undeniable'.[92] More recently, Timothy Irish Watt's function and lexical word tests on the play led him to conclude that Shakespeare wrote the Countess scenes, but that the scenes describing the French wars are by an unknown writer.

So the question remains to a large degree intractable, yet many contemporary stylometric practitioners more or less agree both that the play has multiple authors, and that Shakespeare is highly likely to be among them, a position endorsed by this edition. How, why, and when Shakespeare came to be involved in the play, when it was written, by whom it was first performed, and who the co-author/s was/were are all things we shall probably never know for certain unless more historical, as opposed to stylistic, stylometric, impressionistic or interpretive evidence emerges. And yet to venture a hypothesis, it seems likeliest that Shakespeare was working with Derby's Men in the brief winter season of 1593–94, during which *Richard III* debuted, when he contributed his scenes. We feel it is impossible to state dogmatically whether *Edward III* was written originally in collaboration or whether Shakespeare was revising or adding to an earlier substrate text. Marlowe and Greene were dead by then, so revision/addition is the only answer if they are present and if the rough date of Shakespeare's involvement is right. Kyd, Peele and Nashe were still alive so collaboration is also possible, though we could equally be looking at another dramatist about whom, because of the extremely slender records of the pre-1594 theatre business, we know nothing. But we here present the surviving text of *Edward III* as a play by Shakespeare – whom we feel is almost certainly the hand behind 1.2.90–166, 2.1, 2.2 and 4.4 – and at least one other unidentified writer.

The Spanish Tragedy (c.1587, revised c.1597–98?)

Shakespeare had been working within the narrow world of the professional theatres for around three years when Thomas Kyd, almost certainly the author of *The Spanish Tragedy*, died in August 1594, possibly as a slow result of injuries sustained under torture. Christopher Marlowe, who had shared lodgings with Kyd, had met his well-documented, grisly and mysterious end in a Deptford tavern some fifteen months earlier.[93] With the passing of the two former friends and colleagues, who had developed the conventions of the literary-dramatic model that Shakespeare was to inherit and take to the most precipitous heights in our language, the first great flowering of talent behind the English secular stage was gone. Boy companies privately performing courtly comedies by John Lyly and his imitators had dominated the early to mid 1580s, but 1587 seems to mark the tipping point towards the repertories of the adult companies performing on the public stage, a move heralded by two of the most lasting and influential works in English drama.[94] *The Spanish Tragedy*, along with Marlowe's *Tamburlaine* (1587), is the seminal work of the Elizabethan theatres. It holds its own for rhetorical power, affect and skilful dramatic modulation with anything the early professional playwrights were to produce, and remained in the repertory for decades after it was written. Ben Jonson, who has been linked to it as a revising author, complained of its continued popularity nearly thirty years later in his 1614 satirical comedy *Bartholomew Fair*. Kyd revolutionized drama in his depiction of dynamic, sometimes visceral and grotesque onstage action, his use of the soliloquy as a medium for synthesizing intense psychological experience into stage narrative, and in his powerful revivification of the blank verse medium, overhauling with a muscular rhetorical sophistication both the starchy philosophizing of Senecan imitators and the crudities of the 'rhyming mother wits' mocked in the *Tamburlaine* prologue.

The standard translation of Seneca's collected tragedies into English had appeared between 1559 and 1581, and its influence on academic plays written for private and court performance – plays such as Sackville and Norton's *Gorboduc* (1561), which followed the sententious, moralizing patterns of Senecan drama very closely – was strong.[95] English revenge tragedy was nothing new when Kyd came along, yet his innovations saw a previously meditative, aphorism-laden and somewhat static approach to its life on stage radically and immediately changed. Gone was the simple narrative trajectory of rise and fall, the tragic hero as caricature driving moral fables about the precariousness of Fortune. *The Spanish Tragedy* tightened the focus onto the human soul collapsing under the pressures of court politics, psychological turmoil, and a terrible weight of private responsibility to the un-revenged dead. It paved the way for the ensuing fifty-five-year proliferation of drama in England, and made Shakespeare's career as a playwright possible. Influence in Shakespeare seems to happen, for the most part, obliquely. Charting it frequently requires perceptive close reading, beyond blanket observations about manipulation of source material, to suggest how images, words and themes might have fired his imagination and made their way into the very mood and fabric of his work. Of no other writer is this truer than the Roman poet Ovid, from whom Shakespeare absorbed the spirit of shape-shifting which drove his theatrical craft from the very beginning.[96] The title-page epigraph of *Venus and Adonis*, one of the only instances of Shakespeare speaking, albeit through Ovid, about artistic principles, seems to suggest Ovid's influence partly as provider of source material but almost certainly also as poetic muse.[97] Arguably Shakespeare's first great dramatic creation, Richard Gloucester, announces that he can:

> ...add colours to the chameleon,
> Change shapes with Proteus for advantages,
> And set the murderous Machiavel to school. (*Henry VI Part 3*, 3.2.192–4)

Proteus comes direct from *Metamorphoses*, though Shakespeare knew that theatrical performance itself was metamorphic; an actor has only to don a prop crown and inhabit a complex characterization to become a king before the eyes of an audience. Yet a more pragmatic recourse to the influence of Kyd and the university playwrights is rather easier to chart in these *Henry VI* plays, channelling much of their solid structure and heightened language, ranging from the powerfully affective to the faintly histrionic. Early Shakespearean blank verse is also closer to Kyd's formal patterning – full of such heavily-wielded stock devices as anaphora, hyperbole, simile, repetition – than the more experimental idiosyncrasies of his later work, and the emphasis on bloody and spectacular stage business abounds in both writers' work at this time, as it does in *Locrine* and many others like it. It did not take long for Shakespeare to get comfortable within this model and seek to outgrow it, even to offer satirical commentary on its tropes. The classical revenge fantasy he wrote with George Peele in the early 1590s, *Titus Andronicus*, affectionately parodies the escalatory, Grand-Guignol motifs of blood and thunder tragedies in the Marlovian and Kydian moulds. Shakespeare must surely have known Kyd, and they may even have felt a close affinity in the early days of the territorial University Wits (as with Shakespeare, we have no evidence that Kyd attended university). Thomas Nashe referred to Kyd as a 'shifting companion' or deceitful rogue in insinuating that his *Hamlet* was plagiarized from Seneca, apparently attempting to undermine his reputation in much the same way as Greene tried to do to Shakespeare three years later in calling him an 'upstart crow'.[98]

Greene, who died just before those words were printed in late 1592, never knew how emphatically his criticisms were about to be answered. Around a year later Shakespeare finished *Richard III*, a dizzying hybrid of the technical bedrock he had inherited from Kyd and the Ovidian-inspired ideology of morphic innovation that was to become a more dominant feature of his originality in later works. Shakespeare had at last produced a masterpiece that set him apart, yet he seemingly retained affection for the man who had helped show him the way. Although we know next to nothing about Shakespeare's private thoughts and personal relationships, it seems he must have seen something in Kyd's work that he liked and that he wanted to develop. The question of the Ur-*Hamlet*'s existence aside, many critics have drawn parallels between *The Spanish Tragedy*'s Hieronimo as the prototypical revenger on the professional stage and Hamlet as the supreme realisation of the character type. Furthermore, Lukas Erne has pointed out other ways in which Shakespeare's 1590s tragedies drew practical and thematic inspiration from Kyd's works, with *Titus Andronicus* closely following *The Spanish Tragedy*'s structure, *Romeo and Juliet* being only the second play to place a love conflict at the centre of a tragedy after Kyd's *Solomon and Perseda*, and *Julius Caesar* covering the same historical period as *Cornelia*, which also features a dialogue between Brutus and Cassius, who proffers Caesar's ambitions as a reason for effecting his death.[99]

All this speculation is intended as something of a foreword of context to the rather baffling prospect that Shakespeare seems likely to be present as an authorial hand in one of the extant versions of *The Spanish Tragedy*, despite external evidence seeming to militate heavily against such a judgement. The question revolves around a group of five passages – 2.5.46–104; 3.2.68–77; 3.11.2–48; 3.13.1–179; and 4.4.170–219 – apparently added as part of a revival sometime between 1592 and 1602, possibly in 1597. The play was first printed without the Additions in 1592 with no authorial attribution on the title page, information that is also lacking from the nine other early printings of 1594, 1599, 1602, 1603, 1610, 1615, 1618, 1623 and 1633. Only one copy of the 1592 text, the most authoritative version of the play as originally performed, survives. It was published by Edward White, who, as discussed in the *Arden of Faversham* entry, did so spuriously; copyright in *The Spanish Tragedy* then lay with Abel Jeffes, whom we know to have illicitly printed *Arden* that year before being imprisoned on 7 August. It is not clear whether Jeffes got around to making good on his ownership of *The Spanish Tragedy* by having it printed before his incarceration. If so, no copies survive. Lukas Erne posits that they are likely to have existed, but this is guesswork only.[100] Jeffes reprinted the play in 1594 and 1599, with only very minor differences to White's 1592 imprint. By 1602 the copyright had passed to Thomas Pavier, who was to have a much greater role in the Shakespeare apocrypha story.[101] The Quarto he printed that year was the first to contain the additional passages, amounting to some 320 extra lines, and all six subsequent reprints derive from this expanded text.

The only reason we have to attribute the original play to Kyd at all is found in Thomas Heywood's *Apology for Actors* (1612), which makes reference to the writing of 'M. *Kid* in the *Spanish* Tragedy'. As a piece of contemporary external evidence it may seem a little belated to be sure; Heywood, who was born sometime in the early 1570s, could have been as young as twelve when the play was written, but nonetheless his testimony seems within the limits of plausible living memory and its authority is by and large trusted. Not only did Kyd's name remain unassociated during the period of the professional theatres with printed editions of the work that had helped to shape their existence, but the neglect also lasted into the Restoration and beyond. Shakespeare was named as the play's author in the notoriously unreliable catalogue Edward Archer appended to Middleton, Massinger and Rowley's *The Old Law* in 1656, which contains many wildly inaccurate ascriptions to Shakespeare and cannot be taken as authoritative. The next time Kyd was identified as the author anywhere happened to be in a work with a scholarly, as opposed to commercial, impetus, Thomas Hawkins' three-volume Oxford study *The Origin of the English Drama* (1773), which cited the Heywood reference as the sole authority. We know nothing of the play's original performances in 1587 – company or venue – and even the dating is a best guess many scholars accept based on the combined facts that the play is imitated in *The Misfortunes of Arthur*, performed before Elizabeth at Gray's Inn on 28 February 1588; that it makes no mention of the 1588 Spanish Armada, a huge influence on the drama in its wake; and that we know *Tamburlaine* was performed that year. Jonson, in *Bartholomew Fair*, alludes to it being 'five and twenty or thirty years' old, yielding a date range of 1584–89, though *Tamburlaine* has exerted a gravitational pull in decisions to nominate 1587, a neat narrative in that both plays were responsible for driving the revolution in adult professional performance. The development of drama in the 1580s must have been a far more complex picture than we know about, though the haziness of the records has left us with the image of it exploding onto the scene from almost nothing in 1587 through these two works. It is an image in part perpetuated by the undeniable potency and influence of Kyd and Marlowe's writing at this time.

The first performances of the play that we do know about took place under the auspices of Strange's Men in early 1592, some five years later, at the beginning of Henslowe's period of record keeping for the newly refurbished Rose theatre. Henslowe never referred to it by its familiar title, opting always for the moniker 'Jeronimo' (in various spellings). It has been supposed that he was referring to the play first printed in 1605 called 'THE FIRST PART OF Jeronimo. With the Warres of Portugall, and the life and death of Don Andraea', a prequel to the events of Kyd's play, with which it seems to have been paired in performances on 13 and 14 and 30 and 31 March, 22 and 24 April and 21 and 22 May 1592.[102] It seems likelier, however, that this was the play Henslowe named variously 'the comodey of doneoracio', 'doneoracio' or 'the comodey Jeronymo', ending as it does with Horatio's triumph alongside Andrea's death, and being therefore fitter at least in this regard than Kyd's play for a 'comedy' tag. It is clearly distinct from the play named only 'Jeronimo' by Henslowe, which is almost certainly *The Spanish Tragedy*. There is no evidence of it being performed by the Admiral's company again, so its life on stage seems to have begun and ended with Strange's. It is almost certain that Edward Alleyn played Hieronimo for the sixteen performances of *The Spanish Tragedy* up to 22 January 1593, a period that saw the company relying heavily on revivals of other old classics such as Robert Greene's *Friar Bacon* (1589) and Marlowe's *The Jew of Malta* (1589), in which Alleyn would have reprised his old role as Barabas.[103] He could conceivably have been the original Hieronimo in 1587 although we cannot know this; he would certainly have played the part when the

Admiral's Men revived it again over twelve performances at the Rose between 7 January and 19 July 1597, and once by an amalgam of the Admiral's and Pembroke's on 13 October 1597.[104] Alleyn, Strange's star actor in 1592, went on to become the leading player of the Admiral's and Richard Burbage's main rival following the reorganization of the constantly shifting companies of the early 1590s within London into the Chamberlain's/Admiral's duopoly in 1594. The purpose of discussing Burbage is that he is said to have played Hieronimo, and establishing the likely date may also help to account for Shakespeare's presence (or lack thereof) in the 1602 imprint.

The murky details of Shakespeare's possible affiliations with Derby's (as Strange's became in September 1593) company in the early 1590s are further examined in the essay on *Edward III*. The piece of evidence not discussed there is the fact that the title page of the 1594 Quarto of *Titus Andronicus* credits Derby's, Pembroke's and Sussex's (in that order) as the companies that performed it. Many have argued this is a chronological list of Shakespeare's affiliations, although Sussex's Men, by whom the play was certainly performed on 24 January 1594 as evidenced by Henslowe, employed members of both Derby's and Pembroke's in that brief winter season, and the list may therefore be referencing all patrons connected with this particular performance, rather than a list of different companies through whose hands the play had variously passed. However, the Second Quarto changes the order to Pembroke's, Derby's, Sussex's, adding the Chamberlain's, and Martin Wiggins suggests this is a correction to the chronology, perhaps by one involved with the play.[105] Strange's/Derby's had been on a long provincial tour when Henslowe was able to showcase Sussex's at the Rose for the six-week period between December 1593 and February 1594, the cold winter causing the devastating plague of 1593 to abate. Wiggins hypothesizes that Shakespeare brought *Titus* with him when he joined Derby's and that they may also have performed it briefly when the theatres reopened, though we do not know where they resided for the final few months of their existence.

Both companies were working for Henslowe at this time, yet we have no evidence of Derby's returning to the Rose after the reopening, despite Henslowe being Alleyn's father-in-law by then. Shakespeare was not necessarily a member of Sussex's, who performed *Titus* unaided, and we have no indications of an amalgamation with Derby's. We also have evidence of Sussex's performing *The Jew of Malta*, another Derby's play, suggesting Henslowe was free to exploit certain links between them. The theatres closed again from early February until 1 April, when Shakespeare's energies would have been devoted to writing *The Rape of Lucrece* for his literary patron, the Earl of Southampton. On 16 April his dramatic patron, the Earl of Derby, was to die, and in May the Chamberlain's company, in which Shakespeare became a shareholder, was formed. But when Strange's performed *The Spanish Tragedy* at the Rose on 14 March 1592, having performed 'harey vj' eleven days earlier, Shakespeare and Burbage were north of the river at the Theatre, owned by Richard's father James, enjoying both the patronage of the Earl of Pembroke and popular success with Shakespeare's *Contention* plays, which we now know as *Henry VI Part 2* and *Part 3*.[106] Strange's owned nothing of Shakespeare's during 1592 according to Henslowe's records. Perhaps the short months between autumn 1593 and early 1594, when *Richard III* was the likely play with which he announced his arrival at Derby's, could also have afforded him time to contribute scenes to a revival text of *Henry VI Part 1* and, perhaps, *The Spanish Tragedy*.

Yet it is unlikely Burbage played the part at this time; even if he followed Shakespeare to Derby's Alleyn was still top dog. It is not inconceivable that Shakespeare could have supplied the Additions at this time, Burbage simply playing the part at a later date. The 1594 and 1599 Quartos were essentially reprints of the 1592 text, and the style of the Additions does have the feel of an earlier Shakespeare, with the main tenor of their plot – Hieronimo's boundary-flirting madness as feigned revenge strategy/real reaction to the death of a child – something Shakespeare had explored forcefully in *Titus*. Other critics have however pointed to the theme of madness in *Hamlet* as potential grounds for dating the Additions closer to 1599–1600, the company eager to exploit the success of Shakespeare's play.[107] G. E. Bentley contended, apropos of revivals, that 'the refurbishing of old plays in the repertory seems to have been the universal practice in the London theatres from 1590 to 1642'.[108] In other words, when an old play was revived for an audience it was almost always reworked to some degree. It is conceivable the additional passages could have been written by Kyd himself in 1592 and did not make it into the first imprints, as Andrew Cairncross suggested, though we have no reason to assume that this is the case based on extant textual witness or stylistic evidence.[109] The 1592 imprint itself might also be a revision of the 1587 text, which we cannot test or verify, though the Additions in any case seem to postdate 1592. The 1597 revival is the only one we have evidence for, so if they were written for that why is Shakespeare contributing passages for his rival company? *Sir Thomas More* is likewise placed with the Admiral's through longstanding critical tradition, which many have struggled to consolidate with the strong internal evidence for Shakespeare's presence as a contributing author. Yet in this case the question may not even be relevant. As Brian Vickers contends:

> Since *The Spanish Tragedy* had been played in London from about 1587 to 1588, and published in 1592 with no declaration on its title-page associating it with a theatre company, then, according to Elizabethan pragmatic practices neither Strange's nor the Admiral's Men could claim it as their exclusive property, and other companies were free to perform it.[110]

John Webster's Induction to the 1604 imprint of Marston's *The Malcontent*, written originally for the Children of Paul's, provides a useful analogue. It has Burbage, Henry Condell, William Sly, John Lowin and John Sincler playing themselves in a discussion of their acquisition of their rivals' work:

SLY   I wonder you would play it, another company having interest in it.
CONDELL   Why not Malevole in folio with us as Jeronimo in decimo-sexto with
           them? They taught us a name for our play: we call it one for another.

Malevole is the lead character in Marston's play, and the folio and decimo-sexto formats clearly allude wittily to adults and children as well as to the idea of publication. E. K. Chambers felt that Henslowe's records provided proof that the Admiral's were the exclusive owners of *The Spanish Tragedy*, and that 'the King's could hardly have laid claim to it'.[111] He therefore felt Webster was more likely referencing *Jeronimo Part 1*, though G. K. Hunter disagreed, claiming the Children would have been unlikely to have filched such an obscure play, Kyd's being far more worth their while.[112] He also points out, rightly, that this does not prove the King's Men's ownership of it, though Brian Vickers contends that: 'some proprietorial attitude is surely displayed by "us" and "them". Perhaps *The Spanish Tragedy* was by then considered common (or at least shareable) property.'[113]

The evidence linking performances of the play to Shakespeare's company or rather performances of Hieronimo to Burbage is found, somewhat weakly at first, in a student play performed at Cambridge in 1601 called *The Second Return From Parnassus*, in which Burbage features as a character. He is depicted in one scene advising a student how to carry a powerful lead performance, and suggests the young man's voice 'would serve for Hieronimo', before offering a rendition of a line – 'Who calls Hieronimo from his naked bed?' – himself. This is an intriguing link, though it does not prove that Burbage had played the part by then. In Ben Jonson's repeated formulations, in the prologue to *Cynthia's Revels* (1601) as well as in *Bartholomew Fair*, *The Spanish Tragedy* was almost a byword for antiquated bombast and an index of shabby audience taste. The Burbage character in *Parnassus* seems to be proffering Hieronimo as a role requiring a certain kind of booming overture in delivery, and the point may therefore be that the audience would recognize a hammy actor (in the author's view) reciting the hammiest role, not necessarily one he was known for playing. However, Burbage's epitaph eighteen years later unequivocally links him to it:

No more young Hamlet, old Hieronimo,
Kind Lear, the grievèd Moor, and more beside,
That lived in him, have now forever died.

If we believe this we therefore know that Burbage played the part with the Chamberlain's/King's company by 1619, and, if we choose to interpret the *Parnassus* evidence as confirmation, by 1601. So if Burbage is linked to the play, then Shakespeare is too. If we follow the growing consensus among stylistic analysts that he wrote the Additions, are we looking, in the 1602 text, at the acting version of the Chamberlain's company, with the part of Hieronimo expanded for their star actor?

It had long been assumed that Ben Jonson was the author of the Additions based on two pieces of evidence in Henslowe, the first of which records a payment of forty shillings to him on 25 September 1601 'upon writtting of his adicians in geronymo', with a further advance of ten pounds on 22 June 1602 'in earneste of A Boocke called Richard crockbacke & for new adicyons for Jeronymo'.[114] Yet in addition to the argument that the sums of money advanced were in excess of what a writer would expect to be paid for three hundred lines' worth of material, another piece of evidence severely contradicts the likelihood of Jonson's additions (if indeed he ever wrote them) being those preserved by the 1602 imprint. The famous 'Painter' scene is parodied in John Marston's *Antonio and Mellida*, which features a painting bearing the date 1599, stating also that its subject is twenty-four years old, Marston's age that year.[115] This suggests it was intended as a joking authorial self-portrait, and dates the play almost certainly to that year and *The Spanish Tragedy* Additions, therefore, to then at the latest. Both *Antonio and Mellida* and its sequel, *Antonio's Revenge* (1600), were entered in the Stationers' Register on 24 October 1601 and published in 1602. Anne Barton, in an attempt to account for Jonson's authorship of the Additions, argued that the Painter parody was a last-minute insert by Marston, and that Jonson, 'stung by the attacks of critics who felt ... Kyd's play had been more coherent in its original form', likewise added a last-minute rejoinder in his *Cynthia's Revels* prologue, mocking an unnamed dullard who 'sweares ... That the olde Hieronimo, (*as it was first acted*) was the onely best, and Judiciously-pend Play of Europe'.[116] Lukas Erne, however, points out that Jonson's play was entered in the Stationers' Register on 23 May 1601 and printed that year, and that Barton's chronology 'does not square with the facts'.[117]

Jonson seems to be hinting at revision of the play by 1601 through the phrase 'as it was first acted'. He could conceivably have known about Henslowe's intention to ask him to revise the play in May that year (even though the first advance payment is recorded in September), and we could be witnessing a typical Jonsonian stance on the version containing none of his writing as inferior, though this is mere speculation. As stated earlier, we don't know if Jonson ever provided Henslowe with the Additions, and being involved with *The Spanish Tragedy* may even have been a sensitive subject for him in 1601–02, at the height of the 'War of the Theatres', in which Thomas Dekker, in *Satiromastix* (1601), mockingly alludes to the play's place in Jonson's past:

'thou hast forgot how thou amblest in leather pilch by a play-wagon, in the highway, and took'st mad Hieronimo's part, to get service among the mimics'. (4.1.161–5)

Jonson may have played Hieronimo, in a lowly touring production to boot – in much of his later work he seeks to distance himself from playing and to emphasize himself as an author – and he may not have wanted to reopen associations with the play. It is also conceivable that he wrote additions that were simply never printed, though the combined *Antonio and Mellida* and *Parnassus* evidence suggest that the 1599–1601 allusions to the play's adaptation and Burbage's links to it were a current conversation. The record of the 1597 revival in Henslowe marks the play 'ne', an omnipresent notation in the *Diary* about which scholars cannot come to a consensus, especially, as Erne notes, because it 'is not consistent in meaning'.[118] However, many take it to mean 'ne[w]', and if Henslowe is calling *The Spanish Tragedy* new in 1597 we can at least hypothesize that this signals revision. Is this the version for which Shakespeare provided material? Or could there even have been a separate revival by the Chamberlain's in or shortly before 1599 (which would make more sense if we imagine Burbage taking the lead role)? The 1602 text claims on its title page that it has been: 'Newly corrected, amended, and enlarged with new additions of the Painters part, and others, as it hath of late been diuers times acted.' The payments to Jonson in 1601–02 seem to act as evidence that the Admiral's would have been performing it then as many critics suggest, though considering Vickers' point about the lack of restrictions on performing the play the 1602 text could still be the Chamberlain's version while alluding to recent performances by the Admiral's. The Quarto seems more concerned with luring potential book buyers by advertising additions to a classic play and mainstay of the stage than with linking its popularity to any specific company or author.

Yet the payments to Jonson, while apparently confirming performance of the play by the Admiral's at this time, do not confirm that the Additions in the 1602 text are his. That they were, had in the main been almost unthinkingly averred since 1790, when Edmond Malone partially transcribed Henslowe's papers, misplaced for a long time in the College of God's Gift Library, Dulwich, which Alleyn himself founded in 1619. Jonson's authorship was for many the natural conclusion, the newly publicized evidence seeming so conclusive. Coleridge, however, in 1833 rejected the idea on stylistic grounds, suggesting moreover that the Additions 'are very like Shakespeare', each one thematically revisited 'in full form and development' elsewhere in the Shakespeare canon. Although several scholars, including William Gifford, Isaac Reed, F. S. Boas, W. W. Greg and E. K. Chambers have privileged the Henslowe evidence, attribution to Jonson has in large part been rejected, following Coleridge, on the perceived grounds that the Additions bear no stylistic relationship to his known writing. Percy Simpson, one of the twentieth century's most significant editors of Jonson, argued that the interiority, psychological nuance and depth of feeling in the Additions' depiction of Hieronimo's grief is lacking completely from the scenario in Jonson's *The Case is Altered* in which Count Ferneze laments the death of a son. In Simpson's estimation, Jonson's treatment of the character's emotional experience is 'competent and well expressed, but without one rare touch, one penetrating or memorable trait'.[119] Nonetheless, two of Jonson's major biographers in recent decades, Anne Barton and David Riggs, reopened the case for him, both focusing on the fact that he lost his infant daughter, Mary, in 1601, and arguing that the subject of a father's grief for a child would naturally find creative expression in his work at this time.

And yet, the chronological problems detailed above notwithstanding, such biographical speculation of the ilk claiming that Shakespeare's private feelings about the death of his son in 1596 are reflected in *King John*, does not supply a solid foundation upon which to build a literary case. We might equally argue, if the Additions do date from around 1597–99, that Shakespeare is the likely author, though again such assumptions about the expression of biographical experience in art are unhelpful. As Lukas Erne comments, 'it seems a biographer's fallacy to build an argument on "Jonson's heart" rather than on the material pressures of the stage business'.[120] No recent editor of Jonson or of *The Spanish Tragedy* has assigned the scenes to him; Philip Edwards rejected the idea and the new *Cambridge Edition of the Works of Ben Jonson* relegates the scenes to the dubia section, deeming his authorship of them 'unlikely'.[121] Of other candidates that have been explored, Thomas Hawkins in 1773 suggested the Additions had been 'foisted in by the players', relegating them to the footnotes in his edition. Charles Lamb in 1808 restored them to the main body of the text, calling them the 'very salt of the old play', and proposed John Webster as their author (a proposition that at least seems to work circumstantially in that Webster was writing for Henslowe in 1602, his greatest successes beginning a decade later). Edward Fitzgerald in the late nineteenth century echoed the Webster theory, as did Swinburne, though it has gained no real subsequent purchase. H. W. Crundell and R. G. Howarth in a series of *Notes and Queries* articles from 1933 to 1941 proposed Dekker, though again this has found very limited acceptance. The only candidate to whom scholars have seemed continually to return in the last half-century has been Shakespeare.

The four major Shakespeare proponents have been C. Van Heyningen, Warren Stevenson, Hugh Craig and, most recently, Brian Vickers. Van Heyningen wrote a short article asserting Shakespearean authorship of the passages in 1961, without going into any real evidential detail. Warren Stevenson, however, published a lengthy study eight years later as an extension of the work of his doctoral thesis. He performed parallel passage analysis of the Additions against the works of Shakespeare, using a concordance and the *OED* as references, though failed to provide what many attributionists since Muriel St Clair Byrne refer to as 'negative checks' (checking the results against the oeuvres of other writers to gain a true sense of the uniqueness, or not, of a word or phrase). Nonetheless, he came up with several matches that bear strong resemblance to ideas and images unique to Shakespeare. In 2008 he published a monograph expanding capaciously upon his previous work, though again merely developing parallel passage evidence. Brian Vickers has recently undertaken two lengthy studies of verbal parallels between the Additions and other works, using what he refers to as 'trigrams', parallels consisting of three words or more, as the chief category of evidence. Unlike Stevenson he has utilized online literary databases to expand exponentially the range of negative check evidence. His first article compared the Additions with sixty-four plays written between 1580 and 1595, though it was criticized for the incompleteness of negative check evidence resulting from this date range.[122] He has since expanded the study to encompass more than four hundred plays and masques dating across the whole period of the early professional theatres (1580–1642), finding more than one hundred unique matches listed in full in an appendix to the article between Shakespeare's plays and the Additions, which, in Vickers' reckoning, 'amounts to decisive evidence for [Shakespeare's] authorship'.[123] He also notes that the verbal textures of the Additions 'have more in common, in terms of language and subject matter, with plays from the first half of his career'.[124]

Hugh Craig undertook a component word analysis of the Additions in 1992, looking at function and lexical words in the 2,656-word-long sample they comprise.[125] His article was aimed specifically at testing the passages against the Shakespeare and Jonson canons, taking the fifty most common words from nine well-attributed works for each writer. Jonson was found to favour the function words *or, of* and *all* quite clearly, Shakespeare *me, thou, this* and *my*. The results suggested Shakespeare as the more likely author, though Craig admitted the tests' main shortcoming was their limiting to two authors, and that 'the added scenes might still prove to be more like some third author than like Shakespeare'.[126] He returned to the question in 2009 in a chapter in a co-authored monograph extolling the development of the kinds of computer-aided linguistic profiling tests that were somewhat in their infancy when his first foray into the question was made.[127] This time Craig extended the range to two hundred function words and five hundred lexical words from a corpus of 136 plays from 1576 to 1642, using 1,021 blocks of text (2,500 words long in each case) as samples, with the tests shown to have a 93 per cent success rate at correctly indentifying Shakespeare passages as Shakespeare. In these tests Craig examined the Additions against the canons of Jonson, Dekker, Webster, Peele, Lyly, Marlowe, Greene, Heywood, Fletcher and Middleton, noting that 'in each case the Additions were placed with Shakespeare rather than with the other author'.[128] Again, however, he concluded with a healthy circumspection, the tests showing the Additions to be 'like

Shakespeare, but not to the point that all doubt is removed'.[129] He also checked Stevenson's parallels, noting many to be unsatisfactory as markers of Shakespearean authorship, but that some 'cannot be matched anywhere else in *English Verse Drama*'.[130] Among the most striking are in Hieronimo's attempt to find out about the moonshine on the night of Horatio's murder: 'She should have shone: search thou the book' (3.13.48), which, Craig notes, affords a combination of words in a particular sense – 'a heavenly body "shining" with a calendar "book"' – paralleled only in *Richard III*'s 'he disdains to shine, for by the book / He should have braved the east an hour ago' (5.3.281–2).[131] Similarly, when Hieronimo instructs the Painter how to depict the murderers he tells him to 'let their eyebrows jutty over' (3.13.142), a combination of words and sense that appears elsewhere only in *Henry V*'s 'let the brow o'erwhelm it / As fearfully as doth a galled rock / O'erhang and jutty his confounded base' (3.1.11–13). And Hieronimo's phrase, again from the same scene, 'minutes jarring' (3.13.156) recalls *Richard II*'s 'My thoughts are minutes, and with sighs they jar' (5.5.51). A phrase repeated verbatim is found in Addition 3 in the lines '... there is Nemesis, and Furies / And things called whips' (3.11.41–2), recalling *Henry VI Part 2*'s '... have you not / Beadles in your town and things called whips?' (2.1.139–40). This, however, falls into the category of parallels Craig suggests as 'so obvious that they may well have been intended as allusions, or even as parodies' and may not therefore be suggestive of a common creative source.[132]

The other major recent contributor to discussions of the play has been Lukas Erne, though his book was only partially concerned with the authorship of the Additions. He remained non-committal on the subject, and moreover felt that, apart from the Painter scene, the Additions 'do nothing to improve Kyd's play' and that they 'belong' in appendices, not integrated into the working text.[133] This may be a little dismissive, though it identifies a feature of the Additions that will need to be addressed by attributionists: that of the uneven nature of their poetic and verbal textures. Erne identifies 'metrical deficiencies', and contends, following Edwards, who suggested they may have come from actors, that the copy Pavier obtained may have been 'an imperfect and partial transcript of the added material'.[134] He cites two verbal borrowings – one from *Titus Andronicus* in Addition IV and one from *Doctor Faustus* in Addition V – as potential evidence of memorial reconstruction, the actors supplementing material their faulty memories could not provide with lines from other plays. Craig, however, points out that an actors' report still does not rule out Shakespeare as original author. Moreover, it is not only the Painter scene (Addition IV) that stands out. It should be clear to most readers that the dynamics in the poetic and dramatic modulation of Addition III, in its skilful development of psychological slippage under the pressure of grief in a lengthy soliloquy, are of a different quality to the workmanlike fashion in which Additions I, II and V present character and convey information. Philip Edwards felt the 'literary quality' of these other three 'is slight' and that they 'do much damage to Kyd's careful unfolding of plot and character'.[135] Of course it is perfectly possible that Shakespeare wrote them, their poor quality notwithstanding. But the discrepancy – both between the other two Additions and the rest of Shakespeare's known work – does raise questions. Edwards declared the authorship of all the Additions unknown, while Clara Calvo and Jesús Tronch suggest there are 'sufficient grounds to link the author of the fourth addition with Shakespeare'.[136]

It would make sense that whoever wrote some of the Additions wrote them all, but equally there are evident differences in poetic style and tone which are difficult to ignore and to explain, and which require further investigation. Yet on balance we feel there is a wealth of stylistic, stylometric and impressionistic evidence suggesting that Shakespeare is the likeliest of all known early dramatists to have written Additions III and IV. Even that is not definitively settled, just as the question of dating remains mysterious; but we here suggest that the most influential tragedy of the earliest days of the professional theatres came, in time, to include material by their most famous son. It may be somewhat romantic, though not implausible, to see a discreet act of homage on Shakespeare's part, beyond the simple pragmatic expediency of serving his company's needs: in the *Venus and Adonis* epigraph Shakespeare subsumed his own voice into a literary mentor's lines in an act that seems somehow both an acknowledgement of, and an attempt to repay, an artistic debt.

Thomas Lord Cromwell (c.1599–1602)

Thomas Lord Cromwell was the first of the plays that came to be classed as 'Shakespeare apocrypha' to be printed after the Chamberlain's Men's move to the Globe theatre in 1599. This move seemingly coincided with a company decision to withhold from the presses any new plays by their star dramatist, and we can see a definite demand on the part of audiences to read, and for publishers to supply, printed plays by Shakespeare in the 1600s, the decade in which the most lastingly controversial title-page ascriptions to him were made.[137] Four came from within the Chamberlain's/King's repertory, beginning with *Cromwell*, and followed by *The London Prodigal*, *A Yorkshire Tragedy* and *Pericles*, with one other, *The Puritan*, coming from within the ranks of Paul's Boys.[138] *The Puritan* partners *Cromwell* in Globe-era apocrypha in that it refers only suggestively to its author, one 'W. S.', while the other three name Shakespeare explicitly. It was not linked to Shakespeare through company ownership which is likely to account for the fudged ascription, though why *Cromwell* received similar treatment is harder to explain.[139] Shakespeare would have been the most natural 'W. S.' to associate with the penning of plays for the Chamberlain's in 1602 when *Cromwell* was first printed, as whoever was responsible for the information no doubt well knew. Perhaps they also knew that he had not written it, and wanted to hide behind the relative safety they hoped the ambiguous attribution would afford. We might observe that of these five plays only *Cromwell*'s printing predates 1603, when Shakespeare's company came under the patronage of King James and Shakespeare became the pre-eminent dramatist in the country, though his name was relatively hot property before this, having appeared several times on the title pages of plays that he did write prior to and including 1602. Plausible deniability of a knowingly spurious claim therefore seems the more likely scenario here. *Cromwell* was entered in the Stationers' Register to William Cotton on 11 August 1602, though no mention of authorship was made in the note:

> William Cotton   Entred for his Copie vnder the handes / of master JACKSON and master waterston Warden A booke called the lyfe and Deathe of the Lord Cromwell, as yt was lately Acted by the Lord Chamberleyn his servantes ... vj^d

It went to press some time later that year, with the authorial information in place, though perhaps the oddest thing to note is that the publisher named on the title page was now William Jones:

> THE / True Chronicle Hi- / storie of the whole life and death / of *Thomas* Lord *Cromwell*. / As it hath beene sundrie times pub- / *likely Acted by the Right Hono-* / rable the Lord Chamberlaine / *his Seruants*. / Written by W.S. / Imprinted at London for William Iones, and are / to be solde at his house neere Holburne con- / duict, at the signe of the Gunne. / 1602.

W. W. Greg suggests the entry to Cotton may have been made in error as the play was not claimed as part of his stock until 1617, some years after his death.[140] The cryptic authorial attribution was reiterated on the title page of the 1613 reprint, and the company information was updated from Chamberlain's to King's. *Cromwell* was included in the Third Folio, based seemingly on the authority of the early Quartos, and was reprinted in the Fourth. Shakespeare was named as the author of 'Cromwell's History', presumably the same play, in the catalogues of Edward Archer (1656) and Francis Kirkman (1661/71), and Nicholas Rowe included it in his 1709 edition of Shakespeare. Robert Walker issued it separately in 1734 as 'A Tragedy. By Shakespear. [*sic*]' within his collection of cheap, small-format editions of individual Shakespeare plays, yet despite this plethora of early acceptance of Shakespeare's authorship, mostly, it must be said, commercially driven, resistance to the idea has subsequently proved both widespread and strong. No other eighteenth-century editor of Shakespeare accepted the attribution, with Pope, Rowe's successor, intoning in his 1725 edition:

> I make no doubt to declare that those wretched plays, *Pericles, Locrine, Sir John Oldcastle, Yorkshire Tragedy, Lord Cromwell, The Puritan*, and *London Prodigal*, cannot be admitted as his.

Towards the end of the century Edmond Malone dismissed the play in even stronger terms:

> To vindicate Shakespeare from having written a single line of this piece would be a waste of time. The poverty of language, the barrenness of incident and the inartificial conduct of every part of the performance, place it rather perhaps below the compositions of even the second-rate dramatic authors of the age in which it was produced.[141]

Yet no critic's pen has been as steeped in gall as Swinburne's when denouncing the attribution to Shakespeare and evaluating the play on purely impressionistic grounds:

> *Thomas Lord Cromwell* is a piece of such utterly shapeless, spiritless, bodiless, soulless, senseless, helpless, worthless rubbish, that there is no known writer of Shakespeare's age to whom it could be ascribed without the infliction of an unwarrantable insult on that writer's memory.[142]

Attribution to Shakespeare found favour in the nineteenth century with Ludwig Tieck and A. W. Schlegel, 'to their lasting discredit' according to C.F. Tucker Brooke, who denounced them as a critical movement of 'romantic satellites', somewhat cheaply packaged within a xenophobic portrayal of a group of 'Germans all...incapable of appreciating the delicacies of English style'.[143] Nonetheless, a survey of their track record throughout these essays somewhat bears out Brooke's accusation that they were given frequently to 'wild attributions', this one surely chief among them. W. G. Simms argued against Shakespeare's authorship, while Henry Ulrici felt *Cromwell* a very early Shakespearean effort, written before 1592, and Max Moltke likewise allowed for the possibility of Shakespeare's involvement. F. G. Fleay, employing the kind of guesswork so characteristic of much of his scholarship, nominated Michael Drayton, while A. F. Hopkinson adjudged it the work of Greene, partly revised by Shakespeare. Serious attempts to connect the play to Shakespeare, however, did not survive into the twentieth century, and it has not since been included in any Shakespeare edition or series. As Gary Taylor noted:

> The external evidence is weak, and the internal evidence tells strongly against Shakespeare's authorship of all or part; no one this century has supported attribution to Shakespeare.[144]

Only A. W. Titherley – whose view was warped towards authorship conspiracy rather than any serious stylistic study – proposed Shakespeare, the pseudonym, he believed, of William Stanley, sixth Earl of Derby.[145] Tucker Brooke included it in his edition of *The Shakespeare Apocrypha*, though dismissed Shakespearean attribution. E. K. Chambers, Arthur Acheson, Clara Longworth de Chambrun, Irving Ribner and Jonathan

Hope all likewise rejected claims for Shakespeare's authorship. The debates do not extend much further than this, and the sparsity of this list of scholars owes much to the fact that Shakespearean non-involvement in this play has seemed so cut-and-dried that little serious consideration of the question has been attempted. William R. Bowden supported attribution to Thomas Heywood in 1951, first proposed by Richard Farmer around 1780, though nothing connects Heywood with the King's Men before 1634. Irving Ribner noted in the play some resemblances to Heywood in its 'bourgeois sentiments', but felt there was no real evidence for his hand.[146] Arthur Melville Clark dismissed claims for Heywood on the basis that the play was, he felt, too poor to be his, and J. M. Robertson threw out the case for Drayton on the same grounds, a judgement echoed by Bernard H. Newdigate. Ribner also rejected Wentworth Smith and William Sly as other 'W. S.' candidates. Such judgements serve as a very strong index of the almost complete lack of credibility attached to any Shakespeare attribution, and help explain the absence of any attempt to reopen the debate since the 1890s. Tucker Brooke pointed to the play's structural shortcomings, and seemed tacitly to imply that the mess was either the product of incompetent or multiple authorship:

> The scenes of *Cromwell* are disconnected and undramatic to such a degree that the real plot cannot be said to begin before the close of the third Act.[147]

Baldwin Maxwell took up and expanded Brooke's comment, arguing that the play was either originally in multiple parts, here condensed together; that it was originally collaborative; or that it was begun by one dramatist, and completed by another. He felt the point of division comes at the end of 2.5, though contrary to Brooke made a lengthy case arguing that the play up to that point is skilfully constructed and purposefully sequential, while the latter half falls away into mere episodes with no sense of unity.

Probably the most useful scholarly work on *Cromwell* has been in establishing its date, which has shed light on a set of creative circumstances that might help suggest potential authors, although more stylometric investigation is required. It has often been linked to two lost *Cardinal Wolsey* plays of 1601, for which payments are recorded in Henslowe's *Diary* to Henry Chettle, Anthony Munday, Michael Drayton, and Wentworth Smith. Acheson thought *Cromwell* was an early 1580s play, and came up with a hugely complicated transmission scenario in which it made its way from Oxford's Men to the Chamberlain's via Pembroke's, was revised by Dekker, passing to Henslowe where it was used by the aforementioned writers as a source for the *Wolsey* plays, before finally being released to the press in 1602. Robert Boies Sharpe argued that it was an older play revived by the Chamberlain's company in 1601, while Baldwin Maxwell felt that it was actually composed around the same time as the *Wolsey* plays and *Sir Thomas More*, a view recently echoed by John Jowett.[148] Maxwell also saw borrowings from *Julius Caesar* and *Henry V*, concluding that it must therefore postdate 1599, and that the likely authors of this apparently collaborative play were to be found among those who had produced the other entries in this mini-vogue for drama about Henry VIII's chancellors: Munday, Chettle, Heywood, Dekker, and Wentworth Smith. Dekker and Shakespeare have been eliminated as candidates by Jonathan Hope's sociolinguistic analysis, as have Marlowe, Middleton and Fletcher. Hope judged the regulation rate of the auxiliary 'do' evidence for Cromwell extraordinarily low, and while the relative marker evidence was quite standard, the extreme result throughout the play in the former category makes collaboration, in Hope's view, highly unlikely, and Shakespearean authorship out of the question. He also notes that such extreme evidence means that 'if there are any extant plays by the writer of *Thomas Lord Cromwell*, and they are sampled at some point in the future, it should be relatively easy to identify him or her'. Ward Elliott and Robert Valenza's tests ruled out Shakespeare in strong terms, the play scoring thirteen rejections in their evaluation, where none of the twenty-nine acknowledged baseline canonical Shakespeare plays they tested scores more than two.[149]

Serious stylometric analysis investigating the identity of the actual author(s), beyond eliminating Shakespeare from the list of suspects, has been largely lacking, mainly because the play has otherwise proved to be of little interest. Hopefully its appearance in this volume might reignite attempts to test it against the canons of more marginal writers from c.1600, which is almost certainly when it was written. Perhaps 'W.S.' does indeed refer to the actual author, Wentworth Smith or another, though ambiguity allowing for an interpretive attribution to Shakespeare is surely intended. The identification of his company as the play's owners, which there is little reason to doubt, seems to support this, and the likelihood that Shakespeare was involved collaboratively in a very broad sense is strong. He probably attended rehearsals, overlooked the script, conversed with or advised the author, and spoke some of the play aloud in performance. But he did not write it. Nonetheless, *Thomas Lord Cromwell* offers us a unique insight into the company's non-Shakespearean repertory around the turn of the seventeenth century, which may have included a play on a similar theme to which Shakespeare was, just a few years later, to contribute a substantial revision: the dangerously controversial *Sir Thomas More*.

Sir Thomas More (c.1600?, revised c.1604)

The manuscript of *Sir Thomas More*, a play that was never printed and apparently never even performed, is one of the most precious artefacts to survive from the early professional theatres because it almost certainly contains the only dramatic writing we have in Shakespeare's own hand. It is housed in the British Library as MS. Harley 7368, and, owing to its uniqueness and fragility, may not be handled without very special permission, though one of the Hand D pages, believed to be Shakespeare's, is frequently placed on display to the public. How it survived is something of a mystery, though its provenance is traceable to 1728 when the London book collector John Murray donated it to Edward Harley, Third Earl of Oxford and Lord Mortimer. Harley, in turn, after binding it with another manuscript play, *The Humorous Lovers*, bequeathed it in 1753 to the British Museum, along with the rest of his vast manuscript collection, though interest in it as a possible Shakespearean relic would not be stirred for more than a century after. The insights offered by *The Booke of Sir Thomas Moore* into the workings of early play composition, and of collaborative playwriting more specifically, are profound, and yet the difficulties thrown up by its chaotic state are perhaps even greater. It is not the only dramatic manuscript to survive from the period, though Stanley Wells notes that it is 'probably the untidiest, [and] most heavily revised', and continues:

> It represents a troubled and ultimately abandoned attempt on the part of various authors to create a script, interrupted by the censorial intervention of the Master of the Revels, Edmund Tilney...The basic manuscript is a fair copy made by the dramatist Anthony Munday (1560–1633) of a text in which he may have collaborated with Henry Chettle (c.1560–c.1607). Alterations and additions were made by Chettle, Thomas Dekker (c.1572–1632), very probably William Shakespeare, and probably Thomas Heywood (c.1573–1641). A theatre scribe annotated parts of the manuscript, and some of the revisions exist in transcripts he wrote out...Shakespeare's authorship of the majority of [Act 2 Scene 4], first proposed in 1871, has been accepted by most scholars on the basis of handwriting and of the evidence of dramatic and linguistic style. His contribution shows him as a thoroughgoing professional sharing with colleagues whose work he respected in an essentially collaborative enterprise.[150]

A thoroughgoing professional Shakespeare undoubtedly was, yet we perhaps see another side to his playwriting in his contribution to *Sir Thomas More*, which cannot be considered a straightforward act of collaboration, but rather part of a highly unusual *post hoc* salvage attempt. The impetus behind all of the additions and revisions seems to have been, ostensibly at least, to tackle the objections raised by Tilney to the original play. It seems the chief reason behind the unusually large number of revising authors and the consequent untidiness of the manuscript has to do with the play's subject matter, although Scott McMillin demonstrated that simple theatrical expediency was also a factor. His account of doubling shows that the number of parts is reduced by the revisions and, among other things, transitions between scenes and time for costume changes were better allowed for.[151] Nonetheless, *Sir Thomas More* dramatizes the life and downfall of the famous Catholic martyr, executed at the command of Henry VIII for refusing to sanction Henry's divorce from Katherine of Aragon and consequently his break from Rome, albeit that these matters are handled in as veiled and euphemistic a manner as possible. Clearly this was not fit matter for public staging in post-Reformation England under Henry's daughter, Elizabeth, whose 1559 proclamation 'Prohibiting Unlicensed Interludes and Plays, Especially on Religion or Policy' came shortly on the heels of her accession in November the previous year. Elizabeth was returning England to Protestantism after her half-sister Mary's gruelling five-year re-establishment of Roman Catholicism, which earned her the ominous soubriquet 'Bloody Mary'. Religion was a tinderbox and public performances – sermons, plays, ballad singing, street preaching – were sources of fire.

As the professional theatres grew in London in the 1570s, the matter of 'Interludes and Plays' became a far more serious threat and the Revels Office became increasingly important. In 1573 the office of the Master of the Revels grew in its influence to become effectively official state censor. It was held by Edmund Tilney from 1579 until his death in 1610, so the presence of his hand on the Original Text is of no help whatsoever in narrowing the possible date range of the play and its Additions, the limits of which almost all scholars set at early 1590s to mid 1600s. Perhaps the most curious thing about Tilney's interventions is the fact that he seemed most concerned with the 'Ill May Day' riots episode, marking for deletion only small parts of the lengthy portion of Original Text following the Additions which deal with More's resistance to Henry's reformation of the English Church and his subsequent execution. This may be because he felt he had seen enough to deny the play licence by then anyway; one of the few definite calls for deletion he makes later in the manuscript is the point in Act 4 scene 2 at which we are given indirectly to understand that More is refusing to sign the Act of Succession, a key piece of Reformation legislation recognizing the legitimacy of the heirs of Henry and Anne Boleyn. This means that the play is effectively dramatizing a rejection of Elizabeth's right to the English throne and her place as the head of its Church, a symbolic moment that could not be staged under any circumstances. It is therefore likely that Tilney had reached his limit and was no longer willing to work with the dramatist(s) in preparing the play for performance. That this is true may be suggested by the fact that earlier in the manuscript he offers detailed instruction for revision as a precondition for allowing the script, which he still clearly saw as an option at that point. In the margin alongside the first nineteen lines of text he has written:

Leaue out... / ye insurrection / wholy w^t / ye Cause ther off & / begin w^t S^r Th: / Moore att ye mayors sessions / w^t a reportt afterwards / off his good servic' / don being' Shriue off Londō / vppō a mutiny Agaynst y^e / Lūbards only by A shortt / reportt & nott otherwise / att your own perilles / E Tyllney.[152]

The plural 'perilles' does not necessarily furnish proof that the Original Text was written collaboratively as plays were thought of as the product of companies rather than authors. The rioting episode would nonetheless have contributed strongly to Tilney's final decision, taking as he does especial care to call for the revision of 'strangers' and 'Frenchmen' to the more politically neutral 'Lombards'.[153] The early to mid 1590s in London saw religious hostilities from the citizen classes towards the community of continental Protestant exiles dwelling in the city, as well as famine-provoked uprisings, which has led to the popular conclusion that the play was written at that time. Yet the Original Text and Additions, as we will see, more probably date to c.1600 and c.1604 respectively, with Tilney's comments – perhaps not so much responding to a current problem as taking steps to avoid reawakening a dormant one – made shortly after the Original Text's composition. The play seemingly lay on the shelf for four years before the revisers came in to try and rework it for the stage, though astonishingly they did not comply with Tilney's requests, retaining the insurrection and drafting in no less a dramatist than Shakespeare to expand upon it. The Original Text was prepared as a 'fair copy', a neat, legible copy of messy authorial drafts, by the dramatist Anthony Munday, and the manuscript he submitted to Tilney comprised sixteen, or maybe seventeen, leaves of paper – technically referred to as 'folios' – measuring approximately 32 × 21 cm, thirteen of which survive: folios 3–5, 10, 11, 14, 15 and 17–22.[154] There are seven discernible hands present in the surviving manuscript (including additions/revisions) which have been identified, provisionally in some cases, as follows:

Original Text

Hand S – Anthony Munday, plus marginal annotations and deletions in the hand of *Edmund Tilney*, Master of the Revels

Additions/Revisions

Hand A – Henry Chettle (Addition I)

Hand B – Thomas Heywood? (Additions II and VI)

Hand C – Playhouse Scribe; he merely copied the work of other dramatists in some scenes and annotated the manuscript in others. The job of identifying the authors behind the passages copied in his hand has therefore proved even more difficult (Additions II, III, IV and V)

Hand D – William Shakespeare (Addition II)

Hand E – Thomas Dekker (Addition IV)

A breakdown of the authorial hands behind the Additions, as well as their location in this edition, is as follows:

Addition I – Henry Chettle [4.5.60–130]

Addition II – Thomas Heywood? [2.2]; Henry Chettle (transcribed in **Hand C**) [2.3]; William Shakespeare [2.4.1–148]

Addition III – William Shakespeare? (transcribed in **Hand C**) [3.2.1–21]

Addition IV – Thomas Dekker [3.2.22–266]; lines 22–239 are in **Hand C** and 240–66 in **Hand E**, though Dekker is the likely author of the entire Addition

Addition V – William Shakespeare/Thomas Heywood? (transcribed in **Hand C**) [3.3]

Addition VI – Thomas Heywood? [4.1.276–323]

Tilney's hand is not present in any of the Additions which may mean that he was never presented with the expanded manuscript that survives, or that he made the decision not to license the revised play before even lifting his pen to it. An understanding of Tilney's role in all of this, as well as of the arguments for authorship that follow, will rely on an ability to visualize the physical manuscript as it now survives, including Additions, and G. Harold Metz's description is compact and elegant:

The manuscript comprises a total of twenty-two leaves of which the first two are the original vellum wrapper, a double leaf extracted from a fifteenth century Latin breviary, on one page of which is inscribed '*The Booke of Sir Thomas Moore*', in ornamental italic letters. Thirteen of the leaves contain most of the original text of the play, but there are two lacunae, one probably representing the loss of two leaves (after fol. 5) and the other possibly the loss of one leaf (after fol. 11). The remaining leaves contain additions to the play, some of which represent replacements for the text on the lost leaves, while others constitute revisions or expansions of, or insertions into, the extant original text. Alterations and deletions are marked in the original version, some of which are minor, some substantial, and not all of the additions and revisions are properly integrated into the text.[155]

The Additions comprise two groups: the first, folios 6–9, was intended to replace the material at the first lacuna described by Metz; the second group comprises folios 12–13 (second lacuna) and folio 16. Each group also contains one addition slip pasted on to pages from the Original Text (11* and 13*). The one major anomaly is folio 6, known as Addition I, which is wrongly placed in the manuscript. As Peter Blayney notes :

> It contains a long speech by More in the hand of Henry Chettle, and is designed to replace two deleted speeches on 19a [i.e. the first side of folio 19]. Since there are two intervening speeches which have not been marked for deletion, it is not immediately obvious how this is to be fitted in. As on 7a, the text is confined to one side of the leaf by writing the last few lines in the margin, the verso [i.e. the 'b' side] being blank.[156]

It is known as Addition I because of where it appears in the manuscript, even though its correct placing – adding to Act 4 scene 5 in which More reflects on his banishment from court – ought to make it Addition VI. It is itself substantially revised by Chettle (see gloss on 4.5.64 and 4.5.113). Blayney notes that there are two speeches not marked for deletion on 19a which complicate its insertion into the manuscript, referring to the small section:

> *Catesbie.* Sir, we haue seene farre better dayes, then these.
> *Moore.* I was the patrone of those dayes, and knowe,
>   those were but painted dayes, only for showe,
>   then greeue not you to fall with him that gaue them.

This portion of text, unlike the two large blocks on either side of it, has no deletion line next to it in the margin, yet some editors including Jowett treat the whole section as intended for deletion, seeing the removal of these lines as implicit in Tilney's instruction.[157] Gabrieli and Melchiori privilege the Original Text marked for deletion over the Addition.[158] The problem is resistant to easy resolution and relies heavily on friable editorial interpretation. Addition II is the whole section that fills the first lacuna (folios 7–9) dealing with the 'ill May Day' riots. Folio 7a is a rewrite of material deleted on 5b and is in Hand B. It does indeed squeeze its final few lines into the margin as Blayney says, although unlike 6b, 7b is not blank, containing a new scene in Hand C, which is likely to have been written by Chettle on stylistic evidence.[159] Folios 8 and 9a are written in Hand D, believed to be that of William Shakespeare, and deal with More's quelling of the rebellion. Hand C marks for deletion five lines on 9a leading up to the phrase 'Tell me but this', also in his hand, at 2.4.114. Blayney adds:

> 9b deserves special mention, having been described as blank by every commentator since Dyce in 1844, which is not quite true. In the upper left-hand corner appears, quite plainly, the speech-prefix 'all.' in

Hand D. Below this, and slightly to its left, another 'a' has been begun, but smudged out before it was finished.[160]

The notation 11* refers to an addition slip containing a speech by More in Hand C, pasted over the deletions on the lower half of 11b (part of the Original Text). It has frequently been argued, and is likely, that this speech in which More reflects on the fickleness of worldly power and fortune is also by Shakespeare, copied out by the scribe; it is known as Addition III. Addition IV marks the beginning of the second group and follows immediately after, comprising folios 12 and 13; it is written in Hand C until halfway down 13b and finished off by Hand E. As Blayney notes, the scene 'once finished halfway down 13b, but the final "exit." has been crossed out by Thomas Dekker, who has filled the rest of the page with an extension of the final dialogue'.[161] Although the Addition is written in two different hands, its authorship is generally attributed entirely to Dekker. It describes two episodes that show More as both human and humanist, counselling the Bishop of Winchester's ruffian servant, Faulkner, to cut his hair, and, in a scene in which two of Holbein's famous subjects meet, trading wit and mutual respect with the intellectual reformer, Erasmus. Addition V, like Addition III, is a slip pasted on to a page of the Original Text, in this case 14a, the underlying text of which is heavily crossed out. The slip is referred to as 13* as it is more properly part of the previous addition. According to Blayney:

> since the new scene does not properly connect with what follows in the original, a small scrap of paper containing a soliloquy by More in Hand C, fol. 13*, has been pasted over the deleted material at the bottom of 14a in an attempt to provide better continuity.[162]

It is likewise in the hand of the playhouse scribe, and is very difficult to attribute to an author given its brevity, though John Jowett in his edition argues that it is also the work of Shakespeare, possibly revised by Heywood. The Messenger's speech preceding More's 'Why, this is cheerful news ...' (3.3.6) has been copied out in the margin of page 14a/13* by Hand C, the rough draft of which appears in isolation halfway down 16b. Folio 16 (Addition VI) is entirely in Hand B (Heywood?), and, apart from this draft speech, is designed as an elaboration of action that appears on 17a in the Original text (the performance of *The Marriage of Wit and Wisdom*), so it is, like folio 6, misplaced. Folio 17a features the marginal direction 'Enter To the players wth a reward' in Hand C and a reference mark to the relevant folio 16.

The other major additional contribution to the play is a series of speeches for a 'Clown' added into the margins of 10a, 10b and 11a by Hand B, who also added Clown material into his reworked 5b material on 7a. Identification of Hand B as Thomas Heywood has not met with universal approval, and Eric Rasmussen has suggested that one of the supporting arguments for Heywood's authorship, that Hand B must be a composing playwright brought in to add comic material, is not justified, and that the speeches are likely to be transcriptions of what the company's clown actor improvised onstage in the original performances.[163] John Jowett, however, argues that the scenario Rasmussen describes – in which *Hand B* could be a theatre functionary – is 'not plausible', adding:

> A revision on this scale would, by the evidence of Henslowe's *Diary* and all else that we know about the production of play texts, normally be handed to a professional dramatist. There is no evidence for scribes, book-keepers or other theatre personnel taking on this role. Hand B is a composing writer ... He was capable of writing lively and effective comic dialogue that includes humour and word-play. He was alert to social nuance, aware of dramatic tradition, and able to produce resonant metatexual reference. His diction was broad and discriminating, strong in idiomatic inflexion, asseverations and proverbial

references ... The passages as a whole therefore offer far more than an approximation to, or transcription of, improvised clownage.[164]

Again, identification is difficult, though Heywood is here proposed as the most likely candidate. Neither Tilney nor Munday's hands appear in any of the revisions, and all other identifiable interventions by second hands in the manuscript are as follows:

Hand C – (i) alteration of some speech prefixes in Addition II (in both the Heywood and Shakespeare sections), (ii) the marginal note *Et tu Erasmus an diabolus* at 13a (3.2.176, omitted in this edition), a page in Hand C anyway, (iii) a direction for music ('Waits play hautbois') at 14b (4.1.76), (iv) an added entrance direction including an actor's name ('Mess[enger] T Goodal') at 13* (3.3.0)

Hand E (Dekker) – a phrase at 13a which reads 'I am ipse' (3.2.221)

Tilney – deletion marks in 3a, 3b, 5a (with the marginal note 'Mend yᶦˢ' against Shrewsbury's first speech in 1.3, the word *Englishe* replaced by *man*, and the words *straunger* and *ffrencheman* replaced by the more noncommittal *Lombard* (1.3.37, 49, 53)), 10b, 17b (with marginal note *all altr* (at 4.2.94, omitted in this edition), signalling that the whole passage concerned with More's refusal to sign the Act of Succession and his resignation had to be altered)

The authorship of the play – the Original Text

The discussion so far has focussed mainly on the handwriting in the manuscript, but now turns to the question of the composing agents behind it. John Jowett points out that there are 'no known examples from the period of a dramatist copying a play in which he had no hand'.[165] The Original Text of the play is entirely in Anthony Munday's hand, which has led to a general acceptance that he is at least a co-author, but there is no scholarly consensus regarding his sole authorship. It has been argued that Munday, a virulent anti-Catholic spy, could not have had a hand in a play that seems to sympathize with a Catholic martyr, and that he merely copied it out at the instruction of the authorities and under assurance that he would be free from recrimination, producing a fair copy under the guise of a regular act of theatrical collaboration in order to work with, identify, and ultimately entrap the actual authors. This conspiracy theorizing in order to remove Munday from the list of the play's authors is purely hypothetical and has been seen as paranoid fabrication to advance the claims of others, most significantly Shakespeare, from whom the Catholic question is never far these days, and not in accordance with stylistic evidence linking parts of the work strongly to Munday. Marlowe has been suggested as a plotter of the play, but this is dependent on a dating no later than 1593, which is another matter of scholarly dispute. Thomas Merriam, in a number of articles ranging over thirty years, has argued for Shakespeare's sole authorship of the Original Text, though he is virtually alone in this conviction.[166]

F. G. Fleay, the pioneering though frequently unreliable nineteenth-century Renaissance drama scholar, proposed Thomas Lodge as the author of the Original Text in 1893, finding support from A. F. Hopkinson in 1902. The New Bibliography, an early twentieth-century academic movement devoted to a more rigorous, 'scientific' approach to textual study, provided the breakthrough with the application of palaeographical scrutiny to the manuscript. W. W. Greg, arguably the most prolific of all textual bibliographers, felt initially that it was a scribal copy, which could not have been authorial as it contained transcription errors. He felt an author would hardly have been likely to have trouble with his own writing when preparing the fair copy, and so referred to the hand of the Original Text as 'Hand S', shorthand for the anonymous scribe he believed was responsible for copying it. However, in 1913 he stated the belief that Munday was the likely author and transcriber of the play after noticing that the handwriting was the same as that in Munday's manuscript play *John a Kent and John a Cumber*, which was published in the Tudor Facsimile Texts series in 1912, a year after Greg's Malone Society edition of *Sir Thomas More*.[167] Since then no one has doubted Munday's penmanship of the Original Text, but the matter of his authorship, sole or collaborative, has proved controversial. Greg's view that Munday was at least the play's part-author was corroborated by the great palaeographer, Sir Edward Maunde Thompson, while Samuel Tannenbaum felt that Munday had written it alone.[168] Greg later began increasingly to come round to the idea that the play was collaborative, the transcription errors explained by the fact that Munday, one of the authors, had trouble with the work of his co-author(s).[169] G. Harold Metz offers the following summary of the errors noted by Greg (Metz's parenthetical references are keyed to Greg's Malone Society edition of the play):

> The most significant of these indications is the meaningless word *fashis* (l. †1847, p. 61) where the sense undoubtedly requires *fashion*. Greg drew attention to this in his Malone Society edition and explained it as a misreading of *fashiō*. 'This is quite an easy mistake, for the two [endings] resemble one another closely in some hands but it is a mistake of which it is almost impossible to suppose that an author would be guilty in copying his own work' (p. xvi). Perhaps of equal significance is the presence of duplicate endings to the play (ll. †1956–64, pp. 64–5; and ll. †1965–86, p. 65). It is scarcely conceivable that the original author would have transcribed into his fair copy his own two endings as they presumably stood in his foul papers, the first of which he would probably have previously rejected.[170]

MacDonald Jackson's 1963 article took Greg's 1911 argument to task to argue that transcription errors could occur within an author's copying of his own work, and affirmed that Munday probably was part-author of the Original Text; both arguments were reiterated by Richard Beebe in 1971. E. H. C. Oliphant argued for multiple authors, perceiving the Original Text to operate on three distinct levels of stylistic quality: one was 'somewhat old-fashioned', one 'much jerkier and less regular', and the other 'much finer and more impressive verse than either of the others'.[171] He ascribed the three sections to Hands S, B and A (Munday, Heywood? and Chettle) respectively. G. B. Harrison broadly concurred, though proposed Dekker as third author instead of Chettle. R. C. Bald came down somewhere between the two, taking Oliphant's three authors and proposing Dekker as a reviser. Harold Jenkins felt that Munday could have collaborated with Chettle 'since Chettle was a close friend of Munday from 1592 ... but the case is by no means clear'.[172] Bald agreed with Oliphant on the three authors, and felt that Dekker may have been brought in afterwards as a reviser.[173] J. M. Nosworthy concluded that Munday collaborated with Chettle and Dekker, eliminating Hands B, C and D as they were, respectively, unidentified, unlikely to collaborate being only a scribe, and currently beyond discussion 'since Shakespeare's *locus standi* has yet to be ascertained'.[174] A. C. Partridge analysed the use of contractions, spelling, grammar, punctuation and vocabulary of each of the playwrights in light of Oliphant's study and came round to endorsing Oliphant's view of the three collaborators (Munday, Chettle and Heywood). Peter Blayney also argued that the first stage of the play's composition after its plotting was the drafting of scenes by 'several playwrights, probably including Munday, Chettle and Heywood'.[175] I. A. Shapiro and David M. Bergeron argued for Munday's sole authorship, while John Jowett proposed Henry Chettle's presence in the Original Text, allowing for the possibility of Oliphant's claim that Chettle was solely responsible for scenes 10–13 (Act 4 scenes 2–5), and arguing for his presence elsewhere as well.[176] He notes:

> [My] own earlier study advocating collaboration between Munday and Chettle examines orthographical forms, asseverations, rhyme words, verbal parallels, and other evidence, identifying Scs 1, 6, 7, 8, 10 and 13 as those that show a convergence of features suggesting Chettle rather than Munday. This

investigation has been endorsed by Vickers, and strengthened by [MacDonald] Jackson, who finds the putative Chettle scenes to be more advanced in their placement of mid-line pauses than the Munday scenes. Marina Tarlinskaja has also studied strong syntactic breaks in verse-lines, and comes to broadly similar conclusions: she attributes to Munday Scs 2, 3, 7, 9 (23–312), 14, 16 and 17.[177]

But Jowett also notes that the claims of Merriam and Hope complicate the ascription. Merriam argued that the Chettle identifiers are also not uncharacteristic of Munday's work, while the high incidence of feminine endings is inconsistent with Chettle's other works but not with Munday's or, crucially, with Shakespeare's, whom he continues to advocate as the author of the Original Text.[178] Louis Marder, influenced by Merriam's stylometric work, proposed Shakespeare as the author of everything, additions and revisions included, and tentatively speculated that the different hands meant that the other writers may have been merely transcribing Shakespeare's foul papers. M. W. A. Smith's stylometric analysis ruled out Shakespeare as possible author of the Original Text, while Jonathan Hope's sociolinguistic survey 'suggests that there are at least two hands at work in the original scenes of the play (1–17) – with scenes 3, 7, 8b, 9, 10 apparently representing the work of a less regulated author or authors. This experimental division is supported by relativization evidence, which would also discriminate between these and the other original scenes'.[179] The case for the authorship of the Original Text is not comfortably resolved, although Munday's (at least) part-authorship seems fairly solid. His transcription of the play means that the presence of his co-author (if indeed there was one) has been obscured in much the same way as the 'veil of print' muddies the boundaries between co-authors in collaborative printed plays.

The authorship of the Additions/revisions

Scholars now agree absolutely that Hand A and Hand E are those of Henry Chettle and Thomas Dekker respectively (who are, like Hands B and D, the composing authors as well as the calligraphers of the passages in their hands). These attributions rest partly on clear handwriting evidence. Greg argued that Dekker, who made two moderately substantial autograph entries in Henslowe's Diary, was behind Hand E, which many scholars including Sir George Warner, E. H. C. Oliphant, Harold Jenkins, David J. Lake, MacDonald Jackson, Gary Taylor, Vittorio Gabrieli, Giorgio Melchiori and John Jowett have confirmed. Similarly, Samuel Tannenbaum identified Hand A with Chettle after the publication of Greg's English Literary Autographs, which contained facsimiles of Chettle's calligraphy, enabling him to make the comparison. This found favour with the same group of scholars, as well as T. W. Baldwin, R. B. McKerrow, C. J. Sisson, J. M. Nosworthy, and Anthony G. Petti. Some, including Melchiori, have worried that there is not enough of Chettle's non-collaborative, un-adapted work extant with which to make a stylistic comparison.[180] However, analysis has been performed on the surviving pieces of writing that can be identified as Chettle's, and critics such as H. Dugdale Sykes, Muriel St Clare Byrne, Harold Jenkins and John Jowett have developed a strong sense of his poetic style. It is from this that the attribution to Chettle of the portion of Addition II in Hand C has been made.[181] As for Hand E, Gabrieli and Melchiori note:

> Hand E is undoubtedly Thomas Dekker's, a younger man than Chettle...The objections to his authorship, based on his youth and on the fact that his name appears in Henslowe's Diary only after 1598, are as weak as those raised on the same grounds against the identification of hand B with Heywood.[182]

Stylistic evidence for Dekker, as largely outlined by David J. Lake and MacDonald Jackson, is also very strong, and there are many stylistic indicators in the passage in Dekker's hand as well as the rest of Addition IV in Hand C to suggest his authorship.[183]

Hand B has already been discussed as one of the two controversial ascriptions, though the weight of scholarly consensus rests with Thomas Heywood. Greg admitted ignorance of the identity of the hand in his 1911 edition of the play, though in 1923 suggested Heywood on the strength of similarities he noted between Hand B and Heywood's manuscript play *The Captives*. However, he also noted differences and urged caution on the matter, feeling unhappy with the ease with which the attribution became accepted in the wake of Samuel Tannenbaum's pushy account of 1927 (C. J. Sisson concurred in print with Tannenbaum the same year). Greg published a riposte urging for the case to be considered not proven in 1928, which led to a period of greater scepticism. R. A. Law and J. M. Nosworthy ruled against Heywood, while Harold Jenkins shared Greg's caution but felt Heywood was certainly a possibility. Anthony G. Petti revived the Heywood attribution in 1977, which, despite resistance from Thomas Merriam and Eric Rasmussen, has been on the whole accepted as, at least, the most likely of any that we have. Scholars who have favoured the attribution in the last twenty years include Gary Taylor, Vittorio Gabrieli, Giorgio Melchiori, Brian Vickers, Stanley Wells and John Jowett (who provides stylistic parallels in favour of the ascription in his edition).[184]

Tannenbaum claimed that Hand C was Kyd's, though W. W. Greg, T. W. Baldwin, R. B. McKerrow and C. J. Sisson rebutted him. Anthony G. Petti thought Dekker the hand responsible, although this theory died as it was born. Greg was the first to make the identification, based on handwriting evidence, that Hand C was a scribe, the same who prepared a surviving fragmentary plot which Greg conjecturally identified as *Fortune's Tennis Part 2*, and dated to the winter of 1597–98, ascribing it to the Admiral's Men. It has been largely accepted that Greg was right in that C seems not to have been a composing author, and makes notes and modifications consistent with the work of a company scribe. His overall role in the attempt to revive the play was significant, however, and Jowett suggests that he 'assisted and guided' the revising dramatists in a project in which none of them had 'oversight of the whole process'.[185] The major passages he copied have, with varying degrees of surety, been ascribed among the four revisers thus: Addition II by Chettle, III by Shakespeare, IV by Dekker and V, possibly, by Shakespeare/Heywood, though there has been much disagreement about Greg's identification of the company for whom Hand C worked and therefore for whom the play was written. Gary Taylor argues that:

> If Greg's identification of the hand, or of the company, or of the date, were incorrect, we should have no particular reason for assigning the *More* manuscript to Henslowe...Moreover, even if Greg is right about Hand C and *2 Fortune's Tennis*, such evidence only establishes that in 1597-8 the scribe was working for Henslowe; at some other time he may have been working for the King's men. Actors and playwrights, about whom we have more information, certainly did switch companies from time to time, and our complete ignorance of the day-to-day operations of the King's men makes it impossible to pass judgement on such possibilities.[186]

The play is mainly given to the Admiral's because Munday, Chettle, Heywood and Dekker were company stalwarts during the late 1590s, named in numerous entries in Henslowe as authors and co-collaborators. This has sat uncomfortably with the theory that Shakespeare, who was firmly established as a Chamberlain's dramatist in the late 1590s, was involved with the play. It has been impossible to determine the dates of both the Original Text, and, to a lesser degree of difficulty, of the Additions. Many scholars keen on insisting upon Shakespeare's involvement, including Gabrieli and Melchiori, have argued that everything must date from before 1594, the play having been written for Strange's Men, with whom they believed Shakespeare was involved in the hazy, early years of his career before the company eventually split into the Chamberlain's/Admiral's duopoly in 1594. The early date has been seen as essential to the argument for Shakespeare's involvement, in spite of the fact that Heywood would have been about nineteen years old at the time proposed, and Chettle is not known to have worked as a dramatist before 1598. However, Hand C also prepared the plot of *The Seven Deadly Sins* which, David Kathman has argued, 'was prepared for the Lord Chamberlain's Men in about 1597–98, around the same time this company was first performing such plays as *The Merchant of Venice* and *Henry IV Part1* and *Part 2*.[187] If this is the case, then we might have a reason for Shakespeare's involvement in the play that does not rely on an early dating: that his company was reviving the play, and may even have been responsible for it in the first place. John Jowett's edition of the play argues for a c.1600 dating of the Original Text, showing how parts of it are influenced by Shakespeare's *Julius Caesar*, and noting that the period 1598–1600 saw the height in market interest for performances and publications of history plays. He also notes that around this time:

> Writers associated with the Admiral's Men, accustomed to collaboration and working in a more populist vein, developed plays about non-royalty as an alternative specialisation. From the records of Henslowe's *Diary*, covering 1598-1603, we find a significant proportion of plays of this type, many of them written wholly or partly by Chettle or Munday.[188]

Jowett lists no fewer than fifteen such plays from the pages of Henslowe at this time, twelve of which involved Chettle, Munday, or both, and argues that the play is linked with the Admiral's *1 & 2 Cardinal Wolsey* (1601) and the Chamberlain's play *Thomas Lord Cromwell* (1602) in 'a distinct sub-group of plays of around 1600 about Henry VIII's chancellors'.[189] He also follows Taylor's observation that dramatists could and did move between companies at times, noting that the payment records (or lack thereof) in Henslowe show that Munday and Chettle 'were both available to work for another company between 19 June 1600 and 31 March 1601'.[190] This argument puts the composition of the Original Text at a later date than has ever been proposed, and also tentatively ascribes it to the Chamberlain's Men (a good possible reason why the play is not mentioned in Henslowe). Furthermore, it has been proposed, by Gary Taylor and MacDonald Jackson especially, that the Additions were written as late as 1604, which has proved significant apropos of Shakespeare especially in terms of stylistic congruity with the works he is known to have written around that time, as well as works he had already written.[191] It also shares strong parallels of dramatic situation with *Julius Caesar* and *Coriolanus* especially, both of which similarly deal with orators attempting to influence an unruly mob.[192] The related vocabulary is significant, and Jowett has shown that Hand D's phrase 'peace ho' occurs eleven times in Shakespeare, mainly in *Caesar* and *Coriolanus* in 'attempts to silence a tumultuous crowd', while occurring only three times in all other drama from the period.[193] The phrase 'Friends, masters, countrymen' at 2.4.25 also clearly echoes *Julius Caesar*. Jackson's pause pattern tests in the verse of Hand D concluded that their distribution 'clearly places Shakespeare's addition in the period from *Twelfth Night* (1601–2) to *Macbeth* (1606)'.[194] Jackson also used the works of Hartmut Ilsemann, who 'counted the number of words in every speech in the entire dramatic works. He discovered that in plays written up till about 1599 the speech-length most frequently used was of nine words and that thereafter it fell to four words. He connects this change with the opening of the Globe and Shakespeare's greater artistic involvement in productions'.[195] Jackson argues that a more sophisticated approach to using this observation towards charting Shakespeare's development is needed, but that it nonetheless yields interesting results, and that it suggests that the Hand D section can be dated around 1603–04:

Hand D's addition to the manuscript play *Sir Thomas More* is widely believed to be by Shakespeare, but its composition has been assigned to a range of dates from the Revels edition's 1593–4 to the Oxford Shakespeare's 1603–4. Hand D's pages have twelve speeches of 3–6 words and seven of 7–10 words, giving a percentage of 62.3 for the shorter speeches. Chronologically this associates Hand D with such plays as *Timon of Athens* (1605) with 62.8, *Troilus and Cressida* (1602) with 62.9, and *Othello* (1603–4) with 63.6. Moreover, the most frequent speech-length is of four words: there are six four-word speeches, and no more than three speeches of any other specific word length. The figures are far more consistent with a composition date of about 1603–4 than with one of about 1593–4.[196]

For many who agree that the early dating of the revisions is wrong, the likelihood of Shakespeare's involvement in the play, given what we know of his company standing by c.1604, the complete lack of evidence of him ever acting as a mere patcher of texts, or of him ever working with anyone but the Chamberlain's/King's company after 1594, has proved difficult to accept. We still cannot say for certain which company the play was written for, though we can say that whoever wrote the Hand D passage was doing a lot more for the play than merely patching it up. Critics have seized on many reasons for scepticism regarding Shakespeare's involvement, and yet when we remove from the question biographical context and perceptions of Shakespeare as an authorial figure, and focus entirely on the linguistic and palaeographic evidence (as many other critics have done), arguments for his presence seem difficult to refute.

Hand D – William Shakespeare?

Richard Simpson first put forward the case for Shakespeare's part-authorship of *Sir Thomas More* in 1871. Since Simpson, the sheer number of commentators interested in the Hand D passage means that a complete survey of all the ideas and arguments relating to it is almost impossible here. There are two Additions in particular which have stirred interest regarding Shakespeare's potential authorship: the portion of Addition II in Hand D (folios 8a and b, and 9a), believed to be Shakespeare's own, and Addition III, which has been copied out by Hand C. Addition II.D has been linked to Shakespeare for over a hundred years, with strong arguments put forward in favour of the ascription on both palaeographical and stylistic grounds. Handwriting is tricky evidence in Shakespeare's case as we only have six of his accepted signatures with which to compare the passage, though many thoughtful and sensitive analyses of vocabulary, style, cadence and dramatic mood have strengthened the idea in many scholarly circles that Shakespeare is indeed the author we are looking at. There have been two major collections of essays on the subject, both of which arrived at the broad conclusion that Shakespeare is more likely than not to have been involved in the play and to be the author of the Hand D passage.[197] There follows a list which attempts to be as exhaustive as possible of those who have ruled in favour of Shakespeare (in chronological order):[198] James Spedding, A. W. Ward, A. F. Hopkinson, C. F. Tucker Brooke, E. Maunde Thompson, A. W. Pollard, R. W. Chambers, G. B. Harrison, T. W. Baldwin, R. B. McKerrow, C. J. Sisson, E. K. Chambers, Caroline Spurgeon, H. W. Crundell, E. E. Willoughby, D. C. Collins, Clara Longworth de Chambrun, Richard Flatter, R. C. Bald, F. P. Wilson, Peter Alexander, Harold Jenkins, J. M. Nosworthy, John Dover Wilson, John Munro, A. S. MacNalty, E. A. J. Honigmann,[199] S. Schoenbaum, Thomas Clayton, Peter W. M. Blayney, Karl P. Wentersdorf, G. Blakemore Evans, T. H. Howard-Hill, Philip Brockbank, Giles E. Dawson, David J. Lake, William H. Matchett, Anthony G. Petti, MacDonald Jackson, Steven Urkowitz, J. H. P. Pafford, Charles Hamilton, P. J. Croft, R. E. Alton, Gary Taylor, Charles R. Forker, John W. Velz, Vittorio Gabrieli, Giorgio Melchiori, Thomas Merriam, Brian Vickers, J. J. M. Tobin, Timothy Irish Watt and John Jowett. There have also been notable opponents to the attribution, though fewer than those who have supported it, namely F. J. Furnivall, F. G. Fleay, B. A. P.

Van Dam, L. L. Schücking, Samuel Tannenbaum, S. R. Golding, R. L. Eagles, Paul Deutschberger, Stirling Brents, Albert Feuillerat, Ralph H. Lane, I. A. Shapiro, Paul Ramsay, Carol Chillington, Ward Elliott, Robert Valenza and Gerald Downs, while Madeleine Doran, R. A. Huber, and Paul Werstine have all advised that the case is unproven.

W. W. Greg, noting skill, commanding wit and passion in the writing that was distinct from the rest of the play, was nonetheless unwilling at first to pronounce in either direction. He noted that he wasn't as impressed with it as others had been, but said he found it 'an eminently reasonable view that would assign this passage to the writer who, I believe, foisted certain of the Jack Cade scenes into the second part of *Henry VI*'.[200] However, convinced by the palaeographic conclusions of E. Maunde Thompson in 1916 and 1923, he came to support the attribution to Shakespeare in a number of scholarly articles ranging throughout the rest of his life. Addition II.D, purportedly in Shakespeare's autograph, can be analysed palaeographically in a way that Addition III cannot. MacDonald Jackson states that 'Hand D cannot be identified as that of any other Renaissance dramatist whose handwriting has survived', building on Giles E. Dawson's 1990 article, 'Shakespeare's Handwriting', for support, in which Dawson compared the Hand D passage with letters and documents from the Elizabethan and Jacobean periods by over 250 different writers. Astonishingly, he found four orthographic features in Shakespeare's six acknowledged signatures which are totally unique, not found in any other document examined by Dawson except for the Hand D passage, in which all four features (a 'spurred *a*', a unique *w* form, a strange flourish in the *k* formation, and unique upstrokes in the *w* and *m* of Shakespeare's sixth signature) appear. As Jackson argues, 'the odds against finding another document that, like Hand D, bears all four Shakespearean oddities must be astronomical'.[201]

In addition to this, the passage contains strong spelling evidence to bolster the case for Shakespeare's authorship. John Dover Wilson's 1923 article on the matter listed spellings within the Hand D section that were only to be found elsewhere in printed works of Shakespeare.[202] Some of Wilson's words have been shown to be ineffective in the light of the broader searches offered by databases such as LION and EEBO. Jackson, however, has shown that six of them, although not entirely unique, are strong evidence for Shakespeare: *argo* ('ergo', *Henry VI Part 2*), *scilens* ('silence', Quarto *Henry IV Part 2*), *Iarman* ('German', Quarto *Henry IV Part 2*), *elamentes* ('elements', Quarto *Love's Labour's Lost*), *a levenpence* ('eleven pence', Quarto *Love's Labour's Lost*), and *deule* ('devil', Folio *Henry V*). Of these, Jackson argues, only *Iarman* appears elsewhere in sixteenth- and seventeenth-century English drama (once in the manuscript play *John of Bordeaux*, attributed to Robert Greene). *Elamentes* appears in two much earlier poems, as does *scilens*, while *deule* appears in the fifteenth-century religious play *The Wisdom That Is Christ*, and in two medieval poems. *A leven* for eleven is common, but *a levenpence* is uniquely Shakespearean. *Argo* ('argal') is only found once in Thomas Middleton's *The Phoenix* outside Shakespeare. So although they are not entirely without precedent, their usage within Shakespeare's lifetime is limited to one appearance of *Iarman* and one of *argo* in two other works. The fact that all six appear in Shakespeare, however, firmly bolsters the likelihood of his presence. Thomas Merriam also notes eight collocations in the passage unique to Shakespeare: *vppon thipp* ('upon the hip', *The Merchant of Venice*), *peace scilens* (*Julius Caesar*), *bloody tymes* (*Henry VI Part 3*), *hath Chidd* (*A Midsummer Night's Dream*), *woold feed on on* [sic] *another* (*Coriolanus*), *those same hands* (*King John*), *com to* [sic] *short of* (*Henry VIII*) and *and lyke as* (*Henry VI Part 1*, *Troilus and Cressida*).[203] As he also notes, contrary to Jackson, although the spelling *scilens* is not exclusive to Shakespeare, appearing as it does in two other plays from the period, the combination of this very rare spelling appearing within a unique Shakespeare collocation is powerfully suggestive of his authorship.

Quarto *Henry IV Part 2* is almost certainly a text set from authorial papers, in which *scilens* occurs no fewer than sixteen times. Wilson noted in addition that Hand D had an occasional tendency to omit the terminal *e* from words ending in -*ce* (*obedienc, offyc, ffraunc*), in -*ge* (*charg*), and -*ne* (*ymagin*), a habit Shakespeare apparently shared, adding further reinforcement to the claims for his hand.[204] Jackson has listed all the words in the passage shown by Literature Online to have no spelling matches elsewhere, including the three words lacking terminal *e* exemplified above: *adicion, aucthoryty, ffraunc, inhumanyty, liom, obedienc, obedyenc, offyc, parsnyp, qualllyfy, shreef, shrevaltry, supposytion, sylenct, thappostle* and *ynnovation*, and Merriam notes that *adicion* also resembles First Quarto *King Lear*'s 'addicions', which has no spelling matches elsewhere in Elizabethan or Jacobean drama. Spelling and punctuation in early modern books is erratic by modern standards anyway, reflective of an emergent, unsystematized bibliographical and orthographical culture, with pages and even sentences varying forms of the same words, especially if set by more than one compositor, or if the compositor was influenced by the copy from which he was working, in addition to occasionally regularizing its spellings himself. Yet the Hand D manuscript passage is extraordinarily idiosyncratic and sloppy, even by the standards of the time, and it is certainly strange to think of our greatest composing author bogged down in the more basic mechanics of writing.

Carol Chillington argued for John Webster being the author of Addition II.D, prompting detailed attacks on her theory from Charles R. Forker and Gary Taylor.[205] John Jowett argues for Shakespeare on the basis of stylistic analysis of the passage's orthography and imagery in comparison with accepted works of Shakespeare, and R. W. Chambers, Caroline Spurgeon and Karl P. Wentersdorf all provided compelling parallels of imagery, theme, language and dramatic situation and structure between Addition II.D and other acknowledged works of Shakespeare.[206] The attribution of the passage to Shakespeare has been vindicated by its repeated inclusion in various complete editions of Shakespeare, including Riverside, Oxford, Norton and the RSC, with the Second Edition of *The Oxford Shakespeare* in 2005 becoming the first complete works to include the full text of the play. In 'Date and Authorship', MacDonald Jackson presented detailed Literature Online evidence to bolster the argument that Shakespeare is Hand D.[207] He searched phrases and collocations within the passage and within Addition III, noting all those with links with five or fewer plays first performed within the 1590–1610 date range. Of the fifteen plays with four links or more, ten were by Shakespeare.[208] Timothy Irish Watt performed lexical word tests on the Hand D passage, establishing a list of 108 unusual words that do not appear in 60 per cent of the corpus of 136 well-attributed, single-author plays used for comparison.[209] The play with the highest proportion of shared vocabulary was *Othello*, and seven of the ten plays with the highest proportions were by Shakespeare. Ward Elliott and Robert Valenza, however, using their 'silver bullet' methods of computer-aided testing, came to the conclusion that Hand D is non-Shakespearean, and yet their results, showing only two rejections, contrast sharply with those for the play as a whole, and place the passage very close to acceptable Shakespeare territory by their standards. Jackson rebutted them in 'Is "Hand D" of *Sir Thomas More* Shakespeare's?', calling into question their methods of statistical interpretation, as did Watt, who claimed the findings of their tests were compromised by the limits of their control samples. Jonathan Hope's sociolinguistic analysis of the passage (as well as Addition III) was inconclusive as the passages were too short for the methods he devised to prove telling.[210]

The case of the authorship of Addition II.D, relying as it does on the accumulation of deductive reasoning, is not solved definitively, though the majority of opinion leans towards Shakespeare, as it does with Addition III. Of the latter, Peter Blayney notes that it 'presents a special problem':

That the speech it contains is by Shakespeare is tolerably obvious, and that it is a finer piece of writing than anything else in the play is equally so. Yet outstanding as it is from a literary viewpoint, it is virtually useless dramatically, for it neither fits the context in which it is placed, nor any other point in the play.[211]

The attribution has not been seen as 'tolerably obvious' by all, though Taylor reasons that:

> The status of Addition III is less certain, because it exists only in a transcription by Hand C, leaving us wholly dependent upon verbal parallels in a much briefer passage. No one who doubts Shakespeare's authorship of II.D will be persuaded by the meagre evidence for attributing Addition III to him. However, if one accepts his presence among the adapters, he seems more likely than the other available candidates to have written the speech.[212]

Scholars who have accepted the attribution include Richard Simpson, A. F. Hopkinson, C. F. Tucker Brooke, E. K. Chambers, R. C. Bald, H. W. Crundell, R. W. Chambers, J. M. Nosworthy, A. S. MacNalty, Harold Jenkins, Peter W. M. Blayney, G. Blakemore Evans, Gary Taylor, Vittorio Gabrieli, Giorgio Melchiori, Brian Vickers, J. J. M. Tobin and John Jowett. Jowett notes numerous unique parallels of 'phrasing and ideation' between the Addition III passage and the works of Shakespeare, dismissing the other contributors on opposite grounds of negative attribution, and concluding that:

> Shakespeare is far likelier to have written the speech than any of the other dramatists in the play, and it would be remarkable if equal parallels could be adduced in the work of any other dramatist of the period.[213]

He goes further to suggest that Addition V (also in **Hand C**) was written by Shakespeare and revised by Heywood, and analyses the place and functionality of the speeches within the play more usefully than Blayney. In this as a whole we see Shakespeare taking:

> major responsibility for the play's re-emergence as a potential theatre work. Not least, he develops the presentation of More himself, who is uniquely eloquent in Sc. 6, and is given the privilege of partly personal and partly choric soliloquies in Adds III and V. The short soliloquies are key points of transition in the episodic middle scenes.[214]

Jowett's Addition V theory is compelling, and the unfolding critical dialogue surrounding its acceptance will be very interesting to chart as more analysis is performed on it. This edition nevertheless proposes that Shakespeare is the author of the Hand D passage in Addition II (2.4.1–148), and of Addition III (3.2.1–21), and that the question of his involvement in Addition V (3.3) needs to be taken very seriously. As we have seen, many critics keen to verify Shakespeare's presence have opted for an early (i.e. early 1590s) dating, but if the original play dates from c.1600, as Jowett provocatively and persuasively suggests, and the revisions from c.1604, the circumstances and extent of Shakespeare's involvement become far more difficult to explain. Perhaps we can assume that Elizabeth's death in 1603 and James' accession, bringing about the end of the Tudor dynasty, provided a platform for the play's owners to try once more to get it on the stage. But that power transition also brought about Shakespeare's instatement as the pre-eminent dramatist in the country when his company came under the patronage of the king himself. Why would he need or want to contribute passages to a play blighted by potentially dangerous controversy, especially one that, although unlikely, may not even have originally been written for his company? Shakespeare shows himself consistently to be an astute handler of political material, which makes even stranger the idea of his involvement in a play that puts such matters ultimately beyond his control, albeit that his main contribution characteristically articulates moral counsel and social correction through a skilful and sustained cultivation of empathy. And yet, as strong as these theoretical objections are to the idea of Shakespeare's presence as a revising author in *Sir Thomas More*, there, it seems, he is. The play does not survive as a printed book but as a uniquely complex manuscript. Its physical form is as essential to an understanding of Shakespeare the writer and to a reappraisal of what we think we know about early theatre history as anything the play as a work of literature could tell us. It is like nothing else in the Shakespeare canon, and is a baffling spanner in the works of conventional narratives about how early theatre was made and how Shakespeare helped to make it.

The London Prodigal (c.1604)

If we are to believe the title-page information of the 1605 Quarto imprint of *The London Prodigal*, then we know that at one time, at least, the play was owned and performed by Shakespeare's company:

> THE / LONDON / Prodigall. / As it was plaide by the Kings Maie- / sties feruants. / By *William Shakefpeare*, / LONDON. / Printed by T.C. for *Nathaniel Butter*, and / are to be fold neere *S. Austins* gate, / at the figne of the pyde Bull. / *1605.*

That this apparently happened in their incarnation as the King's, as opposed to the Chamberlain's, has been cited as evidence for *Prodigal*'s Jacobean dating. Yet it really only tells us the company's name at the time of the Quarto's publication and that they had apparently performed the play within the last two years (which doesn't preclude its being written before then). Trust in any title-page statement here might ultimately be undermined by the arresting claim made for Shakespeare's authorship – this, in fact, is the most unambiguous contemporary attribution to Shakespeare of all the plays in this volume. While the majority of scholars have seen little reason to doubt the King's Men's ownership of *Prodigal*, even though no other evidence links them to it, scepticism has understandably prevailed in the matter of its being entirely by Shakespeare. We might argue that print consumers wishing to buy a copy of a popular play they had seen would be less likely to know who had written it than where they had seen it, and therefore which company had performed it. Whether Nathaniel Butter, who also published *King Lear* in 1608, possibly against the wishes of Shakespeare's company, was acting on this principle is of course mere speculation, but it is likely that Shakespeare's name, an attractive selling point in the book trade by the early 1600s, was intended to add value to a product about which one truth had already been told. At a time when the King's Men were apparently withholding their Shakespeare stock from the press, Butter might have felt that he could exploit the vagaries of authorial origin in the wake of their greatly reduced presence in the bookshops and satisfy the demand for new Shakespeare plays in print through *The London Prodigal*.

Despite the limited evidence, *Prodigal* is almost universally considered to be Jacobean. Several critics, among them Ludwig Tieck, F. G. Fleay, Richard Simpson and A. F. Hopkinson, have argued for a 1580s to early 1590s dating in order to assert Shakespeare's authorship, but such opinion has failed to shape the prevailing consensus. Edmond Malone, the great eighteenth-century Shakespeare scholar, looked within the play for dating evidence, arguing that Sir Arthur Greenshield's mention of his station as commander 'under the King' and his suggestion that Oliver should be pressed 'for the wars' help supply chronological limits for *Prodigal*'s composition. James VI of Scotland was proclaimed King James I of England on 24 March 1603 (Elizabeth died earlier that same day), and the hostilities with Spain, into which he was very quickly thrust, were not quelled until a peace was ratified between the two nations on 19 August 1604. Of course, the farthest limit for *Prodigal*'s composition is set at its 1605 publication, so Malone's conclusion that the wars referred to are those with Spain, accepting that the play was written with a King on the throne, is entirely reasonable.[215] The word 'King' could easily have replaced 'Queen', however, as has several times been suggested, though attempting to spy historical facts through a fictional narrative is not our only, or indeed our likeliest, recourse for establishing a date. There are far stronger reasons for thinking the play Jacobean when we locate with greater precision its generic characteristics within the ever-changing repertories of the early theatres, and *Prodigal*'s can be comfortably contextualized within the King's Men's repertory at the particular historical moment at which it was apparently written and performed. Although squarely non-Shakespearean in many of its formal and linguistic characteristics, *The London Prodigal* is nonetheless entirely commensurate in its plot concerns with the surviving output of the King's Men from the two-year window of 1603–05, which for Shakespeare saw the creation of what many critics from the nineteenth century onwards have dubbed his mini-sequence of 'problem comedies': *Measure for Measure* and *All's Well that Ends Well*.

Yet before attempting a detailed picture of the immediate contexts of *Prodigal*'s production, it is important to see it within a broader model of continuity and change. The term 'Jacobean city comedy' is now almost a part of the vernacular since it was popularized by Brian Gibbons in the 1960s, the 'Jacobean' part of the formulation every bit as significant as 'city' or 'comedy'. Many critics tend to associate these dark, cynical anatomies of greed, lust, criminality and corruption as something that came in the wake of the Golden Age of Elizabeth. In them an emergent societal order is being stretched to breaking point through the combined tensions of free enterprise and mercantilism on the one hand and an ailing aristocracy on the other, fuelling the desperate, acquisitive spirit in almost every character that enters the fray. Writers like Ben Jonson and Thomas Middleton pushed at the barriers of the 'humours' plays and the early model citizen plays of the 1590s to create murky representations of London as a seething stew, ballooning out of control, the moral squalor matching the septic environmental kind. *Prodigal* also has its ancestral roots in 'humours' plays, which became hugely popular around 1597 with George Chapman's *A Humorous Day's Mirth*, though the writer most associated with the genre is Jonson.[216] Personalities typically accorded with the medical humours, characters distilled down to the mere embodiments of impulses and fitted with such improbable monikers as Delirio, Shift, Sordido and Fastidious Brisk (from Jonson's *Every Man Out of His Humour* (1599)). In *Prodigal* we have the bullish Spurcock, the sexual innuendo value bolstered by his forename 'Lancelot', the indecisive Weathercock and the foppish Civet, and such tactics are not entirely alien to Shakespeare. The somewhat misfit *The Merry Wives of Windsor* (1597–1600?) is set near London and centres on neo-bourgeois citizens, including such aptly-named characters as the weedy Slender, the oafish Shallow, and the simple Simple. It sidesteps explicit commentary on current affairs by its links to the *Henry IV* plays, which are the closest Shakespeare ever came to 'city comedy' by virtue of their part-London setting, albeit set in the past. The seedy urban texture conjured in *Measure for Measure*, a play apparently set very much in the present, has frequently been seen as Shakespeare's real entry into the city comedy milieu, though again the standard act of Shakespearean displacement is built in with the action removed to Vienna.[217]

All of this is very different from *The London Prodigal*, a play interested in the here and now in a way that Shakespeare never was. Shakespeare's 1590s comedies, in fact most comedy from the Chamberlain's and Admiral's repertories, took the form of what many commentators have termed 'romantic adventure plays', which typically involve an individual or couple hindered from a particular state of being, usually a love match, by the wider mores of society, having to spend the play patiently suffering through the obstacles that bar them until they at last achieve happiness. They also often feature escapist, fantastical settings – the forest worlds of *A Midsummer Night's Dream* or *As You Like It*, for instance – though importantly Shakespearean romantic adventure was fully conscious of the potential outlined in Nabokov's quip that one letter is all that separates the comic from the cosmic. Shakespeare always compromised the sentimentalism that could easily attend such material, darkening and ethically complicating the mood of even the most silvery farce with the spectre of damaging behaviour, dangerous desire, or death. Think of the cruel treatment of the Mechanicals at the hands of the scoffing nobles in *A Midsummer Night's Dream*, the narrowly averted rape in *The Two Gentlemen of Verona*, and the announcement of the French king's passing in *Love's Labour's Lost*. Nonetheless, in spite of such moral complexity, we see the tonal register and thematic focus of Shakespearean comedy change dramatically into the 1600s. Many critics from the Victorian period onwards argued that Shakespeare was experiencing a personal crisis, a dark period of his life, as a way of explaining the venom and pessimism of plays like *Troilus and Cressida*, traditionally seen as the other problem play, composed sometime around 1602, an ensemble-driven mood piece without a hero, rotten with sexual disgust and interpersonal cynicism. Yet one historical fact about the theatrical culture in the very early part of the decade is likelier to take us towards the real root cause.

Shakespeare's 'problem comedies' were entirely redolent of a wider theatrical trend at a specific moment at the turn of the century, most famously alluded to in *Hamlet*'s 'little eyases' sequence (2.2.307–27). Rosencrantz and Guildenstern were referring pointedly to the boy players who had returned to the London stage in 1599 at the Blackfriars playhouse and whose repertory, rife with sexual innuendo and biting political satire, was becoming popular enough to pose a serious commercial threat to the Chamberlain's Men in the very early 1600s. Paul Yachnin has written of a 'project of institutional identity formation at a particularly lively juncture in the history of the theatre' when Shakespeare was working on these plays.[218] He argues that those writing for the boy companies – Jonson, Middleton, John Marston and George Chapman – conceived of themselves and of their audiences as constituting 'the artistic and moral heart of the nation', presenting plays designed to 'punish the immorality of the members of the civic establishment'.[219] It was, he argues, a climate that forced the adult companies to rethink the tone of their comic drama, and forced Shakespeare in particular, in a tricky situation given his role as chief dramatist in the King's company from 1603 onwards, to 'think beyond the absolutism of Jacobean rule' and employ 'a high level of inventiveness' in his treatment of power and politics.[220] What we see in Shakespeare at this time is a response to city comedy and to the prevailing culture of topical satire, but one that employs a far more inventive and enigmatic 'orchestration of ideology' than a work like *Prodigal*.[221]

The boy companies, then, provoked an anxious reaction insomuch as we see in the adult companies a gradual but definite response to their rivals' success within their own repertories. One play that sprang from this culture of antagonism provides us with a further narrowing of the question of *Prodigal*'s origins. Around late 1602 to early 1603 John Marston wrote *The Malcontent* for the Children of Paul's, a play that was to prove paradigmatic to the preoccupations of comedy throughout the following year. It dramatized a deposed and banished duke, Altofronto, returning to court 'disguised as a railing satirist' thus enabling him 'to expose vices that would otherwise remain hidden' and eventually bring about the downfall of the play's malefactor, Mendoza.[222] The play was a huge commercial success. It was quickly bought up by the King's Men, adapted for the adult stage by John Webster, and followed by a rash of disguised duke plays from several major companies in London, including Marston's *Parasitaster, or The Fawn* (1604), Middleton's *The Phoenix* (1604), John Day's *Law Tricks* (1604), and, of course, Shakespeare's *Measure for Measure* (1604). Although not a duke, Old Flowerdale's disguise as his son's servant, Kester, allowing him to see at first-hand his son's profligacy and deceit, is a major device in *Prodigal*, cited as a reason to link the play to Shakespeare at this time. Shakespeare was not alone in employing the trope, of course, but there are other clear links to his company's repertory interests.

Robert Y. Turner, writing of the evolution of comedy in the London theatres at the turn of the seventeenth century, notes that 'innovations of comical satire' were beginning to take over in the 1601–04 timeframe.[223] Roslyn Knutson locates a subspecies within this wider trend in a 'formula of domestic relations' manifesting itself in the King's repertory in the form of prodigal son and enforced marriage narratives.[224] Comedy now demanded tougher moral examinations of its protagonists, and dissolute young men authoring their own downfalls were put in the place of romantic heroes whose only job was to weather the storms of adversity. G. K. Hunter has described the formulae typical to comedy's new interest in the hedonistic and cruel spirit attempting to rise above the template of social norms, finding repentance through the love of the wife he does not deserve.[225] Knutson situates Shakespeare's *All's Well that Ends Well* within a body of King's Men plays from 1603–07 that deal with prodigality and enforced marriage: namely *The Fair Maid of Bristow*, *A Yorkshire Tragedy*, *The Miseries of Enforced Marriage*, and, of course, *The London Prodigal*. *Prodigal* has the outrageous yet ultimately penitent Flowerdale and his enforced marriage to Luce, as well as the unwelcome attempts to make Delia take a husband. Shakespeare famously explored the theme in *All's Well*, with the disloyal Bertram's enforced marriage to Helen, the woman he at first cannot abide, but later penitently accepts, while in *Measure* we have Angelo's to Mariana, Lucio's to Kate Keepdown, a prostitute carrying his child, and possibly – the great ambiguity which ends the play – Isabella's to the Duke himself. We also see in Luce's disguise in *Prodigal*, by which she shames and converts Flowerdale, a plot device similar to the bed tricks in *Measure* and *All's Well*, though again this is not exclusive to Shakespeare.

We might observe that 'prodigal son narrative' is a little loose and inaccurate apropos *All's Well*: granted, Bertram is a rakish philanderer, but the strict sense of spendthrift-cum-penitent does not apply to him.[226] He does not exhaust his means and he crucially does not beg for forgiveness: as in *Measure*, the ambiguity of his acceptance of Helen, addressed as it is to the King and weighted with a conditional 'if', is quite unlike the tidy resolution of Flowerdale's conversion. Notwithstanding, he exemplifies completely the shift in emphasis from 1590s romantic comic heroes. Between them *Measure* and *All's Well* cover all these sordid motifs of surveillance incognito, abused political authority, and sexual deception, and we can perhaps conclude that *The London Prodigal* made sense in thematic terms as a Shakespeare play to a 1605 audience of print consumers, or at the very least as a play that Shakespeare's company would have been likely to produce. A modern audience lacking these contexts will inevitably begin to judge the play's Shakespearean-ness through subjective judgements about linguistic and dramatic qualities. But is *Prodigal* a typical Shakespeare comedy, or, indeed, does it bear any of the hallmarks of Shakespeare's writing?

There is a dark cynicism at work in the comedy of Flowerdale's rejection of Luce, his telling her to 'turn whore' to make her living, and his lying about her death to his maidservant (actually Luce in disguise), yet critics have struggled more widely to locate the grainier ethical examinations so typical of Shakespearean drama that overgo the final neat moralizing of plays like *Prodigal*. C. F. Tucker Brooke, in something of the spirit of censure, felt that 'Shakespeare's catholicity and psychological insight are conspicuously absent, and every principle of his dramatic morality is outraged in the treatment of the prodigal's career'.[227] Richard Proudfoot notes that *Prodigal* 'is fairly well supplied with moments of Shakespearean reminiscence or premonition', and concedes to having been 'fleetingly reminded' while reading it of *Love's Labour's Lost*, *Henry V*, *Hamlet*, *Troilus and Cressida*, *All's Well*, *Othello*, *Measure for Measure* and *Timon of Athens*.[228] He notes that 'affinities of plot or situation'[229] with *Othello*, *All's Well* and *Measure* (recent plays in 1603–04) all appear in scene 13, and of the forty verbal parallels he identifies between Shakespeare's works and the play, twenty-five appear in three scenes – 8, 9 and, again, 13 – singled out by Jonathan Hope's tests as differing stylistically from the rest of the play. This could of course reflect Shakespearean influence as much as Shakespearean authorship; *Prodigal* was produced, as far as we know, in repertory with *Measure* and *All's Well* – probably slightly before *All's Well* – and it seems more likely that this is a play written with Shakespeare in the room, as it were, rather than at the writing desk. The stylistic and stylometric work that has been done on *Prodigal* all bears out the sensation that the writing has the broad feel of skilful-yet-generic early-modern playwriting rather than the profound heights of Shakespeare's more accomplished work; Shakespeare's writing, although the most famous of the period, makes up only a small proportion of the surviving whole.

The 1605 Quarto was *Prodigal*'s first and only imprint in that format. The editors of the First Folio did not share Nathaniel Butter's belief in Shakespeare's authorship of *Prodigal*, though it was included in the second edition of the 1664 Third Folio and in the 1685 Fourth Folio. Shakespeare was also named as the play's author in the catalogues published by Rogers and Ley, Edward Archer (both 1656) and Francis Kirkman (1661). Gerard Langbaine and Charles Gildon, prominent men of letters at the end of the seventeenth century, both coolly asserted Shakespeare's authorship, and their judgement stood for a time. Nicholas Rowe included it in his 1709 edition of Shakespeare, the first to be founded on scholarly as well as commercial principles, as did Alexander Pope in the 1728 second edition of his. This presumably had more to do with his publisher Jacob Tonson's interests than his own wishes as in his introduction he casts it and the other apocryphal plays included as 'wretched', asserting that they 'cannot be admitted as [Shakespeare's]'. No other edition of the period followed suit, and non-acceptance of the attribution became something of a scholarly orthodoxy among the major eighteenth-century editors, with Lewis Theobald, Sir Thomas Hanmer, Samuel Johnson, Edward Capell and George Steevens excluding it from their canons. Edmond Malone produced a supplement to the Johnson-Steevens edition in 1780, including *Prodigal* in a second volume of apocryphal works which he took pains to disavow as Shakespeare's. He claimed merely to be offering an interested public properly edited versions of these disputed works so that the question of their real authorship might be usefully and more readily advanced. Malone, it should be noted, was 'the first and perhaps greatest scholar in what we might call authentication studies', and his edition marks the first serious attempt to move the question beyond dismissive catcalling.[230] Matthew Draper produced an adapted version in 1731 called *The Spendthrift*, claiming Shakespeare as the author of the play on which his was based.

Into the nineteenth century the attribution to Shakespeare was supported by Ludwig Tieck, Max Moltke, F. G. Fleay, and A. F. Hopkinson, and more tentatively allowed by W. G. Simms and Richard Simpson. Fleay, however, in 1886, recanted, a decade after his original pronouncement, and over the following five years published work championing first Robert Armin and then Michael Drayton as the authors (the latter attribution being castigated as 'irresponsible' by Bernard H. Newdigate fifty years later). William Hazlitt, Charles Knight and Francois Victor Hugo, son of the great writer, and translator of Shakespeare into French, rubbished the attribution, while A. W. Ward, more productively, corroborated by endorsing Thomas Heywood. Henry Ulrici believed the play to be the product of Munday in collaboration with at least one other unidentified dramatist. De Winter, in his 1905 edition of Ben Jonson's *The Staple of News*, became the first to propose *Prodigal* as an early effort by Shakespeare's pedantic, pugnacious rival, though the theory did not carry. Tucker Brooke somewhat sceptically allowed either Dekker or Marston as the most likely authors, a view echoed by Baldwin Maxwell, while Marie Thérèse Jones-Davies and Santha Devi Arulanandam went one further to propose Dekker. Tucker Brooke pointed out that the attribution would only be possible if Dekker 'could plausibly be shown to have written for the King's Players just before 1605', when indeed we know him to have been writing for Prince Henry's.[231] The mysterious connection forged between him and Shakespeare's company through the additions to *Sir Thomas More* around 1604, however, perhaps suggests that anything is possible. Charles Barber looked at a rare use of the word 'honour' as evidence of Thomas Middleton's authorship, noting that *Prodigal* yielded 'negative results'.[232] Other proposals included G. S. Greene's suggestion of George Wilkins, Michel Grivelet's of Thomas Heywood, and a few half-hearted attempts to restate the argument for Shakespeare from Ernst Von Kamnitzer, Henri Ghéon, and Clara Longworth de Chambrun.

Gary Taylor, writing in 1987, stated: 'No serious scholar has taken the attribution [to Shakespeare] seriously; but no convincing alternative has been offered'.[233] Perhaps no serious scholar had taken it seriously, but at that time no one had tried seriously to offer grounds more relative for disbelief in the attribution either. That same year, T. B. Horton completed a PhD thesis examining function words as a way of discriminating between the authorial hands of Shakespeare and John Fletcher, the playwright who was to succeed Shakespeare as the King's principal dramatist in the early 1610s, and who collaborated with him on *Cardenio*, *Henry VIII* and *The Two Noble Kinsmen*.[234] Horton became the first person in the play's long critical history, stretching back effectively to 1605, to propose Fletcher's authorship. Perhaps the most unusual thing about this is the fact that all the work of the last two decades seems mutually reinforcing in suggesting that a young Fletcher, hitherto unconsidered as a candidate, is in fact the play's most likely author. Thomas Merriam undertook detailed stylometric analysis of the play as part of a PhD thesis on the Shakespeare canon in 1992 and his conclusions, essentially supporting those of Horton, would come to be restated in almost all subsequent inquiries.[235] Mainly using parallels between *Prodigal* and Fletcher's known work, and looking at the characteristic use of oaths and contractions appearing in the play within the oeuvres of several writers active at the time, including Middleton, Dekker, Shakespeare, Fletcher and Wilkins, Merriam calculated that Fletcher was more likely to have authored *Prodigal* than Shakespeare by 50×10^{27} to 1; Fletcher over Middleton by 4×10^{27} to 1; and Fletcher over Wilkins by 7×10^{13} to 1. Dekker was ruled out by the fact that the contractions in the play only show themselves in his work prior to 1599.

He returned to the question in collaboration with Robert Matthews, this time upping the statistical ante to employ neural networking techniques, developed by statisticians as a way of processing data in much the same way as biological neural networks, emulating the central nervous system and its axons, dendrites and synapses. It is described as a non-linear statistical data-modelling tool, which is used to model complex relationships between inputs and outputs or to find patterns in data.[236] Again, it relied essentially on the sets of discriminators developed by Horton and the function words used by Gary Taylor in his stylometric work on the Oxford Shakespeare, pushing the Fletcher and the Shakespeare data, measured against one-thousand-word samples from several of their undisputed works, through five ratios in a series of computer-aided tests. The results strongly suggested Fletcher's authorship of the whole play, though Merriam and Matthews also noted that at the level of individual acts statistical confusion crept in and that by their calculations Shakespeare was the likely author of Act 1, as Horton had suggested. The obvious weakness of these tests, of course, is that only Shakespeare and Fletcher were tested, while the reliability of the methods on the level of individual acts is thrown troublingly into question by the fact that the results show that Fletcher is the likely author of Acts 3 and 4 of *The Tempest*. This, they acknowledge, is 'apparent misclassification'.[237]

Still, the case for Fletcher remains strong, as was reconfirmed by Matthews when he teamed up with David Lowe to apply Radial Basis Functions to the stylometric data for *Prodigal*.[238] RBF networks, they claimed, do not suffer from the same confusion within local minima as the 'Multi-Layer Perceptrons' used in Matthews' work with Merriam, meaning that statistically 'noisy' sections can be analysed more clearly. Their results again supported the conclusion that *Prodigal* 'is predominantly Fletcherian, though with some Shakespearian influences', but their overall ruling was for Fletcher.[239] Jonathan Hope's sociolinguistic analyses furthered the notion that *Prodigal* was in fact collaborative, though his findings detected a different distribution of co-authorship. The auxiliary 'do' percentage for the play as a whole (86 per cent) puts it out of both Shakespeare and Fletcher's ranges (Fletcher is 90+ per cent, while Shakespeare 'never exceeds 84', and 'no other author shows a regulation rate below 85'). The three scenes in the play that differed from the rest in Hope's auxiliary 'do' tests (8, 9, and 13, which he terms *LPA*) fall uniquely within Shakespeare's range, and, he argues, 'cannot be by Fletcher'. By separating them and measuring them against the rest of the play (*LPB*) we get figures of 81 per cent and 90 per cent respectively, meaning that 'section B certainly could be by Fletcher, and section A by Shakespeare'. As for relative marker evidence, Hope notes that the evidence from section A strongly contradicts Shakespearean authorship ('the "who" and "which" rates for these scenes, and indeed the whole play, are far below his usual rates'), though does not rule out Fletcher, and also includes the possibilities of Middleton and Dekker. He concludes:

> Although the sample sizes are small ... it may be worth noting that there are no differences in terms of relativisation between section A and B. Given the gap between them in terms of auxiliary 'do' evidence, I would not want to question the dual authorship of these sections, but it may be the case that one of the collaborators 'corrected' his partner's relatives in a final version.[240]

Ward Elliott and Robert Valenza's tests on the play as a whole put it well outside the range they would expect for Shakespeare.[241] *Prodigal* has sixteen discrete rejections, a figure which they claim puts the play in 'another galaxy' from Shakespeare. Their tests do not seek to identify alternative authors, however, merely to ascertain what Shakespeare did or did not write. Richard Proudfoot has argued that incredulity arising from the Shakespeare ascription has caused the play to be marginalized in the popular imagination, and that the plethora of candidates shows the fruitlessness of authorial investigation apropos *Prodigal*:

> Either the evidence is more than usually slippery, the attempts at attribution more than usually lacking in rigour, or the question of authorship is the wrong question to address to this play.[242]

Nonetheless, he follows Hope's analysis of the play's pattern of co-authorship, while at the same time tacitly disavowing Shakespeare's involvement:

> I take it that *The London Prodigal* represents the workmanlike norm of playwriting for the King's Men in the early years of the reign of James I ... If the play may be seen as having been written for rapid learning, rehearsal, and production, it may likewise have been written at some speed, one author composing the 895 lines of scenes 8, 9, and 13, while the other wrote the 1,062 lines of the remaining 10 scenes. One or other would then have done some tidying (with less than 100 percent success) – and there was a play fitted ... We are unlikely ever to know the nature and extent of Shakespeare's participation in the communal act of producing this play, whether as dramatist, dramaturge, plotter, actor, or sponsor of the play with his colleagues, but we are inescapably faced with a claim that he did in some way contribute to that production and that it took place early in the reign of James I.[243]

Acceptance of *Prodigal* as a King's Men play means that Shakespearean contact in one form or another is almost inevitable, but establishing the extent of that contact remains unlikely. All stylometric results suggesting his authorial presence seem specious without further investigation, suffering either self-negation, as with Hope's tests, or the shaky confidence inspired by methodologies that at times produce palpably wrong results (Fletcher's hand in *The Tempest* in Merriam and Matthews' work). In spite of generic affinities, *Prodigal*'s poetic features diverge sharply from Shakespeare's solo-authored writing at almost every stage of his career, while internal evidence for Fletcher is bedevilled by the fact that we have no record of him having written for the stage prior to 1606 (even then, his first three plays were written for boy companies in private theatres).[244] The first we know he wrote for the adult professional stage was *Philaster* (1609), for Shakespeare's company, and though his authorship of *Prodigal* is by no means impossible – he would have been twenty-five in 1604 – we nonetheless have a five-year gap during which he had no evident ties to adult drama to explain away. These are all questions that admit no comfortable answers, though the current stylometric consensus seems to agree that there is no stronger candidate to whom to attribute *Prodigal* than Fletcher, apparently in collaboration with another, who, it seems, is highly unlikely to be Shakespeare. The play does reflect the interests of Shakespeare's company at a time in which some of his traditionally more challenging playwriting was undertaken; yet the author(s) of *The London Prodigal* produced a fine comedy that does not deserve to be overshadowed by the question of Shakespeare's involvement. Rather, it deserves the attention both of new theatre audiences and of serious students of the evolution of comic writing, including Shakespeare's, in the early Jacobean period.

A Yorkshire Tragedy (1605)

When considering Shakespeare's authorship of *A Yorkshire Tragedy* it is perhaps worth remembering that he seems to have been a writer heavily predisposed towards the avoidance of controversy in his work. Shakespeare took consistent care to duck any current religious or political turmoil, maintaining, ostensibly at least, clear geographical and/or temporal distance in his narrative settings. While some of his contemporary playwrights were imprisoned, even killed, for the boldness of their writing, Shakespeare passed consistently from under the gaze of the Elizabethan and Jacobean authorities. It is odd, then, to find his name attached to a play that does something thoroughly un-Shakespearean in its choice of subject matter. It narrates the terrible real-life events that had taken place at Calverley Hall, West Yorkshire, on 23 April 1605, when one Walter Calverley, the head of the ancient and respected household, carried out a violent and premeditated attack on his wife and two eldest children, badly wounding her and murdering his infant sons, aged four and eighteen months. He was apprehended en route to kill his youngest son, at wet-nurse with a neighbour at the time, and on 5 August that year was convicted and pressed to death. While Shakespeare's acknowledged canon shows him never to have been a topical writer, *A Yorkshire Tragedy* partakes fully in the grim gossip spreading in the wake of the scandal, apparently penned and performed within weeks of the killings.[245] It is far more, however, than a mere penny dreadful put on its feet. MacDonald Jackson allows it a 'satisfying psychological complexity', and describes its handling of Husband's descent into madness in terms that might recall Othello or Leontes:

> it depicts with force and understanding a man in the grip of what a modern clinician might diagnose as paranoid schizophrenia, which develops rapidly from 'fearful melancholy' (ii.21) to psychotic violence.[246]

It can have been written no earlier than 12 June 1605, when its source pamphlet, *Two Most Unnatural and Bloody Murders*, was entered in the Stationers' Register to Nathaniel Butter, and, as it seems to know nothing of Calverley's execution, could well have been finished before the conclusion of the case. Stanley Wells notes that this could simply mean the playwright was working only from the pamphlet, which we must assume was printed shortly after its entry in the Register.[247] Henslowe's *Diary* shows evidence of many full-length plays being written within a month or less, and *A Yorkshire Tragedy*, at just over 700 lines, about a third the length of a standard five-Act play, could easily have been composed in this short time. Thomas Pavier's 2 May 1608 entry in the Stationers' Register asserting his right to print it, however, is the earliest extant evidence both of its existence and of Shakespeare's supposed authorship:

Master Pavyer   Entered for his Copie vnder the handes / of master WILSON and master Warden *Seton* / A booke Called *A Yorkshire Tragedy* written / by WYLLIAM SHAKESPERE.... vj

Sometime later that year Pavier issued the First Quarto edition, repeating the authorial attribution on the title page, its authenticity apparently bolstered by the naming of the King's Men as the company which had performed the play:

A / YORKSHIRE / Tragedy. / *Not so New as Lamentable* / and true. / *Acted by his Maiesties Players at* / the *Globe.* / *Written by W. Shakspeare* / AT LONDON / Printed by R.B. for *Thomas Pauier* and are to bee sold at his / shop on Cornhill, neere to the exchange. / 1608.

And yet the attribution to Shakespeare is the only supporting evidence for the ascription of *A Yorkshire Tragedy* to the King's Men, and vice versa. We could be dealing with two mutually-reinforcing, albeit fraudulent, pieces of information and this possibility must be acknowledged before we can consider any subsequent recapitulations of the same statements – of which there are several – as meaningful. Immediately preceding the text of our play is the heading: 'ALL'S ONE, / OR / One of the foure Plaies in one, called / a York-shire Tragedy: as it was plaid / by the Kings Maiesties Plaiers.' There is no other evidence that these 'four plays in one' existed, but there seems no strong reason to doubt it, and the suggestion helps to account for the play's length. Gary Taylor argues this means it 'was thus originally only one act of a four-act anthology or variety show, and the subject, genre, and authorship of the other parts remain unknown'.[248] He has elsewhere suggested that Shakespeare could have written one of the other short plays, perhaps explaining the attribution to him.[249] Again, however, this depends on the acceptance of the King's Men ascription. Two Stationers' Register transfers of 4 August 1626 and 8 November 1630 circumstantially link Shakespeare, and, by extension, the King's Men, to the play, as does a transfer of several Shakespeare plays on 21 August 1683. Shakespeare is also identified as the play's author in Edward Archer and Francis Kirkman's untrustworthy play catalogues of 1656 and 1661/71, though more significantly it appeared in the Third Folio (1664), and was reprinted in the Fourth (1685). There is, however, little to suggest that the selection of plays with which the Third Folio attempted to add to the Shakespeare canon was based on any other criteria than the title-page attributions of their earliest printings. The Calverley story is elsewhere attached to Shakespeare's company through George Wilkins' play on the same theme, *The Miseries of Enforced Marriage* (1606), though the information Pavier supplied in 1608 is likely to be the authority for all other seventeenth-century attributions of *A Yorkshire Tragedy* to Shakespeare. Pavier's word, though, is badly undermined by the play's second imprint, or rather the context in which it appeared.

In 1619 he attempted to publish a collection of ten 'Shakespeare' Quartos (the others being *Henry VI Part 2* and *Part 3*, *Pericles*, *The Merchant of Venice*, *The Merry Wives of Windsor*, *King Lear*, *Henry V*, *A Midsummer Night's Dream*, and *Sir John Oldcastle Part 1*). Although he was technically within his rights to do so, holding the licence for some of the plays, while licences for some had expired, the King's Men seem to have taken legal action to thwart his efforts.[250] After their intervention, rather than ceasing all activity on the project, Pavier apparently continued to work on the remaining volumes, antedating those he had not printed when the injunction came through. Some volumes, including *A Yorkshire Tragedy*, are correctly dated to 1619, but *Henry V* and *King Lear* were dated 1608, with *The Merchant of Venice*, *A Midsummer Night's Dream*, and *Sir John Oldcastle Part 1* dated to 1600. Pavier was apparently trying to authenticate the latter four volumes by aligning them with an historical truth about their printing histories: these are indeed the years in which they were first printed, which he clearly knew. But *Henry V* and *Oldcastle* represent the worst excesses of his duplicity, as he himself had published the Second Quarto of *Henry V* (1602) and still owned the rights, and was the publisher of the 1600 Quarto of *Oldcastle*, which bore no authorial attribution, and which was ascribed to the Admiral's company on its title page, as was the reprint. Whether or not Pavier knew the identity of *Oldcastle*'s actual authors – Robert Wilson, Michael Drayton, Anthony Munday, and Richard Hathaway – in 1600 is impossible to determine, but he is likely to have known that Shakespeare was the principal dramatist for the Chamberlain's (later King's) company at that time.[251] He certainly knew it in 1608 when he published the First Quarto of *A Yorkshire Tragedy*, just as he knew it in 1619 when he falsely attributed *Oldcastle* to Shakespeare. This is not a character assassination intended to discredit Pavier's attribution to Shakespeare of *A Yorkshire Tragedy*, but a series of observations to assert that he was not above unscrupulous dealings, and that any title-page information he supplies cannot be taken at face value. Furthermore, *A Yorkshire Tragedy* appeared in print at a time when there was a very definite pattern of Shakespeare's plays being withheld from publication by the King's Men. If company assets were being protected, and Shakespeare's name dissociated from cheap printed editions after 1600, it seems hard to imagine circumstances in which the King's Men would authorize the title-page attribution, even if he had written it. The fact that it appeared in print at all at this time, coupled with its non-appearance in the First Folio, argues against the validity of the attribution, although *Pericles* is a potential corrective.

Scholarly opinion has predictably proved somewhat divided. Of the great eighteenth-century editors, Nicholas Rowe stood alone in including the seven apocryphal plays from the Third Folio in his Shakespeare canon; Pope, Theobald, Hanmer, Warburton, Johnson, Capell, Steevens and Malone remained unconvinced. Belief in the Shakespeare attribution reached its height in the nineteenth century, with George Steevens, A. W. Schlegel, Henry Ulrici, W. G. Simms, Max Moltke, J .P. Collier, F. G. Fleay, A. F. Hopkinson, and A. W. Ward all allowing for the possibility that he had indeed written all or part. Swinburne, a notable objector, nonetheless deeply admired the play's power, judging it 'unsurpassed for pure potency of horror'.[252] From the turn of the twentieth century through to the 1970s attribution to Shakespeare was largely dismissed, usually on general impressionistic grounds. J. A. Symonds, J. O. Halliwell-Phillipps, C. F. Tucker Brooke, E. K. Chambers and Baldwin Maxwell all ruled against, and the play's exclusion from all major editions of Shakespeare buttresses the judgement. A notable exception and standalone theory came from Marc Friedlaender, who felt that Shakespeare was responsible for the problematic, and, as many critics argue, incongruous first scene, and was complicit in the otherwise fraudulent attribution. Sylvia D. Feldman and Richard Proudfoot, in the Malone Society edition of the play, argued that it 'differs so entirely from the other plays written by Shakespeare from 1605 to 1608 that it seems very unlikely to be wholly or even largely his'.[253] Alternative candidates were sought both from within the ranks of writers provably working for the King's Men during the 1600s, as well as from outside, on the assumption that it may not be a King's play or that it may be by a writer who was not regularly employed by the company. Bertram Dobell, H. Dugdale Sykes and Keith Sturgess looked tentatively to Wilkins, with Dobell and Sturgess allowing for the possibility that Shakespeare could subsequently have revised the efforts of his *Pericles* co-author. Sidney Lee suggested Thomas Heywood or Cyril Tourneur, and A. M. Clark concurred on the Heywood attribution, looking to generic similarities with his great domestic tragedy, *A Woman Killed with Kindness*, written for Worcester's Men in 1603.

Heywood, as far as we know, did not work for the King's Men before 1634, and Jackson is quick to dismiss both him and Wilkins on stylistic grounds, stating: 'The cosy-minded Heywood is the last man I should look to as author of *A Yorkshire Tragedy*, and the evidence for Wilkins is worthless'.[254] Tourneur, author of *The Atheist's Tragedy* (printed in 1611 and performed by an unknown company), was proposed on the strength of Edward Archer's attribution to him of *The Revenger's Tragedy*, a King's Men play printed in 1607 bearing many similarities of style and tone to *A Yorkshire Tragedy*. W. W. Greg conjectured that Archer's connection between the two may have been as superficial as the similarity in title, but, notwithstanding, Tourneur's supposed authorship of *Revenger's* stood as a critical orthodoxy, as did the ascription of *Atheist's* to the King's Men. This all changed between 1975 and 1979 when David J. Lake and MacDonald Jackson built upon the work of Mark Eccles and Peter B. Murray to develop detailed stylometric cases proving beyond almost all doubt that *Revenger's* was in fact the work of a young Thomas Middleton, who until 1605 had been involved with Paul's Boys writing smart, cosmopolitan, urban satires such as *Michaelmas Term*, *A Trick to Catch the Old One*, and *A Mad World, My Masters*.[255] Eccles' 1931 article had established linguistic profiling for Middleton around the use of idiomatic expressions ('give him his due', 'the best is', 'Troth, you say true') and highly characteristic contractions (*h'as, sh'as, 't'as, 't'ad, uppo'th'*) in his acknowledged canon to all but prove his hand in *The Puritan*, another Paul's play, published in 1607 and attributed, like *Locrine* and *Thomas Lord Cromwell*, to 'W. S.' on its title page.[256] E. H. C. Oliphant had in fact first suggested in 1927 that Middleton could have written *A Yorkshire Tragedy*, though for many years his theory had lain by the wayside, deemed the product of critical clutching at straws. But the link with *Revenger's* put Middleton in the frame of the King's Men's repertory several years before he was – until then – known to have worked with them, and a new candidate was available to be tested seriously for the authorship of *A Yorkshire Tragedy*.[257]

Middleton was not a regular King's dramatist, and could have written the play for Paul's Boys, although it seems hard to imagine a play of such savage intensity being performed effectively by children. They were not incapable of depictions of violence, as Marston's *Antonio and Mellida* and *Antonio's Revenge* attest (c.1599–1600), but the repertory of their plays thereafter until the company's disbandment around 1608 is biased exclusively towards comedy, and neither of Marston's plays matches the claustrophobic horror of *A Yorkshire Tragedy*. It may also be noted that during 1605–06, when the play is likely to have been written, the King's Men were heavily engaged in performing tragedies – the surviving plays from these two years are *Timon of Athens*, *King Lear*, *Macbeth*, *The Revenger's Tragedy*, *The Miseries of Enforced Marriage*, with *Volpone* the only comedy – strengthening the likelihood that it was written for them. Further points of contact between Middleton and the King's Men can be drawn in 1605 to strengthen the inferential conclusion that he could have authored the play and that it probably does belong to their stable. As early as 1876 F. G. Fleay noted resemblances between *Timon of Athens* (1605) and *Revenger's*, a conclusion developed in 1909 by E. H. C. Oliphant, who felt *Timon* must be multi-authored and that the tone of the non-Shakespearean 3.1 – as he judged it – was of a piece with *Revenger's*.[258] Since then, Lake, Jackson, R. V. Holdsworth, Brian Vickers and John Jowett have all strongly demonstrated that Middleton was Shakespeare's co-author on *Timon*, with Jowett also finding verbal and intellectual parallels between the Middletonian sections of the play and *Two Most Unnatural and Bloody Murders*: 'In the pamphlet, Walter Calverley indulges in profligacy that is described in phrases echoed in the language of *Timon of Athens*'.[259] Jackson also notes that 'the mingling of imagery of finance, sex, and disease in *A Yorkshire Tragedy*' is a characteristic vehicle of Middleton's satire, strongly present in *Timon of Athens*. Middleton went on to adapt Shakespeare's *Macbeth*, probably around 1616, possibly because he felt uniquely placed to be able to do so, having written *Revenger's* for the King's Men the same year as Shakespeare's darkest tragedy (both 1606), and having collaborated with him on *Timon* the year before. Furthermore, a biographical link to the play's narrative interest drawn by Taylor is that: 'like Calverley in 1605, Middleton's stepfather in 1595 had allegedly attempted to murder his wife (Middleton's mother), so the playwright had firsthand experience of conjugal violence'.[260]

Lake had no problems with Middleton's presence in the play, but felt his singular authorship was thrown into doubt by the play's first scene, which he, and many critics before him, judged to be incongruous with the tone and integrity of the wider narrative. Fleay and Sykes felt that the whole play was an unused draft of the latter half of Wilkins' *Miseries*, with Sykes contending that Scene 1 fitted into the middle of Wilkins' play. Jackson judged Baldwin Maxwell's analysis to have 'systematically demolished' Sykes' argument, and, in spite of Lake's claim that the scene is 'anomalous and detachable', he mounted a lengthy defence for its being considered an organic part of the play. He began by responding to Sturgess' objections that the scene:

> is not based verbally on the pamphlet; its characters are named; its low comedy is not single-mindedly concerned with the play's plot; and it suggests details of the story contradicted by or unconnected with the rest of the play.[261]

Jackson dismisses the first two points on the basis that the servants' names, Oliver, Ralph and Sam, are as depersonalized as Tom, Dick and Harry, or Husband, Wife and Master, and that many other plays, such as *Macbeth*, have moments of low comedy (the Porter scene) that can seem tangential to the main flow of the narrative (45). The first and last of Sturgess' points he adjudges to be the real 'heart of the matter', and proceeds at length to demonstrate how the scene in fact:

> represents a skilful and economical handling of that portion of the narrative least amenable to dramatization, and any minor ambiguities in *A Yorkshire Tragedy* about place and circumstance are inherent in the pamphlet itself.[262]

Jackson's survey is probably the most detailed consideration of the scene's place in the play, and makes a compelling case that *A Yorkshire Tragedy* is authorially and structurally all of a piece, though the case is not settled for good and all. Both Lake and Jonathan Hope noted sections of the play that were, in Hope's phrase, 'not entirely Middletonian', with Hope suggesting some possible textual interference to explain the irregularities in his relativization evidence.[263] Lake argued strongly in favour of Middleton's authorship of certain scenes within the play, though felt that it was probably multi-authored, conjecturally apportioning the scenes in three tiers thus:

> Middleton: Scenes i-iii.a (to the end of the husband's first speech on B4), vi-x.a (to S.D. *Children laid out*, D2v).

> X (i.e. an unknown author): Scenes iii.b, v, x.b.

> Mixed (Middleton, X, perhaps Shakespeare): Scene iv.[264]

Nevertheless, where he identifies Middleton, the evidence is strong:

> To go no further than three contractions, *t'as*, *upo'th'*, and *'em*, I can state that the class of known authors writing in 1600–1620 for the London stages who use *t'as* and *upo'th'* even once as well as *'em* more often than *them* in even one play is a class with one member only – Middleton.[265]

The stylometric evidence for Middleton was supported and expanded upon by Jackson, who argued for Middleton's sole authorship. He noted that *upo'th* appears in two early Middleton plays written just prior to *A Yorkshire Tragedy*, *A Mad World...* (× 6) and *Michaelmas Term* (× 2). Looking first at the rates of occurrence of six favoured Middleton contractions – *I'm* (6), *I'd* (1), *I've* (0), *on't* (1), *ne'er* (5), *e'en* (4) – and then noting thirty-two further instances of contractions he habitually employs – *'em* (5), *i'th'* (5), *o'th'* (4), *ha'* (2), *'tas* (1), *h'as* (2), *'t* (13) – Jackson argued that these rates of occurrence, especially in a play one third the normal length, and especially containing as they do certain features exclusive to Middleton, pointed in only one direction:

The pattern as a whole is more strongly suggestive of Middleton than any other dramatist I have examined. Certainly Wilkins is a most unlikely author of the play, if the linguistic data means anything at all...No play by Shakespeare exhibits anything approaching *A Yorkshire Tragedy*'s ratio of 16 *has* to *hath*: Shakespeare always prefers *hath*. *I'm*, used 6 times in *A Yorkshire Tragedy*, appears only 12 times within the whole Shakespeare canon, and 4 of these examples are in the Fletcher scenes of *Henry VIII*. In its linguistic minutiae *A Yorkshire Tragedy* is all of a piece. The pointers to Middleton's authorship are no less clear in the opening scene than in the rest of the play: in scene i *has* (twice) and *does* are used, whereas *hath* and *doth* are not, and *'em, i'th'* (twice), *is't, in't, e'en, ne'er,* and *on't* appear. The linguistic evidence is thus in agreement with the literary evidence which I have adduced: scene i is an intrinsic part of the play, of which Middleton is the probable author.[266]

Lake and Jackson's work was not universally accepted, however. A. C. Cawley and Barry Gaines, the play's editors in the Revels series, expressed scepticism towards the practice of stylometric analysis in general, and also deemed Lake and Jackson's results magnified because of the play's relatively short length, a problem acknowledged by Lake and Jackson. While they contended that 'no definitive conclusion concerning the principal author seems possible', they nonetheless left the door open for Shakespearean involvement, suggestively quoting Baldwin Maxwell's suggestion that Shakespeare might have 'introduced here and there lines which he thought might render the play more effective'.[267] Roger Holdsworth's respected stylometric work on Middleton's hand in *Timon* seven years later, however, supported Middletonian authorship of *A Yorkshire Tragedy*, which he followed up a year later in detailed and decisive terms.[268] Ward Elliott and Robert J. Valenza's tests ruled Shakespeare out entirely, though they did not propose alternative authorship. The play's inclusion in the 2007 Oxford Middleton, a volume that has dramatically advanced studies of Middleton's authorial persona, was a clear, definitive endorsement of the work of Lake, Jackson, Holdsworth and others on the part of the editors.[269]

When Baldwin Maxwell undertook his *Studies in the Shakespeare Apocrypha* in 1956, he contended that: 'A convincing identification of the author or authors of *A Yorkshire Tragedy*, if it is ever to be accomplished, must await our clearer knowledge of what were the peculiar characteristics of the various Jacobean dramatists.'[270] This, indeed, was the very work undertaken by scholars such as Lake, Jackson, and Holdsworth on the play. And unlike so many cases of stylometric analysis that lead to what Schoenbaum termed 'diminishing returns' or even blind alleys, we are in this case extremely lucky that, for pure linguistic idiosyncrasy, Middleton's 'peculiar characteristics' present themselves far more clearly and consistently than do those of almost all other early modern dramatists. The job of placing Middleton within the King's Men around the time this play was written – linking him to *Timon* and *Revenger's* – was likewise done purely on internal, stylometric grounds; a job that we could not hope to do with anything like the degree of confidence we have were Middleton's authorial fingerprints not so bold. Jackson has more recently reiterated a long list of Middletonian habits that have been subjected to wider comparative analysis than his 1979 study thanks to the use of the online database LION.[271] He describes the authorial profile as an 'identikit of features' which Middleton uses at 'above-average rates', noting that 'when doubtful texts are matched against it, the likeness is sometimes so perfect that we can confidently associate them with our man'.[272]

For those seeking certainty about the authorship of the plays herein then, *A Yorkshire Tragedy* might be among the most satisfying, unless you wish to think it the work of Shakespeare. The irregularities noted by Lake and Hope may leave the door open to another author's limited presence, which may or may not be Shakespeare's, but equally Jackson has offered strong justification for single authorship. Whether the statements Pavier issued in 1608 were the result of a genuine mix up (if we accept the four-plays-in-one theory); a best guess or default attribution (he may not have known the author, but knew the play's provenance and that Shakespeare was the chief King's dramatist); or a cynical marketing ploy, his attribution to Shakespeare obscured the predominant hand's identity for nearly four hundred years. Middleton had written tragedies at the very start of his career before turning his attentions to comedy.[273] During 1605–06, however, he evidently enjoyed a three-play, albeit uncredited, return to the darker genre with the King's Men, even getting to collaborate directly with Shakespeare in late 1605 on *Timon of Athens*.[274] And it seems almost certain that union was brought about by the young prodigy forcing the old master's attention on the strength of his impressive, savage, breakthrough debut for the company: *A Yorkshire Tragedy*.[275]

Mucedorus (c.1590–91, revised c.1610)

Mucedorus was the most popular printed play in early modern England, and yet nobody knows when, by whom, or for whom it was first written. Something of a trite comedic romance from the early days of the professional stage in London, it nonetheless transcended the bounds of limited favour we might expect for such a vehicle and ran to fourteen editions by the time Parliament had closed the doors on the public theatres in 1642. It was reprinted three more times between c.1656 and 1668, making seventeen imprints in total, yet it was some twenty years in the wake of its inception before interest in the play began to snowball. The first edition appeared in 1598, essentially reprinted in the second (1606) as Leo Kirschbaum – who also argued that both were based on actors' memorial reports – demonstrated.[276] The third edition of 1610, however, was apparently prepared from an authoritative manuscript and was fleshed out with new additions by a King's company dramatist: 'as it was acted before the Kings Maiestie at White-hall on Shroue-sunday night. By his Highnes Seruantes vsually playing at the Globe'. There are two main tiers to the *Mucedorus* authorship debate, concerning firstly the author of the A-text (1598, 1606) and secondly the author of the Additions to the B-text, involving most obviously a prologue and masque-like insertion into the Epilogue written in homage to the king, and an expansion of the role of the clown character, Mouse. Could something regarding the possibility of Shakespearean involvement help account for the huge increase in the play's popularity following the appearance of this substantially revised text, on which all subsequent reprints were based, on booksellers' stalls? The fact that the Quarto makes no attempt to exploit Shakespeare's name suggests not; the attribution that really seems to have changed things was the newfound association with the king. As George F. Reynolds notes:

> The decisive events in the history of the popularity of *Mucedorus* are clear from its record: the change in its fortune came with the performances in London by the King's men, and the publication of the B text [Q3]. Before these events the play was a badly worn antique; after them it became a unique success.[277]

This alone cannot explain the phenomenon, as many printed plays of limited readership declared auspices with the King's Men on their title pages. Most critics attempting the question of the A-text's authorship have been united in the sense that the play is formulaic and thoroughly un-Shakespearean, and yet this may in fact have been the bedrock of its massive resurgence. Paul Kreuzer suggests that rife conventionality – the hero prince and heroine princess, the loyal friend, the villain, the comic fool – made it 'a friendly play' for Jacobean audiences, sharing in the romance mode that had become *de rigueur* at the end of the 1600s, reflected in the King's company's repertory in all of Shakespeare's works at this time.[278] We see the motifs of the wild man, Bremo, paralleled in *The Tempest*'s Caliban and the more primitive pastoral of the Wales scenes in *Cymbeline*, as well as the bear familiar from *The Winter's Tale*. Ben Jonson's *Masque of Oberon* also calls for two white bears to draw Oberon's chariot, and it has been argued that real polar bears may have been used in both it and *Mucedorus* (see 2.110–16).[279] Thus the play may have held a disarming charm in its simple comedy while being at the same time – with the new affiliation, the Prologue and reworked Epilogue – potently symbolic of royal power, a somewhat heady combination driving its appeal beyond the norm.

The 1598 edition lacked authorial or company attribution of any kind on a title page also declaring the play to have been 'sundrie times plaide in the honorable Cittie of London'. Many have put the date of original composition much earlier, with F. G. Fleay suggesting 1588 based on the fact that the 'honourable city of London' as performance venue was to his mind only seen elsewhere on the title pages of Queen's Men plays, giving *The Troublesome Reign of King John* (1591) as an example. It also appears on the title pages of *Fair Em* (1591?, Strange's) and *Edward II* (1594, Pembroke's) in the early 1590s and on many others at later dates, chiefly royal entertainments and civic pageants.[280] Fleay's surmise that *Mucedorus* began with the Queen's Men has never been resolved and the original company remains obscure, yet his guess may be a good one. Martin Wiggins suggests that as the title page does not mention the Chamberlain's it is unlikely to be theirs, and was therefore almost certainly in existence by 1594 when the duopoly was formed, its absence from Henslowe's records suggesting it was not an Admiral's play either. Pre-1594, Henslowe evidence again argues against Strange's, and, probably, Sussex's, for whom we also have a short repertory sample in the *Diary*.[281] If it was Pembroke's it might have come to the Chamberlain's in 1594, but, again, title-page evidence suggests not. Which leaves the Queen's Men, a likelihood made stronger by the suggestion of a court performance at which Elizabeth was in attendance in the play's final scene. The c.1590–91 dating is a guess based on the above, on the sense of the play's very early style, and on the fact that it uses for plot Sir Philip Sidney's *Arcadia*, first printed in 1590.[282] F. G. Fleay also suggested that the structural arrangement for performance by eight actors was indicative of an early work, though he placed it c.1587. Robert Greene is the author most often associated with the handful of attributed Queen's Men plays, along with Thomas Lodge and George Peele. The company's extant histories about *King John*, *Henry V*, *King Leir* and *Richard III* – all of which Shakespeare was to rework – are still unattributed. As we will see though, no writer has been confidently or sustainedly linked with the A-text's authorship.

Richard T. Thornberry has pointed out that the Second Quarto includes very minor alterations, switching all the Elizabeth references to the recently crowned James.[283] He argues for an accompanying performance between 1604–06 on the basis of this, which would suggest that the King's Men had acquired it by this time, though the changes could just as easily have been made in the printing house as by any dramatic author or company, as Wiggins points out.[284] The 1610 text, however, does include substantial reworking for performance, adding a Prologue and three new scenes, and revising the endings of the final scene and the Epilogue. It also provides evidence of a performance before James at Whitehall on Shrove Sunday that year, which, in old, Annunciation-style dating would have technically been 20 February 1609, the New Year falling on 25 March, with the Quarto printed sometime thereafter. This seems a more likely scenario than the performance having taken place on 3 February, the date of Shrove Sunday the following year, with the printing then rushed out before 24 March, though we cannot rule this out.[285] We do not know when the King's Men acquired the play, but one of their dramatists most certainly added material to it. Exactly when this happened is not easy to determine either, though a c.1610 dating allows for the possibility that composition may have begun late 1609. Teresa Grant's article on the white bears worked into the Mouse material (scene 2) shows that they are likely to be those whose capture in Lapland in April/May 1609 was recorded by Jonas Poole, who also tells us they were brought to England by 30 May that year, most probably before they had been weaned.[286] This means they would have been hand-reared by humans and would have been tame enough to appear (at least one of them, anyway) in a performance of *Mucedorus* the following February. Going by the logic of the printing date, the period between 1 January and 20 February is quite short, and it would have been normal at this time anyway for the company to iron out plays before a private, paying audience in their Blackfriars repertory before taking them to court.[287] The material in the play's Epilogue, which seems to combine both anti-masque disorder and masque-like resolution by the attendant monarch, was clearly written exclusively for the court performance designated by the title page. But it is entirely possible that the rest of the additional passages were written late 1609 to early 1610, with the play first performed sans Prologue and Epilogue at the Blackfriars. If, however, Shrove Sunday 1611 is implied, then the Additions were probably composed later in 1610. We cannot therefore be entirely confident about their date, though the question of when seems easier to establish than that of who.

Among King's Men dramatists Shakespeare is the obvious, and, naturally, the most desirable candidate, though if the adaptation was commissioned for a royal performance their premier writer of courtly entertainments was Jonson. Of the eleven court masques played at Whitehall in the time between James' accession in 1603 and the company's performance of *The Tempest* there in 1611, Jonson had written eight. The Jacobean court lavished huge sums of money on entertainments, enough, in fact, to have severely depleted the holdings of the royal Exchequer by the time the ill-fated Charles I ascended the throne. Continued expensive masquing with Parliament-raised funds was to be one of the divisive factors accelerating the onset of the Civil War. King's Men writers were frequently commissioned to provide masques and similar entertainments, and it may be significant for Shakespearean authorship, or at least for his company's involvement, that *Mucedorus*, a court romance from the early 1590s, was being resurrected at this time. Shakespeare never wrote masques, though his late plays, often classed as romances, reflect something of the taste for grandiose masque-like entertainment in their style and subject matter, the company's repertory surely in large part influenced by their patron's tastes. Court performances of plays by Shakespeare, which he would have attended, were nothing unusual, but the *Mucedorus* Epilogue includes an expansion of the Second Quarto's sycophantic, allegorical paean to the monarch of the kind at which Jonson excelled and in which Shakespeare never indulged. Such circumstantial factors, nonetheless, will not do for an authorial attribution, and Jonson has never been proposed as the play's reviser on stylistic grounds.

Apart from the King's Men connection, the principal early foundation on which claims for Shakespearean authorship rest is the play's inclusion in a one-off volume of plays bound together under the title 'Shakespeare Vol. 1', apparently for the personal edification of Charles I. It has been a longstanding scholarly misapprehension, based on the unverified recycling of critical statements, that the volume belonged to the library of Charles II, and that it contained only three plays: *Merry Devil*, *Fair Em* and *Mucedorus*. However, Peter Kirwan has recently demonstrated that it actually belonged to the elder Charles, and that it originally contained eight plays, *The Puritan*, *Thomas Lord Cromwell*, *The London Prodigal*, *Love's Labour's Lost* and *Sir John Oldcastle* being the other five.[288] It passed into the ownership of the great eighteenth-century actor-manager David Garrick, and two scholars and famous Shakespeare editors of the time, Edward Capell and George Steevens, both attested to its ownership by Charles I (Capell also catalogued Garrick's collection). Steevens erroneously named Charles II as the owner in three footnotes in a 1793 Variorum edition, and the misattribution was preserved from then on. The volume finally ended up in the British Museum, and was 'broken up in the 1840s on the orders of Anthony Panizzi'.[289] As Kirwan notes, this is surely the earliest attempt to compile works we could loosely conceive of as Shakespeare apocrypha, albeit the inclusion of *Love's Labour's Lost* is tricky to explain. Yet the volume's existence alone constitutes very weak evidence upon which to base an attribution of *Mucedorus* to Shakespeare. Not all the plays within it named an author, and it seems that the rationale in part for the way it was split has to do with attribution: *Mucedorus*, *Merry Devil* and *Fair Em* are the only plays from the collection never to have named Shakespeare, either explicitly or suggestively, on their title pages. Their inclusion is therefore much harder to explain than the five plays that do.[290]

Mucedorus was not included in any of the Folio reprints or any eighteenth-century Shakespeare edition. It featured in Tucker Brooke's *The Shakespeare Apocrypha*, one of the many works to repeat the Charles II error, claiming that the volume of three plays stood mainly as 'a commentary on Shakespeare knowledge after the Restoration'.[291] Following Kirwan though, our sense of its actual auspices needs to be readjusted to within about a decade of the First Folio. Some of the title pages in fact date from the early 1630s, showing that it was not merely the long theatrical drought of the Interregnum that generated the culture of fanciful statements regarding Shakespeare's authorship. Yet Tucker Brooke's observation is also essentially true: the 1650s and 1660s saw many wildly inaccurate attributions, nowhere more prevalent than in the play catalogues produced by Edward Archer and Francis Kirkman in 1656 and 1661 respectively, both of which gave *Mucedorus* unequivocally to Shakespeare. The Charles I volume's treatment in modern scholarship serves as a potent reminder that recycled, unchecked statements in print are not made accurate through the mere fact of their repetition. Tucker Brooke, incidentally, did not support the attribution to Shakespeare, describing *Mucedorus* and *Fair Em* as:

> productions that bear the mark of vagabondage on every feature. Yet, for the reader of today, these plays, distinctly the weaklings of the flock, possess an attractiveness of their own by very virtue of their dull impersonality, because they display so little of the individual author and so much of the vulgar dramatic taste.[292]

Brooke felt it was not even authored by any known dramatist of the period but by an obscure, unexceptional-yet-competent disciple of the University Wits, which, Paul Kreuzer suggests, has been 'the generally accepted twentieth-century solution to the problem of [*Mucedorus*'] authorship'.[293] This view was echoed by C. R. Baskerville, V. B. Heltzel and A. H. Nethercot, who included *Mucedorus* in their 1934 collection *Elizabethan and Stuart Plays*, one of only two publications of the play since Brooke. The other was James Winny's *Three Elizabethan Plays* (1959), which rejected the idea of Shakespearean involvement outright, though, as Kirschbaum would do, pointed to textual deficiencies to propose the text was either 'carelessly transcribed in the printing-house' or co-written, one of the two authors being 'imperfectly acquainted with blank verse form'. In any case, no known author has been more than half-heartedly linked to the A-text; Fleay rejected most known playwrights of the early theatres, leaving open only the possibility of Thomas Lodge:

> As to authorship, the Induction is, I think, by the same hand as that to [*A*] *Warning for Fair Women*; there are many coincidences in expression with Marius and Sylla, and the 'cooling card' [13.104] trade-mark is found in Sc. 17. No other author but Lodge is known in connexion with the 1587 Queen's men who could have written it; it is certainly not by Marlow [*sic*], Peele, Green [*sic*], or Dekker.[294]

Despite Fleay's dismissive stance, Robert Greene is the author most commonly proposed in the extremely rare instances that any attempt at attribution, outside Shakespeare, has been made. Malone suggested it in 1821, though J. Churton Collins disagreed. The theory was nonetheless recapitulated in 1931 by Arthur Acheson, who also believed the text was later revised, and there, in effect, ends the attribution history of *Mucedorus* to Greene. Alden Brooks suggested, in *Will Shakespere and the Dyer's Hand* (1943), a Greene/Lodge collaboration with some help from Shakespeare, whom he felt – as the punning title of his book unfortunately asserts – was Edward Dyer. Freiherr von Freisen proposed George Peele in 1876, though he found no support, and Ludwig Tieck, over a number of years in the early nineteenth century, made the outright lunge at Shakespeare. Only A. W. Titherly, in his 1952 study *Shakespeare's Identity*, followed suit, noting similarities of vocabulary and dramatic situation in *Mucedorus* within the acknowledged works of Shakespeare. However, he felt the Additions – which if anything are the most likely Shakespearean material – were by another author, though, as has been noted previously, he was a proponent of William Stanley, the sixth Earl of Derby as the 'real' Shakespeare. Among the critics to reject Shakespearean authorship of the A-text explicitly are J. P. Collier, Richard Simpson, C. F. Tucker Brooke, A. F. Hopkinson, Gary Taylor, Ward Elliott and Robert Valenza, though Collier, Simpson and Hopkinson all argued for Shakespeare's authorship of the B-text Additions, while Charles Knight, Henry Tyrrell, F. G. Fleay, Karl Warnke and Ludwig Proescholdt, E. Soffé, A. W. Ward, George F. Reynolds and Elliott and Valenza took the opposite view. The hands of John Day, George Wilkins and Thomas Heywood were suspected by J. C. Maxwell, who argued elsewhere for the possibility that the author of the non-Shakespearean portion of *Pericles* – who is now accepted to be Wilkins – was also responsible for the *Mucedorus* Additions. In spite of one definite collaboration with Shakespeare a couple of years before, there is still nothing conclusively tying Wilkins to the *Mucedorus* Additions. John Peachman noted several striking parallels between *Mucedorus* and *Guy of Warwick*, another anonymously authored play, which therefore tells us nothing about the identity of the hand that may be behind both.[295] Leo Kirschbaum, in *The Texts of Mucedorus*, claimed that the Wild Man is modelled on Lust in *The Faerie Queene*, Book IV, Canto vii, not published until 1596, which could suggest revision in the two years leading up to the Quarto's publication, or even a later date for the play, though the idea has not subsequently been taken up.

Richard Preiss interestingly argued that the play's authorlessness, certainly from the Third Quarto onwards, was a deliberate strategy on the part of the King's Men to secure their repertory.[296] George Buc gained control of the censorship of printed playbooks from the Church Court of High Commission in 1606 and a loophole arose whereby provincial companies could use printed copies of plays for performance, though still could not use company manuscripts. *Mucedorus*, Preiss argues, was the King's Men's way of turning this into a marketing advantage; by releasing to the public this frippery of a play to which they had no strong connection, certainly not in the sense of authorial property, they were effectively sanctioning a 'utopian idea of theatre that they legitimated and that reciprocally legitimated them, a magic kingdom everyone had a right, and the means, to experience'.[297] In other words, people were getting the chance to perform what the London professionals performed. This, Preiss continues, accounts for the many subsequent reprints that all retain a company name and a performance venue that had both long since vanished when some of the last reprints were issued. He concludes:

> Regardless of what he may have contributed to it, in no meaningful sense was Shakespeare ever the author of *Mucedorus*, nor did the King's Men wish to be so either; they merely authored its authorlessness – an authorlessness that worked, in all respects other than ownership, exactly like authorship itself. The faithful promiscuity of every intervening edition from 1610 to 1668 attests to the runaway success of that experiment...By a nice coincidence, the name 'Mucedorus' itself meant 'gift of the muses' – and here, quite literally, a play finally anonymous.[298]

It is a clever piece of criticism doing much justice to the fact that the play's enormous popularity and charming magical simplicity have somehow divorced it from more pragmatic scholarly attempts to solve questions of provenance and authorship. Preiss may well be right about the company's unwitting part in creating this critical ceasefire, though the fact remains that behind this apparent act of artistic self-negation lies an author or authors. These lines did not write themselves, in spite of their symbolic effect, and the only King's Men authors we know to have been working around 1609–10 likely to perform such revisions are Francis Beaumont, John Fletcher, Ben Jonson and William Shakespeare.

The only serious consideration of the possibility that Shakespeare is in fact involved remains MacDonald Jackson's 1964 article 'Edward Archer's Ascription of *Mucedorus* to Shakespeare' in which he made the case, on the basis of stylistic and dramatic similarities with Shakespeare's known work, for his contribution to a court performance sometime between 1606 and 1610.[299] Of Addition III, scene 10, Jackson notes (references added):

> The diction resembles that of Shakespeare's late period. Words ending in '-ure', like 'parture' [10.23], abound in *Troilus and Cressida*, and 'affectious' [10.24] is a typically Shakespearean Latinism. 'Molestation' [10.7] is an uncommon word which he uses only in *Othello*... The first instance of 'extolment' [10.35] recorded by the *OED* is from *Hamlet*. The coinage 'young-fed' [10.29] is the sort of compound Shakespeare was fond of creating. The use of the noun instead of the infinitive 'to conceal', in 'what my breast vowed concealment' [10.26], has a Shakespearian flavour.[300]

Perhaps the most poetically arresting moment among the Additions occurs in the revised Epilogue in the lines:

> COMEDY   Envy, spit thy gall,
>   Plot, work, contrive, create new fallacies.
>   Teem from thy womb each minute a black traitor
>   Whose blood and thoughts have twin conception.
>   Study to act deeds yet unchronicled,
>   Cast native monsters in the moulds of men,
>   Case vicious devils under sancted rochets,
>   Unhasp the wicket where all perjureds roost
>   And swarm this ball with treasons. Do thy worst!
>   Thou canst not, hell-hound, cross my star tonight,
>   Nor blind that glory where I wish delight. (lines 16–26)

It is undoubtedly the point at which the play finds another gear linguistically, the imagery crammed into these ten lines suddenly bursting at the seams with strange, violent concepts, in contrast to the leisurely flow of the quaint versifying and comic prose dominating the language up to that point. The words 'unchronicled' and 'unhasp', for instance, are striking, these being the earliest recorded uses of both in the *Oxford English Dictionary*, which may be of deeper significance in light of Alfred Hart's observation that Shakespeare had a particular propensity for coinages formed with the addition of the negative 'un-' prefix, as Jackson points out.[301] Jackson examined ten non-Shakespeare plays comprising works by Jonson, Marston, Beaumont and Fletcher, Tourneur, Middleton, Webster, Heywood, Dekker and Rowley, in which he found a total of thirteen new 'un-' words, while *Hamlet* alone has seventeen, showing Shakespeare statistically more likely to be behind the two uses here than these other writers. 'Sancted' is also a coinage the *OED* attributes to this scene, with *Macbeth* and *All's Well* the other two earliest examples. However, it dates *Mucedorus* 1598, apparently in ignorance of the fact that this passage was written *c.*1610, meaning this could certainly be Shakespeare using a favoured word at around this phase of his work. Jackson also notes Hart's observation that the habitual turning of nouns ('saint') into new participles ('sancted' or 'sainted') was 'peculiar to Shakespeare'.[302] The first use the *OED* records of the noun 'bench' as a verb, as in the Prologue, is in *King Lear*, and the use of 'swarm' (Epilogue 24) as a causative verb here is the earliest example according to Jackson. He views the passage as 'rich in new and rare words as only the work of Shakespeare, as a dramatist, customarily is'.[303] The final piece of evidence he offers is a lengthy and compelling demonstration that, among certain image clusters that apparently formed in Shakespeare's mind, that of a 'goose' in the sense of 'whore' nearby images of a key being turned or door being opened, as with a punter gaining covert ingress into a brothel, is strong and recurrent, appearing in *1 Henry VI*, *Love's Labour's Lost*, *Troilus and Cressida*, *King Lear*, *Macbeth* and *Coriolanus*. Here we have the reference to a goose (Epilogue 30) within a few lines of 'Unhasp the wicket' (line 23), another intriguing detail supporting the possibility of Shakespearean thought within the imagery here. Jackson concludes upon the relative inadequacy of the Additions compared with Shakespeare's best work, noting that the job of patching a play of 'humble stock' would not have been the kind of thing to 'stimulate [Shakespeare's] powers to any great achievement'.[304] But he nonetheless reasons that they have many points of contact with the more unexceptional features of Shakespeare's late style: 'If a short scene from *Cymbeline*, IV.iii, for instance, had appeared as an insertion in such a play as *Mucedorus*, I doubt whether anyone would have recognized its author.'[305]

Ward Elliott's tests on the play as a whole noted eleven Shakespeare rejections, strongly counter-indicating his authorship, though he has recently noted that the Additions show only two rejections.[306] The verse portion makes up some 1,300 words, the standard blocks into which they split plays being units of 1,500 words, and in the thirteen usable tests for a portion this short it fails twice. Five out of 140 control blocks of definite Shakespeare verse show this many rejections, and while the number is very low, it is nonetheless still possible that Shakespeare wrote this passage by the standards of Elliott's tests. In spite of adjudging the likelihood 'improbable but not impossible', he reiterates the continuous assessment evidence for the play as a whole and the opinions of the 'golden ear' panel to strongly refute Shakespearean authorship. And yet the most plausible Shakespearean involvement in *Mucedorus* is confined to the Additions, so the fact that they show as many rejections as a small percentage of acknowledged Shakespeare passages is certainly noteworthy. Of course the sample size is smaller than an entire Shakespeare play, but it is clear that the additional passages behave differently from the rest of *Mucedorus* in these tests. Both they and Jackson's analyses situate the passages close to Shakespeare's acceptable norms, and the possibility therefore remains that he wrote them.

By way of closure, it is exciting to note that Jackson, in collaboration with Hugh Craig, is revisiting his old theory through a detailed computer-aided stylometric project, due for publication c.2016. The case is very much in need of reopening; Literature Online and similar databases can test the uniqueness or literary provenance of a word much more accurately than the *OED*, and until such work is done on the passages we cannot claim with any kind of certainty that Shakespeare was their author. His authorship of the A-text is not seriously expected based on stylistic incongruities, probable company auspices, and the likely date of the play's composition. Shakespeare seems to have begun his playwriting career no earlier than 1591, almost certainly with Pembroke's Men, and the first play he wrote, *Henry VI Part 2*, displays strongly in its poetry and action many of the characteristics we associate with his drama throughout his career. The majority of *Mucedorus*, on the one hand, seems far more akin to the styles of late 1580s to early 1590s writers such as Greene, who may indeed have been the play's original author. The question of Shakespeare penning the Additions, on the other hand, is intriguing. Certainly the change in company ownership supports the possibility, as do certain stylistic features, and this shop-worn relic of a play may well have become the greatest publishing success enjoyed by any acting troupe in Renaissance England after the period's greatest writer reworked it. It is curious to consider, however, that if he did his involvement would almost certainly have been as obscured to the legions of readers who bought the refurbished *Mucedorus* as it remains to us.

Cardenio (1612); *Double Falsehood* (1727)

In 2010 *Double Falsehood* caused something of a media stir with its high-profile publication in the Arden Shakespeare series, hailed in broadsheets and tabloids alike as the Bard's lost play newly found. Among those with barely the time or the energy even for *Hamlet* in their lives, such hyperbolic sound bites no doubt bespoke good, albeit not lastingly important, news. Yet another, admittedly select, audience was riven by this symbolic act of canonical inclusion. To them *Double Falsehood or The Distressed Lovers* was Lewis Theobald's infamous work of 1727 (printed 1728), which, he claimed, was an adaptation of a then-unknown Shakespeare play he had come to own in manuscript form. It is based on episodes found in Parts 3 and 4 of Cervantes' *Don Quixote*, and scholars and amateurs have hotly debated the likelihood of it containing any Shakespeare ever since it first appeared. A current consensus led chiefly by Brean Hammond, David Carnegie and Gary Taylor, with which we happen to agree, deems that likelihood acceptable, yet direct access to Shakespeare is not possible with the text we have, which is a palimpsest of perhaps up to three different layers of overwriting.[307] Theobald's Preface states that the most authoritative manuscript from which he worked – he in fact claimed to have three, possibly four – was 'of above sixty years' standing, in the handwriting of Mr Downes, the famous old prompter; and as I am credibly informed, was early in the possession of the celebrated Mr Betterton, and by him designed to have been ushered into the world'. This means that we must look for Shakespeare's stylistic habits through the white noise of John Downes as scribe – and scribes could often iron out authorial tics in accordance with their own habits – the actor Thomas Betterton as potential adapter of the text Downes prepared, and Theobald as adapter of Betterton's manuscript of uncertain origins and second-hand authority. The usual problems for stylometric analysis are therefore both intensified and multiplied, more so because we have every reason to believe that the supposed source text, *Cardenio*, was originally the product of a collaboration between Shakespeare and John Fletcher, though we have only uncertain evidence on which to base even this attribution.

We can prove that in 1613 the King's Men owned and performed a play with a title likely to be *Cardenio*, the name of a character in Cervantes' novel, first published in English in 1612 in a translation by Thomas Shelton. The King's Treasurer's accounts for 20 May and 9 July 1613 record payments to Shakespeare's company for performances at court of a play referred to as 'Cardenno' and 'Cardenna' in the respective entries. The latter entry refers to a special performance of the play for the Duke of Savoy's Ambassadors on 8 June, while the 20 May Chamber Account entry lists six plays in all, including *Much Ado about Nothing*, which were probably part of the annual winter court revels that took place between Christmas and Shrovetide. Gary Taylor has attempted a detailed reconstruction of the likeliest date range of these performances, narrowing it to 9–21 February.[308] The accounts show a notably heavy volume of masquing around Shrovetide as part of the celebrations for Princess Elizabeth's marriage to Frederick V, the Elector Palatine, on 14 February, perhaps suggesting the theatrical performances may more likely have been closer to Christmas. In either case, *Cardenio* must have been written in 1612, as we would expect any new plays taken to court by the company at this time to have been in their Blackfriars repertory for some weeks first.[309] Nothing in either of the accounts, however, is said about authorship. There is nothing unusual about this; who wrote the play is not at issue here, rather the fact that the company had performed it and needed to be paid. Still, there is great frustration caused by knowing that at least one person involved in the recorded transaction, King's Men actor and business manager John Hemings, to whom the payments were made, would have known what we wish so earnestly to know: the playwright or playwrights responsible, and, indeed, the play's contents.

Forty years later, on 9 September 1653, publisher and bookseller Humphrey Moseley entered in the Stationers' Register 'The History of Cardenio, by Mr Fletcher & Shakespeare.' Moseley, for reasons unknown, apparently did not publish whatever text he had in his possession, but the evidence is tantalizing, and a chain of reasoning can be employed in support of the attribution's authenticity. First of all, as Taylor points out,

> Moseley can hardly have been aware of the court payments, which independently attribute the play to Shakespeare's company at the very time when he was collaborating with Fletcher on *All Is True* [i.e. *Henry VIII*] and [*The Two Noble*] *Kinsmen*. Although Moseley could have known of the claim of collaboration on *Kinsmen*, he could not have dated it, and there is no evidence that Fletcher's share in *All Is True* was common knowledge in the seventeenth century.[310]

In other words, all Moseley could have had to go on regarding the fact that Shakespeare and Fletcher ever collaborated was the 1634 Quarto of *The Two Noble Kinsmen* (1613–14). *Henry VIII* (1613) was printed only in the First Folio (1623, reprinted in the Second Folio, 1632), which attributed everything therein solely to Shakespeare. Moseley would not have been able to date either *Kinsmen* or *Cardenio*, so the fact that he is claiming the two playwrights were collaborating at a time when we know they were, but he didn't, increases the likelihood that the attribution is right. Both Moseley's entry and the 1613 accounts serve independently to suggest Moseley's manuscript was of the same play, whether or not his authorial ascription was correct, though the King's Men connection suggests it probably was. Shakespeare had been the company's principal dramatist for the best part of twenty years, and Fletcher was now taking over the role, a fact to which their three collaborations at this time seem to attest, of which *Cardenio* is likely to have been the earliest.[311]

It is perhaps interesting that Fletcher is named first in Moseley's entry, given that Fletcher's writing held a greater appeal to later seventeenth-century readers and playgoers than did the tortuous difficulties of Shakespeare's late style. Fletcher and Jonson were the only two playwrights from the halcyon days of the theatre to be honoured by having bookshops named after them in the Interregnum, which may again speak of the more Fletcherian interest in the play during the 1650s. Indeed, Shakespeare's plays came to be performed more often than not in heavily adapted versions after the reopening of the theatres in the Restoration into the eighteenth and nineteenth centuries, which works in favour of *Double Falsehood*'s authenticity. We can also see specific links between Shakespeare and Fletcher collaborations and Betterton's Duke's company, who performed *The Rivals*, William Davenant's adaptation of *The Two Noble Kinsmen*, and *Henry VIII* in the 1660s. Gordon McMullan points out that *Henry VIII* was one of the few Shakespeare plays – and it would have been assumed to be solely his thanks to the Folio – that was successful in an unadapted form during the Restoration.[312] Of course, this may be because Fletcher's share is so large that the play's style held its appeal, which would suggest that audiences were indeed drawn to writing style rather than authorial name. The Shakespeare portions of *Henry VIII* are also arguably not as syntactically tricky as those of *Kinsmen*, and *The Rivals* provides an analogue for Betterton's possible treatment of *Cardenio*, excising as it does most of the difficult Shakespearean text of the first and fifth Acts of *Kinsmen*, and changing the principal character names.

Whatever Theobald may have been able to conclude about the extent of Betterton's work on the play, it was nonetheless still perfectly normal by the standards of the time that he should seek to adapt the old play he believed Shakespeare's rather than to present it in its original state, more so if we consider Brean Hammond's point that he was likely to have received more revenue from performances of the piece if he was its part-author in the sense of adapter.[313] We do not know if Theobald had any knowledge of Moseley's entry in the Stationers' Register, though John Freehafer and Brean Hammond have argued that he did, which might suggest that his ascription to Shakespeare alone reflects the fact that by the 1720s, in spite of the frequent adaptation of his works, Shakespeare had risen to an almost deific status, with Fletcher seen as a mere contemporary.[314] Of course, Theobald could have fabricated a *Cardenio* play based only on Moseley's entry, with no knowledge of the existence of the 1613 evidence, about which he seems not to have known. Perhaps importantly for belief in Theobald and for confirmation of Moseley's *Cardenio* attribution, however, is Theobald's acknowledgement that 'others' had sceptically pronounced the play closer in style to Fletcher than to Shakespeare. Such independent impressionistic conclusions – Theobald never publicly admitted Fletcher as a co-author – seem to suggest that the manuscript did preserve the work of at least one of the supposed original authors.

Belief in Theobald's claims could have been secured fairly easily had he simply produced the shadowy manuscript to the public gaze; he claims to have shown it to some 'Great Judges' in his preface, but he is not actually known to have shown it to anyone. It is certainly not beyond the realms of possibility that a century-old theatrical manuscript could have survived to him, as evidenced by the case of *Sir Thomas More* (bequeathed to Edward Harley, coincidentally, also in 1728). Theobald was not only a dramatist, but also a fine textual scholar, publishing an edition of the works of Shakespeare in 1733, five years after *Double Falsehood* premiered at Drury Lane. His adaptation did not appear in the edition, but neither, incredibly, did the hitherto unpublished original version of *Cardenio*, a coup that any editor of Shakespeare could only dream of bringing about. Again, however, while seeming almost impossible to us, this can perhaps be explained by the paradoxical standards of the day, in which theatrical Shakespeare veered heavily towards adaptation, and the textual study of Shakespeare, chiefly through Theobald, in fact, towards faithful representation of what he wrote in the earliest versions of his plays. We must also acknowledge Theobald's, and the age's, reverence for pure, non-collaborative Shakespeare in textual scholarship. In the preface to his second edition of *Double Falsehood*, Theobald seemed less sure of Shakespeare's sole authorship, and may perhaps have omitted *Cardenio* from his edition on the grounds that he believed it to be a collaborative work. In fact, Edmund King argues plausibly that Theobald, who was engaged in a war of words with his rival Shakespeare editor, the poet Alexander Pope, came to fear the embarrassment of not having been able to tell that the play he professed Shakespeare's in fact contained material by Fletcher, and, probably, Betterton, and so wanted to cover all traces.[315]

The first edition of *Double Falsehood* prints George II's 1727 issue of copyright in the play to Theobald for a term of fourteen years, though as John Freehafer points out, when in 1728 Theobald 'sold *Double Falsehood* to John Watts…like most authors of his day, he did not reserve his right to a second term of copyright, but sold the play outright…After 1728, therefore, Theobald could not have published the play without Watts's consent.'[316] Clearly we might inquire whether the unadapted manuscript was affected by the copyright, but King argues that the Shakespeare edition's publisher, Jacob Tonson, is more likely than Theobald to have made the decision regarding what went in and what was left out. Tonson published, and owned the copyright to, Pope's 1728 edition, and wanted merely to maintain the limits of that secure canon and have new editors revise the apparatus in future editions, so that copyright extension could be avoided and Tonson could maintain his right in publishing Shakespeare. He would have had two copyright problems to deal with by trying to secure *Double Falsehood* for inclusion in the volume, so the decision to exclude it seems perfectly natural. Furthermore, Theobald seems to have known the manuscript may have been adapted by Betterton, and may have felt that the best he could do was to present the already impure text he had in as appealing a manner as possible as an oddity rather than as a new addition to the canon. All three early editions of *Double Falsehood* (two in 1728, one in 1763) claim on their title pages that it was '*Written originally by W. Shakespeare; and now revised and adapted to the stage by Mr. Theobald*', so there is no attempt to claim the presentation of an unsullied Shakespeare original. As we have seen, however, modification of Shakespeare's difficult language was actually a selling point. Again, a near impossibility by modern standards is perhaps not so strange when considered within unfamiliar historical contexts.

Yet even after we have explained away what at first sight seems an insurmountable obstacle to belief in Theobald's story, others remain. There is the apparent unlikelihood of Theobald having his hands on not just one copy of this lost Shakespeare play, but several – one of which, as recorded in a contemporary newspaper report, had supposedly come into the collections of the Covent Garden playhouse library by 1770, yet must have been lost in 1808 when the building burned down. Harriet Frazier argued forcefully that Theobald never in fact owned any at all, and that his play, like *Vortigern*, William Henry Ireland's 1796 fabrication of a play by Shakespeare he claimed to have discovered, was a forgery. In fact, Pope had argued bitterly that Theobald had forged the play in the wake of Theobald's 1726 *Shakespeare Restored*, which severely and justly critiqued Pope's edition of Shakespeare. The venom Pope directed at Theobald did not end there: he made him chief among the Dunces in his *Dunciad* (1728), in spite of the fact that he adopted many of Theobald's corrections in the second printing of his Shakespeare edition the same year, showing that his forgery argument may have more to do with private resentment than objective judgement. The argument has found recent support, however, from Jeffrey Kahan, who deemed the play's transmission history to be so dubious as to almost rule out entirely the possibility of it being a Shakespeare/Fletcher collaboration, though his treatment of evidence in building his argument has been called seriously into question by Hammond.[317]

Tiffany Stern has since prepared a detailed rebuttal of Shakespearean involvement in the play, stimulated chiefly by Arden's inclusion of it in their Shakespeare series.[318] After surveying all the evidence relating to the play's supposed transmission history – including doubts that 'Cardenna' actually denotes a play called *Cardenio* at all – and showing how it can equally be read as spurious, she points out, among other things, that Theobald was a Fletcher editor, a Cervantes 'fanatic', and prolific plagiaristic playwright who frequently turned to old English plays, or, just as often, to old Spanish ones and to *Don Quixote* for his plots. She also argues he was 'an acknowledged professor of Shakespearean style, with a keen sense of Shakespeare's "melody" and diction…Whether or not Theobald had a manuscript when he was working on *Double Falsehood*, that text can be expected to sound "Shakespearean".'[319] She remains ultimately undogmatic about the forgery argument, though asserts it is 'a more likely possibility than has been conceded'.[320] Although we feel that the weight of circumstantial external evidence combined with internal evidence suggesting both Shakespeare and Fletcher's authorship in separate parts of the play argues against forgery, Stern's arguments are nonetheless a timely and important intervention in the discussion informing the not inconsiderable degree of caution we attach to that judgement.

Others doubtful of Shakespeare's hand in *Double Falsehood* have deemed it more probable that Theobald had acquired an old play along with the narrative that it was the work of Shakespeare, as he seems to suggest himself, which was simply misguided. Whether or not Theobald had multiple copies, however, looks likely to remain a mystery, yet in spite of his many objectors, there has been a parallel scholarly consensus that the play he presented was in fact likely to have been originally by Fletcher and, probably, Shakespeare. Gamaliel Bradford Jr crucially pointed out that Theobald's play contained many direct verbal echoes of Shelton's 1612 translation of *Don Quixote* specifically, which was a significant milestone in determining the origins of the text Theobald produced.[321] John Freehafer's seminal article in favour of the tangled truth of Theobald's claims expanded upon this by comprehensively checking all of the early editions of *Don Quixote* to establish that Shelton's text did in fact most closely resemble lines in the play, and Bradford's list of parallels was expanded, bolstering the argument. The significance of this has been amplified by Brean Hammond, who points out not only that Theobald knew Spanish well, but also that:

The sale catalogue of Theobald's library specifies Spanish-language versions of *Don Quixote* corresponding to the first 1605 edition and another dated 1611. It does not list Shelton, suggesting that Theobald got his *Quixote* in the original and is therefore less likely to be responsible for the play's close verbal echoes of Shelton's translation.[322]

So the likelihood that Theobald was in fact telling the truth increased dramatically in the light of Freehafer's work, which was expanded again by A. Luis Pujante.[323] Freehafer did much to chart the likely features of the original, including the Cervantine character names that must have underlain Theobald's such as, of course, Cardenio for Theobald's Julio, as well as the probable length of the play and the evidence for condensed or missing scenes and plot threads (the play is half the length of the other two Shakespeare/Fletcher collaborations, *Henry VIII* and *Kinsmen*):

> *Double Falsehood* opens with an aged duke's concern over the worthiness of his two sons to succeed him – a favourite theme that Shakespeare might have developed at length; but this theme is introduced with evident loss of context, and it is scarcely referred to again. In the same scene the duke arranges to employ Julio as 'An honest spy upon' his younger son's 'Riots', but the spying that must have followed is absent from the existing play. Further evidence of cutting is provided by the fact that Fabian, Lopez, and Gerald (who shares the name of the schoolmaster in *The Two Noble Kinsmen*) appear briefly in the play, but not in the dramatis personae; their brief parts apparently represent a remnant of a comic underplot that has been largely expunged.[324]

Gary Taylor also posits some of the Jacobean features of the original manuscript, showing that, for one thing, naming the villain Henriquez would have been out of the question for Shakespeare or Fletcher in 1612–13 after the death of King James' eldest son and heir apparent, Prince Henry, on 6 November 1612.[325] Therefore the name – which exists nowhere else in Shakespeare – is a feature of adaptation, arguing against forgery. Taylor points to the unusual lack of song and spectacle in the play, features of both Shakespeare's late plays, and his and Fletcher's *Kinsmen* in particular, and the 'spectacular musical pantomimes' Theobald was known for writing.[326] The text twice calls for funeral ceremonies that never appear, which Taylor interprets as a possible measure to distance the play from Thomas D'Urfey's 1694 *Comical History of Don Quixote*, a pantomimic and musical extravaganza. This may mean the, or a, manuscript that came to Theobald was in fact adapted after this date, and not in the 1660s as has frequently been assumed. David Carnegie analysed the pattern of adaptation in two other plays Theobald reworked for the stage, Webster's *The Duchess of Malfi* – called *The Fatal Secret* in Theobald's version – and Shakespeare's *Richard II*.[327] In comparing them against the surviving originals he attempts to deduce how *Cardenio* might once have looked. Acknowledging the problems of sample size (only two plays) and prior adaptation, he nonetheless suggests that features characteristic of Theobald's work, informed as he was by the tastes of his age, include the imposition of the dramatic unities of time, place and action. We may note that the first three Acts of *Double Falsehood* are set largely in and around Julio's village and the latter two in the mountains, where we would expect Shakespeare and Fletcher, as in *All is True* and *Kinsmen*, to have alternated more fluidly between both settings, probably over a longer timeframe. Carnegie also highlights a deliberate reduction in dramatic complexity in order for Theobald to best provide 'rational and moral entertainment' for his audience, and, on the subject of poetic register linked to this principle, continues:

> whenever the dialogue becomes inflated, over-explicit, and developed as epic similes we may more strongly suspect the presence of Theobald's hand. The last ten lines or so of every act and scene are especially likely to be his, and to weaken the source text into thin generality and sentimentality.[328]

As for attempts to see past Theobald to the division of authorial labour in the original *Cardenio*, evidence for Shakespeare has proved trickier than for Fletcher. The supposed Shakespearean portion, widely believed to be the first half of the play, has been so heavily cut and rewritten that many have felt it yields insufficient grounds on which to build an attribution. E. K. Chambers, one of the great twentieth-century authorities on early drama, stated:

> I cannot find a single passage which compels a belief in Shakespeare. Here and there are lines which might be his in no inspired mood. But what possible criterion can distinguish, through the veil of adaptation, second- or third-rate work of Shakespeare from that of a contemporary disciple, or even from what Theobald himself, with his mind steeped in Shakespeare, might write.[329]

Yet many subsequent developments in the practice of stylometry have forced reappraisals of this traditionally dismissive view, starting chiefly with Cyrus Hoy's pioneering works in the 1950s to establish a complex authorial profile for Fletcher which has been used to identify traits of his hand in the play, largely in the second half (verb forms like *has* over *hath*, for example – Shakespeare preferred the opposite – and the contractions *i'th*, *o'th*, *h'as* for *he has*, to name a few). Brean Hammond's edition of the play tabulates Fletcherian characteristics within the play using Hoy's lists, as well as a table for the occurrence of feminine endings (pentameter lines with one extra syllable) which were also characteristic of Fletcher, although this is weaker evidence as Shakespeare's use of feminine endings is at its highest in the mature phase of his career.[330] Hammond's results are suggestive of the pattern almost all investigators have found; that is, many Fletcherian characteristics in the second half of the play, with a different pattern in the first. Although the Shakespeare section is muddy, the play seems certainly to be a collaborative effort on this evidence alone, which works against Theobald (or Fletcher) as sole author, and bolsters the tricky external attribution evidence outlined above. Stephan Kukowski pushed Hoy's work further, and identified many Fletcherian traits in the verse's imagery and vocabulary, concurring that the play is likely to be authentic in its claims of being based on an older original, and that Fletcher's hand predominates over Shakespeare's, particularly in the second half of the play.[331] Jonathan Hope's 'sociolinguistic' analysis concluded that:

> nothing in the auxiliary 'do' or relativisation evidence conflicts strongly with the notion that *Double Falsehood* is an eighteenth-century adaptation of a collaboration between Shakespeare and Fletcher ... Generally, both types of evidence support the suggestion of most studies that the early parts of *Double Falsehood* (up to and including 2.02) are those with most evidence for Shakespeare's presence.[332]

He adds the caveat, however, that 'it seems highly likely that most scenes in *Double Falsehood* mix material from different scenes of any original text: we should not expect to be able to produce scene-by-scene ascriptions of *Double Falsehood* to its putative grandparents'.[333] Thomas Merriam and Robert Matthews employed what, to all but the most accomplished statistician, seems like cryptically elaborate linguistic testing on the play, using pattern-analysis techniques developed in the field of neural science. Their conclusions broadly mirrored those detailed above, with the exception that they also found Shakespeare strongly present in Act 4. Michael Wood's 2003 study of Shakespeare argued that an extant manuscript song called 'Woods, Rocks, & Mountaynes' by the King's Men's lutenist, Robert Johnson, from around the time of the original *Cardenio*, was probably used in the play, based on the similarity of the lyrical content to a moment in the narrative in Shelton's translation of *Don Quixote* at which music is called for.[334] Although caution on this point has been stressed by other critics, it remains tantalizing and brilliantly insightful, and, as Brean Hammond points out, one attempt to pour cold water on Wood's claim noted that the song bears more similarities to songs in other Fletcher plays than those in Shakespeare, apparently in ignorance of the fact that the play was a supposed collaboration between the two.[335] Again, the evidence, while conjecturally connected, works plausibly to suggest that *Cardenio* was indeed a Shakespeare/Fletcher work, and that Theobald was indeed working from an ancestral version of it. In a *Times* interview in April 2010, Professor Hammond revealed that his hunch about the original collaboration was that Shakespeare probably wrote the first half, and Fletcher the rest, also acting as reviser of the whole play. Tiffany Stern's article economically summarizes the findings of two recent stylometric studies, by MacDonald Jackson and Richard Proudfoot, noting:

> Jackson's thorough and varied tests find a concentration of diverse features 'indicative of a Shakespearean palimpsest' but he is cautiously surer that he has identified Fletcher in the play ... Proudfoot's consideration of polysyllable use at the ends of lines likewise concludes that *Double Falsehood* contains 'traces of authorship by Fletcher and Shakespeare, but also, to a lesser degree, of their adaptor, Theobald'.[336]

She also records, however, that neither searches for any other writers in their tests, though her article was in advance of the book's publication; Jackson in fact tests against Beaumont, while Proudfoot tests against Beaumont, Chapman, John Day, Dekker, Nathan Field and Middleton. A major book by Roger Chartier, published just at the time of writing, reviews all the evidence in detail, and, while remaining circumspect on any conclusions about authorship or legitimacy, contributes strongly to the discussion through a theory-driven book history tracing the literary figure Cardenio from the early printings of *Don Quixote*, through Shakespeare and Fletcher's putative work together, through other surviving dramatic adaptations, and, of course, through Theobald.[337] It goes a long way towards our understanding of past attitudes towards reading, literary authorship, and textual 'authority', and helps provide plausible cultural contexts for the baffling – to modern sensibilities – story behind this play's supposed provenance. Ambiguities have been raised by recent high-profile adapted stagings taking the name of the supposed Shakespeare and Fletcher original, of which Peter Kirwan notes:

> While several productions entitled *Cardenio* have been performed in recent years, such as those by Stephen Greenblatt and Charles Mee (American Repertory Theatre, Cambridge MA, 2008), Gary Taylor (Wellington, 2009) and Gregory Doran (Royal Shakespeare Company, 2011), it should be borne in mind that these are conjectural reconstructions based on a combination of Shelton's *Don Quixote* and Theobald's *Double Falsehood*, and thus bear no direct historical relation to the lost play.[338]

Without question, much of what *Double Falsehood* is comes from Theobald's pen, and yet it seems highly probable that we are also looking, albeit through a glass darkly, at a partial survival of the lost *Cardenio*. What that play was in its original form we shall almost certainly never know. But the authorial voices that remain distantly in Theobald's adaptation – a significant Fletcherian contribution in the latter half of the play, and a smattering of Shakespeare in the former – along with a cumulative weight of other kinds of circumstantial evidence suggest to us that it did exist, and that *Double Falsehood* is in some way based upon it. We might also observe that the two surviving collaborations between the two dramatists, unadapted as they are, have proved extremely difficult to untangle and apportion, even to admit as canonical in the case of *The Two Noble Kinsmen*. *Cardenio* is therefore a play likely, even in its original state, to have been atypically Shakespearean in its structural and stylistic makeup. It marked a return to dramatic authorship for Shakespeare following his apparent swansong with *The Tempest* in November 1611, and inaugurated his most consistent period of writing as a collaborative author. Whether he was helping to groom his young successor or attempting to come back from a retirement of sorts remains mysterious; he was certainly not writing out of financial necessity, and we can derive little insight from their surviving work together in

Henry VIII and *Kinsmen*. Whatever really happened, the fact remains that Shakespeare's role within the King's Men had changed when he came to collaborate on *Cardenio* in, probably, the latter half of 1612. He would never work alone on a play again.

PLAYS EXCLUDED FROM THIS EDITION

Fair Em (c.1591?)

Fair Em, first published in an undated Quarto, has been variously attributed to Shakespeare, Robert Greene, Robert Wilson, and Anthony Munday, without any positive identification. Shakespeare is by far the least likely of the four based simply on stylistic comparisons, though the likelihood for Greene is diminished severely by the fact that he ridiculed lines from the last scene and attacked the unknown author in his pamphlet *Farewell to Folly* (1591). There is no apparent suggestion of collaborative authorship either. The earliest authority for a Shakespearean attribution to this play comes from its inclusion in a volume from Charles I's personal library entitled 'Shakespeare. Vol. I', which has come to be viewed as very weak external evidence. It was included in Tucker Brooke's 1908 edition of *The Shakespeare Apocrypha*, though he rather crisply described it as 'a thoroughly childish and inartistic production', and doubted there was 'even the slightest probability of the play's Shakespearian origin'.[339] The Quarto identifies Strange's Men on the title page as the company that first performed it. Lord Strange became Lord Derby on 25 September 1593, so the play must predate this. Shakespeare seems never to have been associated with Strange's Men prior to 1593, though Greene was.[340] *Fair Em* is the only play in which William the Conqueror features as a character, and much has been made about the dubious anecdote of Shakespeare, Burbage, and the courtesan, though this seems a very weak hook upon which to hang an argument for Shakespeare's authorship of, or participation in, the play. The lawyer John Manningham's diary for 1602–03 attests:

> Upon a time when Burbage played Richard the Third there was a citizen grew so far in liking with him, that before she went from the play she appointed him to come that night unto her by the name of Richard the Third. Shakespeare, overhearing their conclusion, went before, was entertained and at his game ere Burbage came. Then, message being brought that Richard the Third was at the door, Shakespeare caused return to be made that William the Conqueror was before Richard the Third.[341]

The joke also does not depend on Shakespeare having played William the Conqueror, as it is punning on Shakespeare and Burbage's own names, with the king theme coming off the back of Burbage having played Richard III. In short, it neither precludes nor provides suitable evidence for Shakespeare's involvement in *Fair Em*, though his involvement as an actor would be far more likely than his involvement as an author. Elliott and Valenza's computerized testing established twenty-two Shakespearean rejections for *Fair Em*, the highest of any play along with *Locrine* and *The Second Maiden's Tragedy*.

Edmond Ironside (c.1593?)

Edmond Ironside exists in a single manuscript of unknown date, company ownership, and authorship. It was not included in Tucker Brooke's *Apocrypha* volume, though Eric Sams' edition of the play sought to vindicate the work of Ephraim Everitt, who ascribed it to Shakespeare in his 1954 monograph *The Young Shakespeare: Studies in Documentary Evidence*.[342] Sams heralded *Ironside* as 'Shakespeare's Lost Play' and alienated many critics with the self-righteousness of his prose, but nonetheless produced many compelling parallels with early Shakespeare. However, many of these come from *Titus Andronicus*, *Edward III* and *Henry VI Part 1*, all plays dogged with co-authorship controversies. The argument also largely rests on Sams' 1588 dating for the manuscript, attempting to place it before anything included in the 1623 Folio, which Gary Taylor describes as 'certainly not certain, and probably not probable'.[343] Taylor also notes that the number of real similarities between *Ironside* and Shakespeare's early work merits further investigation, as does Hope, though both are ultimately very doubtful of Shakespeare's authorship. Randall Martin's work shows influences on *Ironside* by *Venus and Adonis* and Shakespeare's *Henry VI* plays (not the other way around), which, if correct, would be 'fatal to the plausibility of the attribution' in Taylor's words.

Everitt claimed the manuscript was in Shakespeare's hand throughout, which Charles Hamilton confirmed, though this was based on comparison with many autographs boldly claimed to be in Shakespeare's hand which have not been verified, or taken seriously, in any subsequent scholarship. Hamilton is elsewhere seen as something of a fanciful Shakespearean attributionist (see entry on *The Second Maiden's Tragedy* below). Taylor's list of function word tests in three apocryphal plays – *Arden of Faversham*, *Edward III* and *Edmond Ironside* – shows that *Ironside* deviates furthest from the mean for the acknowledged works of Shakespeare. In fact, Shakespeare is more likely to have written many of Marlowe's works than *Ironside* on this basis: 'No single complete text in the Shakespeare canon, whether good or bad, whether of single or disputed authorship, is in its overall totals as anomalous as *Ironside*'.[344] Similarly, Matthew Smith's 'Principal Component Analysis' of the distribution of function words in the play shows a marked separation from other plays of Shakespeare in the early 1590s, which, he argues, eliminates 'any vestige of a case for introducing *Ironside* to the Shakespeare canon'.[345] Elliott and Valenza's tests give *Ironside* twelve discrete rejections.

Sir John Oldcastle Part 1 (1600)

Philip Henslowe's *Diary* provides us with the evidence that *The First Part of Sir John Oldcastle* was written by Anthony Munday, Michael Drayton, Robert Wilson, and Richard Hathway, and completed on 16 October 1599. Shakespeare's *Henry IV Part 1* (1597) was famously controversial for its naming of Falstaff as Sir John Oldcastle in its first performances, which the company was forced to alter in light of objections raised by the Cobham family, Oldcastle's ancestors. This is presumably part of the reason *Oldcastle* came to be ascribed to Shakespeare. The First Quarto of 1600 named no author on the title page, but named the Admiral's Men as the company that had performed it, as we would expect from its appearance in Henslowe's account books. Thomas Pavier, publisher of *A Yorkshire Tragedy* in 1608, which also sought to cash in on Shakespeare's name, published a spurious collection of Shakespeare and pseudo-Shakespearean Quartos in 1619, which were, interestingly, printed by William Jaggard, one of the publishers of the First Folio. *Oldcastle* was included in Pavier's collection, falsely dated to 1600 and attributed to Shakespeare on the title page. The dating was presumably intended to aid credibility in the attribution, giving the book a counterfeit historical authority, and fudging a connection between the play and Shakespeare's *Henry IV* plays, all written some twenty years earlier. Pavier was apparently once again keen to exploit Shakespeare based on the marketability of his name, which carried a greater appeal in 1619 than that of any of the actual authors. No stylistic evidence in the play speaks at all strongly in Shakespeare's favour (eleven rejections in Elliott and Valenza's tests), though in this case the external evidence for his non-involvement is rock solid. Nonetheless, Mark Dominik has argued at length for Shakespeare's authorial hand in the play.[346] It appeared in the Third Folio (1664), and was reprinted in the Fourth (1685).

The Merry Devil of Edmonton (c.1602)

The Merry Devil of Edmonton has been attributed primarily, though inconclusively in all cases, to Shakespeare, Thomas Dekker, Michael Drayton and Thomas Heywood. Of these, Dekker seems the most likely candidate, though the case remains unproven. There is also no reason to think the play is collaborative based on stylistic evidence. Nonetheless, the 1608 Quarto's ascription to the King's Men is confirmed both by its Stationers' Register entry – never a guarantee of more trustworthiness than the claims made by published texts anyway – and, crucially, by a Revels Account entry of 15 May 1618. Also of significance is the fact that the Quarto does not attribute the play to Shakespeare, or to any author, meaning that we do not have the same reason to question the company attribution as we have with the texts of *The London Prodigal* and *A Yorkshire Tragedy*. The evidence linking *Merry Devil* to Shakespeare's company, therefore, is very strong; but the evidence linking it to Shakespeare's pen is very weak. The principal foundation on which the claim rests is the play's inclusion in a one-off volume of plays bound together under the title 'Shakespeare. Vol. 1', apparently for the personal edification of Charles I, which is hardly strong evidence.[347] It is in clear dialogue with Shakespeare's *The Merry Wives of Windsor* (c.1597–98), both through the formula of its title and through the fact that both:

> share an out-of-town setting; a drunken and criminal Sir John; a night-time woodland scene featuring the hunting of deer (literal or figurative); parents thwarted in a forced marriage attempt; and an inn as primary setting.[348]

We know it existed by 1602 as it is mentioned that year in Thomas Middleton's *Black Book*. Middleton alluded to the play again in *A Mad World My Masters* (c.1606), apparently referring to a dramatic episode missing from the extant play, which also suggests that the text we have may have been abridged from that of the original performances. We know that Middleton was paid in 1602 to write material for a revival of *Friar Bacon and Friar Bungay*, apparently based on the same prose pamphlet, *The Famous History of Friar Bacon*, from which *Merry Devil* derived its plot.[349] These 'superstition' plays, popular in the early 1590s, were enjoying a return to vogue at this time, with Marlowe's *Doctor Faustus* also being revived at the Fortune theatre that year, perhaps further prompting *Merry Devil*'s composition.[350] *Merry Devil* seems to belong to this brief return to popularity of an old genre, mixing into it some of the characteristics of a popular Shakespearean comedy (Host Blague is also apparently influenced by the Host in Shakespeare's play).

The entry on *The London Prodigal* notes the shift in Shakespeare's comic writing around 1603–04, when his company came under the King's patronage, but even by 1602 Shakespeare had moved on to darker, stranger, more musical comedies built around the cerebral style of their new principal comedian, Robert Armin. While Will Kempe would most likely have personated all of Shakespeare's great rumbustious comic characters from the mid 1590s – Bottom, Dogberry, perhaps Falstaff – Armin's talents gave rise to the creation of more abstruse, intellectual clown characters such as Touchstone, Feste, and, later, the Fool in *King Lear*. By c.1602 Shakespeare, having created Feste, was busy setting the limits of the wise fool with vinegar in his veins at their most extreme verge in the figure of Thersites in *Troilus and Cressida*. *Merry Devil* has Shakespearean analogues but is seemingly arriving at the party around five years too late. It has been excluded from every major series of editions of Shakespeare, and was roundly rejected from the Shakespeare canon on stylistic grounds by Ward Elliott and Robert Valenza.[351] Dekker has been the subject of the most compelling scholarly case to date, in William A. Abrams' 1942 edition of the play, which made a lengthy and convincing case for his authorship.[352] Abrams reviewed the cases for Drayton, Heywood and Shakespeare before going on to present many perceived parallels between *Merry Devil* and Dekker's acknowledged work. This mainly took the form of parallel passages, as well as similarities in dramatic style, plotting and characterization, without a more forensic analysis of language, though his study predates the innovations of Cyrus Hoy in that area.[353]

No real stylistic analysis on the play has been done in the last fifty years, and no convincing alternative author proposed. Gary Taylor described Dekker as 'the only candidate to have achieved any currency', while MacDonald Jackson, in 2006, suggested *Merry Devil*'s author was 'probably Dekker'.[354]

Thomas of Woodstock (c.1604–10?)

Michael Egan's major study of *Thomas of Woodstock* claims that it is an early 1590s play, by Shakespeare, and effectively a dry run for *Richard II* (the play narrates the story of Woodstock, Duke of Gloucester, whose mysterious death hangs heavy over the first scene of Shakespeare's *Richard II*).[355] Corbin and Sedge, in their edition of the play, similarly opt for an early 1590s dating.[356] Egan attempts to show how we may see in the play, for example, early model sketches of Shakespeare's later use of Holinshed's *Chronicles* for *Richard II*, and of *Much Ado about Nothing*'s doltish law officer, Dogberry, in the character of Master Ignorance. Acceptance of this, however, depends entirely on the play's early dating, and MacDonald Jackson has argued, based on extremely convincing stylometric parallels, for the play being an early Jacobean work by Samuel Rowley (not to be confused with William Rowley).[357] Rowley's name appears in Henslowe's records several times from 1597 onwards, though he cannot be proven to have been involved in playwriting prior to 1601. David J. Lake proposed, based on the appearance of oaths used in the manuscript, that it must have been Jacobean, dated between 1604–10, and Jackson corroborated this, going initially for an early dating of *c*.1604-5, which he later more permissively expanded to 'the period 1598–1609'.[358] In either case, however, the play postdates *Richard II*, and both the parallels found in the use of source material, and in a notable character, mean that the influence is working in the other direction, and Rowley is in fact imitating Shakespeare. Both Jackson and Lake have noted more stylistic similarities between *Woodstock* and Rowley's only acknowledged extant play, *When You See Me, You Know Me*, than with any other early modern play. Jackson offers strong refutation of several of Egan's key points and performs a verse analysis 'which shows that the play cannot possibly have been written by Shakespeare, but which tends to confirm Samuel Rowley's authorship and a seventeenth-century date'.[359]

The surviving manuscript itself is certainly Jacobean – a different issue from the date of the play's composition, which has led to speculation that it could be a revision of an earlier play – and was perhaps used much later in a revival, as it names actors in marginal prompter's directions, apparently members of Prince Charles II's company, indicating c.1630s performance. The names are written in shorthand and are unidentifiable to any degree of certainty, but they do seem to suggest a company attribution that deals another powerful blow to the idea of Shakespeare's authorship of the play. *Woodstock* has twenty discrete rejections in Elliott and Valenza's tests, an extremely high figure counter-indicating Shakespeare by their reckoning. Louis Ule and John Baker have performed stylometric tests on the play and claim that it bears a closer relationship to the works of Shakespeare and Marlowe than to *When You See Me*.[360] Corbin and Sedge, in their edition, do not declare Shakespearean authorship, but reason that the play's style is not a million miles away from early Shakespeare, though this of course rests on the argument that the manuscript is late 1580s/early 1590s, and not early/mid to late 1600s, as seems to be the case.

The Puritan, or The Widow of Watling Street (1606)

The 1607 Quarto attested that the play was written by 'W. S.', and that it was 'Acted by the Children of Paules'. This company attribution alone works strongly against Shakespeare's involvement, and nobody has ever really agreed that the style of the play is reminiscent of Shakespeare's works. There is an almost unanimous scholarly consensus now that *The Puritan* is the work of Thomas Middleton. Efforts have been made to link the play to other writers with the same initials – Wentworth Smith, William Stanley, William Smith and William Sly – to no avail. Mark Eccles wrote an excellent article in favour of Middleton in 1931 which has never been seriously challenged, and the work of Lake and Jackson has bolstered the attribution to the point of virtual solidity.[361] It is also in Taylor and Lavagnino's edition of Middleton's *Collected Works*. *A Yorkshire Tragedy*, another play now accepted as mainly Middleton's, was attributed to Shakespeare, suggesting that the 'W. S.' ascription was likewise intended to boost sales by implying the King's principal playwright as author. Indeed, most of the apocryphal plays in Quarto naming Shakespeare date from the first decade of the seventeenth century, saying more about his popularity at this time than about his actual activities as a writer. *Thomas Lord Cromwell* is likewise a thoroughly un-Shakespearean play attributed to 'W. S.', but we have chosen to exclude *The Puritan* on the grounds that it was not performed by Shakespeare's company and is apparently non-collaborative. *The Puritan* can also be said to be a thoroughly Middletonian play in its generic unity with the city comedy fare produced by Jacobean boy companies.

It was first unambiguously attributed to Shakespeare by Edward Archer in 1656, and was included in the Third Folio in 1664, reprinted in the Fourth (1685). It also featured in Tucker Brooke's *Apocrypha* volume in 1908. Hope felt there were certain problems with the Middleton attribution, but that the evidence of his tests worked 'strongly against Shakespearean authorship'.[362] Interestingly, on 9 September 1653 a play called 'The Puritan Maid, modest Wife & Wanton Widdow by Mr. Tho: Midleton' was entered in the Stationers' Register for Humphrey Moseley, though it is considered to be a lost play, both because the entry is not a transfer but apparently for a never-before-printed play, and because the characters mentioned in the title do not fit the personnel of *The Puritan*. The attribution to Middleton is not necessarily correct either. Moseley printed many of Middleton's works during the Interregnum, and may conceivably – and this is a remote hypothesis – have been exploiting Middleton's name based on his knowledge of the author's penning of a similar play, in the same way Pavier tried to exploit Shakespeare's over *Oldcastle*. No surviving seventeenth-century source links *The Puritan* to anyone's hand but Shakespeare's, though we can never know about the word-of-mouth knowledge Moseley could have been privy to.

The Second Maiden's Tragedy (1611)

Barker and Schoenbaum advanced claims for Middleton's authorship in the early to mid-twentieth century and in the 1970s David Lake and MacDonald Jackson noted many stylistic discriminators in the play that are consistent with the acknowledged, solo-authored works of Middleton.[363] The play exists only as a manuscript, in a scribal hand, though Lake has shown the copyist retained many of Middleton's favoured forms. Thomas Goffe, George Chapman and William Shakespeare are named as authors on the last leaf in different, unidentified hands, all much later than the 1611 date of composition (which is verified by the presence of the then Master of the Revels George Buc's handwriting and dating, approving the play for performance by the King's Men). None of these authorial attributions, especially to Shakespeare, has been taken seriously, though E. B. Everitt stands virtually alone in supporting it.[364] During the nineteenth century the play was variously ascribed to Webster, Massinger, Tourneur and Middleton, and since the turn of the twentieth century only the latter two have been considered serious candidates. Tourneur was proposed mainly on the basis of the play's many striking parallels with *The Revenger's Tragedy*, an anonymous King's Men play printed in 1606, which was assumed to be Tourneur's because of his authorship of the similar *Atheist's Tragedy* (1611). Nobody really knows enough about Tourneur to be able to say with any certainty for which company he wrote *Atheist's*, though his authorship of it is not in doubt. However, *Revenger's* is now fairly uncontroversially accepted as also being by Middleton, thanks largely to the work of Lake and Jackson, detailing the similarities in style between it and *Second Maiden's*. Anne Lancashire's edition of *Second Maiden's* (1978) also proposed Middleton as the most likely author, based on her independent corroborations of pre-existing scholarly work.[365] It is included in Taylor and Lavagnino's edition of Middleton's *Collected Works*.

As for Shakespearean involvement, Eric Rasmussen argued that nine words in the margin of one of the five addition slips in the manuscript were written by Shakespeare. He also argued for Shakespearean authorship of the additions, which, although copied by a scribe, retained Shakespearean 'fingerprints' in several of their verbal forms. Jackson replied very quickly with the counter-argument that, in fact, most of these forms are statistically far more likely to be Middletonian, and that in subjective terms the additions feel much closer to Middleton's verse than Shakespeare's.[366] Jackson also argued, as others had done, that the additions were by Middleton and copied by a scribe who preserved Middleton's, not Shakespeare's, verbal forms. *A Yorkshire Tragedy*, included in this volume, is another King's Men play likely to be by Middleton, though conflicting evidence in the work of Lake and Hope leaves open the small possibility of a second author's involvement, who may have been Shakespeare. Although the external evidence it provides for Shakespeare's authorship is weak, it inaugurated a period when the two writers worked closely together, which certainly gave rise to direct collaboration on *Timon of Athens*. *Second Maiden's*, although a later King's play, offers no reason to suppose on internal evidence that it is not the work of Middleton alone, with only one flimsy and heavily postdated suggestion of Shakespearean involvement, hence its exclusion here.

The play has also been identified as Shakespeare and Fletcher's lost *Cardenio* by Charles Hamilton, though his book is eccentric in its argumentation, based on stretched palaeographical analyses.[367] He compared the manuscript with the handwriting in Shakespeare's will, which he claimed was all Shakespeare's, despite there being differences and a good deal of deterioration in its legibility, which he attempted to explain by asserting that the poet had a stroke halfway through the document's composition. Nobody has really taken Hamilton's work seriously, and the likelihood of *Cardenio* surviving, at least partially, through *Double Falsehood* – another play included in this volume – is far greater.

The Birth of Merlin (1622)

The Birth of Merlin carries the most clear-cut case for exclusion from this volume, with strong evidence suggesting that it was composed six years after Shakespeare's death. A record in the private collection of Revels papers owned by Henry Herbert, the Master of the Revels 1623–73, shows that his predecessor, Sir John Astley, licensed a play called *The Childe hath founde his Father* in 1622, describing it as a 'New Play, acted by the Princes Servants at the Curtayne'. *Merlin* was first published in 1662 by Francis Kirkman as 'The Birth of Merlin: or, *The Childe hath found his Father*', with the title page attributing it to '*William Shakespear*, and *William Rowley*'. The Master of the Revels' job was to license plays for the stage, making sure they contained no seditious matter, and no play could be performed without it first being submitted to him. If the play was therefore not new, Astley was hardly likely to have described it as such having presumably just licensed it, so what he says about it seems to be far more trustworthy than doubtful. The portion of Herbert's papers within which this entry resides was not discovered until the mid 1990s in a document referred to as the Burn transcript, found in the collections of Yale University Library. Its contents were first published in 1996, effectively ending for good and all the speculation regarding Shakespeare's part-authorship of the play.[368]

Merlin is widely regarded to be, in part at least, by William Rowley, possibly in collaboration with another writer. Rowley is most famous for co-authoring *The Changeling* (1622) with Thomas Middleton for the Lady Elizabeth's company, though MacDonald Jackson has demonstrated that Middleton could not have been his collaborator on *Merlin*, and Gary Taylor asserts that 'linguistic evidence also clearly rules out Fletcher'.[369] Rowley was not involved with the King's Men before 1623, a fact consistent with the date and company attribution Astley provides. Mark Dominik was the only scholar to support the Shakespeare and Rowley attribution in the last century, hypothesizing that it was written 1613–15, and basing his argument on what he perceived to be stylistic similarities with the works of both writers.[370] His study, however, was published in 1985, and would come to be crucially undermined by the discovery of the Herbert evidence ten years later. Hope's linguistic tests also ruled against Shakespearean involvement.

ACKNOWLEDGEMENTS

My principal acknowledgement is to Jonathan Bate for taking the chance, for the trust shown and for the tactful guidance. A special debt of gratitude must also be extended to the following, who have offered generous support in my work leading up to this project, or have variously read, commented on, proofed and improved immeasurably the work herein: Neil Allan, Brandon Chua, Hugh Craig, Marcus Dahl, Paul Edmondson, Brean Hammond, Peter Holbrook, MacDonald Jackson, John Jowett, Peter Kirwan, Ross Knecht, Peter Orford, Lene Petersen, Paul Prescott, Eric Rasmussen, Jan Sewell, Peter J. Smith, Terry Stone, Marina Tarlinskaja (who generously sent me a copy of her book), Gary Taylor, Yu Umemiya, Sir Brian Vickers, Stanley Wells, Martin Wiggins – whose advice and encouragement I shall struggle to repay – and Henry Woudhuysen. I must also thank the many textual, attribution and apocrypha scholars past and present named throughout these essays who supplied the tools and the materials to make my work possible, chiefly W. W. Greg, Cyrus Hoy and Richard Proudfoot. Jill Levenson and Anne Lancashire's study in *Predecessors of Shakespeare* (1973) was of particular value. All errors, infelicities and things of darkness that remain I of course acknowledge mine. José Pérez Díez and Helen Osborne were immeasurably kind, and Erin Sullivan has made it all worthwhile. Lizz Ketterer was, as always, happy for me when I got this commission. I wish more than anything she were still here to see this book. All that is good in what I have written I dedicate affectionately to them.

The entire team is deeply grateful to Tracey Dando for her extraordinary copy-editing skills – and for noticing many small errors that had escaped several pairs of editorial eyes.

SELECTED FURTHER READING

The following is a list of some essential texts for those wishing to further their sense of the practices and underlying concepts of stylistic and stylometric analysis, of the arguments surrounding the Shakespeare canon, and of authorial attribution in original documents. A wider and more specific set of references can be found in the footnotes accompanying individual entries. Many allusions to nineteenth- and early-twentieth-century works of criticism not recorded are gathered in the expansive bibliography appended to C. F. Tucker Brooke's *The Shakespeare Apocrypha* (1908), free to read online courtesy of The University of Toronto Library (see below).

Boyd, Brian, and MacDonald P. Jackson, eds, *Words That Count: Essays on Early Modern Authorship in Honor of MacDonald P. Jackson*, University of Delaware Press, 2004.

Brooks, Douglas A., ed., *The Shakespeare Apocrypha*, The Edwin Mellen Press, 2007.

Carnegie, David, and Gary Taylor, eds, *The Quest for Cardenio: Shakespeare, Fletcher, Cervantes, & the Lost Play*, Oxford University Press, 2012.

Chambers, E. K., *William Shakespeare: A Study of Facts and Problems*, Oxford University Press, 1930.

Craig, Hugh, and Arthur F. Kinney, eds, *Shakespeare, Computers, and the Mystery of Authorship*, Cambridge University Press, 2009.

Doran, Gregory, *Shakespeare's Lost Play: In Search of Cardenio*, Nick Hern Books, 2012.

Elliott, Ward E. Y., and Robert J. Valenza, 'And Then There Were None: Winnowing the Shakespeare Claimants' in *Computers and the Humanities* 30 (1996): 191–245, available online at: www.claremontmckenna.edu/pages/faculty/welliott/archived.htm.

—— 'Oxford by the Numbers: What are the Odds that the Earl of Oxford Could Have Written Shakespeare's Poems and Plays?', *Tennessee Law Review* 72 (2004): 323–453; available online at: www.claremontmckenna.edu/pages/faculty/welliott/select.htm.

Erne, Lukas, *Shakespeare and the Book Trade*, Cambridge University Press, 2013.

Farmer, Alan B., and Zachary Lesser, *Database of Early English Playbooks*, http://deep.sas.upenn.edu/.

Foakes, R. A., ed., *Henslowe's Diary*, Cambridge University Press, 2002.

Foster, Donald, *Author Unknown: On the Trail of Anonymous*, Henry Holt and Co., 2000.

Gurr, Andrew, *Shakespeare's Opposites*, Cambridge University Press, 2009.

—— *The Shakespeare Company: 1594–1642*, Cambridge University Press, 2004.

Hope, Jonathan, *The Authorship of Shakespeare's Plays: A Sociolinguistic Study*, Cambridge University Press, 1994.

Howard-Hill, T. H., ed., *Shakespeare and Sir Thomas More*, Cambridge University Press, 1989.

Jackson, MacDonald P., *Studies in Attribution: Middleton and Shakespeare*, Insitut Für Anglistik und Amerikanistik, 1979.

—— *Defining Shakespeare: Pericles as Test Case*, Oxford University Press, 2003.

—— 'Early Modern Authorship: Canons and Chronologies', in Gary Taylor and John Lavagnino, with MacDonald P. Jackson, John Jowett, Valerie Wayne and Adrian Weiss, eds, *Thomas Middleton and Early Modern Textual Culture*, Oxford University Press, 2007, pp. 80–97.

Jowett, John, *Shakespeare and Text*, Oxford University Press, 2007.

Knutson, Roslyn Lander, *The Repertory of Shakespeare's Company 1594–1613*, University of Arkansas Press, 1991.

Lake, David J., *The Canon of Thomas Middleton's Plays*, Cambridge University Press, 1975.

Love, Harold, *Attributing Authorship*, Cambridge University Press, 2002.

Petersen, Lene B., *Shakespeare's Errant Texts*, Cambridge University Press, 2010.

Proudfoot, Richard, *Shakespeare: Text, Stage & Canon*, The Arden Shakespeare, 2001.

Rosenbaum, Ron, *The Shakespeare Wars: Clashing Scholars, Public Fiascoes, Palace Coups*, Random House, 2008.

Schoenbaum S., *Internal Evidence and Elizabethan Dramatic Authorship*, Edward Arnold Ltd., 1966.

Stern, Tiffany, *Documents of Performance in Early Modern England*, Cambridge University Press, 2009.

Tarlinskaja, Marina, *Shakespeare's Verse*, Peter Lang Inc., 1987.

Taylor, Gary, 'The Canon and Chronology of Shakespeare's Plays', in Stanley Wells and Gary Taylor, with John Jowett and William Montgomery, eds, *William Shakespeare: A Textual Companion*, Oxford University Press, 1987, pp. 69–144.

Tucker Brooke, C. F., ed., *The Shakespeare Apocrypha*, Oxford University Press, 1908, available online at: http://archive.org/details/shakespeareapoc00broouoft.

Vickers, Brian, *Shakespeare, Co-Author*, Oxford University Press, 2002.

—— *'Counterfeiting' Shakespeare*, Cambridge University Press, 2002.

—— *Shakespeare, A Lover's Complaint, and John Davies of Hereford*, Cambridge University Press, 2007.

Wiggins, Martin, in association with Catherine Richardson, *British Drama 1533–1642: A Catalogue*, 10 Vols (projected), Oxford University Press, 2012–.

NOTES

1. The authorship question is much too broad to discuss in any depth here, but excellent, scholarly and rational discussions of the subject can be found in James Shapiro, *Contested Will*, Faber and Faber, 2010, and Paul Edmondson and Stanley Wells, eds, *Shakespeare Beyond Doubt*, Cambridge University Press, 2013. Shapiro's book contains a full bibliography, including texts arguing against Shakespeare's authorship.

2. Fredson Bowers, *On Editing Shakespeare and the Elizabethan Dramatists*, University of Pennsylvania Library, 1955, p. 87.

3. MacDonald P. Jackson, *Defining Shakespeare: Pericles as Test Case*, Oxford University Press, 2003, p. 150.

4. Those interested in trying it for themselves can take the test at http://goldenear.cmc.edu/ge/.

5. Richard Proudfoot, *Shakespeare: Text, Stage & Canon*, The Arden Shakespeare, 2001, p. 89.

6. See MacDonald P. Jackson, *Studies in Attribution: Middleton and Shakespeare*, Insitut Für Anglistik und Amerikanistik, 1979; Cyrus Hoy, 'The Shares of Fletcher and His Collaborators in the Beaumont and Fletcher Folio I–VII', *Studies in Bibliography* 8–9, 11–15 (1956–62): 129–46, 143–62, 85–106, 91–116, 77–108, 45–67, 71–90.

7. Jonathan Hope, *The Authorship of Shakespeare's Plays: A Sociolinguistic Study*, Cambridge University Press, 1994.

8. See David J. Lake, *The Canon of Thomas Middleton's Plays*, Cambridge University Press, 1975.

9. Gary Taylor, 'The Canon and Chronology of Shakespeare's Plays', in Stanley Wells and Gary Taylor, with John Jowett and William Montgomery, eds, *William Shakespeare: A Textual Companion*, Oxford University Press, 1987, pp. 69–109.

10. John Burrows, 'A Second Opinion on "Shakespeare and Authorship Studies in the Twenty-First Century"', *Shakespeare Quarterly* 63:3 (2012), 355–92, at p. 363.

11. A full analysis of the techniques and quirks of Shakespeare's style is impossible here, but excellent, readable introductions can be found in David Crystal's *Think On My Words*, Cambridge University Press, 2008, and Russ McDonald's *Shakespeare and the Arts of Language*, Oxford University Press, 2001.

12. Ward E. Y. Elliott and Robert J. Valenza, 'And Then There Were None: Winnowing the Shakespeare Claimants', *Computers and the Humanities* 30 (1996): 191–245, at p. 198.

13. Anthony Graham-White, *Punctuation and Its Dramatic Value in Shakespearean Drama*, University of Delaware Press, 1995, p. 67.

14. Burrows, 'A Second Opinion', p. 367.

15. See entry on *The Spanish Tragedy* for a discussion of Kyd and Marlowe's influence.

16. Martin Wiggins ed., *A Woman Killed With Kindness and Other Plays*, Oxford World's Classics, 2008, pp. viii–ix.

17. See Anne Lancashire and Jill Levenson, 'Anonymous Plays', in Terence P. Logan and Denzell S. Smith, eds, *The Predecessors of Shakespeare: A Survey and Bibliography of Recent Studies in English Renaissance Drama*, University of Nebraska Press, 1973. Much of the information on the history of the attribution of the plays discussed in these essays is heavily indebted to Lancashire and Levenson's study.

18. Further evidence is provided by a performance of an apparently old play called *Hamlet* being performed at Newington Butts in 1594, and by Thomas Lodge's mocking reference in *Wit's Misery and the World's Madness* (1596) to a rather histrionic ghost, 'which cried so miserably at the Theatre, like an oyster-wife, "Hamlet, revenge"'.

19. Martin L. Wine, ed., *Arden of Faversham*, The Revels Plays, Methuen, 1973, p. lxxxii.

20. Kenneth Muir, *Shakespeare as Collaborator*, Methuen, 1960, p. 3.

21. Martin White, ed., *Arden of Faversham*, The New Mermaids, Ernest Benn Ltd, 1982, p. xiii.

22. White, *Arden of Faversham*, p. xvii.

23. Martin Wiggins, ed., *A Woman Killed with Kindness and Other Domestic Plays*, Oxford World's Classics, 2008, p. 285. For the allusion see *The Spanish Tragedy* (2.5.1).

24. Wiggins, *A Woman Killed with Kindness*, pp. xxxvi–xxxvii.

25. Wiggins, *A Woman Killed with Kindness*, pp. 286–7.

26. Wiggins, *A Woman Killed with Kindness*, p. 284.

27. W. W. Greg, 'Shakespeare and *Arden of Faversham*', *Review of English Studies* 21 (1945): 134–36.

28. C. F. Tucker Brooke, ed., *The Shakespeare Apocrypha*, Oxford University Press, 1908, p. xiv.

29. Tucker Brooke, *The Shakespeare Apocrypha*, p. xiv.

30. Tucker Brooke, *The Shakespeare Apocrypha*, p. xv.

31. E. H. C. Oliphant, 'Problems of Authorship in Elizabethan Dramatic Literature', *Modern Philology* 8:3 (1911): 411–59, at p. 420.

32. Oliphant, 'Problems of Authorship', p. 420.

33. Samuel Schoenbaum, *Internal Evidence and Elizabethan Dramatic Authorship*, Edward Arnold Ltd, 1966, p. 137.

34. Russell A. Fraser and Norman Rabkin, eds, *Drama of the English Renaissance 1: The Tudor Period*, Macmillan, 1976, p. 411.

35. Alexander Leggatt, '*Arden of Faversham*', *Shakespeare Survey* 36 (1983): 121–33, at p. 133.

36. Wells and Taylor, *William Shakespeare: A Textual Companion*, p. 88.

37. See MacDonald P. Jackson, 'Shakespearean Features of the Poetic Style of *Arden of Faversham*', *Archive Fur Das Studium Der Neueren Sprachen und Literaturen* 230 (1993): 279–304; Jayne M. Carroll and MacDonald P. Jackson, 'Shakespeare, *Arden of Faversham*, and Literature Online', *The Shakespeare Newsletter* 26 (Spring 2004): 3–4, 6; MacDonald P. Jackson, 'Shakespeare and the Quarrel Scene in *Arden of Faversham*', *Shakespeare Quarterly* 57 (2006): 249–93; MacDonald P. Jackson, 'Compound Adjectives in *Arden of Faversham*', *Notes and Queries* 53 (2006): 51–4.

38. Carroll and Jackson, 'Shakespeare, *Arden of Faversham*', p. 3.

39. Jackson, 'Compound Adjectives in *Arden of Faversham*', p. 53.

40. Jackson, 'Compound Adjectives in *Arden of Faversham*', p. 54.

41. Jackson, 'Shakespeare and the Quarrel Scene in *Arden of Faversham*', p. 270.

42. Ward E. Y. Elliott and Robert J. Valenza, 'Oxford by the Numbers: What are the Odds that the Earl of Oxford Could Have Written Shakespeare's Poems and Plays?', *Tennessee Law Review* 72 (2004): 323–453, at p. 404.

43. Jackson, 'Shakespeare and the Quarrel Scene in *Arden of Faversham*', p. 274.

44. Brian Vickers, 'Thomas Kyd, Secret Sharer', *Times Literary Supplement*, 18 April 2008, pp. 13–15.

45. MacDonald P. Jackson, 'New Research on the Dramatic Canon of Thomas Kyd', *Research Opportunities in Renaissance Drama* 47 (2008): 107–27, at p. 124.

46. Hugh Craig and Arthur F. Kinney, eds, *Shakespeare, Computers, and the Mystery of Authorship*, Cambridge University Press, 2009, p. 89.

47. Craig and Kinney, *Shakespeare, Computers*, p. 99.

48. Macdonald P. Jackson, 'Gentle Shakespeare and the Authorship of *Arden of Faversham*', *The Shakespearean International Yearbook* 11 (2011): 25–40.

49. Jackson, 'Gentle Shakespeare', pp. 36–7.

50. Wiggins, *A Woman Killed with Kindness*, p. vii.

51. Alfred Harbage, *Annals of English Drama – 975–1700* (Revised by S. Schoenbaum), Methuen & Co. Ltd, 1964.

52. Jackson, 'Gentle Shakespeare', p. 37.

53. Jane Lytton Gooch, ed., *The Lamentable Tragedy of Locrine*, Garland Publishing, Inc., 1981, especially pp. 27–32.

54. Baldwin Maxwell, *Studies in the Shakespeare Apocrypha*, King's Crown Press, 1956, p. 26.

55. Laurie E. Maguire, 'The Craft of Printing (1600)', in David Scott Kastan, ed., *A Companion to Shakespeare*, Blackwell Publishing, 1999, pp. 434–49, at p. 443.

56. Maguire, 'The Craft of Printing', p. 444.

57. Leonard R. N. Ashley, *Authorship and Evidence: A Study of Attribution and the Renaissance Drama Illustrated by the Case of George Peele (1556–1596)*, Genève Librairie Droz, 1968, p. 67.

58. Peter Philip Kirwan, 'Shakespeare and the Idea of Apocrypha: Negotiating the Boundaries of the Dramatic Canon', unpublished PhD thesis, University of Warwick (2011), pp. 185–6.

59. G. K. Hunter, *English Drama 1586–1642: The Age of Shakespeare*, Oxford University Press, 1997, pp. 50–1.

60. Sonia Massai, 'Shakespeare, Text and Paratext', *Shakespeare Survey* 62 (2009): 1–11.

61. See entry on *Sir Thomas More* for further information on Edmund Tilney.

62. The page is trimmed along the edge; the material in brackets was conjecturally supplied by W. W. Greg in 'Three Manuscript Notes by Sir George Buc', *The Library* 12 (1931): 307–21.

63. Chambers had dismissed the evidence in *The Elizabethan Stage*, Clarendon Press, 1923, but recanted in *William Shakespeare: A Study of Facts and Problems*, Oxford University Press, 1930. Greg, 'Three Manuscript Notes by Sir George Buc'. R. C. Bald, 'The *Locrine* and *George-a-Greene* Title Page Inscriptions', *The Library* 12 (1931): 295–305.

64. See C. F. Tucker Brooke, *The Tudor Drama*, Houghton Mifflin Company, 1911, p. 191.

65. Jonathan Bate, *Soul of the Age: The Life, Mind and World of William Shakespeare*, Penguin, 2008, p. 403.

66. Peter Berek, '*Locrine* and *Selimus*', in *Dictionary of Literary Biography Vol. 62: Elizabethan Dramatists*, Gale Research Company, 1987, pp. 369–72.

67. The one exception is Lyly's *The Woman in the Moon* (1591–94?), but as Lyly exclusively wrote comedies and classical legends for private boys' companies he is probably the least likely of the three.

68. Tucker Brooke, *The Shakespeare Apocrypha*, p. xvii.

69. See Brian Vickers, *Shakespeare, Co-Author*, Oxford University Press, 2002.

70. Tucker Brooke, *The Shakespeare Apocrypha*, p. xix.

71. Tucker Brooke, *The Shakespeare Apocrypha*, p. xx.

72. Gooch, *Locrine*, p. 29.

73. Proudfoot, *Shakespeare: Text, Stage & Canon*, p. 81.

74. Proudfoot, *Shakespeare: Text Stage & Canon*, p. 83.

75. See John Jowett, ed., *Richard III*, The Oxford Shakespeare, 2000, p. 12.

76. Michael Dobson and Stanley Wells, eds, *The Oxford Companion to Shakespeare*, Oxford University Press, 2001, p. 124.

77. Giorgio Melchiori, ed., *Edward III*, New Cambridge Shakespeare, 1998, p. 9.

78. Wells and Taylor, *William Shakespeare: A Textual Companion*, p. 137. See also Karl Wentersdorf, 'The Authorship of *Edward III*', unpublished PhD thesis, University of Cincinatti (1960); MacDonald P. Jackson, '*Edward III*, Shakespeare, and Pembroke's Men', *Notes and Queries* 210 (1965): 329–31.

79. Wells and Taylor, *William Shakespeare: A Textual Companion*, p. 137.

80. Melchiori, *Edward III*, p. 9.

81. Richard Proudfoot, '*The Reign of King Edward the Third* (1596) and Shakespeare', *Proceedings of the British Academy* 71 (1985): 159–85, at p. 162.

82. See John Dover Wilson, ed., *The Second Part of King Henry VI*, The New Shakespeare, Cambridge University Press, 1952, pp. xii–xiii.

83. *Henry VI Part 2* and *Part 3* were called *The First Part of the Contention of the Two Famous Houses of York and Lancaster* and *The True Tragedy of Richard Duke of York* in their earliest printings in 1594 and 1595 respectively.

84. Randall Martin, ed., *Henry VI Part Three*, The Oxford Shakespeare, 2001, pp. 361–78.

85. James R. Siemon ed., *Richard III*, The Arden Shakespeare, 2009, pp. 461–63.

86. Martin Wiggins in association with Catherine Richardson, *British Drama 1533–1642: A Catalogue*, 10 Vols (projected), Oxford University Press, 2012–, Vol. 3, No. 952.

87. Tucker Brooke, *The Shakespeare Apocrypha*, p. xxii.

88. Eric Sams, ed., *Shakespeare's Edward III*, Yale University Press, 1996, p. 203.

89. Brian Vickers, 'Review of Giorgio Melchiori's Cambridge edition of *Edward III*', *Yearbook of English Studies* 30 (1999): 301–2, at p. 301.

90. Thomas Merriam, 'Marlowe Versus Kyd as Author of *Edward III* I.i, III and V', *Notes and Queries* 56 (2009): 549–51, at p. 551.

91. Wells and Taylor, *William Shakespeare: A Textual Companion*, p. 137.

92. Melchiori, *Edward III*, p. 17.

93. Marlowe's stabbing to death on 30 May 1593, ostensibly in a brawl over a 'reckoning' or bill, is believed by some to have been perpetrated by the Elizabethan authorities for the dangerous sedition of his works. Kyd and Marlowe's shared lodgings were searched leading to Kyd's arrest and questioning under at least the threat of torture about heretical papers found there. Marlowe was arrested on 18 May, released shortly thereafter, and was awaiting trial when he was murdered.

94. Debate still rages about the date of *The Spanish Tragedy*; 1587 is the traditional view, though several scholars contend it could be as early as 1586.

95. See Martin Wiggins, *Shakespeare and the Drama of his Time*, Oxford University Press, 2000, especially chapter 2, and Bate, *Soul of the Age*, pp. 400–7.

96. See the *Edward III* entry for a discussion on the likely chronology of Shakespeare's earliest plays. For the most complete exploration of Ovid's influence on Shakespeare see Jonathan Bate, *Shakespeare and Ovid*, Oxford University Press, 1993.

97. The epigraph, from Ovid's *Amores*, reads '*Vilia miretur vulgus: mihi flavus Apollo / Pocula Castalia plena ministret aqua*', which translates roughly as 'Let what is cheap excite the marvel of the crowd; for me may golden Apollo minister full cups from the Castalian fount.'

98. See the entry on *Arden of Faversham* on Nashe and Kyd. *Greene's Groatsworth of Wit* (1592) is likely to be – at least in part – a forgery by Henry Chettle, to whom the insult to Shakespeare is often ascribed.

99. Lukas Erne, *Beyond The Spanish Tragedy: A Study of the Works of Thomas Kyd*, Manchester University Press, 2001, p. 5.

100. Erne, *Beyond The Spanish Tragedy*, p. 119.

101. See the entry on *A Yorkshire Tragedy*.

102. See Andrew Gurr, *Shakespeare's Opposites*, Cambridge University Press, 2009, p. 186.

103. See R. A. Foakes, ed., *Henslowe's Diary* (Second Edition), Cambridge University Press, 2002, pp. 17–19, and Carol Chillington, *Documents of the Rose Playhouse*, Manchester University Press, 1984, p. 50.

104. See Foakes, *Henslowe's Diary*, pp. 51–60, and Wiggins, *British Drama 1533–1642*, Vol. 2, No. 783.

105. Wiggins, *British Drama 1533–1642*, Vol. 3, No. 928.

106. See the entry on *Edward III* for details.

107. See Clara Calvo and Jesús Tronch, eds, *The Spanish Tragedy by Thomas Kyd*, Arden Early Modern Drama, 2013, pp. 319–28.

108. G. E. Bentley, *The Profession of Dramatist in Shakespeare's Time 1590–1642*, Princeton University Press, 1971, p. 263.

109. Andrew S. Cairncross, ed., *The First Part of Hieronimo* and *The Spanish Tragedy*, Regents Renaissance Drama, 1967.

110. Brian Vickers, 'Identifying Shakespeare's Additions to *The Spanish Tragedy* (1602): A New(er) Approach', *Shakespeare* 8:1 (2012): 13–43, at p. 16.

111. E. K. Chambers, *The Elizabethan Stage*, Vol. 3, Clarendon Press, 1923, p. 396.

112. G. K. Hunter, ed., *The Malcontent*, Manchester University Press, 1975.

113. Vickers, 'Identifying Shakespeare's Additions', p. 17.

114. See Foakes, *Henslowe's Diary*, pp. 182, 203.

115. See MacDonald P. Jackson and Michael Neill, eds, *The Selected Plays of John Marston*, Cambridge University Press, 1986, p. 509.

116. Anne Barton, *Ben Jonson, Dramatist*, Cambridge University Press, 1984, p. 16.

117. Erne, *Beyond The Spanish Tragedy*, p. 121.

118. Erne, *Beyond The Spanish Tragedy*, p. 120.

119. C. H. Herford and Percy and Evelyn Simpson, *Ben Jonson*, 11 Vols, Oxford University Press, 1925–53, Vol. 2, p. 242.

120. Erne, *Beyond The Spanish Tragedy*, pp. 121–2.

121. Philip Edwards, ed., *The Spanish Tragedy by Thomas Kyd*, Manchester University Press, 1986; David Bevington, Martin Butler and Ian Donaldson, eds, *The Cambridge Edition of the Works of Ben Jonson*, 7 Vols, Cambridge University Press, 2012, vol. 1, p. 92.

122. Brian Vickers, 'Shakespeare and Authorship Studies in the Twenty-First Century', *Shakespeare Quarterly* 62:1 (2011), 106–42; see also Burrows, 'A Second Opinion', and Calvo and Tronch, *The Spanish Tragedy by Thomas Kyd*, pp. 319–28.

123. Vickers, 'Identifying Shakespeare's Additions', p. 31.

124. Vickers, 'Identifying Shakespeare's Additions', p. 31.

125. D. H. Craig, 'Authorial Styles and the Frequencies of Very Common Words: Jonson, Shakespeare, and the Additions to *The Spanish Tragedy*', *Style* 26 (1992): 199–220.

126. Craig, 'Authorial Styles and the Frequencies of Very Common Words', p. 215.

127. Craig and Kinney, *Shakespeare, Computers*. Craig also makes the case against Jonson in the 'Dubia' section of the Electronic Edition of Bevington et al., *The Cambridge Edition of the Works of Ben Jonson*.

128. Craig and Kinney, *Shakespeare, Computers*, p. 178.

129. Craig and Kinney, *Shakespeare, Computers*, p. 179.

130. Craig and Kinney, *Shakespeare, Computers*, p. 169.

131. Craig and Kinney, *Shakespeare, Computers*, p. 169.

132. Craig and Kinney, *Shakespeare, Computers*, p. 167.

133. Erne, *Beyond The Spanish Tragedy*, p. 126.

134. Erne, *Beyond The Spanish Tragedy*, p. 120.

135. Edwards, *The Spanish Tragedy*, p. lxi.

136. Calvo and Tronch, *The Spanish Tragedy*, p. 328.

137. For a discussion of this see especially Lukas Erne, *Shakespeare and the Book Trade*, Cambridge University Press, 2013.

138. See section 'Plays Excluded from This Edition', on *The Puritan*, the only other apocryphal play, apart from *Locrine*, to suggest Shakespearean authorship on its title page in this way. Shakespeare's part-authorship of *Pericles* is, of course, no longer controversial.

139. Proudfoot, *Shakespeare: Text, Stage & Canon*, p. 71.

140. See W. W. Greg, *Bibliography of the English Printed Drama to the Restoration*, Oxford University Press, 1939–59 (4 Vols), Vol. 1, p. 189. The Stationers' Register records a transfer of the rights in the play from William Jones (II) to John Browne (sen.) on 16 December 1611, who paid Thomas Snodham to print it for him two years later.

141. Edmond Malone, *Supplement to Shakespeare* (1780), quoted in Tucker Brooke, *The Shakespeare Apocrypha*, p. xxix.

142. A. C. Swinburne, *A Study of Shakespeare*, Chatto and Windus, 1880, p. 232.

143. Tucker Brooke, *The Shakespeare Apocrypha*, p. viii.

144. Wells and Taylor, *William Shakespeare: A Textual Companion*, p. 135.

145. See also the entry on *Arden of Faversham*.

146. Irving Ribner, *The English History Play in the Age of Shakespeare*, Methuen, 1965, p. 206.

147. Tucker Brooke, *The Shakespeare Apocrypha*, p. xxviii.

148. See the entry on *Sir Thomas More*.

149. Elliott and Valenza, 'Oxford by the Numbers', p. 402.

150. Stanley Wells and Gary Taylor, with John Jowett and William Montgomery, eds, *The Oxford Shakespeare: The Complete Works* (Second Edition), Oxford University Press, 2005, p. 813.

151. Scott McMillin, *The Elizabethan Theatre and 'The Book of Sir Thomas More'*, Cornell University Press, 1987.

152. 'Leave out the insurrection wholly with the cause thereof and begin with Sir Thomas More at the Mayor's sessions, with a report afterwards of his good service done being Sheriff of London upon a mutiny against the Lombards – only by a short report and not otherwise, at your own perils. E Tilney.'

153. See John Jowett, ed., *Sir Thomas More*, The Arden Shakespeare, 2011, pp. 41-47.

154. Folios 1–2 are the vellum wrapper.

155. G. Harold Metz, '"Voice and Credyt": The Scholars and *Sir Thomas More*', in T. H. Howard-Hill, ed., *Shakespeare and Sir Thomas More*, Cambridge University Press, 1989, pp. 11–44, at p. 13.

156. Peter W. M. Blayney, 'The *Booke of Sir Thomas Moore* Re-examined', *Studies in Philology* 69:2 (1972): 167–91, at p. 169.

157. Jowett, *Sir Thomas More*.

158. Vittorio Gabrieli and Giorgio Melchiori, eds, *Sir Thomas More*, The Revels Plays, Manchester University Press, 1990.

159. See Giorgio Melchiori, 'The *Booke of Sir Thomas Moore*: A Chronology of Revision', *Shakespeare Quarterly* 36 (1986): 291–308, at p. 306.

160. Blayney, 'Sir Thomas Moore Re-examined', p. 168.

161. Blayney, 'Sir Thomas Moore Re-examined', p. 168.

162. Blayney, 'Sir Thomas Moore Re-examined', p. 168.

163. Eric Rasmussen, 'Setting Down What the Clown Spoke: Improvisation, Hand B, and *The Book of Sir Thomas More*', *The Library* 6:13 (1991): 126–36.

164. Jowett, *Sir Thomas More*, pp. 435–6.

165. Jowett, *Sir Thomas More*, p. 419.

166. Louis Marder in 1980 published work influenced by Merriam's stylometric analyses (first published in 1981) claiming all of the play, revisions included, was Shakespeare's. Marder speculated that the different hands meant the other writers may merely have been transcribing Shakespeare's foul papers.

167. This has led some critics to refer subsequently to the hand as 'Hand M'. See W. W. Greg, ed., *The Book of Sir Thomas More*, The Malone Society, 1911.

168. Samuel A. Tannenbaum, *'The Booke of Sir Thomas Moore': A Bibliotic Study*, New York, 1927.

169. W. W. Greg, 'The Handwritings of the Manuscript,' in A. W. Pollard, ed., *Shakespeare's Hand in the Play of Sir Thomas More*, Cambridge University Press, 1923, pp. 41–56.

170. Metz, '"Voice and Credyt"', pp. 17–18.

171. E. H. C. Oliphant, 'Sir Thomas More', *Journal of English and Germanic Philology* 18 (1919): 226–35.

172. See W. W. Greg, *The Book of Sir Thomas More*, The Malone Society Reprints, 1961, with a supplement by Harold Jenkins, pp. xvi–xvii.

173. R. C. Bald, 'The Booke of *Sir Thomas More* and its Problems', *Shakespeare Survey 2* (1949): 44–65.

174. J. M. Nosworthy, 'Shakespeare and *Sir Thomas More*', *Review of English Studies* 6 (1955): 12–25.

175. Blayney, '*Sir Thomas Moore* Re-examined', p. 190.

176. John Jowett, 'Henry Chettle and the Original Text of *Sir Thomas More*', in T. H. Howard-Hill, ed., *Shakespeare and Sir Thomas More*, Cambridge University Press, 1989, pp. 131–49; Jowett, *Sir Thomas More*.

177. Jowett, *Sir Thomas More*, pp. 422–3. See Vickers, *Shakespeare, Co-Author*, especially pp. 34–43. Both Jackson and Tarlinskaja's studies are forthcoming.

178. Thomas Merriam, 'Did Munday compose *Sir Thomas More?*', *Notes and Queries* 235 (1990): 175–8. Thomas Merriam, 'Orthographic changes in *John a Kent* and Hand M of *More*', *Notes and Queries* 251 (2006): 475–8.

179. Hope, *The Authorship of Shakespeare's Plays*, p. 155.

180. Presumably this judgement is in response to the uncertain nature of the Quarto of Chettle's only surviving solo-authored play, *Hoffman* (1603, printed 1631), which was evidently revised for a revival. Harold Jenkins, in his Malone Society edition of the play, notes that in the Quarto the character Otho 'is always so called in the first scene, where he makes his single appearance in the play. But elsewhere he is sometimes referred to as Charles (ll. 1226, 1229, 1314). The metre shows that Charles was the name originally used, and the half-hearted attempt to replace it was no doubt due to its occurrence in the English royal house. A change would be urgent upon any revival after 1612, when Prince Charles became heir to the throne' (p. vii). See also Gurr, *Shakespeare's Opposites*, pp. 115–19.

181. Muriel St Clare Byrne, 'Bibliographic Clues in Collaborate Plays', *The Library* 4, Vol. 13 (1932): 21–48; Jowett, 'Henry Chettle and the Original Text of *Sir Thomas More*'; John Jowett, 'Johannes Factotum: Henry Chettle and *Greene's Groatsworth of Wit*', *PBSA* 87 (1993): 453–86; John Jowett, 'Notes on Henry Chettle', *Review of English Studies* 45 (1994): 384–8, 517–22; H. R. Hoppe, 'The Bad Quarto of *Romeo and Juliet*: A Bibliographical and Textual Study', *Cornell Studies in English* 36 (1948); Sidney Thomas, 'Henry Chettle and The First Quarto of *Romeo and Juliet*', *Review of English Studies* 1 (1950): 8–16; John Jowett, 'Romeo and Juliet', in Stanley Wells and Gary Taylor, with John Jowett and William Montgomery, eds, *William Shakespeare: A Textual Companion*, Oxford University Press, 1987, pp. 288–90; John Jowett, 'Henry Chettle and the First Quarto of *Romeo and Juliet*', *PBSA* 92 (1998): 53–74; Harold Jenkins, *The Life and Work of Henry Chettle*, Sidgwick and Jackson Ltd, 1934; Harold Jenkins, 'The 1631 Quarto of The Tragedy of Hoffman', *The Library* 5, Vol. VI (1951–52): 88–99.

182. Gabrieli and Melchiori, *Sir Thomas More*, p. 22.

183. Metz, '"Voice and Credyt"', p. 19.

184. Jowett, *Sir Thomas More*, pp. 433–7.

185. Jowett, *Sir Thomas More*, p. 6.

186. Gary Taylor, 'The Date and Auspices of the Additions to *Sir Thomas More*', in T. H. Howard-Hill, ed., *Shakespeare and Sir Thomas More*, Cambridge University Press, 1989, pp. 101–29, at p. 103.

187. David Kathman, 'Reconsidering The Seven Deadly Sins', *Early Theatre* 7 (2004): 13–44, at p. 14.

188. Jowett, *Sir Thomas More*, pp. 425–6.

189. Jowett, *Sir Thomas More*, p. 426.

190. Jowett, *Sir Thomas More*, p. 431.

191. Both Elliott/Valenza and Tarlinskaja agree that the Hand D passages are not consistent with early Shakespeare, but highly consistent with later Shakespeare.

192. R. W. Chambers, 'The Expression of Ideas – Particularly Political Ideas – in the Three Pages and in Shakespeare', in A. W. Pollard, ed., *Shakespeare's Hand in the Play of Sir Thomas More*, Cambridge University Press, 1923, pp. 142–87.

193. Jowett, *Sir Thomas More*, p. 443.

194. See Taylor, 'The Date and Auspices of the Additions to *Sir Thomas More*', p. 120.

195. MacDonald P. Jackson, 'A New Chronological Indicator for Shakespeare's Plays and for Hand D of *Sir Thomas More*', *Shakespeare Survey* 59 (2006): 69–78, at p. 304.

196. Jackson, 'A New Chronological Indicator for Shakespeare's Plays', p. 306.

197. A. W. Pollard, ed., *Shakespeare's Hand in the Play of Sir Thomas More*, Cambridge University Press, 1923; T. H. Howard-Hill, ed., *Shakespeare and Sir Thomas More*, Cambridge University Press, 1989.

198. Many in this list have published several articles on the matter, so their order of appearance relates to their earliest work.

199. Honigmann's main argument was that while it probably was Shakespeare, II.D is mainly full of rhetorical commonplaces and may even include lines by someone else that Shakespeare merely copied out. He felt that Addition III was nearer to poetic distinction, but neither example represented Shakespeare – who wasn't likely to have taken seriously the job of patching a play of average quality by other writers – at his best.

200. W. W. Greg, ed., *The Book of Sir Thomas More*, The Malone Society, 1911, p. viii.

201. MacDonald P. Jackson, 'Is "Hand D" of *Sir Thomas More* Shakespeare's? Thomas Bayes and the Elliott-Valenza Authorship Tests', *EMLS* 12:3 (2007); Giles E. Dawson, 'Shakespeare's Handwriting', *Shakespeare Survey* 42 (1990): 119–28.

202. John Dover Wilson, 'Bibliographical Links between the Three Pages and the Good Quartos', in A. W. Pollard, ed., *Shakespeare's Hand in the Play of Sir Thomas More*, Cambridge University Press, 1923, pp. 113–41.

203. Thomas Merriam, 'Some Further Evidence for Shakespeare's Authorship of Hand D in *Sir Thomas More*', *Notes and Queries* 53 (2006): 65–6.

204. Charles R. Forker, 'Webster or Shakespeare? Style, Idiom, Vocabulary, and Spellings in the Additions to *Sir Thomas More*', in T. H. Howard-Hill, ed., *Shakespeare and Sir Thomas More*, Cambridge University Press, 1989, pp. 151–70.

205. Carol Chillington, 'Playwrights at Work: Henslowe's, not Shakespeare's, *Book of Sir Thomas More*', *English Literary Renaissance* 10 (1980): 439–79; Taylor, 'The Date and Auspices of the Additions to *Sir Thomas More*'; Forker, 'Webster or Shakespeare?'

206. Caroline F. E. Spurgeon, 'Imagery in the *Sir Thomas More* Fragment', *Review of English Studies* 6 (1930): 257–70; Karl P. Wentersdorf, 'Linkages of Thought and Imagery in Shakespeare and *More*', *Modern Language Quarterly* 34 (1973): 384–405.

207. MacDonald P. Jackson, 'The Date and Authorship of Hand D's Contribution to *Sir Thomas More*: Evidence from Literature Online', *Shakespeare Survey* 59 (2006): 69–78.

208. *Julius Caesar* 9, *Antony and Cleopatra* 8, *Coriolanus* 8, *Othello* 6, *As You Like It* 5, *Cymbeline* 4, *King Lear* 4, *The Merchant of Venice* 4, *Much Ado about Nothing* 4, *Twelfth Night* 4.

209. Timothy Irish Watt, 'The Hand-D Addition to The Book of Sir Thomas More', in Hugh Craig and Arthur F. Kinney, eds, *Shakespeare, Computers, and the Mystery of Authorship*, Cambridge University Press, 2009. The plays in the corpus are listed pp. 213–20.

210. See Hope, *The Authorship of Shakespeare's Plays*, pp. 140–5, 154–5.

211. Blayney, '*Sir Thomas Moore* Re-examined', pp. 178–9.

212. Taylor, 'The Date and Auspices of the Additions to *Sir Thomas More*', pp. 101–29, at p. 125.

213. Jowett, *Sir Thomas More*, p. 456.

214. Jowett, *Sir Thomas More*, p. 458.

215. The introduction to Paul Edmondson's unpublished PhD thesis edition of the play provides an invaluable, detailed account of the play's probable date (University of Birmingham, 2001).

216. See Wiggins, *Shakespeare and the Drama of his Time*, pp. 53–78. Jonson's *Humour* plays accelerated the genre's popularity, and the principles of its comedic style were the very fabric of his later, darker city comedies.

217. In fact, Gary Taylor and John Jowett have argued that the play, with its host of Italianate names, was originally set in Italy. The location was probably changed to Vienna by Thomas Middleton to forge a more contemporary link to the events of the Thirty Years' War (1618–48) when he adapted it sometime between 1619 and 1623. See Gary Taylor and John Jowett, *Shakespeare Reshaped*, Oxford University Press, 1993.

218. Paul Yachnin, 'Shakespeare's Problem Plays and the Drama of His Time', in Richard Dutton and Jean E. Howard, eds, *A Companion to Shakespeare's Works Vol. 4 – The Poems, Problem Comedies, Late Plays*, Blackwell, 2003, p. 53.

219. Yachnin, 'Shakespeare's Problem Plays', p. 51.

220. Yachnin, 'Shakespeare's Problem Plays', p. 66.

221. Yachnin, 'Shakespeare's Problem Plays', p. 66.

222. Wiggins, *Shakespeare and the Drama of his Time*, pp. 106–7.

223. Robert Y. Turner, 'Dramatic Conventions in *All's Well That Ends Well*', *PMLA* 75 (1960): 497–502, at p. 497.

224. Roslyn Lander Knutson, *The Repertory of Shakespeare's Company 1594–1613*, University of Arkansas Press, 1991, p. 173; see also p. 115.

225. Hunter, *English Drama 1586–1642*, pp. 378–87.

226. As Brian Vickers and Marcus Dahl point out in '*All's Well that Ends Well*: An Attribution Refuted', *Times Literary Supplement*, 11 May 2012, pp. 14–16, a rebuttal to Laurie Maguire and Emma Smith, 'Many Hands: A New Shakespeare Collaboration?', *Times Literary Supplement*, 20 April 2012, pp. 13–15, who argue that *All's Well that Ends Well* was a collaboration between Shakespeare and Thomas Middleton. At the time of writing the question cannot be considered resolved, but, for the purposes of the present discussion, we accept *All's Well* as a King's Men play associated with Shakespeare, displaying the 'innovations of comical satire' Turner describes.

227. Tucker Brooke, *The Shakespeare Apocrypha*, p. xxx.

228. Richard Proudfoot, 'Shakespeare's Most Neglected Play', in Laurie E. Maguire and Thomas L. Berger, eds., *Textual Formations and Reformations*, University of Delaware Press, 1998, pp. 149–57, at p. 156.

229. Proudfoot, 'Shakespeare's Most Neglected Play', p. 156.

230. John Jowett, 'Shakespeare Supplemented', in Douglas A. Brooks, ed., *The Shakespeare Apocrypha*, Edwin Mellen Press, 2007, p. 53.

231. Tucker Brooke, *The Shakespeare Apocrypha*, p. xxx.

232. Charles Barber, 'A Rare Use of the Word *Honour* as a Criterion of Middleton's Authorship', *English Studies* 38 (1957): 161–8, at p. 168.

233. Wells and Taylor, *William Shakespeare: A Textual Companion*, p. 138.

234. T. B. Horton, 'The Effectiveness of the Stylometry of Function Words in Discriminating Between Shakespeare and Fletcher', unpublished PhD thesis, University of Edinburgh (1987).

235. Thomas Van Ness Merriam, 'Modelling a Canon: A Stylometric Examination of Shakespeare's First Folio', unpublished PhD thesis, King's College, University of London (1992).

236. Thomas V. N. Merriam and Robert A. J. Matthews, 'Neural Computation in Stylometry I: An Application to the Works of Shakespeare and Fletcher', *Literary and Linguistic Computing* 8 (1993): 203–9.

237. Merriam and Matthews, 'Neural Computation in Stylometry I', p. 207.

238. David Lowe and Robert Matthews, 'Shakespeare Vs. Fletcher: A Stylometric Analysis by Radial Basis Functions', *Computing in the Humanities* 29 (1995): 449–61.

239. Lowe and Matthews, 'Shakespeare Vs. Fletcher', p. 458.

240. Hope, *The Authorship of Shakespeare's Plays*, p. 115.

241. Elliott and Valenza, 'Oxford by the Numbers'.

242. Proudfoot, 'Shakespeare's Most Neglected Play', p. 152.

243. Proudfoot, 'Shakespeare's Most Neglected Play', pp. 154–6.

244. *The Woman Hater* (1606) for Paul's Boys, and *Cupid's Revenge* (1608) and *The Faithful Shepherdess* (1609) for the Children of the Queen's Revels.

245. Even the events of *Arden of Faversham*, if Shakespeare was involved, took place forty years before the play was written and were narrated in Holinshed's *Chronicles*, from which the play drew its principal source.

246. Jackson, *Studies in Attribution*, p. 48.

247. Stanley Wells, 'A Yorkshire Tragedy' in 'Works Included in this Edition: Canon and Chronology', in Gary Taylor and John Lavagnino, with MacDonald P. Jackson, John Jowett, Valerie Wayne and Adrian Weiss, eds, *Thomas Middleton and Early Modern Textual Culture*, Oxford University Press, 2007, p. 355.

248. Gary Taylor, 'Thomas Middleton', in *Oxford Dictionary of National Biography*, http://www.oxforddnb.com/view/printable/18682.

249. Wells and Taylor, *William Shakespeare: A Textual Companion*, p. 141.

250. Sonia Massai, in *Shakespeare and the Rise of the Editor*, Cambridge University Press, 2007, argues that Pavier's deception was not aimed at other stationers or at the acting company – who in all likelihood approved of his project because it provided good advertising for their forthcoming Folio venture – but at readers, trying to give the impression of a 'nonce' collection; that is, a collection that seemed to gather old as well as new imprints within a volume in order to whet readers' appetites for a new collected edition of Shakespeare. Whoever the deception was aimed at, Pavier's unreliability as a source of information remains.

251. Henslowe's records provide us with the evidence for the play's authorship.

252. Swinburne, *A Study of Shakespeare*, p. 144.

253. Sylvia D. Feldman and G. R. Proudfoot, eds, *A Yorkshire Tragedy (1608)*, The Malone Society Reprints, 1973, p. vi.

254. Jackson, *Studies in Attribution*, p. 46.

255. Lake, *The Canon of Thomas Middleton's Plays*; Jackson, *Studies in Attribution*.

256. Mark Eccles, 'Middleton's Birth and Education', *Review of English Studies* 7 (1931): 431–41. *The Puritan* appeared in the Third Folio along with *A Yorkshire Tragedy*.

257. See also the entry on *The Second Maiden's Tragedy* in the section 'Plays Excluded in this Edition', below.

258. See MacDonald P. Jackson, 'Early Modern Authorship: Canons and Chronologies', in Gary Taylor and John Lavagnino, with MacDonald P. Jackson, John Jowett, Valerie Wayne and Adrian Weiss, eds, *Thomas Middleton and Early Modern Textual Culture*, Oxford University Press, 2007, pp. 80–97.

259. John Jowett, ed., *Timon of Athens*, The Oxford Shakespeare, 2004, p. 6.

260. Taylor, 'Thomas Middleton'.

261. Keith Sturgess, ed., *Three Elizabethan Domestic Tragedies*, Penguin, 1969.

262. Jackson, *Studies in Attribution*, p. 46.

263. Hope, *The Authorship of Shakespeare's Plays*, p. 126.

264. Lake, *The Canon of Thomas Middleton's Plays*, p. 172.

265. Lake, *The Canon of Thomas Middleton's Plays*, p. 166.

266. Jackson, *Studies in Attribution*, p. 51.

267. A. C. Cawley and Barry Gaines, eds, *A Yorkshire Tragedy*, The Revels Plays, Manchester University Press, 1986, pp. 5–6, quoting Maxwell, *Studies in Shakespeare the Apocrypha*, p. 186.

268. Roger Holdsworth, 'Middleton's Authorship of *A Yorkshire Tragedy*', *Review of English Studies* 45 (1994): 1–25.

269. Elliott and Valenza, 'Oxford by the Numbers', p. 403; Gary Taylor and John Lavagnino, with MacDonald P. Jackson, John Jowett, Valerie Wayne and Adrian Weiss, eds, *Thomas Middleton: The Collected Works*, Oxford University Press, 2007, pp. 452–66; Taylor and Lavagnino, *Thomas Middleton and Early Modern Textual Culture*, pp. 355–6, 592–7.

270. Maxwell, *Studies in the Shakespeare Apocrypha*, p. 196.

271. See Jackson, 'Early Modern Authorship', p. 84.

272. Jackson, 'Early Modern Authorship', pp. 84–5.

273. Henslowe's account books record payments to Middleton for the provisionally titled *The Chester Tragedy*, on behalf of Worcester's Men, in 1602, the play switching to the ownership of the Admiral's along with its change in title to *Randall, Earl of Chester*. Middleton also collaborated on *Caesar's Fall* for the Admiral's that same year.

274. See note 226.

275. For the chronology of Middleton's works see 'Works Included' in Taylor and Lavagnino, *Thomas Middleton and Early Modern Textual Culture*, pp. 335–443. The editors place *A Yorkshire Tragedy* immediately before *Timon* in 1605.

276. Leo Kirschbaum, 'The Texts of *Mucedorus*', *Modern Language Review* L (1955): 1–5.

277. George F. Reynolds, '*Mucedorus*, Most Popular Elizabethan Play?', in Josephine W. Bennett, Oscar Cargill and Vernon Hall, eds, *Studies in the English Renaissance Drama*, New York University Press, 1959, pp. 248–68, at p. 257.

278. Paul G. Kreuzer, '*Mucedorus*', in *Dictionary of Literary Biography Vol. 62: Elizabethan Dramatists*, Gale Research Company, 1987, pp. 373–83, at p. 374.

279. Teresa Grant, 'White Bears in *Mucedorus*, *The Winter's Tale* and *Oberon, The Fairy Prince*', *Notes and Queries* 48:3 (2001): 311–13.

280. See Alan B. Farmer and Zachary Lesser's *Database of Early English Playbooks*, http://deep.sas.upenn.edu/.

281. See the entry on *The Spanish Tragedy*.

282. Martin Wiggins, private communication.

283. Richard T. Thornberry, 'A Seventeenth-Century Revival of *Mucedorus* in London before 1610', *Shakespeare Quarterly* 28:3 (1977): 362–4.

284. Wiggins, *British Drama 1533–1642*, Vol. 3, No. 884.

285. Wiggins, *British Drama 1533–1642*, Vol. 3, No. 884.

286. Grant notes that polar bear cubs are born in November/December and weaned between July and September of their first year. Even if Poole's bears were eighteen months old (i.e. from the previous year's litter) they would still have been relatively small and lacking in the aggression that comes at sexual maturity at around four or five years of age. Grant's article also records that Henslowe and Alleyn were issued with a royal warrant on 20 March 1610/11 to keep them (Grant, 'White Bears in *Mucedorus*', p. 311).

287. See also the entry on *Cardenio/Double Falsehood*.

288. Peter Kirwan, 'The First Collected "Shakespeare Apocrypha"', *Shakespeare Quarterly* 62:4 (2011): 594–601.

289. Kirwan, 'The First Collected "Shakespeare Apocrypha"', p. 595.

290. The British Library copy of *Oldcastle* that was in the collection has apparently been sold off, so there is no way of knowing whether it was the 1600 copy, lacking authorial attribution, or the 1619 reprint, falsely dated to 1600 and attributed to Shakespeare. Nonetheless, by the time the collection was compiled a copy of the play attributed to Shakespeare was in circulation.

291. Tucker Brooke, *The Shakespeare Apocrypha*, p. vii.

292. Tucker Brooke, *The Shakespeare Apocrypha*, p. vi.

293. Kreuzer, '*Mucedorus*', p. 373.

294. F. G. Fleay, *Chronicle of the English Drama*, 2 Vols, Reeves and Turner, 1891, Vol. 2, p. 50.

295. John Peachman, 'Links Between *Mucedorus* and *Guy Earl of Warwick*', *Notes and Queries* (53:4) 2006: 464–7.

296. Richard Preiss, 'A Play Finally Anonymous', in Douglas A. Brooks, ed., *The Shakespeare Apocrypha*, The Edwin Mellen Press, 2007.

297. Preiss, 'A Play Finally Anonymous', p. 128.

298. Preiss, 'A Play Finally Anonymous', p. 129.

299. MacDonald P. Jackson, 'Edward Archer's Ascription of *Mucedorus* to Shakespeare', *Journal of the Australasian Universities Language and Literature Association* 22 (1964): 233–48.

300. Jackson, 'Edward Archer's Ascription of *Mucedorus* to Shakespeare', p. 236.

301. Jackson, 'Edward Archer's Ascription of *Mucedorus* to Shakespeare', p. 238.

302. Jackson, 'Edward Archer's Ascription of *Mucedorus* to Shakespeare', p. 239. See also Alfred Hart, 'Shakespeare and the Vocabulary of *The Two Noble Kinsmen*', *Review of English Studies* X (1934): 274–87, at p. 284.

303. Jackson, 'Edward Archer's Ascription of *Mucedorus* to Shakespeare', p. 239.

304. Jackson, 'Edward Archer's Ascription of *Mucedorus* to Shakespeare', p. 245.

305. Jackson, 'Edward Archer's Ascription of *Mucedorus* to Shakespeare', p. 245.

306. Elliott and Valenza, 'Oxford by the Numbers'; Ward Elliott, 'Notes from the Claremont Shakespeare Clinic', *The Shakespeare Newsletter* 61:3 (Winter 2011/12): 105–12.

307. Brean Hammond, ed., *Double Falsehood*, The Arden Shakespeare, 2010; David Carnegie and Gary Taylor, eds, *The Quest for Cardenio: Shakespeare, Fletcher, Cervantes, & the Lost Play*, Oxford University Press, 2012.

308. Gary Taylor, 'The Embassy, The City, The Court, The Text: *Cardenio* Performed in 1613', in David Carnegie and Gary Taylor, eds, *The Quest for Cardenio: Shakespeare, Fletcher, Cervantes, & the Lost Play*, Oxford University Press, 2012, pp. 287–308.

309. I am grateful to Martin Wiggins for pointing this out in a private communication.

310. Wells and Taylor, *William Shakespeare: A Textual Companion*, pp. 132–3.

311. *Henry VIII* was playing when the Globe burned down on 29 June 1613, and was described by Sir Henry Wotton, who recorded the event, as a 'new play' at the time. *The Two Noble Kinsmen*'s Prologue speaks of 'our losses', believed to be an allusion to the Globe, while Ben Jonson alludes several times to 'Palamon' in *Bartholomew Fair* (1614), another apparent reference to the play. *Kinsmen*'s morris dance was also apparently borrowed from Francis Beaumont's *Masque of the Inner Temple and Gray's Inn* that was performed on 20 February 1613.

312. Gordon McMullan, ed., *Henry VIII*, The Arden Shakespeare, 2000.

313. Hammond, *Double Falsehood*, p. 87.

314. John Freehafer, '*Cardenio*, by Shakespeare and Fletcher', *PMLA* 84:3 (1969): 501–13; Hammond, *Double Falsehood*. On Shakespeare's rise to pre-eminence in the eighteenth century see Michael Dobson, *The*

Making of the National Poet: Shakespeare, Adaptation, and Authorship, 1660–1769, Oxford University Press, 1992.

315. Edmund G. C. King, 'In the Character of Shakespeare: Canon, Authorship, and Attribution in Eighteenth-Century England', unpublished PhD thesis, University of Auckland (2008), pp. 152–7.

316. Freehafer, '*Cardenio*, by Shakespeare and Fletcher', p. 505.

317. Jeffrey Kahan, ed., *Shakespeare Imitations, Parodies and Forgeries: 1710–1820*, 3 Vols, Routledge, 2004; see Hammond, *Double Falsehood*, pp. 88–9.

318. Tiffany Stern, '"The Forgery of Some Modern Author"?: Theobald's Shakespeare and Cardenio's *Double Falsehood*', *Shakespeare Quarterly* 62:4 (2011): 555–93.

319. Stern, '"The Forgery of Some Modern Author"?', pp. 576–7.

320. Stern, '"The Forgery of Some Modern Author"?', p. 592.

321. Gamaliel Bradford Jr, 'The History of Cardenio by Mr Fletcher and Shakespeare', *Modern Language Notes* 25 (1910): 51–6.

322. Hammond, *Double Falsehood*, p. 81.

323. A. Luis Pujante, '*Double Falsehood* and the Verbal Parallels with Shelton's *Don Quixote*', *Shakespeare Survey* 51 (1998): 95–105.

324. Freehafer, '*Cardenio*, by Shakespeare and Fletcher', p. 505.

325. Taylor, '*Cardenio* Performed in 1613', pp. 287–308.

326. Taylor, '*Cardenio* Performed in 1613', p. 307.

327. David Carnegie, 'Theobald's Pattern of Adaptation: *The Duchess of Malfi* and *Richard II*', in David Carnegie and Gary Taylor, eds, *The Quest for Cardenio: Shakespeare, Fletcher, Cervantes, & the Lost Play*, Oxford University Press, 2012, pp. 180–91.

328. Carnegie, 'Theobald's Pattern of Adaptation', p. 191.

329. Chambers, *William Shakespeare: A Study of Facts and Problems*, Vol. 1, p. 542.

330. Hammond, *Double Falsehood*, pp. 102–3. See, for example, Russ McDonald, *Shakespeare's Late Style*, Cambridge University Press, 2006, and Marina Tarlinskaja, *Shakespeare's Verse*, Peter Lang Inc., 1987, pp. 182–4.

331. Stephan Kukowski, 'The Hand of John Fletcher in *Double Falsehood*', *Shakespeare Survey* 43 (1991): 81–9.

332. Hope, *The Authorship of Shakespeare's Plays*, p. 100.

333. Hope, *The Authorship of Shakespeare's Plays*, p. 100.

334. Michael Wood, *In Search of Shakespeare*, BBC Books, 2003, p. 315; '"A Sound from Heaven": New Light on Shakespeare's *Cardenio*', unpublished essay, 2001 (see Hammond, *Double Falsehood*, pp. 328–35).

335. Hammond, *Double Falsehood*, pp. 328–35.

336. Stern, '"The Forgery of Some Modern Author"?', p. 586. The essays to which she refers are MacDonald P. Jackson, 'Looking for Shakespeare in *Double Falsehood*: Stylistic Evidence' and Richard Proudfoot, 'Can *Double Falsehood* (1727–8) be Merely a Forgery by Lewis Theobald?', both in David Carnegie and Gary Taylor, eds, *The Quest for Cardenio: Shakespeare, Fletcher, Cervantes, & the Lost Play*, Oxford University Press, 2012.

337. Roger Chartier, *Cardenio between Cervantes and Shakespeare: The Story of a Lost Play*, Polity Press, 2013.

338. Peter Kirwan, 'Cardenio', in Lost Plays Database, www.lostplays.org/index.php/Cardenio.

339. Tucker Brooke, *The Shakespeare Apocrypha*, p. xxxix.

340. See the entries on *The Spanish Tragedy* and *Edward III*.

341. Quoted in Chambers, *William Shakespeare: A Study of Facts and Problems*, Vol. 2, p. 212.

342. Eric Sams, ed., *Shakespeare's Edmund Ironside: The Lost Play*, Wildwood House, 1986; E. B. Everitt, *The Young Shakespeare: Studies in Documentary Evidence, Volume 2*, Rosenkilde and Bagger, 1954.

343. Wells and Taylor, *William Shapkespeare: A Textual Companion*, p. 138.

344. Wells and Taylor, *William Shapkespeare: A Textual Companion*, p. 88.

345. Matthew W. A. Smith, '*Edmund Ironside*', *Notes and Queries* 238 (1993): 202–5.

346. Mark Dominik, *A Shakespearean Anomaly: Shakespeare's Hand in Sir John Oldcastle*, Alioth Press, 1991.

347. See the entry on *Mucedorus*.

348. Kirwan, 'Shakespeare and the Idea of Apocrypha', p. 135.

349. Taylor and Lavagnino, *Thomas Middleton: The Collected Works*, p. 37.

350. See Kirwan, 'Shakespeare and the Idea of Apocrypha'.

351. Elliott and Valenza, 'Oxford by the Numbers'.

352. William A. Abrams, ed., *The Merry Devil of Edmonton*, Duke University Press, 1942.

353. See the introductory essay on *Authorship and Attribution*.

354. Wells and Taylor, *William Shakespeare: A Textual Companion*, p. 139; Jackson, 'Shakespeare and the Quarrel Scene in *Arden of Faversham*', p. 282.

355. Michael Egan, ed., *The Tragedy of Richard II, Part One: A Newly Authenticated Play by William Shakespeare*, 4 Vols, Edwin Mellen Press, 2006.

356. Peter Corbin and Douglas Sedge, *Thomas of Woodstock or King Richard the Second, Part One*, The Revels Plays, Manchester University Press, 2002.

357. MacDonald P. Jackson, 'Shakespeare's *Richard II* and the Anonymous *Thomas of Woodstock*', *Medieval and Renaissance Drama in England* 14 (2001): 17–65; MacDonald P. Jackson, 'Shakespeare's *Richard II* and the anonymous *Thomas of Woodstock*', *Research Opportunities in Renaissance Drama* (2007): 67–100.

358. David J. Lake, 'Three Seventeenth-Century Revisions: *Thomas of Woodstock*, *The Jew of Malta*, and *Faustus B*', *Notes and Queries* 228 (1983): 133–43.

359. Jackson, 'Shakespeare's *Richard II* and the Anonymous *Thomas of Woodstock*', p. 68.

360. See Louis Ule, *A Concordance to the Shakespeare Apocrypha*, 3 Vols, Georg Olms Verlag AG, 1987.

361. Eccles, 'Middleton's Birth and Education'; Lake, *The Canon of Thomas Middleton's Plays*; Jackson, *Studies in Attribution*.

362. Hope, *The Authorship of Shakespeare's Plays*, p. 122.

363. Richard H. Barker, 'The Authorship of *The Second Maiden's Tragedy* and *The Revenger's Tragedy*', *Shakespeare Association Bulletin* 20 (1945): 56–60; Samuel Schoenbaum, *Middleton's Tragedies: A Critical Study*, Columbia University Press, 1958.

364. E. B. Everitt, *The Young Shakespeare: Studies in Documentary Evidence, Volume 2*, Rosenkilde and Bagger, 1954. Everitt actually claimed that Shakespeare co-wrote the play with Middleton.

365. Anne Lancashire, ed., *The Second Maiden's Tragedy*, The Revels Plays, Manchester University Press, 1978.

366. Eric Rasmussen, 'Shakespeare's Hand in *The Second Maiden's Tragedy*', *Shakespeare Quarterly* 40:1 (1989): 1–26; MacDonald P. Jackson, 'The Additions to *The Second Maiden's Tragedy*: Shakespeare or Middleton?', *Shakespeare Quarterly* 41:3 (1990): 402–5.

367. Charles Hamilton, *Cardenio, or, The Second Maiden's Tragedy*, Glenbridge Publishing, 1994.

368. N. W. Bawcutt, ed., *The Control and Censorship of Caroline Drama: The Records of Sir Henry Herbert, Master of the Revels 1623–73*, Oxford University Press, 1996.

369. Jackson, *Studies in Attribution*; Wells and Taylor, *William Shakespeare: A Textual Companion*, p. 135.

370. Mark Dominik, *William Shakespeare and The Birth of Merlin*, Philosophical Library, 1985.

FROM SCRIPT TO STAGE
Interviews by Peter Kirwan

12. Love in *Arden*
'Then with thy lips seal up this new-made match' (8.150)
Alice Arden (Hedydd Dylan) and her lover Mosby (Daniel Llewelyn-Williams) in Terry Hands' 2010 production of
Arden of Faversham for Clwyd Theatr Cymru. Designer Martyn Bainbridge. Nobby Clark © Clwyd Theatr Cymru

TERRY HANDS ON DIRECTING *ARDEN OF FAVERSHAM*

Terry Hands studied at the University of Birmingham and the Royal Academy of Dramatic Art. In 1964 he established the Liverpool Everyman Theatre. He became joint Artistic Director of the Royal Shakespeare Company with Trevor Nunn in 1978, and was sole Artistic Director from 1986 to 1991. In 1997 he became Artistic Director and Chief Executive of Clwyd Theatr Cymru. He has directed *Arden of Faversham* three times: for the RSC in 1982, for Schauspielhaus Zürich in 1992 and for Clwyd Theatr Cymru in 2010, the last of which he discusses here.

How important (if at all) is the question of authorship to you as a director?

TH: As a director authorship is rarely of any importance. Occasionally it can point to familiar themes or background influences of family, education or society but, in general, the play itself provides all relevant information.

The play appeals throughout to 'simple truth', and is based on chronicles. Did the factual story of Arden (insofar as we can trust the sources) influence your production? Is it the 'naked tragedy' that Franklin's Epilogue claims?

TH: Franklin gives the usual apologies: 'Gentlemen, we hope you'll pardon this naked tragedy, / Wherein no filed points are foisted in / To make it gracious to the ear or eye'. For once the Epilogue is pretty accurate. A play about greedy peasants is unlikely to be refined. On the other hand the psychosexual relationships between Arden, Alice, Mosby are very complex. The 'simple truth' of the chronicle is only of value in emphasizing where the author has diverged.

The play is usually described as 'domestic tragedy' but also sometimes as 'black comedy'. How did you approach the task of balancing the comic elements with the more serious? Is there a point where the play stops being funny?

TH: The play is both 'domestic tragedy' and black comedy. There is no 'court', no 'wit', no aristocracy (save Cheyne – a minor Lord) and it is also very funny. Elizabethan drama uniquely favours the tragi-comedy. Only an Elizabethan dramatist would put a fool into *King Lear*, for instance, or a death threat into *The Merchant of Venice*. If metaphysical poetry was 'heterogeneous ideas yoked with violence together' then Elizabethan theatre was heterogeneous genres.

Related to this, how did you approach the several aborted and unsuccessful murder plots? Do they provoke genuine tension, or should an audience be expecting them to fail?

TH: Each murder attempt is a masterpiece of comic invention. Tension is built, held and exploded, whether 'amateur', as in the case of Alice, Mosby and Clarke, or professionally incompetent, as in the case of Black Will and Shakebag. But through it all the author constantly reminds us that our subject is murder, not a game. He adds the eerie Ferryman, Reede's curse, the hallucinatory appearance of Alice and Mosby in each other's arms, dreams. By the time Arden is really killed the audience is shocked. The author is adept at creating surprise – in this case, by finally willing the public into believing the deed will never happen.

How sympathetic is Arden? Both in relation to his cuckoldry and to his activities as landowner, his own culpability and ethics are relatively unfixed. How did your production treat him?

TH: Arden himself is a peasant made rich through hard work and ruthless self-interest. He is 'greedy gaping still for gain'. A successful bully. But he does love Alice. His suffering is real and his attempts to please her

13. Conspiracy in *Arden*
'I have vowed my Master Arden's death' (3.170)
Shakebag (Dyrfig Morris), Greene (Wayne Chater), Michael (Steven Meo) and Black Will (Brendan Routh) in Terry
Hands' 2010 production at Clwyd Theatr Cymru. Nobby Clark © Clwyd Theatr Cymru

very moving. As the Americans might say, he is pussy-whipped. I use a coarse term to describe a coarse play. The characters have their feet in the mud and their eyes not on the stars, as with Shakespeare, but on wealth. We played him as uxurious and doting. There is a kind of hyperactive madness that informs the end of the play, an abandonment of reason. It overwhelms Alice and especially Arden.

The play's title page instructs us to look upon Alice as 'disloyal and wanton', 'a wicked woman'. What options did you and the actor experiment with for her presentation? Can she be a sympathetic character?

TH: Alice is, as the title page tells us, a disloyal and wanton wife, a wicked woman. She is a murderess. If we regard simply her attempts to kill Arden there can be no sympathy nor even interest. Her actions are criminal and cruel. What makes the character fascinating is her evident allure, and the sexual drive behind her behaviour.

Unlike pretty well every other character in the play Alice is not peasant based. She is a gentlewoman. Greene is shocked to hear that Arden uses her unkindly. 'Respects he not your birth,/ Your honourable friends, nor what you brought?/ Why, all Kent knows your parentage and what you are.' She is half her workaholic husband's age and bored. Unquestionably she lusts after Mosby but she loves Arden.

The exploration of this complex, sometimes perverse, sometimes childish triangle is unique in Elizabethan literature. It prefigures Middleton's Beatrice-Joanna in *The Changeling* and carries elements of the Henry/ Margaret relationship in *Henry VI Part 2.* As Margaret mourns over the head of her lover Suffolk Henry, her husband, observes sadly: 'I fear me, love, if that I had been dead, / Thou wouldst not have mourned so much for me.' To which she replies: 'No, my love, I should not mourn, but die for thee.' The author of *Arden of Faversham* makes this father/daughter/husband/wife syndrome the psychoanalytic centre of his play. Not just what happened but how and why. He details the games and role-playing, the excitement and reversals. It is not simply 'the unsatiable desire of filthy lust'.

The domestic hierarchies of the play are quite richly drawn, and your production gave a good deal of prominence to Michael in particular (especially in the night-time bungled murder attempt). What is the role of the lower-status characters like Michael and Susan?

TH: The other characters serve mainly to facilitate the structural mechanics of the play. Susan and Michael, the domestics, are more intimately involved with the main triangle. Susan, Mosby's sister, is a pawn offered variously to promote Alice and Mosby. She is genuinely innocent, even simple, and offers a clear contrast to Alice's confused machinations. Michael is more central. He echoes the play's themes of greed and murder: 'For I will rid mine elder brother away:/ And then the farm of Bolton is mine own.' He wants Susan and more importantly he bridges the world of Black Will and Alice. He also heightens the tension as a frightened onlooker to several of the murder attempts. His soliloquies are crucial to the audience's understanding of the real issues and emotions underpinning the hectic fantasies of Arden, Alice and Mosby.

There are an extraordinary number of financial transactions going on in the play, both to do with land and in blood money. There's also an economy of 'love', at least in the justifications made by several characters for their actions. What were the driving forces in your production? Is there space for love within the play?

TH: The love interests of the play are either lustful or financially motivated. Love as empathy, caring or compassion is entirely absent. Only Arden loves unwisely and too well – but then he is both cuckold and wittol.

Critics have pointed out several logical discrepancies in the play, such as Greene's letter to Alice reporting events that happened after it was written; and Michael recognizing Black Will despite never having met him. Did you feel the need to address these in performance?

TH: The play is tightly written and contains only one logical discrepancy – Greene's letter to Alice. In performance the moment passes unremarked. Because we are party to the incidents, we naturally assume they have been recorded. Michael has not previously met Black Will but he has heard of him. Black Will, like the Kray twins, is notorious. Michael's sudden recognition that he is in the presence of the great man is good writing. A boy's excitement at meeting a celebrity hero.

The bulk of the play builds towards Arden's murder. How does the play change following the act itself? What are the challenges of the final few scenes of cover-up, capture and repentance?

TH: The play runs one hour and fifty minutes without an interval. With Arden's death, about ten minutes from the end, the play returns from frenzied speculation to panic stricken reality. Where to put the body, how to clean up, how to escape discovery. Like children, Alice and Mosby have not thought beyond the deed itself. Inevitably they are apprehended and the Epilogue solemnly records their final words and exhaustion. Musically the play is superbly orchestrated. Visually, in an all-white world of snow, the characters are shown as they really are: children whose fevered games have gone too far.

Given the apparently didactic purpose of the play as voiced by the title page, what did you make of the numerous ambiguities – Bradshaw's condemnation, the disappearance of Clarke, the curse of Dick Reede? What is the play expecting of its audience?

TH: Given the commercial puff of the title page the author is surprisingly liberal in his inclusion of final details in the Epilogue. Bradshaw is innocent and wronged, Clarke dispensable, Michael in love with Susan and Alice in love with Arden. Was it just a *crime passionnel* or an other-worldly justice operating through Reede's curse? The author sets out to entertain his audience – which I would define as to interest, to instruct and occasionally to amuse. He succeeds.

And finally, do you have an opinion on whether Shakespeare was involved in this play?

TH: I cannot see any evidence of Shakespeare in any part of the play, and nor could three different casts of experienced actors. The singularity of purpose, the tightly-associated sub-plots, the peasant society, indeed the major theme, murder, are all unShakespearean. So too the role-playing and toying with the audience.

14. Murder in *Arden*

'See, Mistress Arden, where your husband lies.' (16.1)

Susan (Cathy Finlay) and Alice (Jenny Agutter, kneeling) over the body of Arden (Bruce Purchase) in Terry Hands' 1982 RSC production at The Other Place, Stratford-upon-Avon. Reg Wilson © Royal Shakespeare Company

Scene 8 has been quoted as demonstrating the possibility of collaboration. It is a lover's quarrel. Such rows either lead to sex, or preclude it (the slammed bedroom door) or are, as in this case, the act of sex itself. I can't find anything similar in Shakespeare and the destruction of the prayer-book is more daring than even Marlowe's burning of the Qu'ran in *Tamburlaine*.

Why can we not celebrate a remarkable play by a remarkable author who, to our loss, and for whatever reason, wrote nothing else?

JAMES WALLACE ON DIRECTING *LOCRINE*

James Wallace is an actor and director, and trained at Central School of Speech and Drama. He became involved with Shakespeare's Globe's 'Read Not Dead' project in 1998, and in the fifteen years since has acted in or directed over seventy plays by Shakespeare's contemporaries. He has written about the experience in *Shakespeare's Globe: A Theatrical Experiment*, edited by Christie Carson and Farah Karim-Cooper (Cambridge, 2008).

Here, James discusses his 1999 staging of *Locrine* as part of Shakespeare's Globe's 'Read Not Dead' series.

How important is the question of authorship to you as a director?

JW: When we staged *Locrine* back in 1999, we didn't think that it was by Shakespeare, but even a hint that he might have been somehow involved of course added a bit of interest, a bit of curiosity. The Read Not Dead project is designed to stage all of the plays by Shakespeare's contemporaries, so my job was just to put the play on, regardless of authorship. So I wasn't primarily interested in the play because it's by 'W.S.', but because it's part of early modern drama.

Could you say a little about the context of Read Not Dead, in which *Locrine* happened?

JW: Shakespeare's Globe initiated the Read Not Dead project to give readings to all of the surviving professional plays from the opening of The Theatre in 1576 to the closure of all the theatres in 1642. The main purpose is to stick all of these plays up on their feet and to give them a chance to live in front of an audience, otherwise, for the most part, they'd never be done. I've learned a lot doing it; it helps to see a bigger picture, to stop seeing Shakespeare as an isolated genius, to understand that he was part of a big conversation that was going on between writers, actors, and audiences, and the general culture of the time. I hope my understanding of Shakespeare is better for seeing him in that context. We rehearse the play in a day, with professional actors, from 10 a.m., and put it on at 3 p.m. to a mixed audience of academics, students, other actors and directors, and members of the public.

Locrine was performed in the old Globe Education building in Bear Gardens. It had central double doors, two side doors, the side walls slightly angled out towards the audience, steps up either side, and a very small stage with a short rail around the front, and a gallery along the top – the basics of an indoor Elizabethan-Jacobean stage, and very intimate. The stage lighting was very simple, just three spotlights and one general flood. The audience were lit as well as the stage, so the actors were constantly aware of them, but the space concentrated things onto the actors and the words. We would use entrances and exits rather than sitting the whole cast on stage throughout, so that you could see how many people were supposed to be on stage at any one time, and we used very basic props.

Read Not Deads are script in hand, so the performances feel quite improvised. The actors have to make bold, clear choices, just go on stage and do it, and try to act in the moment. Luckily, the audiences are very smart, very forgiving! If you get things right they're very appreciative, if you mess things up they will laugh and be very appreciative of that too, so they really would be 'piecing out our imperfections'. I've just been listening to the recording of it and there are so many places where words are transposed, mixed up, spoonerisms (some of which are quite funny), some lines missed out, actors stumbling over words – it's very rough. We only had a budget of £50 for props or bits of costume, so it was definitely 'poor' theatre, but done with the spirit of everybody just trying to give something to the Globe project, make the play live in the moment, and see what would happen.

One of the immediate problems for a small-scale production of this play is its classical framework with Chorus and dumb shows. Did you stage those?

JW: I did stage them. In the script it's clear that the dumb shows would happen and then Até would speak. I made the choice to combine them, so while Até spoke, for the first half of those speeches the dumb show was played out by actors in masks. I was very lucky to have two musicians from the Globe playing early modern instruments. They were great, and really added an epic quality to it, a slightly old-fashioned feel. Certainly Até introducing the drama adds a layer of theatricality to it; you always know you're being presented with a play. The actress that I cast as Até, Lisa Gornick, has a very striking face, like a more angular Bette Davis (if she'll forgive the comparison), with big staring eyes, and she was dressed all in black. I wanted Até to be severe, to create some kind of frisson of impending doom. The acting out of the dumbshows had its limits – the crocodile and the snake were a rubber crocodile and a rubber snake – but the audience kind of forgave that, they knew we were marking the space rather than presenting it as it would have originally been done. I also left Ate on for a bit longer sometimes. After her first speech she stayed on stage observing the scene. I had placed Brutus' bed within the 'withdrawal space' created by the gallery jutting out, supported by two small columns, over the central doors. There were red curtains hung there, which Até drew around Brutus when he died.

Brutus is unusual in the early modern drama as a major role who dies in the opening scene! How significant was he to your production?

JW: We doubled him with Oliver, I think. I remember watching that beginning scene with Brutus and thinking that it's very slow dramatically. He has these long 'epic' speeches that try to give themselves some kind of power through the invocation of mythical names, and with the slow plod of the verse and rather obvious rhetorical devices it was quite a tough beginning.

Do the classical allusions pose a problem for a modern audience?

JW: Probably, but I think the biggest issue is just that they are very long speeches; it's not dramatic action, or cause and effect psychology. We did cut Até's long Latin speech! I suppose four hundred years ago there must have been a pleasure in hearing these strange names spoken on stage. I think it's deliberately written to sound a little old fashioned even then, an epic British genesis myth, like *The Aeneid,* that traces our history back to Troy. I wonder if that was part of the point of the play, perhaps performed by the Queen's Men, who were propagandizing, mythologizing, creating a sanctioned history, to allow audiences to think of themselves as equal with the Trojans, of London as 'Troynovant'.

Might the tribute to the Queen at the end of the play be seen as part of this as well?

JW: It's pretty blatant, isn't it? And there's the excoriation, the insulting of foreign invaders too. I wonder if there was an enjoyment of the evocation of these mystical, mythical, ancient British names, which perhaps can have a dramatic and epic effect precisely because you don't quite recognize or get them. It adds to the mystery. People would be used to that in church, hearing things they didn't quite understand, names they weren't familiar with, but which were delivered with godly seriousness. We see it also in *Henry IV Part 2,* where Pistol loves quoting names and classical allusions which he's obviously got from the theatre. It would be interesting to know how far the writer was deliberately coining words for the audience's delight, or whether they were deliberately antiquated. If you listen to the recording in the Globe's archives, it's slightly like stepping back in time. The older actors are very declamatory. Sometimes it's tedious, sometimes it's fun. There's a lot of rhetorical power in the play, and if we had been better at playing the rhetoric, I think parts of the play could be quite exciting to listen to – if you've got some experience in tub-thumping, it's there to be thumped.

Despite the long speeches, the play is also very driven by plot.

JW: It's very succinct. The first half ran an hour and ten minutes, the second fifty minutes, so 'two hours' traffic'. There's very little fat on it, despite the long opening speeches. It doesn't feel like someone swimming down from university and just writing a play with little experience of the professional stage. It's very theatrical, very honed. It wouldn't have been 'newly set forth, overseen and corrected' if it didn't have a performance history, so rough edges would have been knocked off in that.

How did you stage the ghosts?

JW: I simply asked for a slight whitening of the face. They were gentle ghosts, somewhere in the background, who don't do very much other than observe and torment. I think back to echoes of other plays like *Richard III*, the kind of thing John Marston mocks in *Antonio's Revenge*. I do wonder how much the play is written in a deliberately old style. I was struck reading George Peele's [a candidate for the authorship of *Locrine*] *David and Bethsabe* how much that play seems to be written in deliberately difficult language. The language is not like his other plays, so it seems to me to be a deliberate choice to write something a little archaic, a bit biblical, and the same decisions seems to have been made in *Locrine* to create a more mythic, stately kind of speech.

And yet this stately speech is undercut by a very prominent clown figure, in Strumbo.

JW: I think the clown is written for a professional clown. It's quite an achievement for one writer, if he has written all of this play including the clown's part. It seems like a well-honed routine. It requires an audience's previous knowledge of the clown for him to come in and instantly have that comic rapport, and a clown's previous knowledge of his audience. He provides variety, but he also brings the play's themes home to an amphitheatre audience who would have suffered in times of war. There are similar things in [the anonymous play] *The True Tragedy of Richard III*, which has a wonderful speech where a young page comes on and describes the blood-soaked battlefield, and it's suddenly not about rich aristocratic men asserting their rights, it's about the suffering of ordinary people. Strumbo doesn't have that emotional depth, but I think he's very necessary – in between those long, serious speeches he's a bit of light relief.

The play's stage directions are remarkably full for a play of this era. It's a very visual play – did you have opportunity to play with those visual pictures?

JW: I tried to create as much of a sense of them as I could in a day. With it being a sort of primordial drama, we had weapons, some swords but mostly wooden clubs. The actors were just in black trousers and shirtsleeves. For the dumbshows, we put people in masks. I tried to make the battles stylized, and as simple as possible, because obviously that wasn't something we could choreograph fully in a day. The two armies lined up on either side of the stage, and then, when battle commenced, both sides took one step forwards, shouting out, brandishing their weapons, so that the audience knew there would have been a battle scene there and could imagine what that might have been. We didn't follow the stage directions literally – the actor who played Humber, wouldn't have had his 'hair down' or have had 'bloodied hands'. We tried to use sound a lot. For the ghosts, we used music to underscore their appearances, to create a sense of the eerie.

How did your production handle Locrine? He's a title character but takes a long time to enter fully into the action.

JW: Alan Cox played Locrine and he was fantastic. He chewed up the furniture, as they say, while he was playing it, but he did it very well. The play needs that approach in order to work. Alan's brilliant at following the rhetorical rhythms of the speeches. They require the actor to be able to demand the audience's attention, to build the energy to the climaxes. Alan would have just come on stage and done his stuff, I think. He played the scene, played the audience, followed his instincts. It's important to capture the change in Locrine from Mars to Venus, and he did this very well. I remember there being a strong sexual charge between him and Estrild [Michele Monks]. I deliberately cast a very strong Estrild, very beautiful, very forceful, a no-nonsense, feminist kind of woman, to catch her nobility and her strength of the character.

Is Estrild a villain? There are some similarities to Tamora in *Titus Andronicus*, but her 'crimes' are of a very different nature.

JW: Certainly she encourages Humber in the early scenes. Her lament when she's captured maintains her dignity within that situation. Her choice to then become Locrine's lover is very quick, but it's understandable on a political level that if you've lost one king as a husband you'll take another on. That scene has echoes of *Richard III*. It seems a bit harsh to a modern audience that Locrine and Estrild die, but I suppose they have to die for their sins. I remember our audience had a sympathy for their love, and for Locrine's love of her. Even though it's wrong, betraying his wife, he does genuinely love Estrild. He's immediately struck by her beauty, strength, dignity, loyalty, and he wants her. It's interesting how the language becomes like John Lyly's at this point. Romantic desire and sex are attractive on the stage, sex is attractive to us in the audience, and it's difficult to judge it on an objective, moral level when it's so effective dramatically.

Does the final death, of the innocent daughter, complicate these judgements further?

JW: Yes, hers is an innocent death. For the drownings we used confetti, little dark-blue tissue-paper squares which were thrown up into the air and walked through as they fell, which gave the deaths a kind of poetry. The actress who played Sabren [Liza Hayden] was much shorter than anyone else on stage, which lent an innocence, a vulnerability to her, which helped her death work. It had a seriousness and a delicacy to it. And there's a smartness to the ending, as you realize that you are being given the supposed reason for the naming of the River Severn, a geographical etymology. However, the ending seems perfunctory, it just seems to happen. It doesn't feel particularly earned. It's as if it's just the closing of another chapter, a presentation of a mythical fact as it happened.

Do you think there is any Shakespeare in it?

JW: Maybe. If there are any lines, then they might be found in Hubba and Humber's speeches, some of which seem to me to be more Shakespearean than the rest. If (a big if) a young Shakespeare was in it, he would have been unlikely to have played any of the old characters, wouldn't have been Locrine. He could be William, or Hubba or Thrasimachus, possibly Albanact, or just a captain, but one of the younger men. If he was playing Hubba he might have wanted to buff up the lines in his own scenes!

We like to think that genius springs forth fully formed, but there's something in the idea that Shakespeare in his youth, his apprenticeship, might have got a bit lost in rhetoric and the supposed dramatic power of classical names, and that only in subsequent plays could he really start working on psychological depth. It's possible that some of this could be juvenilia, and that he realized very quickly what was missing. But the thing is, overall, it's really not very good, so I don't suppose many people would want to claim it for Shakespeare. Perhaps he might have just been responsible for tidying up someone else's work.

From the whole Read Not Dead project, we've realized how collaborative early modern drama was. We've been reminded how much Shakespeare's plays were written in collaboration, with Middleton and Fletcher and Marlowe and Peele, in *Pericles* with George Wilkins, in *Thomas More* with Dekker and Heywood and Munday; and how completely collaborative these plays are – the actors are adapting their parts to themselves, cutting lines, changing lines, repeating lines to suit themselves. The plays are written for specific actors and their tics or demands or vocal skills or styles. And the whole thing is commercial and in both collaboration and competition with itself, so it's all part of a big conversation.

Would you do much different with it if you had the chance to revisit it?

JW: Yes. It was only the second reading I'd staged. I hope that we'd have more confidence with it, with the language, and that we'd play it faster. It would work better if the rhetoric had been followed more strongly than we often did, because, in a way, that's its main driver, and it then directs itself. It's not the greatest poetry in the world, but in terms of the rousing speeches, there's some more fun to be had with the ranting and raving. It's very much material for actors with a real feel for the rhetoric, and a full production could have a field day with that.

CAROLINE FABER AND DAVID RINTOUL ON PLAYING IN *EDWARD III*

Caroline Faber is a stage and screen actress whose Shakespeare roles include Lady Capulet and Goneril (both for Headlong Theatre) and the Countess in *Edward III* and Emilia in *The Malcontent* as part of the RSC's award-winning Jacobethan season. Her television credits include *Merlin*, *Disconnected*, *Foyle's War* and others.

David Rintoul studied at Edinburgh University and then went on a scholarship to RADA. He has been an actor for over forty years, playing leading parts on film, television, radio and theatre, including spells with the National Theatre, Shakespeare's Globe and the Royal Shakespeare Company.

David and Caroline talk here about their roles in Anthony Clark's 2002 production of *Edward III* for the RSC in Stratford-upon-Avon and London.

How important (if at all) is the question of authorship to you as an actor?

DR: It's fascinating, yes, I think it's interesting. It's difficult to tell – when I've been in dual authorship plays such as *The Changeling*, I found it very difficult there to tell which was Middleton, which was Rowley, and so on. *Edward III* is fascinating. I do think it could be an entire piece of revised Shakespeare juvenilia.

CF: In the case of Edward III it was exciting to think that parts of it might be written by Shakespeare, that you were perhaps unearthing undiscovered treasure. It certainly felt that parts of the play were written by someone who had a great deal of depth and humanity and other parts were more workmanlike. I like the idea though that Shakespeare possibly wrote it with a contemporary of his, that it was a young Shakespeare testing his dramatic prowess in a few scenes (perhaps the Countess scenes). With this production, doing it at the RSC and in Stratford it felt somehow momentous and magical that it 'might be' Shakespeare. But it was more important that we made the play live and exhilarating for an audience, whoever the writer or writers may be. Before the audition, working on the Countess scenes I remember thinking they felt vivid and lively and full of the complexity of Isabella's scenes in *Measure for Measure*. It seemed to just jump off the page and I found I had an immediate connection to the Countess. Her strength, wit, cleverness and moral certitude thrilled me.

15. King Edward III tries to seduce the Countess
'Didst thou not swear to give me what I would?' (2.1.246)
Edward III (David Rintoul) propositions the Countess of Salisbury (Caroline Faber) in Anthony Clark's 2002 RSC
production at the Swan Theatre, Stratford-upon-Avon. Malcolm Davies Collection © Shakespeare Birthplace Trust

The production coincided with the first publication of the play in a major Shakespeare series, and many media responses looked forward to the opportunity to 'test' the attribution in performance. Did you feel a responsibility in this regard?

CF: In many ways I felt excited to 'test' this attribution myself, to see if in performance it felt to myself, other company members and indeed the audience, like Shakespeare. There is a malleability, shape-shifting quality to many Shakespearean characters, I think. They can take lots of messing around with, deconstructing, endless reinterpretations, can be set in different milieu, periods, etc. *Edward III* felt in lots of ways like a history play with this extraordinary warped love story at the centre of it, so it didn't feel it needed to be relocated in another time. I also think that the beauty of doing this old play that had so rarely been performed was that it felt like you were creating the characters for the very first time, that the audience didn't know the fate of the Countess as they know the fate of Lady Macbeth. You didn't have the pressure of the shadow of another previous interpretation looming large before you, there was no great theatrical antecedent. This was luxurious and a privilege really, because it's rare, at the RSC, that you get to create a Shakepearean heroine for the first time.

DR: The production had an excitement about it because the RSC very cheekily said it's by Shakespeare, so it got that conversation going. There was a buzz about it that, to be honest, perhaps the play itself didn't fully merit. But it was quite a sexy show to do because of all the interest. The pressure wasn't to make it 'Shakespearean' but to make a good job of it. And we had a very strong company that year for the 'Jacobethan' season. The play fitted the Swan. There are quite a lot of two-handers: the Countess scenes, the Lodowick scenes, which tend to be better than the large public scenes.

Do you have an opinion on whether Shakespeare was involved in this play?

DR: The received opinion, which is probably sensible, is that Shakespeare had a hand in the Countess scenes but not much else elsewhere; then maybe. But if you were to date it as some scholars do around the time of *A Midsummer Night's Dream*, it's a fairly low level of sophistication in construction. The language is quite beautiful at times, though also quite clunky. It's a bit jazzier than Marlowe, but not as jazzy as Shakespeare. But possibly early Shakespeare. I feel that if it had a later date, the oration would be different, that the Countess scenes, for example, would be stronger and stand out even more. I don't know.

CF: I don't know whether Shakespeare wrote parts of this play, but lots of people who saw it certainly felt that he did write parts of it. To me it felt that the fervour and intensity of the Countess scenes could be the hand of Shakespeare. I felt that although we had endeavoured to play it straight the scenes could take a lot of 'play' within them. I found it easy to create it afresh every night because it felt substantial and fully rounded and intriguing. The Countess scenes were psychologically complex and this felt like Shakespeare to me, it certainly wasn't Marlowe! Some nights I felt I got on it and it just played itself and other nights I would have to circumnavigate my way cleverly around it; it was always a rollercoaster and always challenging to play.

What were your director's intentions for the overall feel of the production?

CF: I liked that Tony Clark, the director, wanted to keep it simple, to let the play sing through its words rather than do a huge directorial flourish on it. This allowed the audience to judge for itself how like Shakespeare it felt. It felt intrinsically medieval and I know Tony Clark wanted to play up to this with an almost fairytale-like design, the first image of the Countess was almost Rapunzel-like. I was sat on a high chair looking down on the Scots in a white dress with long Pre-Raphaelite tresses.

DR: The production came together at quite short notice following the departure of a previous director, so Tony Clark and I came to it with *tabula rasa*. The way I played and imagined Edward – the central figure who unifies the different aspects of the play – was a very driven obsessive man who focused that obsession and could quite easily shift the obsession to something else if it's not working out that way. Tony had two of us, the French King and I, atop tennis umpires' ladders, watching during the war scenes. I thought that's fair enough, but I thought he was a fighter, and I daubed my face with some fake blood, which someone pointed out made me look like Gorbachev, to say that he is a warrior.

But it's not just a play about warfare, as central to the second half you have the great moral dilemma of the son. Is it just brutishness that says just let him fight in the vanguard, the most violent part of the battle, and let him get on with it? To modern sensibilities that's bad parenting! But I imagined the parallel with a senior RAF officer in World War II whose son flies Spitfires. Does he pull the son out of the action? Of course not, he lets him get on with it, and that's the honourable thing for the boy to do, that's what he has to do. The play is unified by this character's bullishness. Thump Scots – fail; try to hump Countess – fail; try to thump French – main plot of play. Let's thump them.

Critics often remark on the relative detachment of the 'Countess' scenes from the rest of the play. Did you have an impression of your scenes linking to the wider arcs of the play? The Countess never shares the stage with her husband, who appears later in the play – was the connection necessary?

CF: The Countess scenes certainly felt different from the rest of the play, an interlude from the battles, a moment of retreat, but the scenes themselves became a battle between the Countess and the King, a battle to possess her in his case and to hold onto her virtue in hers. It felt like a play within the play almost, but somehow its emotional heart too. We had a short rehearsal period so not enough time to explore the relationship between the Countess and her husband with improvisation for example, although the marriage, its vows and her love for him were key to her ability to defy and counterattack the King in his relentless pursuit of her. I thought a lot in rehearsals about her brilliantly vehement loyalty to her husband and felt this was really why she was able to stand up to the King, because her relationship with her husband was so important to her and something she would never willingly betray.

DR: There is a line towards the end of the play after Salisbury comes back on, and the king replies to whatever Salisbury says, in the Queen's presence 'We thank thee for thy service, valiant earl, / Challenge our favour for we owe it thee.' Saying it in the presence of the Queen, who may well know about the attempted affair, and to Salisbury who may know about it – it implies, you know what I'm talking about, I know what I'm talking about, my wife knows what I'm talking about. It's very interesting to play it that way. As a king he owes Salisbury who's been fighting, but it's interesting to play it the other way. I think we *just* make the connection between Salisbury and his wife, even though we never see them on stage together, and the audience got it without us needing to flag it in an obvious way.

How did you approach the character of the Countess?

CF: I saw her as a kind of warrior of virtue and loyalty, so besieged or not she stood firm against assaults from all quarters, whether imprisoned in her castle by the Scots or cornered by the King. She is wily enough to use her wit to mock the Scots when they threaten to possess her. She overhears a conversation when they betray their weaknesses and uses them against them, refusing to be a 'spoil' of war. 'After the French ambassador, my liege, / And tell him that you dare not ride to York: / Excuse it that your bonny horse is lame.' I loved that she uses her wit and intelligence to avoid being raped by a King. They can lock her up physically but mentally she is always free, her intelligence never besieged. She rises to the occasion and shines most brightly in the moments when she is most threatened.

What kind of man is Edward in the Countess scenes?

DR: Crudely, he's a hunter of men and a hunter of women, and when he fails to thump the Scots because the Scots bugger off, there's this other splendid creature to conquer as it were. He's an obsessive, I think, thrown into a terrific moral quandary by his lust. Loyalty comes up an awful lot in the play. You're a loyal subject, your duty is to make the King happy, so sleep with me. He even tries to force the father to pimp for said daughter. But the questions of allegiance, loyalty, pulling rank, all of those are very interesting in the play.

Related to the latter, was there a mutual attraction between the two? What is at stake in Edward's pursuit of the Countess?

CF: I think she is attracted to him, that he has the power to free her from the Scots, that he is a king and a handsome one at that; her speech when she persuades him to stay has a sexual undertone but I think she is using her charm to thank him really in the only way she knows how, with honesty and openness and intelligence, and that she never intended it to go as far as it does. She wants to be the most brilliant hostess and wants to welcome him in the proper way. We get a sense that she is unsure quite how to do this before he arrives, when she says 'How may I entertain his majesty, / To show my duty and his dignity?' She wants to do the right thing but is naturally a little intimidated at first that she is entertaining a king.

Of course she finds him bright and articulate and a welcome relief from the barbarous Scots and her father but she knows it's an attraction that must have its boundaries. It is the King that gets carried away, I think she loves her husband and will not risk that for a brief encounter, even with a king. Honour and virtue are more important to her and when he threatens to risk both their marriages for the fulfilment of sexual desire, she finds that unattractive and amoral.

DR: Caroline, Tony and I talked a lot about whether she is just repulsed by this man and his advances, or is the attraction in fact mutual, which I was very much trying to encourage, because I think that makes the scenes very much stronger, so she is resisting herself as well as him. And Edward is fighting the attraction too, so they're both fighting it. He doesn't fight it that strongly, but I think you do have a sense of him, however far back, as a Christian king whose morality comes for nothing, by default. From the English point of view the morality is meant to be part of his persona, and they're judging him.

There is a certain amount of comedy in the Countess scenes, but also some potentially distressing moments. Did the scenes need some levity?

DR: I would say it is a rather humorous play, and we did get laughs out of it, especially the Lodowick scene, which was always extremely funny. But it's a tricky old play and a tricky old character, because he's definitely a warrior king, he's a bit of a thug and very decisive. In the first scene when he knows the Scots are up in arms he completely changes plan, decides tasks, etc. He's a warrior king, and then there's this extraordinary poetic outburst immediately after he sees the Countess, which already seems to be at odds with his military focus.

CF: The comedy comes from the Countess's quick-wittedness, her ability to overcome any vulnerabilities she may feel with wordplay and humour; even when the situation becomes dark and threatening she finds the strength to use words and her morality to fight her corner. I always played the scene straight and never for comedy though. I think she finds herself in a situation where she has to use her depth and integrity to get herself out of something she will possibly regret her entire life, so it required much levity and truthful playing.

There are very serious aspects to this scene: the main character attempting to force a woman into sleeping with him, and the father having to become complicit in that seduction. How did you handle these aspects?

CF: I felt that the Countess was incredibly close to her father, that he taught her much of her ways of perceiving the world and that her morality comes from him. He tells her he is not speaking as himself when he broaches the subject of her surrendering to Edward: 'I am not Warwick as thou thinkst I am, / But an attorney from the court of hell'. Nonetheless, I think it is incredibly painful to hear these words from his mouth and that he has been unable to persuade the King otherwise, but she then shows him that she will not do it and this confirms how he really feels about the situation. I think she knows he has been put in an appalling situation and that it is up to her to change it by getting herself out of it. By the end of the scene they are both united against the King's desires and this makes her subsequent defiance in the scene a little easier.

DR: I didn't worry too much about sympathy for the King – if he comes off unsympathetic, so be it. Around the time of the Armada, there were a lot of fairly core presumptions to be attacked and exploited. How much our sensibility on decisive/thuggish kings differs from Elizabethan sensibilities on decisive/thuggish kings I don't know! Maybe they would see such a man as more admirable than we. He did win great English victories, his son certainly did as well. With his father being Edward II, a very indecisive man who met a very sticky end, he's determined not to go down that road.

How prepared is the Countess to kill herself? Do you see connections to Shakespeare's other self-willed women (assuming he wrote the scene)?

CF: I think she would kill herself for her beliefs, that her chastity belt of knives is an embodiment of how strongly she feels about defending her honour, but I think in her heart she hopes that the King will be moved by her words. I felt the stakes had to be that high, in order for the drama of the scene to work and the King's volte-face to have true impact.

Does Edward achieve any kind of satisfaction by the play's end?

DR: The final line is quite ludicrous: 'three kings, two princes, and a queen', which is amusingly clunky. I suppose he is, in the end, but you kind of feel him slightly fading back out of focus in the writing. He's merciful to the burghers, but only at the Queen's prompting, I think he's not particularly bothered. What the author wants us to think of the man is interesting, because I think we see here Shakespeare the ironist. The questioning of Edward III's behaviour is good, with King David brought on simply for humiliation (presumably a decision that would have angered James). It's not a simply patriotic play.

MICHAEL BOYD ON DIRECTING *THE SPANISH TRAGEDY*

Michael Boyd was appointed Artistic Director of the Royal Shakespeare Company in 2002, and over the next ten years he oversaw the transformation and rebuilding of the Royal Shakespeare Theatre, the successful staging of the Complete Works and World Shakespeare Festivals (2006–07 and 2012), the RSC's New York Residency in 2011 and *Matilda the Musical* in Stratford and the West End of London. His own productions at the RSC included the award-winning History Cycles of 2001–02 and 2006–08. He was a trainee director at the Malaya Bronnaya Theatre in Moscow and in 1985 was the founding Artistic Director of the Tron Theatre, Glasgow, which he ran for eleven years. He talks here about his 1997 RSC production of *The Spanish Tragedy* at the Swan Theatre, The Barbican and on tour.

What drew you, as a director, to *The Spanish Tragedy*?

MB: It read like a very angry play. I found myself outraged at the casual violence and abuse of power at court, and thought I might be able to pass on some of the raw impact of that to the audience.

The play explores the same wild, transgressive cruelty as Tarantino and contemporary exploitation movies. It makes you giddy with grief and horror, desecrates the vocabulary and grammar of morality plays and courtly love, and provokes a rictus grin in the face of humanity so reduced. The murderous Babel of the play within the play, Hieronimo's grotesque self-mutilation, and the chilling final lines, recall the many hells of his near namesake Bosch.

Three aspects of the play struck me as carrying it beyond the confines of sensationalist entertainment:

- The play seemed to have a purpose, conscious or unconscious, beyond the titillation of spectacular violence, to incite dissent. Such vividly articulated anger and outrage would be dangerous on the public stage, and inevitably spill into the political discourse of a deeply divided England. If a Knight Marshall cannot receive justice, how can we arm ourselves against tyranny?

- The forensic rigour of Kyd's portrait of a human subjected to insupportable stress may offer little sentimental comfort, but it arms the audience to fight their own worst fears. (It also makes it more possible for *Lear* and *Endgame* to be written.)
- Although no alternative to revenge is offered within the action of *The Spanish Tragedy*, the absurd, crazed nature of Hieronimo's retribution, and the despairing, 'endless tragedy' prescribed at the end of the play, surely dramatizes the inadequacy of Revenge as a response to evil or injustice. Kyd's very shredding of the moral map paradoxically elicits a deeply moral and compassionate reaction.

From a theatrical point of view I could also see fascinating insights into *Hamlet*, and great parts for favourite actors like Peter Wight (Hieronimo), Siobhan Redmond (Bel-imperia), Robert Glenister (Lorenzo) and Darrell D'Silva (Balthazar). I was initially concerned at the static and creaky nature of the Revenge/Don Andrea framing device, but quickly became excited by the idea of Revenge as a masked figure, revealed to be Hieronimo as the self-consuming cycle of revenge recommenced, in our production, at the close of the evening.

16. Hieronimo and the hanged Horatio
'Alas, it is Horatio, my sweet son!' (2.5.14)
Hieronimo (Peter Wight) discovers the body of Horatio (Tristan Sturrock) in Michael Boyd's 1997 RSC production at
the Swan Theatre, Stratford-upon-Avon. Malcolm Davies Collection © Shakespeare Birthplace Trust

How do the 1602 additions affect the play on the stage? How did you decide whether or not to incorporate them in your performance text? Most editions continue to choose to print them separately, implicitly preferring the unity of the earlier version.

MB: The additions are all in themselves extremely effective and share an ease of writing, a vivid, dense simplicity and a natural flow. They do feel like the work of Shakespeare in his maturity. They don't, however, serve the natural and necessary momentum of the play. They often duplicate and expand on the mood and action of the original, and proved hard to incorporate in rehearsal. I was only able to include the unmissable episode with the painter, Don Bazardo, by stealing space from the petitioner scene. By replacing the formulaic 'senex' Don Bazulto with the far more colourful painter, I was also able to avoid a duplication of grieving father parallels which neither Kyd nor the author of the additions could possibly have intended.

The play is dominated by Hieronimo, who is implicated in all the additions. Addition IV in particular extends the sequence of his 'madness'. How did you and your actor (Peter Wight) approach the character?

MB: On the one hand, Peter Wight is and was a robust, intelligent, and utterly humane performer (who has also for instance made terrific naturalistic work with Mike Leigh on screen) and Hieronimo is the admired, respected, and effective Knight Marshal of the Royal Court: Shakespeare's Humphrey of Gloucester, for instance, owes a debt to Hieronimo's painstaking concern for petitions from the common people. It was important for us and for Kyd to present a strong hero; a credible figure at court who had the resources to secure justice by fair means in a just society.

On the other hand, Peter and I had worked on many projects together, including our dramatization of Gogol's absurd nightmare, *The Nose*, and we knew that we shared a strong understanding of the dark comedy that can result from humanity cracking under pressure, from madness. The true meaning of Chekhov's 'laughter through tears' is born out of Gogol, and that's what we sought in our rehearsal room for *A Spanish Tragedy*.

Hieronimo's commissioning of the impossible painting from Don Bazardo in Addition IV is at once a compassionate study in obsession, an inspiration for the mock trial scene in *Lear*, and a glorious self-aware hymn to the power of theatre as an art form superior to painting.

What is the tone of Hieronimo's long speeches (such as Addition III) in performance? These are not always soliloquies, but often cut across other characters entirely. Does he need extra speeches?

MB: We loved Addition III and were sad to cut it at a late stage of rehearsal. We felt it was an exquisite expansion on what the audience already knew, and that it did not move the action forward with the ferocious and relentless economy of the base text. That said, the frightening reversals of emotion and sudden contradiction of clear and recognizable positions on fatherhood are telling symptoms of Hieronimo's mind straining to make sense of a world that is not what it seems. You can hear his heart breaking with the sickening clarity of a breaking bone.

Finally, do you have an opinion, as a director, on whether Shakespeare may have written the additional passages?

MB: It would make perfect sense if they were by Shakespeare, and it would also make sense if Shakespeare felt a responsibility towards this play that had such a profound and evident influence on his own work. Directing the play now, in the light of recent scholarship, I would probably try even harder to integrate the 1602 additions into Kyd's original script.

Rereading both [versions] to make notes for this edition, listening consciously for Shakespeare's voice, I nonetheless hear him far more frequently in Kyd's script than in the additions. I hear Margaret, Suffolk, Richard, Anne, Elizabeth, Hal, and Kate in the rhythms of Balthazar and Bel-imperia. I hear the laments of Pyramus and Thisbe in those of Hieronimo for Horatio, and Shakespeare's insidious vocabulary of corruption in Pedringano's celebration of his gold. Titus and Lear and Hamlet all go through Hieronimo like a stick of rock. I hear Lear again, as well as Ophelia, in Isabella's perfect short scene with her maid, and Margaret again in Isabella's dying curses. I even hear Iago in Hieronimo's final resolution of muteness.

In short, I think there's far more Shakespeare in his debts to Kyd, than even in these lines which could indeed be penned by him in person.

ROBERT DELAMERE ON DIRECTING *SIR THOMAS MORE*

Robert Delamere is an award-winning writer and director of theatre, television and opera. From 2008 to 2009 he was Creative Director of Amnesty International (UK). He is Co-Founder and CEO of Digital Theatre, producing quality recordings of major plays for a broader audience. He talks here about his 2005 RSC production of *Thomas More*.

17. Nigel Cooke as Thomas More addressing the rioters
'Look, what you do offend you cry upon' (2.4.57)
Thomas More (Nigel Cooke) addresses the rioters in Robert Delamere's 2005 RSC production at the Swan Theatre, Stratford-upon-Avon. Malcolm Davies Collection © Shakespeare Birthplace Trust

How important is the question of authorship to you as a director?

RD: I think it's about trying to understand the different tones, the different language use, which you play with as a director. There was a sort of knowledge that different parts came from different authors. There were different parts of the play that were already very dynamic and dramatically effective, and I felt that we had to authorize the whole production to bring the disparate text elements together. So it's key but it's about being attuned to the different tones and voices to best serve the play.

Considering the fragmented and multilayered nature of the manuscript itself, was it difficult to pull together a workable performance script?

RD: It was quite a lot of work. Some scenes are almost indecipherable, such as the one with the players that is reminiscent of the Mechanicals in *A Midsummer Night's Dream*. We turned it into a German cabaret scene, because we were having to test the comedy to ask what it was addressing, what was funny, what was the thematic importance to the whole piece. Other scenes, such as the Erasmus and Faulkner episodes, which have important character purposes but don't necessarily contribute to the main narrative drive, got cut during the run. You have to dip in and out of the play to find the unifying ideas and themes, and then a unifying aesthetic to create a bigger world for the production to exist within.

Was there a pressure in debuting such a little-known play as 'Shakespeare's banned play'?

RD: There was a feeling that it was important to address the fullness of the text in the opening of these pieces, at least at the start of the run. I felt some artistic responsibility for making sure people didn't go 'Ah, *this* is why it's his unknown piece'! So there was a sense of personal responsibility to the piece, and then a kind of responsibility towards the audience that followed.

The play itself is very episodic. What are the challenges of this kind of history play, which skates over so many different historical moments?

RD: One poor actor was playing about nineteen parts! Apart from the complexity of trying to understand how to cast it and how to balance out the casting, there's a danger of creating the Tudor pageant: this happened, then that happened, and of course you already know from history books and school that this is what occurred. I had a very clear fear when I started, from the time when I was an assistant director in my first job on *Henry VIII*, that 'Tudor bling' would get in the way of the narrative at the heart of the drama. It's the narrative I was interested in and certainly seemed to be what Shakespeare was interested in in the scene we believe he wrote: the moral authority of the figure who can influence a crowd. I really wanted to pare it down, so it was about the ethical and moral and character issues: what is conscience, the individual versus the state? I felt the need for people to be respected in a position of conscience even if it's not what's accepted in the state at the time or what common normal humanist values would say. That's how I came to be Creative Director of Amnesty International a short time after; it led from *Thomas More*. We have to get away from historical characterization and character and try to get into the actual human drama.

That feeds into the way you started the production – could you tell us about that? You started it with an image of refugees and the company?

RD: I was thinking, where is the comparative state apparatus, without being too specific? The designer and I were looking through photographic material around the fall of the Berlin Wall and the emergence of characters making noble gestures, sacrifices, some dying, in a context where the state was very strong.

I decided to create a troop who were playing out this play, a bit like in Augusto Boal's work or medieval drama where the play is performed on behalf of the community. It becomes a moral lesson, to try to have an audience respond to it and say what would I do in that situation? The aim was to create an emotional space, an atmospheric space of a burnt, broken world. In the actual historical period the state was in trouble, there were dozens of people being hung, and today you can see the Syrian situation, where people are protesting against values and people are sacrificed or murdered or put under false trial. This is how the state operates against the individual conscience, so let us find a metaphor of a troop performing this play for themselves. It was about creating an appropriate environment.

And a very international environment, as opposed to the focus on 'Englishness' which often informs productions of the history plays.

RD: I think that's right, and it's very easy to see the potential production disappearing down an historical alleyway where you're looking at a very proficient Tudor kaleidoscope of music, sound, images and clothing where people say, I'm very satisfied, this is exactly how I imagined it would be. I didn't want people to play the game of historical identification with it. 'Oh now this is going to happen, now this is going to come in, I've worked it out.' I really wanted it just to be about people and human character and what different people do, what one daughter does and what a different one does; how they react to all the different moral choices throughout the play, leading the audience to the great moral choice at the end.

Does the ambiguity over what More's 'fault' is help with that? The fact that the 'articles' are never specified?

RD: The audience knows what's happening and, because they're unspecified, it felt like if we absolutely hammered it historically into its appropriate dress, that those issues may sing out dangerously for the play and turn it into a pageant. That's one of the reasons Nigel [Cooke, who played More] was so good – he had the flintiness and attitude and backbone to make sense of why he would stand his ground, and he was able to inhabit the character's clarity of vision and humanity. The end of the play was one of the most successful bits of staging because it was a man alone with his conscience. It's like the Martin Luther King idea that a man's religion is whatever is most important to him, so we didn't take it from a historically religious perspective, but more from a spiritual perspective. The issues were of character and selfhood who am I being in relation to the state apparatus at this point? We were trying to make sure that steps towards what seems to be inevitable are properly expressed and inhabited for the audience. I wanted an audience to feel at the end that this was literally a man who was laying down his life for his beliefs. It's not something that people do very often in a western society, so try to give it as much space and dignity as possible, which is why we stripped out all the Tudor bling, to focus on human actions.

Part of his humanity is also his humour. How did you balance this with the need for dignity?

RD: It's creating counterpoint to human gravitas. He can't appear pompous or holier-than-thou or self-satisfied, and as C. S. Lewis says, 'Joy is the serious business of Heaven.' There's a sort of spiritual naturalness to the idea of joy which can sit alongside weightier issues, and I think gets played out in the scene with the family where there is a playful, jovial attitude, and then the state arrives and removes him and he has to turn into the compassionate father, from the playful father. The shifts were quite key. Using black humour to alleviate the tension could be seen as bad, but it's actually about how one person can manage to get their soul around the idea of the ultimate sacrifice. For the people who aren't motivated in the same way this is difficult to comprehend – why would you abandon your children and your wife for an idea that could be easy to let go; surely it's about surviving?

The family scenes became very important to me, trying to put this man in context. This is one of the first dramatic explorations of domesticity as we understand it, rather than the more iconic relationships Shakespeare works through parents and children. It's a whole household, and it means we're dealing with the domestic environment, and the removal of the man from that environment and what that does. It seems to me that the writers were wondering what it must be like for someone to be taken from their family. They are the emotional ballast that stimulates the idea for an audience that he's leaving real relationships behind. There are many Christ parallels – the garden of Gethsemane, for example.

This then continues into the scene with the servants following their master's departure.

RD: It was a great scene, and very important for expressing the love that he is experiencing from and inspiring in other people. It also made more sense of the end, where there's a woman talking to the executioner. Every encounter is a relationship, so let's explore what that is. Is there shame? Was there embarrassment? Just by their presence, it raises questions of morality and values. It's a good way of exploring remarkable characters, putting them in a social and domestic context, humanizing them rather than elevating and aggrandizing the character.

This seems to recur throughout the play, where More is equally comfortable interacting with lower-status characters and lords.

RD: That's where the collective troop idea at the beginning helped. It's the emotional idea of a community – that this person can seem to affect numerous people. Whether in a moment of meeting or in a lifetime of love and marriage, you affect and impact on people, your actions have consequences. And yet there's a state apparatus, a state vision, as in Syria at the moment, which means that human conduct, human propriety or international law don't matter because there's a bigger motivating factor, which is the protection of the state system. I thought that rigidity of the state system against the fluidity of the human community felt to me to be interesting as a parallel.

That would lead to talking more about the early riot scenes. Did your production take a stance on the actions of the rebels?

RD: I tried not to make a judgement call on it. It wasn't 'about' the rioting as such, and it's the same debate that's happening at the moment about the riots [this interview took place shortly after the London riots of summer 2011]. Everyone's got a different opinion about why that moment occurred, but actually, there are no definite politician's statements, no simple combination of factors, and so I didn't want to be judgemental here. I wanted to stage it in as raw a manner as possible because otherwise More's dampening of the riot makes no sense. I think there is a spirit of chaos that exists in humanity once the opportunity is taken to abandon our moral systems and the values of humane society. The play's quite specific about what the circumstances are – drink, violence against women, that sort of thing.

We see some of these grievances at the very start, and then the mob develops a life of its own?

RD: It's the rule of the mob, and I looked at that idea a lot – how do mobs occur, what are the tipping points, when does it become about the collective act of chaos rather than about the individual. I'm sure in the recent riots there were individual acts of protest, and then it moved past the individual voice. It became a borrowing that spread throughout the city and to other cities. And sometimes it was opportunistic, and that's what the playwrights seem to be saying in *Thomas More*. More is someone who's arguing 'Go back to the individual issues, go back to stop this destroying of values and community.'

So with that said, what did you make of John Lincoln's hanging? It's a powerful moment, but is it heroic or a failure?

RD: There can be false heroes. I try not to come down on either side. There are two very different value systems that operate in very different ways. In a sense one is spiritually absolutist and one is politically absolutist; I die for what I believe in, and there are very many parallels. In a very obvious way you can ask, do you find Malcolm X's encouragement of violence against the system more persuasive that Martin Luther King's more spiritual leadership. It's a place full of ambiguity and I remember saying to the actor, whatever you do, don't put your chin up, don't aggrandize. This is your last statement on earth, and everything you say is said in the fullness of an era where words are your truth and your word is your bond.

You mentioned earlier difficulties with the central set-piece, *The Marriage of Wit and Wisdom*, which became one of the production's most memorable moments – how did you stage this interlude?

RD: We talking about George Grosz and German political cartoonists from the '30s, and from the back of those conversations about mid twentieth-century Europe we found a way of piecing it together. By evoking the Weimar Republic, we're in an era of state oppression, where the fight for personal and individual freedom becomes relevant.

It looked like *The Blue Angel*, in a way! We had cabaret-style, pop-cultural versions of the Weimar era, and an actor came down dressed as Marlene Dietrich doing a 'number', and then the dumb show played out. It seemed to make sense that there was a festivity in this moment and it became more powerful than it possibly could have been because it had metaphorical references rather than being merely the comic interlude. I didn't want it to be an interlude. It's got to have thematic relevance to the whole piece.

It's a very telling scene, because of course More jumps in to this play and takes over it. Was this significant?

RD: There's a technique I use which is based on an Italian psychoanalyst, Roberto Assagioli, who founded psychosynthesis where people play multiple roles. He takes someone like Thomas More: the buffoon, the clown, the player, the joy-seeker, the light-hearted fool, and asks how we can humanize this person as much as possible. How can we use *The Marriage of Wit and Wisdom* to see someone who can both hold an office of state and pick up a karaoke machine? I was very nervous of it becoming a slightly po-faced interpretation of a religious or semi-religious figure, which would be dramatically inert.

I remember I chose *Thomas More* because these issues fascinate me about how you become who you are. I wanted to find something to grapple with, and I think it can be a very moving and profound drama. It leaks a bit because it's constructed by multiple hands, but the core ideas which we worked out in our performance script are that it's quite filmic, which is why we set it in a burned-out cinema. There's something fundamentally cinematic about the biographical approach, the way it moves from the domestic world to a riot in London, from an attempted rape to the lords at dinner. This is deeply filmic in a sense, and yet it has this overall great narrative backbone and character journey. It almost obeys the Jungian steps, or any kind of film theory way of reviewing film narratives. It's the journey of the hero via a series of revelatory incidents. It's like the first film as well as the first domestic play.

Finally, do you think Shakespeare had much to do with this play?

RD: Yes, I do, clearly. Not all of it, and not as an overall editor. There's the riot scene, and maybe also the final speech of Lincoln. It operates a bit like film does at the moment, where someone writes a version of it, and then it gets rewritten by hired guns. Most films are like that, multi-written, but the core idea's so good that it works.

NIGEL COOKE ON PLAYING THOMAS MORE

Nigel Cooke is a stage and screen actor. He trained at Bristol Old Vic Theatre School and has performed in a number of Shakespeare productions for the RSC, Shakespeare's Globe, Liverpool Everyman and Regent's Park. He recently appeared in the BBC's *Hollow Crown* series. He talks here about playing the title role in Robert Delamere's 2005 RSC production of *Thomas More*.

How important is the question of authorship to you as an actor?

NC: Not hugely. I'll take the words on their own merit. I go along with the belief that some of *Thomas More* was written by Shakespeare. I didn't research it, so it was just instinct. Apart from the 'strangers' speech which I think is generally reckoned to be written by him, there's also the farewell speech to Erasmus which struck me as having a ring of Will about it. It was just a hunch!

The original manuscript for the play is physically fragmented and authored by several different hands, whereas you were working from a coherent script. How aware were you of the extent of collaboration?

NC: I was aware that up to the council scene where More refuses to sign the papers it was a very fragmented, episodic play. Not so much in the style of writing, but simply in terms of its structure. Apart from the Lincoln sub-plot, every scene puts More with a different set of people dealing with, for the most part, circumstances that have no apparent connection. Whether Munday, Chettle, Heywood, et al. wrote each scene by 'committee' or they went off and individually took responsibility for single scenes – who knows? It wasn't something that occupied me. What occupied me was simply trying to honour the tone of each scene.

I did a play at the Lyric Hammersmith – *A Thousand Stars Explode in the Sky* – which was written collaboratively by three writers: David Eldridge, Simon Stevens and Robert Holman. From simply reading the play, its multiple authorship wasn't at all apparent. However, they attended rehearsals. We didn't know who had written which bits. (In fact they were almost at pains to conceal that information from us.) But with them present clues emerged and you could piece together who had written what, and how the writing matched aspects of their personalities.

Had Munday et al. been in the rehearsal room maybe the same would have applied.

More is the through-line who unites a very episodic play. What are the responsibilities and challenges of that?

NC: Just as with any other leading part you've got to drive the thing. You have to take responsibility for being the play's motor. My take on any leading role is that the less you do in terms of sticking on bits of characterization, the better. Particularly for the part of More who is ultimately his own nemesis. The only significant antagonist is the offstage king. So, for my money, if you want to win the audience's sympathy you've got to be as much yourself as possible. Otherwise, whether the audience consciously knows it or not, they're going to smell artifice.

You rely on all the other bits, the peripatetic nature of all the characters he goes to, for shape, sound and colour. You rely on the supporting characters to do exactly that: support you. With any luck you get yourself into a state where you can be as free and uninhibited as possible, where you can really *inhabit* More, as opposed to 'playing' or 'acting' him. When you are genuinely uninhibited and alive to the moment, I think you are capable of producing genuine surprise and excitement.

How much did the historical figure of More, or more recent popular imaginings of him, affect your performance?

NC: Very little. It's a one-sided pro-More play and that's what you have to do. For all the pro-Morers out there, I'm sure there are as many anti-Morers. In fact, a number of people would nobble me after the show and, whilst being tactfully complimentary about the production and my performance, they were very keen to let me know that their view of More was considerably less flattering than the play's depiction of him. 'He was a nasty little shit', was one comment that springs to mind.

As I've said, I didn't do a lot of research, but I did read Peter Ackroyd's *The Life of Thomas More*, which was fantastic. And from that, I got two big things. First was the idea of London in the 1500s being like Istanbul, with hundreds of churches, bells ringing – the huge presence of religion. It was normal, and people grew up with it, and that was a way into regarding More, for all his 'extraordinariness', as normal. Secondly, it gave me a great insight into the massive energy More must have had. He'd be up praying before the crack of dawn, he seemed to manage on about three hours of sleep. Praying, writing, praying, studying, teaching his children Latin and music, praying, teaching himself music, praying. Not to mention his job and slaughtering Protestants (I think his wife must have had a pretty raw deal!). So instead of seeing him as a deeply contemplative and reflective sage (which is actually what my vague pre-knowledge of him was) I wanted to present him more like a cheery milkman on his rounds at 0400 hours, whistling, quipping with the odd passer-by. Busy, busy, busy doing his duty. Now, I don't have that sort of energy for free. But I do know that with a couple of strong espressos down me in the morning I get an hour or so of a 'supercharged Nigel' in which I get more things done than in the rest of the day. So I just had to imagine myself like that all the time.

The pro- and anti-Morers are irrelevant in a way. Ideally, as with any play, I think you should be aiming it at people who come to it with the least pre-knowledge. You don't presume anything. You let the play speak for itself, and let people who have no prefixed idea about who or what More was work it out for themselves. And I imagine those people who have little or nil pre-knowledge of either the play or the historical figure get a simple story of a highly motivated, decent man whose obstinacy gets the better of him. That's his big flaw.

The debate between obstinacy and integrity is key to stories about More. What was your take on that?

NC: I had to think that *he thought* he was acting on absolute integrity; that he felt he could do no other thing. That doesn't and shouldn't stop someone thinking, 'Well what an obstinate man, to abandon his wife and children.' There was no doubt in my mind that More's faith was at the heart of all his actions. His faith and his desire to prove to His Maker (and/or himself) that his faith was absolute.

One of the interesting things about the character is that he interacts with people at all levels. How did you approach that? Does he alter himself in moving between different groups?

NC: It goes from that idea that he was an extremely energetic man. When you see extremely energetic people, the way they take to other people can be extraordinary. Very immediate. I think More does alter himself. I think we all do, to some degree, according to whom we are with. If at times he appears to ingratiate, I don't think he's trying to be ingratiating. With the Players, for example, we see his unfulfilled desire to perform. More's a *doer*. He hears they have an actor missing, and there's a glee and excitement at having the opportunity to do something. And that desire to do is exactly the same impulse as when he jumps in to quell the rioting mob. But it brings out a completely different aspect of his personality.

With the Faulkner scene, the idea, never properly realized in our production, was to trick the audience into thinking a genuine drunk had crashed his way from the street and onto the stage. For a moment you should have wondered whether the actor or More was dealing with the situation.

Both the historical figure and the character of this play are known for their wit. But his humour might also be seen as quite cruel, particularly as he's being taken away from his family. How did you handle his wit?

NC: Humour is a way of dealing with the situation. It's a defence mechanism really, isn't it? And maybe that's what it was with More at times – when he was emotionally unable to deal with the situation. A lot of the time, people who are constantly making a crack or a joke at something, they're blocking something else. But also, you have to give him the benefit of the doubt and say that perhaps he really delighted in wisecracking for its own sake and as a way of opening channels with people. I was aware that his humour had the potential of being extremely irritating. (And maybe it was for some people!) And I think that that was a spur to me thinking 'Don't be hanging around trying to get laughs here there and everywhere, just crack on.'

I didn't try to make More too complex. Massive achievers are not necessarily massively complex. They're hugely driven, but no more or less complex than the average milkman or Nigel ...

How connected is he to the people and events around him?

NC: To both people and events I think *he thinks* he's fairly connected. How much his wife felt he was connected to her would be a different tale. But yes, by and large, I think he's definitely connected and engaged with people and events.

The moment I think he's more More than ever, when he's most connected to himself and the event facing him, is just before he gets to the chopping block. He's been wisecracking with his guard, and he suddenly realizes that this is the place. There's a half line there which I stretched out. I gave myself a massive pause. I thought – I'd pretty much rattled through the play, I hadn't hung around, and I consciously did that because it needed to be driven, there's no central antagonism, and it fitted with my take on More's energy. It had to keep moving until that moment, 'Is this the place?' I think that's a good bit of writing, and it certainly fired up my imagination. For all his bonhomie and joviality, there is a sense that it could have all been a bit of an act and that in all his zipping around and doing good and believing things, he hasn't really, *really* taken stock of what or who he is, what he's doing, where he's going and why. So the purposeful espresso-fuelled milkman becomes an indecisive dog circling its basket, not knowing the most comfortable way to lie down. I think that's his biggest moment of connection. It doesn't last long because he's quickly back into wisecracking with Surrey and Shrewsbury and then the Hangman.

Is there any significance to what happens to More beyond the personal? Is it just one man's story, or does it stand for a wider set of political concerns?

NC: I didn't feel the wider significance. Whether the production told that or not, that he was the voice that stood up against the establishment, I didn't feel it was my job. More reacts to the moment – when he talks to the rioters, that's about him seizing the moment. And about being a good mediator and persuasive speaker, it's not about being a dissenting voice.

That's the scene that stands out, not only because of Shakespeare's probable authorship. How did you play that scene? Is he an authority, or one of the people?

NC: Though massively educated, his origins were relatively humble. At heart he was very much one of the people. He relates to them as equals, but the writing also distinguishes him from them. In that scene in particular he's got some great rhetoric, heightened language, which marks him out. But the instinct is as one of the people, and that's what allows him to take the opportunity to urge them to do unto others what you would have done unto you.

I remember in rehearsals feeling that it shouldn't all suddenly stop, that the rioters shouldn't suddenly and magically be pacified, that there was a genuine job of persuasion to do. And that's quite hard to do convincingly. As with Antony reading the will in *Julius Caesar*, it's very hard for the unscripted mob (especially over a long run of a play) to stay alive theatrically. There's a danger of it becoming a rather dead set-piece. So I felt very reliant on everyone else's input and welcomed the other actors to feel free to shout over me, spit at me, ignore me or whatever it took for them to feel they were an active part of the scene. The secret to staging that sort of mob scene, I think, is to make sure you calibrate everybody's levels of dissent. You should get the full spectrum between the one who wants to agree most and the one who wants to disagree most. If that's achieved, the actor playing More (or Antony) has the easier job in a way.

Is it just about his words, or is there a physicality to his energy and eloquence at all?

NC: Well, with a ten-stone weakling of the man like me playing him, there's always going to be a limitation. I couldn't make him a hugely imposing figure of a man. I could, however, put a spring in my step and make him quite nippy and physically alert. And good voice production helps. By 'good' I essentially mean 'relaxed'. Relaxed, so that according to the demands you can be as loud, soft, aggressive, urgent, gentle, as you like.

When we first see him in prison, I wondered how he would have passed all that time – given that he'd been deprived of his books, etc. He would have talked to his warders as much as they'd allow him. And he would have prayed of course, but rather than that obvious image I decided to show him taking exercise. Press-ups or the like wouldn't have been right, so I decided to have him doing a headstand – sort of yoga I suppose. In some way testing himself physically. I thought it gave a sense of a man who could never let the grass grow beneath his feet and an ability to keep calm, no matter what the circumstances. I thought the headstand was a practical and also slightly mystical gesture that physicalized his passive resistance. It meant more to me than simply praying.

Did you have a lot of freedom in that sense? Especially in a role which doesn't have as much baggage of past performances.

NC: Yes. Absolutely. I was very fortunate in that Robert Delamere, the director, gave me great freedom. (I think he was quite fortunate too, because I think I came up with some good ideas!) But it's up to you to use that freedom wisely, otherwise you can end up pissing off the director and/or the rest of the company. But if you do use it wisely, your opinion in the rehearsal room is tacitly accorded more weight. And I think that's right. If you are in almost every scene of the play, you tend to gain a far greater oversight of the play than if you are only in the odd scene.

And yes, it's great to have the chance to put a mark on a role and not be compared to a host of past performances. In playing More I realized that if I wasn't as free as a bird, I was nothing; and in that freedom comes the chance to really make a role your own.

As a PS, I also pondered a fair bit on what effect his name had on him. Ripe for punning of course, was it also a spur to do more. Always go that bit further, and his death was the ultimate way to prove his faith.

STEPHEN UNWIN ON DIRECTING *A YORKSHIRE TRAGEDY*

Stephen Unwin read English at Cambridge, where he directed many student productions, including an award-winning production of *Measure for Measure* that transferred to the Almeida. For much of the 1980s he was Associate Director at the Traverse Theatre, Edinburgh, and in the early 1990s he became Resident Director at the National Theatre Studio. In 1993 he founded English Touring Theatre. He is currently Artistic Director of the Rose Theatre in Kingston. He talks here about his studio production of *A Yorkshire Tragedy*, performed in January 1987 in the Cottesloe, National Theatre, London.

How important is the question of authorship to you as a director?

SU: Only in the most simple, practical way. I directed a Noel Coward play called *This Happy Breed* in 2011 that's hardly ever done, which I loved doing, and it's such a completely different world from standard Coward. I used to remember that it is the same mind [behind the play] and some of the same kinds of things are evident. With [*A Yorkshire Tragedy*], not being a textual scholar, I had and still have no idea whether it's by Shakespeare. Reading it again I think it's a very wonderful play. Having directed *The Changeling* a couple of years ago I thought I perhaps recognized Middleton in it, but that's pure instinct.

Can you tell us a bit about the context of the production, within the National Theatre Studio strand of work?

SU: It was 1987 when the NT Studio was run by Peter Gill, and I was there for a while, part of the family, part of the furniture. Peter was always interested in the realism in Elizabethan and Jacobean writing, the working-class realism above all, which is something I'm still obsessed by and writing a book on. I said to him, what about *A Yorkshire Tragedy*? Isn't that an interesting play in terms of realism, social realism?

It's not quite a working-class voice because they're not all working-class characters, but it has a rawness which the theatre industry in general during the high Thatcherite times was not really doing. I was drawn to that, and I still am. It's a dramatized pamphlet, and I love that! The sense that it really did happen, or some version of it. Personally, with Shakespeare, I get a bit fed up with the fairies and spirits, and even with the kings and queens, and this is more like domestic drama. So there was something about the context, what Peter Gill has always stood for and what I was learning from him as a young director, that seemed a kind of extension of those things which had been interesting me.

Did the historical source material play any part in this?

SU: I must have read the pamphlet, and I suppose the actors would have read it. I think it's important to get a sense of the context. Re-reading it, it's about money! That's the most important thing in the play. There's this small-time aristocrat in a small-time house in the middle of the wilds of Yorkshire, deep, rural Yorkshire. I love the fact he's not grand, he's not the Earl of Northumberland, he's just ... gentry. And that's the sort of people for whom cash flow was important. I think the fact that there was a true-life account gave us a sense of immediacy. I think that, for the modern theatre, the problem with Renaissance theatre is how metaphorical it sometimes is, and what's fascinating about this is how unmetaphorical it is. This is like something from the *Henry* plays, or the tougher end of Shakespeare. This is like Williams in *Henry V*, that kind of world, rather than Titania.

Even the characters and locations are anonymized.

SU: That helps! It was staged in the Cottesloe, and we just put in a rough, tough wooden floor, and a few real bits of heavy Elizabethan furniture. I do remember something about the English tradition of domestic violence. I'd just done *Look Back in Anger*. There's a bit in that play where they have a fight, she falls over and burns her arm with an iron, and it's completely unidealistic – it's anti-idealistic, completely materialistic, and it says what actually happens in a domestic situation: a woman gets a burned arm. What's interesting is that *A Yorkshire Tragedy* has got the same kind of quality. Reading it again, I thought that the violence should be really realistic, realistically bloody. Not fancifully bloody, not over-designed bloody, but you should find it unbearable that these kids are being cut and the wife is stabbed, and people are beaten up. Casting a real child contributed to this.

How did you depict the violence? How did the production look?

SU: We did as much as we could. If we did it again, I'd want it to be more horrible, messier: the chairs knocked over, people being hurt. It needs to get to that. We thought the Master of the College should turn up, and be a really tough character. We had Elizabethan ruffs, very simple Elizabethan clothes – we didn't take it too far. I'd want those to have real 3D texture. It was important it be on a very simple wooden floor. For the scene when the Wife is in bed, we brought on a simple iron bed. The lighting was just a bright white light – very Brechtian, very simple.

One of the things we did do was have two Yorkshire actors – Stephen Petcher and Mary Jo Randle, and they performed in Yorkshire voices, which is something I've always been interested in, as RP isn't the only voice for Shakespeare. I'm not sure if I did it again if that's right, because it can end up sounding like a coal miner and his wife, and I'm not sure how appropriate that would be now – but it felt very right in the '80s.

The danger is not getting the class right. You want to give the impression of 'small-time' – that when he goes to London he's completely anonymous. He might be a big figure in his small bit of Yorkshire, but when he goes to London no one knows who he is. He's not the Earl of Northumberland, he's not a Percy – because if he was, they wouldn't be going broke.

How far does that feed into his actions in the play? Between the references to devils, bastardy, money worries, what are his motivations?

SU: Those are all part of the play's realism, how a man like that would think about the world. I was surprised by the play's date, because I kept feeling that it's a really Elizabethan play, but it's Jacobean! I think the mentions of devils capture its provincialism, and I think its provincialism is really interesting. That first scene with the servants is fantastic. I was thinking if I did it again I'd want to move that scene, but you can't. It's such a rich flavoured scene, and then you don't really see them again.

It's an anomalous scene: it's the only one not based on the pamphlet, the only one with named characters who then don't appear again.

SU: I remember feeling that it was brilliantly written, and we had a hugely interesting time doing it. It feeds into what I'm interested in with serving characters in Shakespeare's time – they're not comic relief, they're hugely realistic textured bits of writing. And I think that's true, but then the play feels like it totally changes tone in scene 2. You almost think that there is a bigger play being worked up here and that those characters are going to have some life and be important, and then they essentially disappear.

Is that jump in tone important?

SU: It's all part of it being a fragment, I guess. I'm not saying it's a fragment of a bigger play, but it does feel like there's something missing, or that there was an ambition to write a bigger play. The title page says it's one of 'four Plays in one'. I could see the play being done without the first scene. It wouldn't make any difference apart from that that scene's got some really wonderful writing in it. We had a small cast, so when it called for other servants we did bring these guys back on stage. Those guys were there and then crept through.

There's a more recent fragment, Georg Büchner's *Woyzeck*, a short play from the 1830s about a common man, a soldier, who kills his wife. It's the beginning of modern drama, and it's written in that really intense, simple, energized language that also characterizes *A Yorkshire Tragedy*. I was really struck by a line repeating 'bastards' here – 'Bastards, bastards, bastards: begot in tricks, begot in tricks.' What I love about that kind of writing is it shows the character is limited and intense. It's not fancy, it's 'Bastards, bastards'. It's so raw.

How important is it to keep up the play's momentum? It's one of the fastest sequences of action in the early modern drama.

SU: You've got to go fast, and that's one of the things that's challenging about it. You've also got to be careful. With a play like this, if you over-freight it in the theatre with endless alien psychological explanations, or endless alien naturalistic elements, I think it collapses. There are elements which are naturalistic, like having a drink or a table or chair, but you can't overload it. The play isn't Ibsen! It's remorseless, it's got to be loud, and then it's over in three quarters of an hour. The Husband is a particularly hard part in terms of the action. It's hard to show the Husband being thrown off a horse. In our production the audience heard a horse and then he just tumbled onto the stage, which is probably what they would have done on the early modern stage.

How do you balance a character like the Husband in performance? You mentioned an interest in serving characters, and the servants here are the other characters who seem to interact most with the Wife.

SU: In *King Lear*, it's the servants during the blinding of Gloucester who stab Cornwall and change history as a result. Their relationship with their masters or mistresses is sophisticated and they put up with an awful lot, but then suddenly, eventually, they don't. That's an unspoken contract between masters and servants, and all these plays show that. The servants care about the Wife because they know she's being abused.

What do we make of the final scene, of forgiveness and repentance?

SU: I think that the final scene is quite playable, the remorse. You need to have two children covered in blood: it's got to feel like a murder. I don't know how you do it. When he kisses them and he says 'I'll kiss the blood' – if done well, it's an astonishingly powerful theatrical image, just as powerful as the moment when you see Gloucester's blinded eyes for the first moment, if there's a lot of blood and he gets a lot of blood on his face. What I want to do now is make sure those sorts of things come across. The Wife's line 'Dearer than all is my poor husband's life' demonstrates the rawness of the writing. It wouldn't work in a posh voice, it's consonantal and tough. I think the way we do Shakespeare needs to learn from this more.

The forgiveness is entirely playable. Again, if you overlaid it with alien emotion it would be naff. You could say it's a bit preposterous, as she's nearly been killed, but people do plead, the world is full of women who are beaten up by their husbands and don't report them to the police. And of course the world says – he's dead. And that's the funny thing, if there wasn't the realism of the world – if she 'won', you wouldn't believe it. The law is the law, and you kill your kids, and you're going to hang – and that's what that last line says. Capital punishment was everywhere.

Most of the other characters appear very briefly. Did they have a choric function, or did the actors play them as individuals?

SU: They were reasonably individual. We had two big guys – the Master and the Gentleman who actually beats up the Husband. The actors were both big, white-haired, impressive men, and we deliberately made them powerful. You want to play the power stuff for real, because it's not psychological. When the Master says 'your hopeful brother / At the university', you've got to feel the full force of disapproval of an older man who's dignified.

That fits interestingly with what you were saying earlier about the sense that the Husband is primarily important in his own mind.

SU: I think that's right. The Gentleman who beats him up is maybe from the next town along, where he's a big guy, of real distinction. The Husband (played by Stephen Petcher in our production) is troubled, has a natural sense of trouble, finds life difficult – he's got responsibilities but he just can't cope, his head is popping. And then these older, more dignified men are telling him he's messing it up, but he's pushing through.

How did the Wife handle this presentation of the Husband? In some ways she draws on the stock type of the Patient Grissel figure, and yet she's far from passive.

SU: The Wife (Mary Jo Randle in our production) has got some dignity. She can speak. Look at that first speech! It's a brilliant speech. The Husband is violent and dangerous. There's some old wisdom about beating your wife and servants, and the more you beat the more they bear. You've got to give it some kind of social context: it's his castle, he's at home, this is how he runs it. He feels he can beat his wife, he just can't kill her. That's what's difficult for us to understand. This is why it needs the intervention of the other men, to demonstrate that he doesn't actually have the power in that setting that he assumes.

Is the claustrophobia of that setting important?

SU: I should think so. It's a domestic interior atmosphere, not that I'd put great walls around it, but it needs a table and chair. You just need a few very real objects and some very viscerally real figures and what you believe is real blood. The simplest images are the most powerful, but it's an actor's play. It provides a little bit of a model for some of the things that are occasionally forgotten about in the way Shakespeare is staged. That domestic realism, that earthiness, that raw power. Blood and wood, sky and money: the basic building blocks of what happened on that brilliant open stage.

Do you think Shakespeare had anything to do with it?

SU: Probably not, but I've no idea! As someone who's read a lot of Shakespeare and Middleton, my instinct was – that's Middleton. Funnily enough, if anything seems Shakespeare, it's the first scene. There's something about those servants that can feel Shakespearean, but then the Wife's monologue reminds me of Beatrice-Joanna in *The Changeling*, the straightforward interiority that Middleton manages to do. But that's only a guess!

ALEX HASSELL ON PLAYING IN *CARDENIO*

Alex Hassell is a stage and screen actor. He trained at the Central School of Speech and Drama, and has since taken roles for the RSC, Shakespeare's Globe, Hampstead Theatre and many others. His screen work includes *Calendar Girls*, *Anonymous* and *Cold Mountain*. He talks here about his role as Fernando in Gregory Doran's 2011 RSC production of *Cardenio*.

As an actor, does it matter to you who wrote the play you are performing in?

AH: On some levels, as an actor, no it doesn't matter. As a person being very excited about Shakespeare, of course I am interested to know if there are new works by Shakespeare. I am quite evangelical about my belief in iambic pentameter and verse structure, so knowing something was by Shakespeare would make me trust that more. You think, if I don't understand this, it's because I'm not clever enough to understand it, because Shakespeare does know what he's talking about, so I have to lift myself to understand why it is particularly written in a way I don't currently understand. Whereas if it's not Shakespeare, you can get to a point where you just think this is a bit knotty, a bit weak, and you might need to try and help it along or paper over a crack. So in that way I suppose it makes a difference.

When rehearsing the play, did the company have any sense of which sections of the text are attributed to different authors?

AH: No we didn't. One of the things I loved about this production is that we treated it like a new play. There was one scene where Ollie [Rix] who plays Cardenio and I felt like there wasn't enough of our relationship before I betray him, so we added a new scene – so I know there are some bits which aren't Shakespeare! It wasn't like we just made up words. A brilliant thing Greg did was that he sourced text from other plays by

Shakespeare, or based on Cervantes, filched bits here and there, so it was more like we were editing than writing new bits.

The RSC production went back to Cervantes, especially in the change of names. In *Double Falsehood* your character is Henriquez, in your production it's Fernando. Did you work with Cervantes?

AH: I read the Cardenio story, but I didn't read *Double Falsehood* because, as an actor, I feel that if I read too much around the text, you start to put things into what you're doing that aren't in your script – intentions, shades, ideas of a character – which might take you further away from looking at precisely what you have in your play. I find it very useful not to pre-judge characters, and so to read other works where they might be read from a judging standpoint is not helpful. In Cervantes he seems to be a very bad person. A scholar told us there's a charm to the character, that at the end it's alright and they laugh about it, so there's some sort of wink or sparkle in the stories about him, which I suppose made me feel that it was okay not to try to forgive him, to be brave enough to downplay his heinous actions without trying to apologize for them.

How did you interpret the central action, the seduction/rape of Dorothea?

AH: I only interpret it through his eyes. As me, I don't think he gives her any option at all, so I think even though he didn't physically force her, it's rape. But it's not helpful at all to base the choices of my character on my own beliefs. One has to think about what he wants and what he's capable of. He shapes his morality through the play, even his ideas about what he thinks is factually happening. I think he thinks at that moment that she is in love with him, and that she just doesn't know it in the way he knows it. So he thinks he's doing something that is okay, or he doesn't think at all. I try not to think too much about why, because the characters *are* doing it. And in life you don't always know why you're doing things, especially if they're as extreme as what Fernando does, on the edges of what is right or wrong. I just try to do it and believe each line that I'm saying.

In this production, with Fabian and Lopez cut, the post-seduction justification scene was played as soliloquy. Who were you trying to convince?

AH: I always take soliloquies as being to the actual audience, but that the actual audience shift about as being your conscience, your selves. It's useful in any soliloquies to be thinking about what you're contradicting in the minds of other people. It's useful for me to know they've seen that and are thinking I'm morally reprehensible, and to try to either explain to them that I don't think it was morally reprehensible or to stick two fingers up to them if they think that about it. What's interesting in that speech is that Fernando seems to have a kind of scientific or emotional distance. He manages to look at his actions and consider them from many angles, and decide not to feel bad about it, which is very interesting. I wanted to avoid being a pantomime villain. When I first read the script, I was so confused by his actions, it didn't seem there was a clear line through it, and I really wanted to keep that confusion intact. If I was making any attempt to make him forgivable, it's that his actions are so confused that inside one might think there's a lot of turmoil going on.

I think in terms of playing to the audience, convincing them, I think it's an interesting journey to go from 'No, come on, you all saw it, I did.' Because you can read it, with her kissing him back, that he's not forcing her, there's a gap in his mind that he can crawl into, that she wasn't doing it at gunpoint. It allows the audience to think about their own positions.

Your character ties together the love plot and has close bonds with Dorothea, Lucinda and Cardenio. How does Fernando manage these relationships?

AH: It changes. I definitely think there's something about him that desires closeness and contact. These are the three main connections you get. As you perform, you start trying to weave together a 'how does he feel about these people?' and then you try to forget it, so it moves about. Stalking was something we talked about. He decides he's in love with someone or wants something from someone, and then decides that they feel the same way. And it changes in an instant, especially in the case of Lucinda, and it's no coincidence that it's his best friend's girl. There's a very self-destructive streak.

The worst thing he could do at that moment is fall in love with his best friend's girl, because of what he's just done to Dorothea and because of how much he and Cardenio mean to each other, so it's no coincidence that he deliberately seeks to head to Cardenio's hometown. But I don't think he thinks he's deliberately picking the worst possible person. He convinces himself that she's giving him signals, but that comes and goes as well.

With Cardenio, again, one tries not to judge it. There could be many reasons he would feel a deep and real relationship and affection. There could be much to read from the idea that he's using him for gratification and for being looked up to and being made to feel special. I certainly do feel and try to convince Ollie of the fact that I genuinely feel for him and this is a real friendship. But very quickly he turns to talking about himself, and Cardenio becomes an audience to that. What I love about the character is that it is so layered. In Cardenio there isn't often subtext – he's saying what he thinks and feels. In Fernando, there's an enormous amount of subtext all the time.

As part of the complexities of the character, your performance also got a lot of laughs.

AH: When we were rehearsing, we didn't know what sort of play it was. We were stunned at how funny audiences found it, and particularly how funny they found some of the stuff I was doing. Greg challenged me to make Fernando absolutely unapologetic, and challenge the audience to love and be charmed by this absolute bastard and feel conflicted that they wanted me to do more bad things because they enjoyed watching me do it! If it's just a romp, and you're just enjoying someone being bad, then you're not thinking about what's happening and you're not taking a stance as an audience member. It's a line that I'm continually trying to walk. He manipulates people without them knowing they're being manipulated. It's difficult to know how much of that is me playing it and how much is the writing.

We've been playing a lot in the first balcony scene with how much Dorothea loves him, as in the source. When I have taken away his charisma and just played it plainly, it becomes a very different production. I think our production has been partly built around the idea that Fernando is a burning force, a big ball of energy that ravages through the play, so I have to take that as read and enjoy that. I've been conflicted sometimes with how much I should enjoy it. You have to love Fernando, in a sense, in our production, but I'd be interested to see how different productions handled it.

Speaking of the ball of energy, could you talk me through the end of your production, where Fernando decides to try to kill Cardenio in front of the Duke? What's the thinking at this stage?

AH: This wasn't in the script originally, we added it later. There didn't seem to be anything between Fernando and Cardenio in the final scene. We explored whether that was a good thing or whether that left things up in the air. Greg felt that there needed to be more of a resolution, that the audience would want to see him get his comeuppance. One could read that this person who has strived so hard to get what he wants, and has been painted into a corner by this little kid – what's he going to do now? He's backed into a corner and flips, he gets Lucinda and tries to escape! It's a series of desperate acts, as in our added scene showing him jump out of the coffin in the convent to abduct Lucinda. If one were to think about these actions, they're not good plans! One has to take it that he thinks that these are going to solve his problems, and this is revealing of his state of mind.

18. Ravishment in *Cardenio*

'True, she did not consent; as true, she did resist; but still in silence all. 'Twas but the coyness of a modest bride, not the resentment of a ravished maid.' (2.1.26–8)

Dorothea [Violante] (Pippa Nixon) and Fernando [Henriquez] (Alex Hassell) in Gregory Doran's 2011 RSC production of *Cardenio* at the Swan Theatre, Stratford-upon-Avon. Ellie Kurttz © Royal Shakespeare Company

Is this also the thinking behind the opening of the play, which sees Fernando enter and lie down momentarily in his father's open coffin?

AH: That was another later invention. The story is that the coffin is my father's, which he will go into when he dies, and that I am looking at it and thinking about our relationship and the distance between us, and that he'll die soon and I'm the second son, but also I'm thinking about my own mortality. I realized that one could excuse Fernando's actions through grief. His mother's not in the play – what if she was dead, and his father was going to die, and that these desperate actions were an attempt to cling onto something, someone? That if he meets someone and feels something for them he wants to consume them, so Cardenio and Dorothea and Lucinda are all consumed by him in the hope that this will somehow fill a void.

And does it fill a void? Is there a sense of reconciliation or resolution for Fernando at the play's end?

AH: The end is the most difficult bit for me. Dorothea is the absolute embodiment of virtue. She offers herself to Fernando, and if he wants any chance of survival, emotionally or morally, he'd better tie himself to her as hard as he can and promise, and believe, that he's going to change and that she's the person to help him do that. But then it's up to audiences to decide whether it's possible or not! We talked about whether he might be lying, but also about the aspiration to goodness and decided that, whether he's changed or not, he certainly wants to try. I think that the key is that Dorothea believes he's a good person. No one in the play has said anything nice about him, so for him to hear that is the turning point.

Many people don't believe the repentance. People seem to feel, watching it, that he's not going to be able to change, that it won't be a happy marriage. This is a pleasure of doing this, being the first person to play this version of the character, because you don't have to deal with the baggage of what other people have done with or made of the character. The audience has no idea what's about to happen so they're not comparing you with other performers. They're actually surprised by what's happening and get different things from the performance. Greg felt that he wanted it to be hopeful. He didn't want to sully it, but he wanted to make sure there was an ability to believe in hope.

Finally, do you think Shakespeare had anything to do with the play?

AH: I don't think he wrote it. Maybe he had a hand in some bits. I don't think it reads like Shakespeare. I do think it's really good and the writing's good, but there's a difference between 'really good' and Shakespeare. There are lots of Shakespearean things that may well have been things which were in all plays of that period, or might have been filched from the best bits of Shakespeare, but primarily this was a production that we put together ourselves as a company.

GREGORY DORAN ON DIRECTING *CARDENIO*

Gregory Doran is Artistic Director of the Royal Shakespeare Company. He studied at Bristol University and the Bristol Old Vic Theatre School. He began his career as an actor before becoming associate director at Nottingham Playhouse. He played some minor roles in the RSC ensemble before beginning to direct for the company. He has made a particular mark with several of Shakespeare's lesser-known plays and the revival of works by his contemporaries. For this edition, Gregory was interviewed about his 2011 'reimagining' of *Cardenio*, based partly on *Double Falsehood*.

For Gregory Doran, the question of who wrote 'Shakespeare' is ultimately secondary to the fact that we have the plays. The question is one of academic interest, and not to be highlighted in performance, as Doran has learned from experience on other collaborative dramas such as *All is True/Henry VIII*: the play's the thing, as Hamlet tells us. Yet the very nature of a hypothetical authorial collaboration cannot help but influence the direction that the research for a production takes. Examples such as Anthony Munday of early modern 'plotters' suggest modes of collaboration that go beyond the identification of specific contributions, and it frees the modern director to consider modes of adaptation rather than adhering slavishly to an unreachable idea of an 'authentic' play.

Doran returned to Thomas Shelton's 1612 translation of *Don Quixote*, the source that would have been available to Shakespeare and Fletcher around the time that they are believed to have written the play of *Cardenio*. The plot takes a great deal of unwinding, as it is told backwards in flashbacks. To create a dramatically effective piece requires substantial reworking, and the experience of unpacking Shelton's translation, Theobald's *Double Falsehood* and other of the Spanish sources allowed Doran to live through a version of the process of creating a play from disparate narrative sources. In effect, Doran's main work in creating a 'reimagined' version of *Cardenio* was as a plotter, creating a way of telling the story that would speak to its new audience.

Part of the role of the plotter is to determine what the necessary cuts and additions are, which necessarily entails some degree of subjectivity, as the significant differences between Doran's version and other recent attempts at reconstruction by Gary Taylor, Bernard Richards and others demonstrates. Nonetheless, Doran's intuition as an experienced director of early modern plays gave him a clear sense of what the differences would be between the prose *Cardenio* and Shakespeare and Fletcher's play. As Theobald did in *Double Falsehood*, he believes Shakespeare and Fletcher would have omitted the framing story of Quixote and Sancho Panza, but that Fletcher in particular would have pushed for the addition of the two fathers, Camillo and Don Bernard. He cannot imagine a Renaissance version of the play that would not have staged Fernando [Henriquez in *Double Falsehood*] seducing Dorothea [Violante] in between Acts 1 and 2. Other added scenes included Fernando's invasion of the convent to which Lucinda [Leonora] had fled, bursting out of a coffin and bundling the screaming girl into it, a scene mirrored in several plays by Fletcher, Thomas Middleton and others; and scenes hearkening back to *The Two Gentlemen of Verona* that went further in embellishing the relationship between Cardenio [Julio] and Fernando, in order to raise the significance of the betrayal that occurs. These scenes exist in Shelton's translation, narrated by the characters, and the challenge was to render them into iambic pentameter.

The other imperative was the needs of a modern audience. Doran's production was never considered a 'reconstruction' of the play, but a twenty-first-century 'reimagining' which could focus on aspects that Doran and his audience would find interesting but would not have been Shakespeare or Fletcher's priorities. This allowed the vestiges of a sub-plot (Fabian and Lopez) to be omitted and more attention given to the psychological complexity and nuances of the four central characters.

The production pursued Doran's interest in the Spanish context, explored with the aid of Antonio Álamo, the play's Spanish dramaturge. Setting the play in the Spanish Golden Age brought the rigid social structures of the play to the fore. Within the seventeenth-century Spanish context, a woman in Dorothea's position, having lost her virginity, would have been considered a non-person in society, unable to marry again. Doran heightened her situation for explication to a modern audience by emphasizing the sanctity of the troth-plight sworn by Fernando before a statue of the Virgin Mary and a witness, Dorothea's serving maid, adding weight to her subsequent pursuit of Fernando that inevitably recalls Helena's pursuit of Bertram in *All's Well that Ends Well*.

Within the Spanish context, the social strata of the play became very clear. Don Bernardo's family were imagined as social climbers, with the father clutching at the possibility of a match with a Duke's son, while Camillo and his family were considered rather lower middle-class. Huge gates, based on those of the rood screen in Toledo Cathedral, acted as physical divisions that frequently parted Lucinda and Cardenio. Doran also insisted on there being a clear step down to Dorothea's village life, given colour by the introduction of a noisy fiesta and fireworks that framed the seduction scene. Fernando's incursion into that environment thus pointed up the perverted sense of entitlement engendered by his rank.

In researching other seventeenth-century versions of the Cardenio story, Doran noticed that in the final scene, when Fernando sees Cardenio, the two men fight. Cervantes, in *Don Quixote*, was more constrained by the conventions of Spanish literature, which require a certain amount of submission to Fernando as the nobleman and Cardenio's social superior. As Doran's company rehearsed, using Theobald's text, it became clear that this was dramatically inert and left Cardenio almost silent and inactive. For a modern British audience, the automatic assumption of social superiority is uncomfortable. The company experimented with several ideas and eventually settled on staging a conflict initiated by Fernando but quickly run by Cardenio, much stronger as a working man than his noble opponent. There was also a need to strengthen the rationale for redemption and forgiveness, which still (as in plays such as *The Two Gentlemen of Verona* and *All's Well that Ends Well*) presents difficulties for a modern audience. Doran added a major new speech for Dorothea that served to justify and complicate her role, challenging her husband but still expressing love for him.

In the best performances, Dorothea's speech would reduce Alex Hassell [playing Fernando, interviewed above] to tears, allowing an audience to begin to buy in to his contrition. Within a modern context, the question of audience sympathy for Fernando was made thorny by the fraught question of what constitutes rape; a question posed by Fernando to himself in the integral speech immediately after the seduction, retained from *Double Falsehood*. During some performances, when Fernando asked himself 'Was it a rape then?', some audience members would spontaneously answer 'Yes!' The question of his persuasiveness, and of the extent of his coercion of Dorothea, needed to be carefully handled if the audience were not to be instructed to sympathize with a rapist.

For Doran, the line between seduction and rape became one of impulsiveness. In this production, while Fernando's endeavours to break into her apartment and apply pressure were reprehensible, his actions were imagined to be those of a man who believes entirely in what he says and does at the time. He leapt at the opportunity offered by Dorothea who suggests '*If we were to be married...*' and, in that moment, utterly committed to the idea of marrying her; a resolution that saw both enter willingly into the contract, but which was broken in the cold light of day by his impulse to the next action. In this, Doran aligned Dorothea's situation with that of Helena's, the abandoned loving wife, 'bitten and flung away' like an apple (a line borrowed from another Fletcher play), and thus contextualizing her continued pursuit of his oath.

The passion of the scene was echoed in the Spanish fiesta, paid for by Fernando to turn Dorothea's environment into a party area that would create the right atmosphere, a direct reference to August Strindberg's *Miss Julie*, with the unseen encounter represented by coarse puppets with oversized phalluses. Doran's intention was not to make the seduction scene politically correct, but rather to paint Fernando as someone who takes what he wants – impulsive, spoiled and addicted to pleasure, attractive to an audience in the same way that Richard III appeals even as he repels, but with the sincerity in the immediate moment that mitigates his wild inconsistencies and mood shifts throughout the play.

The free adaptation of the play allowed Cardenio's character to be similarly embellished, finding justifications for his behaviour throughout. For Doran, Cardenio was initially passive, bullied by his father and deliberately misinterpreted by his girlfriend in scenes that were extended to play on the comedy of a modern, realistic relationship. By refusing to idealize Cardenio and Lucinda's relationship through their arguments and misunderstandings, the company were able to turn the play's turning point, the attempted marriage of Lucinda to Fernando, into a realistically untidy crisis point. In the pressure of the moment, Lucinda was unable to find the knife that she had concealed for the final eventuality, and as a result of panic stammered out an acceptance of the marriage before fainting. In a departure from *Double Falsehood*, Cardenio did not interrupt the wedding but watched, passive. His madness came as a result of his feelings of guilt and confusion, unleashing the strength and dynamism that had hitherto been repressed.

All of these decisions were part of the work that Doran and a committed, engaged group of collaborators felt was necessary to turn Theobald's sentimental eighteenth-century play into a believable, dramatically effective twenty-first-century play that also paid tribute to Shakespeare and Fletcher's work. Doran's foregrounding of Pedro [Roderick] was key to this. As one of the few characters with no precedent in *Don Quixote*, Doran identified Pedro as an important piece of dramatic functioneering, a cousin to Camillo of *The Winter's Tale*. Importantly, he is kept somewhat apart from the main action, serving to enable the play's conclusions and reunifications rather than taking a share in them himself.

19. Disguise in *Cardenio*
'I have found a suff'ring true companion' (4.2.118)
Cardenio [Julio] (Oliver Rix) encounters the disguised Dorothea [Violante] (Pippa Nixon) in Gregory Doran's 2011 RSC
production of *Cardenio* at the Swan Theatre, Stratford-upon-Avon. Ellie Kurttz © Royal Shakespeare Company

Doran's *Cardenio* was, ultimately, an attempt to create a new play that was a palimpsest of all the sources while remaining true to its own moment of performance, its company and its audience. In rewriting and adaptation, a misplaced sense of authenticity to a lost original is less productive than adherence to the best version of the story for its new audience. It was this ethos that prompted the play's tagline 'Shakespeare's lost play *reimagined*'. This sense of responsibility to the audience was rewarded by the creation of an atmosphere almost unique to RSC audiences in Stratford-upon-Avon, in which the majority of audiences did not know the story or what would happen next. For director and company, the ability to adapt freely and keep an audience in suspense was a liberation, introducing this tangentially 'Shakespearean' play not as a heritage item but as a living and surprising theatrical event.

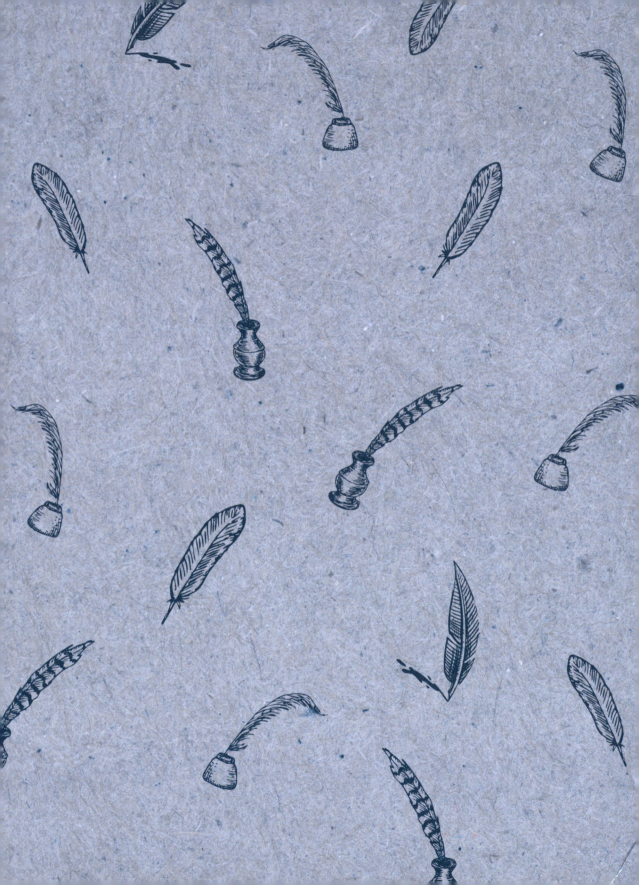